FUNDAMENTALS

OF

LEGAL RESEARCH

By

STEVEN M. BARKAN
Director of Library and Information Services and Professor of Law
University of Wisconsin Law School

ROY M. MERSKY
Late Harry M. Reasoner Regents Chair in Law and Director of Research
The Jamail Center for Legal Research, Tarlton Law Library
University of Texas School of Law

DONALD J. DUNN
Late Dean and Professor of Law
University of LaVerne College of Law

NINTH EDITION

FOUNDATION PRESS
2009

THOMSON REUTERS

© 1977, 1981, 1985, 1987, 1990, 1994, 1998, 2002 FOUNDATION PRESS

© 2009 By THOMSON REUTERS/FOUNDATION PRESS

> 195 Broadway, 9th Floor
>
> New York, NY 10007
>
> Phone Toll Free 1–877–888–1330
>
> Fax (212) 367–6799
>
> foundation–press.com

Printed in the United States of America

ISBN 978–1–59941–218–4

TEXT IS PRINTED ON 10% POST CONSUMER RECYCLED PAPER

This book is dedicated

To the memory of my colleagues and friends

Roy M. Mersky (1925–2008)
and
Donald J. Dunn (1945–2008)

To my parents

Ruth Hoffman Barkan
and
Irving Barkan

And to my children

Davida Fernandez-Barkan
and
Daniel Fernandez-Barkan

S.M.B.

He [or She] Who Cites His [or Her] Source,
Begins Deliverance to the World

Mishnah, Avot. VI

PREFACE

Fundamentals of Legal Research has a distinguished history as both a teaching tool and a guide to legal research. Since the first edition in 1956, its authors have resisted making the book a comprehensive manual of legal resources. The authors have always intended it to be a text for students learning to do legal research.* At the same time, *Fundamentals of Legal Research* offers a comprehensive description of legal research sources.

Every chapter of the text has been revised to reflect changes in the resources and methods of legal research. This edition includes a new chapter introducing the forms and processes of legal writing (Chapter 3). The eighth edition's chapter on constitutions has been reorganized and expanded to cover research in constitutional law and the U.S. Supreme Court (Chapter 8). Annotated law reports (*A.L.R.*) are treated as secondary sources and relocated accordingly (Chapter 17).

This edition retains many of the features that have been popular over the years. The familiar outline format, the many footnote references that enable students to pursue subjects in greater depth, and the organization of chapters remain. The chapters in *Fundamentals of Legal Research* have been ordered to reflect a "jurisprudential" approach to teaching legal research. Resources are presented in the order that reflects how law students typically are taught to conceptualize law. Since most law students begin the study of law by reading and analyzing judicial opinions, the book begins with a discussion of the process of publishing court reports and the methods for locating them. The examination of court reports is followed by chapters on other primary sources of law, then by secondary sources, and then by specialized chapters on research in international and human rights law, legal research in the United Kingdom, electronic legal research, legal citation form, and research in tax law.

Fundamentals of Legal Research also can be used effectively to support a "process" approach to teaching legal research in which resources are presented in the order in which lawyers tend to conduct research—secondary authority before primary authority, etc. Instructors using a process approach can begin with introductory chapters 1, 2, and 3, and then cover secondary sources in chapters 16, 17, 18, and 19, before covering primary sources.

Assignments to Accompany Fundamentals of Legal Research, 9th and *Legal Research Illustrated, 9th* is available as a separate pamphlet.

---

* This is actually the thirteenth edition of FUNDAMENTALS OF LEGAL RESEARCH. The numbering of editions was reinitiated in 1977 with a change in authorship. For a history of this and other legal research textbooks, see my review of a previous edition of FUNDAMENTALS OF LEGAL RESEARCH. Steven M. Barkan, *On Describing Legal Research* (Book Review of FUNDAMENTALS OF LEGAL RESEARCH (2d ed. 1981) by J. Myron Jacobstein & Roy M. Mersky), 80 MICH. L. REV. 925 (1982).

These assignments, edited by Mary Ann Nelson of the University of Iowa, are designed to help students understand the resources described in this book.

There are, of course, challenges in producing a book that describes legal research in an era dominated by electronic resources. Legal research is more complicated than ever before. There are more resources from which to choose and more variations in media, cost, quality, durability, and reliability of resources. In any given context, a researcher might not have access to many of the resources that are discussed in this book.

Although legal research has always been an evolving field, the print-on-paper environment was relatively static in comparison to today's dynamic electronic environment. New resources are regularly reaching the market and existing resources are frequently changing their coverage, design, ownership, names, methods of access, and functionality. At best, a book about legal research can provide no more than the proverbial snapshot of the research environment at a point in time—in our case, December 31, 2008. Today's researcher must understand that despite many changes, research skills are adaptable from one resource to another, and the fundamentals of legal research are constant.

STEVEN M. BARKAN
Madison, Wisconsin

April 2009

ACKNOWLEDGMENTS

The influences of Donald J. Dunn and Roy M. Mersky permeate this book. Both men were colleagues, mentors, and friends to me—and to most of the contributors to *Fundamentals of Legal Research*. Their immeasurable contributions have left indelible marks on legal research instruction, the profession of academic law librarianship, and legal education.*

For over 50 years, *Fundamentals of Legal Research* has been a work-in-progress. This edition builds on the work of Professors Ervin H. Pollack, J. Myron Jacobstein, Roy M. Mersky, Donald J. Dunn, and numerous contributing authors. Along with the primary and contributing authors, the law library staffs at Ohio State, Stanford, Texas, and Western New England have supported the research and development of this book. I refer the reader to the authors' acknowledgments in previous editions for listings of these contributors.

I express my appreciation to the following people who supported my work on the ninth edition of *Fundamentals of Legal Research*.

The staff of the University of Wisconsin Law Library, especially Bonnie Shucha, Head of Reference, for sharing her expertise on many aspects of modern legal research; Bill Ebbott, Assistant Director for Public Services; Sunil Rao, Foreign Law Librarian; Erin Schlicht, Evening/Weekend Supervisor; Eric ("ET") Taylor, Evening Reference Librarian; and Steve Weber, Reference Intern, for providing reference and research support.

Dean Kenneth B. Davis, Jr. and the faculty and administration of the University of Wisconsin Law School for sustaining an environment that values and nurtures many types of legal research and scholarship.

Gwyn Anderson, formerly of the Tarlton Law Library, Jamail Center for Legal Research, University of Texas School of Law, for supporting in so many ways the authors of, and contributors to, *Fundamentals of Legal Research* over the years.

---

* *See* Roy M. Mersky, *Memorial: Donald J. Dunn (1945–2008)*, 100 LAW LIBR. J. 601 (2008); Terry Martin, *Roy Martin Mersky, 1925–2008*, 28 (1) THE ALL–SIS NEWSLETTER, Fall 2008, at 19, available at http://www.aallnet.org/sis/allsis/newsletter/28_1/Mersky.htm; *In Memoriam: Professor Roy M. Mersky, 1925–2008*, http://www.utexas.edu/law/news/2008/050708_mersky.html.

ACKNOWLEDGMENTS

The following people were primarily responsible for preparing specific chapters or sections of this edition. I am grateful for their contributions and for their commitment to this project.

Melissa Bernstein, Reference Librarian, Tarlton Law Library, Jamail Center for Legal Research, University of Texas School of Law (Chapters 16, 17, 19).

Mary A. Hotchkiss, Director of Academic Advising and Senior Lecturer, University of Washington School of Law (Chapter 3).

Richard Leiter, Library Director and Professor, University of Nebraska College of Law (Chapters 9, 10).

Daniel W. Martin, Director of the Law Library and Professor of Law, Loyola Law School, Los Angeles (Appendix A).

David McClure, Tarlton Fellow, Tarlton Law Library, Jamail Center for Legal Research, University of Texas School of Law (Glossary).

Mary Ann Nelson, Executive Law Librarian, University of Iowa Law Library (Assignments and Instructor's Manual).

Pat Newcombe, Associate Director, Western New England College School of Law Library (Chapter 24).

Jane O'Connell, Interim Coordinator of Public Services, Tarlton Law Library, Jamail Center for Legal Research, University of Texas School of Law (Chapter 20).

George H. Pike, Director of the Barco Law Library and Assistant Professor of Law, University of Pittsburgh School of Law (Chapter 23).

Jonathan Pratter, Foreign and International Law Librarian, Tarlton Law Library, Jamail Center for Legal Research, University of Texas School of Law (Chapter 21, Appendix C).

Jeanne F. Price, Director of the Law Library and Associate Professor of Law, William S. Boyd School of Law, University of Nevada, Las Vegas (Chapter 15).

Gail Levin Richmond, Professor, Nova Southeastern University Shepard Broad Law Center (Chapter 25). In addition, Gail, proofreader *par excellence*, meticulously proofread the entire book.

Bonnie Shucha, Head of Reference, University of Wisconsin Law Library (Chapters 11, 18, Appendix B).

Keith Ann Stiverson, Director of the Law Library, Chicago–Kent College of Law (Chapter 13).

ACKNOWLEDGMENTS

Mary Whisner, Reference Librarian, Gallagher Law Library, University of Washington School of Law (Chapter 3).

Stephen Young, Reference Librarian, Judge Kathryn J. DuFour Law Library, Catholic University of America, Columbus School of Law (Chapter 22).

The staff of Foundation Press, especially John Bloomquist, Publisher; Jim Coates, Senior Attorney Editor; and Sharon Pizzi, Senior Publishing Specialist, supported this project with enthusiasm. I am grateful for their courtesy, patience, and expertise. I also express my appreciation to the publishers' representatives who provided information about their products and services.

Fundamentals of Legal Research is a book for students learning to do legal research. Therefore, I thank and acknowledge law librarians and all teachers of legal research, both in and out of the classroom. Their efforts to teach law students and lawyers how to find the information upon which legal decisions are made contribute to the betterment of our legal system. Their suggestions and feedback for improving this book will always be appreciated.

In closing, I join in the words of Don and Roy from the previous edition:

> Finally, we thank all of the law students who read and use the book and who continue to sustain our intellectual interests and curiosity. We are gratified when lawyers indicate that the book they used in their first-year legal research class or in an advanced course in legal research is still in their personal library, and that they continue referring to it. All of those comments truly give us a sense of pride and humility. Ultimately, we are grateful for having the opportunity to make our contributions to the body of legal literature.

STEVEN M. BARKAN

*

SUMMARY OF CONTENTS

*

TABLE OF CONTENTS

TABLE OF CONTENTS

GLOSSARY OF TERMS USED IN LEGAL RESEARCH*

This glossary of terms is limited in scope, and the definitions of words are restricted in meaning to their legal or legal research context. Words whose meanings conform to general usage and are obvious are omitted from the list, e.g., Index.

ACQUITTAL—

the verdict in a criminal trial in which the defendant is found not guilty.

ACT—

an alternative name for statutory law. When introduced in a legislature, a piece of proposed legislation is typically described as a "bill." After a bill is enacted, the terms "law" and "act" may be used interchangeably to describe it. An act has the same legislative force as a joint resolution but is technically distinguishable, being of a different form and introduced with the words "Be it enacted" instead of "Be it resolved."

ACTION—

the formal legal demand of one's rights from another person brought in court.

ADJUDICATION—

the formal pronouncing or recording of a judgment or decree by a court.

ADMINISTRATIVE AGENCY—

a governmental authority, other than a legislature or court, which issues rules and regulations or adjudicates disputes arising under designated statutes and regulations. Administrative agencies usually act under authority delegated by the legislature.

ADMINISTRATIVE LAW—

law that governs, and is promulgated by, governmental administrative agencies other than courts or legislative bodies. These administrative agencies derive their power from legislative enactments and are subject to judicial review.

ADVANCE SHEETS—

current pamphlets containing the most recently reported opinions of a court or the courts of several jurisdictions. The volume and page numbers usually are the same as in the subsequently bound volumes of the series, which cover several of the previously issued advance sheets.

---

* This glossary was revised by David McClure, Tarlton Fellow at the Tarlton Law Library, Jamail Center for Legal Research, University of Texas School of Law. Previous versions were revised by Fred R. Shapiro, Associate Librarian for Collections and Access, Yale Law School.

ADVISORY OPINION—

an opinion rendered by a court at the request of the government or an interested party that indicates how the court would rule on a matter should adversary litigation develop. An advisory opinion is thus an interpretation of the law without binding effect. The International Court of Justice and some state courts will render advisory opinions; the Supreme Court of the United States will not.

AFFIDAVIT—

a written statement or declaration of facts sworn to by the maker, taken before a person officially permitted by law to administer oaths.

ALWD CITATION MANUAL—

a manual of legal citation form prepared by the Association of Legal Writing Directors.

ALTERNATIVE DISPUTE RESOLUTION—

the process of resolving disputes through such means as mediation or arbitration rather than through litigation.

AMICUS CURIAE—

means, literally, "friend of the court." A person or entity with strong interest in or views on the subject matter of a dispute involving other parties that petitions the court for permission to file a brief in the case, ostensibly on behalf of one of the parties, but actually to suggest a rationale consistent with its own views.

ANNOTATIONS—

(1) Statutory: brief summaries of the law and facts of cases interpreting statutes passed by Congress or state legislatures that are compiled in codes; or (2) Textual: expository essays of varying length on significant legal topics chosen from selected cases or statutes, which are often published together with the essays.

ANSWER—

the pleading filed by the defendant in response to the plaintiff's complaint.

APPEAL PAPERS—

the record of lower court proceedings and briefs filed by attorneys with courts for the purpose of appealing a lower court's actions in a litigated matter.

APPELLANT—

the party who requests that a higher court review the actions of a lower court. Compare with APPELLEE.

APPELLATE COURT—

a court that has legal authority to review the actions and decisions of a lower court or an administrative agency on appeal.

APPELLEE—

the party against whom an appeal is taken (usually, but not always, the winner in the lower court). It should be noted that a party's status as appellant or appellee bears no relation to his, her or its status as plaintiff or defendant in the lower court.

ARBITRATION—

the hearing and settlement of a dispute between opposing parties by one or more neutral and non-judicial third parties. The third parties' decision is often binding by prior agreement of the opposing parties. Arbitration is an alternative to litigation as a means of resolving disputes.

ATTORNEY GENERAL OPINION—

an opinion issued by the chief counsel of the federal government or a state government at the request of the president, a state governor or other governmental official on behalf of a state or federal agency interpreting the law for the requesting official or agency in the same manner as a private attorney would for his or her client. The opinion is not binding on a court but is usually accorded some degree of persuasive authority.

AUTHORITY—

that which can bind or influence a court. Case law, legislation, constitutions, administrative regulations, and writings about the law are all legal authority. See PRIMARY AUTHORITY; MANDATORY AUTHORITY; PERSUASIVE AUTHORITY.

BILL—

a legislative proposal introduced in a legislature. The term distinguishes unfinished legislation from enacted law.

BLACK LETTER LAW—

an informal term indicating the basic principles of law generally accepted by the courts and/or embodied in the statutes of a particular jurisdiction.

BLOG—

an abbreviated version of the term "web log," it typically describes a website that features a running log of posted messages in reverse chronological order discussing current news or individual thoughts and opinions on a particular topic. Readers are often invited to post comments or questions to messages published on the blog. Blogs on legal topics are often referred to as "blawgs."

BLUEBOOK—

a commonly-used manual of legal citation form compiled by the editors of the *Harvard Law Review*, *Yale Law Journal*, *Columbia Law Review*, and *University of Pennsylvania Law Review*. The full title is *The Bluebook: A Uniform System of Citation*.

BOOKMARK

a function on Web browsers and social bookmarking programs that enables the user to save or mark the URL of a website so that it can be accessed directly in the future.

BOOLEAN LOGIC—

a form of search strategy used in databases, such as *Westlaw* and *LexisNexis*. In a Boolean search, connectors such as AND, OR, and NOT are used to construct a complex search command. The command "fungible and gasoline" for example, retrieves documents in which the term "fungible" and the term "gasoline" both appear. Compare with NATURAL LANGUAGE.

BRIEF—

(1) in American law practice, a written statement prepared by the counsel arguing a case in court. It contains a summary of the facts of the case, the pertinent laws, and an argument of how the law applies to the facts supporting counsel's position; (2) a summary of a published legal opinion prepared for the purpose of studying the opinion in law school.

BRIEFS AND RECORDS—

See APPEAL PAPERS.

CALENDAR—

a list or schedule that states the order in which cases are to be heard during a term of court.

CALR—

an acronym for Computer–Assisted Legal Research. *LexisNexis*, *Loislaw*, and *Westlaw* are CALR services.

CAPTION—

See STYLE OF A CASE.

CASE IN POINT—

a judicial opinion which deals with a fact situation similar to the one being researched and substantiates a point of law to be asserted. It is also referred to as "case on all fours."

CASE LAW—

the law of reported judicial opinions as distinguished from statutes or administrative law.

CASEBOOK—

a textbook used to instruct law students in a particular area of law. The text consists of a collection of judicial opinions, usually from appellate courts, and notes by the author(s).

CAUSE OF ACTION—

a claim in law and in fact sufficient to bring a case to court; the grounds of an action. (Example: breach of contract.)

CD–ROM—

an acronym for "compact disc–read only memory." A compact disc is a digital storage device approximately 4 inches in diameter on which data is coded to be scanned by a laser beam and transmitted to a computer monitor. A large volume of data can be stored on such a device.

CERTIORARI—

a writ issued by a higher court to a lower court requiring the latter to produce the records of a particular case tried therein. It is most commonly used to refer to the Supreme Court of the United States, which uses the writ of certiorari as a discretionary device to choose the cases it wishes to hear. The term's origin is Latin, meaning "to be informed of."

CHARTER—

a document issued by a governmental entity that gives a corporation legal existence. A corporation's charter may be referred to as the "articles of incorporation" or the "certificate of incorporation," depending on the terminology used in the state where the corporation was incorporated.

CITATION—

the reference to authority necessary to substantiate the validity of an argument or position. Citations to authority and supporting references are both important and extensive in any form of legal writing. Citation form is also given emphasis in legal writing, and early familiarity with a manual of legal citation form, such as *The Bluebook* or the *ALWD Citation Manual*, will stand the law student in good stead.

CITATORS—

books or online services that provide the subsequent judicial history and interpretation of reported cases or lists of cases and legislative enactments construing, applying, or affecting statutes. Citators indicate where a specific source (cited source) is cited by another source (citing source). In the United States, the most widely used citators are *Shepard's* and *KeyCite*.

CITED CASE—

a case that is referred to by other cases.

CITING CASE—

the case that refers to the cited case.

CIVIL LAW—

(1) Roman law embodied in the Code of Justinian, which is the basis of law in most Latin American countries and most countries of Western Europe other than Great Britain and is the foundation of the law of Louisiana and Quebec; (2) the law concerning noncriminal matters in both common law and civil law jurisdictions, such as those described in (1).

CLAIM—

(1) the assertion of a right, as to money or property; (2) the accumulation of facts that give rise to a right enforceable in court.

CLASS ACTION—

a lawsuit brought by a representative party on behalf of a group, all of whose members have the same or a similar grievance against the defendant.

CODE—

in popular usage, a compilation of statutory laws. In a code, the current statutory laws, together with judicial decrees having the force of law, are rewritten and arranged in classified order by subject. Repealed and temporary acts are eliminated and the revision is reenacted. See also COMPILED STATUTES; CONSOLIDATED STATUTES; REVISED STATUTES.

CODIFICATION—

the process of collecting and arranging systematically, usually by subject, the laws of a state or country.

COLLABORATIVE SOFTWARE—

software that facilitates the cooperative efforts of individuals in business and social settings. Examples of collaborative software include email, voicemail, calendar software, videoconferencing, discussion boards, wikis, and social networking websites. It is sometimes also referred to as "social software."

COLLECTIVE INTELLIGENCE—

the theory that higher levels of intelligence and understanding result from the collaborative and competitive efforts of interconnected groups of people.

COMMON LAW—

the basis of the Anglo–American legal systems. English common law was largely customary law and unwritten, until discovered, applied, and reported by the courts of law. In theory, the common law courts did not create law but rather discovered it in the customs and habits of the English people. The strength of the judicial system in pre-parliamentary days is one reason for the continued emphasis in common law systems on case law. In a narrow sense, common law is the phrase still used to distinguish case law from statutory law.

COMPILED STATUTES—

in popular usage, a code. Technically, it is a compilation of acts printed verbatim as originally enacted but in a new classified order. The text is not modified; however, repealed and temporary acts are omitted. See also CODE; CONSOLIDATED STATUTES; REVISED STATUTES.

COMPLAINT—

the plaintiff's initial pleading. Under the Federal Rules of Civil Procedure, it is no longer full of the technicalities demanded by the common law. A complaint need only contain a short and plain statement of the claim upon which relief is sought, an indication of the type of relief requested, and an indication that the court has jurisdiction to hear the case.

CONNECTOR—

See BOOLEAN LOGIC.

CONSOLIDATED STATUTES—

a compilation of statutes arranged in classified order by subject and subdivided as necessary into parts, articles, chapters, and sections for clarity and consistency of style. In the process of preparing consolidated statutes, all temporary and repealed statutes are deleted. A collection of statutes is sometimes referred to in popular usage as "consolidated laws," "compiled statutes," "revised statutes," or a "code." See also CODE; COMPILED STATUTES; REVISED STATUTES.

CONSOLIDATING STATUTE—

a law that gathers various statutes on a certain topic and organizes them into a single statutory act, making minor textual revisions and eliminating repealed and temporary acts in the process.

CONSTITUTION—

the system of fundamental principles by which a political body or organization governs itself. Most national constitutions are written; the English and Israeli constitutions are unwritten.

COOKIE—

a small data file created by a website and stored on a user's computer with information about the user and the user's preferences and browsing patterns when using the Internet.

COUNT—

a separate and independent claim. A civil petition or a criminal indictment may contain several counts.

COUNTERCLAIM—

a claim made by a defendant against a plaintiff in a civil lawsuit; it constitutes a separate cause of action.

COURT DECISION—

the disposition of a case by a court. See OPINION.

COURT RULES—

rules of procedure promulgated to govern civil and criminal practice before the courts.

CREATIVE COMMONS—

a non-profit organization that seeks to promote a balance in society between full copyright protections for creative works under the copyright laws and the lack of copyright protections for works in the public domain. To encourage the sharing of creative works while still providing certain copyright protections for authors, Creative Commons has developed a range of licenses where authors can choose to permit and restrict use of their creative works in various ways.

DAMAGES—

monetary compensation awarded by a court for an injury caused by the act of another. Damages may be actual or compensatory (equal to the amount of loss shown), exemplary or punitive (in excess of the actual loss given to punish the person for the malicious conduct that caused the injury), or nominal (a trivial amount given because the injury is slight or because the exact amount of injury has not been determined satisfactorily).

DATABASE—

a collection of information organized for rapid retrieval by computer. In legal research, it usually refers to a commercial service that may be searched online. A full-text database provides the complete text of documents such as judicial opinions or newspaper articles. *Westlaw* and *LexisNexis* are full-text databases. A bibliographic database provides citations or abstracts of articles, books, reports, or patents.

DECISION—

See COURT DECISION.

DECREE—

a determination by a court of the rights and duties of the parties before it. Formerly, decrees were issued by courts of equity and distinguished from judgments, which were issued by courts of law. See EQUITY.

DEFENDANT—

the person against whom a civil or criminal action is brought.

DEMURRER—

a means of objecting to the sufficiency in law of a pleading by admitting the actual allegations made, but disputing that they frame an adequate legal claim. A demurrer is more commonly referred to in most jurisdictions today as a "motion to dismiss for failure to state a claim."

DICTUM—

See OBITER DICTUM.

DIGEST—

an index to reported cases, providing brief, unconnected statements of court holdings on points of law, which are arranged by subject and subdivided by jurisdiction and courts.

DIGITAL LIBRARY—

an organized collection of materials and documents in an electronic format that may be stored, retrieved, and viewed.

DIGITAL REPOSITORY—

an electronic database maintained for the purpose of depositing, preserving, and providing access to scholarly research, scholarship, and other digital content.

DIGITIZATION—

the act of converting audio or video signals or physical objects into binary code that can be viewed, edited, and stored on a computer.

Various methods of scanning and recording are used in the digitization process.

DISCUSSION BOARDS—

online forums dedicated to particular topics or issues where individuals may post questions and comments and read postings by others. Discussion boards are typically asynchronous, i.e., individuals are not required to be online at the same moment in order to participate in the discussion. Discussion boards are sometimes also referred to as "forums," "newsgroups," or "Internet discussion boards (IDBS)."

DOCKET NUMBER—

a identifying number, sequentially assigned by the court clerk at the outset of a lawsuit submitted to the court for adjudication.

DVD—

an acronym for "digital video disc" or "digital versatile disc." It is a type of CD–ROM that is capable of storing more video and audio data than other CD–ROMs due to its high recording density.

E–BOOK—

a book that is in an electronic format and may be accessed online, through a computer network database, or through a hand-held electronic device that is often referred to as a "reader."

E–COMMERCE—

the activity of exchanging goods and services by electronic means, typically via the Internet.

E–JOURNAL—

a journal that is in an electronic format and may be accessed online, through an electronic network, CD–ROM, or DVD.

E–LEARNING—

learning that takes place by electronic means, typically via the Internet. It may take various forms, such as distance learning or distributed learning, and it may be led by an instructor or a computer in a synchronous or asynchronous fashion or some combination thereof.

EN BANC—

a session in which the entire bench of the court will participate in the decision rather than the regular quorum. It is common for an appellate court to have more members than are necessary to hear an appeal. In the United States, the federal circuit courts of appeals usually sit in groups of three judges but for important cases may expand the bench to nine members, when they are said to be sitting en banc.

ENCYCLOPEDIA—

a work containing expository statements on principles of law, topically arranged, with supporting footnote references to cases and statutes on point.

EQUITY—

justice administered according to fairness as contrasted with the strictly formulated rules of common law. It is based on a system of rules and principles that originated in England as an alternative to the harsh rules of common law and that were based on what was fair in a particular situation. One sought relief under this system in courts of equity rather than in courts of law.

EXECUTIVE AGREEMENT—

an international agreement, not a treaty, concluded by the president without senatorial consent on the president's authority as commander-in-chief and director of foreign relations. The distinction between treaty and executive agreement is complicated and believed by some to be of questionable constitutionality, but the import of such agreements as that of Yalta, Potsdam, the Algiers Accords, the North American Free Trade Agreement (NAFTA), and the General Agreement on Tariffs and Trade (GATT), among many others, is unquestionably great.

EXECUTIVE ORDER—

an order issued by the president under specific authority granted to the president by Congress. There is no precise distinction between a presidential proclamation and an executive order; however, a proclamation generally cover matters of widespread interest, and an executive order often relates to the conduct of government business or to organization of the executive branch of government. Every act of the president authorizing or directing the performance of an act, in its general context, is an executive order. See PRESIDENTIAL PROCLAMATION.

EXTRANET—

a secure, password-protected website designed by a company or other organization as part of its internal computer network to share information with selected individuals involved with the company or organization, such as clients or vendors.

FICHE—

See MICROFICHE.

FINDLAW—

a portal on the World Wide Web (http://www.findlaw.com) providing links to a wide range of law-related information. *FindLaw* is owned by

Thomson Reuters, but much of the information accessible through the portal is free of charge.

FORM BOOKS—

books containing sample instruments that are helpful in drafting legal documents.

FORMS OF ACTION—

conventions that governed common law pleadings and were the procedural devices used to give expression to the theories of liability recognized by the common law. Failure to analyze the cause of the action properly, to select the proper theory of liability and to choose the appropriate procedural mechanism or forms of action could easily result in being thrown out of court. A plaintiff had to elect his or her remedy in advance and could not subsequently amend the pleadings to conform to his or her proof or to the court's choice of another theory of liability. According to the relief sought, actions were divided into three categories: real actions were brought for the recovery of real property; mixed actions were brought to recover real property and damages for injury to it; personal actions were brought to recover debts or personal property, or for injuries to personal, property, or contractual rights. The common law forms of action were usually considered to be eleven in number: trespass, trespass on the case, trover, ejectment, detinue, replevin, debt, covenant, account, special assumpsit, and general assumpsit.

FULL–TEXT—

See DATABASE.

GIF—

an acronym for "graphics interchange format." It is a common format for encoding image files to be displayed on the World Wide Web.

GIS—

an acronym for "geographic information system" or "geospatial information system." It is a computer system designed to collect, store, analyze, and display data that is spatially referenced to Earth in order to consider complicated issues relating to natural resources, the environment, and society.

GPS—

an acronym for "global positioning system." It is a navigating system that utilizes electronic receivers and satellites orbiting the Earth to precisely determine the location of its users.

GRAND JURY—

a jury of six to twenty-three persons that sits permanently for a specified period and hears criminal accusations and evidence, and then determines whether indictments should be made. Compare with PETIT JURY.

HEADNOTE—

a brief summary of the legal rule or significant facts in a case that precedes the printed opinion in reports.

HEARINGS—

proceedings extensively employed by both legislative and administrative agencies to elicit facts or to make authorized determinations. Adjudicative hearings of administrative agencies can be appealed in a court of law. Investigative hearings are often held by congressional committees prior to enactment of legislation, and are important sources of legislative history.

HEINONLINE—

a database containing page images and searchable text of legal journals and other legal materials. *HeinOnline* is produced by the William S. Hein & Co.

HOLDING—

the declaration of the conclusion of law reached by the court as to the legal effect of the facts of the case.

HOLOGRAPH OR OLOGRAPH—

a will, deed, or other legal document that is entirely in the handwriting of the signer.

HORNBOOK—

the popular reference to a basic or rudimentary treatise that reviews a certain field of law in summary, textual form, as opposed to a casebook that is designed as a teaching tool and includes many reprints of judicial opinions.

INDICTMENT—

a formal accusation of a crime made by a grand jury at the request of a prosecuting attorney.

INFORMATION—

an accusation based not on the action of a grand jury but rather on the affirmation of a public official.

INJUNCTION—

a judge's order that a person do or, more commonly, refrain from doing, a certain act. An injunction may be preliminary or temporary, pending trial of the issue presented, or it may be final if the issue has already been decided in court.

INSTANT MESSAGING—

a form of communication that allows users who are on the Internet at the same time to engage in a real-time conversation or "chat" by exchanging short, typed messages.

INTERNET—

a worldwide system of thousands of interconnected computer networks using the TCP/IP protocols. The Internet facilitates various data communication services.

INTRANET—

a restricted-access internal computer network that facilitates information sharing internally within a company or organization.

ISP—

an acronym for "internet service provider." An ISP is a company that provides Internet access to those who subscribe to its services, typically for a fee.

JUDGMENT—

See COURT DECISION.

JURISDICTION—

(1) the power given to a court by a constitution or a legislative body to make legally binding decisions over certain persons, property, or subject matter, or (2) the geographical area in which a court's decisions or legislative enactments are binding.

JURISPRUDENCE—

(1) the science or philosophy of law; (2) a collective term for case law as opposed to legislation.

KEY NUMBER—

a category of the major indexing system devised for American case law, developed by West Publishing Company. The key number is a permanent number given to a specific point of law.

LAW REVIEW/LAW JOURNAL—

a legal periodical. The term "law review" usually describes a scholarly periodical edited by students at a law school.

LEGISLATIVE HISTORY—

information embodied in legislative documents and other materials that provides background information and insight into the purpose and intent of statutes. Citations and dates of legislative enactments, amendments, and repeals of statutes are sometimes imprecisely identified as legislative histories. More accurate designations of these citations of legislative changes, as included in codes, are historical notes or amendatory histories.

LEXISNEXIS—

a division of Reed Elsevier Inc. *LexisNexis* is a CALR service providing the full text of court decisions, statutes, administrative materials, law review articles, Supreme Court briefs, and other items. Key-word searches, Boolean searches, natural language searches, segment searches, and citator searches are available.

LIABILITY—

the condition of being responsible either for damages resulting from an injurious act or for discharging an obligation or debt.

LIBEL—

(1) written or visual defamation of a person's character. Compare with SLANDER; (2) in an admiralty court, the plaintiff's statement of the cause of action and the relief sought.

LIBRARY 2.0—

a model for library service that emphasizes Web 2.0 technologies, online services, and increased interaction, participation and feedback from library users. Virtual reference services, personalized online public access catalogs (OPACs), and publicly accessible online materials play a prominent role in the Library 2.0 model.

LISTSERV—

an electronic mailing list for individuals who desire to discuss items or issues of shared interest with others. Individuals subscribe to a listserv through a central email service that forwards email messages to all subscribers.

LITIGATE—

to bring a civil action in court.

LOISLAW—

a subsidiary of Wolters Kluwer Law & Business. *Loislaw* is a CALR service providing the full text of court decisions, statutes, administrative materials, and other sources.

LOOSELEAF SERVICES AND REPORTERS—

publications that contain federal and state administrative regulations and decisions or subject treatment of a legal topic. They traditionally consist of separate, perforated pages or pamphlet-sized inserts in special binders, simplifying frequent insertion or substitution of new material. Many looseleaf services and reporters are now also available online.

MANDATORY AUTHORITY—

authority that a given court is bound to follow. Mandatory authority is found in constitutional provisions, legislation, and judicial opinions. Compare with PERSUASIVE AUTHORITY.

MEMORANDUM—

(1) an informal record; (2) a written document that may be used to prove that a contract exists; (3) an exposition of all the points of law pertaining to a particular case (referred to as a "memorandum of law"); or (4) an informal written discussion of the merits of a matter pending in a lawyer's office, usually written by a law clerk or junior associate for a senior associate or partner (referred to as an "office memorandum").

METADATA—

Data that describes other data. Metadata often provides information on electronic resources and documents by describing characteristics of them, such as their content, condition, location, structure, formatting, date and time of creation, modification history, and other relevant attributes. Metadata plays an important role in organizing and archiving data. Attorneys often utilize software to remove hidden metadata from drafts of contract documents that they do not want disclosed to adversarial parties in contract or other negotiations.

MICROFICHE—

a sheet of film, usually 4 x 6 inches or 3 x 5 inches in size, containing miniaturized photographic images of printed text. The term "fiche" is synonymous with microfiche. "Ultrafiche" is a type of microfiche containing images that are reduced by a factor of 90 or more.

MICROFILM—

a film containing miniaturized photographic images of printed text. This is usually in a reel, but may also be in a cartridge or cassette form.

MICROFORM—

a general term describing miniaturized reproduction of printed text on film or paper. Microfilm and microfiche are specific types of microform.

MODEL CODES—

codes formulated by various groups or institutions to serve as model laws for legislatures. They are intended to improve existing laws or unify diverse state legislation.

MOOT POINT—

a point that is no longer a subject of contention and that is raised only for the purpose of discussion or hypothesis. Many law schools conduct moot courts where students gain practice by arguing hypothetical or moot cases.

MOTION—

a formal request made to a court pertaining to any issue arising during the pendency of a lawsuit.

MP3—

an acronym for "MPEG audio layer 3." It is a standard used to compress audio signals into a digital format for storage and transmission. It is a popular standard for converting, storing, and accessing music files.

NATIONAL REPORTER SYSTEM—

the collection of reporters published by West, which attempts to publish and digest all cases of precedential value from all state and federal courts.

NATURAL LANGUAGE—

an online database search strategy using normal English-language sentences or phrases instead of Boolean commands. Compare BOOLEAN LOGIC.

NEXIS—

the general and business news database of *LexisNexis*, a division of Reed Elsevier Inc. *Nexis* provides the full text of newspaper, magazine and newsletter articles, wire-service stories, and other items.

NISI PRIUS—

generally, a court where a case is first tried, as distinguished from an appellate court.

NOTER UP—

(1) the term used in the British Commonwealth countries for a citator; or (2) the name of the updating service for *Fundamentals of Legal Research* and *Legal Research Illustrated*.

OBITER DICTUM—

an incidental comment, not necessary to the formulation of the decision, made by the judge in his or her opinion. Such comments are not binding as precedent.

OFFICIAL REPORTS—

court reports directed by statute. Compare with UNOFFICIAL RE-PORTS.

OPEN ACCESS—

a publication model in which scientific and scholarly research is made available for free on the World Wide Web.

OPEN ID—

an open and decentralized computer standard that allows Internet users to create a single digital identity that can be utilized to log on to numerous websites supporting OpenID logins, rather than having a separate username and password for each website.

OPEN SOURCE—

a design method for computer programs in which the source code of the programs is made freely available to the public for others to use, modify, and distribute.

OPINION—

an expression of the reasons why a certain decision (the judgment) was reached in a case. A majority opinion is usually written by one judge and represents the principles of law that a majority of his or her colleagues on the court deem operative in a given decision; it has more precedential value than any of the following. A separate opinion may be written by one or more judges in which he, she, or they concur in or dissent from the majority opinion. A concurring opinion agrees with the result reached by the majority, but disagrees with the precise reasoning leading to that result. A dissenting opinion disagrees with the result reached by the majority and thus disagrees with the reasoning and/or the principles of law used by the majority in deciding the case. A plurality opinion (called a "judgment" by the Supreme Court) is agreed to by less than a majority as to the reasoning of the decision, but is agreed to by a majority as to the result. A per curiam opinion is an opinion by the court that expresses its decision in the case but whose author is not identified. A memorandum opinion is a holding of the whole court in which the opinion is very concise.

ORAL ARGUMENT—

a spoken presentation of reasons for a desired decision directed to an appellate court by attorneys for the parties.

ORDINANCE—

the equivalent of a municipal statute, passed by the city council and governing matters not already covered by federal or state law.

PAMPHLET SUPPLEMENT—

a paperbound supplement to a larger bound volume, usually intended to be discarded eventually.

PARALLEL CITATION—

a citation reference to the same case printed in two or more different reports.

PDF—

an acronym for "portable document format." It is a file format developed by Adobe Systems Incorporated that preserves the page layout, graphics, fonts, and appearance of the original source document.

PER CURIAM—

literally, "by the court." Usually a short opinion written on behalf of the majority of the court but whose author is not identified. It may be accompanied by concurring or dissenting opinions.

PERIODICAL—

a publication appearing at regular intervals. Legal periodicals include law school publications, bar association publications, commercially published journals, and legal newspapers.

PERMANENT LAW—

an act that continues in force for an indefinite time.

PERSUASIVE AUTHORITY—

a law or reasoning which a given court may, but is not bound to, follow. For example, decisions from one jurisdiction may be persuasive authority in the courts of another jurisdiction. Compare with MANDATORY AUTHORITY.

PETIT JURY—

a group of six, nine, or twelve persons that decides questions of fact in civil and criminal trials. Compare with GRAND JURY.

PETITION—

a formal, written application to a court requesting judicial action on a certain matter.

PETITIONER—

the person presenting a petition to a court, officer, or legislative body; the one who starts an equity proceeding or the one who takes an appeal from a judgment.

PLAINTIFF—

the person who brings a lawsuit against another.

PLEA BARGAINING—

the process whereby the accused and the prosecutor in a criminal case work out a mutually satisfactory disposition of the case. It usually involves the defendant's pleading guilty to a lesser offense or to only one or some of the counts of a multi-count indictment in return for a lighter sentence than that possible for the graver charge.

PLEADINGS—

the technical documents by which parties to a dispute frame the issue for the court. The plaintiff's complaint or declaration is followed by the defendant's answer; subsequent papers may be filed as needed.

POCKET SUPPLEMENT / POCKET PART—

a paperbound supplement to a book, inserted in the book through a slit in its back cover. Depending on the type of publication, it may have textual, case, or statutory references keyed to the original publication.

PODCAST—

a combination of the terms "iPod™" and "broadcast," it refers to a digital audio or video recording available on the Internet for downloading to a personal computer or portable media player.

POPULAR NAME TABLE—

a table listing popular names by which certain cases or statutes have become known, and identifying for each popular name the official name and citation of the case or statute.

PORTAL—

a website that is a starting point for users when they connect to the Web from which they can access other websites, databases, and electronic resources.

POWER OF ATTORNEY—

a document authorizing a person to act as another's agent.

PRECEDENT—

See STARE DECISIS.

PRELIMINARY PRINTS—

the name given to the advance sheets of the official *United States Reports*.

PRESENTMENT—

in criminal law, a written accusation made by the grand jury without the consent or participation of a prosecutor.

PRESIDENTIAL PROCLAMATION—

a declaration issued under specific authority granted to the president by Congress. Generally, it relates to matters of widespread interest. Some proclamations have no legal effect but merely are appeals to the public, e.g., the observance of American Education Week. See EXECUTIVE ORDER.

PRIMARY AUTHORITY—

the law itself: constitutions, statutes, case law, ordinances, and administrative regulations issued pursuant to enabling legislation. Primary authority may be either mandatory or persuasive. All other legal writings are secondary authority and are never binding on courts. See AUTHORITY; MANDATORY AUTHORITY; PERSUASIVE AUTHORITY.

PRIVATE LAW—

(1) an act that relates to a specific person, or (2) that body of law that concerns relations between private parties rather than governmental powers and functions. Compare PUBLIC LAW.

PROCEDURAL LAW—

the law which governs the operation of the legal system, including court rules and rules of procedure, as distinguished from substantive law.

PUBLIC LAW—

(1) an act that affects the public as a whole. It may be: (a) general (applicable to each person in the jurisdiction); (b) local (applicable to a specific geographic area); or (c) special (concerning an entity charged with a public interest), or (2) that body of law that concerns governmental powers and functions rather than relations between private parties.

RATIO DECIDENDI—

the point in a case that determines the result—the basis of the decision.

RECORD—

the documentation, prepared for an appeal, of the trial court proceedings (pleadings, motions, transcript of examination of witnesses, objections to evidence, rulings, jury instructions, opinion, etc.).

RECORDS AND BRIEFS—

See APPEAL PAPERS.

REGIONAL REPORTER—

a unit of the *National Reporter System* that reports state court cases from a defined geographical area.

REGULATIONS—

rules or orders issued by various governmental departments to carry out the intent of the law. Agencies issue regulations to guide the activity of their employees and to ensure uniform application of the law. Regulations are not the work of the legislature and do not have the effect of law in theory. In practice, however, because of the intricacies of judicial review of administrative action, regulations can have an important effect in determining the outcome of cases involving regulatory activity. United States Government regulations appear first in the *Federal Register*, published five days a week, and are subsequently arranged by subject in the *Code of Federal Regulations*.

RELIEF—

the remedy or redress sought by a complainant from a court.

REMAND—

the act of sending back for further proceedings, as when a higher court sends a case or claim back to a lower court.

REMOTE ACCESS—

the ability to use a computer in one location to connect and access information and files from a computer or network in a different location.

REPORTS—

(1) court reports—published judicial decisions organized on the basis of jurisdiction, court, period of time, subject matter, case significance, or some other grouping; and (2) administrative reports or decisions—published decisions of an administrative agency.

RESOLUTION—

a formal expression of the opinion of a rule-making body adopted by the vote of that body.

RESPONDENT—

the party who makes an answer to a bill in an equity proceeding or who contends against an appeal.

RESTATEMENTS OF THE LAW—

systematic restatements of the existing common law in certain areas, published by the American Law Institute since 1923. The restatements are valuable secondary research sources, but are not binding as law.

REVISED STATUTES—

in popular usage, a code. It is a collection of statutes that has been reorganized by subject matter and modified, as necessary, in order to create a harmonious body of law, while preserving the intent and meaning of each statute as originally enacted. In the process of preparing the revised statutes, all temporary and repealed acts are deleted. See also CODE; COMPILED STATUTES; CONSOLIDATED STATUTES.

RSS—

an acronym for "rich site summary" or "really simple syndication." It is a data format for distributing Web content in real-time. RSS feeds are available for blogs, news, judicial opinions, legislation, scholarly publications, and more. See also RSS READER.

RSS READER—

an online service that downloads and aggregates RSS data feeds in a format that users can read and share. See RSS.

RULES OF COURT—

the rules regulating practice and procedure before the various courts. In most jurisdictions, these rules are issued by the individual courts or by the highest court in that jurisdiction.

SANCTION—

(1) to assent to another's actions; (2) a penalty for violating a law.

SCOPE NOTE—

a notation appearing below a topic heading in a publication that delimits and identifies the content of the topic.

SEARCH ENGINE—

the hardware or software designed to search data for specific information. On the Internet, a search engine is a coordinated set of programs that seeks out website pages, indexes them, and enables searches for indexed pages to be run.

SECONDARY AUTHORITY—

See PRIMARY AUTHORITY.

SECTION LINE—

the subject of a key number in West's key number digests, printed after the key number.

SESSION LAWS—

laws enacted by a legislature that are published in bound or pamphlet volumes after adjournment of each regular or special session.

SHEPARDIZING—

a trademark of Reed Elsevier Properties Inc., descriptive of the general use of its Shepard's publications and citator services.

SLIP LAW—

a legislative enactment published in pamphlet or single sheet form immediately after its passage.

SLIP OPINION—

an individual judicial opinion published separately soon after it is decided.

SMS—

an acronym for "short message service." It is a wireless messaging service that allows users to send and receive short text messages to and from mobile devices. SMS messages are typically referred to as "text messages."

SOCIAL BOOKMARKING—

the act of saving and categorizing websites of personal interest through a Web-based bookmarking program that is open and accessible to others, rather than saving such sites on a personal Web browser. Social bookmarking facilitates the sharing of Internet bookmarks by allowing individuals to search and review each other's bookmarks and to add bookmarks saved by others to their own collections.

SOCIAL MEDIA—

the various Internet technologies and tools that users employ to interact and participate with others and to create and exchange content online.

SOCIAL NETWORKING—

in the online environment, it refers to the phenomena of individuals making social connections with other individuals and groups through a variety of Internet websites and other online social media.

SQUIB—

a very brief rendition of a single case or a single point of law from a case. Compare with HEADNOTE.

STAR PAGINATION—

a scheme in unofficial print and electronic editions of court reports used to show where the pages of the text of the official edition begin and end.

STARE DECISIS—

the common law doctrine that states that when a court has formulated a principle of law as applicable to a given set of facts, it will follow that principle and apply it in future cases where the facts are substantially the same. It connotes the decision of present cases on the basis of past precedent.

STATUS TABLE—

gives the current status of a bill or court proceeding.

STATUTES—

acts of a legislature. Depending upon its context in usage, a statute may mean a single act of a legislature or a body of acts that are collected and arranged according to a scheme or for a session of a legislature or parliament.

STATUTES AT LARGE—

the official compilation of acts passed by the U.S. Congress. The arrangement is currently by Public Law number, and by chapter number in pre–1951 volumes. This is the official print of the law for citation purposes where titles of the *United States Code* have not been enacted into positive law.

STATUTES OF LIMITATIONS—

laws setting time limits after which a dispute cannot be taken to court.

STATUTORY INSTRUMENTS—

English administrative regulations and orders. The term applies especially to the administrative rules published since 1939, supplementing the English administrative code, Statutory Rules and Orders.

STATUTORY RULES AND ORDERS—

English administrative regulations and orders.

STREAMING MEDIA—

digital audio or video files that are transmitted over the Internet in a consistent flow that allows the user to hear or view the files as they are in the process of being downloaded rather than waiting for entire files to download.

STYLE OF A CASE—

the parties to a lawsuit as they are written in the heading at the beginning of a written court document. Also known as the caption of a case.

SUBPOENA—

a court order compelling a witness to appear and testify in a certain proceeding.

SUBSTANTIVE LAW—

the law which establishes rights and obligations, as distinguished from procedural law, which is concerned with rules for establishing their judicial enforcement.

SUMMONS—

a notice delivered by a sheriff or other authorized person informing a person that he or she is the defendant in a civil action, and specifying a time and place to appear in court to answer to the plaintiff.

SUPERSEDE—

to displace or to supplant one publication or its segment with another.

SUPREME COURT—

(1) the court of last resort in the federal judicial system (the Supreme Court of the United States also has original jurisdiction in some cases); (2) in state judicial systems, except New York and Massachusetts, the highest appellate court or court of last resort.

SYLLABUS—

See HEADNOTE.

TABLE OF CASES—

a list of cases, arranged alphabetically by case names, with citations and references to the body of the publication where the cases are found or treated.

TABLE OF STATUTES—

a list of statutes with references to the body of the publication where the statutes are treated or construed.

TAGGING—

the act of assigning key-words, phrases or labels to pieces of data to assist users in processing or retrieving the data at a later time. It is a popular component of many social media and Web 2.0 applications.

TEMPORARY LAW—

an act that continues in force for a limited period of time.

TERM OF COURT—

the period of time prescribed by law during which a court holds session. The court's session may actually extend beyond the term. It often includes a reference to the time when the term begins. For example, the October Term of the Supreme Court of the United States, which is now the only term during which the Court sits, lasts from October to June or July.

TIFF—

an acronym for "tagged image file format." It is a common file format for storing and exchanging digital images, and is compatible with many image processing computer applications.

TRANSCRIPT OF RECORD—

the printed record compiled in each case of the proceedings and pleadings necessary for the appellate court to review the history of the case.

TREATISE—

a book-length exposition, which may be critical, evaluative, or interpretative, on a legal subject. Usually it is more thorough and authoritative than an encyclopedia article.

TREATY—

an agreement between two or more sovereign nations.

ULTRAFICHE—

See MICROFICHE.

UNIFORM LAWS—

proposed statutes drafted for adoption by the several states in the interest of uniformity. A considerable number of uniform laws on various subjects have been approved by the National Conference of Commissioners on Uniform State Laws (NCCUSL), and have been adopted by jurisdictions in the United States and its possessions. An example of a uniform law is the Uniform Commercial Code, which has been adopted, with some modifications, by forty-nine states.

UNIFORM SYSTEM OF CITATION—

See BLUEBOOK.

UNOFFICIAL REPORTS—

court reports published without statutory direction. They are not distinguished from official reports on grounds of varying quality or accuracy of reporting.

URL—

an acronym for "uniform resource locator." A URL is a standard address for a resource or site on the Internet. A URL such as http://www.tiddlywinks.com describes the access method used (http) and the location of the server hosting the site (www.tiddlywinks.com). The most common use of a URL is to enter it into a Web browser such as *Internet Explorer* or *Firefox*.

USER–GENERATED CONTENT—

online content that is created by individual users of websites, rather than by professional producers and editors of media content, such as broadcasting companies. Increased availability of Internet access and user-friendly software tools have led to an increase in user-generated content. Common examples of such content include blogs, wikis, and podcasts.

VENUE—

the particular geographical area where a court with jurisdiction may hear a case.

VERDICT—

the finding or decision of a jury in a civil or criminal case on the questions of fact submitted for their judgment.

VIRTUAL WORLD—

an online space that simulates the real world or creates a new fantasy world in which users interact with others through graphical representations of themselves known as "avatars." Virtual worlds have increasingly drawn the attention not only of individuals, but of educational institutions and business entities. An example of a virtual world is *Second Life*.

WEB—

See WORLD WIDE WEB.

WEB 2.0—

a concept describing the perceived transition of the World Wide Web from the first generation of websites that primarily offered static content to a second generation of Web-based services, such as social networking sites, blogs, and wikis, that encourage interaction, input, and collaboration by and among users.

WEB APPLICATION—

a computer application that is designed to run on an Internet web server and be viewed and accessed by users through an Internet web browser.

WEBCAST—

a live broadcast of an event, such as a training session, meeting, conference, or other multimedia presentation, transmitted over the Internet.

WEB PUBLISHING—

the process of preparing and uploading content that is to be displayed on the World Wide Web utilizing Internet tools and technology.

WESTLAW—

the CALR service produced by Thomson Reuters. *Westlaw* provides the full text of court decisions, statutes, administrative materials, *ALR* annotations, law review articles, Supreme Court briefs, and other items. Key-word searches, Boolean searches, natural language searches, field searches, and citation searches are available.

WI–FI—

an acronym for "wireless fidelity." It refers to wireless networking technology that utilizes radio waves to transmit Internet data within a relatively small area.

WIKI—

a website that facilitates collaboration and collective group effort in developing documents and other online content by allowing individual users to quickly edit, delete, supplement, and modify content published on the website. The term derives from the phrase "wiki wiki," which means "quick" in the Hawaiian language.

WORLD WIDE WEB OR WEB—

a global information retrieval system using hypertext links to connect text, graphic, sound, and multimedia files across the Internet. The Web is the major medium for publishing information on the Internet.

WRIT—

a written order, of which there are many types, issued by a court and directed to an official or party, commanding the performance of some act.

ZIP—

a common computer format for compressing digital files into a smaller size, which facilitates user storage and transmission of the files over the Internet.

*

FUNDAMENTALS

OF

LEGAL RESEARCH

*

Chapter 1

AN INTRODUCTION TO LEGAL RESEARCH

Legal research is the process of identifying and retrieving the law-related information necessary to support legal decision-making. In its broadest sense, legal research includes each step of a course of action that begins with an analysis of the facts of a problem and concludes with the application and communication of the results of the investigation.

Many types of information are needed to support legal decision-making. Although this book focuses on information sources that are concerned explicitly with law, legal decisions cannot be made out of their economic, social, historical, and political contexts. Today, legal decisions often involve business, scientific, medical, psychological, and technological information. Consequently, the process of legal research often involves investigation into other relevant disciplines.

This chapter, an introduction to legal research, explains why researchers seek certain types of information. This chapter explains the basic jurisprudential model upon which legal resources are designed, created, and collected, and introduces materials that are covered more comprehensively in subsequent chapters.

SECTION A. SOURCES OF LAW

American law, like the law of other countries, comes from a variety of sources. In the context of legal research, the term "sources of law" can refer to three different concepts. In one sense, the term sources of law refers to the origins of legal concepts and ideas. Custom, tradition, principles of morality, and economic, political, philosophical, and religious thought may manifest themselves in law. Legal research frequently must extend to these areas, especially when historical or policy issues are involved.

The term sources of law can also refer to the governmental institutions that formulate legal rules. The United States incorporates one national (federal) government, fifty autonomous state governments, and the local government of the District of Columbia. Although there are some variations in their structures, each of these governments has legislative, executive, and judicial components that interact with one another. Because all three branches of government "make law" and create legal information that is the subject of legal research, researchers must understand the types of information created by each branch and the processes through which that information is created.

Finally, sources of law can refer to the published manifestations of the law. The books, electronic databases, microforms, optical disks (CD–ROMs and DVDs), and other media that contain legal information are all sources of law.

1. The Nature of Legal Authority

Legal authority is any published source of law setting forth legal rules, legal doctrine, or legal reasoning that can be used as a basis for legal decisions.[1] In discussions about legal research, the term *authority* is used to refer both to the types of legal information and to the degree of persuasiveness of legal information.

When the term is used to describe types of information, legal authority can be categorized as *primary* or *secondary*.[2] Primary authorities are authorized statements of the law formulated by governmental institutions. Such authorities include the written opinions of courts (case law), constitutions, legislation, rules of court, and the rules, regulations, and opinions of administrative agencies. Secondary authorities are statements about the law and are used to explain, interpret, develop, locate, or update primary authorities. Treatises, articles in law reviews and other scholarly journals, *American Law Reports (A.L.R.)* annotations, restatements of the law, and looseleaf services are examples of secondary authorities.[3]

When the term is used to describe the degree of persuasiveness of legal information, authority is an estimation of the power of information to influence a legal decision. In this sense, authority can be termed *binding* (also called *mandatory*), meaning that a court or other decision-maker believes the authority applies to the case before it and must be followed; or authority can be considered *persuasive*, meaning that a decision-maker can, if so persuaded, follow it.

Only primary authority can be binding; but some primary authority will be merely persuasive, depending on the source of the authority and its content. Secondary authority can never be binding, but can be persuasive. The application of legal authority to individual problems is a complex and often controversial process. Variations in the facts of individual cases enable judges, influenced by their own philosophies and perspectives, to exercise wide discretion in interpreting and applying legal authority.[4]

2. The Common Law Tradition

The American legal system, like those of most English-speaking countries, is part of the *common law* tradition. The common law is the body of law that originated and developed in England and spread to those countries that England settled or controlled. Historically, the common law was considered to be the "unwritten law" and was distinguished from the

---

[1] Thomas B. Marvell, Appellate Courts and Lawyers 129 (1978).

[2] When used in this sense, the terms *authority* and *source* are interchangeable.

[3] Other types of relevant information, such as historical, economic, and social science information, are also sometimes referred to as secondary authorities. Such materials are often sources of law and thus used in legal argument.

[4] For an excellent, but dated, explanation of why courts cite authority and a discussion of the authority of various legal sources, see John Henry Merryman, *The Authority of Authority,* 6 Stan. L. Rev. 613 (1954). For an examination of how one noted jurist used authority, see William H. Manz, *Cardozo's Use of Authority: An Empirical Study,* 32 Cal. W. L. Rev. 31 (1995).

"written," or statutory, law. The common law was an oral tradition derived from general customs, principles, and rules handed down from generation to generation and was eventually reflected in the reports of the decisions of courts. The English common law arrived in America with the colonists who used it as a basis for developing their own law and legal institutions.[5] English common law is still cited as authority in American courts.[6]

The common law tradition should be contrasted with the *civil law* tradition, which is based on Roman law and predominates in continental Europe and other western countries. Common and civil law systems differ in their theories about the sources of law, the relative persuasiveness of the sources, and the ways in which the sources are used in legal reasoning. For example, in legal systems that are part of the civil law tradition, the legislature creates a comprehensive code of legal principles that represents the highest form of law, and there is a presumption that code provisions apply to every legal problem.[7] In common law systems, there is no presumption that statutes or codes cover all legal problems; many legal principles are discoverable only through the "unwritten," or common law.

3. Case Law and the Doctrine of Precedent[8]

a. *Structure of the Court System.* On the federal level, and in the states, there are hierarchical judicial systems in which some courts have jurisdiction, or control, over other courts. The typical court structure consists of three levels,[9] and it is important to understand what types of information are created at each level and where that information can be found.

Trial courts are courts of original jurisdiction that make determinations of law and of fact, with juries often making the determinations of fact. Documents prepared by the parties, called *pleadings* (complaint, answer, interrogatories, among others) and *motions*, are filed before, during, and after a trial; *exhibits* are submitted into evidence during the trial; and a *record* (or transcript) is made. Although pleadings, motions, exhibits, and records were usually only available directly from the court in which the litigation was conducted, some of these documents now are obtainable electronically from various governmental and commercial sources. After a trial, the trial court issues a judgment or decision and sometimes a written opinion; the opinions of trial courts are infrequently published, reported, or otherwise made generally available to the public.[10]

---

[5] For general histories of American law, see LAWRENCE M. FRIEDMAN, A HISTORY OF AMERICAN LAW (3d ed. 2005); LAWRENCE M. FRIEDMAN, AMERICAN LAW IN THE 20TH CENTURY (2002); and KERMIT L. HALL, THE MAGIC MIRROR: LAW IN AMERICAN HISTORY (2d ed. 2008).

[6] *See* Chapter 22 of this book for a discussion of basic legal research in the United Kingdom.

[7] JOHN HENRY MERRYMAN, THE CIVIL LAW TRADITION 23–25 (3d ed. 2007).

[8] Case law is discussed extensively in the following chapters of this book: Chapter 4, Court Reports; Chapter 5, Federal Court Reports; Chapter 6, State Court Reports and the National Reporter System; and Chapter 7, Digests for Court Reports.

[9] A chart included in Chapter 4, Section D, of this book depicts the federal judicial system and a typical state judicial system.

[10] Many legal researchers are surprised to learn that written opinions are not issued in all cases, and that only a small percentage of written opinions are published and reported. For a more complete discussion of this subject, see Chapter 4, Section A, of this book.

Intermediate appellate courts, often called circuit courts or courts of appeal,[11] have authority over lower courts within a specified geographical area or jurisdiction. Appellate courts generally will not review factual determinations made by lower courts, but will review claimed errors of law that are reflected in the record created in the lower courts. Appellate courts accept written *briefs* (statements prepared by the counsel arguing the case) and frequently hear *oral arguments*. Some large law libraries collect copies of the briefs filed in appellate courts. Intermediate appellate courts often issue written opinions that are sometimes published and found in law libraries and electronic sources. Many appellate courts have the discretion to determine on a case-by-case basis whether to publish opinions. Rules of court in each jurisdiction specify whether "unpublished" opinions can be cited as authority.

A court of last resort, typically called a supreme court, is the highest appellate court in a jurisdiction. State courts of last resort are the highest authorities on questions of state law, and the Supreme Court of the United States is the highest authority on questions of federal law. Many libraries make available in paper or electronic format copies of the briefs and records filed in the Supreme Court of the United States and of the court of last resort in the state in which they are located. Transcripts of the oral arguments in these courts also are available in some law libraries and on the Internet. Courts of last resort usually issue written opinions that are almost always published, collected by libraries, and made available electronically.

b. *Federal and State Jurisdiction.* There are some matters over which a state or federal court have exclusive jurisdiction and some matters over which a state court has concurrent jurisdiction with the federal courts. Federal courts can, in some instances, decide questions of state law; state courts can, in some instances, decide questions of federal law. For both the beginning law student and the experienced attorney, it can be difficult to determine which matters are questions of federal law, which are questions of state law, and which can be subjects of both. In researching any particular problem, legal information of various types may be needed from both state and federal sources.

c. *Precedent.* In the early history of English law, the custom developed of considering the decisions of courts to be *precedents* that would serve as examples, or authorities, for decisions in later cases with similar questions of law. Under what has come to be called the *doctrine of precedent,* the decision of a common law court not only settles a dispute between the parties involved but also sets a precedent to be followed in future cases.[12] According to an older, now discredited, theory, judges merely declared what had always been the law when they decided a case. It is now generally

---

[11] Some states have no intermediate appellate courts; appeals go directly to the courts of last resort in these states.

[12] The bare skeleton of an appeal to precedent is easily stated: "The previous treatment of occurrence X in manner Y constitutes, *solely because of its historical pedigree,* a reason for treating X in manner Y if and when X again occurs." Frederick Schauer, *Precedent,* 39 STAN. L. REV. 571 (1987). For a discussion of the early development of the doctrine of precedent, see M. ETHAN KATSH, THE ELECTRONIC MEDIA AND THE TRANSFORMATION OF LAW 33–39 (1989).

acknowledged that judges often create new law when applying precedent to current problems.

The doctrine of precedent is closely related to three other concepts represented by the Latin terms *stare decisis, ratio decidendi,* and *dictum.*

Stare decisis, literally "to stand on what has been decided," is the principle that the decision of a court is binding authority on the court that issued the decision and on lower courts in the same jurisdiction for the disposition of factually similar controversies. In the hierarchical federal and state court systems, therefore, the decisions of a trial court can control future decisions of that trial court, but they do not control other trial courts or appellate courts. Appellate courts can bind themselves and lower courts over which they have appellate jurisdiction, but appellate courts cannot bind other appellate courts at the same level.[13]

The *ratio decidendi* is the holding or the principle of law on which the case was decided. It is the *ratio decidendi* that sets the precedent and is binding on courts in the future. Unlike legislatures, American courts do not promulgate general propositions of law, nor do they respond to hypothetical questions. Rather, courts decide actual cases and controversies, and the rules they announce are tied to specific fact situations. Therefore, the *ratio decidendi,* or rule of the case, must be considered in conjunction with the facts of the case.

In contrast, *dictum* (or *obiter dictum*) is language in an opinion that is not necessary to the decision. *Dictum* comes from the Latin verb *decire,* "to

[13] For the views of a former U.S. Supreme Court justice regarding the importance of *stare decisis,* see Lewis F. Powell, Jr., *Stare Decisis and Judicial Restraint,* 47 WASH. & LEE L. REV. 281 (1990). *See also* William N. Eskridge, Jr., *The Case of the Amorous Defendant: Criticizing Absolute Stare Decisis for Statutory Cases,* 88 MICH. L. REV. 2450 (1990); Lawrence C. Marshall, *Contempt of Congress: A Reply to the Critics of an Absolute Rule of Statutory Stare Decisis,* 88 MICH. L. REV. 2467 (1990); David K. Koehler, *Justice Souter's "Keep–What–You–Want–and–Throw–Away–the–Rest" Interpretation of* Stare Decisis, 42 BUFF. L. REV. 859 (1994); Amy L. Padden, *Overruling Decisions in the Supreme Court: The Role of a Decision's Vote, Age, and Subject Matter in the Application of Stare Decisis After* Payne v. Tennessee, 82 GEO. L.J. 1689 (1994); Robert C. Wigton, *What Does It Take to Overrule? An Analysis of Supreme Court Overrulings and the Doctrine of Stare Decisis,* 18 LEGAL STUD. F. 3 (1994). For an empirical study of why justices of the Supreme Court of the United States chose to alter precedent during a 47–year period, see SAUL BRENNER & HAROLD J. SPAETH, STARE INDECISIS: THE ALTERATION OF PRECEDENT ON THE SUPREME COURT, 1946–1992 (1995). For an article that argues that justices are not influenced by landmark precedents with which they disagree, see Jeffrey A. Segal & Harold J. Spaeth, *The Influence of* Stare Decisis *on the Votes of United States Supreme Court Justices,* 40 AM. J. POL. SCI. 971 (1996), which is a portion of an entire issue devoted to *stare decisis.* For the economic effect of *stare decisis,* see Thomas R. Lee, *Stare Decisis in Economic Perspective: An Economic Analysis of the Supreme Court's Doctrine of Precedent,* 78 N.C. L. REV. 643 (2000).

For an extensive sociological inquiry into the importance of precedent, including the need for attention to computer technology, see SUSAN W. BRENNER, PRECEDENT INFLATION (1991); Susan W. Brenner, *Of Publication and Precedent: An Inquiry into the Ethnomethodology of Case Reporting in the American Legal System,* 39 DEPAUL L. REV. 461 (1990). *But see* Michael Wells, *The Unimportance of Precedent in the Law of Federal Courts,* 39 DEPAUL L. REV. 357 (1990). For an attempt to describe precedent and its applications, see Ruggero J. Aldisert, *Precedent: What It Is and What It Isn't; When Do We Kiss It and When Do We Kill It?* 17 PEPP. L. REV. 605 (1990). *See also* Lawrence C. Marshall, *"Let Congress Do It": The Case for an Absolute Rule of Statutory Stare Decisis,* 88 MICH. L. REV. 177 (1989); Note, *Constitutional Stare Decisis,* 103 HARV. L. REV. 1344 (1990); Evan H. Caminker, *Why Must Inferior Courts Obey Superior Court Precedents?,* 46 STAN. L. REV. 817 (1994).

say," and refers to what is "said by the way," that which is not essential to the holding of the court. Although language categorized as *dictum* is not binding on future courts, it might be persuasive. Yesterday's *dictum* may develop into today's doctrine.

It is often difficult to distinguish the *ratio decidendi* of a case from *dictum*. The determination of what is the *ratio decidendi,* and what is *dictum,* is a focus of much legal analysis and is often the critical point of legal argument.

Courts have much leeway in interpreting cases put forth as binding precedent.[14] No two cases are exactly the same, and, on one or more points, every case can be distinguished from others. Generally, a case is considered binding if it shares the same significant facts with the case at issue and does not differ in any significant facts from the instant case. Furthermore, similar issues must be presented in the two cases and the resolution of those issues must have been necessary to the decision in the previous case (otherwise, the words of the court would be *dictum*). Courts can reject cases put forth as binding authority by distinguishing the cases on their facts or issues, thus finding that the previous cases are different from the instant case in some significant way.[15] In some situations, a court can avoid being bound by a previous case by finding that the rule put forth in the previous case is no longer valid and overruling it.

The doctrine of precedent assumes that decisions of common law courts should be given consideration even if they are not binding. Accordingly, researchers often look to relevant decisions in other states, jurisdictions, and even other common law countries. Cases that are not directly on point may contain principles or legal theories on which legal arguments can be based. Decisions that are not binding, either because they have different fact situations or because they are from another jurisdiction, can be persuasive because of the depth of analysis and quality of reasoning in the opinion. Among other factors that can determine the persuasiveness of a non-binding opinion are the location and position of the court that issued the opinion, the identity of the jurist writing the opinion, the agreement (or lack thereof) among individual members of the court (i.e., unanimous decisions versus split decisions), and subsequent judicial and academic treatment of the opinion.

Policy considerations supporting the doctrine of precedent include the resulting fairness, as it encourages similar cases to be treated similarly; the predictability and stability it encourages within the legal system; and its efficiency in terms of time and energy as it enables decision-makers to take

---

[14] In a chapter entitled "The Leeways of Precedent," Karl Llewellyn presented "a selection of [sixty-four] available impeccable precedent techniques" used by courts to follow, avoid, expand, or redirect precedent. KARL N. LLEWELLYN, THE COMMON LAW TRADITION: DECIDING APPEALS 77–91 (1960).

[15] *See generally* Kent Greenawalt, *Reflections on Holding and Dictum,* 39 J. LEGAL EDUC. 431 (1989). The practice of judges writing separately, generally in the hopes of laying the groundwork for a reversal or to demonstrate why one rationale may be better than another, is becoming commonplace. For some observations on this trend, see Laura Krugman Ray, *The Justices Write Separately: Uses of the Concurrence by the Rehnquist Court,* 23 U.C. DAVIS L. REV. 777 (1990); and Ruth Bader Ginsburg, *Remarks on Writing Separately,* 65 WASH. L. REV. 133 (1990).

advantage of previous efforts and prior wisdom.[16] Critics argue that a reliance on precedent can result in a rigid and mechanical jurisprudence that can force us to treat unlike cases as if they were similar; that the doctrine of precedent can perpetuate outmoded rules; and that its inherently conservative nature can impede the law from being responsive to new social needs.[17]

Notwithstanding these criticisms, the doctrine of precedent remains the foundation upon which our models of legal research are constructed. The written opinions of courts, particularly appellate courts, are the "stuff" of legal argument and the major source of legal doctrine. Consequently, they are the primary, but certainly not the only, objects of legal research. Law libraries and legal electronic databases are filled with published court opinions, along with secondary sources and index tools to help researchers find, interpret, and update opinions that are relevant to particular fact patterns.

4. Legislation and the Interpretation of Statutes[18]

a. *Legislation.* A *statute,* sometimes referred to as legislation, is a positive statement of legal rules enacted by a legislature. In comparison, a *constitution* is the fundamental body of principles, most often written, by which a political body, such as a nation or state, governs itself. Because many of the basic concepts and techniques of statutory and constitutional research are similar, they can be discussed together at an introductory level. However, American constitutional law, both federal and state, is a pervasive and specialized subject; including it in a general discussion of legislation should not obscure either its importance or its uniqueness.

In English law, the king enacted the earliest statutes with the concurrence of his council; later, the role of statute-maker was assumed by Parliament. In the United States, statutes are enacted by the legislative branch and signed into law by the chief executive. The growth of statutory law has reflected the impact of the industrial revolution, as it became apparent that a jurisprudence based only on judicial decisions could not meet the needs of a growing, dynamic society. Situations developed in which answers were needed that were not found in court reports, or the answers found in court reports either no longer met current needs, or resulted in actions that were considered unjust.

Statutes, and collections of statutes arranged by subject called *codes,* have become very important in common law systems; and American law combines both statutory and case law. Statutes are used to create new areas of law; to fill gaps in the law; and to change court-made rules. However, unlike civil law systems, in the American legal system there is no presumption that a statute will apply to every legal problem or that codes are comprehensive statements of the law.

[16] *See* John Henry Merryman, *The Authority of Authority, supra* note 4, for a discussion of the benefits of following precedent.

[17] *See* Steven M. Barkan, *Deconstructing Legal Research: A Law Librarian's Commentary on Critical Legal Studies,* 79 LAW LIBR. J. 617 (1987).

[18] Constitutions and legislation are discussed in the following chapters of this book: Chapter 8, Constitutional Law and the Supreme Court of the United States; Chapter 9, Federal Legislation; Chapter 10, Federal Legislative Histories; Chapter 11, State and Municipal Legislation.

b. *Statutory Interpretation.* Courts play predominant roles in interpreting and applying statutes and in extending the law to subjects not expressly covered by statutes. The legislature may state a general legal rule in the form of a statute, but it is the judiciary that interprets the general rule and applies it to specific cases. Under the doctrine of precedent, it is the statute as *interpreted by the courts* that is applied in the next case. In theory, if the legislature disagrees with the way a court has interpreted a statute, the legislature should revise the statute.[19]

Statutory interpretation is an important part of legal research.[20] Researchers must not find only the statutes applicable to a problem, but also must find information that will help determine what the statutes mean and how they should be applied. After looking for the "plain meaning" of the words of a statute,[21] and applying traditional canons or principles of statutory interpretation to the text of the statute,[22] researchers resort to a number of approaches to statutory interpretation.

An important method of statutory interpretation is to look for judicial opinions that have construed the specific statute. The persuasiveness of interpretive opinions depends on the similarity of facts involved and on the courts issuing the opinions. Legislatures sometimes pass laws that are designed to reflect existing common law rules; in such situations judicial opinions that pre-date the statute are useful aids to interpretation.

Researchers often attempt to identify the legislature's purpose in passing a statute and the legislature's intended meaning for specific statutory provisions. To do this, researchers look at the *legislative history* of the statute—documents, such as the original bill and revisions thereto, revised versions of bills and legislative debates, hearings, reports, and other materials, created by the legislature while the statute was under consideration—for evidence of legislative purpose and intent.[23] Although controversy exists over their proper use,[24] legislative histories are often consulted by lawyers and judges and are frequently used in legal argument.

Researchers also search for cases from other jurisdictions that have interpreted similar statutes. Although these opinions are not binding

---

[19] Guido Calabresi, A Common Law for the Age of Statutes 31–34 (1982).

[20] On statutory construction in general, see F. Reed Dickerson, The Interpretation and Application of Statutes (1975); Norman J. Singer, Statutes and Statutory Construction (6th ed. 2000); Kent Greenawalt, Legislation: Statutory Interpretation: 20 Questions (1999); and William N. Eskridge, Jr. et al., Legislation and Statutory Construction (2000). For a variety of views on the role of statutory construction, see *Symposium on Statutory Interpretation*, 53 SMU L. Rev. 1 (2000).

[21] Some states have "plain meaning" statutes that attempt to limit courts in their interpretation of statutes that are unambiguous on their face. For an example, see Or. Rev. Stat. § 174.010 *et seq.* (2007).

[22] Karl Llewellyn provided an extensive listing of canons of construction to demonstrate that, since legal arguments suggest that there can be only one correct meaning of a statute, there are two opposing canons on every point. Karl N. Llewellyn, *supra* note 14, at 521–35.

[23] The usual components of a legislative history are described in detail in Chapter 10 of this book.

[24] *See* Peter C. Schanck, *An Essay on the Role of Legislative Histories in Statutory Interpretation*, 80 Law Libr. J. 391, 414 (1988); Philip P. Frickey, *From the Big Sleep to the Big Heat: The Revival of Theory in Statutory Interpretation*, 77 Minn. L. Rev. 241 (1992); James J.

authority, well-reasoned opinions from other courts can be very persuasive. This approach is consistent with the doctrine of precedent, under which the decisions of other common law courts may be considered, even if they are not binding.

5. Administrative Law[25]

The third major institutional source of law is the executive branch of government. The President of the United States and the governors of the states issue orders and create other documents with legal effect. Executive departments and offices, and administrative agencies, establishments, and corporations all create legal information.

Administrative agencies, which exist on the federal and state levels, are created by the legislative branch of government and are usually part of the executive branch. A number of independent agencies, establishments, and corporations exist within the executive branch but are not considered to be executive departments.[26] For the most part, federal agencies handle matters of federal law and state agencies handle matters of state law, but there is often interaction between federal and state agencies. Administrative agencies conduct activities that are in nature both legislative and adjudicative, as well as executive. Under the authority of a statute, these agencies often create and publish rules and regulations that further interpret a statute. Agencies may also make determinations of law and fact in controversies arising under the statute and, like courts, publish opinions.

Administrative law can be a very complex area to research. Not only will researchers need to find, interpret, and update the rules, regulations, and decisions created by the administrative agency, but they will also need to find, interpret, and update the legislation the agency is administering and judicial opinions that interpret those rules, administrative adjudications, and legislation.

SECTION B. THE MATERIALS OF LEGAL RESEARCH

Published legal resources can be divided into three broad categories: (1) primary sources or authorities;[27] (2) secondary sources; and (3) index, search, or finding tools. All of these "published" legal resources can appear in more than one format, including printed books, electronic databases, digital images, microforms, compact disks (CD–ROMs and DVDs), videos, and audiocassettes. Many resources contain more than one type of information and serve more than one function. For example, some electronic

---

Brudney, *Congressional Commentary on Judicial Interpretations of Statutes: Idle Chatter or Telling Response?*, 93 Mich. L. Rev. 1 (1994). *But see* J. Myron Jacobstein & Roy M. Mersky, *Congressional Intent and Legislative Histories: Analysis or Psychoanalysis?*, 82 Law Libr. J. 297 (1990). *See also* Chapter 10 of this book.

[25] Research in administrative law is discussed in Chapter 13 of this book.

[26] The Federal Communications Commission, the Interstate Commerce Commission, and the Securities and Exchange Commission are among the many independent federal establishments and corporations. The United States Government Manual contains a complete list of executive agencies, independent establishments, and government corporations. A wealth of information about and from all branches of the federal government is available at the Government Printing Office website, *GPO Access*, at http://www.access.gpo.gov.

[27] As noted earlier, the terms *authorities* and *sources* are interchangeable when referring to types of legal materials.

resources and looseleaf services include both primary authority and secondary materials; they are, at the same time, designed to be finding tools. An understanding of how legal materials are structured and organized (regardless of the media in which they are published) is necessary to effective legal research.

1. Primary Sources

As noted earlier in this chapter, primary sources are authoritative statements of legal rules by governmental bodies. They include opinions of courts, constitutions, legislation, administrative regulations and opinions, and rules of court. Because many primary sources are published in the order they are issued with little or no subject access, secondary sources and indexing tools are needed to identify and retrieve them.

2. Secondary Sources[28]

Secondary sources are materials about the law that are used to explain, interpret, develop, locate, or update primary sources. These sources are published both in paper and electronic formats. The major types of secondary sources are treatises, restatements, looseleaf services, legislative histories, law reviews and other legal periodicals, legal encyclopedias, *American Law Reports (A.L.R.) annotations, and legal dictionaries. Secondary sources can be interpretive and may contain textual analysis, doctrinal synthesis, and critical commentary of varying degrees of persuasiveness. Depending upon the reputation of the author or publisher, some secondary sources, such as restatements, scholarly treatises, and journal articles, are often persuasive to a court.[29] In contrast, practice manuals and legal encyclopedias have little persuasive value but are useful for basic introductions to subjects, for concise or "black letter" statements of legal rules, and for practical advice. Secondary sources can be used as finding tools to locate other information. For example, cases cited in treatises, law review articles, and encyclopedias can lead to other cases.*

3. Index, Search, and Finding Tools[30]

Index, search, and finding tools help locate or update primary and secondary sources. The major types of finding tools are digests (to locate cases discussing similar points of law), annotations in annotated statutes and codes,[31] citators, and legal periodical indexes. Index, search, and finding tools are *not* authority and should never be cited as such.

[28] Secondary sources are discussed in the following chapters of this book: Chapter 10, Federal Legislative Histories; Chapter 14, Looseleaf Services; Chapter 16, Legal Encyclopedias; Chapter 17, American Law Reports; Chapter 18, Legal Periodicals and Indexes; Chapter 19, Treatises, Restatements, and Model Codes; and Chapter 20, Practice Materials and other Resources.

[29] It should be noted, however, that the writings of legal scholars are generally not held in the same high levels of esteem in common law systems as in civil law systems. *See* JOHN HENRY MERRYMAN, *supra* note 7, at 56–60.

[30] In this book, index, search, and finding tools are discussed in conjunction with the resources they are designed to locate. Two chapters, however, are devoted to specific finding tools: Chapter 7, Digests for Court Reports; and Chapter 15, Citators.

[31] Do not confuse annotated statutes, which have brief annotations, or "squibs," describing cases that interpret statutory provisions, and annotated reports, such as A.L.R., which have lengthy interpretive annotations of cases.

Looseleaf services and computer-assisted legal research (CALR) systems, such as *Westlaw* and *LexisNexis*, are among the most valuable finding tools. They must be distinguished from other finding tools because they contain the full text of primary authorities, as well as materials from secondary sources.

4. American Law Publishing

a. *Proliferation of Materials.* In the colonial period of American history, law books were extremely scarce and consisted mostly of English law reports. The most extensive law book collections numbered from 50 to 100 volumes.[32] As the country spread westward and the economy changed from agrarian to industrial, greater demands were made upon courts and legislatures, and the body of American legal literature grew proportionately.[33]

Extraordinary growth has occurred in the quantity of primary legal materials. During the period from 1658 to 1896 American courts reported 500,000 decisions;[34] by 1990 there were 4,000,000 reported decisions. By 2000, the number exceeded 6,000,000. In 1950, 21,000 cases were published, and it is estimated that over 220,000 cases are now published annually. Congress and the state legislatures produce huge amounts of statutory law every year, and federal and state administrative agencies produce thousands of rulings and regulations. Many of these primary authorities are published in multiple sources. The quantities of secondary sources and other law-related materials have expanded proportionately. The flood of legal publications has caused concern to the legal profession for over 100 years, but little has been done to stem the proliferation of legal materials.[35]

b. *Official and Unofficial Publications.* American legal resources, whether books, electronic databases, or other media, can be divided into those that are *official,* and those that are *unofficial.* This distinction is important but often misunderstood. An official publication is one that has been mandated by statute or governmental rule. It might be produced by the government, but does not have to be. Citation rules[36] often require both official and unofficial citations, but the authority of official and unofficial publications is equivalent.

Unofficial publications of cases, statutes, and regulations are often more useful than official publications. Unofficial publications of primary

---

[32] ALBERT J. HARNO, LEGAL EDUCATION IN THE UNITED STATES 19 (1953); LAWRENCE M. FRIEDMAN, A HISTORY OF AMERICAN LAW 474–82 (3d ed. 2005). For thorough discussions of early American law book publishing, see ERWIN C. SURRENCY, A HISTORY OF AMERICAN LAW PUBLISHING (1990); and Jenni Parrish, *Law Books and Legal Publishing in America, 1760–1840,* 72 LAW LIBR. J. 355 (1979).

[33] For an indication of the growth in size of academic law libraries, see J. Myron Jacobstein & Roy M. Mersky, *An Analysis of Academic Law Library Growth Since 1907,* 75 LAW LIBR. J. 212 (1982); GLEN-PETER AHLERS, THE HISTORY OF THE LAW SCHOOL LIBRARY IN THE UNITED STATES: FROM LABORATORY TO CYBERSPACE (2002).

[34] 1 CENTURY DIGEST iii (1897).

[35] For a discussion of the problems of excessive reporting, see J. Myron Jacobstein, *Some Reflections on the Control of the Publication of Appellate Court Opinions,* 27 STAN. L. REV. 791 (1975).

[36] *See* Chapter 24 for a discussion of legal citation form.

authorities are published more quickly and usually include editorial features and secondary information that help interpret the primary sources, along with important locating or finding tools.

c. *Law Publishers.* Private publishers traditionally have dominated American law publishing; the decade of the 1990s began a period of mergers, acquisitions, and consolidation for the publishing industry. Many of the trade names under which resources were originally published have been retained. Although the law publishing industry is dominated by a relatively small number of large publishers, the advent of the Internet and the World Wide Web has led to a plethora of both public and private electronic publishing ventures of varying degrees of reliability, accuracy, and comprehensiveness.

The largest private publisher of legal information is the Thomson Reuters Corporation, which acquired the West Publishing Company and several other legal publishers formerly known as the West Group.[37] Thomson Reuters produces the *National Reporter System* (the largest and most comprehensive collection of federal and state judicial opinions), the *American Digest System,* an electronic research service called *Westlaw,* annotated statutes, treatises, legal encyclopedias, law school textbooks, and many other resources. The West Publishing Company, which developed its resources around a theory of comprehensive reporting, has played such an important role in legal publishing that some scholars claim West influenced the development of American law.[38] Among the trade names acquired by Thomson Reuters are: Bancroft Whitney; Banks Baldwin; Clark Boardman Callaghan; Foundation Press; Lawyers Cooperative Publishing; and Thomson/West; West Publishing Company; and West Group.[39]

Other major commercial legal publishers, and some of the trade names under which they publish, include: Reed Elsevier (Anderson; Butterworths; Lexis Law Publishing; LexisNexis; Matthew–Bender; Shepard's); Wolters Kluwer Law & Business (Aspen; CCH); and the Bureau of National Affairs (BNA).[40]

5. Evaluating Legal Resources

When inspecting and evaluating legal resources, it is important to determine and understand the purposes the resources were designed to serve. An awareness of the functions, features, interrelationships, strengths, and weaknesses of resources, whether they are traditional paper resources or electronic resources, is valuable for effectively conducting legal research. Is the resource part of a set, or is it designed to be used with other resources? Does it have finding tools or special features, such as

[37] Foundation Press, the publisher of this book, is a subsidiary of Thomson Reuters.

[38] *See* GRANT GILMORE, THE AGES OF AMERICAN LAW 58–59 (1977); Robert C. Berring, *Full–Text Databases and Legal Research: Backing into the Future,* 1 HIGH TECH. L.J. 27 (1986); Steven M. Barkan, *Can Law Publishers Change the Law?* 11(3/4) LEGAL REFERENCE SERVICES Q., 1991, at 29.

[39] To avoid confusion that might result from the various brand names that have been applied in recent years to Thomson Reuters products (West, West Group, Thomson/West, Thomson Reuters, etc.), this book identifies the publisher of these products as "West," unless otherwise noted.

[40] An extensive listing of law publishers and their corporate affiliations can be found at http://www.aallnet.org/committee/criv/resources/tools/list/.

indexes and tables? Is the text searchable electronically? How is the resource updated, and when was it last updated? The credibility of the author, editor, publisher, or producer should be considered, together with the types of authority (primary and secondary) included and the potential persuasiveness of the authority. With the expansion of resources available on the World Wide Web, evaluating resources for accuracy, credibility, and currency is increasingly important.[41]

SECTION C. AN ESSENTIAL SKILL

In 1992, a special task force of the American Bar Association on law schools and the legal profession issued a report that stated that "[i]t can hardly be doubted that the ability to do legal research is one of the skills that any competent practitioner must possess."[42] That report also stated that "[i]n order to conduct legal research effectively, a lawyer should have a working knowledge of the nature of legal rules and legal institutions, the fundamental tools of legal research, and the process of devising and implementing a coherent and effective research design."[43]

Furthermore, the ABA's *Model Rules of Professional Conduct* provide: "A lawyer shall provide competent representation to a client. Competent representation requires the legal knowledge, skill, thoroughness, and preparation reasonably necessary for the representation."[44]

Clearly, a lawyer must be able to research the law to provide competent representation. In addition to issues of professional responsibility, questions relating to competency in legal research may arise in legal malpractice actions in which an attorney is sued for failing to know "those plain and elementary principles of law which are commonly known by well-informed attorneys, and to discover the additional rules which, although not commonly known, may readily be found by standard research techniques."[45] Issues relating to an attorney's competence in legal research also have been raised in claims for malicious prosecution,[46] and in claimed violations of the Sixth Amendment right to effective assistance of counsel.[47]

The ability to use fundamental legal research tools and to implement an effective and efficient research plan must become part of every lawyer's training if she or he is to provide competent representation and uphold the standards of the legal profession.

[41] Chapter 23 provides additional discussion of evaluating resources available on the Internet.

[42] LEGAL EDUCATION AND PROFESSIONAL DEVELOPMENT: AN EDUCATIONAL CONTINUUM, REPORT OF THE TASK FORCE ON LAW SCHOOLS AND THE PROFESSION: NARROWING THE GAP 163 (1992). This is most often referred to as the *MacCrate Report* after its chair, Robert MacCrate. The full text of the section of the report discussing legal research is reproduced in Appendix F of this book.

[43] *Id.*

[44] MODEL RULES OF PROFESSIONAL CONDUCT, Rule 1.1 (1983).

[45] Smith v. Lewis, 13 Cal. 3d 349, 530 P.2d 589, 118 Cal. Rptr. 621 (1975). In this malpractice case, the plaintiff received a judgment of $100,000 against the defendant lawyer in connection with his negligence in researching the applicable law.

[46] *See, e.g.,* Sheldon Appel Co. v. Albert & Oliker, 47 Cal. 3d 863, 765 P.2d 498, 254 Cal. Rptr. 336 (1989) (plaintiff in a malicious prosecution action unsuccessfully arguing, among other things, that lack of probable cause for an action may be established by showing that the former adversary's attorney failed to perform reasonable legal research before filing a claim).

[47] *See, e.g.,* People v. Ledesma, 43 Cal. 3d 171, 729 P.2d 839, 233 Cal. Rptr. 404 (1987).

Chapter 2

THE LEGAL RESEARCH PROCESS*

Legal research is as much art as science; it calls for strategy as well as serendipity. There are many approaches to legal research, and there is no single, or best way to conduct legal research. Methods vary according to the nature of the problem and depend on the researcher's subject expertise and research skills.

Approaches to legal research also may be shaped by the availability of research materials. Knowledge of alternative research tools is valuable, because researchers do not always have access to all of the different paper, microform, or electronic resources described in this book. Moreover, preferred resources do not, at times, produce the expected results.

Regardless of one's level of expertise in a particular field of law, a lawyer encounters problems involving unfamiliar subjects. The capacity to solve legal problems rapidly and accurately is developed best by constructing a systematic approach to legal research.

The processes of legal research and legal writing are closely related.[1] Legal research is often wasted if the results are not communicated effectively. Legal research informs legal writing, and legal writing is meaningless without accurate content. Many differing viewpoints exist about how the disciplines of legal research and legal writing interrelate. Some researchers prefer to conduct most of their research before beginning to write. Others prefer to write as they conduct their research.

This chapter presents a general approach to legal research that can be modified and applied to most problems and can be merged with various approaches to legal writing. The approach is resource-neutral in that it can be applied to research in books, electronic resources, or a combination of media. In the end, researchers must develop research and writing methodologies that are most effective for their needs.

A GENERAL APPROACH TO LEGAL RESEARCH

A general approach to legal research, which can be modified to accommodate most problems, can be broken down into four basic steps. These are:

---

* The general approach to legal research described in this chapter was conceptualized by Professor Ervin Pollack in the first and second editions of this book. *See* ERVIN H. POLLACK, FUNDAMENTALS OF LEGAL RESEARCH 13–20 (1956); ERVIN H. POLLACK, FUNDAMENTALS OF LEGAL RESEARCH 14–18 (2d ed. 1962).

[1] *See* Chapter 3 for an introduction to the forms and processes of legal writing.

STEP 1. Identify and analyze the significant facts.

STEP 2. Formulate the legal issues to be researched.

STEP 3. Research the issues presented.

STEP 4. Update.

This discussion focuses on each of these steps individually; each step, however, is closely related to the others. Legal research, moreover, is rarely a linear process. It often is necessary to revisit previous steps and revise and refine previous work.

1. STEP 1: Identify and Analyze the Significant Facts

The researcher's first task is to identify and analyze the facts of the problem. Some facts have legal significance; others do not. The process of legal research begins with compiling a descriptive statement of legally significant facts. It is often difficult for a beginner to identify significant facts and to discard insignificant ones. Consequently, when researching a problem in an unfamiliar area of the law, it is usually best to err on the side of over-inclusion rather than exclusion.

Factual analysis is the first step in identifying the legal issues that will be researched. Factual analysis also enables a researcher to locate access points to the available resources. Which volumes are relevant? Which subjects should be consulted in indexes and tables of contents? Which words should be used in an initial search of an electronic database? Which websites should be examined? An experienced researcher is able to identify issues and appropriate subjects; the beginning researcher, who does not have the experience to examine a fact pattern and readily categorize it and formulate legal issues, needs to devote more time and attention to this activity.

Inexperienced legal researchers might tend to skim over the facts and immediately begin researching. No productive research can be done outside a particular fact pattern. Most controversies are over facts, not law; and cases are most often distinguished on their facts. Rules stated by courts are tied to specific fact situations, and they must be considered in relation to those facts. Because the facts of a legal problem control the direction of research, the investigation and analysis of facts must be incorporated into the research process. Taking the time to identify relevant facts and writing them down in some narrative form is usually a worthwhile investment of time and energy.

The TARP Rule. A useful technique is to analyze facts according to the following factors:

T–Thing or subject matter;

A–Cause of **action** or ground of defense;

R–Relief sought;

P–Persons or **parties** involved in the problem.

Thing or subject matter. The place or property involved in a problem or controversy may be important. Thus, when a consumer is harmed after taking a prescription drug, the drug becomes an essential fact in the dispute.

Cause of action or ground of defense. Identify the claim that might be asserted or the defense that might be made. For example, the cause of action might involve a breach of contract, negligence, intentional infliction of emotional distress, or some other legal theory giving rise to litigation.

Relief sought. What is the purpose of the lawsuit? It might be a civil action in which the party bringing the suit is seeking monetary damages for an injury, or an action in which a party is asking the court to order another party to do a specific act or to refrain from doing a specific act. Alternatively, the litigation may be a criminal action brought by the state.

Persons or parties involved in the problem; their functional and legal status and relationship to each other. The parties or persons might be individuals, or might be a group that is significant to the solution of the problem or the outcome of the lawsuit. Similarly, the relationship between the parties, such as exists between husband and wife or employer and employee, might be of special importance.

2. STEP 2: Formulate the Legal Issues to Be Researched

This is the initial intellectual activity that presumes some knowledge of the relevant substantive law and, consequently, the point at which inexperienced legal researchers are most likely to have trouble. The goal is to classify or categorize the problem into, first general, and then increasingly specific, subject areas and to begin to hypothesize legal issues. For example, is this a matter of civil or criminal law? Federal or state law? Does the litigation involve contracts or torts, or both? If torts, is it a products liability or a negligence case? Problems are often not easily compartmentalized; problems can fall into more than one category, and categories affect each other.

a. *Get an Overview.* To assist in formulating issues, it is useful to consult general secondary sources for an overview of relevant subject areas. These sources can include national legal encyclopedias, a state encyclopedia, treatises, looseleaf services, or one or more subject periodicals or journals. The best choice varies according to the researcher's background, but it is wise to start with the most general and work to the more detailed and specific. These secondary sources can provide valuable background information and can direct a researcher to issues and to primary sources. Be sure to note any constitutional provisions, statutes, administrative regulations, and judicial and administrative opinions cited by these sources. At this preliminary stage of research, these secondary sources provide background information and help formulate issues; they are the tools, not the objects of research.

Writing a clear, concise statement of each legal issue raised by the significant facts is an important and difficult task. Failure to frame all issues raised by a particular set of facts can result in incomplete and inadequate research. It is better, when framing the issues, for a beginner to err on the side of formulating too many issues. Insignificant issues can always be eliminated after they have been thoroughly investigated, and overlapping issues can be consolidated.

b. *Create an Outline.* Once statements of the issues have been drafted, they should be arranged in a logical pattern to form an outline. Logically related issues might be combined as sub-issues under a broader main issue. Issues that depend upon the outcome of other issues should be arranged accordingly. The outline should be expanded, modified, and revised as research progresses. As a particular issue is researched, it might be found to be too broad; the statement of the issue should then be narrowed. It might also be necessary at times to split an issue into two, or to divide an issue into sub-issues. Alternatively, an original issue might be deemed too narrow and unlikely to lead to any relevant information. In such instances, the issue should be broadened. Many times, during the process of research, it becomes apparent that issues not originally considered are relevant. The task of framing issues is, thus, an ongoing one.

3.　STEP 3: Research the Issues Presented

After the facts are analyzed and the probable issues are framed, it is time to begin researching the first issue.

a. *Organize and Plan.* Although serendipity can play an important role in legal research, good legal researchers, as a rule, are systematic, methodical, and organized, and they keep good records. Every researcher must develop a system for taking and organizing notes.

For each issue, decide which sources to use, which sources not to use, and the order in which sources should be examined. A good practice would be to write down all sources to be consulted for each issue, even if sources are repeated. As relevant information is found, its source and relevance should be recorded, and the legal research outline accordingly expanded. Maintaining an accurate list of sources consulted, terms and topics checked, and updating steps taken prevents inefficient uses of time and omissions of crucial information.

Frequently, it is not possible to research each issue completely before moving on to the next issue. It is common to move back and forth between issues, revising and refining them. As a general practice, it is best to research each issue completely before moving to the next issue. The ongoing nature of legal research emphasizes the importance of good note taking, record-keeping, and organization.

It is often very tempting to include information in a written product that has taken many hours to develop, but which ultimately is irrelevant to a proper analysis of the issues. Any number of legal research leads may ultimately prove to be irrelevant to a resolution of the issues; irrelevant information detracts from, and often masks, analysis that is directly on point.

b. *Identify, Read, and Update All Relevant Constitutional Provisions, Statutes, and Administrative Regulations.* Identifying and reading relevant constitutional provisions, statutes, and administrative regulations provides the framework on which the rest of the research is built. These primary sources can be identified in several ways.

● *Statutory Compilations.* Statutory compilations almost always include tables of contents and indexes listing the subjects and topics covered by the statutes. Because relevant statutory provisions are often found in several places in the compiled statutes, consult both the table of contents and the index.

● *Electronic Legal Research.* The full text of the *United States Code, Code of Federal Regulations, Federal Register*, and statutes of the states are available on the Internet free of charge and are also available on *Westlaw*, *LexisNexis*, and other fee-based electronic sources.

● *Secondary Sources.* Secondary sources, such as encyclopedias, treatises, looseleaf services, and law review articles, commonly cite relevant constitutional provisions, statutes, and administrative regulations. Depending upon the scope of the inquiry, secondary sources that focus on the law of one state or on federal law may prove especially valuable. Electronic versions of many secondary sources are available on *Westlaw*, *LexisNexis*, and other commercial electronic services.

It will not always be easy to identify all relevant statutes at the beginning of a research project. Indexing problems sometimes make it difficult to match concepts with indexing terms. Sometimes issues are too vague or underdeveloped to ensure that relevant statutes are identified. Accordingly, research involving relevant constitutional provisions, statutes, and administrative regulations should be continually undertaken and issues and strategies modified accordingly.

c. *Identify, Read, and Update All Relevant Case Law.* After relevant constitutional provisions, statutes, and administrative regulations are identified and read, case law that interprets and applies those forms of enacted law, as well as other case law that is relevant to the fact situation, must be located.

Do not limit research to cases that support a particular position. A competent researcher anticipates both sides of an argument and identifies cases that result in contrary conclusions. In many situations, the same case can be interpreted to support both sides of an issue; the argument may involve the question of whether the holding is to be broadly or narrowly applied, or whether the facts of the cases can be distinguished. It is common, however, for sides to argue that entirely different lines of cases are controlling.

The goal, at this stage of research, is to compile a comprehensive, chronological list of relevant opinions for each issue. Because no two cases are exactly alike, it is unlikely for a researcher to find cases with identical fact patterns to the situation at hand. The most relevant judicial opinions come from the same court or superior appellate courts in the jurisdiction in question, as they are the only cases that are potentially binding. Next in importance are judicial opinions, which might be persuasive, from other courts and jurisdictions dealing with similar facts, statutes, and issues. Even if binding, authoritative cases are located, persuasive authority from other jurisdictions might support an argument, particularly if the opinions are from well-known and respected judges. Reading cases chronologically can reveal background information that is not necessarily repeated in each case, show the development of the case law, and point to the ''lead'' case that is cited in other opinions.

Cases that interpret statutes can be identified in several ways.

● *Annotated Statutes and Codes.* Annotated statutes and codes list interpretive cases after each statutory provision.

● *Treatises and Looseleaf Services.* Treatises and looseleaf services, particularly if they involve the law of a state being researched or a federal law that is the topic of an inquiry, cite cases that interpret the statutes they discuss.

Citators. Citation services, such as *Shepard's* and *KeyCite*, can provide a list of cases that have cited the statute.

● *Computer–Assisted Legal Research (CALR).* Materials available in *Westlaw* and *LexisNexis* and in other electronic resources can be searched for cases that have cited a particular statute.

● *Other Sources.* A.L.R. annotations and legal encyclopedias often can provide relevant case citations. Relevant cases providing statutory interpretation can also be identified with finding tools, such as digests, which contain a subject arrangement of abstracts of cases that can be accessed through a table of contents and a descriptive-word index.

Once a relevant case is identified, other cases on the same subject can be located through several techniques. These techniques include: tracing the key numbers used in that case through West's digests or *Westlaw* to find other cases with the same key numbers; using *KeyCite, Shepard's,* and CALR systems as citators to find other citing cases; and consulting the tables of cases in treatises, looseleaf services, encyclopedias, and digests.

As each case is read and briefed, its full citation, parallel citations, judge and court issuing the opinion, date of the decision, relevant facts, holding, summary of the court's reasoning, key numbers assigned, and sources cited by the court should be recorded. Each case should be incorporated into the legal research outline.

d. *Refine the Search.* After primary sources are identified, read, and organized, secondary sources can be used to refine the search and expand the argument. Invariably, new cases and lines of argument appear. Treatises, law review articles, and restatements of the law are not binding authority, but they can be persuasive and can provide ideas on how best to utilize the primary sources. If the problem involves a statute, the legislative history might suggest the legislature's intent in passing the act and the problem the law was intended to remedy. Historical, social, economic, and political information can put legal arguments in their proper context and can support policy arguments.

4.   STEP 4: Update

The importance of updating legal research warrants special attention. Law changes constantly. Legislatures pass new statutes and modify old ones. Each appellate court decision creates new law, refines the law, reaffirms the law, or changes the law; researchers must be aware of the most recent decisions on the subject they are researching. Research that is current today may be out of date tomorrow. Few lawyers would disagree that failure to update legal research can be careless and negligent, and sometimes leads to disastrous results.

Citation services, such as *KeyCite* and *Shepard's*, should be used to update the status of cases, statutes, and regulations; electronic databases, such as *Westlaw* and *LexisNexis*, should be consulted, as well as pocket parts and supplements, looseleaf services, and advance sheets, to determine whether the authorities have been interpreted or modified, or whether new cases, statutes, or regulations have been published.

5. When to Stop

The question of when to stop researching is a difficult one. With experience, researchers develop insight into the point at which further legal research is unproductive. In many instances an obvious repetition of citations or absence of new information suggests that enough research has been done. However, there is no uniform rule on how extensive research should be, and knowing when to stop is a skill that only develops over time.

Occasionally, researching a problem in all conceivable sources is needless, unwarranted, or repetitious. It is possible to over-research a problem. All cases are not of equal importance; much information is redundant. Including too much information can obscure important points. Furthermore, many simple problems do not call for exhaustive research. Common sense and professional insight play significant roles in legal research.

In the last analysis, research skills are measured as much by the knowledge of what can be omitted as by which research materials are used and how they are used. The attorney's stock in trade is time; a skilled legal researcher knows how to use it wisely.[2]

---

[2] For an in-depth discussion of when to stop researching, see Christina L. Kunz, *Terminating Research,* 2 Persp.: Teaching Legal Res. & Writing 2 (1993).

Chapter 3

COMMUNICATING RESEARCH RESULTS THROUGH WRITING*

———————

This chapter briefly describes the types and forms of legal writing, describes common strategies for legal writing, discusses the general process of legal writing, and provides a list of selected legal writing sources.

SECTION A.   INTRODUCTION

As observed in the previous chapter, the processes of legal research and legal writing are closely related. A written product is very often the goal of performing research, and the quality of research fundamentally affects the quality of writing. And of course, legal analysis is intertwined as well, for a researcher who does not understand what question to answer does not identify relevant sources, and a writer who does not think clearly cannot write clearly.

Because writing is so intimately connected with research, this chapter presents a broad overview of the types of and general process of legal writing. Complete coverage of the craft of legal writing is beyond the scope of this research book. For that the reader is referred to the many excellent resources on the nuts and bolts of legal writing, as well as its theory and rhetoric (see the end of the chapter for a selective list).

Legal writing begins with research and analysis. A piece of legal writing must convince the reader that the writer understands the problem discussed; that the writer has identified the issues and sub-issues and the key facts and the unknowns; that the writer has researched and analyzed the relevant law; and that the writer has considered the appropriate arguments and counterarguments. Above all, the writing must persuade the reader that the writer's conclusions are valid.

SECTION B.   TYPES OF LEGAL WRITING

Lawyers (and other legal writers, from law students to judges) produce many different types of written work, for different audiences and different purposes. A fundamental distinction among the types is that between *objective* writing and *persuasive* writing. In objective or predictive writing, the author provides a neutral analysis of the law governing a certain situation and predicts the likely outcome. For example, a summer associate in a law firm might write an office memorandum to a supervising attorney

———————

* Mary A. Hotchkiss, Director of Academic Advising and Senior Lecturer, University of Washington School of Law, and Mary Whisner, Reference Librarian, Gallagher Law Library, University of Washington School of Law, wrote this chapter.

addressing one issue facing a client, exploring possible legal claims and defenses, and predicting how a court would resolve them, whether favorably or unfavorably for the client. Persuasive writing, on the other hand, is analysis with an agenda. The writer's goal is to convince or persuade the reader to make a particular decision. For example, if the client is sued, then the attorney might prepare a motion for summary judgment with a memorandum of law that tries to convince the judge to rule for the client.

It is important to note that objective and persuasive analysis and writing are closely related. In an objective document, the writer analyzes the arguments of both sides in order to predict the outcome. In a persuasive document, the writer still needs to address and resolve the arguments of both sides—this time, in order to advocate one position and counter the opposing arguments. This is why the approach to research suggested in Chapter 2 advised researchers not to limit their research to cases that support a particular position. Both objective and persuasive legal writing follow certain conventions, such as citing authority for statements of law.

SECTION C.　FORMS OF LEGAL WRITING

1.　Memoranda

Memoranda are generally written for an internal audience (a supervising attorney within a firm or agency or, in the case of a bench memo, a judge). They analyze a legal problem, presenting both sides objectively. An objective memo should provide the reader with a balanced analysis of key authorities governing a legal issue.

Suppose a firm is considering whether or not to take on a case. To evaluate chances of success and to advise the client about her options, the lawyers need to research the applicable law. A senior lawyer might assign to an associate or a summer clerk the task of researching and writing a memorandum that outlines the facts and summarizes the law in the area, looking at both sides of the issue. The memo should state the facts that are assumed and areas where further investigation would be important. The memo should cite cases and other legal authority, carefully working through the legal analysis. A sample outline is below. (In some offices or for some projects, supervising attorneys prefer other formats.)

The senior attorney will use the memo to help make a decision. It will also go in a file as the basis of later work. Sometimes attorneys write memos to themselves—or to the file—with varying levels of formality, for just the same purposes.

[Illustration 3–1]

SAMPLE MEMORANDUM OUTLINE

To:
From:
Date:
Re: *Should include name of client, nature of matter or claim, and procedural status, if appropriate.*

I. **Question(s) Presented** – *Should identify the legal issue starting with the claim, crime, or defense, and summarizing the key facts relating to the disputed issue.*

II. **Brief Answer(s)** – *Should respond directly to the question presented and provide an objective summary of the analysis, indicating degree of certainty.*

III. **Statement of Facts** – *Should include the relevant facts in chronological order. May also suggest unknown facts that may be important to the issue.*

IV. Discussion
   a. Begin with an inclusive, introductory, thesis paragraph that states the issues and predicts an outcome without analyzing the law. (The thesis establishes the "road map" for the analysis.)
   b. First issue (sample): Is a demonstrator vehicle used by the dealer's sales staff covered under Washington State's Lemon Law which covers only "new motor vehicles"?
      i. Present the authority (rule + support)
         1. describe cases and explain how the rule has worked in previous cases
         2. include cases that demonstrate what scenarios will and will not satisfy the rule
      ii. Rule application (may include counter-arguments)
   c. Second issue: XXX
      i. Present the authority (rule + support)
         1. describe cases and explain how the rule has worked in previous cases
         2. include cases that demonstrate what scenarios will and will not satisfy the rule
      ii. Rule application (may include counter arguments)
   d. Continue the structure as needed.

V. **Conclusion** – *Should recap your conclusions and restate your prediction on the outcome of the matter. The conclusion should not introduce new material or simply repeat the brief answer(s).*

2. Client or Opinion Letters

Client or opinion letters are written for an outside audience (a client). Their goal is to explain the law in plain English. A well-written client letter should provide sufficient information and options for the client to make an informed decision.

Typically a client letter begins with an opening paragraph that restates the client's question and provides a brief answer. The paragraphs that follow review the relevant facts and explain the relevant law. Then the writer outlines various options available to the client. If needed, the letter may request additional information from the client. A closing paragraph summarizes the letter. The letter should ensure that the reader understands issues of attorney-client confidentiality. A warning to the client not to share the letter with other readers will preserve the confidentiality.

[Illustration 3–2]

SAMPLE CLIENT LETTER

Ross, Marsh & Foster
Attorneys at Law
Marysville, WA 98270

March 20, 2008

Ms. Becky Smith
Box 215
Marysville, WA 98270

Dear Ms. Smith:

I have researched the possibility that the dealer will be required to replace or repurchase your 2006 Ford Explorer. The failure of the car's power steering is considered a serious safety defect under the Washington State Lemon Law (Wash. Rev. Code § 19.118.010). In my opinion we can make a strong argument that the dealer's actions to date do not meet either the manufacturer's or the statutory warranty. While I cannot guarantee that a court will agree with this opinion, I am optimistic that a lawsuit would be successful if you wish to proceed.

Before I explain the law and your various options, I would like to review the facts. When you purchased the Explorer, it had been used as a dealer's demonstrator vehicle. It was still under the manufacturer's warranty.

[The text of other key facts, explanation of the law, and various remedies have been deleted.]

Please talk these options over with your family and friends and give me a call if you have any questions or concerns. *Please note that you should not show this letter to them in order to preserve attorney-client confidentiality.* After you have had a chance to think over the options, please set up an appointment so I can help you decide which remedy to pursue. We need to make a decision no later than July 31, 2008, because there is a time limit by which we must initiate litigation.

Sincerely yours,

---

3. Demand Letters

Demand letters are letters in which a lawyer explains his or her client position and requests that the recipient take some action (or risk being sued). These letters are moving along the continuum from objective towards persuasive writing. A demand letter by its nature requires a level, professional tone.

The general structure of a demand letter is an opening paragraph, introducing the dispute and relevant facts, followed by an explanation of the client position. The letter should make a specific demand and delineate the consequences of noncompliance.

[Illustration 3–3]

SAMPLE DEMAND LETTER

Ross, Marsh & Foster
Attorneys at Law
Marysville, WA 98270

June 1, 2008

Ford Motor Company
Customer Relationship Center
P.O. Box 6248
Dearborn, Michigan 48126

Certified Mail – Return Receipt Requested

Dear Customer Relationship Representative:

On September 9, 2006, Ms. Becky Smith purchased a 2006 Ford Explorer from Sheehy Ford in Marysville, Washington, for $27,090. Within three months she started experiencing significant problems with the power steering. The dealer "fixed" the problem three times (January 2007, May 2007, and September 2007).

[Text with additional facts has been deleted.]

Failure of power steering on a vehicle is considered a serious safety defect under the Washington State Lemon Law (Wash. Rev. Code § 19.118.010). Based on the above facts, demand is hereby made that you refund the sum of $27,090 to Ms. Smith in full.

Please be advised that failure to comply with this request may subject you to the following remedies available under Washington law: actual damages; civil penalty up to twice the actual damages; and court costs and attorneys fees.

Sincerely yours,

4. Litigation Documents

Litigation documents are varied. For instance, a *complaint* initiates a case by alleging facts and asking for relief; an *answer* responds to the complaint (perhaps by denying the facts); a *motion for summary judgment* asks a court to rule on some or all of the legal issues in a case before trial, based only on affidavits and stipulated facts; a *memorandum of points and authorities* in support of a motion (also known as brief in support of a motion) presents legal arguments; and an *appellate brief* argues for the reversal or affirmance of a trial court decision. The goal of each of these documents is ultimately to convince a judge to rule in the client's favor.

It is beyond the scope of a legal research text to describe the formats and rhetorical standards for all of these documents. For now, let us simply emphasize that all of these documents depend upon sound research and analysis. In fact, if the claims in a complaint are not supported by existing law or by a non-frivolous argument for the extension or modification of existing law, then the attorney who signs the complaint may be liable for sanctions.[1]

---

[1] *See, for example,* Fed. R. Civ. P. 11 and corresponding state rules. For a discussion of cases in which judges criticize attorneys for inadequate research, among other things, see Mary Whisner, *When Judges Scold Lawyers,* 96 LAW LIBR. J. 557 (2004).

5. Transactional Documents

Transactional documents are documents that themselves have legal effect. They are termed "transactional" because they implement transactions. For example, *contracts* spell out the terms of a sale or other agreement—and potentially make a party liable if it breaches the contract; *leases* provide for the length of time something will be rented, the amount one party must pay the other, which party is responsible for repairs, and so on—and, again, a party can be liable if it does not abide by the terms of the document. In a sense, one could consider a lease to be a special type of contract—a contract for one party to rent property to another in exchange for rent. Other special types of contracts include employment contracts, licenses, and retainer agreements. *Wills, trusts*, and other estate planning tools are also considered transactional documents, even though the recipient of the property that is transferred might not be aware of the "transaction" until many years after the document is written.

6. Academic Writing

Academic writing includes formal scholarship in treatises, monographs, and periodicals. Examples of this genre of legal writing can fall anywhere on the spectrum from objective to persuasive. Some treatise authors, for instance, take a very strong position on what the law should be, while others adopt a more descriptive approach.[2]

Scholarly legal writing tends to be heavily footnoted, citing some authority to support almost every proposition. The footnotes are a boon for researchers but contribute to the impression that these works are not ideal beach reading.

Traditionally, law reviews have used the term "article" only for articles written by professionals—generally professors, lawyers, and judges. Articles can discuss doctrinal law or more theoretical issues. Like treatises, they can be strongly opinionated or more objective. The pieces by students are typically (but not always) shorter than articles and are usually called "notes," "comments," or "recent developments." Many law reviews also have a section for book reviews.

While these traditional forms of writing still predominate in law reviews, recent decades have seen new forms included in law reviews, such as personal narratives, fictional narratives, and poetry.[3]

7. Other Legal Writing

Other legal writing can include a wide array of materials aimed at lawyers and other legal researchers. Lawyers develop outlines, checklists, or guides in various areas, often to support a presentation for a continuing legal education (CLE) program. Lawyers also write manuals, handbooks, and deskbooks—materials aimed at practitioners. Others write opinion pieces, commentary, and editorials for legal newspapers and bar association publications. These works are less scholarly than law reviews and treatises.

[2] For a discussion of treatises, see Chapter 19.

[3] For a discussion of legal periodicals, see Chapter 18.

Some lawyers also write for publication in new media, such as firm web pages and blogs.

SECTION D. COMMON STRATEGIES FOR LEGAL WRITING

As discussed above, there are a number of common forms of legal writing—memoranda, client letters, briefs, and so on. Some writing strategies serve writers well across the different forms. First, begin with threshold issues. For example, the question of liability will not matter if the court does not have jurisdiction over the dispute or the statute of limitations has run. The rules of dividing property upon divorce do not need to be explained if the parties' marriage was invalid.

Another common strategy is to discuss simple issues before complex issues. Often these simple issues lay the groundwork for the more intricate issues. Using the example from above, in a divorce, the distribution of a jointly owned savings account is a much simpler issue than child custody.

Legal issues and arguments are often complex. A writer can help the reader by using rhetorical devices that serve as roadmaps and signposts. In a memorandum or brief, the "questions presented" section gives readers a roadmap to what follows. In a memorandum or brief, the subheadings or point headings serve as signposts to guide readers. In a client letter, the introductory paragraph serves as a roadmap and, depending on the length of the letter, subheadings provide additional pointers. Similarly, in a law review article, an introduction or abstract serves as a roadmap.

To guide the readers through their arguments, good legal writers use a thesis paragraph at the beginning of each complex issue to outline the sub-issues. Navigational headings at the beginning of each major section serve as signposts.

Note that the outline you use to organize your notes as you are researching does not bind you to that order when you write. Even though you research a particular issue first, you might choose to discuss it last—e.g., because another issue would be dispositive.

SECTION E. THE GENERAL PROCESS OF WRITING

1. How the Writing Project Shapes Research

A researcher can become more efficient by bearing in mind the written product he or she hopes to create. There are several ways in which the anticipated work product should shape the research:

a. *The writing project affects the length, depth, or breadth of the research.* What issues will be discussed? What sort of support will be needed for each? How thorough should the work be? For example, an article in a bar journal might say, "At least a dozen states have adopted laws allowing doctors to apologize to patients without the apology being introduced as evidence in a civil trial," and provide no specific citations, while a law review article would need citations to each state's code.

b. *The writing project affects the notes the researcher takes.* For example, if one is writing a brief in a jurisdiction that requires parallel citations to cases in an official and a regional reporter, then one should include the parallel citations in notes. If a writing project is going to take a semester instead of a day, one might take more thorough notes, writing down the dates that different sources were consulted to make it easier to bring everything up to date before the project is finalized.

c. *The writing project can affect the order of the research.* For instance, finding a clear, determinative answer to a jurisdictional question might obviate (or at least reduce) the need to research other questions.

d. *The writing project affects the types of sources consulted.* A seminar paper might be greatly enhanced by material from history and economics that would seldom be cited in a practice manual.

2. Organizational Devices

Effective organization and good note-taking aid research, analysis, and writing. Many devices exist for organizing the multitude of cases, statutes, regulations, and other authorities one needs for a major research and writing project. Some are low-tech (e.g., drawing a grid on a legal pad, using separate legal pads or creating separate documents for separate issues). Students with a technical bent might prefer to use software to help them organize their notes (e.g., creating an outline in word processing with hypertext links to cases). While no one method works for everyone, it is important to have *some* method to keep track of the sources you have consulted and the index terms or searches you have tried, what you found, and how current the material was.[4] Researchers should always note the information that will be needed for correct citation form later. Research notes do not have to be in polished form but these notes should record the critical elements: author, title, date, reporter citation, court, etc.[5]

a. *A Structured Research Log.* Using a structured research log encourages researchers to think strategically about their research and writing process. For example, the few moments spent in preliminary analysis, writing down the primary issue, key facts, and words and phrases, and determining the jurisdiction and level of prior knowledge, rather than going online immediately, will save both time and money. The notes that document the relevant primary sources are critical to developing one's legal analysis. However, it is not enough to take notes; whatever note-taking method is adopted, researchers should routinely review their notes as a way to organize both their writing and their follow-up research. These routine reviews can also be used as time- and project-management tools. When working on a project, one needs to set aside sufficient time for researching, drafting, additional research, revising, editing, verification, and proofreading. While there is no substitute for experience in determining the appropriate mix of research and writing time, using a research log helps even novice writers think through the process more strategically. Here is a sample research log template:

---

[4] *See* Penny A. Hazelton et al., *Develop the Habit: Note–Taking in Legal Research*, 4 PERSP.: TEACHING LEGAL RES. & WRITING 48 (1996); Peter Jan Honigsberg, *Organizing the Fruits of Your Labor: The Honigsberg Grid*, 4 PERSP.: TEACHING LEGAL RES. & WRITING 9 (1996); and Mary Whisner, *Managing a Research Assignment*, 9 PERSP.: TEACHING LEGAL RES. & WRITING 9 (2000).

[5] For a discussion of legal citation form, see Chapter 24.

[Illustration 3–4]

SAMPLE RESEARCH LOG: LEMON LAW PROJECT

Preliminary Analysis – Identify the issue(s), key facts, words & phrases for searching, and jurisdiction, and assess your prior knowledge related to the project

<u>Initial Issue Statement</u>: When a car sold under warranty by a dealership has been repeatedly repaired does the consumer have the right to demand that the dealership buy back or replace the car?

<u>Key facts</u>: Vehicle purchased in 2006 for $27,090. 12,000 miles on odometer; had been used as a dealership demonstrator. Still under manufacturer's warranty. Problems with power steering. Numerous unsuccessful repairs. Dealership beginning to ignore client's complaints.

<u>Words and Phrases</u>: Vehicle, Automobile, Warranty, Purchaser, Consumer, Consumer Protection, Defect, Lemon Law, Repair, Replace, Refund

<u>Jurisdiction</u>: Washington State

<u>Knowledge Assessment:</u> Took Contracts; talked briefly about warranties and remedies. Know nothing specific about Lemon Law or Washington State consumer protection

Project_details – Date project is due; requester's name and contact information; estimate of time to spend on the project; sensitivity to client's needs and budget; format of final work product, etc.

General Plan – Notes from intake from assigning attorney: consult secondary sources for general overview and citation to relevant primary sources. To save time, use state-based practitioner materials when available. Then follow up, first examining relevant statutes in an annotated code and then examining relevant case law. Refine your analysis and update your authorities while you research.

---

b. *Case Analysis Chart.* Another organizational tool many researchers find effective during the analytical, prewriting stage is developing a case analysis chart. A case analysis chart allows the comparison of cases across categories of procedure, facts, and holdings. This helps the researcher see analogies and distinctions among cases and spot patterns of fact scenarios that satisfy or don't satisfy a legal rule. As an organizational tool, the case analysis chart assists researchers in condensing and tracking key information about a given group of cases.[6]

---

[6] *See* Tracy McGaugh, *The Synthesis Chart: Swiss Army Knife of Legal Writing*, 9 Persp.: Teaching Legal Res. & Writing 80 (2001).

[Illustration 3–5]

SAMPLE CASE ANALYSIS CHART: LEMON LAW

Case Title and Citation	*Chrysler Motors v. Flowers*, 116 Wash. 2d 208	*Ford Motor Co. v. Barrett*, 115 Wash. 2d 556	*Meyers v. Volvo*, 852 A.2d 1221
Court & Date	WA Sup. Ct. 1991	WA Sup. Ct. 1990	Pa. Superior 2004
Procedural Posture	Review of Summary Judgment	Superior Ct affirmed arbitration board; State AGO intervened to defend statute	Review of Summary Judgment
Is vehicle covered under the statute?	Yes, if car is new or under 24,000-mile warranty limitation	Ford conceded defect but contested statute's constitutionality	Volvo qualifies as "new motor vehicle" under PA Automobile Lemon Law
Previously titled?	No	No	No
Warranty in effect?	Yes	Yes	Yes
Number of repairs?	Eight	unknown	Four
Sent to arbitration?	Yes	Yes	Not applicable under PA

    c. Approaches to Organization. Effective legal writing must synthesize multiple authorities (and accurately cite them) to support its analysis. One common organizational tool is IRAC (Issue, Rule, Application, Conclusion). The outline of the rule of law forms the outline of the analysis. For each issue and sub-issue, the writer identifies the rules of law and any elements that must be met. Next the writer applies the rule to the key facts, showing how these facts meet (or do not meet) the required elements. Finally, the author states a conclusion. The writer also determines whether cases or authorities that go against her position can be distinguished.

    Although IRAC is a common tool, it is not the only one,[7] nor is it always appropriate. One expert on legal writing describes IRAC as a "form of deductive reasoning appropriate to an objective analysis in an office memorandum" and CRAC, "Conclusion, Rule, Application of the legal rule to facts, and Conclusion," as the paradigm appropriate for advocacy.[8] Another legal writing expert advocates using CruPAC: "Conclusion, *Ru*le, *P*roof of Rule, *A*pplication, and *C*onclusion" (restate if complicated).[9]

    d. Prewriting. There are many models for the drafting process. Most legal writers begin with prewriting during the initial research and analysis stage. Prewriting includes categorizing your research into sections and

---

[7] For a discussion of variations of the IRAC structure, see Mary Beth Beazley, *Point/Counterpoint: Use of IRAC-type Formulas—Desirable or Dangerous?*, SECOND DRAFT, Nov. 1995, at 1.

[8] CHARLES R. CALLEROS, LEGAL METHOD AND WRITING 329 (5th ed. 2006).

[9] RICHARD K. NEUMANN, JR., LEGAL REASONING AND LEGAL WRITING: STRUCTURE, STRATEGY, AND STYLE 100 (5th ed. 2005).

subsections. This step will be simplified if you outlined your issues as you were conducting your research, as recommended in Chapter 2. For instance, in the Lemon Law example, there are two basic issues: (1) Is a demonstrator vehicle used by the dealer sales staff covered under Washington State Lemon Law? and (2) Is the specific problem a substantial defect? During the prewriting stage the writer might work on one issue at a time. Prewriting includes setting out a basic thesis statement as well as outlining key points and inserting relevant citations or excerpts within the outline. The first draft provides the basic structure, in a rough, imperfect form. The draft should identify the primary audience and lay the foundation for the reader. Effective legal research and writing requires multiple drafts, to develop both content and organization. The rewriting process builds on the rough draft and subsequent drafts, focusing on content revision and the large-structure organization. The editing process reviews the document at the sentence level, and polishes the tone and style. The final step is careful proofreading.

e. Conclusion. Whether a document is predictive or persuasive it should: (1) be tailored to a specific audience and purpose; (2) include the relevant law and facts; (3) use coherent, single-issue paragraphs; (4) provide clear distinctions among issues and sub-issues; and (5) provide a complete analysis that answers the reader's questions. For in the end, the goal of legal writing is communicating research results to the reader. That is what matters most. The processes of research, analysis, and writing are highly interdependent; effective legal writing begins with careful legal research and sound analysis. This broad overview is designed only to introduce various forms and strategies for written communication. Mastering the art and craft of legal writing is a lifelong challenge.

SECTION F. SELECTED LEGAL WRITING RESOURCES

- Linda H. Edwards, *Legal Writing: Process, Analysis, and Organization* (4th ed. 2006).
- Bryan Garner, *The Elements of Legal Style* (2d ed. 2002).
- Bryan Garner, *The Redbook: A Manual on Legal Style* (2006).
- Tom Goldstein, *The Lawyer's Guide to Writing Well* (2d ed. 2002).
- Margaret Z. Johns, *Professional Writing for Lawyers* (2002).
- Terri LeClercq, *Guide to Legal Writing Style* (3d ed. 2004).
- Diana V. Pratt, *Legal Writing: A Systematic Approach* (4th ed. 2004).
- Theresa J. Reid Rambo & Leann J. Pflaum, *Legal Writing by Design: A Guide to Great Briefs and Memos* (2001).
- Pamela Samuelson, *Good Legal Writing: Of Orwell and Window Panes*, 46 U. Pitt. L. Rev. 149 (1984).
- Wayne Schiess, *Better Legal Writing: 15 Topics for Advanced Legal Writers* (2005).
- Eugene Volokh, *Academic Legal Writing: Law Review Articles, Student Notes, Seminar Papers, and Getting on Law Review* (2d ed. 2005).
- Richard C. Wydick, *Plain English for Lawyers* (5th ed. 2005).

Chapter 4

COURT REPORTS

This chapter discusses how judicial opinions are published and reported, the segments of a reported judicial opinion, the differences between official and unofficial reports, the elements of judicial reporting, the organization of court reports, and abbreviations and citations for court reports.

SECTION A. THE REPORTING OF JUDICIAL OPINIONS

1. Introduction

The doctrine *stare decisis,* discussed in Chapter 1, Section A–3 of this book, has as its premise that courts are to adhere to judicial precedent. Reliance on prior judicial decisions is the foundation of the common law. Lawyers and judges are expected to turn to established judicial authorities and rules of law as the bases for formulating legal arguments and deciding cases. Access to "case law"—the aggregate of reported cases that form a body of jurisprudence, as distinguished from statutory and administrative law—is, therefore, crucial to legal research. Consequently, the editing, publishing, and distribution of judicial opinions have special characteristics in American law.

Court reports are compilations of judicial opinions, most often from state and federal appellate courts, arranged according to some grouping, such as jurisdiction, court, period of time, or subject matter. Today, the word "reporter" is often used synonymously with court reports.

When a court makes a determination about the outcome of a case, it may issue an opinion in which it states the reasons for its decision. Technically speaking, the *decision* of a court only signifies the action of the court and is indicated by the words *Affirmed, Reversed, Remanded,* or similar words or phrases. The *opinion* provides the explanation for the decision. In common practice, the terms *opinion* and *decision* are often used interchangeably.[1]

The first volume of state appellate court reports was published in 1789, with the reports of the Supreme Court of the United States commencing officially in 1817. The numbers of published reports have proliferated dramatically since that time. More than 7,000,000 reported United States judicial opinions are now in published form, and over 200,000 new American cases are reported each year from more than 600 courts. Most of these published opinions are from federal and state appellate courts. Justice

---

[1] For a discussion of the difference between *decision of the court* and *opinion of the court,* see Rogers v. Hill, 289 U.S. 582, 587 (1933). *See also* Towley v. King Arthur Rings, Inc., 40 N.Y.2d 129, 351 N.E.2d 728, 386 N.Y.S.2d 80 (1976).

Holmes once observed that, "It is a great mistake to be frightened by the ever-increasing number of reports. The reports of a given jurisdiction in the course of a generation take up pretty much the whole body of law, and restate it from the present point of view. We could reconstruct the corpus from them if all that went before were burned."[2]

Information technology has added another dimension to the publication of legal information. The development of two major electronic storage and retrieval systems, *LexisNexis* and *Westlaw*, both launched in the 1970s, allowed for full-text searching of judicial opinions and numerous other types of law-related materials. The number of providers of electronic legal information constantly increases. More recent technology, such as the Internet and the World Wide Web, CD–ROM (compact disk-read only memory), and digital imaging, also has greatly expanded access to the full text of cases and other materials. At times, a researcher's needs can be satisfied by relying exclusively on either electronic sources or on bound court reporters; at other times the best results are achieved by using both.[3]

2. The Court System

Each jurisdiction has its own system of court organization. Although there may be differences in detail, the typical structures are the same. [Illustration 4–1] In general, there are trial courts and appellate courts. The former are the courts in which the trial is held (courts of first instance or original jurisdiction). Here the parties appear, witnesses testify, and evidence is presented. Usually, questions of fact in dispute are determined and applicable rules of law are applied.

Ordinarily, cases decided by state trial courts are not reported. Only a few states, such as New York, Ohio, Pennsylvania, and Virginia, publish some trial court opinions, but those selected are few in number and represent only a very small portion of the total cases heard by the trial courts. By contrast, many opinions of federal district courts (federal trial courts) are published.[4]

After the trial court reaches its decision, the losing party has a right of appeal to an appellate court on errors of law. Each state has a final court of appeals or court of last resort. Forty states and Puerto Rico also have intermediate appellate courts.[5] Generally, the appellate court can only address claimed errors of law, and its decision in each case is based on the trial court record, e.g., pre-trial proceedings, exhibits, and the trial transcript. Appellate courts do not receive new testimony or decide questions of fact, and in most states only the appellate courts issue written opinions.

---

[2] OLIVER WENDELL HOLMES, *The Path of the Law, in* COLLECTED LEGAL PAPERS 167, 169 (1920 & photo reprint 1985).

[3] Electronic legal research, often referred to as computer-assisted legal research (CALR), is discussed in detail in Chapter 23 of this book.

[4] Federal court reports are discussed in Chapter 5.

[5] For detailed information on the activities of state courts, see STATE COURT CASELOAD STATISTICS: ANNUAL REPORT, produced jointly by the Conference of State Court Administrators and the National Center for State Courts, available at: http://www.ncsconline.org/D_Research/csp/CSP_Main_Page.html.

See also latest COUNCIL OF STATE GOVERNMENTS, THE BOOK OF THE STATES (1935–).

When a case is appealed to an appellate court, both parties submit written briefs that contain a summary of the facts and arguments on the relevant points of law. The court may hear oral arguments by the attorneys. The court then issues an opinion in which it states the reasons for its decision. If an intermediate appellate court decides the case and the losing party believes its position is legally correct, this appellate court decision may be appealed to the court of last resort for further determination. Not all appellate court opinions are published (nor are all decisions accompanied by opinions), and publication procedures differ in the various appellate courts.

3. Publishing and Reporting Judicial Opinions

Generally, the order of publication of judicial opinions is determined by dates of decision and not by other factors, such as the subject of the opinion. Opinions may be published separately in either paper or electronic format as *slip opinions* soon after they are decided. Usually, each *slip opinion* is paginated separately, contains no syllabus or editorial enhancements, and is not indexed.

After the issuance of slip opinions, the most common method of publishing opinions is as *advance sheets*. These pamphlets contain a number of recently decided cases. They are consecutively paged, are published as quickly as they can be assembled after the decisions are issued, and after publication of a sufficient number (typically three to five issues), they are cumulated into a bound volume that uses the same page numbers as the *advance sheets*. This process provides prompt, permanent citations to opinions. The features of the cases in the *advance sheets* are similar to those included in bound volumes. Some jurisdictions do not publish *advance sheets*. Electronic sources, of course, merge new cases with existing ones and can distribute opinions as soon as they are received and processed, eliminating the need for *slip opinions* and *advance sheets*.

4. Official and Unofficial Reports

Because the text of judicial opinions is not copyrighted,[6] numerous sets of court reports are published by commercial publishers. These sets either duplicate the opinions in the official reports, include cases not officially published, or both. If the publication of court reports is sanctioned by statute or court rule, those reports are referred to as *official reports.* [Illustration 4–2] In some instances, these publications are produced under government supervision; in other situations, the official report may have ceased and an existing commercial publication has been designated as the official source. Those reports published without legislative or judicial authority are referred to as *unofficial reports,* i.e., commercial or private publications. Neither term reflects superior quality or accuracy, because the text of the opinions reported in both should be identical. Unofficial publications often are more useful research tools because they typically have editorial enhancements and appear much more quickly than official reports. [Illustrations 4–2 through 4–5]

---

[6] Wheaton v. Peters, 33 U.S. (8 Pet.) 591 (1834). *See also* Banks v. Manchester, 128 U.S. 244 (1888).

5. Published and Unpublished Decisions

Justice Holmes' comments notwithstanding, the tremendous growth in the number of cases has led to attempts to restrict the number of cases that are reported.[7] Many judges, lawyers and legal scholars believe that far too many opinions that do not merit permanent publication are, nevertheless, written, published, and reported. They argue that many published cases make no doctrinal clarifications or advancements. Although important to the parties, these cases add little or nothing to our understanding of the law.

Some courts and legislatures have attempted to control the publication of judicial opinions by limiting publication to those opinions that (1) enunciate a new rule of law or change or modify an existing rule; (2) apply an established rule of law to a new or significantly different fact situation; (3) involve a legal issue of continuing public interest; (4) criticize existing law; (5) resolve an apparent conflict of authority; or (6) contribute to the legal literature by collecting relevant case law or reciting legislative history.[8] Many of these courts also have "non-citation" rules that prohibit citing opinions not specifically marked "For Publication."[9]

Non-citation rules have been criticized by some members of the bench and bar, and there is a movement to loosen or eliminate these rules and permit the citation of unpublished opinions for their persuasive value.[10] Advocates for liberalizing or eliminating non-citation rules argue that unpublished opinions are widely available and are, in fact, relied on by

[7] The value of selective reporting of appellate court opinions has caused considerable debate. For an historical survey, see J. Myron Jacobstein, *Some Reflections on the Control of the Publication of Appellate Court Opinions*, 27 STAN. L. REV. 791 (1975). For additional views, see Richard L. Neumeier, *Unpublished Opinions: Their Threat to the Appellate System*, BRIEF, Spring 1988, at 22; Keith H. Beyler, *Selective Publication Rules: An Empirical Study*, 21 LOY. U. CHI. L.J. 1 (1989); Jenny Mockenhaupt, Comment, *Assessing the Nonpublication Practice of the Minnesota Court of Appeals*, 19 WM. MITCHELL L. REV. 787 (1993); Boyce F. Martin, Jr., *In Defense of Unpublished Opinions*, 60 OHIO ST. L.J. 177 (1999); *Citation of Unpublished Opinions: The Appellate Judges Speak* (Panel Discussion), 74 FORDHAM L. REV. 1 (2005).

For the practice of some state supreme courts to "depublish" opinions of intermediate appellate courts, see Philip L. Dubois, *The Negative Side of Judicial Decision Making: Depublication as a Tool of Judicial Power and Administration on State Courts of Last Resort*, 33 VILL. L. REV. 469 (1988); Stephen R. Barnett, *Making Decisions Disappear: Depublication and Stipulated Reversal in the California Supreme Court*, 26 LOY. L.A. L. REV. 1033 (1993); Gerald F. Uelman, *Publication and Depublication of California Court of Appeals Opinions: Is the Eraser Mightier Than the Pencil?*, 26 LOY. L.A. L. REV. 1007 (1993); and William H. Manz, *The Citation Practices of the New York Court of Appeals, 1850–1993*, 43 BUFF. L. REV. 121 (1995).

[8] George M. Weaver, *The Precedential Value of Unpublished Judicial Opinions*, 39 MERCER L. REV. 477 (1988). *See also* William L. Reynolds & William M. Richman, *An Evaluation of Limited Publications in the United States Courts of Appeals: The Price of Reform*, 48 U. CHI. L. REV. 573 (1981). In Anastasoff v. United States, 223 F.3d 898 (8th Cir. 2000), a panel of the Eighth Circuit held that its rule providing that unpublished opinions are not precedent was unconstitutional under Article III of the Constitution of the United States. *See also* Dione Christopher Greene, Note, *The Federal Courts of Appeals, Unpublished Decisions, and the "No–Citation Rule,"* 81 IND. L.J. 1503 (2006).

[9] *See, for example*, WISCONSIN STATUTES, Rules of Appellate Procedure, Section 809.23, which lists the criteria for publishing opinions and limits citation of unpublished opinions.

[10] Federal Rule of Appellate Procedure 32.1 now permits citation of unpublished opinions issued on or after January 1, 2007.

lawyers and judges; non-citation rules reduce the likelihood that similar cases will be treated in a similar manner and, therefore, work against the interests of justice; and public policy favors expanded citation practices. Those favoring retaining non-citation rules argue that non-citation rules work well to limit the number of published opinions; and the elimination of non-citation rules would increase the cost of legal research, create new professional obligations for lawyers, and increase the work of the court.[11]

The increased availability of unpublished opinions makes this an important issue for the courts. Researchers should ascertain the rules of each court on the question of whether or not unpublished opinions may be cited as persuasive authority.

6. The Organization of Court Reports

The most extensive collection of bound judicial opinions is West's *National Reporter System.* The *National Reporter System,* which began in approximately 1880, is composed of numerous units that group together cases from the federal courts, state courts by region and by state, and specialized courts. Court reports are organized in several different ways:

a. *By Jurisdiction*

The reports of a particular court are issued chronologically in a numbered series, such as the *New York Reports* or the *Illinois Appellate Court Reports* or the *United States Reports.* In some instances, the reports of both the highest state court and its intermediate appellate court are published in the same set of reports, such as in the *California Reporter.*

b. *By Geography*

Regional reporters group the opinions of geographically adjacent states. For example, the *North Western Reporter* includes cases from the appellate courts of Iowa, Michigan, Minnesota, Nebraska, North Dakota, South Dakota, and Wisconsin.[12]

c. *By Subject*

Sets of specialized subject law reports contain cases dealing with a specific subject. Examples of these subject reports are *Labor Law Reports, United States Tax Reporter,* and *United States Patents Quarterly.*

7. Judicial Opinions on the Internet

The rapid development of the Internet and the World Wide Web provides new ways to access judicial opinions. In many instances, courts make their opinions available via the Internet simultaneously with their release to publishers. This enables individuals to obtain these opinions at little or no cost and offers an additional means for accessing this information.[13]

---

[11] Beth Ermatinger Hanan, *To Cite or Not to Cite: Should Wisconsin Permit Citing of Unpublished Opinions?*, 81(8) WISCONSIN LAWYER, Aug. 2008, at 25.

[12] The components of the *National Reporter System* are discussed in Chapters 5 and 6 of this book.

[13] A listing of especially useful websites is provided in Chapter 23.

A note of caution is appropriate when dealing with opinions located using a search engine on the free Internet. Even if they are posted on a court's website, these opinions often lack the editorial review and the enhancements found with proprietary electronic sources. Typically, only the most recent cases are available because retrospective coverage is limited. Some Internet sources containing court reports are entirely reliable. However, there also are sources in which the cases have not been carefully proofread, the arrangement is difficult to discern, and a newer, edited version will replace an older one. When citation to legal authority is critical, the open or free Internet usually is not yet the best source to cite.

SECTION B.   THE SEGMENTS OF COURT OPINIONS

An American court case typically includes the following segments. [Illustrations 4–2 and 4–3]

1.   Name or Title of the Case

Cases generally are identified by the names of the parties to a lawsuit. This is sometimes referred to as the "style of the case" or "caption." Examples are:

Carol Berry, Plaintiff v. Richard M. Green, Defendant—in the table of cases (a listing of cases typically arranged in alphabetical order) as *Berry v. Green*.

In re Berry—in the table of cases as *Berry, In re*. These are judicial proceedings in which there are no adversarial parties. Such designations usually denote a bankruptcy case, probate case, guardianship matter, a contempt case, disbarment proceeding, or *habeas corpus* case.

Ex parte Berry—in the table of cases as *Berry, Ex parte*. This is a special proceeding for the benefit of one party only.

State on the relation of Berry v. Green—in the table of cases as *State ex rel. Berry v. Green*. These cases involve extraordinary legal remedies, e.g., *mandamus*, prohibition, *certiorari, quo warranto*, or *habeas corpus*.

State v. Berry—in the table of cases as *State v. Berry*. This a suit by the state in its representative capacity as the party wronged by a criminal act. In some reporters the criminal cases are arranged in alphabetical order under the names of the respective states. *People* or *Commonwealth* is used in some states instead of *State*. If the United States brings the suit, it is captioned, for example, as *United States v. Berry*. To aid with location, cases of this nature also may be listed in the table of cases as *Berry, State v.* or *Berry, United States v.*

In maritime law, a suit may be brought against a ship, e.g., *The Caledonia*.

Cases involving the seizure of commodities refer to the commodity as a party, e.g., *United States v. 37 Photographs*.

Usually the plaintiff and defendant names remain in that order when cases are appealed by the defendant. However, in some states the order is reversed, and the appellant is listed first.

2. Citation

The citation to the case usually appears near the name of the case in a reporter. The publisher often includes parallel citations to other sources in which the case is published.

3. Docket Number

A docket number is the numerical designation assigned to each case by a court, e.g., No. 02–1145, or some similar numbering sequence. It is the means of identifying the case before a decision is reached. Appellate briefs often are organized by docket number in law library collections.

4. Date of Decision

This is the date on which the decision was rendered, and generally it appears after the docket number in the reported case.

5. Prefatory Statement

The prefatory statement explains the nature of the case, its disposition in the lower court, the name of the lower court and sometimes its judge, and the disposition of the case in the appellate court, e.g., *Affirmed* or *Reversed.*

6. Syllabus or Headnote

Headnotes, or syllabi, are brief summaries of the points of law, usually accompanied by relevant facts bearing on that point of law. They are typically drafted by editors or reporters employed by the court, although in a few states they are prepared by the judges who rendered the decisions. Each headnote represents a point of law extracted from the case, and the number of headnotes varies from case to case. Headnotes cannot be relied on as authority; the actual case must be consulted.[14]

The syllabi or headnotes are useful in allowing the reader to grasp relatively quickly the legal issues discussed within the opinion and then to locate these issues within the case. They also help in locating other cases involving the same or similar points of law.[15] [Illustrations 4–2 and 4–4]

7. Names of Counsel

The names of counsel for both parties to a suit precede the opinion of the court.

8. Statement of Facts

A statement of the facts in the case usually follows the names of counsel.

---

[14] The Ohio Supreme Court has gone farther than most courts in giving a special status to the syllabus. Ohio's Supreme Court Rules for the Reporting of Opinions provide that "[t]he law stated in a Supreme Court opinion is contained within its syllabus (if one is provided), and its text, including footnotes." Ohio S. Ct. Rep. Op. Rule 1(B)(1). "If there is disharmony between the syllabus of an opinion and its text or footnotes, the syllabus controls." Rule 1(B)(2).

[15] Syllabi and headnotes are discussed in more detail in Chapter 7.

9. Opinions of the Court

As previously mentioned, most judicial opinions that are published are those of appellate courts. Every appellate court has at least three judges,[16] and in some jurisdictions appellate courts may have five, seven, nine, or more judges. The *opinion* of the court is the explanation of the court's decision, the latter being the conclusion or result in a controversy. The *majority opinion* is written by one member of the court and represents the principles of law that a majority of the judges deem operative in a given decision.

A member of the majority, while agreeing with a decision, may disagree with its reasoning. That judge then may write a *concurring opinion* elaborating his or her reasoning. When a number of judges join an opinion that does not represent the opinion of a majority of judges on the court, but is joined by a greater number of judges than any other opinion written with respect to the case, that opinion is known as a *plurality opinion.*

The views of the minority generally are expressed by a *dissenting opinion,* which is written by one of the dissenting judges. An opinion in *accord* with the dissent is written by a dissenting judge when he or she agrees with the conclusions and results of the dissent, but disagrees with its reasoning. The judges, each expressing different views, may render several dissenting opinions independently.

Dissenting and concurring opinions are not the law in a case; they are not binding as precedent. They assume the characteristics of *dicta* and serve merely as persuasive authority. The controlling opinion may later be overruled and a dissenting or concurring opinion might then be accepted as the correct statement of the law.

A *per curiam opinion* is an opinion of the entire majority as distinguished from an opinion written by a specific judge. In some courts, e.g., New York Court of Appeals, a *per curiam* opinion may present a discussion of the issues in the case. In other courts, e.g., Supreme Court of the United States, this type of opinion may only give the conclusion without any reasoning.[17] A *memorandum opinion* is a very brief opinion by the entire court; it may simply consist of a statement of the court's holding. A *rescript opinion* is an appellate court's decision, typically unsigned, that is sent down to the trial court for a specific action. An *advisory opinion* is a nonbinding opinion rendered by a court at the request of the government or an interested party that indicates how the court would likely rule if the matter were to come before it.

Two additional elements, mentioned in Chapter 1 of this book, merit reiteration. The first is the *ratio decidendi,* or the point in a case that

---

[16] Many appellate courts sit in panels smaller than the full court. When the full court meets, it is referred to as an *en banc* proceeding. See Neil D. McFeeley, *En Banc Proceedings in the United States Courts of Appeals,* 24 IDAHO L. REV. 255 (1987–88).

[17] For discussion of the decline in the use of the *per curiam* opinion by the Supreme Court of the United States, see Stephen L. Wasby et al., *The Per Curiam Opinion: Its Nature and Functions,* 76 JUDICATURE 29 (1992). *See also* Stephen L. Wasby et al., *The Supreme Court's Use of Per Curiam Dispositions: The Connection to Oral Argument,* 13 No. ILL. U.L. REV. 1 (1992). For a recent overview, see Laura Krugman Ray, *The Road to* Bush v. Gore: *The History of the Supreme Court's Use of the Per Curiam Opinion,* 79 NEB. L. REV. 517 (2000).

determines the result. In other words, it is the basis of the decision, explicitly or implicitly, stated in the opinion. The second is *obiter dictum*. This is a collateral statement contained in the opinion that does not relate directly to the result of the case. *Dictum,* therefore, is an official, incidental comment made by a judge in his or her opinion that is not necessary to the formulation of the decision and is not binding as precedent.

10. Decision, with Judgment or Decree

This refers to the actual disposition of the case by the court. Thus, a *decision* is noted by such terms as *Affirmed, Reversed, Modified,* etc. Often the words *decision* and *judgment* are used synonymously. A *decree,* typically issued in equity or admiralty actions, announces the legal consequences of the facts as determined by the court.

11. Features of Bound Volumes of Reports

As described above, opinions are cumulated in bound volumes or incorporated into electronic databases. The bound volumes typically include many of the following features:

- A table of cases contained in the volume.
- A table of statutes interpreted in the cases reported in the volume (until 2000 for West reporters).
- Various types of opinions: (1) written by a judge (majority, plurality, dissenting, or concurring); (2) *per curiam;* (3) memorandum; and (4) rescript and advisory.
- The cases are cumulated from advance sheets and have the same volume and page numbers as the advance sheets.
- Table of cases decided without opinions.
- Subject index or digest of the cases reported.
- Judicial definition of words and phrases used in the cases reported.
- Recent changes in court rules.
- A list of all judges sitting on the courts covered by the volume.
- Unofficial reports generally contain cross-reference tables to the official reports.

SECTION C.   ILLUSTRATIONS

4–1. Basic Court Structure in the United States
4–2. First Page of a Typical Case as Reported in a Set of Official State Court Reports (51 Mass. App. Ct. 53)
4–3. Last Page of Opinion, 51 Mass. App. Ct. 53, 56
4–4. First Page of a Typical Case as Reported in a Set of Unofficial Reports, 742 N.E.2d 1902 (Same Case as 51 Mass. App. Ct. 53)
4–5. Last Page of Opinion, 742 N.E.2d 1092, 1094
4–6. Typical Statutory Provisions for Publication of Court Reports

[Illustration 4–1]

BASIC COURT STRUCTURE IN THE UNITED STATES

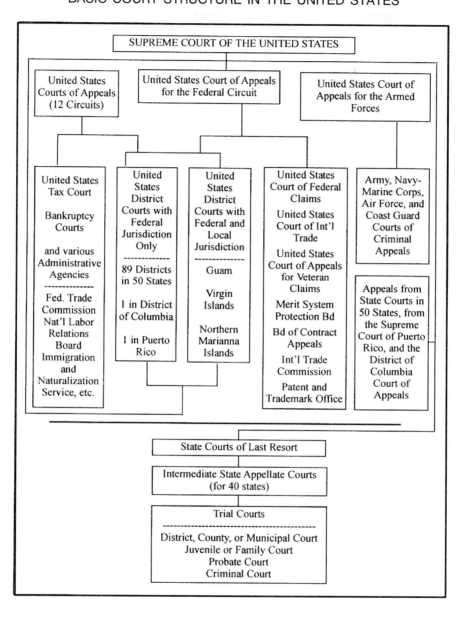

[Illustration 4–2]

FIRST PAGE OF A TYPICAL CASE AS REPORTED IN A SET OF OFFICIAL STATE COURT REPORTS (51 MASS. APP. CT. 53)

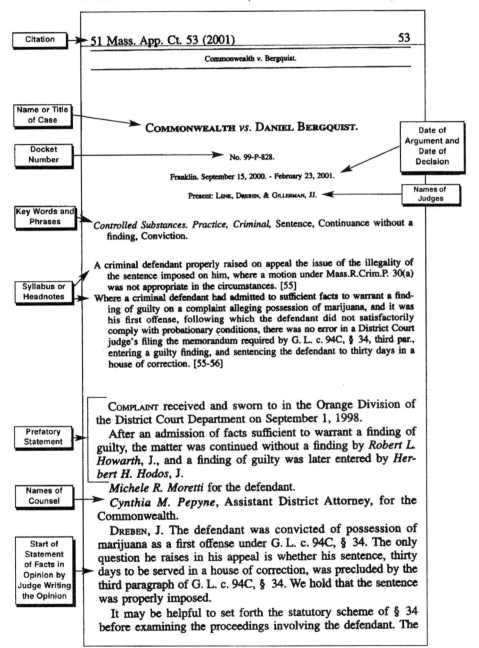

Citation → 51 Mass. App. Ct. 53 (2001)   53

Commonwealth *v.* Bergquist.

Name or Title of Case → COMMONWEALTH *vs.* DANIEL BERGQUIST.

Docket Number → No. 99-P-828.

Franklin. September 15, 2000. - February 23, 2001.

Present: LENK, DREBEN, & GILLERMAN, JJ.

Date of Argument and Date of Decision

Names of Judges

Key Words and Phrases → *Controlled Substances. Practice, Criminal,* Sentence, Continuance without a finding, Conviction.

Syllabus or Headnotes →
A criminal defendant properly raised on appeal the issue of the illegality of the sentence imposed on him, where a motion under Mass.R.Crim.P. 30(a) was not appropriate in the circumstances. [55]

Where a criminal defendant had admitted to sufficient facts to warrant a finding of guilty on a complaint alleging possession of marijuana, and it was his first offense, following which the defendant did not satisfactorily comply with probationary conditions, there was no error in a District Court judge's filing the memorandum required by G. L. c. 94C, § 34, third par., entering a guilty finding, and sentencing the defendant to thirty days in a house of correction. [55-56]

Prefatory Statement →
COMPLAINT received and sworn to in the Orange Division of the District Court Department on September 1, 1998.

After an admission of facts sufficient to warrant a finding of guilty, the matter was continued without a finding by *Robert L. Howarth,* J., and a finding of guilty was later entered by *Herbert H. Hodos,* J.

Names of Counsel →
Michele R. Moretti for the defendant.

Cynthia M. Pepyne, Assistant District Attorney, for the Commonwealth.

Start of Statement of Facts in Opinion by Judge Writing the Opinion →
DREBEN, J. The defendant was convicted of possession of marijuana as a first offense under G. L. c. 94C, § 34. The only question he raises in his appeal is whether his sentence, thirty days to be served in a house of correction, was precluded by the third paragraph of G. L. c. 94C, § 34. We hold that the sentence was properly imposed.

It may be helpful to set forth the statutory scheme of § 34 before examining the proceedings involving the defendant. The

[Illustration 4–3]

LAST PAGE OF OPINION, 51 MASS. APP. CT. 53, 56

---

56   51 Mass. App. Ct. 53 (2001)

Commonwealth v. Bergquist.

Mass. App. Ct. 666, 670 (1998); cf. *Fire Chief of E. Bridgewater* v. *Plymouth County Retirement Bd.*, 47 Mass. App. Ct. 66, 71 (1999), as well as analogous statutory provisions, e.g., G. L. c. 278, § 18, and statutes cited in *Commonwealth* v. *Pyles*, 423 Mass. 717, 723 (1996), and even the statute at bar in its second paragraph, recognize that a continuation without a finding differs from a conviction. See Smith, Criminal Practice and Procedure § 1522. Until such time as a finding of guilty is entered on the docket, there is no conviction. If the defendant had complied with the conditions imposed, the complaint would have been dismissed and he would have avoided the consequences of a criminal conviction on his record. The fact that § 34, third par., provides that even after conviction, upon a successful completion of probation, the case is to be dismissed and the records sealed does not eliminate the distinction between a continuance without a finding and a conviction. Since there was no conviction until the judge entered the guilty finding, the statutory requirement was met by the issuance of a memorandum at that time.

The defendant also suggests that the requirement of a written memorandum in § 34 should be construed as only allowing a judge to forgo imposition of probation rather than justifying a period of incarceration. Not only does such a reading seem implausible, but we also consider this interpretation disposed of by implication in *Commonwealth* v. *Lupo*, 394 Mass. at 649.

Judgment affirmed.

> Portion of Opinion

> Decision

> Note in Illustration 4–5 that the publisher identifies where the page from the official version (in this example page 56) begins in the unofficial version.

[Illustration 4–4]

FIRST PAGE OF A TYPICAL CASE AS REPORTED IN A
SET OF UNOFFICIAL REPORTS, 742 N.E.2d 1092
(SAME CASE AS 51 MASS. APP. CT. 53)

1092 Mass.   742 NORTH EASTERN REPORTER, 2d SERIES

51 Mass.App.Ct. 53

┃₅₃COMMONWEALTH

v.

Daniel BERGQUIST.

No. 99–P–828.

Appeals Court of Massachusetts,
Franklin.

Argued Sept. 15, 2000.

Decided Feb. 23, 2001.

Pursuant to defendant's admission of
facts sufficient to warrant conviction for
possession of marihuana as first offender,
matter was continued without finding by
the District Court Department, Franklin
County, Robert L. Howarth, J. After unsuccessful probationary period, the Court,
Herbert H. Hodos, J., entered judgment of
conviction and sentenced defendant to thirty days to be served in house of correction.
Defendant appealed. The Appeals Court,
Dreben, J., held that trial court was authorized to impose incarceration.

Affirmed.

1. **Habeas Corpus** ⚓296

Where defendant challenged legality
of his sentence, appeal from sentence,
rather than motion for release from unlawful restraint, was proper avenue of relief.
Rules Crim.Proc., Rule 30(a), 43C
M.G.L.A.

2. **Habeas Corpus** ⚓221

A motion for release from unlawful
restraint is available only when a defendant seeks relief from a sentence "which
he is then serving." Rules Crim.Proc.,
Rule 30(a), 43C M.G.L.A.

3. **Criminal Law** ⚓1134(3)

An appeal may properly challenge an
illegal sentence.

4. **Sentencing and Punishment** ⚓2078,
   2079

Continuation without finding was not
"conviction" in prosecution for possession

This is the same case as shown in Illustrations
4-2 & 4-3 as it appears in the *North Eastern
Reporter 2d*, an unofficial set of court reports.

The editorial staff at West prepares the
prefatory statement and headnotes to the left in
this Illustration. Note that these headnotes are
not the same as in the official *Massachusetts
Appeals Court Reports.*

Although the material preceding the opinion of
the court may vary in the unofficial hard copy
reports and computer-retrievable versions from
that in the official reports, the text of the opinion
itself is identical. [See Illustration 4-5]

The differences between the official and
unofficial reports, as well as other features of
court reports, are discussed further in Chapters
4, 5, and 6 of this book.

See Appendix D of this book for a list of states
that have discontinued their official reports.

Michele R. Moretti, Boston, for the defendant.

Cynthia M. Pepyne, Assistant District
Attorney, for the Commonwealth.

Present LENK, DREBEN, &
GILLERMAN, JJ.

DREBEN, J.

The defendant was convicted of possession of marihuana as a first offense under
G.L. c. 94C, § 34. The only question he
raises in his appeal is whether his sentence, thirty days to be served in a house
of correction, was precluded by the third
paragraph of G.L. c. 94C, § 34. We hold
that the sentence was properly imposed.

It may be helpful to set forth the statutory scheme of § 34 before examining the
proceedings involving the defendant. The
┃₅₄first paragraph of § 34 sets forth the
penalties for unlawful possession of certain
drugs, one of which is marihuana. The
penalty for that offense is "imprisonment
in a house of correction for not more than
six months or a fine of five hundred dol-

[Illustration 4–5]

LAST PAGE OF OPINION, 742 N.E.2d 1092, 1094

1094 Mass.   742 NORTH EASTERN REPORTER, 2d SERIES

Commonwealth v. Sanchez, 405 Mass. 369, 379 n. 7, 540 N.E.2d 1316 (1989); *Commonwealth v. Molino,* 411 Mass. 149, 155, 580 N.E.2d 383 (1991). Cf. *Commonwealth v. Lupo,* 394 Mass. at 646–648, 476 N.E.2d 963. Since the defendant has already served his sentence, rule 30(a) is not an option.

[4] The defendant argues that the statute must be construed to mean that if a sentence other than probation is imposed, the memorandum must be filed at the original time of disposition. The judge could not sentence him to the house of correction at a later time by filing a memorandum. The difficulty with the defendant's argument is that the third paragraph of § 34 sets forth the penalty for "any person who is *convicted* for the first time." (Emphasis supplied.) Our cases, e.g., *Commonwealth v. Duquette,* 386 Mass. at 843, 438 N.E.2d 334; *Commonwealth v. Jackson,* 45 Mass.App.Ct. 666, 670, 700 N.E.2d 848 (1998); cf. *Fire Chief of E. Bridgewater v. Plymouth County Retirement Bd.,* 47 Mass.App.Ct. 66, 71, 710 N.E.2d 644 (1999), as well as analogous statutory provisions, e.g., G.L. c. 278, § 18, and statutes cited in *Commonwealth v. Pyles,* 423 Mass. 717, 723, 672 N.E.2d 96 (1996), and even the statute at bar in its second paragraph, recognize that a continuation without a finding differs from a conviction. See Smith, Criminal Practice and Procedure § 1522. Until such time as a finding of guilty is entered on the docket, there is no conviction. If the defendant had complied with the conditions imposed, the complaint would have been dismissed and he would have avoided the consequences of a criminal conviction on his record. The fact that § 34, third paragraph, provides that even after conviction, upon a successful completion of probation, the case is to be dismissed and the records

sealed does not eliminate the distinction between a continuance without a finding and a conviction. Since there was no conviction until the judge entered the guilty finding, the statutory requirement was met by the issuance of a memorandum at that time.

[5] The defendant also suggests that the requirement of a written memorandum in § 34 should be construed as only allowing a judge to forgo imposition of probation rather than justifying a period of incarceration. Not only does such a reading seem implausible, but we also consider this interpretation disposed of by implication in *Commonwealth v. Lupo,* 394 Mass. at 649, 476 N.E.2d 963.

Judgment affirmed.

Compare this illustration with Illustration 4–3. Note that all of page 56 of the *Massachusetts Appeals Court Reports* (vol. 51) is contained on page 1094 of the *North Eastern Reporter 2d* (vol. 742) and that the opinion in both sources is identical.

v.

MECHANICS BANK[2]; James A. Maddalena & others,[3] Third-Party Defendants.

No. 97-P-117.

Appeals Court of Massachusetts, Worcester.

Argued Nov. 17, 1998.

Decided Feb. 23, 2001.

Drawers brought action against depositary bank to recover for crediting their

---

1. G.O.V. Realty Corp. and Govoni Realty, Inc.

2. There is some indication that since the filing of the complaint, Mechanics Bank may have been involved in several mergers and a successor entity may now bear its liabilities. No

formal substitution of parties appears in the record before us.

3. A.R. Davis Associates, Inc., Donald Govoni, Sr., and Donald Govoni, Jr.

[Illustration 4–6]

TYPICAL STATUTORY PROVISIONS FOR PUBLICATION OF COURT REPORTS

Excerpt from West's Ann. Calif. Gov't Code

§ 68902. Publication of official reports.

Such opinions of the Supreme Court, of the courts of appeals, and of the appellate divisions of the superior courts as the Supreme Court may deem expedient shall be published in the official reports. The reports shall be published under the general supervision of the Supreme Court.

Excerpts from McKinney's Consol. Laws of N.Y. Ann. Judiciary Law

§ 430. Law reporting bureau; state reporter

There is hereby created and established the law reporting bureau of the state of New York. The bureau shall be under the direction and control of a state reporter, who shall be appointed and be removable by the court of appeals by an order entered in its minutes. The state reporter shall be assisted by a first deputy state reporter and such other deputy state reporters and staff as may be necessary, all of whom shall be appointed and be removable by the court of appeals.

§ 431. Causes to be reported

The law reporting bureau shall report every cause determined in the court of appeals and every cause determined in the appellate divisions of the supreme court, unless otherwise directed by the court deciding the cause; and, in addition, any cause determined in any other court which the reporter, with the approval of the court of appeals, considers worthy of being reported because of its usefulness as a precedent or its importance as a matter of public interest.

Excerpt from Vernon's Ann. Mo. Stat.

§ 477.231. Designation of private publication as official reports

The supreme court may declare the published volumes of the decisions of the supreme court as the same are published by any person, firm or corporation, to be the official reports of the decisions of the supreme court, and the courts of appeals may jointly make a similar declaration with respect to published volumes of the opinions of the courts of appeals. Any publication so designated as the official reports may include both the opinions of the supreme court and the courts of appeals in the same volume.

SECTION D. ABBREVIATIONS AND CITATIONS OF COURT REPORTS

Court reports are published in numbered sets,[18] with the name of the set reflected in its title; for example, *Illinois Reports* (opinions of the Illinois Supreme Court) or *United States Reports* (opinions of the Supreme Court of the United States) or *Oil and Gas Reporter* (opinions from all U.S.

---

[18] The first American cases were reported by private reporters and are cited to the name of the reporter. In Michigan, for example, the first volume of court reports was reported by Douglass and is cited as 1 Doug. The practice of citing to names or nominative reporters ceased in most jurisdictions during the middle of the nineteenth century.

jurisdictions dealing with the law of oil and gas). In legal writing it is customary, when referring to a court report, to give both the name of the case and its citation in the appropriate court reports. But rather than citing to, for example, Volume 132 of the *Illinois Reports* for the case starting at page 238, a citation is given using a standard format and a standard abbreviation for the set of reports, e.g., 132 Ill. 238, or 498 U.S. 103, or 18 Oil & Gas Rptr. 1083.

There is no universally accepted table of abbreviations or manual of citations. Tables of abbreviations may be located in law dictionaries and in books on legal research.[19] The most widely used citation manual is *The Bluebook: A Uniform System of Citation* (18th ed. 2005), published by the editors of the *Columbia Law Review*, *Harvard Law Review*, *University of Pennsylvania Law Review*, and *Yale Law Journal*. A popular alternative to *The Bluebook* is the *ALWD Citation Manual* (3d ed. 2006), sponsored by the Association of Legal Writing Directors.[20]

To enable researchers to find and give citations to slip opinions and unreported cases, both *Westlaw* and *LexisNexis* provide a standard format for citing recent cases and administrative decisions contained in their databases. These formats are called *Westlaw Cites* and *LEXIS Cites*, respectively. In addition, *Westlaw* and *LexisNexis* provide "star pagination" to indicate the pages where language in the electronic versions appears in West's *National Reporter System* and in the official *United States Reports*.

---

[19] Appendix A of this book is an extensive table of abbreviations.

[20] These two manuals are discussed and compared in Chapter 24.

Chapter 5

FEDERAL COURT REPORTS

Section 1 of Article III of the Constitution of the United States provides that "The judicial Power of the United States, shall be vested in one supreme Court, and in such inferior Courts as the Congress may from time to time ordain and establish." Since the adoption of the Constitution in 1789, Congress has provided for various arrangements of the federal courts.

Since 1880 the federal court system can be described as consisting of three main divisions: Supreme Court of the United States (the highest court); courts of appeals (intermediate appellate courts); and district courts (courts of original jurisdiction or trial courts).[1] [Illustration 5–1]

All written opinions of the Supreme Court of the United States are published in both official and unofficial reports. Most *per curiam* opinions also are published. All written opinions that are designated "for publication" by the courts of appeals are reported in unofficial reports. A large, and increasing, number of federal appellate court opinions that are not designated "for publication" are being reported in electronic legal research services, the *Federal Appendix* (a unit of West's *National Reporter System*), and other sources.[2] Only selected cases of the federal district courts are reported unofficially. Unreported opinions generally are available from the clerks of the court. Appellate court rules and local court rules should be consulted before relying on unpublished or unreported cases as authority.

---

[1] Extensive information about the federal court system, including the jurisdiction of the district courts and the courts of appeals and links to individual court websites, can be found at the U.S. Courts website: http://www.uscourts.gov. For a description of the federal court system, see DANIEL R. COQUILLETTE ET AL., 15 MOORE'S FEDERAL PRACTICE §§ 100–100.45 and Historical Appendix (3d ed.) [hereinafter MOORE'S FEDERAL PRACTICE]. *See also* ERWIN C. SURRENCY, HISTORY OF THE FEDERAL COURTS (1987); ADMINISTRATIVE OFFICE OF THE UNITED STATES COURTS, THE UNITED STATES COURTS: THEIR JURISDICTION AND WORK (1989) [hereinafter THE UNITED STATES COURTS]. The Federal Judicial Center maintains a "History of the Federal Judiciary" on its website at: http://www.fjc.gov/history/home.nsf. This website provides the service record and biographical information for all judges who have served on the various federal courts since 1789. It also contains excellent information on the background of all the federal courts, along with other historical material.

For an exhaustive collection of legislation relating to the federal courts, see CONGRESS AND THE COURTS: A LEGISLATIVE HISTORY (William S. Hein & Co.). Thus far, this multivolume series consists of five compilations of documents: 1887–1977; 1978–1984; 1985–1992; 1993–1998; and 1999–2004.

[2] Federal Rule of Appellate Procedure 32.1 now permits citation of unpublished opinions in federal circuit courts. FRAP 32.1(a) provides that "[a] court may not prohibit or restrict the citation of federal judicial opinions, orders, judgments, or other written dispositions that have been: (i) designated as 'unpublished,' 'not for publication,' 'non-precedential,' 'not precedent,' or the like; and (ii) issued on or after January 1, 2007."

[Illustration 5–1]

GEOGRAPHIC BOUNDARIES OF U.S. COURTS OF APPEALS AND DISTRICT COURTS

Geographic Boundaries
of United States Courts of Appeals and United States District Courts

SECTION A.   UNITED STATES SUPREME COURT REPORTS

Because of the preeminent role of Supreme Court of the United States in our judicial system and the significance of the limited number of cases it decides each year, access to the Court's opinions is fundamental to legal research. These opinions are available in four current, printed sets and several electronic sources.

Bound Reporters:

1. *United States Reports* (official edition) (Government Printing Office), cited U.S.

2. *West's Supreme Court Reporter*, cited S. Ct. or Sup. Ct.

3. *United States Supreme Court Reports, Lawyers' Edition* (LexisNexis; formerly published by Lawyers Cooperative Publishing), cited L. Ed. and L. Ed. 2d.

Looseleaf Reporters:

4. *United States Law Week* (Bureau of National Affairs), cited *U.S.L.W.* Also available electronically from BNA.

Electronic Sources:

5. Computer-assisted research services, such as *Westlaw*, *LexisNexis*, *Loislaw*, *VersusLaw*, and numerous Internet websites.

1. United States Reports (Official Edition)

The *United States Reports* are the official reports for cases decided by the Supreme Court of the United States. Prior to 1817, private reporters published the reports of the Court. The first 90 volumes are cited by the name of the individual ("reporter"), from Dallas through Wallace, who compiled the cases for publication. There were seven of these early reporters, and each time a new reporter was named the volume numbering began anew. Later, these volumes were renumbered consecutively from 1–90. Commencing with volume 91 (1875), the name of the Reporter of Decisions of the Supreme Court was no longer used in citing reports and consecutive numbering of volumes continued. 1 Dallas, although a volume of the *United States Reports,* contains only Pennsylvania cases. The other three volumes of Dallas contain both Supreme Court of the United States and Pennsylvania cases.[3] The seven early reporters, with their abbreviations and volumes and years of coverage, are as follows:

Dallas (Dall.)	4 v.	v. 1–4	U.S.	(1789–1800)
Cranch (Cranch)	9 v.	v. 5–13	U.S.	(1801–1815)
Wheaton (Wheat.)	12 v.	v. 14–25	U.S.	(1816–1827)
Peters (Pet.)	16 v.	v. 26–41	U.S.	(1828–1842)
Howard (How.)	24 v.	v. 42–65	U.S.	(1843–1860)
Black (Black)	2 v.	v. 66–67	U.S.	(1861–1862)
Wallace (Wall.)	23 v.	v. 68–90	U.S.	(1863–1874)

Previously, it was the custom of the Supreme Court of the United States to have one term that started in October and ordinarily adjourned in June or July, with special terms held "whenever necessary." The current rule, effective January 1, 1990, requires the Court to "hold a continuous annual Term commencing on the first Monday in October."

---

[3] Arthur John Keefe, *More Than You Want to Know About Supreme Court Reports,* 62 A.B.A. J. 1057 (1976). *See also* Craig Joyce, Wheaton v. Peters: *The Untold Story of the Early Reporters,* 1985 SUP. CT. HIST. SOC'Y Y.B. 35. For a description of these early reports and the early reporters, see MORRIS L. COHEN & SHARON HAMBY O'CONNOR, A GUIDE TO THE EARLY REPORTS OF THE SUPREME COURT OF THE UNITED STATES (1995). For a listing of the opinions by individual justices, see LINDA A. BLANDFORD & PATRICIA RUSSELL EVANS, SUPREME COURT OF THE UNITED STATES, 1789–1980: AN INDEX TO OPINIONS ARRANGED BY JUSTICE (1983). A 1994 supplement lists opinions of all justices from October 1980 through 1990.

The cases decided by the Supreme Court are officially printed and sold by the United States Government Printing Office and are issued in three formats. Initially, the cases are issued separately as *slip opinions.* Typically, each includes a syllabus and summary of facts prepared by the Reporter of Decisions, is individually paged, contains no index, and is subject to correction by the Court prior to its publication in bound volumes. These *slip opinions* are subsequently compiled, assigned a volume number, and published in a consecutively paged advance sheet known as a *preliminary print*, to which an index is added.

After two or three *preliminary print* pamphlets are published, they are cumulated into a bound volume using the same volume and page numbers as in the *preliminary print.* Three or four bound volumes are issued per term. [Illustrations 5–2 through 5–5] Due to lengthy publication delays by the Government Printing Office, each *preliminary print* is usually two to three years behind schedule. Even worse, the bound volumes run four or five years behind schedule. As a result of the slower publication schedule for the *United States Reports,* and the editorial features in the unofficial reports discussed next, most researchers prefer the unofficial versions to the official one. Fortunately, the Court's electronic-dissemination project, Project Hermes, discussed in Section A–5 of this chapter, allowed for the transmission of its opinions to subscribers in electronic form contemporaneously with the Court's announcement of its decisions.

2. West's Supreme Court Reporter

This set, a unit of West's *National Reporter System,* reproduces the full text of the opinion or opinions for each Supreme Court case. The publisher then adds the many editorial features common to its other sets of law reports, e.g., syllabus, headnotes, topics, and key numbers (West's legal classification system).[4] West's *Supreme Court Reporter* begins with volume 106 (1882) of the official set; therefore, it does not contain the cases reported in volumes 1–105 of the official reports.

Opinions are issued in advance sheets twice a month while the Court is in session and then compiled into interim volumes while the Court is making final corrections to its opinions. After the corrections are made, three bound, permanent volumes containing all the cases of the term replace the interim volumes.[5] The volume and page numbers used in the advance sheets and the interim volumes are the same as those in the later permanent volumes. Because this set uses smaller type than is used in the official reports, two or three volumes of official reports are contained in one volume of West's *Supreme Court Reporter.* [Illustrations 5–6 and 5–7]

3. United States Supreme Court Reports, Lawyers' Edition

This set is published by LexisNexis (formerly published by Lawyers Cooperative Publishing Company) and is in two series. The first series,

---

[4] These various features are discussed in Chapters 6 and 7.

[5] Through volume 79 of West's SUPREME COURT REPORTER, the volumes of the UNITED STATES REPORTS covering a term of the Court could be published in one volume of the West version. As the Court's opinions lengthened, commencing with the October 1959 term, West began publishing the opinions of a term in two books, e.g., volumes 80 and 80A. Commencing with the October 1985 term, coverage expanded to three books, e.g., volumes 106, 106A, and 106B, owing in great part to the separate concurring and dissenting opinions issued by the justices.

which covers 1 U.S. through 351 U.S. (1789–1956), is in 100 volumes; the second series, which restarts its numbering with volume one, commences coverage with 352 U.S. (1956). Current opinions are published twice a month in advance sheets while the Court is in session. These advance sheets contain a "Current Awareness Commentary." The volume number and pagination of the advance sheets are the same as in subsequent bound volumes.

Until volume 78 of *Lawyers' Edition 2d,* two to three volumes of the official reports were published in one volume of this unofficial set. The publisher then began to issue a single bound volume each time a volume of the official set was completed in advance sheet form. Both series reprint the opinions and syllabi in the *United States Reports.* These are supplemented with the editorial treatment given the cases by the publisher, including its own summary of cases and headnotes that precede the opinions.

In addition, and for selected cases only, summaries of attorneys' briefs submitted to the Court and annotations written by the publisher's editorial staff are included in an appendix to each bound volume. Advance sheets do not contain annotations. The annotations are articles or essays on significant legal issues discussed in the reported cases. These are very useful in gaining an understanding of the impact and meaning of the cases. An increase in the number of annotations per volume began with volume 93 of the first series of *Lawyers' Edition.*[6]

Beginning with volume 32 of *Lawyers' Edition 2d*, each volume is updated with an annual pocket supplement in the back of the volume. In order to update volumes 1–31 of *Lawyers' Edition 2d*, two separate pamphlets are published annually. The *Citator Service and Corrections* pamphlet contains brief summaries of the pertinent findings from other Supreme Court decisions that make significant reference to the decisions in volumes 1–31 and provides corrections by the Court to decisions made by the justices after volumes 1–31 were published. The *Later Case Service* pamphlet supplements the annotations in volumes 1–31.

Final bound volumes replace the advance sheets after a volume of *United States Reports* replaces the *preliminary print* pamphlets. These volumes incorporate the *Citator Service* and the *Later Case Service.* These final bound volumes, three per term, also include official reporter pagination, summaries of the briefs, and full listing of counsel.

An annual *Quick Case Table* pamphlet contains an alphabetically arranged table of cases for all the Court's decisions accompanied by opinions. It also includes references to annotations in *Lawyers' Edition 2d* and the various *A.L.R.* series.[7] A six-volume general index, also published as part of *Digest of United States Supreme Court Reports, Lawyers Edition,*[8] provides a comprehensive topical index to cases decided by the Supreme Court of the United States. This index also includes a table of justices, statutory table, and an annotation history table. [Illustrations 5–8 and 5–9]

---

[6] Annotations are also discussed in Chapter 17.

[7] The ALR INDEX, discussed in Chapter 17, also indexes these annotations.

[8] Discussed in Chapter 7 of this book.

4. The United States Law Week

Rapid access to current U.S. Supreme Court cases is available through *United States Law Week*, published by the Bureau of National Affairs, Inc. The publisher receives slip opinions electronically on the day they are handed down, reproduces them, and mails them promptly to subscribers. Opinions also are posted to the *Law Week* website for immediate subscriber access. These Supreme Court cases have few editorial features added to them, but they do allow cases to become available in print form within a week or less after they are released by the Court. For older cases, it is preferable to use one of the three other sets previously discussed.

United States Law Week consists of two looseleaf binders, containing "General Law Sections" and "Supreme Court Sections." The "General Law Sections" binder starts with a two-page "Case Alert," which provides access to the issue's entire contents in alphabetical topical abstracts. This is followed by a summary and analysis prepared by the publisher's editorial staff of significant court opinions. The "Legal News" component gives analysis of selected pre-decisional developments and non-judicial topics and specialized articles of interest to the legal profession. A "General Topical Index" is provided for the contents of this binder.

The "Supreme Court Sections" binder begins with "Supreme Court Today," which contains the following valuable features:

(a) Summary of Orders: A summary of cases acted upon, as well as the lower court holdings that the Supreme Court consented to review, together with the questions presented for review by those cases.

(b) Journal of Proceedings: The minutes of all sessions of the Court held during the week.

(c) Cases Docketed: Includes citations to cases decided in the lower courts and to be heard by the Supreme Court, and the general subject matter of the cases.

(d) Summary of Cases Recently Filed.

(e) Hearings Scheduled: Includes docket number, caption, and brief statement of issues presented.

(f) Arguments Before the Court: A summary of the oral arguments of the more important cases argued each week.

(g) Table of Cases and Case Status Report: Issued every three to four weeks. For most cases the user can determine the status of a case by consulting this table.

(h) A supplemental electronic component provides both "near real time notice and text" of every Supreme Court action, including opinions. It also has a powerful, fully searchable archive.

A separate section contains the Supreme Court opinions from the most recent term. A topical index is published at the outset of the Court's term and cumulated at frequent intervals, with a final cumulative index published shortly after the Court's last session of the term.

5. Electronic Access to Opinions

Westlaw, *LexisNexis*, *Loislaw*, *United States Law Week*, and *VersusLaw* (all fee-based services), among others, provide electronic access to the text of opinions of the Supreme Court of the United States much faster than any of the print publications discussed above. The text of each opinion is transmitted electronically from the Court to the information vendors almost simultaneously with the announcement of the decision from the bench. Cases frequently are available in these online sources within a day, and typically within a few hours, after being announced.

Later, when the *United States Reports* and West's *Supreme Court Reporter* are published, both *Westlaw* and *LexisNexis* add *star pagination* to the text of the opinions to enable users to locate where the pages of these reporters appear on the screen. *LexisNexis* also adds references to *Lawyers' Edition*. *Westlaw* and *LexisNexis* both provide comprehensive coverage dating from the Court's first term in 1790 to the present. *Loislaw* coverage is from 1899; *VersusLaw* coverage is from 1900. In addition, West's *Supreme Court Reporter,* a part of the West CD–ROM Libraries, covers from 1789 forward by including both the official *United States Reports* (volumes 1–105) and the complete *Supreme Court Reporter*. This CD–ROM product can be updated through a subscription to *Westlaw*.

The official website of the Supreme Court posts opinions of the Court on the day they are issued.[9] The Court's official website has opinions beginning with the 2000 term. It also includes the oral argument calendar, court rules, schedules, visitor guides, and bar admission forms.

In 1990, through an initiative called Project Hermes, the Court began transmitting to *LexisNexis*, *Westlaw*, news services, and an educational consortium simultaneously with issuance of opinions from the bench. More extensive coverage of Supreme Court cases is available through the Internet from numerous sources, including the *Legal Information Institute (LII)* of Cornell University Law School,[10] the *Federal Courts Finder*, provided by Emory Law Library,[11] *Justia.com US Supreme Court Center*,[12] and the FindLaw *Supreme Court Center*,[13] a commercial source.

6. Chambers Opinions of the Supreme Court Justices

At the beginning of each term, each Supreme Court justice is assigned to supervise one or more federal judicial circuits. Frequently, when the Supreme Court is not in session, a petition may be directed to a justice in his or her capacity as Circuit Justice. An opinion resulting from such a petition is known as a *chambers opinion*. Before the 1970 term, these chambers opinions appeared only in *Lawyers' Edition* and West's *Supreme Court Reporter*. Starting with the 1970 term, they also appear in the official *United States Reports*.[14] They are included as well in *United States Law Week*, *Westlaw*, *LexisNexis*, *Loislaw*, and *VersusLaw*.

---

[9] http://www.supremecourtus.gov/.

[10] http://www.law.cornell.edu.

[11] http://www.law.emory.edu/index.php?id=2997/index.html.

[12] http://supreme.justia.com/.

[13] http://supreme.lp.findlaw.com/.

[14] ROBERT L. STERN ET AL., SUPREME COURT PRACTICE 847–48 (9th ed. 2007) [hereinafter SUPREME COURT PRACTICE]. *See also* Frederick Bernays Wiener, *Opinions of Justices Sitting in Chambers,*

7. Citing United States Supreme Court Cases

Conventional citation practice calls for citing only to *United States Reports* after these are published, e.g., *Bush v. Gore*, 531 U.S. 98 (2000). The unofficial reporters, West's *Supreme Court Reporter* (S. Ct.) and *United States Supreme Court Reports, Lawyers' Edition* (L. Ed.), which have their own distinct pagination, show the pagination of the *United States Reports*. As when used in the electronic services, this is known as *star pagination*. Both the *Supreme Court Reporter* and *Lawyers' Edition* include in each volume a cross-reference table listing the cases in the *United States Reports* and showing where they are reported in their volumes.

If the case is so recent that it is not yet in the official reporter, the preferred practice is to cite to the *Supreme Court Reporter*, then to *Lawyers' Edition*. For cases even more recent than the *Supreme Court Reporter* or *Lawyers' Edition,* the preferred cite is to *United States Law Week* (U.S.L.W.) or to an electronic version distributed by one of the two major CALR services.

8. Finding Parallel Citations to Supreme Court of the United States Opinions

When the only citation available is to West's *Supreme Court Reporter* or the *United States Supreme Court Reports, Lawyers' Edition,* the citation to the other two sets can be obtained by referring to:

(1) *Shepard's United States Citations: Cases* (print edition).

(2) *Shepard's* or "Get a Document" on *LexisNexis*.

(3) *KeyCite* or "Find by Citation" on *Westlaw*.

(4) *Table of Cases* in one of the digests for federal cases.[15]

SECTION B. LOWER FEDERAL COURT REPORTS

The Supreme Court of the United States deals with a small fraction of the total litigation of the federal court system. With certain exceptions, the Supreme Court selects only the cases it wishes to hear on appeal,[16] and these are relatively few in number. The bulk of the work of the federal courts occurs in the trial courts, i.e., the federal district courts, and in the appeals from them to the United States courts of appeals. These appellate courts are divided into thirteen circuits—eleven numbered circuits, plus the United States Court of Appeals for the Federal Circuit and for the District of Columbia Circuit. Each state and U.S. territory has one or more federal district courts.

In addition, there are federal courts with limited or specialized jurisdiction. The more important of these are the United States Court of Federal

---

49 Law Libr. J. 2 (1956); Marian Boner, *Index to Chambers Opinions of Supreme Court Justices,* 65 Law Libr. J. 213 (1972).

[15] Tables of cases and the *American Digest System* are discussed in Chapter 7 of this book; *Shepard's* is discussed in Chapter 15.

[16] Cases reach the Supreme Court either by writ of *certiorari* or by appeal.

Claims,[17] the United States Court of Appeals for the Federal Circuit (mentioned above),[18] and the United States Tax Court.[19]

1. Privately Published Editions of the Lower Federal Court Reports

Only a few sets of official reports are published for lower federal court opinions, and these are for specialized courts only. No official reports are published exclusively for cases of the federal district courts and the United States courts of appeals. West assumed the responsibility for publishing opinions from these courts, primarily through the federal units of its *National Reporter System.* Until the arrival of electronic legal research services, West's reporters were the only comprehensive sources for accessing these opinions. Most electronic research services now provide access to these opinions.

a. *Federal Cases.* Prior to 1880 and the development of the *National Reporter System,* the opinions of the federal district courts and the circuit courts of appeals were published in many different sets of law reports. In the mid–1890s, West reprinted all previously reported lower federal court opinions in one set of 31 volumes called *Federal Cases.* This set contains 18,313 opinions reported between 1789 and 1879, accompanied by brief notes (annotations) to the cases. Unlike most sets of court reports, in which the cases are arranged chronologically, the cases in this set are arranged alphabetically by case name and are numbered consecutively. Cases are cited by number. Volume 31 is the Digest volume; it includes tables printed on blue paper that cross-reference the citations of the original volumes of reports to *Federal Cases.*

Approximately 15 years before the compilation of *Federal Cases,* West commenced publication of its *National Reporter System,* which has grown to several units over the years. The features of these various units include the use of topics and key numbers and the issuance of opinions in advance sheets that are later cumulated into bound volumes having the same volume and page numbers as the advance sheets.[20]

b. *Federal Reporter.* The *Federal Reporter* began in 1880. It currently contains only cases of the United States courts of appeals (formerly the U.S. circuit courts of appeals). However, over the years the *Federal Reporter* has published cases from other federal courts. It contains federal district court cases until 1932 when the *Federal Supplement* started. Cases from other federal courts that have since been abolished or reorganized also are included in the *Federal Reporter,* namely the United States Circuit Courts,

---

[17] This court was originally named the United States Court of Claims. It was renamed the United States Claims Court by the Federal Courts Improvement Act of 1982, Pub. L. No. 97–164, 96 Stat. 25, effective on October 1, 1982. The United States Claims Court was renamed the United States Court of Federal Claims, as a result of certain provisions of the Federal Courts Administration Act of 1992, Pub. L. No. 102–572, 106 Stat. 4506, effective January 1, 1993.

[18] This court was created by Pub. L. No. 97–164, 96 Stat. 25, effective on October 1, 1982. It is a merger of the Court of U.S. Customs and Patent Appeals and the appellate division of the U.S. Court of Claims. For additional information on this court, see THE UNITED STATES COURT OF APPEALS FOR THE FEDERAL CIRCUIT: A HISTORY 1982–1990 (1991).

[19] For a more detailed description of specialized federal courts, see THE UNITED STATES COURTS, *supra* note 1; 15 MOORE'S FEDERAL PRACTICE §§ 100–100.45 and Historical Appendix, *supra* note 1.

[20] The uses of and features in the *National Reporter System* are discussed in Chapter 6.

Commerce Court of the United States, Temporary Emergency Court of Appeals, United States Emergency Court of Appeals, United States Court of Claims, and United States Court of Customs and Patents Appeals.[21]

The *Federal Reporter* is in three series. The first series ended with Volume 300 in 1924. The second series, consisting of volumes 1–999, covers cases reported in 1924 and continued coverage into 1993. The third series began in the fall of 1993.[22]

Only those opinions that are ordered by the federal courts of appeals to be published are included in the *Federal Reporter 2d* and *3d*. These cases are those deemed by the federal courts to have "general precedential value." All of these courts have rules restricting the number of published opinions.[23] Increasingly, the federal courts are deciding to withdraw their opinions from publication before they are in bound form. To indicate this, the advance sheets contain a "Table of Opinions Withdrawn from Bound Volume."

c. *Federal Appendix*. This set commenced in 2001. Coverage begins January 1, 2001, and includes unpublished opinions of the U.S. courts of appeals. Opinions from the fifth and eleventh circuits are not included. Although these cases may not have value as precedent, they might contain fact situations and applications of value to researchers. Each reported case

---

[21] Cases from the United States Court of Customs and Patents Appeals were reported in the FEDERAL REPORTER, beginning with volume 34 of the second series, until the court was abolished October 1, 1982. The function of that court, as well as that of the appellate division of the former United States Court of Claims, was transferred to the United States Court of Appeals for the Federal Circuit, whose cases are included in the FEDERAL REPORTER. *See supra* note 17 for additional information pertaining to this particular court.

[22] West provided very little by way of explanation about why a FEDERAL REPORTER 3D started after almost seventy years and after volume 999 of FEDERAL REPORTER 2D, other than to say it was "to avoid potential confusion that could arise from a four-digit case volume citation." Matthew Goldstein, *68 Years, 999 Volumes of F.2d End as New Era of F.3d Begins,* N.Y. L.J., October 14, 1993, at 1. No change in format or coverage occurred in this new series. Obviously, having volume numbers that are less than four digits in length saves, over an extended period of time, a tremendous amount of space in both printed citations and electronic storage. As other units in the *National Reporter System* have reached volume 999, they too have started a new numbering series commencing with volume 1. It is unlikely that any unit of the *National Reporter System* will ever have a volume 1000.

[23] For discussion of these policies, see David Dunn, Note, *Unreported Decisions in the United States Courts of Appeals,* 63 CORNELL L. REV. 128 (1977); William L. Reynolds & William M. Richman, *The Non–Precedential Precedent—Limited Publication and No–Citation Rules in the United States Courts of Appeals,* 78 COLUM. L. REV. 1167 (1978); William L. Reynolds & William M. Richman, *An Evaluation of Limited Publication in the United States Courts of Appeals: The Price of Reform,* 48 U. CHI. L. REV. 573 (1981); Donald R. Songer, *Criteria for Publication of Opinions in the U.S. Courts of Appeals: Formal Rules Versus Empirical Reality,* 73 JUDICATURE 307 (1990); Martha J. Dragich, *Will the Federal Courts of Appeals Perish If They Publish? Or Does the Declining Use of Opinions to Explain and Justify Judicial Decisions Pose a Greater Threat?,* 44 AM. U. L. REV. 757 (1995); Elizabeth M. Horton, Comment, *Selective Publication and the Authority of Precedent in the United States Courts of Appeals,* 42 UCLA L. REV 1631 (1995); Ellen Platt, *Unpublished vs. Unreported: What's the Difference?,* 5 PERSP.: TEACHING LEGAL RES. & WRITING 26 (1996); Robert A. Mead, *"Unpublished" Opinions as the Bulk of the Iceberg: Publication Patterns in the Eighth and Tenth Circuit United States Courts of Appeals,* 93 LAW LIBR. J. 589 (2001); and Jon A. Strongman, Comment, *Unpublished Opinions, Precedent, and the Fifth Amendment: Why Denying Unpublished Opinions Precedential Value Is Unconstitutional,* 50 U. KAN. L. REV. 195 (2001).

in the *Federal Appendix* includes a caveat stating: "This case was not selected for publication in the Federal Reporter."

d. *Federal Supplement.* This set began in 1932, when West decided to no longer include federal district court cases and United States Court of Claims cases (from volumes 1 to 181) in the *Federal Reporter.* Coverage of United States Court of Claims cases returned to the *Federal Reporter* in 1960.

Because these are the trial courts within the federal court system, the opinions reported in the *Federal Supplement* are exceptions to the general rule that only appellate court opinions are reported. It must be emphasized, however, that only a very small percentage of the cases heard in the federal district courts are reported in the *Federal Supplement.* The decision whether or not to publish is made by the judge writing the opinion.

The *Federal Supplement,* in addition to its federal district court coverage, also reports cases from the United States Court of International Trade since 1980; the United States Customs Court from 1956 to 1980, when it was replaced by the United States Court of International Trade; the Special Court under the Regional Rail Reorganization Act of 1973; and the Judicial Panel on Multidistrict Litigation since its inception in 1969. A second series of the *Federal Supplement* began in 1998. The last volume of the original series was numbered 999.

Some opinions not published in the *Federal Supplement* may be printed in subject reporters or may be available electronically.

e. *Federal Rules Decisions (F.R.D.).* This set contains opinions of the federal district courts since 1939 that construe the Federal Rules of Civil Procedure and cases since 1946 decided under the Rules of Criminal Procedure. These opinions are not published in the *Federal Supplement.* Similar to other units of the *National Reporter System, F.R.D.* is issued in advance sheets and bound volumes, with headnotes that are classified to West's key number system. In addition to judicial opinions, it also includes articles on various aspects of federal courts and federal procedure. A cumulative index to these articles is in every tenth volume, and a consolidated index for volumes 1–122 is in volume 122.

f. *Military Justice Reporter.* This set, which began in 1975, is the successor to the *Decisions of the United States Court of Military Appeals* and the *Court–Martial Reports* (1951–1975) by other publishers. The *Military Justice Reporter* includes cases of the United States Court of Appeals for the Armed Forces[24] and the Courts of Criminal Appeals[25] of the Army, Navy–Marine Corps, Air Force, and Coast Guard.

g. *Bankruptcy Reporter.* This set began in 1980 as a result of major changes in the bankruptcy laws enacted in 1978.[26] It reports opinions from the United States bankruptcy courts and those cases from the federal district courts that deal with bankruptcy matters, no longer including these

---

[24] The name of this court was changed from the United States Court of Military Appeals, effective October 5, 1994.

[25] The name of these courts was changed from the Courts of Military Review, effective October 5, 1994.

[26] Bankruptcy Reform Act of 1978, Pub. L. No. 95–598, 92 Stat. 2549.

in the *Federal Supplement*. The *Bankruptcy Reporter* also reprints bankruptcy opinions appearing in the *Supreme Court Reporter* and *Federal Reporter 2d* and *3d*, retaining the paginations of these reporters.

h. *Federal Claims Reporter*. This set, which began in 1992, is a continuation of the *United States Claims Court Reporter*, a reporter covering a trial-level federal court created in 1982. It inherited substantially all the jurisdiction and caseload of the United States Court of Claims, a court that had been existence since 1855. In 1992, when the name of the United States Claims Court was changed to the United States Court of Federal Claims, the *United States Claims Court Reporter* was renamed the *Federal Claims Reporter,* commencing with volume 27. This reporter also includes reprints from the *Federal Reporter 2d* and *3d* and the *Supreme Court Reporter* of those cases that have reviewed opinions of the United States Court of Federal Claims.

i. *Veterans Appeals Reporter*. Begun in October 1991, this set contains cases decided in the United States Court of Appeals for Veteran Claims[27] and cases of the United States Court of Appeals for the Federal Circuit and the Supreme Court of the United States, which hear appeals from the decisions of the Court of Appeals for Veterans Claims.

j. *West's Federal Case News*. This is a weekly pamphlet, not a reporter, that summarizes recently decided federal cases even before they are published in advance sheets. This alerting service includes the case name, court, judge deciding the case, filing date, docket number, and essential points of the case.

2. Officially Published Reports of Special Federal Courts

Cases Decided in the United States Court of Claims. Washington, Government Printing Office, 1863–1982. v. 1–231.

Reports of the United States Tax Court. Washington, Government Printing Office, Oct. 1942 to present. v. 1 *et seq*.

Trade Cases Adjudged in the U.S. Court of Appeals for the Federal Circuit. Washington, Government Printing Office, 1996 to present. v. 10 *et seq*. This set partially continues *Cases Decided in the United States Court of Appeals for the Federal Circuit*. Washington, Government Printing Office, 1982–1991. v. 1–9.

United States Court of International Trade Reports. Washington, Government Printing Office, 1980 to present. v. 1 *et seq*. This court was formerly the United States Customs Court, and its cases were reported in *United States Customs Court Reports*, 1938–1980. v. 1–85.

3. Electronic Access

Both *Westlaw* and *LexisNexis* provide comprehensive, full-text coverage of published federal opinions, including those of the various specialized

---

[27] Veterans' Judicial Review Act of 1988, Pub. L. No. 100–687, 102 Stat. 4105. *See* Laurence R. Helfer, *The Politics of Judicial Structure: Creating the United States Court of Veterans Appeals,* 25 CONN. L. REV. 155 (1992). For additional information about this court, see *Veterans Law Symposium,* 46 ME. L. REV. 1 (1994). The name of this court was changed from the Court of Veterans Appeals to the United States Court of Appeals for Veterans Claims in March 1999.

federal courts. These cases are made available electronically with ever-increasing speed, and always prior to their publication in advance sheets. In addition, these two services include many opinions found in looseleaf services and other publications, but that may not be published in a West reporter. For these opinions, the two services note at the start of the electronic version that this case may not be appropriate to rely on as authority. West also makes available a library collection of federal court opinions on CD–ROM. Most other commercial sources, such as *Loislaw*, *FindLaw*, and *VersusLaw*, offer electronic access to federal appellate court opinions, although the retrospective coverage is not as complete nor are the enhancements as extensive as those of *Westlaw* and *LexisNexis*.

In mid–1993, all federal courts of appeals began offering electronic public access via a bulletin board to their slip opinions through a system known either as Appellate Court Electronic Services (ACES) or Electronic Dissemination of Opinions System (EDOS). More recently, several websites have been created that provide access to federal courts of appeals opinions. Excellent sources for links to these opinions are the *Legal Information Institute (LII)* of Cornell University Law School,[28] the *Federal Courts Finder* of Emory Law Library,[29] and *Justia.com*.[30] The opinions found using these, and similar sites, are typically from the mid-1990s forward. Numerous district court opinions and the opinions from various specialized federal courts also can be located using these sites.

4. Citing Lower Federal Court Cases

Because there are no official reports for the federal courts of appeals and the federal district courts, citations are to the three series of the *Federal Reporter*, to the two series of *Federal Supplement*, to *Federal Appendix*, or to the specialized federal reporters.

Examples are:

United States v. One 1987 27 Foot Boston Whaler, 808 F. Supp. 382 (D.N.J. 1992).

In re Bond, 254 F.3d 669 (7th Cir. 2001).

Jones v. West, 12 Vet. App. 383 (1999).

SECTION C. ILLUSTRATIONS

The case of *Solid Waste Agency of Northern Cook County v. United States Army Corps of Engineers* [531 U.S. 159, 121 S. Ct. 675, 148 L. Ed. 2d 576 (2001)] as it is published in:

5–2 to 5–5.	**Advance Sheets (Preliminary Print) of the United States Reports (Official)**
5–6 to 5–7.	**Volume 121 of West's Supreme Court Reporter Interim Volume**
5–8 to 5–9.	**Volume 148 of United States Supreme Court Reports, Lawyers' Edition, 2d Series (LexisNexis)**

---

[28] http://www.law.cornell.edu.

[29] http://www.law.emory.edu/index.php?id=2997/index.html.

[30] http://www.justia.com.

[Illustration 5–2]

SOLID WASTE AGENCY OF NORTHERN COOK COUNTY V. UNITED
STATES ARMY CORPS OF ENGINEERS, AS REPORTED IN THE PRE-
LIMINARY PRINT (ADVANCE SHEETS) OF THE UNITED STATES RE-
PORTS, 531 U.S. 159 (2001)

OCTOBER TERM, 2000   159

Syllabus

SOLID WASTE AGENCY OF NORTHERN COOK COUNTY *v.* UNITED STATES ARMY CORPS OF ENGINEERS ET AL.

CERTIORARI TO THE UNITED STATES COURT OF APPEALS FOR THE SEVENTH CIRCUIT

No. 99–1178.   Argued October 31, 2000—Decided January 9, 2001

Petitioner, a consortium of suburban Chicago municipalities, selected as a solid waste disposal site an abandoned sand and gravel pit with excavation trenches that had evolved into permanent and seasonal ponds. Because the operation called for filling in some of the ponds, petitioner contacted federal respondents, including the Army Corps of Engineers (Corps), to determine if a landfill permit was required under §404(a) of the Clean Water Act (CWA), which authorizes the Corps to issue permits allowing the discharge of dredged or fill material into "navigable waters." The CWA defines "navigable waters" as "the waters of the United States," 33 U.S.C. §1362(7), and the Corps' regulations define such waters to include intrastate waters, "the use, degradation or de-

---

> **This page is taken from the *Preliminary Print* (advance sheets) to the *United States Reports*.**
> **As is customary, indication is given to the court from which the case is being appealed.**
>
> **Note that the docket number, date of argument, and date of decision also are given.**

---

instant site pursuant to that Rule, the Corps refused to issue a §404(a)
permit. When petitioner challenged the Corps' jurisdiction and the merits of the permit denial, the District Court granted respondents summary judgment on the jurisdictional issue. The Seventh Circuit held that Congress has authority under the Commerce Clause to regulate intrastate waters and that the Migratory Bird Rule is a reasonable interpretation of the CWA.

Held: Title 33 CFR §328.3(a)(3), as clarified and applied to petitioner's site pursuant to the Migratory Bird Rule, exceeds the authority granted to respondents under §404(a) of the CWA.   Pp. 166–174.

(a) In *United States* v. *Riverside Bayview Homes, Inc.,* 474 U.S. 121, this Court held that the Corps had §404(a) jurisdiction over wetlands adjacent to a navigable waterway, noting that the term "navigable" is of "limited import" and that Congress evidenced its intent to "regulate at least some waters that would not be deemed 'navigable' under [that term's] classical understanding," *id.,* at 133. But that holding was based in large measure upon Congress' unequivocal acquiescence to, and

[Illustration 5–3]

PAGE FROM 531 U.S. 159, 161

Cite as: 531 U. S. 159 (2001)   161

Syllabus

state activities that substantially affect interstate commerce, raise significant constitutional questions, yet there is nothing approaching a

> **Each case is preceded by a summary and syllabus prepared by the Reporter of Decisions. See also previous illustration.**
>
> **Note the indication as to which justice wrote the majority opinion, which justices joined in the opinion, and which justices dissented. Note also how the names are given of the attorneys involved in the case before the Supreme Court of the United States.**

ministrative deference. Pp. 172–174.

191 F. 3d 845, reversed.

REHNQUIST, C. J., delivered the opinion of the Court, in which O'CONNOR, SCALIA, KENNEDY, and THOMAS, JJ., joined. STEVENS, J., filed a dissenting opinion, in which SOUTER, GINSBURG, and BREYER, JJ., joined, *post*, p. 174.

Timothy S. Bishop argued the cause for petitioner. With him on the briefs were *Kaspar J. Stoffelmayr, Sharon Swingle,* and *George J. Mannina, Jr.*

Deputy Solicitor General Wallace argued the cause for respondents. With him on the brief for the federal respondents were *Solicitor General Waxman, Assistant Attorney General Schiffer, Malcolm L. Stewart,* and *John A. Bryson. Myron M. Cherry* filed a brief for respondents Village of Bartlett et al.*

---

*Briefs of *amici curiae* urging reversal were filed for the State of Alabama by *Bill Pryor,* Attorney General, *Alice Ann Byrne,* Assistant Attorney General, and *Jeffrey S. Sutton;* for the American Farm Bureau Federation et al. by *William G. Myers III;* for Arid Operations, Inc., by *Charles L. Kaiser;* for Cargill, Inc., by *Leslie G. Landau, Edgar B. Washburn,* and *David M. Ivester;* for the Cato Institute et al. by *Theodore M. Cooperstein, William H. Mellor, Clint Bolick, Scott G. Bullock, Timothy Lynch, Robert A. Levy,* and *Ronald D. Rotunda;* for the Center for the Original Intent of the Constitution by *Michael P. Farris* and *Scott W. Somerville;* for the Chamber of Commerce of the United States by *Robert R. Gasaway, Jeffrey B. Clark, Daryl Joseffer,* and *Robin S. Conrad;* for the Claremont Institute Center for Constitutional Jurisprudence by *Edwin Meese III;* for Defenders of Property Rights by *Nancie G. Marzulla;* for the National Association of Home Builders by *Thomas C. Jackson;* for the Nationwide

[Illustration 5–4]

PAGE FROM 531 U.S. 159, 162 (MAJORITY OPINION)

162   SOLID WASTE AGENCY OF NORTHERN COOK CTY.
          v. ARMY CORPS OF ENGINEERS
               Opinion of the Court

CHIEF JUSTICE REHNQUIST delivered the opinion of the Court.

Section 404(a) of the Clean Water Act (CWA or Act), 86 Stat. 884, as amended, 33 U. S. C. § 1344(a), regulates the discharge of dredged or fill material into "navigable waters." The United States Army Corps of Engineers (Corps) has interpreted § 404(a) to confer federal authority over an abandoned sand and gravel pit in northern Illinois which pro-

> This is the fourth page of the *Solid Waste Agency* case illustrating the start of the majority opinion. Note that if *amici curiae* briefs are filed in the case this information also is provided.

these waters, and, if so, whether Congress could exercise such authority consistent with the Commerce Clause, U. S. Const., Art. I, §8, cl. 3. We answer the first question in the negative and therefore do not reach the second.

Petitioner, the Solid Waste Agency of Northern Cook County (SWANCC), is a consortium of 23 suburban Chicago

Public Projects Coalition et al. by *Lawrence R. Liebesman;* for the Pacific Legal Foundation et al. by *Anne M. Hayes* and *M. Reed Hopper;* for the Serrano Water District et al. by *Virginia S. Albrecht* and *Stephen J. Wenderoth;* for the Washington Legal Foundation et al. by *Mark A. Perry, Daniel J. Popeo,* and *Paul D. Kamenar;* for the U. S. Conference of Mayors et al. by *Richard Ruda* and *James I. Crowley;* and for James J. Wilson by *Steven A. Steinbach* and *Gerald A. Feffer.*

Briefs of *amici curiae* urging affirmance were filed for the State of California et al. by *Bill Lockyer,* Attorney General of California, *Richard M. Frank,* Chief Assistant Attorney General, *J. Matthew Rodriguez,* Senior Assistant Attorney General, *Dennis M. Eagan,* Supervising Deputy Attorney General, and *Joseph Barbieri,* Deputy Attorney General, and by the Attorneys General for their respective States as follows: *Thomas J. Miller* of Iowa, *Andrew Ketterer* of Maine, *John J. Farmer, Jr.,* of New Jersey, *W. A. Drew Edmondson* of Oklahoma, *Hardy Myers* of Oregon, *William H. Sorrell* of Vermont, and *Christine O. Gregoire* of Washington; for the Anti-Defamation League et al. by *Martin E. Karlinsky, Steven M. Freeman, Michael Lieberman,* and *Elliot M. Mincberg;* and for Environmental Defense et al. by *Louis R. Cohen* and *Michael Bean.*

Briefs of *amici curiae* were filed for the American Forest & Paper Association et al. by *Russell S. Frye;* for the Center for Individual Rights by *Michael E. Rosman;* for the National Stone Association by *Kurt E. Blase;* and for Dr. Gene Likens et al. by *Michael Bean.*

[Illustration 5–5]

PAGE FROM 531 U.S. 159, 174 (DISSENTING OPINION)

174   SOLID WASTE AGENCY OF NORTHERN COOK CTY.
v. ARMY CORPS OF ENGINEERS
STEVENS, J., dissenting

These are significant constitutional questions raised by respondents' application of their regulations, and yet we find nothing approaching a clear statement from Congress that it intended § 404(a) to reach an abandoned sand and gravel pit such as we have here. Permitting respondents to claim federal jurisdiction over ponds and mudflats falling within the "Migratory Bird Rule" would result in a significant impingement of the States' traditional and primary power over land and water use. See, *e. g., Hess* v. *Port Authority Trans-Hudson Corporation,* 513 U. S. 30, 44 (1994) ("[R]egulation of land use [is] a function traditionally performed by local governments"). Rather than expressing a desire to readjust the federal-state balance in this manner, Congress chose to ["recognize, preserve, and protect the primary responsibil-]

This is the last page of the majority opinion from the *Solid Waste Agency* case. The Supreme Court's decision was to *reverse* the Court of Appeals for the Seventh Circuit. Note that dissenting opinions immediately follow the majority opinion.

significant constitutional and federalism questions raised by respondents' interpretation, and therefore reject the request for administrative deference.[8]

We hold that 33 CFR § 328.3(a)(3) (1999), as clarified and applied to petitioner's balefill site pursuant to the "Migratory Bird Rule," 51 Fed. Reg. 41217 (1986), exceeds the authority granted to respondents under § 404(a) of the CWA. The judgment of the Court of Appeals for the Seventh Circuit is therefore

Reversed.

JUSTICE STEVENS, with whom JUSTICE SOUTER, JUSTICE GINSBURG, and JUSTICE BREYER join, dissenting.

In 1969, the Cuyahoga River in Cleveland, Ohio, coated with a slick of industrial waste, caught fire. Congress re-

---

[8] Because violations of the CWA carry criminal penalties, see 33 U. S. C. § 1319(c)(2), petitioner invokes the rule of lenity as another basis for rejecting the Corps' interpretation of the CWA. Brief for Petitioner 31–32. We need not address this alternative argument. See *United States* v. *Shabani,* 513 U. S. 10, 17 (1994).

[Illustration 5–6]

SOLID WASTE AGENCY OF NORTHERN COOK COUNTY V. UNITED STATES ARMY CORPS OF ENGINEERS, AS REPORTED IN 121 S. CT. 675 (2001) INTERIM VOLUME

SOLID WASTE AGENCY v. ARMY CORPS OF ENGINEERS   675
Cite as 121 S.Ct. 675 (2001)

₁₅₉SOLID WASTE AGENCY
OF NORTHERN COOK
COUNTY, Petitioner,

v.

UNITED STATES ARMY CORPS
OF ENGINEERS, et al.
No. 99–1178.

Argued Oct. 31, 2000.

Decided Jan. 9, 2001.

Consortium of municipalities sued the United States Army Corps of Engineers, challenging Corps' exercise of jurisdiction over abandoned sand and gravel pit on which consortium planned to develop disposal site for nonhazardous solid waste and denial of a Clean Water Act (CWA) permit for that purpose. The United States District Court for the Northern District of Illinois, George W. Lindberg, J., 998 F.Supp. 946, granted summary judgment for Corps on jurisdictional issue, and con-

3. Game ☞3.5

Navigable Waters ☞38

Army Corps of Engineers' rule extending definition of "navigable waters" under Clean Water Act (CWA) to include intrastate waters used as habitat by migratory birds exceeded authority granted to Corps under CWA, and therefore, abandoned sand and gravel pit containing ponds used by migratory birds was not subject to Corps' jurisdiction under CWA. Federal Water Pollution Control Act Amendments of 1972, § 404(a), as amended, 33 U.S.C.A. § 1344(a); 33 C.F.R. § 328.3(a)(3).

4. Statutes ☞219(6.1)

Army Corps of Engineers' rule extending definition of "navigable waters" under Clean Water Act (CWA) to include intrastate waters used as habitat by migratory birds which cross state lines was not entitled to *Chevron* deference; rule raised significant constitutional questions, such as whether Congress had power to regulate

---

This is the first page of the *Solid Waste Agency* case as it appears in West's *Supreme Court Reporter*, an unofficial set. The summary is prepared by the editors.

The seven numbered headnotes in this illustration were prepared by West's editorial staff. The significance of headnotes is discussed in Chapter 7.

---

under CWA to include intrastate waters used as habitat by migratory birds exceeded authority granted to Corps under CWA.

Reversed.

Justice Stevens filed dissenting opinion in which Justices Souter, Ginsburg, and Breyer joined.

1. Statutes ☞217.4

Failed legislative proposals are a particularly dangerous ground on which to rest an interpretation of a prior statute.

2. Statutes ☞220

For purposes of statutory interpretation, subsequent legislative history is less illuminating than contemporaneous evidence.

☞330

Where an administrative interpretation of a statute invokes the outer limits of Congress' power, agency must establish a clear indication that Congress intended that result.

6. Administrative Law and Procedure ☞330

Concern that agency interpretation of a statute exceeds limits of power granted by Congress is heightened where interpretation alters the federal-state framework by permitting federal encroachment upon a traditional state power.

7. Constitutional Law ☞48(1)

Where an otherwise acceptable construction of a federal statute would raise

[Illustration 5–7]

PAGE FROM 121 S. CT. 675, 684 (2001) INTERIM VOLUME

684 121 SUPREME COURT REPORTER 531 U.S. 174

tion of their regulations, and yet we find nothing approaching a clear statement from Congress that it intended § 404(a) to reach an abandoned sand and gravel pit such as we have here. Permitting respondents to claim federal jurisdiction over ponds and mudflats falling within the "Migratory Bird Rule" would result in a significant impingement of the States' traditional and primary power over land and water use. See, *e.g., Hess v. Port Authority Trans–Hudson Corporation,* 513 U.S. 30, 44, 115 S.Ct. 394, 130 L.Ed.2d 245 (1994) ("[R]egulation of land use [is] a function traditionally performed by local governments"). Rather than expressing a desire to readjust the federal-state balance in this manner, Congress chose to "recognize, preserve, and protect the primary responsibilities and rights of States . . . to plan the development and use   of land

ed[175] to that dramatic event, and to others like it, by enacting the Federal Water Pollution Control Act (FWPCA) Amendments of 1972, 86 Stat. 817, as amended, 33 U.S.C. § 1251 *et seq.,* commonly known as the Clean Water Act (Clean Water Act, CWA, or Act).[1] The Act proclaimed the ambitious goal of ending water pollution by 1985. § 1251(a). The Court's past interpretations of the CWA have been fully consistent with that goal. Although Congress' vision of zero pollution remains unfulfilled, its pursuit has unquestionably retarded the destruction of the aquatic environment. Our Nation's waters no longer burn. Today, however, the Court takes an unfortunate step that needlessly weakens our principal safeguard against toxic water.

It is fair to characterize the Clean Wa-

This is the last page of the majority opinion in the *Solid Waste Agency* case. All opinions in West's *Supreme Court Reporter* are identical to those in the official *United States Reports*. Only the editorial material preceding the majority opinion differs.

We hold that 33 CFR § 328.3(a)(3) (1999), as clarified and applied to petitioner's balefill site pursuant to the "Migratory Bird Rule," 51 Fed.Reg. 41217 (1986), exceeds the authority granted to respondents under § 404(a) of the CWA. The judgment of the Court of Appeals for the Seventh Circuit is therefore

Reversed.

Justice STEVENS, with whom Justice SOUTER, Justice GINSBURG, and Justice BREYER join, dissenting.

In 1969, the Cuyahoga River in Cleveland, Ohio, coated with a slick of industrial waste, caught fire. Congress respond-

amended, 33 U.S.C. § 407, Congress had assigned to the Army Corps of Engineers (Corps) the mission of regulating discharges into certain waters in order to protect their use as highways for the transportation of interstate and foreign commerce; the scope of the Corps' jurisdiction under the RHA accordingly extended only to waters that were "navigable." In the CWA, however, Congress broadened the Corps' mission to include the purpose of protecting the quality of our Nation's waters for esthetic, health, recreational, and environmental uses. The scope of its jurisdiction was therefore redefined to encompass all of "the waters of the United States, including the territorial seas." § 1362(7). That

---

8. Because violations of the CWA carry criminal penalties, see 33 U.S.C. § 1319(c)(2), petitioner invokes the rule of lenity as another basis for rejecting the Corps' interpretation of the CWA. Brief for Petitioner 31–32. We need not address this alternative argument.

See *United States v. Shabani,* 513 U.S. 10, 17, 115 S.Ct. 382, 130 L.Ed.2d 225 (1994).

1. See R. Adler, J. Landman, & D. Cameron, The Clean Water Act: 20 Years Later 5–10 (1993).

[Illustration 5–8]

SOLID WASTE AGENCY OF NORTHERN COOK COUNTY V. UNITED STATES ARMY CORPS OF ENGINEERS, AS REPORTED IN ADVANCE SHEETS OF 148 L. ED. 2d 576 (2001)

SOLID WASTE AGENCY OF NORTHERN COOK COUNTY, Petitioner

v

UNITED STATES ARMY CORPS OF ENGINEERS, et al.

⟶ 531 US —, 148 L Ed 2d 576, 121 S Ct —

[No. 99-1178]

Argued October 31, 2000. Decided January 9, 2001.

Decision: Clean Water Act provision (33 USCS § 1344(a)), requiring permit from Army Corps of Engineers for discharge of fill material into navigable waters, held not to extend to isolated, abandoned sand and gravel pit with seasonal ponds which provided migratory bird habitat.

SUMMARY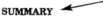

A consortium of suburban municipalities in northern Illinois selected as a solid waste disposal site an abandoned sand and gravel pit with excavation trenches that had evolved into permanent and seasonal ponds. These ponds were intrastate waters that were not adjacent to any bodies of open water. Because the operation called for filling in some of the ponds, the consortium contacted the Army Corps of Engineers (Corps) to determine if a landfill permit was required under § 404(a) of the Clean Water Act (CWA) (33 USCS § 1344(a)), which authorizes the Corps to issue permits allowing the discharge of dredged or fill material into "navigable waters." The CWA defines "navigable waters" as "the waters of the United States" (33 USCS § 1362(7))

This is the first page of the *Solid Waste Agency* case as it appears in an advance sheet of L. Ed. 2d. Formerly published by Lawyers Cooperative Publishing, this set is now published by LexisNexis. The Summary is prepared by the publisher's editorial staff. The omitted page numbers in the citations will be added when the case becomes part of the permanent bound volume.

Rule, the Corps refused to issue a § 404(a) permit. When the consortium brought suit in the United States District Court for the Northern District of Illinois to challenge the Corps' jurisdiction and the merits of the permit denial, the District Court granted the Corps summary judgment on the jurisdictional issue. The United States Court of Appeals for the Seventh Circuit, in affirming, held that (1) Congress had authority under the Federal Constitution's commerce clause (Art I, § 8, cl 3) to regulate intrastate

576

[Illustration 5–9]

PARTIAL PAGES FROM ADVANCE SHEETS OF
148 L. ED. 2D 576, 577 & 579 (2001)

⟶ **HEADNOTES**

Classified to United States Supreme Court Digest, Lawyers' Edition

Environmental Law § 30 — Clear Water Act — Corps of Engineers' jurisdiction — migratory bird rule

1a-1g. Section 404(a) of the Clean Water Act (CWA) (33 USCS § 1344(a)), which requires a permit from the Army Corps of Engineers for the discharge of dredged or fill material into navigable waters, does not extend to an abandoned sand and gravel pit with seasonal ponds which provides habitat for migratory birds, where such ponds are intrastate waters that are not adjacent to any bodies of open water, for (1) holding that such ponds fell under § 404(a) would assume that the use of the word "navigable" does not have any independent significance; (2) the Migratory Bird Rule, by which the Corps extends its jurisdiction over waters which "are or would be used as habitat by migratory birds esced to the Migratory Bird Rule; and (4) construing the CWA as supporting the Migratory Bird Rule would raise significant federal constitutional and federalism questions, as such a construction would result in significant impingement of the states' traditional and primary power over land and water use. (Stevens, Souter, Ginsburg, and Breyer, JJ., dissented from this holding.)

Environmental Law § 30 — Army Corps of Engineers — jurisdiction

2. While the Army Corps of Engineers' jurisdiction under § 404(a) of the Clean Water Act (33 USCS § 1344(a)) extends to wetlands that are adjacent to open water, the text of § 404(a) does not support an extension of jurisdiction where there is no nexus between the wetlands and navigable waters.

This illustration shows examples of headnotes (above, from page 577) in the *Solid Waste Agency* case in L. Ed. 2d as prepared by LexisNexis. Note that they differ from those in West's *Supreme Court Reporter*. "Research References" (below, from page 579) direct the user to related sources in other publications.

RESEARCH REFERENCES ⟵

61C Am Jur 2d, Pollution Control §§ 947 et seq.

33 USCS § 1344(a)

L Ed Digest, Environmental Law § 30; Statutes §§ 107, 112, 152, 156

L Ed Index, Clean Water Act

Annotations:

Supreme Court's views as to construction and application of Federal Water Pollution Control (Clean Water) Act (33 USCS §§ 1251-1376). 84 L Ed 2d 895.

What constitutes "discharge of dredged or fill materials" into navigable waters, so as to be subject to permit requirements under § 404(a) of Federal Water Pollution Control Act (33 USCS § 1344(a)). 72 ALR Fed 703

Criminal proceedings, under § 309(c)(1, 3) of the Federal Water Pollution Control Act (33 USCS § 1319(c)(1, 3), based on violation of § 301(a) of the Act (33 USCS § 1311(a)), prohibiting discharge of pollutants without a permit. 53 ALR Fed 481.

What are "navigable waters" subject to the provisions of the Federal Water Pollution Control Act, as amended (33 USCS §§ 1251 et seq.). 52 ALR Fed 788.

Chapter 6

STATE COURT REPORTS AND THE NATIONAL REPORTER SYSTEM

This chapter discusses state court reports, the *National Reporter System* and its coverage and special features, and methods for citing cases and locating parallel citations.

SECTION A. STATE COURT REPORTS

As indicated in previous chapters, the laws and court rules of the individual states specify the method of publishing state court reports. Case reporters sanctioned by statutes are called *official reports*. Private companies also publish court reports, with or without legislative directives. The private publications of cases that are not legislatively endorsed are called *unofficial reports,* although they are no less accurate than the official reports. The unofficial reports may duplicate the opinions in the official reports or may be the only source of publication.

The unofficial reports fall into two categories. The first consists of those sets that compete directly with the officially published state reports. These reports, which collect cases decided by the courts and publish them in chronological order, usually have more helpful editorial features and faster publication schedules than the official reports. In many states, an unofficial set is a unit of West's *National Reporter System,* which is discussed in the next section of this chapter. The other category is special or subject reports, discussed briefly in this chapter and in more detail in subsequent chapters.

At one time, all states published their judicial opinions in bound volumes of reports, such as the *Michigan Reports.*[1] Those states having intermediate courts of appeals also may have separately bound sets of reports, such as the *Illinois Appellate Reports.*[2] The cases are published chronologically by term of court. An increasing number of states, however, have discontinued publishing official state reports and rely solely on the *National Reporter System* or reports of another commercial publisher as the

---

[1] For additional references to early law reporting in America, see 1784 Conn. Pub. Acts 267; 1–3 Charles Evans, American Bibliography (1903); 4 Isaiah Thomas, History of Printing in America (2d ed. 1874); 1 Charles Warren, History of the Harvard Law School and of Early Legal Conditions in America 203–14 (1908); Mary R. Chapman, Bibliographical Index to the State Reports Prior to the National Reporter System (1977); and Daniel R. Coquillette, *First Flower—The Earliest American Law Reports and the Extraordinary Josiah Quincy, Jr. (1744–1775),* 30 Suffolk U. L. Rev. 1 (1996).

[2] For a listing of states with intermediate courts of appeals, see the latest edition of Council of State Governments, The Book of the States (1935–   ).

official report.[3] In a few instances, a state does not have a designated official set of reports. Increasingly, states are using the Internet to make their court cases available.

In several states, advance sheets or slip opinions often precede the publication of official bound reports. The unofficial print publications always include advance sheets as part of the subscription. In many instances, the fastest means of access is an electronic version.

A court or its reporter of decisions may have the power to select the cases for publication in the official state reports. In the exercise of that power, some less important cases may be eliminated from the official reports.[4]

The Internet has spawned remarkable growth in the ready availability of state case law. Many websites, such as that of the National Center for State Courts, provide links to Web pages and opinions of state courts.[5] These state sites are updated frequently as new court materials become available. The amount of information for each state varies greatly depending upon the speed with which the different governments are entering the electronic age.

In a general survey, such as this, it is not possible to present a detailed study of the reporting system for each state. Legal research guides are available for many states. These guides typically discuss a state's case law research in depth.[6]

SECTION B. NATIONAL REPORTER SYSTEM

The *National Reporter System,* which began in 1879, is published by West. It is the largest and most comprehensive collection of state and federal cases in printed form. It consists of three main divisions: (1) cases of state courts; (2) cases of federal courts; and (3) cases of special courts. There are also subject reporters that extract cases from the various *National Reporter System* units.[7]

The development of the *National Reporter System* has had a profound impact on the method of finding judicial opinions and some suggest on the development of American law.[8] At the inception of the *National Reporter*

[3] *See* Appendix D of this book for a list of states that have discontinued their state reports and a table indicating the year of the first case decided for each state or territory. For a state-by-state guide to published court reports and how they interrelate with the *National Reporter System,* see KEITH WIESE, HEIN'S STATE REPORT CHECKLIST (2d rev. ed. 2000) (A.A.L.L. Legal Research Series, No. 2 looseleaf).

[4] Leah F. Chanin, *A Survey of the Writing and Publication of Opinions in Federal and State Appellate Courts,* 67 LAW LIBR. J. 362 (1974). *See also* Chapters 4 and 5 for discussions of unpublished opinions.

[5] http://www.ncsconline.org/D_KIS/info_court_web_sites.html. *See also* the *State and Local Government on the Net* website: http://www.statelocalgov.net/50states-courts.cfm.

[6] A list of these state guides is published in Appendix B of this book.

[7] *See* Appendix E of this book for a chart showing coverage of the *National Reporter System.*

[8] *See* Thomas A. Woxland, *"Forever Associated with the Practice of Law": The Early Years of the West Publishing Company,* 5(1) LEGAL REFERENCE SERVICES Q., Spring 1985, at 115; Joe Morehead, *All Cases Great and Small: The West Publishing Company Saga,* SERIALS LIBRARIAN, No. 3/4, 1988, at 3. *See also* Robert C. Berring, *Full–Text Databases and Legal Research: Backing into the Future,* 1 HIGH TECH. L.J. 27, 29–38 (1986); Robert C. Berring, *Legal Research*

System, the states and territories in existence at the time, the various federal circuit courts, and the Supreme Court of the United States all published court reports. In fact, some of these publications had been ongoing for almost a century. In the absence of a coherent, uniform means of accessing these materials, the difficulty of finding cases with similar points of law became immense. The *National Reporter System,* in conjunction with West's topic and key number classification system (discussed in the next chapter), brought organization to the chaos resulting from the rapid growth in published court reports by numerous sources. The *National Reporter System* continues to play an important role in legal research, although technological developments have made it possible for case law to be disseminated, stored, and retrieved in new ways.

1. State Court Coverage

The original idea of the *National Reporter System* was to group together cases from several adjacent states. The first of these geographical groupings was the *North Western Reporter,* which began in 1879. By 1887, an additional six groupings—*Pacific, North Eastern, Atlantic, South Western, Southern,* and *South Eastern*—in that order, had been added to make coverage nationwide. [Illustration 6–1]

These seven units are often referred to as regional reporters, although the states included in some groupings are not always what might be expected, e.g., Oklahoma is in *Pacific Reporter,* Michigan is in *North Western Reporter,* etc. These early geographical groupings were likely based on the country's population at the time and the expectation that each regional unit would grow at approximately the same pace. This did not occur, but the regional groupings remained unchanged from when they were originally established, except in those instances when a new state came into existence and needed to be added to a particular group. Today, each regional unit contains several hundred volumes and all are in a second series, except *Pacific* and *South Western,* which are in a third series.[9]

Population growth has, however, altered the coverage of two of the regional reporters. This occurred first in 1888 with the establishment of a separate reporter for New York, the *New York Supplement.* This reporter includes cases from the New York Court of Appeals, which is New York's court of last resort, as well as cases from the lower appellate courts. The only New York cases currently reported in the *North Eastern Reporter* are those of the New York Court of Appeals. In 1960, West began publishing the *California Reporter.* It includes cases from the California Supreme Court and intermediate appellate courts. These intermediate appellate court cases from California are no longer in the *Pacific Reporter.* Both of these state units of the *National Reporter System* are in their second series.

The *National Reporter System* has, since its beginning, reported cases from each state's highest court. Although it now also reports cases from all

---

and Legal Concepts: Where Form Molds Substance, 75 CAL. L. REV. 15 (1987); Robert C. Berring, *Chaos, Cyberspace and Tradition: Legal Information Transmogrified,* 12 BERKELEY TECH. L.J. 189 (1997).

[9] Like the FEDERAL REPORTER 2D and FEDERAL SUPPLEMENT, these units began a new series after reaching volume 999.

state intermediate appellate courts, the inclusion of these cases began at different times. For example, Missouri appellate cases are included in the *South Western Reporter,* beginning with 93 Mo. App. (1902); Illinois appellate cases are contained in the *North Eastern Reporter,* beginning with 284 Ill. App. (1936).

Often it is impractical for attorneys to acquire a regional reporter when what they most often need is access to cases from their state. Consequently, West publishes "offprint" reporters for individual states by reprinting a state's cases from a regional reporter and rebinding them under a new name, e.g., *Texas Cases, Missouri Decisions.* There are approximately 30 publications of this type. These offprints retain the volume number and pagination of the regional reporter. The exception to this is another *National Reporter System* unit, *Illinois Decisions,* in which each volume is paged consecutively. Most states that no longer publish official state reports have adopted the regional reporter that covers their state and the offprint version as their official reports.

Both *Westlaw* and *LexisNexis* provide extensive state court coverage. Although there is no uniform date for how far back this coverage extends, coverage for most states exists at least since the 1940s. For many states, the coverage is much more extensive, often dating from the late 1800s. Information about the scope of coverage is available online and through print publications of these two vendors. The retrospective coverage of state case law of other electronic research services varies from state to state. In addition, West publishes collections of state reports on CD–ROM. These products allow for hypertext linking whereby a researcher can highlight a case citation and jump automatically to a screen displaying the cited case. These CD–ROM products can be updated through a subscription to *Westlaw*.

2. Federal Court and Special Court Coverage

West's federal court coverage began only a year after its first regional reporter in 1879. Today, five units of the *National Reporter System* cover the various federal courts—*West's Supreme Court Reporter, Federal Reporter* (F., F.2d, F.3d), *Federal Appendix* (F. App.), Federal *Supplement* (F. Supp., F. Supp. 2d), and *Federal Rules Decisions.* Another four units contain cases from specialized federal courts—*Bankruptcy Reporter, Military Justice Reporter, Federal Claims Reporter,* and *Veterans Appeals Reporter.*[10] Like the regional reporters, reports from the federal units of the *National Reporter System* are available in *Westlaw, LexisNexis,* and other CALR services.

3. Coverage of Specialized Subjects

In addition to the federal, state, and regional reporters mentioned above, West also publishes specialized subject reporters such as the *Education Law Reporter, Social Security Reporting Service,* and *United States Merit Systems Protection Board Reporter.* Although the publisher does not

---

[10] These various federal units of the *National Reporter System* are discussed in Chapter 5 of this book.

consider these sets to be part of its *National Reporter System,* they often reprint cases contained in it.

4.   Features of the National Reporter System

As described, the *National Reporter System* contains the full text of cases decided by the various state and federal courts. West adds numerous editorial enhancements that facilitate research. These common features, discussed below, make it possible for researchers to find cases from all the states, as well as those decided in the federal courts on the same or similar points of law.

When West receives opinions from the courts, its editors prepare headnotes and assign key numbers from its *American Digest System.* West publishes these cases first in advance sheets and then in bound volumes. The key numbers are the basis of the *National Reporter System*'s indexing method, the nature of which is described in Chapter 7 of this book. Bound volumes retain the same volume and page numbers as the advance sheets.[11]

In addition to the opinions and headnotes, the advance sheets and bound volumes of the *National Reporter System* include a synopsis of the case, a digest section containing headnotes and key numbers of the cases covered,[12] a table of cases arranged by state, a table of statutes interpreted by cases covered (ceased at the start of 2000), a list of words and phrases defined in the cases reported, and a table showing cases that have cited the second edition of the American Bar Association's *Standards for Criminal Justice.* From time to time the various units also include proposed changes to or newly approved versions of court rules.

The advance sheets to the reporters contain several current awareness features that are not incorporated into the bound volumes. For example, the state and regional reporters contain summaries of federal cases arising in each state covered by that reporter. "Judicial Highlights," contained in both the state and regional reporters, are features that briefly describe cases of special interest or significance.

5.   Ultra Fiche Edition

West also publishes an ultra fiche edition for each series of the *National Reporter System.* The reduction ratio is 75x and is compatible with lenses covering a range of 67x to 92x. The first, second, and third series are available in this format. Ongoing second and third series are filmed as the hard copy volumes are published, with very little lag time between issuance of the two formats. The shelf space savings allowed by the ultra fiche edition are enormous.

[11] Occasionally after a case has been published in an advance sheet, the judge who wrote the opinion might, for one reason or another, decide that it should not be published and recalls the opinion. In such instances, another case is published in the appendix of a subsequent advance sheet with the same pagination as the withdrawn case. By this means, the original pagination is preserved in the bound volume.

[12] Features such as the digest section in individual volumes are current awareness devices and are repeated in the cumulations of digests on the state, regional, and national levels. Consequently, West does not reproduce these digest sections and some other features when reprinting older volumes.

[Illustration 6–1]

MAP OF THE NATIONAL REPORTER SYSTEM®*
Showing the States in Each Regional Reporter Group

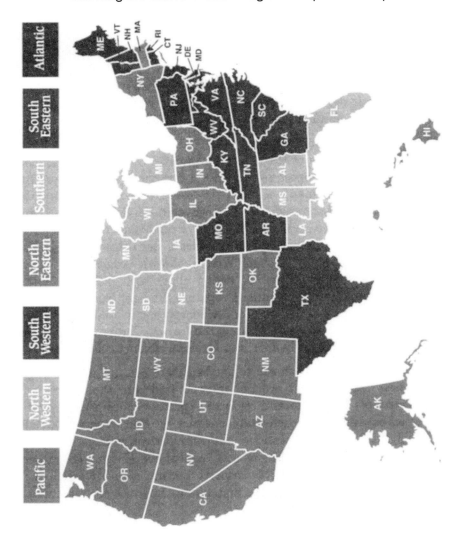

* The National Reporter System also includes:

Supreme Court Reporter
Federal Supplement
West's Bankruptcy Reporter
West's California Reporter
West's Military Justice Reporter
Federal Claims Reporter

Federal Reporter
Federal Rules Decisions
New York Supplement
West's Illinois Decisions
Veterans Appeals Reporter
Federal Appendix

SECTION C. METHODS OF CITING STATE CASES

1. Name of Case

Generally, a citation should contain the name of the case followed by the citation to the case's location either in the official reports, if available, to the corresponding unit or units of the *National Reporter System,* or to both.[13] When both the official and unofficial citations are used, this is referred to as *parallel citation*. The full name of the case appears at the beginning. A short form of the case name usually appears at the top of each subsequent page of the case. Typically, it is the short form (or a slight variation) that is used in the citation, e.g.,

Josephine RAVO, an Infant, by Her Father and Natural
Guardian, Antonio RAVO, Respondent

v.

Sol ROGATNICK, Respondent, and Irwin L. Harris,
Appellant

Its short form title is *Ravo v. Rogatnick.*

2. Early State Reporters

Where the name of a reporter is used in citing an early state report, the preferred practice is to indicate the state and the date. An example is:

Day v. Sweetser, 2 Tyl. 283 (Vt. 1803).

3. Parallel Citations

When a case has been reported in an official state reporter and in a regional reporter, official court rules for the state may require a parallel citation. In such instances, the citation to the state report is given first, followed by the parallel citation to the appropriate regional reporter or reporters. The year the case was decided is then given in parenthesis. Examples are:

Ravo v. Rogatnick, 70 N.Y.2d 305, 514 N.E.2d 1104, 520 N.Y.S.2d 533 (1987).

Izazaga v. Superior Court, 54 Cal. 3d 356, 815 P.2d 304, 285 Cal. Rptr. 231 (1991).

Commonwealth v. Jaime, 433 Mass. 575, 745 N.E.2d 320 (2001).

When there is no official set of state reports or where there is no local court rule to the contrary, citation is given first to where it is reported in the *National Reporter System* followed by an indication of the court and year of decision in parenthesis. An example is:

Apex Towing Co. v. Tolin, 41 S.W.3d 118 (Tex.2001).

---

[13] For state court documents, the 18th edition of THE BLUEBOOK: A UNIFORM SYSTEM OF CITATION requires parallel citations only for cases decided by courts of the state in which the documents are being submitted or if required by local court rules. The ALWD CITATION MANUAL requires parallel citations if it is required by local court rules. However, courts do not necessarily follow either citation manual. It is essential, therefore, to check the appropriate court rules to determine proper citation form. Citation form is discussed extensively in Chapter 24.

4. Finding Parallel Citations to State Court Opinions

Frequently, a researcher has only the citation to a case in an official state report or a regional or state unit of the *National Reporter System* and needs to find the parallel citation. This can be accomplished in several ways.

a. *State Citation to National Reporter System Citation.* When only the state citation is available, refer to one of the following:

(1) *National Reporter Blue Book.* This set, published by West, lists all state citations, alphabetically by state, and gives for each state citation its parallel citation in the appropriate unit or units of the *National Reporter System.* This set consists of bound volumes that are kept current by annual cumulative pamphlets.

(2) *Shepard's Citations* (print edition) for the state.

(3) *Shepard's* or "Get a Document" on *LexisNexis.*

(4) *KeyCite* or "Find by Citation" on *Westlaw.*

(5) The *Table of Cases* in the appropriate state or regional digest.

b. *National Reporter System Citation to State Citation.* When only the citation to a volume of the *National Reporter System* is available, refer to one of the following:

(1) *Shepard's Citations* (print edition) for the appropriate regional and state reporter unit.

(2) *Shepard's* or "Get a Document" on *LexisNexis.*

(3) *KeyCite* or "Find by Citation" on *Westlaw.*

(4) The *Table of Cases* in the appropriate state or regional digest, or *Table of Cases* volumes in the appropriate unit of the *American Digest System.*

(5) *Star Pagination in the National Reporter System.* The volumes of the *National Reporter* System usually contain the parallel citation to official reports. As early as 1922, West provided "star pagination," or parallel pagination, from the texts of opinions in its *New York Supplement* to the corresponding pages in the official *New York Reports.* Star pagination allows the researcher to find "jump cites" or "pinpoint cites" to textual matter within the body of the case. Although this feature is still included for a few cases, the delay of most states in publishing their official reports, when coupled with West's speed in publishing the *National Reporter System,* often makes star pagination impossible in the print editions.

[Illustration 6–2]

PAGE FROM THE NATIONAL REPORTER BLUE BOOK

93 NEW YORK REPORTS, SECOND SERIES

N.Y.2d Page	N.Y.S.2d Vol.	Page	N.E.2d Vol.	Page	N.Y.2d Page	N.Y.S.2d Vol.	Page	N.E.2d Vol.	Page	N.Y.2d Page	N.Y.S.2d Vol.	Page	N.E.2d Vol.	Page
1	686	743	709	452	729	697	538	719	897	897[1]	690	176	712	114
14	686	750	709	459	750	697	866	720	86	904	690	501	712	668
23	686	754	709	463	758	697	869	720	89	904[1]	690	177	712	115
29	686	756	709	465	768	698	594	720	870	904[2]	690	177	712	115
34	687	598	710	244	781	698	590	720	866	904[3]	690	177	712	115
42	687	601	710	247	790	698	601	720	878	906	691	377	713	411
48	687	604	710	250	821	687	615	710	261	907[1]	691	377	713	411
60	687	609	710	255	823	687	615	710	261	907[2]	691	377	713	411
73	688	90	710	655	825	687	617	710	263	907[3]	691	377	713	411
80	688	101	710	665	827	687	622	710	268	907[4]	691	377	713	412
86	688	105	710	669	828	687	618	710	264	908	690	510	712	676
90	688	96	710	660	828[2]	687	622	710	268	908[1]	691	378	713	412
99	688	107	710	671	828[3]	687	622	710	268	908[2]	691	378	713	412

> The *National Reporter Blue Book* consists of a main bound volume, permanent bound supplements, and a cumulative supplement updating the latest permanent bound volume. This *Blue Book* contains tables showing volume and page of the *National Reporter System* volume for every case found in the corresponding state reports.
>
> In this example, if one had only the citation to 93 N.Y.2d 90, the table can be used to locate the citation of this case in the *New York Supplement 2d* and *North Eastern 2d*.

N.Y.2d Page	N.Y.S.2d Vol.	Page	N.E.2d Vol.	Page	N.Y.2d Page	N.Y.S.2d Vol.	Page	N.E.2d Vol.	Page	N.Y.2d Page	N.Y.S.2d Vol.	Page	N.E.2d Vol.	Page
239	689	660	711	958	842	689	1	711	187	932	693	67	715	95
249	689	692	711	970	845[1]	688	490	710	1089	933[2]	694	345	716	181
254	689	689	711	967	845[2]	688	490	710	1089	934	693	502	715	504
261	689	695	711	972	845[3]	688	490	710	1089	936	693	69	715	96
273	689	701	711	978	846[2]	688	490	710	1089	938	693	502	715	504
282	690	495	712	662	846[4]	688	491	710	1090	939	693	66	715	93
296	690	489	712	656	846[5]	688	491	710	1090	942	693	70	715	98
307	690	517	712	682	846[6]	688	491	710	1090	944	693	503	715	505
314	690	520	712	686	847	688	491	710	1090	944[1]	693	502	715	504
322	690	524	712	689	847[6]	688	492	710	1091	944[2]	693	502	715	505
327	690	527	712	692	859[1]	689	13	711	198	944[3]	693	503	715	505
334	690	475	712	644	860	688	94	710	659	945[1]	693	503	715	505
343	690	478	712	647	862	689	13	711	198	945[2]	693	504	715	506
352	690	483	712	652	864	689	13	711	198	945[3]	693	504	715	506
361	690	503	712	669	867	689	13	711	198	946	694	337	716	172
368	690	506	712	673	868[1]	689	14	711	199	946[1]	693	504	715	506
375	690	512	712	678	868[1]	689	679	711	958	946[2]	693	504	715	507
382	690	854	712	1220	869[1]	689	14	711	199	948	694	342	716	177
398	690	863	712	1228	869[2]	689	14	711	199	949	694	338	716	173
416	690	874	712	1238	869[3]	689	14	711	200	952	694	342	716	177
424	691	372	713	406	881[1]	689	424	711	638	952[2]	694	343	716	178
433	692	638	714	851	881[2]	689	424	711	638	953[1]	694	343	716	178
454	692	649	714	861	882[1]	689	424	711	638	953[2]	694	343	716	178
465	693	63	715	91	882[2]	689	425	711	639	953[3]	694	344	716	179
471	693	77	715	104	882[3]	689	425	711	639	954[1]	694	344	716	179
477	693	71	715	99	883[1]	689	425	711	639	954[2]	694	344	716	179
487	693	81	715	107	883[2]	689	426	711	640	954[3]	694	344	716	180
499	693	87	715	113	883[3]	689	426	711	640	955[1]	694	345	716	180
508	693	91	715	117	884	688	479	710	1078	956[1]	694	346	716	181
517	693	475	715	479	884[1]	689	426	711	640	956[2]	694	346	716	181
525	693	479	715	482	886[1]	689	426	711	640	956[3]	694	346	716	182
531	693	482	715	486	886[2]	689	427	711	641	959	694	340	716	175
539	693	486	715	489	886[3]	689	427	711	641	960	694	346	716	182
554	693	493	715	495	887[1]	689	428	711	642	963	694	347	716	182
564	693	498	715	500	887[2]	689	427	711	641	982[1]	695	740	717	1077
571	693	861	715	1054	887[3]	689	428	711	642	983	695	740	717	1077
584	693	857	715	1050	889	689	687	711	965	986	695	49	716	1094
592	695	39	716	1084	891	689	686	711	964	988[1]	695	740	717	1077
611	695	515	717	674	893	689	685	711	963	988[2]	695	741	717	1078
620	695	715	717	1052	895[1]	690	175	712	113	988[3]	695	741	717	1078
645	695	525	717	684	895[2]	690	175	712	113	989[1]	695	741	717	1078
655	695	520	717	679	895[3]	690	175	712	113	989[2]	695	741	717	1079
664	695	531	717	690	896[1]	690	176	712	114	989[3]	695	742	717	1079
677	697	846	720	66	896[2]	690	176	712	114	989[4]	695	742	717	1079
710	695	730	717	1067	896[3]	690	176	712	114	990	695	537	717	696

Chapter 7

DIGESTS FOR COURT REPORTS

———————

This chapter discusses digests, which traditionally have been one of the most important finding aids for locating judicial opinions. The development of computer-assisted legal research services (CALR), with huge case law databases and powerful search engines, has provided a more effective and efficient method for identifying relevant case law. In some situations, however, a researcher might not have access to a CALR service, or a digest might still be the most efficient way to approach a problem. West is the most prominent producer of case law digests, and the focus of this chapter is on its system.

SECTION A. DIGESTS IN GENERAL

Because our jurisprudential system is based on the doctrine of *stare decisis,* the ability to locate earlier case law on the same or similar points of law is essential to effective legal research. As has been noted, judicial opinions are published in court reports in chronological order rather by subject. Without a method to locate cases by subject, retrieving cases with the same or similar points of law would be time-consuming and difficult.

After cases are decided, editors of commercial publishers analyze the opinions and write brief descriptive abstracts of the various points of law in the opinions. These abstracts are typically referred to as *headnotes* or *digest paragraphs*. Later, these descriptive paragraphs are arranged by subject in a classification system and published in sets known as *digests*.

Digests provide a valuable way to find cases on a specific subject. Digests vary in the types of cases they abstract and organize. Some include only cases from the courts of a single state, one court, or a system of courts; others include cases from a group of neighboring states; and some include cases on only one broad subject. One is comprehensive, and includes cases from all federal and state appellate courts. In this chapter we focus primarily on the digests published by West that work in conjunction with its *National Reporter System*.

Because digests are finding aids that serve as a means of locating cases by subject, they have no legal authority and are never cited as such. Do not rely on the text of the digest paragraphs for the theory of a case; instead use them as a means for obtaining citations to cases. Digest paragraphs are necessarily brief and can fail to suggest the reasoning behind the court's decision and important factors that affected the decision, factors that may have a specific bearing on the problem. *In all instances, researchers should read the actual opinion from which the digest paragraph was developed.*

SECTION B.   WEST'S KEY NUMBER DIGESTS

1.   The Classification System

When the *National Reporter System* began in the late nineteenth century, West Publishing Company, as it was then known, realized that users of its reporters needed a means to locate by subject the many points of law set forth in the chronologically arranged cases. To answer this need, West developed its own unique subject classification of law, with each subject receiving its own "topic" and "key number." Editors created digest paragraphs abstracting the points of law in the cases, assigned appropriate topics and key numbers to the paragraphs, and arranged these digest paragraphs according to its system of classification. The result was the *American Digest System*, a massive set of materials in several units. It is described by West as a "master index to all of the case law of our country." It contains the headnotes, with their corresponding topics and key numbers, from every unit of the *National Reporter System*.

West's classification system divides the subject of law into seven main classes: Persons; Property; Contracts; Torts; Crimes; Remedies; and Government. Each class is divided into subclasses and each subclass into topics. Each of the over 400 topics corresponds to a legal concept. [Illustration 7–1] Topics are then divided into subdivisions with each subdivision being assigned a key number. The amount of key numbers assigned within topics varies from a few to many hundreds. Digest paragraphs, with their topic and key numbers, are cumulated and published in multivolume sets of digests.

2.   The Key Number System

The process undertaken by West in developing its key number digests starts with receipt of an opinion directly from the court. That opinion is assigned to a West editor. Assume the editor receives the Illinois opinion for *Kasin v. Osco Drug, Inc.* The editor reads and analyzes the case and, in this instance, writes three headnotes, with each headnote representing a particular point of law addressed in the case. [Illustration 7–2] Over 500,000 new headnotes are written each year.

In this example, an editor decides that one of the three headnotes derived from the *Kasin* case deals with "drugs." The editor consults the list of over 400 topics and assigns to the headnote the topic *Drugs and Narcotics*. The next step is the assignment of a particular key number or key numbers. The editor examines a detailed outline of subdivisions within the topic *Drugs and Narcotics*. This outline, discussed more fully in Section D–2 of this chapter, is referred to as the *Analysis*.

After consulting this outline, the editor determines that the headnote deals with manufacturers of drugs, a subject which corresponds to key number 18. The topic *Drugs and Narcotics*, therefore, receives key number 18. The same steps are followed for the other two digest paragraphs. One is assigned two topics—*Drugs and Narcotics*, key number 18, and *Physicians and Surgeons*, key number 15(8). The third digest paragraph is also classified under the topic *Drugs and Narcotics* and is assigned key number 19. After the editorial work is complete, the case, immediately preceded by the topics, key numbers, and digest paragraphs, is published in the appropriate unit or units of the *National Reporter System.* [Illustration 7–2] These topics, key numbers, and digest paragraphs are then incorporated into the appropriate sets of key number digests.

A set of brackets surrounding a number in the text of the published opinion, e.g., [3], indicates the language in the opinion that corresponds to the headnote. [Illustration 7–3] This enables a researcher interested in the point of law discussed in a particular headnote to go directly to that part of the case from which the headnote is derived. As indicated above, at times a headnote is classified to more than one topic. In such instances, all appropriate topics and key numbers are shown.[1]

3. Common Features of West's Key Number Digests

West's key number digests have the following common features in addition to topics and key numbers:

a. *Descriptive–Word Index* volume(s). This source is described in Section D–1, below.

b. *Table of Cases* volume(s). This source is described in Section D–3, below.

c. *Words and Phrases.* This is an alphabetical listing that contains words and phrases that have been judicially defined. These definitions are subsequently compiled in a multivolume set entitled *Words and Phrases.* It is discussed in Section M–1 of this chapter.

d. *Supplements.* Digests are periodically updated by replacement volumes, pocket supplements, interim pamphlet supplements, and later bound volumes and advance sheets of the West reporters.

e. *Numerical References to Topics.* The pocket supplements and recently published volumes of digests contain numerical references to topics that can be used in *Westlaw* searches for cases with the topic and within specified key numbers.

SECTION C. KEY NUMBERS AND DIGEST PARAGRAPHS IN WESTLAW

Cases dated after 1931 are searchable electronically in *Westlaw* with the key number system. It is possible to search, for example, the topic *Drugs and Narcotics,* key number 18, and retrieve all cases classified under this point of law since 1932; to restrict the search to a particular period of time; or to add a specific search term, such as *manufacturer,* to the query. Key number searching in *Westlaw* often eliminates the task of searching in the more recent paper key number digests. *Westlaw* and a companion CD–ROM product both include powerful hypertext features in case headnotes. A researcher can "jump" directly to the related text in the opinion or jump from the text directly to the related headnote. [Illustration 7–4][2]

---

[1] For an article exploring the strengths and weaknesses of West's digests, see Fritz Snyder, *The West Digest System: The Ninth Circuit and the Montana Supreme Court,* 60 Mont. L. Rev. 541 (1999).

[2] Electronic legal research is discussed in Chapter 23.

In *Westlaw*, topics are converted to a numerical equivalent that corresponds to the alphabetically arranged topics used in the key number digests. [Illustration 7–1] The key number symbol is converted to the letter "k." [Illustration 7–4] Information indicating *Westlaw*'s numerical equivalents to the West topic and key numbers is available online and in numerous print publications, including the more recent key number digest volumes.

The most recent innovation using the key number system in *Westlaw* is *KeySearch*. *KeySearch* is an electronic research tool that helps the user locate cases and secondary sources within a specific area of law. A researcher selects a legal issue from an organized hierarchy powered by the West key number system, and then *KeySearch* creates the query using relevant key numbers and their unique concepts. *KeySearch* includes approximately 10,000 legal issues that are used in running queries.

SECTION D. CONDUCTING RESEARCH USING A STATE KEY NUMBER DIGEST

To demonstrate how to use a key number digest, we can focus on the use of a state digest. Because most features in a state key number digest are common to all key number digests, an understanding of the methods of using a state digest is transferable to the comprehensive and cumbersome-to-use *Decennial Digests* and *General Digests*, discussed in Section G of this chapter, and to the various specialized West digests. An understanding of the digest system also is extremely helpful in conducting *Westlaw* research.

West publishes a key number digest for almost every state.[3] A typical state key number digest consists of digest paragraphs for all reported appellate opinions of the state, including federal court opinions that arose in or were appealed from that jurisdiction. Some West state digests have special features unique to a particular state, such as references to law review articles from law schools in the state. [Illustration 7–6] Researchers should examine carefully the state digest available for their state and familiarize themselves with any special features.

Assume the following hypothetical problem, which will serve as the basis for discussion and most of the illustrations used later in this and other chapters of this book:

> Fran went to the doctor complaining of abdominal pain. The doctor correctly diagnosed the problem as acute gastritis and prescribed a relatively common medicine as treatment. Fran followed the directions for taking the drug provided by the pharmacist and the treating physician. Within a few days, Fran became ill and jaundiced. Shortly thereafter, Fran suffered complete liver failure requiring a transplant. All of these events occurred in Illinois. Who, if anyone, is liable for Fran's suffering?

Before beginning to research any legal problem, the researcher first must determine the important issues involved, and it might be necessary to conduct preliminary or background research in order to formulate the legal

---

[3] West publishes key number digests for every state except Delaware, Nevada, and Utah. A few states have digests available from other publishers.

issues.[4] One issue might involve the duty, if any, of the pharmaceutical company that manufactured the drug to warn Fran of the adverse side effects of the drug. Other issues may relate to the potential liability of both the physician and pharmacist.

In order to find the law applicable to this situation, the researcher might begin search for appellate court opinions with the same or similar facts. If only Illinois appellate case reporters were available, it would be necessary to examine individually hundreds of volumes to determine if any cases were on point. If a relevant Illinois case could not be located, it then would be necessary to search for cases from other states. Because of their subject arrangement, digests reduce the laborious task of having to search for cases in court reports volume by volume.

In our earlier discussion, we explained how the West editors prepare topics, key numbers, and headnotes. With more than 400 topics and over 100,000 key numbers in use in West digests, learning how to find the appropriate topics and key numbers is very important for successful case finding. Four common methods are provided for finding topics and key numbers within the various key number digests. Thereafter, the researcher must update the topics and key numbers to find the most recent information.

1.   The Descriptive–Word Method

The *Descriptive–Word Index (DWI)* is a highly detailed, alphabetically arranged, subject index to the contents of the key number digests. This index is often the best starting point for research, unless a relevant case or the particular topic and key number is already known. The *DWI* includes *catchwords* or descriptive words relating to the legal issues covered by the digests. This *Descriptive–Word Index,* often in several volumes, is a part of each key number digest.

Using the *Descriptive–Word Index* successfully requires analysis of the legal issues and often the ability to think in both broad and narrow terms and to shift perspective from the general to the specific. It might prove helpful at this point to review the *TARP Rule* discussed in Chapter 2 of this book.

Let us examine the hypothetical problem presented previously to see how the *Descriptive–Word Index* to the *Illinois Digest 2d* is used to locate topics and key numbers for finding cases dealing with the liability of a manufacturer for making drugs that cause injury. When using this index, the first entry to consult should be a specific word or phrase relevant to the fact situation being researched.

In our fact situation, a specific word is *manufacturer.* An examination of this word in the *Descriptive–Word Index* to the *Illinois Digest 2d* reveals the following entry:

---

[4] *See* Chapter 2 for a general approach to the research process.

[See Illustration 7–5]

MANUFACTURERS AND MANUFACTURING COMPANIES

DRUGS and medicine, civil liability.

Drugs & N 18

These references indicate that the topic *Drugs and Narcotics,* key number 18, contains digest paragraphs that address the legal issue being researched.

2. Analysis or Topic Method

As mentioned in Section B–1 of this chapter, over 400 topics are used in West's key number digests. Each topic is subdivided in outline form, setting forth the main headings and subdivisions to which key numbers are assigned.

These outlines are published at the start of each topic in the various key number digests. Two preliminary sections, "Subjects Included" and "Subjects Excluded and Covered by Other Topics," are set forth immediately before the detailed outline. [Illustration 7–7] Reading this "scope note" is often helpful in determining if the research is being conducted in the proper topic. The topical outline that follows, which is the key number classification scheme for that topic, is titled the *Analysis.*

The *Analysis* sections under the topics *Drugs and Narcotics* and *Physicians and Surgeons* were used in establishing the key numbers for the headnotes in *Kasin v. Osco Drug, Inc.,* a case important in resolving our hypothetical problem. By carefully scanning the *Analysis,* a researcher often can see details in coverage that might not have come to mind in the initial assessment of a legal issue and, thus, identify the most specific key number (or additional key numbers) to use. Section lines, preceded by the key numbers, indicate the content of each key number under a topic. [Illustration 7–8]

Use of the *Analysis* method generally requires certainty that the topic selected is the appropriate one, as well as a thorough understanding of West's key number classification.[5] Use of this method is often most successful when combined with the *Descriptive–Word Index* method.

3. Table of Cases Method

Each key number digest includes, in one or more volumes, *Table of Cases* volumes that list the parties to all cases included in the digest by both plaintiff and defendant name. The *Table of Cases* is arranged alphabetically. Each case listing includes the citation and the topics and key numbers under which the case has been digested and any subsequent case history. For example, if the researcher has determined that *Kasin v. Osco Drug, Inc.,* is relevant to the issue and the case citation is not available, the *Table of Cases* provides both the citation to that case and the topics and key numbers assigned to that case. [Illustration 7–9] Once the pertinent topic and key numbers are identified, the *Analysis* can be consulted for other relevant key numbers.

---

[5] WEST'S ANALYSIS OF AMERICAN LAW, issued annually, reproduces the entire key number classification system in one paperback volume. It incorporates the latest changes and additions made to West's key number system.

4. An Alternative Method for Locating Topics and Key Numbers

Frequently, a citation to a case is located that suggests it contains a relevant point of law. Such citations might be found in almost any legal source, e.g., a law review article, another case, a set of annotated statutes, a treatise, or an encyclopedia. Rather than attempting to find similar cases using any of the three methods previously described, it is sometimes more practical to go immediately to the unit of the *National Reporter System* containing the cited case that has been identified. If, after reading the case, a determination is made that it is relevant to the research, one should note all relevant topics and key numbers under which any part of the case has been classified. A researcher can then go directly to any of West's key number digests and look under the same topics and key numbers and find other digest paragraphs involving similar issues of law.

5. Updating West's Key Number Digests

Because digest paragraphs originate as headnotes in the advance sheets of the *National Reporter System,* updating research using the key number classification in print sources requires the researcher to consult the advance sheets of the relevant reporter. After locating an appropriate topic and key number in the bound volume of a digest, e.g., *Illinois Digest 2d*, the researcher must next check under the same topic and key number in the pocket supplement to that volume and in any interim pamphlets. A table, usually entitled *Closing with Cases Reported in*, is located in the front of the latest supplementation, typically on the back of the title page. This "closing table" indicates the last volume covered in each *National Reporter System* unit included in the digest.

For example, a closing table in *Illinois Digest 2d* includes references similar to the following:

Closing with Cases Reported in

Illinois Decisions	254 Ill.Dec. 298
North Eastern Reporter, Second Series	747 N.E. 2d 338
Supreme Court Reporter	121 S.Ct. 1752
Federal Reporter, Third Series	248 F. 3d 1186
Federal Supplement, Second Series	137 F.Supp. 2d
Federal Rules Decisions	200 F.R.D. 51
Bankruptcy Reporter	261 B.R. 321
Illinois Court of Claims	46 Ill.Ct.Cl.

After a researcher determines the extent of coverage of the digest, the next step is to check under this topic and key number in the digest section found in the *back* of any later bound volumes of reporters covering the jurisdiction being researched. The last step is to check the digest paragraphs found in the *front* of each advance sheet to these reporters. Only West's *Supreme Court Reporter* cumulates its digest paragraphs in the last advance sheet for a volume. A *Westlaw* topic and key number search for cases reported after the most recent available print resource would produce the most recent decisions.

SECTION E. KEY NUMBER DIGESTS FOR FEDERAL CASES

Whenever a researcher is aware that the research problem involves issues that would be decided in a federal court, research may be effectively conducted in a federal digest. Several key number digests are published for federal judicial opinions.

1. West's Federal Practice Digest, 4th

This set includes digests of cases from 1984 to present for all federal courts.[6] Its special features include:

a. Under each key number, cases are arranged by court and are listed in reverse chronological order. Cases decided by the Supreme Court of the United States are listed first, followed by cases from the courts of appeals, and, finally the district courts (arranged alphabetically by jurisdiction).

b. The digest paragraphs include information as to whether a case has been *affirmed, reversed,* or *modified.*

c. A complete numerical listing of all patents adjudicated for the period covered by this digest is found under the topic *Patents,* key number 328.

d. An alphabetical table of all *Trade–Marks and Trade Names Adjudicated* is included in the *Trade Regulation* volume at key number 736.

e. Each topic and key number can be linked to its numerical equivalent in *Westlaw.*

2. Earlier Federal Digests

Federal cases prior to 1984 are available in the following:

a. *West's Federal Practice Digest, 3rd,* December 1975 to the beginning of *West's Federal Practice Digest, 4th.*

b. *West's Federal Practice Digest, 2nd,* 1961–November 1975.

c. *Modern Federal Practice Digest,* 1939–1960.

d. *Federal Digest,* all federal cases prior to 1939.

3. United States Supreme Court Digest

Because the Supreme Court of the United States plays such a significant role in the American legal system, a digest that contains only its cases can be extremely useful. West publishes a multivolume set, which includes the Supreme Court digest paragraphs in the *American Digest System* and in the various West federal digests.

SECTION F.   REGIONAL KEY NUMBER DIGESTS

Four sets of regional key number digests are published that correspond to four sets of the regional reporters of the *National Reporter System.*

---

[6] Publication of West's Federal Practice Digest, 4th began in 1989. No "bright line" exists as to its scope of coverage or of that of West's Federal Practice Digest, 3rd, which it continues. For example, some volumes of the 3rd, issued in 1975 when this set began, covered cases through November 1975 and were never revised. These volumes contained pocket supplementation that included cases decided from December 1975 into 1983. Other volumes of the 3rd were revised at various times, the last issued in 1983. As new volumes of the 4th were published, they incorporated the supplementation to the 3rd. This means that some volumes in the 4th contain cases from December 1975, while others have coverage commencing in 1983. Therefore, specifically for the period December 1975 through 1983, both the 3rd and 4th *must* be consulted to assure comprehensive coverage. For cases from 1984 forward, only the 4th must be consulted.

Other regional digests have ceased over time, presumably due to an inadequate subscription base. Regional digests are arranged under the topic and key number classification and include abstracts of all reported cases for each of the states in the region. The digest paragraphs under each key number are arranged alphabetically by the states included within the digest. The regional digests that continue to be published are:

Atlantic Digest, First and Second Series

North Western Digest, First and Second Series

Pacific Digest, Five series[7]

South Eastern Digest, First and Second Series

SECTION G. DECENNIAL AND GENERAL DIGESTS

1. Comprehensive Nature

The *American Digest System* has as its core a massive set of materials in several units known as *Decennial Digests* and their companion volumes containing later information, the *General Digest*. These units contain every topic, key number, and digest paragraph ever assigned to cases reported by West. If research requires examining every case ever reported on a particular point of law, the only recourse is to use the *Decennial Digests*. Another way to think of this is as follows: if a key number digest paragraph is located in a state or federal digest or a specialized digest, that same digest paragraph also is contained in a volume of a *Decennial Digest* or the *General Digest*.

The process of developing a *Decennial Digest* unit begins with the publication of a volume of the *General Digest*. The *General Digest* is published in bound volumes, with a new volume issued approximately once a month. Each volume consists of *all* the headnotes taken from *all* the units of the *National Reporter System* for the period covered. These headnotes are arranged alphabetically by topic, and then under each topic numerically by key number.

If no further cumulation took place, digests of all the cases, arranged topically, would be in the bound volumes of the *General Digest*. Therefore, to find all the cases dealing with a particular topic, e.g., *Drugs and Narcotics*, it would be necessary to examine each one of hundreds of bound volumes. To avoid this problem, in 1906 West cumulated into one alphabetical arrangement all the topics and headnotes contained in all *General Digest* volumes from 1897 to 1906. This set is called the *First Decennial Digest*. By examining a volume of the *First Decennial* containing a particular topic and key number, all cases decided involving a particular point of law and decided during the period from 1897 to 1906 can be located.

This process of systematically cumulating a set of the *General Digest* into a new *Decennial* has taken place every ten years since 1897. Starting with the *Ninth Decennial,* the publisher began to issue the decennials in multiple parts, with each part covering a designated period of years. An advantage of this arrangement is that a researcher has fewer volumes of

---

[7] Volumes in these series are not designated as 1st, 2d, etc. Rather, each series indicates the first volume of the PACIFIC REPORTER or PACIFIC REPORTER 2D included in the set.

the *General Digest* to examine. The latest decennial published is the *Eleventh Decennial Digest, Part 3,* covering 2004–2007. A *General Digest, Twelfth Series* is underway, beginning with 2008.

Thus, given a topic and key number, one can start with the *First Decennial* and proceed through the *Eleventh, Part 3,* and the ongoing volumes in the *General Digest, Twelfth Series*, to locate all cases on a point of law under a particular topic and key number from 1897 to several weeks ago.[8]

Since each volume in the *General Digest* contains digest paragraphs covering only a short period of time, there may be as many as 60 volumes to search before they are cumulated and replaced by a new decennial. To avoid the necessity of examining a volume of the *General Digest* that does not include a particular key number, the publisher includes a cumulative *Table of Key Numbers* in every volume of the *General Digest*. These tables indicate those volumes of the *General Digest* that contain cases assigned to a particular key number. The table is cumulative in ten-volume increments, and then starts a new cumulation. [Illustration 7–10]

2. Century Edition

It is possible to find all cases from 1658, the date of the first reported American case, as cases from 1658 to 1896 are digested in a publication entitled *Century Edition*. Because the *National Reporter System* did not exist during this period, the *Century Edition* does not contain key numbers. A different topical arrangement was used. For example, the topic *Drugs and Narcotics*, key number 18, in the decennials stands for *Civil Liability of Manufacturers*. In the *Century Edition, Drugs and Narcotics* 18 is listed under the heading of *Druggists*, and more specifically, under the sections *Persons Purchasing or Using Articles Sold or Dispensed* and *Actions for Damages*, which are digested under Section Numbers 8 and 9.[9]

3. Scope of Coverage

The sets in the *American Digest System* are:

Century Digest	1658–1896	50 vols.
First Decennial	1897–1906	25 vols.
Second Decennial	1907–1916	24 vols.
Third Decennial	1916–1926	29 vols.
Fourth Decennial	1926–1936	34 vols.
Fifth Decennial	1936–1946	52 vols.
Sixth Decennial	1946–1956	36 vols.
Seventh Decennial	1956–1966	38 vols.

[8] In the decennials and the GENERAL DIGEST, cases are arranged hierarchically, beginning with those of the Supreme Court of the United States and followed by the lower federal courts, with the most recent case listed first in each grouping. Federal case headnotes are followed by headnotes for cases decided by state courts. These cases are arranged alphabetically by state and hierarchically by court, with the most recent case listed first in each grouping.

[9] In both the first and second decennials, cross-references are made from the decennial key numbers to the subject classification used in the CENTURY EDITION, with the cross-references in the second being more complete. If one locates a point of law in the CENTURY EDITION, key numbers for later cases on the same point of law can be located by consulting a pink reference table in volume 21 of the FIRST DECENNIAL.

Eighth Decennial	1966–1976	50 vols.
Ninth Decennial, Part 1	1976–1981	38 vols.
Ninth Decennial, Part 2	1981–1986	48 vols.
Tenth Decennial, Part 1	1986–1991	44 vols.
Tenth Decennial, Part 2	1991–1996	64 vols.
Eleventh Decennial, Part 1	1996–2001	64 vols.
Eleventh Decennial, Part 2	2001–2004	62 vols.
Eleventh Decennial, Part 3	2004–2007	62 vols.
General Digest, 12th Series	2008 +	in progress

SECTION H. KEEPING THE KEY NUMBER SYSTEM CURRENT

West attempts to keep its key number system current with the changes and developments in law by adding new topics and by expanding or reclassifying existing topics.

1. Adding New Topics

When the original key number classification system was prepared in 1897, no provisions were made for cases dealing with damages resulting from a jet breaking the sound barrier or for the control and regulation of nuclear energy. Consequently, to cover these and other new areas of law, West occasionally adds new topics to its key number classification. Recently, for example, two new topics—*Child Custody* and *Child Support*—were added. These new topics collected the child custody and child support issues that were previously classified to three topics: *Divorce*; *Infants*; and *Parent and Child*. When a new topic is added, it is first published in the advance sheets to the *National Reporter System*.

2. Reclassifying and Expanding Topics

At times, key numbers are reclassified or revised in order to adapt to changing circumstances. For example, the topics *Bankruptcy* and *Federal Civil Procedure* were recently reclassified, i.e., existing key numbers were reassigned to new key numbers in order to reflect changes in the federal laws governing these areas.

At other times, existing topics are expanded as additional issues emerge in the area over time. For example, until about forty years ago, all headnotes dealing with issues concerning liability of sellers of prescription drugs, an issue relevant to our research problem, received the topic *Druggists* and the key number 9. When reclassification or expansion occurs, key number translation tables, set forth near the start of the topic in the digest indicate new key numbers that replace old ones and vice versa. [Illustration 7–11]

3. Updating Using Westlaw

Westlaw updates changes in topics and key numbers automatically for all key numbers from 1932 forward. A researcher can retrieve all relevant cases under a current key number even though some of those cases may have been previously classified under a different key number. [Illustration 7–12]

SECTION I. ILLUSTRATIONS: FINDING TOPICS AND KEY NUMBERS

[Illustration 7–1]

PAGE FROM ALPHABETICAL LIST OF DIGEST TOPICS USED IN KEY NUMBER SYSTEM

DIGEST TOPICS

See, also, Outline of the Law by Seven Main Divisions of Law preceding this section.

The topic numbers shown below may be used in WESTLAW searches for cases within the topic and within specified key numbers.

1	Abandoned and Lost Property	42	Assumpsit, Action of	79	Clerks of Courts
2	Abatement and Revival	43	Asylums	80	Clubs
		44	Attachment	81	Colleges and Universities
4	Abortion and Birth Control	45	Attorney and Client	82	Collision
		46	Attorney General	83	Commerce
5	Absentees	47	Auctions and Auctioneers	83H	Commodity Futures Trading Regulation
6	Abstracts of Title	48	Audita Querela		
7	Accession	48A	Automobiles	84	Common Lands
8	Accord and Satisfaction	48B	Aviation	85	Common Law
9	Account	49	Bail	88	Compounding
		50	Bailment		

Over 400 topics are in the *American Digest System*. These topics are used in creating headnotes. See next illustration. This listing of digest topics is in the front of each volume of a key number digest. The numbers to the left of the topics can be used in accessing the topics on *Westlaw*. This is discussed in Section C of this chapter.

	and Procedure	61	Breach of Marriage Promise		Protection
16	Admiralty			93	Contempt
17	Adoption	62	Breach of the Peace	95	Contracts
18	Adulteration	63	Bribery	96	Contribution
19	Adultery	64	Bridges	97	Conversion
20	Adverse Possession	65	Brokers	98	Convicts
21	Affidavits	66	Building and Loan Associations	99	Copyrights and Intellectual Property
23	Agriculture				
24	Aliens	67	Burglary		
25	Alteration of Instruments	68	Canals	100	Coroners
		69	Cancellation of Instruments	101	Corporations
26	Ambassadors and Consuls			102	Costs
		70	Carriers	103	Counterfeiting
27	Amicus Curiae	71	Cemeteries	104	Counties
28	Animals	72	Census	105	Court Commissioners
29	Annuities	73	Certiorari		
30	Appeal and Error	74	Champerty and Maintenance	106	Courts
31	Appearance			107	Covenant, Action of
33	Arbitration	75	Charities	108	Covenants
34	Armed Services	76	Chattel Mortgages	108A	Credit Reporting Agencies
35	Arrest	76A	Chemical Dependents		
36	Arson			110	Criminal Law
37	Assault and Battery	76H	Children Out-of-Wedlock	111	Crops
38	Assignments			113	Customs and Usages
40	Assistance, Writ of	77	Citizens	114	Customs Duties
41	Associations	78	Civil Rights	115	Damages

XV

[Illustration 7–2]

PAGE FROM KASIN V. OSCO DRUG, INC., 728 N.E.2D 77 (ILL.APP. 2000)

KASIN v. OSCO DRUG, INC.   Ill. **77**
Cite as 728 N.E.2d 77 (Ill.App. 2 Dist. 2000)

granting summary judgment in favor of the State and we remand this cause for the defendant to receive a jury trial on his

> **This is the first page of *Kasin v. Osco Drug, Inc.*, a case relevant to our research problem. Three headnotes were assigned to this case. Notice how each headnote has been assigned a topic or topics and a specific key number or key numbers.**
>
> **See next illustration.**

concurring.

312 Ill.App.3d 823
245 Ill.Dec. 346

Clarence KASIN and Paul Kasin,
Plaintiffs–Appellants,

v.

OSCO DRUG, INC., Defendant–
Appellee.

No. 2–99–0356.

Appellate Court of Illinois,
Second District.

April 12, 2000.

Pharmacy customer and his brother, whose kidney had been transplanted into the customer, sued the pharmacy for negligence, alleging that, in dispensing a prescription drug, the pharmacy had negligently advised the customer of the drug's side effects, including possible kidney failure. The Circuit Court, Lake County, John R. Goshgarian, J., granted summary judgment against the pharmacy, and plaintiffs appealed. The Appellate Court, Bowman, J., held that, by voluntarily undertaking to list some of a drug's side effects, a pharmacy did not assume a duty to list all possible side effects, so as to remove it from the protection of the learned intermediary doctrine.

Affirmed.

1. Drugs and Narcotics ⬅19

By voluntarily undertaking to list some of a drug's side effects, a pharmacy did not assume a duty to list all possible side effects, so as to remove it from the protection of the learned intermediary doctrine regarding side effects it did not list; side effects listed by the pharmacy constituted the extent of its undertaking.

2. Drugs and Narcotics ⬅18

Physicians and Surgeons ⬅15(8)

"Learned intermediary doctrine" provides that manufacturers of prescription drugs have a duty to warn prescribing physicians of a drug's known dangerous propensities and that physicians, in turn, using their medical judgment, have a duty to convey the warnings to their patients.

See publication Words and Phrases for other judicial constructions and definitions.

3. Drugs and Narcotics ⬅18

Learned intermediary doctrine precludes the imposition of a duty upon drug manufacturers to warn patients directly of a drug's known dangerous propensities.

Charles A. Cohn, Erwin Cohn, Cohn & Cohn, Chicago, for Clarence Kasin and Paul Kasin.

Eric J. Parker, Ridge, Ridge & Lindsay, Waukegan, for Osco Drug Inc., Corp.

Presiding Justice BOWMAN delivered the opinion of the court:

Plaintiffs, Clarence and Paul Kasin, brought a negligence action in the circuit court of Lake County against defendants, Dr. James A. Gross and Osco Drug, Inc. (Osco). Subsequently, Dr. Gross was dismissed with prejudice. As to Osco, plaintiffs alleged that in dispensing the prescription drug Daypro Osco had negligently advised Clarence Kasin of the side effects of the drug when it failed to advise him "of symptoms to be aware of

[Illustration 7–3]

PAGE FROM 728 N.E.2D 77, 79 (ILL.APP. 2000)

KASIN v. OSCO DRUG, INC.   Ill. **79**
Cite as 728 N.E.2d 77 (Ill.App. 2 Dist. 2000)

tled to judgment as a matter of law. *Cramer v. Insurance Exchange Agency*, 174 Ill.2d 513, 530, 221 Ill.Dec. 473, 675 N.E.2d 897 (1996). The existence of a duty owed by t~~he defendant to a plaintiff~~ a question of l~~aw for the court to decide~~ on a motion fo~~r summary judgment.~~ ~~Ja~~cob v. Greve, 2~~~~ Ill.Dec. 671, 6~~~~ court's review ~~of~~ a summary jud~~gment.~~ *Mutual Insura~~nce~~* App.3d 495, 5~~0~~~~, 233 Ill.Dec. 428, 698~~ N.E.2d 271 (1998).

> This is another page of *Kasin v. Osco Drug, Inc.* It illustrates how headnotes are developed. The bracketed numbers are inserted by the editors. Each section so bracketed has been condensed into a corresponding headnote for the point of law in each bracketed section.
>
> **See next illustration.**

[1–3] Plaintiffs first contend that Osco's voluntary undertaking to provide an information or a warning sheet with a prescription drug removed it from the protection of the "learned intermediary doctrine." The learned intermediary doctrine provides that manufacturers of prescription drugs have a duty to warn prescribing physicians of a drug's known dangerous propensities and that physicians, in turn, using their medical judgment, have a duty to convey the warnings to their patients. *Kirk v. Michael Reese Hospital & Medical Center*, 117 Ill.2d 507, 517, 111 Ill.Dec. 944, 513 N.E.2d 387 (1987). The doctrine precludes the imposition of a duty upon drug manufacturers to warn patients directly. *Kirk*, 117 Ill.2d at 519, 111 Ill.Dec. 944, 513 N.E.2d 387. The doctrine also has been applied to exempt pharmacies and pharmacists from giving warnings to patients. See *Fakhouri v. Taylor*, 248 Ill.App.3d 328, 187 Ill.Dec. 927, 618 N.E.2d 518 (1993); *Leesley v. West*, 165 Ill.App.3d 135, 116 Ill.Dec. 136, 518 N.E.2d 758 (1988).

Plaintiffs concede that absent Osco's voluntary undertaking it would have been shielded from liability by the learned intermediary doctrine but argue that because Osco voluntarily undertook to warn of some side effects of Daypro it was removed from the protection of the doctrine. Conversely, Osco maintains that pursuant to our supreme court's decision in *Frye v. Medicare–Glaser Corp.*, 153 Ill.2d 26, 178

Ill.Dec. 763, 605 N.E.2d 557 (1992), it was protected by the doctrine.

In *Frye* a pharmacist voluntarily undertook to affix to a prescription drug a label ~~that~~ might cause ~~drowsiness. Plaintiff~~ sued both the ~~pharmacist and the druggi~~st under a voluntary ~~undertaking theor~~y of liability. ~~Plaintiff alleged~~ that neither ~~the physician nor the phar~~macist had the ~~drug's serio~~us side effects ~~and further alleg~~ed that once they undertook to warn of dangerous side effects they undertook to warn of all potential dangers involved in taking the drug. The supreme court rejected plaintiff's argument and found that the defendants' liability depended upon the extent of their undertaking.

Osco asserts that the court in *Frye* determined that a pharmacist was still protected by the learned intermediary doctrine even though the pharmacist offered a warning to a consumer of a drug's dangerous propensities. To support this assertion Osco relies on a statement made by the *Frye* court, in *dicta*. The statement followed the court's rejection of the plaintiff's argument that the pharmacist's placement of a "drowsy eye" label on the prescription drug container might mislead a consumer into believing that drowsiness was the only side effect of the drug. The court stated:

> "In our opinion, consumers should principally look to their prescribing physician to convey the appropriate warnings regarding drugs, and it is the prescribing physician's duty to convey these warnings to patients." *Frye*, 153 Ill.2d at 34, 178 Ill.Dec. 763, 605 N.E.2d 557.

In so stating, the court made no reference to the learned intermediary doctrine. Given the context in which the statement was made, we are not persuaded that the statement indicated that the court had concluded that a pharmacist is protected by the learned intermediary doctrine even if the pharmacist voluntarily undertakes to warn a consumer of some side effects.

[Illustration 7–4]

SCREEN PRINT FROM WESTLAW SHOWING HEADNOTES

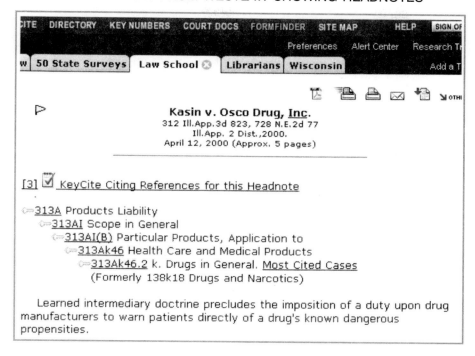

[Illustration 7–5]

PAGE FROM DESCRIPTIVE–WORD INDEX, ILLINOIS DIGEST 2D

MANHOLES
56 Ill D 2d—648

References are to Digest Topics and Key Numbers

MANHOLES—Cont'd

MUNICIPAL liability for injuries. Mun Corp 767, 783
  Pleading and proof. Mun Corp 816(10)
  Question for jury. Mun Corp 821(1, 13, 14, 19, 22)
  Unimproved street. Mun Corp 759(5)
OBSTRUCTION. Mun Corp 777
STREETS and highways—
  Injuries. Mun Corp 783
WATER company's liability for pedestrian's injury when manhole lid tilted. Waters 195

MANICURE PARLORS

WOMEN employees, operator permitting to massage male patrons' genitals, sufficiency of evidence. Nuis 86

MANIFEST

MANUAL DELIVERY

See this index Delivery

MANUAL POSSESSION

DEED, necessity that grantee have. Deeds 56(2)

MANUAL TRAINING

BOARD of Education's power to prescribe. Schools 55
COUNTY aid. Counties 153½

MANUAL TRAINING ROOM

WORKSHOP within Workmen's Compensation Act. Work Comp 140

MANUALS

SECURITIES, information as to issuer published in recognized manual affecting validity of securities law exempting resales by brokers—
  Licens 18½(22)
  Statut 47

MANUFACTURERS AND MANUFACTURING

DRUGS, products liability, failure to warn patient. Drugs & N 20

MANUFACTURERS AND MANUFACTURING COMPANIES

ACCOUNT, fiduciary relation between manufacturer and designer. Acct 4
  Evidence. Acct 18
  Theft of design. Acct 7
AIRCRAFT, liability of manufacturer. Aviation 13
ALLOWANCE in lieu of brokerage, manufacturer converting to direct selling. Trade Reg 915
ANIMAL food, liability not limited by privity of contract requirement. Neglig 27
ATTORNEY fees, paneling's noncompliance with city code concealed from hospital. Costs 172
AUTHORIZED dealer agreement, vertical restraints, rule of reason. Monop 17(1.3)
AUTOMOBILE, see this index Automobiles
BAILMENT, goods delivered for manufacture. Bailm 14(2)

MANUFACTURERS AND MANUFACTURING COMPANIES—Cont'd

BANKRUPTCY—
  Action of trespass against party at whose instigation receiver was appointed where court had jurisdiction. Bankr 114(1)
  Damages from petitioner on dismissal of petition. Bankr 99
BANKRUPTCY laws, applicability. Bankr 72
BOUNTIES for manufacturing. Bounties 4, 7
BURDEN of proof on customer reworking manufactured goods in manufacturer's action for manufacture of goods. Bailm 31(1)
BYSTANDERS, injury from defective product, strict liability. Torts 14.1
CLAW hammer manufacturer, hammer defect, products

Defense or indemnification, liability policy. Insurance 435.24(6)
CONTRACTS—
  Certainty as to subject matter. Contracts 9(1)
  Construction. Contracts 201
  Implied contract to manufacture for United States. U S 69(4)
  Mutuality of obligation. Contracts 10(2)
CONTRIBUTION, employer-buyer, strict liability. Contrib 5(6)
CORN picker, injury complaint alleging defect—
  Neglig 111(2)
  Torts 26(1)
COSMETICS, intended for professional use, restraining sales to general public. Inj 89(1)
DANGEROUS products, tort liability. Torts 14.1
DEALERSHIP, cancellation, manufacturer selling directly to end-users. Monop 28(7.4)
DISTRIBUTOR habitually negligent as driver, retention. Autos 197(7)
→ DRUGS and medicine, civil liability. Drugs & N 18
ELECTRIC vaporizer causing burns to infant—
  Burden of proof. Neglig 121.5
  Presumption. Neglig 121.3
  Question for jury. Neglig 136(17)
ELEVATOR of manufacturers as common carriers. Carr 235
EQUAL treatment, sales to competing buyers. Trade Reg 911
EVIDENCE in action against manufacturer of vaporizer, for breach of warranty—
  Neglig 121.3
  Sales 441(2)
EXCISE tax on manufacturers, see this index Excise
EXPLOSIVES. Explos 3, 8
  Illegal or negligent manufacture causing injuries. Explos 8
FOOD—
  Illegal manufacture. Food 13
  Implied warranty. Sales 255
GLASS coffee maker, injury on breaking, res ipsa loquitur doctrine. Neglig 121.3
GOVERNMENT contract, construction and operation. U S 70(1)

> This page illustrates how topics and key numbers can be located by using the *Descriptive-Word Index* to the *Illinois Digest 2d*. In this instance, we begin with a specific word in our fact situation, "manufacturer." Notice the major heading for "Manufacturers and Manufacturing Companies." Notice in the sub-entry "Drugs and medicine, civil liability" that we should consult "Drugs and Narcotics," Key Number 18.
>
> Many times, one will not find an index entry under the particular word or phrase chosen. In such instances, one should search in the *Descriptive-Word Index* under other appropriate words or phrases.

[Illustration 7–6]

PAGE FROM TOPIC, DRUGS AND NARCOTICS, ILLINOIS DIGEST 2D

23 Ill D 2d—1

DRUGS & NARCOTICS ⟜18

DRUGS AND NARCOTICS

For other and later cases, see **CHEMICAL DE-PENDENTS**

I. DRUGS AND DRUGGISTS IN GENERAL.

Research Notes

Application for use of new drug; practice under Food, Drug and Cosmetic Law, see West's Federal Practice Manual.

Library references

C.J.S. Drugs and Narcotics §§ 7 et seq., 10 et seq., 27 et seq., 43 et seq., 72 et seq., 84 et seq.

⟜**2. Federal regulation.**
See ⟜2.1.

⟜**2.1. —— In general.**
C.A.7 (Ill.) 2001. Statement in which manufacturers and marketers of over-the-counter and prescription strength forms of stomach acid reliever ranitidine told consumer that he "could not" sub-

⟜**15. —— Revocation or suspension.**
Ill.App. 1 Dist. 2000. Actions of Department of Professional Regulation in seeking either rehearing or order directing State Pharmacy Board to reconsider its recommendation regarding penalty to be imposed against licensed pharmacist who was subject of disciplinary proceeding, and remanding matter, even if not authorized by statute, were not prejudicial to pharmacist, and could not provide basis for reversal, where Board confirmed its initial recommendation on remand. S.H.A. 225 ILCS 85/35.8, 35.9; Ill.Admin. Code title 68, §§ 1110.210(a)(8), 1110.240(g).—Wilson v. Illinois Dept. of Professional Regulation, 250 Ill.Dec. 596, 739 N.E.2d 57, 317 Ill.App.3d 57.

Under Pharmacy Practice Act, Department of Professional Regulation is authorized to request that its Director take action contrary to a recommendation by State Pharmacy Board, as an incident to (1) Department's duty to effectuate the purpose of the Pharmacy Act, and (2) its power to discipline. S.H.A. 225 ILCS 85/11, 30(a), 35.10.—Id.

Department of Professional Regulation acted

When the topic and key number are known, sets of West digests can be consulted to locate cases with the same or similar points of law. It is good research practice to start with the most specific digest for your research problem, e.g., *Illinois Digest 2d*.

Notice how digest paragraphs are reprinted as they originally appeared as headnotes in the reported cases. Notice also how citations are given after the digest paragraph to where the case is reported. West's state key number digests also often contain references to relevant law review articles from that state.

---

scription strength forms of stomach acid reliever ranitidine indicated that two drugs were not the same medications fell within exemption under Illinois Consumer Fraud and Deceptive Business Practices Act (CFA) for actions specifically authorized by federal law, given that, for federal regulatory purposes, two products were different "drugs" and manufacturers and marketers were thus authorized to say they were different "medications," even if statement was confusing as to laypersons. Federal Food, Drug, and Cosmetic Act, § 1 et seq.; 21 U.S.C.A. § 301 et seq.; 21 C.F.R. §§ 310.3(h)(4), 330.1(i); S.H.A. 815 I.L.C.S. 505/10b(1).—Bober v. Glaxco Wellcome PLC, 246 F.3d 934.

⟜**8. —— Prescription drugs.**
Law Rev. 1996. Rationalizing Product Liability for Prescription Drugs: Implied Preemption, Federal Common Law, and Other Paths to Uniform Pharmaceutical Safety Standards. David R. Geiger and Mark D. Rosen.—45 DePaul L. Rev. 395.

⟜**11. State and municipal regulation in general.**
Ill.App. 1 Dist. 2000. Purpose of Pharmacy Practice Act is the protection of the public health, safety, and welfare through regulation of the practice of pharmacy. S.H.A. 225 ILCS 85/1 et seq.—Wilson v. Illinois Dept. of Professional Regulation, 250 Ill.Dec. 596, 739 N.E.2d 57, 317 Ill.App.3d 57.

Law Rev. 1996. Rationalizing Product Liability for Prescription Drugs: Implied Preemption, Federal Common Law, and Other Paths to Uniform Pharmaceutical Safety Standards. David R. Geiger and Mark D. Rosen.—45 DePaul L. Rev. 395.

Const.Amend. 14; S.H.A. 225 ILCS 85/11, 30(a), 35.10.—Id.

Sanction imposed by Director of Department of Professional Regulation in disciplinary proceeding brought against licensed pharmacist who had pleaded guilty to federal felony charge of receipt of misbranded drugs through interstate commerce, under which pharmacist's license was revoked for nine months, followed by 27 months of probation, and license of pharmacy he owned and operated was revoked, was not against manifest weight of the evidence, and was not an abuse of discretion. Federal Food, Drug, and Cosmetic Act, §§ 301(c), 303(a)(2), 21 U.S.C.A. §§ 331(c), 333(a)(2); S.H.A. 225 ILCS 85/11, 30(a), 35.10.—Id.

⟜**18. —— Manufacturers.**
Ill.App. 2 Dist. 2000. "Learned intermediary doctrine" provides that manufacturers of prescription drugs have a duty to warn prescribing physicians of a drug's known dangerous propensities and that physicians, in turn, using their medical judgment, have a duty to convey the warnings to their patients.—Kasin v. Osco Drug, Inc., 245 Ill. Dec. 346, 728 N.E.2d 77, 312 Ill.App.3d 823.

Learned intermediary doctrine precludes the imposition of a duty upon drug manufacturers to warn patients directly of a drug's known dangerous propensities.—Id.

Law Rev. 1996. Defending the pill: Oral contraceptives and strict liability in Illinois. Craig T. Liljestrand.—84 Ill.B.J. 364.

Law Rev. 1982. "Cause in fact" in tort law—A philosophical and historical examination.—31 De Paul L.Rev. 769.

[Illustration 7–7]

PAGE FROM ANALYSIS, DRUGS AND NARCOTICS,
FROM A KEY NUMBER DIGEST

DRUGS AND NARCOTICS

⟶ SUBJECTS INCLUDED

Regulation of the manufacture, dispensing, and sale of medicines and other drugs and devices by pharmacists or others

Civil and criminal liabilities relating to drugs in general

Regulation of the sale, use, etc., of narcotics and hallucinogenic, depressant, and stimulant drugs

Violation of laws relating to such drugs and criminal liability and prosecution therefor

Searches, seizures, and forfeitures relating to such drugs

⟶ SUBJECTS EXCLUDED AND COVERED BY OTHER TOPICS

Commitment and treatment of addicts, see CHEMICAL DEPENDENTS

Insecticides and fungicides, see POISONS

Internal revenue acts generally, offenses and prosecutions under, see INTERNAL REVENUE

Poisons, regulations relating to, see POISONS

For detailed references to other topics, see Descriptive-Word Index

---

Analysis

I. DRUGS AND DRUGGISTS IN GENERAL, ⟜1–40.

II. NARCOTICS AND DANGEROUS DRUGS, ⟜41–198.

    (A) REGULATIONS, ⟜41–60.

    (B) OFFENSES, ⟜61–100.

I.

This illustrates the "Analysis" method of locating topics and key numbers. If a researcher knows that a particular issue deals with *Drugs and Narcotics*, that topic can be consulted immediately in the appropriate volume or volumes of a West digest. After reading the "scope note" for information included, excluded, or covered elsewhere, the next step is to find a relevant key number.

See next illustration.

[Illustration 7–8]

PAGE FROM ANALYSIS, DRUGS AND NARCOTICS, FROM A KEY NUMBER DIGEST

DRUGS & NARCOTICS   23 Ill D 2d—2

I. DRUGS AND DRUGGISTS IN GENERAL.—Continued.

    12. Registration, certificate, or license.

    12.1. —— In general.

    13. —— Necessity.

    14. —— Eligibility and right; licensing boards.

    15. —— Revocation or suspension.

    16. Conduct of business.

    17. Civil liability.

    17.1. —— In general.

    18. —— Manufacturers.

    19. —— Retailers or dispensers.

    20. Actions for damages.

    20.1. —— In general.

    21. —— Evidence.

    22. —— Questions for jury.

    23. Injunction.

    24. Penalties.

    25. Seizure and forfeiture.

    25.1. —— In general.

    26. —— Property subject and grounds.

    27. —— Proceedings.

    28. —— Evidence.

    29. Offenses.

    30. Criminal prosecutions.

    30.1. —— In general.

    31. —— Evidence and questions for jury.

II. NARCOTICS AND DANGEROUS DRUGS.

  (A) REGULATIONS.

    ☞41. Nature and power to regulate.

    42. Statutes and other regulations in general.

    43. Validity of statutes.

    43.1. —— In general.

    44. —— Presumptions and inferences, provisions relating to.

> **This is the second page from the *Analysis* in a key number digest. Note that the outline under "I. Drugs and Druggists In General" Includes the Civil liability of Manufacturers, Key Number 18. It is useful practice to browse the other listings in the outline for additional relevant key numbers.**

    50. Civil liability.

  (B) OFFENSES.

    ☞61. Nature and elements in general.

    62. Illegal possession.

    62.1. —— In general.

    63. —— Elements of offense in general.

    64. —— Knowledge and intent.

    65. —— Constructive possession.

    66. —— Substance and quantity possessed.

[Illustration 7–9]

PAGE FROM TABLE OF CASES, ILLINOIS DIGEST 2D

KARR;

55 Ill D 2d—30

References are to Digest Topics and Key Numbers

Karr; People v., IllApp 2 Dist, 25 IllDec 453, 386 NE2d 927, 68 IllApp3d 1040, habeas corpus gr US ex rel Karr v. Wolff, 556 FSupp 760, vac 732 F2d 615, on remand 1985 WL 2487.—Sent & Pun 537.

Karris; Ray v., CA7 (Ill), 780 F2d 636.—Sec Reg 60.40.

Kartholl, In re Marriage of, IllApp 2 Dist, 97 IllDec 347, 492 NE2d 1006, 143 IllApp3d 228.—Child C 120, 634, 637.

Kasbeer v. Kasbeer, IllApp 2 Dist, 159 NE2d 840, 22 IllApp2d 218.—Child C 7; Child S 24, 25, 60, 91, 556(1), 557(1).

Kasbeer; .Kasbeer v., IllApp 2 Dist, 159 NE2d 840, 22 IllApp2d 218.—Child C 7; Child S 24, 25, 60, 91, 556(1), 557(1).

Kas' Estate, In re, IllApp 1 Dist, 303 NE2d 201, 14 IllApp3d 729.—Joint Adv 1.2(4), 1.15.

K., Ashley, In Interest of, IllApp 1 Dist, 156 IllDec 925, 571 NE2d 906, 212 IllApp3d 849. See Ashley K., In Interest of.

Kasin v. Osco Drug, Inc., IllApp 2 Dist, 245 IllDec 346, 728 NE2d 77, 312 IllApp3d 823.—Drugs & N 18, 19; Phys 15(8).

Kaspar v. Clinton-Jackson Corp., IllApp 1 Dist, 254 NE2d 826, 118 IllApp2d 364.—App & E 1004(1).

Kass v. Resurrection Medical Center, IllApp 1 Dist, 250 IllDec 194, 738 NE2d 158, 316 IllApp3d 1108, reh den. —App & E 1060.1(2.1); New Tr 27; Trial 125(1), 133.2, 133.3.

Kassnel; Adams v., IllApp 1 Dist, 148 NE2d 818, 16 IllApp2d 540.—Trade Reg 257.1.

Kautz v. Kautz, IllApp 1 Dist, 243 NE2d 426, 102 IllApp2d 165.—Child S 340.

Kautz; Kautz v., IllApp 1 Dist, 243 NE2d 426, 102 IllApp2d 165.—Child S 340.

Kavanaugh v. Ford Motor Co., CA7 (Ill), 353 F2d 710.— Trade Reg 871(2), 871(4).

Kavinsky; People v., IllApp 1 Dist, 47 IllDec 90, 414 NE2d 1206, 91 IllApp3d 784.—Sent & Pun 310.

Kavonius v. Industrial Com'n, IllApp 2 Dist, 247 IllDec 279, 731 NE2d 1287, 314 IllApp3d 166, reh den, appeal den 252 IllDec 78, 742 NE2d 328, 192 Ill2d 691.—Work Comp 1187, 1892.

Kawasaki Motors Mfg. Corp., USA; Boland v., IllApp 4 Dist, 243 IllDec 165, 722 NE2d 1234, 309 IllApp3d 645. —App & E 525(1), 970(2), 971(3); Death 21, 75; Evid 560; Pretrial Proc 14.1, 15, 39, 40, 45; Prod Liab 27, 40, 98; Trial 43, 252(2); Witn 267.

Kay v. Kay, IllApp 1 Dist, 318 NE2d 9, 22 IllApp3d 530.— Child C 7, 177, 178, 577, 638.

Kay; Kay v., IllApp 1 Dist, 318 NE2d 9, 22 IllApp3d 530. —Child C 7, 177, 178, 577, 638.

Kaznowski v. City of La Salle, IllApp 2 Dist, 43 NE2d 852, 316 IllApp 115.—App & E 1004(5).

K.B., In re, IllApp 4 Dist, 247 IllDec 866, 732 NE2d 1198, 314 IllApp3d 739.—Infants 156, 157, 158, 178, 180, 181, 196, 232, 247, 248.1, 252.

Kealey v. Carey's Estate, IllApp 1 Dist, 181 NE2d 197, 35 IllApp2d 61.—Theaters 6(36.1).

Kealey v. Kealey, IllApp 5 Dist, 33 IllDec 672, 397 NE2d 5, 77 IllApp3d 962.—Child S 140(2).

> When a researcher knows the name of a case that deals with a relevant point of law, key numbers assigned to that topic can be located by use of the Table of Cases volume(s). See, for example, the listing for *Kasin v. Osco Drug, Inc.* This same information is contained under *Osco Drug, Inc.; Kasin v.* Thus, a case can be located when either the plaintiff or defendant is known. Note also that parallel citations are provided.

Katris v. City of Waukegan, NDIll, 498 FSupp 48.—Civil R 206(2.1).

Katsigiannis; People v., IllApp 2 Dist, 122 IllDec 249, 526 NE2d 508, 171 IllApp3d 1090, 82 ALR4th 337.—Sent & Pun 55, 56, 60.

Katz v. Comdisco, Inc., NDIll, 117 FRD 403.—Sec Reg 154.1.

Katzenbach; Rini v., CA7 (Ill), 403 F2d 697.—Sent & Pun 349, 400.

Katzer v. Katzer, IllApp 1 Dist, 18 IllDec 852, 378 NE2d 316, 61 IllApp3d 299.—Child C 551, 553, 559, 567, 637, 921(1), 923(4).

Katzer; Katzer v., IllApp 1 Dist, 18 IllDec 852, 378 NE2d 316, 61 IllApp3d 299.—Child C 551, 553, 559, 567, 637, 921(1), 923(4).

Kauffman v. International Broth. of Elec. Workers, Local Union No. 461, NDIll, 124 FSupp2d 1127.—Fed Civ Proc 2497.1; Labor 106.1, 108.1, 109, 111, 112, 119.

Kauffman v. Kauffman, IllApp 4 Dist, 333 NE2d 695, 30 IllApp3d 159.—Child C 7, 67, 922(1), 922(2).

Kauffman; Kauffman v., IllApp 4 Dist, 333 NE2d 695, 30 IllApp3d 159.—Child C 7, 67, 922(1), 922(2).

Kauffman; People v., IllApp 4 Dist, 123 IllDec 182, 527 NE2d 645, 172 IllApp3d 1040, appeal den 128 IllDec 895, 533 NE2d 406, 123 Ill2d 563.—Sent & Pun 2037, 2038, 2041.

Kaufman; People v., IllApp 3 Dist, 23 IllDec 674, 384 NE2d 468, 67 IllApp3d 36.—Sent & Pun 31.

3355(1.10), 3355(2.1), 3382.1, 3385, 3420(12), 3423; Work Comp 1846, 1847, 1939.6, 1939.11(1), 2093.

Keathley; People v., IllApp 1 Dist, 248 NE2d 782, 109 IllApp2d 323.—Rob 24.10, 24.40.

Keating; People v., IllApp 2 Dist, 274 NE2d 362, 2 IllApp3d 884, supplemented 276 NE2d 350, 2 IllApp3d 884.—Drugs & N 45.1.

Keating; People v., IllApp 2 Dist, 191 IllDec 531, 624 NE2d 380, 252 IllApp3d 801.—Sent & Pun 85, 90.

Keaton v. Atchison, T. & S. F. Ry. Co., CA7 (Ill), 321 F2d 317.—Fed Cts 896.1.

Keck; People v., IllApp 3 Dist, 168 IllDec 892, 590 NE2d 529, 226 IllApp3d 937, appeal den 176 IllDec 811, 602 NE2d 465, 146 Ill2d 640.—Sent & Pun 2003, 2020, 2021.

Keck, Mahin & Cate, In re, NDIll, 253 BR 530.—Atty & C 26, 62; Bankr 2923, 3568(2), 3782, 3786; Fed Civ Proc 636; Fraud 3, 16; Judgm 634, 720.

Keefe; People ex rel. Legislative Commission on Low Income Housing v., Ill, 223 NE2d 144, 36 Ill2d 460.— Searches 75.

Keefer v. Keefer, IllApp 2 Dist, 245 NE2d 784, 107 IllApp2d 74.—Child C 176, 178, 187, 577, 638.

Keefer; Keefer v., IllApp 2 Dist, 245 NE2d 784, 107 IllApp2d 74.—Child C 176, 178, 187, 577, 638.

Keefer; U.S. v., CA7 (Ill), 464 F2d 1385, cert den 93 SCt 322, 409 US 983, 34 LEd2d 247.—Drugs & N 119.1.

Keehner; Luthy v., IllApp 3 Dist, 45 IllDec 509, 412 NE2d 1091, 90 IllApp3d 127.—Judgm 181(15.1).

For Later Case History Information, see KeyCite on WESTLAW

[Illustration 7–10]

PAGE FROM TABLE OF KEY NUMBERS FROM VOLUME 7, GENERAL DIGEST, 10th SERIES

1611

DOWER AND CURTESY —Cont'd	DRUGS AND NARCOTICS —Cont'd	EASEMENTS—Cont'd	ELECTION OF REMEDIES —Cont'd
☞	☞	☞	
70.1—6	122—3	17(1)—4, 5, 6	5—2, 3, 4, 5, 6, 7
114—6	123.1—4	18(1)—1, 2, 3, 4, 5	7(1)—7
118—6	123.2—1, 2, 3, 4, 5, 6, 7	18(2)—2	9—3
	123.3—7	18(3)—1	14—4, 7
DRAINS	125.1—1, 6	22—1, 3, 6	15—2, 6, 7
☞	126—1, 2, 4, 6, 7	24—1, 4, 6, 7	
17—2	127—1, 4, 5	25—6	**ELECTIONS**
19—1, 2	128—2, 4, 5	26(1)—2, 4, 5, 6	☞
20—1	129.1—1, 2	26(2)—2, 6	1—3, 7
36(2)—6	130—2, 4, 5, 6	27—2, 7	3—4
36(6)—6	131—4, 5, 7	30(1)—1, 2, 3, 4, 6	5—3, 4, 5
45—4, 6	132—1, 2	30(2)—6	7—1
50—2	133—1, 2, 3, 4, 5, 6, 7	30(3)—2, 3	8.1—1
52—4	182.3—6	32—2	9—7
57—1	183(1)—1	33—2	10—1, 4, 5, 6
70—2	183(2)—2, 3, 4, 5	36(1)—1, 2, 3, 4, 5, 6, 7	12(2.1)—3
71—6	183(3)—7	36(3)—1, 2, 3, 4, 5, 6, 7	12(3)—4
82(3)—2	183(4)—2	37—1, 7	12(6)—3, 4, 5, 6
82(5)—2	183(5)—2, 4, 5, 7	38—1, 2, 4, 5, 7	12(8)—3
	183(6)—2, 4, 5, 7	40—1, 2, 4	12(9.1)—3, 4, 7
DRUGS AND NARCOTICS	183.5—1	41—4, 5	12(10)—4, 5
☞	184(1)—2, 4, 5, 7	42—1, 4, 5, 6, 7	15—1
2.1—6, 7	184(2)—1, 4, 7	44(2)—1	21—2
3—6	184(6)—4, 5	48(4)—4, 5	22—3, 4
9—1, 5, 7	185(1)—7	48(6)—1, 2	24—2, 7
10—4, 5, 7	185(2)—2, 4	50—1, 7	27—1
11—2, 4, 5	185(3)—1, 2, 3, 4, 6	51—1, 4, 7	28—4
12.1—4, 5	185(4)—2, 4, 5, 7	53—1	29—3
15—4, 7	185(7)—2, 4	54—1, 2, 4, 5, 6	54—1
16—2	185(8)—4, 5, 7	57—4, 7	105—4, 5
17.1—1, 4, 5, 7	185.5—1, 4, 5, 6, 7	58(1)—4	108—3
18—1, 3, 4, 5, 7	185.10—1, 2, 4, 5, 6, 7	58(2)—4	114.1—6
19—4, 5	187(2)—2, 4, 6	58(3)—1, 4, 7	115—3
20.1—2, 3, 4, !	188(1)—4	61(1)—4, 5	116—2
21—1, 2, 4		61(2)—1, 4, 5	
23—7			
41—7			
42—4, 5			
43.1—1, 2, 3, 4			
45.1—2			
46—2, 4, 6			
47—1, 6			
61—1, 2, 3, 4,			
62.1—2			
63—1, 2, 3, 4,			
64—1, 2, 3, 4,			
65—1, 2, 3, 4, 5, 6, 7	194.1—2, 4, 5, 7		167—1
66—1, 2, 3, 4, 5, 7	195—1, 3, 4, 5, 6, 7	1—3, 4	172—1
67—1, 2, 4, 5, 6, 7	196—2, 3, 4, 5, 6, 7	3—4	177—2
68.1—7		7—3, 7	179—2
69—1, 2, 4, 5, 6	**EASEMENTS**	9(2)—3	186(1)—1
70—2	☞	9(3)—3	188—1
73.1—1, 2, 3, 4, 5, 6, 7	1—1, 2, 3, 4, 5, 6, 7	17—3	197—1
76—1, 2, 4, 5, 6, 7	2—6	19—4	208—2
78—2, 6, 7	3(1)—4, 5, 6	21—3	216.1—1, 4
102.1—1, 2, 4, 5	3(2)—4, 5	36—7	220—2
103—4, 5	5—1, 2, 3, 4, 5, 6, 7	62.1—3	227(1)—1, 4
104—2, 3, 4, 6	6—1, 2, 7	63—3	227(8)—1, 4
106—4, 5	7(0.5)—2, 4, 5	109—7	235—1
107—1, 2, 3, 4, 5, 6, 7	7(5)—3, 6	120(0.5)—3	236—1
108—1, 2, 3, 4, 5, 7	8(1)—1, 2, 4, 5, 6, 7	120(1)—3	239—4
109—1, 2, 3, 4, 5, 6, 7	8(2)—1, 2, 4, 5, 7	124—3	247—1
110.1—1, 2	8(4)—7	132—3	255—2
111—2, 3, 4, 5, 7	9(1)—3, 6		257—4, 5
112—1, 2, 6	10(1)—1	**ELECTION OF REMEDIES**	259—1
114—2, 4, 5, 7	12(1)—2, 3, 4, 5, 7	☞	260—1, 2
116—1, 2, 3, 4, 5, 6, 7	12(2)—2	1—2	262—1
117—1, 2, 3, 4, 5, 6, 7	12(3)—4, 5	2—2, 3	269—1, 4, 6
118—1, 2, 3, 4, 5, 6, 7	14(1)—1, 4, 5, 6, 7	3(1)—1, 2, 6	270—1, 4
119.1—1, 2, 3, 4, 5, 6, 7	15.1—2, 3, 4, 5, 6, 7	3(4)—2	271—1, 2, 4
120—2, 4, 5	16—4, 5, 7	4—3, 6	275—3

> This table, which is cumulative in each volume of the *General Digest* through ten volumes and then starts a new cumulation, allows a researcher to determine which of the volumes contain a particular topic and key number.
>
> The table in this illustration, cumulative for volumes 1-7, indicates that only five of the seven volumes need be consulted for cases dealing with *Drugs and Narcotics*, Key Number 18.

[Illustration 7–11]

PAGE FROM KEY NUMBER TRANSLATION
TABLE IN A KEY NUMBER DIGEST

23 Ill D 2d—7 | DRUGS & NARCOTICS

TABLE 2

KEY NUMBER TRANSLATION TABLE

DRUGS AND NARCOTICS TO PRIOR TOPICS

Drugs and Narcotics Key Number	Prior Topic and Key Number
1	Druggists ☞1, 5, 11
2.1–11	Druggists ☞2, 3, 5
12.1–15	Druggists ☞1–6
16	Druggists ☞5, 6
17.1–19	Druggists ☞8, 9
20.1–22	Druggists ☞9, 10
23	Druggists ☞2, 5
24–26	Druggists ☞2, 5, 11
27, 28	Druggists ☞11
29	Druggists ☞2, 3, 5, 12
30.1, 31	Druggists ☞12
41	Druggists ☞2, 5; Physicians and Surgeons ☞10; Poisons ☞2, 4
42	Druggists ☞2, 3, 5; Poisons ☞2, 4, 9
43.1	Druggists ☞2; Internal Revenue ☞2401; Poisons ☞2, 4
44	Poisons ☞2, 4, 9
45.1	Druggists ☞2; Poisons ☞2–4, 9

Drugs and Narcotics Key Number	Prior Topic and Key Number
	Poisons ☞4, 9
75	Poisons ☞4, 9
76	Custom Duties ☞125; Druggists ☞12; Internal Revenue ☞2401, 2447; Poisons ☞4, 9
77	Customs Duties ☞125; Druggists ☞12; Poisons ☞2, 4, 9
78	Poisons ☞2, 4, 9
101, 102.1	Druggists ☞12; Poisons ☞2, 9
103	Customs Duties ☞134; Internal Revenue ☞2433, 2441; Poisons ☞2, 4, 9
104	Poisons ☞4, 9
105	Internal Revenue ☞2433; Poisons ☞4, 9
106	Customs Duties ☞134; Internal Revenue ☞2448; Poisons ☞2, 4, 9
107	Customs Duties ☞134; Internal Revenue ☞2447

When a topic is expanded or reclassified in a key number digest, a Key Number Translation Table is printed immediately prior to the new topic. This illustration shows that Drugs and Narcotics, Key Numbers 17.1–19 were formerly covered by Druggists, Key Numbers 8 and 9. Frequently, the *Analysis* in earlier editions of digests can be consulted to see a more detailed breakdown of the original topic before it was expanded or reclassified.

Drugs and Narcotics Key Number	Prior Topic and Key Number
	Poisons ☞4, 9
50	Druggists ☞9, 10; Poisons ☞4, 6
61	Druggists ☞2, 5, 12; Poisons ☞2, 4, 9
62.1	Poisons ☞2, 4, 9
63	Druggists ☞2; Poisons ☞4, 9
64	Poisons ☞4, 9
65	Druggists ☞2; Poisons ☞4, 9
66	Poisons ☞2, 4, 9
67	Poisons ☞4, 9
68.1	Druggists ☞2, 12; Poisons ☞2, 4, 9
69, 70	Druggists ☞2; Poisons ☞4, 9
71	Poisons ☞2, 4, 9
72	Poisons ☞4
73.1	Druggists ☞12; Internal Revenue ☞2401; Poisons ☞2, 4, 9
74	Customs Duties ☞125, 134;

Drugs and Narcotics Key Number	Prior Topic and Key Number
112	Internal Revenue ☞2449; Poisons ☞4, 9
113, 114	Poisons ☞2, 4, 9
115.1	Customs Duties ☞134; Internal Revenue ☞2449; Poisons ☞4, 9
116	Poisons ☞4, 9
117	Druggists ☞2, 12; Poisons ☞4, 9
118	Poisons ☞9
119.1	Druggists ☞12; Poisons ☞9
120, 122	Poisons ☞9
123	Customs Duties ☞134; Druggists ☞12; Internal Revenue ☞2447, 2449; Poisons ☞4, 9
124	Customs Duties ☞125, 134; Poisons ☞2, 9
125.1–127	Poisons ☞9
128	Customs Duties ☞134; Internal Revenue ☞2449; Poisons ☞9

[Illustration 7–12]

SCREEN PRINT FROM WESTLAW SHOWING A RECLASSIFIED TOPIC

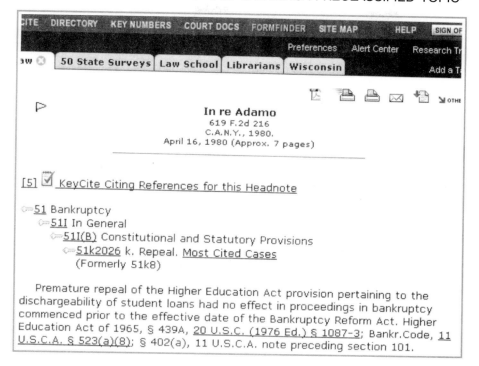

SECTION J.   OTHER SPECIALIZED WEST DIGESTS

1. West's Bankruptcy Digest

This key number digest includes cases from *West's Bankruptcy Reporter* and selected bankruptcy cases from the *Federal Reporter 2d* and *3d* and West's *Supreme Court Reporter.*

2. West's Military Justice Digest

This key number digest includes cases from *West's Military Justice Reporter.*

3. United States Federal Claims Digest

This is a key number digest that includes cases from volumes 1–26 of the *United States Claims Court Reporter* and from volume 27 forward of the *Federal Claims Reporter.*

4. West's Education Law Digest

This publication provides key number digest paragraphs from all cases in the *National Reporter System* on topics relating to education law.

5. West's Veterans Appeals Digest

This is a key number digest that includes cases reported in the *Veterans Appeals Reporter,* and cases from the U.S. Court of Appeals for the

Federal Circuit and the Supreme Court of the United States that review those cases reported in the *Veterans Appeals Reporter*.

6.   United States Merit Systems Protection Board Digest

This publication digests cases involving federal employees and the federal merit system. It uses a classification scheme different from the key number digests.

SECTION K. CHART ILLUSTRATING WEST GROUP'S KEY NUMBER DIGESTS

MASTER INDEX TO ALL CASE LAW

American Digest System

Cases from: U.S. Supreme Court, all lower federal courts, all specialized federal courts, and all state courts

Use:	Chronological Coverage
*Century Digest	1658-1896
First Dicennial	1896-1906
Second Dicennial	1907-1916
Third Dicennial	1916-1926
Fourth Dicennial	1926-1936
Fifth Dicennial	1936-1946
Sixth Dicennial	1946-1956
Seventh Dicennial	1956-1966
Eighth Dicennial	1966-1976
Ninth Dicennial (Part 1)	1976-1981
Ninth Dicennial (Part 2)	1981-1986
Tenth Dicennial (Part 1)	1986-1991
Tenth Dicennial (Part 2)	1991-1996
Eleventh Dicennial (Part 1)	1996-2001
Eleventh Dicennial (Part 2)	2001-2004
Eleventh Dicennial (Part 3)	2004-2007
General Digest (12th Series) (in progress)	2008 +

*The Century Digest indexes cases prior to the start of the National Reporter System. Therefore, digest coverage is more inclusive than reporter coverage.

FEDERAL COURT COVERAGE

Complete Supreme Court coverage
Cases from: *Supreme Court Reporter*
Use: *U.S. Supreme Court Digest*

Complete Federal Court coverage
Cases from: U.S. Supreme Court, all lower federal courts, and all specialized federal courts.
Use: *Federal Practice Digest, 4th*
     (1984 to date)
Federal Practice Digest, 3rd
     (Dec. 1975 to *Fed. Prac. Dig. 4th*)
Federal Practice Digest, 2nd
     (1961 - Nov. 1975)
Modern Federal Practice Digest
     (1939-1960)
Federal Digest

STATE COURT COVERAGE

Individual State Digests

Coverage corresponds to regional digest in which state appears. Note: Some state digests are in a 2d, 3d, or 4th series.
Published for all states except:
Del. (Use: *Atlantic Digest*);
Nev. and Utah (Use: *Pacific Digest*)

Regional Reporter Digests

Cases from: The seven regional reporters, Calif. & N.Y., plus pre-reporter cases.

Use as appropriate:
Atlantic (CT, DE, MD, ME, NH, NJ, PA, RI, VT, DC)
     1st (to 1938)
     2d (1938 to date)
North Western (IO, MI, MN, NE, ND, SD, WI)
     1st (to 1941)
     2d (1941 to date)
Pacific (AK, AZ, CA*, CO, HI, ID, KA, MT, NM, NV, OK, OR, UT, WA, WY)
     1850-1931 (California & Pacific)
     1-100 P.2d
     101-366 P.2d
     367-584 P.2d
     585-to date
South Eastern (GA, NC, SC, VA, WV)
     1st (to 1934)
     2d (1934 to date)

      * * * * *

North Eastern (IL, ID, MA, NY, OH)
     (to 1968)
     CEASED PUBLICATION
     Use: appropriate state digest
Southern (AL, FL, LA, MS)
     (to 1988)
     CEASED PUBLICATION
     Use: appropriate state digest
South Western
     NOT PUBLISHED
     Use: state digests for AR, KY, MO, TN, TX

*Covers all Calif. courts to 1960 and only Cal. Sup. Ct. thereafter. For full coverage since 1960, use *California Digest* Series.

SECTION L. OTHER DIGESTS

Digests are not unique to West publications. Other publishers prepare digest volumes on a variety of topics, and researchers should become familiar with their format and features. Some of these non-West digests are discussed below.

1. **Digest of United States Supreme Court Reports, Lawyers' Edition** (LexisNexis; formerly published by Lawyers Cooperative Publishing Company)

This is a multivolume digest, with annual pocket supplements, to all cases of the Supreme Court of the United States. The digest paragraphs used are collected from those published in the two editions of the *U.S. Supreme Court Reports, Lawyers' Edition.* This digest provides references to this publisher's other publications.

2. **Digests for Looseleaf Services, Topical Reporters, and Other Types of Publications**

Frequently looseleaf services, topical reporters, multivolume treatises, and, on occasion, legal periodicals, provide subject or alphabetically arranged abstracts of cases. At other times, materials are grouped under state or federal code sections. Still other digest volumes use a hybrid of these methods. Since digest volumes are useful finding aids for identifying similar materials, it is always useful to check sets for separate digest volumes and for case abstracts within these volumes.

3. **A.L.R. Digests**

These publications are discussed in Chapter 17, Section B–2 of this book.

4. **Digests for Federal Tax Materials**

See Chapter 25 for a discussion of tax research.

SECTION M. WORDS AND PHRASES AND POPULAR NAME TABLES

1. **Words and Phrases**

Sometimes a research problem involves the definition of certain words or phrases such as, for example, *learned intermediary doctrine,* which was derived from *Kasin v. Osco Drug, Inc.,* in our hypothetical problem. Courts frequently define the meaning of words and phrases to add clarity to their opinions.

Headnotes that contain judicial definitions are reprinted in West's *Words and Phrases,* a multivolume set containing approximately 600,000 alphabetically arranged judicial definitions of legal and non-legal terms. *Words and Phrases* is updated by annual cumulative pocket supplements, which are further supplemented by *Words and Phrases* tables in later bound volumes and advance sheets of the various units of the *National Reporter System.* Most of the key number digests also contain these tables. [See Illustration 7–13 for an example of a page from *Words and Phrases.* See also the second headnote in Illustration 7–2, which indicates that a judicial definition is derived from that headnote.]

2. Popular Name Tables

Frequently, a case becomes better known by a popular name rather than by its actual name. For example, *Cruzan v. Director, Missouri Dept. of Health* is popularly known as the "Right to Die Case." At other times, a group of cases may come to be known collectively by a popular name, such as the "Right to Counsel Cases." When only the popular name of a case or a group of cases is known, it is necessary to consult a table of cases by popular name in order to obtain citations to the actual case or cases. These tables are located in the following sources:

a. *First through Sixth Decennial Digests.* The Table of Cases volume contains a cumulative List of Popular Name Titles in the *American Digest System.* This feature was discontinued with the *Seventh Decennial Digest.*

b. *Tables of Cases by Popular Names* in the various special digests.

c. *Shepard's Acts and Cases by Popular Names.* [Illustration 7–14]

SECTION N.   ILLUSTRATIONS

7–13.   Page From Volume of Words and Phrases
7–14.   Page From Shepard's Acts and Cases by Popular Names

[Illustration 7–13]

PAGE FROM VOLUME OF WORDS AND PHRASES

LEARNED INTERMEDIARY

24A W&P— 142

tient through informed consent, so as to enable patient to use product safely.—Niemiera by Niemiera v. Schneider, 555 A.2d 1112, 114 N.J. 550.—Drugs & N 18.

N.Y.A.D. 3 Dept. 2000. Under doctrine of "learned intermediary," manufacturer of medical device satisfies its duty to warn of potential adverse effects when it adequately warns medical professionals who use the device in treatment of patients; when this occurs, medical professional acts as "learned intermediary" between manufacturer and patient, relieving manufacturer of any responsibility to directly warn patient of potential adverse side effects.—Banker v. Hoehn, 718 N.Y.S.2d 438, 278

> The paragraphs in *Words and Phrases* are essentially the same as the headnotes in the volumes of the *National Reporter System*. The pocket supplements and any supplemental pamphlets should always be checked.
>
> If a researcher needs to determine if other courts have defined a word or phrase, e.g., "learned intermediary doctrine," consulting *Words and Phrases* is a valuable time-saver.

C.A.5 (Miss.) 1999. "Learned intermediary defense" allows manufacturer to discharge its duty to warn by providing information to a third person upon whom it can reasonably rely to communicate the information to the ultimate users of the product or those who will be exposed to its hazardous effects.—Curtis v. M&S Petroleum, Inc., 174 F.3d 661.—Prod Liab 14.

D.S.C. 1988. "Learned intermediary defense" rests on the sufficiency and clarity of warnings given to the trained, licensed physician; if the doctor receives a warning which fully comports with the Food and Drug Administration legal standards, doctrine prevents recovery by a treated patient against the manufacturer.—Tarallo v. Searle Pharmaceutical, Inc., 704 F.Supp. 653.—Drugs & N 18.

Nev. 1994. "Mass immunization" exception to "learned intermediary defense" applied in action against manufacturer of measles, mumps and rubella (MMR) vaccine administered by county health district; physician's advice to infant's mother that "it was time" for infant to receive vaccine was not type of "individualized medical judgment" contemplated by learned intermediary defense. (Per Springer, J., with one Justice concurring, Chief Justice concurring in results and two Justices concurring in part and dissenting in part.)—Allison v. Merck and Co., Inc., 878 P.2d 948, 110 Nev. 762.—Drugs & N 18.

Tex.App.–San Antonio 2001. Under the "learned intermediary defense" to a products liability action, a manufacturer may fulfill its duty to warn by proving that an adequate warning was given to an intermediary who would then pass the warning along to the user.—Coleman v. Cintas

Sales Corp., 40 S.W.3d 544, rehearing denied, and review denied.—Prod Liab 14.

LEARNED INTERMEDIARY DOCTRINE

C.A.5 (La.) 1999. Under "learned intermediary doctrine," seller of medical product has obligation to inform physician of risks of that product.—Theriot v. Danek Medical, Inc., 168 F.3d 253.—Prod Liab 46.

C.A.5 (La.) 1999. Pedicle screw manufacturer's alleged failure to adequately test screws did not preclude summary judgment for seller pursuant to "learned intermediary doctrine" on claim under Louisiana Products Liability Act (LPLA) that seller to adequately warn plaintiff patient's treating an of screw's potential side effects; physician d that he was fully apprised of potential LSA-R.S. 9:2800.52 et seq.—Theriot v. Da- edical, Inc., 168 F.3d 253.—Prod Liab 46.

5 (La.) 1991. Under Louisiana's "learned ediary doctrine," manufacturer has no duty 1 patient but need only warn patient's physi- Willett v. Baxter Intern., Inc., 929 F.2d -Prod Liab 46.

5 (Miss.) 1992. Mississippi follows "learned ediary doctrine," under which manufacturer's to warn patient of product's risk does not product defective or unreasonably dangerous so long as manufacturer adequately warns learned intermediary.—Thomas v. Hoffman-La-Roche, Inc., 949 F.2d 806, rehearing denied 957 F.2d 869, certiorari denied 112 S.Ct. 2304, 504 U.S. 956, 119 L.Ed.2d 226.—Drugs & N 18; Prod Liab 46.

C.A.4 (S.C.) 1992. Under "learned intermediary doctrine," manufacturer's duty to warn extends only to prescribing physician, who then assumes responsibility for advising individual patient of risks associated with drug or device.—Odom v. G.D. Searle & Co., 979 F.2d 1001.—Drugs & N 18.

C.A.5 (Tex.) 1999. Under Texas' "learned intermediary doctrine," when a drug manufacturer properly warns a prescribing physician of the dangerous propensities of its product, the manufacturer is excused from warning each patient who receives the drug; the doctor stands as a learned intermediary between the manufacturer and the ultimate consumer.—In re Norplant Contraceptive Products Litigation, 165 F.3d 374, rehearing denied.—Drugs & N 18.

C.A.4 (Va.) 1999. The "learned intermediary doctrine" provides an exception to the general rule imposing a duty on manufacturers to warn consumers about the risks of their products, and, for products requiring prescription or application by physicians, the doctrine holds that a manufacturer need only warn doctors and not consumers.—Talley v. Danek Medical, Inc., 179 F.3d 154.—Prod Liab 14.

D.Conn. 1999. Under "learned intermediary doctrine" defense to products liability actions, adequate warnings to prescribing physicians obviate the need for manufacturers of prescription products to

[Illustration 7–14]

PAGE FROM SHEPARD'S ACTS AND CASES BY POPULAR NAME

FEDERAL AND STATE CASES CITED BY POPULAR NAME   Roa

Rich Young Ruler Case
192 N.C. 251, 134 S.E. 487

Richardson Valve Case
113 U.S. 157, 28 L. Ed. 939, 5 S. Ct. 513

Richmond, Virginia Case
124 Va. 522, 98 S.E. 643; 256 U.S. 635, 65 L. Ed. 1135, 41 S. Ct. 619

RICO Antiabortion Protest Case
510 U.S. 249, 127 L. Ed. 2d 99, 114 S. Ct. 798 (1994)

RICO Predicate Conviction Case
473 U.S. 479, 87 L. Ed. 2d 346, 105 S. Ct. 3275

Riegelman Case
27 T.C. 833; 253 F.2d 315

Right of Privacy Case
155 Fla. 198, 20 So. 2d 243; 159 Fla. 31, 30 So. 2d 635

Right to Appoint Counsel Case
440 U.S. 367, 59 L. Ed. 2d 383, 99 S. Ct. 1158

Right to Be Heard Case
415 U.S. 452, 39 L. Ed. 2d 505, 94 S. Ct. 1209

Right to Counsel Cases
315 U.S. 791, 86 L. Ed. 1194, 62 S. Ct. 639; 316 U.S. 455, 86 L. Ed. 1595, 62 S. Ct. 1252
469 U.S. 91, 83 L. Ed. 2d 488, 105 S. Ct. 490
51 L. Ed. 2d 424, 97 S. Ct. 1232
116 F.2d 690, 313 U.S. 551, 85 L. Ed. 1222, 61 S. Ct. 835; 315 U.S. 60, 86 L. Ed. 680, 62 S. Ct. 457; 315 U.S. 827, 86 L. Ed. 1222, 62 S. Ct. 629, 62 S. Ct. 637

Right to Die Case
111 L. Ed. 2d 224, 110 S. Ct. 2841

Right-to-Reply Case
418 U.S. 241, 41 L. Ed. 2d 730, 94 S. Ct. 2831

Rights of Involuntarily Committed Persons Case
457 U.S. 307, 73 L. Ed. 2d 28, 102 S. Ct. 2452

Rights of Pretrial Detainees Case
441 U.S. 520, 60 L. Ed. 2d 447, 99 S. Ct. 1861

Rigid Steel Conduit Case
168 F.2d 175; 336 U.S. 902, 93 L. Ed. 1068, 69 S. Ct. 491; 336 U.S. 956, 93 L. Ed. 1110, 69 S. Ct. 888

River Bed Cases
20 F.2d 845
20 F.2d 873; 275 U.S. 552, 72 L. Ed. 421, 48 S. Ct. 115; 275 U.S. 555, 72 L. Ed. 423, 48 S. Ct. 116
121 Tex. 515, 50 S.W.2d 1065; 25 S.W.2d 706

River Rights Cases
199 A.D. 539, 192 N.Y.S. 211; 235 N.Y. 351, 139 N.E. 474, 236 N.Y. 579, 142 N.E. 291; 271 U.S. 364, 70 L. Ed. 992, 46 S. Ct. 569
199 A.D. 552, 192 N.Y.S. 222; 235 N.Y. 364, 139 N.E. 477; 236 N.Y. 578, 142 N.E. 291; 271 U.S. 403, 70 L. Ed. 1009, 46 S. Ct. 581

River Road Case
353 U.S. 30, 1 L. Ed. 2d 622, 77 S. Ct. 635; 353 U.S. 948, 1 L. Ed. 2d 857, 77 S. Ct. 823; 229 F.2d 926

Riverside Mills Case
168 F. 987; 168 F. 990; 219 U.S. 186, 55 L. Ed. 167, 31 S. Ct. 164

Road Cases
30 Tex. 503
30 Tex. 506

Roane-Anderson Case
192 Tenn. 150, 239 S.W.2d 27; 342 U.S. 847, 96 L. Ed. 639, 72 S. Ct. 74; 342 U.S. 232, 96 L. Ed. 257, 72 S. Ct. 257

Chapter 8

CONSTITUTIONAL LAW AND THE SUPREME COURT OF THE UNITED STATES

This chapter discusses researching U.S. constitutional law and the institution of the Supreme Court of the United States, as well as state constitutional law and the constitutions of other countries. The chapter does not include discussions of the reports of the opinions of the Supreme Court or the records and briefs of the Court; they are discussed in other chapters of this book.[1]

SECTION A. THE CONSTITUTION OF THE UNITED STATES

The Constitution of the United States of America, in a formal sense, is the written document that was drafted at Philadelphia in the summer of 1787, plus the amendments that have since been added. The framers of the Constitution did not intend it to be a static document, but rather, as stated by Chief Justice Marshall, "to endure for ages to come, and, consequently, to be adapted to various *crises* of human affairs."[2] Researching problems in constitutional law requires reference to the document itself[3] and to sources that assist in its interpretation.[4] These sources can include the background and record of the Constitutional Convention, interpretations of the Constitution by the Supreme Court of the United States in the more than 530 volumes of its official reports, and commentaries on the Constitution in treatises, monographs, legal periodicals, encyclopedias, and other secondary sources.

1. Judicial Interpretations

a. *Annotated Editions of the Federal Constitution*

Courts, especially the Supreme Court of the United States, frequently interpret provisions of the Constitution of the United States. Some of the most useful sources for identifying and locating citations to these judicial interpretations are the various annotated editions of the Constitution. These publications set forth each article, section, and clause of the Consti-

---

[1] Supreme Court opinions are discussed in Chapter 5 along with other federal court reports. Supreme Court records and briefs are discussed in Chapter 20.

[2] McCulloch v. Maryland, 17 U.S. (4 Wheat.) 316, 415 (1819).

[3] The text of the Constitution and its amendments are readily available. In addition to being included with the official UNITED STATES CODE and the annotated federal codes (discussed in this section), it is typically included in sets of state annotated codes, as well as in constitutional law texts and casebooks, law dictionaries, and a multitude of Internet websites.

[4] For two contrasting approaches to constitutional interpretation, see STEPHEN G. BREYER, ACTIVE LIBERTY: INTERPRETING OUR DEMOCRATIC CONSTITUTION (Knopf 2005), and ANTONIN SCALIA, A MATTER OF INTERPRETATION: FEDERAL COURTS AND THE LAW (Princeton University Press 1997).

tution and its amendments and provide abstracts of the cases and, in some instances, commentary interpreting the provisions of the Constitution.

(1) *United States Code Annotated, Constitution of the United States Annotated* (West). This set, published as part of the *United States Code Annotated (U.S.C.A.)*, consists of unnumbered volumes, supplemented by pamphlets or pocket parts. An index to the Constitution is included at the end of the last volume of the set. Set forth after each article, section, and clause of the Constitution and after each of its 27 amendments are cross-references to pertinent sections in *U.S.C.A.* and references to encyclopedias, law reviews, and treatises.

Notes of Decisions, which are digest paragraphs from all cases that have interpreted a constitutional provision or amendment, follow these references. These notes are preceded by references to West's key number system and relevant encyclopedia section numbers, and then by numbered topics, which enable a user to go directly to the cases digested under those topics. [See Illustrations 8–1 through 8–3 for the method of locating a constitutional provision and the notes of decisions that accompany it.] An electronic version of *U.S.C.A.* is available on *Westlaw.*

(2) *United States Code Service, Constitution* (LexisNexis). This is a separate unit of the *United States Code Service (U.S.C.S.)*. It includes extensive references to articles, annotations, judicial opinions, and other resources that interpret provisions of the Constitution. These Constitution volumes are organized and updated in much the same way as the *United States Code Annotated* and are used in a similar manner, with the last volume containing an index. An electronic version of *U.S.C.S.* is available on *LexisNexis.*

(3) *The Constitution of the United States of America* (Library of Congress ed. 2002, with supplements). This annotated, one-volume edition of the Constitution[5] is prepared by the Congressional Research Service of the Library of Congress, as authorized by a Joint Congressional Resolution.[6] This publication sets forth each article, section, and clause of the Constitution and its amendments. Immediately following each of them, in smaller typeface, is analysis and commentary prepared by the editorial staff. Important cases decided by the Supreme Court of the United States are discussed in the analysis, and citations to the cases are given in the footnotes. [Illustrations 8–4 and 8–5] Frequently, the commentary quotes from the proceedings of the Constitutional Convention, opinions of dissenting justices, and other documents. This volume, unlike the others discussed above, does not attempt to cite or comment on all cases of the Supreme Court of the United States, but refers only to the more significant cases. This is a very useful volume and is often the preferred starting point for

---

[5] The Constitution of the United States of America, S. Doc. No. 17, 108th Cong., 2d Sess. (1996). Although published in 2004, this is known as the 2002 edition. *See* note 6, below.

[6] 2 U.S.C. § 168 (2006). This Joint Resolution provides for a new hard-bound volume every ten years with pocket supplements to be issued biennially. The current 2,608 page edition covers material dated up to June 28, 2002. Although a biennial supplement is published, it typically only supplements the volume to within about a year of the date at the time of its issuance. An electronic version of the current edition is available on the *GPO Access* website: http://www.gpoaccess.gov/constitution/index.html.

research on constitutional questions. It has a detailed index and includes useful tables such as the following:

Proposed amendments pending before the states.

Proposed amendments not ratified by the states.

Acts of Congress held unconstitutional in whole or in part by the Supreme Court of the United States.

State constitutional and statutory provisions and municipal ordinances held unconstitutional or held to be preempted by federal law.

Supreme Court decisions overruled by subsequent decisions.

Table of Cases.

b. *Digests of Federal Court Reports*

Digests of federal cases provide access to additional interpretations of the Constitution.[7] The following digests are discussed in detail in Chapter 7:

(1) *Digest of United States Supreme Court Reports, Lawyers' Edition* (LexisNexis). Volume 17 contains the text of the Constitution together with references to this publisher's relevant headnote topics and sections.

(2) *United States Supreme Court Digest* (West).

(3) *Federal Digest, Modern Federal Practice Digest,* and *West's Federal Practice Digest, 2nd, 3rd,* and *4th* (West).

c. *Annotations.* The annotations in *A.L.R. Federal; U.S. Supreme Court Reports, Lawyers' Edition; A.L.R., A.L.R.2d,* and *A.L.R.3d* (pre–1969) may contain discussions of constitutional issues, in which case the annotations include case references.

d. *Computer-Assisted Legal Research Services.* The text of the U.S. Constitution is available on most computer-assisted legal research services and on numerous websites, e.g., *GPO Access.* Using one of these CALR services, search terms can be combined with sections and clauses of the Constitution to search the full-text and retrieve relevant cases.

e. *Citators. Shepard's* and *KeyCite* provide references to cases citing or construing the Constitution.[8]

2. Secondary Sources

Constitutional commentary by legal scholars is voluminous. Secondary sources, such as monographs, treatises, encyclopedias, and periodical articles, provide analysis of constitutional issues. Some of the most well-known sources are listed below.

a. The six-volume *Encyclopedia of the American Constitution*[9] contains approximately 2,400 articles written by 237 authors, typically lawyers, historians, and political scientists. Arrangement is alphabetical with arti-

---

[7] State and regional digests also contain digest paragraphs for federal cases arising within their jurisdictional coverage.

[8] Citators are discussed in Chapter 15.

[9] (Leonard W. Levy & Kenneth L. Karst eds., 2d. ed. Macmillan Publishing Co. 2000).

cles discussing both broad subjects and individual cases. Some of the articles contain useful bibliographic references.

b. *The Founders' Constitution*[10] is a five volume set (also available on CD–ROM) containing an extensive collection of documents that discuss the text of the Constitution, from the Preamble through the Twelfth Amendment. Volume 1 is arranged by theme and highlights the debate over the principles embodied in the Constitution; volumes 2–4 are arranged to correspond to the text of the Constitution; and volume 5 is devoted to Amendments I–XII.

c. Those interested in researching the 27 amendments to the Constitution should consult *Constitutional Amendments, 1789 to date.*[11] This volume devotes a chapter to each amendment. A final chapter discusses failed amendments.

d. Researchers seeking an extensive listing of sources on the Constitution will want to consult Kermit L. Hall's *A Comprehensive Bibliography of American Constitutional and Legal History, 1896–1979.*[12] This five-volume set contains over 68,000 entries for books, journal articles, and doctoral dissertations. It is divided into seven chapters: general surveys and texts; institutions; constitutional doctrine; legal doctrine; biographical; chronological; and geographical. Also useful is the one-volume *The Constitution of the United States: A Guide and Bibliography to Current Scholarly Research.*[13]

e. While all law dictionaries provide definitions of terms bearing on constitutional law, the two-volume *Constitutional Law Dictionary*[14] is intended specifically for this purpose. Volume 1 is subtitled *Individual Rights;* volume 2 *Governmental Powers.* Each volume contains a summary of approximately 300 cases organized in a subject-matter chapter format. This arrangement is followed by several hundred definitions.

f. Highly regarded contemporary treatises on the subject of constitutional law are Laurence H. Tribe's one-volume *American Constitutional Law;*[15] the five-volume *Treatise on Constitutional Law: Substance and Procedure,*[16] by Ronald D. Rotunda and John E. Nowak; and the three-volume *Modern Constitutional Law,*[17] by William J. Rich and Chester James Antieau. Constitutional law casebooks[18] and legal periodicals[19] also provide analysis and interpretation.

---

[10] (Philip B. Kurland & Ralph Lerner eds., University of Chicago Press 1987).

[11] (Kris E. Palmer ed., Gale 2000).

[12] (Krauss International Pubs. 1984). A two-volume supplement covers 1980–1987.

[13] (Bernard D. Reams, Jr. & Stuart D. Yoak eds., Oceana 1987). This volume is also published as volume 11 of SOURCES AND DOCUMENTS OF UNITED STATES CONSTITUTIONS.

[14] Ralph C. Chandler et al. (ABC–CLIO Information Sources 1985 & 1987). Volume one has been updated with three supplements, bringing coverage through the 1993 Supreme Court term.

[15] (3d ed. Foundation Press 2000).

[16] (4th ed. West 2007). An abridged version is published as CONSTITUTIONAL LAW (7th ed. 2004) and is a part of West's *Hornbook Series.*

[17] (2d ed. West 1997).

[18] A good example is KATHLEEN M. SULLIVAN & GERALD GUNTHER, CONSTITUTIONAL LAW (16th ed. Foundation Press 2007).

[19] Almost all legal periodical will publish articles on constitutional issues. Some, however, are devoted to these topics, such as the University of Minnesota's CONSTITUTIONAL COMMENTARY, Seton Hall University's CONSTITUTIONAL LAW JOURNAL, GEORGE MASON CIVIL RIGHTS LAW JOURNAL, HARVARD CIVIL RIGHTS–CIVIL LIBERTIES LAW REVIEW, HASTINGS CONSTITUTIONAL LAW QUARTERLY,

3. Historical Sources

When faced with the task of interpreting the meaning of a provision or clause of the Constitution, ascertaining the meaning of the words used by the framers is often important. This may necessitate consulting sources that preceded the adoption of the Constitution, such as documents of the Continental Congress or the Articles of Confederation.[20] These sources can be located in the Library of Congress Legislative Reference Service's *Documents Illustrative of the Formation of the Union of the American States.*[21] Also useful is *Documentary History of the Constitution of the United States of America, 1786–1870.*[22] Indispensable are the essays of Madison, Jay, and Hamilton published as *The Federalist.*[23] Thurston Green, *The Language of the Constitution: A Sourcebook and Guide to the Ideas, Terms, and Vocabulary Used by the Framers of the United States Constitution*, discusses the language used in drafting the Constitution.[24]

While the Constitutional Convention did not keep official records of its secret sessions, the most widely accepted source for insights into the debates is Max Farrand's three-volume *Records of the Federal Constitution of 1787.*[25] For understanding the ratification process by the states, a valuable source is *Elliot's Debates.*[26] The *Documentary History of the Ratification of the Constitution*,[27] is the most comprehensive and up-to-date source of the history of the ratification of the U.S. Constitution. Courts, at

University of Pennsylvania's JOURNAL OF CONSTITUTIONAL LAW, TEXAS FORUM ON CIVIL LIBERTIES, and WILLIAM AND MARY BILL OF RIGHTS JOURNAL. Legal periodicals are discussed in Chapter 17 of this book.

[20] Many of these sources, as well as other sources on the historical development of the Constitution, are available on *Westlaw* in the *Bicentennial of the Constitution* (BICENT) database. The BICENT database, however, is not available under the general law school subscription.

[21] H.R. DOC. NO. 398, 69th Cong., 1st Sess. (1935). *See also* SOL BLOOM, FORMATION OF THE UNION UNDER THE CONSTITUTION (1935). For background on the Articles of Confederation, see William F. Swindler, *Our First Constitution: The Articles of Confederation*, 67 A.B.A. J. 166 (1961). For documents pertaining to the adoption of the Bill of Rights, see BERNARD SCHWARTZ, THE BILL OF RIGHTS: A DOCUMENTARY HISTORY (Chelsea House 1971, 2 vols.), and THE COMPLETE BILL OF RIGHTS: THE DRAFTS, DEBATES, SOURCES, AND ORIGINS (Neil H. Cogan ed., Oxford University Press 1997).

[22] U.S. Bureau of Rolls and Library of the Department of State (1894–1905; reprinted in 1965 by Johnson Reprint Corp.).

[23] THE FEDERALIST has been published in many editions. *See also* JAMES MADISON, THE PAPERS OF JAMES MADISON (Henry D. Gilpin ed., 1840).

[24] (Greenwood Press 1991).

[25] (Yale University Press 1911). A supplement was prepared in 1987 by James H. Hutson. *See also* THE FOUNDERS' CONSTITUTION, *supra* note 10; WILBOURN E. BENTON, 1787: DRAFTING THE U.S. CONSTITUTION (Texas A & M University Press 1986, 2 vols.).

[26] JONATHAN ELLIOT, THE DEBATES, RESOLUTIONS, AND OTHER PROCEEDINGS, IN CONVENTION, ON THE ADOPTION OF THE FEDERAL CONSTITUTION (1827). This set has appeared in many editions with different titles and somewhat different content, all known generally as *Elliot's Debates*. The most complete edition was published in five volumes in 1937.

[27] (Merrill Jensen ed., State Historical Society of Wisconsin 1976– , 22 volumes to date).

times, also turn to these historical sources for support in their opinions interpreting the Constitution.[28] The Library of Congress maintains a website, *Primary Documents in American History: United States Constitution*, that contains many primary source documents, relevant external links, and bibliographies about the adoption of the Constitution.[29]

SECTION B. ILLUSTRATIONS

Problem: **In a products liability case where suit was brought against a prescription drug manufacturer, *Abbot v. American Cyanamid Co.*, 844 F.2d 1108 (4th Cir. 1988), the issue related to defective design and failure to warn. Does federal law preempt state common law liability?**

Illustrations

8–1.   **Page from Volume Containing Index to Constitution: U.S.C.A.**

8–2.   **Page from a Constitution Volume: U.S.C.A.**

8–3.   **Page Showing Notes of Decisions from a Constitution Volume: U.S.C.A.**

8–4 to   **Pages from The Constitution of the United States of**
8–5.   **America (Library of Congress)**

---

[28] *See, e.g.,* Morrison v. Olson, 487 U.S. 654, 674 (1988) (citing RECORDS OF THE FEDERAL CONVENTION OF 1787 (Max Farrand ed., 1966)); Welch v. Texas Dept. of Highways, 483 U.S. 468, 481 n.10 (1987) (citing ELLIOT'S DEBATES, 2d ed. 1861); Atascadero State Hosp. v. Scanlon, 473 U.S. 234, 271 (1985) (Brennan, J., dissenting) (citing DOCUMENTARY HISTORY OF THE RATIFICATION OF THE CONSTITUTION).

[29] http://www.loc.gov/rr/program/bib/ourdocs/Constitution.html.

[Illustration 8–1]

PAGE FROM VOLUME CONTAINING INDEX TO CONSTITUTION: U.S.C.A.

CONSTITUTION OF THE UNITED STATES   **LETTERS**

JUDICIAL OFFICERS
See, also, Judges or Justices, generally, this index
Oath to support Constitution, **Art. 6, cl. 3**

JUDICIAL POWER
Vested in Supreme and inferior courts, **Art. 3, § 1**

JUDICIAL PROCEEDINGS
See Actions and Proceedings, generally, this index

JURISDICTION
Controversy to which judicial power of U.S. extends, **Art. 3, § 2, cl. 1**
Crime, fugitives to be removed to State having, **Art. 4, § 2, cl. 2**
New State not to be erected within another State, **Art. 4, § 3, cl. 1**
Original and appellate of Supreme Court, **Art. 3, § 2, cl. 2**
Supreme Court, **Art. 3, § 2, cl. 2**
   Ambassadors, and other public ministers and consuls, cases affecting, **Art. 3, § 2, cl. 2**
   Inferior courts, judicial power vested in, **Art. 3, § 1**
   Original jurisdiction, **Art. 3, § 2, cl. 2**
   Where State is party, **Art. 3, § 2, cl. 2**

JURY
Common law,
   No fact tried by jury shall be re-examined except according to, **Am. 7**
   Rules adhered to, **Am. 7**
   Trial by jury,
     According to rules of, suits involving

KING
Office holder accepting present, title, etc., from, **Art. 1, § 9, cl. 8**

LABOR
Due in one State not to be abrogated in another, **Art. 4, § 2, cl. 3**

LANDS
Congress to have power over land owned by U.S., **Art. 1, § 8, cl. 17**
Judicial power and controversies for land claims, **Art. 3, § 2, cl. 1**
Private Lands or Property, generally, this index

LAWS
Bills, generally, this index
Cases arising under laws of U.S., judicial power extends to, **Art. 3, § 2, cl. 1**
Congress shall make necessary laws, **Art. 1, § 8, cl. 18**
Congress to provide,
   Call in militia to execute, **Art. 1, § 8, cl. 15**
   Punishing offenses against Law of Nations, **Art. 1, § 8, cl. 10**
President's duty regarding executing laws of U.S., **Art. 2, § 3**
State judges to be bound by law of the land, **Art. 6, cl. 2**
Supreme Court to have appellate jurisdiction as to law, **Art. 3, § 2, cl. 2**
What constitutes supreme law of the land, **Art. 6, cl. 2**

LAWYERS
Attorneys and Counselors, generally, this index

The first step in researching a problem involving the United States Constitution is to look in the volume containing the index to the Constitution. For the problem under research, Article 6, Clause 2 should be examined.

Grand Jury, generally, this index
Impartial, in all criminal prosecutions, **Am. 6**
Impeachment, jury trial not required, **Art. 3, § 2, cl. 3**
Re-examination after jury trial, restrictions, **Am. 7**
Suits at common law, **Am. 7**
Trial by, in controversies involving value over twenty dollars, **Am. 7**
Writs of error, re-examination after jury trial, restrictions, **Am. 7**

JUST COMPENSATION
Private property not to be taken for public use without, **Am. 5**

JUSTICE
Constitution to establish, **Preamble**
Fugitives From Justice, generally, this index
Judges or Justices, generally, this index

KEEPING ARMS
Right not to be infringed, **Am. 2**

LEGISLATURES OF STATES
Amendments, application for or ratification, **Art. 5**
Consent of, required,
   By U.S. in purchasing, **Art. 1, § 8, cl. 17**
   In forming new States, **Art. 4, § 3, cl. 1**
May apply for or ratify amendments, **Art. 5**
Members of, to take oath to support Constitution, **Art. 6, cl. 3**
President, limiting holding office to two terms, ratification of article concerning, **Am. 22, § 2**
Senators and Representatives, regulation, election of, **Art. 1, § 4, cl. 1**
United States to protect States against invasion, **Art. 4, § 4**

LETTERS
Marque and reprisal,
   Power of Congress to grant, **Art. 1, § 8, cl. 11**
   States, prohibited from issuing, **Art. 1, § 10, cl. 1**

1049

[Illustration 8–2]

PAGE FROM A CONSTITUTION VOLUME: U.S.C.A.

Art. 6 SUPREME LAW OF LAND   **Cl. 2**

WESTLAW ELECTRONIC RESEARCH

See WESTLAW guide following the Explanation pages of this volume.

Clause 2. Supreme Law of Land

This Constitution, and the Laws of the United States which shall be made in Pursuance thereof; and all Treaties made, or which shall be made, under the Authority of the United States, shall be the supreme Law of the Land; and the Judges in every State shall be bound thereby, any Thing in the Constitution or Laws of any State to the Contrary notwithstanding.

LIBRARY REFERENCES ←

Law Reviews

Adjudication of federal causes of action in state court. Martin H. Redish and John E. Muench, 75 Mich.L.Rev. 311 (1976).

> This shows the text of the constitutional provision covering federal supremacy in a Constitution volume of the *United States Code Annotated*. Note the references to additional useful sources. This set and the *United States Code Service* are kept current by annual pocket supplements and subsequent pamphlets.

Texts and Treatises

Federal common law, see Wright, Miller & Cooper, Federal Practice and Procedure: Jurisdiction § 4514.

Federal preemption, see Rotunda, Nowak & Young, Treatise on Constitutional Law: Substance and Procedure §§ 12.1 to 12.4.

Relations of state and federal courts, see Wright, Miller & Cooper, Federal Practice and Procedure: Jurisdiction § 4201 et seq.

Treaties and executive agreements, see Tribe, American Constitutional Law § 4–4.

WESTLAW ELECTRONIC RESEARCH

See WESTLAW guide following the Explanation pages of this volume.

NOTES OF DECISIONS

I.   GENERALLY 1–30
II. FEDERAL LAWS AS SUPREME 31–90
III. TREATIES AS SUPREME 91–130
IV. STATE LAWS OR ACTS DISPLACED BY SUPREME LAW—GENERALLY 131–170
V.   FEDERAL INSTRUMENTALITIES AND PROPERTY GENERALLY 171–210
VI. TAXATION OF FEDERAL INSTRUMENTALITIES AND PROPERTY 211–260
VII. MISCELLANEOUS LAWS OR ACTS 261–430
VIII. STATE JUDGES BOUND BY SUPREME LAW 431–458

For Detailed Alphabetical Note Index, see the Various Subdivisions.

555

[Illustration 8–3]

PAGE SHOWING NOTES OF DECISIONS FROM
A CONSTITUTION VOLUME: U.S.C.A.

Cl. 2   **SUPREME LAW OF LAND**   **Art. 6**

I. GENERALLY

Subdivision Index

Constitution as supreme
   Generally 2
   Foreign relations and intercourse
     3
   Labor activities 4
Federal district courts, persons bound
   by supreme law 6
Foreign relations and intercourse, Con-
   stitution as Supreme 3
International law 9
Labor activities, Constitution as su-
   preme 4
Persons bound by supreme law
   Generally 5
   Federal district courts 6
   State legislatures 7

courts for enforcement of federal law which state deems penal. Robinson v. Norato, 1945, 43 A.2d 467, 71 R.I. 256.

2. Constitution as supreme—Generally

Under this clause that the Constitution and laws made in pursuance thereof shall be the supreme law of the land, it is of the very essence of supremacy to remove all obstacles to its action within its own sphere, and so to modify every power vested in subordinate governments as to exempt its own operations from their own influence. Public Utilities Commission of State of Cal. v. U.S., Cal.1958, 78 S.Ct. 446, 355 U.S. 534, 2 L.Ed.2d 470, rehearing denied 78 S.Ct.

After the text of each clause of the Constitution are digest paragraphs of all cases that have interpreted the clause. These paragraphs are preceded by an index to these paragraphs.

---

   preme law 7
United States Supreme Court, persons
   bound by supreme law 8

American Digest System
  Nature and authority of constitutions, see Constitutional Law ⇐1.

Encyclopedias
  Constitution as supreme law of the land, see C.J.S. Constitutional Law § 3.

1. Purpose

The purpose of this clause was to avoid the disparities, confusions and conflicts that would follow if the federal government's general authority were subject to local controls. U.S. v. Allegheny County, Pa., Pa.1944, 64 S.Ct. 908, 322 U.S. 174, 88 L.Ed. 1209.

This clause was intended to eliminate right of any state to regulate operations of federal government without its express consent. U.S. v. State Corp. Commission of Com. of Va., D.C.Va.1972, 345 F.Supp. 843, affirmed 93 S.Ct. 912, 409 U.S. 1094, 34 L.Ed.2d 682.

This clause was intended to apply only in case of conflict between federal Constitution, acts and treaties and state Constitution and laws, and does not compel a state to provide, at its own expense,

preme law of land and cannot be curtailed, circumvented, or extended by a state procedure merely because it will apply some doctrine of private right. Garner v. Teamsters, Chauffeurs and Helpers Local Union No. 776 (A.F.L.) Pa.1953, 74 S.Ct. 161, 346 U.S. 485, 98 L.Ed. 228.

The United States Constitution and the laws passed pursuant to it are the supreme laws of the land, binding alike upon states, courts, and the people, anything in the Constitution or laws of any state to the contrary notwithstanding. Testa v. Katt, R.I.1947, 67 S.Ct. 810, 330 U.S. 386, 91 L.Ed. 967.

This Constitution is the supreme law of the land, and no Act of Congress is of any validity which does not rest on authority conferred by that instrument. U.S. v. Germaine, Me.1878, 99 U.S. 508, 9 Otto. 508, 25 L.Ed. 482. See, also, Choctaw Indians, 1870, 13 Op.Atty.Gen. 357; Trial of Andrew Johnson, 176.

The government thus established and defined is to some extent a government of the states in their political capacity but, it is also, for certain purposes, a government of the people; within the scope of its powers, as enumerated and defined, it is supreme and above the states, but beyond, it has no existence. U.S. v. Cruikshank, La.1876, 92 U.S. 550, 2 Otto. 550, 23 L.Ed. 588.

[Illustration 8–4]

PAGE FROM THE CONSTITUTION OF THE UNITED STATES
OF AMERICA (LIBRARY OF CONGRESS)

PRIOR DEBTS, NATIONAL SUPREMACY, AND OATHS OF OFFICE

ARTICLE VI

Clause 1. All Debts contracted and Engagements entered into, before the Adoption of this Constitution, shall be as valid against the United States under this Constitution, as under the Confederation.

PRIOR DEBTS

There are no annotations to this clause.

Clause 2. This Constitution, and the Laws of the United States which shall be made in Pursuance thereof; and all Treaties made, or which shall be made, under the Authority of the United States, shall be the supreme Law of the Land; and the Judges in every State shall be bound thereby; any Thing in the Constitution or Laws of any State to the Contrary notwithstanding.

NATIONAL SUPREMACY

Marshall's Interpretation of the National Supremacy Clause

Although the Supreme Court had held, prior to Marshall's appointment to the Bench, that the supremacy clause rendered null and void a state constitutional or statutory provision which was inconsistent with a treaty executed by the Federal Government,[1] it was left for him to develop the full significance of the clause as applied to acts of Congress. By his vigorous opinions in *McCulloch v.*

> This one-volume edition of the Constitution sets forth the full text of each Article, Section, and Clause of the Constitution and its Amendments. Analysis and commentary follow immediately, in smaller type.

or in any manner control, the operations of the constitutional laws enacted by Congress to carry into execution the powers vested in

---

[1] Ware v. Hylton, 3 Dall. (3 U.S.) 199 (1796).
[2] 4 Wheat. (17 U.S.) 316 (1819).
[3] 9 Wheat. (22 U.S.) 1 (1824).

[Illustration 8–5]

PAGE FROM THE CONSTITUTION OF THE UNITED STATES OF AMERICA (LIBRARY OF CONGRESS)

918   ART. VI—PRIOR DEBTS, SUPREMACY CLAUSE, ETC.

Cl. 2—Supremacy of the Constitution, Laws, Treaties

the general government. This is, we think, the unavoidable consequence of that supremacy which the Constitution has declared."[4] From this he concluded that a state tax upon notes issued by a branch of the Bank of the United States was void.

In *Gibbons v. Ogden*, the Court held that certain statutes of New York granting an exclusive right to use steam navigation on the waters of the State were null and void insofar as they applied to vessels licensed by the United States to engage in coastal trade. Said the Chief Justice: "In argument, however, it has been contended, that if a law passed by a State, in the exercise of its acknowledged sovereignty, comes into conflict with a law passed by Congress in pursuance of the Constitution, they affect the subject, and each other, like equal opposing powers. But the framers of our Constitution foresaw this state of things, and provided for it, by de-

Analysis of the Supremacy Clause by the editors of the volume. Footnotes contain citations to cases mentioned in the analysis.

to such acts of the State legislatures as do not transcend their powers, but though enacted in the execution of acknowledged State powers, interfere with, or are contrary to the laws of Congress, made in pursuance of the Constitution, or some treaty made under the authority of the United States. In every such case, the act of Congress, or the treaty, is supreme; and the law of the State, though enacted in the exercise of powers not controverted, must yield to it."[5]

Task of the Supreme Court Under the Clause: Preemption

In applying the supremacy clause to subjects which have been regulated by Congress, the primary task of the Court is to ascertain whether a challenged state law is compatible with the policy expressed in the federal statute. When Congress legislates with regard to a subject, the extent and nature of the legal consequences of the regulation are federal questions, the answers to which are to be derived from a consideration of the language and policy of the state. If Congress expressly provides for exclusive federal dominion or if it expressly provides for concurrent federal-state jurisdiction, the task of the Court is simplified, though, of course, there may still be doubtful areas in which interpretation will be necessary. Where Congress is silent, however, the Court must itself decide

[4] 4 Wheat. (17 U.S.) 436 (1819).

[5] 9 Wheat. (22 U.S.), 210–211 (1824). See the Court's discussion of *Gibbons* in Douglas v. Seacoast Products, 431 U.S. 265, 274–279 (1977).

SECTION C. RESEARCHING THE SUPREME COURT OF THE UNITED STATES

This section describes some of the most well-known resources focusing on the Supreme Court of the United States as an institution. The Supreme Court's official website contains Court rules, opinions since 1991, orders since 2003, *The Journal of the Supreme Court of the United States* since 1993, transcripts of oral arguments since 2000, docket, and current calendar. The website also provides an overview of the Court and brief biographies of current justices.[30]

In addition to the Court's website, the Court's decisions also are available on numerous websites, such as Cornell Law School's Legal Information Institute Supreme Court Collection[31] and *FindLaw's* Supreme Court Center.[32] The Supreme Court Historical Society website provides historical information regarding the Court and brief biographies of all Supreme Court justices.[33]

SCOTUS Blog is a rich source of information, commentary, and analysis about the Court, especially for pending and recently decided cases.[34] The blog is written by a panel of expert authors, primarily from private law practice. The site contains links to relevant websites, such as the Court's own sites, sources of Supreme Court opinions, and other Court-related blogs. *SCOTUS Wiki*, a new project linked to *SCOTUS Blog*, provides extensive information about cases scheduled for argument before the Court.[35]

Preview of United States Supreme Court Cases, published by the American Bar Association's Public Education Division, is a periodical that publishes essays written by scholars about selected cases pending on the Court's calendar, but not yet argued. These essays provide excellent background and analysis of the cases the Court subsequently will decide.

1. Reference and Research Guides

CQ Press, formerly Congressional Quarterly, Inc., publishes numerous reference books about the Supreme Court, including the following:

a. Lawrence Baum, *The Supreme Court* (9th ed. 2006). This volume provides an introduction to the Court with chapters focusing on the Court, the justices, cases, decision-making, policy outputs and the Court's impact.

b. Joan Biskupic & Elder Witt, *The Supreme Court at Work* (2d ed. 1997). This volume provides a brief history of the Court along with profiles of justices and an explanation of Court procedure and traditions.

c. Lee Epstein, Jeffrey A. Segal, Harold J. Spaeth & Thomas G. Walker, *The Supreme Court Compendium: Data, Decisions, and Develop-*

---

[30] http://www.supremecourtus.gov.

[31] http://supct.law.cornell.edu/supct/.

[32] http://supreme.lp.findlaw.com/.

[33] http://www.supremecourthistory.org.

[34] http://www.scotusblog.com/wp/.

[35] http://www.scotuswiki.com/index.php?title=Main_Page.

ments (4th ed. 2006). This volume is filled with interesting summary tables on such matters as trends in Supreme Court decision-making, post-confirmation activities of the Court, and the political and legal environments in which the Court operates.

d. *The Supreme Court, A to Z* (Kenneth Jost ed., 4th ed. 2006). This single-volume work has brief entries on constitutional issues and individual justices. Arranged alphabetically, use of the volume is aided by an extensive index, a compilation of Court milestones and a selected bibliography.

e. Fenton S. Martin & Robert U. Goehlert, *How to Research the Supreme Court* (1992). Focused on researching Supreme Court materials primarily in a print environment, a bibliography with specific entries for every justice is included in addition to information regarding primary and secondary sources.

f. Fenton S. Martin & Robert U. Goehlert, *The U.S. Supreme Court: A Bibliography* (1990). This volume provides an extensive listing of works about the Court and its members.

g. D.G. Savage, *Guide to the U.S. Supreme Court* (4th ed. 2004). The two-volume set provides an in-depth narrative overview of the workings and history of the Court.

Important works from other publishers include:

a. *Encyclopedia of Supreme Court Quotations* (Christopher A. Anzalone ed., M.E. Sharp 2000). Important quotes from Supreme Court opinions are organized by topic. A keyword index aids in locating quotes.

b. Shelley L. Dowling & Mary C. Custy, *The Jurisprudence of the United States Constitutional Interpretation: An Annotated Bibliography* (Fred B. Rothman & Co., Inc. 1999). Print primary and secondary materials are the focus with additional information on electronic resources.

c. Jill Ann Duffy & Elizabeth A.L. Lambert, *Researching the Supreme Court of the United States: Available Resources for Commonly Asked Questions,* 18(2) LEGAL REFERENCE SERVICES Q., 2000, at 25. An especially valuable article devoted to various aspects of Supreme Court research.

d. Kermit Hall, *The Oxford Companion to the Supreme Court of the United States* (2d ed. Oxford University Press 2005). This single volume, encyclopedic compilation includes more than 400 alphabetically arranged summaries on important cases decided by the Court, legal terms and concepts, justices, important court personnel and practitioners.

e. Gary Hartman, Roy M. Mersky & Cindy L. Tate, *Landmark Supreme Court Cases* (Facts on File 2006). Over 350 of the most important and influential Supreme Court cases are summarized in this volume.

f. Jethro K. Lieberman, *A Practical Companion to the Constitution: How the Supreme Court Has Ruled on Issues from Abortion to Zoning* (University of California Press 1999). With a dictionary-style arrangement, key words, terms, and concepts defined and addressed by the Supreme Court are contained in this volume.

g. Lisa Paddock, *Facts about the Supreme Court of the United States* (Facts on File 1996). This volume is organized by Chief Justice and has information about individual justices, significant cases, and the political composition of the Court.

h. *Supreme Court of the United States: A Bibliography with Indexes* (George A. Rutland, ed., Nova Science Publishers 2006). A bibliography of print primary and secondary sources about the Court and individual justices.

i. *Encyclopedia of the Supreme Court* (Davis Schultz ed., Facts on File 2005). This alphabetically arranged volume includes entries on famous cases, legal terms, and profiles of justices.

j. Robert J. Wagman, *The Supreme Court: A Citizen's Guide* (Pharos Books 1993). This volume provides an introduction to the Supreme Court with chapters on how the Court works, the history of the Court, important decisions of the Court, and brief biographical information on justices.

2. Histories of the Court

The following list is a brief selection from the numerous general histories that have been written of the Court:

a. Chester James Antieau, *Our Two Centuries of Law and Life 1775–1975: The Work of the Supreme Court and the Impact of Both Congress and the Presidents* (William S. Hein & Co. 2001). The volume focuses on the interaction of Supreme Court decisions with presidential and congressional actions.

b. Hampton L. Carson, *The Supreme Court of the United States: Its History* (John W. Huber 1891). This classic work was written to commemorate the 100th anniversary of the Supreme Court.

c. *The Supreme Court of the United States: Its Beginnings & Its Justices, 1790-1991* (Commission on the Bicentennial of the United States Constitution 1992). This volume contains extremely brief biographical sketches of every justice and an accompanying portrait.

d. *The Oliver Wendell Holmes Devise: History of the Supreme Court of the United States* (Paul A. Freund & Stanley Katz eds., Cambridge University Press 1971, ongoing). The most scholarly and comprehensive history of the Court; 12 of the projected 14 volumes are available.

e. Peter Irons, *A People's History of the Supreme Court* (2d ed. Penguin 2006). This volume provides an accessible history of the Court, focusing on the Court's most well-known decisions.

f. *The Documentary History of the Supreme Court of the United States, 1789–1800* (Maeva Marcus & James R. Perry eds., Columbia University Press). This multivolume set gathers all original materials to reconstitute the record of the first eleven years of the Court.

g. William H. Rehnquist, *The Supreme Court* (rev. ed. Knopf 2001). An accessible history of the Supreme Court written by Chief Justice Rehnquist.

h. Jeffrey A. Segal, Harold J. Spaeth & Sara C. Benesh, *The Supreme Court in the American Legal System* (Cambridge University Press 2005). This volume examines both the history of the Supreme Court and its relationship with lower courts.

i. Robert Shnayerson, *The Illustrated History of the Supreme Court of the United States* (Harry N. Abrams 1986). Numerous portraits, photographs and reproductions of historical documents are included in this introductory history of the Court.

j. Charles Warren, *The Supreme Court in United States History* (rev. ed. Little Brown 1926). This volume puts the work of the Court in historical and political contexts and covers the Court up to 1918.

The following journals focus on the history and work of the Court:

a. *The Docket Sheet* (1959 to 1995). Published quarterly by the Supreme Court's Public Information Office, this publication includes a wealth of Supreme Court trivia and other items on more esoteric aspects of the Court and its work.

b. The *Journal of Supreme Court History* (formerly *Yearbook of the Supreme Court Historical Society,* 1976–1990; Blackwell Publishing 1990–present). Published three times annually by the Supreme Court Historical Society, this journal provides in-depth articles on former justices and their Courts.

c. *The Supreme Court Historical Society Quarterly* (1978–present). Published quarterly by the Supreme Court Historical Society, this pamphlet publishes current awareness articles about the Court and upcoming Society events along with short articles focusing on the Court's history.

3. Case Selection and Decision–Making

As the Supreme Court grants review to such a small percentage of the cases in which it is requested, the Court's selection of cases has been a focus of much research. The following list of works focuses on the factors that influence Supreme Court case selection and decision-making:

a. *Supreme Court Decision Making: New Institutionalist Approaches* (Cornell W. Clayton & Harold Gillman eds., University of Chicago Press 1999).

b. Felix Frankfurter & James M. Landis, *The Business of the Supreme Court: A Study in the Federal Judicial System* (Macmillan 1928).

c. Lisa A. Kloppenberg, *Playing It Safe: How the Supreme Court Sidesteps Hard Cases and Stunts the Development of Law* (N.Y.U. Press 2001).

d. Richard L. Pacelle, Jr., *The Transformation of the Supreme Court's Agenda: From the New Deal to the Reagan Administration* (Westview Press 1991).

e. H.W. Perry, Jr., *Deciding to Decide: Agenda Setting in the United States Supreme Court* (Harvard University Press 1991).

f. Doris M. Provine, *Case Selection in the United States Supreme Court* (University of Chicago Press 1980).

g. David W. Rohde & Harold L. Spaeth, *Supreme Court Decision Making* (W.H. Freeman & Co. 1976).

h. Bernard Schwartz, *Decision: How the Supreme Court Decides Cases* (Oxford University Press 1996).

4. Biographies and Profiles

Numerous works provide biographical information about the justices. The titles listed below are merely a few of the general biographical works on the Court.

a. *The Supreme Court and Its Justices*, (Jesse H. Choper ed., American Bar Association 2001). A collection of essays about the Supreme Court and its members including essays by Chief Justices Earl Warren and William H. Rehnquist and Justices Tom C. Clark and Lewis F. Powell, Jr.

b. Clare Cushman, *The Supreme Court Justices: Illustrated Biographies, 1789–1995* (Congressional Quarterly 2d ed. 1996). The single-volume reference provides in-depth biographies on justices from John Jay through Ruth Bader Ginsburg and Stephen G. Breyer.

c. Henry Flanders, *The Lives and Times of the Chief Justices of the Supreme Court of the United States* (T. & J.W. Johnson & Co. 1881, 2 vols.). This set provides in-depth information on early Chief Justices.

d. Leon Friedman & Fred L. Israel, *The Justices of the United States Supreme Court: Their Lives and Major Opinions* (Chelsea House 1997, 5 vols.). Perhaps the most comprehensive work, this multivolume set is organized by each justice's date of appointment to the Court. In addition to providing detailed biographical information, a selected bibliography is included for each justice.

e. Timothy L. Hall, *Supreme Court Justices: A Biographical Dictionary* (Facts on File 2001). Biographical sketches of every justice, organized by date of appointment to the Court. Also includes recommended readings for additional information on each justice.

f. *Biographical Encyclopedia of the Supreme Court: The Lives and Legal Philosophies of the Justices* (Melvin Urofsky ed., CQ Press 2006). The alphabetically arranged volume provides profiles on every justice accompanied by a brief bibliography and a list of noteworthy opinions.

g. *Memorials of the Justices of the Supreme Court of the United States* (Roger F. Jacobs ed., Fred B. Rothman & Co. 1981). This volume reprints the speeches given at the Bar of the Supreme Court to mark the death of a Justice.

5. Confirmation Hearings

The ideological and philosophical beliefs of a particular justice can be explored by examining transcripts of hearings held during the confirmation process. The hearings are published by the Government Printing Office and distributed to depository libraries. They also are reprinted in *The Supreme Court of the United States: Hearings and Reports on Successful and Unsuccessful Nominations of Supreme Court Justices by the Senate Judiciary Committee* (William S. Hein & Co.), compiled by J. Myron Jacobstein and Roy M. Mersky. This is an ongoing set that contains the text of confirmation hearings and related committee reports. Coverage begins with the 1916 nomination of Louis D. Brandeis and runs, to date, through the nomination of Samuel Alito.

6. Personal Papers

The website of the Supreme Court Historical Society suggests a number of sources for locating the personal papers of the justices.[36] The most comprehensive source of information about the location and accessibility of papers of the justices is Alexandra K. Wigdor, *The Personal Papers of the Supreme Court Justices: A Descriptive Guide* (Garland Pub. 1986).

7. Ratings and Statistical Studies

The seminal work in the area of rating and studying the justices of the Supreme Court of the United States and their opinions is Albert P. Blaustein & Roy M. Mersky, *The First One Hundred Justices: Statistical Studies on the Supreme Court of the United States* (Archon Books 1978). More recently, William D. Pederson and Norman W. Prozier have edited *Great Justices of the U.S. Supreme Court: Ratings and Case Studies* (P. Lang 1993).

SECTION D.   STATE CONSTITUTIONS

Each state has its own constitution, and many states have adopted different constitutions at different times over the years. A state's constitution is the highest primary legal authority for the state, except for those matters controlled by federal law.

Research regarding a state constitution often involves reference to both historical documents that led to its adoption and state and federal judicial opinions that interpret it.[37] A provision of a state's constitution may not have been interpreted by the courts of that state. In such instances, it might be useful to see how the courts of another state have interpreted a similar provision in its constitution.

Judicial opinions interpreting provisions of a state's constitution can be located in ways similar to those for the U.S. Constitution discussed in Section A–1 of this chapter. These include computer-assisted legal research services, the digest paragraphs accompanying the annotated version of the state constitution, state digests, *Shepard's Citations* and *KeyCite*, and *A.L.R. Annotations*. Likewise, treatises,[38] casebooks,[39] legal periodical arti-

---

[36] http://www.supremecourthistory.org/06_research/06_a02.html.

[37] For a listing of over 2,100 entries relating to the literature of state constitutions, see BERNARD D. REAMS, JR. & STUART D. YOAK, THE CONSTITUTIONS OF THE STATES: A STATE-BY-STATE GUIDE AND BIBLIOGRAPHY TO CURRENT SCHOLARLY RESEARCH (Oceana Publications 1987). This volume is also published as volume 5 of SOURCES AND DOCUMENTS OF UNITED STATES CONSTITUTIONS, Second Series.

[38] *Reference Guides to the State Constitutions of the United States* is a series by Greenwood Press that covers each of the states in a separate volume. Each volume contains an overview of the history and development of one state's constitution, the text of the state's constitution with a section-by-section analysis, a bibliographic essay, a table of cases, and an index. A separate volume discusses common themes and variations in constitutional development. A separate index to the 51 volumes completes the set. *See also* JAMES A. GARDNER, INTERPRETING STATE CONSTITUTIONS: A JURISPRUDENCE OF FUNCTION IN A FEDERAL SYSTEM (2005); G. ALAN TARR, UNDERSTANDING STATE CONSTITUTIONS (1998).

[39] *See, for example*, ROBERT F. WILLIAMS, STATE CONSTITUTIONAL LAW: CASES AND MATERIALS (4th ed. 2006).

cles,[40] and state legal encyclopedias can assist with constitutional interpretation. State-specific legal research guides typically discuss researching that state's constitution.[41]

1. Historical Sources

The process of adopting a new state constitution usually begins with the convening of a state constitutional convention. The records, journals, proceedings, and other documents from state constitutional conventions can provide valuable information about the intended meanings and interpretations given to state constitutions by their framers. *State Constitutional Conventions, Commissions, and Amendments,* a microfiche collection published by Congressional Information Service (CIS), which covers the period from 1776 through 1978, is the most comprehensive source of documents for all of the states.[42] *Sources and Documents of United States Constitutions,*[43] compiled by William F. Swindler, reprints in chronological order the major constitutional documents of each state.

2. Texts of State Constitutions

a. *Volumes of state codes and revised statutes.* A common source for the text of a state constitution is the published volumes of the state code or revised statutes.[44] Annotated versions of state statutes commonly have a volume devoted to the state constitution. This constitution volume ordinarily contains the current text, the text of previously adopted versions, and digest annotations. Many states also publish an un-annotated edition of their state constitution in pamphlet form.

b. State government websites typically provide the text of that state's constitution.[45]

c. *Constitutions of the United States: National and State.*[46] This multivolume looseleaf set, which also is available in searchable electronic

[40] The RUTGERS LAW JOURNAL publishes an annual issue devoted to state constitutional law, including a section on "Developments in State Constitutional Law"; coverage began with 1988 cases.

[41] *See* Appendix B for a listing of state-specific legal research guides.

[42] Two bibliographies provide access to this set: CYNTHIA E. BROWNE, STATE CONSTITUTIONAL CONVENTIONS FROM INDEPENDENCE TO THE COMPLETION OF THE PRESENT UNION, 1776–1959: A BIBLIOGRAPHY (Greenwood Press 1973); CONGRESSIONAL INFORMATION SERVICE, STATE CONSTITUTIONAL CONVENTIONS, 1959–1978: AN ANNOTATED BIBLIOGRAPHY (1981, 2 vols.).

[43] Oceana (1973–79, 11 vols. in 12 books). Volume 11, a bibliography, was added to this set in 1988. *See supra* note 13. A Second Series began in 1982. Older, but still useful titles for tracing the historical development of state constitutions, are BENJAMIN PEARLEY POORE, CHARTERS AND CONSTITUTIONS (1878); FRANCIS NEWTON THORPE, FEDERAL AND STATE CONSTITUTIONS (1909); NEW YORK CONSTITUTIONAL CONVENTION COMMITTEE, 3 REPORTS: CONSTITUTIONS OF THE STATES AND UNITED STATES (1938). Although the Poore and Thorpe volumes are out of date, they are helpful for their parallel studies of state constitutions. The last item, although never brought up-to-date, is still useful for its index volume to the constitutions of all of the states. *See also* WALTER FAIRLEIGH, THE REVISION AND AMENDMENT OF STATE CONSTITUTIONS (1910); ALBERT LEE STURM, A BIBLIOGRAPHY ON STATE CONSTITUTIONS AND CONSTITUTIONAL REVISION, 1945–1975 (1975).

[44] State codes are discussed in Chapter 11. State constitutions, which accompany the state codes, are available on most CALR services.

[45] *See, for example*:

http://www.leginfo.ca.gov/const.html (California).

http://www.dos.state.ny.us/info/cons2004.htm (New York).

http://tlo2.tlc.state.tx.us/txconst/toc.html (Texas).

http://www.legis.state.wi.us/rsb/2wiscon.html (Wisconsin).

[46] (Oceana 1974–).

format on the Web, collects the texts of the constitutions of the United States and all U.S. states and territories. It is kept current by supplements. Formerly produced by the Columbia University Legislative Drafting Research Fund, this service now is maintained by the Oceana Editorial Board.[47]

d. Robert L. Maddex, *State Constitutions of the United States.*[48] This one volume work explains and compares each of the fifty state constitutions. It provides supplemental materials, including an overview of state constitutions, comparative tables, "new rights" such as privacy and victim's rights, and "special provisions" such as the environment and home rule, etc.

SECTION E. FOREIGN CONSTITUTIONS

To locate the constitutions of foreign countries, consult the twenty volume *Constitutions of the Countries of the World.*[49] This set, which is edited by the Max Planck Institute, is published in looseleaf format with a separate pamphlet for each country. The constitutions for 192 countries are arranged alphabetically and include explanatory notes, commentaries, and annotated bibliographies. For countries where there is not an official English version, an English translation is provided. The introduction in chapter 1 of this set provides bibliographical references to previous compilations of constitutions. Supplements are issued periodically to keep each constitution up-to-date.

A companion set is *Constitutions of Dependencies and Territories.*[50] This multivolume looseleaf set contains pamphlets of the constitutions of the world's dependencies and territories. Each pamphlet contains the nation's constitutional provisions that define the relationship between the state and its dependencies and territories, as well as commentary and an annotated bibliography. When a *territory* achieves the status of a nation-state, its constitution is incorporated into *Constitutions of the Countries of the World.*

Both *Constitutions of the Countries of the World* and *Constitutions of Dependencies and Territories* are available by subscription in electronic versions on the Web. With the online versions, it is possible to search the full text of constitutions by country, or group of countries; by specific time period; and by type of document.

[47] One method of locating comparative state constitutional provisions is through the INDEX DIGEST OF STATE CONSTITUTIONS (Columbia University, Legislative Drafting Research Fund, 2d ed., Oceana 1959), a companion to CONSTITUTIONS OF THE UNITED STATES: NATIONAL AND STATE. The *Index Digest* is arranged alphabetically by subject; each subject heading includes references to similar constitutional provisions of the states. Although this volume has been updated only through 1967, it can still be useful, because many provisions of state constitutions do not change frequently. An attempt to provide a comprehensive subject index to all state constitutions began in 1980 when Columbia University's Legislative Drafting Research Fund issued FUNDAMENTAL LIBERTIES AND RIGHTS: A FIFTY STATE INDEX as part of its CONSTITUTIONS OF THE UNITED STATES: NATIONAL AND STATE. This was followed in 1982 by LAWS, LEGISLATURES, LEGISLATIVE PROCEDURE: A FIFTY STATE INDEX.

[48] (2d ed. CQ Press 2005).

[49] (Albert P. Blaustein & Gisbert H. Flanz eds., Oceana Publications 1971 to present).

[50] (Philip Raworth ed., Oceana Publications 1998 to present).

Also helpful is Congressional Quarterly's *Constitutions of the World,*[51] which serves as a guide to the constitutions and constitutional histories of eighty nations, selected for their political and constitutional importance.

The University of Bern maintains an International Constitutional Law (ICL) Project website that makes available the English texts of approximately 90 national constitutions.[52] The site also provides background information about the countries for which it has constitutions, as well as for more than 40 countries for which it does not have constitutions. Also provided are many useful links to other websites with information relevant to international and comparative constitutional law. The ICL website is not updated as frequently as *Constitutions of the Countries of the World*, the subscription service discussed above.

See also the website of the Constitution Society, which provides the full text of numerous national constitutions, many with English translations.[53]

[51] ROBERT L. MADDEX, CONSTITUTIONS OF THE WORLD (3d ed. CQ Press 2008).

[52] http://www.servat.unibe.ch/law/icl/index.html.

[53] http://www.constitution.org/cons/natlcons.htm.

Chapter 9

FEDERAL LEGISLATION*

Article I, Section 8, of the United States Constitution enumerates the powers of Congress, and provides the authority for Congress to make all laws necessary and proper for carrying into execution the enumerated powers, as well as other powers vested in Congress.

The Senate and the House of Representatives meet in two-year periods. Each year is a session and the two-year period is known as a Congress. The period in which Congress met, for example, during 2000–2001, is known as the 107th Congress. The 1st Congress actually took place over three calendar years, 1789–91. Under the Constitution, Congress must meet at least once a year.[1]

This chapter presents a discussion of enacted federal legislation and sources for locating these materials. Today, many websites provide links and portals to legislative documents.[2] This chapter provides references to electronic sources that contain legislative materials. Chapter 10 of this text, "Federal Legislative Histories," discusses the various documents generated during the legislative process, the sources to use to locate these documents, and sources containing finding aids that help in locating them.

SECTION A. THE ENACTMENT OF FEDERAL LAWS

Before discussing the various ways federal legislation is published, a brief description of the legislative process is necessary.[3] At any time during

---

* Richard Leiter, Library Director and Professor at the University of Nebraska College of Law revised this chapter with the assistance of Steven M. Weber, graduate student at the University of Wisconsin School of Library and Information Studies and Reference Intern at the University of Wisconsin Law Library. Bonnie L. Koneski–White, formerly of the Western New England College School of Law Library, wrote previous versions of this chapter.

Note: This chapter contains many references to *GPO Access*, the U.S. Government Printing Office (GPO) system for distributing federal government information over the World Wide Web. After this book went into production, GPO announced that it will replace *GPO Access* with its new *Federal Digital System* (*FDsys*) during 2009. GPO plans to maintain *GPO Access* until the migration to *FDsys* is complete. After that, searches using a *GPO Access* URL will automatically be redirected by the system to *FDsys*.

[1] U.S. CONST. art. I, § 4, cl. 2.

[2] For example, *FirstGov*, http://www.usa.gov, is an official United States government portal to more than 47 million pages of government information, services, and online transactions. The Government Printing Office website, http://www.gpoaccess.gov/, provides access to officially printed government documents, including federal legislation, committee prints, congressional reports and hearings, the UNITED STATES CODE, CONGRESSIONAL RECORD, and federal regulatory material.

[3] For more detailed statements on the enactment of federal laws, see CHARLES W. JOHNSON, HOW OUR LAWS ARE MADE, H.R. DOC. No. 93, 108th Cong., 1st Sess. (2003), also available in PDF

a congressional session, representatives and senators can introduce legislation in their respective branch of Congress. Upon introduction, each proposed law is called a *bill* or a *joint resolution*.[4] The first bill in the House of Representatives in each Congress is labeled *H.R. 1*, with all subsequent bills numbered sequentially. Similarly, the first bill introduced in the Senate is labeled *S. 1*.

After a bill passes the house in which it was introduced, it is sent to the other house for consideration.[5] If approved in identical form,[6] it is then sent to the president for signing. If the president signs it, the bill becomes a law. If the president vetoes a bill,[7] Congress can override the veto with a two-thirds vote in both houses of Congress.[8] Under the Constitution, a bill sent to the president also becomes law if the president does not either sign or veto it within ten days of receiving the bill.[9] Bills introduced but not passed during a specific Congress do not carry over to the next Congress. Sponsors who want the new Congress to consider the bill must submit it as a new bill.

After a bill becomes law, it is sent to the archivist, who is directed to publish all laws so received.[10] The archivist classifies each law as either a

---

and html formats at http://thomas.loc.gov/home/lawsmade.toc.html [hereinafter How Our Laws Are Made]; Robert B. Dove, Enactment of a Law: Procedural Steps in the Legislative Process, S. Doc. No. 20, 97th Cong., 1st Sess. (1982). Updated, electronic versions of this publication in PDF and html format are available at http://thomas.loc.gov/home/enactment/enactlawtoc.html (1997). *See also* Congressional Quarterly, Inc., Guide to Congress (6th ed. 2007) [hereinafter Guide to Congress]; Robert U. Goehlert & Fenton S. Martin, Congress and Law-Making: Researching the Legislative Process (ABC–CLIO, 2d ed. 1989).

[4] Most legislation is introduced as a *bill*. A *joint resolution* may also be used, but there is no practical difference between the two, and the two terms are used interchangeably. *Concurrent resolutions* are used for non-legislative matters that affect the operations of both houses. *Simple resolutions* are used for non-legislative matters concerning the operation of either house. Bills, joint resolutions, and concurrent resolutions are published in the United States Statutes at Large; simple resolutions appear in the Congressional Record. How Our Laws Are Made, *supra* note 3, at 5–8.

[5] At this stage, a proposed piece of legislation ceases technically to be called a bill, but rather is an *act*, indicating it is an act of one body of Congress. However, it is still popularly referred to as a bill. Once a bill or joint resolution passes the house in which it was introduced, including changes made during floor action, it must be certified as accurate by either the Secretary of the Senate or the Clerk of the House of Representatives (depending upon the house in which it was passed). Once certified, this document (printed on blue paper) is known as an *engrossed bill*.

[6] Once a bill or joint resolution passes the Senate and House of Representatives in identical form, it is certified as an official copy by the chief officer of the house in which it originated and is signed by the Speaker of the House of Representatives and the Senate President *pro tempore*. Once the document is ready for the president's signature, it is known as an *enrolled bill* and is printed on parchment paper.

[7] For a list of presidential vetoes, see Gregory Harness, Presidential Vetoes, 1789–1988, S. Pub. 102–12 (1992); Zoe Davis, Presidential Vetoes, 1989–2000, S. Pub. 107–10 (2001). The full-text of each of the reports may be found at the Senate website at http://www.senate.gov/reference/reference_index_subjects/Vetoes_vrd.htm. In addition, the website tracks presidential vetoes since 2001.

[8] U.S. Const. art. I, § 7, cl. 2.

[9] *Id.*

[10] 1 U.S.C. § 106(a); *See also* 44 U.S.C. §§ 709–711. Executive Order No. 10530, ch. 47, Codification of Presidential Proclamations and Executive Orders 935, 936 (1989 comp.)

public law or a private law. A *public law* affects the nation as a whole or deals with individuals as a class, and relates to public matters. A *private law* benefits only a specific individual or individuals. Private laws deal primarily with matters relating to claims against the government or with matters of immigration and naturalization.[11]

The first law to pass a Congress is designated as either Public Law No. 1 (e.g., Pub. L. No. 107–1), or Private Law No. 1 (e.g., Priv. L. No. 107–1), with 107 designating the Congress. Each succeeding public or private law is numbered sequentially throughout the two-year life of a Congress.

SECTION B. PUBLICATION OF FEDERAL LAWS

1. Recent Public Laws

The United States Government Printing Office issues the first official publication of a law in the form of a *slip law*. [Illustration 9–1] Each is separately published and may be one page or several hundred pages in length. Slip laws are available in all libraries that are depositories for U.S. government publications[12] and in other libraries that subscribe to these publications. Other sources commonly consulted for the text of recently enacted public laws are:

a. *United States Code Congressional and Administrative News*. This set, which began in 1941 with the 77th Congress, 1st Session, is published by West. During each session of Congress, West publishes monthly pamphlets that contain the full-text of all public laws. Each monthly pamphlet contains a cumulative subject index and a cumulative Table of Laws Enacted. After each session of Congress, the pamphlets are reissued in bound volumes.

b. *United States Code Service, Advance Service*. LexisNexis publishes these monthly pamphlets, containing newly enacted public laws, in connection with the *United States Code Service*. This Advance Service contains a cumulative index arranged in alphabetical order.

c. *LexisNexis, Loislaw,* and *Westlaw*.[13] These online services include the text of recently enacted and retrospective public laws.

d. *THOMAS*.[14] This electronic resource from the Library of Congress lists all public laws since the 93rd Congress. Each entry includes the bill number, its sponsor(s), committee action, and relevant report numbers. In addition, when available, *THOMAS* provides access to the full-text of proposed bills and a direct link to the full text of the public law from GPO.

e. *GPO Access*.[15] The Government Printing Office's website sets forth the text of all laws enacted beginning with the 104th Congress, 1995–96. To

---

(*available at* http://www.archives.gov/federal-register/codification/). *See also* 44 U.S.C. §§ 709–711 (2000).

[11] For a complete discussion of private bills and laws, see GUIDE TO CONGRESS, *supra* note 3, at 526–27.

[12] There are approximately 1,250 depository libraries. For a complete listing, see the annual FEDERAL DEPOSITORY LIBRARY DIRECTORY, which is usually published in the fall of each year, or http://www.gpoaccess.gov/libraries.html.

[13] Computer-assisted legal research services are discussed in Chapter 23.

[14] http://thomas.loc.gov.

[15] http://www.gpoaccess.gov/plaws/.

guarantee authenticity, public laws beginning with the 110th Congress are digitally signed.

f. *LexisNexis Congressional.* *LexisNexis Congressional* is an extensive Web-based service offering access to a wealth of congressional documents and information including that produced by Congressional Information Service, Inc. The base edition of this electronic resource contains the full text of laws from the 91st Congress to the present.[16]

g. *Specialized Looseleaf Services.* Publishers often provide pamphlet reproductions of public laws for selected "important" legislation that relates to the subject covered by the looseleaf service.[17]

2. United States Statutes at Large[18]

At the end of each session of Congress, all slip laws, both public and private, are published in numerical order as part of the set entitled *United States Statutes at Large.* Public and private laws are set forth in separate sections of the volumes. Accordingly, all of the laws enacted since 1789 are contained in the many volumes of this set. [Illustration 9–2] The *United States Statutes at Large* (Stat.) is the authoritative source for the text of federal laws.

Because publication of the *United States Statutes at Large* did not commence until 1846, legislation enacted prior to that year was published retrospectively. Consequently, volumes 1–5 cover the public laws and volume 6 the private laws for the 1st through 28th Congresses (1789–1845), with volumes 7 and 8 devoted exclusively to treaties.[19] The publication pattern for volumes 9 through 49 differs from that currently followed. Volume 9 covers the 29th–31st Congresses; volumes 10 through 12 cover two Congresses each (32nd–37th); and volumes 13 to 49 cover one Congress each (38th–74th). The current pattern of one numbered volume per session began in 1936 with the 75th Congress, 1st Session.[20]

It is important to keep in mind that the laws in *United States Statutes at Large* are arranged in chronological order rather than by subject. Moreover, amendments to a law may appear in different volumes from the volume containing the law being amended. For example, a law passed in 1900 appears in volume 31 of *United States Statutes at Large.* If Congress amended that law in 1905, the amendment would appear in volume 34. Some laws have been amended numerous times. To obtain the full and current text of such a law, the *United States Statutes at Large* volume

---

[16] *LexisNexis Congressional* is described more fully in Chapter 10, Sections D, E, and H.

[17] Looseleaf services are discussed in Chapter 14.

[18] *A Century of Lawmaking for a New Nation, U.S. Congressional Documents and Debates,* http://memory.loc.gov/ammem/amlaw/lawhome.html, contains 18 volumes of the United States Statutes at Large for the first 43 Congresses, 1789–1875, at http://memory.loc.gov/ammem/amlaw/lwsl.html.

[19] *See* Chapter 21 for a discussion of treaties.

[20] For a concise historical explanation of the development of United States Statutes at Large, its significance, and a complete bibliographic listing of the set, see Curt E. Conklin & Francis Aclund, An Historical and Bibliographic Introduction to the United States Statutes at Large (1992). *See also* Larry M. Boyer, Checklist of United States Session Laws, 1789–1873 (1976).

containing the original law must be examined, together with subsequent volumes in which amendments to that law appear.

Each volume of *United States Statutes at Large* has its own subject index, and beginning in 1991, a popular name index as well. From 1957 through 1976, each volume contained tables listing previous public laws affected by the public laws published in that volume. Beginning with volume 33, marginal notes indicate House or Senate bill numbers, public law numbers, and dates of enactment. *United States Statutes at Large* also contains interstate compacts. Regrettably, bound copies of *United States Statutes at Large* are approximately one Congress (or two years) behind in publication. When published, the *United States Statutes at Large* volume supersedes the slip laws for that volume.

SECTION C. CODIFICATION OF FEDERAL LAWS

The chronological publication of congressional laws creates obvious problems determining the statutory provisions on any given subject. Therefore, the laws passed by Congress have been rearranged in a manner that accomplishes three objectives: (1) to collate the original law with all subsequent amendments, reflecting the deletion or addition of language made by those amendments; (2) to gather together all laws on the same subject or topic; and (3) to eliminate all repealed, superseded, or expired laws. This process is called *codification*.[21]

1. United States Revised Statutes

The first codification of the *United States Statutes at Large* was the *Revised Statutes of the United States*.[22] This first codification is known as either the *Revised Statutes of 1873* (reflecting the last year of laws contained in this code), as the *Revised Statutes of 1874* (reflecting the code's date of enactment), or as the *Revised Statutes of 1875* (reflecting the publication date of the code). This chapter refers to this codification as "*Revised Statutes of 1875.*"

Because *United States Statutes at Large* had no cumulating subject index, the difficulty in research was apparent. In 1866, President Andrew Johnson, pursuant to congressional authorization, appointed a commission to extract from the volumes of the *United States Statutes at Large* all public laws that were still in force and were of a general and permanent nature. The next step was to rewrite each public law and all its amendments in one sequence by incorporating amending language and removing deleted language. Laws were then arranged by topics in titles, and then further subdivided into chapters and sections. Title 14, for example, contained all legislation concerning the judiciary; Title 64 contained all legislation on bankruptcy. All titles were then arranged in one volume, a subject index prepared, and the volume published as the *Revised Statutes of 1875.*

---

[21] For a discussion of the process involved in codification, see Charles S. Zinn, *Revision of the United States Code,* 51 LAW LIBR. J. 388 (1958). For a discussion of the relationship between the UNITED STATES CODE and the UNITED STATES STATUTES AT LARGE, see Michael J. Lynch, *The U.S. Code, The Statutes at Large, and Some Peculiarities of Codification,* 16(2) LEGAL REFERENCE SERVICES Q., 1997, at 69.

[22] Ralph H. Dwan & Ernest R. Feidler, *The Federal Statutes—Their History and Use,* 22 MINN. L. REV. 1008, 1012–13 (1938) [hereinafter Dwan & Feidler].

Revised Statutes of 1875 was introduced in Congress as a bill, which subsequently became a public law. Incorporated into the bill that Congress passed was a title specifically repealing each previously enacted public law that had been incorporated into *Revised Statutes of 1875*.[23] Accordingly, the codification of all of the public laws enacted between 1789 and 1873 still in force and of a general nature became positive law. Because the codification was positive law, it no longer was necessary to refer to the *United States Statutes at Large*.

Unfortunately, the first publication of *Revised Statutes of 1875*, known as the first edition, was subsequently discovered to contain many inaccuracies and unauthorized changes in the law.[24] In 1878, Congress authorized a second edition of *Revised Statutes*. This second edition included legislation passed since 1873; deleted sections that were repealed since 1873; and corrected the errors inadvertently incorporated into the first edition.

The second edition indicated changes to the text of the first edition through the use of brackets and italics. It is important to note that Congress never enacted the second edition of *Revised Statutes* into positive law, and all changes indicated in it are only *prima facie* evidence of the law. Although several attempts were made to adopt a new codification, it was not until 1924 that Congress authorized the publication of a codification of federal laws.[25]

2. United States Code (U.S.C.)

Prior to 1926, one volume of the *Revised Statutes of 1875* and 24 subsequent volumes of *United States Statutes at Large* contained the positive law for federal legislation. In 1926, the *United States Code,* prepared under the auspices of special committees of the House and Senate, was published. This codification included all sections of *Revised Statutes of 1875* that had not been repealed as well as all public and general laws still in force that were included in the *United States Statutes at Large* volumes dated after 1873.

These laws were then arranged into 50 titles and published as the *United States Code,* 1926 edition.[26] Between 1927 and 1933, cumulated bound supplements were issued each year. In 1934, Congress issued a new edition of the *United States Code*, the 1934 edition, which incorporated the cumulated supplements to the 1926 edition. Every six years a new edition is published with cumulative supplements issued during the intervening years. The *United States Code* is thus the "official" codification of federal public laws of a general and permanent nature that are in effect at the time of publication.

Unlike the *Revised Statutes of 1875,* the *United States Code* was never submitted to Congress and enacted into positive law in its entirety. Instead,

[23] REVISED STATUTES OF THE UNITED STATES, 1873–74, Act of June 22, 1874, tit. LXXIV, §§ 5595–5601, at 1085 (1878).

[24] Dwan & Feidler, *supra* note 22, at 1014–15.

[25] For a discussion and bibliography of federal laws before 1926, see Erwin C. Surrency, *The Publication of Federal Laws: A Short History,* 79 LAW LIBR. J. 469 (1987).

[26] *See* Preface at 44, Pt. 1 Stat. at v (1926).

in 1974, Congress created the Office of the Revision Counsel[27] and directed that office to revise the *United States Code* title by title. It was contemplated that each title would be submitted to Congress for enactment into positive law. To date, however, fewer than one-half of the titles have been enacted into positive law.[28] Thus, when using the *United States Code,* it is important to ascertain if the a particular title has been enacted into positive law. Those titles not yet enacted are *prima facie* evidence of the law.[29] Should there be a conflict between the wording in the *United States Code* and the *United States Statutes at Large,* the latter will govern.[30] The end of each *United States Code* section includes a historical note that lists *United States Statutes at Large* citations, public law numbers, date of original enactment, and any amendments. [Illustrations 9–4 and 9–8]

Some additional features of the *United States Code* are as follows:

a. A multivolume general index.

b. Historical notes that provide information on amendments or other public laws' effect on sections of the *United States Code.*

c. Cross-references to other sections of the *United States Code* that contain related matters or that refer to specific sections of the *U.S.C.*

d. A table of "Acts Cited by Popular Name," in which public laws are listed alphabetically by either the short titles assigned by Congress or by the names by which the laws have become known. Citations are provided to the *United States Code* and to *United States Statutes at Large.*

e. Volumes that include tables providing the following information:

(1) Table 1 indicates where titles of the *United States Code* that have been revised and renumbered since the 1926 edition appear within the current edition of the *U.S.C.*

(2) Table 2 provides references to the current edition of the *U.S.C.* from the *Revised Statutes of the United States of 1878.*

---

[27] The principal duty of this Office is "to develop and keep current an official and positive codification of the laws of the United States," 2 U.S.C. § 285a (2006), and "[t]o prepare . . . one title at a time, a complete compilation, restatement, and revision of the general and permanent laws of the United States. . ." 2 U.S.C. § 285b(1) (2006).

[28] Titles enacted into positive law are 1, 3, 4, 5, 9, 10, 11, 13, 14, 17, 18, 23, 28, 31, 32, 35, 36, 37, 38, 39, 40, 44, 46, and 49. Title 10 eliminated title 34; and the enactment of Title 31 repealed Title 6. Title 6 is now entitled Domestic Security. A list of titles reenacted as positive law can be found in the following sources: (1) after the title page of the volumes of the *United States Code;* (2) after Section 204(e) of Title 1 of the UNITED STATES CODE, the UNITED STATES CODE ANNOTATED (U.S.C.A.), and the UNITED STATES CODE SERVICE (U.S.C.S.); and (3) inside the front cover of bound volumes of the U.S.C.S.

[29] 1 U.S.C. § 204(a) (2006) provides that: "The matter set forth in the edition of the Code of Laws of the United States current at any time shall, together with the then current supplement, if any, establish *prima facie* the laws of the United States, general and permanent in their nature, in force on the day preceding the commencement of the session following the last session the legislation of which is included: *Provided, however,* That whenever titles of such Code shall have been enacted into positive law the text thereof shall be legal evidence of the laws therein contained, in all the courts of the United States, the several States, and the Territories and insular possessions of the United States."

[30] For an interpretation of 1 U.S.C. § 204(a), see United States v. Welden, 377 U.S. 95, 98 n.4 (1964). *See also* North Dakota v. United States, 460 U.S. 300 (1983); United States v. Wodtke, 627 F. Supp. 1034, 1040 (N.D. Iowa 1985), *aff'd,* 871 F.2d 1092 (8th Cir. 1988).

(3) Table 3 lists the public laws in *United States Statutes at Large* in chronological order and indicates where each section of a public law is contained in the current edition of the *United States Code*.

(4) Another table provides information on internal cross-references within the *United States Code*.

(5) Additional tables indicate where other materials, e.g., Presidential executive orders, are referenced in the current edition of the *United States Code*.

The volumes containing tables are updated by the annual cumulative supplements to the *United States Code*.

3.　Annotated Editions of the United States Code

The *United States Code* is printed and sold by the U.S. Government Printing Office; publication often is slow, particularly the issuance of supplements, which are seldom available until a year or more after the end of a session of Congress.

Furthermore, the meaning of a statute passed by a legislative body is not always clear, and a court must frequently interpret the language used in the statute. Because judicial opinions interpreting statutes are often sought, publishers have created annotated codes which provide digests of court opinions interpreting or deciding the constitutionality of specific code sections. Two annotated editions of the *United States Code* currently are published privately: *United States Code Annotated* (West) and *United States Code Service* (LexisNexis).

The annotated editions of the *United States Code* have many advantages over the official edition. These advantages include: (1) publication of each title in one or more separate volumes; (2) updating of the entire set through publication of annual cumulative pocket supplements and, when necessary, recompiled volumes; (3) publication of pamphlets during the year updating the pocket supplements; (4) more detailed indexing [Illustration 9–3]; (5) inclusion of annotations of judicial opinions interpreting each *Code* section; and (6) citations to the *Code of Federal Regulations*.[31]

a.　*United States Code Annotated (U.S.C.A.).* U.S.C.A., published by West, sets forth the text of legislation as it appears in the *United States Code*. Thus, it contains the same features that were listed in Section C–2 of this chapter. [Illustrations 9–5, 9–6, and 9–7]

Many enhancements have been included by the publisher to supplement those features found in the official version of the *United States Code*. Most important are the Notes of Decisions, which provide digests of cases that interpret a particular section of the *Code*. These digests are popularly referred to as annotations. Notes of Decisions are organized under an alphabetical subject index that precedes the actual annotations.

Other features of the *U.S.C.A.* are as follows:

(1) References to other West publications and to topics and key numbers that can assist researchers in finding additional cases and other pertinent materials.

---

[31] This publication is discussed in Chapter 13.

(2) The multivolume General Index, which is issued annually in paperback form. At the end of each title of the *U.S.C.A.* there is a separate index for that title.

(3) Supplementary pamphlets include those public laws enacted since the last supplementation of a title and that affect sections of that title. Public laws are classified to particular *Code* sections. The most recent Notes of Decisions also are included for *Code* sections that have been construed by the courts since the last pocket supplements were published.

(4) The Popular Name Table for Acts of Congress is located in the last volume of the General Index. [Illustration 9–11] This listing is arranged alphabetically by popular name, with references provided to both *United States Statutes at Large* and to the *Code*. This popular name table is cumulatively updated by means of the pamphlets discussed in (3), above. Also, many titles of the *U.S.C.A.* contain tables entitled "Popular Name Acts," which provide an alphabetical listing of public laws within that title and references to sections of that specific title. If there is more than one volume, these tables are located in the first volume of the title.

The General Index to *U.S.C.A.* also includes, in the proper alphabetical location, the public law by popular name. Most frequently, the researcher is referred to the Popular Name Table for Acts of Congress in the last volume of *U.S.C.A.*'s General Index. Occasionally, a direct reference is given to a *Code* section.

(5) The *U.S.C.A.* contains many of the same tables contained in the *United States Code*. These tables are located in separate volumes and are updated by means of pocket and pamphlet supplementation as described above.

b.   *United States Code Service (U.S.C.S.).* This set is published by LexisNexis. Like *U.S.C.A., U.S.C.S.* provides the same features found in the *United States Code,* e.g., historical notes and cross-references are set forth in a section entitled "History; Ancillary Laws and Directives," which follows each section of the *Code.* [Illustrations 9–8 and 9–9]

U.S.C.S., unlike *U.S.C.A.*, follows the text of public laws as they appear in *United States Statutes at Large.* Therefore, if a title has not been enacted into positive law, the user of *U.S.C.S.* will have the authoritative language. If the editors of *U.S.C.S.* believe that clarification of the language of the public laws included in the set is necessary, they provide clarifying information through the use of brackets (inserting words or references) or explanatory notes.

U.S.C.S. provides, in its Interpretive Notes and Decisions, "pertinent" digests of judicial opinions and federal administrative agency decisions that interpret or construe a public law or a particular section of a public law.

An "analytical" index, which precedes the actual digest of cases and administrative decisions, enables users to focus their research. The Later Case and Statutory Service pamphlets, issued three times a year, update the Interpretive Notes and Decisions between the release of annual pocket supplements.

Other features of the *U.S.C.S.* include:

(1) References to other publications, including those of LexisNexis, and to relevant law review articles. These references are set forth in a section entitled Research Guide.

(2) A multivolume General Index is kept current by a General Index Update pamphlet.

(3) The *Cumulative Later Case and Statutory Service* that indicates public laws enacted since the last supplementation of a specific title that affect sections of that title. This *Cumulative Later Case and Statutory Service* is issued three times a year.

(4) The Table of Acts by Popular Name is a table of enacted laws that are arranged alphabetically by popular name. Additionally, the popular name table provides references to *United States Statutes at Large* and to *U.S.C.S.* It is updated by the *United States Code Service, Advance Service,* discussed in section B–1–b of this chapter.

The General Index also includes the popular names of public laws. However, unlike *U.S.C.A.*, *U.S.C.S.* provides citations to relevant sections or cross references to given subjects in the General Index when they are contained in the *U.S.C.S.*

(5) Additional tables similar to those as described for *U.S.C.* These tables are contained in separate volumes labeled as such and are updated by means of pocket and pamphlet supplementation as described above.

c. *Summary and Comparison: Annotated Editions of the United States Code.* Both *U.S.C.A.* and *U.S.C.S.* follow the same citation pattern as the official *United States Code*; a citation to the *United States Code* can be located in either of the two annotated sets.[32] As noted above, only certain titles of the *United States Code* have been enacted into positive law. The *U.S.C.A.* uses the text as it appears in the *United States Code,* while the *U.S.C.S.* follows the text as it appears in *United States Statutes at Large.* Thus, when using *U.S.C.A.*, it may be necessary at times to check the text of *United States Statutes at Large* for those titles that are still only *prima facie* evidence of the law.

Both *U.S.C.A.* and *U.S.C.S.* contain digests of cases interpreting sections of the *United States Code.* Each set is updated by annual pocket supplements, monthly pamphlets, and, when necessary, by replacement volumes. Each version contains editorial materials that refer to other publications. The *U.S.C.A.* contains more annotations than the *U.S.C.S.* Both sets are easier to use, more current, and better indexed than the *United States Code.* However, when only the text of the *Code* is needed, it may be simpler to consult the official *United States Code.* [See Illustrations 9–3 through 9–9, which show the use of various sets of the *U.S. Code.*]

Both annotated codes include volumes containing the United States Constitution and various court rules.[33]

[32] For a discussion of these two sets, see Jeanne Benioff, *A Comparison of Annotated U.S. Codes,* 2(1) Legal Reference Services Q., Spring 1982, at 37.

[33] These subjects are discussed in Chapters 8 and 12.

4. Access to the Code in Electronic Format

a. *LexisNexis. LexisNexis* contains the *Code* as published in the *U.S.C.S.* Each section of a *Code* title contains the full text of the law, a complete history of the *Code* section showing sources and derivations of the law including any amendments, and a list of research references and interpretive notes. Each *Code* section is updated to include the new material in paper supplementation. Information regarding each section's currency is included. *LexisNexis Congressional* also contains the text of the *U.S. Code*.

b. *Westlaw. Westlaw* contains the *Code* as published in the *U.S.C.A.* The USC database provides the unannotated version. A related materials directory in *Westlaw* enables the user to update the *Code* section; to view historical notes, references, and tables; and to find notes of decisions. The USCA database contains the text of the *Code,* annotations, and a popular name table. The *Code* section can be updated, and notes, references, and tables can be viewed, by using the update feature.

c. *Loislaw.* The official text of the *United States Code* is available.

d. *Internet Sources* (other than Web-accessible, fee-based services).

(1) The *Legal Information Institute* at Cornell University has the full-text of the latest edition of the *United States Code.*[34] An RSS feed for each title enables researchers to stay current.

(2) *GPO Access* contains the *United States Code.*[35]

(3) U.S. House of Representatives, Office of the Law Revision Counsel, provides a website where the full-text of individual titles of the *Code* can be downloaded or searched.[36]

SECTION D.   ILLUSTRATIONS

---

[34] http://www.law.cornell.edu/uscode/.

[35] http://www.gpoaccess.gov/uscode.

[36] http://uscode.house.gov/.

9–8 to

9–9.   Pages from Title 15, U.S.C.S. § 661

[Illustration 9–1]

SLIP LAW–106TH CONGRESS

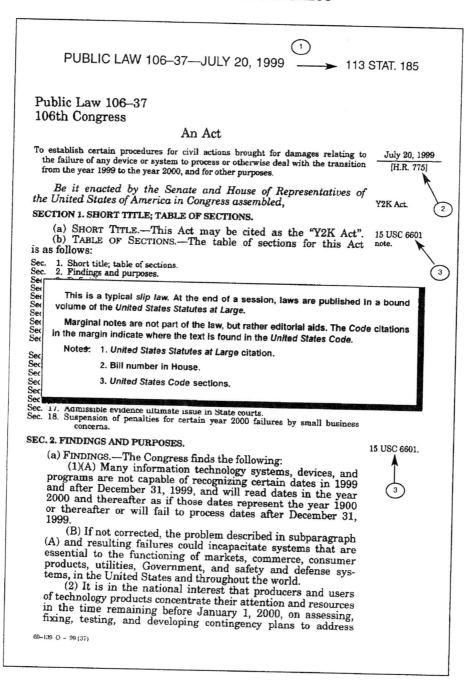

[Illustration 9–2]

PAGE FROM 106 UNITED STATES STATUTES AT LARGE

PUBLIC LAW 102-366—SEPT. 4, 1992   106 STAT. 1019

(2) within 180 days after the date of enactment of this Act, publish in the Federal Register final rules and regulations implementing this Act, and enter such contracts as are necessary to implement this Act and the amendments made by this Act.

SEC. 416. BUY AMERICA.

Section 102 of the Small Business Investment Act of 1958 (15 U.S.C. 1661) is amended by adding at the end the following: "It is the intention of the Congress that in the award of financial assistance under this Act, when practicable, priority be accorded to small business concerns which lease or purchase equipment and supplies which are produced in the United States and that small business concerns receiving such assistance be encouraged to continue to lease or purchase such equipment and supplies.".

15 USC 661.

SEC. 417. STUDIES AND REPORTS.

(a) SBA ANNUAL REPORT.—Section 308(g) of the Small Business Investment Act of 1958 (12 U.S.C. 687(g)) is amended by adding at the end the following new paragraph:

15 USC 687.

"(3) In its annual report for the year ending on December 31, 1993, and in each succeeding annual report made pursuant to section 10(a) of the Small Business Act, the Administration shall include a full and detailed description or account relating to—

"(A) the number of small business investment companies the Administration licensed, the number of licensees that have

> 15 U.S.C. § 661 was amended in 1992. Frequently, a single public law may simultaneously amend sections of various titles of the U.S.C.

"(B) the amount of government leverage that each licensee received in the previous year and the types of leverage instruments each licensee used;

"(C) for each type of financing instrument, the sizes, geographic locations, and other characteristics of the small business investment companies using them, including the extent to which the investment companies have used the leverage from each instrument to make small business loans, equity investments, or both; and

"(D) the frequency with which each type of investment instrument has been used in the current year and a comparison of the current year with previous years.".

(b) REPORT OF THE COMPTROLLER GENERAL.—Not later than 4 years after the date of enactment of this Act, the Comptroller General of the United States shall transmit to the Committees on Small Business of the House of Representatives and the Senate a report that reviews the Small Business Investment Company program (established under the Small Business Investment Act of 1958) for the 3-year period following the date of enactment of this Act, with respect to each item listed in section 308(g)(3) of the Small Business Investment Act of 1958, as amended by subsection (a).

15 USC 681 note.

SEC. 418. NO EFFECT ON SECURITIES LAWS.

Nothing in this Act (and no amendment made by this Act) shall be construed to affect the applicability of the securities laws, as that term is defined in section 3(a)(47) of the Securities Exchange Act of 1934, or any of the rules and regulations thereunder, or

15 USC 661 note.

[Illustration 9–3]

PAGE FROM VOLUME OF GENERAL INDEX TO THE U.S.C.A.

FINDING A FEDERAL LAW

Problem: Find the section of the law dealing with the declaration of policy for investing in small businesses.

Step 1. Check the index to *U.S.C.*, *U.S.C.A.*, or *U.S.C.S.* This will indicate that this topic is covered in 15 U.S.C. § 661.

[Illustration 9–4]

PAGE FROM UNITED STATES CODE

PART B—SURETY BOND GUARANTEES

SUBCHAPTER I—GENERAL PROVISIONS

§ 661. Congressional declaration of policy

It is declared to be the policy of the Congress and the purpose of this chapter to improve and stimulate the national economy in general and the small-business segment thereof in particular by establishing a program to stimulate and supplement the flow of private equity capital and long-term loan funds which small-business concerns need for the sound financing of their business operations and for their growth, expansion, and modernization, and which are not available in adequate supply: *Provided, however*, That this policy shall be carried out in such manner as to insure the maximum participation of private financing sources.

sistance under this chapter, when practicable, priority be accorded to small business concerns which lease or purchase equipment and supplies which are produced in the United States and that small business concerns receiving such assistance be encouraged to continue to lease or purchase such equipment and supplies."

SHORT TITLE OF 2004 AMENDMENT

Pub. L. 108–232, § 1, May 28, 2004, 118 Stat. 649, provided that:"This Act [amending section 697e of this title] may be cited as the 'Premier Certified Lenders Program Improvement Act of 2004'."

SHORT TITLE OF 2001 AMENDMENT

Pub. L. 107–100, § 1, Dec. 21, 2001, 115 Stat. 966, provided that: "This Act [amending sections 636, 683, 687d, 687e, and 697 of this title, section 1833a of Title 12, Banks and Banking, and section 1014 of Title 18, Crimes and Criminal Procedure, and enacting provisions set out as notes under sections 636, 683, and 697 of this title] may be cited as the 'Small Business Investment Company Amendments Act of 2001'."

SHORT TITLE OF 2000 AMENDMENT

Pub. L. 106–554, § 1(a)(8) [§ 1(a)]. Dec. 21, 2000, 114 Stat. 2763, 2763A–653, provided that: "This section [enacting part B of subchapter III of this chapter, amending section 683 of this title, section 109 of Title 11, Bankruptcy, and section 1464 of Title 12, Banks and Banking, and amending provisions set out as a note under section 631 of this title] may be cited as the 'New Markets Venture Capital Program Act of 2000'." •

Pub. L. 106–554, § 1(a)(9) [title III, § 301], Dec. 21, 2000, 114 Stat. 2763, 2763A–684, provided that: "This title [enacting section 697g of this title, amending sections 695 to 697 and 697e of this title, enacting provisions set out as a note under section 697g of this title, and repealing provisions set out as a note under section 697e of this title] may be cited as the 'Certified Development Company Program Improvements Act of 2000'."

Pub. L. 106–554, § 1(a)(9) [title IV, § 401], Dec. 21, 2000,

Step 2. Locate the title and section referred to in the index. Ordinarily, one would consult the latest edition of *U.S.C.* and its cumulative supplements, or one of the two annotated codes.

This illustration shows how this law appears in the *U.S.C.*

Note how at the end of § 661 (as is the case with all *U.S.C.* sections) citations are given to the section in the *United States Statutes at Large*. § 661 was first passed in 1958 and amended in 1992.

REFERENCES IN TEXT

This chapter, referred to in text, was in the original "this Act", meaning Pub. L. 85–699, which enacted this chapter, amended sections 77c, 77ddd, 80a–18, 633 and 636 of this title, and sections 217 [now 212], 218 [now 213], 221 [now 216], 657, 1006 and 1014 of Title 18, Crimes and Criminal Procedure, repealed section 352a of Title 12, Banks and Banking, and enacted notes set out under this section and section 352a of Title 12. Sections 212 and 213 of Title 18, as renumbered by Pub. L. 87–849, were subsequently repealed. For complete classification of this Act to the Code, see Short Title note set out below and Tables.

AMENDMENTS

1992—Pub. L. 102–366 inserted at end "It is the intention of the Congress that in the award of financial as-

SHORT TITLE OF 1992 AMENDMENT

Section 401 of title IV of Pub. L. 102–366 provided that: "This Act [probably means "This title", amending this section and sections 662, 682, 683, 685 to 687, 687b, and 687l of this title, enacting provisions set out as notes under this section and sections 681 and 687b of this title, and amending provisions set out as a note under section 631 of this title] may be cited as the 'Small Business Equity Enhancement Act of 1992'."

SHORT TITLE OF 1988 AMENDMENT

Pub. L. 100–590, title II, § 201, Nov. 3, 1988, 102 Stat. 3007, provided that: "This title [amending sections 694b and 694c of this title and enacting provisions set out as notes under section 694b of this title] may be cited as the 'Preferred Surety Bond Guarantee Program Act of 1988'."

[Illustration 9–5]

PAGE FROM TITLE 15 U.S.C.A. § 661

Ch. 14B SMALL BUSINESS INVESTMENT 15 § 661

- update your research with the most current information
- expand your library with additional resources
- retrieve direct history, precedential history and parallel citations with the Insta-Cite service

For more information on using WESTLAW to supplement your research, see the WESTLAW Electronic Research Guide, which follows the Explanation

---

SUBCHAPTER I—GENERAL PROVISIONS

§ 661. Congressional declaration of policy

It is declared to be the policy of the Congress and the purpose of this chapter to improve and stimulate the national economy in general and the small-business segment thereof in particular by establishing a program to stimulate and supplement the flow of private equity capital and long-term loan funds which small-business concerns need for the sound financing of their business operations and for their growth, expansion, and modernization, and which are not available in adequate supply: *Provided, however,* That this policy

> This illustration and the next show references to the *United States Statutes at Large* and the historical notes summarizing the effect of the amendment on the original public law.

chapter shall be so administered that any financial assistance provided hereunder shall not result in a substantial increase of unemployment in any area of the country.

It is the intention of the Congress that in the award of financial assistance under this chapter, when practicable, priority be accorded to small business concerns which lease or purchase equipment and supplies which are produced in the United States and that small business concerns receiving such assistance be encouraged to continue to lease or purchase such equipment and supplies.

(Pub.L. 85–699, Title I, § 102, Aug. 21, 1958, 72 Stat. 689; Pub.L. 102–366, Title IV, § 416, Sept. 4, 1992, 106 Stat. 1019.)

HISTORICAL AND STATUTORY NOTES

Revision Notes and Legislative Reports

1958 Acts. House Report No. 2060 and Conference Report No. 2492, see 1958 U.S. Code Cong. and Adm. News, p. 3678.

1992 Acts. House Report No. 102–492 and Statement by President, see 1992 U.S. Code Cong. and Adm. News, p. 891.

References in Text

This chapter, referred to in text, was in the original "this Act", meaning Pub.L. 85–699, which enacted this chapter, amended §§ 77c, 77ddd, 80a–18, 633 and 636 of this title, and §§ 217 [now 212], 218 [now 213], 221 [now 216], 657, 1006 and 1014 of Title 18, Crimes and Crimi-

673

[Illustration 9–6]

PAGE FROM TITLE 15 U.S.C.A. § 661

---

15 § 661 COMMERCE AND TRADE Ch. 14B

nal Procedure, repealed § 352a of Title 12, Banks and Banking, and enacted notes set out under this section and § 352a of Title 12. For complete classification of this Act to the Code, see short title set out below and Tables.

Amendments

1992 Amendments. Pub.L. 102–366 inserted at end "It is the intention of the Congress that in the award of financial assistance under this chapter, when practicable, priority be accorded to small business concerns which lease or purchase equipment and supplies which are

681, 683, 684, and 686 of this title] may be cited as the 'Small Business Investment Act Amendments of 1972'."

1967 Amendments. Section 201 of Pub.L. 90–104, title II, Oct. 11, 1967, 81 Stat. 269, provided that: "This title [amending sections 681, 682, 683, 684, 686, 687, 687b, and 692 of this title] may be cited as the 'Small Business Investment Act Amendments of 1967'."

1966 Amendments. Section 1 of Pub.L. 89–779, Nov. 6, 1966, 80 Stat. 1359, provided: "That this Act [enacting sections 687e, 687f, 687g, and 687h of this title

> These "Historical and Statutory Notes," continued from the prior illustration, show the intent of the 1992 amendments and the short title of the act.

supplies."

Short Title

1994 Amendments. Pub.L. 103–403, Title V, § 501, Oct. 22, 1994, 108 Stat. 4198, provided that: "This title [enacting section 697f of this title and provisions set out as a note under section 697f of this title] may be cited as the 'Small Business Prepayment Penalty Relief Act of 1994'."

1992 Amendments. Section 401 of Pub.L. 102–366 provided that: "This Act may be cited as the 'Small Business Equity Enhancement Act of 1992'." "This Act" probably refers to this title, meaning Title IV of Pub.L. 102–366, Sept. 4, 1992, 106 Stat. 1007, which amended this section and sections 662, 682, 683, 685, 686, 687, 687b, and 687l of this title, enacted provisions set out as notes under this section and sections 681 and 687b of this title, and amended provisions set out as notes under section 631 of this title. For complete classification of Pub.L. 102–366 to the Code, see Short Title of 1992 Amendments note set out under section 631 of this title and Tables.

1988 Amendments. Pub.L. 100–590, Title II, § 201, Nov. 3, 1988, 102 Stat. 3007, provided that: "This title [amending sections 694b and 694c of this title and enacting provisions set out as notes under section 694b of this title] may be cited as the 'Preferred Surety Bond Guarantee Program Act of 1988'."

1972 Amendments. Section 1 of Pub.L. 92–595, Oct. 27, 1972, 86 Stat. 1314, provided: "That this Act [enacting sections 687i and 687j of this title and amending sections 80a–18, 633, 636, 662,

may be cited as the 'Small Business Investment Act Amendments of 1966'."

1964 Amendments. Section 1 of Pub.L. 88–273, Feb. 28, 1964, 78 Stat. 146, provided: "That this Act [enacting section 687d and amending sections 682, 686, and 687 of this title] may be cited as the 'Small Business Investment Act Amendments of 1963'."

1961 Amendments. Section 1 of Pub.L. 87–341, Oct. 3, 1961, 75 Stat. 752, provided: "That this Act [enacting sections 687a, 687b, and 687c of this title, amending sections 633, 662, 681, 683 to 687, and 696 of this title, and enacting provisions set out as notes under sections 631 and 686 of this title] may be cited as the "Small Business Investment Act Amendments of 1961"."

1960 Amendments. Section 1 of Pub.L. 86–502, June 11, 1960, 74 Stat. 196, provided: "That this Act [amending sections 662, 681, 682 and 684 of this title, and section 26–610 of the District of Columbia Code, 1973 edition] may be cited as the "Small Business Investment Act Amendments of 1960"."

1958 Acts. Section 101 of Pub.L. 85–699 provided in part that: "This Act [enacting this chapter, amending sections 77c, 77ddd, 80a–18, 633 and 636 of this title, and sections 217 [now 212], 218 [now 213], 221 [now 216], 657, 1006 and 1014 of Title 18, Crimes and Criminal Procedure, repealing section 352a of Title 12, Banks and Banking, and enacting notes set out under this section and former section 352a of title 12] may be cited as the 'Small Business Investment Act of 1958'."

[Illustration 9–7]

PAGE FROM TITLE 15 U.S.C.A. § 661

Ch. 14B   SMALL BUSINESS INVESTMENT   15 § 662

Effect of Small Business Equity Enhancement Act of 1992 on Securities Laws

Section 418 of title IV of Pub.L. 102–366 provided that: "Nothing in this Act [probably means "this title", see Short Title of 1992 Amendment note above] (and no amendment made by this Act) shall be construed to affect or apply to—

"Notwithstanding any law, rule, regulation or administrative moratorium, except as otherwise expressly provided in this Act [probably means "this title", see Short Title of 1992 Amendment note above], the Small Business Administration shall—

"(1) within 90 days after the date of

> The important difference in the annotated sets of the *Code* is the digest of court cases after each section of the *Code*. These digests assist in interpreting the meaning of the *Code* section.
>
> Also illustrated are other research aids available in *U.S.C.A.*

---

supersede or limit the jurisdiction of the Securities and Exchange Commission or the authority at any time conferred under the securities laws."

Regulations

Section 415 of title IV of Pub.L. 102–366 provided that:

"(2) within 180 days after the date of enactment of this Act, publish in the Federal Register final rules and regulations implementing this Act, and enter such contracts as are necessary to implement this Act and the amendments made by this Act."

LIBRARY REFERENCES ◄────────

Administrative Law

Margin stock defined—

Credit by banks for the purpose of purchasing or carrying, see 12 CFR § 221.2.

Securities credit other than banks, brokers, or dealers, see 12 CFR § 207.2.

Programs, see West's Federal Practice Manual § 2062.

Small business investment companies, see 13 CFR § 107.20.

American Digest System

United States ⬡53(8), 82.

Encyclopedias

C.J.S. United States §§ 70, 122.

NOTES OF DECISIONS ◄────────

Private right of action   2
Purpose   1

---

1. Purpose

This chapter was passed for purpose of making loans available to those engaging in comparatively small enterprises who cannot obtain adequate borrowed funds through customary financial institutions. First Louisiana Inv. Corp. v. U. S., C.A.5 (La.) 1965, 351 F.2d 495.

Purpose of this chapter is to produce financing for small businesses for long term loans. Hernstadt v. Programs for Television, Inc., N.Y.City Ct.1962, 232 N.Y.S.2d 683, 36 Misc.2d 628.

2. Private right of action

There exists no private right of action under Small Business Investment Act. Hooven-Dayton Corp. v. Center City Mesbic, Inc., S.D.Ohio 1996, 918 F.Supp. 193.

§ 662. Definitions

As used in this chapter—

(1) the term "Administration" means the Small Business Administration;

[Illustration 9–8]

PAGE FROM TITLE 15 U.S.C.S. § 661

---

15 USCS § 661   Commerce and Trade

GENERAL PROVISIONS

§ 661. Congressional declaration of policy

It is declared to be the policy of the Congress and the purpose of this Act to improve and stimulate the national economy in general and the small-business segment thereof in particular by establishing a program to stimulate and supplement the flow of private equity capital and long-term loan funds which small-business concerns need for the sound financing of their business operations and for their growth, expansion, and modernization, and which are not available in adequate supply: Provided, however, That this policy shall be carried out in such manner as to insure the maximum participation of private financing sources.

It is the intention of the Congress that the provisions of this Act shall be so administered that any financial assistance provided hereunder shall not result in a substantial increase in unemployment in any area of the country. It is the intention of the Congress that in the award of financial assistance under this Act, when practicable, priority be accorded to small business concerns which lease or purchase equipment and supplies which are produced in the United States and that small business concerns receiving such assistance be encouraged to continue to lease or purchase such equipment and supplies.

(As amended Sept. 4, 1992, P. L. 102-366, Title IV, § 416, 106 Stat. 1019.)

HISTORY; ANCILLARY LAWS AND DIRECTIVES

Amendments:

1992. Act Sept. 4, 1992 added the sentence beginning "It is the intention of the Congress in the award . . .".

Short title:

Act Aug. 21, 1958, P. L. 85-699, Title I, § 101, 72 Stat. 689; April 5, 1999, P. L. 106-9, § 2(d)(3), 113 Stat. 18, provides: "This Act [15 USCS §§ 661 et seq. generally; for full classification, consult USCS Tables volumes] may be cited as the 'Small Business Investment Act of 1958'.".

Act Nov. 3, 1988, P. L. 100-590, Title II, § 201, 102 Stat. 3007, provides: "This title may be cited as the 'Preferred Surety Bond Guarantee Program Act of 1988'.".

Act Sept. 4, 1992, P. L. 102-366, Title IV, § 401, 106 Stat. 1007, provides: "This Act [title] may be cited as the 'Small Business Equity Enhancement Act of 1992'.". For full classification of such Title, consult USCS Tables volumes.

Act Oct. 22, 1994, P. L. 103-403, Title V, § 501, 108 Stat. 4198, provides: "This title may be

---

> **This shows the text of 15 U.S.C.S. § 661, as amended, historical background relating to the law, and ancillary laws and directives. *U.S.C.S.* uses the text of the public law as it appears in the *United States Statutes at Large.***
>
> **See next illustration.**

---

the 'New Markets Venture Capital Program Act of 2000'.".

Act Dec. 21, 2000, P. L. 106-554, § 1(a)(9), 114 Stat. 2763 (enacting into law § 301 of Title III of H.R. 5667 (114 Stat. 2763A-__), as introduced on Dec. 15, 2000), provides: "This title [adding 15 USCS § 697g, and amending 15 USCS §§ 695, 696, 697, and 697e] may be cited as the 'Certified Development Company Program Improvements Act of 2000'.".

Act Dec. 21, 2000, P. L. 106-554, § 1(a)(9), 114 Stat. 2763 (enacting into law § 401 of Title IV of H.R. 5667 (114 Stat. 2763A-__), as introduced on Dec. 15, 2000), provides: "This title [amending 15 USCS §§ 662, 682, 683, and 687b] may be cited as the 'Small Business Investment Corrections Act of 2000'.".

Other provisions:

Implementation of the Small Business Equity Enhancement Act of 1992. Act Sept. 4, 1992, P. L. 102-366, Title IV, § 415, 106 Stat. 1018, provides:

"Notwithstanding any law, rule, regulation or administrative moratorium, except as otherwise expressly provided in this Act [Title IV of Act Sept. 4, 1992, P. L. 102-366; for full classification, consult USCS Tables volumes], the Small Business Administration shall—

"(1) within 90 days after the date of enactment of this Act, publish in the Federal Register proposed rules and regulations implementing this Act and the amendments made by this Act [Title IV of Act Sept. 4, 1992, P. L. 102-366; for full classification, consult USCS Tables volumes]; and

"(2) within 180 days after the date of enactment of this Act, publish in the Federal Register final rules and regulations implementing this Act [Title IV of Act Sept. 4, 1992, P. L. 102-366; for full classification, consult USCS Tables volumes], and enter such contracts as are necessary to implement this Act and the amendments made by this Act.".

Effect of Small Business Equity Enhancement Act of 1992 on securities laws. Act Sept. 4, 1992, P. L. 102-366, Title IV, § 418, 106 Stat. 1019, provides: "Nothing in this Act (and no

2

[Illustration 9–9]

PAGE FROM TITLE 15 U.S.C.S. § 661

SMALL BUSINESS INVESTMENT   **15 USCS § 662**

amendment made by this Act) [Title IV of Act Sept. 4. 1992, P. L. 102-366; for full classification, consult USCS Tables volumes] shall be construed to affect the applicability of the securities laws, as that term is defined in section 3(a)(47) of the Securities Exchange Act of 1934 [15 USCS § 78c(a)(47)], or any of the rules and regulations thereunder, or otherwise supersede or limit the jurisdiction of the Securities and Exchange Commission or the authority at any time conferred under the securities laws.''.

CODE OF FEDERAL REGULATIONS

This section is no longer cited as authority for:
13 CFR Part 116.

RESEARCH GUIDE

Federal Procedure:

10A Fed Proc L Ed, Economic Development §§ 27:181, 187, 190, 193–195, 198, 202, 213, 217, 219.

Am Jur:

17 Am Jur 2d, Consumer and Borrower Protection § 185.
69 Am Jur 2d, Securities Regulation—Federal (1993) §§ 107. 498.

INTERPRETIVE NOTES AND DECISIONS

Small Business Administration did not exceed its statutory authority by improper implementation of a standard operating procedure in action brought by businesses ''graduated'' from Small Business Administration's program in accordance with criteria established by regulation where regulation is not arbitrary, unreasonable, erroneous, or inconsistent exercise of power, despite argument that businesses were economically more viable than other program participants and more worthy of continued support. Roberts Constr. Co. v United States Small Business Admin. (1987, DC Colo) 657 F Supp 418.

Small business owner's claim against SBA and specialized small business investment company which financed it must fail, where owner claims company violated, and SBA failed to enforce, various regulations under Small Business Investment Act (15 USCS §§ 661 et seq.), because Act does not expressly create private right of action, and its language and legislative history intend enforcement to be undertaken solely by SBA. Hooven-Dayton Corp. v Center City Mesbic (1996, SD Ohio) 918 F Supp 193.

> **This illustrates the "Research Guide" and the annotations ("Interpretive Notes and Decisions"), which are editorial enhancements to the annotated sets of the Code. The pocket supplement should always be consulted for any additional amendments.**

(A) an investment by a venture capital firm, investment company (including a small business investment company) employee welfare benefit plan or pension plan, or trust, foundation, or endowment that is exempt from Federal income taxation—

    (i) shall not cause a business concern to be deemed not independently owned and operated regardless of the allocation of control during the investment period under any investment agreement between the business concern and the entity making the investment;

    (ii) shall be disregarded in determining whether a business concern satisfies size standards established pursuant to section 3(a)(2) of the Small Business Act [15 USCS § 632(a)(2)]; and

    (iii) shall be disregarded in determining whether a small business concern is a smaller enterprise; and

(B) in determining whether a business concern satisfies net income standards established pursuant to section 3(a)(2) of the Small Business Act [15 USCS § 632(a)(2)], if the business concern is not required by law to pay Federal income taxes at the enterprise level, but is required to pass income through to the shareholders, partners, beneficiaries, or other equitable owners of the business concern, the net income of the business concern shall be determined by allowing a deduction in an amount equal to the sum of—

    (i) if the business concern is not required by law to pay State (and local, if any) income taxes at the enterprise level, the net income (determined without regard to this subparagraph), multiplied by the marginal State income tax rate (or by the combined State and local income tax rates, as applicable) that would have applied if the business concern were a corporation; and

    (ii) the net income (so determined) less any deduction for State (and local) income taxes calculated under clause (i), multiplied by the marginal Federal income tax rate that would have applied if the business concern were a corporation;

(6) [Unchanged]

(7) the term ''license'' means a license issued by the Administration as provided in section 301 [15 USCS § 681];

3

SECTION E. POPULAR NAMES FOR FEDERAL LAWS

Federal legislation is often referenced by its popular name, a name sometimes given to a statute by the public or media. The popular name may describe the legislation (e.g., Gold Clause Act) or may refer to its authors (e.g., Taft–Hartley Act).

The tables of popular names of federal laws are designed to provide citations to acts when only the popular names are known. [Illustrations 9–10, 9–11, and 9–12] In addition to *U.S.C.*, *U.S.C.A.*, and *U.S.C.S.*, the following sources also provide popular name tables:

1. *Shepard's Acts and Cases by Popular Names.* This source is discussed in Chapters 7 and 15 of this book.

2. *United States Code Congressional and Administrative News.* Since the 77th Congress, 2d Session, 1942, this source contains a table called Popular Name Acts for each session of Congress.

SECTION F. TABLES FOR FEDERAL LAWS

As noted, federal laws are first published in chronological order in the volumes of *United States Statutes at Large.* A particular law may cover one topic or may include matters on several different topics. Another law may amend one or several previous laws. Some are public laws of a general and permanent nature and are codified in the *U.S.C.*

This method of enacting and publishing laws makes it necessary to have tables that enable a researcher to trace each section of a law as it appears in *United States Statutes at Large* and to determine whether a particular section has been codified and, if so, its citation in the *U.S.C.* For example, assume a researcher is interested in Section 3(2) of Pub. L. No. 101–376. In order to ascertain this section's location in the *U.S.C.*, the researcher must consult the appropriate table of public laws. [Illustration 9–13]

From time to time, a particular title of *U.S.C.* is completely revised with entirely new section numbers. Tables permit researchers to translate citations from the old title to the section numbers in the revised title. [Illustration 9–14]

Each of the three previously described sets containing the *Code* includes one or more volumes that contain cross-reference tables that serve various purposes. These tables include the following:

1. *Revised Title.* Revised Title tables indicate where sections of former titles of the *Code* that have been revised are now incorporated in the *Code.*

2. *Revised Statutes of 1878.* This table indicates the location of sections of *Revised Statutes* in the *Code.*

3. *United States Statutes at Large.* This table shows where public laws published in *United States Statutes at Large* are found in the *Code.*

SECTION G.   ILLUSTRATIONS: POPULAR
NAMES AND TABLES

[Illustration 9–10]

PAGE FROM SHEPARD'S ACTS AND CASES BY POPULAR NAMES

FEDERAL AND STATE ACTS CITED BY POPULAR NAME   Rye

Rural Zoning Enabling Act (County)
Mich. Comp. Laws Ann., 125.201 et seq.

Rural/Downstate Health Act
Ill. Rev. Stat. 1991, Ch. 111 1/2, § 8051 et
seq.

Rush Unsafe Buildings Law
N.Y. Local Laws 1973, Town of Rush, p.
2878

Russell Act (Business Licenses)
Ohio Laws Vol. 80, p. 129

Russell Amendment
J

Ru
S

> Frequently, a public law will become known by a popular name.
> When only the popular name is known, popular name tables
> enable the actual citations to be found. *See, e.g.,* Ryan White
> Comprehensive AIDS Resources Emergency Act of 1990.
>
> **See next two illustrations.**

Russian Friendship Treaty
Haw. Session Laws 1870, p. 83, June 19,
1869

Russian Roulette Act (Taxation)
Fla. Stat. Ann., 194.101

Rutgers, The State University Act
N.J. Stat. Ann., 18A:65-1 et seq.

Ryan Act (Drug Users)
Mich. Comp. Laws Ann., 335.201 et seq.

**Ryan Act (Teacher Preparation and
Licensing)**
Cal. Education Code 1976, § 44200 et seq.

Ryan Liquor Control Act
N.Y. Alcoholic Beverage Control Law
(Consol. Laws Ch. 3B) § 101b

Ryan Master Teacher Act
Cal. Education Code 1976, § 44490 et seq.

**Ryan White Comprehensive AIDS
Resources Emergency Act of 1990**
Aug. 18, 1990, P.L. 101-381, 42 U.S. Code
§ 201 nt.
May 20, 1996, P.L. 104-146, 42 U.S. Code
§ 201 nt.

Ryder Act (Revaluation of Property)
Wash. Rev. Code Ann., 84.41.010 et seq.

Rye Park Act
N.Y. Laws 1907, Ch. 711

993

[Illustration 9–11]

PAGE FROM POPULAR NAME TABLE IN U.S.C.A. ANNUAL INDEX

1195   **POPULAR NAME TABLE**

Rural Local Broadcast Signal Act
   Pub.L. 106–113, Div. B, § 1000(a)(9) [Title II (§§ 2001, 2002], Nov. 29, 1999, 113 Stat. 1536,
      1501A–544 (47 § 338 note)

Rural Post-Roads Act
   See Federal Aid Acts

Rural Rehabilitation Corporation Trust Liquidation Act
   May 3, 1950, ch. 152, 64 Stat. 98 (7 § 1001 note; 40 §§ 440 to 444)

Rural Small Business Enhancement Act of 1990
   Pub.L. 101–574, Title III, Nov. 15, 1990, 104 Stat. 2827 (5 § 601 note; 15 §§ 631 note, 631b,
      636, 648, 653, 653 note, 654)

Rural Telecommunications Improvements Act of 1990
   Pub.L. 101–624, Title XXIII, Subtitle F, Nov. 28, 1990, 104 Stat. 4038 (7 §§ 901 notes, 918,
      924 to 928, 932, 935, 936. 939, 945, 946, 946 note, 948, 950)

~~Rural Telephone Cooperative Associations ERISA Amendments Act of 1991~~

**This is a typical page from the Popular Name Table in the Index volumes of *U.S.C.A.*
This example shows the findings for the same popular name in the previous illustration.**

Russell-Overton Amendment
   Sept. 16, 1940, ch. 720, § 9, 54 Stat. 892 (50 App. § 1158)

Ryan White CARE Act Amendments of 1996
   Pub.L. 104–146, May 20, 1996, 110 Stat. 1346 (5 § 4103 note; 42 §§ 201 note, 294n, 300d,
      300cc note, 300ff–11, 300ff–11 note, 300ff–12 to 300ff–18, 300ff–21 to 300ff–23,
      300ff–26, 300ff–27, 300ff–27a, 300ff–28 to 300ff–31, 300ff–33, 300ff–33 note, 300ff–34 to
      300ff–37, 300ff–47 to 300ff–49, 300ff–51, 300ff–52, 300ff–54, 300ff–55, 300ff–64,
      300ff–71, 300ff–74, 300ff–76 to 300ff–78, 300ff–84, 300ff–101, 300ff–111)
   Pub.L. 106–345, Title V, § 503(b), Oct. 20, 2000, 114 Stat. 1355 (42 § 300ff–22)

Ryan White CARE Act Amendments of 2000
   Pub.L. 106–345, Oct. 20, 2000, 114 Stat. 1319 (see Tables for classification)

Ryan White Comprehensive AIDS Resources Emergency Act of 1990
   Pub.L. 101–381, Aug. 18, 1990, 104 Stat 576 (42 §§ 201 note, 284a, 286, 287a, 287c–2, 289f,
      290aa–3a, 299c–5, 300x–4 note, 300ff, 300ff–1, 300ff–11, 300ff–11 note, 300ff–12 to
      300ff–18, 300ff–21 to 300ff–30, 300ff–41 to 300ff–46, 300ff–46 note, 300ff–47 to
      300ff–55, 300ff–61 to 300ff–67, 300ff–71 to 300ff–76, 300ff–80, 300ff–80 note, 300ff–81
      to 300ff–90, 300aaa to 300aaa–13)

SAA
   See Safety Appliance Acts

SAA
   See Suits in Admiralty Act

Sabbatino Amendment
   See Hickenlooper Amendment

Saccharin Study and Labeling Act
   Pub.L. 95–203, Nov. 23, 1977, 91 Stat. 1451 (21 §§ 301 note, 321, 343, 343a; 42 §§ 218 note,
      289*l*–1 note)
   Pub.L. 96–273, June 17, 1980, 94 Stat. 536 (21 § 348 note)
   Pub.L. 97–42, § 2, Aug. 14, 1981, 95 Stat. 946 (21 § 348 note)
   Pub.L. 98–22, § 2, Apr. 22, 1983, 97 Stat. 173 (21 § 348 note)
   Pub.L. 99–46, May 24, 1985, 99 Stat. 81 (21 § 348 note)
   Pub.L. 100–71, Title I, July 11, 1987, 101 Stat. 431 (21 § 348 note)
   Pub.L. 104–180, Title VI, § 602, Aug. 6, 1996, 110 Stat. 1594 (21 § 348 note)
   Pub.L. 106–554, § 1(a)(1) [Title V, § 517], Dec. 21, 2000, 114 Stat. 2763, 2763A–73 (21
      § 343a)

Saccharin Study and Labeling Act Amendment of 1981
   Pub.L. 97–42, Aug. 14, 1981, 95 Stat. 946 (21 §§ 301 note, 348 note)

Saccharin Study and Labeling Act Amendment of 1983
   Pub.L. 98–22, Apr. 22, 1983, 97 Stat. 173 (21 §§ 301 note, 348 note)

[Illustration 9–12]

PAGE FROM POPULAR NAME TABLE FROM TITLE 42, U.S.C.A.

POPULAR NAME ACTS

Popular Name	Sections
Rural Housing Amendments of 1983	1441 note, 1471, 1472, 1472 note, 1474, 1476, 1479 to 1487, 1490, 1490a, 1490a note, 1490c, 1490e to 1490g, 1490i to 1490o
Ryan White Comprehensive AIDS Resources Emergency Act of 1990	201 note, 284a, 286, 287a, 287c–2, 289f, 290aa–3a, 299c–5, 300x–4 note, 300ff, 300ff–1, 300ff–11 note, 300ff–11 to 300ff–18, 300ff–21 to 300ff–30, 300ff–41 to 300ff–46, 300ff–46 note, 300ff–47 to 300ff–49a, 300ff–50, 300ff–51 to 300ff–55, 300ff–61 to 300ff–67, 300ff–71 to 300ff–76, 300ff–80 note, 300ff–80 to 300ff–90

This page from the Popular Name Table within Title 42 of the *U.S.C.A.* shows the findings for the same popular name in the two previous illustrations.

Popular Name	Sections
	300g to 300g–6, 300h to 300h–7, 300i, 300i–1, 300j to 300j–3, 300j–4 to 300j–9, 300j–11, 300j–21 to 300j–25
Safe Drinking Water Act Amendments of 1986	201 note, 300f, 300g–1 to 300g–6, 300g–6 notes, 300h to 300h–2, 300h–4 to 300h–7, 300i, 300i–1, 300j, 300j–1 note, 300j–1 to 300j–4, 300j–7, 300j–11, 6939b, 6979b
Safe Drinking Water Amendments of 1977	201 note, 300f, 300f notes, 300g–1, 300g–3, 300g–5, 300h, 300h–1, 300j to 300j–2, 300j–4, 300j–6, 300j–8, 300j–10, 7401 note, 7410, 7411, 7413, 7414, 7416, 7419, 7420, 7426, 7472 to 7475, 7478, 7479, 7502, 7502 notes, 7503, 7506, 7521, 7522, 7525, 7541, 7545, 7549, 7602, 7604, 7607, 7623 note, 7625a, 7626
SARA	See Superfund Amendments and Reauthorization Act of 1986
School Lunch Act	See National School Lunch Act
School Lunch and Child Nutrition Amendments of 1986	1751 note, 1752, 1755, (1758, 1760) and notes, 1761, 1762a,

LXXXIV

[Illustration 9–13]

PAGE FROM TABLES VOLUME, U.S.C.S.

103 Stat			STATUTES AT LARGE					101st Cong

Left half

Pub. L.	Section	Stat. Page	USCS Title Section	Status
101-366—Cont'd			1990 August—Cont'd	
	102(b)	431	38 prec. 4141	Added
			38 4141	Added
		435	38 4142	Added
	102(c)	436	38 4107(e)(1)	Amd.
	102(d)		38 prec. 4101	Amd.
	103	437	38 4107(e)(5)	Amd.
	104		38 4141 nt.	New
	201(a)(1)		38 620C	Added
	201(a)(2)	438	38 prec. 601	Amd.
	201(b)		38 620C nt.	New
	2*2(a)		38 5051	Amd.
	202(b)(1)		38 5053(a)	Amd.
	202(b)(2)		38 5053(b)	Amd.
	203(1)	439	38 4114(a)(3)(A)	Amd.
	203(2)		38 4114(a)(3)(C)	Amd.
	204		38 612A nt.	Amd.
	205(a)(1)		38 prec. 4351	Amd.
			38 4351	Added
		440	38 4352	Added
			38 4353	Added
			38 4354	Added

Right half

Pub. L.	Section	Stat. Page	USCS Title Section	Status
101-371		453	Spec.	Un-class.
101-372		454	Spec.	Un-class.
101-373		455	Spec.	Un-class.
101-374	1	656	42 201 nt.	New
	2(a)		42 290aa-12(a)	Amd.
	2(b)(1)		42 290aa-12(d)	Rpld.
	2(b)(2)		42 290aa-12(a)- (g)	
			[(c), (e), (f)]	Redes.
	2(b)(3)		42 290aa-12(c), (d)	Added
	2(c)(1)		42 290aa-12(g)(1)	Amd.
	2(c)(2)		42 290aa-12(g)(3)	Amd.
	2(c)(3)	457	Appn.	Un-class.
	2(d)		Spec.	Un-class.
	2(e)		42 290aa-12 nt.	New

> This table lists all public laws and indicates where each section has been codified in the *U.S.C.* For example, Section 3(2) of Pub. L. 101–376 can be located in Title 5, § 7701(j) in the *U.S.C., U.S.C.A,* or *U.S.C.S.*

Left half (lower)

Pub. L.	Section	Stat. Page	USCS Title Section	Status
	205(c)(2)		38 4303(a)(1), (b)	Amd.
	205(c)(3)		38 4304(1)(A), (2) (D), (5)	Amd.
	206(a)		38 1784A	Added
	206(b)	442	38 1434 nt.	New
	206(c)		38 prec. 1770	Amd.
	206(d)		5 552a nt.	New
	207		38 1622 nt.	New
	208(a)	443	38 1791(b)	Amd.
	208(b)		38 1791 nt.	New
	209		Spec.	Un-class.
101-367	1, 2	445	Spec.	Un-class.
101-368	1	446	42 201 nt.	New
	2(a)(1)		42 247b(j)(2)	Amd.
	2(a)(2)		42 247b(k)(2)(A)- (D)	Amd.
	2(b)		42 247b(l)	Added
	2(c)		42 247b(j)(2)	Amd.
101-369	1	448	9 prec. 301	Amd.
			9 301	Added
			9 302	Added
			9 303	Added
		449	9 304	Added
			9 305	Added
			9 306	Added
			9 307	Added
	2	450	9 prec. 1	Amd.
	3		9 301 nt.	New
101-370	1	451	49 Appx. 1475(d)(4)	Added
	2		49 Appx. 1357(g)	Amd.
	3	452	49 Appx. 1482 nt.	New

Right half (lower)

Pub. L.	Section	Stat. Page	USCS Title Section	Status
			1990 August 17	
101-376	1	461	5 7501 nt.	New
	2(a)		5 7511	Amd.
	2(b)	462	5 4303(e)	Amd.
	2(c)		5 4303 nt.	New
	3(1)		5 7701(k)((j))	Redes.
	3(2)		5 7701(j)	Added
	4	463	5 4303 nt.	New
101-377	1	464	16 430g-4	New
	2		16 430g-5	New
	3	465	16 430g-6	New
	4		16 430g-7	New
	5	466	16 430g-8	New
	6	467	16 430g-9	New
	7		16 430g-10	New
101-378	Title I			
	101	468	Spec.	Un-class.
	Title II			
	201		Spec.	Un-class.
	202		Spec.	Un-class.
	203	469	Spec.	Un-class.
	204		Spec.	Un-class.
	205(a)	470	16 1132 nt.	Amd.
	205(b)		Spec.	Un-class.
	Title III			
	301(1)	471	43 1629c(d)(1)(A)	Amd.
	301(2)		43 1629c(d)(2)(B) (i)(d)(2)(B)]	Redes.

400

[Illustration 9–14]

PAGE FROM TABLES VOLUME, U.S.C.S.

T 38   REVISED TITLES

TITLE 38—VETERANS' BENEFITS

[This title was enacted into law by Act Sept. 2, 1958, P. L. 85-857, § 1, 72 Stat. 1105. This table shows where sections of former Title 38 are incorporated in revised Title 38]

Title 38 Former Sections	Title 38 New Sections	Title 38 Former Sections	Title 38 New Sections
1–3	Omitted	16b	5203
4	214	16c	5204
5–9	Omitted	16d	5205
10	215	16e	5206
11	201, 210(b)	16f	5207
11a	101(1), 210(a), 210(b)	16g	5208
11a-1	Omitted	16h	601(4), 5209
11a-2	211(a)	16i	5210
11a-3	233	16j	Omitted
11b	5006	17	5220
11c–11d-1	Omitted	17a	5221
11e	214	17b	5222
11f	Omitted	17c	5223
11g	202	17d	5224
11h	3303	17e	5225
11i	5014	17f	5226
11j	233(1), (2)	17g	5227
11k	233(4)	17h	5228
11*l*	3204	17i	Omitted
12	Omitted	17j	210(c)

> When a title of the *U.S.C.* is revised with new section numbering, a table similar to this one is prepared and can be consulted in the Tables volumes of the various sets containing the *Code.*

Title 38 Former Sections	Title 38 New Sections	Title 38 Former Sections	Title 38 New Sections
13e	4206	34	902
13f	4207	35	Omitted
13g	4208	36	3102(b)
14	5101	37	101(4)
14a	5102	38	107(a)
14b	5103	39, 39a	505
14c	5104	41	3002
14d	5105	42–49	Omitted
14e	214	49a	3107
15	4101	50	3020
15a	4102	51–57	Omitted
15b	4103	58	See 3011
15c	4104	71–75	Omitted
15d	4105	76	111(a)–(c)
15e	4106	77	111(d)
15f	4107	91–95	Omitted
15g	4108	96	See 3021
15h	4109	97	Omitted
15i	4110	101	3402, 3403
15j	4111	102	3404
15k	4112	103	3405
15*l*	4113	104	Omitted
15m	4114	111	3404
15n	4115	112–116	Omitted
16	5201	121–124	Omitted
16a	5202	125	3301

92

SECTION H. FEDERAL LEGISLATION: RESEARCH PROCEDURE

1. Public Laws in Force

To determine whether any *Code* sections pertain to a given topic, the following procedures may be used:

a. *Index Method.* Check first the general index to one of the sets of the *Code.* As both *U.S.C.A.* and *U.S.C.S.* have more current indexes, it is usually better to start with either of these sources rather than with the official *U.S.C.* The index will direct the researcher to the *Code* title under which the subject being researched will be found. Next, check the index to the individual *Code* title in either of the annotated editions. The individual *Code* Title indexes may provide better guides to the subject matter of the title than the entries located in the general index.

b. *Topic or Analytic Method.* If the researcher is familiar with a *Code* title that includes the topic under research (e.g., bankruptcy or copyright), it may be useful to obtain the volumes covering the title and consult the outline or "table of contents" preceding the relevant title. This table of contents sets forth headings for each section and, therefore, can narrow the research path.

c. *Definition Method.* The general indexes of all three sets of the *Code* include a main entry, "Definitions." Under this main entry are sub-entries consisting of all terms defined within the *Code.* This method may be a quick way to access particular *Code* provisions. For example, if the research involves labor relations and the researcher consults the Definitions entry in the General Index and the sub-entry *supervisor* to determine if *supervisor* is defined in the *Code,* the following relevant entries are noted:

Supervisor,

> Labor management relations, 29 § 142
>
> > Federal employees, 5 § 7103
> >
> > Federal Service, 5 § 7101 note, Ex. Ord. No. 11491
> >
> National Labor Relations Act, 29 § 152

Similar information is found in the *U.S.C.A.* and the *U.S.C.S.*

2. Public Laws No Longer in Force

If a researcher wants to find public laws that are no longer in force, the following indexes should be consulted:

a. Middleton G. Beaman & A.K. McNamara, *Index Analysis of the Federal Statutes, 1789–1873* (1911).

b. Walter H. McClenon & Wilfred C. Gilbert, *Index to the Federal Statutes, 1874–1931* (1933).

To locate the full-text of public laws no longer in force, superseded editions of the *U.S.C.* can be consulted. As noted above, the *U.S.C.* began in 1926 and, since 1934, has been published every six years with annual cumulative supplements issued between editions. Many law libraries retain these superseded editions or have them in microform. A microfiche collection of historical compilations of federal laws, *Hein's Early Federal Laws* (1992), can be consulted to locate federal laws from the eighteenth and nineteenth centuries.

3. Private, Temporary, and Local Laws

Occasionally, a researcher may need to locate a private, temporary, or local law that was never included in the *U.S.C.* These laws are contained in *United States Statutes at Large* and can be consulted if the date of enactment is known. If this date is not known, it becomes more difficult to locate such laws. The *Consolidated Index to the Statutes at Large of the United States of America from March 4, 1789 to March 3, 1903,* may be used to find laws within the period covered. After that period the volumes of *United States Statutes at Large* must be checked individually.

One of the volumes included in the *United States Code Service, Notes to Uncodified Laws and Treaties,* contains interpretive notes and decisions for laws that were not classified in the *U.S.C.* or that were classified in the *U.S.C.* but subsequently eliminated. The text of the law is not included.

4. Shepard's Citations and KeyCite

Shepard's Citations (both in print and electronic formats) can be used to determine the history and treatment of a federal statute. *KeyCite* also can be used in much the same way.[37]

---

[37] *Shepard's Citations* and *KeyCite* are discussed in detail in Chapter 15 of this book.

Chapter 10
FEDERAL LEGISLATIVE HISTORIES*

This chapter discusses federal legislative histories, including their sources and documents. Specifically, the chapter identifies the most typical documents created during the legislative process; lists sources of previously compiled legislative histories; describes methods for identifying and then locating the documents of a legislative history if a compiled legislative history is not available; and indicates methods for tracking the legislative process.[1]

SECTION A. LEGISLATIVE HISTORIES IN LEGAL RESEARCH

A law is the means by which a legislative body expresses its intent to declare, command, or prohibit some action. Traditionally, *legislative history* is the term designated to describe the documents that contain the information considered by the legislature during the process of enacting legislation. One purpose of compiling a legislative history, therefore, is to facilitate an understanding of the considerations leading to the enactment of a law or the failure of a bill to become law. In connection with pending legislation, researchers may need to determine the current status of proposed legislation and to locate documents generated during the progress of the legislation through Congress. The status of pending legislation is important to certain groups if they want to influence the pending legislation as it becomes law.

A legislative history is most frequently used to determine the intent of a legislative body in passing a law or to determine the meaning of specific language used in a law. Courts and advocates often use legislative histories when interpreting statutes.[2] Differences of opinion exist about the extent to

---

* Richard Leiter, Library Director and Professor at the University of Nebraska College of Law revised this chapter with the assistance of Steven M. Weber, graduate student at the University of Wisconsin School of Library and Information Studies and Reference Intern at the University of Wisconsin Law Library. Bonnie L. Koneski–White, formerly of the Western New England College School of Law Library, wrote previous versions of this chapter.

Note: This chapter contains many references to *GPO Access*, the U.S. Government Printing Office (GPO) system for distributing federal government information over the World Wide Web. After this book went into production, GPO announced that it will replace *GPO Access* with its new *Federal Digital System* (*FDsys*) during 2009. GPO plans to maintain *GPO Access* until the migration to *FDsys* is complete. After that, searches using a *GPO Access* URL will automatically be redirected by the system to *FDsys*.

[1] This chapter focuses exclusively on federal legislative histories. The documents necessary to compile a state legislative history are often more difficult to obtain and rarely as extensive as those at the federal level. Chapter 11 of this book discusses state legislative histories. Chapter 9 of this book, Federal Legislation, discusses the published sources of federal legislation.

[2] "But, while the clear meaning of statutory language is not to be ignored, 'words are inexact tools at best,' . . . and hence it is essential that we place the words of a statute in their proper context by resort to the legislative history." Tidewater Oil Co. v. United States, 409 U.S. 151, 157 (1972).

which courts should use legislative histories.[3] This conflict has led to a re-examination of legislative histories as a subject in law school legal research

[3] *See, e.g.,* Schwegmann Bros. v. Calvert Distillers Corp., 341 U.S. 384, 395 (1951) (Justice Jackson in a concurring opinion indicating that "we should not go beyond Committee reports"), *reh'g denied*, 341 U.S. 956 (1951); National Small Shipments Traffic Conference, Inc. v. Civil Aeronautics Board, 618 F.2d 819, 828 (D.C.Cir. 1980) (court warns against the manufacture of legislative histories). *But see* Schwenke v. Secretary of Interior, 720 F.2d 571, 575 (9th Cir. 1983) (reversing the lower court for failure to consider legislative history of the statute in question). *See also Conference on Statutory Interpretation: The Role of Legislative History in Judicial Interpretation: A Discussion Between Kenneth W. Starr and Judge Abner J. Mikva,* 1987 DUKE L.J. 361.

An increasingly vocal group of federal judges led by Justice Antonin Scalia of the Supreme Court of the United States argues that legislative history has become an unreliable guide to congressional intent because lobbyists and congressional staff members so often distort it. *See* Charles Rothfeld, *Read Congress's Words, Not Its Mind, Judges Say,* N.Y. TIMES, Apr. 14, 1989, at B5, col. 3; Charles Tiefer, *The Reconceptualization of Legislative History in the Supreme Court,* 2000 WIS. L. REV. 205. *See also* Elizabeth A. Liess, Comment, *Censoring Legislative History: Justice Scalia on the Use of Legislative History in Statutory Interpretation,* 72 NEB. L. REV. 568 (1993); Arthur Stock, Note, *Justice Scalia's Use of Sources in Statutory and Constitutional Interpretation: How Congress Always Loses,* 1990 DUKE L.J. 160. *See generally* U.S. DEPARTMENT OF JUSTICE, OFFICE OF LEGAL POLICY, USING AND MISUSING LEGISLATIVE HISTORY: A RE-EVALUATION OF THE STATUS OF LEGISLATIVE HISTORY IN STATUTORY INTERPRETATION 120 (1989), which offers four basic principles intended to "reinforce certain traditional axioms of statutory analysis, consistent with original meaning jurisprudence." For a look at the use of legislative history during a Supreme Court term, see Stephanie Wald, *The Use of Legislative History in Statutory Interpretation Cases in the 1992 U.S. Supreme Court Term; Scalia Rails but Legislative History Remains on Track,* 23 SW. U. L. REV. 47 (1993). *See also,* John F. Manning, *Textualism and Legislative Intent,* 91 VA. L. REV. 419 (2005) and John F. Manning, *Deriving Rules of Statutory Interpretation from the Constitution,* 101 COLUM. L. REV. 1648 (2001).

For discussions of the use, misuse, abuse, or appropriateness of legislative histories in judicial decision-making, see Anthony D'Amato, *Can Legislatures Constrain Judicial Interpretation of Statutes?,* 75 VA. L. REV. 561 (1989); GEORGE A. COSTELLO, SOURCES OF LEGISLATIVE HISTORY AS AIDS TO STATUTORY CONSTRUCTION (1989); Jeffrey J. Soles, *Changing the Past: The Role of Legislative History in Statutory Interpretation,* United States ex rel. Bergen v. Lawrence, 6 COOLEY L. REV. 361 (1989); George A. Costello, *Reliance on Legislative History in Interpreting Statutes,* CRS REV., Jan.–Feb. 1990, at 29; Louis Fisher, *Statutory Interpretations by Congress and the Courts,* CRS REV., Jan.-Feb. 1990, at 32; Edward Heath, *How Federal Judges Use Legislative History,* 25 J. LEGIS. 95 (1999); Patricia M. Wald, *The Sizzling Sleeper: The Use of Legislative History in Construing Statutes in the 1988–89 Term of the United States Supreme Court,* 39 AM. U. L. REV. 277 (1990); Nicholas S. Zeppos, *Legislative History and the Interpretation of Statutes: Toward a Fact–Finding Model of Statutory Interpretation,* 76 VA. L. REV. 1295 (1990); Leigh Ann McDonald, *The Role of Legislative History in Statutory Interpretation: A New Era After the Resignation of Justice William Brennan?,* 56 MO. L. REV. 121 (1991); Stephen Breyer, *On the Uses of Legislative History in Interpreting Statutes,* 65 S. CAL. L. REV. 845 (1992); William T. Mayton, *Law Among the Pleonasms: The Futility and Aconstitutionality of Legislative History in Statutory Interpretation,* 41 EMORY L.J. 113 (1992); W. David Slawson, *Legislative History and the Need to Bring Statutory Interpretation Under the Rule of Law,* 44 STAN. L. REV. 383 (1992); Jack Schwartz & Amanda Stakem Conn, *The Court of Appeals at the Cocktail Party: The Use and Misuse of Legislative History,* 54 MD. L. REV. 432 (1995); Randall W. Quinn, *The Supreme Court's Use of Legislative History in Interpreting the Federal Securities Laws,* 22 SEC. REG. L.J. 262 (1994). For a discussion of how legislative history has been used in one specialized area of the law, see Gregory E. Maggs, *The Secret Decline of Legislative History: Has Someone Heard a Voice Crying in the Wilderness?,* 1994 PUB. INT. L. REV. 57. *See also* Bernard W. Bell, *R–E–S–P–E–C–T: Respecting Legislative Judgements in Interpretive Theory,* 78 N.C. L. REV. 1253 (2000); Adrian Vemeule, *The Cycles of Statutory Interpretation,* 68 U. CHI. L. REV. 149 (2001); JOSEPH L. GERKIN, WHAT GOOD IS LEGISLATIVE HISTORY? JUSTICE SCALIA IN THE FEDERAL COURTS OF APPEALS (William S. Hein & Co. 2007).

courses.[4] These controversies are more academic than practical, however, because the use of legislative histories is a well-established aspect of contemporary litigation.

Components of a legislative history are any documents that contain evidence of the intent of the members of Congress for enacting a law. The language of a bill as introduced in the legislature and subsequent amendments to it may explain the success or failure of the bill to become law. Reports of legislative committees to which the bill was assigned, hearings and debates about the bill, and other documents prepared in connection with the bill's progress through Congress may provide insights on the purpose of the law or the meaning of specific language in the law. Ancillary documents, such as presidential messages, as well as blogs and podcasts produced by legislators and political parties also can provide useful information about the purposes of legislation.

SECTION B.   DOCUMENTS RELEVANT TO FEDERAL LEGISLATIVE HISTORIES

Before compiling a federal legislative history, researchers should familiarize themselves with the documents that may be relevant to establishing legislative intent. These documents are typically found in federal government depository libraries, through commercial electronic sources, through free Internet websites (especially those of the federal government), and for purchase from the Government Printing Office.

1. Congressional Bills

A proposed piece of legislation is introduced as a bill or a joint resolution in either the House of Representatives, where it is assigned an H.R. or H.J. Res. number, or the Senate, where it is assigned either an S. or S.J. Res. number.[5] This number stays with the bill until it is passed or until the end of the Congress in which it was introduced. When a bill is amended, it usually is reprinted with the amending language; less frequently, the amendment or amendments are printed separately. A comparison of the language of the bill as introduced, its subsequent amendments, and the final language of the bill as passed (the public law), may reveal legislative intent because of the insertion or deletion of language.[6]

The researcher should identify and obtain each of the following documents that exist in connection with the legislation being researched:

[4] *See, e.g.,* Peter C. Schanck, *An Essay on the Role of Legislative Histories in Statutory Interpretation,* 80 LAW LIBR. J. 391 (1988); J. Myron Jacobstein & Roy M. Mersky, *Congressional Intent and Legislative Histories: Analysis or Psychoanalysis?,* 82 LAW LIBR. J. 297 (1990); Peter C. Schanck, *The Only Game in Town: Contemporary Interpretive Theory, Statutory Construction, and Legislative Histories,* 82 LAW LIBR. J. 419 (1990). For references to additional sources regarding the uses of legislative histories, see Peter C. Schanck, *The Use of Legislative Histories in Statutory Interpretation: A Selected and Annotated Bibliography*, 13(1) LEGAL REFERENCE SERVICES Q., 1993, at 5.

[5] *See* Chapter 9, notes 3 and 4.

[6] United States v. St. Paul M. & M. Ry. Co., 247 U.S. 310, 318 (1918). *See also* Donovan v. Hotel, Motel & Restaurant Employees and Bartenders Union, Local 19, 700 F.2d 539, 543 n.4 (9th Cir. 1983).

a. The bill as originally introduced in the House or Senate.

b. Amended forms of the bill by the first house.

c. The bill as it passed in the originating body and as introduced into the other house.

d. The bill as amended by the second house.

e. The bill as it is passed by the second house.

f. The bill as amended by a conference committee of the House and Senate.

g. The public law.

2. Committee Reports

After a bill is introduced in either the House or the Senate, it is assigned to one or more committees that have jurisdiction over the bill's subject matter.[7] The committee's task is to consider the bill and to decide whether or not to recommend its passage. If passage is not recommended, or if no action is taken during the Congress in which the bill was introduced, the bill "dies in committee." If the committee recommends passage, it does so in a written committee report that usually sets forth: the revised text of the bill, if any; the changes made in committee; an analysis of the intent and the content of the proposed legislation; and the rationale behind the committee's recommendation.

When the house in which it was first introduced approves the bill, it is sent to the other house and again assigned to an appropriate committee or committees where it receives similar consideration.[8] When both houses pass a bill, but in different versions, a conference committee is convened in order to reconcile the different versions of the bill. The conference committee consists of a group of Representatives and Senators; the activities of the committee are restricted to reconciling differing language in the respective versions of the bill. The conference committee issues a conference committee report, which contains recommendations for reconciling the differences between the two bills and a statement explaining the effect of the actions.

Committee reports are considered to be among the most important documents in determining the legislative intent of Congress because they reflect the understanding of those members of Congress closely involved in studying the subject matter and drafting the proposed legislation.[9] [Illustration 10–1]

---

[7] Committee assignments may be discovered in two ways. First, the initial version of the bill that appears on the *THOMAS* website, http://thomas.loc.gov/home/bills_res.html, contains the committee assignment in the header of the document. In addition, CCH's CONGRESSIONAL INDEX contains a list of all bills introduced in each Congress. This list includes all sponsors of the bill and the bill's initial committee assignments.

[8] After a bill passes one house, it is thereafter referred to as an *act*. An act only becomes a law if it successfully makes its way through the entire legislative process as described in this chapter.

[9] GWENDOLYN B. FOLSOM, LEGISLATIVE HISTORY: RESEARCH FOR THE INTERPRETATION OF LAWS 33 (1972). *See also* Zuber v. Allen, 396 U.S. 168, 186 (1969); Stevenson v. J.C. Penney Co., 464 F. Supp. 945, 948–49 (N.D. Ill. 1979).

The researcher should, therefore, also identify and obtain each of the following documents that exist for the bill under consideration:

a. The reports of the committees of both houses to which the bill was assigned.

b. The report, if any, of the conference committee of the House and Senate. This report is usually issued as a House report.[10]

3. Committee Hearings

Hearings, which may be held by the committees of the House and Senate, are generally of two types. A hearing may be held to investigate matters of general concern, such as AIDS or the use of steroids in athletics. These hearings may or may not result in legislation. The second type of hearings, usually related to proposed legislation, is the more prevalent. These hearings are held after a bill is assigned to a congressional committee.

The primary function of the second type of hearing is to provide committee members with information that may be useful in their consideration of the bill. Interested persons and experts on the subject matter of the bill may be invited or subpoenaed to express their opinions or answer questions about the bill's purpose or effect and may suggest changes or amendments to the bill. In most, but not all, instances, transcripts of the hearings are published. When published, a hearing document contains the transcript of testimony, the questions posed by committee members and the answers provided by witnesses, statements and exhibits submitted by interested parties, and occasionally the text of the bill that is the subject of the hearing.

Hearings are not held on all legislation, nor are all transcripts of hearings published. Moreover, hearings that are pertinent to the intent of a public law may have been held during a session of Congress prior to the one in which the law was enacted. Hearings also might have been held on proposed legislation that contains provisions similar to those of the law being researched. Therefore, it is often useful to extend the search for hearings beyond a particular congressional session or for legislation other than that under consideration. This is especially true if either no hearings were held or if hearings were not published for the legislation being researched.

Committee hearings are technically not part of a legislative history since they do not contain congressional deliberations, but rather, the views of non-legislators. Often senators and members of the House of Representatives may themselves offer testimony. Hearings, therefore, should be consulted when available because they frequently contain information helpful to understanding why Congress adopted or did not adopt certain language.

---

[10] Under the rules of Congress, the conference report is also to be printed as a Senate report. This requirement frequently is waived by the unanimous consent of the Senate. ROBERT B. DOVE, ENACTMENT OF A LAW: PROCEDURAL STEPS IN THE LEGISLATIVE PROCESS, S. DOC. NO. 20, 97th Cong., 1st Sess. (1981). This version of the document is the last one published in print. An updated, electronic version of this publication in html and PDF formats can be found at http://thomas.loc.gov/home/enactment/enactlawtoc.html (1997).

The researcher should identify and obtain each of the following documents, if they exist:

a.   Hearings held by the committees to which the bill was assigned.

b.   Hearings from previous congressional sessions concerning the subject matter of the bill being researched.

c.   Hearings on related bills or bills containing similar provisions that may have been held in prior Congresses and the Congress in question.

4. Congressional Debates

Debate on a bill on the floor of the House or Senate can take place at almost any time during the legislative process, but most frequently the debate occurs after a bill has been reported out of the committee to which it was assigned.[11] During the debates, legislators may propose amendments, argue for and against the bill and its amendments, and discuss and explain ambiguous or controversial provisions. Some authorities claim that floor statements of legislators on the substance of a bill under discussion ought not be considered by courts as determinative of congressional intent.[12] The courts, however, generally do give some weight to such statements, especially when made by the bill's sponsors, whose stated intention is to clarify or explain the bill's purpose.[13] Such statements are published in the *Congressional Record* and are usually included as an integral part of legislative histories.[14]

Therefore, the researcher should identify and obtain the debates, if any, on the floor of both houses of Congress. [Illustration 10–8]

---

[11] Most public laws are passed without ever being debated on the floor of Congress. Usually, only bills of great public interest receive such debate.

[12] As Justice Holmes noted: "We do not inquire what the legislature meant; we ask only what the statute means." Oliver Wendell Holmes, *Theory of Legal Interpretation*, 12 Harv. L. Rev. 417, 419 (1898–99).

[13] S & E Contractors, Inc. v. United States, 406 U.S. 1, 13 n.9 (1972); Federal Energy Admin. v. Algonquin SNG, Inc., 426 U.S. 548, 564 (1976). *But see* State of Ohio v. United States Environmental Protection Agency, 997 F.2d 1520, 1532 (D.C. Cir. 1993); Lori L. Outzs, *A Principled Use of Congressional Floor Speeches in Statutory Interpretation*, 28 Colum. J.L. & Soc. Probs. 297 (1995).

[14] The Congressional Record may not truly reflect what was actually said on the floor of either house of Congress, since members have the right to correct their remarks before publication. Studies have shown that this privilege is generally not abused, as the majority of revisions are syntactical or otherwise within the bounds of propriety. Prior to 1978, members of Congress were allowed to insert remarks into the Congressional Record that were not delivered on the floor of either house without any indication that this was the process followed. Effective March 1, 1978, Congress changed its rules to provide that statements in the Congressional Record were to be identified when no part of them was spoken on the floor of either house of Congress. In such instances, a *bullet* symbol (●) precedes and follows the statement. If, however, any part of a statement was delivered orally, the entire statement appears without the symbol. 124 Cong. Rec. 3852 (1978). Commencing with vol. 132, no. 115, of the Congressional Record (September 8, 1986), the House of Representatives abolished the *bullet* symbol and substituted instead the use of a different style of typeface to indicate material inserted or appended. [Illustration 10–8] The Senate, however, has retained the *bullet* symbol. *See* Joe Morehead, *Into the Hopper: Congress and the Congressional Record: A Magical Mystery Tour*, 13 Serials Libr. 59 (1987). *See also* Donald J. Dunn, *Letter to the Editor*, 14 Gov't Publications Rev. 113 (1987) (updating a part of Michelle M. Springer, *The Congressional Record: "Substantially a Verbatim Report"?*, 13 Gov't Publications Rev. 371 (1986)).

5. Committee Prints

Committee prints are special studies about specific subjects prepared for the use and reference of congressional committees and their staffs. These publications vary in nature, such as bibliographies, analyses of similar bills on a subject, and excerpts from hearings.[15]

The researcher should identify and obtain those committee prints that may have some relation to the legislation under consideration.

6. Presidential or Executive Agency Documents

Occasionally, other documents are relevant to a legislative history but because Congress does not produce these documents, they are not, strictly speaking, sources of legislative intent. These other documents may consist of presidential messages or reports and documents of federal agencies. The president of the United States or members of an executive agency, who usually act through the president, often send proposed legislation to Congress for consideration. Presidential messages or executive agency memoranda may accompany the proposal to Congress. These documents explain the purpose of, and describe the president's or agency's intent in proposing the legislation.[16]

After a bill passes Congress, it is sent to the president. If the president signs or vetoes the legislation, the president may add a signing statement or veto message incorporating the president's rationale for the action taken on the legislation.[17]

[15] Often, only a limited number of committee prints, for the use of the committee members, are printed. Committee prints have recently become more available through the Depository Program, though indexing is often incomplete. All committee prints, from the 105th Congress (1997–98), are available online at http://www.gpoaccess.gov/cprints.

[16] The presidential messages and memoranda are contained in the WEEKLY COMPILATION OF PRESIDENTIAL DOCUMENTS and the PUBLIC PAPERS OF THE PRESIDENT. Occasionally, they may be located as House or Senate documents. Agency memoranda are more difficult to find. They are sometimes transmitted to Congress along with an accompanying communication from the president proposing legislation and may be inserted in congressional hearings. The majority of these documents will not, however, be available in depository collections. The agency may have to be contacted.

[17] The role of presidential signing statements in a legislative history is discussed in Frank B. Cross, *The Constitutional Legitimacy and Significance of Presidential Signing Statements*, 40 ADMIN. L. REV. 209 (1988); Brad Waites, Note, *Let Me Tell You What You Mean: An Analysis of Presidential Signing Statements*, 21 GA. L. REV. 755 (1987); Kathryn M. Dressayer, Note, *The First Word: The President's Place in "Legislative History"*, 89 MICH. L. REV. 399 (1990); William D. Popkin, *Judicial Use of Presidential Legislative History: A Critique*, 66 IND. L.J. 699 (1991); Kristy L. Carroll, Comment, *Whose Statute Is It Anyway?: Why and How Courts Should Use Presidential Signing Statements When Interpreting Federal Statutes*, 46 CATH. U. L. REV. 475 (1997). *See also* Marc N. Garber & Kurt A. Wimmer, *Presidential Signing Statements as Interpretations of Legislative Intent: An Executive Aggrandizement of Power*, 24 HARV. J. ON LEGIS. 363 (1987); Mark R. Killenbeck, *A Matter of Mere Approval? The Role of the President in the Creation of Legislative History*, 48 ARK. L. REV. 239 (1996).

For an excellent discussion of recent usage of presidential signing statements, see Charlie Savage, "Bush Challenges Hundreds of Laws," BOSTON GLOBE, April 30, 2006. The article has been available at the GLOBE website at http://www.boston.com/news/nation/articles/2006/04/30/bush_challenges_hundreds_of_laws/.

See also Note, *Context–Sensitive Deference to Presidential Signing Statements*, 20 HARV. L. REV. 597 (2006). In 2006 the American Bar Association created a Task Force on Presidential

The researcher needs to identify and obtain each of the following presidential documents:

a. Presidential or executive agency reports accompanying proposed legislation sent to Congress by the president.

b. Presidential signing statements or veto messages.

7. Blogs and Podcasts

Both major parties, as well as individual legislators, lobbyists, think tanks, political action committees, and influential commentators use blogs and podcasts to discuss policy positions and to describe, comment upon, criticize and support various legislative initiatives.[18] Blogs and podcasts can be revealing sources of information about the intent and meaning behind various legislative initiatives. Blogs may be most easily found by using a Web search engine such as *Google*. Podcasts may be easily found in the same manner or by using a podcast aggregator such as *iTunes*, the largest single source of links to political podcasts.

SECTION C. CHART: DOCUMENTS OF FEDERAL LEGISLATIVE HISTORIES

The documents that may be created during the legislative process that may be relevant to a federal legislative history are identified in the following chart.

Signing Statements & the Separation of Powers Doctrine. The task force's recommendations can be found at http://www.abanet.org/op/signingstatements/.

[18] For an example of a senator's blog, see http://dodd.senate.gov/index.php?q=blog/1.

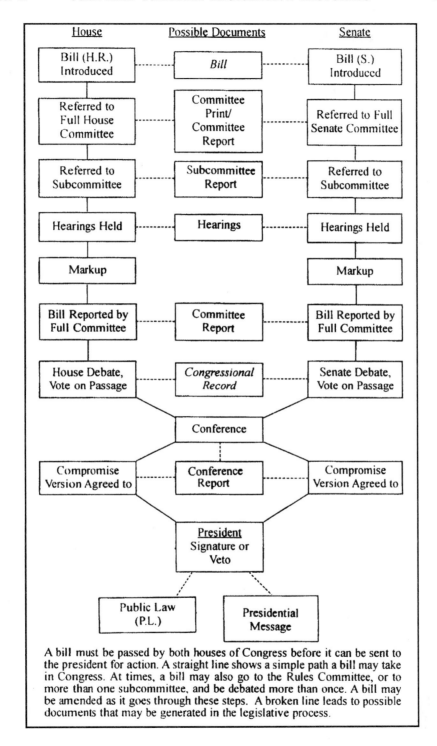

House	Possible Documents	Senate
Bill (H.R.) Introduced	*Bill*	Bill (S.) Introduced
Referred to Full House Committee	Committee Print/ Committee Report	Referred to Full Senate Committee
Referred to Subcommittee	Subcommittee Report	Referred to Subcommittee
Hearings Held	Hearings	Hearings Held
Markup		Markup
Bill Reported by Full Committee	Committee Report	Bill Reported by Full Committee
House Debate, Vote on Passage	*Congressional Record*	Senate Debate, Vote on Passage

Conference

| Compromise Version Agreed to | Conference Report | Compromise Version Agreed to |

President
Signature or Veto

| Public Law (P.L.) | Presidential Message |

A bill must be passed by both houses of Congress before it can be sent to the president for action. A straight line shows a simple path a bill may take in Congress. At times, a bill may also go to the Rules Committee, or to more than one subcommittee, and be debated more than once. A bill may be amended as it goes through these steps. A broken line leads to possible documents that may be generated in the legislative process.

SECTION D.   COMPILED FEDERAL LEGISLATIVE HISTORIES

Identifying and then locating the various documents that are needed for a legislative history can be time-consuming and laborious. For some laws, legislative histories have been compiled and published. Using compiled legislative histories may save considerable time and effort.

This section is divided into two parts. The first lists sources of compiled legislative histories for specific laws. The compiled legislative histories that are listed in these sources identify the specific documents of the legislative history and in some cases provide those documents. The second part of this section identifies sources of compiled legislative histories with the relevant documents.

1. Listings of Compiled Legislative Histories

The following sources indicate whether a compiled legislative history might exist for a specific law. These sources do not contain the text of the documents comprising a legislative history.

a. *Sources of Compiled Legislative Histories: A Bibliography of Government Documents, Periodical Articles, and Books.*[19] This resource, available both in print as a looseleaf service and on *HeinOnline* in its U.S. Federal Legislative History Library, provides references to print and electronic sources that contain compiled legislative histories for major laws. Its definition of a compiled legislative history is the collection in one place of "either the texts of legislative documents pertaining to a statute or citations to the necessary legislative documents."[20] Coverage begins with the first Congress in 1789. Its checklist, which is arranged chronologically by Congress and then by public law number, indicates which legislative documents are contained or referenced in the publication or electronic service listed. Indexes provide access by author and title and by name of the public law.

b. *Union List of Legislative Histories.*[21] This publication, compiled by the Law Librarians' Society of Washington, D.C., Legislative Research Special Interest Section, provides information on compiled legislative histories commercially produced or compiled in-house by librarians in the Washington, D.C. area and held by the law libraries in that region. Supplemented in 2002, the list's coverage is from the 1st Congress through the 107th Congress, 2002.

c. *Monthly Catalog of United States Government Publications.* This comprehensive index to publications of the federal government provides information on legislative histories compiled by agencies of the federal government. The print version of this publication was discontinued in December 2004. It is now available electronically at the Government Printing Office website as the *Catalog of U.S. Government Publications.*[22]

---

[19] Nancy P. Johnson, Sources of Compiled Legislative Histories: A Bibliography of Government Documents, Periodical Articles, and Books (AALL Publication Series, No. 14, 1979) (updated periodically).

[20] *Id.* at i.

[21] (Law Librarians' Society of Washington, D.C., Inc. 2000; Supp. 2002). *See also* Kevin P. Gray, Legislative History Union List (Chicago Association of Law Libraries 2001).

[22] The Monthly Catalog of United States Government Publications is available electronically from July 1976 at http://catalog.gpo.gov. Listed documents that are available electronically contain a hot link within the citation to allow direct access.

d. *Federal Legislative Histories: An Annotated Bibliography and Index to Officially Published Sources* (1994). Compiled by Bernard D. Reams, Jr., the 255 entries in this annotated bibliography cover congressional, executive agency, and special commission sources published from 1862 through 1990. The annotations describe the types of documentation in a work, contain notes about citations and paginations of original documents, and refer to the location of texts in *United States Statutes at Large*. It includes numerous indexes.

e. *HeinOnline*'s U.S. Federal Legislative History Title Collection. This database in *HeinOnline*'s U.S. Federal Legislative History Library contains the full-text of, as of this writing, approximately 75 compiled legislative histories collected from many different sources, including individuals, law firms and federal agencies. Also included is a well known, but out of print work by Eugene Nabors, *Legislative Reference Checklist: The Key to Legislative Histories from 1789–1903* (Fred B. Rothman 1982).

2. Sources of Compiled Legislative Histories

The sources described below list, identify, or cite to documents that are generated as a bill travels through Congress and in many cases reproduce the documents themselves, either in print, microform, or an electronic format.

a. *Congressional Information Service, Inc. (CIS)*. This publication, commencing in 1970, has simplified the method of compiling a federal legislative history. CIS provides indexes to locate legislation where some action has occurred after the introduction of a bill. Abstracts are provided that give a brief synopsis of the document resulting from a specific step in the progress of the bill. If the bill is enacted as a public law, this set provides a compiled legislative history by giving citations to the documents comprising the legislative history. A companion microfiche component reproduces many of the documents needed to determine the intent of the public law.

LexisNexis Congressional, a Web-based service, provides an electronic version of the *CIS Index/Abstracts* and online access to some documents in the CIS microfiche collection.[23]

---

[23] The base edition of *LexisNexis Congressional* (formerly known as *Congressional Universe*) provides access to: index/abstracts for documents, prints, reports and published hearings, 1970–present; legislative histories, 1969–present; committee hearings, selected transcripts, and full-text statements, 1988–present; committee prints, selected full text, 1993–2004; committee reports full text, 1990–present; House and Senate documents (electronic versions) full text, 1995–present; GAO report abstracts, 2004–present; CONGRESSIONAL RECORD daily edition, 1985–present; bill texts and tracking, 1989–present; public law texts, 1988–present; U.S. CODE; CODE OF FEDERAL REGULATIONS, 1981–present; FEDERAL REGISTER, 1980–present; campaign finance data, 1987–present; key votes data, 1987–present; member financial disclosures, profiles, and voting records; political news; hot bills and hot topics; committee rosters and schedules. There are two optional modules to *LexisNexis Congressional*: (1) Historical Indexes, 1789–1984 (*e.g.*, the CIS U.S. Serial Set Index (1789–1969)); U.S. Congressional Hearings Index (1834–1969); Unpublished House Committee Hearings Index (1833–1972); Unpublished Senate Committee Hearings Index (1824–1984); U.S. Congressional Committee Prints Index (1830–1969); and U.S. Senate Executive Documents & Reports Index (1817–1969). (2) U.S. STATUTES AT LARGE, 1789–present. LexisNexis also produces several large digital collections of congressional documents that are described in Section H of this chapter.

For legislation enacted since 1970, the CIS print, microfiche, and Web-based services are the quickest and most efficient method of locating citations to, and the full-text of, many of the documents that comprise a legislative history. The frequency of publication, thoroughness of the indexing, citation to all relevant documents, and the availability of microfiche or electronic access to the full-text of many documents make this an invaluable source. The components of the set are described below.

(1) *CIS/Index.* This monthly component consists of two parts, an abstract and an index pamphlet. The abstract pamphlet of the *CIS/Index* contains entries that briefly describe the format and scope of the hearings, reports, committee prints, and other congressional publications, such as House and Senate documents, included in the *Index.* For hearings, the abstract provides not only a synopsis of the testimony but also the name, affiliation, and perspective of the witness. The abstract pamphlet to the *CIS/Index* is cumulated annually as the *CIS Annual/Abstracts.*

The index pamphlet contains detailed indexes by subject, title, bill, report, document, hearing, and print number. Each index entry includes an accession number that references a specific publication in the abstract volume. [Illustration 10–3] The index pamphlet of the *CIS/Index* is cumulated quarterly and annually, and the *CIS Annual Index* is cumulated every four years.

LexisNexis Congressional parallels this coverage by providing the index and abstracts for committee hearings, reports, documents, and prints from 1970 to the present.

(2) *Legislative Histories of U.S. Public Laws.* From 1970 to 1983, each CIS Annual volume contained a section on legislative histories for public laws passed during the year. Starting in 1984, this section became a separate volume, *Legislative Histories of U.S. Public Laws.* Each public law is listed and citations are given to the bill number, committee reports, hearings, *Congressional Record,* and other documents that may be relevant to a legislative history. Through the use of indexes and the annual *Legislative Histories of U.S. Public Laws,* references to public laws can be found by the popular name or title of a law, by the subject matter of the law, or by bill number.

The *Legislative History* volumes contain histories in two formats. For laws identified as major legislation (based on the criterion that the law may be the subject of litigation in which interpretation of its provisions may be important), the citations to congressional committee publications also include the CIS abstracts. Additional citations are provided to all relevant bills and debates. [Illustration 10–2] Both formats provide citations to presidential signing statements or veto messages.

For laws not classified as major legislation, entries do not include the full abstracts but, instead, references to the abstracts. Related bills are not cited, and debate citations are limited to those provided from the slip law.[24]

LexisNexis Congressional also provides this information through its legislative history section (1969 to present). Starting in 1969, it includes

---

[24] Slip laws are discussed in Section E–1 of this chapter and in Section B–1 of Chapter 9.

"abbreviated" legislative histories. From 1999, *Congressional Universe* includes full legislative histories for all public laws.

(3) *CIS/Microfiche Library,* 1970 to present. For bills that have become public laws, this component provides a microfiche reprint of the bills, hearings, reports, committee prints, and congressional documents related to the enacted legislation.

b. *LexisNexis. LexisNexis* provides legislative histories for selected bankruptcy, estate, tax, securities, environmental, and banking statutes and for appropriation laws for various agencies. The documents included vary with each legislative history.

c. *United States Code Congressional and Administrative News (USCCAN).* In addition to the tables in the *United States Code Congressional and Administrative News* discussed below, *USCCAN* contains a finding aid list and the text of some documents relevant to a federal legislative history.

This set is published by West, and is issued in monthly pamphlets during each session of Congress. After each session of Congress, the monthly pamphlets are reissued in bound volumes. All public laws for each session of Congress are included; a separate volume sets forth legislative histories.

Immediately before the reprint of the selected committee reports and other documents, if applicable, *USCCAN*'s legislative history section provides researchers with citations to all committee and conference reports, references to the dates of consideration and passage of the bill in both houses, and citations to any presidential signing statements. [Illustration 10–1]

Prior to the 99th Congress (1985–86), *USCCAN* usually printed only a House report or a Senate report. Starting with the 99th Congress, it also included any statement that the president made upon signing the law. *USCCAN* has recently included joint explanatory statements and statements by legislative leaders for laws that the editors view as major legislation. These statements often contain citations to the *Congressional Record.*

USCCAN is available in many law libraries and provides a simple method of obtaining one of the most important documents of a legislative history, the committee report.

d. *Westlaw. Westlaw*'s "Legislative History—U.S. Code" file in its "U.S. Federal Materials" library contains all legislative history published in *USCCAN* from 1948 through 1989. Beginning in January 1990, the Legislative History file contains the full-text of all congressional reports, including those for bills that did not become law. *Westlaw* contains selective legislative histories, prepared by the law firm of Arnold & Porter, for major public laws. Examples of areas covered are pensions, environment, banking, bankruptcy, and securities. The documents included vary with each legislative history. *Westlaw* also will be adding legislative histories that were compiled by the General Accounting Office (see next entry).

e. *GAO Legislative History Collection.* This is an outstanding collection of legislative histories compiled by what was the General Accounting

Office, now the Government Accountability Office. The GAO began compiling legislative histories for departmental use in 1921, and over the years has compiled over 20,000 histories in hard copy. In 1990, the GAO contracted with the Remac Information Corporation to create a microfiche collection of the entire set. Remac produced microfiche copies of about half of the set (67th through 96th Congresses; 1921–1980) when publication ceased. There was a very limited distribution of the microfiche set. The GAO continued to compile legislative histories through the 104th Congress, 1st session, 1995. There are plans to digitize the entire set and make it available on *Westlaw*.

f. *Public Laws, Legislative Histories.*[25] From the 96th Congress through the 100th Congress, this microfiche set made available the House and Senate bill as introduced, the reported House bill, Senate bill, or both, committee reports, conference reports, if any, committee prints, slip laws, and relevant legislative debate as reported in the *Congressional Record.* All enactments are indexed by subject, public law number, and bill number. This set includes a compiled legislative history for every public law.

g. *Looseleaf Services, Treatises, and Other Compiled Legislative Histories.* Many looseleaf services and treatises dealing with specific areas of the law, e.g., securities, tax, and labor, may contain compiled legislative histories for laws related to their subject. Other publications may have as their sole purpose the compilation of a federal legislative history.

h. *CQ.com On Congress.* This web-based service of Congressional Quarterly includes the text of bills, committee reports, the *Congressional Record*, and testimony. Supplementary information is provided, including citations to articles discussing a bill in selected commercial publications.

SECTION E.   IDENTIFYING THE DOCUMENTS OF A LEGISLATIVE HISTORY (IF A COMPILED LEGISLATIVE HISTORY IS NOT AVAILABLE)

If a compiled legislative history cannot be located, or if information is needed about a legislative bill that has not been enacted as law, researchers will need to identify the materials that were created as the bill worked its way through the legislative process.

The first step in this process is to create a list of documents related to the public law, the legislation that was not enacted, or the pending bill. The sources described below provide information, references, or citations to the documents typically generated during the legislative process.

1.   Slip Laws/United States Statutes at Large

Since 1975, there is a legislative summary at the end of each slip law. It provides citations to the bill that became the public law, to the committee reports, to the dates of consideration and passage of the bill by both houses of Congress, and to presidential statements, if any. Although the slip laws provide the volume number of the *Congressional Record* for dates of consideration and passage of the bill, there are no page references. When

---

[25] Commerce Clearing House published this set, which covered 1979–1988. It ceased publication in 1988.

the slip laws are compiled in *United States Statutes at Large*, this information is retained. [Illustration 10–7]

From 1963 to 1974, *United States Statutes at Large* contains a Guide to Legislative History of Bills Enacted into Public Law. The Guide includes the references now provided at the end of the slip law, except that references to presidential statements were first included in 1971 for the 91st Congress, 2d Session.

Each slip law sets forth the number of the bill that eventually was enacted and reprinted in the slip law. Since the 58th Congress in 1903, each public law reprinted in *United States Statutes at Large* references its corresponding original bill number.[26]

2. United States Code Congressional and Administrative News (USCCAN)

The monthly pamphlets of *USCCAN* contain a Legislative History Table that provides information on bills that have become public laws. The tables are cumulated in the annual bound volume. These legislative history tables, which are arranged by public law number, provide citations to *United States Statutes at Large,* bill number and committee reports, and references to dates of consideration and passage of the bill. The information provided for committee reports includes committee report numbers and abbreviated references to the committees of the House and Senate, and the conference committee, if any. For dates of consideration and passage of the bill, *USCCAN* references the volume of the *Congressional Record*, along with the dates when the House and Senate took these actions.

3. Congressional Record

Although this publication is discussed in detail later in this chapter, several features are highlighted here because of their usefulness for identifying documents that are part of federal legislative histories.

(a) *History of Bills and Resolutions.*[27] The *History of Bills and Resolutions* is a section of the bi-weekly index to the daily edition of the *Congressional Record*. This section is divided by chamber and arranged by bill number. It includes a brief digest of the legislation, the name of the sponsor, and the committee to which the legislation was referred. Also included are references to debates, committee reports, and dates of passage. Page references are provided to the daily *Congressional Record* where the activity is reported. [Illustration 10–5] Although this section covers only bills acted upon during the two weeks covered by the index, coverage for any bill so included is complete back to the date of the bill's introduction. A cumulative "History of Bills and Resolutions" for each session of Congress is a part of the annual Index to the bound set of the *Congressional Record*.

---

[26] Bill numbers for laws passed prior to 1903 can be located in EUGENE NABORS, LEGISLATIVE REFERENCE CHECKLIST: THE KEY TO LEGISLATIVE HISTORIES FROM 1789–1903 (1982).

[27] *History of Bills Online* available via *GPO Access*, at http://www.gpoaccess.gov/hob, provides the same information as the print version. The online coverage begins with volume 129 of the CONGRESSIONAL RECORD, in 1983. Coverage for the current session is updated daily.

GPO Access provides access to this information on its website, under the category History of Bills.[28]

(b) *History of Bills Enacted into Public Law.* This table appears in the annual Daily Digest volume of the bound *Congressional Record.* It includes the same information as does the *History of Bills and Resolutions,* except that it does not include entries for sponsors or debates. As its name implies, this table only covers bills that have become public laws.

Both history tables in the *Congressional Record* provide citations to bill numbers. The history table in the bi-weekly index provides information on pending bills, on bills that did not become public law, and on bills that were enacted into public law.

(c) *THOMAS. THOMAS,* a website maintained by the Library of Congress, contains a database called *Bill Summary & Status (BSS)* that provides a short description of the activity on a bill and links to detailed information about the bill's progress through Congress, including references to floor actions, *Congressional Record* page references, the text of the bill, sponsors, the CRS summary, and Congressional Budget Office cost estimates. *BSS* coverage begins with the 93d Congress, 1973–1974.[29]

4. Congressional Index

This two-volume looseleaf service, published by Commerce Clearing House, (CCH), is updated weekly while Congress is in session and for several weeks thereafter until all public bills and resolutions sent to the president have been acted upon. New volumes are issued for each Congress.

A digest indicates the contents of each bill introduced in Congress. There are status tables for pending bills in the Senate and in the House. The status tables set forth actions taken on the bill and provide committee report numbers and, most importantly, note if hearings were held and on what dates. [Illustration 10–4]

Subject and sponsor indexes are provided for bills and public laws. An Enactment—Vetoes section contains tables by public law number, by bill number, by the name of the law, and by author of the law, as well as a list of vetoes. The *Congressional Index* also contains a table of companion bills, tables of voting records of congressional members by bill and resolution number, and a list of treaties, reorganization plans, and pending nominations.

Because of its weekly supplementation, the *Congressional Index* is an excellent source for obtaining information about pending and enacted legislation. Older volumes can be consulted to gather information on bills that failed enactment.

5. House and Senate Calendars

The calendars chronicle the activity of bills as they travel through Congress. These calendars provide bill numbers and can be used to trace action on pending legislation, public laws, and bills that did not become law.

---

[28] http://www.gpoaccess.gov/hob/index.html.

[29] The *Bill Summary & Status* database can be found at http://thomas.loc.gov/bss.

(a) *Calendars of the United States House of Representatives and History of Legislation.*[30] This is the "calendar" of the House of Representatives, but it actually consists of five calendars to which House bills may be assigned. It is printed each day the House is in session. Although the title refers only to the House, it serves as an index to all legislation that has been reported by the committees and acted upon by either or both chambers. Senate resolutions not of interest to the House and special House reports are excluded.

Each issue of the calendars is cumulative. A subject index for both House and Senate legislation reported by a committee and acted upon by either or both of the chambers is printed in the calendars on the first legislative day of the week that the House is in session. It does not list hearings and debates comprehensively.

The section of the calendars entitled "History of Bills and Resolutions: Numerical Order of Bills and Resolutions Which Have Been Reported to or Considered by Either or Both Houses," divides the pending legislation by chamber and then again by the form of legislation. It provides the current status and legislative history of all activity on each piece of legislation on which some action has been taken. Information on hearings is not provided. Entries are arranged by bill or resolution number.

(b) *Senate Calendar of Business.*[31] This calendar is less useful for tracing the current status of Senate legislation because it is not cumulative and has no index. However, a General Orders section covers all Senate legislation by bill number, title, and report number.

6. House and Senate Journals

The House and Senate journals, unlike the *Congressional Record,* are constitutionally mandated and are the official records for the proceedings of Congress. Both journals are published at the end of each session; they have subject indexes and History of Bills and Resolutions sections. The *House Journal* is available on the *GPO Access* website.[32] Historical collections of both the House and Senate journals from 1789 to 1875 are available on the Library of Congress website.[33]

7. Digest of Public General Bills and Resolutions

The *Digest of Public General Bills and Resolutions* was published by the Congressional Research Service (CRS) of the Library of Congress from 1936 until the 102d Congress in 1990. Accordingly, this resource is helpful for historical research. The *Digest* provides information on bills enacted into public law, bills that were pending, and bills not enacted as public

---

[30] The HOUSE CALENDAR from the 104th Congress to the present can be found at http://www.gpoaccess.gov/calendars/house/index.html.

[31] The SENATE CALENDAR from the 104th Congress to the present can be found at http://www.gpoaccess.gov/calendars/senate/index.html.

[32] The HOUSE JOURNAL may be found at http://www.gpoaccess.gov/hjournal; coverage is from 1991 through 1999. The SENATE JOURNAL is not available on this site.

[33] *See* http://memory.loc.gov/ammem/amlaw/lwhj.html (House) and http://memory.loc.gov/ammem/amlaw/lwsj.html (Senate).

laws. The *Digest*, issued annually in two volumes, is divided into three parts.

The first part summarizes the provisions of the legislation on which some action occurred after the bill was introduced. This part is further divided into "Public Laws" and "Other Measures Receiving Action." The "Public Laws" section includes digests and legislative histories of enacted laws. The "Other Measures" section discusses current bills with their legislative histories.

The second part includes digests of bills and resolutions where no action was taken after the measure was introduced and assigned to a committee. Indexes by sponsor and co-sponsor, short title, subject, and identical bills comprise the third part.

8.   LexisNexis Congressional Digital Collections

Researchers with access to one or more components of the *LexisNexis Congressional* digital backfiles will find them extremely useful for identifying and retrieving legislative history materials.[34] The full text of the documents in these collections is fully searchable, making it possible to identify documents by bill, public law, sponsor, subject, citation, and many other descriptors.

SECTION F.   ILLUSTRATIONS: IDENTIFYING DOCUMENTS

Compiling Legislative History for H.R. 457, 106th Cong., 1st Sess.

10–1.   **Pages from 1999 USCCAN Legislative History Volume Showing Legislative History Listing for Pub. L. No. 106–56 and Senate Report No. 106–143**

10–2.   **Page from 1999 CIS/Annual Legislative Histories Volume for Pub. L. No. 106–56**

10–3.   **Page from 1999 CIS/Index**

10–4.   **Page from House Status Table from Congressional Index (CCH)**

10–5.   **Page from 1999 Congressional Record Bi–Weekly Index**

---

[34] The components of the LexisNexis Digital Collections are: *Congressional Hearings Digital Collection*; *Congressional Record Permanent Digital Collection*; *U.S. Serial Set Digital Collection*; and *Congressional Research Digital Collection*. These collections are also discussed in Section H of this chapter.

[Illustration 10–1]

PAGES FROM 1999 USCCAN LEGISLATIVE HISTORY VOLUME SHOWING LEGISLATIVE HISTORY LISTING FOR PUB. L. NO. 106–56 AND SENATE REPORT NO. 106–143

ORGAN DONOR LEAVE ACT

PUBLIC LAW 106-56, see page 113 Stat. 407

⟶ **DATES OF CONSIDERATION AND PASSAGE**

House: July 26, 1999

Senate: September 8, 1999

Cong. Record Vol. 145 (1999)

**House Report (Government Reform Committee)
No. 106-174, June 8, 1999
[To accompany H.R. 457]**

⟶ **Senate Report (Governmental Affairs Committee)
No. 106-143, September 8, 1999
[To accompany H.R. 457]**

The Senate Report is set out below.

ORGAN DONOR LEAVE ACT OF 1999

* * * * * * * *

I. PURPOSE AND SUMMARY

The purpose of H.R. 457, the Organ Donor Leave Act of 1999, is to provide federal employees with paid leave not exceeding 30 days in any calendar year to serve as an

---

Legislative histories are included in a separate section or volume of *USCCAN*. This is the first page of the legislative history of Pub. L. No. 106-56. Notice how, at the top of the page, reference is made to committee reports and to the dates of consideration and passage.

While *USCCAN* is useful and widely available, it does not set forth the text of all documents of a legislative history. *USCCAN* reprints the House or Senate report and the conference report, if any. Since 1986, it includes the text of presidential signing statements. See next page of illustration.

The Federal Government, the nation's largest employer, should lead by example and make it easier for Federal employees to become donors.

[page 2]

73

[Illustration 10–1 cont'd]

PAGES FROM 1999 USCCAN LEGISLATIVE HISTORY VOLUME SHOWING PRESIDENTIAL SIGNING STATEMENT FOR H.R. 457

ORGAN DONOR LEAVE ACT

PUBLIC LAW 106-56

For text of Act see page 113 Stat. 407

⟶ **STATEMENT BY PRESIDENT OF THE UNITED STATES**

STATEMENT BY PRESIDENT WILLIAM J. CLINTON UPON SIGNING H.R. 457

34 Weekly Compilation of Presidential Documents 1817,
September 24, 1999

Today, I am pleased to sign into law H.R. 457, the "Organ Donor Leave Act," which would enhance the Federal Government's leadership role in encouraging organ donations by making it easier for Federal employees to become donors.

Currently, more than 65,000 Americans are awaiting an organ transplant. Last year, almost 5,000 Americans died while waiting for an organ to become available. This amounts to an average of 13 citizens each day. Many of these deaths could have been prevented if t̶ ┌───┐ ple tool to help address │ **When the president signs a piece of legislation, the** │ ations by Federal emplo │ **president may add a signing statement, such as this one,** │ │ **incorporating the reasons for signing the legislation.** │ └───┘

In 1997, my Administration launched the National Organ and Tissue Donation Initiative, which included new efforts by the Federal Government to increase awareness among Federal employees of the need for organ and tissue donation. The Department of Health and Human Services, in partnership with the Office of Personnel Management, has implemented a Government-wide campaign to encourage Federal employees to consider organ donation and, as the country's largest employer, to set the example for the private sector as well as other public organizations.

H.R. 457 builds on my Administration's long-standing commitment to increasing organ donations nationwide. Under current law, a Federal employee may use up to 7 days of paid leave each year, other than sick leave or annual leave, to serve as a donor. Recent surveys of doctors and hospitals indicate that the current 7-day limit is clearly insufficient for recovery from organ donation surgery. This bill increases the amount of paid leave available to Federal employees who donate organs for transplants, providing up to 30 days of paid leave, in addition to annual and sick leave, for organ donation.

In addition to our current efforts, my Administration will go forward in the coming weeks with the framework for an organ allocation system that will serve patients better. Our approach, which has been validated by the Institute of Medicine, calls for improved allocation policies to be designed by transplant professionals, not by the Government, and

[Illustration 10–2]

PAGE FROM 1999 CIS/ANNUAL LEGISLATIVE HISTORIES VOLUME FOR PUB. L. NO. 106–56

Public Law 106-56   **113 Stat. 407**

Organ Donor Leave Act

September 24, 1999

Public Law

1.1   Public Law 106-56, approved Sept. 24, 1999. (H.R. 457)

(CIS99:PL106-56   1 p.)

"To amend title 5, United States Code, to increase the amount of leave time available to a Federal employee in any year in connection with serving as an organ donor, and for other purposes."
Increases the amount of paid leave time available to Federal employees who serve as organ donors.

P.L. 106-56 Reports ← (1)

106th Congress

2.1   H. Rpt. 106-174 on H.R. 457, "Organ Donor Leave Act," June 8, 1999.

(CIS99:H403-20   5 p.)
(Y1.1/8:106-174.)

(2)

Recommends passage of H.R. 457, the Organ Donor Leave Act, to increase the amount of paid leave time available to Federal employees who serves organ donors.

2.2   S. Rpt. 106-143 on H.R. 457, "Organ Donor Leave Act," Aug. 27, 1999.

(CIS99:S403-10   iii + 4 p.)
(Y1.1/5:106-143.)

Recommends passage of H.R. 457, the Organ Donor Leave Act, to increase the amount of paid leave time available to Federal employees who serve as organ donors.
H.R. 457 is related to S. 1334.

P.L. 106-56 Bills

106th Congress

ENACTED BILL

3.1   H.R. 457 as introduced Feb. 2, 1999; as reported by the House Government Reform Committee June 8, 1999; as passed by the House July 26, 1999; as reported by the Senate Governmental Affairs Committee Aug. 27, 1999.

96   CIS/INDEX Legislative Histories

---

(3)   COMPANION BILL ← (3)

3.2   S. 1334 as introduced.

P.L. 106-56 Debate ← (4)

145 Congressional Record
106th Congress, 1st Session - 1999

4.1   July 26, House consideration and passage of H.R. 457, p. H6360.

4.2   Sept. 8, Senate consideration and passage of H.R. 457, p. S10637.

P.L. 106-56 Miscellaneous   (6)

8.1   Weekly Compilation of Presidential Documents, Vol.

This page is from *CIS Legislative Histories* volume for Pub. L. 106-56. CIS does not reproduce in full the various documents that are part of a legislative history. Rather, it only provides abstracts with full citations to the actual documents. The set is especially useful because it cites all relevant congressional documents for each public law.

CIS gives the following information either in abstract or citation, to:

1. all House, Senate, and conference reports issued that are related to the public laws;

2. the bill that was enacted and companion bills;

3. debates on bills in the *Congressional Record*;

4. all hearings held on or related to the public law;

5. presidential messages; and

6. committee prints.

[Illustration 10–3]

PAGE FROM 1999 CIS/INDEX

Index of Subjects and Names

Oster, Clinton V., Jr.

Organ Donor Leave Act
Organ donation by Fed employees, leave time increase, H403–20, S403–10, PL106–56

Organ Procurement and Transplantation Network Amendments
Organ donation and transplant program, extension and revision, H273–23

Organ transplants
see Medical implants and transplants

Organisation for Economic Cooperation and Development
"Maintaining Prosperity in an Ageing Society", S141–3.2
Unemployment intl trends and implications, review, J842–10

Organization for Economic Cooperation and Development
Foreign investment nondiscriminatory treatment, Organization for Economic Cooperation and Dev agreement, issues review, H461–57
Foreign officials bribery, intl convention implementation, H271–39
Shipbuilding intl trade agreement approval and implementation, S261–5

Organization for Interi
Income tax treatment and multinatl corpo income, revision, S

Organization for Secur Europe
Belarus human rights political devs, review, J891–9
Europe political devs and human rights issues, Commission on Security and Cooperation in Europe newsletter, J892–9, J892–14, J892–19, J892–21, J892–27
Helsinki Agreement human rights commitments implementation, Warsaw meeting rpt, J892–6
Human rights protection, field missions role, Organization for Security and Cooperation in Europe seminar rpt, J892–28
Turkey human rights conditions; Organization for Security and Cooperation in Europe 1999 summit in Turkey, J891–7

Organization Resources Counselors
Occupational health and safety programs revision, H341–99.2

Organizations of Academic Family Medicine
DOL, HHS, and Educ Dept programs, FY2000 approp, H181–66.4

Organized crime
Bosnia-Herzegovina peace efforts status rpt, Pres communic, H460–7
Bosnia-Herzegovina peace efforts status rpt, Pres message, H460–41
Cocaine trafficking organization ops in NYC, H521–33
Colombia drug traffickers property in US, access and transactions prohibition extension, Pres message, H460–54
Colombia economic sanctions status rpt, Pres message, H460–20, H460–55
Drug abuse problem in central Fla and treatment and prevention strategies review, H401–73.2
Drug control efforts in Caribbean area and Latin Amer, H461–65.2
"Drug Kingpins Moved Millions as N.J. Lawmakers Stood By", H241–6
Drug money laundering through Colombia peso brokers, S961–23

Drug trafficking from Mexico into US, law enforcement cooperation review, H401–5.2, S961–16.1
Drug trafficking interdiction efforts in Caribbean area and Fla, S961–13.3
FBI programs, FY2000 approp, H181–70.2, S181–40.5
FBI programs, FY99 approp, S181–3.3
Foreign drug traffickers property in US, access and transactions prohibition estab, H433–3, PL106–120
Intl crime, FBI programs review, S181–14.3
Intl crime informants visa program, extension, PL106–104
Justice Dept Organized Crime Drug Enforcement Task Force programs, FY2000 approp, H181–70.3
Labor union members democratic rights, impediments review, H341–128
Natl security threats to US from Russia, issues review, H571–3.1
Nigerian organized crime groups, activities review, H461–18
Teamsters union expenditures and 1996 election rerun, Fed monitoring activities, H341–46
Teamsters union financial transactions, review, H341–49, H341–59

involvement, H341–47
Teamsters union 1996 election investigation, H342–2, H342–3
Teamsters union 1996 election rerun, Fed oversight, H341–57, H341–100
Teamsters union 1996 election rerun, funding issues, H341–40
Trafficking of persons, prevention and victim protection program estab, H463–12

Organized Crime Control Act
see also Racketeer Influenced and Corrupt Organizations Act

Organized labor
see Labor unions

O'Riley, Paloma
Year 2000 computer problems, consumer implications, H701–22.1

Orlando, Fla.
Solar-powered car race opening ceremonies, US Capitol grounds use, H753–17

Orlando, James E.
Airline and airport security issues and improvement strategies review, H751–17.1

Ornelas, Leroy
Milk mktg order program revision, H161–35.3

Ornish, Dean M.
Complementary and alternative medicine, issues review, H401–58.2, H401–58.3

O'Rourke, Mary
Elem and secondary educ aid programs, extension and revision, S431–23.2

Orphan Medical, Inc.
Drugs used to facilitate sexual assaults, review, H271–49.4

Orr, Clair
Elem and secondary educ improvement strategies review, H341–45.2

Orr, Kevyn D.
Bankruptcy laws applicable to individual and commercial debtors, revision, H521–69.3

Orr, Mark Z.
Trade agreements compliance by foreign countries, monitoring and enforcement issues, review, S361–38.2

Orr, Scott J.
Global climate change intl treaty, economic implications for US, H401–37.8
Small business compliance with environmental regulations, Fed assistance programs, S721–1.1

Orr, Stephen A.
Mining on public lands, laws revision, S311–5.3

Orsello, William
Mont reservoir land conveyance, S321–4.1

Orser, Oakley
Bankruptcy laws applicable to individual debtors, revision, S241–25.1

Orszag, Jonathan M.
Indian economic dev programs estab, S411–24.1

Orszag, Peter R.
Social security reform, implications of ... ystems, H781–54.6

... ed by land grants from ... rocedures estab,

... gis and Musculoskeletal and Skin Diseases programs, FY2000 approp, H181–39.8

Ortiz, Solomon P.
Judgeship nominations, S521–14.6

Orton Dyslexia Society
"Informed Instruction for Reading Success: Foundations for Teacher Preparation", H341–66.4

Orton, William T.
Legis br programs, FY2000 approp, H181–12.12

Orum, Paul
Toxic substances airborne release risk mgmt program, EPA info dissemination issues, H271–46.3
Toxic substances airborne release risk mgmt program, EPA info dissemination regulations estab, H271–62.2

Osage County, Okla.
Okla lands conveyance, H751–16

Oscar, Kenneth J.
Army procurement and R&D programs, FY99 authorization, H571–12.3

OSHA/DOE/Argonne Pilot Partnership on External Regulation of Worker Safety
"Core Group Report", H701–12.1

O'Shea, Kevin
Estate tax rules revision, H721–30.2

Osman, Ronald E.
Medicare fraud by insurance cos in contracts admin, review and prevention efforts, H271–109.3

Osteoporosis
Age-related disability and chronic disease effects, prevention, and research status, S141–19.1
Osteoporosis research, prevention, and treatment advances review, S181–24

Oster, Clinton V., Jr.
Airline industry competition issues, H751–6.7

> In the 1999 *CIS/Index*, the Index of Subjects and Names, one can locate references under the title of Public Law No.106-56.

[Illustration 10–4]

PAGE FROM HOUSE STATUS TABLE FROM CONGRESSIONAL INDEX (CCH)

35,010 **Status of House Bills** ◄ 101 1-5-2001
See also Status at pages 34,101 and 34,501.
For digest, see "Bills" and "Resolutions" Divisions.

Ordered reptd w/o amdts by Small Business Com
. . . . 2/3/99
Reptd w/o amdts, H Rept 106-11, Pt 1, by Small
Business Com 2/8/99
Passed under suspension of rules by 2/3 vote (413
to 0; H Leg 13) 2/9/99

★ 440
Introduced 2/2/99
Ref to H Small Business Com 2/2/99
Ordered reptd w/o amdts by Small Business Com
. . . . 2/3/99
Reptd w/o amdts, H Rept 106-12, by Small
Business Com 2/8/99
Passed under suspension of rules by 2/3 vote (411
to 4; H Leg 12) 2/9/99
Ref to S Small Business Com 2/22/99
Small Business Com discharged 3/25/99
Amdts adopted (Voice) 3/25/99
Passed by S (Voice) 3/25/99
H agreed to amdts by S (Voice) 4/12/99
Sent to President 4/15/99
Signed by President 4/27/99
Public Law 106-22 (113 Stat 36) 4/27/99

★ 441
Introduced 2/2/99
Ref to H Judiciary Com 2/2/99
Approved w/o amdts by Immigration Subcom
. . . . 3/18/99
Ordered reptd w/o amdts by Judiciary Com
. . . . 3/24/99
Passed under suspension of rules by 2/3 vote
(Voice) 5/24/99
Ref to S Judiciary Com 5/25/99
Ordered reptd w/o amdts by Judiciary Com
. . . . 6/24/99
Reptd w/o amdts, w/o written rept, by Judiciary
Com 6/24/99
Amdts adopted (Voice) 10/22/99
Passed by S (Voice) 10/22/99
H agreed to amdts by S (Voice) 11/2/99
Sent to President . . . .
Signed by President . . . .
Public Law . . . .

Introduced . . . .
Ref to H

Approved w/o amdts by National Parks Subcom
. . . . 2/25/99
Ordered reptd w/o amdts by Resources Com
. . . . 3/3/99
Reptd w/o amdts, H Rept 106-66, by Resources
Com 3/17/99
Passed under suspension of rules by 2/3 vote
(Voice) 4/12/99
Ref to S Energy Com 4/13/99
Ordered reptd w/o amdts by Energy Com
. . . . 5/19/99
Reptd w/o amdts, S Rept 106-68, by Energy Com
. . . . 6/7/99
Passed by S (Voice) 11/19/99
Sent to President 11/30/99

Signed by President 12/7/99
Public Law 106-131 (113 Stat 1678) 12/7/99

454
Introduced 2/2/99
Ref to H Judiciary Com 2/2/99
Reptd w/o amdts, H Rept 106-711, Pt 4, by
Judiciary Com 10/19/00

456
Introduced 2/2/99
Ref to H Judiciary Com 2/2/99
Hrgs by Immigration Subcom 5/18/99
Approved w/amdts by Immigration Subcom
. . . . 6/22/99
Ordered reptd w/amdts by Judiciary Com
. . . . 7/20/99
Reptd w/amdts, H Rept 106-270, by Judiciary
Com 7/29/99

★ 457
Introduced 2/2/99
Ref to H Govt Reform Com 2/2/99
Approved w/o amdts by Civil Service Subcom
. . . . 5/13/99
Ordered reptd w/o amdts by Govt Reform Com
. . . . 5/19/99
Reptd w/o amdts, H Rept 106-174, by Govt
Reform Com 6/8/99
Passed under suspension of rules by 2/3 vote
(Voice) 7/26/99
Ref to S Govt Affairs Com 7/27/99
Ordered reptd w/o amdts by Govt Affairs Com
. . . . 8/3/99
Reptd w/o amdts, S Rept 106-143, by Govt
Affairs Com 8/27/99
Passed by S (Voice) 9/8/99
Sent to President 9/14/99
Signed by President 9/24/99
Public Law 106-56 (113 Stat 407) 9/24/99

★ 459

This Status Table in the *Congressional Record Index* (CCH) for 1999-2000 lists all bills introduced during the 106th Congress and gives citations to committee reports. Date references for hearings are provided.

. . 2/2/99
. . 2/2/99

. 4/14/99
Com
. 4/21/99
ommerce
Com 4/28/99
Passed under suspension of rules by 2/3 vote
(Voice) 5/4/99
Ref to S Energy Com 5/5/99
Hrgs by Water Subcom 5/27/99
Ordered reptd w/o amdts by Energy Com
. . . . 6/16/99
Reptd w/o amdts, S Rept 106-97, by Energy Com
. . . . 6/24/99
Passed by S (Voice) 11/19/99
Signed by President 12/6/99
Public Law 106-121 (113 Stat 1637) 12/6/99

460
Introduced 2/2/99

H 440

©2001, CCH INCORPORATED

[Illustration 10–5]

PAGE FROM 1999 CONGRESSIONAL RECORD BI–WEEKLY INDEX

HOUSE BILLS   H.B. 17

H.R. 443—A bill to amend the Packers and Stockyards Act, 1921, to make it unlawful for any stockyard owner, market agency, or dealer to transfer or market nonambulatory cattle, sheep, swine, horses, mules, or goats, and for other purposes; to the Committee on Agriculture.
By Mr. ACKERMAN (for himself, Mr. Shays, Ms. Kilpatrick, Mr. Smith of New Jersey, Mr. Campbell, Mrs. Johnson of Connecticut, Mr. Sherman, Mr. Wexler, Mr. Lewis of Georgia, Mr. Abercrombie, Ms. Pelosi, Mr. Payne, Mr. Wynn, Mr. Delahunt, Mr. Brown of California, Mr. Farr of California, Mr. Moran of Virginia, Ms. DeGette, Mr. Traficant, Mrs. Tauscher, Mr. Deutsch, Mr. Waxman, Ms. Rivers, Ms. Lee, Mr. Filner, Mrs. Lowey, Mr. Frank of Massachusetts, Mr. Kucinich, Mr. Berman, Mr. ...

H.R. 444 ...

... benef ... gram ... the C ...
By Ms. ... and ...

H.R. 445 ... Act ... the utilization of certain debit cards; to the Committee on Banking and Financial Services.
By Mr. BARRETT of Wisconsin (for himself and Mr. Vento), H375 [2FE]

H.R. 446—A bill to amend the Internal Revenue Code of 1986 to eliminate tax subsidies for ethanol fuel; to the Committee on Ways and Means.
By Mr. BENTSEN, H375 [2FE]

H.R. 447—A bill to establish the Lands Title Report Commission to facilitate certain home loan mortgages; to the Committee on Banking and Financial Services.
By Mr. BEREUTER, H375 [2FE]
Cosponsors added, H419 [3FE]

H.R. 448—A bill to provide new patient protections under group health plans; to the Committees on Commerce; Education and the Workforce; Ways and Means; the Judiciary.
By Mr. BILIRAKIS (for himself, Mr. Hastert, Mr. Upton, Mr. Talent, Mr. Goodling, Mr. Gillmor, Mr. Cunningham, Mr. English of Pennsylvania, Mr. Goss, Ms. Pryce of Ohio, Mr. Hill of Montana, Mr. Armey, and Mr. Oxley), H375 [2FE]

H.R. 449—A bill to authorize the Gateway Visitor Center at Independence National Historical Park, and for other purposes; to the Committee on Resources.
By Mr. BORSKI (for himself, Mr. Weldon of Pennsylvania, and Mr. Brady of Pennsylvania), H375 [2FE]
Cosponsors added, H645 [11FE]

H.R. 450—A bill to amend the Trade Act of 1974 to establish procedures for identifying countries that deny market access for agricultural products of the United States; to the Committee on Ways and Means.
By Mr. CAMP (for himself, Mr. Gutknecht, and Mr. Pomeroy), H375 [2FE]

H.R. 451—A bill to amend the Balanced Budget and Emergency Deficit Control Act of 1985 to provide for a sequestration of all budgetary accounts for fiscal year 2000 (except Social Security, Federal retirement, and interest on the debt) equal to 5 percent of the OMB baseline; to the Committee on the Budget.
By Mr. CAMPBELL, H375 [2FE]

H.R. 452—A bill to provide off-budget treatment for the receipts and disbursements of the land and water conservation fund, and to provide that the amount appropriated from the fund for a fiscal year for Federal purposes may not exceed the amount appropriated for that fiscal year for financial assistance to the States for State purposes; to the Committees on the Budget; Resources.
By Mr. CAMPBELL, H375 [2FE]
Cosponsors added, H539 [9FE], H645 [11FE]

H.R. 453—A bill to amend the Animal Welfare Act to ensure that all dogs and cats used by research facilities are obtained legally; to the Committee on Agriculture.
By Mr. CANADY of Florida (for himself, Mr. Hyde, Ms. Jackson-Lee of Texas, Mr. Gilman, Mr. Murtha, Mr. Campbell, Mr. DeFazio, Mr. Holden, Mr. Lewis of Georgia, Mr. Rothman, Mr. Saxton, Mr. Shays, Mr. Hinchey, Ms. Pelosi, Mr. Klecrka, Mr. Smith of New Jersey, Ms. Rivers, Mr. Moran of Virginia, Mr. Tierney, Mr. Wexler, Mr. Blumenauer, Mr. Sherman, and Ms. Woolsey), H375 [2FE]

...Torres, Mr. Brown of California, Mr. Kilpatrick, Mr. Bonior, Mr. McDermott, Mr. Towns, Mr. McGovern, Ms. Jackson-Lee of Texas, Mr. Lantos, Ms. Eshoo, Mr. Lucas of Kentucky, Mrs. Jones of Ohio, Mr. Filner, and Ms. DeGette), H375 [2FE]
Cosponsors added, H461 [4FE], H645 [11FE]

H.R. 456—A bill for the relief of the survivors of the 14 members of the Armed Forces and the one United States civilian Federal employee who were killed on April 14, 1994, when United States fighter aircraft mistakenly shot down 2 United States helicopters over Iraq; to the Committee on the Judiciary.
By Mr. COLLINS, H375 [2FE]

H.R. 457—A bill to amend title 5, United States Code, to increase the amount of leave time available to a Federal employee in any year in connection with serving as an organ donor, and for other purposes; to the Committee on Government Reform.
By Mr. CUMMINGS (for himself, Ms. Norton, Ms. Kilpatrick, Mr. Bentsen, Mrs. Morella, Mr. Ford, Ms. Rivers, Mr. Underwood, Mr. Frost, and Mrs. Jones of Ohio), H375 [2FE]

H.R. 458—A bill to amend title XIX of the Social Security Act to allow States to use the funds available under the State children's health insurance program for an enhanced matching rate for coverage of additional children under the Medicaid Program; to the Committee on Commerce.
By Ms. DUNN of Washington (for herself, Mr. McDermott, Mr. Dicks, Mr. Hastings of Washington, Mr. Nethercutt, Mr. Metcalf, Mr. Smith of Washington, Mr. Inslee, and Mr. Baird), H375 [2FE]

H.R. 459—A bill to extend the deadline under the Federal Power Act for FERC Project No. 9401, the Mt. Hope Waterpower Project; to the Committee on Commerce.
By Mr. FRELINGHUYSEN (for himself and Mr. Pallone), H375 [2FE]

H.R. 460—A bill to amend title 5, United States Code, to provide that the mandatory separation age for Federal firefighters be made the same as the age that applies with respect to Federal law enforcement officers; to the Committee on Government Reform.
By Mr. GALLEGLY, H375 [2FE]

H.R. 461—A bill to amend rule 11 of the Federal Rules of Civil Procedure regarding representations made to courts by or on behalf of, and court sanctions applicable with respect to, prisoners; to the Committee on the Judiciary.

By Mr. GALLEGLY (for himself, Mr. Salmon, Mr. Royce, Mr. Sherman, Mr. Stump, Mr. Horn, Mr. Cunningham, Mr. Rogan, Mr. Bachus, Mr. Hayworth, Mr. Ney, Mr. Traficant, Mrs. Tauscher, Mr. Ehrlich, and Mr. Nethercutt), H375 [2FE]

H.R. 462—A bill to clarify that governmental pension plans of the possessions of the United States shall be treated in the same manner as State pension plans for purposes of the limitation on the State income taxation of pension income; to the Committee on the Judiciary.
By Mr. GEKAS (for himself, Mr. McCollum, Mr. Mica, and Mr. Romero-Barcelo), H375 [2FE]

H.R. 463—A bill to amend the Federal Election Campaign Act of 1971 to protect the equal participation of eligible voters in campaigns for election for ... Administration ...

... and ...

... enue Code ... education; ...

... Mr. Paul, ... of New ... Frost, Mr. ... Young of ... Morella, Mr. ... ntosh, Mr. ... Mr. Barton of Texas, Mr. McHugh, Mr. Schaffer, Mr. Shows, Mr. Armey, Mr. Thornberry, Mr. Rogan, Mr. Combest, Mr. Buyer, and Mr. Scarborough), H375 [2FE]

H.R. 465—A bill to direct the Foreign Trade Zones Board to expand Foreign Trade Zone No. 143 to include an area of the municipal airport of Chico, California; to the Committee on Ways and Means.
By Mr. HERGER, H375 [2FE]

H.R. 466—A bill to make improvements in the Black Lung Benefits Act; to the Committee on Education and the Workforce.
By Mr. HOLDEN (for himself, Mr. Wise, Mr. Mascara, Mr. Kanjorski, Mr. Murtha, and Mr. Boucher), H375 [2FE]

H.R. 467—A bill to amend section 313(p)(3) of the Tariff Act of 1930 to allow duty drawback for Methyl Tertiary-butyl Ether ("MTBE"), a finished petroleum derivative; to the Committee on Ways and Means.
By Mr. SAM JOHNSON of Texas, H375 [2FE]

H.R. 468—A bill to establish the Saint Helena Island National Scenic Area; to the Committee on Resources.
By Mr. KILDEE (for himself and Mr. Stupak), H376 [2FE]

H.R. 469—A bill to amend title 18, United States Code, to provide penalties for certain crimes relating to day care providers in or affecting interstate or foreign commerce; to the Committee on the Judiciary.
By Mr. LAZIO of New York (for himself, Mr. Shows, Mr. Horn, Mr. Gilman, and Mr. Barcia of Michigan), H376 [2FE]

H.R. 470—A bill to amend title XIX of the Social Security Act to extend the higher Federal medical assistance percentage for payment for Indian Health service facilities to urban Indian health programs under the Medicaid Program; to the Committee on Commerce.
By Mr. McDERMOTT (for himself, Mr. Dicks, Mr. Frost, Mr. Filner, and Mrs. Capps), H375 [2FE]

H.R. 471—A bill to amend title 49, United States Code, to grant the State of New York authority to allow tandem trailers to use Interstate Route 787 between the New York State Thruway and Church Street in Albany, New York; to the Committee on Transportation and Infrastructure.
By Mr. McNULTY, H376 [2FE]

H.R. 472—A bill to amend title 13, United States Code, to require the use of postcensus local review ...

> Legislative history information can be located using the History of Bills and Resolutions Table in the *Congressional Index*.
>
> This table gives the history of all bills introduced into each session of Congress. It refers to all relevant documents, except hearings.
>
> These tables are located in the bound annual index volumes of the *Congressional Record*, and in the bi-weekly index of unbound issues. H.B. in this illustration stands for History of Bills and Resolutions.

SECTION G. ILLUSTRATIONS: DOCUMENTS

[Illustration 10–6]

H.R. 457, 106th CONGRESS, 1ST SESS., AS PRINTED IN CONGRESSIONAL RECORD

H6360   CONGRESSIONAL RECORD — HOUSE   *July 26, 1999*

assured by the archivist that any cases where privacy is a concern, such as an individual who testified on conditions of anonymity, would be honored and such files would not be made public.

Mr. Speaker, the end of the Cold War has resulted in the discovery of literally hundreds of documents which had previously been out of reach behind the Iron Curtain. I see no need for the House to maintain a veil of secrecy over its Select Committee files, especially when such information may provide some insight into the fate of some of the more than 2,000 service members who still remain unaccounted for from the Vietnam conflict.

Accordingly, I ask my colleagues to join in supporting this worthy legislation which would bring the House rules on this subject into accord with those of our counterpart committee in the Senate.

Mr. THOMAS. Mr. Speaker, I have no further requests for time, and I yield back the balance of my time, once again thanking the gentleman from New York for this resolution.

"(2) not to exceed 30 days of leave under this section to serve as an organ donor.".

(c) TECHNICAL AMENDMENTS.—(1) The second section 6327 of title 5, United States Code (relating to absence in connection with funerals of fellow Federal law enforcement officers) is redesignated as section 6328.

(2) The table of sections at the beginning of chapter 63 of title 5, United States Code, is amended by adding after the item relating to section 6327 the following:

"6328. Absence in connection with funerals of fellow Federal law enforcement officers.".

The SPEAKER pro tempore. Pursuant to the rule, the gentlewoman from Illinois (Mrs. BIGGERT) and the gentleman from Maryland (Mr. CUMMINGS) each will control 20 minutes.

The Chair recognizes the gentlewoman from Illinois (Mrs. BIGGERT).

GENERAL LEAVE

Mrs. BIGGERT. Mr. Speaker, I ask unanimous consent that all Members may have 5 legislative days within which to revise and extend their remarks on H.R. 457.

The SPEAKER pro tempore. Is there

Illinois General Assembly and personally signed up every legislator on our driver's license on the back.

Illinois is one of the few States with an organ/tissue donor registry. In Illinois, this registry makes use of the existing driver's license and ID card database to identify individuals who are willing to be organ or tissue donors after death. Since October 1992, everyone applying for or renewing an Illinois driver's license or identification card is asked if they want to participate in this registry.

The response has been terrific. Approximately 3 million Illinoians have joined the registry and nearly 100,000 more enroll each month. The average participation rate statewide is 38 percent compared to a national average of 13 percent, and some counties have reported participation rates of over 70 percent.

The bottom line is when we make it easier for individuals to become organ donors, more people will become donors. H.R. 457 is an important step to-

> From the indexes or tables shown in previous illustrations, the researcher should now have citations to (1) bill number, (2) reports, and (3) *Congressional Record.*
>
> This illustration shows H.R. 457 as introduced during the 106th Congress, 1st session.

The SPEAKER pro tempore (Mr. PEASE). The question is on the motion offered by the gentleman from California (Mr. THOMAS) that the House suspend the rules and agree to the resolution, House Resolution 172.

The question was taken; and (two-thirds having voted in favor thereof) the rules were suspended and the resolution was agreed to.

A motion to reconsider was laid on the table.

ORGAN DONOR LEAVE ACT

Mrs. BIGGERT. Mr. Speaker, I move to suspend the rules and pass the bill (H.R. 457) to amend title 5, United States Code, to increase the amount of leave time available to a Federal employee in any year in connection which serving as an organ donor, and for other purposes.

The Clerk read as follows:

H.R. 457

Be it enacted by the Senate and House of Representatives of the United States of America in Congress assembled,

SECTION 1. INCREASED LEAVE TIME TO SERVE AS AN ORGAN DONOR.

(a) SHORT TITLE.—This Act may be cited as the "Organ Donor Leave Act".

(b) IN GENERAL.—Subsection (b) of the first section 6327 of title 5, United States Code (relating to absence in connection with serving as a bone-marrow or organ donor) is amended to read as follows:

"(b) An employee may, in any calendar year, use—

"(1) not to exceed 7 days of leave under this section to serve as a bone-marrow donor; and

tion; but whenever we have a chance to highlight this important issue, we should do so.

More than 54,000 people are currently on the organ transplant waiting list, and about 4,000 each year die while waiting for a transplant. I believe that Congress should do whatever it can do to encourage our citizens to consider becoming organ or bone marrow donors and that the Federal Government should be a leader in this effort.

The Organ Donor Leave Act does that. Mr. Speaker, the least we can do for those who are giving so much of themselves is to give them the time to rest and recover with their families as they save the lives of others.

H.R. 457 will make it easier for Federal employees to become organ donors by providing those who donate organs with 30 days of paid leave in any calendar year. Under current law, employees are permitted to take 7 days of leave in order to donate bone marrow or organs.

H.R. 457 retains the 7-day leave period for bone marrow donors but increases the leave available to organ donors to 30 days. This leave is separate and distinct from the annual or sick leave available to Federal employees.

Mr. Speaker, my home State of Illinois has been a leader in organ and tissue donation through our Secretary of State's office. In fact, I signed up as a potential organ donor when our Secretary of State, now Governor George Ryan, came to the House floor of the

Mr. Speaker, I want to thank the gentlewoman from Illinois (Mrs. BIGGERT) for her kind comments, and certainly I want to thank the chairman of the committee, the gentleman from Indiana (Mr. BURTON), and our ranking member, the gentleman from California (Mr. WAXMAN), as well as the chairman of the Subcommittee on Civil Service, the gentleman from Florida (Mr. SCARBOROUGH), for making sure that we moved in a bipartisan effort to bring this bill to the floor of the House.

Mr. Speaker, I introduced already 457, the Organ Donor Leave Act, because it supports Federal employees who make the lifesaving decision to become living organ or bone marrow donors by granting them additional leave time to recover from making the donation.

In the last 20 years, important medical breakthroughs have allowed for a larger number of successful organ and tissue transplants and a longer survival rate for transplant recipients. In many cases, transplantation is the only hope for thousands of people suffering from organ failure or in desperate need of corneas, skin, bone, or other tissue.

Despite the success rate of organ transplants, the need for donated organs and tissues continues to outpace the supply. Currently, however, 60,000 Americans are waiting for life-saving transplants. Tragically, every day 12 people die while waiting for a transplant. Every 16 minutes another name is added to the waiting list. This is a

[Illustration 10–7]

PUB. L. NO. 106–56 AS PRINTED AS A SLIP LAW

PUBLIC LAW 106–56—SEPT. 24, 1999   113 STAT. 407

Public Law 106–56
106th Congress

An Act

To amend title 5, United States Code, to increase the amount of leave time available to a Federal employee in any year in connection with serving as an organ donor, and for other purposes.

Sept. 24, 1999
[H.R. 457]

Be it enacted by the Senate and House of Representatives of the United States of America in Congress assembled,

Organ Donor Leave Act.

SECTION 1. INCREASED LEAVE TIME TO SERVE AS AN ORGAN DONOR.

    (a) SHORT TITLE.—This Act may be cited as the "Organ Donor Leave Act".

5 USC 6301 note.

    (b) IN GENERAL.—Subsection (b) of the first section 6327 of title 5, United States Code (relating to absence in connection with ...

> Note how the slip law refers to (1) the date the bill became law and (2) the bill that became law. The text of the public law as it appears here can be compared to the introduced bill to determine legislative intent, if amendments were made.
>
> Since 1975, a brief summary at the end of each slip law (3) provides references or citations to some documents that may be relevant to the legislative history of a public law.

title 5, United States Code (relating to absence in connection with funerals of fellow Federal law enforcement officers) is redesignated as section 6328.

    (2) The table of sections at the beginning of chapter 63 of title 5, United States Code, is amended by adding after the item relating to section 6327 the following:

"6328. Absence in connection with funerals of fellow Federal law enforcement officers.".

Approved September 24, 1999.

LEGISLATIVE HISTORY—H.R. 457:

HOUSE REPORTS: No. 106–174 (Comm. on Government Reform).
CONGRESSIONAL RECORD, Vol. 145 (1999):
    July 26, considered and passed House.
    Sept. 8, considered and passed Senate.
WEEKLY COMPILATION OF PRESIDENTIAL DOCUMENTS, Vol. 35 (1999):
    Sept. 24, Presidential statement.

[Illustration 10–8]

PAGE FROM DEBATES ON H.R. 457, 106th CONGRESS, 1st SESS., IN CONGRESSIONAL RECORD

July 26, 1999   CONGRESSIONAL RECORD—HOUSE   **H6361**

solvable problem and the Federal Government and its employees can help.

In December of 1997, Vice President AL GORE and Health and Human Services Secretary Donna Shalala launched a national organ and tissue donation initiative. In 1998, after the first full year of the initiative, organ donations increased 5.6 percent, the first substantial increase since 1995. During 1998, HHS issued a new regulation to ensure that hospitals worked collaboratively with organ procurement organizations in identifying potential donors and approaching their families.

HHS has conducted a national conference aimed at identifying the most effective strategies to increase donation and transplantation. In conjunction with dozens of partner organizations in the private and volunteer sectors, HHS has worked to increase the awareness of the need for organ and tissue donation.

Recognizing that Federal employees also have a role to play, I first introduced the Organ Donor Leave Act last

I urge all Members to give their support to this very, very important legislation.

Mr. Speaker, I reserve the balance of my time.

Mrs. BIGGERT. Mr. Speaker, I reserve the balance of my time.

Mr. CUMMINGS. Mr. Speaker, I yield myself such time as I may consume.

Mr. Speaker, one of the arguments that is often made about transplantation is that there are two types. One is where, of course, a person dies and their organs are used. And the other is where the person is still living.

A lot of people wonder why is it so important that organs be transplanted from living people. I mean, do not get me wrong, those who have died are very important also. But the living are very important because of the following reasons.

The time shown from harvesting of an organ until the time of transplantation is as follows: If a person dies and it is a heart transplantation, it would be 4 to 6 hours; heart and lung 4 to 6

walk. Explore every corner of my brain. Take my cells if necessary, and let them grow so that, some day, a deaf girl will hear the sound of rain against her window. Burn what is left and scatter the ashes in the winds to help the flowers grow. If you must bury something, let it be my fault, my weaknesses and all the prejudices against my fellow man.

"Give my sins to the devil. Give my soul to God. If by chance you wish to remember me, do it with a kind deed or word to someone who needs you. If you do all I have asked, I will live forever.

"Make a miracle, be an organ donor."

Mr. Speaker, I yield back the balance of my time.

Mrs. BIGGERT. Mr. Speaker, I yield myself the balance of my time.

Mr. Speaker, I would like to thank the distinguished gentleman from Maryland (Mr. CUMMINGS) for introducing this legislation and working to bring this bill to the floor.

I also want to thank the gentleman

The discussion of a pending bill by members of Congress may be useful in determining congressional intent. The researcher should ascertain whether such discussion occurred in either house of Congress.

The House of Representatives uses a different style typeface in the Congressional Record *to indicate material inserted or appended; the Senate uses a bullet (•) symbol.*

The Organ Donor Leave Act is supported by the American Society of Transplantation, the largest professional transplant organization in the United States.

In a letter expressing their support for the bill, the AST stated that "a lack of leave time has served as a significant impediment and disincentive for individuals willing to share the gift of life."

Currently, Federal employees may use up to 7 days of leave in each calendar year to serve as an organ or bone marrow donor. Yet, experience has shown that an organ transplant operation and postoperative recovery for living donors may take as long as 6 to 8 weeks.

In order to address this disparity, I worked with the Office of Personnel Management and the Department of Health and Human Services in drafting this legislation to increase the amount of leave that may be used for organ donation to 30 days.

The amount of leave that may be used for bone marrow donation will remain at 7 days because that is generally viewed to be adequate.

Under this legislation, donors will not have to be concerned with using their personal sick or annual leave for these vital medical procedures because the leave granted is in addition to what they routinely earn.

Ultimately, this bill will benefit the 62,000 people who are on the organ transplant waiting list.

that I just spoke of.

Finally, let me just say this. While we are talking here about the organ donations from those who are living, there is a very fitting quote that comes from Stephanie Kristine Crosse of the University of Dayton School of Law where she talked about organ donation. Although this talks about donations of the dead, I think that it still says a lot for donations.

She says, "The day will come when my body will lie upon a white sheet, neatly tucked under four corners of a mattress, located in a hospital busily occupied with the living and the dying. At a certain moment a doctor will determine that my brain has ceased to function and that, for all intents and purposes, my life has stopped.

"When that happens, do not attempt to instill artificial life into my body by use of a machine. And don't call this my deathbed. Let it be called the bed of life, and let my body be taken from it to help others lead fuller lives.

"Give my sight to the man who has never seen a sunrise, a baby's face, or love in the eyes of a woman. Give my heart to a person whose own heart has caused nothing but endless days of pain. Give my blood to the teenager who was pulled from the wreckage of his car so that he might live to see his grandchildren play. Give my kidneys to one who depends on a machine to exist from week to week.

"Take my bones, every muscle, every fiber, and every nerve in my body and find a way to make a crippled child

portant step forward in making the Federal Government a leader by example and encouraging our citizens to become organ or bone marrow donors.

I urge all Members to vote for 457 and make it easier for Federal employees to help save a life through organ donation. The Congressional Budget Office has determined that this bill will not have a significant impact on the Federal budget.

I urge all Members to strongly support H.R. 457.

Mr. STARK. Mr. Speaker, I rise today in strong support of H.R. 457, the "Organ Donor Leave Act." This legislation will assure that federal employees have an adequate amount of leave if they choose to undertake organ or bone marrow donation.

Over 50,000 people are currently awaiting an organ transplant, but because of a national shortage, over 4,000 people die each year for lack of a suitable organ. Research points to a clear need for incentive programs and public education concerning organ donation. We need to use every possible option to increase the number of donated organs. This legislation is one way to meet this goal.

Currently, federal employees may use up to 7 days of leave to serve as an organ or bone marrow donor. However, experience indicates the need for additional time for organ transplant operation and post-operative recovery for living donors—up to six or eight weeks in many cases. The "Organ Donor Leave Act" increases the amount of leave that federal employees may use to serve as an organ donor to 30 days.

This legislation also goes hand-in-hand with the "Gift of Life Congressional Medal Act of

SECTION H.   OBTAINING THE DOCUMENTS
OF A LEGISLATIVE HISTORY

Previous sections of this chapter discussed sources that allow a researcher to identify which documents relevant to the legislative history of a specific law exist. This section describes where the full text of these documents can be located. As a general rule, most legislative history materials, from the 1990s to the present, can now be found either on the *THOMAS* website[35] or on *GPO Access*.[36] These sites are now the quickest way to access the documents needed for a legislative history. However, absent a compiled legislative history, identifying and locating older materials will depend on access to some of the resources listed below, whether in print or electronic format.

1. Public Bills

The print resources, listed below are of particular use for historical research. The online sources are preferred sources for modern legislation.

a. *United States Congress Public Bills and Resolutions.* Traditionally, bills were distributed to federal depository libraries. At the end of each session, depositories would receive the collection of bills on microfiche. The United States Government Printing Office ceased publication of this microfiche set in 2000 with the 106th Congress, 2d Session. The microfiche set contains the text of all public bills and resolutions, including amendments, introduced in both houses of Congress from the 96th Congress to the 106th Congress. Access to this set is provided by the *Microfiche Users Guide/Bill Finding Aid.* The *Guide* may refer to a public bill or resolution that has not been provided in the microfiche set.

Since 2000, the Government Printing Office has been distributing copies of bills to depository libraries only sporadically. The expectation is that patrons interested in reading or tracking the status of new bills can do so more quickly through either the Library of Congress' *THOMAS* website or the *GPO Access* website, both of which are mentioned below.

b. *CIS/Microfiche Library.* From 1970, CIS provides reprints of bills that have become public laws.

c. *Public Laws—Legislative Histories on Microfiche.* From 1979 through 1988, bills can be located in this collection.

d. *GAO Legislative History Collection.* For selected legislation that has become public law, reprints of relevant bills and amendments are available on microfiche. This source and years of coverage is described above in Section D–2–e.

e. *Congressional Record.* Occasionally, the text of a bill, especially if amended on the floor of either house during discussion or debate, may be printed in the *Congressional Record.*

f. *Committee Reports.* Committee reports often reprint bills, as amended by committees, for those bills being reported out of committee.

---

[35] http://thomas.loc.gov/.

[36] http://www.gpoaccess.gov/legislative.html.

Committee reports reprinted in the *United States Code Congressional and Administrative News (USCCAN)* do not include the text of the bill, even if it was included in the original report.

g. *Electronic Services.* The following electronic services provide the most timely access to recent congressional materials.

(1) *GPO Access* (free service). The website of the U.S. Government Printing Office provides Congressional Bills,[37] a database containing all bills from the 103d Congress, 1993–1994, forward. The database is updated daily when the House or Senate is in session.

(2) *THOMAS* (free service).[38] This website, by the Library of Congress, provides:

(a) the full text of bills beginning with the 101st Congress, 1989, and summaries of all bills introduced in either the House or Senate beginning in 1973;

(b) access to the Bill Summary & Status (BSS) section that provides links to everything about a bill except the full text: sponsors, *Congressional Record* references, and links to all floor actions and reports, to name a few. This section also will provide links to full text versions of the bill or public law if available.

(3) *CQ.com On Congress* (fee-based service). Bills from the 104th Congress forward are available through this Web-based service.

(4) *Westlaw* (fee-based service). Provides the full-text of all bills beginning with the 104th Congress, 1995–1996. The bills from each Congress may be searched separately or combined.

(5) *LexisNexis* (fee-based service). Provides the full-text of all bills beginning with the 101st Congress, 1989–1990. The bills from each Congress may be searched separately or combined.

(6) *LexisNexis Congressional* (fee-based service). The base edition of this service provides texts of bills since 1989.

2. House, Senate, and Conference Committee Reports

The sources listed in paragraphs a–g, below, are generally the best sources for historical research. The online sources listed in paragraph h., however, are the preferred sources for modern legislation.

a. *CIS.* Reports from 1970 to present for bills that have become public law can be found in the *CIS Microfiche Library.*

b. *United States Code Congressional and Administrative News.* From 1941, *USCCAN* selectively reprints committee reports for bills that became public laws.

c. *Serial Set.* Committee reports are reprinted in the official series and the commercial set published by Congressional Information Services,

---

[37] http://www.gpoaccess.gov/bills.

[38] http://thomas.loc.gov or http://www.thomas.gov. *THOMAS* links to the *GPO Access* website to provide many documents in PDF format.

Inc. (CIS). Also available electronically in the *LexisNexis U.S. Serial Set Digital Collection.*[39]

d.   *GAO Legislative Histories.* Committee reports for bills that became public laws are available for selected laws.[40]

e.   *Public Laws—Legislative Histories on Microfiche.* This set, produced by Commerce Clearing House (CCH), makes available Senate, House, and conference committee reports for public laws enacted during the 96th through 100th Congresses.

f.   *Looseleaf Services and Treatises.* Committee reports for specialized areas of legal research may be reproduced for subscribers to these services.

g.   *Congressional Record.* This publication may occasionally contain committee reports, although this is not the standard method of publication.

h.   *Electronic Services.* The following services provide the most timely access to recent congressional materials.

(1) *GPO Access* (free service). This website's Congressional Reports page includes the full-text of all reports issued by Congress beginning with the 104th Congress, 1995–1996.

(2) *THOMAS* (free service). Provides selected House and Senate committee reports, including conference and joint committee reports, from the 104th Congress, 1995–1996, forward.

(3) *CQ.com On Congress* (fee-based service). Committee reports for bills from the 104th Congress, January 4, 1995, forward are available.

(4) *Westlaw* (fee-based service). *Westlaw* includes all committee reports printed in *USCCAN* since 1948. From 1990, *Westlaw* contains all committee reports, even for bills that did not become law.

(5) *LexisNexis* (fee-based service). Provides House and Senate reports for legislation since 1990.

(6) *LexisNexis Congressional* (fee-based service). The base edition provides committee reports from 1990 forward. A comprehensive collection is available in the *LexisNexis U.S. Serial Set Digital Collection.*

3.   Congressional Debates

Although the *Congressional Record* contains much more than the debates that occur on proposed legislation, it is the primary source for the transcripts of debates and votes on pending legislation. When using the *Congressional Record,* the researcher should be acquainted with its history and pattern of publication.

a.   *Predecessors to the Congressional Record.*[41] The predecessors to the *Congressional Record* are the *Annals of Congress,* 1789–1824 (1st to 18th Cong., 1st Sess.); the *Register of Debates,* 1824–1837 (18th Cong., 2d Sess. to 25th Cong., 1st Sess.); and the *Congressional Globe,* 1837–1873 (25th

---

[39] The Serial Set is discussed in Section H–6 later in this chapter.

[40] This source and years of coverage are described above in Section D–2–e.

[41] The predecessors to the CONGRESSIONAL RECORD can be found on the Library of Congress' *American Memory* website, *A Century of Lawmaking for a New Nation, U.S. Congressional Documents and Debates,* at http://memory.loc.gov/ammem/amlaw/.

Cong., 2d Sess., to 42d Cong., 2d Sess.). The early volumes of the *Congressional Globe* contain abridged versions of the proceedings of Congress. The *Congressional Record* began in 1873 with the 43d Cong., 1st Sess.

b. *Congressional Record Daily Edition.* The *Congressional Record* is published daily while either chamber is in session. It consists of four sections: the proceedings of the House of Representatives and the Senate (including debates) in separate sections; the Extension of Remarks (reprints of articles, editorials, book reviews, and tributes); and the Daily Digest, since the 80th Congress. The Daily Digest summarizes the day's proceedings, lists actions taken and laws signed by the president that day, and provides very useful committee information. [Illustrations 10–6 and 10–8]

Each section of the daily *Congressional Record* is paginated consecutively during each session of Congress. Each page in each section is preceded by the following letter prefix: S–Senate; H–House; E–Extension of Remarks; and D–Daily Digest.

An index to the *Congressional Record* is published every two weeks and provides access in a single alphabetical listing by subject, name of legislator, and title of legislation. These indexes are non-cumulative.

c. *Congressional Record Permanent Edition.* A permanent, bound edition of the *Congressional Record* is published after the end of each session of Congress. Publication of paper and microfiche copies of these editions is behind schedule. The permanent edition is generally the most authoritative source for research.

The permanent edition differs from the daily edition in that it does not use the same method of pagination, but rather integrates all material into one sequence. Also, the permanent edition does not contain the Extensions of Remarks from 1955 to 1968.

The permanent edition includes an index that provides access by subject, sponsor, and bill number. The Daily Digest section of each of the daily editions of the *Congressional Record* is cumulated in one volume of the permanent edition.

d. *Electronic Sources.* The following electronic sources provide the most timely access to recent congressional materials.

(1) *GPO Access* (free source). Coverage of the *Congressional Record* (daily edition) begins in 1994. An index to the *Congressional Record*, updated daily when Congress is in session, dates back to 1992.[42] The bound permanent edition of the *Congressional Record* is available only for 1999–2001.[43]

(2) *THOMAS* (free source). This website of the Library of Congress contains the full text of the daily edition of the *Congressional Record* beginning with the 101st Congress (1989–1990). The Keyword Index begins with the 104th Congress (1995).[44]

---

[42] http://www.gpoaccess.gov/crecord/index.html.

[43] http://www.gpoaccess.gov/crecordbound/index.html.

[44] http://thomas.loc.gov/home/r110query.html.

(3) *CQ.com On Congress* (fee-based service). Full text is available from the 104th Congress, January 4, 1995, forward.

(4) *Westlaw* (fee-based service). Coverage is available beginning with the 99th Congress, 1985–1986.

(5) *LexisNexis* (fee-based service). Coverage is available beginning with the 99th Congress, 1985–1986.

(6) *LexisNexis Congressional* (fee-based service). The base edition provides coverage beginning with the 99th Congress, 1985–1986. The *Lexis-Nexis Congressional Record Permanent Digital Collection* provides access from 1873 through 1997.

4. Hearings

Hearings relating to bills can be difficult to locate. In addition to the references provided above, the following resources may provide information useful for locating reprints of both published and unpublished hearings:

a. *Congressional Information Service (CIS).*

(1) Since 1970, CIS publications have provided citations to all Senate and House hearings. CIS produces the full-text of all Senate and House hearings in microfiche, including appendices to the hearings.

(2) *CIS US Congressional Committee Hearings Index.* This index identifies published hearings from 1833 to 1969. The microfiche component provides the text of hearings published within the time frame covered by this index.

(3) *CIS Index to Unpublished US Senate Committee Hearings.* This index identifies unpublished Senate hearings from 1823 to 1976. The microfiche component to the set provides the text of the hearings.

(4) *CIS Index to Unpublished US House of Representatives Committee Hearings.* This index enables a researcher to find the citation to an unpublished hearing and to locate the text of the hearing in the microfiche component. Coverage is from 1833 to 1968.

b. *LexisNexis Congressional* (fee-based). The base edition provides selected congressional hearing transcripts from 1988 to present. The *Lexis-Nexis Congressional Hearings Digital Collection* includes full transcripts of both published and unpublished hearings, along with all related proceedings, such as oral statements, committee questions, and discussion, from 1833 to the present.

c. *LexisNexis* (fee-based). Hearing summaries from 1993 are provided through the Federal Document Clearing House Congressional Hearings Summaries.

d. *Westlaw* (fee-based). Transcripts of oral and written testimony before committees of the U.S. Congress, January 1993 to present.

e. *GPO Access.* In the *Congress Congressional Hearings* file[45] all hearings released to the GPO from the committees are available in full-text beginning with the 104th Congress, 1995–1996.

---

[45] http://www.gpoaccess.gov/chearings/index.html.

f. *CQ.com On Congress* (fee-based). This web product provides verbatim transcripts of House and Senate committee hearings from the 104th Congress, January 4, 1995, forward. Witness lists and prepared statements are available.

g. Websites for the House of Representatives[46] and the Senate[47] contain links to committee websites, which post hearings.

h. *Index of Congressional Committee Hearings (not confidential in character) prior to January 3, 1935 in the United States Senate Library.*

i. *Cumulative Index of Congressional Committee Hearings (not confidential in character) from Seventy–Fourth Congress (January 3, 1935) through Eighty–Fifth Congress (January 3, 1959) in the United States Senate Library.*

j. *Shelflist of Congressional Committee Hearings (not confidential in character) in the United States Senate Library from Eighty–Sixth Congress (January 7, 1959) through Ninety–First Congress (January 2, 1971).*

k. *Congressional Hearings Calendar: An Index to Congressional Hearings by Date, Committee/Subcommittee, Chairman, and Title,* 1985 to present. The purpose of these compilations is to provide a means of identifying recently held hearings that may not yet be covered by document indexes. The *Calendar* index also provides different access points than does *CIS,* e.g., date of hearing, name of committee and subcommittee, and name of the chair presiding over the hearing. This is especially helpful for multi-part hearings, making only one look-up necessary.

l. *Monthly Catalog of United States Government Publications.* Now published electronically as *Catalog of U.S. Government Publications.* This index provides references to hearings held on specific legislation. The paper version of this index was discontinued in December 2004; coverage in the electronic version goes back to 1976.[48]

5. Committee Prints

The following sources provide access to committee prints:

a. *CIS US Congressional Committee Prints Index* and microfiche component. This multivolume Index identifies committee prints from 1830 to 1969. The microfiche component reprints these documents.

b. *Congressional Information Service (CIS).* From 1970 forward, the *CIS Index and Abstracts* volumes identify committee prints. The CIS microfiche library provides reprints of the documents.

c. *Serial Set.* If a committee print is designated as a House or Senate document, it is available in the official *Serial Set* or in the CIS commercial version of this set. The CIS commercial series is complete through 1969 and is then continued by the CIS microfiche library, above.

---

[46] A list of House Committees can be found at http://www.house.gov. From this page, you can click on the Committees link.

[47] A list of Senate Committees can be found at http://www.senate.gov. From this page, you can click on the Committees link.

[48] http://catalog.gpo.gov/.

d. *LexisNexis Congressional.* The base edition contains selected full text committee prints from 1993 to 2004. As a part of its *Congressional Research Digital Collection,* LexisNexis is creating a collection of the full text of all committee print documents in two files: one that will cover 1830–1969, and another that will cover 1970 to the present.

e. *LexisNexis.* Contains selected documents from the 104th Congress, 1995–1996, to March 2004.

f. *GPO Access.* All prints are available in full text beginning with the 105th Congress, 1997–1998.[49]

6. The Serial Set

The *United States Congressional Serial Set,* published by the Government Printing Office, has been known by various titles since its inception in 1789. According to the latest publication schedule, the *Serial Set* is about four years behind schedule.[50]

Although the *Serial Set* includes numerous publications of the federal government and some non-governmental organizations, the relevant publications for legislative histories that it contains are the committee reports and the presidential messages relevant to specific legislation.

From the 84th through the 95th Congresses, House and Senate reports on public and private bills were available in bound volumes entitled "Miscellaneous Reports" by type of bill. Beginning with the 96th Congress, all reports are compiled and arranged in numerical sequence in bound volumes. Presidential messages can be found in the House and Senate Documents section of the *Serial Set.* Occasionally, a committee print may be classified as a House or Senate document and can be found in this set.

The *GPO Access* website contains documents and reports from the *Serial Set* from the 104th Congress to the present.[51]

Congressional Information Services, Inc., publishes the *CIS US Serial Set Index,* covering 1789–1969, along with microfiche that provide access to the documents located through the *Index.* Also available is a four-volume Index by Reported Bill Numbers. Electronically, the *Serial Set Index* is an optional module of *LexisNexis Congressional.*

The *LexisNexis U.S. Serial Set Digital Collection,* when completed, will be a comprehensive digital collection of the full text of the *U.S. Serial Set.* The collection has been completed through 1969; content for 1970–2009 is scheduled to be added in 2009. Future content will be added as it is available.

7. Presidential Documents

The statements that the president issues when sending proposed legislation to Congress or when signing or vetoing a bill are available in the following sources.

[49] http://www.gpoaccess.gov/cprints.

[50] The publishing schedule can be found at http://www.gpoaccess.gov/serialset/schedule/.

[51] http://www.gpoaccess.gov/serialset/index.html.

a. *Weekly Compilation of Presidential Documents.*[52] *The Weekly Compilation* is issued each Monday and includes the text of many presidential documents. Of particular importance to compilers of legislative histories are veto messages, signing statements, messages to Congress, and the list of acts approved by the president. Each issue contains an index. Prior to volume 31, number 1, January 9, 1995, a cumulative index was published in each issue. From 1995, indexes have been issued quarterly and distributed separately. Semiannual and annual cumulative indexes also are published. *HeinOnline* contains the full set of this title.[53]

b. *Public Papers of the Presidents.*[54] This annual series began with President Hoover's administration. The series is being compiled contemporaneously and retrospectively. Prior to 1977, *Public Papers* was an edited version of the *Weekly Compilation.* However, beginning with the administration of President Carter and continuing through the volume for 1988–89, the last year of President Reagan's administration, the set includes all of the material printed in the *Weekly Compilation of Presidential Documents.* Beginning in 1989, the first year of the administration of President George Herbert Walker Bush, Proclamations and Executive Orders are not reproduced. Rather, a table refers the user to the appropriate issue of the *Federal Register* in which those documents are published. The papers of President Roosevelt are not part of this series; they are, however, published commercially.[55] *HeinOnline* contains the full set of this title.

The final volume for each year of an administration contains an index. A cumulative index for each administration is commercially published under the title *Cumulated Indexes to the Public Papers of the Presidents of the United States.*[56]

Issues of *Public Papers* and the *Weekly Compilation* are available through *LexisNexis* from March 24, 1979. *Westlaw* publishes the full text of the *Weekly Compilation* from January 2000. *GPO Access* carries the full text beginning in 1991.

c. *United States Code Congressional and Administrative News.* Since 1986, *USCCAN* reprints, in the legislative history volumes of the set, the text of presidential signing statements. The presidential signing statements that are reprinted in *USCCAN* also are available through *Westlaw.*

d. *Additional Sources.* Presidential messages also can be found in the *Congressional Record,* the House and Senate *Journals,* and in the *Serial Set* if considered a House or Senate document. The White House website has a collection of presidential documents.[57]

---

[52] The National Archives and Records Administration site, available through *GPO Access,* contains the WEEKLY COMPILATION from 1993, at http://www.gpoaccess.gov/wcomp.

[53] *See* Chapter 18, Section A–6–b, for a description of *HeinOnline.*

[54] This publication is available from 1991, at http://www.gpoaccess.gov/pubpapers.

[55] THE PUBLIC PAPERS AND ADDRESSES OF FRANKLIN D. ROOSEVELT (New York: Random House 1938–50).

[56] This publication is discussed in Chapter 13, Section H–6–b, of this book.

[57] http://www.whitehouse.gov/.

SECTION I.   CHART: FINDING AIDS AND
SOURCES FOR DOCUMENTS

This chart identifies documents, finding aids, and some of the sources in which the documents may be located. For more detailed information on these items and others that have ceased publication and are not included in this chart, refer to the preceding sections in this chapter.

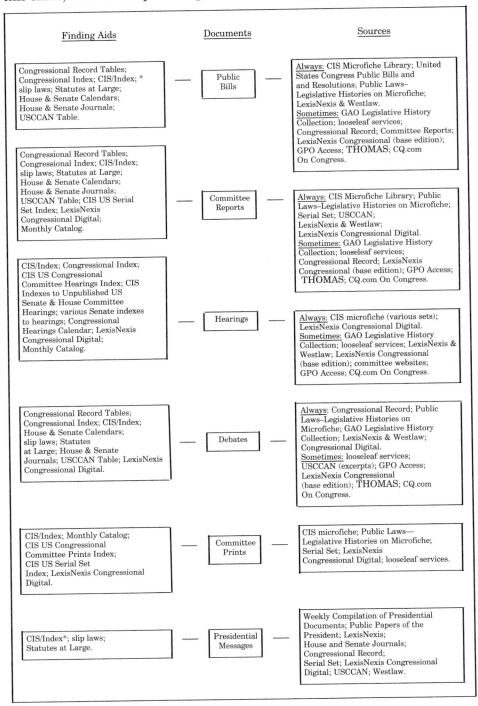

Finding Aids | Documents | Sources

Public Bills

Finding Aids: Congressional Record Tables; Congressional Index; CIS/Index; * slip laws; Statutes at Large; House & Senate Calendars; House & Senate Journals; USCCAN Table.

Sources: Always: CIS Microfiche Library; United States Congress Public Bills and and Resolutions; Public Laws–Legislative Histories on Microfiche; LexisNexis & Westlaw. Sometimes: GAO Legislative History Collection; looseleaf services; Congressional Record; Committee Reports; LexisNexis Congressional (base edition); GPO Access; THOMAS, CQ.com On Congress.

Committee Reports

Finding Aids: Congressional Record Tables; Congressional Index; CIS/Index; slip laws; Statutes at Large; House & Senate Calendars; House & Senate Journals; USCCAN Table; CIS US Serial Set Index; LexisNexis Congressional Digital; Monthly Catalog.

Sources: Always: CIS Microfiche Library; Public Laws–Legislative Histories on Microfiche; Serial Set; USCCAN; LexisNexis & Westlaw; LexisNexis Congressional Digital. Sometimes: GAO Legislative History Collection; looseleaf services; Congressional Record; LexisNexis Congressional (base edition); GPO Access; THOMAS; CQ.com On Congress.

Hearings

Finding Aids: CIS/Index; Congressional Index; CIS US Congressional Committee Hearings Index; CIS Indexes to Unpublished US Senate & House Committee Hearings; various Senate indexes to hearings; Congressional Hearings Calendar; LexisNexis Congressional Digital; Monthly Catalog.

Sources: Always: CIS microfiche (various sets); LexisNexis Congressional Digital. Sometimes: GAO Legislative History Collection; looseleaf services; LexisNexis & Westlaw; LexisNexis Congressional (base edition); committee websites; GPO Access; CQ.com On Congress.

Debates

Finding Aids: Congressional Record Tables; Congressional Index; CIS/Index; House & Senate Calendars; slip laws; Statutes at Large; House & Senate Journals; USCCAN Table; LexisNexis Congressional Digital.

Sources: Always: Congressional Record; Public Laws–Legislative Histories on Microfiche; GAO Legislative History Collection; LexisNexis & Westlaw; Congressional Digital. Sometimes: looseleaf services; USCCAN (excerpts); GPO Access; LexisNexis Congressional (base edition); THOMAS; CQ.com On Congress.

Committee Prints

Finding Aids: CIS/Index; Monthly Catalog; CIS US Congressional Committee Prints Index; CIS US Serial Set Index; LexisNexis Congressional Digital.

Sources: CIS microfiche; Public Laws— Legislative Histories on Microfiche; Serial Set; LexisNexis Congressional Digital; looseleaf services.

Presidential Messages

Finding Aids: CIS/Index*; slip laws; Statutes at Large.

Sources: Weekly Compilation of Presidential Documents; Public Papers of the President; LexisNexis; House and Senate Journals; Congressional Record; Serial Set; LexisNexis Congressional Digital; USCCAN; Westlaw.

SECTION J. TRACKING PENDING LEGISLATION

In addition to the sources previously described, the following online sources allow researchers to track the progress of pending legislation and, in most cases, to identify documents generated during the bill's progress.

1. BILLCAST

BILLCAST, published by Information for Public Affairs, Inc., provides a forecast report for public bills pending in the current Congress. The report gives a brief summary of the bill's purpose and predictions of the bill's chance of passing in committee and on the floor. *BILLCAST* for the current Congress, as well as archival information, is available through *Westlaw* and *LexisNexis*.

2. Bill Tracking Reports

a. *Westlaw.* A database contains summaries and status information relating to current federal legislation. A public bill is covered through each step of the legislative process. An archive provides information up to 1991; some state material also is included.

b. *LexisNexis.* Bill tracking summaries provide an ongoing update of the status of bills pending in both houses of the current Congress. Each summary contains a synopsis of the bill, its introduction date, committee referrals, and a complete legislative chronology, including references to the *Congressional Record*.

c. *CQ.com On Congress.* Tracking legislative activity is a strong point of this service, which also provides e-mail alerts to those following specific pending legislation.

d. *LexisNexis Congressional Universe.* This Web service tracks federal bills from 1989 forward.

e. *THOMAS.* This website, maintained by the Library of Congress, provides information about the status of pending legislation. It can be searched in a variety of ways such as keyword, number, sponsor, and committee.

3. Congressional Quarterly Materials

Congressional Quarterly, Inc., and its partner, CQ Press, are prolific publishers of materials dealing with all branches of the federal government. Some publications particularly relevant to federal legislative histories are highlighted in this section.

a. *CQ Weekly.* This magazine of congressional news contains summaries of major legislation and public policy issues. Although coverage is not comprehensive, *CQ Weekly,* previously *Congressional Quarterly Weekly Report*, is valuable because of its extensive analysis and background discussion of laws and legislative issues.

b. *CQ Almanac.* Published at the end of each session of Congress, *CQ Almanac* provides information of permanent research value on congressional activity during that year. *CQ Almanac* provides an excellent narrative overview of the legislative history of major bills passed. It is a good starting point to determine whether or not a specific section of the bill became a part of the law.

c. *Congress and the Nation.* This publication began as a project to cumulate and summarize information in individual *CQ Almanacs.* The set is comprised of many volumes, with each covering a span of years. The publication currently evaluates and assesses the politics and legislation for the period of time covered.

d. *CQ Daily Monitor.* This daily reporting service provides information on legislation currently before Congress.

e. *CQ.com On Congress.* A Web-based service that includes the text of bills, committee reports, the *Congressional Record*, and testimony. Supplementary information includes selected references to articles discussing the legislation.

Chapter 11

STATE AND MUNICIPAL LEGISLATION*

State and local governments enact legislation that regulates conduct within these jurisdictions. These primary authority sources and the finding aids used to research issues relating to state and municipal legislation are the subjects of this chapter.[1]

The enactment, organization, and publication of federal and state statutes are very similar. The differences that do exist among the statutes of the states are mostly in terminology rather than substance. Each state has a state legislature and, with the exception of Nebraska, each has an upper and lower house similar to the Senate and the House of Representatives of the United States Congress. In general, the legislative process for the passage of state laws is similar to that previously described for federal laws.

State legislatures meet in either annual or biennial sessions. Information for individual states regarding terminology, frequency of session, and other pertinent information on state legislatures is available in the latest edition of *The Book of the States*.[2]

SECTION A. SESSION LAWS

Each state publishes a series of bound volumes containing all of the laws passed during each session of its legislature. These volumes are often generally titled *session laws,* although some states use other names, such as *acts (and resolves), statutes,* or *laws.* By whatever name they are published, these session laws include public laws (those that relate to the public as a whole), as well as private, temporary, local, and appropriation acts. State session laws are published chronologically by order of adoption, much like the *United States Statutes at Large,* and are issued in bound form after the legislative session is over. Many states also publish their laws in *slip* form soon after they are passed.[3] Additionally, recently enacted laws are frequently published by private companies in advance sheets as part of a subscription to an annotated state code. [Illustration 11–1]

---

* This chapter was revised and updated by Bonnie Shucha, Head of Reference, University of Wisconsin Law Library.

[1] The primary purpose of this chapter is to introduce the methods of locating state statutes. After the relevant statute has been found, however, it is often necessary to determine its proper application. For this latter purpose, see NORMAN J. SINGER, STATUTES AND STATUTORY CONSTRUCTION (7th ed. 2007). For a discussion of federal legislation, see Chapter 9 of this book.

[2] COUNCIL OF STATE GOVERNMENTS, THE BOOK OF THE STATES (1935–).

[3] The term *slip* refers to the fact the laws are printed individually on separate slips of paper before their inclusion in the bound session laws.

SECTION B.   CODIFICATION OF STATE LAWS

In addition to session laws, which are arranged chronologically, each state also produces a set of statutes that have extracted the session laws and reorganized them topically for ease of use (similar to the subject arrangement of the *United States Code*). [Illustration 11–2] The terms *revised, compiled, consolidated,* and *code* are often used to describe such sets of currently enforceable statutes.

In some states, compilations of laws are published under official auspices; in others, by private publishers; and, in some states, there are both official and unofficial sets of codes.[4] Some state codes have been enacted into positive law; others are only *prima facie* evidence of the law. In the latter case, positive law continues to be set forth in the volumes of the session laws. An important point to remember is that each state has a set of session laws and at least one current code. The set being used should be examined carefully to note its features, method of publication, and frequency and method of updating its contents. Because state codes contain public acts only, the private, temporary, local, and appropriation acts are available exclusively in the session laws.

The following features are common to many sets of state codes:

1. Constitutions

Each state code contains the state constitution currently in force, usually with annotations, as well as the text of previous constitutions. The text of the Constitution of the United States, typically unannotated, is usually included as well.

2. Tables

Each state code has tables, usually in a separate volume, that cross-reference from session laws to code sections [Illustration 11–3], and many have tables that relate older state codifications to the current one and a table of popular names of state acts.

3. Indexes

All sets of state codes contain a separate subject index for use in locating materials within the entire set. [Illustration 11–4] These indexes may provide the popular names of state acts if this information is not provided in a separate table. In addition, most of these sets also contain an index at the end of each subject grouping, or title, within the set.

---

[4] For articles dealing with the codification of state laws, see Gunther A. Weiss, *The Enchantment of Codification in the Common–Law World,* 25 Yale J. Int'l L. 435 (2000); Lewis Grossman, *Codification and the California Mentality,* 45 Hastings L.J. 617 (1994); Barbara C. Salken, *To Codify or Not to Codify—That Is the Question: A Study of New York's Efforts to Enact an Evidence Code,* 58 Brook. L. Rev. 641 (1992); Shael Herman & David Hoskins, *Perspectives on Code Structure: Historical Experience, Modern Formats, and Policy Considerations,* 54 Tul. L. Rev. 987 (1979); Diana S. Dowling, *The Creation of the Montana Code Annotated,* 40 Mont. L. Rev. 1 (1979); and John H. Tucker, Jr., *Tradition and Technique of Codification in the Modern World: The Louisiana Experience,* 25 La. L. Rev. 698 (1965).

4. Text of Statutes

Each state code contains the currently (as of the date of publication) enforceable public laws of a general nature arranged by subject. [Illustration 11–2]

5. Historical Notes

Historical references, which follow the text of each statute, provide citations to the session laws from which the statute was derived. Since many states have had several codifications of their laws over time, citations frequently are given to a previous codification's version of the current law.

6. Annotations

At least one annotated code is published for each state and in some instances there are two, each by a different publisher. Some are very similar in appearance to the *U.S.C.A.* or the *U.S.C.S.* and include such information as notes of decisions, citations to law review articles, legal encyclopedias, and other research aids, and cross-references to related code provisions. [Illustration 11–2] Some codes include pamphlet "advance annotation services" containing the latest topically arranged materials prior to their incorporation into the pocket supplements.

7. Rules of Court

State codes typically contain the rules of court, which detail the procedural requirements for presenting matters before the various courts within the state.[5] Usually, a separate "rules" pamphlet, issued annually, accompanies the set.

SECTION C. FINDING STATE LEGISLATION

1. Session Laws

All states publish print session law volumes, but these are usually not available until well after the end of the legislative session. Therefore, most states also publish slip laws in pamphlet form; some states also make them available electronically via their websites.[6] Recently enacted laws are also frequently published by private companies in advance sheets as part of a subscription to an annotated state code.[7]

Sessions laws are available electronically in *Westlaw* and *LexisNexis*. Both systems have the laws from the last legislative session as well as some older laws, generally from the early 1990s to the present. The years of

---

[5] Court rules are discussed in Chapter 12 of this book.

[6] The National Conference of State Legislatures offers a directory of the legislative content that each state makes available on the Internet. The list is available at http://www.ncsl.org/public/leglinks.cfm. In addition, the LEGISLATIVE SOURCE BOOK from the Law Librarians' Society of Washington, D.C., has a list of state legislatures, laws, and regulations. This list, which includes both Web links and contact information, is available at http://www.llsdc.org/state-leg/.

[7] For information about the availability of slip laws, advance legislative services, advance annotation services, and electronic versions of state documents, see WILLIAM H. MANZ, GUIDE TO STATE LEGISLATION, LEGISLATIVE HISTORY, AND ADMINISTRATIVE MATERIALS (7th ed. 2008) (AALL Publication Series, no. 61).

coverage vary by state. In addition, *Westlaw* and *LexisNexis* have current and archival bills and bill tracking.

HeinOnline and *Loislaw* also offer electronic session laws for all fifty states from the late 1990s to the present. Dates of coverage vary by state, with new laws added as they are published. The session laws in *HeinOnline* are arranged by state, then by year; keyword searching is not available. Conversely in *Loislaw,* laws can be searched individually or collectively for all states; browsing, however, is not available.

In addition, William S. Hein & Co., publishes state session laws on microfiche. *Session Laws of American States and Territories* is a comprehensive microfiche collection covering 1775 to present. Years of coverage vary by state.

2. Codes

When researching state legislation, a researcher is usually attempting to determine if there is a current state statutory provision on a particular subject, e.g., driver's license eligibility. The first step in the research process is to examine carefully the state code in question and become familiar with its organization.

When using the code in print, consulting the index should enable the researcher to find the applicable provision. [Illustration 11–4] To ensure currency, the method of supplementation should be noted (e.g., revised replacement volumes, pocket supplements, bound cumulative supplements, or advance pamphlets), and any updated sources should be checked for the most recent enactments.

There are times when only the name of an act is known, be it the actual name or the popular name. Many state codes index acts by name, either in a separate table or incorporated into the code's index. [Illustration 11–5] *Shepard's Acts and Cases by Popular Names* is also helpful for locating citations when only the name of the act is known.[8]

Both *Westlaw* and *LexisNexis* make available electronically the current codes for all states, the District of Columbia, and the territories. These state statutory databases within *Westlaw* and *LexisNexis* can be searched individually or collectively for all states or browsed by table of contents. [Illustration 11–6] Materials made available through advance legislative services, i.e., the most recently enacted legislation, are also available on *Westlaw* and *LexisNexis*. Several other commercial publishers, including *Loislaw, VersusLaw,* and *Fastcase,* also provide electronic access to state statutory codes.[9]

LexisNexis StateCapital is a powerful resource for researching state legislation.[10] The service provides access to state bills and bill tracking, codes, constitutions, proposed and enacted administrative regulations, newspapers of record, articles about legislative issues affecting the states, and legislature membership. Users can search for information about one state, any combination of states, or all states.

---

[8] *See* Chapter 15 for additional discussion of *Shepard's.*

[9] These services are discussed in more detail in Chapter 23.

[10] *LexisNexis StateCapital* is not included in the standard law school *LexisNexis* service. It is a separate product available from *LexisNexis.*

All 50 states now make their state codes available electronically on the Internet.[11] There are several sources that provide free and easy access to these state materials. *American Law Sources Online (ALSO!)*,[12] from Law-Source, Inc., is a portal which provides links to sources of state and federal law that are freely available on the Internet. Content is organized geographically with a separate page for each state containing links to session laws, codes, bills, judicial opinions, regulations, court rules, local legislation, and more.

Public Library of Law,[13] powered by *Fastcase*, also offers links to state codes, regulations, court rules, and more. It also features a collection of state and federal judicial opinions. Other portals to state legislation are Cornell's *Legal Information Institute*,[14] *FindLaw*,[15] and *lexisONE*.[16]

At times, a research problem involves an act that has been repealed or is no longer in force. To locate these superseded acts, consult either a version of the code that was in effect when the law was in force or the session law volume that contains the text of the act as originally passed by the legislature.

Superseded State Statutes and Codes from William S. Hein & Co., is a comprehensive microfiche collection that contains volumes of annotated codes which were replaced by later volumes in sets that are currently published. "Superseded," as used in this collection, does not suggest that all laws in a replaced volume are inoperative; however, some of them will be.

SECTION D. ILLUSTRATIONS FOR STATE LEGISLATION

11–1. Page from the 2000 Washington Legislative Service (Session Law)

11–2. Page from the 2002 Pocket Supplement, Revised Code of Washington Annotated (Statute)

11–3. Page from a Transfer Table in the Washington Legislative Service

11–4. Page from an Index Volume, Revised Code of Washington Annotated

11–5. Page from the Popular Name Table, West's Wisconsin Statutes Annotated

11–6. Screen Print, Wisconsin Statutes–Annotated, Table of Contents, Westlaw

---

[11] There is concern that the codes that states have made available on the Web may not be accurate or authentic representations. A 2007 study conducted by the American Association of Law Libraries found that a significant number of state legal resources on the Internet are labeled *official* but none are *authenticated* or afford ready authentication by standard methods. AMERICAN ASSOCIATION OF LAW LIBRARIES ACCESS TO ELECTRONIC LEGAL INFORMATION COMMITTEE AND WASHINGTON AFFAIRS OFFICE, STATE-BY-STATE REPORT ON AUTHENTICATION OF ONLINE LEGAL RESOURCES (March 2007), http://www.aallnet.org/aallwash/authenreport.html.

[12] http://www.lawsource.com/also/.

[13] http://www.plol.org.

[14] http://www.law.cornell.edu/statutes.html.

[15] http://www.findlaw.com/casecode/.

[16] http://www.lexisone.com/.

[Illustration 11–1]

PAGE FROM THE 2000 WASHINGTON LEGISLATIVE SERVICE (SESSION LAW)

Ch. 111	REGULAR SESSION

COURTS—COURTS OF LIMITED JURISDICTION— STATE–WIDE WARRANT PROCESSING

CHAPTER 111

S.H.B. No. 2799

AN ACT Relating to granting state-wide warrant jurisdiction to courts of limited jurisdiction; amending RCW 3.66.010, 3.66.060, 3.66.070, 3.46.030, 3.50.020, and 35.20.030; and creating new sections.

BE IT ENACTED BY THE LEGISLATURE OF THE STATE OF WASHINGTON:

NEW SECTION. **Sec. 1.** The administrator for the courts shall establish a pilot program for the efficient state-wide processing of warrants issued by courts of limited jurisdiction. The pilot program shall contain procedures and criteria for courts of limited jurisdiction to enter into agreements with other courts of limited jurisdiction throughout the state to process each other's warrants when the defendant is within the processing court's jurisdiction. The administrator for the courts shall establish a formula for allocating between the court processing the warrant and the court that issued the warrant any moneys collected and costs associated with the processing of warrants.

Sec. 2. RCW 3.66.010 and 1984 c 258 s 40 are each amended to read as follows:

(1) The justices of the peace elected in accordance with chapters 3.30 through 3.74 RCW are authorized to hold court as judges of the district court for the trial of all actions enumerated in chapters 3.30 through 3.74 RCW or assigned to the district court by law; to hear, try, and determine the same according to the law, and for that purpose where no special provision is otherwise made by law, such court shall be vested with all the necessary powers which are possessed by courts of record in this state; and all laws of a general nature shall apply to such district court as far as the same may be applicable and not inconsistent with the provisions of chapters 3.30 through 3.74 RCW. The district court shall, upon the demand of either party, impanel a jury to try any civil or criminal case in accordance with the provisions of chapter 12.12 RCW. No jury trial may be held in a proceeding involving a traffic infraction.

(2) A district court participating in the program established by the office of the administrator for the courts pursuant to section 1 of this act shall have jurisdiction to take recognizance, approve bail, and arraign defendants held within its jurisdiction on warrants issued by any other court of limited jurisdiction participating in the program.

Sec. 3. RCW 3.66.060 and 1984 c 258 s 44 are each amended to read as follows:

The district court shall have jurisdiction: (1) Concurrent with the superior court of all

Sec. 4. RCW 3.66.070 and 1991 c 290 s 2 are each amended to read as follows:

All criminal actions shall be brought in the district where the alleged violation occurred: PROVIDED, That (1) the prosecuting attorney may file felony cases in the district in which the county seat is located, (2) with the consent of the defendant criminal actions other than those arising out of violations of city ordinances may be brought in or transferred to the district in which the county seat is located, and (3) if the alleged violation relates to driving, or being in actual physical control of, a motor vehicle while under the influence of intoxicating

     Additions are indicated by underline; deletions by strikeout

[Illustration 11–2]

PAGE FROM THE 2002 POCKET SUPPLEMENT, REVISED CODE OF WASHINGTON ANNOTATED (STATUTE)

COURTS OF LIMITED JURISDICTION   **3.66.020**

This Illustration is from the 2002 pocket supplement to West's *Revised Code of Washington Annotated*. Notice how the session law that was passed two years before (See Illustration 11-1) was incorporated into the state code. Notice also how a citation is given to the session law from which § 3.66.010 was codified.

Following the text of each session of a statute, citations are provided to: (1) "Historical and Statutory Notes"; (2) "Library References" that index articles from law reviews published in the state and references to encyclopedias, digests, and treatises; and (3) "Notes of Decisions" from all federal and state cases and Attorney General opinions that have cited and interpreted this section of the statute.

jury to try any civil or criminal case in accordance with the provisions of chapter 12.12 RCW. No jury trial may be held in a proceeding involving a traffic infraction.

(2) A district court participating in the program established by the office of the administrator for the courts pursuant to RCW 2.56.160 shall have jurisdiction to take recognizance, approve bail, and arraign defendants held within its jurisdiction on warrants issued by any other court of limited jurisdiction participating in the program.

[2000 c 111 § 2; 1984 c 258 § 40; 1979 ex.s. c 136 § 20; 1961 c 299 § 112.]

Historical and Statutory Notes ◄───────

2000 Legislation
Laws 2000, ch. 111, § 2, inserted the subsection numbering; and, added subsec. (2).

Library References ◄───────

Trials, verdicts, see Wash.Prac. vol. 4A, Orland, CRLJ 49.

Notes of Decisions ◄───────

Municipal court 7
Powers, generally 6

─────────

4. Transfer of venue
Seastrom v. Konz (1976) 86 Wash.2d 377, [main volume] 544 P.2d 744.

6. Powers, generally
This section delineating general powers of district courts does not give district

courts the power to appoint special prosecuting attorneys. Ladenburg v. Campbell (1990) 56 Wash.App. 701, 784 P.2d 1306.

7. Municipal court
RCWA 3.66.010 authorizing county district court judges to sit as municipal court judges did not permit district court judge to sit as municipal judge without mayoral appointment. Nollette v. Christianson (1990) 115 Wash.2d 594, 800 P.2d 359.

3.66.020. Civil jurisdiction

If the value of the claim or the amount at issue does not exceed fifty thousand dollars, exclusive of interest, costs, and attorneys' fees, the district

[Illustration 11–3]

PAGE FROM A TRANSFER TABLE IN THE WASHINGTON
LEGISLATIVE SERVICE

TABLE 1—CUMULATIVE

REVISED CODE OF WASHINGTON— AMENDMENTS, REPEALS, ADDITIONS, ETC.

Listing the Chapters and Sections of the Revised Code of Washington and the Revised Code of Washington Annotated affected by the Laws of 2000, published in the 2000 Washington Legislative Service.

RCWA and RCW Sec.	Effect	2000 Chap.	Sec.
1.16.050	Amended	60	1
2.24.040	Amended	73	1
3.46.030	Amended	111	5
3.50.020	Amended	111	6
3.50.090	Amended	55	1
3.66.010	Amended	111	2
3.66.020	Amended	49	1
3.66.060	Amended	111	3
3.66.070	Amended	111	4
4.64.030	Amended	41	1
6.27	Section added	72	6
6.27.005	Amended	72	1

When only a citation to a state session law is available, a transfer table may be consulted to locate where a particular section of a session law is within the state's code. These tables are usually included in a volume of the state's code as well as in the back of the legislative service pamphlets. For example, this illustration shows that Chapter 111, Sec. 2 of the 2000 legislative session amended § 3.66.010 of the *RCW.*

Sometimes an individual session law will deal with several Different matters, as does Chapter 111. In these instances, notice how the session law is incorporated into several sections of the code.

9.94A.110	Reenacted and amended	75	8
9.94A.120	Reenacted and amended	28	5
		43	1
9.94A.130	Amended	28	9
9.94A.135	Amended	28	27

T1–1

[Illustration 11–4]

PAGE FROM AN INDEX VOLUME, REVISED CODE OF WASHINGTON ANNOTATED

DISTRICT

> When attempting to locate a state statute by subject, the index to the state code should be consulted.
> This Illustration shows how the Index to the *Revised Code of Washington* is used to locate the powers and duties of the district courts, the subject of Illustrations 11-1 through 11-3.

559

[Illustration 11–5]

PAGE FROM THE POPULAR NAME TABLE, WEST'S WISCONSIN STATUTES ANNOTATED

POPULAR NAME TABLE

Funds transfers, Uniform Commercial Code, 410.101 et seq.
General Municipality Law, 66.0101 et seq.
Hazardous Substances Labeling Act, 100.37
Hazardous Waste Management Act, 291.001 et seq.
Hospital Regulation and Approval Act, 50.32 et seq.
Housing Authorities Law, 66.1201
Housing Authority for Elderly Persons Law, 66.1213
Huber Law, 303.08

Nonprobate Transfers on Death Act, 705.10 et seq.
Nonprofit Association Act, 184.01 et seq.
Nonstock Corporation Law, 181.0103 et seq.
Oil Inspection Act, 168.01 et seq.
Open Meeting Law, 19.81 et seq.
Open Records Act, 19.31 et seq. ◄
Organized Crime Control Act, 946.80 et seq.
Out of state parolee supervision, 304.13
Partnerships, 178.01 et seq.
Photographic Copies of Business and Public Records as Evidence Act, 889.29

POPULAR NAME TABLE

Funds transfers, Uniform Commercial Code, 410.101 et seq.
General Municipality Law, 66.0101 et seq.
Hazardous Substances Labeling Act, 100.37
Hazardous Waste Management Act, 291.001 et seq.
Hospital Regulation and Approval Act, 50.32 et seq.
Housing Authorities Law, 66.1201
Housing Authority for Elderly Persons Law, 66.1213
Huber Law, 303.08

Nonprobate Transfers on Death Act, 705.10 et seq.
Nonprofit Association Act, 184.01 et seq.
Nonstock Corporation Law, 181.0103 et seq.
Oil Inspection Act, 168.01 et seq.
Open Meeting Law, 19.81 et seq.
Open Records Act, 19.31 et seq. ◄
Organized Crime Control Act, 946.80 et seq.
Out of state parolee supervision, 304.13
Partnerships, 178.01 et seq.
Photographic Copies of Business and Public Records as Evidence Act, 889.29

> Many state codes index acts by name, either in a separate table or incorporated into the code's index.
>
> For example, if one knows that Wisconsin has enacted the Open Records Act, the citation to the act can be found by consulting the popular name table.

seq.
Investment securities, Uniform Commercial Code, 408.101 et seq.
Joint Obligations Act, 113.01 et seq.
Judicial Notice of Foreign Law Act, 902.02
Juvenile Justice Code, 938.01 et seq.
Lease of goods, Uniform Commercial Code, 411.101 et seq.
Letters of credit, Uniform Commercial Code, 405.101 et seq.
Living wills, 154.01 et seq.
Long Arm Statute, 801.05
Management of Institutional Funds Act, 112.10
Marital Property Act, 766.01 et seq.
Megans Law, 301.45
Mental Health Act, 51.001 et seq.
Metallic Mining Reclamation Act, 293.01 et seq.
Military Justice Code, 21.37
Model Real Estate Time Share Act, 707.02 et seq.
Motor club service, 616.71 et seq.
Motor vehicle insurance, Safety Responsibility Law, 344.12 et seq.
Motor vehicles,
　Consumer Lease Act, 429.101 et seq.
　Safety Responsibility Law, 344.22
　Title and Antitheft Law, 342.01 et seq.
Multifamily Dwelling Code, 101.971 et seq.
Municipal Electric Company Act, 66.0825
Municipal Employment Relations Act, 111.70 et seq.
Municipal Law, 66.0101 et seq.
Navigable Waters Protection Law, 281.31
Negotiable instruments, Uniform Commercial Code, 403.102 et seq.

Rules of evidence, 901.01 et seq.
Safe place statute, 101.11
Safety Responsibility Law, 344.12 et seq.
Sales, Uniform Commercial Code, 402.101 et seq.
Secured Creditors Dividends in Liquidation Proceedings Act, 128.25
Secured transactions, Uniform Commercial Code, 409.101 et seq.
Securities Law, 551.01 et seq.
Securities Ownership by Minors Act, 54.92
Seller of Checks Law, 217.01 et seq.
Sex Crimes Law, 975.001 et seq.
Soldiers and Sailors Civil Relief Act, 45.53
Soldiers and Sailors Relief Act, 21.75
Stacking Statute (insurance), 631.43
State Defense Force Act, 21.025
State Employment Labor Relations Act, 111.80 et seq.
Stop and Frisk Law, 968.24, 968.25
Tax Increment Law, 66.1105
Theft, Vehicle Title and Antitheft Law, 342.01 et seq.
Title and Antitheft Law, motor vehicles, 342.01 et seq.
TOD security registration, 705.21 et seq.
Town mutuals, 612.01 et seq.
Trade Secrets Act, 134.90
Transboundary Pollution Reciprocal Access Act, 299.33
Transfers on Death Law, 854.01 et seq.
Transfers to Minors Act, 54.854 et seq.
Trusts, Uniform Common Trust Fund Act, 223.055 et seq.
Turnpike Corporation Act, 182.30 et seq.
Unclaimed Property Act, 177.01 et seq.
Unfair Sales Act, 100.30

1198

[Illustration 11–6]

SCREEN PRINT, WISCONSIN STATUTES–ANNOTATED, TABLE OF CONTENTS, WESTLAW

SECTION E.   COMPARATIVE STATE STATUTORY RESEARCH

When a researcher is interested in comparing a particular law of one state with that of another or comparing similar laws of all states, searching each state code individually may be required. Unfortunately, state statutes are not organized according to comparable indexing or classification schemes, and they might use different descriptive language. Therefore, it can be very difficult to find substantially similar statutory provisions from different states.

Fortunately, several sources have pulled together state statutes on particular subjects. Some of those sources are described below.

1.   Indexes

Treatises, legal periodical articles, and other secondary sources are often good sources for multi-state comparisons of state laws. Especially helpful is *Subject Compilations of State Laws*,[17] a bibliography of articles,

---

[17] Cheryl Rae Nyberg & Carol Boast, Subject Compilations of State Laws: An Annotated Bibliography (1984–).

books, government documents, looseleaf services, court opinions and websites that compare state laws on hundreds of subjects. Coverage begins with 1979. It is updated annually in print and quarterly in *HeinOnline*.

Statutes Compared: A U.S., Canadian, Multinational Research Guide to Statutes by Subject[18] may also be useful for locating sources of state statutory comparisons. In addition to U.S. material, this annotated bibliography also indexes international sources.

2. Fifty–State Surveys

The increasing availability of fifty-state surveys has vastly simplified comparative statutory research. These surveys compile the statutory, and oftentimes regulatory, provisions covering a designated topic for all 50 states. In the last few years, both *Westlaw* and *LexisNexis* have added fifty-state survey databases. The surveys include charts comparing the laws of each state, the citation to the statute or regulation, and the subject matter and/or details about the laws.

Another source for fifty-state surveys is *National Survey of State Laws*.[19] This volume also offers charts that allow users to make basic state-by-state comparisons of current state laws for various legal topics. Content from *National Survey of State Laws* is available electronically in *Westlaw's 50 State Survey* database.

Some surveys are available on the Internet. On their *50–State Legislative Tracking Web Resources* site,[20] the National Conference of State Legislatures has hundreds of fifty-state compilations on a wide range of topics. *Wex*, from Cornell's Legal Information Institute, offers a topical index to state statutes.[21] Approximately 40 topics are covered, with links to the states with statutes related to those topics.

3. Looseleaf Services

Many looseleaf services provide full texts, or abstracts of, or tables of citations to, state statutes dealing with a specific subject. For example, Commerce Clearing House's *Inheritance, Estate and Gift Tax Reporter* includes separate volumes that set forth the text of state laws from all states on wills, trusts, and estates.[22]

4. Martindale–Hubbell Law Digest

For many years, this digest of state laws was a part of the *Martindale-Hubbell Law Directory* in print. The full fifty-state digest is now only available on CD–ROM from *Martindale-Hubbell* or online through *LexisNexis*. Individual states are available in paperback from Amazon.com.[23]

---

[18] JON S. SCHULTZ, STATUTES COMPARED: A U.S., CANADIAN, MULTINATIONAL RESEARCH GUIDE TO STATUTES BY SUBJECT (2d ed. 2001).

[19] RICHARD A. LEITER, NATIONAL SURVEY OF STATE LAWS (1993).

[20] http://www.ncsl.org/programs/lis/lrl/50statetracking.htm.

[21] http://topics.law.cornell.edu/wex/state_statutes.

[22] Looseleaf services are discussed in Chapter 14 of this book.

[23] *Martindale-Hubbell* is discussed more fully in Chapter 20 of this book.

SECTION F.   STATE LEGISLATIVE HISTORIES

Attempting to compile a legislative history for a state law in a manner similar to that described in Chapter 10 for federal laws is often difficult and, at times, is impossible. As a general rule, state legislatures do not publish their debates, committee reports, or transcripts of hearings held before legislative committees. Yet, the need for these sources is often just as great, because state laws can contain provisions that are vague and ambiguous and need clarification.[24]

The most accessible official documents are the state Senate and House journals. These journals usually contain only brief minutes of the proceedings and final votes on legislation.[25] A few states may issue reports of a state law revision commission or the reports of special committees of the legislature for selected laws. If a state has an annotated code, the notes should be examined carefully to see if reference is made to documents of this type.

Local newspapers may also be useful sources for legislative history research. News stories, articles, interviews, and editorials written around the time that the legislation was proposed and enacted may help illustrate legislative intent.

Often, guidance for research in state legislative history is available in the state legal research guides listed in Appendix B of this book or from librarians with knowledge of sources within the state. Some states maintain "working documents" or copies of legislative history materials that are only available through a visit to the state's legislative library.[26] In many instances, however, extrinsic aids for determining legislative intent are not available, and one must rely on the language of the act by using the ordinary rules of statutory construction.

SECTION G.   INTERSTATE COMPACTS

The United States Constitution provides that "No State shall, without Consent of Congress ... enter into any Agreement or Compact with another State...."[27]

In an early interpretation of this clause, the Supreme Court of the United States held that the Constitution prohibited all agreements between states unless consented to by Congress.[28] However, in a subsequent case, the Court changed its position and held that congressional consent was not necessary for agreements or compacts that did not increase the political

---

[24] To determine which state documents are available, see MANZ, *supra* note 7. For information on the legislative process for each state, see STATE LEGISLATIVE SOURCEBOOK: A RESOURCE GUIDE TO LEGISLATIVE INFORMATION IN THE FIFTY STATES (annual). Also useful is José R. Torres & Steve Windsor, *State Legislative Histories: A Select, Annotated Bibliography*, 85 LAW LIBR. J. 545 (1993).

[25] Maine and Pennsylvania, however, have legislative journals that record actual legislative debate and parallel the CONGRESSIONAL RECORD in form and content.

[26] Contact information for state legislative libraries appears in the Law Librarians' Society of Washington, D.C.'s LEGISLATIVE SOURCE BOOK available at http://www.llsdc.org/state-leg/. The site also lists contact information for commercial sources for state legislative research.

[27] U.S. CONST. art. I, § 10, cl. 3.

[28] Holmes v. Jennison, 39 U.S. (14 Pet.) 540 (1840).

powers of the states or interfere with the supremacy of the United States.[29] Normally, however, interstate agreements or compacts are formally enacted by the legislatures of the states involved and are then submitted to Congress for its consent.[30]

Until about 1900, most interstate compacts dealt with boundary disputes between states. Since then, compacts have more commonly been used to resolve, through cooperation, problems common to two or more states, such as flood or pollution control, or the establishment of a port authority.

1. Publication of Interstate Compacts

The texts of interstate agreements are set forth in the session laws of the respective states and in *United States Statutes at Large,* since they involve agreements among the states involved.

A complete listing of compacts is in *Interstate Compacts & Agencies,* published periodically by the Council of State Governments.[31] It contains the following information:

  a. Title, abstract, and state list for each compact;

  b. Subject index;

  c. List of compacts by state; and

  d. List of compacts no longer enforced

The most up-to-date information regarding interstate compacts is available from the Council of State Governments website.[32] This site indexes all interstate compacts known to exist.

Each biennial edition of *The Book of the States,* also published by the Council of State Governments, contains a chapter on current developments in interstate compacts and a selective listing of the more significant agreements.

2. Locating Judicial Opinions on Interstate Compacts

  a. *Digests.* Digests of cases involving interstate compacts are under *States*, Key Number 6, in the West digests and under States, Territories & Possessions § 52 in the *Digest of the United States Supreme Court Reports, Lawyers' Edition.*

  b. *State Code Annotated Editions.* The practice of including the text of compacts in state codes varies. The indexes to the code of each state should be consulted.

---

[29] Virginia v. Tennessee, 148 U.S. 503, 518 (1893). *See also* United States Steel Corp. v. Multistate Tax Commission, 434 U.S. 452 (1978).

[30] Interstate compacts do not have to be formally enacted by Congress. *See* the annotation to Art. 1, § 10, cl. 3, *in* THE CONSTITUTION OF THE UNITED STATES OF AMERICA: ANALYSIS AND INTERPRETATION 402–07 (Libr. of Cong. 1992 ed.). *See also* FREDERICK L. ZIMMERMAN & MITCHELL WENDELL, THE LAW AND USE OF INTERSTATE COMPACTS (2d ed. 1976); PAUL T. HARDY, INTERSTATE COMPACTS: THE TIES THAT BIND (1982); Kevin J. Heron, *The Interstate Compact in Transition: From Cooperative State Action to Congressionally Coerced Agreements,* 60 ST. JOHN'S L. REV. 1 (1985); Jill Elaine Hasday, *Interstate Compacts in a Democratic Society: The Problem of Permanency,* 49 FLA. L. REV. 1 (1997).

[31] COUNCIL OF STATE GOVERNMENTS, INTERSTATE COMPACTS & AGENCIES (2003).

[32] http://www.csg.org/programs/ncic/database/.

c. *Citators.* The statutes volumes or sections of the appropriate *Shepard's Citations* can be used to Shepardize state code, session law, and *United States Statutes at Large* citations.

SECTION H.   MUNICIPAL OR LOCAL GOVERNMENT LEGISLATION

Traditionally, the various forms of local government are known as *municipal corporations* or *municipalities.* Municipalities are instruments of the state and have only such powers as are granted to them by the state. These powers vary from state to state, and the constitution and statutes of the state in which the municipality is located must be examined to ascertain a municipality's scope of authority.

1.   Municipal Charters

In general, a municipality operates under a charter, which is the basic document setting forth its power. Usually the charter has been adopted by the voters of a municipality and is analogous to a state constitution. The form of publication varies and, in the larger cities, may include bound volumes.

2.   Ordinances

Ordinances are the legislative enactments of local jurisdictions, as passed by their legislative body, e.g., the city council, county commissioners, or board of supervisors. Ordinances are to municipalities what session laws are to the federal and state governments. In larger cities, ordinances are first published in an official journal and may be separately published in *slip* form. In smaller communities, they are frequently published in the local newspaper.

3.   Codes

Municipal codes are codifications of ordinances. They generally contain only ordinances in force at the time of publication and are usually classified and arranged by subject. Many municipalities are now publishing their codes, ordinances, and charters on the Internet.[33] The Seattle Public Library maintains a nationwide list of links to municipal code resources available online.[34] *American Law Sources Online* also includes links to municipal and county codes, if available, for each state.[35]

Very few municipal codes are published in print. Most often, these are for cities, rather than townships or counties, and may not be supplemented

---

[33] Most municipal ordinances on the Internet are made available through code publishing companies. These include American Legal Publishing, Code Publishing Company, General Code Publishers, LexisNexis Municipal Codes, Municipal Code Corporation, Quality Code Publishing, and Sterling Codifiers.

Some municipalities offer additional legislative documents on the Internet through *Legistar. Legistar* is a legislative management software package that helps municipalities manage the flow of documents through the legislative process. These documents (ordinances, resolutions, reports, committee minutes, etc.) are then made available on the Internet. *See, for example*: http://www.legistar.com/legistar/clients_leg.html.

[34] http://www.spl.org/default.asp?pageid=collection_municodes.

[35] http://www.lawsource.com/also/.

in a timely fashion. When municipal codes are not published in print or available electronically, it may be necessary to go to the seat of government and examine the ordinances on file there. The local public library may also maintain a copy of the code.

4. Interpretations of Municipal Charters and Ordinances

Most municipal codes do not include annotations of opinions interpreting the charters and ordinances. The following sources are useful in obtaining judicial opinions for municipal legislation:

a. *State Digests*. Judicial opinions interpreting ordinances or charters are included in state digests. The location of the appropriate West key numbers or paragraph numbers under which such opinions are abstracted can be located through the use of the index or topical outlines to the digest.

b. *Treatises*. Both McQuillin's *The Law of Municipal Corporations*[36] and *Antieau on Local Government Law*[37] are useful in locating judicial opinions. Helpful in understanding and drafting ordinances are *Municipal Ordinances: Text and Forms*[38] and *Municipal Legal Forms with Commentary*.[39]

---

[36] Eugene McQuillin, The Law of Municipal Corporations (3d ed.).

[37] Sandra M. Stevenson & Chester James Antieau, Antieau on Local Government Law (2d ed.).

[38] Byron S. Matthews & Thomas Alexander Matthews, Municipal Ordinances: Text and Forms (2d ed.).

[39] Ralph J. Moore, Municipal Legal Forms with Commentary (1999).

Chapter 12

COURT RULES AND PROCEDURES

This chapter describes the resources that provide and explain rules and procedures for the conduct of matters in courts. Rules of courts control the operation of the courts and the conduct of the litigants appearing before them. The sources discussed in this chapter deal with the procedures for initiating and defending a case; the procedures and methods for appealing cases to appellate courts; and the procedures within appellate courts. Court rules relate to matters such as the filing of complaints, assignment of cases, methods of appeal, and the proper means for making motions that are required during the many phases of litigation. Some rules are as basic as those specifying the format that must be followed in preparing a document. Other rules, such as those establishing time limitations, control whether or not a matter can proceed. In general, the purposes of court rules are to establish uniform procedures; to provide parties to a lawsuit with information and instructions on matters pertaining to judicial proceedings; and to aid the court in conducting its business. These sources include legislation, rules promulgated by courts, judicial opinions construing these rules and legislation, and legal forms used in court proceedings.

The advent of the Internet and the World Wide Web has made court rules from both federal and state courts easily accessible. Federal and state courts and/or bar associations have posted current electronic versions of the rules of court for that jurisdiction on the Web. These rules can be accessed directly by searching with a standard Web browser or by accessing a website, such as *LLRX.com*,[1] *American Law Sources Online (ALSO!)*,[2] the *Public Library of Law*,[3] or the *Legal Information Institute* at Cornell University Law School,[4] which aggregates court rules. The fee-based computer-assisted legal research services, such as *LexisNexis*, *Westlaw*, and *Loislaw*, also make available court rules. Rules of court also are available in many print sources.

SECTION A. FEDERAL COURT RULES: SOURCES, INTERPRETATIONS, ANALYSIS, AND FORMS

1. In General

The power of a court to promulgate court rules is found either in its inherent authority or in constitutional or statutory provisions. For exam-

---

[1] *LLRX.com* has aggregated most, if not all, rules of court that have been posted to the Web; see http://www.llrx.com/courtrules.

[2] http://www.lawsource.com/also/.

[3] http://www.plol.org.

[4] http://www.law.cornell.edu.

ple, Section 17 of the Judiciary Act of 1789 gave the federal courts the authority to promulgate rules relating to the orderly conduct of their business. Federal statutory language, found primarily in Title 28 of the *United States Code (U.S.C.)*, mandates some procedural requirements for the courts.

Federal court rules and procedures can be grouped into four categories: (1) rules of general application that are national in scope; (2) rules for specific federal courts, such as for the Supreme Court of the United States and the bankruptcy and admiralty courts; (3) "local" rules for individual courts within the federal court system; and (4) statutory requirements found in Title 28 of the *United States Code*.

Four sets of rules of general application in the federal courts have been promulgated: the Federal Rules of Civil Procedure, effective September 16, 1938; the Federal Rules of Criminal Procedure, effective March 21, 1946; the Federal Rules of Appellate Procedure, effective July 1, 1968; and the Federal Rules of Evidence, effective July 1, 1975.

In addition, various federal courts have rules specific to their operations. For example, filing a motion in the U.S. Court of International Trade may involve a different process from filing a motion in the U.S. Court of Federal Claims. "Local" rules often add procedural requirements or limitations. For example, one federal district court may permit television in the courtroom; another may not. Additionally, separate statutes, and judicial interpretations of these statutes, can control matters of court procedure.

Court rules often are available in both unannotated and annotated versions.

2. Unannotated Rules

a. *Electronic Sources.* As noted above, the rules of most federal courts have been posted to the Internet and are easily accessible either directly or through an aggregating website such as LLRX.com.

Westlaw, *LexisNexis*, and *Loislaw* provide online access to the federal rules. *Westlaw* contains the most recent versions of rules appearing in the *U.S.C.*, updated by any recent amendments to those rules. These include the four sets of rules of general application and the various rules of the specialized courts. *LexisNexis* contains the four sets of rules of general application, as well as the Advisory Committee Notes. Some of the other federal court rules are also included. *Loislaw* has a full collection of general, special, and local rules of federal courts.

b. *United States Code.* The text of the Federal Rules of Criminal Procedure is set forth in the Appendix to Title 18 of the *United States Code*; the text of the Federal Rules of Civil Procedure, Appellate Procedure, and Evidence, as well as the rules for some of the specialized federal courts, are contained in the Appendix to Title 28 of the *U.S.C.* Other sets of court rules accompany the particular *U.S.C.* title covering specific subjects, e.g., Bankruptcy, Title 11; Copyright, Title 17.

The *U.S.C.* also includes Judicial Conference Advisory Committee Notes. These notes are provided by the committee that drafted the original rules, and also include notes by any subsequent committees that proposed changes to the rules. These notes can prove especially helpful in interpreting the meaning and intent of the rules.

Because of the delay in publishing the *U.S.C.*, other privately produced sources often are more useful, especially for recent rules changes:

c. *Federal Procedure, Lawyers Edition* (West, formerly published by Lawyers Cooperative Publishing). This large set reproduces in several pamphlets the complete text of rules of general application and Advisory Committee notes, along with several other sets of specialized rules. Additional volumes contain the rules adopted by each of the circuit courts of appeals and the district courts within each circuit.

d. *Federal Rules Service* (West, formerly published by Lawyers Cooperative Publishing). This set, discussed in Section A–5–b of this chapter, contains a "Finding Aids" volume that includes the Federal Rules of Civil and Appellate Procedure along with a cumulative table of cases construing these rules and a supplemental word index.

e. *Cyclopedia of Federal Procedure,* 3d ed. (West, formerly published by Lawyers Cooperative Publishing). The texts of the various rules, without the Advisory Committee notes, are in volume 16A (Parts 1 and 2), "Rules," of this set.

f. *Pamphlet Editions.* West publishes annually a pamphlet that contains various federal rules and related statutory provisions. In addition, in connection with the state statutory compilations published by West and LexisNexis, pamphlets are issued annually that contain the federal district court and appellate court rules for the corresponding courts in that state.

g. *Reporters of Federal Cases.* When changes to major rules are proposed or adopted, they are published in the advance sheets to West's *Supreme Court Reporter, Federal Reporter 3d, Federal Supplement 2d,* and *Federal Rules Decisions.* The advance sheets to the *U.S. Code Congressional and Administrative News* contain amendments to the rules for all courts. The bound *Federal Rules Decisions* also include rule changes, preliminary drafts of proposed changes, proposed amendments, congressional acts concerning court rules, and the publisher's editorial comments.

3. Annotated Rules

Four sources provide annotated versions of federal rules:

a. *United States Code Service* (LexisNexis). The various court rules are in unnumbered volumes entitled "Court Rules." The text of each rule is set forth, followed by annotations of cases involving the rule. [Illustrations 12–1 and 12–2] The notes following the rules include comments from the Advisory Committee, as well as references to law review articles and to appropriate sections of other publications by LexisNexis. This compilation of rules is especially useful for its historical references.

b. *United States Code Annotated* (West). The annotated rules in this set correspond to the arrangement of the *United States Code*. Some rules follow, for example, Titles 18 and 28. Each rule is followed by editorial annotations and Advisory Committee notes. Newer volumes also contain information for *Westlaw* searches and citations to law review articles and other secondary sources. [Illustrations 12–3 and 12–4]

c. *Digest of United States Supreme Court Reports, Lawyers Edition* (LexisNexis). This set includes several "Court Rules" volumes containing the rules for all federal courts, the Advisory Committee notes, references to other publications, and annotations of cases decided by the Supreme Court of the United States that interpret the rules.

d. *Moore's Federal Rules Pamphlets* (Matthew Bender/LexisNexis). Published annually in three volumes, these pamphlets contain the four sets of rules of general application, the rules for the Supreme Court of the United States, and a few selected statutory provisions. Excerpts from the Advisory Committee notes, annotations of leading cases, and references to the multivolume treatise, *Moore's Federal Practice,* also are provided.

4. Statutory Provisions Relating to Court Procedure

Statutory provisions addressing court procedure are in various titles of the *U.S.C.* Perhaps the most notable are the venue and *habeas corpus* provisions in Title 28. These statutory provisions are referenced in treatises and often are in pamphlets that include the federal rules of general application.

5. Federal Rules Interpreted by the Courts

After rules are promulgated, litigation frequently occurs concerning the meaning of the rules and their applicability to specific situations. When involved in research on federal procedure, it is common to need to locate judicial opinions that interpret the rules. The following West sources are useful for this purpose:

a. *Federal Rules Decisions. Federal Rules Decisions (F.R.D.)* is a unit of West's *National Reporter System* that contains cases of the federal district courts since 1939 that interpret the Federal Rules of Civil Procedure and cases since 1946 that interpret the Federal Rules of Criminal Procedure. These cases are not published in the *Federal Supplement.* Similar to other units of the *National Reporter System, F.R.D.* is issued in advance sheets and bound volumes, with headnotes that are classified in West's key number system. In addition to judicial opinions, the set also includes articles on various aspects of federal courts and federal procedure. A cumulative index to these articles is in every tenth volume, and a consolidated index for volumes 1–122 is in volume 122.

b. *Federal Rules Service* (formerly published by Callaghan). This set is useful when searching for judicial opinions construing the Federal Rules of Civil Procedure and the Federal Rules of Appellate Procedure. It is in three sections:

(1) *Federal Rules Service* reporter.

First Series, 1939–1958

Second Series, 1958–1985

Third Series, 1985 to present

The Third Series is kept current with monthly advance sheets.

(2) *Federal Rules Digest*, 3d ed., 1973 to present (formerly published by Callaghan). This multivolume digest classifies all judicial opinions from

April 1954 to present that appear in the *Federal Rules Service*. Headnotes are organized using the publisher's "Findex" system of rule subdivisions, which enables a user to pinpoint a rule of interest and go directly to digest sections listing pertinent cases. Abstracts of cases from 1938 to 1954 are located in the four volumes of *Federal Rules Digest*, 2d ed.

(3) *Finding Aids* volume. This volume includes a word index to the Federal Rules of Civil Procedure and Appellate Procedure. The full text of the Rules of Civil Procedure and the Rules of Appellate Procedure is also set forth in the Finding Aids volume, together with the Findex outline (in which numbered rule subdivisions are related to specific digest sections) following each rule.

c. *Federal Rules of Evidence Service* (formerly published by Lawyers Cooperative Publishing Company). This set is useful when searching for civil and criminal cases from all federal courts that have interpreted the Federal Rules of Evidence. The format is similar to that of the *Federal Rules Service,* in that the set contains a case reporter (covering September 1975 to present), a digest, and a Finding Aids volume with the Findex feature.

d. *Federal Rules of Evidence Digest*. This set, arranged by rule number, abstracts cases that have been decided under a particular rule number.

6. Treatises

Many treatises pertain to the practice and procedures of the federal courts. They generally contain the text of appropriate statutes and federal rules that are the subject of the treatise. Typically, the text of each rule is followed by an analysis of that rule; citations to judicial opinions are given in the footnotes. The multivolume sets discussed below, some of which are encyclopedic in nature, are useful in obtaining commentary on federal practice: Additional treatises and books of forms can be located by checking the catalog in a law library.

a. *Cyclopedia of Federal Procedure*, 3d ed. (West, formerly by Lawyers Cooperative Publishing Company).

b. *Federal Procedure, Lawyers Edition* (West, formerly by Lawyers Cooperative Publishing).

c. Charles Alan Wright & Arthur R. Miller, *Federal Practice and Procedure*, 3d ed. (West) This is perhaps the most frequently cited source on federal practice and procedure. [Illustration 12–5]

d. *Moore's Federal Practice,* 3d ed. (Matthew Bender/LexisNexis; 4 vols, looseleaf).

e. *Federal Litigation Guide* (Matthew Bender/LexisNexis).

f. *Orfield's Criminal Procedure Under the Federal Rules,* 2d ed. (West, formerly by Lawyers Cooperative Publishing).

g. *Weinstein's Federal Evidence*, 2d ed. (Matthew Bender/LexisNexis; 6 volumes, looseleaf).

7. Form Books

Model instruments or forms used in federal practice are published in resources that relate the federal rules to the forms or instruments which they require. These forms contain terms, phrases, and other essential details needed by attorneys filing documents in federal courts. The resources discussed in this section are multivolume practice form books.[5]

a. *Bender's Federal Practice Forms*. This is a looseleaf publication with annotations and cross-references to *Moore's Federal Practice*, 3d ed. The forms cover civil and criminal rules.

b. *Nichols Cyclopedia of Federal Procedure Forms* (West, formerly by Lawyers Cooperative Publishing). The forms are annotated and cover civil and criminal rules, as well as rules promulgated by certain administrative agencies.

c. *West's Federal Forms*. This set, covering both civil and criminal forms for use in the federal courts, is annotated and includes references to *Federal Practice and Procedure*, 3d ed.

d. *Federal Procedural Forms, Lawyers Edition* (West, formerly by Lawyers Cooperative Publishing). This set provides civil and criminal forms for use in all federal courts, as well as for adversary and rulemaking proceedings before administrative agencies.

8. Historical Sources

At times, it may be necessary to go beyond the text of the rules, the Advisory Committee notes, judicial interpretations, and secondary sources. The following sources are especially helpful in providing historical information about the federal rules:

a. *Records of the U.S. Judicial Conference: Committees on Rules of Practice and Procedures, 1935–1988* (Congressional Information Service). This major compilation, updated periodically, gathers together the minutes and transcripts of meetings, deskbooks, correspondence, and comments of committees established by the Supreme Court of the United States to draft new rules of practice and procedures for the federal district and appellate courts.[6]

b. *Drafting History of the Federal Rules of Criminal Procedure* (Madeleine Wilken & Nicholas Triffin comp., William S. Hein & Co., 1991). This set provides a "legislative history" of the Federal Rules of Criminal Procedure. It includes a reproduction of the four-volume *Comments, Recommendations, and Suggestions Concerning the Proposed Rules of Criminal Procedure* originally used by the committee members. In addition, the set contains previously unpublished preliminary drafts, letters and Supreme Court memoranda, successive preliminary drafts of the Rules of

---

[5] Form books are discussed in Chapter 20.

[6] This collection, consisting of over 4,000 pieces of microfiche, is organized by committee into the following groupings: Standing Committee on Rules 1935–91; Committee on Civil Procedure 1935–91; Committee on Admiralty Procedure 1952–88; Committee on Criminal Procedure 1941–91; Committee on Appellate Procedure, 1958–91; Committee on Bankruptcy 1949–91; and Committee on Evidence 1959–96. Three printed indexes provide access to the set: "List of Documents"; "Index by Rule Topics"; and "Index by Names of Individuals and Organizations."

Criminal Procedure, the Final Committee report, and final approved Federal Rules of Criminal Procedure. Various finding aids facilitate research.

c. *The Federal Rules of Evidence: Legislative Histories and Related Documents* (James F. Bailey, II & Oscar M. Trelles, III, comp., William S. Hein & Co., 1980). This four-volume collection contains materials from the American Law Institute, the National Conference of Commissioners on Uniform State Laws, and the Judicial Conference of the United States, as well as congressional hearings and legislation relating to the Federal Rules of Evidence.

SECTION B. FEDERAL COURT RULES OF SPECIFIC APPLICABILITY, INCLUDING LOCAL RULES

The Supreme Court of the United States, federal courts of appeals, federal district courts, and various specialized courts have promulgated court rules. These rules apply only to the court adopting them and are mainly concerned with its operation. These include court-specific rules for filing motions and preparing briefs, as well as other rules dealing with the procedure of the court. The rules for the various federal courts are contained in the following publications:

1.   Rules for the Supreme Court of the United States

The most widely used treatise for practice in the Supreme Court of the United States is Robert L. Stern et al., *Supreme Court Practice* (9th ed. 2007), with periodic pamphlet updates. The Rules for the Supreme Court of the United States are available on the Supreme Court's website[7] and many other sources.

2.   Rules for the Courts of Appeals

a. *Federal Procedure, Lawyers Edition* (West). This set includes pamphlets setting forth the rules for the various federal courts and specialized courts. Separate pamphlets are available for the first through the eleventh circuits. These pamphlets also include the rules adopted by the district courts within the circuit.

b. *Federal Local Court Rules*, 2d ed. (West). This set is discussed in Section B–3–a, below.

c. Rules volumes following Title 18 and Title 28 for the *U.S.C.*, the *U.S.C.A.*, and the *U.S.C.S.*

d. *Digest of United States Supreme Court Reports, Lawyers' Edition.*

e. Most courts issues rules in pamphlet form and post them to the World Wide Web.

3.   Rules for the Federal District Courts

a. *Federal Local Court Rules*, 2d ed. (West). This five-volume, unannotated looseleaf set contains all the rules currently in force for all the federal district courts. Rules are arranged alphabetically by state, and the volumes are updated as amendments and new rules are issued. [Illustration 12–6] The fifth volume contains the rules for the courts of appeals.

---

[7] http://www.supremecourtus.gov/ctrules/ctrules.html.

b. Many of the federal district courts also issue their court rules in pamphlet form and via the Internet.

4. Rules for the Specialized Federal Courts

a. *Federal Procedure, Lawyers Edition.* This set, discussed above in Section B–2–a, sets forth rules for the specialized courts, e.g., admiralty, bankruptcy, copyright, international trade, and tax.

b. Rules volumes following Title 18 and Title 28 for the *U.S.C.*, the *U.S.C.A.*, and the *U.S.C.S.*

c. *Digest of United States Supreme Court Reports, Lawyers' Edition* (includes the rules for multidistrict litigation, international trade, tax, armed forces, and federal claims).

SECTION C. COURT RULES FOR STATE COURTS

The methods of publication of the rules of courts vary from state to state.[8] In most states, court rules are published in the state code, in separate rules pamphlets, or in the state case reports. Court rules for many state courts are available on the Internet, either on the state website, the state bar association website, or the court's own website. The *LLRX.com* website aggregates state court rules from the various sites where they have been posted. The fee-based computer-assisted research services, such as *Loislaw*, *LexisNexis*, and *Westlaw*, also make available state court rules.

Treatises on state civil and criminal practice are published for many states. They can be located using the catalog of a law library.

SECTION D. CITATORS

Electronic citation services, such as *KeyCite* and *Shepard's*, track citations of federal and state court rules.[9] In print, *Shepard's Federal Rules Citations* includes citations to the Federal Rules of Civil Procedure, Criminal Procedure, Appellate Procedure, and Evidence, as well as the rules of the U.S. Supreme Court, U.S. courts of appeals and district courts, and many specialized federal courts. Citing sources include decisions of the U.S. Supreme Court and lower federal courts, state court decisions published in regional reporters, articles in selected law reviews, and *A.L.R.* annotations. *Shepard's United States Citations—Statutes* includes citations to federal court rules. Also, citations to federal court rules mentioned in major law reviews and legal periodicals can be obtained by referring to *Shepard's Federal Law Citations in Selected Law Reviews*. The state units of *Shepard's* include citations to state and federal cases that have cited state court rules.

[8] For a table of sources for state court rules for each state, the District of Columbia, and the territories of the United States, see Betsy Reidinger & Virginia Till Lemmon, *Sources of Rules of State Courts*, 82 LAW LIBR. J. 761 (1990). *See also* JACK B. WEINSTEIN, REFORM OF COURT RULE-MAKING PROCEDURES (1977). If one is available, also check the relevant state legal research manual. See Appendix B of this book for a listing of these state legal research guides.

[9] Citators are discussed in Chapter 15 of this book.

SECTION E.   ILLUSTRATIONS

Problem: Assume that your research involves determining whether two or more criminal indictments can be tried together. See Illustrations 12–1 through 12–5. Assume further that you need to determine if the trial can be
televised in the Northern District of Florida. See Illustration 12–6.

[Illustration 12–1]

PAGE FROM A U.S.C.S. RULES VOLUME CONTAINING RULE 13, FEDERAL RULES OF CRIMINAL PROCEDURE

Rule 12.3   RULES OF CRIMINAL PROCEDURE

INTERPRETIVE NOTES AND DECISIONS

Rule's disclosure requirement does not unfairly interfere with constitutional right to compulsory process for obtaining witnesses; it does not prohibit compulsory process, but merely requires compliance with simple disclosure rules to guarantee that all parties will receive fair trial, and requirement is consistent with court's duty to ensure fair and orderly trial. United States v Seeright (1992, CA4 Md) 978 F2d 842, 36 Fed Rules Evid Serv 1399.

Government had no reason to make inquiries of particular law enforcement agencies regarding defendant's alleged cooperation with them where they were not listed among those defendant submitted pursuant to Rule 12.3. United States v Roach (1994, CA8 Ark) 28 F3d 729, 40 Fed Rules Evid Serv 1341.

Fact that rule refers only to belief, not to reasonableness, does not mean that reasonableness of belief is not element of defense; rule is procedural and elements of defense are found in federal common law dealing with substance of defense. United States v Burrows (1994, CA9 Cal) 36 F3d 875, 94 CDOS 7427, 94 Daily Journal DAR 13663.

Defendant is not entitled to raise in pretrial motion question whether government breached agreement with him if agreement provides defense to liability for crimes charged in indictment; resolution of that question requires trial of general issue and is not properly decided in pretrial motion. United States v Doe (1995, CA2 NY) 63 F3d 121, subsequent app (1996, CA2 Conn) 103 F3d 234, 25 Media L R 1211.

Rule 12.3(a)(1) of FRCrP is constitutional and must be complied with, even though alleged heroin importers asserting authorization defense challenge rule mandating pretrial notice of that defense on Fifth Amendment and Due Process grounds, because (1) there is nothing incriminatory about giving notice of defense to be offered at trial, (2) nothing is compelled since defendants are not under any compulsion to pursue defense, and (3) rule triggers discovery of witness names and addresses but grants defendants reciprocal discovery rights. United States v Abcasis (1992, ED NY) 785 F Supp 1113, request den (1992, ED NY) 811 F Supp 828, 37 Fed Rules Evid Serv 913.

Rule 13. Trial Together of Indictments or Informations

The court may order two or more indictments or informations or both to be tried together if the offenses, and the defendants if there is more than one, could

> After the text of the rule are historical notes from the Advisory Committee and cross-references and citations to related sources of the publisher, as well as to other secondary sources. For some rules, scholarly commentary is provided.

Other provisions:

Notes of Advisory Committee. This rule is substantially a restatement of existing law, 18 U.S.C. [former] § 557 (Indictments and presentments; joinder of charges); *Logan v United States*, 144 U.S. 263, 296, 12 S. Ct. 617, 36 L. Ed. 429; *Showalter v United States*, 260 F. 719 (C.C.A. 4th), cert. den., 250 U.S. 672, 40 S. Ct. 14, 63 L. Ed. 1200; *Hostetter v United States*, 16 F2d 921 (C.C.A. 8th); *Capone v United States*, 51 F.2d 609, 619–620 (C.C.A. 7th).

CROSS REFERENCES

Joinder of offenses and defendants, USCS Rules of Criminal Procedure, Rule 8.
Relief from prejudicial joinder, USCS Rules of Criminal Procedure, Rule 14.

RESEARCH GUIDE

Federal Procedure:

24 Moore's Federal Practice (Matthew Bender 3d ed.), Trial Together of Indictments or Informations §§ 613.01 et seq.

28 Moore's Federal Practice (Matthew Bender 3d ed.), Procedure for Misdemeanors or Petty Offenses § 658.20.

9 Fed Proc L Ed, Criminal Procedure §§ 22:571, 1000, 1008.

20 Fed Proc L Ed, Internal Revenue § 48:1375.

[Illustration 12–2]

PAGE OF ANNOTATIONS FOR RULE 13, U.S.C.S., FROM A RULES VOLUME, FEDERAL RULES OF CRIMINAL PROCEDURE

RULES OF CRIMINAL PROCEDURE   **Rule 13, n 4**

Am Jur:
1 Am Jur 2d, Actions § 136, 137.

Forms:
7 Fed Procedural Forms L Ed, Criminal Procedure (1994) § 20:415.

Annotations:
Joinder of offenses under Rule 8(a), Federal Rules of Criminal Procedure. 39 ALR Fed 479.

What constitutes "series of acts or transactions" for purposes of **Rule 8(b)** of Federal Rules of Criminal Procedure, providing for joinder of **defendants** who are alleged to have participated in same series of acts or transactions.

> Following the explanatory notes and various references to related sources, annotations ("Interpretive Notes and Decisions") of cases are set forth that have interpreted the rule.

TEXTS:
Cook, Constitutional Rights of the Accused: Pretrial Rights.
Orfield, Criminal Procedure Under the Federal Rules.

Law Review Articles:
Procedure. 18 Litig 5, Spring 1992.

INTERPRETIVE NOTES AND DECISIONS

1. Generally
2. Constitutionality
3. Relationship with other rules
4. —FRCrP 8
5. —FRCrP 14
6. Discretion of court
7. Offenses that could have been joined
8. —Prejudice
9. —Same or similar acts
10. —Connected acts or transactions
11. —Conspiracy and substantive offenses
12. —Separate offenses
13. —Consent of defendant
14. Defendants that could have been joined
15. —Same offense
16. —Common scheme
17. —Conspiracy and substantive offenses
18. Judgment and sentence
19. Appeal and review
20. —Harmless error

1. Generally

Indictments that are consolidated become, in legal effect, separate counts of one indictment. Dunaway v United States (1953) 92 US App DC 299, 205 F2d 23.

Identity of parties in both indictments is not prerequisite to consolidation. United States v Samuel Dunkel & Co. (1950, CA2 NY) 184 F2d 894, cert den (1951) 340 US 930, 95 L Ed 671, 71 S Ct 401.

Rule 13 is designed to promote economy and efficiency and to avoid multiplicity of trials where this can be achieved without substantial prejudice to

rights of defendants to fair trial. Daley v United States (1956, CA1 Mass) 231 F2d 123, 56-1 USTC ¶ 9405, 49 AFTR 392, cert den (1956) 351 US 964, 100 L Ed 1484, 76 S Ct 1028.

2. Constitutionality

Trial of defendant before one jury upon indictment for unlawful sale of narcotics in which 11 separate offenses are charged is not denial of due process of law. Brandenburg v Steele (1949, CA8 Mo) 177 F2d 279.

Joint trial of defendants charged with conspiracy does not violate standards of due process. United States v Keine (1971, CA10 Colo) 436 F2d 850, cert den (1971) 402 US 930, 28 L Ed 2d 864, 91 S Ct 1531.

3. Relationship with other rules

Where joinder of offenses is improper under Rules 8 and 13, relief from joinder should be granted under Rule 14 and failure to do so is not harmless error under Rule 52. United States v Graci (1974, CA3 Pa) 504 F2d 411.

Unless indictment has been transferred under Rule 21, court may not order indictment pending in another district consolidated with case pending in court's district. United States v Sklaroff (1971, SD Fla) 323 F Supp 296.

4. —FRCrP 8

Consolidation, on government's motion, of 3 separate indictments against 1 defendant, being of same or similar character is permissible under language of

[Illustration 12–3]

PAGE FROM U.S.C.A. TITLE 18 APPENDIX CONTAINING RULE 13, FEDERAL RULES OF CRIMINAL PROCEDURE

Rule 12.4   **RULES OF CRIMINAL PROCEDURE**

Research References

Forms

5. West's Federal Forms § 7502. Dis...

Like the set shown in Illustrations 12–1 and 12–2, this set sets forth the rule and then provides references to related sources of the publisher, as well as to various secondary sources.

WESTLAW ELECTRONIC RESEARCH

See Westlaw guide following the Explanation pages of this volume.

Notes of Decisions

Organizational victims 1

1. Organizational victims

Government's failure to disclose information regarding the organizational victims, under plain error standard of review, did not affect defendant's substantial rights in prosecution for passing counterfeit checks, where district judge had notice of organizational victims without disclosure statement since they were identified in superceding indictment. U.S. v. Henderson, C.A.8 (Mo.) 2006, 440 F.3d 453, rehearing and rehearing en banc denied, certiorari denied 127 S.Ct. 270, 166 L.Ed.2d 208. Criminal Law ⚖ 1035(2)

Rule 13.   Joint Trial of Separate Cases

The court may order that separate cases be tried together as though brought in a single indictment or information if all offenses and all defendants could have been joined in a single indictment or information.

(As amended Apr. 29, 2002, eff. Dec. 1, 2002.)

ADVISORY COMMITTEE NOTES

1944 Adoption

This rule is substantially a restatement of existing law 18 U.S.C. § 557 (Indictments and presentments; joinder of charges); *Logan v. United States,* 144 U.S. 263, 296, 12 S.Ct. 617, 36 L.Ed. 429; *Showalter v. United States,* 4 Cir., 260 F. 719 certiorari denied, 250 U.S. 672, 40 S.Ct. 14, 63 L.Ed. 1200; *Hostetter v. United States,* 8 Cir., 16 F.2d 921; *Capone v.* *United States,* 7 Cir., 51 F.2d 609, 619, 620, C.C.A.7th.

2002 Amendments

The language of Rule 13 has been amended as part of the general restyling of the Criminal Rules to make them more easily understood and to make style and terminology consistent throughout the rules. These changes are intended to be stylistic only.

LIBRARY REFERENCES

American Digest System

Criminal Law ⚖620, 622.
Key Number System Topic No. 110.

Corpus Juris Secundum

CJS Criminal Law § 803, Consolidation of Trials of Multiple Defendants Separately Charged.

608

[Illustration 12–4]

PAGE OF ANNOTATIONS FOR RULE 13 FROM U.S.C.A. TITLE 18 APPENDIX, FEDERAL RULES OF CRIMINAL PROCEDURE

Rule 13　　　　　　　　**RULES OF CRIMINAL PROCEDURE**

Federal Procedure, Lawyers Edition § 22:1083, Relief from Prejudicial Joinder under Fed. R. Crim. P. 14(a).

Federal Procedure, Lawyers Edition § 22:2210, Consolidation Order under Fed. R. Crim. P. 13.

1A Wright & Miller: Federal Prac. & Proc. § 212, Several Offenses.

16A Wright & Miller: Federal Prac. & Proc. App. A, Orders of the Supreme Court of the United States Adopting and Amending the Appellate Rules.

19A Wright & Miller: Federal Prac. & Proc. App SUPR. CT. ORDERS, Orders of the Supreme Court of the United States Adopting and Amending Rules.

WESTLAW ELECTRONIC RESEARCH

See Westlaw guide following the Explanation pages of this volume.

Notes of Decisions

Generally　1
Abuse of discretion, discretion of court
　8
Conspiracy and substantive offenses
　10-14
　　Generally　10
　　Drug offenses　11
　　Fraud　12
　　Miscellaneous offenses　14
　　Transportation in interstate commerce　13

L.Ed.2d 819.　Criminal Law ☞ 622.7(2); Criminal Law ☞ 622.7(5)

Test as to whether separately indicted defendants may be jointly tried is whether they could have been jointly indicted. King v. U.S., C.A.1 (Mass.) 1966, 355 F.2d 700.　Criminal Law ☞ 622.6(1)

Single joint trial of several defendants may not be had at expense of defendant's right to fundamentally fair trial.　U.S. v.

> **Annotations ("Notes of Decisions") of cases interpreting the rule are set forth after explanatory notes, various references to related sources, and the outline of the "Notes of Decisions."**

Drug offenses, conspiracy and substantive offenses　11
Duty of court　6
Fraud, conspiracy and substantive offenses　12
Identity of parties　17
Miscellaneous offenses, conspiracy and substantive offenses　14
Nature of consolidation process　4
Power of court　5
Purpose　3
Same or connected transactions　16
Similarity of consolidated charges　15
Time for motion　19
Transportation in interstate commerce, conspiracy and substantive offenses　13
Use of evidence against codefendant　18
Waiver　20

1.　Generally

There is substantial public interest in joint trial of persons charged with committing same offense or with being accessory to its commission.　U.S. v. Camacho, C.A.9 (Ariz.) 1976, 528 F.2d 464, certiorari denied 96 S.Ct. 2208, 425 U.S. 995, 48

N.D.Ill.1990, 754 F.Supp. 1101, enforcement granted in part, set aside in part 754 F.Supp. 1197, vacated in part on reconsideration 754 F.Supp. 1206, clarified 764 F.Supp. 1248, reconsideration denied 764 F.Supp. 1252.　Criminal Law ☞ 622.6(2)

Law generally favors joint trial for reasons of judicial economy and presentation of the whole of an alleged illegal operation at one time.　U.S. v. Mandel, D.C.Md.1976, 415 F.Supp. 1033.　Criminal Law ☞ 620(1)

2.　Construction with other rules

This rule has no relation to rule 8(a) of these rules providing that more than one offense may be included in one indictment, nor does phrase "single indictment" in this rule mean one sentence, or change effect of being indicted for three separate crimes whether in one indictment or separately.　U.S. v. Koury, C.A.6 (Ohio) 1963, 319 F.2d 75.

This rule must be read with rule 8(b) of these rules authorizing two or more defendants to be charged in the same information, if they allegedly participated in

[Illustration 12–5]

PAGE FROM C. WRIGHT & A. MILLER, FEDERAL PRACTICE
AND PROCEDURE, CONTAINING RULE 13, FEDERAL
RULES OF CRIMINAL PROCEDURE

RULE 13. TRIAL TOGETHER OF INDICTMENTS OR INFORMATIONS

§ 215 History and Purpose of the Rule
§ 216 Trying Indictments or Informations Together

Text of Rule 13

The court may order that separate cases be tried together as though brought in a single indictment or information if all offenses and all defendants could have been joined in a single indictment or information.

As amended Apr. 29, 2002, eff. Dec. 1, 2002.

ADVISORY COMMITTEE NOTES

The Advisory Committee Notes to this rule and its amendments are set out in Appendix C of Volume 3C.

§ 215. History and Purpose of the Rule

Rule 13 was part of the original criminal rules, and at the time of adoption it reflected a restatement of existing law.[1] The pre-rules statute that governed this topic, which went back to 1853, permitted the joinder of charges in an indictment and the consolidation of indictments for trial.[2] The original drafters avoided using the term "consolidation" in the Rule as had been used in the statute, hoping to avoid any technical or ambiguous meanings connected with the words "consolidated" and "consolidation."[3] The phrase "tried together" is used instead, although courts continue to use

---

[Section 215]

[1]**Restatement of existing law** ‹

295–296, 36 L.Ed. 429.

See generally Lester B. Orfield, Consolidation in Federal Criminal Procedure, 1961, 40 Or.L.Rev. 318.

[2]**Prior statute**

The statute, formerly 18 U.S.C.A. § 557 and now repealed,

provided: "When there are several charges against any person for the same act or transaction, or for two or more acts or transactions con-

whole may be joined in one indictment in separate counts; and if two or more indictments are found in such cases, the court may order them to be consolidated."

[3]**Term consolidation avoided**

Page from C. Wright & A. Miller, *Federal Practice and Procedure*, setting forth the text of the rule. Thereafter, the authors present commentary regarding the rule. Other treatises on the federal rules often do likewise.

[Illustration 12–6]

PAGE FROM FEDERAL LOCAL COURT RULES (FLORIDA)

FLORIDA (ND)   Loc. R. 77.2

magistrate judge conduct any or all proceedings in the case and order the entry of a final judgment. The notice shall state that the parties are free to withhold their consent without adverse substantive consequences.

(2) *Execution of Consent.* Any party who consents to trial of any or all of the civil case by a magistrate judge must execute a consent form and return it to the office of the clerk of the court within forty-five (45) days of the date of service of the notice. The form shall not be returned if the party does not consent. No magistrate judge, district judge, or other court official may attempt to coerce any party to consent to the reference of any matter to

> **Rule 77.1 of the Federal District Court, Northern District of Florida, pertains to television in the courtroom. The rules for each federal district court are contained in this set. When rules for a particular court are amended or added, the publisher supplies a new set of up-to-date rules for that court.**

shall be referred to the full-time magistrate judge assigned to the case, and notice thereof shall be made a part of the file, with copies furnished to the parties.

(B) Misdemeanor Cases.

(1) If the defendant consents to disposition of a misdemeanor or petty offense case by a magistrate judge or if consent is not required pursuant to 28 U.S.C. § 636(a), the magistrate judge shall proceed as provided in Fed. R. Crim. P. 58. If the defendant does not consent to disposition of the case by a magistrate judge in cases requiring such consent, the magistrate judge shall:

(a) If the prosecution is on a complaint charging a misdemeanor other than a petty offense, proceed as provided in Fed. R. Crim. P. 5(c) and 5.1.

(b) In all other cases, order the defendant to appear before a district judge for further proceedings on notice, fix appropriate conditions of release under 18 U.S.C. § 3142, and appoint counsel for eligible defendants under 18 U.S.C. § 3006A.

Adopted effective April 1, 1995. Amended effective October 1, 1999; July 15, 2005.

RULE 77.1 PHOTOGRAPHS; BROADCASTING OR TELEVISING

Except as provided in N.D. Fla. Loc. R. 77.2, the taking of photographs or the broadcasting or televising of judicial proceedings is prohibited, except that a judge may authorize:

(A) the use of electronic or photographic means for the presentation of evidence or for the perpetuation of a record; and

(B) the broadcasting, televising, recording, or photographing of investiture, ceremonial, naturalization, or other special proceedings.

In order to facilitate the enforcement of this rule, no photographic, broadcasting, television, sound or recording equipment of any kind, except that of court personnel or other employees of the United States on official business in the building, will be permitted in any part of any building where federal judicial proceedings of any kind are usually conducted or upon the exterior grounds thereof, unless such is done with the approval of one of the judges of this court.

Adopted effective April 1, 1995.

RULE 77.2   VIDEO OR TELEPHONE TRANSMISSIONS IN CIVIL CASES

(A) Hearings and Conferences. In the discretion of the judicial officer, conferences and hearings, including evidentiary hearings, may be held in civil cases by means of video or telephonic transmission from remote locations.

Chapter 13

ADMINISTRATIVE LAW*

This chapter explains the manner in which the rules, regulations, and adjudications of federal administrative agencies are published and the means of locating these materials. The chapter also discusses presidential documents and state administrative materials.

SECTION A. INTRODUCTION: FEDERAL ADMINISTRATIVE REGULATIONS AND DECISIONS

Administrative law has been defined as:

[T]he law concerning the powers and procedures of administrative agencies, including especially the law governing judicial review of administrative action. An administrative agency is a governmental authority, other than a court and other than a legislative body, which affects the rights of private parties through either adjudication, rule-making, investigating, prosecuting, negotiating, settling, or informally acting. An administrative agency may be called a commission, board, authority, bureau, office, officer, administrator, department, corporation, administration, division, or agency.[1]

The power to issue regulations[2] and to adjudicate disputes is delegated to administrative bodies by Congress.[3] The increasing complexity of American society, especially industry and government, brought about a tremendous increase in the number of administrative agencies and the number of publications produced by them. Ordinarily, Congress delegates to an administrative office or agency the power to issue rules and regulations, and sometimes the power to hear and settle disputes arising under particular statutes. After the administrative body has been established, the issuance of rules and regulations involves a fairly simple process, much different

---

* Keith Ann Stiverson, Director of the Law Library at Chicago–Kent College of Law, revised this chapter, which was written for an earlier edition of this book by Bonnie L. Koneski–White, formerly of Western New England College School of Law Library.

Note: This chapter contains many references to *GPO Access*, the U.S. Government Printing Office (GPO) system for distributing federal government information over the World Wide Web. After this book went into production, GPO announced that it will replace *GPO Access* with its new *Federal Digital System* (*FDsys*) during 2009. GPO plans to maintain *GPO Access* until the migration to *FDsys* is complete. After that, searches using a *GPO Access* URL will automatically be redirected by the system to *FDsys*.

1 KENNETH CULP DAVIS, ADMINISTRATIVE LAW AND GOVERNMENT 6 (2d ed. 1975).

2 Procedures that affect the rulemaking process and recent developments in rulemaking are explained in JEFFREY S. LUBBERS, A GUIDE TO FEDERAL AGENCY RULEMAKING (4th ed. 2006).

3 For a discussion of congressional authority to delegate legislative power to agencies, see 1 JACOB A. STEIN ET AL., ADMINISTRATIVE LAW § 3.03 (2006).

from the enactment of a statute and the corresponding legislative process. Some agencies have additional powers. For instance, the National Labor Relations Board (NLRB) not only promulgates regulations, but also is authorized to adjudicate disputes between management and labor unions; the results of its adjudications are published in a format similar to court reports.

All administrative regulations are issued under authority delegated to the agency by a federal statute or by authority of a Presidential Executive Order.

There are several different types of actions that may be taken by federal agencies: the issuance of rules and regulations; orders; licenses; advisory opinions; and decisions. A brief description of each follows:

(1) *Rules and regulations.* Rules and regulations (the terms are often used interchangeably) are statements of general or particular applicability made by an agency and are designed to implement, interpret, or prescribe law or policy. Rules and regulations that were properly promulgated have the same practical legal effect as statutes.

(2) *Orders.* An order describes the final disposition of an agency matter (other than rulemaking, but including licensing).

(3) *Licenses.* Licenses include permits, certificates, or other forms of permission.

(4) *Advisory opinions.* Advisory opinions contain agency advice regarding contemplated action; these opinions are not binding and serve only as authoritative interpretations of statutes and regulations.

(5) *Decisions.* Many federal agencies are empowered to adjudicate controversies arising out of the application of statutes and administrative rules and regulations. The results of these adjudications are issued as decisions of the agencies. Special boards of review, hearing examiners, or other officers perform the adjudication function.

SECTION B.   HISTORICAL BACKGROUND: PUBLICATION OF FEDERAL REGULATIONS

Before 1936, no official source for publication of rules and regulations of federal agencies existed; nor, indeed, were such agencies required to make their rules and regulations available to the public. Accordingly, there was no easy way to determine if any proposed action was prohibited by a federal agency. In fact, in one well-known instance, a case, *Panama Refining Co. v. Ryan,*[4] reached the Supreme Court of the United States before the Attorney General realized that the action was based on a regulation that had been revoked prior to the time the original action had begun.[5]

In 1935, as a result of the *Panama Refining* case, Congress passed the Federal Register Act,[6] providing for the publication of the *Federal Register.*

---

[4] 293 U.S. 388 (1935).

[5] *See* Note, *The Federal Register and the Code of Federal Regulations—A Reappraisal,* 80 Harv. L. Rev. 439 (1966).

[6] Ch. 417, 49 Stat. 500 (1935) (codified as amended at 44 U.S.C. §§ 1501–1511).

The *Federal Register* was first published in 1936. Any administrative rule or regulation that has general applicability and legal effect must be published in the *Federal Register*. The definition of a document that has "general applicability and legal effect" is as follows:

> ... [A]ny document issued under proper authority prescribing a penalty or course of conduct, conferring a right, privilege, authority, or immunity, or imposing an obligation, and relevant or applicable to the general public, members of a class, or persons in a locality, as distinguished from named individuals or organizations. . . .[7]

As a consequence, since 1936 the *Federal Register* has published, in chronological order, every regulation having general applicability and legal effect, and amendments thereto, promulgated by federal agencies that are authorized by Congress or the president to issue rules and regulations.

Had the *Federal Register* continued year after year with no subject access, then the ability to locate regulations would have been compromised, and researchers would not have been much better off than they were before the *Panama Refining* case. Fortunately, in 1937, Congress amended the Federal Register Act[8] and provided for a systematic method to codify and provide subject access to these regulations. The *Code of Federal Regulations (CFR)*, first published in 1938, bears the same relationship to the *Federal Register* as the *United States Code* bears to *United States Statutes at Large*. Over the years it has been published at different intervals and in different formats, but since 1968 the *CFR* has been published annually, in quarterly installments.

Despite the fact that by 1937 a regular vehicle existed for the publication and compilation of agency rules and regulations, the process and procedures of agency rulemaking remained an enigma to the public. In 1946, Congress addressed this situation by passing the Administrative Procedure Act,[9] which granted the public the right to participate in the rulemaking process by requiring agencies to publish notice of their proposed rulemaking in the *Federal Register* and by giving the public the opportunity to comment on proposed regulations.

Subsequently, three additional laws were enacted to enhance the public's access to agency information. The Freedom of Information Act of 1966[10] requires that agencies publish in the *Federal Register*: (1) descriptions of their organizations, including those agency employees from whom the public may obtain information; (2) rules of procedure and general applicability; and (3) policy statements and interpretations. The Government in the Sunshine Act of 1976[11] requires agencies to publish notices of most meetings in the *Federal Register*.

---

[7] 1 C.F.R. § 1.1 (2007). It is often difficult to determine precisely which documents the government is required to publish in the FEDERAL REGISTER. For a discussion of this problem, see Randy S. Springer, Note, *Gatekeeping and the* Federal Register: *An Analysis of the Publication Requirement of Section 552(a)(1)(D) of the Administrative Procedure Act,* 41 ADMIN. L. REV. 533 (1989).

[8] Ch. 369, 50 Stat. 304 (1937) (codified as amended at 44 U.S.C. § 1510).

[9] Ch. 324, 60 Stat. 237 (1946) (codified as amended in scattered sections of 5 U.S.C.).

[10] Pub. L. No. 89–487, 80 Stat. 250 (1966) (codified as amended at 5 U.S.C. § 552).

[11] Pub. L. No. 94–409, 90 Stat. 1241 (1976) (codified as amended at 5 U.S.C. §§ 551–52, 556–57; 5 U.S.C. app. § 10; 39 U.S.C. § 410).

In 1980, Congress passed the Regulatory Flexibility Act,[12] which dictates that agencies publish in the *Federal Register*, each October and April, an agenda (known as a flexibility agenda), briefly detailing (1) the subject of any rule that the agency expects to propose or promulgate which would have a significant economic impact on a substantial number of small entities, (2) a summary of the rules being considered, their objectives, the legal basis for issuance, and (3) the name and telephone number of an agency official knowledgeable about the rule. These flexibility agendas are published in the *Federal Register* as the "Unified Agenda."

SECTION C. SOURCES OF FEDERAL REGULATIONS

1. The Federal Register[13]

The *Federal Register* is published Monday through Friday (except on federal holidays) and its contents are required to be judicially noticed.[14] All issues in a given year constitute a single volume with consecutive pagination throughout the year. In recent years, each volume of the *Federal Register* has exceeded 70,000 pages (the 2006 volume was nearly 80,000 pages). In addition to chronologically published rules and regulations of federal agencies [Illustration 13–9], issues of the *Federal Register* contain the following features:

a. *Contents.* At the front of each issue is a table of contents in which agencies are listed alphabetically. Under the name of each agency, the documents appearing in that issue are arranged by category, and page numbers are provided.

b. *CFR Parts Affected in This Issue.* Discussed in Section E–1–b below.

c. *Presidential Documents.* Discussed in Section H below.

d. *Proposed Rules.* This section contains notices of proposed rules and regulations. Its purpose is to give interested persons an opportunity to participate in the rulemaking process prior to the adoption of final rules.

e. *Notices.* This section of the *Federal Register* contains documents other than rules or proposed rules that are of interest to the public, e.g., grant application deadlines, and the filing of petitions and applications. Since 1996, notices of meetings, required by the Government in the Sunshine Act, are included this section. Before 1996, those notices appeared in a separate section entitled "Sunshine Act Meetings."

f. *Unified Agenda of Federal Regulations.* The Regulatory Flexibility Act requires that agencies publish flexibility agendas in April and October that describe the regulatory actions they are developing. Each agency lists its rules in four groups: (1) Advance Notice of Proposed Rulemaking; (2) Proposed Rule Stage; (3) Final Rule Stage; and (4) Completed Actions. The Unified Agenda is organized by agency. Information is provided on govern-

---

[12] Pub. L. No. 96–354, 94 Stat. 1164 (1980) (codified as amended at 5 U.S.C. §§ 601–612 (2006)).

[13] Additional information is provided in Office of the Federal Register, The Federal Register: What It Is and How to Use It (rev. ed. 1992).

[14] 44 U.S.C. § 1507 (2006).

mental or private entities that might be affected by the planned regulations.

g. *Reader Aids.* This section appears at the end of the *Federal Register* and lists telephone numbers for information and assistance, online resources, a parallel table of *Federal Register* pages for the month, a cumulative table of *CFR* parts affected during the month, and a List of Public Laws, setting forth those bills from the current session of Congress that have recently become law. The Monday issue contains a CFR Checklist of the current *CFR* Parts.

h. *Special Sections.* To accommodate the duplication and distribution needs of issuing agencies, some agency documents are published in separate sections near the end of each issue, rather than in the appropriate sections.

i. *Electronic Access.* In addition to the print and microfiche copies available from the federal government, an Internet version of the *Federal Register* on *GPO Access* is published by authority of the Administrative Committee of the Federal Register. The electronic version is updated by 6:00 a.m. each day that the *Federal Register* is published, and includes both the text and graphics from Volume 59, Number 1 (January 2, 1994) to the present day.[15]

2. The Code of Federal Regulations (CFR)[16]

The *Code of Federal Regulations* is the codification of the rules and regulations first published in the *Federal Register,* with all regulations and amendments that are currently in force brought together by subject. The *CFR* is *prima facie* evidence of the text of the documents,[17] and consists of 50 titles (similar, but not identical to, the arrangement of the *United States Code*). Titles are subdivided into chapters, subchapters, parts, and sections and is cited by title and section, e.g., 42 C.F.R. § 405.501. [Illustrations 13–3 and 13–4] Each year, the volumes of *CFR* are issued in a binding color different from the previous year, making it easier to spot the current year on the shelf. The titles are updated on a quarterly basis according to the following schedule:

Title 1 through Title 16, as of January 1

Title 17 through Title 27, as of April 1

Title 28 through Title 41, as of July 1

Title 42 through Title 50, as of October 1

Therefore, at most times during the year, the "current" CFR is a combination of volumes in this year's color, last year's color, and a few volumes from previous years that had no changes.

Each new volume contains the text of regulations then in force, incorporating those promulgated during the preceding 12 months, and deleting those that have been revoked. All regulations first published in the *Federal Register* and currently in force are rearranged by subject and

---

[15] http://www.gpoaccess.gov/fr/.

[16] For a detailed history of the publication of the earlier editions of the *Code of Federal Regulations,* see ERVIN H. POLLACK, FUNDAMENTALS OF LEGAL RESEARCH 366–72 (3d ed. 1967).

[17] 44 U.S.C. § 1510(e).

agency in the fifty titles of the *CFR*. For example, the regulations issued by the Federal Communications Commission, and still in force, are in Title 47 of the *CFR* and are updated through October 1.

In early 2007, West began publishing an unofficial but annotated version of *CFR* entitled *West's Code of Federal Regulations Annotated*, which supplements the text of the regulations with case summaries and other materials. On *Westlaw*, the same product in electronic form is known as RegulationsPlus.

3. Looseleaf Services

Looseleaf services, discussed in Chapter 14, may contain documents published in the *Federal Register* and the *Code of Federal Regulations*. These services often contain better indexes than the corresponding print government publications and have other features that are helpful to the researcher.

Consequently, when it is necessary to research administrative law, it may be helpful to determine whether or not a looseleaf service covers the topic being researched, and to use that service as a starting point. Within the past few years, a number of specialized looseleaf services have been published as online, Web-based products, saving the expense of labor-intensive filing and presumably enabling the publisher to update the materials more easily. The looseleaf approach, or its electronic equivalent, can be especially helpful in regulation-intensive areas of the law.

4. Electronic Sources

The following Web-based electronic resources can be extremely helpful in locating regulations:

a. *LexisNexis.* The *Federal Register* is available through *LexisNexis* from July 1, 1980, to the present, and the *Code of Federal Regulations* is available from 1981 to the present. The *CFR* and *Federal Register* can be searched in a combined file.

b. *LexisNexis Congressional*, a separate database of legislative and regulatory information, includes the *Federal Register* from 1980 to the present and the *Code of Federal Regulations* from 1981 to the present.

c. *Westlaw.* In *Westlaw*, rules and regulations, proposed rules, notices, and Unified Agenda documents published in the *Federal Register* are available, with an historical database that dates back to 1936. *West's Code of Federal Regulations Annotated* is a new (2007) resource that should greatly enhance regulatory research.

d. In addition to the well-known, fee-based legal databases listed above, there are less expensive online legal databases, such as *LoisLaw* and *VersusLaw*, which also include the *Federal Register* and the *CFR*.

e. *HeinOnline.* Scanned PDF images of the *Federal Register* from 1936 to the present, and the *Code of Federal Regulations* from 1938 to the present (1992–97 currently includes only Title 37) are available in this fee-based online service, which also includes presidential material. *HeinOnline* posts these documents to its site soon after they appear on the GPO website.

f.   Free access to an unofficial but very current electronic version of the CFR is available on GPO Access.[18]

g.   Free access to PDF files of the *Federal Register* from 1994 to the present is available from *GPO Access*.[19]

h.   Free access to PDF files of the *Code of Federal Regulations*[20] from 1996 and the Unified Agenda[21] from 1997 also are available on *GPO Access*.

5.   Other Sources

Selected regulations are also published in the monthly pamphlet supplements to the *United States Code Congressional and Administrative News* (West) and in the *United States Code Service*, Advance Service (LexisNexis).

SECTION D.   FINDING FEDERAL REGULATIONS

Because the *Federal Register* and the *Code of Federal Regulations* are the official sources for federal agency regulations, they will be emphasized in this discussion.

Whether or not research is begun in the *Federal Register* or the *Code of Federal Regulations* depends upon the date of the regulation in question. If the regulation was issued recently, that is, later than the scope of coverage of the appropriate *Code of Federal Regulations* volume, research should begin in the *Federal Register*. If, however, the regulation was not recently enacted or amended, or if the date of the amendment's enactment is not known, the starting point should be the *Code of Federal Regulations*. These two sources are accessed differently.

It is important to find the regulation in the *Federal Register* because for final rules of any economic significance, that is where the agency is required to explain that it considered alternatives to the rule and provide other relevant information. This analysis often discusses in great detail how the rule will be applied. Similarly, for proposed rules, the agency may include a discussion of why a rule is needed along with the proposed text. This discussion usually is more helpful than the text itself in understanding the rule.

1.   Access to the Federal Register

a.   *Federal Register Index.* This official index, a slim volume arranged alphabetically by agency, is issued every month. Each issue of the *Federal Register Index* cumulates that year's previous monthly indexes, and the December issue is the final index of the year. Because each issue of the *Index* is not distributed until several weeks after the month it covers, the contents of each issue of the *Federal Register* published after the last monthly *Index* must also be consulted. The *Index* and contents are not very

[18] http://ecfr.gpoaccess.gov.

[19] http://www.gpoaccess.gov/fr/.

[20] http://www.gpoaccess.gov/cfr/index.html.

[21] http://www.gpoaccess.gov/ua/index.html.

detailed; at times, it may be difficult to find a regulation if one does not know the issuing agency.

b. *CIS Federal Register Index.* This commercially published index, which began in 1984, provided comprehensive coverage for all issues of the *Federal Register,* but it ceased publication in 1998, so is no longer useful except for historical research. It includes indexes by subject and name, *CFR* section numbers affected, federal agency docket number, Calendar of Effective Dates, and Comment Deadlines.

2. Access to the Code of Federal Regulations

a. *CFR Index and Finding Aids.* This single volume accompanies the *CFR* and is revised annually.[22] It provides several access points to the *CFR.*

(1) *Index.* This alphabetical index includes entries for both subjects and agency names. The subject terms used in the index are taken from the thesaurus developed by the Office of the Federal Register.[23] Use of this thesaurus ensures that, although different agencies may use different terms to describe the same concept, references to all of those terms will be gathered together under one subject heading. For example, one agency may use the word *compensation* in its regulations, while another might use *pay,* and yet a third, *salaries.* By using the thesaurus, references to all three of these regulations will appear in the index under the subject heading *Wages.*

The *Index* provides references to the appropriate title of the *CFR* and to the specific part within the title, but not to specific sections. [Illustration 13–1]

(2) *Parallel Table of Authorities and Rules.* This table lists rulemaking authority for regulations codified in the *CFR.* [Illustration 13–2] If the law or presidential document that authorized the issuance of regulations is known, this table shows where administrative regulations promulgated under such authority can be found in the *CFR.* The table also includes statutory citations which are noted as being interpreted or applied by regulations codified in the *CFR.* The citations are divided into four segments: *U.S.C.,* by title and section; *U.S. Statutes at Large,* by volume and page number; public law, by number; and presidential documents, by document number. Within each segment, citations are arranged in numerical order.

(3) *List of Agency-Prepared Indexes Appearing in Individual CFR Volumes.* This list enables the researcher to locate agency-prepared (and therefore, presumably more extensive) indexes published in various volumes of the *CFR.*

3. Regulations No Longer in Force

It is often necessary to determine the regulations that were in force as of a particular date. If prior editions of *CFR* are available, one may simply consult the edition that was current on the appropriate date. Many librar-

---

[22] LexisNexis publishes the CFR Index and Finding Aids volume as a supplement to the United States Code Service.

[23] The thesaurus is available online at http://www.archives.gov/federal-register/cfr/thesaurus.html.

ies keep superseded editions of *CFR* in print copy or in microform. Regulations no longer in force can also be located in the electronic sources listed in Section C–4, above.

One might also begin by locating the applicable subject matter in the current edition of *CFR*. Each *CFR* section sets forth the date and *Federal Register* citation for the adoption of each section, and the same information for each subsequent amendment of that section. Researchers may therefore determine whether the present language of the section was in effect at the applicable time and may find the original language in the *Federal Register* if the section has been amended.

The following official publications also provide *CFR* citations that allow one to find the precise text of regulations that were in force on any given date during the years covered. There are four separate compilations thus far: *Code of Federal Regulations List of Sections Affected: 1949–1963; 1964–1972; 1973–1985;* and *1986–2000.* In early 2008, only the 1986–2000 compilation was available electronically at *GPO Access.*[24] For changes after the last compilation, each volume of the *CFR* contains a *List of CFR Sections Affected* that appears at the end of the volume.

SECTION E.   UPDATING REGULATIONS

After locating a regulation, further research is necessary to determine whether the regulation has been amended or revoked. If the regulation was amended or revoked or if a new regulation has been promulgated, the *Federal Register* contains the documentation. The sources described below aid in retrieving citations to the *Federal Register* where changes to regulations are published.

1. Sources

a. *LSA: List of CFR Sections Affected.*[25] This publication is issued monthly and includes finalized and proposed changes to regulations adopted since the latest publication of the *CFR*. The December issue cumulates all changes for Titles 1–16; the March issue contains all changes for Titles 17–27; the June issue lists changes for Titles 28–41; and the September issue indicates changes for Titles 42–50. [Illustration 13–6] For changes to regulations that have become final, the *LSA* is arranged by *CFR* title and section and sets forth the nature of the changes, e.g., "revised," and provides page number references to the *Federal Register*. [Illustration 13–6] For proposed changes, the *LSA* is arranged by title and part with reference to the applicable *Federal Register* page numbers. [Illustration 13–7] A separate section of the *LSA* updates the *Parallel Table of Authorities and Rules*.

b. *CFR Parts Affected.* Each issue of the *Federal Register* contains a section near the front that lists *CFR Parts Affected in This Issue.* However, this section is incorporated in the cumulative list in the Reader Aids section. The section in the front of the *Federal Register* should be consulted

[24] http://www.gpoaccess.gov/lsa/compilation.html.

[25] The LSA, available in print, is also available in electronic form, covering 1997 to the present, through *GPO Access:* http://www.gpoaccess.gov/lsa/index.html.

if one must review each issue of the *Federal Register* to ascertain if a specific regulation has changed.

Each issue of the *Federal Register* also includes a list of *CFR Parts Affected* in the Reader Aids section. The list is cumulative for one calendar month. [Illustration 13–10] The lists near the front of the issue and the list in the Reader Aids section give page number references to the *Federal Register*.

c. *Converting Page Number References to Specific Issues of the Federal Register.* If a particular regulation has been affected, a reference to the appropriate *Federal Register* is set forth in the *LSA* and/or the list of *CFR Parts Affected*. This reference is to the page number of the *Federal Register* on which the amendment, proposed amendment, or removal appears. To find the issue of the *Federal Register* in which the change appears, use the conversion table in the *Federal Register Index* or the *LSA*, whichever is more current. [Illustration 13–8] If the page number does not appear in the *Index* or *LSA* conversion table, one must turn to the last issue of each month of the *Federal Register* published since the *Index* or the *LSA* and use the conversion tables in the Reader Aids section. [Illustration 13–10]

d. *Shepard's Code of Federal Regulations Citations.* To ascertain whether a federal court has ruled on the constitutionality or validity of a regulation, this print unit of *Shepard's Citations* may be consulted. However, it is far more likely that a researcher will have access to a Web-based electronic citator, either *Shepard's* via *LexisNexis*, or *KeyCite* via *Westlaw*.[26]

e. A federal government website, *Regulations.gov*, which became available in 2003, describes itself as "the public face of the U.S. government's eRulemaking Initiative." The site enables the public to find, view, and comment on federal regulatory actions online. The site purports to be the "source for all regulations (or rulemakings) issued by U.S. government agencies."[27]

2. Research Methodology

The need to update regulations depends on the published source of the regulation in question.

If the regulation was found in the *CFR,* the researcher should first use the most current *LSA*. It is important to note the publication date on the cover of the *CFR* volume in which the regulation was found in order to cover the appropriate time period. Since the *LSA* is issued monthly, a further check must be made in the cumulative *List of CFR Parts Affected* in the *Federal Register* for any later changes. Therefore, note the coverage of the *LSA* used, and check the *List of CFR Parts Affected* in the last issue of each subsequent month, including the current month, of the *Federal Register*.

If the regulation was found in the *Federal Register*, and if the latest issue of *LSA* is for a month *later* than the month of the issue of the *Federal Register* in which the regulation appears, first use the *LSA* that covers the period from the date of the issue of the *Federal Register* in which the

[26] Citators are discussed in Chapter 15 of this book.

[27] http://www.regulations.gov/search/index.jsp.

regulation was found. Since the *LSA* is issued monthly, a further check must be made for any later changes in the cumulative list of *CFR Parts Affected* in the *Federal Register*. Therefore, note the coverage of the particular *LSA* used, and check the list of *CFR Parts Affected* in the last issue of each subsequent month, including the current month, of the *Federal Register*.

If the regulation was found in an issue of the *Federal Register* and if the latest *LSA* available is for a month *prior* to the month of the issue of the *Federal Register* in which the regulation appears, check the *List of CFR Parts Affected* in the last issue of the month of the *Federal Register* in which the regulation was found and the *List of CFR Parts Affected* in the last issue of each subsequent month, including the current month, of the *Federal Register*.

If the regulation appears in an issue of the *Federal Register* for the current month, check the *List of CFR Parts Affected* in the last available issue of the current month's *Federal Register* to be as up to date as possible. Electronic updating in the various databases, including *LexisNexis*, *Westlaw*, and *GPO Access*, can be done in a few keystrokes rather than a protracted search for all the print resources.

SECTION F. ILLUSTRATIONS: FEDERAL REGISTER AND CODE OF FEDERAL REGULATIONS

Problem: Find regulations pertaining to notice requirements under the labeling proceedings for alcoholic beverages.

[Illustration 13–1]

PAGE FROM CFR INDEX AND FINDING AIDS VOLUME

CFR Index

Conduct on Pentagon Reservation, 32 CFR 234

Drunk and drugged driving, 32 CFR 62b

Drug and alcohol abuse prevention, 34 CFR 86

Energy Department, human reliability program, 10 CFR 712

Federal and federally assisted alcohol and drug abuse treatment programs, confidentiality of patient records, 42 CFR 2

Alcohol and alcoholic beverages

Commercial driver's license program, State compliance, 49 CFR 384

Commercial driver's license standards, requirements and penalties, 49 CFR 383

Controlled substances and alcohol use and testing, 49 CFR 382

Driving of commercial motor vehicles, 49 CFR 392

Longer combination vehicles driver and driver instructor qualifications, 49 CFR 391

Step 1:
To research the problem presented in this section, consult the Index in the *CFR Index and Finding Aids*. The reference is to Title 27, Part 13. See next illustration.

Pilots, flight instructors, and ground instructors, 14 CFR 61

Certification and operations, domestic, flag, and supplemental operations, operating requirements, 14 CFR 121

Commuter and on-demand operations and rules governing persons on board such aircraft, operating requirements, 14 CFR 135

Federal employees' health and counseling programs, 5 CFR 792

Federal Railroad Administration, railroad safety, alcohol and drug use control, 49 CFR 219

Federal Transit Administration, alcohol misuse and prohibited drug use prevention in transit operations, 49 CFR 655

Highway safety programs
Alcohol-impaired driving prevention programs, incentive grant criteria, 23 CFR 1313
Motor vehicles operation—
Intoxicated minors, 23 CFR 1210
Intoxicated persons, 23 CFR 1225
Repeat intoxicated driver laws, 23 CFR 1275
National minimum drinking age, 23 CFR 1208

Marine safety
Marine investigation regulations, personnel action, 46 CFR 5
Operating a vessel while intoxicated, 33 CFR 95

Motor carrier safety

Homeless Providers Grant and Per Diem Program, 38 CFR 61

Medical benefits, 38 CFR 17

State homes, grants to States for construction or acquisition, 38 CFR 59

Alcohol and alcoholic beverages
See also Beer; Gasohol; Liquors; Wine

Alcohol beverage dealers, 27 CFR 31

Alcohol, tax free distribution and use, 27 CFR 22

Alcoholic beverages
Basic permit requirements under Federal Alcohol Administration Act, distilled spirits and wine nonindustrial use, distilled spirits bulk sales and bottling, 27 CFR 1
Commercial bribery, 27 CFR 10
Consignment sales, 27 CFR 11
Exclusive outlets, 27 CFR 8
Health warning statement, 27 CFR 16
Labeling proceedings, 27 CFR 13
Tied house, 27 CFR 6

Armed services military club and package stores, 32 CFR 261

Customs and Border Protection Bureau
Air commerce regulations, aircraft liquor kits, 19 CFR 122
Drawback on customs duties, 19 CFR 191

Denatured alcohol and rum
Distribution and use, 27 CFR 20
Formulas, 27 CFR 21

Distilled spirits, wine, and beer, imports, 27 CFR 27

67

[Illustration 13–2]

PAGE FROM PARALLEL TABLE OF AUTHORITIES AND RULES, CFR INDEX AND FINDING AIDS VOLUME

CFR Index

26 U.S.C. (1986 I.R.C.)—Continued	CFR
9034	11 Part 9034
9035	11 Part 9035
9036	11 Part 9036
9037	11 Part 9037
9038	11 Parts 201, 9038
9039	11 Parts 201, 9031—9039
9801	26 Part 54
9806	26 Part 54
9833	26 Part 54
27 U.S.C.	
202	27 Parts 6, 8, 10, 11
203—204	27 Part 1
203	27 Parts 26, 251, 252
204	27 Part 71
205	27 Parts 4—13, 16, 26, 179, 197, 251, 252
206	27 Part 1
211	27 Part 1

28 U.S.C.—Continued	CFR
	40 Part 23
	46 Part 502
2343—2344	40 Part 23
2401—2402	32 Part 536
2401 note	49 Part 229
2402	32 Part 842
2412	34 Part 21
2461	14 Part 13
	18 Part 385
	20 Parts 356, 702
	30 Parts 723, 845
	32 Part 269
	46 Part 506
	49 Part 224
2461 note	5 Parts 2634, 2636
	10 Parts 2, 13, 207, 218, 430, 501, 601, 820, 1013, 1017, 1050

Step 1a: An alternative method of finding regulations in the CFR.

There are times when the *U.S.C.* citation to the statute that delegated the authority to issue regulations is known. In such instances, the Parallel Table of Authorities and Rules in the CFR Index and Finding Aids volume can be used to locate citations to regulations in the *CFR*. For example, the statutory authorization for labeling proceedings for alcoholic beverages is found at 27 U.S.C. § 205.

	501, 503, 504, 506, 509—511, 513, 522—524, 527, 540—545, 547—553, 570—572, 600—603, 1216
	48 Part 2819
509	28 Parts 27, 36, 64, 80, 549, 551
510	28 Parts 27, 36, 549, 551
	48 Parts 2801—2810, 2812—2817, 2822, 2824, 2825, 2828—2835, 2845, 2852, 2870
513	32 Part 516
515—519	28 Parts 0, 17, 27
515	28 Parts 600—602
	32 Part 516
515—518	28 Part 9
524	28 Part 9
528	28 Part 45
530B	28 Part 77
534	28 Parts 16, 20
	32 Part 635
534 note	32 Part 637
543	28 Parts 600, 603
	32 Part 516
586	28 Part 58
1346	28 Part 543
	32 Parts 536, 842
1498	10 Part 782
1608	22 Part 93
1733	22 Part 131
1746	8 Part 3
	30 Part 870
	34 Part 690
1784	22 Part 92
1821—1825	28 Part 21
1821	22 Part 713
1823	32 Part 534
2112	5 Part 2429
	21 Parts 10, 12—16
	29 Parts 101, 2200

	594, 595, 597, 598
	33 Parts 27, 326
	34 Part 36
	40 Parts 19, 27
	45 Part 672
	49 Parts 107, 171, 209, 213, 214, 215—216, 217, 218, 220—225, 228, 230—241, 244, 1503
2671—2680	14 Part 1261
	22 Part 511
	28 Part 543
	32 Part 536
	38 Part 14
	39 Part 912
	43 Part 22
2671—2672	32 Part 842
2672	5 Part 177
	10 Parts 14, 1014
	13 Part 114
	14 Part 15
	15 Part 2
	20 Part 429
	22 Part 304
	24 Part 17
	28 Part 14
	29 Parts 15, 100
	31 Part 3
	32 Part 1280
	33 Part 25
	34 Part 35
	40 Part 1620
	45 Part 35
	46 Part 204
	49 Part 1
2674—2680	32 Part 842
2675	14 Part 15
2679	10 Part 14

[Illustration 13–3]

PAGE FROM TITLE 27 OF CFR

Pt. 13

Julien, Sancerre, Santenay, Saumur, Savigny or Savigny-les-Beaunes, Tavel, Touraine, Volnay, Vosne-Romanee, Vouvray.

(c) *Italy:* Asti Spumante, Barbaresco, Barbera d'Alba, Barbera d'Asti, Bardolino, Barolo, Brunello di Montalcino, Dolcetto d'Alba, Frascati, Gattinara, Lacryma Christi, Nebbiolo d'Alba, Orvieto, Soave, Valpolicella, Vino Nobile de Montepulciano.

(d) *Portugal:* Dao, Oporto, Porto, or Vinho do Porto.

(e) *Spain:* Lagrima, Rioja.

PART 13—LABELING PROCEEDINGS

Subpart A—Scope and Construction of Regulations

Sec.
13.1   Scope of part.
13.2   Delegations of the Administrator.
13.3   Related regulations.

Subpart B—Definitions

13.11   Meaning of terms.

Subpart C—Applications

13.20   Forms prescribed.
13.21   Application for certificate.
13.22   Withdrawal of applications.
13.23   Notice of denial.
13.25   Appeal of qualification or denial.
13.26   Decision after appeal of qualification or denial.
13.27   Second appeal of qualification or denial.

27 CFR Ch. I (4–1–06 Edition)

13.72   Effective dates of revocations.
13.73   Effect of revocation.
13.74   Surrender of certificates.
13.75   Evidence of receipt by TTB.
13.76   Service on applicant or certificate holder.
13.81   Representation before TTB.
13.91   Computation of time.
13.92   Extensions.

Subpart G—Appeals Concerning Other Agencies' Rules

13.101   Appeals concerning use of the term "organic."

AUTHORITY: 27 U.S.C. 205(e), 26 U.S.C. 5301 and 7805.

SOURCE: T.D. ATF–406, 64 FR 2129, Jan. 13, 1999, unless otherwise noted.

EDITORIAL NOTE: Nomenclature changes to part 13 appear by T.D. ATF–449, 66 FR 19085, Apr. 13, 2001.

Subpart A—Scope and Construction of Regulations

§ 13.1   Scope of part.

The regulations in this part govern the procedure and practice in connection with the issuance, denial, and revocation of certificates of label approval, certificates of exemption from label approval, and distinctive liquor bottle approvals under 27 U.S.C. 205(e) and 26 U.S.C. 5301. The regulations in this part also provide for appeal procedures when applications for label approval, exemptions from label ap-

---

Step 2:

Refer to Title 27, Part 13 of the *CFR* as located using Step 1. After each part, a detailed list of sections is given. In this instance, Section 13.11 is relevant. Note how at the end of Subpart G the statutory authorization is noted. See next illustration for text of Section 13.11.

13.45   Final decision after appeal.

Subpart E—Revocation by Operation of Law or Regulation

13.51   Revocation by operation of law or regulation.
13.52   Notice of revocation.
13.53   Appeal of notice of revocation.
13.54   Decision after appeal.

Subpart F—Miscellaneous

13.61   Publicity of information.
13.62   Third-party comment on certificates.
13.71   Informal conferences.

beverage labels. See § 13.101.

[T.D. ATF–406, 64 FR 2129, Jan. 13, 1999, as amended by T.D. ATF–483, 67 FR 62858, Oct. 8, 2002]

§ 13.2   Delegations of the Administrator.

The regulatory authorities of the Administrator contained in this part are delegated to appropriate TTB officers. These TTB officers are specified in TTB Order 1135.13, Delegation of the Administrator's Authorities in 27 CFR Part 13, Labeling Proceedings. You

[Illustration 13–4]

PAGE FROM TITLE 27 OF CFR

Alcohol and Tobacco Tax and Trade Bureau, Treasury   **§ 13.11**

may obtain a copy of this order by accessing the TTB Web site (*http:// www.ttb.gov*) or by mailing a request to the Alcohol and Tobacco Tax and Trade Bureau, National Revenue Center, 550 Main Street, Room 1516, Cincinnati, OH 45202.

[T.D. TTB–44, 71 FR 16924, Apr. 4, 2006]

§ 13.3 Related regulations.

The following regulations also relate to this part:

7 CFR Part 205—National Organic Program
27 CFR Part 1—Basic Permit Requirements Under the Federal Alcohol Administration Act, Nonindustrial Use of Distilled Spirits and Wine, Bulk Sales and Bottling of Distilled Spirits
27 CFR Part 4—Labeling and Advertising of Wine
27 CFR Part 5—Labeling and Advertising of

27 CFR Part 16—Alcoholic Beverage Health Warning Statement
27 CFR Part 19—Distilled Spirits Plants
27 CFR Part 24—Wine
27 CFR Part 25—Beer
27 CFR Part 26—Liquors and Articles from Puerto Rico and the Virgin Islands
27 CFR Part 27—Importation of Distilled Spirits, Wines, and Beer
27 CFR 28—Exportation of Alcohol
27 CFR Part 71—Rules of Practice in Permit Proceedings

[T.D. ATF–483, 67 FR 62858, Oct. 8, 2002, as amended by T.D. TTB—8, 69 FR 3829, Jan. 27, 2004]

Subpart B—Definitions

§ 13.11 Meaning of terms.

Where used in this part and in forms prescribed under this part, where not otherwise distinctly expressed or manifestly incompatible with the intent thereof, terms shall have the meaning ascribed in this subpart. Words in the plural form shall include the singular, and vice versa, and words importing the masculine gender shall include the feminine. The terms "include" and "including" do not exclude things not enumerated that are in the same general class.

Act. The Federal Alcohol Administration Act.

Administrator. The Administrator, Alcohol and Tobacco Tax and Trade Bureau, Department of the Treasury, Washington, DC.

Applicant. The permittee or brewer whose name, address, and basic permit number, or plant registry number, appears on an unapproved Form 5100.31, application for a certificate of label approval, certificate of exemption from label approval, or distinctive liquor bottle approval.

Appropriate TTB officer. An officer or employee of the Alcohol and Tobacco Tax and Trade Bureau (TTB) authorized to perform any functions relating to the administration or enforcement of this part by TTB Order 1135.13, Delegation of the Administrator's Authori-

beer for sale.

Certificate holder. The permittee or brewer whose name, address, and basic permit number, or plant registry number, appears on an approved Form 5100.31, certificate of label approval, certificate of exemption from label approval, or distinctive liquor bottle approval.

Certificate of exemption from label approval. A certificate issued on Form 5100.31 which authorizes the bottling of wine or distilled spirits, under the condition that the product will under no circumstances be sold, offered for sale, shipped, delivered for shipment, or otherwise introduced by the applicant, directly or indirectly, into interstate or foreign commerce.

Certificate of label approval. A certificate issued on Form 5100.31 that authorizes the bottling or packing of wine, distilled spirits, or malt beverages, or the removal of bottled wine, distilled spirits, or malt beverages from customs custody for introduction into commerce, as long as the project bears labels identical to the labels affixed to the face of the certificate, or labels with changes authorized by the certificate.

279

208-103 D-10

Step 2 cont'd:
This shows the text of Section 13.11 as it appears in Title 27 of the *CFR*.

[Illustration 13–5]

TITLE PAGE FROM LSA: LIST OF CFR SECTIONS AFFECTED PAMPHLET

Code of Federal Regulations

LSA
List of CFR Sections Affected

November 2006

Title 1–16
Changes January 3, 2006
through November 30, 2006

Title 17–27
Changes April 1, 2006
through November 30, 2006

Title 28–41
Changes July 1, 2006
through November 30, 2006

Title 42–50
Changes October 1, 2006
through November 30, 2006

Step 3:
   Title 27 of the CFR is revised annually as of April 1. Hence, it must be ascertained if any changes have subsequently occurred. This is accomplished by using this list. It is issued monthly, with the December, March, June, and September issues consisting of an annual cumulation as indicated on the title page.

[Illustration 13–6]

PAGES FROM LSA: LIST OF CFR SECTIONS AFFECTED PAMPHLET

NOVEMBER 2006   **75**

CHANGES APRIL 1, 2006 THROUGH NOVEMBER 30, 2006

5.4 Revised 16921
5.11 Amended 16921
5.22 (k)(1), (2) and (l)(2) amended
....16922
5.23 (a)(2) amended.........................16922
5.26 (b) amended 16922
5.28 Introductory text amended
....16922
5.32a Added; interim 42268
5.32b Added; interim 42268
5.33 (g) amended 16922
5.34 (a) amended 16922
5.35 (a) amended 16922

nated as (c)(12) through (22);
new (c)(11) added 34527
9.157 (b) introductory text and
(c)(13) through (18) revised;
(b)(41) and (42) amended;
(b)(43) added 34524
9.194 Added 33242
9.195 Added 40414
9.196 Added 40414
9.197 Added 40414
9.198 Added 40414
9.199 Added 40414
9.200 Added 40414

Step 4:
   Note that section 13.11 of Title 27 has been amended. This addition was first printed at page 16924 of the 2006 *Federal Register*. This should be read for the text of the addition.

5.55 (a), (b) and (c) amended 16922
5.65 (a)(4), (5) and (g) amended
....16922
6.5 Revised...................................16922
6.6 (a) through (c)(3) amended 16922
6.11 Amended................................16922
7.3 (a) amended; (b) revised 16922
7.5 Revised...................................16922
7.10 Amended................................16923
7.20 (c)(1) amended.........................16923
7.22a Added; interim 42269
7.22b Added; interim 42269
7.23 (b) amended 16923
7.24 (g) amended 16923
7.25 (a)(1) amended.........................16923
7.29 (a)(4), (5) and (d) amended
....16923
7.31 (a), (b) and (c) amended 16923
7.41 (a) amended 16923
7.54 (a)(4) and (5) amended.............16923
8.5 Revised...................................16923
8.6 (a) through (c)(3) amended 16923
8.11 Amended................................16923
9.3 (a) amended 16923
9.11 Amended................................16923
9.32 (a) revised 66455
9.46 (b) and (c) revised 34531
9.59   (c)(13)   revised;   (c)(14)
through (19) redesignated as
(c)(16) through (21); new
(c)(14) and (15) added 34527
9.75 (b) introductory text and
(c)(10) through (16) revised;
(b)(40) and (41) amended;
(b)(42) and (43) added 34524
9.139 (c)(9) and (10) revised;
(c)(11) through (21) redesig-

10.5 Revised..................................16923
10.6 (a) through (c)(3) amended
....16924
10.11 Amended...............................16924
11.5 Revised..................................16924
11.6 (a) and (b) amended.................16924
11.11 Amended...............................16924
12.1 Amended................................16924
12.3 (a) and (b) amended.................16924
12.31 Introductory text amended
....16924
13.2 Revised 16924
13.11 Amended 16924
13.20 (a) amended; (b) revised 16924
13.21 (a) and (b) amended 16925
13.22 Amended 16925
13.23 Amended 16925
13.25 (a) and (b) amended 16925
13.26 (a) and (b) amended 16925
13.27 (a), (b) and (c) amended 16925
13.41 Amended 16925
13.42 Amended 16925
13.43 (a) and (b) amended 16925
13.44 (a) and (b) amended 16925
13.45 (a) and (b) amended 16925
13.51 Amended 16925
13.52 Amended 16925
13.53 Amended 16925
13.54 (a) and (b) amended 16925
13.61 (a)(2), (b) and (d) amended
....16925
13.62 Amended 16925
13.71 (a) and (b) amended 16925
13.72 (b) amended..........................16925
13.74 Amended 16925
13.75 Heading amended 16925
13.76 (a) amended..........................16925

[Illustration 13–7]

PAGES FROM LSA: LIST OF CFR SECTIONS AFFECTED PAMPHLET

88   **LSA—LIST OF CFR SECTIONS AFFECTED**

CHANGES APRIL 1, 2006 THROUGH NOVEMBER 30, 2006

TITLE 27 Chapter I—Con.

70.482 (a) introductory text and
  (d)(1)(i) amended 16963
70.483 Amended 16963
70.484 Amended 16963
70.485 (a) and (d)(1) amended..........16963
70.486 Amended 16963
70.504 (c)(2) amended...................16963
70.506 Amended 16963
70.507 (g) amended 16963
70.602 (a) and (b)(1) introductory
  text amended...........................16963
70.606 Introductory text amended
 16963
70.608 Amended 16963
70.609 Amended..........................16963
70.701 (a)(1), (2), (c), (d)(1), (2)
  heading, (i)(A), (B), (iii)(B),
  (C), (D), (iv)(A), (B) and (C)
  amended 16963
70.702 (c) amended......................16963
70.801 Amended 16963
70.802 (c) through (g) amended........16963
70.802 (g) amended 16964
70.803 (b)(1), (2), (c), (d) introductory text, (3), (e) heading, (1)
  through (5) introductory

71.63 Amended 16965
71.64 (a), (b) and (c) amended.........16965
71.65 Amended 16965
71.70 Amended 16965
71.71 Amended 16965
71.72 Amended 16965
71.73 Amended 16965
71.75 Amended 16965
71.78 Amended 16965
71.79 (b) amended 16965
71.80 Amended 16965
71.85 Amended 16965
71.95 Amended 16965
71.96 Amended 16965
71.97 Amended 16965
71.98 Amended 16965
71.99 Amended 16965
71.100 Amended 16965
71.105 Amended 16965
71.106 Amended 16965
71.107—71.110 Undesignated cen-
  ter heading removed.................16965
71.107 Amended 16965
71.107a Heading, (a) introductory
  text, (2) and (3) amended 16965
71.108 (a) and (b) amended.............16966

Step 5:
  The *LSA* should also be consulted to ascertain if proposed rules may be relevant.

71.25 Amended 16965
71.26 Amended 16965
71.27 Amended 16965
71.29 Amended 16965
71.31 Amended 16965
71.35 Amended 16965
71.36 Amended 16965
71.37 Amended 16965
71.38 Amended 16965
71.45 Amended 16965
71.46 Amended 16965
71.48 Introductory text amended
 16965
71.49 Amended 16965
71.49a Introductory text amend-
  ed..16965
71.49b Introductory text and (c)
  amended 16965
71.55 (a) amended.........................16965
71.57 Amended 16965
71.59 Amended 16965
71.60 (a), (b) and (c) amended.........16965
71.61 Amended 16965
71.62 Amended 16965

71.118 Amended 16966
71.126 Amended 16966
71.129 Amended 16966

Chapter II—Bureau of Alcohol, Tobacco, Firearms, and Explosives, Department of Justice (Parts 400—699)

555.141 (a)(10) added 46101

Proposed Rules: ◄

4 ....42329, 54943
5 ....42329, 54943
7 ....42329, 54943
9 ......25795, 37870, 40458, 40465, 53612, 65432,
                                                  65437
40 62506
41 62506
44 62506
45 62506
555 46174

[Illustration 13–8]

PAGE FROM LSA'S TABLE OF FEDERAL REGISTER ISSUE PAGES AND DATES SHOWING VOLUME 71 FEDERAL REGISTER (2006)

TABLE OF FEDERAL REGISTER ISSUE PAGES AND DATES   125

2006

71 FR Page

Page	Date	Page	Date
		15005–15320	27
		15321–15556	28
		15557–16013	29
1–230	Jan. 3	16015–16192	30
231–536	4	16193–16476	31
537–872	5	16477–16689	Apr. 3
873–1387	6	16691–16972	4
1389–1471	9	16973–17334	5
1473–1681	10	17335–17689	6
1683–1914	11	17691–17965	7
1915–2133	12	17967–18159	10
2135–2451	13	18161–18588	11
2453–2855	17	18589–19096	12
2857–2989	18	19097–19426	13
2991–3203	19	19427–19619	14
3205–3407	20	19621–19803	17
3409–3752	23	19805–19982	18
3753–4032	24	19983–20334	19
4033–4230	25	20335–20515	20
4231–4449	26	20517–20862	21
4451–4804	27	20863–23854	24
4805–4973	30	23855–24550	25
4975–5153	31	24551–24801	26
5155–5578	Feb. 1	24803–25057	27
5579–5775	2	25058–25482	28
5777–5965	3	25483–25738	May 1
5967–6190	6	25739–25917	2
6191–6331	7	25919–26188	3
6333–6660	8	26189–26407	4
6661–6971	9	26409–26673	5
6973–7392	10	26675–26815	8

Step 6:

This table lists pages of the Federal Register and shows the date of the Federal Register in which the pages are located. Page 16924 is found in the April 4, 2006 Federal Register.

See next illustration.

Page	Date	Page	Date
10411–10603	Mar. 1	29757–30046	24
10605–10830	2	30047–30261	25
10831–11133	3	30263–30558	26
11135–11286	6	30559–30791	30
11287–11504	7	30793–31068	31
11505–12117	8	31069–31914	June 1
12119–12276	9	31915–32263	2
12277–12612	10	32265–32414	5
12613–12989	13	32415–32799	6
12991–13241	14	32801–33145	7
13243–13523	15	33147–33373	8
13525–13735	16	33375–33592	9
13737–13921	17	33593–33988	12
13923–14087	20	33989–34230	13
14089–14353	21	34231–34505	14
14355–14628	22	34507–34786	15
14629–14793	23	34787–35141	16
14795–15003	24	35143–35371	19

[Illustration 13–9]

PAGE FROM VOLUME 71, FEDERAL REGISTER

16924 Federal Register / Vol. 71, No. 64 / Tuesday, April 4, 2006 / Rules and Regulations

Street, Room 1516, Cincinnati, OH 45202.

§ 10.6 [Amended]

■ 34. Amend § 10.6 as follows:

■ a. In paragraph (a) remove the word "Director" each place it appears and add, in its place, the word "Administrator".

■ b. In paragraph (b), the heading of paragraph (c), and paragraphs (c)(1), (c)(2) and (c)(3), remove the reference to "ATF" each place it appears and add, in its place, a reference to "TTB".

■ 35. Amend § 10.11 as follows:

■ a. Remove the definitions of "Appropriate ATF officer" and "Director".

■ b. Add, in alphabetical order, definitions of "Administrator" and "Appropriate TTB officer" to read as

add, in its place, the word "Administrator".

■ b. In paragraph (b) remove the reference to "ATF" each place it appears and add, in its place, a reference to "TTB".

■ 39. Amend § 11.11 as follows:

■ a. Remove the definitions of "Appropriate ATF officer" and "Director".

■ b. Add, in alphabetical order, definitions of "Administrator" and "Appropriate TTB officer" to read as follows:.

§ 11.11   Meaning of terms.

*   *   *   *   *

Administrator. The Administrator, Alcohol and Tobacco Tax and Trade Bureau, Department of the Treasury, Washington, DC.

§ 13.2   Delegations of the Administrator.

The regulatory authorities of the Administrator contained in this part are delegated to appropriate TTB officers. These TTB officers are specified in TTB Order 1135.13. Delegation of the Administrator's Authorities in 27 CFR Part 13, Labeling Proceedings. You may obtain a copy of this order by accessing the TTB Web site (*http://www.ttb.gov*) or by mailing a request to the Alcohol and Tobacco Tax and Trade Bureau, National Revenue Center, 550 Main Street, Room 1516, Cincinnati, OH 45202.

■ 46. Amend § 13.11 as follows:

■ a. In the definition of "Applicant" remove the reference to "ATF F 5100.31" and add, in its place, a reference to "Form 5100.31".

Step 7:

This is the page from the *Federal Register* on which the revision to Section 13.11 is published.

Bureau, Department of the Treasury, Washington, DC.

Appropriate TTB officer. An officer or employee of the Alcohol and Tobacco Tax and Trade Bureau (TTB) authorized to perform any functions relating to the administration or enforcement of this part by TTB Order 1135.10, Delegation of the Administrator's Authorities in 27 CFR Part 10, Commercial Bribery.

*   *   *   *   *

PART 11—CONSIGNMENT SALES

■ 36. The authority citation for part 11 continues to read as follows:

Authority: 15 U.S.C. 49–50; 27 U.S.C. 202 and 205.

■ 37. Revise § 11.5 to read as follows:

§ 11.5   Delegations of the Administrator.

Most of the regulatory authorities of the Administrator contained in this part are delegated to appropriate TTB officers. These TTB officers are specified in TTB Order 1135.11, Delegation of the Administrator's Authorities in 27 CFR Part 11, Consignment Sales. You may obtain a copy of this order by accessing the TTB Web site (*http://www.ttb.gov*) or by mailing a request to the Alcohol and Tobacco Tax and Trade Bureau, National Revenue Center, 550 Main Street, Room 1516, Cincinnati, OH 45202.

§ 11.6   [Amended]

■ 38. Amend § 11.6 as follows:

■ a. In paragraph (a) remove the word "Director" each place it appears and

of the Administrator's Authorities in 27 CFR Part 11, Consignment Sales.

*   *   *   *   *

PART 12—FOREIGN NONGENERIC NAMES OF GEOGRAPHIC SIGNIFICANCE USED IN THE DESIGNATION OF WINES

■ 40. The authority citation for part 12 continues to read as follows:

Authority: 27 U.S.C. 205.

§ 12.1   [Amended]

■ 41. Amend § 12.1 by removing the word "Director" and adding, in its place, the word "Administrator".

§ 12.3   [Amended]

■ 42. Amend § 12.3 as follows:

■ a. In paragraph (a) remove the word "Director" and add, in its place, the word "Administrator".

■ b. In paragraphs (a) and (b), remove the reference to "ATF" each place it appears and add, in its place, a reference to "TTB".

§ 12.31   [Amended]

■ 43. Amend the introductory text of § 12.31 by removing the word "Director" and adding, in its place, the word "Administrator".

PART 13—LABELING PROCEEDINGS

■ 44. The authority citation for part 13 continues to read as follows:

Authority: 27 U.S.C. 205(e), 26 U.S.C. 5301 and 7805.

■ 45. Revise § 13.2 to read as follows:

in its place, a reference to "Form 5100.31".

■ d. In the definitions of "Certificate holder," "Certificate of exemption from label approval," and "Certificate of label approval," remove the reference to "ATF F 5100.31" and add, in its place, a reference to "Form 5100.31".

■ e. In the definition of "Liquor bottle" remove the reference to "ATF" and add, in its place, a reference to "TTB".

■ f. Add, in alphabetical order, definitions of "Administrator", "Appropriate TTB officer", and "TTB" to read as follows:

§ 13.11   Meaning of terms.   ←

*   *   *   *   *

Administrator. The Administrator, Alcohol and Tobacco Tax and Trade Bureau, Department of the Treasury, Washington, DC.

Appropriate TTB officer. An officer or employee of the Alcohol and Tobacco Tax and Trade Bureau (TTB) authorized to perform any functions relating to the administration or enforcement of this part by TTB Order 1135.13, Delegation of the Administrator's Authorities in 27 CFR Part 13, Labeling Proceedings.

*   *   *   *   *

TTB. The Alcohol and Tobacco Tax and Trade Bureau, Department of the Treasury, Washington, DC.

*   *   *   *   *

■ 47. Amend § 13.20 as follows:

■ a. In paragraph (a) remove the reference to "ATF" and add, in its place, a reference to "TTB".

■ b. Revise paragraph (b) to read as follows:

[Illustration 13–10]

PAGE FROM VOLUME 71, FEDERAL REGISTER–
LIST OF CFR PARTS AFFECTED

i

Reader Aids

Federal Register

Vol. 71, No. 64

Tuesday, April 4, 2006

CUSTOMER SERVICE AND INFORMATION

Federal Register/Code of Federal Regulations

General Information, indexes and other finding aids	202–741–6000
Laws	741–6000
Presidential Documents	
Executive orders and proclamations	741–6000
The United States Government Manual	741–6000
Other Services	
Electronic and on-line services (voice)	741–6020
Privacy Act Compilation	741–6064
Public Laws Update Service (numbers, dates, etc.)	741–6043
TTY for the deaf-and-hard-of-hearing	741–6086

ELECTRONIC RESEARCH

World Wide Web

Full text of the daily Federal Register, CFR and other publications is located at: **http://www.gpoaccess.gov/nara/index.html**

Federal Register information and research tools, including Public Inspection List, indexes, and links to GPO Access are located at: http://www.archives.gov/federal_register/

for change settings); then follow the instructions

PENS (Public Law Electronic Notification Service) is an e-mail service that notifies subscribers of recently enacted laws.

To subscribe, go to **http://listserv.gsa.gov/archives/publaws-l.html** and select *join or leave the list (or change settings)*; then follow the instructions.

FEDREGTOC-L and **PENS** are mailing lists only. We cannot respond to specific inquiries.

Reference questions. Send questions and comments about the Federal Register system to: **fedreg.info@nara.gov**

The Federal Register staff cannot interpret specific documents or regulations.

FEDERAL REGISTER PAGES AND DATE, APRIL

16477–16690	3
16691–16972	4

CFR PARTS AFFECTED DURING APRIL

At the end of each month, the Office of the Federal Register publishes separately a List of CFR Sections Affected (LSA), which lists parts and sections affected by documents published since the revision date of each title.

3 CFR

Proclamations:	
7992	16685
7993	16687
7994	16689
7995	16969
7996	16971

6 CFR

Proposed Rules:	
5	16519

7 CFR

Proposed Rules:	
301	16711

14 CFR

39	16477, 16691

27 CFR

1	16918
4	16918
5	16918
6	16918
7	16918
8	16918
9	16918
10	16918
11	16918
12	16918
13	16918
16	16918
17	16918
18	16918
19	16918
20	16918
21	16918
22	16918
24	16918
25	16918
26	16918
27	16918
28	16918
29	16918
30	16918
31	16918
40	16918
44	16918
45	16918
46	16918
53	16918
70	16918

71	16918

28 CFR

Proposed Rules:	
540	16520

29 CFR

11	16664
500	16664
501	16664
516	16664
519	16664
531	16664
536	16664
547	16664
548	16664
549	16664
550	16664
552	16664
57	16664
70	16664
71	16664
72	16664
75	16664
77	16664
90	16664
250	16859

33 CFR

100	16488
117	16489, 16491, 16492
Proposed Rules:	
100	16525
117	16527, 16529
165	16531

36 CFR

251	16614, 16622
Proposed Rules:	
Ch. I	16534

40 CFR

18	16699
80	16492
280	16862
261	16862
264	16862
265	16862
266	16862
268	16862
270	16862

Step 8:

The *List of CFR Parts Affected* indicates changes made during the year to the *CFR*. To ascertain further changes, one should check the *CFR Parts Affected* table in the last issue of the *Federal Register* for months subsequent to the most recent *LSA*. Note the table of *Federal Register* pages and dates.

SECTION G. OTHER SOURCES OF INFORMATION ABOUT ADMINISTRATIVE AGENCIES

1. The United States Government Manual

This handbook, published by the Office of the Federal Register, is revised annually and contains general information about Congress and the federal judiciary. *GPO Access* has the most current version and contains older editions of *The United States Government Manual*.[28] The major emphasis of *The United States Government Manual* is on the executive branch and regulatory agencies. Each department and agency is concisely described, with citations to the enabling statute that created the department or agency. A description of functions and authority, names of government officials, and listings of major publications are provided.

The *Manual* includes several appendices. One appendix lists all abolished and transferred agencies, with an indication of what happened to the functions for which they had responsibility. For example, under *Civil Service Commission, U.S.*, it is noted that the agency has been re-designated as the *Merit Systems Protection Board* and its functions transferred to the *Board* and to the *Office of Personnel Management* by the Reorganization Plan No. 2 of 1978.

Other appendices list commonly used abbreviations and acronyms, and all agencies, in alphabetical order, that appear in the *CFR*. Separate indexes for name and agency/subject are provided.

2. Federal Regulatory Directory

The *Federal Regulatory Directory*[29] can be used to augment information contained in *The United States Government Manual*. Discussions of the topics of regulations and current issues involving federal administrative agencies, as well as extensive profiles of the largest and most important agencies, are included. Summary information on most other federal agencies is also provided.

3. Federal Yellow Book and Federal Regional Yellow Book

These titles, two in a series of directories that are updated semiannually, provide website information, email addresses, and telephone numbers for government officials.[30]

4. USA.gov

This federal government web site, *USA.gov*,[31] which began several years ago as *FirstGov.gov*, is a one-stop site for federal, state, and local government websites. There is an A–Z agency list on the home page as well as links to state, local, and tribal government home pages.

SECTION H. PRESIDENTIAL DOCUMENTS

Most rules and regulations are the result of activities of federal agencies operating under powers delegated by Congress. The president also has the authority to issue documents that have legal effect. This authority is constitutional, statutory, or sometimes both. This section describes the types of presidential documents and the sources in which documentation of presidential activities may be found.

---

[28] The UNITED STATES GOVERNMENT MANUAL is available free, from 1995 to the present, at http://www.gpoaccess.gov/gmanual/index.html. *HeinOnline*, a fee-based service, has PDF images of this publication from 1935 to the present.

[29] (CQ Press 12th ed. 2005).

[30] Published by Leadership Directories, Inc., these titles and the rest of the series are also available as a fee-based electronic database.

[31] http://www.usa.gov.

1. Proclamations and Executive Orders[32]

Proclamations and Executive Orders have been widely used by presidents to exercise their authority. Proclamations are generally addressed to the entire nation, and their content frequently relates to ceremonial or celebratory occasions. Executive Orders are generally used by the president to direct and govern the activities of government officials and agencies. [Illustration 13–11]

Proclamations and Executive Orders appear in both print and electronic form in the following titles:

a.   The *Federal Register*

b.   The *Weekly Compilation of Presidential Documents*

c.   Title 3 of the *CFR* and compilation volumes of Title 3

d.   *Public Papers of the Presidents* (until January 1989)

e.   *United States Code Congressional and Administrative News,* Advance pamphlets

f.   *United States Code Service,* Advance Service

g.   *The American Presidency Project,* created in 1999, now includes more than 85,000 documents related to the study of the presidency.[33]

h.   *LexisNexis* and *Westlaw. Westlaw* contains Executive Orders issued since 1936 and all other presidential documents from the *Federal Register* since 1984. *LexisNexis* contains presidential documents from 1980 to the present.

i.   *HeinOnline* includes a Presidential Library with PDF images of the complete file of *Weekly Compilation of Presidential Documents, Public Papers of the Presidents,* and a variety of other materials.

j.   Proclamations also may be found in *United States Statutes at Large.*

k.   The White House home page[34] contains all White House documents released during the current administration, including Executive Orders and Presidential Proclamations. [Illustration 13–12] In addition, the other electronic research sources described in Section C–4 (above) contain presidential documents that are included in the *Federal Register* and the *CFR.*

2. Codification of Presidential Proclamations and Executive Orders

The Office of the Federal Register began publication of the *Codification of Presidential Proclamations and Executive Orders* in 1979, but

---

[32] For a detailed study, see HOUSE COMM. ON GOVERNMENT OPERATIONS, 85TH CONG., 1ST SESS., EXECUTIVE ORDERS AND PROCLAMATIONS: STUDY OF A USE OF PRESIDENTIAL POWERS (Comm. Print 1957). *See also* KENNETH R. MAYER, WITH THE STROKE OF A PEN: EXECUTIVE ORDERS AND PRESIDENTIAL POWER (2001). For research help, see Donna Bennett & Philip Yannarella, *Locating Presidential Proclamations and Executive Orders—A Guide to Sources,* 5(2/3) LEGAL REFERENCE SERVICES Q., Sum./Fall 1985, at 177; Mary Woodward, *Executive Orders: A Journey,* 10(3) LEGAL REFERENCE SERVICES Q., 1990, at 125.

To locate Executive Orders issued prior to the publication of the *Federal Register,* see NEW YORK CITY HISTORICAL RECORDS SURVEY, PRESIDENTIAL EXECUTIVE ORDERS, NUMBERED 1–8030, 1862–1938 (1944); NEW JERSEY HISTORICAL RECORDS SURVEY, LIST AND INDEX OF PRESIDENTIAL EXECUTIVE ORDERS: UNNUMBERED SERIES, 1789–1941 (1944).

[33] http://www.presidency.ucsb.edu/index.php.

[34] http://www.whitehouse.gov.

suspended publication in 1995. Its purpose was to provide in one source Proclamations and Executive Orders that have general applicability and continuing effect. This codification takes all the previously published Proclamations and Executive Orders still in force and arranges them by subject. Amendments to the original documents are incorporated in the text.

The codification is arranged in fifty titles corresponding to those of the *Code of Federal Regulations*, and covers the period April 13, 1945, through January 20, 1989. A "Disposition Table" at the back of the volume lists all Proclamations and Executive Orders issued, with their amendments, and indicates their current status and chapter designations, where applicable. The codification was widely distributed, but is now out of print. It is available on the Internet.[35]

3. Reorganization Plans

By the provisions of 5 U.S.C. §§ 901–912 (2000), the president is authorized to examine the organization of all agencies and make changes that provide for better management of the executive branch of the government. The president is authorized to submit proposed reorganization plans to both houses of Congress. Proposed reorganization plans are published in the *Congressional Record*. A reorganization plan becomes effective if the president accepts the joint resolution passed by the House and the Senate that approves the plan submitted by the president.

Reorganization plans are published, as approved, in the *Federal Register,* Title 3 of the *CFR, United States Statutes at Large,* and 5 *U.S.C.* Appendix. The *Congressional Record* is the best source for plans not approved by Congress.

4. Other Presidential Documents

In addition to the documents discussed above, the president issues Administrative Orders, such as findings, determinations, and memoranda; Executive Agreements; and messages to Congress and signing statements. Administrative Orders are published in the *Federal Register* and in Title 3 of the *Code of Federal Regulations*. The American Presidency Project contains an enormous amount of information, and has organized everything from inaugural addresses to signing statements in one website.[36]

5. Presidential Nominations

A list of presidential nominations submitted to the Senate is set forth at the end of each issue of the *Weekly Compilation of Presidential Documents*. The White House website lists nominations by name and by date.[37] Each issue of the *Congressional Record's Daily Digest* for the Senate contains the names of those nominated and those confirmed by the Senate.

6. Compilations of Presidential Documents

The following sources provide comprehensive collections of presidential documents:

[35] http://www.archives.gov/federal-register/codification/.

[36] http://www.presidency.ucsb.edu/index.php.

[37] http://www.whitehouse.gov/news/nominations/.

a. *Weekly Compilation of Presidential Documents*. This title is published every Monday and contains statements, messages, and other presidential materials released by the White House during the preceding week. An index of Contents is set forth at the beginning of each issue for documents included in that issue. Until 1995, each issue also contained a cumulative subject index and name index for the previous issues of the current quarter. An annual index is divided into names and subjects. Since 1995 (volume 31, no. 1), indexes are issued quarterly and distributed separately; there are no more cumulative indexes in each issue. Other finding aids include: lists of laws approved by the president; nominations submitted to the Senate; and a checklist of White House releases. The print version is no longer widely available because it is no longer distributed free to depository libraries.

The National Archives and Records Administration site available through *GPO Access* contains the *Weekly Compilation of Presidential Documents* from 1993.[38]

b. *Public Papers of the Presidents*.[39] This print series starts with the administration of President Hoover. It is published annually in one or more volumes and includes a compilation of the Presidents' messages to Congress, public speeches, news conferences, and public letters. The final volume for each year contains a cumulative index to the volumes published during the year. After all volumes for an administration are published, a commercial firm publishes a cumulative index for that president.[40] The papers of President Franklin Roosevelt and some of the earlier presidents, not part of the *Public Papers* series, have been published commercially.

Beginning with the 1977 volumes, which cover the first year of President Carter's administration, and continuing through the volume for 1988–89, the last year of President Reagan's administration, the set includes all of the material printed in the *Weekly Compilation of Presidential Documents*. Beginning in 1989, the first year of the administration of President George Herbert Walker Bush, Proclamations and Executive Orders are not included. Instead, a table refers the user to the appropriate issues of the *Federal Register* in which the documents are published.

c. *The American Presidency Project* is the largest online compilation of presidential documents, with more than 85,000 items.[41] It includes the contents of the *Public Papers of the Presidents*, all Executive Orders from 1826 to the present, all Proclamations from 1789 to the present, and the *Weekly Compilation of Presidential Documents* from 1977 to the present. It also includes obscure data, such as "Number of Requests of Congress in State of the Union Addresses" and "List of Acknowledged Guests Sitting in House Galleries" during the State of the Union Address. There is also an audio/video archive and links to all the presidential library websites.

---

[38] http://www.gpoaccess.gov/wcomp/index.html.

[39] This publication is available from *GPO Access*, covering 1991 to the present, at http://www.gpoaccess.gov/pubpapers/index.html.

[40] THE CUMULATED INDEXES TO THE PUBLIC PAPERS OF THE PRESIDENTS OF THE UNITED STATES (KTO Press 1977–79; Krauss International Publications 1979–81; Bernan Press 1995).

[41] http://www.presidency.ucsb.edu/index.php.

d. *Title 3 of the Code of Federal Regulations.* Presidential documents required to be published in the *Federal Register* are compiled in Title 3 of the *CFR*. Before 1976, compilation volumes of Title 3 were published covering varied time periods. Since 1976, a compilation volume has been published annually. Unlike the other yearly codifications of agency regulations, each compilation of Title 3 is a unique source of presidential documents rather than an updated codification, therefore, each compilation of Title 3 is a permanent reference source.

7. Updating Presidential Documents

The use of *Shepard's Code of Federal Regulations Citations,* mentioned in Section E–1–d above, also applies to Presidential Proclamations, Executive Orders, and Reorganization Plans. It bears repeating that print citators, such as a unit of *Shepard's Citations,* rarely are seen now; the most current citators are electronic databases, the best known of which are *Shepard's* (*LexisNexis*) and *KeyCite* (*Westlaw*). Presidential documents included in Title 3 can be updated using the *LSA* (see Section E–1–a). See also Section C–4 above for electronic resources.

SECTION I. ILLUSTRATIONS: PRESIDENTIAL DOCUMENTS

13–11. Screen Print, Example of Presidential Executive Order
13–12. Screen Print, White House Website

[Illustration 13–11]

SCREEN PRINT, EXAMPLE OF PRESIDENTIAL EXECUTIVE ORDER

75047

Federal Register

Vol. 71, No. 242

Monday, December 18, 2006

Presidential Documents

Title 3—

The President

Executive Order 13418 of December 14, 2006

Amendment to Executive Order 13317, Volunteers for Prosperity

By the authority vested in me as President by the Constitution and the laws of the United States of America, and to add combating malaria as one of the objectives of the global prosperity agenda, it is hereby ordered that section 1(a) of Executive Order 13317 of September 25, 2003, is amended by:

(a) striking ", and stemming the spread of HIV/AIDS." and inserting in lieu thereof ", stemming the spread of HIV/AIDS and controlling malaria."; and

(b) striking ", and the Middle East Partnership Initiative." and inserting in lieu thereof ", the Middle East Partnership Initiative, and the President's Malaria Initiative.".

THE WHITE HOUSE,
December 14, 2006.

[Illustration 13–12]

SCREEN PRINT, WHITE HOUSE WEBSITE

The White House home page, http://www.whitehouse.gov, includes links to presidential proclamations, Executive Orders, etc.

SECTION J.   FEDERAL ADMINISTRATIVE DECISIONS

1. Agency Decisions

Many federal administrative agencies also serve an adjudicatory function and, in performing this function, issue decisions.[42] The Federal Communications Commission, for example, is authorized by statute to license radio and television stations. It also has the authority to enforce its regulations concerning the operations of these stations. When stations allegedly violate the terms of the statute or regulations, the Federal Communications Commission can hear charges and issue decisions.

---

[42] Many of the mysteries about various administrative law courts are explained in Harold H. Bruff, *Specialized Courts in Administrative Law,* 43 ADMIN. L. REV. 329 (1991).

Decisions of administrative agencies are published, not in the *Federal Register,* but in separate sources.[43] Decisions can be published in print or electronically by the U.S. Government Printing Office (*GPO Access*), the agency itself,[44] and/or commercial publishers.

a. *Government Publication of Decisions of Federal Administrative Agencies.* Print versions of some of these publications are available in law libraries and in public and university libraries that are official depositories of the U.S. Government Printing Office. The format, frequency, and method of publication vary from agency to agency. Generally, agency publications are issued infrequently and are poorly indexed. Some print sets include indexes and digests in the back of each volume. For other sets, separate indexes and digests are published. Some sets of federal administrative decisions have an advance sheet service. Some agency decisions are available from *GPO Access* or from agency websites.

b. *Commercial Publication of Decisions of Federal Administrative Agencies.* Commercial publishers often reprint agency decisions in looseleaf services, which often are accompanied by bound, sequentially numbered volumes of decisions. *LexisNexis* has a combined library of federal agency decisions, in addition to subject-specific libraries containing decisions of individual agencies. *Westlaw* has topical databases that contain agency decisions.[45]

2. Judicial Review of Agency Decisions

After an agency has issued an administrative decision, it may be appealed to the federal courts. The decisions resulting from these appeals may be found by consulting the following sources:

a. *West's Federal Practice Digest, 4th,* and its predecessor sets.

b. *United States Supreme Court Digest, Lawyers' Edition* or *U.S. Supreme Court Digest.*

c. *American Digest System* if the preceding digests are not available.

d. Check either *Shepard's Citations* or *Westlaw's KeyCite.*

e. *Treatises on administrative law.*

f. *Looseleaf services.*

g. *LexisNexis* and *Westlaw.*

3. Examples of Currently Published Official Decisions of Federal Agencies

a. Federal Communications Commission. *Reports* [1st Series], vol. 1–45 (1934–1965); [2d Series], vol. 1–104 (1965–1986). Continued by: *FCC Record,* vol. 1 *et seq.* (1986 to present).

b. Federal Trade Commission. *Decisions,* vol. 1 *et seq.* (1915 to present).

c. National Labor Relations Board. *Decisions and Orders,* vol. 1 *et seq.* (1935 to present).

---

[43] For a selected list of official federal administrative reports and decisions, see THE BLUEBOOK: A UNIFORM SYSTEM OF CITATION 196–97 (18th ed. 2005).

[44] A University of Virginia website maintains a list of agency decisions on the Internet; see http://www.lib.virginia.edu/govdocs/fed_decisions_subject.html.

[45] Looseleaf services are discussed in Chapter 14 of this book; electronic legal research is discussed in Chapter 23.

d. Securities and Exchange Commission. *Decisions and Reports*, vol. 1 *et seq.* (1934 to present).

As noted elsewhere in this chapter, websites of government agencies often contain decisions, rules and regulations, and other documents pertinent to the agencies. Quite often in recent years, material will be available on the agency website that will never be published in print form.

SECTION K. STATE ADMINISTRATIVE REGULATIONS AND DECISIONS

Although comprehensive research in state administrative law is difficult due to the varied publication policies of the states, the proliferation of websites and electronic resources makes state administrative materials more widely available than they were in the past.[46] In addition, recent publications assist in locating print and electronic resources.[47]

1. State Regulations

The regulations of state agencies are published in a variety of formats. In some states administrative regulations are officially codified and published in sets similar to the *Code of Federal Regulations*. These may be supplemented by a publication similar to the *Federal Register*. In other states, each agency issues its own regulations, and research inquiries must be directed to the appropriate agency. State regulations are increasingly being made available free through state websites.[48]

2. State Administrative Decisions

Many state agencies also publish their decisions. Most commonly, the decisions of unemployment compensation commissions, tax commissions, and public utility commissions are published. Like state regulations, state agency decisions are increasingly being added to *Westlaw* and *LexisNexis* and made available through websites.

3. Research in State Administrative Law

a. Check the state code to determine if the state has an Administrative Procedure Act and if the method for publication of regulations is prescribed therein.

b. Check the state's organization manual to determine those agencies that issue regulations or decisions.

c. Consult a legal encyclopedia or administrative law treatise if published for the state.

---

[46] Both *LexisNexis* and *Westlaw* contain a wide variety of state materials; there is also a separate Web-based product devoted to state laws and regulations, *LexisNexis State Capital Universe.* Cornell's *Legal Information Institute* has a directory of the states that links to all the primary source materials that are available for each state, at http://www.law.cornell.edu/ states/listing.html.

[47] *See, e.g.,* STATE ADMINISTRATIVE LAW BIBLIOGRAPHY: PRINT AND ELECTRONIC SOURCES (Cheryl Rae Nyberg ed., 2000); WILLIAM H. MANZ, GUIDE TO STATE LEGISLATIVE AND ADMINISTRATIVE MATERIALS (AALL Publication Series, No. 61, 2002).

[48] State websites can be found alphabetically through the main federal government website, http://www.usa.gov, and also through the Cornell *Legal Information Institute* site, http://www. law.cornell.edu.

d. Consult a state legal research manual, if available.[49]

e. Consult electronic and Internet sources to determine if state administrative regulations or agency decisions are available.

---

[49] *See* Appendix B of this book for a listing of state-specific guides to legal research.

Chapter 14

LOOSELEAF SERVICES

Looseleaf services provide timely and up-to-date access to information in specific areas of law. These services typically bring together in one source various types of primary and secondary authority, as well as finding tools. They are called "looseleaf" services because they are published in binders, rather than as bound books, so that superseded pages can easily be removed and new pages inserted.

In recent years, the content of many looseleaf services has been made available electronically in full text on the Internet directly from publishers as well as through computer-assisted legal research services such as *Lexis-Nexis*, *Westlaw*, and *Loislaw*. The electronic format allows levels of currency, access, and precise searching that were not available with print resources.

SECTION A. BENEFITS OF LOOSELEAF SERVICES

To research a problem in the law of taxation, for example, a researcher might need to locate not only relevant statutes and judicial opinions but also administrative regulations of the Internal Revenue Service and the Treasury Department, rulings of the Commissioner of Internal Revenue, news releases, technical information publications, and other agency documents. Looseleaf services can provide access to many of these different types of sources. Most looseleaf services attempt to consolidate into one source the statutes, regulations, judicial opinions, agency decisions, and commentary on a particular legal topic and then facilitate access to this material through detailed indexes and other finding aids.

In some areas of law, such as taxation and other areas of administrative law, there is a greater need for frequent updating. Looseleaf services can be updated much more quickly with additional or replacement pages and new releases than can publications updated by pocket parts, supplemental pamphlets, or replacement volumes.

The looseleaf format allows for creativity in the ways materials are organized. Furthermore, most looseleaf services include current awareness information, which can include news of proposed legislation, pending agency regulations, court and agency decisions, and even informed rumor. They also frequently contain forms, summaries of professional meetings, calendars of forthcoming events, and other news relevant to researchers or practicing attorneys in the field.

There are three basic types of looseleaf services: (1) those in which new pages are *interfiled* with existing materials; (2) those in *newsletter* format for which each issue is added to a binder sequentially and chronologically;

257

and (3) those using a combination of the two formats. Traditionally, looseleaf publications prepared by a publisher's editorial staff (as opposed to named authors), regardless of the publication's format, have had standardized publication schedules, typically weekly, biweekly, or monthly. By contrast, looseleaf services produced by named authors, which are more like treatises, usually are updated with interfiled materials less frequently on an "as needed" basis.[1]

The notion that looseleaf services are exclusively paper products no longer is valid. Looseleaf publishers are producing electronic versions of many, if not most, of their services. The electronic versions are available on the Internet directly from the publishers and also, in some cases, via electronic research services such as *LexisNexis* and *Westlaw*. Rather than requiring subscribers to file pages mailed by the publisher, electronic services are updated immediately when new materials are added, deleted, or changed. In addition, many looseleaf treatises by named authors are published in electronic versions. Because they require less frequent updating, these materials also work well as CD–ROM publications. An electronic full-text version of a looseleaf service is the most efficient source for updated materials and offers the most precise searching capabilities. The efficiency of updating, ease of access and use, and searching capabilities of electronic services will make them increasingly valuable research tools.[2]

Commerce Clearing House (CCH), a part of Wolters Kluwer Law & Business, and the Bureau of National Affairs (BNA) have been leading publishers of staff-prepared looseleaf services. Research Institute of America (RIA), a part of Thomson Reuters, is a major publisher of tax and accounting services prepared by its editorial staff.[3] Matthew Bender & Company, Inc., a part of LexisNexis, continues to be the largest publisher of treatises by named authors, including such notable works as *Moore's Federal Practice, Benedict on Admiralty,* and *Powell on Real Property.*[4] West and LexisNexis also publish numerous looseleaf services.

This chapter highlights only those features that are common to most interfiled and newsletter looseleaf services. Particular attention is given to representative publications of CCH and BNA because of the large number of looseleaf services produced by these two companies.

---

[1] Treatises are discussed in Chapter 19 of this book.

[2] The best method for determining whether or not a particular publication is available in electronic format is to consult the publisher's website or print catalog. The online and paper content guides for *Westlaw, LexisNexis,* or *Loislaw* will indicate the services available via that research service. Also helpful is the "Electronic Format Index" in LEGAL LOOSELEAFS IN PRINT (Arlene L. Eis comp. & ed.). This is an annual publication that lists approximately 3,600 titles by over 240 publishers. This source includes information on the number of volumes in a looseleaf set, price, frequency, cost of supplementation, and Library of Congress classification number. It is arranged alphabetically by title and includes publisher, subject, and electronic format indexes.

[3] For example, the Research Institute of America publishes the popular UNITED STATES TAX REPORTER and a number of other looseleaf services in the tax, estate planning, and business areas.

[4] Matthew Bender's web-based *Authority–On–Demand* includes the electronic versions of many Matthew Bender treatises.

The convenience, currency, frequency, and indexing of looseleaf services often make them the best place to begin researching many types of legal problems. In many rapidly developing areas of the law, such as privacy, the environment, and consumer protection, a looseleaf service may be the only extensive research tool available.[5]

SECTION B. CHARACTERISTICS OF LOOSELEAF SERVICES

1. Interfiled Looseleafs in General

Most topical looseleaf services, in which new pages replace older pages rather than supplementing existing ones, have the following common characteristics:

a. Full text of the statutes on the topic, often with significant legislative history;

b. Either full text or abstracts of relevant judicial opinions and administrative agency decisions;

c. Editorial commentary and explanatory notes;

d. Topical indexes;

e. Tables of cases and statutes;

f. Finding lists for statutes, cases, and administrative materials;

g. Indexes to current materials and cumulative indexes; and

h. Current reports summarizing recent developments.

Interfiled looseleaf publications typically are issued weekly, biweekly, or monthly.

2. Newsletter Looseleafs in General

Most topical looseleaf services in the newsletter format, in which updates are filed sequentially and chronologically, have the following common characteristics:

a. News and editorial comments of general interest;

b. Explanations of recent state and federal developments and recent developments in particular areas within the broad subject;

c. Text of, or excerpts from, major legislation, judicial opinions, administrative regulations, and agency decisions; and

d. Subject and table of cases indexes.

These newsletter publications also typically are issued weekly, biweekly, or monthly.

3. Commerce Clearing House (CCH) Services

a. *Print Services.* Commerce Clearing House (CCH) publications are typically of the type in which pages are interfiled. Examples include the *Copyright Law Reporter, Federal Securities Law Reporter, Products Liability Reporter,* and *Trade Regulation Reporter.* CCH publications range from

---

[5] For assistance in identifying relevant looseleaf services, see LEGAL LOOSELEAFS IN PRINT, *supra*, note 2.

those that consist of one binder to those that consist of a dozen or more binders.

CCH publications begin with an introductory section that discusses the use and organization of the service. The importance of this section cannot be over-emphasized. A careful reading of it can save the researcher much time and frustration. Volumes are divided into sections by tab cards. These tabs offer quick access to major topic headings. Typically, there is a comprehensive Topical Index to the full service. In addition, some services have special indexes to specific topics or volumes. The quality of the indexing is generally quite high, as the publisher strives to provide as many access points as possible.

The indexes are made more useful by the unique, dual numbering system employed by the publisher. Under this system, in addition to regular pagination, a paragraph number is assigned to each topic area. Materials organized under one paragraph number may consist of as little as one textual paragraph or as many as fifty or more pages. This flexibility of format allows for frequent additions and deletions to the text without disrupting the indexing system. Research can begin by consulting one of the indexes, which will reference the appropriate paragraph numbers where relevant information can be found. In looseleaf services, page numbers often are used only as guides for filing new pages and removing old ones.

The volumes containing the CCH editorial commentary and explanations, various reference materials, laws and regulations, and forms are typically referred to as "compilation" volumes. Full text of new judicial opinions and agency rulings, often supplied as part of the looseleaf service, generally are placed in a separate volume or section from the compilation volume(s).

Each case or ruling is commonly assigned its own paragraph number that can be located in several ways. Most services have tables of cases, statutes, and administrative regulations. When a citation to a case, statute, or administrative regulation is available, research can begin by consulting the appropriate table and obtaining the paragraph number where the cited material is discussed. Special indexes cross-reference materials found under the paragraph numbers to materials concerning current developments.

Materials summarizing current developments are often included in weekly bulletins that accompany new pages sent from the publisher. These bulletins are usually retained as part of the service and can be valuable research tools themselves. [Illustrations 14–1 through 14–4 show examples of a typical CCH looseleaf service.]

Often a CCH service that systematically reports judicial opinions or agency decisions is accompanied by a separate, bound reporter.[6] For example, CCH's widely used *Standard Federal Tax Reporter* includes a binder labeled "U.S. Tax Cases—Advance Sheets." These advance sheets are

---

[6] As was noted in Chapter 5 of this book, federal district court opinions are reported selectively. Cases not officially reported sometimes are published in one or more subject looseleaf services, as well as in the *National Reporter System's* FEDERAL APPENDIX, computer-assisted legal research services, and on the Internet. Consequently, it is worthwhile to check the table of cases of looseleaf services for cases not reported in the FEDERAL SUPPLEMENT.

cumulated into bound volumes twice a year, with the "Advance Sheet" volume always containing only the most recent materials.

In general, the successful use of CCH looseleaf services requires the researcher to follow the following three steps:

1. Locate the topic or topics being researched by consulting the Topical Index to the service.

2. Read carefully all materials under paragraph numbers referenced in the Topical Index. When abstracts of cases are available, citations to cases should be noted so that the full text can be read.

3. Consult the appropriate index or indexes to current materials.

b. *Electronic Services.* CCH's electronic offerings are divided into two networks: the *CCH Internet Research NetWork* and the *CCH Internet Tax Research NetWork*—both are available by subscription. The *CCH Internet Research NetWork* includes CCH's services in the following broad categories: securities; exchanges & SROs; corporate governance; corporation & business organization law; investment management; mergers & acquisitions; international business; banking; capital changes; antitrust & trade regulation; insurance coverage litigation; products liability & safety; government contracts; intellectual property, computer & Internet law; federal energy guidelines; transportation law; commodities & derivatives; and trial attorneys. *Loislaw* also is accessible through this network

The *CCH Internet Tax Research NetWork* includes services in the following broad categories: accounting & audit; federal tax; state tax; state business income tax; sales/property tax; financial & estate planning; wealth management; tax practice areas; pension & payroll; international tax; and other tools to assist practitioners. Both of CCH's research networks provide "Tracker" news services.

4. Bureau of National Affairs (BNA) Services

a. *Print Services.* The Bureau of National Affairs (BNA) is another major publisher of looseleaf services. As a general rule, its organizational principles differ from those of CCH. BNA's typical format consists of one or more three-ring binders in which periodic issues (or releases) are filed. Unlike CCH, the issues generally do not contain individual pages to be interfiled with existing text, but instead consist of pamphlet inserts numbered sequentially and filed chronologically. Thus, there is no provision for revision of earlier issues. This format allows for the service to be issued quickly. Examples of these publications are *Antitrust & Trade Regulation Report, Securities Regulation & Law Report,* and *Patent, Trademark & Copyright Journal.*

Many differences exist among BNA's numerous publications and services. Some of BNA's looseleaf services consist of several separate components, usually including a summary and analysis of major developments, the text of pertinent legislation, and the full text or abstracts of judicial opinions. Important speeches, government reports, book reviews, and bibliographies also may be included. Each of these components is generally filed behind its own tab divider. Examples of services providing this type of information are *United States Law Week,*[7] *Criminal Law Reporter,* and *Family Law Reporter.*

BNA services feature cumulative indexes that offer topical access to material. Because current issues supplement earlier issues, paragraph numbers are not needed, and simple pagination is used. Case tables are provided for each service. For some of its services, BNA periodically supplies special storage binders for old issues, so that the main volumes always contain current material. Regardless of whether the service is issued as a single newsletter or in several pamphlet-type components, it is intended to keep the researcher fully informed of developments in the subject area.

Some services, by BNA and other publishers, include state law sections. These generally are arranged by state, with the paragraph numbers assigned uniformly to the same topic for each state. In some instances, *all-state* charts are published that provide state-by-state comparisons of specific legislation. [Illustration 14–5]

One of BNA's most comprehensive looseleaf services is its *Labor Relations Reporter.* This set, together with its *Environment Reporter* and *Occupational Safety & Health Reporter,* is arranged differently from most other BNA services. *Labor Relations Reporter* includes the following segments:

Labor Management Relations (federal)

Labor Arbitration and Dispute Settlements

Wages and Hours

Fair Employment Practices

State Labor Laws

Individual Employment Rights

Americans with Disabilities

These looseleaf volumes contain relevant statutes, regulations, and judicial opinions. Periodically, reports of court cases are removed from the looseleaf volumes and reprinted in bound volumes, e.g., *Labor Arbitration Reports* and *Wage and Hour Cases.* Each series has its own index and digest, in which the cases are classified according to BNA's own classification scheme.

The entire *Labor Relations Reporter* set is unified by a two-volume looseleaf "Master Index" and a two-volume looseleaf "Labor Relations Expediter." [Illustrations 14–6 through 14–9 show the use of one component of the *Labor Relations Reporter.*]

b. *Electronic* Services. BNA makes its many looseleaf publications available in electronic format on the Internet.[8] Subscriptions to the electronic BNA services are obtained directly from the publisher; some of the BNA services also are available on *LexisNexis* and *Westlaw.* BNA's electronic services, like its print services, can be grouped in several broad subject areas: corporate law & business; employee benefits; employment & labor

---

[7] Discussed in Chapter 5, Section A–4, of this book.

[8] http://www.bna.com.

law; environment, health & safety; health care; human resources; intellectual property; litigation; tax & accounting; and international materials. BNA offers, depending on the service, monthly, weekly, and/or daily email "highlights" updating services.

SECTION C.   ILLUSTRATIONS

Illustrations Using CCH Products Liability Reporter

Problem: What constitutes adequate warning about the potential dangers of a product's design?

[Illustration 14–1]

PAGE FROM TOPICAL INDEX, CCH PRODUCTS LIABILITY REPORTER

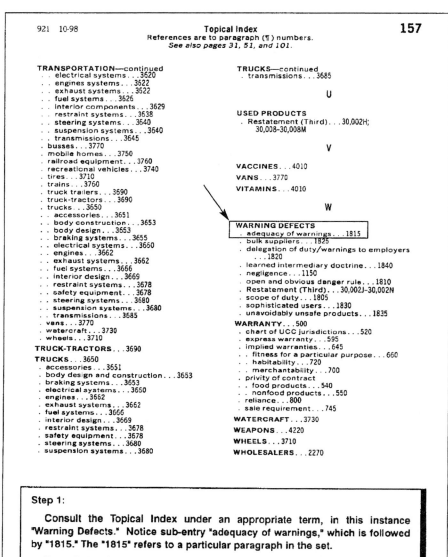

921   10-98   **Topical Index**   **157**
                        References are to paragraph (¶) numbers.
                           See also pages 31, 51, and 101.

TRANSPORTATION—continued
.. electrical systems...3620
.. engines systems...3622
.. exhaust systems...3622
.. fuel systems...3626
.. interior components...3629
.. restraint systems...3638
.. steering systems...3640
.. suspension systems...3640
.. transmissions...3645
. busses...3770
. mobile homes...3750
. railroad equipment...3760
. recreational vehicles...3740
. tires...3710
. trains...3760
. truck trailers...3690
. truck-tractors...3690
. trucks...3650
.. accessories...3651
.. body construction...3653
.. body design...3653
.. braking systems...3655
.. electrical systems...3650
.. engines...3662
.. exhaust systems...3662
.. fuel systems...3666
.. interior design...3669
.. restraint systems...3678
.. safety equipment...3678
.. steering systems...3680
.. suspension systems...3680
.. transmissions...3685
. vans...3770
. watercraft...3730
. wheels...3710

TRUCK-TRACTORS...3690

TRUCKS...3650
. accessories...3651
. body design and construction...3653
. braking systems...3653
. electrical systems...3650
. engines...3662
. exhaust systems...3662
. fuel systems...3666
. interior design...3669
. restraint systems...3678
. safety equipment...3678
. steering systems...3680
. suspension systems...3680

TRUCKS—continued
. transmissions...3685

U

USED PRODUCTS
. Restatement (Third)...30,002H;
   30,008–30,008M

V

VACCINES...4010

VANS...3770

VITAMINS...4010

W

WARNING DEFECTS
. adequacy of warnings...1815
. bulk suppliers...1825
. delegation of duty/warnings to employers
   ...1820
. learned intermediary doctrine...1840
. negligence...1150
. open and obvious danger rule...1810
. Restatement (Third)...30,002J–30,002N
. scope of duty...1805
. sophisticated users...1830
. unavoidably unsafe products...1835

WARRANTY...500
. chart of UCC jurisdictions...520
. express warranty...595
. implied warranties...645
.. fitness for a particular purpose...660
.. habitability...720
.. merchantability...700
. privity of contract
.. food products...540
.. nonfood products...550
. reliance...800
. sale requirement...745

WATERCRAFT...3730

WEAPONS...4220

WHEELS...3710

WHOLESALERS...2270

Step 1:

Consult the Topical Index under an appropriate term, in this instance "Warning Defects." Notice sub-entry "adequacy of warnings," which is followed by "1815." The "1815" refers to a particular paragraph in the set.

Note that a looseleaf service index typically is sophisticated. This same information might be indexed under a different key word or phrase, such as "Design Defects" or "Product Defects." Note also that there are separate indexes in the set for prior cases and for the most recent material not yet integrated into the larger indexes.

See next illustration for Step 2.

Products Liability Reports

WHO

[Illustration 14–2]

PAGE FROM COMPILATION VOLUME, CCH
PRODUCTS LIABILITY REPORTER

---

981   2-2001   **Warning Defects**   **4221**

¶ 1815   ADEQUACY OF WARNINGS

Once a duty to warn is established, which is generally a question of law, the adequacy or sufficiency of the warning must be established. The question of adequacy is most often a question of fact for the jury.

Under strict products liability, a product carrying an inadequate warning is defective because it is unreasonably dangerous to the user or consumer in the absence of an adequate warning. The adequacy of any warning is measured by what warning would be reasonable under the circumstances, which is technically a general negligence standard.

The content of a warning that would discharge a seller's responsibility to the user is one that, if followed, would render the product safe for users. Factors that must be considered by a jury include consumer expectations as to how the product operates, how complicated the product is, the severity and likelihood of harm to which the user will be subject if the product is not properly used, and whether a warning is feasible and likely to prevent injury.

To fulfill this duty, the manufacturer or supplier may be required to list specific dangers inherent in the product or in its use on the product's label or instruction manual. If the product must be used in a certain way to avoid injury, the instructions

> **Step 2:**
>
> Consult the paragraph number referred to in the Topical Index, i.e., "¶ 1815." Most CCH looseleaf services provide a brief discussion of the subject of the paragraph, in this instance "Adequacy of Warnings."
>
> Following the general discussion under the paragraph number, there is frequently an alphabetical listing of "Annotations by Jurisdiction" or "Annotations by Topic."
>
> See next illustration.

When a warning is given, the seller may reasonably assume that it will be read and heeded. A product bearing such a warning, which is safe for use if it is followed, is not in a defective condition, nor is it unreasonably dangerous.

Inadequacy of warning is treated under the *Restatement (Third) of Torts: Products Liability* § 2, Comment *i* (see ¶ 30,002J).

Hypersensitive or Idiosyncratic Users. Warnings by a product manufacturer or seller are not necessarily inadequate because they do not specifically warn an allergic user; it is generally sufficient to warn of known dangers. Some decisions have limited liability where there has not been an "appreciable" number of users suffering an adverse reaction. However, where the severity of the potential injury is great, even if the risk to the ordinary user is slight, a duty to warn may be imposed, and warnings may be inadequate based on failure to warn of a slight risk of severe injury. This topic is discussed by the *Restatement 3d* at Comment *k* (see § 30,002L).

Annotations to ¶ 1815 Appear by Jurisdiction Below, as Follows:

Alabama	.01	Colorado	.06
Alaska	.02	Connecticut	.07
Arizona	.03	Delaware	.08
Arkansas	.04	District of Columbia	.09
California	.05	Florida	.10

[Illustration 14–3]

PAGE FROM COMPILATION VOLUME, CCH
PRODUCTS LIABILITY REPORTER

4222   **Strict Liability**   981   2-2001

.01 Alabama.—Whether a warning to a tester of a high-pressure vessel not to stand in front of a pipe stopper during a hydrostatic test adequately apprised the tester of the risk of injury and death presented by the mismatching of the jaws securing the stopper was a question of fact. The tester sustained a fatal head injury when the stopper became dislodged and shot off of one of the vessel's pipes during the test. [SJ]'

> *Hicks v. Commercial Union Ins. Co.* (AlaSCt 1994) PRODUCTS LIABILITY REPORTS ¶ 14,023, 652 So2d 211.

Manufacturer's warnings that were included on the labels, decals, instructions, and hang tag that accompanied a kerosene heater, as well as in the ow[...]
ni[...]
an[...]
ha[...]
os[...]
tu[...]
pri[...]

from the purchaser's use of gasoline to fuel the heater. The purchaser had read the instructions and warnings before using the heater and failed to heed them. [SJ]

> *Yarbrough v. Sears, Roebuck & Co.* (AlaSCt 1993) PRODUCTS LIABILITY REPORTS ¶ 13,745, 628 So2d 478.

Warnings given by a manufacturer of a silicone breast implant understated the risks of the implant's rupturing during a surgical procedure.

> *Toole v. McClintock* (11thCir 1993) PRODUCTS LIABILITY REPORTS ¶ 13,606, 999 F2d 549; *2d opin* (11thCir 2000), *sub nom. Toole v. Baxter Healthcare Corp.*, PRODUCTS LIABILITY REPORTS ¶ 15,971.

Whether warnings by the manufacturer of a multipiece wheel assembly, which had propensity to explode when a tire was being inflated on it, were adequate was a jury question. A tire changer

died when he inflated a tire. The wheel assembly exploded, and he was struck by pieces of the wheel rim. The assembly parts were not imprinted with a warning and were not color-coded to prevent mismatching. The changer had no access to manuals or charts to insure that parts he was using were matching parts. [SJ]

> *Reynolds v. Bridgestone/Firestone, Inc.* (11thCir 1993) PRODUCTS LIABILITY REPORTS ¶ 13,477, 989 F2d 465.

Warnings on packages of cigarette lighters that the lighters should be kept out of the reach of, or away from, children were inadequate as a matter of law. An action was brought by the parents of a 4-year-old child who died in a fire she allegedly [...]

> **Starting with paragraph 1815.01 are digests of all cases, arranged alphabetically by state, dealing with "Adequacy of Warnings."**
>
> **Be sure to read the relevant cases in their entirety. Notice how citations are given to both the CCH reporter and to the *National Reporter System*.**

LIABILITY REPORTS ¶ 13,163, 597 So2d 1336.

In an action brought by the estate of a tractor owner who was killed when his tractor tipped over and landed on him, the warning supplied by the manufacturer in the owner's manual that the tractor should not be operated without a roll guard was inadequate as a matter of law. A jury question remained as to whether the danger of the tractor's rollover propensity was obviated by the manufacturer's warning.

> *Deere & Co. v. Grose* (AlaSCt 1991) PRODUCTS LIABILITY REPORTS ¶ 12,957, 586 So2d 196.

A manufacturer and a seller of a one-person motorcycle adequately warned of the dangers associated with carrying passengers on the vehicle as a matter of law. Thus, a 14-year-old passenger who disregarded the manufacturer's warnings could not recover damages for a leg injury he sustained while being driven on the motorcycle.

' [SJ] *indicates a post-1992 summary judgment ruling.*

¶ 1815.01

[Illustration 14–4]

PAGE FROM CUMULATIVE INDEX, CCH
PRODUCTS LIABILITY REPORTER

979   1-2001   **Cumulative Index to Prior Decisions**   **11,103**
                       See also Cumulative Index to Current Decisions

From Compilation   **To Current Decisions**
Paragraph No.   **Paragraph No.**

1770	.05	Design defect claim involving assault rifle not allowed (CalCtApp)	15,872
	.14	Employer's addition of safety device to envelope machine (NDIll)	15,875
	.19	No evidence of laundry unit safety device's feasibility (GaCtApp)	15,938
	.36	Issue as to truck bunk bed's lack of safety device (EDPa) (applying Ohio law)	15,856
	.39	Jury issue as to truck bunk bed's lack of safety device (EDPa)	15,856
1780	.15	Jury properly instructed on defective design in cigarette case (IndCtApp)	15,846
	.49	Issue as to pesticide's unavoidably unsafe character (WashSCt) ans'g cert ques fr (9thCir)	15,931
1805	.07	No duty to warn of beer consumption levels' effects (DConn)	15,913
	.21	No heeding presumption for cigarette smoker who knew of dangers (DMd)	15,883
	.22	Snowblower maker has no continuing duty to warn remote purchasers (MassAppCt)	15,825
	.31	Recycling plant conveyor maker has warning duty as component supplier (2dCir) (applying NJ law)	15,881
	.33	Brush chipper maker's successor could have independent duty to warn (WDNY)	15,917
	.36	Jury issue as to truck bunk bed's lack of warnings (EDPa) (applying Ohio law)	15,856
	.36	Smoking dangers not common knowledge from 1950 to 1965 (6thCir)	15,857
	.36	Failure-to-warn instruction correct in air bag defect claim (6thCir)	15,898
	.39	Jury issue as to truck bunk bed's lack of warnings (EDPa)	15,856
	.41	Smoker's claims allowed based on pre-1964 conduct (DRI)	15,827
1810	.21	Cigarettes' dangers open and obvious, common knowledge (DMd)	15,883
	.33	Jury issue as to worker's actual knowledge of tire rim danger (NYAppDiv)	15,873
	.36	Firearms' dangers open and obvious in municipality's claim (OhioCtApp)	15,880
	.36	Dangers of cigarette smoking matter of common knowledge (6thCir)	15,899
	.39	SUV cargo area danger not open and obvious (EDPa)	15,912
1815	.09	No proof that hormone maker inadequately warned of birth defects (DDC)	15,921
	.14	Jury issue as to adequacy of envelope machine's warnings (NDIll)	15,875
	.19	Pickup truck manual adequately warned about air bag nondeployment (EDLa)	15,939
	.28	Propane gas seller adequately warned of odorant fade danger (8thCir)	15,945
	.31	Recycling plant conveyor maker provided adequate warnings (2dCir) (applying NJ law)	15,881
	.36	Failure-to-warn instruction correct in air bag defect claim (6thCir)	15,898
	.37	Issue as to adequacy of water sports vest's warnings (10thCir)	15,946
	.39	Jury issue as to pneumatic nail gun's adequacy of warnings (EDPa)	15,821
	.39	Jury issue on adequacy of SUV's warning on riding in cargo area (EDPa)	15,912
1830	.28	Propane gas seller has no duty to warn sophisticated users (8thCir)	15,945
	.37	Issue as to duty to warn experienced mechanic of lift's use (OklaCtCivApp)	15,936
1835	.09	Synthetic hormone deemed unavoidably unsafe product (DDC)	15,921

> A researcher must determine if any relevant cases were decided after those appearing in the main (compilation) volume. This is accomplished by consulting the cross-reference tables that contain current materials.

Parties

2130	.05	Nuclear power worker's spouse could be foreseeable bystander (9thCir)	15,864
	.05	Firefighter's rule bars claim v. semiautomatic assault rifle maker (CalCtApp)	15,872
	.36	Municipality cannot bring claims against firearms makers (OhioCtApp)	15,880
2220	.11	Issue as to forklift assembler's liability as manufacturer (GaCtApp)	15,922
2230	.31	Recycling plant conveyor maker has warning duty as component supplier (2dCir) (applying NJ law)	15,881
	.45	Water pump maker not liable for finished spa's defects (TexCtApp)	15,887
2240	.26	Insufficient proof of workbridge maker's identity (8thCir)	15,862
	.33	Question as to market share liability of handgun makers (2dCir) ques cert to (NYCtApp)	15,882
	.36	Municipality must specify firearms makers, defects in claims (OhioCtApp)	15,880
	.37	Semi-tractor frame lift sufficiently identified (OklaCtCivApp)	15,936
2245	.33	Exceptions do not apply to brush chipper maker's successor (WDNY)	15,917
2260	.11	Pharmacist, pharmacy not subject to strict liability (GaCtApp)	15,851
	.47	Utility did not sell electricity that caused house fire (VtSCt)	15,914
	.49	Swimming pool trade association owes duty to consumers (WashCtApp)	15,894
	.51	Reconditioner could be liable for crane's new ladders (WisSCt)	15,876

Products Liability Reports

Illustrations Using BNA Fair Employment Practices
(FEP) Division of Labor Relations Reporter

Problem: Can attorneys' fees be collected for the work of paralegals and law clerks?

[Illustration 14–5]

PAGE FROM BNA LABOR RELATIONS REPORTER, FAIR EMPLOYMENT PRACTICES ALL–STATES VOLUME

451:108   STATE FAIR EMPLOYMENT PRACTICE LAWS   No. 923

State Family Leave Laws/Rules Exceeding Federal FMLA Requirements

Comparison Chart — The chart that follows shows those states that have family related leave mandates in *excess* of those contained in the federal Family and Medical Leave Act. Footnotes indicate those states that provide such leave for public employees only and any separate maternity, parental, school, or adoption leave provisions.

The first three categories of the chart relate to a state's family medical leave act or rule. The fourth category relates only to a state's separate maternity, parental, school, or adoption leave provisions. When this benefit applies only to state employees, it is followed by a pound symbol (#).

STATE MANDATES BEYOND FMLA

STATE (# means public employees only)	Length of Leave (More than 12 weeks)	Minimum Number of Employees (Fewer than 50)	Employee's Qualification (Fewer)	Separate Maternity* Parental** School*** Adoption****
Alabama	none	none	none	yes* #
Alaska#	yes	yes	yes	none
Arizona	none	none	none	yes** #
Arkansas	none	none	none	yes* #
California	none	none	none	yes*/ **/ ***
Colorado#	yes	none	none	yes****
Connecticut	yes	none	yes	none

> Several looseleaf services include coverage for state laws. In some, comparison charts are published showing how different states have dealt with a particular issue through legislation, as is shown in this illustration. Occasionally, a chart will show where the laws on a topic for various states are located in the looseleaf service.

Georgia	none	none	none	none
Hawaii	none	none	yes	yes*
Idaho	none	none	none	yes* #
Illinois	none	none	none	yes***/ ****#
Indiana	none	none	none	yes* #
Iowa	none	none	none	yes*
Kansas#	yes	none	none	none
Kentucky#	yes	none	none	yes****
Louisiana	none	none	none	yes*/ ***
Maine	none	yes	none	none

[Illustration 14–6]

PAGE FROM BNA MASTER INDEX TO LABOR RELATIONS REPORTER CONTAINING FAIR EMPLOYMENT PRACTICES (FEP) OUTLINE OF CLASSIFICATIONS

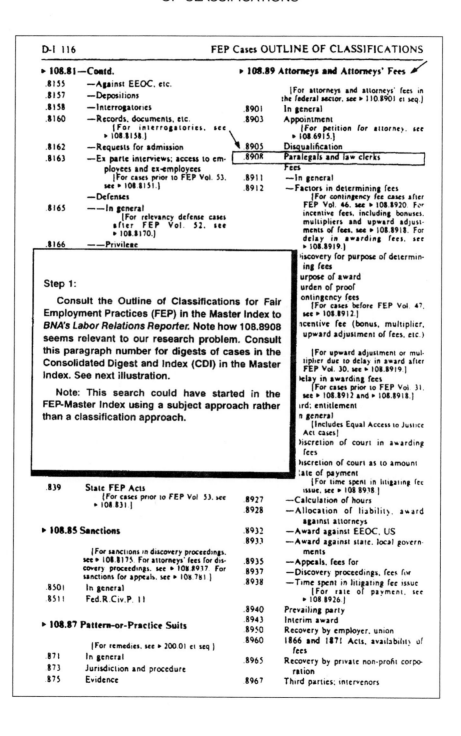

D-I 116   FEP Cases OUTLINE OF CLASSIFICATIONS

▶ **108.81—Contd.**   ▶ **108.89 Attorneys and Attorneys' Fees**

.8155   —Against EEOC, etc.

.8157   —Depositions   [For attorneys and attorneys' fees in
.8158   —Interrogatories   the *federal sector,* see ▶ 110.8901 et seq.]
.8160   —Records, documents, etc.   .8901   In general
         [For interrogatories, see   .8903   Appointment
         ▶ 108.8158.]   [For petition for attorney, see
.8162   —Requests for admission   ▶ 108.6915.]
.8163   —Ex parte interviews; access to em- .8905   Disqualification
         ployees and ex-employees   .8908   Paralegals and law clerks
         [For cases prior to FEP Vol. 53,   Fees
         see ▶ 108.8151.]   .8911   —In general
         —Defenses   .8912   —Factors in determining fees
.8165   ——In general   [For contingency fee cases after
         [For relevancy defense cases   FEP Vol. 46, see ▶ 108.8920. For
         after FEP Vol. 52, see   incentive fees, including bonuses,
         ▶ 108.8170.]   multipliers and upward adjust-
.8166   ——Privilege   ments of fees, see ▶ 108.8918. For
                                                    delay in awarding fees, see
                                                    ▶ 108.8919.]

Step 1:

Consult the Outline of Classifications for Fair Employment Practices (FEP) in the Master Index to *BNA's Labor Relations Reporter.* Note how 108.8908 seems relevant to our research problem. Consult this paragraph number for digests of cases in the Consolidated Digest and Index (CDI) in the Master Index. See next illustration.

Note: This search could have started in the FEP-Master Index using a subject approach rather than a classification approach.

                                         iscovery for purpose of determin-
                                          ing fees
                                         urpose of award
                                         urden of proof
                                         ontingency fees
                                          [For cases before FEP Vol. 47,
                                          see ▶ 108.8912.]
                                         ncentive fee (bonus, multiplier,
                                          upward adjustment of fees, etc.)

                                          [For upward adjustment or mul-
                                          tiplier due to delay in award after
                                          FEP Vol. 30, see ▶ 108.8919.]
                                         lelay in awarding fees
                                          [For cases prior to FEP Vol. 31,
                                          see ▶ 108.8912 and ▶ 108.8918.]
                                         ird; entitlement
                                         n general
                                          [Includes Equal Access to Justice
                                          Act cases]
                                         iscretion of court in awarding
                                          fees
                                         iscretion of court as to amount
                                         late of payment
                                          [For time spent in litigating fee
                                          issue, see ▶ 108.8938.]
.839   State FEP Acts   .8927   —Calculation of hours
         [For cases prior to FEP Vol 53, see .8928   —Allocation of liability, award
         ▶ 108.831.]   against attorneys
                                         .8932   —Award against EEOC, US
                                         .8933   —Award against state, local govern-
▶ **108.85 Sanctions**   ments
                                         .8935   —Appeals, fees for
         [For sanctions in discovery proceedings, .8937   —Discovery proceedings, fees for
         see ▶ 108.8175. For attorneys' fees for dis- .8938   —Time spent in litigating fee issue
         covery proceedings, see ▶ 108.8937. For   [For rate of payment, see
         sanctions for appeals, see ▶ 108.781.]   ▶ 108.8926.]
.8501   In general   .8940   Prevailing party
.8511   Fed.R.Civ.P. 11   .8943   Interim award
                                         .8950   Recovery by employer, union
                                         .8960   1866 and 1871 Acts, availability of
▶ **108.87 Pattern-or-Practice Suits**   fees
                                         .8965   Recovery by private non-profit corpo-
         [For remedies, see ▶ 200.01 et seq.]   ration
.871   In general   .8967   Third parties; intervenors
.873   Jurisdiction and procedure
.875   Evidence

[Illustration 14–7]

PAGE FROM BNA MASTER INDEX TO LABOR RELATIONS REPORTER CONTAINING FAIR EMPLOYMENT PRACTICES (FEP) CUMULATIVE DIGEST AND INDEX (CDI)

A732   85 FEP Cases   Final CDI

▶ **108.871** (Contd.)
public interest in eliminating employment discrimination. —*Reid v. Lockheed Martin Aeronautics Co.* (DC NGa) 85 FEP Cases 602

▶ **108.8901**   Failure of unsuccessful former employee to oppose employer's bill of costs is not evidence of bad faith that would entitle employer to sanctions, since 28 U.S.C. §1920 states that costs will be allowed of course to prevailing party that files bill of costs, there is no dispute that employer is prevailing party, and unless former employee had reason to challenge reasonableness or amount of costs it would have been indication of bad faith, or at least indication that he intended to harass employer, for him to have challenged employer's bill of costs. —*Kron v. Moravia Central School District* (DC NNY) 85 FEP Cases 1414

Counsel representing female employee of CIA will not be permitted to attend federal district court's in camera review of CIA director's cl[...]
details co[...]
and statut[...]
in unclassi[...]
ee's reque[...]
and files, [...]
has been [...]
would per[...]
vit. —*Til[...]*
Cases 404[...]

Attorne[...]
client for [...]
negligent f[...]
42 U.S.C[...]
caused hir[...]
those obta[...]
cially esto[...]
he would [...]
ages unde[...]
despite co[...]
position on matter throughout earlier action, where attorneys were not parties in that action, and issue of whether former client had claim under §1981 was never addressed on merits. —*Olmsted v. Emmanuel* (Fla DistCtApp) 85 FEP Cases 651

White former employee who recovered damages under Title VII but who was precluded from seeking additional damages under 42 U.S.C. §1981 because of his attorneys' negligent failure to raise §1981 as basis for relief in pretrial statement cannot show, for purpose of his malpractice action, that reasonable person could have found that he would have prevailed on §1981 claim but for attorneys' negligence, where he had alleged that he had been discharged

in retaliation for complaining to superiors about employment practices that discriminated against blacks, but federal court of appeals had ruled in earlier case that §1981 did not apply to claimant who did not allege that discrimination against him was due to his race. *Id.*

▶ **108.8908**   Lodestar amount of attorneys' fees of $1,096,412.60, which includes $25,920 for work of paralegals and externs, will not be reduced simply because it is larger than amount recovered by 11 employees who accepted offers of judgment, where each of them has received substantial recovery that is not just nuisance value settlement, some remain employed by employer and some have retained right to press forward with other claims, their attorneys performed well, and fees are not some large multiple of recovery. —*Kitchen v. TTX Co.* (DC NIll) 85 FEP Cases 96

▶ **108.8911**   Attorneys' fees were properly [...]ved that em[...]
[...] for assisting
[...]OC charges,
[...]ld have been
[...] attendance
[...]d Corp. (CA
[...]
[...]n for award
[...]nsidered un-
[...] filed within
[...]s required by
[...]e that judg-
[...]t of appeals
[...] not address
[...]nctive relief,
[...]aterials were
[...]n-final judg-
[...]s (DC NGa)

▶ **108.8912**   Federal dist. court properly awarded $150,837 in attorneys' fees to exemployee who prevailed on his ADA claim, where court found that his attorneys' lodestar value accurately reflected complexity and novelty of case, that ability and reputation of attorneys was accurately reflected in their customary billing rates, and that result obtained justified lodestar value. —*Giles v. General Electric Co.* (CA 5) 11 AD Cases 844

Federal district court properly awarded $150,837 in attorneys' fees to former employee who prevailed on his ADA claim, where his attorneys' lodestar value accurately reflected complexity and novelty of case, ability and reputation of attorneys was

---

Step 2:

Note how 108.8908 digests cases dealing with the question of awarding attorneys' fees to non-lawyers employed by attorneys.

The search must be updated by consulting any supplemental indexes.

Full texts of the digested cases are in the volumes entitled *Fair Employment Practices* (FEP) Cases. Note that the case is located in volume 85 of FEP Cases. This case is published first in the looseleaf "Cases" binder of the FEP volumes and later in a bound volume.

See next illustration.

[Illustration 14–8]

PAGE FROM A VOLUME OF BNA FAIR EMPLOYMENT PRACTICES CASES

Kitchen v. TTX Company   85 FEP Cases 97

non-attorney work such as photocopying, where attorney's presence at depositions was necessary for effective preparation of trial team and made her more effective in reviewing documents, her presence probably resulted in lower total fee request because her rate was lower than those of other attorneys, and counsel were reasonable in time spent on letter writing and non-attorney work; moreover, hours billed by employer's counsel, which do not include valuable and time consuming efforts by employer's in-house counsel, ex-

whose opinion was ultimately barred, where such compilation was reasonable in that it was gathered to assist expert in his attempt to establish that race played role in promotions within employer.

[9] Costs ▶ 108.901

Employees who accepted offers of judgment are entitled to award of $12,680 for creation of demonstrative exhibits, despite employer's contention that it did not know about

---

Step 3:

This is the start of the full text of the opinion referenced in the previous Illustration. Read the full text of digested cases located through indexes. In the problem given, only one case is relevant. Note how the publisher provides headnotes that enable the researcher to go directly to the point in the case being researched, in this instance headnote 7.

See next illustration.

▶ 108.8926

Hourly rate for employees' attorneys will be determined with reference to number of years of practice, their overall experience during those years, fees that other courts have set in past, observation of their performance, and evidence submitted pertaining to fees for other similar practitioners; one attorney who requested rate of $325 per hour is entitled to $295 per hour, another attorney who also sought $325 per hour will be awarded $240 per hour, and third attorney, who sought $190 per hour, will be awarded $185 per hour.

[7] Attorneys' fees 108.8908 ▶ 108.8912 108.8921

Lodestar amount of attorneys' fees of $1,096,412.60, which includes $25,920 for work of paralegals and externs, will not be reduced simply because it is larger than amount recovered by 11 employees who accepted offers of judgment, where each of them has received substantial recovery that is not just nuisance value settlement, some of them remain employed by employer and some have retained right to press forward with other claims, their attorneys performed well for them, and fees are not some large multiple of recovery.

[8] Costs ▶ 108.901

Costs associated with compilation of statistical data, which was performed by husband of one of employees' attorneys, are reimbursable, even though data were compiled for use in statistical analysis by employees' expert

penses, including taxi cab fares and some deposition transcripts, that their attorneys are unable to document, since attorneys have responsibility to account for their expenses.

———

H. Candace Gorman and Gregory X. Gorman (Law Office of H. Candace Gorman), Chicago, Ill., for plaintiffs.

John Yo-Hwan Lee (Ross & Hardies), Chicago, Ill., and Terrence C. Newby, Thomas P. Kane, and David M. Wilk (Oppenheimer, Wolff & Donnelly), St. Paul, Minn., for defendant.

Full Text of Opinion

WAYNE R. ANDERSON, District Judge.

This case is before the Court to resolve the petition for fees filed by H. Candice Gorman, Gregory X. Gorman and Catherine Caporusso, the attorneys for the plaintiffs in this action. Each of the eleven plaintiffs accepted a Rule 68 Offer of Judgment made to each of them by the defendant TTX Company, their employer. The parties submitted extensive briefs and the Court conducted a hearing over four days with respect to this issue. The petitioners requested $1,308,153 in attorneys' fees and $54,127.46 as reimbursement for expenses. We have concluded that the defendant should pay to them a total of $1,096,412.60 as fair and reasonable attorneys' fees and $51,357.66 as reimbursement for expenses.

[Illustration 14–9]

PAGE FROM A VOLUME OF BNA FAIR EMPLOYMENT PRACTICES CASES

85 FEP Cases 100   Kitchen v. TTX Company

(We note, parenthetically, that the hours billed by defense counsel to TTX exceeded the hours for which plaintiffs' attorneys have sought compensation, and the dollars paid to defense counsel exceed the amount requested by the plaintiffs' attorneys. Moreover, during the course of this lawsuit the Court observed that in-house counsel for TTX made extremely valuable and time consuming contributions to the defense of the case; none of this in-house counsel time was included in the billings made by defense counsel to TTX. Although these observations are certainly not decisive with respect to the Court's determination of the reasonableness of the request made by plaintiffs' attorneys, they are a very strong indicator that the time spent and the amount requested by the attorneys for the plaintiffs are well within the realm of reasonableness.)

[6] We have determined the hourly rate for all three attorneys with reference to the number of years they have practiced, their overall

is larger than the recovery and we determine that the total fee award is $1,059,260.60.

V. *Costs*

TTX challenges the bill of costs in several ways. TTX argues that the expenses associated with Christopher Ross' services should not be compensated. Second TTX argues that they should not have to pay for the demonstrative exhibits. Third, TTX argues that they should not have to pay for the expenses which plaintiffs' attorneys cannot document. Finally, TTX argues that, based on whether all plaintiffs are prevailing parties, it should only pay a pro rata share of the remaining expenses.

[8] Christopher Ross, H. Candice Gorman's husband, compiled statistical data for use by plaintiffs' expert Dr. Skoog. Dr. Skoog prepared a statistical analysis which attempted to establish that race played a role in promotions within TTX. Although the Magistrate Judge ultimately barred the use of Dr. Skoog's opin-

Bracketed numbers in the text of the opinion, in this example [7], identify the location that served as the topic of the headnote.

H. Candice Gorman is entitled to $295 per hour, Gregory X. Gorman is entitled to $240 per hour and Catherine Caporusso is entitled to $185 per hour. Multiplying the number of hours by the hourly rate results in a lodestar figure of $1,070,492.60. In addition, plaintiffs are entitled to the reasonable sum of $25,920 for the work of paralegals and externs. Therefore, the total fee lodestar is $1,096,412.60.

[7] Finally, we must determine whether the fee is reasonable given the degree of success obtained. We believe the fee is reasonable. There is no mechanical rule requiring that a reasonable attorneys' fee be no greater than the recovery. *Connolly v. National Sch. Bus Serv. Inc.*, 177 F.3d 593, 597 [80 FEP Cases 92] (7th Cir. 1998). We have considered the question of proportionality. All plaintiffs have received a substantial recovery. Furthermore, some of the plaintiffs remain employed by TTX and some have retained their rights to press forward with other claims. As we noted above, the offers of judgment do not represent nuisance value settlements, all plaintiffs prevailed and the plaintiffs' attorneys performed well for their clients. Finally, the argument for reducing the lodestar is most compelling if the fees are some large multiple of the recovery. *Id.* That is not the case here. Therefore, we will not reduce the lodestar simply because it

plaintiff for the services of Christopher Ross.

[9] TTX argues that it did not know about the demonstrative exhibits when it made the offers of judgment. TTX made the offers on the eve of trial. Plaintiffs were reasonably preparing for a jury trial by creating demonstrative exhibits for the jury. This is a reasonable practice and TTX has advanced no authority to suggest that the touchstone of awarding costs is whether defendant was aware of the expenditure. Therefore, we award plaintiffs $12,680 for the creation of demonstrative exhibits.

[10] TTX argues that plaintiffs should not be compensated for expenses which plaintiffs cannot document. We agree. Plaintiffs' attorneys have been unable to document several expenses including taxi cab fares and some deposition transcripts. Plaintiffs' attorneys have a responsibility to account for their expenses. Because they are unable to do so here, we grant defendant's objection and disallow $2,769.80 in expenses.

TTX's final argument is that plaintiffs should only be entitled to fees for the prevailing plaintiffs. Because we determined above that all plaintiffs prevailed in this action, we will not consider whether we would have divided the expenses on a pro rata basis. Plaintiffs' attorneys are entitled to all the reasonable fees.

Chapter 15

CITATORS*

Law is a discipline that looks both backward and forward. In advising clients, drafting agreements, arguing cases before a court, proposing legislation, and analyzing legal developments, lawyers refer to cases, statutes, regulations, and secondary sources. They rely upon those sources to reflect the law on a particular subject at a particular point in time. Lawyers may be interested in determining the sources of a particular law or legal theory; they look backward from a particular source to find earlier discussions of the same issue. Or, researchers may wish to determine how an issue articulated in an authority has been addressed by subsequent authorities; attorneys look forward to see citations to the original authority in more recent materials. To find those sources of a law or legal theory, lawyers look to the document at hand; they read citations and note footnote and bibliographic references. Lawyers consult citation services, also called citators, to determine how a particular legal authority has been cited by other authority and if it has been followed or dismissed.

Legal citation services (citators) identify where a specific source (cited authority, case, or statute) has been cited in another source (citing authority). A citation service can indicate the kind of treatment an authority has received. Citation services are not unique to the discipline of law. But, because our legal system is based on the doctrine of precedent, the idea that similar fact situations should result in similar legal outcomes, and because we rely on judicial and statutory precedent to ensure similar outcomes, citation services can play a more integral role in legal research than they do in many other disciplines. The adverse consequences of citing to, and relying on, a judicial holding that has been criticized or overturned can be serious. Courts have little sympathy for attorneys who fail to ensure the continuing validity of the authorities they cite.[1] The use of legal citation services enables attorneys to ensure that the authorities they rely on continue to represent "good" law.

As legal thinking becomes more interdisciplinary and more international, the sources used by attorneys and scholars to make legal arguments correspondingly expand. So, in addition to looking backward and forward, legal researchers increasingly look sideways—they seek to broaden their research across disciplines, jurisdictions, and audiences, and, more and

---

* Jeanne F. Price, Director of the Law Library and Associate Professor of Law, William S. Boyd School of Law, University of Nevada, Las Vegas, wrote this chapter.

[1] *See, for example*, McCarthy v. Oregon Freeze Dry, Inc., 976 P. 2d 566, 567 (Or. App. 1999): "The trial court denied the motion, concluding that the mistake alleged—failure to 'Shepardize' a key case—was not excusable. Plaintiff appealed, we affirmed without opinion, and the Supreme Court eventually denied review."

more frequently, they may need to consult citation services or alternatives to those services outside traditional legal research resources.

This chapter explores traditional legal citation services—*LexisNexis'* *Shepard's* and *Westlaw's KeyCite*—and considers more briefly both citation services outside the legal domain and alternatives to citation services that may enable researchers to accomplish similar objectives, but within a larger universe of information.

SECTION A.   USES AND FUNCTIONS OF CITATION SERVICES

By identifying sources that have cited a particular authority, citation services serve two primary functions: (1) they enable researchers to assess the validity and strength of the cited authority, and (2) they provide a means of expanding research across jurisdictions and types of sources.

Citators indicate the prior and subsequent history of a cited authority. For any particular cited case, a citator will provide a reference to that case in a lower court or in any court prior to the date of the original cited case (i.e., the case's prior history), and will provide references to that case in appellate courts and, in fact, in any court that considers that same case subsequently to the date of the original cited case (i.e., the case's subsequent history).

SECTION B.   ILLUSTRATION: USES AND FUNCTIONS
OF CITATION SERVICES

15–1.   Print from KeyCite Showing the Direct History of a Case

[Illustration 15–1]

PRINT FROM KEYCITE SHOWING THE DIRECT HISTORY OF A CASE

Consider *City of Chicago v. Terminiello*, 79 N.E. 2d 39 (Ill. 1948), a case decided by the Illinois Supreme Court in 1948. [Illustration 15–1] That case's *prior* history includes two reported cases:

— first, a decision by the Illinois Supreme Court in January 1947 (*City of Chicago v. Terminiello*, 71 N.E. 2d 2 (Ill. 1947)—in that case, the court determined that it did not have jurisdiction absent a particular finding by the trial court); and

— second, a decision by an Illinois appellate court in June 1947 (*City of Chicago v. Terminiello*, 74 N.E. 2d 45 (Ill. App. Ct. 1947)).

The *subsequent* history of *City of Chicago v. Terminiello*, 79 N.E. 2d 39, the 1948 Illinois Supreme Court case, includes three reported decisions:

— first, the decision by the United States Supreme Court in December 1948 to grant certiorari in Mr. Terminiello's case (*Terminiello v. City of Chicago*, 335 U.S. 890 (1948));

— second, a United States Supreme Court decision (*Terminiello v. City of Chicago*, 337 U.S. 1, 65 S. Ct. 894 (1949)) reversing the 1948 Illinois Supreme Court case; and

— third, the decision of the United States Supreme Court not to rehear the case (*Terminiello v. City of Chicago*, 337 U.S. 934 (1949)).

Citation services provide references to the *direct* history of a case—its prior and subsequent history. By tracing how a case has been interpreted and applied by later courts, researchers can determine whether or not a particular case is still "good" law.

Beyond a case's direct history, citators provide references to cases, administrative adjudications, law review articles, other secondary sources, and, in some instances, court documents (e.g., petitions, pleadings, motions, and briefs) that cite the case. To the extent that a particular case is relevant to a research question, authorities that cite that case may be equally, or even more, relevant. Moreover, the nature and quantity of courts and opinions that cite a particular judicial authority provide a researcher with some indication of the importance of that authority. If a case has been cited frequently (and favorably) by a variety of appellate courts, its influence is strong and it is probably important to cite to that case in any argument involving the issue it discusses. Judges, practitioners, and scholars all value comprehensive research; use of citation services is one way of ensuring thoroughness.

Similarly, for legislation, citators can provide information about prior versions of a statute, as well as subsequent legislative activities that affect the validity of that statute. Materials that reference the statute—from legislative history materials to law review articles to cases and other statutes that cite the statute—also will be included in statute citators. Similarly, information provided by citators for regulatory materials may include historical information (i.e., regulatory documents that evidence the regulation's adoption and amendment) and references to cases, administrative documents, and secondary sources that cite the regulation.

Citation services also provide citation information about some secondary sources. That information includes references to primary authority (usually cases and administrative decisions) and secondary authority that cite the secondary source. Among secondary sources, law review articles are most comprehensively represented in legal citation services, as cited authorities and as citing references. Coverage of other secondary sources is much more limited.

SECTION C.   HISTORY AND FORMATS
OF CITATION SERVICES

Except for a few looseleaf services that provided citation information in specialized areas of law, prior to the late 1990s there existed only one comprehensive legal citation service, *Shepard's Citations*. From its beginnings in the late nineteenth century as a case citation service, *Shepard's Citations* evolved to include constitutions, statutes, administrative rules and regulations, administrative adjudications, court rules, law review articles, restatements, and individual patents. The jurisdictions covered in the print versions of *Shepard's* included the United States, both federal and state, and Canada. In its print version, *Shepard's* was (and continues to be) published in several different units. Each unit of *Shepard's* provides similar information with respect to the different authorities it covers and retains a distinctive organization, format, and system of notation.

The use of *Shepard's Citations* to update and verify legal authority became so established that lawyers commonly refer to that process as "Shepardizing."[2] In the late 1990s *Shepard's Citations* was acquired by Reed Elsevier and by 1998 *Shepard's* was included in the electronic collection of another Reed Elsevier product, *LexisNexis*. In 1997 *Westlaw* introduced its own electronic citation service, *KeyCite*. *LoisLaw*, another general research service, includes its own citator, *GlobalCite*, which provides more limited citation information than either *KeyCite* or *Shepard's*.

The marriage of digital technology and citation services is a happy one. Tasks that were time-consuming and tedious in print format have been made far easier in an electronic environment. The rapidity of updating, improved interface, graphical representation of concepts and chronology, and elimination of multiple sources, all combine to make use of electronic citation services far more efficient than use of the traditional print services. That said, attorneys might find themselves in situations without access to electronic resources. Furthermore, an understanding of the development and structure of the print version of *Shepard's* can provide insights into the use and functionality of the electronic versions of *Shepard's* and *KeyCite*. The focus of this chapter is on the digital version of *Shepard's* and on *KeyCite*, but descriptions and explanations of the print versions of *Shepard's* also are included.

SECTION D.   ELECTRONIC CITATORS:
SHEPARD'S AND KEYCITE

Citators identify where a specific authority or source ("cited" authority or source) has been cited by another authority or source ("citing" authority or source). This information enables researchers (1) to determine how the cited authority has been treated by subsequent citing authorities, and (2) to find other authorities relevant to the issues discussed in the cited authority.

1. Common Features

a. *Validating Authority vs. Finding Other Relevant Authority.* Shepard's distinguishes between these functions by offering two options in the

---

[2] The term "Shepardize" is a registered trademark of Reed Elsevier Properties, Inc.

Shepard's interface—"*Shepard's* for Validation" or "*Shepard's* for Research." [Illustration 15–2] "*Shepard's* for Validation"—or what *LexisNexis* calls the KWIC view of citing references—includes, for cases, subsequent appellate history and only those citing references that have been assigned analytical notations. For example, for the U.S. Supreme Court case of *Terminiello v. City of Chicago*, 337 U.S. 1 (1949), "*Shepard's* for Validation" includes the case's subsequent history (the denial of rehearing by the United States Supreme Court at 337 U.S. 934) and more than 150 citing references that include some sort of analytical notation assigned by *Shepard's* that describes the court's treatment of the *Terminiello* case. [Illustration 15–3]

By contrast, "*Shepard's* for Research"—or what *LexisNexis* terms the "FULL" view of citing references—includes, for cases, references to all prior and subsequent history, all cases that refer to the cited source, whether or not they merit editorial annotation, annotations to statutes that cite the case, and secondary sources that cite that Shepardized case. So, for the *Terminiello* case, "*Shepard's* for Research" includes both prior and subsequent history for the Supreme Court case, as well as references to more than 750 cases and more than 800 secondary sources (law review and bar journal articles, *American Law Reports* annotations, and treatises) that have cited the case. [Illustration 15–4]

Similarly, for statutes, "*Shepard's* for Validation" (the "KWIC" format) points to legislative history documents and sets forth cases and administrative adjudications that have been assigned analytical notations. "*Shepard's* for Research" references the legislative history documents pertaining to a particular statute and all cases, administrative materials, and secondary sources that have cited the statute.

For regulations, "*Shepard's* for Validation" references administrative and other primary authorities that have been assigned analytical notations describing the treatment of the regulation, while "*Shepard's* for Research" includes citations to all primary and selected secondary authorities that have cited the regulation.

Westlaw's *KeyCite* provides two alternatives that allow researchers to limit the number and nature of citing references retrieved for any authority. A researcher may elect to limit *KeyCite* results to "history" or to retrieve all citing references. If the researcher's purpose is to ascertain the validity of a case, there is an additional option available. For cases, *KeyCite* provides (1) the "full" history of the case (which includes prior and subsequent history, as well as "negative" citing references—i.e., those references to which some sort of negative analytical comment is attached); (2) the case's direct (i.e., only prior and subsequent) history, portrayed in a graphical display; or (3) all citing references (cases, administrative materials, secondary sources, and court documents that cite the original case). [Illustration 15–5]

For statutes, *KeyCite* provides a "history" option (references to legislative history documents and public laws which have affected the statute); a "graphical statutes" option (access to proposed legislation which may affect the statute; selected prior versions of the statute; and selected legislative history documents); and the "citing references" option (citations to all cases and administrative materials; selected secondary sources; and selected court documents which have cited the statute). [Illustration 15–6] Similarly, *KeyCite's* "history" option for regulations includes references to administrative materials that have finalized the administrative action or amended the regulations. The "citing references" option provides citations to primary authorities which have cited the regulation and to selected secondary sources.

b. *Notation of Analytical Treatment and Assignment of Cautionary Signals.* The fact that one authority cites an earlier authority often indicates that the citing authority recognizes the persuasiveness and rationale of the prior authority. However, not every citation to an authority is one of endorsement or approval. An authority may be criticized by a subsequent decision or secondary source; the prior authority may be distinguished from the case at hand; or the cited authority may be cited in a dissenting opinion (which, by implication, might indicate that the majority opinion did not agree with the holding or reasoning of the cited authority). In the most extreme case, one authority may cite another only to expressly reverse it. In determining the validity of a particular source, a researcher must be able to identify quickly those subsequent authorities that criticize or distinguish it. Both *Shepard's* and *KeyCite* provide substantive notations that indicate the nature of the treatment received by a cited authority.

Shepard's categorizes citing references and, for cases, denominates those references as including "cautionary," "questioned," "positive," or "neutral" analyses. [Illustration 15–7] A citing case that is categorized under the "cautionary" label has superseded, overruled, not followed, criticized, or distinguished the cited authority. Similarly, *KeyCite* groups some citing references under a "negative cases" label; negative cases include those that overturn, abrogate, supersede, recognize the reversal of, distinguish, criticize, or decline to extend the holding of the cited case. [Illustration 15–8]

These analyses of subsequent authorities enable both *Shepard's* and *KeyCite* to assign substantive labels to cited primary authorities. Those labels provide some indication of the strength and validity of the cited source. *KeyCite* assigns labels to judicial decisions, selected administrative decisions, patents, statutes, and regulations. *Shepard's* assigns labels primarily to adjudications and selected administrative materials. *KeyCite's* labels range from a red flag (indicating, for cases, that the authority is no longer "good" law with respect to at least one of the issues it discusses) to a green "C" (denoting that the case has neither direct history nor negative citing references). [Illustration 15–9] Similarly, *Shepard's* assigns symbols to authorities ranging from a red stop sign (an indication of "strong" negative treatment) to a green plus sign (a representation that the citing references have a positive impact on the validity of the cited case). [Illustration 15–10]

It is important to note that the symbols assigned to particular authorities by *Shepard's* and *KeyCite* are merely labels that reflect judgments made by the editors of services about the strength of an authority. A diligent researcher always will investigate the subsequent treatment of any cited case. A red flag associated with a case or other authority does not mean that it cannot be cited. The authority may have been criticized for reasons or issues quite distinct from those for which it is cited. The assignment of negative symbols should be understood to be an indication that these authorities require more thorough exploration.

Another indication of the subjective nature of the symbols assigned by *Shepard's* and *KeyCite* is the fact that those two citation services often assign very different labels to the same authority. For example, a 1998 federal district court case, *Piacentini v. Levangie*, 998 F. Supp. 86 (D. Mass. 1998), is assigned a yellow cautionary flag by *KeyCite* (indicating some negative treatment) and a green plus sign by *Shepard's* (a representation that subsequent citing references have a positive impact on the authority of the case). Similarly, the United States Supreme Court case, *Miranda v. Arizona*, 384 U.S. 436 (1966), is assigned a red stop sign by *Shepard's* and a yellow cautionary flag by *KeyCite*. Again, researchers should not overemphasize the significance of symbols assigned by citators to particular authorities; there is no substitute for reading and analyzing an authority on which reliance is placed.

c. *Sorting and Filtering Retrieved References.* As a method for finding other relevant sources, citation searches for a popular or well-known case or statute can yield an unworkable number of citing authorities. For example, there are more than 56,000 *KeyCite* results for *Miranda v. Arizona*, and more than 10,000 results in *Shepard's* for Securities and Exchange Commission Rule 10b–5. The efficient use of a citation service requires that researchers use methods to narrow results retrieved according to defined parameters.

Both *Shepard's* and *KeyCite* provide mechanisms for limiting citing references; the nature of the limitations depends on the type of cited authority. The *Shepard's* mechanism for limiting citing references is the "Focus" feature; in *Westlaw*, the feature is simply "*KeyCite* Limits." [Illustrations 15–11 and 15–12] In both services, citing references to all cited authorities may be limited by date. For most types of authority, *Shepard's* and *KeyCite* allow citing references to be restricted by jurisdiction and type of authority or document. Both services also allow the user to impose a requirement that particular words or phrases appear in the full text of the citing reference.

For checking citations to cases, *Shepard's* and *KeyCite* both enable the user to limit citing references (at least cases as citing references) to those that address particular substantive legal issues discussed in the cited authority. *LexisNexis* and West headnotes are the vehicles that make this limitation possible. *Shepard's* allows researchers to limit citing references to those cases that discuss issues described in particular *LexisNexis* headnotes associated with the cited case, and to some extent, to issues described in West and other headnotes. Similarly, *KeyCite* can limit citing references to those authorities citing a case for the proposition described in specific West headnotes.

d. *Notification of New Citations.* Having found a relevant authority, an attorney might want to be made aware of every newly issued authority that cites it. Both *Shepard's*, through its *Shepard's Alert* service, and

KeyCite, through *KeyCite Alert,* allow researchers to set up automatic email notification services that inform the user whenever a particular authority is cited.

2.   Differences and Distinctions

a.   *Coverage of Cited Authorities and Citing References.* The task of a citation service is a straightforward one: given an authority, identify other authorities or documents that make reference to it. *Shepard's,* the first legal citation service, was developed as a tool for updating case law. *Shepard's, KeyCite,* and other legal citation services, now include other types of primary authority and secondary authority as well, and more types of authorities continue to be integrated into these services.

Citation coverage of secondary sources, apart from law review articles, in both *Shepard's* and *KeyCite* is far from complete. As *Shepard's* and *KeyCite* continue to expand, it is likely that more secondary sources, ranging from practitioner treatises to current awareness materials to news and business resources, will be incorporated into these citation services, both as cited authorities and as citing references. As more secondary sources are incorporated into *Shepard's* and *KeyCite,* the two services will become more distinctive.[3] It will be increasingly important to check both citation services to ensure comprehensive results.

b.   *Classification of Search Results.* As noted above, both *Shepard's* and *KeyCite* enable researchers to categorize or filter retrieved results according to various parameters. Date and jurisdiction are limits common to both services; document type is a separate category in *KeyCite,* while the concept of document type is often incorporated into the jurisdiction filters in *Shepard's.*

For judicial authority, both services allow researchers to restrict results to those cases that discuss particular substantive issues; this is accomplished by incorporating limits based on headnotes. Those headnotes, however, may refer to different topic classifications. *KeyCite* headnote references are to the West headnotes appearing in the *National Reporter System,* which incorporate the key number system. *Shepard's* headnote limitations are to the *LexisNexis* headnotes and Search Advisor organization. Historically, *Shepard's* also had included limitations based on West headnotes, officially published headnotes, and, for United States Supreme Court cases, headnotes published in *United States Supreme Court Reports, Lawyers' Edition.* It is likely that *Shepard's* will remove references to West headnotes, but will continue to incorporate the officially published headnotes and headnotes from *United States Supreme Court Reports, Lawyers' Edition* (in addition to the *LexisNexis* headnotes).

Shepard's also allows researchers to limit results based on the treatment of the cited authority by the citing references. So, for example, filtered search results might include only those references in which the authority is cited in a dissenting or concurring opinion. [Illustration 15–13]

---

[3] Currently, for example, *KeyCite* includes at least some court documents in retrieved citing references; *Shepard's* does not include court documents among citing references.

KeyCite also categorizes cases that are citing references according to a "depth of treatment" concept. [Illustration 15–14] Citing cases are labeled as either "examining" a cited authority (discussing the case in some depth, usually involving at least a printed page of discussion), "discussing" an authority (including an analysis of more than a paragraph, but less than a printed page), "citing" an authority (incorporating some brief—less than a paragraph long—discussion of the cited authority), or "mentioning" a cited reference (including the authority as one of several in a string citation). Citing cases that merely mention an authority probably are of far less utility to a researcher than authorities that discuss a case in depth. The depth of treatment limitation enables a researcher to retrieve cases that have actually considered the authority and analyzed it in varying degrees of depth.

c. *Manipulation and Display of Results.* *Shepard's* and *KeyCite* retrieve citing references and display those results in different formats. *Shepard's* provides a summary of results at the beginning of the display, followed by direct history and then judicial authority, organized by jurisdiction and level of court. [Illustration 15–15] *KeyCite* organizes judicial authorities that are "positive" citing references by depth of treatment categories. [Illustration 15–16] Both services allow users to manipulate the results retrieved by applying filters; the order and appearance of those filtered results defaults, for judicial authorities, to, in *Shepard's*, reverse chronological order, and, in *KeyCite*, depth of treatment categories. As digital citation services continue to evolve and improve, we can expect that users will gain more flexibility in manipulating, sorting, and filtering results.

3. Using LexisNexis and Westlaw as Citators

Digital formats and sophisticated search engines enable the *LexisNexis* and *Westlaw* databases to be used as citators.[4] Although new types of cited and citing authorities continue to be added to the citation services, many authorities and sources are not included. Researchers wanting to find citing references in authorities that are not included in *Shepard's* or *KeyCite* can simply search for all of part of a citation within a *LexisNexis* or *Westlaw* database.

For example, *KeyCite* retrieves more than 200 secondary source citing references, not including law review articles, for 26 C.F.R. 1.213–1, a Department of the Treasury income tax regulation. Those secondary source citing references include practitioner oriented materials published by BNA and RIA, as well as other treatises and current awareness materials specific to taxation. On the other hand, Shepardizing 26 C.F.R. 1.213–1, in *Lexis-Nexis* results in a relatively small number of secondary sources among the retrieved results, and almost all of those are law review articles. The LexisNexis system includes a large number of well-recognized practitioner-oriented publications in the tax area, but those publications are not currently among the citing references retrieved by *Shepard's*. A search for the term "1.213–1" within tax-specific secondary sources on *LexisNexis* will presumably retrieve texts that cite that regulation. Indeed, searching for

---

[4] *See also* Chapter 23 for an additional discussion of the use of CALR services as citators.

"1.213–1" within a tax treatises database on *LexisNexis* results in additional citing references, displayed in an easy to understand format. [Illustration 15–17]

Researchers should note that it is possible to run a citation check in a full-text database simply by searching for all or part of a citation within the documents in that database. The results may not be analyzed, organized, or displayed in an easily understood or convenient format, but the results should at least indicate how and in what documents a particular authority has been cited.

SECTION E. ILLUSTRATIONS: SHEPARD'S AND KEYCITE

[Illustration 15–2]

SCREEN PRINT SHOWING "SHEPARD'S FOR VALIDATION"
AND "SHEPARD'S FOR RESEARCH" OPTIONS

[Illustration 15–3]

SCREEN PRINT SHOWING "SHEPARD'S FOR VALIDATION" VIEW

[Illustration 15–4]

SCREEN PRINT SHOWING "SHEPARD'S FOR RESEARCH" VIEW

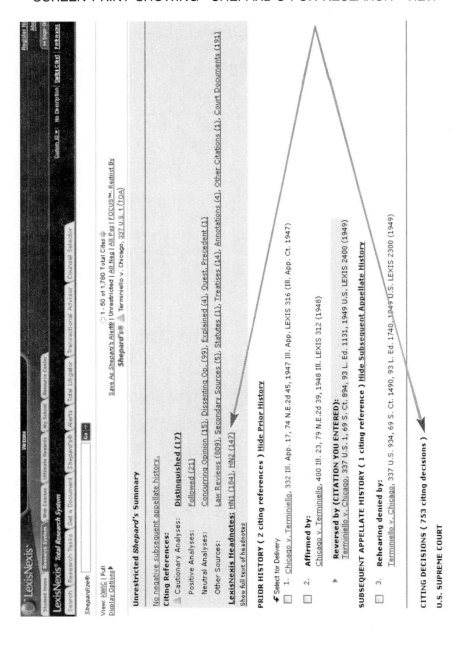

[Illustration 15–5]

SCREEN PRINT SHOWING KEYCITE OPTIONS AVAILABLE FOR A CASE

[Illustration 15–6]

SCREEN PRINT OF KEYCITE GRAPHICAL STATUTES DISPLAY

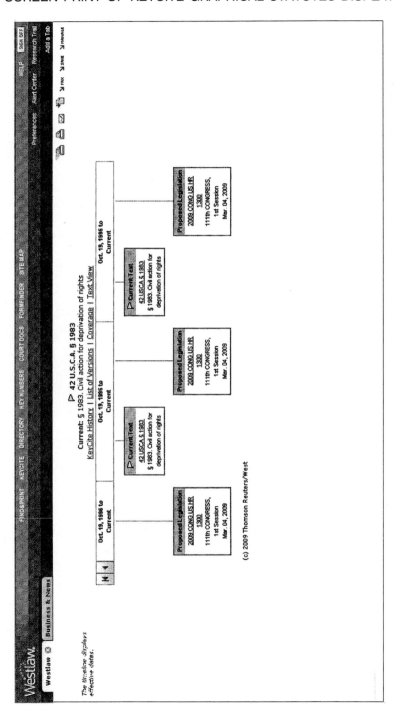

(c) 2009 Thomson Reuters/West

[Illustration 15–7]

SCREEN PRINT SHOWING SHEPARD'S SUMMARY AND CLASSIFICATION OF CITING REFERENCES

LexisNexis™ *Total Research System*

Search | Research Tasks | Get a Document | Shepard's® | Alerts | Total Litigator | Transactional Advisor | Counsel Selector

Student Home | Research System | Web Courses | Ultimate Rewards | My School | Resource Center

Welcome

Register Now
About
Sign Off
Custom ID ▼ : No Description : Switch Client : Preferences : Live Support

Shepardize®:   Go ↑

View: KWIC | **Full**
Display Options ▶

Save As Shepard's Alert® | **Unrestricted** | All Neg | All Pos | FOCUS™- Restrict By

Signal: ⚠ Caution: Possible negative treatment
Trail: **Unrestricted**

Shepard's® ⚠ Terminiello v. Chicago, 337 U.S. 1 (TOA)

↕ **1 - 50** of 1,780 Total Cites ⇧

Terminiello v. Chicago, 337 U.S. 1, 69 S. Ct. 894, 93 L. Ed. 1131, 1949 U.S. LEXIS 2400 (1949)

SHEPARD'S SUMMARY

Unrestricted *Shepard's* Summary

No negative subsequent appellate history.

Citing References:

⚠ Cautionary Analyses: **Distinguished (17)**

Positive Analyses: Followed (21)

Neutral Analyses: Concurring Opinion (15), Dissenting Op. (99), Explained (4), Quest. Precedent (1)

Other Sources: Law Reviews (809), Secondary Sources (5), Statutes (1), Treatises (14), Annotations (4), Other
                            Citations (1), Court Documents (191)

LexisNexis Headnotes: HN1 (184), HN2 (147)

Show full text of headnotes

PRIOR HISTORY (2 citing references) Hide Prior History

↳ Select for Delivery

☐ 1. Chicago v. Terminiello, 332 Ill. App. 17, 74 N.E.2d 45, 1947 Ill. App. LEXIS 316 (Ill. App. Ct. 1947)

☐ 2. **Affirmed by:**

[Illustration 15–8]

SCREEN PRINT SHOWING KEYCITE CITING REFERENCES WITH NEGATIVE CASES LISTED FIRST

Westlaw.
Business & News

FIND&PRINT KEYCITE DIRECTORY KEY NUMBERS COURT DOCS FORMFINDER SITE MAP
Preferences Alert Center Research Trail
HELP
SIGN OFF
Add a Tab
OTHER

Result List
1 Doc
Full Screen List

Links for
69 S.Ct. 894

KeyCite citation:
GO

KeyCite

▷ Some negative history but not overruled KeyCite

Full History
Direct History
(Graphical View)
→Citing References
Monitor With KeyCite Alert

Full-Text Document
• Case Outline

Petitions, Briefs & Filings

ResultsPlus™   View All Results

Am.Jur.2d: Constitutional Law
1. First Amendment Rights [497 559]. Freedom of
Speech and Press [450 530]. "Clear and Present
Danger" Doctrine: Generally Application in Specific
Factual Situations

ALR
2. Validity, Construction, and Application of Fair
Labor Standards Act-Supreme Court Cases

Corpus Juris Secundum: Constitutional
Law
3. Limitations and Restrictions on Right. Regulation
of Speech by Government. Clear and Present
Danger Doctrine

View All Results

List of ResultsPlus Publications

Table of Authorities

West Key Numbers

KeyCite

Terminiello v. City of Chicago
337 U.S. 1, 69 S.Ct. 894
U.S. 1949,
May 16, 1949

Citing References
(Showing 3006 documents)

Negative Cases (U.S.A.)

SELECT TO PRINT, EMAIL, ETC.

Declined to Extend by
☐ ▷1 Brazos Valley Coalition for Life, Inc. v. City of Bryan, Tex., 421 F.3d 314, 326 (5th Cir.(Tex.) Aug 15, 2005) (NO. 04-20201) ★ ★ HN: 3 (S.Ct.)

Distinguished by
☐ ▷2 Lyttle v. Killackey, 546 F.Supp.2d 583, 595+ (N.D.Ill. Mar 13, 2008) (NO. 07 C 1406) ★ ★ ★ HN: 2,4 (S.Ct.)
☐ ○3 World Wide Street Preachers' Fellowship v. City of Grand Rapids, 2007 WL 1462130, *11+ (W.D.Mich. May 16, 2007) (NO. 107-CV-57) ★ ★ ★ ★ HN: 2,4,5 (S.Ct.)
☐ ○4 Wise v. Com., 641 S.E.2d 134, 138, 49 Va.App. 344, 344 (Va.App. Feb 27, 2007) (NO. 2385-05-4) ★ ★ HN: 4 (S.Ct.)
☐ ○5 Doe v. Perry Community School Dist., 316 F.Supp.2d 809, 824+, 188 Ed. Law Rep. 275, 275+ (S.D.Iowa Apr 29, 2004) (NO. 4:04-CV-40161) ★ ★ ★ HN: 2,3,4 (S.Ct.)
☐ ○6 State v. Chima, 463 P.2d 802, 805+, 23 Utah 2d 360, 363+ (Utah Jan 09, 1970) (NO. 11639, 11640) ★ ★ ★ HN: 4
☐ ○7 Locke v. Vance, 307 F.Supp. 439, 446 (S.D.Tex. Dec 19, 1969) (NO. CIV 69-H-430) ★
☐ ○8 People v. Radich, 279 N.Y.S.2d 680, 685, 53 Misc.2d 717, 721 (N.Y.City Crim.Ct. May 05, 1967) ★ ★ HN: 6 (S.Ct.)
☐ ○9 U.S. v. Woodard, 376 F.2d 136, 143 (7th Cir.(Ill.) Apr 04, 1967) (NO. 15566, 15567) ★
☐ ▷10 National Ass'n for Advancement of Colored People v. Overstreet, 142 S.E.2d 816, 830, 221 Ga. 16, 34 (Ga. Apr 20, 1965) (NO. 22814) ★

Positive Cases (U.S.A.)
★ ★ ★ ★ Examined

☐ ▷11 Virginia v. Black, 123 S.Ct. 1536, 1540+, 538 U.S. 343, 345+, 155 L.Ed.2d 535, 535+, 71 USLW 4263, 4263+, 03 Cal. Daily Op. Serv. 2954, 2954+, 2003 Daily Journal D.A.R. 3767, 3767+, 16 Fla. L. Weekly Fed. S 203, 203+ (U.S.Va. Apr 07, 2003) (NO. 01-1107) ★★ HN: 1,4,5 (S.Ct.)
☐ ▷12 Zwicker v. Boll, 270 F.Supp. 131, 139+ (W.D.Wis. Jun 06, 1967) (NO. 67-C-36) ★★ (in dissent) HN: 2,3,4 (S.Ct.)
☐ ▷13 Marks v. City of Anchorage, 500 P.2d 644, 646+ (Alaska Jun 23, 1972) (NO. 1560) ★★ HN: 2,3,4 (S.Ct.)

Limit KeyCite Display

[Illustration 15–9]

SCREEN PRINT OF STATUS FLAGS IN KEYCITE

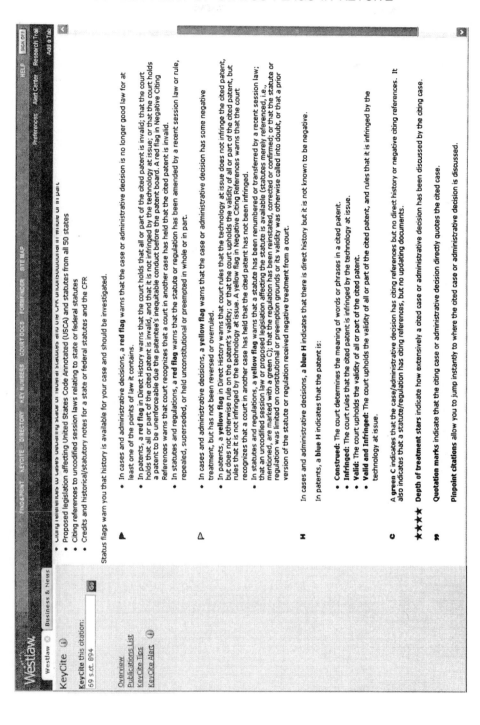

[Illustration 15–10]

SCREEN PRINT OF SHEPARD'S SIGNALS LEGEND

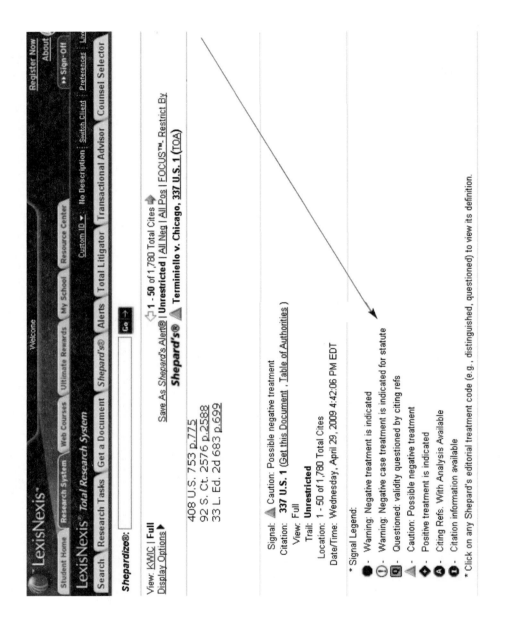

[Illustration 15–11]

SCREEN PRINT OF SHEPARD'S FOCUS RESTRICTIONS

[Illustration 15–12]

SCREEN PRINT SHOWING KEYCITE LIMITS OPTIONS

Westlaw | Business & News

FIND&PRINT   KEYCITE   DIRECTORY   KEY NUMBERS   COURT DOCS   FORMFINDER   SITE MAP

HELP   SIGN OFF

Preferences   Alert Center   Research Trail

Add a Tab

KeyCite Alert Limits
for: 69 S.Ct. 894

▲ Headnotes
▲ Locate
▲ Jurisdiction
▲ Document Type
▲ Depth of Treatment

Click one or more limits above to help restrict your citing references.

[Apply] [Cancel]

KeyCite Alert Limits Tips

Document Type

Cases
☑ Highest court
☑ Other courts

Secondary sources
☑ ALR annotations
☑ Law reviews
☑ KeyRules
☑ Andrews Litigation Reporters
☑ Others

Administrative Materials
☑ Administrative Decisions
☑ Federal Register

Publication
[_____]
(e.g. S.Ct., F.Supp.)

Court Documents
☐ Verdict & Settlement Summaries
☑ Appellate Petitions, Motions & Filings
☑ Appellate Briefs
☐ Joint Appendices
☑ Oral Arguments
☑ Trial Pleadings
☑ Expert Testimony
☑ Trial Depositions & Discovery
☑ Trial Motions, Memoranda & Affidavits
☐ Trial Transcripts
☑ Trial Filings
☑ Jury Instructions
☑ Proposed Orders, Agreements & Settlements
☑ Verdicts, Agreements & Settlements

Copyright © 2009, Thomson Reuters. | Privacy | Customer Service: 1-800-REF-ATTY (1-800-733-2889) | Help

[Illustration 15–13]

SCREEN PRINT SHOWING SHEPARD'S ANALYSIS OPTIONS

[Illustration 15–14]

SCREEN PRINT SHOWING KEYCITE DEPTH OF TREATMENT SYMBOLS

[Illustration 15-15]

SCREEN PRINT SHOWING CITING REFERENCES IN SHEPARD'S

[Illustration 15–16]

SCREEN PRINT SHOWING CITING REFERENCES IN KEYCITE

[Illustration 15–17]

SCREEN PRINT SHOWING RESULTS IN LEXISNEXIS SECONDARY SOURCE DATABASE

LexisNexis™ *Total Research System*

Search | Research Tasks | Get a Document | *Shepard's®* | Alerts | Total Litigator | Transactional Advisor | Counsel Selector

Student Home | Research System | Web Courses | Ultimate Rewards | My School | Resource Center

Welcome

Register Now | About | Sign Out | History

Custom ID ▼: No Description | Switch Client | Preferences | Live Support | Sign Out

FOCUS™ Terms "1.213-1"

View: **Cite** | KWIC | Full | Custom

Source: Legal > Secondary Legal > Area of Law Treatises > **Tax Analysts Tax Publications**
Terms: **"1.213-1"** (Edit Search | Suggest Terms for My Search)

Search Within | Original Results (1 - 202) | Go | Advanced...

◁ 1 - **10** of 202 ▷
Save As Alert | Hide Hits

✔ Select for FOCUS™ or Delivery

1. 2009 TNT 37-49 TAXPAYER ADVOCATE PROPOSES SOLUTIONS TO BURDENS ON TAXPAYERS. (Section 401(k) -- Cash or Deferred Arrangements;) (Release Date: FEBRUARY 26, 2009) (Doc 2009-4252), Statutes, Legislation, and Legislative History; IRS Testimony 13402 words, TAX NOTES TODAY, FEBRUARY 27, 2009 FRIDAY
... Treas. Reg. section **1.213-1**(a)(1), the amount ...

2. 2009 TNT 18-10 COURT FINDS SOME OF INDIVIDUAL'S EXPENSES DEDUCTIBLE, BUT NOT AS BUSINESS EXPENSES. (Joseph H. Schenker v. Commissioner) (T.C. Summ. Op. 2009-17) (United States Tax Court) (Section 162 -- Business Expenses;) (Release Date: JANUARY 29, 2009) (Doc 2009-1936), Court Documents; Court Opinions 6347 words, TAX NOTES TODAY, JANUARY 30, 2009 FRIDAY
... Income. Further, section **1.213-1**(h), Income Tax ...

3. 2009 TNT 4-17 NURSE NOT ALLOWED VARIOUS DEDUCTIONS DUE TO LACK OF DOCUMENTATION. (Stella A. DeVito v. Commissioner) (T.C. Summ. Op. 2009-5) (No. 5821-07S) (United States Tax Court) (Section 213 -- Medical Expense;) (Release Date: JANUARY 07, 2009) (Doc 2009-310), Court Documents; Court Opinions 3583 words, TAX NOTES TODAY, JANUARY 8, 2009 THURSDAY
... Sec. 213(a); sec. **1.213-1**(a)(3), Income ...
... defect or illness. Sec. **1.213-1**(e)(1)(ii), ...

4. 2008 TNT 248-9 SPERM DONOR NOT ENTITLED TO MEDICAL EXPENSE DEDUCTIONS. (William Magdalin v. Commissioner) (T.C. Memo. 2008-293) (No. 7880-07) (United States Tax Court) (Section 213 -- Medical Expense) (Release Date: DECEMBER 23, 2008) (Doc 2008-27096), Court Documents; Court Opinions 2999 words, TAX NOTES TODAY, DECEMBER 24,

SECTION F. CITATORS IN PRINT: SHEPARD'S CITATIONS

Shepard's Citations began in the late 1800s. Originally, it served as a tool for updating case law. *Shepard's* expanded to include citators for constitutions, statutes, administrative rules, regulations, administrative adjudications, court rules, law review articles, restatements, and individual patents. Currently, *Shepard's* in print covers all United States jurisdictions, federal and state, as well as Canadian jurisdictions.

Shepard's traditionally has been published in print in several different units. Some units collect resources by jurisdiction (e.g., *Shepard's Texas Citations, Shepard's Federal Citations*); some by reporter (e.g., *Southwestern Reporter Citations*); others by type of authority (e.g., *Shepard's Federal Rules Citations, Shepard's Law Review Citations*); and still others by subject matter (e.g., *Shepard's Bankruptcy Citations*). Each unit provides similar information about cited authorities and retains the very distinctive *Shepard's* organization, format, and notation system. After a researcher has mastered *Shepard's* organization and notation system, use of the printed volumes of *Shepard's* is relatively straightforward, albeit time-consuming. For the uninitiated, however, the use of *Shepard's* in print can seem daunting.

1. Common Features of Shepard's

Each hardbound and paperbound volume of *Shepard's* (on the spine, cover, title page, or in the prefatory material) sets forth the authorities for which citing references are given. A section titled "The Citations Included in This Volume" or "Scope of Citing Sources" sets forth the authorities from which citing references are taken. [Illustration 15–18] Also included in the prefatory material are lists of abbreviations for authorities and of abbreviations or symbols that describe the history and treatment [Illustration 15–19] of a cited source. This latter section, the list of analytical abbreviations, may, if the citing references include both cases and statutes, be divided into sections that deal with, respectively, analytical abbreviations for cases (e.g., symbols that represent "affirmed," "criticized," "followed") and analytical abbreviations for statutes (e.g., symbols for "amended," "limited," "renumbered"). Unless researchers are very familiar with *Shepard's*, they often will find themselves moving between the main part of *Shepard's* and this analytical abbreviation list in order to understand the notations affixed to the citing references.

The substantive part of *Shepard's* follows this prefatory material and consists of abbreviated citations to the cited sources; beneath each cited source is a list of citing references. [Illustration 15–20] Parallel citations are set forth first within the list of citing references; they appear within parentheses. Any prior and subsequent history references immediately follow. The remainder of the list of citing references is arranged by jurisdiction or source and chronologically within jurisdiction or source. Citing references that are primary authorities always precede citations to secondary sources. Prior and subsequent history references, as well as citing references that *Shepard's* editors have determined treat the cited source in a particular way (e.g., affirming it, amending it, criticizing it, limiting it) are preceded by the letter abbreviation that denotes such treatment.

The extent to which judges and scholars rely on a given authority can be more or less intuited by a quick glance at the list of citations and their corresponding analytical abbreviations following a cited source. Some cited sources have only a small number of citing references. Others are followed by page after page of citing references without preceding abbreviation.

2. Updating Shepard's Citations

Locating the most recent citing references and subsequent history can be a complex task in the print version of *Shepard's*. Each unit of *Shepard's* consists of a number of hardbound and paperbound volumes. The number of hardbound volumes in any unit reflects the scope of the sources covered and the length of time during which a unit has been published.

For example, at the time of writing, *Shepard's Federal Citations*, a case citations service, is in its ninth edition. The federal citations series consists of 38 hardbound volumes, each dated 2006. These 38 volumes cover, as cited authorities, (1) decisions appearing in all volumes (up to the 2006 date of publication) of *Federal Cases, Federal Reporter, Federal Reporter 2d Series, Federal Reporter 3d Series, Federal Appendix, Federal Supplement, Federal Supplement 2d Series, Federal Rules Decisions, Court of Claims Reports, Claims Court Reporter*, and *Federal Claims Reporter,* and (2) unpublished decisions of the federal district courts and Court of Federal Claims (identified by their *LexisNexis* citation). For series that have not been so recently reissued in new editions, *Shepard's* may also publish one or more supplemental hardbound series which update the last edition. Supplemental hardbound series are not cumulative. In order to find all citing references to a source originally referenced in an edition that has since been supplemented by one or more hardbound series, a researcher must check the last published full edition and each of the supplemental hardbound series.

There also are paperbound supplements that update the hardbound volumes. *Shepard's* paperbound supplements are uniformly published with, among other colors, golden, red, blue, or gray covers. Golden-covered volumes are annual, semi-annual, or quarterly supplements. Red-covered supplements are cumulative updates to those golden-covered volumes; blue supplements, issued only for a very few units, are "express" supplements that update red-covered pamphlets. Gray-covered paperbound volumes provide case name access to citations.

The frequency of publication of paperbound supplements varies among *Shepard's* units. Some units are updated monthly, others three times each year, and still others quarterly. Depending upon the time of year in which research is conducted, the number of paperbound supplements will vary. Hardbound volumes of *Shepard's* may contain, in prefatory material, an indication of editions or series that precede or are contemporaneous with the volumes referenced. [Illustration 15–21] The cover of each paperbound supplement lists associated volumes that should also be reviewed. In order to thoroughly update a citation, it is necessary to consult all relevant hardbound volumes and paperbound supplements.

3. Shepard's Citations for Different Types of Authorities

Because different types of authorities have different types of subsequent history and are cited for different purposes, there are a number of differences in notation among *Shepard's* units that cover different types of authorities. For each type of cited authority (e.g., cases), notation is consistent across the different units of *Shepard's*.

a. *Shepard's Case Citators*. Citing references in *Shepard's* case citators may be preceded by letter notations. These letter notations are either *history* notations or *treatment* notations. History notations are appended to citing references to the same litigation in different procedural stages (e.g., dismissing the case, modifying its holding, reversing or superseding it). Treatment notations, on the other hand, indicate how a cited authority is discussed in unrelated cases. These unrelated cases, however, may affect the validity of the cited source and may nullify the cited source as authority. Treatment notations include "criticized," "limited," "distinguished," "explained," "questioned," and "overruled." If a citing reference merely cites to a case without treating it in one of the ways noted by *Shepard's* editors (as signified by the analytical letter notations), the citing reference is simply set forth, without any preceding notation.

Although cases may discuss any number of different points of law, a researcher may be interested in finding only those cases that discuss a particular point of law. To indicate the particular point of law discussed in a citing reference, *Shepard's Citations* has used numbered superscript notations within the citing reference. These superscript notations refer to the West headnote number in the cited source. For example, suppose a researcher Shepardizes a case that lists among its citing references, 838FS[21] 1019, 866FS[4] 223, and 866FS[6] 223. From those superscript notations, it is understood that the case set forth at 838 F. Supp. 1019 references the cited case for the point of law discussed in West headnote 21 of the cited case. And, the case set forth at 866 F. Supp. 223 references the cited case for the propositions of law described in headnotes numbered 4 and 6 of the cited case. If a researcher was interested only in the point of law discussed in the first headnote of the original case, he or she could safely ignore these three citing references.

Shepard's has discontinued including headnote superscript notations for newly issued authorities; print volumes of *Shepard's* will continue to include West headnote references only for those cited authorities and citing references published before this change in policy. *Shepard's* case citators also include citing references to *American Law Reports* annotations; these appear at the end of the list of citing references. In selected case citators, citing references include a number of law reviews.

If a reported case does not appear in any of the printed volumes of *Shepard's* that covers the relevant reporter, that case has neither parallel citations nor prior or subsequent history and has not been cited by any other court or source tracked by *Shepard's*.

Special note should be made of the three *Shepard's* citators covering United States Supreme Court opinions. There is a separate citator unit for each of the three reporters that publish opinions of the Supreme Court. Apart from parallel citations, each of those units includes citing references to subsequent Supreme Court opinions only in the particular reporter covered by that unit of *Shepard's*. For example, citing references in *Shepard's United States Citations, Supreme Court Reporter* include citations only to the *Supreme Court Reporter*. Parallel citations are given to each of the other two reporters.

Each unit of West's regional reporters corresponds to a unit of *Shepard's Citations*. For example, *Shepard's Southwestern Citations* covers cited sources reported in the *South Western Reporter*. Citing references within these regional *Shepard's* units are taken from all regional and federal reporters and *American Law Reports* annotations. *Shepard's* regional reporter citators often are divided into volumes, each volume consisting of several hardbound books.

Individual *Shepard's Citations* units exist for each state, the District of Columbia, Puerto Rico, Guam, the Northern Mariana Islands, and the U.S. Virgin Islands. Each of these sets includes a part that contains state (or district or territory) cases as cited sources. Citing references within these jurisdictional citators are in some ways more limited and in others more comprehensive than their counterparts in the regional reporter citators. Individual state citators include citing references only to federal cases and state cases of courts within that jurisdiction. For example, if a New Jersey court cited a New York Court of Appeals case, that New Jersey case would not be included in *Shepard's New York Court of Appeals Citations*, although it would be included among the citing references for the New York case in the *Shepard's Atlantic Reporter Citations* unit. State citators also include, in contrast to the regional reporter citators, citing references to law reviews published within the state and a selected number of nationally recognized law reviews.[5] If an article in the *Harvard Law Review* cited that New York Court of Appeals case, that article would be included as a citing reference in *Shepard's New York Court of Appeals Citations*, but not in *Shepard's Atlantic Reporter Citations*. (It's easy to see why the electronic version of *Shepard's* eliminates much of the complexity of traditional Shepardizing.)

b. *Shepard's Constitutions, Statutes, Rules and Regulations Citators.* *Shepard's Citations* for legislative and regulatory authority enables a researcher to determine the continued enforceability of those authorities. Perhaps more importantly, these citators direct researchers to cases and secondary authority that interpret and apply particular statutory or regulatory provisions. *Shepard's* provides an overview of the treatment and interpretation of legislative and regulatory language by different jurisdictions.

Citing references in *Shepard's* statutory and regulatory citators are to other statutes and rules that amend or affect the operation of the provision in question, to cases that construe the provision, and to selected secondary sources. Abbreviations appended to citing references are of three kinds, form abbreviations (indicating what type of action is represented by a particular citing reference—e.g., amendment, executive order, resolution, etc.); operation abbreviations (indicating the effect of a particular citing reference on the cited source—e.g., repealed, revised, supplementing, etc.); and judicial abbreviations (indicating judicial action taken with respect to

[5] These are CALIFORNIA LAW REVIEW, COLUMBIA LAW REVIEW, CORNELL LAW REVIEW, GEORGETOWN LAW JOURNAL, HARVARD LAW REVIEW, LAW AND CONTEMPORARY PROBLEMS, MICHIGAN LAW REVIEW, MINNESOTA LAW REVIEW, NEW YORK UNIVERSITY LAW REVIEW, NORTHWESTERN LAW REVIEW, STANFORD LAW REVIEW, TEXAS LAW REVIEW, UCLA LAW REVIEW, UNIVERSITY OF CHICAGO LAW REVIEW, UNIVERSITY OF ILLINOIS LAW REVIEW, UNIVERSITY OF PENNSYLVANIA LAW REVIEW, VIRGINIA LAW REVIEW, WISCONSIN LAW REVIEW, and YALE LAW JOURNAL.

the cited source—e.g., void, unconstitutional, constitutional). [Illustration 15–22]

References to other statutory or regulatory authority that affects the cited source is set forth first among citing references. Cases construing the authority in question follow, organized by jurisdiction, within jurisdiction, by level of court, and, within court level, chronologically. Citing references to secondary authority follow. [Illustration 15–23]

Shepard's Federal Statute Citations is a multivolume set that includes, as cited authority, the *United States Constitution*, the *United States Code* (beginning with the 1928 edition), *Statutes at Large*, Supreme Court rules, bankruptcy and admiralty rules, federal circuit rules, Federal Rules of Evidence and of Appellate, Civil and Criminal Procedure, Tax Court rules, certain miscellaneous rules, and federal sentencing guidelines. Citing references are to federal cases and the *Statutes at Large*. Secondary sources included as citing references are annotations from the *United States Supreme Court Reports, Lawyers' Edition.*

Federal regulatory material is covered in a separate unit, *Shepard's Code of Federal Regulations Citations*. Because the *Code of Federal Regulations* is so frequently amended, each citing reference indicates a year. That year represents either (as indicated by appropriate symbols) the date of the *Code of Federal Regulations* provision cited or, if such a date is not included in the citing reference material, the date of the citing reference itself. [Illustration 15–24] The *Code of Federal Regulations* citators include as citing references federal and state cases, nationally recognized law reviews, and *American Law Reports* and *United States Supreme Court Reports, Lawyers' Edition* annotations. Analytical abbreviations precede citing references that have addressed the validity of regulatory provisions. Decisions of federal or state regulatory bodies are not included as citing references. Some subject-specific *Shepard's* citators (discussed below) do include reference to those administrative proceedings.

State legislative and administrative materials form a separate part of each state's *Shepard's* unit. State statutes are generally covered in each of these units, but administrative codes usually are not. Citing references are to federal cases, state cases from the jurisdiction covered by the citator, law reviews published in the state, nationally recognized law reviews, and annotations in the *American Law Reports* and *United States Supreme Court Reports, Lawyers' Edition*. In addition to legislative authority, many state *Shepard's* units cover court rules and jury instructions, and some include municipal charters and ordinances as well. Municipal charters are arranged alphabetically by municipality in those *Shepard's* state units that do include them, with topical arrangement within each municipality. Ordinances are arranged by subject. Separate detailed topical indexes exist for both municipal charters and ordinances.

c. *Shepard's for Secondary Sources. Shepard's Law Review Citations* enables a researcher to locate cases and other law review articles that have cited a particular article. A researcher who has located an especially relevant case on a developing area of law is well served by consulting *Shepard's* to determine if courts and commentators have cited the article. Moreover, some idea of the article's influence can be gleaned by simply looking at the number of citing references. Unfortunately, because there are no analytical abbreviations that accompany these citing references in *Shepard's Law Review Citations*, the researcher cannot quickly determine if the articles are cited in a positive or negative manner.

Almost 200 law reviews and bar journals are included as cited sources in *Shepard's Law Review Citations*. By far the majority are university-published reviews, but there also is a smattering of bar association and legal society journals. Citing references are to federal and state cases and law reviews.

4. Shepard's Citations for Particular Types of Materials or Specific Subjects

Separate units of *Shepard's Citations* cover specific types of materials, such as the *Code of Federal Regulations Citations* and *Shepard's Law Review Citations*, both discussed previously. Other citators of this type are covered elsewhere in this book.[6] An especially valuable source for identifying popular names of cases and acts is *Shepard's Acts and Cases by Popular Names*. For example, if a researcher only knows that a series of cases is commonly referred to as the "Right to Counsel Cases," the citations for this line of cases are provided in this citator set. Similarly, if a researcher needs to locate the "Ryan White Comprehensive AIDS Resources Emergency Act of 1990," this unit of *Shepard's* will provide citations to the actual legislation.

Other units of *Shepard's Citations* cover specific areas of law and combine types of authority and jurisdictions. These subject-specific citators often set forth parallel citations to commercially published looseleaf services. Moreover, the subject-specific citators include many more secondary sources as citing references than do the regional or jurisdictional units of *Shepard's*. Because new subject-specific citators appear from time to time and others cease to be published, the following list is meant only to be representative of those available.

Shepard's Bankruptcy Citations

Shepard's Criminal Justice Citations

Shepard's Employment Law Citations

Shepard's Environmental Law Citations

Shepard's Federal Energy Law Citations

Shepard's Federal OSHA Citations

Shepard's Federal Tax Citations

Shepard's Immigration and Naturalization Citations

Shepard's Intellectual Property Law Citations

Shepard's Labor Arbitration Citations

Shepard's Labor Law Citations

Shepard's Military Justice Citations

---

[6] For example, SHEPARD'S FEDERAL RULES CITATIONS is discussed in Chapter 12, Section D; SHEPARD'S RESTATEMENTS OF THE LAW CITATIONS is discussed in Chapter 19, Section D; and SHEPARD'S FEDERAL CITATIONS IN SELECTED LAW REVIEWS is discussed in Chapter 18, Section F.

Shepard's Professional and Judicial Conduct Citations

Shepard's Uniform Commercial Code Case Citations

Shepard's Uniform Commercial Code Citations

Shepard's United States Administrative Citations

When providing citing references to a variety of different types of authorities, these subject-specific citators follow the same system of abbreviations and arrangement used in the other units of *Shepard's*.

5.   Shepard's: Electronic vs. Print Formats

The electronic version of *Shepard's* available from LexisNexis simplifies many of the complexities of the print versions. The electronic version of *Shepard's* is not divided into units and, consequently, updating by referring to multiple sources is unnecessary; a single *Shepard's* interface allows access to all citing references. Using the electronic *Shepard's* eliminates the need to memorize the myriad symbols and abbreviations that appear in the print version. The electronic version includes more cited and citing sources, and offers customizable results.

The electronic version is updated more frequently than the print version. Citing references set forth in the electronic *Shepard's* probably will outnumber those in the print product. Moreover, when updating the citation history of a source, the user of the print version of *Shepard's* is limited to the last paper supplement published (although a telephone updating service is available). The electronic version, on the other hand, is updated as soon as the authorities are included in the *LexisNexis* database. A citing reference will appear in the list of references for a particular source even before the *Shepard's* editors have analyzed the document to determine whether analytical abbreviations are appropriate.

All of this considered, however, if a researcher does not have access to electronic resources and needs to do a citation check, *Shepard's Citations* is the only comprehensive print citation service for state and federal authorities.

SECTION G.   ILLUSTRATIONS: CITATORS IN PRINT: SHEPARD'S CITATIONS

[Illustration 15–18]

PAGE FROM SHEPARD'S CITATIONS INDICATING
SOURCES OF CITING REFERENCES

THE CITATIONS INCLUDED IN THIS VOLUME
APPEAR IN

Pacific Reporter, Vols. 1P–855 P2d
United States Reports, Vols. 1–493
United States Supreme Court Reports, Lawyers' Edition, 1LE–113 LE
Supreme Court Reporter, Vol. 1–109
Federal Cases, Vols. 1–30
Federal Reporter, Vols. 1F–13F3d
Federal Supplement, Vols. 1–839
Federal Rules Decisions, Vols. 1–151
Bankruptcy Reporter, Vols. 1–161
Claims Court Reporter, Vols. 1–26
Federal Claims Reporter, Vols. 27–29
Military Justice Reporter, Vols. 1–37
Atlantic Reporter, Vols. 1At–634 A2d
California Reporter, Vols. 1 Car–21 CaR2d
New York Supplement, Vols. 1 NYS–592 NYS2d
Northeastern Reporter, Vols. 1 NE–625 NE
Northwestern Reporter, Vols. 1 NW—508 NW
Southeastern Reporter, Vols. 1 SE–436 SE
Southern Reporter, Vols. 1 So–620 SO
Southwestern Reporter, Vols. 1 SW–866 SW
American Bar Association Journal, Vols. 41–78

and in annotations of

United States Supreme Court Reports, Lawyers' Edition, Vols. 93 LE–113 LE
American Law Reports,, Vols. 1 AR–18 AS
American Law Reports, Federal, Vols. 1–117

> **Introductory material to each hardbound and paperbound volume of *Shepard's Citations* includes a section identifying the authorities from which the citing references are culled.**

[Illustration 15–19]

PAGE FROM SHEPARD'S CITATIONS SHOWING ABBREVIATIONS FOR AUTHORITIES

HISTORY AND TREATMENT ABBREVIATIONS

Abbreviations have been assigned, where applicable, to each citing case to indicate the effect the citing case had on the case you are Shepardizing. The resulting "history" (affirmed, reversed, modified, etc.) or "treatment" (followed, criticized, explained, etc.) of the case you are Shepardizing is indicated by abbreviations preceding the citing case reference. For example, the reference "f434F2d872" means that there is language on page 872 of volume 434 of the *Federal Reporter*, Second Series, that indicates the court is "following" the case you are Shepardizing. Instances in which the citing reference occurs in a dissenting opinion are indicated in the same manner. The abbreviations used to reflect both history and treatment are as follows.

History of Case

a	(affirmed)	The decision in the case you are Shepardizing was affirmed or adhered to on appeal.
cc	(connected case)	Identifies a different case from the case you are Shepardizing, but one arising out of the same subject matter or in some manner intimately connected therewith.
D	(dismissed)	An appeal from the case you are Shepardizing was dismissed.
m	(modified)	The decision in the case you are Shepardizing was changed in some way.
p	(parallel)	The citing case is substantially alike or on all fours, either in law or facts, with the case you are Shepardizing.
r	(reversed)	The decision in the case you are Shepardizing was reversed on appeal.
s	(same case)	The case you are Shepardizing involves the same litigation as the citing case, although at a different stage in the proceedings.
S	(superseded)	The citing case decision has been substituted for the decision in the case you are Shepardizing.
US	cert den	Certiorari was denied by the U.S. Supreme Court.
US	cert dis	Certiorari was dismissed by the U.S. Supreme Court.
US	cert gran	Certiorari was granted by the U.S. Supreme Court.
US	reh den	Rehearing was denied by the U.S. Supreme Court.
US	reh dis	Rehearing was dismissed by the U.S. Supreme Court.
v	(vacated)	The decision in the case you are Shepardizing has been vacated.

Treatment of Case

c	(criticized)	The citing case disagrees with the reasoning/decision of the case you are Shepardizing.
d	(distinguished)	The citing case is different either in law or fact, for reasons given, from the case you are Shepardizing.
e	(explained)	The case you are Shepardizing is interpreted in some significant way. Not merely a restatement of facts.
Ex	(Examiner's decision)	The case you are Shepardizing was cited in an Administrative Agency Examiner's Decision.
f	(followed)	The citing case refers to the case you are Shepardizing as controlling authority.
h	(harmonized)	An apparent inconsistency between the citing case and the case you are Shepardizing is explained and shown not to exist.
j	(dissenting opinion)	The case is cited in a dissenting opinion.
L	(limited)	The citing case refuses to extend the holding of the case you are Shepardizing beyond the precise issues involved.
o	(overruled)	The ruling in the case you are Shepardizing is expressly overruled.
q	(questioned)	The citing case questions the continuing validity or precedential value of the case you are Shepardizing.

Introductory material to each hardbound and paperbound volume of *Shepard's Citations* includes a list of abbreviations for authorities and a list of abbreviations or symbols that describe the history and treatment of a cited source.

[Illustration 15–20]

PAGE FROM SHEPARD'S CITATIONS SHOWING CITED SOURCES AND CITING REFERENCES

Vol. 445		UNITED STATES REPORTS			
423SE174		944F2d395	22AkA238	672P2d537	431So2d1010
Wash	Cir. 2	f 963F2d1064	26AkA182	685P2d187	443So2d202
96Wsh2d47	632F2d1011	e 516FS721	27AkA266	709P2d918	448So2d1242
98Wsh2d820	643F2d59	542FS613	30AkA67	Conn	455So2d1047
105Wsh2d323	643F2d64	564FS718	606SW362	191Ct438	463So2d1167
114Wsh2d249	700F2d784	619FS1567	622SW179	193Ct629	478So2d451
633P2d875	806F2d384	633FS261	652SW44	195Ct508	478So2d495
659P2d467	810F2d368	Cir. 9	725SW579	197Ct690	488So2d82
715P2d126	j 811F2d767	f 636F2d1174	730SW253	198Ct259	494So2d246
787P2d551	846F2d839	f 636F2d1180	738SW425	198Ct262	494So2d251
W Va	f 2F3d1243	653F2d410	749SW313	200Ct332	502So2d1359
172WV71	e 492FS1229	735F2d335	753SW863	201Ct552	574So2d204
172WV456	529FS652	d 735F2d337	762SW400	213Ct716	Ga
303SE709	f 529FS653	810F2d884	771SW292	222Ct683	246Ga333
307SE625	549FS358	811F2d1236	782SW594	1CtA387	248Ga130
Wis	565FS1422	j 856F2d1245	862SW238	2CtA14	249Ga378
143Wis2d548	611FS487	d 939F2d1347	Calif	13CtA417	254Ga670
152Wis2d759	626FS1374	993F2d1450	30C3d826	14CtA503	260Ga234
174Wis2d526	f 633FS502	993F2d1451	30C3d839	25CtA288	166GaA104
422NW635	649FS6	530FS123	41C3d102	25CtA425	166GaA107
449NW333	732FS354	588FS558	44C3d919	465A2d326	166GaA492
497NW788	819FS1205	745FS605	107CA3d148	473A2d314	166GaA493
Wyo	f 821FS118	790FS1482	118CA3d398	475A2d337	173GaA750
622P2d1345					77GaA680
66Cor805					32GaA12
94HLR117					1SE481
79McL115					1SE597
81McL157					0SE447
87McL163					3SE313
90McL917					4SE919
91McL934					8SE225
65MnL1036					3SE603
75MnL916	f 678F2d1206	Cir. DC	207CA3d1388	570A2d178	340SE650
75NwL1129	744F2d381	920F2d946	214CA3d840	594A2d989	354SE652
67NYL478	Cir. 5	924F2d1093	161CA3S27	594A2d1014	391SE400
67AE1322s	633F2d420	955F2d715	165CaR580	610A2d1231	Haw
	644F2d1176	681FS918	173CaR485	630A2d1062	64Haw122
—463—	669F2d279	747FS66	178CaR879	D C	637P2d1103
	672F2d561	CIT	180CaR89	288ADC136	Idaho
United States	712F2d943	787FS1472	180CaR619	293ADC387	106Ida216
v Crews	732F2d410	10MJ645	180CaR627	432A2d735	106Ida223
1980	889F2d583	12MJ391	184CaR464	436A2d1310	109Ida391
	f 905F2d889	13MJ344	187CaR698	475A2d1130	110Ida528
(63LE537)	574FS804	25MJ49	188CaR680	486A2d738	110Ida610
(100SC1244)	Cir. 6	28MJ786	194CaR3	488A2d1330	677P2d529
s 369A2d1063	j 652F2d630	83TCt343	199CaR513	498A2d245	677P2d536
s 389A2d277	930F2d525	Ala	206CaR784	525A2d610	707P2d502
445US592	Cir. 7	397So2d243	207CaR798	533A2d250	716P2d1300
f 445US956	650F2d129	398So2d415	221CaR397	534A2d302	716P2d1382
f 449US914	717F2d423	429So2d660	221CaR831	569A2d132	Ill
467US444	739F2d1275	434So2d840	222CaR619	599A2d1110	89Il2d189
j 467US688	863F2d1342	434So2d841	223CaR574	614A2d1279	89Il2d528
468US805	f 896F2d260	434So2d847	239CaR435	629A2d546	89Il2d535
472US468	f 549FS208	587So2d1092	239CaR436	634A2d415	98Il2d52
472US471	565FS370	Alk	245CaR359	Fla	84Il2A1020
j 472US475	697FS1045	656P2d582	255CaR682	384So2d712	86Il2A694
103FRD225	746FS786	Ariz	263CaR50	389So2d264	88Il2A1117
Cir. 1	814FS1396	127Az212	265CaR85	389So2d267	89Il2A1058
621F2d451	d 814FS1399	619P2d484	640P2d755	391So2d330	89Il2A1066
j 621F2d459	Cir. 8	Ark	640P2d763	397So2d976	93Il2A277
628F2d706	d 650F2d130	270Ark672	710P2d898	400So2d463	100Il2A388
630F2d845	671F2d298	274Ark104	751P2d418	401So2d1365	101Il2A950
632F2d913	700F2d1169	295Ark411	Colo	402So2d20	102Il2A541
665F2d409	730F2d543	296Ark229	200Col512	405So2d464	102Il2A957
668F2d36	738F2d920	314Ark252	616P2d133	412So2d942	103Il2A601
678F2d379	785F2d616	8AkA332	628P2d151	420So2d341	105Il2A814
610FS379	809F2d466	20AkA135	635P2d217	420So2d645	151Il2A112
638FS477	924F2d738	21AkA112	660P2d1288	421So2d42	

> The substantive part of *Shepard's Citations* consists of abbreviated citations to the cited sources. Beneath each such cited source is a list of citing references.

[Illustration 15–21]

PAGE FROM SHEPARD'S CITATIONS VOLUME
SHOWING PRIOR VOLUMES

Volumes/Supplements You Should Consult

Shepard's United States Citations consists of permanent hardbound volumes that are supplemented with soft-covered supplements. If you purchased the master set of *Shepard's United States Citations* your library should contain, and you should consult when Shepardizing a case, the following hardbound volumes:

Bound Volumes:

1.1–1.12	(United States Reports);
2.1–2.12	(United States Supreme Court Reports, Lawyers' Edition);
3.1–3.11	(Supreme Court Reporter); and
4	(Parallel Reference Tables).

If you purchased only the *Supreme Court Reporter* subset, your library should contain the following hardbound volumes:

Bound Volumes:

1.1–1.2	(United States Reports)
3.1–3.11	(Supreme Court Reporter) and
4	(Parallel Reference Tables)

The cover of the most recent supplement to this publication lists all supplements that should be included in your library and consulted during your search.

If You Do Not Have the 1994 Revision

If you do not have the 1994 revision of *Shepard's United States Citations* your library should contain the following:

Hardbound Books
Volumes 1A, 1B, 1C, 2A, 2B, 2C (19
Volumes 3, 4, 5, 6 (1984)
Volumes 7A, 7B (1984–1986 Supplei
Volumes 8, 9, 10, 11, 12 (1986–1988
Volumes 13, 14, 15, 16, 17 (1988–19
Volumes 18, 19 (1990–1991 Supplen
Volumes 20, 21, 22 (1991–1993 Supp
Volumes 1.9, 1.10, 2.9, 2.10, 3.8, 3.9
Volumes 1.11, 2.11, 3.10 (1998 Supp
Volumes 1.12, 2.12, 3.11 (2000 Suppl

Softcover Books
January 1994 Semiannual Cumulative S
October 1, 1994 Cumulative Supplem

> To ensure that the researcher is aware of all hardbound volumes and paperbound supplements in a citator set, *Shepard's Citations* provides, in the prefatory material to each hardbound volume, a section entitled "What Your Library Should Contain" or Volumes/Supplements You Should Consult," identifying all volumes that precede or are contemporaneous with the volume referenced. The cover of each paperbound supplement also sets forth "What Your Library Should Contain."

[Illustration 15–22]

PAGE FROM SHEPARD'S FEDERAL STATUTE CITATIONS SHOWING ABBREVIATIONS

ABBREVIATIONS—ANALYSIS

Form of Statute

Amend.	Amendment	J.R.	Joint Resolution
Appx.	Appendix	No.	Number
Art.	Article	p	Page
C or Ch.	Chapter	¶	Paragraph
CA	Code Amendments	P.L.	Public Law
Cl.	Clause	Res.	Resolution
C. R.	Concurrent Resolution	§	Section
Ex. Ord.	Executive Order	St.	Statutes at Large
Ex. or		Stand.	Standard
Ex. Sess.	Extra Session	Subd.	Subdivision
GRP	Governor's Reorganization Plan	Sub ¶	Subparagraph

Operation of Statute

Legislative

A	(amended)	Sta
Ad	(added)	Ne
E	(extended)	Pro

> **Introductory material to *Shepard's* citators covering statutory and regulatory authority sets forth the abbreviations used: form abbreviations; operation abbreviations; and judicial abbreviations.**

to a later statute, or allowance of additional time for performance of duties required by a statute within a limited time.

GP	(granted and citable)	Review granted and ordered published.
L	(limited)	Provisions of an existing statute declared not to be extended in their application to a later statute.
R	(repealed)	Abrogation of an existing statute.
Re-en	(re-enacted)	Statute re-enacted.
Rn	(renumbered)	Renumbering of existing sections.
Rp	(repealed in part)	Abrogation of part of an existing statute.
Rs	(repealed and superseded)	Abrogation of an existing statute and substitution of new legislation therefor.
Rv	(revised)	Statute revised.
S	(superseded)	Substitution of new legislation for an existing statute not expressly abrogated.
Sd	(suspended)	Statute suspended.
Sdp	(suspended in part)	Statute suspended in part.
Sg	(supplementing)	New matter added to an existing statute.
Sp	(superseded in part)	Substitution of new legislation for part of an existing statute not expressly abrogated.

Judicial

C	Constitutional.	V	Void or invalid.
U	Unconstitutional.	Va	Valid.
Up	Unconstitutional in part.	Vp	Void or invalid in part.

[Illustration 15–23]

PAGE FROM SHEPARD'S FEDERAL STATUTE CITATIONS SHOWING CITED STATUTES AND CITING REFERENCES

UNITED STATES CODE 1970 Ed.   TITLE 15 § 78o-3

TITLE 15	Cir. 4	277FS446	**Subsec. a**	414US128	**§ 78o**
	234F2d769	366FS660	**Subd. 1**	10LE391	**Subsec. b**
	110FS836	Cir. 4	Cir. 2	38LE354	**Subd. 4**
§ 16	140FS165	234F2d769	141F2d242	83SC1247	Cir. 2
Subsec. b	Cir. 6	110FS836	196FS218	94SC383	609F2d580
Rn Subsec i	358F2d864	140FS165	335FS142	Cir. 2	**Subsec. c**
[88St1706	575F2d1169	C 201FS207	471FS391	141F2d242	**Subd. 5**
Cir. 2	194FS574	12LE1208n	Cir. 3	302F2d714	Ad 78St574
463FS986	Cir. 7	12LE1223n	468FS1178	370F2d119	436US105
Cir. 9	321F2d826	**Subd. 5**	Cir. 7	371F2d662	56LE153
591F2d68	509F2d293	R 89St801	350FS1123	391F2d556	98SC1705
§ 45	Cir. 9	351US311	**Subd. 2**	451F2d838	Cir. 2
Subsec. a	283F2d88	100LE1215	Cir. 2	453F2d1214	414F2d93
Subds. 2 to 5	311F2d764	76SC941	141F2d244	498F2d1307	**§ 78o-3**
377US386	113FS31	Cir. 1	196FS218	520F2d1279	**Subsec. a**
428US608	12LE1208n	351F2d939	**Subd. 3**	522F2d153	**Subd. 1**
12LE394	12LE1213n	Cir. 2	373US352	548F2d61	Cir. 2
49LE1160	12LE1214n	244F2d682	10LE397	572F2d356	141F2d244
84SC1274	12LE1216n	396F2d398	83SC1254	227FS519	**Subsec. b**
96SC3126	12LE1218n	522F2d1243	Cir. 2	287FS773	**Subd. 3**
Cir. 2	12LE1224n	122FS333	302F2d714	344FS140	422US732
192FS781	**Subd. 3**	192FS779	169FS218	346FS218	45LE512
193FS283	R 89St801	192FS781	287FS766	352FS715	95SC2430
Cir. 3	377US389	193FS283	352FS715	366FS1265	Cir. 2
444F2d1015	12LE397	214FS937	Cir. 3	373FS140	141F2d244
198FS776	84SC1274	366FS660	327FS495	377FS523	**Subd. 4**
Cir. 6	Cir. 2	Cir. 3	468FS1178	387FS176	Cir. 2
575F2d1170	244F2d682	317FS252	**Subd. 4**	394FS1303	316F2d137
Cir. 7	396F2d398	Cir. 4	373US357	403FS1031	344F2d6
350FS626	522F2d1248	234F2d769	41FRD147	411FS618	Cir. 4

> **Shepard's** statutory and regulatory citators provide references to statutory and regulatory authority that affects the cited sources, followed by references to cases construing the authority in question, and then by references to secondary authority.

Cir. 9	317FS248	Cir. 7	Cir. 5	633FS1256	413F2d832
703F2d343	403FS645	321F2d834	486FS1339	Cir. 7	430F2d675
Cir. 10	Cir. 4	Cir. 9	**Subsec. c**	250FS562	19ARF38n
546F2d328	234F2d769	283F2d92	414US130	362FS858	19ARF81n
96A3644n	240F2d688	703F2d343	38LE353	389FS1154	19ARF122n
96A3661n	110FS836	12LE1208n	94SC383	Cir. 9	¶ A
Subd. 2	140FS165	12LE1218n	Cir. 1	203F2d632	Cir. 10
R 89St801	173FS436	**Subd. 6**	246F2d312	534F2d179	389FS679
351US311	C 201FS207	Rn Subd 2	Cir. 2	**Subsec. f**	**Subd. 5**
377US389	Cir. 7	[89St801	302F2d714	Cir. 2	Cir. DC
100LE1215	509F2d293	Cir. DC	451F2d838	509F2d865	374FS103
12LE397	Cir. 9	636F2d1322	453F2d1214	**§ 78h**	**Subd. 10**
76SC941	283F2d88	767F2d966	287FS774	**Subsec. b**	Cir. 3
84SC1274	12LE1208n	Cir. 6	320FS193	R 89St109	C 557F2d1012
96FRD455	12LE1213n	20BRW129	394FS1303	Cir. 2	Cir. 5
Cir. 2	12LE1214n	Cir. 9	Cir. 5	553F2d751	434FS591
244F2d682	12LE1220n	618F2d64	551F2d632	387FS180	**Subsec. e**
396F2d398	12LE1224n	**§ 53**	Cir. 6	425FS213	R 89St128
522F2d1243	**Subd. 4**	**Subsec. b**	506FS1197	428FS491	422US701
112FS268	R 89St801	Rn Subsec c	Cir. 7	19ARF15n	45LE494
122FS333	Cir. 2	[87St576	389FS1154	19ARF41n	95SC2434
192FS783	244F2d682	**§ 78f**	Cir. 9	**Subsec. c**	**Subsec. f**
193FS285	396F2d398		416FS167	Rn Subsec b	R 89St128
214FS938	522F2d1249	Cir. 2	**Subsec. d**	[89St109	**Subsec. g**
277FS446	128FS457	471FS390	373US342	**Subsec. d**	A 78St577
366FS652	145FS58			A&Rn Subsec c	*Continued*
Cir. 3				[89St109	
444F2d1011					
233FS826					
317FS248					

[Illustration 15–24]

PAGE FROM SHEPARD'S CODE OF FEDERAL REGULATIONS CITATIONS SHOWING CITED CFR SECTIONS AND CITING REFERENCES

CODE OF FEDERAL REGULATIONS   **TITLE 9**

§ 318.8
Cir. 10
516FS345△1981

§ 318.9
Cir. 9
C353FS439△1973

§ 318.10
Cir. 2
568F2d248*1977
Ariz
559P2d1076*1976
Mich
364NW767*1984
381NW406*1984
477NW133△1991

§ 318.10(a)
Ariz
559P2d1077*1976
Del
517A2d708*1985

§ 318.10(a)(1)
Mich
477NW132△1991

§ 318.10(b)
Ariz
559P2d1078*197(
Del
517A2d708*198(

§ 318.10(c)(1)
Cir. 2
568F2d248*1977

§ 319.1(e)
Cir. 6
468F2d86△1972

§ 319.2
Cir. 8
Va631F2d1357*1980
U484FS553*1979
Cir. DC
631F2d973*1980

§ 319.3
Cir. DC
V420FS757△1976

§ 319.5
Cir. DC
749F2d53*1979

§ 319.5(a)
Cir. DC
Va749F2d52*1984
Calif
259CaR537△1989
4CaR2d155*1990
822P2d1302*1990

§ 319.5(d)
Cir. 9
353FS445△1973

§ 319.6
Cir. DC
749F2d53*1979
Calif
4CaR2d155*1990
822P2d1302*1990

§ 319.6(c)
Cir. DC
Va749F2d56△1984

§ 319.6(d)
Cir. DC
Va749F2d56△1984
Calif
259CaR538△1989

§ 319.7(a)(2)
Cir. 5
468F2d88△1972

§ 319.7(c)(3)
Cir. 5
468F2d88△1972

§ 319.15(c)
Cir. 8
631F2d1363△1980
Calif
259CaR538△1989

§ 319.15(e)
Cir. 8
631F2d1363△1980

Cir. 8
631F2d1363△1980
484FS549*1979

§ 319.104
Cir. 9
781FS1462*1989

§ 319.104(b)
Calif
147CaR538*1977
149CaR444*1977

§ 319.104(d)
Calif
147CaR538*1977
149CaR444*1977

§ 319.106
Cir. 6
Up493FS1009△1980

§ 319.106(c)(5)
Cir. 6
Up493FS1009△1980

§ 319.106(c)(6)
Cir. 6
Up493FS1009△1980

§ 319.106(c)(7)
Cir. 6
493FS1009△1980

§§ 319.140 to 319.181
Cir. 6
468F2d87△1972

§ 319.140
Cir. 6
468F2d85△1972
550FS290△1982

§ 319.141
Cir. 6
468F2d85△1972

§ 319.142
Cir. 6
468F2d85△1972

§ 319.143
Cir. 6
468F2d85△1972

§ 319.144
Cir. 6
468F2d85△1972

§ 319.160
Cir. 6
468F2d87△1972

§ 319.180
Cir. 2
369FS1199*1973

Cir. 8
550FS291△1982

§ 319.181
Cir. 6
468F2d85△1972
Cir. 8
631F2d1363△1980
484FS549*1979

§ 319.182(b)
Cir. DC
749F2d56△1984

§ 319.300
77McL215*1978

§ 319.700(a)(3)(iv)
Cir. 8
631F2d1363△1980

§ 320.4
Cir. 9
353FS441△1973

§ 325.1
Cir. 8
685F2d257*1980

§ 325.1(c)
Cir. 7
589F2d283*1978
Cir. 8
685F2d257*1980

§ 327.2
Cir. DC
556FS355△1982

§ 327.2(a)(1)
Cir. 5
992F2d1373△1993

§ 327.2(a)(2)(i)
Cir. DC
556FS356△1982

§ 327.2(a)(2)(ii)
Cir. DC
556FS356△1982

§ 327.2(a)(2)(ii)(h)
Cir. DC
727F2d1159△1984

§ 327.2(a)(3)
Cir. DC
727F2d1159*1983
556FS356△1982

§ 327.3
Cir. 1
653FS399△1986

§ 327.3(a)
Cir. DC
727F2d1159*1983
345FS1206*1971

§ 327.6(k)
Cir. DC
345FS1206*1971

§§ 327.7 to 327.17
Cir. 8
271FS431△1967

§ 327.8
Cir. DC
345FS1206*1971

§ 327.10(b)
Cir. DC
345FS1207*1971

§ 327.10(c)
Cir. DC
345FS1206*1971

§ 327.21(a)
Cir. DC
345FS1206*1971

§ 327.21(a)(2)
Cir. DC
345FS1206*1971

§ 327.21(b)
Cir. DC
345FS1206*1971

§ 331.2
Cir. 6
786F2d753△1986

§ 335.23–2
Cir. 1
563F2d500△1977

§ 335.40
Cir. 5
704FS105*1987

Part 381
Cir. 5
790FS1286*1984

> *Shepard's Code of Federal Regulations Citations* includes as citing references federal and state court cases, nationally recognized law reviews, and *A.L.R.* and *Lawyers' Edition* annotations.

SECTION H. OTHER CITATION SERVICES

As legal citation services, the electronic *Shepard's* and *KeyCite* are unrivaled in their nearly comprehensive coverage of primary authority, the depth of their secondary sources, their currency, and their efficiency and ease of use. Other citation services exist in specialized practice areas (usually in areas regulated by federal administrative agencies). These services may provide very useful alternatives to *Shepard's* and *KeyCite*. Subject-specific citators provide parallel citations to (usually practitioner-oriented) materials. They may also include esoteric administrative materials, as well as important and well recognized secondary authorities, among citing references. Subject-specific citators allow for a variety of citation formats and provide access to a wide range of administrative and secondary authority as citing references.[7]

Both law practice and legal scholarship are increasingly interdisciplinary and international in nature. Consequently, it is common to see citations in primary and especially secondary authority to other than traditional legal research resources. At the same time, more and more non-law publications are citing legal scholarship. We can expect resources like *LexisNexis* and *Westlaw* to continue to expand their content with materials not traditionally included in the legal research process. And resources concentrating on disciplines other than law can be expected to include more traditional legal research materials. Citation services that make connections among these diverse research resources will become increasingly important and valuable.

The *Social Sciences Citation Index* has long served as a citation service for materials published in the social sciences. *ISI Web of Knowledge*, the electronic resource which has evolved from the original print *Social Sciences Citation Index,* now incorporates both science and arts and humanities citation indexes. Recently, a number of law reviews have been incorporated into this index, and selected law review articles appear both as cited and citing references. Interdisciplinary resources, such as the *Social Sciences Citation Index*, provide examples of other means for expanding perspectives on issues and determining the influence of particular secondary authorities.[8]

---

[7] For example, tax-specific citators are discussed in Chapter 25.

[8] A traditional method of assessing the influence of a secondary authority has been to consider the number of times that it has been cited and the nature of citing references. Law review articles that have been cited frequently or favorably by courts (especially appellate courts and courts of last resort) and other commentators gain a certain luster; their authors' repute and prestige are enhanced. Traditionally, citations offered a quantifiable measure of influence that was not available for other uses of authority. For example, how often a particular article was read, as opposed to cited. The advent of digital technologies and electronic resources has enabled new ways of assessing an article's influence. Resources such as the *Legal Scholarship Network*, a component of the *Social Sciences Research Network* (http://ssrn.com/), enable rankings of law review articles and working papers based on the number of times an article is downloaded. As digital resources and the technologies associated with them continue to improve, we can expect more sophisticated ranking mechanisms to develop, perhaps based on a combination of a number of factors (citations and downloads being just two of those possible criteria).

Chapter 16

LEGAL ENCYCLOPEDIAS*

Previous chapters have focused on the primary sources of the law—judicial opinions, constitutions, statutes, and court rules—and various finding and verification aids for these sources—indexes, digests, citators, and other legal materials that enable a researcher to find both the source and status of the law. The amount of primary source materials has become so large that secondary sources play significant roles in identifying and explaining the law. In this and the next four chapters, discussion focuses on secondary sources of the law. These secondary sources consist of legal encyclopedias, periodicals, treatises, restatements, and other miscellaneous sets of law books. Starting research with secondary sources is often a preferred practice.

An individual beginning a research project often lacks even the most basic knowledge necessary to identify and research the legal issues involved. At other times, a refresher in broad concepts is needed. Legal encyclopedias, discussed in this chapter, are very useful for objective background information and as sources of leads to other materials.

SECTION A. INTRODUCTION

Legal encyclopedias are written in narrative form, arranged alphabetically by subject, and contain footnote references to cases on point. In most instances, they are non-critical in approach and do not attempt to be analytical or evaluative. Instead, they simply state general propositions of law, with introductory explanations. These features make legal encyclopedias popular and useful research tools. However, courts and attorneys exaggerate their usefulness when citing a legal encyclopedia as authority rather than merely as an expository introduction to a subject.

In most research problems, it is necessary to go beyond such general sources. A summary citation or annotation frequently will not fully reflect all aspects of the case; the facts of the problem at hand usually are distinguishable from those in the cited cases; and the case may no longer be good law. In most instances, the cases cited must be read, analyzed, and KeyCited or Shepardized, and statutory sources must be checked to ascertain whether the rules of law apply in the particular jurisdiction.

These criticisms should not detract from the appropriate purposes and functions of legal encyclopedias. These publications are excellent introductory guides to the law. They can be effective means to identify relevant issues, index terms and topics, key numbers, statutes, and cases. So long as

* This chapter was revised by Melissa Bernstein, Reference Librarian, Tarlton Law Library, Jamail Center for Legal Research, University of Texas School of Law.

their limitations are kept in mind and legal encyclopedias are not relied upon as the final authority for legal propositions, they can be valuable research tools.

SECTION B. CURRENT GENERAL ENCYCLOPEDIAS

1. Corpus Juris Secundum (C.J.S.)

Corpus Juris Secundum has been published by West since 1936 and includes both procedural and substantive law. As its original subtitle indicated, *C.J.S.* was intended initially to be "a complete restatement of the entire American law as developed by all reported cases." It aimed at citing all reported cases in its footnotes. However, in the mid–1980s, West abandoned its attempt to cite every case and adopted a new approach reflecting a different scope of coverage for revised volumes—"a contemporary statement of American law as derived from reported cases and legislation." *C.J.S.* no longer attempts to reference every case and now provides some discussion of federal and state statutory law.

C.J.S. is a massive set consisting of 101 numbered volumes and over 150 actual books (some volumes consist of more than one book). *C.J.S.* supersedes its predecessor, *Corpus Juris.*[1] Over 400 broad topics, which are listed at the beginning of each volume, are covered in *C.J.S.* Each topic is subdivided into many sections. Preceding each discussion of a point of law, i.e., one of the subdivision topics, is a brief summary of the prevailing rule of law. This "black letter" statement is followed by text expounding upon that point of law. Footnote references are arranged hierarchically by federal court and then alphabetically by state. [Illustration 16–2] Newer volumes include "Annotation References" after the initial topic outline which cite to relevant subjects in *West's ALR Digest* and *ALR Index.*[2]

C.J.S. includes cross-references relating its titles and sections to the corresponding West key number digest permitting easy entry into the *American Digest System.* West topics and key numbers and secondary authority sources are noted under "Research References," which precede each section's discussion in both the main volumes and in the annual cumulative pocket supplements.

C.J.S. has a multivolume, soft-cover General Index that is issued annually. Each volume also has a separate index to each of the topics contained in it. When a topic is covered in more than one book, the topic index is at the end of the last book that includes that topic, e.g., *Drugs and Narcotics* is covered in volumes 28 and 28A, and the index is in volume 28A.

Research in *C.J.S.* is similar to that described in Chapter 7 of this book for digests. *C.J.S.*'s General Index uses the familiar descriptive-word approach. A researcher might alternatively choose to begin research in the appropriate volume. For example, if one is interested in the subject of *products liability*, the index volumes can be bypassed and the search

---

[1] Although CORPUS JURIS SECUNDUM supersedes the text of CORPUS JURIS, occasionally the footnotes in CORPUS JURIS SECUNDUM refer to CORPUS JURIS rather than repeating the citations that appear in the older set.

[2] Annotated law reports (A.L.R.) are discussed in Chapter 17 of this book.

started immediately by consulting the volume that contains the topic *Products Liability*. If the researcher is not initially able to determine the broad topic of the law in which the issue is discussed, begin the research in the index volumes. At the beginning of each topic is an outline and classification for the organization of that topic. [Illustration 16–1]

C.J.S. is updated by replacement volumes and annual cumulative pocket supplements. The pocket supplements may include rewritten text, citations to cases decided since the publication of the original volumes, and references to secondary sources. Replacement volumes are published when significant sections of the text require rewriting or when the pocket supplements become extensive and unwieldy. Each replacement volume contains a correlation table that relates sections in the older volume to the corresponding section in the replacement volume. Volumes covering the Internal Revenue Code are issued annually. *C.J.S.* is available on *Westlaw*.

2. American Jurisprudence 2d (Am. Jur. 2d)

American Jurisprudence 2d, originally published by the Lawyers Cooperative Publishing Company until West acquired that publisher, is a noncritical, textual statement of substantive and procedural law, arranged under more than 430 topics which are divided into subtopics. It contains 83 numbered volumes and approximately 140 actual books and supersedes the earlier edition, *American Jurisprudence*. The editorial philosophy consistently underlying *Am. Jur. 2d* is to set forth points of law, together with discussions of those legal subjects and citations to controlling cases that interpret and construe those points of law. Citations to these selected cases are set forth in footnotes.

Each entry in *Am. Jur. 2d* starts with an outline of the topic and is followed by "Research References." This section includes references to the corresponding West key number digest, as well as relevant *Westlaw* databases, primary authority, *A.L.R.* citations and other *Am. Jur.* publications (discussed in Section B–3 below) "Research References" also appears in each subsection, again noting West topics and key numbers and *A.L.R.* citations. The publishers contrast *Am. Jur. 2d*, a source of the law in breadth, with *A.L.R.*, a source of the law in depth. The former is useful in obtaining a quick answer to a problem that may then be explored further in *A.L.R.*

Like *C.J.S.*, *Am. Jur. 2d* can be searched using either a topical index or descriptive-word approach. *Am. Jur. 2d* has a multivolume, soft-cover index that is issued annually. The last volume of this index contains a popular name table. A separate index covering the contents of each volume is set forth at the end of each book. Like *C.J.S.*, when a topic is covered in more than one book, the topic index is at the end of the last book that includes that topic. There is also a General Index Update pamphlet which covers replacement volumes published after the printing of the General Index. [Illustrations 16–3 and 16–4]

Other features of *Am. Jur. 2d* include:

a. *Greater (as compared with C.J.S.) emphasis placed on statutory law, federal procedural rules, and uniform state laws.* Federal statutory law germane to a topic is noted, while state statutory law is covered in a more general way (without reference to the specific laws of each state). A separate annual volume, Table of Laws and Rules, relates the *United States Code Annotated,* the *United States Statutes at Large,* the *Code of Federal Regulations,* the Federal Rules of Civil Procedure, the Federal Rules of Criminal Procedure, the *United States Sentencing Commission Guidelines Manual,* and the International Court of Justice decisions to section discussions within *Am. Jur. 2d.* A "Table of Statutes and Rules Cited" in the front of each volume indicates citations to federal statutes and rules in that volume.

b. *Annual volumes focusing on the Internal Revenue Code.* This material is contained in the Federal Taxation volumes.

c. *Annual pocket supplements and periodically revised volumes that update the set.* When a volume is revised, the revision contains a "Table of Parallel References" relating subjects in previous editions to references in the current volume.

The *American Jurisprudence 2d New Topic Service,* a looseleaf volume, covers (1) new topics of law that have developed after the printing of the main volumes and (2) substantial changes in the already published encyclopedic articles. For example, this service contains articles on "Limited Liability Companies" and "Real Estate Time Sharing." The general index to *Am. Jur. 2d* includes references to this service. An annual cumulative supplement updates the new topics and provides a table of statutes and rules cited. When new bound volumes are issued, these topics are incorporated into the full set and removed from the looseleaf volumes. *Am. Jur. 2d* is available on *Westlaw* and *LexisNexis.*

d. The *American Jurisprudence 2d Desk Book,* another feature of *Am. Jur. 2d,* functions as a legal almanac of miscellaneous data and information.[3]

3. American Jurisprudence: Related Resources

After the substantive law of the problem under investigation is identified, multivolume sets related to *Am. Jur. 2d* can provide additional information needed to prepare a case for trial. These sets are:

a. *American Jurisprudence Proof of Facts, 1st, 2d & 3d.* This set is now in its 3d series, with each series a continuation of the previous one. Collectively, the three series exceed 140 volumes. The purpose of *Proof of Facts* is to provide a guide for lawyers in the organization and preparation of materials for trial and in the examination of witnesses. It is designed to assist lawyers in obtaining information from clients, taking depositions, writing briefs, and otherwise preparing for trial. Each article within *Proof of Facts* contains "Research References" which cite to relevant articles in both *Proof of Facts* and *Am. Jur. Trials,* an article outline and index, and checklists and planning guides designed to assist in the establishment of the facts in issue. A multivolume, soft-cover index to the three series is published annually. The three series in the set are updated with annual pocket supplements, and by adding new volumes to the 3d series. It is available on *Westlaw* and as a CD–ROM product. The series is accompanied by a medical dictionary for attorneys, which is supplemented by pamphlets.

---

[3] The DESK BOOK is discussed in more detail in Chapter 20 of this book.

b. *American Jurisprudence Trials.* This set is a treatise on trial practice. The first six volumes cover matters common to all types of trial practice. The remaining volumes, entitled *Model Trials*, deal with the handling of specific types of trials, e.g., personal injury, business-related, and criminal. Unlike *Am. Jur. 2d* and the other related sets, the publisher's editorial staff does not write *Trials*. Rather, an experienced trial lawyer authors each topic in the set. This set is accompanied by a separate soft cover index and is updated by annual pocket supplements. It is available on *Westlaw* and as a CD–ROM product.

c. *American Jurisprudence Pleading and Practice Forms Annotated* and *American Jurisprudence Legal Forms 2d.* These two sets contain forms useful in conducting trials and in other aspects of a lawyer's practice.[4]

4. West's Encyclopedia of American Law, 2d ed.

This encyclopedia, published by Thomson Gale in 2005, is directed toward the non-lawyer. Consisting of 13 volumes and containing nearly 5,000 entries, *West's Encyclopedia of American Law* 2d ed. replaces *The Guide to American Law: Everyone's Legal Encyclopedia* (1983). Entries consist of terms, concepts, events, movements, cases, and persons significant to United States law. Included among the many entries are definitions, cross-references, sidebars, biographies, milestones in the law, graphics, tables, and bibliographies. "In Focus" pieces, accompanying some entries, provide additional facts, details, and arguments on particularly important or controversial issues. Sidebars highlight material in some entries. Volumes 1 through 10 each have their own index. Three appendix volumes contain relevant historical materials. Volume 11, Milestones in the Law, focuses on landmark U.S. Supreme Court cases such as *Brown v. Board of Education* and *Miranda v. Arizona*. Volume 12 contains select primary documents from various periods of history such as the Magna Carta, Stamp Act, Articles of Confederation, Missouri Compromise, and documents from the Civil Rights era. Volume 13 contains a dictionary and an index to the set. An annual *American Law Yearbook*, updating the set, has been published since 1998.

SECTION C. ILLUSTRATIONS: ENCYCLOPEDIAS

Legal encyclopedias, such as *Corpus Juris Secundum* and *American Jurisprudence 2d*, can be useful tools to identify relevant issues, index terms and topics, key numbers, statutes, and cases.

Problem: Do prescription drug manufacturers have a duty to warn?

Corpus Juris Secundum

16–1. Page from Volume 28 of C.J.S. Showing Topic Outline: Drugs and Narcotics

16–2. Page from Topic: Drugs and Narcotics § 60, 28 C.J.S. (1996)

American Jurisprudence 2d

16–3. Page from an Am. Jur. 2d General Index volume Showing Topic: Products Liability

16–4. Page from Topic: Products Liability § 1124, 63A Am. Jur. 2d

---

[4] Form books are discussed in more detail in Chapter 20 of this book.

[Illustration 16–1]

PAGE FROM VOLUME 28 OF C.J.S. SHOWING TOPIC OUTLINE: DRUGS AND NARCOTICS

---

28 C.J.S.   **DRUGS AND NARCOTICS**

II. **DRUGS, DRUGGISTS, MANUFACTURERS, AND OTHER DISPENSERS IN GENERAL; GOVERNMENTAL AGENCIES**—Cont'd

    § 28.   —— Judicial review; pre-enforcement review and relief—p 522

  B. REGULATION OF DRUG STORES, PHARMACIES, AND PHARMACISTS—p 527

    § 29.   Regulation in general—p 527

      30.   Appointment and powers of pharmacy board—p 531

      31.   Licensing requirements in general—p 535

      32.   Persons subject to regulations—p 537

      33.   Premises to which regulations applicable—p 538

      34.   Drugs and medicines within regulations—p 539

> The most common method of locating relevant sections in *C.J.S.* is by consulting the annual General Index volumes. Sometimes, it may be easier to take a topical approach. In this instance, by consulting the Topic Outline or "Analysis" for Drugs and Narcotics, it quickly becomes apparent that the matter under research is covered in § 60.
>
> See next illustration.

      42.   Discipline of licensees; revocation or suspension of license or permit; reinstatement—p 550

      43.   —— Proceedings—p 553

      44.   —— Judicial review—p 558

  C. CONDUCT OF BUSINESS AND CIVIL LIABILITY—p 561

    1. *Druggists, Pharmacists, and Other Dispensers*—p 561

    § 45.   Conduct of business—p 561

      46.   —— Warranties—p 563

      47.   —— Validity of contracts—p 563

      48.   Duties and liabilities—p 564

      49.   —— Degree of care and skill required—p 566

      50.   —— Failure to observe statutory regulations—p 568

      51.   —— Delivering deleterious for harmless drug—p 568

      52.   —— Failure to notify customer or physician of dangerous character of drug—p 569

      53.   —— Want of care in filling prescriptions—p 570

      54.   —— Sale of patent or proprietary medicines—p 572

      55.   —— Negligence of clerks and employees—p 572

    2. *Manufacturers and Wholesalers; Governmental Agencies and Compensation Programs*—p 573

    § 56.   Duties; nature and grounds of liability in general—p 573

      57.   —— Strict liability—p 576

      58.   —— Alternate theories of liability; diethylstibestrol (DES) cases—p 579

      59.   Preparation and testing of drugs—p 583

      60.   Warning of dangers—p 584

      61.   —— To whom warnings must be provided—p 588

      62.   —— Adequacy of warnings—p 591

See also General Index

449

[Illustration 16–2]

PAGE FROM TOPIC: DRUGS AND NARCOTICS § 60, 28 C.J.S. (1996)

§ 59 DRUGS AND NARCOTICS   28 C.J.S.

samples[81] or for failure to subject his products to tests under conditions similar to those which they may foreseeably be exposed and which may produce deleterious effects.[82] Premature marketing of a drug without sufficient testing is not justified where there is no epidemic or need warranting the risk and other products are already available to the medical profession which satisfactorily accomplish that which the new drug was designed to do.[83] The public policy favoring the availability of prescription drugs does not provide drug manufacturers with immunity from liability stemming from their failure to conduct adequate research and testing prior to the marketing of their products.[84]

It has been held that the liability of a producer for injury caused by the use of an impure drug does not depend on the manufacturer's knowledge or lack of knowledge of the impurity.[85] On the other hand, under a statute providing that a drug is adulterated if it contains any filthy substance, a manufacturer is not liable for jaundice caused by a virus which could not be seen, described or discovered except from its ultimate result, since the virus was held not to be a filthy substance under the

statute.[86] or in not exercising due care in matters not governed by regulations.[87]

A manufacturer may not be held liable for failure to manufacture a product for a particular age group, where injury resulted from administration of an overdose to a young child, on prescription of a physician.[88]

§ 60. Warning of Dangers

A drug manufacturer or wholesaler will be liable for injury to a user of the drug distributed by him if he fails to give an adequate warning of the dangers involved in its use.

Library References

Drugs and Narcotics ⊕17–18.

Generally, a manufacturer or wholesaler of drugs is under a duty to give warning of the dangers incident to using the drugs he sells or distributes.[89] A warning need be given, however, only where the situation calls for it.[90]

The duty to warn applies even where danger threatens only a small number[91] or small percent-

---

This illustration shows the start of a discussion of cases dealing with the duty of prescription drug manufacturers to warn. Preceding each discussion in a section is a brief summary, in bold type, of the prevailing rule of law, the so-called "black letter" law.

This volume 28 was published in 1996 and uses the new *C.J.S.* format. Volumes in this format are said to represent "a contemporary statement of American law as derived from reported cases and legislation," which is the current philosophy West follows in publishing *C.J.S.*

---

affirmed 411 F.2d 48—Yarrow v. Sterling Drug, Inc., D.C.S.D., 263 F.Supp. 159, affirmed 408 F.2d 978.

Ill—Fornoff v. Parke Davis & Co., 434 N.E.2d 793, 61 Ill.Dec. 438, 105 Ill.App.3d 681.

Ind.—Carmen v. Eli Lilly & Co., 32 N.E.2d 729, 109 Ind.App. 76.

La.—Cobb v. Syntex Laboratories, Inc., App. 1 Cir., 444 So.2d 203.

Miss.—Wyeth Laboratories, Inc. v. Fortenberry, 530 So.2d 688.

Mo—Krug v. Sterling Drug, Inc., 416 S.W.2d 143.

failure to warn as violation of statute

Failure to provide adequate warnings of known risks associated with normal use of a drug violates the Federal Food, Drug, and Cosmetic Act and the New York Education Law.

U.S.—Ezagui v. Dow Chemical Corp., C.A.N.Y., 598 F.2d 727.

90. N.Y.—Glucksman v. Halsey Drug Co., Inc., 1 Dept., 553 N.Y.S.2d 724, 160 A.D.2d 305, 163 A.D.2d 163.

91. Conn.—Tomer v. American Home Products Corp., 368 A.2d 35, 170 Conn. 681.

[Illustration 16–3]

PAGE FROM AN AM. JUR. 2D GENERAL INDEX VOLUME
SHOWING TOPIC: PRODUCTS LIABILITY

AMERICAN JURISPRUDENCE 2d

PRODUCTS LIABILITY—Cont'd
Warnings—Cont'd
  dissemination—Cont'd
    Restatement of Torts 2d provisions, **Prod Liab** § 1187
    ultimate users, **Prod Liab** § 1190
  distributors and wholesalers, dissemination, **Prod Liab** § 1197
  documentary evidence, **Prod Liab** § 1236, 1237
  drug manufacturers, postsale or continuing duty to warn, **Prod Liab** § 1167
  duty to warn, **Prod Liab** § 1123-1170
  economic losses, **Prod Liab** § 1926
  employers, **Prod Liab** § 1173, 1196
  evidence
    generally, **Prod Liab** § 1215-1258
    absence of other accidents, **Prod Liab** § 1227
    adequacy of warning, questions of law or fact, **Prod Liab** § 1219
    advertising, **Prod Liab** § 1239
    burden of proof, **Prod Liab** § 1215, 1240
    causation, generally, **Prod Liab** § 1240-1258
    documentary evidence, **Prod Liab**

PRODUCTS LIABILITY—Cont'd
Warnings—Cont'd
  FDA regulations, **Prod Liab** § 1186, 1203
  foreseeability
    dissemination of warnings, **Prod Liab** § 1188
    knowledge of defendant, below in this group
    questions of law or fact, **Prod Liab** § 1217
  form and expression
    generally, **Prod Liab** § 1175-1186
    FDA regulations, compliance with, **Prod Liab** § 1186
    instructions for use, **Prod Liab** § 1176
    misleading or ambiguous language, **Prod Liab** § 1182
    Model Uniform Product Liability Act, **Prod Liab** § 1178
    readable and conspicuous language, **Prod Liab** § 1180
    reasonableness test, **Prod Liab** § 1179
    specificity, **Prod Liab** § 1183
    statutes, compliance with, **Prod Liab** § 1185, 1186

PRODUCTS LIABILITY—Cont'd
Warnings—Cont'd
  other instrumental party
    generally, **Prod Liab** § 1154-1165, 1246-1258
    actual knowledge of danger, **Prod Liab** § 1161, 1162
    adequate warning would have altered conduct, evidence that, **Prod Liab** § 1253
    adequate warning would not have altered conduct, evidence that, **Prod Liab** § 1254, 1255
    children, open and obvious dangers, **Prod Liab** § 1159
    inability to read warning, **Prod Liab** § 1251
    knowledgeable or sophisticated parties, **Prod Liab** § 1163-1165
    open and obvious dangers, **Prod Liab** § 1156-1160
    ordinary users, dangers generally known to, **Prod Liab** § 1155
    plaintiff or other party did not heed available warning, evidence that, **Prod Liab** § 1252
    plaintiff or other party did not read available warning, evidence that,

> **The annual General Index to *Am. Jur. 2d* will lead the researcher to where the topic being researched is covered in *Am. Jur. 2d*.**
>
> **See next illustration.**

knowledge of defendant, questions of law or fact, **Prod Liab** § 1217
knowledge or conduct of plaintiff or other instrumental party, below in this group
obviousness of danger, questions of law or fact, **Prod Liab** § 1218
other accidents, **Prod Liab** § 1224-1227
presumption that warnings will be read and heeded, **Prod Liab** § 1241-1244
professional groups, notice to, **Prod Liab** § 1239
questions of law or fact, **Prod Liab** § 1216-1219, 1245
rebuttal of presumption that warnings will be read and heeded, **Prod Liab** § 1244
recalls, **Prod Liab** § 1238
strict liability, subsequent remedial measures, **Prod Liab** § 1229
subsequent remedial measures, **Prod Liab** § 1228-1232
substantial similarity, other accidents, **Prod Liab** § 1225
ultimate issues, expert testimony, **Prod Liab** § 1223
expert, manufacturer held to knowledge of, **Prod Liab** § 1140
expert testimony, **Prod Liab** § 1221-1223, 1856
expression. Form and expression, below in this group

§ 1251
industry standards, **Prod Liab** § 1235
instructions for use, **Prod Liab** § 1136-1138, 1176
instructions to jury, **Prod Liab** § 1220
intermediaries. Dissemination, above in this group
knowledgeable or sophisticated parties, **Prod Liab** § 1163-1165
knowledge of defendant
  generally, **Prod Liab** § 1139-1153
  allergies to product, **Prod Liab** § 1151
  alteration of product, **Prod Liab** § 1149
  expert, manufacturer held to knowledge of, **Prod Liab** § 1140
  foreseeability, generally, **Prod Liab** § 1145-1153
  intended or normal uses as foreseeable, **Prod Liab** § 1146
  misuse, **Prod Liab** § 1148
  nonmanufacturing suppliers, **Prod Liab** § 1142
  state of the art defense, **Prod Liab** § 1143, 1144
  testing and other investigations, duty to acquire knowledge through, **Prod Liab** § 1141
  third parties, acts of, **Prod Liab** § 1147
  unusually susceptible consumers, **Prod Liab** § 1150-1153
knowledge or conduct of plaintiff or

§ 1247
prescriptions, **Prod Liab** § 1249, 1255
professionals as knowledgeable or sophisticated parties, **Prod Liab** § 1165
proximate cause, actual knowledge of danger, **Prod Liab** § 1162
questions of law or fact, **Prod Liab** § 1218
workplace settings, plaintiff or other party did not read available warning, **Prod Liab** § 1250
learned-intermediary doctrine
  generally, **Prod Liab** § 1200-1214
  Center for Disease Control, vaccines, **Prod Liab** § 1211
  conduct or independent of intermediary, **Prod Liab** § 1202
  contraceptives, **Prod Liab** § 1208, 1209
  FDA regulations providing for direct warning to user, **Prod Liab** § 1203
  individualized medical judgment, **Prod Liab** § 1201
  mass immunizations, **Prod Liab** § 1210-1212
  nurses, **Prod Liab** § 1207
  pharmacists, **Prod Liab** § 1206
  physicians, generally, **Prod Liab** § 1205
  treating and prescribing physicians, **Prod Liab** § 1204
  vaccines, **Prod Liab** § 1210-1213

[Illustration 16–4]

PAGE FROM TOPIC: PRODUCTS LIABILITY § 1124, 63A AM. JUR. 2D

§ 1123 PRODUCTS LIABILITY 63A Am Jur 2d

An adequate warning is one that is reasonable under the circumstances.[56] A warning may be inadequate in factual content, the expression of facts, or in the method by which it is conveyed.[57]

Warnings cases also often involve duties to provide adequate instructions for safe use of a product.[58] A product distributed without adequate warnings or instructions is sometimes said to have a "marketing defect."[59] Failure to provide an adequate warning has also been treated as a design defect.[60]

§ 1124. Failure to warn may render product defective

A manufacturer has a duty to warn with respect to latent dangerous characteristics of the product, even though there is no "defect" in the product itself.[61] A failure to warn of such a latent danger will, without more, cause the product to be unreasonably dangerous as marketed.[62] In such a case, a product, although faultlessly manufactured and designed, may be defective when placed

---

56. Love v Wolf (3rd Dist) 226 Cal App 2d 378, 38 Cal Rptr 183; Wooderson v Ortho Pharmaceutical Corp., 235 Kan 387, 681 P2d

(applying Louisiana law); Jackson v Coast Paint & Lacquer Co. (CA9 Mont) 499 F2d 809 (among conflicting authorities noted on other grounds

---

> Notice that *Am. Jur. 2d* contains fewer footnotes than *C.J.S.*, even after the change in *C.J.S.'s* editorial philosophy. Also notice the reference to *A.L.R.*, where additional cases can be located. *Am. Jur. 2d* provides a useful way to find *A.L.R.* annotations.
>
> Note: Both *Am. Jur. 2d* and *C.J.S.* have annual pocket supplements. A researcher should always remember to check these supplements for references to later sources.

As to the adequacy of warnings, generally, see §§ 1175 et seq.

58. Frey v Montgomery Ward & Co. (Minn) 258 NW2d 782; Andersen v Teamsters Local 116 Bldg. Club (ND) 347 NW2d 309, CCH Prod Liab Rep ¶ 9971.

59. USX Corp. v Salinas (Tex App San Antonio) 818 SW2d 473, CCH Prod Liab Rep ¶ 13028, writ den (Feb 19, 1992) and rehg of writ of error overr (Apr 22, 1992).

60. Byrd v Proctor & Gamble Mfg. Co. (ED Ky) 629 F Supp 602, CCH Prod Liab Rep ¶ 11059 (applying Kentucky law); C & S Fuel, Inc. v Clark Equipment Co. (ED Ky) 552 F Supp 340, CCH Prod Liab Rep ¶ 9664 (applying Kentucky law); Taylor v General Electric Co., 208 NJ Super 207, 505 A2d 190, CCH Prod Liab Rep ¶ 10945, certif den 104 NJ 379, 517 A2d 388.

61. Miles v Olin Corp. (CA5 La) 922 F2d 1221, CCH Prod Liab Rep ¶ 12724, 32 Fed Rules Evid Serv 55, reh den (CA5) 1991 US App LEXIS 4833; Scott v Black & Decker, Inc. (CA5 La) 717 F2d 251, CCH Prod Liab Rep ¶ 9792

v Nalco Chemical Co., 150 Mich App 294, 388 NW2d 343, CCH Prod Liab Rep ¶ 11041, app den 426 Mich 881 and (criticized on other grounds in Dewitt v Morgen Scaffolding (CA6 Mich) 1996 US App LEXIS 6111); Streich v Hilton-Davis, Div. of Sterling Drug, 214 Mont 44, 692 P2d 440, CCH Prod Liab Rep ¶ 10324, 40 UCCRS 109; Outboard Marine Corp. v Schupbach, 93 Nev 158, 561 P2d 450; Bellotte v Zayre Corp., 116 NH 52, 352 A2d 723; Perfetti v McGhan Medical (App) 99 NM 645, 662 P2d 646, 35 UCCRS 1472, cert den 99 NM 644, 662 P2d 645; Robinson v Reed-Prentice Div. of Package Machinery Co., 49 NY2d 471, 426 NYS2d 717, 403 NE2d 440, CCH Prod Liab Rep ¶ 8658; Harris v Northwest Natural Gas Co., 284 Or 571, 588 P2d 18; Harris v Northwest Natural Gas Co., 284 Or 571, 588 P2d 18; Walton v Avco Corp., 530 Pa 568, 610 A2d 454, CCH Prod Liab Rep ¶ 13227; Ilosky v Michelin Tire Corp., 172 W Va 435, 307 SE2d 603, CCH Prod Liab Rep ¶ 9705.

Annotations: Failure to warn as basis of liability under doctrine of strict liability in tort, 53 ALR3d 239.

62. Garside v Osco Drug, Inc. (CA1 Mass)

SECTION D. STATE ENCYCLOPEDIAS

Some states have legal encyclopedias devoted to their own laws, with most published by West. These are:

California Jurisprudence, 3d

Florida Jurisprudence, 2d

Georgia Jurisprudence

Indiana Law Encyclopedia

Maryland Law Encyclopedia

Michigan Civil Jurisprudence

New York Jurisprudence, 2d

Ohio Jurisprudence, 3d

Summary of Pennsylvania Jurisprudence, 2d

South Carolina Jurisprudence

Texas Jurisprudence, 3d

Some of these encyclopedias are modeled after *Am. Jur. 2d,* while others follow the format of *C.J.S.* Most of these encyclopedias are available on *Westlaw*, and some are available on *LexisNexis*. Some are also available in CD–ROM format.

Encyclopedias are available from other publishers for Illinois, Michigan, New Hampshire, Pennsylvania, Puerto Rico, Tennessee, and Virginia/West Virginia; they are available on *LexisNexis*.

SECTION E. SPECIFIC SUBJECT ENCYCLOPEDIAS

Several smaller legal encyclopedias that are national in scope focus on specific legal subjects. The four-volume *Encyclopedia of Crime and Justice* (Macmillan Reference USA 2002) contains almost 300 topical encyclopedic essays by named scholars covering a range of issues affecting criminal behavior and society's responses to it. The *Encyclopedia of the American Judicial System: Studies of the Principal Institutions and Processes of Law* (Charles Scribner's Sons 1987) is a three-volume work containing 88 encyclopedic essays by named scholars that provide historical accounts and discussions of substantive law, institutions and personnel within the legal system, the judicial process, and constitutional law. The *Encyclopedia of the American Constitution*, 2d ed., is discussed in Chapter 8, Section A–2 of this book.

Also encyclopedic in nature is the four-volume *Great American Court Cases* (The Gale Group 1999), which profiles almost 800 judicial proceedings under the broad headings of Individual Liberties, Criminal Justice, Equal Protection and Family Law, and Business and Government. *Great American Lawyers: An Encyclopedia* (ABC–CLIO 2001) is a two-volume work that provides essays about the lives of 100 great American lawyer-litigators.

Chapter 17
AMERICAN LAW REPORTS (A.L.R.)*

The Lawyers Cooperative Publishing Company began producing the *American Law Reports* (*A.L.R.*) series in 1919; the series is currently published by West.[1] *A.L.R.* is sometimes referred to as a "selective reporter" of appellate court opinions, meaning that its editors select and publish only what they believe to be the most significant judicial opinions—those that are representative of an important legal issue or that expand or change the law in some significant way. With these opinions, the editors provide lengthy *annotations*, which are encyclopedic essays that collect opinions germane to the particular point of law and then, using those cases, discuss and analyze that point of law in depth. It is the annotations, rather than the selectively reported opinions, that are most valuable to researchers. Identifying an *A.L.R.* annotation on point can save significant amounts of research time in identifying and synthesizing the issues and the law relevant to a problem. As is the case with legal encyclopedias, however, *A.L.R.* annotations are best viewed as introductory secondary sources and finding tools and are not as authoritative and persuasive as scholarly treatises or journal articles.

SECTION A. A.L.R. AND A.L.R. FED.

Approximately 10 separate annotations are published in each volume of *A.L.R.* The summary of contents of each volume lists the annotations within that volume. [Illustration 17–1]

1. The American Law Reports are currently in eight series.[2]

(a) Federal 2d Series (*A.L.R. Fed. 2d*), 2005 to present. This series is broader in scope than *A.L.R. Fed.*; it includes both federal and internation-

---

* This chapter was revised by Melissa Bernstein, Reference Librarian, Tarlton Law Library, Jamail Center for Legal Research, University of Texas School of Law.

[1] For many years, Lawyers Cooperative Publishing Company (and its related company, Bancroft Whitney Company) published AMERICAN LAW REPORTS. Lawyers Cooperative Publishing had its own system of research tools, known as the *Total Client Service Library*. In contrast to West's practice of comprehensive reporting, Lawyers Cooperative Publishing reported opinions selectively, on the theory that most judicial opinions did not merit reporting. In 1996, Thomson Corporation acquired Lawyers Cooperative Publishing, as well as West Publishing Company, and several other legal publishers and established the West Group, thus bringing together two traditional law publishing competitors. In 2008, Thomson Corporation and Reuters Group PLC combined to form Thomson Reuters. For more on the contrasting historical philosophies of Lawyers Cooperative Publishing and West Publishing, see Steven M. Barkan, *Can Law Publishers Change the Law?*, 11(3/4) LEGAL REFERENCE SERVICES Q., 1991, at 29–35.

[2] The AMERICAN LAW REPORTS replace the LAWYERS' REPORTS ANNOTATED (L.R.A.). For information about this set, three sets collectively known as the *Trinity Series,* and other earlier sets of annotated reports, see ERVIN H. POLLACK, FUNDAMENTALS OF LEGAL RESEARCH 116–17 (3d ed. 1967).

al topics, recognizing the increased globalization of the practice of law. At the beginning of each volume is a list of subjects annotated in that volume. The illustrative cases reported in the volume follow all the annotations in that volume. This set includes references to *West's ALR Digest*, which has been reclassified to correspond to the West key number system, as well as legal encyclopedias *Am. Jur. 2d* and *C.J.S.*; suggested *Westlaw* databases; an expanded list of related annotations in all series of *A.L.R.*; jurisdictional tables of cited statutes and cases; and references to secondary sources, such as law reviews, treatises, and practice aids. An annual four-volume pamphlet set, the *ALR Federal Tables*, lists cases covered in *A.L.R. Fed.* and *A.L.R. Fed. 2d* and provides both a volume-by-volume listing of annotation titles and annotation history tables that indicate when annotations have been superseded or supplemented.

(b) Federal (*A.L.R. Fed.*), 1969 to 2005, 200 volumes. This series discusses federal topics only and was developed because of the increasing amount and importance of federal case law. In volumes 1–110, the illustrative case immediately precedes the related annotation. Commencing with volume 111 (1993), the illustrative cases reported in the volume follow all the annotations in that volume. Beginning in 1996 when West took over publication, references to West's key number system and to West's other legal encyclopedia, *C.J.S.*, were included.[3] Also included are suggested electronic search queries; jurisdictional tables of cited statutes and cases; and references to secondary sources, such as law reviews, treatises, and practice aids. An annual four-volume pamphlet set, the *ALR Federal Tables*, lists cases covered in *A.L.R. Fed.* and *A.L.R. Fed. 2d* and provides both a volume-by-volume listing of annotation titles and annotation history tables that indicate when annotations have been superseded or supplemented.

(c) Sixth Series (*A.L.R.6th*), 2005 to present. This series covers constitutional and state topics and includes several enhancements. For example, the Sixth Series includes references to *West's ALR Digest*, which has been reclassified to correspond to the West key number system, as well as legal encyclopedias *Am. Jur. 2d* and *C.J.S.*; suggested *Westlaw* databases; an expanded list of related annotations in all series of *A.L.R.*; jurisdictional tables of cited statutes and cases; and references to secondary sources, such as law reviews, treatises, and practice aids. It also includes the standard features contained in most *A.L.R.* series—illustrative cases, outlines, annotations, indexes, and references to other West publications. The illustrative cases reported in each volume follow all the annotations in that volume.

(d) Fifth Series (*A.L.R.5th*), 1992 to 2005, 125 volumes. This series covers state topics only and includes enhancements not found in some of the earlier series discussed below. The Fifth Series includes references to West digest key numbers as well as legal encyclopedias *Am. Jur. 2d* and *C.J.S.*; detailed electronic search queries; jurisdictional tables of cited statutes and cases; and references to secondary sources, such as law

---

[3] Because AM. JUR. also was published by Lawyers Cooperative Publishing Company, the first series of A.L.R. began including references to AM. JUR. When West took over AM. JUR. 2D, it began including references to both of its legal encyclopedias, AM. JUR. 2D and C.J.S.

reviews, treatises, and practice aids. The standard features contained in most *A.L.R.* series can also be found—illustrative cases, outlines, annotations, indexes, and references to other West publications. The illustrative cases reported in each volume follow all the annotations in that volume.

(e) Fourth Series (*A.L.R.4th*), 1980–1992, 90 volumes. This set covers state topics only and contains the traditional *A.L.R.* series features, including illustrative cases, outlines, annotations, indexes, and references to related publications. The illustrative case immediately precedes the related annotation. The same enhancements included in *A.L.R.5th* and in *A.L.R. Fed.* are added to the pocket supplements of *A.L.R.4th*. A separate paperback book, *Electronic Search Queries and West Digest Key Numbers for Annotations in ALR 4th*, contains the materials referenced in its title.

(f) Third Series (*A.L.R.3d*), 1965–1980, 100 volumes. This series covers both state and federal topics for the period from 1965 to 1969. After *A.L.R. Fed.* began in 1969, coverage in *A.L.R.3d* was limited to state topics. It includes the traditional features found in the more recent *A.L.R.* series.

(g) Second Series (*A.L.R.2d*), 1948–1965, 100 volumes. This series covers both state and federal topics and includes the standard features found in the later *A.L.R.* series.

(h) First Series (*A.L.R.*), 1919–1948, 175 volumes. Coverage and features are the same as in *A.L.R.2d*.

2. A.L.R. Annotations in Electronic Format

A.L.R. annotations are available on *Westlaw* and *LexisNexis*. *Westlaw*'s ALR database includes the full text of annotations from all eight series of *A.L.R.* along with the *ALR Index*; the full text of example cases is not included in the database but is generally available by hyperlink elsewhere on *Westlaw*. The database also features *electronic annotations (e-annos)*, which are special annotations available online. These *e-annos* may be included in subsequent *A.L.R.* volumes. The *Westlaw* ALRDIGEST database includes the case headnotes from reported cases for annotations in all the *A.L.R.* series organized according to West key number topics.

The *LexisNexis* ALR database contains the full text of the annotations included in the Second, Third, Fourth, Fifth, Sixth, Federal and Federal Second Series of *A.L.R.* The ALR database is accessible under Legal; Secondary Legal; Jurisprudences, ALR & Encyclopedias.

SECTION B.   FINDING A.L.R. ANNOTATIONS

Finding *A.L.R.* annotations and demonstrating their value is best evidenced with an example and illustrations. Recall the hypothetical problem set forth at the start of Chapter 7, Section D of this book and the reference to the *learned intermediary doctrine*.

In *Edwards v. Basel Pharmaceuticals*, a case decided by the Supreme Court of Oklahoma,[4] the widow of a smoker who died of a nicotine-induced heart attack as a result of smoking cigarettes while wearing two nicotine patches brought a products liability action against the patch manufacturer. The publisher determined that this case [Illustration 17–2] was significant

---

[4] 933 P.2d 298 (Okla.1997).

in any discussion of the duty of a drug manufacturer to warn customers of dangers associated with its products and the role of the "learned intermediary doctrine." Accordingly, an editor prepared a 140–page annotation entitled *Construction and Application of Learned–Intermediary Doctrine.* [Illustration 17–3]

In preparing this annotation, the editor researched the entire area of the law covered by the topic of the annotation, collected cases from all jurisdictions that related to the annotation, and wrote the annotation, incorporating the many editorial features common to the *A.L.R.* series. This annotation, as with all *A.L.R.* annotations, discusses all sides of the cases involving an issue, presents general principles of law deduced from the cases, and gives exceptions to, and qualifications, distinctions, and applications of those principles. [Illustrations 17–4 through 17–7]

1. Index Method

The first step in locating an *A.L.R.* annotation in print is to consult the multivolume, subject-arranged *ALR Index*. This set indexes all annotations in all the *A.L.R.* series except the First Series. It gives almost 300,000 direct references to the nearly 15,000 annotations in these series. A single volume *ALR Table of Laws, Rules and Regulations*, part of the *ALR Index*, provides citations to every annotation in which these sources are mentioned. The *ALR Index* is updated by annual pocket supplements; in the current set, these supplements cover *A.L.R.5th, A.L.R.6th, A.L.R. Fed.*, and *A.L.R. Fed. 2d.*

A separate, one-volume *ALR Federal Quick Index* includes references to all annotations in *A.L.R. Fed.* and *A.L.R. Fed. 2d* It is updated periodically with a pocket supplement. An annual one-volume *ALR Quick Index* for *A.L.R.3d, 4th, 5th,* and *6th* reproduces the references found in the *ALR Index*.

In our example above, one term to look up in the *ALR Index* might be "products liability." [Illustration 17–8]

2. Digest Method

The new *West's ALR Digest* reclassifies previously published *A.L.R.* digests according to the West key number system and covers all series of *A.L.R.* It is updated by pocket part or pamphlet supplement. These digests are classified into over four hundred topics arranged alphabetically. Under each topic are digest paragraphs (headnotes) from cases reported in the entire *A.L.R.* family, along with a listing of the annotations that deal with the particular subject in question. [Illustration 17–9]

3. Electronic Format Method

The annotations in *A.L.R.* through *A.L.R.6th, A.L.R. Fed.*, and *A.L.R. Fed. 2d* are on *Westlaw* in its ALR database; the annotations in *A.L.R.* other than the First Series are available on *LexisNexis* under Legal; Secondary Legal; Jurisprudences, ALR & Encyclopedias. Annotations can be located through Boolean and natural language searches, together with the access mechanisms available for printed copies of *A.L.R.* annotations are retrieved automatically on *Westlaw* when one searches all federal cases or all state cases. From a retrieved annotation, a researcher can go directly to a cited case, statute, related *A.L.R.* annotation, or other sources by clicking its hypertext link. *Westlaw* updates the First Series annually; the remaining series are updated weekly by adding relevant new cases. *Lexis-Nexis* updates its ALR database on a less regular schedule. Updating these citations through *KeyCite* on *Westlaw* is discussed in Section C–3–c of this chapter.

Most of the *A.L.R.* series are available in two CD–ROM products entitled *A.L.R. on LawDesk.* The federal series contains all annotations published in *A.L.R. Fed., A.L.R. Fed. 2d,* and in *A.L.R.3d* dealing with federal matters. The state series contains all of *A.L.R.3d, 4th, 5th,* and *6th* (volumes 1–forward) and the *ALR Index.* These products enable a user to "jump" directly to the articles and sections needed.

SECTION C. HOW A.L.R. IS KEPT CURRENT

1. Upkeep Service

Once an *A.L.R.* annotation is found, further steps must be taken to locate cases subsequent to those cited in the annotation. Over the years, the publisher has developed several different methods of updating its various *A.L.R.* series.

a. *A.L.R.3d, 4th, 5th, 6th, Fed., Fed. 2d.* Each volume of these series has an annual cumulative pocket supplement. After reading an annotation in any of these series, it is necessary to check the pocket supplement for later cases. Abstracts of cases are related directly to the relevant sections of the annotation. Since new volumes are published for *A.L.R.6th* and *A.L.R. Fed 2d.* after the pocket supplements are issued, one must examine the contents page or "subjects annotated" section in all later bound volumes to assure complete coverage.

b. *A.L.R.2d.* This series is kept current with a multivolume *A.L.R.2d Later Case Service,* with each volume covering two to four volumes of the 100 volumes in *A.L.R.2d.* This *Later Case Service* provides digests of cases and then relates them directly to the relevant sections of the *A.L.R.2d* annotations. This set is updated with annual pocket supplements and occasional revised volumes. Thus, to update an *A.L.R.2d* annotation, both the bound *Later Case Service* and its supplement must be checked.

c. *A.L.R.* (First Series). This series is kept current through a cumbersome nine-volume set entitled the *A.L.R. Blue Book of Supplemental Decisions.* Each "permanent" volume covers a different span of years.[5] Each volume lists citations to all cases on the same topic as the annotations, but provides no discussion of the cases. The set is supplemented with an annual pamphlet, making it necessary to consult eleven separate sources to fully update an annotation in *A.L.R.* (First Series).

2. Superseding and Supplementing Annotations

a. *Superseding Annotations.* Frequently, a topic of law of an *A.L.R.* annotation is completely changed by later cases. For example, an annotation in an early volume of *A.L.R.* might show that there is little likelihood

---

[5] As of December 2008, the most recent volume is for 2001–2004.

that one would be convicted of cruelty to animals. Subsequently, statutes are enacted, cases interpret those statutes, and the law changes. The editors may then decide to rewrite and publish in a later *A.L.R.* volume a *superseding* (replacement) annotation. Sometimes only a part of a previous annotation is superseded.

b. *Supplementing Annotations.* This method was used most frequently in *A.L.R.* and *A.L.R.2d.* In such instances, a new annotation was written that supplemented the original one. Therefore, for comprehensive coverage both annotations must be read together as if they are one annotation.

3. Locating the Most Recent Annotations

a. *Annotation History Table.* Whenever a researcher has a citation to an *A.L.R. Annotation,* to avoid wasting time by reading an obsolete annotation or one not fully covering a topic, the researcher should always first check to see if an annotation has been *superseded* or *supplemented.* This is done either by checking the citation in the appropriate *A.L.R.* upkeep volume, or by using the Annotation History Table located in back of each volume of the *ALR Index.* This table gives the history of annotations in all of the *A.L.R.* series. Its use is best shown with the excerpt below:

ANNOTATION HISTORY TABLE

12 ALR 111 Supplemented 37 ALR2d 453	**13 ALR 17** Supplemented 39 ALR2d 782	**13 ALR 1465** Superseded 3 ALR5th 370
12 ALR 333 Superseded 7 ALR2d 226	**13 ALR 151** Superseded 46 ALR2d 1227	**14 ALR 240** Superseded 51 ALR2d 331
12 ALR 596 Superseded 57 ALR2d 379	**13 ALR 225** Superseded 13 ALR4th 1060	**14 ALR 316** Superseded 11 ALR3d 1074

This example indicates that 12 A.L.R. 111 and 37 A.L.R.2d 453 should be read together as if they are a single annotation, and then updated for later cases using the *A.L.R.2d Later Case Service* as previously described.

Suppose, however, that the researcher has found a citation to 82 A.L.R.2d 794, an annotation on cruelty to animals. By checking the Annotation History Table in the *ALR Index,* it would be noted that this annotation is *superseded* as indicated below and that only the later annotation should be consulted:

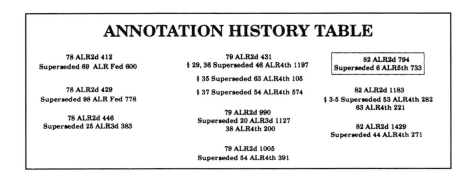

ANNOTATION HISTORY TABLE

78 ALR2d 412 Superseded 69 ALR Fed 600	**79 ALR2d 431** § 29, 36 Superseded 46 ALR4th 1197	**82 ALR2d 794** Superseded 6 ALR5th 733
	§ 35 Superseded 63 ALR4th 105	
78 ALR2d 429 Superseded 98 ALR Fed 778	§ 37 Superseded 54 ALR4th 574	**82 ALR2d 1183** § 3-5 Superseded 53 ALR4th 282 63 ALR4th 221
78 ALR2d 446 Superseded 25 ALR3d 383	**79 ALR2d 990** Superseded 20 ALR3d 1127 38 ALR4th 200	**82 ALR2d 1429** Superseded 44 ALR4th 271
	79 ALR2d 1005 Superseded 54 ALR4th 391	

b. *A.L.R. Alerts.* Review *A.L.R. Alerts* for *A.L.R. 6th* and *A.L.R. Fed. 2d* on the *A.L.R.* website.[6]

c. *KeyCite. KeyCite,* available on *Westlaw,* provides electronic citation validation and verification services. Upon entering an *A.L.R.* citation into this service, the researcher retrieves citations to all supplementing or superseding annotations.

d. *Latest Case Service Hotline.* Each pocket supplement lists a toll free number that can be used to obtain citations to any relevant cases decided since the last supplement.

SECTION D.   ILLUSTRATIONS: LOCATING AND UPDATING A.L.R. ANNOTATIONS

[6] http://west.thomson.com/products/books-cds/A.L.R./alerts/.

[Illustration 17–1]

CONTENTS OF AN A.L.R.5TH VOLUME

Contents of This Volume

Near the front of each volume is the contents, which lists the annotations contained within. Following the contents are several pages containing "Subjects Annotated" in this volume, which is an alphabetical subject guide to the annotations in the volume.

[Illustration 17–2]

START OF OPINION IN A.L.R.5TH

SUBJECT OF ANNOTATION

Beginning on page 1

Construction and application of learned-intermediary doctrine

---

Alpha EDWARDS, Personal Representative of the Estate of
John T. Edwards, Deceased,
Plaintiff-Appellant

v

BASEL PHARMACEUTICALS, a DIVISION OF CIBA-
GEIGY CORPORATION,
Defendant-Appellee

Supreme Court of Oklahoma

March 4, 1997

933 P2d 298, Prod Liab Rep (CCH) P 14894, 57

A case representative of the subject of each *A.L.R.* annotation in
an *A.L.R.* volume is also reported in that same volume. When citing
to an *A.L.R.* annotation, reference is to the annotation, not the
representative case. Immediately preceding the first page of the
case are digest paragraphs classified to the *ALR Digest*. This
annotation is classified under Products Liability §§ 4, 100, and 104.

result of smoking cigarettes while wearing two nicotine patches
brought products-liability action against patch manufacturer. The
United States Court of Appeals for the Tenth Circuit certified question. The Supreme Court, Summers, V.C.J., held that compliance
with Food and Drug Administration (FDA) warning requirements
does not necessarily satisfy manufacturer's common-law duty to
warn consumer.

Question answered.

793

[Illustration 17–3]

FIRST PAGE OF ANNOTATION, 57 A.L.R.5TH 1

57 ALR5th 1

CONSTRUCTION AND APPLICATION OF LEARNED-INTERMEDIARY DOCTRINE

by
Diane Schmauder Kane, J.D.

The learned-intermediary doctrine provides that the manufacturer or supplier of a prescription drug has no legal duty to warn a consumer of the dangerous propensities of its drug, as long as adequate warnings are provided to the prescribing physician. The doctrine has been extended to encompass medical devices and equipment that can be sold only through a physician or a physician's prescription. In certain cases, however, the courts have created exceptions to this doctrine and have ruled that the manufacturer or supplier has a duty to warn consumers directly of the risks associated with the use of its product. In Edwards v. Basel Pharmaceuticals, 933 P.2d 298,
~~Prod. Liab. Rep. (CCH) ¶ 14894, 57 A.L.R.5th 793 (Okla~~

> This is the first page of the annotation in 57 A.L.R.5th 1. This prefatory paragraph, a feature that began with A.L.R.5th, briefly describes the subject of the annotation. For A.L.R.5th, the illustrative cases used with the annotations are published toward the back of the volume following all annotations in that volume. For the earlier *A.L.R.* series, the case immediately precedes the annotation.

ability, despite the fact that the manufacturer adequately may have warned the decedent's physician of the risks associated with its patch. This annotation collects and analyzes those cases in which the courts have discussed or applied the learned-intermediary doctrine in the context of a failure-to-warn claim brought against the manufacturer or supplier of a prescription drug, device, or product.

Edwards v. Basel Pharmaceuticals is fully reported at page 793, infra.

1

[Illustration 17–4]

FIRST PAGE OF OUTLINE TO ANNOTATION, 57 A.L.R.5TH 1

LEARNED-INTERMEDIARY DOCTRINE   57 ALR5th
57 ALR5th 1

TABLE OF CONTENTS

Research References
Index
Jurisdictional Table of Cited Statutes and Cases

ARTICLE OUTLINE

I. PRELIMINARY MATTERS

§ 1. Introduction
    [a] Scope
    [b] Related annotations
§ 2. Summary and comment
    [a] Generally
    [b] Practice pointers

II. APPLICABILITY OF DOCTRINE TO PARTICULAR PRODUCTS

§ 3. Prescription drugs other than contraceptives, smoking-cessation drugs, or investigational drugs
§ 4. Vaccines
    [a] Doctrine held applicable
    [b] Doctrine held inapplicable—mass-immunization exception

This is the first page of a detailed outline of the annotation. It follows the prefatory paragraph shown in Illustration 17-3. Notice that while this annotation covers the point specific to the *Edwards* case, it covers numerous other issues as well. The outline enables a researcher to turn immediately to a section being researched and find relevant discussion and cases.

    [f] Norplant
§ 6. Medical devices designed for surgical implantation in the human body
§ 7. Blood and blood products
§ 8. Smoking-cessation drugs and products
    [a] Doctrine held applicable
    [b] Doctrine held inapplicable
§ 9. Investigational drugs
§ 10. Prescription drugs withdrawn from market

2

[Illustration 17–5]

PAGE SHOWING RESEARCH REFERENCES
FOR ANNOTATION, 57 A.L.R.5TH 1

57 ALR5th   Learned-intermediary Doctrine
                        57 ALR5th 1

63 Am Jur 2d, Products Liability § 337

Practice Aids

9 Am Jur Pl & Pr Forms (Rev), Drugs and Controlled Substances, Forms
   53, 55

20A Am Jur Pl & Pr Forms (Rev), Products Liability, Forms 211–213, 215,
   219–222

7 Am Jur Proof of Facts 3d 1, Injuries from Drugs

7 Am Jur Proof of Facts 3d 225, Defective Design of Golf Cart

49 Am Jur Proof of Facts 2d 125, Teratogenic Drugs

47 Am Jur Proof of Facts 2d 227, Manufacturer's Failure to Warn
   Consumer of Allergenic Nature of Product

6 Am Jur Proof of Facts 2d 175, Manufacturer's Duty to Warn Ultimate
   User Directly of Product-Connected Danger

Digests and Indexes

ALR Digest, Drugs and Druggists § 2

ALR Digest, Products Liability §§ 100, 143

ALR Index, Drugs and Narcotics; Drugstores and Druggists; Food and
   Drug Administration; Food, Drug, and Cosmetic Act; Intermediaries;
   Manufacturers and Manufacturing; Medical Equipment and Supplies;
   Physicians and Surgeons; Prescription Drugs; Products Liability; Side

Following the outline, the *A.L.R.* annotations include "Research
References" to other West publications, as well as to sources by
other publishers. In earlier series, these references were in a box
on the first page of the annotation.

RESEARCH SOURCES

The following are the research sources that were found to be helpful
in compiling this annotation.

Encyclopedias

25 Am Jur 2d, Drugs and Controlled Substances §§ 239, 241

63 Am Jur 2d, Products Liability §§ 327, 337

28 CJS, Drugs and Narcotics §§ 61–65

Texts

Am Law Prod Liab 3d §§ 32:32–32:42, 89:1–89:9, 90:3–90:6

Law Review Articles

Marvinney, How Courts Interpret A Manufacturer's Communications to
   Consumers: The Learned Intermediary Doctrine, 47 Food and Drug
   L.J. 69

5

[Illustration 17–6]

LAST PAGE OF INDEX TO ANNOTATION, 57 A.L.R.5TH 1, AND START OF JURISDICTIONAL TABLE

57 ALR5th   LEARNED-INTERMEDIARY DOCTRINE
57 ALR5th 1

Vaccines, §§ 4, 12[b], 18, 20[a], 21[b], 24, 25[a], 30[a, c, d], 32

Venous thrombosis, § 21[a]

Ventilator, § 11[a]

Veterinarians and veterinary prescriptions, §§ 12, 20, 30[a]

Viral hepatitis, § 7

Vision and eyes, §§ 5[a], 11[b], 13, 16, 22[a], 23[a], 28, 33

Voluntary direct warning to consumer by manufacturer, § 31[c]

Weight-control drug, §§ 27[a], 28

Who is learned intermediary, §§ 17-20, 23[a]

Withdrawn from market, prescription drugs which have been, § 10

X-ray equipment and radiology, §§ 11[a], 14

Jurisdictional Table of Cited Statutes and Cases*

UNITED STATES

21 CFR § 130.45(e)(3). See § 31[b]
21 CFR § 201.105. See § 30[a]
21 CFR § 310.501. See § 5[a, b]
21 CFR § 310.502. See § 5[d]

A.L.R.5th annotations include a detailed index that can lead to specific points in the annotation. Note that Illustration 17-4 referenced § 8 of the annotation. See next illustration. If the researcher is interested in "who is a learned intermediary," reference would be to §§ 17-20, and 23[a] as shown above. Lengthy annotations in earlier series also contain as index.

The jurisdictional table, found in *A.L.R.5th*, provides citations to statutes and cases relevant to the annotation. This information is much more detailed than in earlier series.

(S.D.N.Y. 1995)—§ 29

Hill v. Searle Laboratories, a Div. of Searle Pharmaceuticals, Inc., 884 F.2d 1064, Prod. Liab. Rep. (CCH) ¶ 12250 (8th Cir. 1989)—§ 6

Hurley v. Lederle Laboratories Div. of American Cyanamid Co., 863 F.2d 1173 (5th Cir. 1988)—§ 22[b]

Reyes v Wyeth Laboratories, 498 F.2d 1264 (5th Cir. 1974)—§ 4[c]

* Statutes, rules, regulations, and constitutional provisions bearing on the subject of the annotation are included in this table only to the extent, and in the form, that they are reflected in the court opinions discussed in this annotation. The reader should consult the appropriate statutory or regulatory compilations to ascertain the current status of relevant statutes, rules, regulations, and constitutional provisions.

For federal cases involving state law, see state headings.

11

[Illustration 17–7]

PAGE FROM ANNOTATION, 57 A.L.R.5TH 1

---

§ 7   LEARNED-INTERMEDIARY DOCTRINE   57 ALR5th
57 ALR5th 1

of a blood-clotting agent failed to adequately warn of the risks of contract-ing the AIDS virus from its product. The court explained simply that a pharmaceutical manufacturer is required to warn physicians or other medical personnel authorized to prescribe drugs by state law of all rea-sonably foreseeable risks associated with the use of the product.

In Doe v American Nat'l Red Cross (1994, DC Md) 866 F Supp 242

Notice how § 8 of the annotation discusses cases dealing with prescription smoking-cessation medication. The jurisdictional table, partially shown in Illustration 17-6, can be used to identify relevant cases and statutes from any state. For example, under Oklahoma the table indicates that *Edwards v. Basel Pharmaceuticals*, the illustrative case chosen for this annotation, is discussed under §§ 2[b]. 8[b], and 31[b].

§ 1 of an annotation gives its scope and then lists related annotations.

ated with prescription drugs extends only to the attending physician, and not to the patient.

§ 8. Smoking-cessation drugs and products

[a] Doctrine held applicable

In the following case involving a prescription smoking-cessation medica-tion, the court held that the learned-intermediary doctrine was applicable and that, therefore, the manufacturer of the product had no obligation to warn the user directly of the side effects associated with its product.

A failure-to-warn claim brought against the manufacturer of Nicorette tablets, a smoking-cessation medication, by the administratrix of the estate of a participant in a smoking-cessation program was governed by the learned-intermediary doctrine, concluded the court in Tracy v Merrell Dow Pharmaceuticals, Inc. (1991) 58 **Ohio St 3d** 147, 569 NE2d 875, CCH Prod Liab Rep ¶ 12950, reversing the judgment of the court below. Prior to entering the smoking-cessation program, which was an investiga-tional drug study, the decedent underwent a screening by a physician who was participating in the study. The doctor physically examined the decedent, finding no evidence of heart disease. The decedent did not, however, tell the doctor about his heavy smoking habits or the fact that he previously had been hospitalized for alcoholism. The decedent was given a written agreement which included a warning against the use of alcohol or other drugs while taking the Nicorette tablets, and the doctor warned

[Illustration 17–8]

PAGE FROM A.L.R. INDEX

ALR INDEX

PRODUCTS LIABILITY—Cont'd
Indemnity—Cont'd
    third person, manufacturer's or seller's
       right to contribution or indemnity
       from user of product causing injury
       or damage to third person, and vice
       versa, **28 ALR3d 943**
Independent contractors
    crop dusting, liability for injury caused
       by spraying or dusting of crops, **37
       ALR3d 833**
    government-contractor defense to state
       products liability claims, **53
       ALR5th 535**
    latent defects in materials used,
       liability for, **61 ALR3d 792**
Indorser of product, liability of product
    indorser or certifier for product-caused
    injury, **39 ALR3d 181**
In personam jurisdiction over nonresident
    manufacturer or seller under long-arm
    statutes, **19 ALR3d 13**
Inspections, see group Testing and inspec-
    tion in this topic
Instructions to jury
    alternative instructions, necessity and
       propriety of instructing on alterna-
       tive theories of negligence or breach
       of warranty, where instruction on
       strict liability in tort is given in
       products liability case, **52 ALR3d
       101**
    fires, res ipsa loquitur as to cause of or
       liability for real-property fires, **21
       ALR4th 929**
Insurance
    generally, **45 ALR2d 994**
    causation of injury, insurance coverage
       as extending only to product-caused
       injury to person or other property, as
       distinguished from near product fail-
       ure, **91 ALR3d 921**
    clause excluding products liability
       from coverage of liability insurance
       policy, **54 ALR2d 518**
    completed operations, see group
       Completed operations in this topic
    event triggering liability insurance
       coverage as occurring within period
       of time covered by liability insur-

PRODUCTS LIABILITY—Cont'd
Insurance—Cont'd
    ance policy where injury or damage
    is delayed—modern cases, **14
    ALR5th 695**
    premises liability insurance, coverage
       of premises liability insurance
       extending to liability for injuries or
       damage caused by product sold or
       rented by insured and occurring
       away from insured premises, **62
       ALR3d 889**
    sistership clause of policy excepting
       from coverage cost of product recall
       or withdrawal of product from mar-
       ket, validity and construction of, **32
       ALR4th 630**
    workers' compensation, see group
       Workers' compensation in this topic
Intermediaries
    learned-intermediary, construction and
       application of learned-intermediary
       doctrine, **57 ALR5th 1**
    seller as affected by failure of
       subsequent party in distribution
       chain to remedy or warn against
       defect of which he knew, **45
       ALR4th 777**
Joint tortfeasors, manufacturer and dealer
    or distributor as joint or concurrent
    tortfeasors, **97 ALR2d 811**
Judgment in action against seller or sup-
    plier of product as res judicata in action
    against manufacturer for injury from
    defective product, **34 ALR3d 518**
Jurisdiction
    admiralty, products liability claim as
       within admiralty jurisdiction, **7 ALR
       Fed 502**
    long arm statutes, see group Long arm
       statutes in this topic
    personal jurisdiction over nonresident
       manufacturer of component
       incorporated in another product, **69
       ALR4th 14**
Knowledge, see group Notice and knowl-
    edge in this topic
Labor and employment
    contribution or indemnity, right of
       manufacturer or seller to contribu-

Consult POCKET PART for Later Annotations

516

[Illustration 17–9]

PAGE FROM WEST'S ALR DIGEST

DRUGS AND DRUGGISTS § 1

Consult pocket part for later cases

§ 3 —Violation of statute
§ 4 —Negligence of employee
§ 5 —Contributory negligence
§ 6 Criminal liability for injuries
§ 7 Narcotics and controlled substances, generally
§ 8 —Prescription, distribution, and sale of dangerous drugs by medical practitioners and druggists
§ 9 —Possession and use of drugs, controlled substances, and drug paraphernalia

§ 10 —Sale, distribution, and manufacture of controlled substances
§ 11 —Transportation of controlled substances
§ 12 —Fraud, forgery, and falsehood in obtaining or distributing controlled substances
§ 13 —Miscellaneous offenses and violations
§ 14 —Civil commitment; rehabilitation programs

TABLE OF PARALLEL REFERENCES

The following table shows where the subject matter of changed sections in the original topic *Drugs and Druggists* is now treated in the new topic *Drugs and Druggists*. Consult the new topic scheme for detail and for matter not appearing in the original topic.

Original §	New §	Original §	New §
§ 1.5	§§ 7-13	§ 1.6	§ 14

§ 1 Generally

Text References:

21 Am Jur 2d, Criminal Law §§ 167-171; 25 Am Jur 2d, Drugs, Narcotics, and Poisons

21 Am Jur Proof of Facts 1, Side Effects of Drugs; 25 Am Jur Proof of Facts 567, Negligent and Deceptive Practices in Diagnosis and Treatment of Cancer; 26 Am Jur Proof of Facts 723,

Notice how the outline of the topic *Drugs and Druggists* directs the researcher to the proper location in the digest. Notice also the references to the other sources, including annotations.

13 Federal Procedure, L. Ed, Food, Drugs, and Cosmetics §§ 35:1-35:111, 35:155-35:218, 35:280-35:313, 35:328, 35:375-35:378, 35:389-35:425, 35:513 et seq.

Practice References:

9 Federal Procedural Forms, L. Ed, Food, Drugs, and Cosmetics §§ 31:1 et seq.

8 Am Jur Pl & Pr Forms (Rev), Criminal Procedure, Forms 1 et seq., 255-258; 9 Am Jur Pl & Pr Forms (Rev), Drugs, Narcotics, and Poisons, Forms 1 et seq.; 12 Am Jur Pl & Pr Forms (Rev), Food, Forms 21-24; 19A Am Jur Pl & Pr Forms (Rev), Physicians, Surgeons, and Other Healers, Forms 153, 156-158, 253-257; 20A Am Jur Pl & Pr Forms (Rev), Products Liability, Forms 211, 212, 218, 219, 222

7A Am Jur Legal Forms 2d, Drugs, Narcotics, and Poisons §§ 93:1-93:5, 93:10; 8A Am Jur Legal Forms 2d, Food §§ 120:1, 120:2, 120:51, 120:52; 15 Am Jur Legal Forms 2d, Products Liability §§ 209:1, 209:2

3 Am Jur Proof of Facts 127, Cancer; 4 Am Jur Proof of Facts 549, Drugs; 7 Am Jur Proof of Facts 479, Malpractice; 13 Am Jur Proof of Facts 391, Criminal Drug Addiction and Possession; 14 Am Jur Proof of Facts 211, Cosmetics;

357, Locating Medical Experts; 6 Am Jur Trials 109, Basis of Medical Testimony; 7 Am Jur Trials 1, Drug Products Liability and Malpractice Cases; 8 Am Jur Trials 573, Defense of Narcotics Cases; 9 Am Jur Trials 59, Food Seizure Litigation; 12 Am Jur Trials 1, Products Liability Cases; 14 Am Jur Trials 619, Juvenile Court Proceedings; 16 Am Jur Trials 471, Defense of Medical Malpractice Cases; 17 Am Jur Trials 1, Drug Products Liability and Malpractice Cases

USCS, Constitution, Amendments 1, 5, 8, 9, and 14; 21 USCS §§ 1 et seq.

L Ed Digest, Constitutional Law §§ 431, 458; Drugs, Narcotics and Poisons §§ 1-10; Evidence § 362; Food §§ 1, 1.5, 2, 4-10; Health § 1.5; Privacy § 1

Annotations:

State and local administrative inspection of and administrative warrants to search pharmacies, 29 ALR4th 264

Right of medical patient to obtain, or physician to prescribe, Laetrile for treatment of illness—state cases, 5 ALR4th 178

Products liability: diethylstilbestrol (DES), 2 ALR4th 1091

185

Chapter 18

LEGAL PERIODICALS AND INDEXES*

Legal periodicals can be extremely valuable secondary sources in legal research. Their value typically lies in the depth to which they analyze and criticize a particular topic and the extent of their footnote references to other sources. During the nineteenth century, legal periodicals greatly contributed to improving the image of the legal profession in America.[1] With the proliferation of legislation and judicial opinions, legal periodicals in the twenty-first century play an increasingly important role in keeping researchers current in developing areas of the law and in providing information on specialized areas of the law. With the rapid growth of electronic legal research services and the Internet, legal periodicals are increasingly more accessible.

The legal periodical is an important and useful secondary authority containing articles, frequently by specialists, on specific legal topics. The articles are either critical or expository in nature and their scholarly interpretations are relied on frequently by American courts and lawyers.[2] Legal periodicals can be classified into five types of publications: (1) law reviews published by law schools; (2) subject, special interest, and interdisciplinary journals (frequently commercially published); (3) bar association periodicals; (4) legal newspapers; and (5) legal newsletters.[3] A variety of specialized indexes provide access to these publications. The various types of legal periodicals and finding aids used in accessing the contents of these legal periodicals are the subjects of this chapter.

* This chapter was revised and updated by Bonnie Shucha, Head of Reference, University of Wisconsin Law Library.

[1] MAXWELL H. BLOOMFIELD, AMERICAN LAWYERS IN A CHANGING SOCIETY, 1776–1876, at 142–43 (1976). For a brief account of legal periodicals in nineteenth-century America, see LAWRENCE M. FRIEDMAN, A HISTORY OF AMERICAN LAW 481–482 (3d ed. 2005). Additional sources that deal with the early history of legal periodicals in the United States include Marion Brainerd, *Historical Sketch of American Legal Periodicals*, 14 LAW LIBR. J. 63 (1921), and Roscoe Pound, *Types of Legal Periodical*, 14 IOWA L. REV. 257 (1929). For an extensive history of law school reviews, see Michael I. Swygert & Jon W. Bruce, *The Historical Origin, Founding, and Early Development of Student–Edited Law Reviews,* 36 HASTINGS L.J. 739 (1985), and Michael L. Closen & Robert J. Dzielak, *The History and Influence of the Law Review Institution*, 30 AKRON L. REV. 15 (1996).

For a list of legal periodicals of the nineteenth century and their dates of publication, see LEONARD N. JONES, AN INDEX TO LEGAL PERIODICAL LITERATURE vii–x (1888); 2 *id.* at vii–x (1899). These volumes are part of JONES & CHIPMAN'S INDEX TO LEGAL PERIODICALS, which is discussed in section B–1 of this chapter.

[2] ERVIN H. POLLACK, FUNDAMENTALS OF LEGAL RESEARCH 151 (1956).

[3] For additional breakdowns of categories and for recommendations of titles that should be in a broad-based legal periodical collection, see Donald J. Dunn, *Law, in* MAGAZINES FOR LIBRARIES 601 (Cheryl LaGuardia, ed. 16th ed. 2008).

SECTION A. LEGAL PERIODICALS

1. Law School Reviews/Journals

A periodical published by a law school most often is called a *review,* although *journal* is also widely used, e.g., *Harvard Law Review, Michigan Law Review, Yale Law Journal.* The two terms are used interchangeably. In the United States, student editors typically control the editorial policy and management of law reviews. Students forming the membership of law reviews are commonly chosen on the basis of their academic record, through a writing competition, or by a combination of the two. These students "on law review" write articles and edit each other's work, evaluate for potential publication the writings submitted by academics and practitioners, and then edit those pieces accepted for publication.

The typical law review is published quarterly, although some are issued annually and others as often as eight times a year. The parent institution usually subsidizes the cost of publication and sells subscriptions at a modest price, with circulation frequently limited to law libraries, alumni, and members of the bar within the jurisdiction where the review is published.[4]

These publications generally consist of two or more major sections. The first section consists of articles on various topics, usually written by law professors and occasionally by practitioners or academics from other disciplines. These articles are typically lengthy, scholarly in nature, and might have a substantial impact in changing the law or in charting the course for newly developing fields of law.[5] Frequently, a law review issue is devoted to a symposium on a particular subject[6] or contains an annual review of the work of a particular court.

The second section, often called "Notes and Comments," is written by law students; the notes consist of critical analyses of recent judicial opinions or legislation [Illustration 18–1], while the comments consist of surveys or critiques of selected subjects of contemporary importance. Many journals also publish book reviews written by legal scholars. These book reviews are critical, detailed expositions that frequently venture beyond an assessment of the book to include the reviewer's personal opinion about the issues raised in the book. These book reviews are frequently lengthy and extensively documented.

Law reviews sometimes also contain "Commentary" sections.[7] These commentaries, which typically undergo little or no student editing and, therefore, can be published more quickly than other pieces, often set forth

---

[4] The HARVARD LAW REVIEW has the largest circulation at approximately 7,500. Most law school law reviews have fewer than 1,500 subscribers. *See* Dunn, *supra* note 3.

[5] *See, e.g.,* Samuel D. Warren & Louis D. Brandeis, *The Right to Privacy,* 4 HARV. L. REV. 193 (1890); William L. Prosser, *The Assault upon the Citadel (Strict Liability to the Consumer),* 69 YALE L.J. 1099 (1960); Akhil Reed Amar, *The Bill of Rights as a Constitution,* 100 YALE L.J. 1131 (1991).

[6] *See* Jean Sefanck, *The Law Review Symposium Issue: Community of Meaning or Reinscription of Hierarchy?,* 63 U. COLO. L. REV. 651 (1992).

[7] For an example of this practice, see *Commentary,* 24 CONN. L. REV. 157 (1991), which contains seven brief articles.

a scholar's position on a controversial topic. Commentaries are sometimes followed in the same or a subsequent issue with responses from other scholars challenging those views. Commentary sections are sometimes entitled "Essays" or "Correspondence."

Historically, law reviews were general in subject; today, only a law school's so-called "flagship" review or journal typically remains general in nature. "Secondary" reviews on specialized subjects, e.g., civil rights, constitutional law, dispute resolution, environmental law, international law, and taxation, or reviews that are interdisciplinary in nature, e.g., law and economics, law and society, law and medicine, etc., now predominate.[8]

Law school reviews have had a high degree of success in providing students with a meaningful research and writing experience,[9] while also serving as a forum for the contributions of the foremost legal scholars.[10] It is not uncommon for courts, including the United States Supreme Court, to cite or quote from law review articles as well as student notes and comments.[11]

Faculty-edited law reviews, similarly subsidized by law schools, differ from student-edited law reviews in that they are "refereed," i.e., selection of an article for inclusion is based on peer review, often with those participating in the evaluative process not knowing the author of the piece—a so-called "blind" review.[12] Some of these highly respected journals include *The American Journal of Legal History, Journal of Legal Studies, Journal of Law and Economics, Law and History Review,* and *Law and Society Review.*

Much has changed in the world of law review publishing in recent years. Notable is the proliferation of subject-oriented and interdisciplinary journals. In 1941, the number of reviews published by American law

---

[8] *See* Tracey E. George & Chris Guthrie, *Symposium: An Empirical Evaluation of Specialized Law Reviews*, 26 FLA. ST. U. L. REV. 813 (1999). A representative listing of subject specific law reviews is available in the DIRECTORY OF LAW REVIEWS (compiled by Michael H. Hoffheimer, 2006), *available at* http://www.lexisnexis.com/lawschool/prodev/lawreview/.

[9] For more on the value of student-edited law reviews, see James W. Harper, *Why Student–Run Law Reviews?*, 82 MINN. L. REV. 1261 (1997).

[10] *See,* e.g., Fred R. Shapiro, *The Most–Cited Law Review Articles*, 73 CAL. L. REV. 1540 (1985); Fred R. Shapiro, *The Most–Cited Articles from* The Yale Law Journal, 100 YALE L.J. 1449 (1991). A book resulted from the first article: THE MOST-CITED LAW REVIEW ARTICLES (Fred R. Shapiro ed., 1987), which collects and reprints the 24 law review articles that have been most cited in other law review articles. For later citation studies, see Fred R. Shapiro, *The Most–Cited Law Review Articles Revisited*, 71 CHI.-KENT L. REV. 751 (1996), and Fred R. Shapiro, *The Most–Cited Law Reviews*, 29 J. LEGAL STUD. 389 (2000). *See also* THE CANON OF AMERICAN LEGAL THOUGHT (David Kennedy & William W. Fisher III eds., 2006).

[11] For more on judicial citation of law reviews, see Richard A. Mann, *The Use of Legal Periodicals by Courts and Journals*, 26 JURIMETRICS J. 400 (1986), and Louis J. Sirico, Jr., *The Citing of Law Reviews by the Supreme Court: 1971–1999*, 75 IND. L.J. 1009 (2000).

There are some indications that the number of law review articles cited in judicial opinions has declined in recent years. *See* Michael D. McClintock, *The Declining Use of Legal Scholarship by the Courts: An Empirical Study*, 51 OKLA. L. REV. 659 (1998); Blake Rohrbacher, *Decline: Twenty–Five Years of Student Scholarship in Judicial Opinions*, 80 AM. BANKR. L.J. 553 (2006); and Sirico, *supra*, at 1001.

[12] For more on the difference between student-edited and faculty-edited law reviews, see Richard A. Epstein, *Faculty–Edited Law Journals*, 70 CHI-KENT L. REV. 87 (1994).

schools totaled 50.[13] Today, students at approximately 200 American Bar Association-accredited law schools publish in excess of 500 titles.[14] Obviously, many schools publish more than one journal, with Columbia leading the way with 14.[15] As authors want to publish their work in the most respected journals, a fair amount of literature is published that attempts to rate the law reviews.[16]

Another recent development is the movement for "open access" to legal scholarship. The effort to make the law more widely accessible has led to new publication models which offer scholarly content on the Internet at no charge.[17]

Although law reviews have numerous virtues, they are not without their critics.[18] The substance of the criticism is usually aimed at their pedantic style, excessive use of footnotes,[19] and their similarity to each other. Indeed, one member of Congress has even attacked law reviews as having an insidious influence on the Supreme Court of the United States.[20] In spite of these criticisms, law school law reviews serve as important vehicles for the publication of significant legal research, as valuable resources for references to additional sources of information, and as incisive and effective teaching tools.

[13] This number is derived from the listing of law reviews in Frederick C. Hicks, Materials and Methods of Legal Research 207–09 (3d rev. ed. 1942).

[14] Directory of Law Reviews, *supra* note 8.

[15] A list of Columbia Law School's student journals is available at http://www.law.columbia.edu/current_student/Law_Journals.

[16] *See, e.g., Chicago-Kent Law Review Faculty Scholarship Survey*, 65 Chi.-Kent L. Rev. 195 (1989); Janet M. Gumm, *Chicago-Kent Law Review Faculty Scholarship Survey*, 66 Chi.-Kent L. Rev. 509 (1990); and Colleen M. Cullen & S. Randall Kalberg, *Chicago-Kent Law Review Faculty Scholarship Survey*, 70 Chi.-Kent L. Rev. 1445 (1995) (three Chicago–Kent studies ranking the leading law reviews based on frequency of citation, as well as the amount of scholarship by law school faculties in those leading reviews); Robert M. Jarvis & Phyllis Coleman, *Ranking Law Reviews: An Empirical Analysis Based on Author Prominence*, 39 Ariz. L. Rev. 15 (1997); Robert M. Jarvis & Phyllis Coleman, *Ranking Law Reviews by Author Prominence—Ten Years Later*, 99 Law Libr. J. 573 (2007) (two studies ranking student-edited law reviews based on the prominence of the lead article authors); John Doyle, *Ranking Legal Periodicals and Some Other Numeric Uses of the Westlaw and Lexis Legal Periodical Databases*, 23(2/3) Legal Reference Services Q., 2004, at 1 (examines the use of full-text periodical databases on *Westlaw* and *LexisNexis* for statistical analysis, particularly in ranking legal periodicals).

A database containing the results of all of these studies is available at Washington and Lee School of Law's *Law Journals: Submissions and Ranking* site. *See* http://lawlib.wlu.edu/LJ/.

[17] For a further discussion of open access article repositories, see Section A–6–e below.

[18] *See, e.g.,* Fred Rodell, *Goodbye to Law Reviews*, 23 Va. L. Rev. 38 (1936); Fred Rodell, *Goodbye to Law Reviews—Revisited*, 48 Va. L. Rev. 279 (1962); Roger C. Cramton, *"The Most Remarkable Institution": The American Law Review*, 36 J. Legal Educ. 1 (1986); James Lindgren, *Student Editing: Using Education to Move Beyond Struggle*, 70 Chi.-Kent L. Rev. 95 (1994); Richard A. Posner, *The Future of the Student–Edited Law Review*, 47 Stan. L. Rev. 1131 (1995); Harry T. Edwards, *The Growing Disjunction Between Legal Education and the Legal Profession*, 91 Mich. L. Rev. 34 (1992).

[19] The current record, as of December 2008, is 4,824 established by Arnold S. Jacobs, *An Analysis of Section 16 of the Securities Act of 1934*, 32 N.Y.L. Sch. L. Rev. 209 (1987).

[20] 103 Cong. Rec. 16,159–62 (1957) (statement of Rep. Patman) (characterizing legal writing as "an organized form of lobbying").

2. Subject, Special Interest, and Interdisciplinary Legal Journals

As the literature of the law proliferates and reflects the growing complexity of society, it is more difficult for lawyers to remain current with developments of the law and their own particular legal interests. As the law becomes more complex, the practice of law becomes more specialized. Many legal periodicals now target particular subgroups within the legal profession. Law schools publish some of these subject or audience-specific periodicals which are edited by students or faculty members and follow the format of the traditional law review. Nonprofit associations and commercial publishing companies publish others, in ever-increasing numbers. Another recent development is the publication of periodicals devoted to law and its interaction with other disciplines.

a. *Subject Journals.* Journals devoted to one area of law vary in scope from the very practical to the very theoretical. *TAXES—The Tax Magazine* and *Trusts and Estates,* both published commercially, are examples of periodicals aimed primarily at practicing attorneys specializing in specific fields of law. These publications contain articles written by well-known practitioners interpreting the impact of recent legislation and judicial opinions. Many commercially published subject journals contain reviews of books within their subject area. *The American Journal of International Law* and *The American Journal of Comparative Law* are examples of periodicals published under the auspices of learned societies, while *Ecology Law Quarterly,* published at the University of California at Berkeley School of Law, and *The Review of Litigation,* published at the University of Texas School of Law, are typical of subject journals that are similar to traditional law school reviews.

b. *Special Interest Journals.* These periodicals are aimed at those members of the legal community who have similar interests and serve as a means to encourage writing and research within the special area of interest. They include such journals as *The Catholic Lawyer, The Judges' Journal, National Black Law Journal, Berkeley La Raza Law Journal, The Scribes Journal of Legal Writing,* and *Women Lawyers' Journal.*

c. *Interdisciplinary Journals.* These interdisciplinary periodicals reflect the increasing emphasis many law schools and legal and non-legal scholars place on integrating the findings and methods of the social and behavioral sciences with the legal process. Perhaps the most distinguished of this group is *Journal of Law and Economics,* published by the faculty of the University of Chicago School of Law. Other representative titles are *Journal of Law & Politics, Law & Society Review, The Journal of Law and Religion, The Journal of Legal Medicine, Law & Psychology Review,* and *Yale Journal of Law & the Humanities.*

3. Bar Association Periodicals

All states and the District of Columbia have bar associations.[21] In some states, membership is voluntary; in other states, those having what is called an *integrated bar,* membership is a prerequisite to practicing law within the state. Many counties and large cities also have their own local

---

[21] For a complete list of bar associations, see the latest American Bar Association Directory, which is published annually.

bar associations. Most national and state bar associations, sections within these associations, and many local and specialized bar groups publish periodicals. These publications vary in scope from such distinguished periodicals as the *ABA Journal* and *The Record of the Association of the Bar of the City of New York* to those that are little more than newsletters.

The primary purposes of bar association publications are to inform the membership of the association's activities, to comment on pending and recent legislation, and to review current local judicial opinions. Articles in bar association publications tend to focus more on practical aspects of the law, with an emphasis on problem solving, rather than on theoretical issues. These publications serve a different audience and perform a different function than do academic journals. Accordingly, when compared with law reviews, bar association publications generally have less theoretical value, but are more useful when researching subjects of current interest to practitioners.

4. Legal Newspapers

Legal newspapers can be national, state, or local in focus and are frequently available electronically as well as in print form.[22] Two weekly legal newspapers that are national in scope—*Legal Times* and *The National Law Journal*—began in 1978. These legal newspapers contain articles and regular columns pertaining to a variety of issues and are valuable sources for fast-breaking legal developments. The monthly *The American Lawyer,* which began publication in 1979 and is also national in scope, tends to focus on events at large firms. The *Corporate Legal Times*, launched in 1990, is an example of a monthly, national newspaper with a subject focus. *Lawyers Weekly USA,* started in 1993, is a biweekly national newspaper that places special emphasis on the needs of the smaller law firm.

Legal newspapers are published for many states. These are typically issued either weekly or monthly and concentrate on legal matters of particular importance in the state. They often contain articles of both state and national interest, synopses of cases, and reports of disciplinary proceedings. Examples include *The Connecticut Law Tribune, Massachusetts Lawyers Weekly, Wisconsin Law Journal,* and *The Texas Lawyer.*

The legal community within some large cities support newspapers devoted to the legal affairs of that metropolitan area. These local legal newspapers are generally published each business day, and primarily contain information on court calendars and dockets, changes in court rules, legal notices, news about recent changes in legislation and administrative rules, and stories about local judges and lawyers. Some of these larger publications, such as *New York Law Journal* and *The Los Angeles Daily Journal,* also publish reports of current judicial opinions and articles on various legal topics.

5. Newsletters

While the number of subject-matter journals has grown rapidly, the publication of topical newsletters has also expanded dramatically. As law

---

[22] A list of legal newspapers is available in the annual GALE DIRECTORY OF PUBLICATIONS and in a separate volume of the annual ULRICH'S PERIODICALS DIRECTORY.

has become more specialized, subject-matter newsletters by commercial publishers and law firms have flourished. One would be hard-pressed to find a subject area of the law that is not served by at least one newsletter. These publications are typically issued weekly or monthly, consist of only a few pages, and focus on the most recent trends and developments in a particular area of the law. Rarely do they contain an index and even more rarely are they indexed by the major indexing publications. Their value lies in providing the practitioner with current awareness information.[23]

6. Electronic Access to Legal Periodicals

The role electronic legal research vendors and the Internet play in providing access to legal periodical information is notable. Vendors such as *Westlaw*, *LexisNexis*, and *HeinOnline* continue to expand their coverage of legal periodicals. An increasing amount of scholarly content is also freely available on the World Wide Web, both on journal websites and in article repositories such as *SSRN* and *bepress*.

a. *Westlaw and LexisNexis.* The full text of many legal periodical articles is available in *Westlaw* and *LexisNexis*. This means that articles can be searched on both systems using Boolean logic or natural language searches. Since the legal periodical indexes described in the next section of this chapter cannot capture all the nuances of an article in the subject headings assigned to it, full-text electronic access greatly enhances one's ability to locate topics discussed within the articles.

One of the larger databases in *Westlaw* is Law Reviews, Texts & Bar Journals which contains law reviews, bar journals, *American Law Reports*, legal texts and more. The Journals & Law Reviews database is a subset of the larger database. Each law review or journal title can also be searched separately in *Westlaw*.[24]

The largest legal periodicals database in *LexisNexis* is Law Reviews, CLE, Legal Journals & Periodicals, Combined. Smaller subsets, such as the *US Law Reviews and Journals, Combined* database are also available. Like *Westlaw*, each law review or journal title can also be searched separately in *LexisNexis*.[25]

Today, the two electronic legal research vendors follow a similar philosophy as to how legal periodical articles are added to their services. From the beginning, it has been *LexisNexis'* policy to add the complete full-text coverage of each title it carries. Although *Westlaw* currently also offers

---

[23] The best source for identifying commercial publications is the annual LEGAL NEWSLETTERS IN PRINT, which contains over 2,200 titles published in the United States. Published by Infosources Publishing, it is available both in print and electronically. Many commercial newsletters are available electronically via *Westlaw* and *LexisNexis*.

Increasingly, law firm are making their newsletters available via the Internet. There are several repositories for legal newsletters, including *Lexology* (http://www.lexology.com/), *Linex Legal* (http://www.linexlegal.com/), and *Mondaq* (http://www.mondaq.com/).

[24] A directory of *Westlaw* databases is available at http://directory.westlaw.com/.

[25] A directory of *LexisNexis* databases is available at http://w3.nexis.com/sources/.

Note that on both *Westlaw* and *LexisNexis* it is more time and cost efficient to search the smallest database that meets a researcher's needs. *See* Chapter 23 of this book for further explanation.

complete full-text coverage of each of its titles, this is a change from its initial selection policy; until 1994, only selected works of national interest were offered in full text. In both *Westlaw* and *LexisNexis*, dates of coverage for legal periodicals vary from the early 1980s to the most recent issue.

Although coverage is not comprehensive in either *Westlaw* or *LexisNexis*, both continue to add law reviews, journals, and related materials to their services. Coverage is by no means limited to traditional law reviews, as legal newspapers, bar journals, commercial legal periodicals, and newsletters are also included in the databases.

b. *HeinOnline. HeinOnline* is a collaborative project of William S. Hein & Co., and Cornell Information Technologies (Cornell University). It is best known for its Law Journal Library, which offers electronic access to legal periodicals dating back to the first issue of every title it carries. Much of this older content is not available through *Westlaw* and *LexisNexis*. *HeinOnline* includes almost 1,200 legal periodical titles with approximately 19 million pages. All content is available in the original page-image (PDF) which is especially useful for citation checking.

HeinOnline continues to expand its content. In addition to the Law Journal Library, *HeinOnline* offers many other libraries, such as a collection of classic legal texts, state and federal session laws, congressional documents, the *Code of Federal Regulations* and the *Federal Register*, U.S. Supreme Court opinions, a collection of U.S. treaties and more. *HeinOnline* has also recently added *Index to Legal Periodicals Related to Law*, which is discussed in Section E–6 of this chapter.

The *HeinOnline Law Journal Library* provides multiple searching capabilities. In addition to a citation search and a basic full-text keyword search, an advanced search feature is available. Advanced search offers the ability to limit a search by a specific field (title, author, etc.), subject, date, and/or section (articles, comments, notes, etc.). *HeinOnline* also supports Boolean logic (and, or, not), proximity connectors, phrase searching and word truncation.

c. *Index to Legal Periodicals Full Text* (ILP). The *Index to Legal Periodicals*, which began in 1908, is a product of the H.W. Wilson Company. *ILP* indexes approximately 1,025 English language legal periodicals; full text is available for over 325 periodicals. *ILP* is covered in more detail in section B of this chapter.

d. *Internet.* Increasingly, legal scholarship is being made available at no cost on the Internet. Many law schools are simultaneously publishing their journals electronically and in print. A few law reviews are published exclusively on the Internet, e.g., *Richmond Journal of Law & Technology*. This enables users to access these sources electronically without having to rely on costly electronic legal research services.

To bridge the gap between the slow-moving pace of traditional scholarship and the fast-paced world of blogs, several law reviews have created Internet companions to their regular print issues. These companions typically contain very short commentaries on emerging legal issues. *See, e.g., Harvard Law Review Forum*; Michigan Law Review's *First Impressions*; *Northwestern University Law Review Colloquy*; *UCLA Law Review Dis-*

course; University of Pennsylvania Law Review's *PENNumbra*; Virginia Law Review's *In Brief*; *The Yale Law Journal Pocket Part*.

There are several portals to legal journal content available on the Web, including law review directories from the *University of Southern California School of Law*[26] and *FindLaw*.[27] The most robust source, however, is *Current Law Journal Content (CLJC)*[28] from Washington and Lee School of Law. It offers a searchable database of law journal content, tables of contents for issues, and customized delivery via email and RSS.[29] *CLJC* is discussed more in section B–4 of this chapter.

e. *Repositories*. The desire to make the law more widely accessible, combined with the increasing price of journal subscriptions, has fueled the movement for "open access" to legal scholarship. Open access refers to the electronic publication of scholarly content that is made available at no charge without copyright constraints other than attribution.[30] In 2008, Harvard Law School became the first law school to commit to a mandatory open access policy.[31]

Open access content is often distributed through digital scholarship repositories. Many universities have developed such repositories to collect, preserve, and disseminate the intellectual output of the institution. Other repositories are consortial, such as the *NELLCO Legal Scholarship Repository*.[32]

Many of these institutional repositories are built upon tools developed by the *Berkeley Electronic Press (bepress)*.[33] Founded by academics from the University of California at Berkeley in 1999, *bepress* is a private, for-profit corporation which offers a portfolio of products and services to improve scholarly communication.[34] In addition to institutional repositories, bepress also hosts several subject matter repositories. The *bepress* legal repository features approximately 3,500 papers from scholars and researchers at major national and international law departments, firms, and associations.[35] Anyone can download and read these papers at no cost. A free email alert service, which notifies subscribers of new content in specific subject areas, is also available.

[26] http://law.usc.edu/library/resources/journals.cfm.

[27] http://stu.findlaw.com/journals/general.html.

[28] http://lawlib.wlu.edu/CLJC/.

[29] RSS, or really simple syndication, is a format for distributing Web content.

[30] Paul George, *Members' Briefing: The Future Gate to Scholarly Legal Information*, AALL SPECTRUM (April 2005). For more on the open access movement, see Michael W. Carroll, *The Movement for Open Access Law*, 10 LEWIS & CLARK L. REV. 741 (2006); Richard A. Danner, *Applying the Access Principle in Law: The Responsibilities of the Legal Scholar*, 35 INT'L J. LEGAL INFO. 355 (2007).

[31] Press Release, Harvard Law School, Harvard Law Faculty Votes for "Open Access" to Scholarly Articles (May 7, 2008), http://www.law.harvard.edu/news/2008/05/07_openaccess.php.

[32] http://lsr.nellco.org/.

[33] http://www.bepress.com/.

[34] *bepress* also offers article submission and editorial management services and publishes several online journals.

[35] http://law.bepress.com/repository/.

The largest repository of legal scholarship is the *Social Science Research Network (SSRN)*, established in 1994. *SSRN* is a worldwide, for-profit collaborative effort devoted to the rapid dissemination of social science research.[36] *SSRN* is composed of a number of specialized research networks in the social sciences. One of these, the *Legal Scholarship Network (LSN)*, focuses on research related to law, economics, and business. To date, more than 61,000 law-related papers and abstracts have been uploaded to *SSRN*.[37] Most of these are made available to readers at no cost.[38]

SSRN also offers two types of email abstracting services. The first type, sponsored by individual universities, distributes abstracts of new papers published by the school's faculty. Universities pay *SSRN* to distribute this content; readers may subscribe and download papers at no cost. The other type of abstracting service, produced by *SSRN*, selects papers and abstracts submitted to *SSRN* on particular subject areas and distributes them to subscribers.[39] There is a fee to subscribe to this service; however, many institutions purchase a site license for their users.

SECTION B.   COMPREHENSIVE PERIODICAL INDEXES

The usefulness of legal periodicals to legal research depends almost entirely on the researcher's ability to find what articles have been written and where they have been published. Generally, it is necessary to rely on indexes to legal periodical literature for this purpose.

1.   Jones & Chipman's Index to Legal Periodicals

The *Jones & Chipman's Index to Legal Periodicals* was the first index that attempted to provide a comprehensive and systematic index to English language legal periodicals. It is available electronically through *19th Century Masterfile*, a collection of indexes covering nineteenth-century periodicals and newspapers. This electronic edition of *Jones & Chipman's* indexes legal periodicals and Law Report titles from 1786–1922.

The coverage for the print edition of *Jones & Chipman's* is somewhat larger. It contains six volumes which index periodicals published from 1786 to 1937. The first three volumes, which cover the years 1786 to 1907, precede the more extensive *Index to Legal Periodicals* that began in 1908 and is discussed below. Therefore, these first three volumes of *Jones & Chipman's* should be consulted to locate articles prior to 1908.

2.   Index to Legal Periodicals (ILP)

The *Index to Legal Periodicals* was begun in 1908 by the American Association of Law Libraries and was jointly managed by the AALL and the

---

[36] http://www.ssrn.com/.

[37] The primary motivation for many legal scholars to post their works to *SSRN* and *bepress* is to make their new works widely known as quickly as possible. Both services track the number of times papers are downloaded. *SSRN* makes these statistics public whereas only authors can view them on *bepress*. There is no cost to scholars to upload papers in either *SSRN* or *bepress*.

[38] *SSRN* hosts some content provided by other organizations. There may be a fee to access this material.

[39] *SSRN* refers to these abstracts as "subject matter journals."

H.W. Wilson Company for many years. Today it is owned and managed solely by Wilson. Until 1980, *ILP* was the only extensive index of legal periodical articles.

ILP indexes English language legal periodicals published in the United States, Canada, Great Britain, Ireland, Australia, and New Zealand. Journals indexed must regularly publish legal articles of high quality and of permanent reference value.

There are three electronic *ILP* products: *Index to Legal Periodicals Full Text*; *Index to Legal Periodicals & Books*; and *Index to Legal Periodicals Retrospective*. *Index to Legal Periodicals Full Text* indexes approximately 1,050 legal periodicals from 1982 to the present. Books are indexed beginning in 1994. Over 350 periodicals are also available in full text from 1994 to date.

Index to Legal Periodicals & Books presents the same indexing offered in *Index to Legal Periodicals Full Text*, but without links to full-text articles. The same journals are covered. *Index to Legal Periodicals Retrospective* indexes almost 900 legal periodicals from 1908–1981.

The electronic *ILP* products offer an array of fully searchable fields: keyword, subject heading, court case, statute, jurisdiction, personal name, date, title words, article type, publisher, country of publication, or any combination thereof. *ILP* also supports Boolean logic (and, or, not), proximity connectors, phrase searching, word truncation, and natural language searching.

ILP Full Text and *ILP Retrospective* are available exclusively from Wilson via *WilsonWeb*, their Internet product. *Index to Legal Periodicals & Books*, however, is accessible through both *WilsonWeb* and by CD–ROM. The *ILP & Books* index is also available to subscribers of *LexisNexis*, *Westlaw*, and several other services.

The print edition of *ILP* is issued monthly with quarterly and annual cumulations. From 1908 to 1993, the print edition is titled *Index to Legal Periodicals*. Beginning in 1994 when monographs were added to the index, the title was changed to *Index to Legal Periodicals & Books*.

There are four different access points to the print edition of *ILP*.

a. *Subject and Author Index*. Authors and subjects are included in one index with complete citation information under each entry. [Illustration 18–2]

b. *Table of Cases*. The table of cases lists the names of cases (for the time period covered by the issue or volume) that have had a note or comment written on them. [Illustration 18–3]

c. *Table of Statutes*. The table of statutes lists statutes about which a periodical article or book has been written.

d. *Book Review Index*. The book review index lists the author of books reviewed in the periodicals indexed by *ILP*. [Illustration 18–4]

3. Current Law Index (CLI), LegalTrac, and Legal Resource Index (LRI)

These three indexes, formerly produced by Information Access Company and now by Gale Cengage Learning, are published under the auspices of the American Association of Law Libraries (AALL), with an AALL advisory committee assisting with content selection. As described below, the three titles used for these indexes reflect their different formats and, in some instances, slightly different coverage.

The indexes include publications from the United States, Canada, the United Kingdom, Ireland, Australia, New Zealand, and the European Union. The publications are primarily English language, although some French and Spanish titles are also included.

The three indexes are:

a. *Current Law Index (CLI). Current Law Index* is a printed index issued monthly with quarterly and annual cumulations. It indexes approximately 1,000 academic reviews, bar association journals, specialty journals and selected journals in allied disciplines. It covers the years 1980 to the present.

Each of the first seven volumes consists of a single book. Beginning with volume 8 (1987), *CLI* is published in two parts: Part A includes the subject index, while Part B includes an index by author/title and tables of cases and statutes. A four-volume cumulative subject index is available for the years 1991–1995.

CLI offers several different access points:

(1) *Subject Index*. The subject heading list organizes entries by subject, including personal and proper names that are the subject of articles. [Illustration 18–5]

(2) *Author/Title Index*. This section alphabetically lists all articles by author, with full title and periodical citation. [Illustration 18–6]

(3) *Book Reviews*. Book reviews that appear in the periodicals covered by *CLI* are indexed under the author and title of the book and the author of the review.

(4) *Table of Cases*. Judicial opinions that are the subject of case notes are listed under the names of both plaintiff and defendant.

(5) *Table of Statutes*. This table sets forth all statutes cited in articles, by both official citation and popular name. [Illustration 18–7]

b. *LegalTrac. LegalTrac* is Gale Cengage's electronic counterpart to *Current Law Index*. It includes all titles in *CLI* plus several major legal newspapers. Searches can be conducted in "Basic" or "Advanced" formats. A "Basic" search enables the researcher to search keywords from titles, authors, abstracts, and subjects. An "Advanced" search allows the user to limit the search by journal and date and to search within various database fields, such as author, title and subject. *LegalTrac* supports Boolean logic, proximity connectors, phrase searching, and word truncation.

c. *Legal Resource Index (LRI). Legal Resource Index* is the name given to *LegalTrac* when it is made available through third party vendors, such as *Westlaw* and *LexisNexis*. The content available in *LRI* is identical to *LegalTrac,* except that it includes a few additional years of coverage. Coverage for *LegalTrac* and *CLI* begins in 1980 whereas *LRI* extends back to 1977 for select publications.

4. Current Law Journal Content (CLJC)

Current Law Journal Content from Washington and Lee University School of Law is a free service which indexes articles from over 1,350 current law journals.[40] Most journals are indexed from 2005 to the present; *CLJC* is working to extend the index back to 2000.

CLJC collects the journal tables of contents from a mixture of paper and electronic sources compiled by Washington and Lee and the University of Texas Tarlton Law Library. It includes English language publications from the United States, Canada, the United Kingdom, Ireland, Australia, New Zealand, and more.

The tables of contents available in *CLJC* may be browsed by journal name, country, and/or date. *CLJC* supports Boolean searching by keyword, author, title, journal name, and/or date. Results may be sorted alphabetically, chronologically, or by journal score or ranking, as listed in Washington & Lee's *Law Journals: Submissions and Ranking* list.[41] Note that not all journals are ranked.

In addition to citation information for each article, *CLJC* also offers an OpenURL resolver which launches an automated search for the full-text if available in a subscription database such as *HeinOnline*.[42] [Illustration 18–8] Users of *CLJC* may also establish a profile which will allow them to receive a customized weekly email or RSS feed notifying them of new content in their choice of journals.

5. Current Awareness Publications

a. *Current Index to Legal Periodicals (CILP)*. The *Current Index to Legal Periodicals* is produced weekly by the Marian G. Gallagher Law Library of the University of Washington. It indexes law journal articles approximately four to six weeks before they are indexed by commercial sources such as *Current Law Index* or *Index to Legal Periodicals & Books*. Articles are organized within 100 relevant subject headings and complete tables of contents of all journals indexed are included. *CILP* is available both electronically and in print. Recent issues are available on *Westlaw*.

CILP also offers a customizable email service called *SmartCILP* which alerts users to new articles matching their individual research interests. It includes links to the full-text article in *Westlaw* and *LexisNexis* when available.

b. *Contents Pages from Law Reviews and Other Scholarly Journals.* This free service is provided by the Tarlton Law Library at the University of Texas School of Law.[43] This tool helps researchers keep up-to-date about articles in the over 750 law reviews received by the library. A three-month archive is maintained online, after which the articles are available in standard law review indexing services. English-language journals are in-

[40] http://lawlib.wlu.edu/CLJC/.

[41] http://lawlib.wlu.edu/LJ/.

[42] An OpenURL is a type of URL that contains metadata about an article, book or other resource rather than the physical Web location of the item. The OpenURL retains a permanent identification to a resource no matter where it resides.

[43] http://tarlton.law.utexas.edu/tallons/content_search.html.

dexed under two categories, U.S. and non-U.S. Simple keyword searching is available for the archive.

c. *In-house law library publications*. Many libraries, agencies, firms, and other groups of legal professionals publish their own in-house newsletters designed to alert users to the most recent articles in legal periodicals by reproducing their contents pages.

6. Annual Legal Bibliography

Published by the Harvard Law Library from 1961 to 1981, this source indexed both the books and articles the library received. Over 2,000 periodicals were covered.

SECTION C.   ILLUSTRATIONS: LEGAL PERIODICALS AND INDEXES

18–1.   **Page from 65 Missouri Law Review 1101 (2000)**
18–2.   **Page from Subject and Author Index, Index to Legal Periodicals & Books**
18–3.   **Page from Table of Cases, Index to Legal Periodicals & Books**
18–4.   **Page from Book Reviews, Index to Legal Periodicals & Books**
18–5.   **Page from Subject Index, Current Law Index**
18–6.   **Page from Author/Title Index, Current Law Index**
18–7.   **Page from Table of Statutes, Current Law Index**
18–8.   **Screen Print, "Current Law Journal Content," Washington and Lee University School of Law**

[Illustration 18–1]

PAGE FROM 65 MISSOURI LAW REVIEW 1101 (2000)

The Learned Intermediary Doctrine in the Age of Direct Consumer Advertising

Doe v. Alpha Therapeutic Corp.[1]

I. INTRODUCTION

Traditionally drug manufacturers have been excused from the general duty to warn consumers about the risks associated with their products by the learned intermediary doctrine.[2] Though the doctrine has a sound grounding in public policy, drug companies have recently employed marketing strategies that undermine the usefulness of the learned intermediary rule. In *Doe v. Alpha Therapeutic Corp.*, the Missouri Court of Appeals for the Eastern District of Missouri recently addressed whether the learned intermediary doctrine can be used as a defense when a drug company markets a product directly to consumers. This Note discusses the learned intermediary defense and its applicability to drug companies that engage in direct-to-consumer advertising.

II. FACTS AND HOLDING

Doe v. Alpha Therapeutic Corp. was a consolidated lawsuit brought by hemophiliac patients against a pharmaceutical company.[3] As part of their

> This is an example of a relevant student Note located using the *Index to Legal Periodicals & Books* and the *Current Law Index*. Illustrations 18-2, 18-3, 18-5, and 18-6 show how this item can be located.

stepped up efforts to protect hemophilia patients from AIDS. The newsletter also noted that scientists had uncovered evidence that suggested AIDS was not necessarily associated with blood or blood products, even though by the summer of 1983, in the words of the court, "it was clear that AIDS was transmitted through blood and that hemophiliacs were being exposed to the disease through contaminated blood products used to treat their condition."[7]

---

1. 3 S.W.3d 404 (Mo. Ct. App. 1999).
2. For an explanation of the learned intermediary doctrine, see *infra* Part III.A.
3. *Alpha Therapeutic*, 3 S.W.3d at 406-07.
4. *Id.* at 408. Hemophilia is a genetic disease characterized by a deficiency in Factor VIII, a protein that aids blood in clotting. Because hemophiliacs do not have Factor VIII, their blood cannot clot and therefore they are unable to control hemorrhaging. Factor VIII concentrate is manufactured by drawing blood from donors, extracting the Factor VIII protein and concentrating it. *Id.* at 407.
5. *Id.* at 408.
6. *Id.* at 409.
7. *Id.*

[Illustration 18–2]

PAGE FROM SUBJECT AND AUTHOR INDEX, INDEX TO LEGAL PERIODICALS & BOOKS

SUBJECT AND AUTHOR INDEX   225

Lawrence, Susan E., 1957-

See/See also the following book(s):
Law and politics in the Supreme Court: cases and readings; Susan E. Lawrence. rev, 2nd ed Kendall/Hunt Pub. Co 2000 x, 669p 1 map
ISBN 0-7872-6732-5   LC 99-68674

Lawrence, William H.
A lessor's meaningful residual interest: using trac leases as an object lesson; by W. H. Lawrence, J. H. Minan. 33 no3 *UCC L.J.* 291-343 Wint 2001

Lawson, Charles
Patenting genetic materials: old rules may be restricting the exploitation of a new technology. 6 no4 *J.L. & Med.* 373-88 My 1999

Lawson, Gary
The Hobbesian constitution: governing without authority; by G. Lawson, G. Seidman. 95 no2 *Nw. U. L. Rev.* 581-628 Wint 2001

Lawton, Anne
The meritocracy myth and the illusion of equal employment opportunity. 85 no2 *Minn. L. Rev.* 587-662 D 2000

Lawyers *See* Attorneys

Lawyers and reporters; understanding and working with the media; Robert L. Rothman, editor. Section of Litigation, American Bar Association 1999 xxv, 174p
ISBN 1-570-73763-0   LC 99-53908

Laycock, Douglas
The clear and present danger test. 25 no2 *J. Sup. Ct. Hist.* 161-86 200

Lazarus, Theodore
The Maine Clean Election Act: cleansing public institutions of private money. 34 no1 *Colum. J.L. & Soc. Probs.* 79-132 Fall 2000

Lazarow, Herbert I.

When commencing research in an index, always start with the most specific word or phrase. Note how entries for authors and subjects are in one alphabet.

Reflections on legal education. 30 pt2 *Hong Kong L.J.* 329-44 2000

Le Moal-Gray, Michele J.
Distance education and intellectual property: the realities of copyright law and the culture of higher education. 16 no3 *Touro L. Rev.* 981-1035 Spr 2000

Leach, Eric D.
Everything you always wanted to know about digital performance rights but were afraid to ask. 48 no1/2 *J. Copyright Soc'y U.S.A.* 191-291 Fall/Wint 2000

Leach, James A.
Introduction: modernization of financial institutions. 25 no4 *J. Corp. L.* 681-90 Summ 2000

Leadstrom, Nathan D.
Sanders v. American Broadcasting Companies, Inc. [85 Cal. Rptr. 2d 909 (Cal. 1999)]: does it mean the end to the use of hidden cameras in undercover media investigations? 40 no1 *Washburn L.J.* 143-68 Fall 2000

Leahy, Edward R.
The changing face of international arbitration; by E. R. Leahy, C. J. Bianchi. 17 no4 *J. Int'l Arb.* 19-61 Ag 2000

Lear, Bradford B.
The learned intermediary doctrine in the age of direct consumer advertising. 65 no4 *Mo. L. Rev.* 1101-17 Fall 2000

Learned Intermediary doctrine
Drug and device litigation in the 21st century. L. S. Syitak, P. J. Goss. 27 no1 *Wm. Mitchell L. Rev.* 271-98 2000
The gradual enfeeblement of the learned intermediary rule and the argument in favor of abandoning it entirely. J. O. Castagnera, R. R. Gerner. 36 no1 *Tort & Ins. L.J.* 119-46 Fall 2000
Offense or defense? Managing the off-label use claim. P. D. Rheingold, D. B. Rheingold. 37 no3 *Trial* 52-7 Mr 2001
Missouri
Breaking down the boundaries of malpractice law. P. G. Peters, Jr. 65 no4 *Mo. L. Rev.* 1047-53 Fall 2000
The learned intermediary doctrine in the age of direct consumer advertising. B. B. Lear, student author. 65 no4 *Mo. L. Rev.* 1101-17 Fall 2000
New Jersey
Perez v. Wyeth Labs., Inc. [734 A.2d 1245 (N.J. 1999)]: toward creating a direct-to-consumer advertisement exception to the learned intermediary doctrine. Y. D. Fushman, student author. 80 no4 *B.U. L. Rev.* 1161-83 O 2000
A tale of six implants: the Perez v. Wyeth Laboratories [734 A.2d 1245 (N.J. 1999)] Norplant case and the applicability of the learned intermediary doctrine to direct-to-consumer drug promotion. M. S. Berger, student author. 55 no4 *Food & Drug L.J.* 525-74 2000

Leary, Thomas B.
Freedom as the core value of antitrust in the new millennium. 68 no2 *Antitrust L.J.* 545-57 2000

Leary, Virginia A.
Challenging power. Civil society at the gates of the WTO: the view from Geneva. 93 *Am. Soc'y Int'l L. Proc.* 186-9 1999

Leases

See also
Equipment leasing
Eviction

At long last—the final Section 467 regulations. J. R. Shorter, Jr. 53 no2 *Tax Law.* 383-430 Wint 2000
The effect of a cross-default provision on the ability to assume an executory contract or unexpired lease. A. N. Resnick, B. E. Scheler. 32 no3 *UCC L.J.* 338-43 Wint 2000
Real estate leases in bankruptcy: landlord/tenant issues under the Bankruptcy Code. D. S. Kupetz. 2000 *Ann. Surv. Bankr. L.* 79-106 2000/2001
Section 365. L. Afarin. 2000 *Ann. Surv. Bankr. L.* 401-14 2000/2001
Subleases: the same thing as leases, only different. A. L. Herz, R. G. Wohl. 35 no3 *Real Prop. Prob. & Tr. J.* 667-96 Fall 2000
Tax Court precludes Service from considering TRAC provisions, allowing lessees to keep truckin': Peaden v. Commissioner [113 T.C. 116 (1999)] K. McCauley, student author. 53 no2 *Tax Law.* 563-9 Wint 2000

See/See also the following book(s):
Goldman, G. Drafting a fair office lease. 2nd ed American Law Institute-American Bar Association Committee on Continuing Professional Education 2000 xix, 384p forms, 1 computer optical disc (4 3/4 in.)
Australia
Lessee's ancillary rights. P. W. Young. 74 no6 *Austl. L.J.* 384-90 Je 2000

at will. London Baggage Company v. Railtrack Plc April 17, 2000. M. Haley. 2001 *J. Bus. L.* 91-6 Ja 2001
Caveat lessee. P. Giliker. 8 no2 *Tort L. Rev.* 95-9 Jl 2000
Cum grano salis? AGAs and lease renewals under the Landlord and Tenant Act 1954 (Pt.2). P. Luxton. 2001 *J. Bus. L.* 84-91 Ja 2001
Enforcing restrictive covenants in leases: the case of County Hall [Oceanic Village Ltd. v. United Attractions Ltd., [2000] Ch. 234] S. Bridge. 59 pt3 *Cambridge L.J.* 450-3 N 2000
The non-proprietary lease: the rise of the feudal phoenix. M. Dixon. 59 pt1 *Cambridge L.J.* 25-8 Mr 2000
Once upon a time. M. Robinson. 115 *Law Q. Rev.* 389-93 Jl 1999
Unilateral demise by a joint tenant: does it effect a severance? L. Fox. 64 *Conv. & Prop. Law. (n.s.)* 208-28 My/Je 2000
Pennsylvania
Contracts vs. conveyances: a criticism of Stonehedge Square Ltd. Partnership v. Movie Merchants, Inc. [715 A.2d 1082 (Pa. 1998)] L. R. Kerszencwejg, student author. 61 no2 *U. Pitt. L. Rev.* 559-77 Wint 2000

Leawoods, Heather
Gustav Radbruch: an extraordinary legal philosopher. 2 *Wash. U. J. L. & Pol'y* 489-515 2000

Lederer, Fredric I.
The effect of courtroom technologies on and in appellate proceedings and courtrooms. 2 no2 *J. Appellate Prac. & Process* 251-74 Summ 2000

See/See also the following book(s):
Court-martial procedure; Francis A. Gilligan, Fredric I. Lederer. 2nd ed Lexis Law Pub 1999 3 vp forms
ISBN 0-327-04919-7   LC 99-68783

Lee, Jessica

See/See also the following book(s):
The practitioner's guide to Colorado employment law; Sean R. Gallagher & Kathryn E. Miller, managing editors ; Jessica Lee, senior editor. Continuing Legal Education in Colorado 1998 1 v (loose-leaf)p forms
LC 00-710977

Lee, Lawrence L. C.
Taiwan's current banking development strategy: preparing for internationalization by preventing insider lending. 17 no2/3 *UCLA Pac. Basin L.J.* 166-225 Fall 1999/Spr 2000

Lee, Lila
FACT's fantasies and feminism's future: an analysis of the fact brief's treatment of pornography victims. 75 no3 *Chi.-Kent L. Rev.* 785-804 2000

Lee, Maria
Civil liability of the nuclear industry. 12 no3 *J. Envtl. L.* 317-32 2000

[Illustration 18–3]

PAGE FROM TABLE OF CASES, INDEX TO LEGAL PERIODICALS & BOOKS

400   INDEX TO LEGAL PERIODICALS & BOOKS

Dimond v. Lovell, [2000] 2 All E.R. 897
   2001 *J. Bus. L.* 14-32 Ja 2001
Dimsey; R. v., [1999] S.T.C. 846
   59 pt1 *Cambridge L.J.* 42-5 Mr 2000
Director of Immigration; Ling v., [1999] 1 H.K.L.R.D. 315
   10 no1 *Pac. Rim L. & Pol'y J.* 111-46 D 2000
Director of Pub. Prosecutions v. Majewski, [1976] 2 All E.R. 142
   2000 *Crim. L. Rev.* 719-33 S 2000
Director of Public Prosecutions, ex parte Kebilene; R. v., [1999] 3 W.L.R. 972
   59 pt1 *Cambridge L.J.* 1-3 Mr 2000
Dixon, In re, 228 B.R. 166 (W.D. Va. 1998)
   32 no2 *UCC L.J.* 212-18 Fall 1999
Doe v. Alpha Therapeutic Corp., 3 S.W.3d 404 (Mo. Ct. App. 1999)
   65 no4 *Mo. L. Rev.* 1101-17 Fall 2000
Doe v. City of Belleville, 118 S. Ct. 1183 (1998)
   10 no1 *Colum. J. Gender & L.* 125-61 2000
Doe; Nike Can. Ltd. v., [2000] F.C.J. No. 498
   14 no3 *Intell. Prop. J.* 407-10 S 2000
Doe; Santa Fe Indep. Sch. Dist. v., 120 S. Ct. 2266 (2000)
   28 no1 *S.U. L. Rev.* 61-78 Fall 2000
Dombeck; Onda v., 151 F.3d 945 (9th Cir. 1998)
   30 no3 *Envtl. L.* 617-75 Summ 2000
Don King Prods. Inc. v. Warren, [1999] 2 All E.R. 218

Environmental Def. Fund v. EPA, 167 F.3d 641 (D.C. Cir. 1999)
   27 no3 *Ecology L.Q.* 841-83 2000.
EPA; American Trucking Ass'ns, Inc. v., 175 F.3d 1027 (D.C. Cir. 1999)
   27 no3 *Ecology L.Q.* 549-76 2000
   37 no3 *Hous. L. Rev.* 859-92 Fall 2000
   40 no4 *Jurimetrics J.* 485-97 Summ 2000
EPA; Corrosion Proof Fittings v., 947 F.2d 1201 (5th Cir. 1991)
   15 no4 *J.L. & Pol.* 717-45 Fall 1999
EPA; Environmental Def. Fund v., 167 F.3d 641 (D.C. Cir. 1999)
   27 no3 *Ecology L.Q.* 841-83 2000
Epilepsy Found. of Northeast Ohio; NLRB v., 331 N.L.R.B. 92 (2000)
   48 no1 *Fed. Law.* 34-7 Ja 2001
Erie County Retirees Ass'n v. County of Erie, 220 F.3d 193 (3d Cir. 2000)
   26 no4 *Empl. Rel. L.J.* 143-8 Wint 2000
Erie County Retirees Ass'n v. County of Erie, 220 F.3d 193 (3d Cir. 2000)
   13 no4 *Benefits L.J.* 99-104 Wint 2000
Erie R.R. Co. v. Tompkins, 58 S. Ct. 817 (1938)
   58 no2 *Bench & B. Minn.* 17-19 F 2001
Ethics Comm'n v. Keating, 958 P.2d 1250 (Okla. 1998)
   53 no2 *Okla. L. Rev.* 281-97 Summ 2000

> When one knows that a particular case is on point, e.g., *Doe v. Alpha Therapeutic Corp.*, citations to law review articles written about the case can be located in the Table of Cases section of the *Index to Legal Periodicals & Books*. See Illustration 18-1.
>
> *Current Law Index*, see Illustrations 18-5 through 18-7, also contains a Table of Cases.

[2000] 1 H.K.C. 692
   30 pt2 *Hong Kong L.J.* 177-83 2000
Edmond v. Goldsmith, 183 F.3d 659 (7th Cir. 1999)
   53 no2 *Stan. L. Rev.* 491-518 N 2000
Edmonds Inst. v. Babbitt, 42 F. Supp. 2d 1 (D.D.C. 1999)
   21 *Pub. Land & Resources L. Rev.* 201-22 2000
EEOC v. Frank's Nursery & Crafts, Inc., 177 F.3d 448 (6th Cir. 1999)
   2000 no1 *J. Disp. Resol.* 187-97 2000
   30 no4 *U. Mem. L. Rev.* 955-69 Summ 2000
EEOC v. Waffle House, Inc., 193 F.3d 805 (4th Cir. 1999)
   79 no1 *N.C. L. Rev.* 239-305 D 2000
Egan v. Willis, [1998] 158 A.L.R. 527
   28 no3 *Fed. L. Rev.* 549-73 2000
Egypt; Chromalloy Aeroservices v., 939 F. Supp. 907 (D.D.C. 1996)
   10 no2 *Am. Rev. Int'l Arb.* 247-63 1999
Ehlers-Renzi v. Connelly Sch. of the Holy Child, Inc., 224 F.3d 283 (4th Cir. 2000)
   114 no3 *Harv. L. Rev.* 932-9 Ja 2001
Elberg v. Commissioner, unreported (Fed. Ct., Austl., Apr. 20, 1998)
   6 no3 *J.L. & Med.* 213-15 F 1999
Elections Bd. v. Wisconsin Mfr. & Commerce, 597 N.W.2d 721 (Wisc. 1999)
   2000 no5 *Wis. L. Rev.* 1117-48 2000
Ellerth; Burlington Indus., Inc. v. 118 S. Ct. 2257 (1998)
   54 no1 *Vand. L. Rev.* 123-64 Ja 2001
   36 no1 *Willamette L. Rev.* 141-83 Wint 2000
Elvis Presley Trade Marks, In re, [1999] R.P.C. 567
   59 pt1 *Cambridge L.J.* 33-6 Mr 2000
Emison; Growe v., 113 S. Ct. 1075 (1993)
   114 no3 *Harv. L. Rev.* 878-901 Ja 2001
Engvall v. Soo Line R.R. Co., 605 N.W.2d 738 (Minn. 2000)
   27 no2 *Wm. Mitchell L. Rev.* 1233-51 2000
Enmund v. Florida, 102 S. Ct. 3368 (1982)
   32 no3 *Ariz. St. L.J.* 843-96 Fall 2000
Environment Agency; Official Receiver as Liquidator of Celtic Extraction Ltd. v., [1999] 1 All E.R. 746
   12 no2 *J. Envtl. L.* 207-29 2000

FAA; Alaska Prof'l Hunters Ass'n v., 177 F.3d 1030 (D.C. Cir. 1999)
   101 no1 *Colum. L. Rev.* 155-80 Ja 2001
Fabe; United States Dep't of Treasury v. 113 S. Ct. 2202 (1993)
   2000 *U. Chi. Legal F.* 447-72 2000
Falco Fin. Ltd. v. Gough, unreported (Macclesfield County Ct., Gr. Br., Oct. 28, 1998)
   115 *Law Q. Rev.* 360-5 Jl 1999
Falstaff Brewing Corp.; Bloor v., 601 F.2d 609 (2d Cir. 1979)
   44 no4 *St. Louis U. L.J.* 1465-85 Fall 2000
Falwell; Hustler Magazine, Inc. v., 108 S. Ct. 876 (1988)
   35 no4 *Gonz. L. Rev.* 291-317 1999/2000
Faragher v. City of Boca Raton, 118 S. Ct. 2275 (1998)
   54 no1 *Vand. L. Rev.* 123-64 Ja 2001
   36 no1 *Willamette L. Rev.* 141-83 Wint 2000
Farmland Indus., Inc. v. Commissioner, 78 T.C.M. (CCH) 846 (1999)
   53 no4 *Tax Law.* 931-9 Summ 2000
Farrar; Springob v., 514 S.E.2d 135 (N.C. 1999)
   52 no1 *S.C. L. Rev.* 269-85 Fall 2000
Favreau; Productions Avanti Ciné Vidéo, Inc. v. [1999] 177 D.L.R.4th 568
   14 no3 *Intell. Prop. J.* 403-6 S 2000
FBI Foods Inc.; Cadbury Schweppes Inc. v., [1999] 167 D.L.R. 4th 577
   115 *Law Q. Rev.* 376-80 Jl 1999
FCC; Turner Broad. Sys., Inc. v., 114 S. Ct. 2445 (1994)
   22 no3 *Comm. & L.* 1-30 S 2000
FCC; U.S. West, Inc. v., 182 F.3d 1224 (10th Cir. 1999)
   52 no3 *Admin. L. Rev.* 1055-73 Summ 2000
FDA; Brown & Williamson Tobacco Corp. v., 153 F.3d 155 (4th Cir. 1998)
   3 *Quinnipiac Health L.* 133-66 1999/2000
Fedders Corp.; Wanlass v., 145 F.3d 1468 (Fed. Cir. 1998)
   50 no3 *Syracuse L. Rev.* 1151-87 2000
Ferguson v. City of Charleston, 186 F.3d 469 (4th Cir. 1999)
   53 no2 *Stan. L. Rev.* 491-518 N 2000
Ferguson; Plessy v. 16 S. Ct. 1138 (1896)
   25 no1 *J. Sup. Ct. Hist.* 93-111 2000

[Illustration 18–4]

PAGE FROM BOOK REVIEWS, INDEX TO LEGAL PERIODICALS & BOOKS

BOOK REVIEWS

A

Advances in phonetics. 1999
   7 no2 *Forensic Linguistics* 249-61 2000. M. Jessen
Advances in psychology and law. 1997
   7 no2 *Forensic Linguistics* 266-8 2000. I. Clare
Arnaud, A.-J. and Dulce, J. F. Introduction à l'analyse
sociologique des systèmes juridiques. 1998
   40 no3 *C. de D.* 705-13 S 1999. A. Vallières
Asking to die. 1998
   59 pt1 *Cambridge L.J.* 214-16 Mr 2000. J. Keown
Atkinson, D. N. Leaving the bench. 1999
   25 no1 *J. Sup. Ct. Hist.* 112-27 2000. D. G. Stephenson, Jr.
Aufderheide, P. Communications policy and the public interest.
1999
   22 no3 *Comm. & L.* 85-7 S 2000. A. J. Siegel

B

Bainbridge, D. I. Software copyright law. 4th ed. 1999
   Previous ed.: 1997
   8 no3 *Int'l J.L. & Info. Tech.* 383-5 Aut 2000. T. Aplin
Balancing the scales. 1998
   13 *Austl. Feminist L.J.* 143-9 S 1999. N. Puren
Baldwin, J. Small claims in the county courts in England and
Wales. 1997
   19 *Civ. Just. Q.* 94-7 Ja 2000. C. Osborne
Barnford, K. Amending a commercial lease. 1998
   64 *Conv. & Prop. Law. (n.s.)* 277-9 My/Je 2000
Banking litigation. 1999

> Each issue of *ILP* has a separate Book Reviews section. All books that have been reviewed during the time frame covered by that issue of *ILP* are in one alphabet listing the book's author and title. A citation is provided to where the book is reviewed.

   40 no2 *C. de D.* 480-6 Je 1999. D. Lizotte
Behavioral law and economics. 2000
   68 no1 *U. Chi. L. Rev.* 279-303 Wint 2001. D. A. Farber
Benidickson, J. Environmental law. 1997
   79 no1 *Can. B. Rev.* 296-300 F 2000. P. Bowal and N.
Symington
Bentham, J. Legislator of the world. 1998
   59 pt1 *Cambridge L.J.* 207-9 Mr 2000. P. R. Glazebrook
Bentley, A. Eating for victory. 1998
   19 no1 *Law & Hist. Rev.* 214-15 Spr 2001. M. Jacobs
Berman, E. G. and Sams, K. E. Peacekeeping in Africa. 2000
   47 *Naval L. Rev.* 222-5 2000. G. P. Noone
Bessler, J. D. Death in the dark. 1997
   19 no1 *Law & Hist. Rev.* 227-30 Spr 2001. F. A. Allen
Black men on race, gender, and sexuality. 1999
   24 no3/4 *Legal Stud. F.* 733-8 2000. L. F. Harrison
Blackburn, S. Ruling passions. 1998
   6 no1 *Res Publica* 117-25 2000. P. Stratton-Lake
Block, G. Effective legal writing. 5th ed. 1999
   7 *Scribes J. Legal Writing* 175-9 1998/1999/2000. B. R.
Burlingame
The Bluebook. 17th ed. 2000
   6 *Legal Writing* 257-72 2000. M. H. Weresh
Boer, D. P. and others. Manual for the sexual violence risk—
20. 1997
   18 no6 *Behavioral Sci. & L.* 791-8 2000. P. H. Witt
   18 no6 *Behavioral Sci. & L.* 781-9 2000. D. Mossman
Bouchard, C. La personnalité morale démythifiée. 1997
   40 no4 *C. de D.* 956-61 D 1999. J.-F. De Rico
Bowen, W. G. and Bok, D. C. The shape of the river. 1998
   50 no2 *J. Legal Educ.* 284-305 Je 2000. E. Anderson
Braithwaite, J. and Drahos, P. Global business regulation. 2000
   8 no2 *Competition & Consumer L.J.* 197-201 D 2000. J.
Goldring
Brooks, P. Troubling confessions. 2000
   114 no2 *Harv. L. Rev.* 640-7 D 2000
Brown, S. H. Standing against dragons. 1998
   19 no1 *Law & Hist. Rev.* 216-17 Spr 2001. P. Wallenstein
Bruylant, Émile. Minorités et organisation de l'État. 1998
   40 no4 *C. de D.* 947-56 D 1999. A. Vallières
Byers, M. Custom, power, and the power of rules. 1999
   11 no2 *Eur. J. Int'l L.* 439-64 Je 2000. G. J. Simpson

C

Cabana, D. A. Death at midnight. 1996
   19 no1 *Law & Hist. Rev.* 227-30 Spr 2001. F. A. Allen
Canada's founding debates. 1999
   33 no3 *U.B.C. L. Rev.* 870-3 2000. M. Cameron
Canadian health law and policy. 1999
   31 no3 *Ottawa L. Rev.* 165-9 1999/2000. J. D. Blackburn
Carrington, P. D. Stewards of democracy. 1999
   4 no1 *Green Bag (n.s.)* 85-94 Aut 2000. F. A. Allen
Carroll, E. and Mackie, K. International mediation. 2000
   10 no2 *Am. Rev. Int'l Arb.* 265-9 1999. L. E. Dembeck
Carruthers, B. G. and Halliday, T. C. Rescuing business. 1998
   115 *Law Q. Rev.* 520-2 Jl 1999. L. S. Sealy
Carter, I. A measure of freedom. 1999
   59 pt1 *Cambridge L.J.* 205-7 Mr 2000. M. H. Kramer
The Caspian Sea. 2000
   18 no3 *J. Energy & Nat. Resources L* 307-11 Ag 2000. T.
Adams
The centenary companion to Australian Federation. 1999
   59 pt3 *Cambridge L.J.* 638-40 N 2000. C. Bleby
Coates, P. A. Nature. 1998
   27 no2 *Ecology L.Q.* 521-32 2000. R. Hardack
Cohen, M. L. Bibliography of early American law. 1998
   19 no1 *Law & Hist. Rev.* 197-202 Spr 2001. W. S. Bagnall
Cole, D. No equal justice. 1999
   27 no1 *Ohio N.U. L. Rev.* 29-66 2000. H. Gee
Cole, P. The free, the unfree and the excluded. 1998
   6 no3 *Res Publica* 327-36 2000. R. Hull
Communicating uncertainty. 1999
   11 no3 *Risk Health Safety & Env't* 263-5 Summ 2000. D.

   19 no4 *Law & Phil.* 451-64 Jl 2000. D. A. Strauss
Coombe, R. J. The cultural life of intellectual properties. 1998
   19 no1 *Law & Hist. Rev.* 223-5 Spr 2001. L. A. Marovich
Cooper, D. Governing out of order. 1998
   15 no1 *Can. J. L. & Soc'y* 250-2 2000. R. A. Macdonald
Corporate personality in the 20th century. 1998
   58 pt1 *Cambridge L.J.* 247-9 Mr 1999. L. S. Sealy
Cotterrell, R. Émile Durkheim. 1999
   20 no3 *Legal Stud.* 450-4 S 2000. M. Lobban
Cottrell, J. Law of defamation in Commonwealth Africa. 1998
   8 no2 *Tort L. Rev.* 148-51 Jl 2000. M. Tilbury
Craig, P. P. and Búrca, G. de. EU law. 2nd ed. 1998
   59 pt1 *Cambridge L.J.* 223-5 Mr 2000. P. Kunzlik
Crépeau, P.-A. Les principes d'UNIDROIT et le Code civil du
Québec. 1998
   40 no2 *C. de D.* 486-9 Je 1999. A.-M. Burns
Crime and the criminal justice system in Australia. 2000
   33 no3 *Austl. & N.Z. J. Criminology* 365-8 D 2000. R. Sarre
Crosbie, L. Paul's case. 1997
   13 *Austl. Feminist L.J.* 38-65 S 1999. M. San Roque
A culture of corruption. 1999
   33 no3 *Austl. & N.Z. J. Criminology* 362-4 D 2000. S.
Pickering
Currency crises, monetary union, and the conduct of mone-
tary policy. 1999
   32 no4 *N.Y.U. J. Int'l L. & Pol.* 1203-5 Summ 2000. E.
Diamond
Currie, E. Crime and punishment in America. 1st ed. 1998
   27 no1 *Ohio N.U. L. Rev.* 29-66 2000. H. Gee

D

Dangerous liaisons. 1999
   20 no2 *B.C. Third World L.J.* 447-71 Spr 2000. K. S.
Suffredini
Davis, M. Ecology of fear. 1st ed. 1998
   27 no2 *Ecology L.Q.* 537-40 2000. K. Zarlengo
Day, J. N. Urban castles. 1999
   25 no3 *N.Y.U. Rev. L. & Soc. Change* 479-81 1999. L.
Anthes
Dean, M. Governmentality. 1999
   63 no5 *Mod. L. Rev.* 785-8 S 2000. W. T. Murphy

[Illustration 18–5]

PAGE FROM SUBJECT INDEX, CURRENT LAW INDEX

SUBJECT INDEX   **FAIR USE (COPYRIGHT)**

Important case law for France on VAT deduction on lodging and entertainment expenses.(value added tax) by Patrick Donsimoni
    21 Tax Notes International 1742-1743 Oct 16, 2000
Claiming input tax for employee reimbursements.(Australia) by James Johnson
    74 Law Institute Journal 39(3) Oct, 2000
The whittling away of INDOPCO: PNC Bancorp and Wells Fargo.(capitalization of expenditures beyond IRC s. 263's reach) Wells Fargo & Co. v. Commissioner by Jay Frucci and Lisa Kiner
    26 Michigan Tax Lawyer 8-14 July-Sept, 2000
    see also
    Business travel
EXPENSES as tax deductions *see*
    Expense deductions
EXPERIENCES, Stressful life *see*
    Life change events
EXPERIMENTAL design
    Will experimentation invalidate patents granted under the Patent Act post-October 1, 1989?(Canada) by Dale E. Schlosser
    17 Canadian Intellectual Property Review 237-243 Oct, 2000
EXPERIMENTATION on man, Medical *see*
    Human experimentation in medicine
EXPERIMENTS *see*
    Research
EXPERT evidence *see*
    Evidence, Expert
EXPERT testimony *see*
    Evidence, Expert
EXPO 2000
    It's great representing OZ at World Expo: wish every young lawyer could be here, best wishes.(lawyer from Australia) by Cuong Tu
    38 Law Society Journal 16(2) Oct, 2000
EXPORT assembly industry *see*
    Offshore assembly industry
EXPORT controls
    Overview of export controls. by Lilian V. Blageff
    12 International Quarterly 616-690 Oct, 2000
    Liberalization of high performance computer export controls unti... national sec...
Gursky
49 Catholic ...

Economic ... Legal Devel... McGlone an...
34 In...
see also
Technology tr...
EXPORT cre...
    Exporting
Harmon...
17 The E...
EXPORT credits
    Export credi...
EXPORT license
    Export control
EXPORT premiu...
    Export subsidi...
EXPORT restrict...
    Export control
EXPORT sub...
    NFTC dis...
National F...
foreigns sale...
EXPULSION *see*
    Deportation
EXTENSIBLE M...
    language) *see*
    XML (Document markup language)
EXTENUATING circumstances
    An overview of the mitigation of economic damages.(Hot Topics in Employment Law) by Ed Aro and Peter Walsh
    29 Colorado Lawyer 23(5) Oct, 2000
    Mandatory life sentence for second serious offence.(United Kingdom) R. v. Buckland by Annabelle James
    64 Journal of Criminal Law 456-458 Oct, 2000
EXTENUATION (Law) *see*
    Extenuating circumstances
EXTERNAL debts
    Financial crisis in Asia and its effect on power projects: a lesson in practical banking. by Robin J. Gibbons
    28 International Business Lawyer 411(4) Oct, 2000
    Restructuring of project finance debt in emerging markets. by Margaret B. Cole
    28 International Business Lawyer 415(5) Oct, 2000
EXTERRITORIAL crime *see*
    Criminal jurisdiction
EXTERRITORIALITY
    Extraterritoriality and the Supreme Court's assertion of the economic constitution.(Canada) by Stevan M. Pepa
    34 Canadian Business Law Journal 231-268 Dec, 2000

Fishing for the smoking gun: the need for British courts to grant American style extraterritorial discovery requests in U.S. industry-wide tort actions. by Y. Daphne Coelho-Adam
    33 Vanderbilt Journal of Transnational Law 1223 Nov, 2000
Gaining an advantage in European patent infringement litigation. by John Fellas
    22 EIPR: European Intellectual Property Review 546-550 Nov, 2000
Territoriality in Community trade mark matters: the British problem. by Gordon Humphreys
    22 EIPR: European Intellectual Property Review 405-417 Sept, 2000
Eleventh Circuit holds that Federal Trade Commission's franchise rule does not apply extraterritorially to agreement between U.S. company and Argentine citizen. Nieman v. Dryclean U.S.A. Franchise Co. by Kevin C. McCaffrey
    13 New York International Law Review 131-135 Summer, 2000
    see also
    Diplomatic privileges and immunities
EXTINGUISHMENT of debts
    Supreme Court reinstates insolvent S corp double-dip. Gitlitz v. Commissioner by Lee A. Sheppard
    90 Tax Notes 577-582 Jan 29, 2001
    COD income and basis adjustments of partners.(cancellation of debt) by Burgess J.W. Raby and William L. Raby
    89 Tax Notes 1425-1428 Dec 11, 2000
    Debt discharge controversy for owners of S corporations by Mark R. Martin and James E. Tierney
    65 Practical Tax Strategies 331-342 Dec, 2000
    Federal income tax consequences of the discharge of qualified real property business indebtedness. by Martin D. Pollack and Royce E. Oliver III
    16 Tax Management Real Estate Journal 271-287 Oct 4, 2000
    see also
    Compromise and settlement
    Debt
    Limitation of actions

Post-sale duty to warn: a critical cause of action.(Products Liability in the 21st Century) by Kenneth Ross
    27 William Mitchell Law Review 339-359 Winter, 2000
Warning! Failure to read this article may be hazardous to your failure to warn defense.(Products Liability in the 21st Century) by Hildy Bowbeer, Wendy F. Lumish and Jeffrey A. Cohen
    27 William Mitchell Law Review 439-467 Winter, 2000
Trade association liable for negligent standards, Washington court rules. Meneely v. S.R. Smith, Inc. by Jennifer L. Reichert
    36 Trial 17 Nov, 2000
Machine guard removal cases. by Paul A. Scrudato
    36 Trial 30 Nov, 2000

How many times must the question be answered? The application of the learned intermediary doctrine in the Norplant Contraceptive Products Liability Litigation. Norplant Contraceptive Products Liability Litigation, In re by Stacey Leffler Ravetta
    30 Golden Gate University Law Review 331-377 Spring, 2000
State of the art evidence in products liability suits in Maryland. by Patrick R. Buckler
    28 University of Baltimore Law Review 117-191 Fall, 1998
    see also:
    Products liability
    Warning labels

    -Cases
    The learned intermediary doctrine in the age of direct consumer advertising.(Missouri Law)(Case Note) Doe v. Alpha Therapeutic Corp. by Bradford B. Lear
    65 Missouri Law Review 1101-1117 Fall, 2000
FAIR employment practice *see*
    Employment discrimination
FAIR housing *see*
    Housing discrimination
FAIR trade *see*
    Unfair competition (Commerce)
FAIR trade (Tariff) *see*
    Free trade
FAIR trial

---

sonable doubts ...orial) by Kent
135 Dec, 2000 ...m) by Ragveer
Nov 10, 2000
1994, s. 34 -- direct jury in ...n cannot on its ...air - whether v. Gill by D.J.
924 Nov, 2000 ...child care ...d Kingdom by
8(1) Oct, 2000 ...lependent and ...ion of racial ...ghts) Sander v. Ashworth
'68 Sept, 2000 ...and child ...on Human ...nited Kingdom
138 July, 2000 ...of the right to
privacy and compatibility with the right to a fair hearing.(United Kingdom, European Union) Khan v. United Kingdom by Steve Foster and Beverley Steventon
    54 Law Teacher 346-357 Summer, 2000
FAIR trial and free press *see*
    Free press and fair trial
FAIR use (Copyright)
    Is fair for the principal fair for the agent? by Carlo Scallo Lavizzari
    Copyright World 30(7) Dec, 2000
    Mutilating music.(part 3) by Vanita Kohli
    Copyright World 23-24 Nov, 2000
    Mutilating music.(part 2) by Vanita Kohli
    Copyright World 21-24 Oct, 2000
    Caching and copyright: the right of temporary copying. by P. Bernt Hugenholtz
    22 EIPR: European Intellectual Property Review 482-493 Oct, 2000
    The judicial treatment of fair dealing and freedom of expression in Michelin v. C.A.W.(Canada) Cie Generale des Establissements Michelin v. C.A.W. by Gregor P. Binkley
    17 Canadian Intellectual Property Review 225-235 Oct, 2000
    Dropping slugs in the celestial jukebox: congressional enabling of digital music piracy short-changes copyright holders. by David A. Hepler
    37 San Diego Law Review 1165-1200 Fall, 2000

FACSIMILE machines *see*
    Facsimile equipment
FACSIMILE transmission equipment *see*
    Facsimile equipment
FACT and law *see*
    Law and fact
FACTUAL compilation (Copyright) *see*
    Compiled works (Copyright)
FACTUAL compilations (Copyright) *see*
    Compiled works (Copyright)
FACULTY (Education) *see*
    Teachers
FAILURE of banks *see*
    Bank failures
FAILURE to assist in emergencies *see*
    Assistance in emergencies
FAILURE to warn (Law)
    Product liability in Canada: principles and practice north of the border.(Products Liability in the 21st Century) by David S. Morritt and Sonia L. Bjorkquist
    27 William Mitchell Law Review 177-214 Winter, 2000
    The existence of a duty to warn: a question for the court or the jury?(Products Liability in the 21st Century) by George W. Flynn and John J. Laravuso
    27 William Mitchell Law Review 633-651 Winter, 2000
    The ten myths of product liability.(Products Liability in the 21st Century) by Kevin Reynolds and Richard J. Kirschman
    27 William Mitchell Law Review 551-582 Winter, 2000

99

> *Current Law Index* is divided into separate Indexes for Subjects and Author/Title. This illustration is from Subjects. No heading was provided for "Learned Intermediary Doctrine." However, by checking under the heading "Products Liability," a reference is provided to "Failure to warn (Law)." Under this heading are articles relevant to the research. At times, it is necessary to check under several different words and phrases in order to locate the appropriate information.

[Illustration 18–6]

PAGE FROM AUTHOR/TITLE INDEX, CURRENT LAW INDEX

AUTHOR/TITLE INDEX   LEGAL ASPECTS OF THE INFORMATION SOCIETY

LAW for All: An Analysis of Legal Needs in Inner Sydney Today
reviewed by Andrea Durbach in Law for All: An Analysis of Legal Needs in Inner Sydney Today.
25 Alternative Law Journal 312(1) Dec. 2000

LAW for Physicians: An Overview of Medical Legal Issues
by Carl Horn, Donald H. Caldwell Jr. and Christopher Osborn reviewed by Ila S. Rothschild in Law for Physicians: An Overview of Medical Legal Issues.
21 Journal of Legal Medicine 437-443 Sept. 2000

LAW in Action: Ethnomethodological and Conversation Analytic Approaches to Law
by Max Travers and John F. Manzo reviewed by Robert Dingwall in Law in Action: Ethnomethodological and Conversation Analytic Approaches to Law.
25 Law and Social Inquiry 885-911 Summer, 2000

LAW, M.Y.
Genetic polymorphism at three STR loci - CSF1PO, HUMTHO1 and TPOX, and the AMP-FLP locus D1S80 for the Chinese population in Hong Kong.(short tandem repeat)(Announcement of Population Data) by M.Y. Law, D.M. Wong, W.K. Fung, K.L. Chan, C. Li, T.S. Lun, K.M. Lai, K.Y. Cheung and C.T. Chiu
115 Forensic Science International 103-105 Jan 1, 2001

THE Law of Bail in Canada, 2d ed.
by Gary T. Trotter reviewed by Shelagh R. Creagh
25 Canadian Law Libraries 103(1) Mid-Summer, 2000

LAW of Bank Payments, 2d ed.
by Michael Brindle and Raymond Cox reviewed by Andrew Tettenborn
59 Cambridge Law Journal 414-415 July, 2000

THE Law of Comparative Advertising: Directive 97/55/EC in the United Kingdom and Germany
by Ansgar Ohly and Michael Spence reviewed by Anthony Harvey in The Law of Comparative Advertising: Directive 97/55/EC in the United Kingdom and Germany.
25 European Law Review 684-685 Dec, 2000

THE Law of Financial Derivatives in Canada
by Margaret E. Grottenthaler and Philip J. Henderson reviewed by Christopher C. Nicholls in The Law of Financial Derivatives in Canada.
34 Canadian Business Law Journal 288-300 Dec, 2000

A Law of Her Own: The Reasonable Woman as a Measure of Man

LAWTON, Anne
The meritocracy myth and the illusion of equal employment opportunity. by Anne Lawton
85 Minnesota Law Review 587-662 Dec, 2000

LAWYERS and the Rise of Western Political Liberalism: Europe and North America from the Eighteenth to Twentieth Centuries
by Terence C. Halliday and Lucien Karpik reviewed by Charles J. Reid Jr. in Lawyers and the Rise of Western Political Liberalism: Europe and North America from the Eighteenth to Twentieth Centuries.
43 American Journal of Legal History 99-101 Jan, 1999

THE Lawyer's Desk Guide to Preventing Legal Malpractice, 2d ed.
reviewed by Patrick T. O'Rourke
29 Colorado Lawyer 48(3) Dec, 2000

LAWYERS, Gems and Money
by Paul Conroy reviewed by Gerald Acquaah-Gaisie in Lawyers, Gems and Money.
74 Law Institute Journal 36(1) Nov, 2000

THE Lawyer's Guide to Mentoring
by Ida O. Abbott reviewed by Hazel L. Johnson in The Lawyer's Guide to Mentoring.
26 Law Practice Management 56(1) Oct, 2000

LAWYERS in a New South City: A History of the Legal Profession in Birmingham
by Pat Boyd Rumore reviewed by Robert R. Kracke in Lawyers in a New South City: A History of the Legal Profession in Birmingham.
61 The Alabama Lawyer 272(2) July, 2000

LAWYERS, Legislators and Theorists: Developments in English Criminal Jurisprudence, 1800-1957
by Keith J.M. Smith reviewed by Mark Lunney in Lawyers, Legislators and Theorists: Developments in English Criminal Jurisprudence, 1800-1957.
21 Journal of Legal History 139-141 August, 2000

LAY, Donald P.
Law: A Human Process. by Donald P. Lay reviewed by Thomas H. Boyd
73 The Wisconsin Lawyer 38(2) Oct, 2000

LAYCOCK, Douglas
The Supreme Court and religious liberty. by Douglas Laycock
40 Catholic Lawyer 25-37 Summer, 2000

LAYMAN, Robb H.

The Human Rights Act and employment law.(Human Rights Act)(United Kingdom) by David Leckie
45 Journal of the Law Society of Scotland 23(25) Oct, 2000

LEDERER, Fredric I.
The effect of courtroom technologies on and in appellate proceedings and courtrooms. by Fredric I. Lederer
2 Journal of Appellate Practice and Process 251-274 Summer, 2000

LEDERMAN, Leandra
Late returns claiming refunds: negotiating the 'fantastic labyrinth' (statutes of limitations on refund claims) by Leandra Lederman
89 Tax Notes 1053-1061 Nov 20, 2000

LEE, C. David
Legal reform in China: a role for nongovernmental organizations. by C. David Lee
25 The Yale Journal of International Law 363-434 Summer, 2000

LEE, Cynthia Bolt
Deduction for religious education disallowed. by Cynthia Bolt Lee
190 Journal of Accountancy 83 Dec, 2000

LEE, David L.
Age Discrimination Litigation. by L. Steven Platt and Cathy Ventrell-Monsees reviewed by David L. Lee
14 CBA Record 54(2) Oct, 2000

LEE, Evan
Supermarket slotting fees (allowances): are they legal under Sections 2(c) and 2(d) of the Robinson-Patman Act? by Evan Lee
22 Whittier Law Review 577-613 Winter, 2000

LEE, Hye-Seung
Motherless case in paternity testing. by Hye-Seung Lee, Jae Won Lee, Gil-Ro Han and Juck-Joon Hwang
114 Forensic Science International 57-65 Nov 13, 2000

LEE, Jae Won
Motherless case in paternity testing. by Hye-Seung Lee, Jae Won Lee, Gil-Ro Han and Juck-Joon Hwang
114 Forensic Science International 57-65 Nov 13, 2000

LEE, Lita
Facts fantasies and feminism's future: an analysis of

This section of *CLI* serves as an index to articles by author and as an index to book reviews. Note the following:

1. Authors are listed alphabetically with the complete title and citation.

2. Book reviews are listed under both the author and title of the book.

---

reviewed by Stephen G.A. Pitel
34 Canadian Business Law Journal 307-312 Dec, 2000

LAW on the Internet
by Cate Banks and Heather Douglas reviewed by Karen Wheelwright in Law on the Internet.
38 Law Society Journal 84(11) Nov, 2000

by Cate Banks and Heather Douglas reviewed by Sally Kift in Law on the Internet.
25 Alternative Law Journal 260(1) Oct, 2000

LAW Without Enforcement: Integrating Mental Health and Justice
by Nigel Eastman and Jill Peay reviewed by Ralph Sandland in Law Without Enforcement: Integrating Mental Health and Justice.
9 Social & Legal Studies 597-599 Dec, 2000

LAWLESS, Robert M.
The expenses of financial distress: the direct costs of Chapter 11.(bankruptcy law) by Stephen P. Ferris and Robert M. Lawless
61 University of Pittsburgh Law Review 629-669 Spring, 2000

LAWRENCE, Frederick M.
Punishing Hate: Bias Crimes Under American Law. by Frederick M. Lawrence reviewed by Lana Chiarella Vernon
47 The Federal Lawyer 61-2 Nov-Dec, 2000

Punishing Hate: Bias Crimes Under American Law. by Frederick M. Lawrence reviewed by J. M. Dillof
98 Michigan Law Review 1728 May, 2000

LAWRENCE, Jeffrey
The global chill of regulation FD.(SEC regulation regarding securities disclosure) by Jeffrey Lawrence
18 Company and Securities Law Journal 526-530 Oct, 2000

LAWS of the Postcolonial
by Eve Darian-Smith and Peter Fitzpatrick reviewed by Willow D. Crystal in Laws of the Postcolonial.
25 The Yale Journal of International Law 554-557 Summer, 2000

LAWSON, Richard
Late payment directive.(United Kingdom) by Richard Lawson
144 Solicitors Journal 1030(2) Nov 10, 2000

hierarchy (Rotating Centers, Expanding Frontiers: LatCrit Theory and Marginal Intersections) by Sylvia R. Lazos Vargas
33 U.C. Davis Law Review 1451-1501 Summer, 2000

LE Droit Compare
by Pierre Legrand reviewed by Esin Orucu in Le Droit Compare.
49 International and Comparative Law Quarterly 996-997 Oct, 2000

LE Tourneau, Dominique
Raccolta di concordati: 1950-1999. by Jose T. Martin de Agar reviewed by Dominique Le Tourneau
30 Revue Generale de Droit 719-728 Dec, 2000

LEADSTROM, Nathan D.
Sanders v. American Broadcasting Companies: Does it mean the end to the use of hidden cameras in undercover media investigations?(California law)(Case Note) by Nathan D. Leadstrom
40 Washburn Law Journal 143-168 Fall, 2000

LEAHY, Edward R.
The changing face of international arbitration. by Edward R. Leahy and Carlos J. Bianchi
17 Journal of International Arbitration 19-61 August, 2000

LEAR, Bradford B.
The learned intermediary doctrine in the age of direct consumer advertising.(Missouri law)(Case Note) by Bradford B. Lear
65 Missouri Law Review 1101-1117 Fall, 2000

LEARNING Canadian Criminal Law, 7th ed.
by Don Stewart and Ronald Joseph DeLisle reviewed by Wesley W. Smart
25 Canadian Law Libraries 105-106 Mid-Summer, 2000

LEARY, Thomas B.
Freedom as the core value of antitrust in the new Millennium.(The Future Course of the Rule of Reason) by Thomas B. Leary
68 Antitrust Law Journal 545-557 Summer, 2000

LECKIE, David
This time the sky is falling.(Human Rights Act)(United Kingdom) by David Leckie
45 Journal of the Law Society of Scotland 20(2) Oct, 2000

Expert testimony in liquor liability cases. by Paul C. Lee
11 The Practical Litigator 51-58 Sept, 2000

LEE, Roy S.
The International Criminal Court: The Making of the Rome Statute. by Roy S. Lee reviewed by Danesh Sarooshi
49 International and Comparative Law Quarterly 992-994 Oct, 2000

LEECH, Stewart
"With all my worldly goods I thee endow'": the status of pre-nuptial agreements in England and Wales. by Stewart Leech
34 Family Law Quarterly 193-207 Summer, 2000

LEESFIELD, Ira H.
Admissibility of expert testimony: What's next? by Ira H. Leesfield and Mark A. Sylvester
36 Trial 64 Dec, 2000

How to maximize compensatory damages in a personal injury case. by Ira H. Leesfield
11 The Practical Litigator 7-12 Sept, 2000

LEFEVRE, Frank V.
A survey of physician training programs in risk management and communication skills for malpractice prevention. by Frank V. Lefevre, Teresa M. Waters and Peter P. Budetti
28 Journal of Law, Medicine & Ethics 258 Fall, 2000

LEGAL Alchemy
by David L. Faigman reviewed by Anthony J. Mohr in Legal Alchemy.
23 Los Angeles Lawyer 59(2) July-August, 2000

A Legal and Political Interpretation of Article 215(2) (New Article 288(2)) of the Treaty of Rome: The Individual Strikes Back
by Constantin Stefanou and Helen Zanthaki reviewed by Andrea Biondi in A Legal and Political Interpretation of Article 215(2) (New Article 288(2)) of the Treaty of Rome: The Individual Strikes Back.
25 European Law Review 683-684 Dec, 2000

LEGAL Aspects of the Information Society
by Ian Lloyd in Legal Aspects of the Information Society
144 Solicitors Journal 1075(1) Nov 24, 2000

369

[Illustration 18–7]

PAGE FROM TABLE OF STATUTES, CURRENT LAW INDEX

TABLE OF STATUTES

A.B.A. Code of Judicial Conduct
Sweeping reform for small rules? Anti-bias canons as a substitute for heightened scrutiny.
85 Minnesota Law Review 363-449 Dec, 2000

A.B.A. Model Rules of Professional Conduct
ABA to propose revising Model Rules of Professional Conduct.
37 Trial 17 Feb, 2001
Proposed changes to the Model Rules of Professional Conduct.
57 Bench & Bar of Minnesota 16(6) Dec, 2000
The ethics of attorney web sites: updating on Model Rules to better deal with emerging technologies.
13 Georgetown Journal of Legal Ethics 499-519 Spring, 2000
Rule 5.4 Modifying Model Rule 5.4 to allow for minority ownership of law firms by nonlawyers.(A.B.A. Model Rules of Professional Conduct)
13 Georgetown Journal of Legal Ethics 477-498 Spring, 2000

ABA Model Code of Judicial Conduct *see*
A.B.A. Code of Judicial Conduct
ABA Model Rules of Professional Conduct *see*
A.B.A. Model Rules of Professional Conduct
ABE Lincoln Law *see*
False Claims Act
ADA *see*
Americans with Disabilities Act of 1990

ADA Notification Act (Draft)
Which way for the ADA?(Americans with Disabilities Act)
86 ABA Journal 54(4) Dec, 2000

ADMINISTRATIVE Procedure Act
Wrong turn in cyberspace: using ICANN to route around the APA and the Constitution. (Internet Corporation for Assigned Names and Numbers, Administrative Procedure Act)
50 Duke Law Journal 17 Oct, 2000

ADOPTION and Safe Families Act of 1997
Parental rights and the best interests of the child: implications of the Adoption and Safe Families Act of 1997 on dome[...]
8 American Un[...]

ADOPTION Inter[...]
Hague Conventi[...]
Cooperation in [...]
ADR Act of 1998
Alternative Disp[...]
AGE Discriminat[...]
Age discrim[...]

Cash bala[...]
lump-sum dis[...]
Discriminatio[...]
28 Tax Management Compensation Planning Journal 417-418 Dec 1, 2000
Disparate health coverage for Medicare-eligibles violates ADEA.(Age Discrimination in Employment Act)
28 Tax Management Compensation Planning Journal 358-359 Oct 9, 2000
U.S. Supreme Court sets age discrimination proof requirements.(Hot Topics in Employment Law)
29 Colorado Lawyer 37(3) Oct, 2000
Reeves v. Sanderson: United States Supreme Court attempts to clarify plaintiff's burden in 'ADEA' claims.(Reeves v. Sanderson Plumbing Products, Inc.)(Age Discrimination in Employment Act of 1967)
105 Commercial Law Journal 275-286 Fall, 2000
Judicial independence, age-based BFOQs, and the perils of mandatory retirement policies for appointed state judges.(bona fide occupational qualification)(Age Discrimination in Employment Act of 1967)
52 South Carolina Law Review 81-134 Fall, 2000
Supreme Court rules that states are not immune from age discrimination suits.(Case Note)
8 American University Journal of Gender, Social Policy, and the Law 553-565 Spring, 2000

AGREEMENT on Peace, 1993, Israeli-Palestine Liberation Organization
Co-existence without conflict: the implementation of legal structures for Israeli-Palestinian cooperation pursuant to the interim peace agreements.
26 Brooklyn Journal of International Law 591-688 March, 2000

AGREEMENT on Trade-Related Aspects of Intellectual Property Rights
The protection of well-known marks in Taiwan: from case study to general theory.
90 Trademark Reporter 866-888 Nov-Dec, 2000
The winners and the losers: the Agreement on Trade-Related Aspects of Intellectual Property Rights and its effects on developing countries.
23 Houston Journal of International Law 169 Fall, 2000
Taking TRIPS to the Eleventh Amendment: the aftermath of the College Savings cases.(Agreement on Trade-Related Aspects of Intellectual Property Rights)
51 Hastings Law Journal 1003-1045 July, 2000

Competition policy and the stimulation of innovation: TRIPS and the interface between competition and patent protection in the pharmaceutical industry.(Third Annual Latin American Competition and Trade Round Table)
26 Brooklyn Journal of International Law 363-415 March, 2000

AGREEMENT on Trade Related Intellectual Property Rights *see*
Agreement on Trade-Related Aspects of Intellectual Property Rights

AIRLINE Deregulation Act of 1978
Federal preemption by the Airline Deregulation Act of 1978: how do state tort claims fare?
49 Catholic University Law Review 873-902 Spring, 2000

ALABAMA Constitution
Ala. Const. amend. 622, s. 5 The Alabama religious freedom amendment: an interpretive guide.
31 Cumberland Law Review 47-78 Fall, 2000

ALABAMA Rules of Appellate Procedure
What every lawyer should know: recent amendments to the Alabama Rules of Appellate Procedure.
61 The Alabama Lawyer 382(4) Nov, 2000

ALBERTA. Health Care Protection Act 2000
Bill 11, the Canada Health Act and the social union: the need for institutions.(Alberta's Health Care Protection Act 2000)
38 Osgoode Hall Law Journal 39-99 Spring, 2000

ALIEN Tort Statute
Regulating corporate human rights abuses: is Unocal the answer?(National Coalition Government of Burma v. Unocal Inc.)
42 William and Mary Law Review 619 Dec, 2000
Environmental action by an Indonesian citizen challenging mining operations and cultural genocide by United Stats companies failed to state a cause of action of customary international law under the Alien Tort Claims Act.
13 New York International Law Review 141-145 Summer, 2000
[...] research objects of clinical trials in developing

If the name or a statute is known, this index will provide citations to articles dealing with that statute.

The *Index to Legal Periodicals & Books*, see Illustrations 18-2 through 18-4, contains a similar Index.

ALTERNATIVE Dispute Resolution Act of 1998
The Federal Alternative Dispute Resolution Act of 1998 and its impact on federal court practice in Louisiana.(Target ADR)
48 Louisiana Bar Journal 210(4) Oct, 2000
Litigating with the federal government.
20 Construction Lawyer 24(8) Oct, 2000

AMERICAN Competitiveness and Workforce Improvement Act of 1998
American Competitiveness and Workforce Improvement Act of 1998: balancing economic and labor interests under the new H-1B visa program.
85 Cornell Law Review 1673 Sept, 2000

AMERICAN Inventors Protection Act of 1999
The new provisional rights provision.(inventors)
82 Journal of the Patent and Trademark Office Society 742-760 Oct, 2000

AMERICANS with Disabilities Act *see*
Americans with Disabilities Act of 1990

AMERICANS with Disabilities Act of 1990
Disability and the ADA: learning impairment as a disability.(Americans with Disabilities Act)
28 Journal of Law, Medicine & Ethics 410 Winter, 2000
Employer not required to reassign disabled employee, Seventh Circuit rules.
36 Trial 16 Dec, 2000
The Eleventh Amendment and the threat to the Americans with Disabilities Act.(Disability Law)
79 Michigan Bar Journal 1670(3) Dec, 2000
The Americans with Disabilities Act - time to measure the efficacy of this legislation.(Disability Law)
79 Michigan Bar Journal 1664(5) Dec, 2000
Which way for the ADA?(Americans with Disabilities Act)
86 ABA Journal 54(4) Dec, 2000
Chipping away at the ADA. (U.S. Supreme Court decisions narrowing definition of disabled)
36 Trial 48 Dec, 2000
ADA and the Internet: must websites be accessible to the disabled?(Americans with Disabilities Act)
33 The Maryland Bar Journal 34-36 Nov-Dec, 2000
Federal appellate court limits ADA's 'direct threat' defense.(Americans with Disabilities Act of 1990; individuals constituting a threat to the health and safety of employees)
47 The Federal Lawyer 54-2 Nov-Dec, 2000

ADA pre-employment inquiries: What can you do?(Americans with Disabilities Act of 1990)
29 Colorado Lawyer 73(4) Nov, 2000
EEOC issues new guidance for medical exams and questions for employees.
47 The Federal Lawyer 46-47 Oct, 2000
The Americans with Disabilities Act: new definition of disability post-Sutton v. United Air Lines, Inc.(Case Note)
84 Marquette Law Review 251-271 Fall, 2000
Becoming visible: the ADA's impact on health care for persons with disabilities.(The Americans with Disabilities Act: A Ten-Year Retrospective)
52 Alabama Law Review 51-89 Fall, 2000
Legislation that drives us crazy: an overview of 'mental disability' under the Americans with Disabilities Act.(employment law)
31 Cumberland Law Review 91-192 Fall, 2000
Before disability civil rights: Civil War pensions and the politics of disability in America.(The Americans with Disabilities Act: A Ten-Year Retrospective)
52 Alabama Law Review 1-50 Fall, 2000
The shadows of unconstitutionality: how the new federalism may affect the anti-discrimination mandate of the Americans with Disabilities Act.(The Americans with Disabilities Act: A Ten-Year Retrospective)
52 Alabama Law Review 91-192 Fall, 2000
Higher education and the future of disability policy.(The Americans with Disabilities Act: A Ten-Year Retrospective)
52 Alabama Law Review 241-270 Fall, 2000
"For the misdemeanor outlaw": the impact of the ADA on the institutionalization of criminal defendants with mental disabilities.(The Americans with Disabilities Act: A Ten-Year Retrospective)
52 Alabama Law Review 193-239 Fall, 2000
"Must we talk about that reasonable [...] says yes, but is the [...] h Disabilities Act of [...]*
[...] 967-1002 Fall, 2000
[...]e ADA will not ruin [...]h Disabilities Act)
[...] Review 1489-1550 Fall, 2000
[...]Act and its impact on law.(The Americans [...] Retrospective)
[...] 419-423 Fall, 2000
[...]Act and employment: [...]ns with Disabilities [...]
Act: A Ten-Year Retrospective)
52 Alabama Law Review 375-418 Fall, 2000
The Supreme Court's definition of disability under the ADA: a return to the dark ages.(The Americans with Disabilities Act: A Ten-Year Retrospective)
52 Alabama Law Review 321-374 Fall, 2000
Delusions of rights: Americans with psychiatric disabilities, employment discrimination and the Americans with Disabilities Act.(The Americans with Disabilities Act: A Ten-Year Retrospective)
52 Alabama Law Review 271-319 Fall, 2000
ABA's amicus brief in Garrett.(University of Alabama at Birmingham Board of Trustees v. Garrett)
24 Mental and Physical Disability Law Reporter 691(700) Sept-Oct, 2000
The Americans with Disabilities Act ten years later: a framework for the future.
85 Iowa Law Review 1575-1582 August, 2000
Empirical implications of Title I.(Americans with Disabilities Act; accommodating disabled workers)
85 Iowa Law Review 1671-1690 August, 2000
Emerging disability policy framework: a guidepost for analyzing public policy.
85 Iowa Law Review 1691-1806 August, 2000
The Americans with Disabilities Act: a business perspective.
85 Iowa Law Review 1807-1810 August, 2000
New obstacles in the ability of state employees to sue their state employees under the Americans with Disabilities Act.
85 Iowa Law Review 1835-1859 August, 2000
The unintended consequences of the Americans with Disabilities Act.(Panel Discussion)
85 Iowa Law Review 1811-1834 August, 2000
Let them eat cake: diabetes and the Americans with Disabilities Act after Sutton.
52 Stanford Law Review 1829 July, 2000
A victory for employees with disabilities: SSDI benefits do not preclude employment discrimination claims under the ADA.(Cleveland v. Policy Management Systems)
79 Michigan Bar Journal 830(834) July, 2000

[Illustration 18–8]

SCREEN PRINT, "CURRENT LAW JOURNAL CONTENT" WASHINGTON AND LEE UNIVERSITY SCHOOL OF LAW

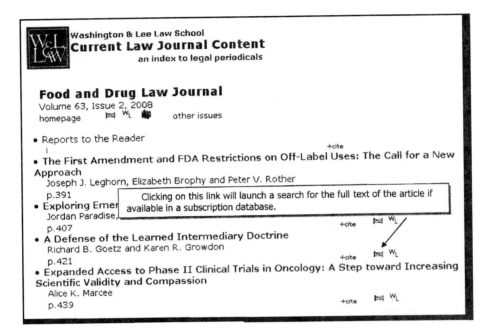

SECTION D.   INDEXES TO FOREIGN PERIODICAL LITERATURE

Periodical indexes focusing on legal journals published in other countries are often useful in legal research. These include:

1.   Index to Foreign Legal Periodicals

The *Index to Foreign Legal Periodicals* (*IFLP*) began in 1960 and is produced by the American Association of Law Libraries. *IFLP* is a multilingual index to articles and book reviews appearing in approximately 470 legal journals published worldwide. It provides in-depth coverage of public and private international law, comparative and foreign law, and the law of all jurisdictions other than the United States, the United Kingdom, Canada, and Australia. *IFLP* also indexes reports, essay collections, yearbooks, and book reviews.

IFLP is published quarterly with an annual cumulation by the University of California Press. In addition, the *IFLP* is available electronically from 1985 to the present via *Ovid Technologies* and *Westlaw*.

2.   Index to Canadian Legal Periodical Literature

The Canadian Association of Law Libraries began publishing the *Index to Canadian Legal Periodical Literature* in 1961 to provide access to the growing number of Canadian legal journals. Articles in Canadian legal periodicals discuss two systems of law, civil and common, in two languages, English and French.

The index, which is available exclusively in print, is arranged by both author and subject. A table of cases and book review index are included.

3. Index to Canadian Legal Literature (ICLL)

This index, which began in 1987, is available in print as part of the *Canadian Abridgement*, a Carswell publication. The *Index to Canadian Legal Literature* is a comprehensive index to Canadian legal articles, books, government publications, case comments, etc., in English and French.

An annual volume is published, which is updated eight times per year. Separate subject and author indexes are provided. *ICLL* is also available electronically on *Westlaw*, *Westlaw eCarswell*, and *Quicklaw*.

4. Legal Journals Index (LJI) and European Legal Journals Index (ELJI)

Legal Journals Index indexes over 400 legal journals from the United Kingdom and Europe. Published by Legal Information Resources Ltd., *LJI* began in 1986. Beginning in 1993, journals devoted to European law were moved to a companion publication, *European Legal Journals Index*. Both titles were discontinued in print in 1999 but are still available electronically.

The LJI database in *Westlaw* contains the content from both *Legal Journals Index* and *European Legal Journals Index*. Both are also part of Sweet & Maxwell's *Current Legal Information* service available via the Internet and CD–ROM.

5. Index to Indian Legal Periodicals

Since 1963 the Indian Law Institute has published the *Index to Indian Legal Periodicals*. This resource indexes periodicals published in India (including yearbooks and other annuals) pertaining to law and related fields. It is issued semiannually with annual cumulations.

6. Index to Legal Periodicals in Israel

This index, published by the Bar–Ilan University Law Library, indexes Israeli legal periodicals and collections of essays. Two print volumes cover the years 1976–1996 and 1997–2002. The index is also available electronically on the Bar–Ilan University Law Library Web site.[44]

SECTION E.　INDEXES TO SPECIFIC SUBJECTS

Several indexes provide access to periodical articles on specific legal subjects. These include:

1. Index to Federal Tax Articles

This index, published by Warren, Gorham & Lamont, covers the literature on federal income, estate, and gift taxation contained in legal, tax, and economic journals, as well as non-periodical publications. Consist-

---

[44] http://www.law.biu.ac.il/library/index.php?id=20&pt=2&pid=13&level=1&lang=2.

ing of separate subject and author indexes, entries are arranged in reverse chronological order under author's name. Three volumes provide retrospective coverage from 1913 to 1974. Since 1974, the indexes are published annually, supplemented on a quarterly basis.

2. Federal Tax Articles

This looseleaf reporter, published by Commerce Clearing House, Inc., contains summaries of articles on federal taxation (income, estate, gift, and excise) appearing in legal, accounting, business, and related periodicals. Proceedings and papers delivered at major tax institutes are also indexed.

Summaries are arranged by Internal Revenue Code section numbers. Separate author and subject indexes are also provided. Cumulative bound volumes, with coverage dating from 1954, are published periodically to make room for current materials in the looseleaf volume. The reporter is updated on a monthly basis.

3. Criminal Justice Periodical Index (CJPI)

Criminal Justice Periodical Index covers criminal justice and law enforcement periodicals published in the United States, England, and Canada. Abstracts are provided for many titles.

The print edition was published by University Microfilms International from 1972 to1998. It features an author index and a subject index, which includes case names. *CJPI* is now available electronically from ProQuest from 1981 to the present.

4. Legal Information Management Index

Legal Information Management Index covers periodicals related to law, librarianship, library management, online and manual research, and related topics. It is published by Legal Information Services.

The print edition began in 1984 and is issued bimonthly with an annual cumulation. It includes keyword, author, and review indexes. The index is also available electronically from Legal Information Services.

5. Annuals and Surveys Appearing in Legal Periodicals: An Annotated Listing

This looseleaf volume indexes surveys appearing in law reviews, bar association journals, and annuals. It is divided into three sections: state surveys; federal court surveys; and subject-specific surveys. Published by William S. Hein & Co., it first appeared in 1987, was revised in 1995 and has annual supplements.

6. Index to Periodical Articles Related to Law

The *Index to Periodical Articles Related to Law* reflected the contributions of other disciplines to the study of law. Edited by Roy M. Mersky and Donald J. Dunn, this index included legal articles of research value that appeared in periodicals not covered by the *Index to Legal Periodicals & Books, Legal Resource Index*, or the *Index to Foreign Legal Periodicals*.

This index, published by Glanville Publishers from 1958 to 2005, was issued quarterly and cumulated annually. Citations are arranged by subject and author. It is available both in print and electronically via *HeinOnline.*

7. Kindex

Subtitled, *An Index to Legal Periodical Literature Concerning Children, Kindex* was published by the National Center for Criminal Justice until 2001. It covers the years 1965 to 2001, emphasizing practical information for those involved in the criminal justice system.

Kindex is available in print or electronically through *HeinOnline.* Access points include a subject index (called a "classification" index) and an author index.

8. Non–Legal Periodical Indexes

Since law affects many other disciplines, it is sometimes necessary to turn to comprehensive indexes that are non-legal in nature to locate general information or to examine legal issues from a non-legal perspective. There are numerous indexes of this type. For example, the H.W. Wilson Company, publisher of *ILP,* also publishes several non-legal indexes, including: *Business Periodicals Index; Humanities Index; Reader's Guide to Periodical Literature* (which covers popular magazines); and *Social Science Index.* These indexes are available commercially on *WilsonWeb. PAIS International,* published by Public Affairs Information Service, Inc., focuses on economics and public affairs and includes several law reviews and government publications in its coverage.

Gale Cengage Learning, publisher of *Current Law Index, LegalTrac,* and *Legal Resource Index,* also publishes a number of non-legal indexes, including *Academic OneFile* (which covers scholarly publications from numerous disciplines) and *General OneFile* (an index somewhat comparable to *Reader's Guide*).

SECTION F. OTHER SOURCES

References to legal periodical articles are frequently found in other sources. Many state codes and the annotated editions of the *United States Code* cite relevant articles in the notes preceding the annotations. Most West digests cite, under the topic and key number, to pertinent law review articles. Similarly, many other West sources, including both national legal encyclopedias, provide references to legal periodical articles.

In addition, citators enable the researcher to locate articles *cited by* courts and other legal periodical articles, as well as articles that *cite to* cases, constitutions, statutes, and rules.[45] This is most easily accomplished through the use of the electronic citators, *Shepard's,* available via *Lexis-Nexis,* and *KeyCite,* available via *Westlaw.*

Several print-based *Shepard's* citators also index law reviews; however coverage may not be as extensive as the electronic citators. *Shepard's Law Review Citations,* with coverage beginning in 1957, provides citations for

[45] Citators are discussed in detail in Chapter 15.

legal periodicals that have been cited in published reports of the state and federal courts and other law reviews. [Illustration 18–9]

Federal Law Citations in Selected Law Reviews lists each time certain nationally recognized law reviews[46] cite to a case in the *U.S. Reports, Federal Reporter, Federal Cases, Federal Supplement, Federal Rules Decisions, Bankruptcy Reporter,* and other lower federal court reporters. It also notes each time any of these reviews cites the U.S. Constitution, any edition of the *United States Code,* or the various federal court rules. Coverage is for articles published since 1973.

The individual state citators provide citations to cases, statutes, constitutions, and court rules that have been cited in the law reviews and bar journals of the state unit being used or by select nationally recognized law reviews. In addition, some of the specialized *Shepard's* citators, e.g., *Federal Tax Citations*, have limited citations to articles.

SECTION G.   ILLUSTRATION: LAW REVIEW CITATIONS IN SHEPARD'S CITATORS

18–9.   Page from Shepard's Law Review Citations

[46] This list of 19 nationally recognized law reviews is provided in Section F of Chapter 15. Note that *Shepard's* on *LexisNexis* indexes substantially more law reviews, approximately 600.

[Illustration 18–9]

PAGE FROM SHEPARD'S LAW REVIEW CITATIONS

TEXAS LAW REVIEW							
72SCL719	38Wsb828	—447—	—951—	—1563—	80MqL460	79TxL849	79TxL152
73TxL1627	98WVL200	49DuLJ752	95McL312	30CnL1355	74TxL1645		24VtL381
73TxL1647		77NCL2051	95McL1097	51HLJ174	74TxL1668	—483—	—1203—
79TxL643		145PaL1427		1999IlLR611	74TxL1801	P R	96McL895
35WML492	**Vol. 74**	86VaL1147	—1039—			1998JTS	70SCL1403
—1627—		43VR203	83Cor403	—1601—	—1943—	[1198	73SCL742
80Cor936	—1—		—1125—	82Cor526	32GaL860	85Cor682	83VaL1566
33GaL1011	193F3d1366	—523—	1998BYU	51StnL76	72NYL800	98CR394	—1301—
49LR192	211BRW551	85CaL440	[144	53StnL248	57OhLJ722	51HLJ310	61LCP(4)45
94McL922	1997BYU	65ChL57	51LR680	74TxL1811	74TxL1645	61LCP(1)26	96McL1326
71NYL299	[804	31CnL716	68MlJ252	107YLJ760	74TxL1665	78NCL1023	77NCL1217
73TxL1650	82Cor774	71CUR14			74TxL1699	75TxL529	72NYL1342
98WVL200	45DR693	47FLR823	—1223—	—1645—	75TxL722	75TxL564	75NYL55
—1647—	33GaL766	95McL729	38W&M446	83Cor106	25WmM670	85VaL1312	146PaL856
73TxL1637	33GaL972	95McL1089	—1227—	31WFL1068		1997WLR	60PitL325
—1653—	85Geo296	—695—	74TxL1198	—1655—		[875	—1413—
97F3d1233	50HLJ264	92F3d1477	—1231—	63ChL1466	**Vol. 75**	—525—	78OLR1051
189FRD352	48LLJ643	20ALJ783	74SCL399	83Cor107	—1—	85Cor682	—1499—
65ChL605	47LR739	30CnL74	—1241—	26FSU963	31CnL480	61LCP(1)26	47EmJ895
33GaL996	97McL973	98CR277	75TxL2	32GaL857	—7—	78NCL1020	83ILR163
83ILR519	57MdL401	111HLR	—1247—	86Geo328	33GaL1027	75TxL559	84MnL909
48RLR623	78NbL873	[2231	74TxL1195	51Mer598	—11—	85VaL1252	75TxL1493
75WsL706	71NYL216	85JlLR6	—1251—	72NYL797	44CLA1007	—559—	—1539—
—1701—	75NYL1632	26SwR1072	41AzL1101	27PLR23	82Cor507	P R	87CaL312
D C	37SAC331	74TxL720	85Geo557	74TxL1645	82Cor1283	1998JTS	83Cor1235
722A2d342	64TnL923	74TxL773	33WFL1041	75TxL763	82Cor1397	[1194	75TxL1497
Pa	30UCD955	74TxL785	1998WLR	75TxL1547	82Cor1473	—571—	76TxL1357
562Pa327	1997WLR	—719—	[915	30UCD491	84Cor349	98CR1149	—1567—
729A2d1148	[740	92F3d1448	—1257—	—1693—	84Cor747	47DuLJ60	49FLR747
755A2d684	—49—	59FS2d953	82ILR498	986FS90	51FLR853	114HLR	32GaL855
	Md	Mich		38AzL1180		[1167	

This unit of *Shepard's* provides a means for "Sheparding" law review articles cited since 1957. Through its use, one can find every time a law review article has been cited by another law review or in a court case.

Tex	—101—	74TxL775	74TxL1201	—1741—	[412	—687—	—1605—
953SW728	85Cor333	75TxL1288	—1297—	74TxL1195	230Wis2d	172F3d1247	99CR1436
30AzSJ386	95McL1090	42WnLJ974	P R	74TxL1666	[138	1999IlLR588	32GaL1041
50BLR318	50Mer448	—773—	1997JTS229	—1783—	579NW651	52StnL1089	75TxL1495
36HUL1171	74TxL111	85ILR102	—1301—	88CaL1113	600NW922	—779—	75TxL1667
43SDR594	32WFL667	26SwR1072	42AzL835	63ChL1508	74NYL128	49DuLJ426	77TxL1411
27SMJ268	—111—	74TxL785	30AzSJ769	1999IlLR450	—189—	77TxL924	—1661—
28SMJ25	85Cor333	—785—	83Cor424	30LoyL195	29EnL804	—907—	Tex
78TxL355	29McGL295	26SwR1072	46DuLJ1023	72NYL801	37IDR64	87CaL1439	977SW337
30UCD955	74TxL101	74TxL777	113HLR	74TxL1645	—215—	67ChL1159	982SW161
—1805—	32WFL667	—795—	[1650	74TxL1831	71CUR1392	50DuLJ519	83Cor883
46AU655	—237—	529US663	51MiL980	86VaL1641	—237—	112HLR	39Wsb379
64GW462	112HLR784	146LE706	76NCL153	—1813—	Wis	[1163	—1699—
1998IlLR356	73NYL1794	120SC1778	33SDL1329	72NYL794	236Wis2d	61LCP(3)95	Tex
32WFL837	83VaL426	1999BYU	—1361—	74NYL634	[237	97McL2263	988SW206
—1821—	—259—	[100	75NYL384	31RJC780	612NW672	74NYL130	29SMJ494
84F3d747	Fla	64ChL484	—1485—	70TLQ1095	114HLR781	146PaL1069	30SMJ5
211BRW576	744So2d494	44CLA763	75OLR971	86VaL476	520kLR69	72SCL350	75TxL1496
Md	49AkL703	98CR427	75TxL3	—1847—	72SCL1129	—989—	—1721—
358Md768	46AU1341	111HLR	—1487—	40AzL603	75TxL1743	971FS68	42AzL24
752A2d243	49DuLJ609	[2220	85Cor1204	82Cor533	1997WLR	86CaL526	99CR1467
Tex	49EmJ91	85ILR7	31RIC787	27Cum572	[448	87CaL116	60LCP(4)42
975SW603	27FSU28	82MnL253	36SDL72	68CUR948	1998WLR	89CaL15	75TxL1498
975SW610	27FSU139	83MnL629	51StnL97	68CUR1002	[116	71CUR928	1998WLR
39AzL597	82MnL727	72NDR480	74TxL1680	68CUR1043	25WmM897	48DuLJ201	[225
44CLA1792	50SMU434	27Pcf1633	74TxL1792	68CUR1095	—293—	49EmJ830	—1765—
44CLA1853	30TTR1357	59PitL813	1997WLR	68CUR1158	125F3d907	111HLR	34FS2d1020
80Cor1027	54W&L765	34SDL251	[384	31GaL798	144F3d1113	97McL465	La
45DR627	38W&M211	26SwR1072	—1527—	32GaL551	56FS2d67	82MnL696	755So2d896
85Geo320	32WFL683	75TxL1290	203F3d710	85ILR646	79FS2d1164	76NCL87	83ILR210
83ILR536	32WFL796	86VaL230	48LLJ23	96McL2213	Okla	60PitL155	58LLR5
94McL912	32WFL887	21VtL761	48LLJ149	—1901—	981P2d1260	40SAC376	58LLR42
94McL1257	25WSR235	—839—	67MlJ614	32AzSJ1283	—375—	35SDL65	96McL1132
29SeH218	—345—	70TuL2134	51StnL119	83Cor105	223BRW294	37SDL1007	37SDL408
73TxL1628	92F3d237	—949—	100WVL570	32GaL857	—435—	52StnL1348	39SoTR93
73TxL1702	58PitL700	76TxL276		1999IlLR449	520kLR165	77TxL930	75TxL1493
37Wsb265							Continued

Chapter 19

TREATISES, RESTATEMENTS, UNIFORM LAWS, AND MODEL ACTS*

This chapter discusses two frequently used categories of secondary sources, legal treatises and restatements of the law. Also discussed are two secondary sources that are intended to provide guidance on the drafting and interpretation of statutes—uniform laws and model acts.

SECTION A.   TREATISES: IN GENERAL

Legal treatises are an important category of secondary authority of law. Treatises are extensive expositions by legal experts on case law and legislation pertaining to a particular doctrinal subject and published in book form.[1] Legal treatises, therefore, include a wide variety of types of publications, ranging from multivolume works and textbooks to shorter monographs. Treatises are typically able treat a subject in greater depth than a legal encyclopedia; treatises are usually less speculative than journal articles.

Legal scholars wrote the first treatises during the period of the early development of the common law. Because few judicial opinions were available as precedent during the formative stages of our legal system, writers such as Lord Coke and William Blackstone played significant roles in the development of the law through their thoughtful, detailed commentaries. The growth of the law resulted in an ever-increasing number of law reports, and treatises organized and synthesized diffuse principles of case law. One commentator has noted that treatises were first written because of the lack of precedents and then because of their over abundance.[2]

During the eighteenth and the early nineteenth centuries in the United States, treatises on English law were an integral part of an American lawyer's library. Gradually, American lawyers and legal scholars, such as James Kent and Joseph Story, began publishing treatises devoted entirely to American law.[3] The American system of federalism has resulted in an increasing number of treatises dealing with the law of a specific state.

---

* This chapter was revised and updated by Melissa Bernstein, Reference Librarian, Tarlton Law Library, Jamail Center for Legal Research, University of Texas School of Law.

[1] Even this most basic definition is subject to some qualification, as many treatises published in book form are also available in electronic format.

[2] GEORGE PATON, A TEXTBOOK OF JURISPRUDENCE 264 (4th ed. 1972). *See* A.W.B. Simpson, *The Rise and Fall of the Legal Treatise: Legal Principles and the Forms of Legal Literature,* 48 U. CHI. L. REV. 632 (1981). For two articles that rank the contributions of scholars to the legal literature, particularly treatises and legal periodical articles, see Fred R. Shapiro, *The Most–Cited Legal Books Published Since 1978,* 29 J. LEGAL STUD. 397 (2000), and Fred R. Shapiro, *The Most–Cited Legal Scholars,* 29 J. LEGAL STUD. 409 (2000).

[3] For a discussion of the development and influence of treatises on American law, see LAWRENCE M. FRIEDMAN, A HISTORY OF AMERICAN LAW 476–81 (3d ed. 2005). *See also* Erwin C. Surrency, *The Beginnings of American Legal Literature,* 31 AM. J. LEGAL HIST. 207 (1987).

1. The Nature of Treatises

Treatises can be broadly classified into four types: (1) treatises that are critical, interpretive, and/or expository; (2) law student texts; (3) practitioner-oriented works; and (4) law for the general public. In most instances, however, particular treatises do not fall neatly into such a classification, and they may include some features of all types. Regardless of how scholarly the work, an experienced researcher would not rely on a treatise without verifying the relevance and accuracy of the underlying authorities.

a. *Critical, Interpretive, or Expository Treatises.* Treatises in this category generally examine an area of law in depth, although they vary in the extent to which they critique, interpret, and explain the law. Some constructively criticize rules of law as presently interpreted by the courts. They might include historical analyses to show that current rules actually had different meanings or interpretations than those presently given by the courts. The author may include an examination of the policy reasons for one or more such rules. Some treatises do not attempt to evaluate rules in relation to underlying policy, but rather attempt to explain the terminology and meaning of the rules as they exist. In these treatises, emphasis is placed upon understanding the law and not upon proposing what the law should be. Some treatises exist primarily as substitutes for digests and are principally used as case finders. These treatises typically consist of survey-type essay paragraphs arranged under conventional subject headings with numerous footnote citations. Usually minimal analysis and synthesis of conflicting cases are the most a researcher can expect to find in them. [Illustrations 19–1 and 19–2]

b. *Student Textbooks.* Student textbooks or hornbooks are typically elementary treatments that include more limited critical and interpretive discussions than those found in full treatises. In fact, the term "hornbook[4] law," is commonly used to refer to basic doctrinal principles of law. [Illustration 19–3] Student hornbooks, however, are useful as case finders because their references are usually selective and limited to landmark cases. Major publishers of student treatises include Foundation Press, LexisNexis Matthew Bender, West, and Wolters Kluwer Law & Business.

c. *Practitioner–Oriented Books.* In recent years, the number of continuing education programs for lawyers has increased significantly. For example, the American Law Institute and American Bar Association Joint Committee on Continuing Legal Education (ALI–ABA), the Practising Law Institute (PLI), and state bar associations hold seminars and symposia on many contemporary subjects that are directed toward practicing lawyers and intended to keep them updated on new developments in law. Many states have their own continuing legal education institutes.[5] It is quite common for such institutes to publish handbooks in conjunction with their programs.

---

[4] A hornbook is a basic or rudimentary primer on a given subject. For the derivation of the word *hornbook,* see 6 THE NEW ENCYCLOPEDIA BRITANNICA, MACROPEDIA 63–64 (15th ed. 1990).

[5] For a listing of continuing legal education courses, consult the ALI–ABA website at http://ali-aba.org.

These volumes, as well as a rapidly increasing number of practice-oriented books by commercial publishers, usually furnish analyses of the law, practical guidance, forms, checklists, and other time-saving aids. These publications often deal with business transactions, personal injuries, commercial and corporate practice, probate practice, trial practice, and other subjects of primary interest to practicing attorneys. West, for example, publishes a *Practitioner Treatise Series.*

d. *Law for the General Public.* Increasingly, non-lawyers are turning to so-called "self-help" books. These publications, which often are met with disdain by the legal community, are intended to help the public conduct some legal affairs without the aid of an attorney, e.g., preparation of a will.[6] Nolo, of Berkeley, California, is the leading publisher of books of this genre. Oceana Publications' *Legal Almanac Series* attempts to describe basic legal issues in simple language. The American Civil Liberties Union has also published several titles targeted for the lay audience. The American Bar Association maintains a LawInfo section on its website described as "your gateway to information on legal topics that affect your daily life."[7]

2. The Characteristics of Treatises

The fundamental characteristics of treatises are essentially the same. Treatises typically contain the following elements:

a. *Table of Contents.* The table of contents sets forth the topical divisions of the treatise, which is usually arranged by chapters and subdivisions.

b. *Table of Cases.* The table of cases lists the cases discussed by the author and provides page number references.

c. *Subject Matter.* The subject matter of the text is contained in the main body of the publication.

d. *Supplementation.* Some treatises are updated and supplemented by pocket parts for insertion in the back of the volume or by separate pamphlets. Other treatises take the form of looseleaf volumes, which allow the removal and replacement of obsolete material. Updated materials indicate recent statutory and case developments. Treatises are increasingly published in looseleaf format.[8]

e. *Index.* An index, setting forth the topics, subtopics, and descriptive words, all arranged alphabetically, and with cross-references among index entries, is typically the last feature found in a treatise.

3. Locating Treatises

The starting point for determining whether or not a library has treatises on a subject or treatises by a specific author is its public catalog. Library catalogs, either electronic or in printed card format, enable a researcher to locate materials by author, title, or subject. Electronic catalogs typically enable users to access information by any word or combina-

---

[6] The best source for identifying this type material is AMBER HEWETT & DIANE MURLEY, LAW FOR THE LAYPERSON: AN ANNOTATED BIBLIOGRAPHY OF SELF-HELP LAW BOOKS (3d ed. 2006).

[7] http://www.abanet.org/lawinfo/home.html.

[8] Looseleaf services are discussed in Chapter 14.

tion of words in the bibliographic record for that item. A useful keyword search is to combine the subject with the word "treatise." Most law libraries use the classification system and subject headings established by the Library of Congress. Users of electronic catalogs can "browse" titles with very similar classification numbers.

Some libraries provide access to the online catalogs of other libraries and online bibliographic databases such as OCLC WORLDCAT. This database includes millions of records describing published works. Librarians also may have access to an array of other sources, both print and electronic, which can assist in locating materials. If an item is identified that is not available in your library, it might be possible to obtain that item through interlibrary loan.

Other methods for identifying treatises on a particular subject or by a specific author include:

a. *Making of Modern Law: Legal Treatises 1800–1926*. Electronic database produced by Gale Cengage Learning. This fully searchable database contains the full text of approximately 22,000 works on United States and British law published from 1800 through 1926. It includes treatises, casebooks, local practice manuals, form books, works for lay readers, pamphlets, letters, speeches, and more.

b. *Rise of American Law*. This is a new electronic collection of legal resources from West covering the period from 1820 to 1970. It provides access to over 1,700 out-of-print volumes in PDF format, including multivolume sets and multiple editions. Searching is by keyword, author, or title.

c. *Bibliography of Early American Law (BEAL)*. This six-volume set, compiled by Morris L. Cohen and published in 1998 by William S. Hein & Co., covers the period from the beginnings of American history up to and including 1860. The over 14,000 items in the set include treatises, bibliographies, commentaries, digests, lectures, polemics, biographies, civil and criminal trials, and numerous other important documents of this period. Eight indexes provide multiple points of access to the set. *BEAL* is also available in CD–ROM.

d. *New York University, School of Law Library, A Catalogue of the Law Collection of New York University* (Julius Marke ed., 1953). This is an excellent source for older treatises and includes book review annotations.

e. Law Books Recommended for Libraries. In the 1960s, the Association of American Law Schools (AALS) undertook a large scale Library Studies Project designed to identify all published treatises and rate their importance to a law school library collection.[9] Arranged under 46 subjects and titled *Law Books Recommended for Libraries*, these lists were published separately in six notebook volumes from 1967 to 1970, with supplements issued for 42 of these subjects from 1974 to 1976. Actual coverage of titles

---

[9] Titles were rated A, B, or C. "A" indicated that the title was "recommended for inclusion in the basic minimum collection." "B" indicated that the title was recommended for "a library which is in the intermediate phase of development and is progressing toward support of a research program and an enriched curriculum which includes seminar offerings." "C" indicated that the title was "recommended for larger libraries with research collections of such quality and scope that they will support original scholarship in considerable depth."

extended only to approximately 1970. The project was discontinued after 1976.

f. *Recommended Publications for Legal Research* (Mary F. Miller ed.), published by William S. Hein & Co., began under different editors, Oscar J. Miller and Mortimer D. Schwartz, as an effort to fill the gap left by the cessation of the AALS Library Studies Project. A separate volume for each year dating back to 1970 was prepared, and each year a new volume is issued covering titles published during the previous year. This publication uses the A, B, and C ratings employed in the AALS project.

g. Kendall F. Svengalis, *Legal Information Buyer's Guide & Reference Manual* (Rhode Island LawPress 12th ed. 2008). This book provides, among other valuable information, a history of legal publishing, information on maintaining a law library (including costs), and ways to evaluate legal materials. In addition to discussing statutes, reporters, digests, legal encyclopedias, and other major legal research tools, this *Guide* provides an annotated listing of legal treatises under approximately 60 subject categories. A separate section contains a practitioner's guide to legal publications by state.

h. *IndexMaster. IndexMaster* is a Web-based subscription service that permits keyword, title, author, and publisher searching of the table of contents and indexes of over 7,000 legal treatises and practice materials.

i. *Law Books and Serials in Print.* This annual publication by Bowker contains over 40,000 titles of legal books, serials, and multimedia publications. A brief descriptive annotation is given for each title.

j. *Law Books in Print. Law Books in Print* was a bibliographic listing of law books in the English language from around the world. It began in 1957 and ended in 1997 with the five-volume 8th edition (coverage was through 1996). It contained separate indexes for author/title, publisher, and subject.

k. *Catalog of Current Law Titles.* This source, published by William S. Hein & Co., began in 1984 as *National Legal Bibliography* and was renamed *Catalog of Current Law Titles* in 1989. The title ceased publication in July 1998. It lists by subject and jurisdiction titles cataloged by over 60 law libraries around the country. A separate section lists those titles cataloged by at least one-fourth of those libraries. A cumulative supplement was issued annually.

l. *Indexes Covering Treatises.* In 1994, the *Index to Legal Periodicals* (*ILP*) added books to the scope of its coverage. Approximately 1,400 book titles are included in each issue of *ILP*. Entries are listed under main entry (author or title) and under subject at the end of the subject entries for articles. *PAIS International* indexes some law-related titles as well, including government publications. The *Index to Canadian Legal Literature*, which began in 1987, is a comprehensive index to Canadian periodical, monographic, and book review literature on law.

m. *Books in Print.* Also useful in locating treatises and other books about law is Bowker's annual *Books in Print. Bowker's Global Books in Print*, the electronic version of this resource, is updated daily and contains books about to be published, as far as six months in advance.

SECTION B. TREATISES: RESEARCH PROCEDURE

1. Case Method

If the name of a leading case on point is known, consult the table of cases of an appropriate treatise to ascertain whether this case is discussed in the book. If so, an examination of the cited pages in the text will reveal a discussion of the subject matter, along with additional cases on point.

2. Index Method

Consult the subject index in the back of the book if the name of a case is not known or if the research is in a particular aspect of a subject. Select an appropriate descriptive word or legal topic to use the index. References will direct the researcher to the text of the publication.

3. Topic Method

The topic method can be used through the table of contents; however, its effectiveness in locating pertinent text depends on the researcher's understanding of the structural subject subdivisions used in that treatise.

4. Definition Method

The index or a separate glossary to the treatise may list words and phrases that are defined and explained in the text.

5. Full–Text Searching (Electronic Versions)

Increasingly, electronic versions of treatises are available in online and CD–ROM formats. Electronic access enables a researcher to search the full text of the work and use strategies unavailable in the print versions. Often it is possible to link, through hypertext, to and from sections in the treatise and to sources cited by that treatise.

SECTION C. ILLUSTRATIONS: TREATISES

Problem: **Does the "learned intermediary doctrine" provide any protections for manufacturers of prescription drug products?**

19–1. **Page from Index to Frumer & Friedman, Products Liability**
19–2. **Page from Frumer & Friedman, Products Liability**
19–3. **Page from Dobbs, The Law of Torts**

[Illustration 19–1]

PAGE FROM INDEX TO FRUMER & FRIEDMAN, PRODUCTS LIABILITY

> To locate a reference to discussion in a treatise, such as Frumer & Friedman, *Products Liability*, of the issue presented in the problem, consult the index.

(Matthew Bender & Co., Inc.)   (Rel.88–7/01 Pub.560)

[Illustration 19–2]

PAGE FROM FRUMER & FRIEDMAN, PRODUCTS LIABILITY

§ 50.04[2]   **PRODUCTS LIABILITY**   50–28

[2]—Who Should Be Warned?

In prescription drug cases, the "nearly universal" rule, which is called the learned intermediary doctrine,[9] is that manufacturers have a duty to warn the physicians, dentists and other health care professionals who prescribe drugs for patients. *See* § 12.08 *above*, for an extensive discussion of this doctrine.

Nevertheless, as also discussed in § 12.08 *above*, in a few states, two specific exceptions to the learned intermediary doctrine have developed. One situation involves mass-immunization with vaccines, where vaccines are administered to everyone, without a balancing of risks as to a specific patient.[10] In a few states, the second exception applies where patients have chosen to utilize a specific type of prescription drug, or prescription device, for birth

---

[9] **The learned intermediary doctrine is nearly universal.** *See, e.g.*:

Arkansas	Hill v. Searle Laboratories, Div. of Searle Pharmaceuticals, Inc., 686 F. Supp. 720, 726 (E.D. Ark. 1988), *aff'd in part and rev'd in part on other grounds*, 884 F.2d 1064, 1070–1072 (8th Cir. 1989), applying Arkansas law ("nearly universal rule"); West v. Searle & Co., 305 Ark. 33, 42, 806 S.W.2d 608, 613 (1991) ("almost universally applied exception").
West Virginia	Pumphrey v. C.R. Bard, Inc., 906 F. Supp. 334, 337 (N.D. W.Va. 1995) (Frumer & Friedman cited; "nearly universal").

> Note that the index leads to a relevant discussion of the issue under research. A typical treatise, such as this one, contains text and then footnote references to cases and other pertinent materials. If supplementation is provided, this material should be consulted for later material.

Iowa	Brazzell v. U.S., 788 F.2d 1352, 1358 (8th Cir. 1986) (swine flu vaccine).
Kansas	Graham v. Wyeth Laboratories, Div. of American Home Prods. Corp., 666 F. Supp. 1483, 1498 (D. Kan. 1987) (DPT vaccine).
Montana	Davis v. Wyeth Laboratories, Inc., 399 F.2d 121, 131 (9th Cir. 1968) (Frumer and Fried cited; Type III Sabin oral polio vaccine).
Nevada	Allison v. Merck & Co., 110 Nev. 762, 776, 878 P.2d 948, 958 (1994) (measles, mumps, rubella vaccine, MMR II).
Oklahoma	Cunningham v. Charles Pfizer & Co., Inc., 532 P.2d 1377, 1381–1382 (Okla. 1974) (Sabin oral polio vaccine).
Pennsylvania	Mazur v. Merck & Co., 964 F.2d 1348, 1357–1360 (3d Cir.), *cert. denied*, 506 U.S. 974, 113 S. Ct. 463, 121 L. Ed. 2d 371 (1992) (measles, mumps, rubella vaccine, MMR II).
Texas	Reyes v. Wyeth Laboratories, 498 F.2d 1264, 1277 (5th Cir.), *cert. denied*, 419 U.S. 1096, 95 S. Ct. 687, 42 L. Ed. 2d 688 (1974) (Sabin oral polio vaccine).

[Illustration 19–3]

PAGE FROM DOBBS, THE LAW OF TORTS

warning could be brighter or bigger does not in itself show that it is inadequate.[18]

English-only warnings. Children, illiterate adults, and adults who read only or mainly a foreign language cannot be warned by an English-only label. In a California case, an aspirin manufacturer targeted Spanish-speaking groups with its Spanish advertising, but its aspirin contained no Spanish warnings that aspirin could cause small children severe neurological damage, blindness, spastic quadriplegia and mental retardation. The court thought that the legislature, by affirmatively requiring warnings in English, negatively implied that no others could be required.[19] A few other cases have gone the other way, considering

> This page is from a treatise written primarily for law students. This particular title is part of the West *Hornbook Series*. Note the footnote references to court cases and secondary sources. Not shown in this illustration are suggested *Westlaw* queries that can be used to research this issue electronically.

altogether and makes federal law the only law on point. The federal statute requiring warnings on cigarette packages is like this. It preempts state tort law that would require a more adequate warning.[21] In broader perspective, the question is whether tort obligations should be decided exclusively by administrative regulations or statutes where they exist.[22]

§ 365. Prescription Drugs, Medical Device Warnings

Prescription drugs, medical devices. Courts almost always hold that a prescription drug manufacturer's warning to the doctor who prescribes a drug is sufficient to warn the doctor's patient as well. If the doctor fails to inform the patient of the risks, the patient has a claim against the doctor, but not against the manufacturer of the drug.[1] This is usually referred to as the learned intermediary doctrine, and it is usually

will ignite leaves or grass, but the only warning was buried in the 100-page owner's manual); cf. Payne v. Soft Sheen Prods., Inc., 486 A.2d 712, 58 A.L.R.4th 15 (D.C. 1985) (chemicals for hair treatment in multiple steps provided warning of burns only at the end of the instructions, after the instructions had guided operator through each step).

18. See General Motors Corp. v. Saenz, 873 S.W.2d 353 (Tex.1993).

19. Ramirez v. Plough, Inc., 6 Cal.4th 539, 25 Cal.Rptr.2d 97, 863 P.2d 167 (1993).

20. Hubbard–Hall Chem. Co. v. Silverman, 340 F.2d 402 (1st Cir.1965) (suggesting skull and crossbones on deadly poison used by agricultural workers); Campos v. Firestone Tire & Rubber Co., 98 N.J. 198, 485 A.2d 305 (1984) ("In view of the unskilled or semi-skilled nature of the work and the existence of many in the work force

who do not read English, warnings in the form of symbols might have been appropriate"). See Marjorie A. Caner, Annotation, Products Liability: Failure to Provide Product Warning or Instruction in Foreign Language or to Use Universally Accepted Pictographs or Symbols, 27 A.L.R.5th 697 (1995).

21. Cipollone v. Liggett Group, Inc., 505 U.S. 504, 112 S.Ct. 2608, 120 L.Ed.2d 407 (1992).

22. See § 373.

§ 365

1. E.g., Stone v. Smith, Kline & French Labs., 447 So.2d 1301 (Ala.1984); Humes v. Clinton, 246 Kan. 590, 792 P.2d 1032 (1990) Restatement of Products Liability § 6 (d). Although the doctor is not chronologically an intermediary between pharmacist and patient, the doctor is the final and

SECTION D. RESTATEMENTS OF THE LAW

In the early part of the twentieth century, prominent American judges, lawyers, and law professors became concerned over two aspects of case law—its growing uncertainty and undue complexity. As a result, in 1923, the American Law Institute (ALI) was founded to address these issues.[10] The objectives of the ALI focused on reducing the number of legal publications that had to be consulted by the bench and bar, simplifying case law by a clear, systematic restatement of it, and diminishing the flow of judicial decisions. The founders feared that the increasing mass of unorganized judicial opinions threatened to break down the common law system of expressing and developing law.[11]

To remedy these problems, the ALI undertook to produce clear and precise restatements of the existing common law that would have "authority greater than that now accorded to any legal treatise, an authority more nearly on a par with that accorded the decisions of the courts."[12]

This was accomplished by eminent legal scholars engaged as reporters for the various subjects to be restated. Each reporter prepared tentative drafts of the particular restatement. These drafts were then submitted to and approved by the members of the ALI. Often, numerous tentative drafts, with the work extending over many years, were prepared before final agreement was reached and a restatement adopted.

Between 1923 and 1944, restatements were adopted for the law of agency, conflict of laws, contracts, judgments, property, restitution, security, torts, and trusts. Since 1957, a second series of restatements have been adopted for agency, conflict of laws, contracts, foreign relations law, judgments, property (landlord & tenant and donative transfers), torts, and trusts.

In 1986, a third series of restatements began with issuance of *Restatement (Third) of the Foreign Relations Law of the United States*. Since 1986, restatements have been adopted for agency, employment law, the law governing lawyers, property (mortgages), property (servitudes), property (wills and other donative transfers), suretyship and guaranty, torts (apportionment of liability, liability for physical and emotional harm, and products liability), trusts (prudent investor rule), and unfair competition. In addition, tentative drafts of additional topics for both the second and third

---

[10] This discussion of the restatements is drawn from the following sources: (1) William Draper Lewis, *History of the American Law Institute and the First Restatement of the Law, in* AMERICAN LAW INSTITUTE, RESTATEMENT IN THE COURTS 1–23 (permanent ed. 1945); (2) HERBERT F. GOODRICH & PAUL A. WOLKIN, THE STORY OF THE AMERICAN LAW INSTITUTE, 1923–1961 (1961); (3) AMERICAN LAW INSTITUTE, THE AMERICAN LAW INSTITUTE 50TH ANNIVERSARY (1973); (4) AMERICAN LAW INSTITUTE, THE AMERICAN LAW INSTITUTE SEVENTY-FIFTH ANNIVERSARY, 1923–1998 (1998); and (5) AMERICAN LAW INSTITUTE, ANNUAL REPORTS. *See also The American Law Institute Restatement of the Law and Codifications, in* 3 PIMSLEUR'S CHECKLISTS OF BASIC AMERICAN LEGAL PUBLICATIONS § V (Marcia S. Zubrow ed. & comp., looseleaf) (AALL Publication Series, No. 4).

[11] Lewis, *supra* note 10, at 1.

[12] *Report of the Committee on the Establishment of a Permanent Organization for the Improvement of the Law Proposing the Establishment of the American Law Institute, in* AMERICAN LAW INSTITUTE, THE AMERICAN LAW INSTITUTE 50TH ANNIVERSARY 34 (1973).

series continue to be issued, likely resulting in additional restatements in the future.[13]

The status of the revision of specific restatements and information pertaining to proposed new restatements can be ascertained from the latest *ALI Annual Reports*, and from its quarterly newsletter, *The ALI Reporter*. ALI's home page[14] includes the status of its publications along with a variety of other useful information.

It had been recommended that state legislatures be required to approve the restatements, not as formal legislative enactments, but as aids and guides to the judiciary so that they will feel free to follow "the collective scholarship and expert knowledge of our profession."[15] This proposal, however, was not adopted by the ALI membership. Nevertheless, many courts give greater authority to the restatements than that accorded to treatises and other secondary sources. In many instances, the restatements are accorded an authority nearly equal that of decided cases.[16]

The first series of the restatements reflected the desire of the ALI's founders that the restatements be admired and adopted by the courts. To this end they deliberately omitted the reporters' citations and references to the tentative drafts upon which the restatement rules were based.

With publication of the second series of the restatements, a decision was made to abandon the idea of the restatements serving as a substitute for the codification of common law. The Second and Third Series sometimes indicate a new trend in the common law and attempt to state what a new rule will or should be.[17] This change in policy is also reflected in the appearance of citations to judicial opinions and to the notes of the reporters. Appendices contain citations to, and brief synopses of, all cases that have cited the restatements. It should be noted that a new restatement on the same topic as an existing one does not supersede the older version. Some courts, in fact, continue to cite earlier restatements.

The frequency with which the restatements are cited by the courts suggests their value and importance to legal research.[18] Restatements not only provide statements of the rules of common law, which are operative in a great number of states, but also are valuable sources for finding cases on point.

Moreover, a comparison of the texts of the restatements and state case law reveals that there are surprisingly few deviations from the common law that are expressed in the restatements. It has been suggested, therefore,

---

[13] For a list of past and present ALI projects, see http://www.ali.org/doc/past_present_ALIprojects.pdf. This list is updated periodically. A listing of current projects can be found at http://www.ali.org/index.cfm?fuseaction=projects.currentprojects.

[14] http://www.ali.org.

[15] Alpheus Thomas Mason, *Harlan Fiske Stone Assays Social Justice, 1912–1923,* 99 U. PA. L. REV. 887, 915 (1951) (quoting from a speech given by Stone).

[16] For a discussion of the precedential authority of the restatements, see James F. Byrne, *Reevaluation of the Restatements as a Source of Law in Arizona,* 15 ARIZ. L. REV. 1021, 1023–26 (1973).

[17] *Id.*

[18] According to the American Law Institute, courts have cited restatements 176,076 times, as of May 1, 2008. The American Law Institute tracks this number internally.

that there is in fact a common law that transcends state lines and prevails throughout the nation.[19] However, courts may at times inaccurately and confusingly state legal rules. Thus, another objective of the restatements is to assist courts in stating doctrinal rules of law more clearly.[20]

1. Features of the Restatements

The various restatements are typically divided broadly into chapters, and further subdivided into narrower titles, and then into numbered discrete sections. Each section begins with a "black letter" **(boldface)** restatement of the law, followed by comments that contain hypothetical illustrations. Reporters' notes are set forth at the end of each section.[21] [Illustrations 19–5 through 19–8] These notes serve as a history of the section and will, if applicable, include the text of the section or sections of earlier restatements that are replaced by this later section.

The following additional features are included in the second and third series of the restatements:

a. *Tables.* These list citations to judicial opinions, statutes, and other authorities referenced in the restatement.

b. *Conversion or Parallel Tables.* These enable a user to locate a section in a tentative draft or prior restatement series within the text in the final restatement.

c. *Cross-references.* These give references to West's key number system and to *A.L.R.* annotations.

2. Indexes

a. *Restatements, First Series.* A one-volume index to all restatements in the first series has been published. Each restatement also has its own subject index.

b. *Restatements, Second Series* and *Third Series.* Some of the older restatements have their own subject index in each volume, covering only the materials in that volume. More recent restatements contain an index in the last volume of the restatement or in a separate volume. [Illustration 19–4] There is no comprehensive index to all restatements.

3. Restatements Cited by Courts

The ALI maintains statistics and information about the number of times the restatements have been cited by courts. For a number of years, this information was contained in a set entitled *Restatements in the Courts.* Issued first as a permanent edition covering 1932 to 1944 and then updated

---

[19] Herbert F. Goodrich, *Restatement and Codification, in* DAVID DUDLEY FIELD: CENTENARY ESSAYS CELEBRATING ONE HUNDRED YEARS OF LEGAL REFORM 241–50 (Allison Reppy ed., 1949).

[20] An exhaustive list of articles on all aspects of the work of the American Law Institute is in the Annual Reports section of the Annual Meeting PROCEEDINGS under the title *The Institute in Legal Literature, A Bibliography.* This listing is also available from ALI's website, *supra* note 14. *See also Symposium on the American Law Institute: Process, Partisanship, and the Restatements of Law,* 26 HOFSTRA L. REV. 567 (1998).

[21] For the first three Restatements (Second), namely agency, torts, and trusts, the reporters' notes are in the appendix volumes accompanying these subjects.

with bound supplements covering from 1945 to 1975, this set indicated, with annotations, each citation by a court to a section of the restatement.

These annotations were subsequently recompiled and added to the individual appendix volumes of the current restatements. New appendix volumes are published periodically. These appendices, prior to being cumulated into bound volumes, are updated either by cumulative pocket supplements or separate annual cumulative supplements, or by semiannual pamphlets entitled *Interim Case Citations.* These interim pamphlets contain only citations and do not include the case synopses found in the pocket supplements and cumulative volumes.

4. Electronic Access to Restatements

Restatements, including current pocket parts, annual supplements, interim case citation pamphlets, and tentative drafts, are available on *Westlaw* in the Restatements of the Law database. Each restatement is also available in its own database. West also publishes the current restatements in a single CD–ROM. Restatements are also available on *LexisNexis* in the Secondary Legal library, Restatements of the Law file. The first series of restatements is not available on *LexisNexis,* nor are the various drafts of the restatements, and the text is searchable separately from case citations.

5. Locating Legal Periodical Articles About the ALI and the Restatements

Articles about the American Law Institute and the restatements can be located though all of the major indexes to legal periodicals: *Index to Legal Periodicals and Books (ILP), Current Law Index (CLI), LegalTrac,* and *Legal Resource Index (LRI).*

6. Shepardizing Restatements

Shepard's Restatement of the Law Citations is devoted entirely to the restatements. This set gives citations to all federal court reports, all units of the *National Reporter System,* and all state court reports that cite to a restatement. [Illustration 19–9] It also includes articles citing the restatements in 19 leading law reviews. Citations to court decisions, law review articles, and other resources such as court documents can also be found by KeyCiting or Shepardizing restatement sections.

7. Restatements in the American Law Institute Archive Publications in Microfiche

The *American Law Institute Archive Publications in Microfiche* (William S. Hein & Co.) is the most exhaustive collection of documents on the ALI and its projects. Its coverage is from 1923, the year of ALI's founding, to the present. This publication includes all ALI *Proceedings, Annual Reports,* minutes, the various drafts of the restatements from inception to completion, the codifications together with their background sources for projects with which the ALI has been associated, and previously unreleased confidential documents. The set is updated annually as of 2009. The collection contains approximately 4,000 documents. A printed guide provides access to these materials. This collection also is available in the

American Law Institute Library on *HeinOnline* and is updated as material is received from the ALI.

SECTION E.   ILLUSTRATIONS: RESTATEMENT (THIRD) OF TORTS: PRODUCTS LIABILITY

Problem: **Does the "learned intermediary doctrine" provide any protections for manufacturers of prescription drugs?**

[Illustration 19–4]

PAGE FROM INDEX TO RESTATEMENT (THIRD) OF TORTS: PRODUCTS LIABILITY

INDEX

LATENCY PERIOD OF HARM
Causation and proportional liability, § **15 Com.** *c*; § **15 RN to Com.** *c*

LAUNDROMAT
Bailment as commercial distribution, dryers, § **20 Com.** *f*

LEARNED INTERMEDIARY RULE
Generally, § **6 Com.** *b*; § **6 RN to Com.** *b*; § **6 RN to Com.** *d*

LEASES
Financing. See Finance Lessors
One who otherwise distributes a product, § **20(b)**; § **20 Com.** *c*; § **20 RN to Com.**
     c
One who sells or otherwise distributes, defined, § **20(b)**
Used product sellers' or distributors' liability for defective used products, short-term
     product leases, § **8 Com.** *j*; § **20 RN to Com.** *c*

LESSORS
One who otherwise distributes a product, lessor as, § **20(b)**; § **20 Com.** *c*; § **20 RN**
     to Com. *c*

In multivolume sets of Restatement 2d and 3d, an index is sometimes in each volume and only covers the topics addressed by that volume; for some sets the index is in the last volume for that subject. Once the appropriate volume is located, typically by reference to the Table of Contents, that volume's index can be used to locate relevant material. In the problem being researched, a likely subject heading to consult is "learned intermediary doctrine" or "learned intermediary rule."

See the next four illustrations for examples of how the restatements are arranged.

LIVESTOCK
"Product," tangible personal property as, § **19 Com.** *b*; § **19 RN to Com.** *b*

LIVING ANIMALS
"Product," tangible personal property as, § **19 Com.** *b*; § **19 RN to Com.** *b*

LONGEVITY
Omission of reasonable alternative rendering product not reasonably safe, § **2 Com.**
     f

LOSS OF EARNINGS
Plaintiff's person, resulting from harm to, § **21 Com.** *b*

LUMBER
"Product," tangible personal property as, § **19 Com.** *b*; § **19 RN to Com.** *b*

M

MAINTENANCE SERVICES
Successor liability for harm caused by successor's own post-sale failure to warn,
     § **13**; § **13 Com.** *b*;

MAINTENANCE
Omission of reasonable alternative rendering product not reasonably safe, § **2 Com.**
     f
Services, distinguished from, § **19 Com.** *f*

MALFUNCTION
Doctrine, § **3 RN 1 to Com.** *b*

MALFUNCTIONS
Economic loss from harm to product itself, § **21 Com.** *d*; § **21 RN to Com.** *d*

[Illustration 19–5]

PAGE FROM RESTATEMENT (THIRD) OF TORTS: PRODUCTS LIABILITY § 6

§ 5 PRODUCTS LIABILITY Ch. 1

ing a partial summary judgment motion to bar claims against a defendant that manufactured a component because genuine issue of material fact existed as to whether defendant was involved in the design); Koonce v. Quaker Safety Prods. & Mfg. Co., 798 F.2d 700 (5th Cir.1986) (applying Texas law).

A component-part manufacturer that does not substantially participate in the integration of the product is not liable under Subsection (b). Courts frequently absolve the compo-

v. Marquess & Nell, Inc. 675 A.2d 620, 627 (N.J.1996); Depre v. Power Climber, Inc., 635 N.E.2d 542, 544 (Ill.App.1994); Noonan v. Texaco, Inc. 713 P.2d 160, 164 (Wyo.1986). These decisions are consistent with the thrust of Subsection (b). In all of the cited cases, the component supplier did not substantially participate in the design of the integrated product and thus would not be subject to liability. Courts appear to be using the concept of lack of "control" as a shorthand method of expressing the

A restatement's "black letter" rule immediately follows the section number.

the integrated product. See e.g., Trevino v. Yamaha Motor Corp., 882 F.2d 182, 184–185, 186 (5th Cir.1989); Artiglio v. General Electric Co., 71 Cal.Rptr.2d 817 (Cal.App.1998); Zaza

seller that does not substantially participate in the integration of the component into the design of the product has no control over the decisionmaking process that brought about the defective product.

§ 6. Liability of Commercial Seller or Distributor for Harm Caused by Defective Prescription Drugs and Medical Devices

(a) A manufacturer of a prescription drug or medical device who sells or otherwise distributes a defective drug or medical device is subject to liability for harm to persons caused by the defect. A prescription drug or medical device is one that may be legally sold or otherwise distributed only pursuant to a health-care provider's prescription.

(b) For purposes of liability under Subsection (a), a prescription drug or medical device is defective if at the time of sale or other distribution the drug or medical device:

(1) contains a manufacturing defect as defined in § 2(a); or

(2) is not reasonably safe due to defective design as defined in Subsection (c); or

(3) is not reasonably safe due to inadequate instructions or warnings as defined in Subsection (d).

144

[Illustration 19–6]

PAGE FROM RESTATEMENT (THIRD) OF TORTS: PRODUCTS LIABILITY § 6

Ch. 1   LIABILITY BASED ON TIME-OF-SALE DEFECTS   § 6

(c) A prescription drug or medical device is not reasonably safe due to defective design if the foreseeable risks of harm posed by the drug or medical device are sufficiently great in relation to its foreseeable therapeutic benefits that reasonable health-care providers, knowing of such foreseeable risks and therapeutic benefits, would not prescribe the drug or medical device for any class of patients.

(d) A prescription drug or medical device is not reasonably safe due to inadequate instructions or warnings if reasonable instructions or warnings regarding foreseeable risks of harm are not provided to:

(1) prescribing and other health-care providers who are in a position to reduce the risks of harm in accordance with the instructions or warnings; or

(2) the patient when the manufacturer knows or has reason to know that health-care providers will not be in a position to reduce the risks of harm in accordance with the instructions or warnings.

(e) A retail seller or other distributor of a prescrip-

> Following the "black letter" rule is a Comment section explaining the purpose of the rule.

(1) at the time of sale or other distribution the drug or medical device contains a manufacturing defect as defined in § 2(a); or

(2) at or before the time of sale or other distribution of the drug or medical device the retail seller or other distributor fails to exercise reasonable care and such failure causes harm to persons.

Comment:

a. History. Subsections (b)(1) and (d)(1) state the traditional rules that drug and medical-device manufacturers are liable only when their products contain manufacturing defects or are sold without adequate instructions and warnings to prescribing and other health-care providers. Until recently, courts refused to impose liability based on defective designs of drugs and medical devices sold only by prescription. However, consistent with recent trends in the case law, two limited exceptions from these traditional rules are generally recognized. Subsection (d)(2) sets forth situations when a prescription-drug or medical-device manufacturer is required to warn the patient directly of risks associated with consumption or use of its product. And

145

[Illustration 19–7]

PAGE FROM RESTATEMENT (THIRD) OF TORTS: PRODUCTS LIABILITY § 6

§ 6   PRODUCTS LIABILITY   Ch. 1

Illustration:

1.   ABC Pharmaceuticals manufactures and distributes D, a prescription drug intended to prolong pregnancy and thus to reduce the risks associated with premature birth. Patricia, six months pregnant with a history of irregular heart beats, was given D during a hospital stay in connection with her pregnancy. As a result, she suffered heart failure and required open-heart surgery. In Patricia's action against ABC, her expert testifies that, notwithstanding FDA approval of D five years prior to Patricia's taking the drug, credible studies published two years prior to Patricia's taking the drug concluded that D does not prolong pregnancy for any class of patients. Notwithstanding a finding by the trier of fact that ABC gave adequate warnings to the prescribing physician regarding the serious risks of heart failure in patients with a history of irregular heart beats, the trier of fact can find that reasonably informed health-care providers would not prescribe D for any class of patients, thus rendering ABC subject to liability.

g.   Foreseeability of risks of harm in prescription drug and medical device cases. Duties concerning the design and marketing of prescription drugs and medical devices arise only with respect to risks of harm that are reasonably foreseeable at the time of sale. Imposing liability for unforeseeable risks can create inappropriate disincentives

Frequently, the Comment section includes hypothetical examples.

risks, insuring against losses due to unknowable risks would be problematic. Drug and medical device manufacturers have the responsibility to perform reasonable testing prior to marketing a product and to discover risks and risk-avoidance measures that such testing would reveal. See § 2, Comments *a* and *m*.

Illustrations:

2.   DEF Pharmaceuticals, Inc., manufactures and distributes prescription drugs. Seven years ago DEF, after years of research and testing, received permission from the FDA to market X, a drug prescribed for the treatment of low-grade infections. Three years later, Jim, age 12, began taking X on his physician's prescription for a recurring respiratory-tract infection. Jim took X for approximately one year. Two years after Jim had stopped taking X, medical research discovered that X causes loss of vision in adolescents. Prior to this discovery DEF had not warned of this risk. Jim has begun to manifest symptoms of the sort caused by the drug. No evidence suggests that DEF's testing of X was substandard, or that any reasonable drug company should have

150

[Illustration 19–8]

PAGE FROM RESTATEMENT (THIRD) OF
TORTS: PRODUCTS LIABILITY § 6

---

§ 6   PRODUCTS LIABILITY   Ch. 1

patients suffering injury for whom the pamphlets would have been effective in avoiding risks of usage.

REPORTERS' NOTE

Comment b. Rationale. Courts have advanced a number of reasons for exclusive reliance on the learned intermediary rule. See, e.g., West v. Searle & Co., 806 S.W.2d 608, 613–14 (Ark.1991) (provider is best assessor of relevant risks and benefits); Brown v. Superior Court, 751 P.2d 470, 478–79 (Cal.1988) (concern that increased liability would drive prices of drugs too high and make them less available); Lacy v. G.D. Searle & Co., 567 A.2d 398 (Del.1989); In re Certified Questions, 358 N.W.2d 873, 883 (Mich.1984) (Boyle, J., dissenting) (in some cases directly warning patient

Merck & Co. v. Kidd, 242 F.2d 592 (6th Cir.) (applying Tennessee law), cert. denied, 355 U.S. 814, 78 S.Ct. 15, 2 L.Ed.2d 31 (1957); Abbott Labs. v. Lapp, 78 F.2d 170 (7th Cir.1935); Hruska v. Parke, Davis & Co., 6 F.2d 536 (8th Cir.1925); Randall v. Goodrich–Gamble Co., 70 N.W.2d 261 (Minn.1955). Comment *k* to § 402A of the Restatement, Second, of Torts reflects this rule: "The seller of [prescription drugs], *with the qualification that they are properly prepared* and marketed, is not to be held to strict liability for unfortunate consequences attending their use" (empha-

> The Reporter's Notes contain information pertaining to the development of the restatement and include references to cases and secondary authorities. These Notes are in the Appendix volumes for the Restatements (Second) of Agency, Torts, and Trusts. For all other Restatements 2d and for all Restatements 3d, these Notes are at the end of each section of the restatement.

Federal Food and Drug Administration (FDA) regulates vaccine manufacturers.... The regulations are quite detailed in their setting of standards for safety, effectiveness and adequate labelling."); Gravis v. Parke–Davis & Co., 502 S.W.2d 863, 870 (Tex.App.1973) ("[The] entire system of drug distribution in America is set up so as to place the responsibility ... upon professional people"). For a useful discussion of the rule and its underlying rationale, see T. Schwartz, Consumer-Directed Prescription Drug Advertising and the Learned Intermediary Rule, 46 Food Drug Cosm. L.J. 829, 830–31 (1991).

Comment c. Manufacturers' liability for manufacturing defects. Prescription drug manufacturers are strictly liable for harm caused by manufacturing defects. See, e.g.,

ball, 77 A. 405 (Me.1910); Burgess v. Sims Drug Co., 86 N.W. 307 (Iowa 1901).

Comment d. Manufacturers' liability for failure adequately to instruct or warn prescribing and other health-care providers. The traditional rule, often referred to as the "learned intermediary rule," holds that manufacturers of prescription drugs discharge their duty of care to patients by warning the health-care providers who prescribe and use the drugs to treat them. See, e.g., DeLuryea v. Winthrop Labs., 697 F.2d 222, 228–29 (8th Cir.1983); Werner v. Upjohn Co., 628 F.2d 848, 858 (4th Cir.1980), cert. denied, 449 U.S. 1080, 101 S.Ct. 862, 66 L.Ed.2d 804 (1981); Lindsay v. Ortho Pharm. Corp., 637 F.2d 87, 91 (2d Cir.1980) (applying New York law). Accord, Salmon v. Parke, Davis

152

[Illustration 19–9]

PAGE FROM SHEPARD'S RESTATEMENT OF THE LAW CITATIONS

TORTS, THIRD (PRODUCTS LIABILITY)					Sec. 13

Sec. 1

Cir. 5
206F3d558
Cir. 9
245BRW135
Haw
92Haw190
989P2d274
N Y
662NE741
639NYS2d261
Tex
16SW134

Comment a
146LE945

R I
733A2d717
Tex
977SW335
2SW258
Wyo
970P2d392
95McL1291

Comment a
Cir. 6
92FS2d753
Cir. 9
197F3d995
Calif
98CaR2d598

Cir. 6
92FS2d753
Kan
268Kan788
999P2d943
N J
155NJ560
164NJ5
317NJS494
709A2d210
715A2d975
722A2d597
751A2d520
N Y
93NY659
662NE743

Reporters Note
Tex
977SW336

Comment m
N Y
662NE737
639NYS2d257

Comment n
Cir. 2
62FS2d823
Iowa
588NW698
Tex
995SW667

Cir. 11
46FS2d1362
N J
161NJ8
313NJS514
713A2d522
734A2d1249
N Y
181NYM371
695NYS2d266

Comment b
Illustration 3
N Y
181NYM370

Comment d

Sec. 10

Cir. 8
75FS2d1011
Cir. 11
190F3d1219
Ill
302IlA888
236IID401
707NE246
Iowa
588NW694
Mass
49MaA305
729NE327

> Each section of the various restatements and the related comments, In this illustration Sec. 6 of the *Restatement (Third) of Torts: Products Liability,* can be Shepardized using *Shepard's Restatement of the Law Citations.*

Sec. 2

146LE945
120SC1937
Cir. 1
84FS2d277
Cir. 2
980FS649
Cir. 5
151F3d334
157F3d314
206F3d552
Cir. 9
69F3d1441
191FRD185
Calif
67CA4th1185
79CaR2d660
98CaR2d592
Ga
494SE756
Iowa
588NW698
Kan
268Kan769
999P2d930
Mo
975SW152
N J
155NJ574
157NJ97
164NJ5
301NJS579
310NJS524
313NJS514
316NJS564
694A2d304
709A2d213
713A2d522
715A2d982
720A2d986
723A2d52
751A2d520

92FS2d753
N J
310NJS518
331NJS162
709A2d210
751A2d580
Tex
2SW257

Comment c
Cir. 5
206F3d551
Cir. 9
69F3d1441
Calif
98CaR2d597
Mass
49MaA305
729NE326

Comment d
146LE945
120SC1937
N J
294NJS69
682A2d733

Comment e
Cir. 2
62FS2d823
Cir. 9
69F3d1441
N J
310NJS518
709A2d210

Comment f
Cir. 1
84FS2d280
Cir. 2
75FS2d228
Cir. 5
157F3d314
206F3d558

Illustration 9
Wis
93NY663
717NE684
695NYS2d525

Illustration 10
N Y
93NY663
717NE684
695NYS2d525

Comment g
Cir. 1
84FS2d278
Kan
268Kan789
999P2d944
Tex
2SW261

Comment i
Cir. 5
206F3d557

Comment j
Tex
967SW351

Comment l
Cir. DC
144F3d845
330ADC202
Cir. 5
157F3d314
206F3d561
Tex
977SW336

Illustration 14
Tex
977SW336

Note
Wis
227Wis2d18
595NW388

Sec. 4
146LE940
120SC1919
Cir. 6
60FS2d671
N J
155NJ569
715A2d979

Comment e
146LE940
120SC1919

Sec. 5
Cir. 1
202F3d379
84FS2d277
Cir. 5
151F3d334
Calif
98CaR2d593
R I
733A2d715
748A2d266

Comment a
Cir. 1
202F3d379
84FS2d277
R I
733A2d716

Sec. 6
Cir. 2
43FS2d256
Cir. 9
191FRD185

Comment e
Cir. 2
214F3d78

Sec. 8
Pa
734A2d19

Comment b
Pa
734A2d19

Comment c
N J
162NJ238
744A2d130
Pa
734A2d19

Comment e
Pa
734A2d20

Comment f
Pa
734A2d20

Comment g
Pa
734A2d20

Comment i
Pa
734A2d20

Sec. 9

Comment c
Ind
730NE663

Comment e
Ind
730NE664

Comment e
729NE327

Sec. 11

Comment a
Ill
302IlA890
236IID402
707NE247

Comment b
Ill
302IlA890
236IID402
707NE247

Sec. 12
Cir. 5
202F3d752
N J
160NJ327
734A2d301
N Y
259NYAD57
696NYS2d531
Tex
16SW134

Comment a
N J
160NJ315
734A2d294

Comment b
Cir. 11
72FS2d1381
N J
153NJ381
160NJ315
709A2d783
734A2d294

SECTION F. UNIFORM LAWS AND MODEL ACTS

1. Uniform Laws

The same law reform movement that led to the creation of the restatements also focused on statutory law and the need, in many instances, for uniform statutes among the states. Toward this goal, the American Bar Association passed a resolution recommending that each state and the District of Columbia adopt a law providing for the appointment of commissioners to confer with commissioners of other states on the subject of uniformity in legislation on certain subjects. In 1892 the National Conference of Commissioners on Uniform State Laws (NCCUSL) was organized, and by 1912 each state had passed such a law. According to the NCCUSL constitution, its object is to "promote uniformity in state law on all subjects where uniformity is desirable and practical."[22]

The National Conference designates an act a *uniform act* when it has a reasonable possibility of ultimate enactment in a substantial number of jurisdictions. The Conference meets once a year and considers drafts of proposed uniform laws. When such a law is approved, the duty of the commissioners is to try to persuade their state legislatures to adopt it. Of course, adoption by the Conference has no legal effect; only subsequent enactment by state legislatures can achieve this result. The Conference has produced over 250 acts and over 100 have been adopted by at least one state. Perhaps the most notable example is the Uniform Commercial Code.

Laws approved by the National Conference of Commissioners on Uniform State Laws are published in the following forms:

a. As separate pamphlets.

b. On the Conference's website (see the discussion in 3–a of this section).

c. In the annual *Handbook* of the National Conference. There is some delay in the publication of this title.

d. In *Uniform Laws Annotated, Master Edition.* This multivolume set, published by West, contains approximately 200 uniform laws. A law must have been adopted by at least one state to be included in this set. [Illustrations 19–10 through 19–12] Volumes are revised periodically and pocket supplements and annual pamphlets issued.

Each section of a uniform law is typically followed by an Official Comment of the Commissioners. In most cases, this is followed by references to law review articles, related West digest topics and key numbers, and *Corpus Juris Secundum* sections. In recently revised volumes and the supplementation, *Westlaw* references also are provided. Each volume contains a detailed index to the laws it contains and indexes may also be found at the end of the volume in which a particular act ends. Tables in both the

---

[22] This document is published annually in the HANDBOOK OF THE NATIONAL CONFERENCE OF COMMISSIONERS ON UNIFORM STATE LAWS AND PROCEEDINGS OF THE ANNUAL MEETING. For a more detailed discussion of the National Conference, see WALTER P. ARMSTRONG, A CENTURY OF SERVICE: A CENTENNIAL HISTORY OF THE NATIONAL CONFERENCE OF COMMISSIONERS ON UNIFORM STATE LAWS (1991); Richard E. Coulson, *The National Conference of Commissioners on Uniform State Laws and the Control of Law–Making—A Historical Essay,* 16 OKLA. CITY U. L. REV. 295 (1991).

bound volumes and the supplements list the states that have adopted each uniform law. [Illustration 19–15] The *Uniform Laws Annotated, Master Edition*, is included in *Westlaw* in the ULA database.

e. *National Conference of Commissioners on Uniform State Laws Archive Collection in Microfiche* (William S. Hein & Co.). This collection, which contains over 2100 documents, includes transcripts of the National Conference's annual meetings and Committee of the Whole meetings, the *Handbooks* from 1892 to date, and successive drafts of uniform laws up to and including the uniform laws as adopted. The microfiche collection is updated annually. As of November 2008, some NCCUSL resources are available on *HeinOnline*, including archive publications and the *Handbook of the NCCUSL and Proceedings of the Annual Conference Meeting*, 1st–114th (1891–2005).

2. Model Acts

A proposed act that does not have a reasonable possibility of uniform adoption is designated as a *model act*. The expectation of the drafters is that parts, but not necessarily all of the act, will be adopted or modified and then adopted by various states. The NCCUSL occasionally drafts some model acts, but this work is most often left to the American Law Institute.[23] Among the more significant of these ALI model acts are the Model Business Corporation Act and the Model Penal Code. The National Conference and the ALI worked jointly on the Uniform Commercial Code.

3. Locating Information About Uniform Laws and Model Acts

a. *The National Conference on Uniform State Laws website*.[24] This is an excellent source for learning about all NCCUSL activities. In addition to detailing legislative status of, and information on, uniform acts (searchable alphabetically and by subject and state), ongoing drafting projects, and topics under discussion, this site provides a link to the NCCUSL electronic archives at the University of Pennsylvania Law School. The archives include the texts of uniform laws, model acts, and related documents.

b. *Handbook of the National Conference of Commissioners on Uniform State Laws*. This annual publication includes discussions of pending legislation, as well as the texts of all uniform laws adopted during that year. Through this *Handbook* a researcher can locate a uniform law, even if it has not been adopted by any state. A complete list of acts approved by the National Conference appears each year in the *Handbook's* appendices. Charts are included that show which states have adopted specific uniform laws and model acts, and the dates of adoption. There is some delay in the publication of this title.

c. *Directory of Uniform Acts and Codes*. This annual pamphlet, published as part of the *Uniform Laws Annotated, Master Edition*, indicates the volume of the *Master Edition* in which a particular law is published. [Illustration 19–13] This directory also includes a state-by-state listing of

---

[23] Documents pertaining to the uniform laws and model acts with which the ALI has been associated are contained in the *American Law Institute Archive Publications in Microfiche* described in Section D–7 of this chapter.

[24] http://nccusl.org.

uniform laws adopted by each state, a list of the Commissioners by state, and a brief subject index to all acts in the set. [Illustration 19–14]

d. *Martindale–Hubbell Law Directory.* One volume (black and gold binding) of this publication[25] includes, on a selective basis, the unannotated text of uniform laws and model acts.

e. *Legal Periodical Articles.* Articles about uniform laws and model acts can be found by checking the major indexes to legal periodicals: *Index to Legal Periodicals* (ILP), *Current Law Index* (CLI), *LegalTrac*, and *Legal Resource Index* (LRI).

SECTION G. ILLUSTRATIONS: UNIFORM LAWS

[25] The *Martindale–Hubbell Law Directory* is discussed in Chapter 20, Section F–1–a.

[Illustration 19–10]

PAGE FROM UNIFORM LAWS ANNOTATED, MASTER EDITION, VOLUME 9, PART II

CONTROLLED SUBSTANCES (1994)◄———   **§ 101**

Section
703. Continuation of Rules; Application to Existing Relationships.
704. Continuing Criminal Enterprise; Civil Action.
705. Statute of Limitations.
706. Uniformity of Application and Construction.
707. Short Title.
708. Severability Clause.
709. Repeals.
710. Effective Date.

WESTLAW Computer Assisted Legal Research

WESTLAW supplements your legal research in many ways. WESTLAW allows you to

> **This is the first page of the Uniform Controlled Substances Act (1994). This Act, which may have relevance to the research problem presented in Sections C and E, is an example of a typical uniform law adopted by the National Conference of Commissioners on Uniform State Laws (NCCUSL).**

For more information on using WESTLAW to supplement your research, see the WESTLAW Electronic Research Guide following the Explanation.

[ARTICLE] 1

DEFINITIONS

Action in Adopting Jurisdictions

Because of the numerous variations resulting from the frequent amendments made to the corresponding sections of text of this Act by the adopting jurisdictions, it is not feasible to note the differences between the official text of this Act and the counterpart texts in the adopting jurisdictions.

§ 101. Definitions.

As used in this [Act]:

(1) "Administer," unless the context otherwise requires, means to apply a controlled substance, whether by injection, inhalation, ingestion, or any other means, directly to the body of a patient or research subject by:

(i) a practitioner or, in the practitioner's presence, by the practitioner's authorized agent; or

(ii) the patient or research subject at the direction and in the presence of the practitioner.

(2) "Controlled substance" means a drug, substance, or immediate precursor included in Schedules I through V of [Article] 2.

17

[Illustration 19–11]

PAGE FROM UNIFORM LAWS ANNOTATED, MASTER EDITION, VOLUME 9, PART II

CONTROLLED SUBSTANCES (1994) 　　　　　　　　　　　**§ 401**

　　　(ii) [50] kilograms or more, but less than [100] kilograms, the person is guilty of a crime and upon conviction [may] [must] be imprisoned for not less than [ ] nor more than [ ] and fined not less than [ ];

　　　(iii) [100] kilograms or more, the person is guilty of a crime and upon conviction [may] [must] be imprisoned for not less than [ ] nor more than [ ] and fined not less than [ ].]

　(h) Except as authorized by law, a person may not knowingly or intentionally possess piperidine with intent to manufacture a controlled substance, or knowingly or intentionally possess piperidine knowing, or having reasonable cause to believe, that the piperidine will be used to manufacture a controlled substance contrary to this [Act]. A person who violates this subsection is guilty of a crime and upon conviction may be imprisoned for not more than [ ], fined not more than [ ], or both.

　[(i) Except as provided in subsection (j), with respect to an individual who is found to have violated subsection (g), adjudication of guilt or imposition of sentence may not be suspended, deferred, or withheld, nor is the individual

After each section of a uniform law, the official Comment of the Commissioners is given explaining that section.

(j) Notwithstanding any other provision of this [Act], the defendant or the attorney for the State may request the sentencing court to reduce or suspend the sentence of an individual who is convicted of a violation of this section and who provides substantial assistance in the identification, arrest, or conviction of a person for a violation of this [Act]. The court shall give the arresting agency an opportunity to be heard in reference to the request. Upon good cause shown, the request may be filed and heard in camera. The judge hearing the motion may reduce or suspend the sentence if the judge finds that the assistance rendered was substantial.

Comment

Except for Section 406, which contains a specific reference to a misdemeanor, criminal penalties throughout the Act are referred to by language "is guilty of a crime and upon conviction may be imprisoned for not more than [ ], fined not more than [ ], or both." States that have a criminal penalty classification system should replace this language with references to their classified penalties, e.g., "is guilty of a class [ ] felony." Actual penalties are not included because it is felt that such a designation is purely a state decision. The penalties imposed under the federal act are found at 21 U.S.C. 841, and additional federal penalties were created by the Anti–Drug Abuse Act of 1986, Public Law 99–570. The criminal penalties in subsection (a) are classified based on the penalties in the federal act, 21 U.S.C. 841(b) as amended by the Anti–Drug Abuse Act of 1986, Public Law 99–570, § 1002 (the "Narcotics Penalties and Enforcement Act of 1986"). In subsection (a)(1) there are no references to amounts of mixtures or substances containing the proscribed controlled substances, and the adopting State should insert amounts appropriate for that State. A reference to an amount is contained in subsection (a)(1)(vii) with respect to marijuana to allow a State that includes this provision to distinguish this provision from subsection (a)(5). Subsections (b), (d), and (e) are based on Florida Statutes Section 893.135. Subsection (c) is based on the offense in the federal act with respect to piperidine, added in 1978 and found in 21 U.S.C. 841(d).

129

[Illustration 19–12]

PAGE FROM UNIFORM LAWS ANNOTATED, MASTER EDITION, VOLUME 9, PART II

CONTROLLED SUBSTANCES (1994)   **§ 302**
Note 3

or who prescribe, will be required to register; however, under subsequent sections they may be exempt from the record-keeping requirements. By registering every

registrants are specifically exempted from the registration requirements since to require otherwise would be extremely burdensome and afford little increase in pro-

> **At the end of each section of a uniform law, references are given to additional research aids. Also, annotations are provided to all court cases citing the section. The supplementation should always be checked for later information.**

designed to eliminate many sources of diversion, both actual and potential.

Common and contract carriers, warehousemen, ultimate users, and agents of

In addition, the annual registration requirement will be a form of check on persons authorized to deal in controlled substances.

Library References

American Digest System
Drugs and Narcotics ⬡12 to 15, 41, 45.

Encyclopedias
C.J.S. Drugs and Narcotics §§ 2 to 6, 30 to 44, 117 to 133, 158, 163, 269.

WESTLAW Electronic Research

138k[add key number].
See, also, WESTLAW Electronic Research Guide following the Explanation.

Notes of Decisions

Generally 2
Corporations 4
Federal action and requirements 3
Nonresidents 5
Part-time pharmacist 6
Purpose 1
Residents and nonresidents 5
Status of unregistered persons and entities 7

---

1. Purpose

Primary purpose of prohibition against dispensing controlled substances is to require practitioners to register with the Commissioner of Public Health and to keep records and maintain inventories. Com. v. Perry, Mass.1984, 464 N.E.2d 389, 391 Mass. 808.

Overall scheme of Controlled Substances Act reveals legislative intent to place limitations on practitioners. People v. Alford, Mich.App.1977, 251 N.W.2d 314, 73 Mich.App. 604, affirmed 275 N.W.2d 484, 405 Mich. 570.

Legislature, in adopting Uniform Controlled Substances Act, intended to come within scheme of complementary federal-state control of distribution of drugs and to create an "interlocking trellis" to assure effectiveness of Act. State v. Rasmussen, Iowa 1973, 213 N.W.2d 661.

Regulations relating to licensing of drug distributors and manufacturers had, as their primary purpose, the protection of the public from dangerous drugs and, although the regulations included a license fee to cover administrative costs, the regulations did not impose a tax. Pharmaceutical Mfrs. Ass'n v. New Mexico Bd. of Pharmacy, N.M.App.1974, 525 P.2d 931, 86 N.M. 571.

2. Generally

When viewed in the context of the Controlled Substances Act as a whole, the right to possess drugs incident to professional use is dependent on compliance with the Act's registration requirement. State v. Mann, R.I.1978, 382 A.2d 1319, 119 R.I. 720.

3. Federal action and requirements

Interest of federal authority in issuing licenses to dispense drugs for purpose of controlling drug abuse clearly outweighs any local interest that Iowa might have in allowing only practitioners registered in state to prescribe in Iowa, and for pharmacists in state to fill prescriptions emanating from out-of-state. State v. Rasmussen, Iowa 1973, 213 N.W.2d 661.

Practitioners registered under Federal Comprehensive Drug Abuse Prevention and Control Act, though not registered in Iowa, and not residents of Iowa, are governed solely by Feder-

[Illustration 19–13]

PAGE FROM UNIFORM LAWS ANNOTATED, DIRECTORY OF UNIFORM ACTS AND CODES

DIRECTORY OF UNIFORM ACTS

This table lists all states alphabetically and indicates under each state which uniform laws or model codes have been adopted by that state. This information is also available on the NCCUSL website at http://www.nccusl.org/nccusl/uniformacts.asp.

2

[Illustration 19–14]

PAGE FROM UNIFORM LAWS ANNOTATED, DIRECTORY OF UNIFORM ACTS AND CODES, TABLE OF JURISDICTIONS LISTING UNIFORM ACTS ADOPTED

TABLE OF JURISDICTIONS LISTING UNIFORM ACTS ADOPTED

List of jurisdictions, in alphabetical order, listing the Uniform Acts or Codes adopted by that particular jurisdiction, and where each may be found in Uniform Laws Annotated, Master Edition.

Each Uniform Act or Code in the Master Edition contains a Table showing the statutory citations of each of the adopting jurisdictions.

ALABAMA

Title of Act	Uniform Laws Annotated Volume	Page
Anatomical Gift Act (1968 Act)	8A	63
Attendance of Witnesses From Without a State in Criminal Proceedings, Act to Secure	11	1
Certification of Questions of Law Act	12	49
Child Custody Jurisdiction and Enforcement Act	9, Pt. IA	649
Commercial Code [1]	1 to 3B	
Common Trust Fund Act	7, Pt. II	181
Condominium Act	7, Pt. II	199
Conservation Easement Act	12	163
Controlled Substances Act (1994)	9, Pt. II	1
Controlled Substances Act (1990)	9, Pt. IV	567
Controlled Substances Act (1970)	9, Pt. IV	643
Criminal Extradition Act	11	97
Declaratory Judgments Act	12	309
Determination of Death Act	12A	589
Disclaimer of Property Interests Act	8A	149
Disposition of Unclaimed Property Act (1966 Act)	8A	207

This table lists all uniform laws contained in the set and shows in which volume the text of the uniform law can be located. The uniform laws are also available on the NCCUSL website at http://www.nccusl.org/nccusl/uniformacts.asp. This website arranges the acts alphabetically, by subject matter, and by state.

Fraudulent Transfer Act	7A, Pt. II	266
Guardianship and Protective Proceedings Act (1982 Act)	8A	439
Insurers Liquidation Act	13	429
Interstate Family Support Act (1996)	9, Pt. IB	235
Limited Liability Company Act (1995)	6A	425
Limited Partnership Act (1976 Act)	6A	1
Management of Institutional Funds Act	7A, Pt. II	475
Mandatory Disposition of Detainers Act	11A	47
Motor Vehicle Certificate of Title and Anti-Theft Act	11A	175
Multiple–Person Accounts Act	8B	165
Nonprobate Transfers on Death Act	8B	191
Parentage Act (1973 Act)	9B	287
Partnership Act (1997 Act)	6	Pocket Part
Photographic Copies of Business and Public Records as Evidence Act	14	185
Principal and Income Act (1997 Act)	7B	131
Securities Act (1956 Act)	7C	102
Simplification of Fiduciary Security Transfers Act	7C	330
Simultaneous Death Act (1940 Act)	8B	267

9

[Illustration 19–15]

PAGE FROM UNIFORM LAWS ANNOTATED, MASTER EDITION, VOLUME 9, PART II, TABLE OF JURISDICTIONS ADOPTING THE UNIFORM CONTROLLED SUBSTANCES ACT

UNIFORM LAWS ANNOTATED

UNIFORM CONTROLLED SUBSTANCES ACT (1994)

1994 ACT

See, also, the 1990 and 1970 Uniform Controlled Substances Acts, infra.

Table of Jurisdictions Wherein Either the 1970, 1990, or 1994 Versions of the Act or a Combination Thereof Has Been Adopted [1]

Jurisdiction	Laws	Effective Date	Statutory Citation
Alabama	1971, No. 140	9–16–1971 *	Code 1975, §§ 20–2–1 to 20–2–190.
Alaska	1982, c. 45	1–1–1983	AS 11.71.010 to 11.71.900, 17.30.010 to 17.30.900.
Arizona	1979, c. 103	7–1–1980	A.R.S. §§ 36–2501 to 36–2553.
Arkansas [2]	1971, No. 590	4–7–1971	A.C.A. §§ 5–64–101 to 5–64–608.
California	1972, c. 1407	3–7–1973	West's Ann.Cal. Health & Safety Code, §§ 11000 to 11651.
Colorado	1981, pp. 707 to 728		West's C.R.S.A. §§ 18–18–101 to 18–18–605.
Connecticut	1967, No. 555	6–21–1967	C.G.S.A. §§ 21a–240 to 21a–308.
Delaware	1972, c. 424	6–13–1972 *	16 Del.C. §§ 4701 to 4796.
District of Columbia	1981, D.C.Law 4–29		D.C.Code 1981, §§ 33–501 to 33–572.
Florida	1973, c. 331	7–1–1973	West's F.S.A. §§ 893.01 to 893.165.

A table, preceding the start of each uniform law, indicates the jurisdictions that have adopted the Act, its effective date, and where it can be located in the state's code and session laws.

Iowa	1971, c. 148	7–1–1971	I.C.A. §§ 124.101 to 124.602.
Kansas	1972, c. 234	7–1–1972	K.S.A. 65–4101 to 65–4164.
Kentucky	1972, c. 226	7–1–1972	KRS 218A.010 to 218A.993.
Louisiana	1972, No. 634	7–26–1972	LSA–R.S. 40:961 to 40:995.
Maine	1975, c. 499	5–1–1976	17–A M.R.S.A. §§ 1101 to 1116.
	1941, c. 251	4–16–1941	22 M.R.S.A. §§ 2383, 2383–A, 2383–B.
Maryland	1970, c. 403	7–1–1970	Code 1957, art. 27, §§ 276 to 303.
Massachusetts	1971, c. 1071	7–1–1972	M.G.L.A. c. 94C, §§ 1 to 48.
Michigan	1978, No. 368	9–30–1978	M.C.L.A. §§ 333.7101 to 333.7545.
Minnesota	1971, c. 937	6–18–1971	M.S.A. §§ 152.01 to 152.20.
Mississippi	1971, c. 521	4–16–1971	Code 1972, §§ 41–29–101 to 41–29–185.
Missouri	1971, H.B. No. 69	9–28–1971	V.A.M.S. §§ 195.010 to 195.320.
Montana	1973, c. 412	7–1–1973	MCA 50–32–101 to 50–32–405.
Nebraska	1971, LB 326	5–26–1971	R.R.S.1943, § 28–401 et seq.
Nevada	1971, c. 667	1–1–1972	N.R.S. 453.011 et seq.
New Jersey	1970, c. 226	1–17–1971	N.J.S.A. 2C:35–1 to 2C:35–23, 2C:36–1 to 2C:36–9, 24:21–1 to 24:21–53.
New Mexico	1972, c. 84		NMSA 1978, §§ 30–31–1 to 30–31–41.
New York	1972, c. 878	4–1–1973	McKinney's Public Health Law §§ 3300 to 3396.
North Carolina	1971, c. 919	1–1–1972	G.S. §§ 90–86 to 90–113.8.
North Dakota	1971, c. 235	7–1–1971	NDCC 19–03.1–01 to 19–03.1–43.
Ohio	1975, p. 269	7–1–1976	R.C. §§ 3719.01 to 3719.99.
Oklahoma	1971, c. 119	9–1–1971	63 Okl.St.Ann. §§ 2–101 to 2–610.

1

Chapter 20

PRACTICE MATERIALS AND
OTHER RESOURCES*

This chapter covers a variety of resources that do not readily fit into any of the categories discussed in previous chapters. Some of these resources are general legal reference sources, form books, jury instructions, law dictionaries and listings of legal abbreviations, directories, collections of quotations, court records and briefs, and attorney general opinions. The final section of this chapter discusses researching the subject of legal ethics.

SECTION A. GENERAL LEGAL REFERENCE SOURCES

Often researchers need information that is not strictly legal, such as statistics, maps, information on state and federal agencies, interest and annuity tables, abbreviations, and addresses and telephone numbers for various groups and organizations. At other times, quick reference may be needed to the U.S. Constitution, the *Model Rules of Professional Conduct*, biographies, bibliographies, and succinct discussions of legal concepts and legal issues. Although no single resource can respond to all legal ready-reference needs, those described below collectively fill the most frequent needs.

a. *American Jurisprudence 2d Desk Book* (West). This volume, with pocket supplements, consists of four parts: historical documents, international agreements, and organizations; federal government and agencies; national statistics; and research and practice aids. It includes such items as federal agency organization charts, population statistics, medical diagrams, compound interest and annuity tables, and tables of weights and measures.[1]

b. Arlene L. Eis, *Legal Researcher's Desk Reference* (Infosources Publishing, biennial). This volume includes addresses and phone numbers for agencies, elected officials, clerks, U.S. attorneys, law publishers, and other law-related organizations, plus finding aids to federal laws and regulations and historical tables on presidents and Supreme Court justices. Subscribers to the print edition now also have access to an electronic version.

---

* This chapter was revised by Jane O'Connell, Interim Coordinator of Public Services, Tarlton Law Library, Jamail Center for Legal Research, University of Texas School of Law.

[1] The AMERICAN JURISPRUDENCE 2D DESK BOOK is a component of the AMERICAN JURISPRUDENCE 2D (AM. JUR. 2D) legal encyclopedia. Other related components include AMERICAN JURISPRUDENCE PROOF OF FACTS and AMERICAN JURISPRUDENCE TRIALS, discussed in Chapter 16, and AMERICAN JURISPRUDENCE LEGAL FORMS and AMERICAN JURISPRUDENCE PLEADING AND PRACTICE FORMS ANNOTATED, discussed later in this chapter.

c. *Law and Legal Information Directory* (Steven Wasserman et al. eds., 18th ed. Gale Research 2007). This volume provides descriptions and contact information for institutions, services, and facilities in the law and legal information industry.

d. *The Lawyer's Almanac* (Aspen Publishers, annual). This volume contains four main sections: (1) The Legal Profession, which provides information on the nation's 700 largest law firms, mandatory continuing legal education (CLE) requirements in the 50 states, bar exam statistics, state bar associations, and ABA leadership; (2) The Judiciary, which includes contact information for federal courts and state supreme courts along with federal litigation statistics; (3) Government Departments and Agencies, which includes contact information for federal agencies and state attorney generals along with where to request vital records for each state; and (4) Commonly Used Abbreviations.

e. *Oxford Companion to American Law* (Kermit Hall ed., Oxford University Press 2002). With 500 entries ranging from broad topics such as environmental law to specific cases such as *Palsgraf v. Long Island Railroad Co.*, this volume aims to provide a contextual overview of American law.

f. Dana Shilling, *Lawyer's Desk Book* (Aspen Publishers, annual). This volume contains topical discussions on such matters as business planning and litigation, contract and property law, financial and credit law, personal planning, tax issues, civil litigation, criminal law, and law office issues.

SECTION B. FORMS

Drafting legal documents such as wills, trusts, and leases is an essential part of law practice. Form books and software provide sample legal documents that can be tailored to specific situations. Today, it is common for practitioners to store documents electronically that have been created for subsequent revision and reuse. Most of the resources described below are available in both book and electronic formats.

1. General Forms

General form books provide forms for all aspects of legal practice and are typically multivolume sets. They are often annotated with references to cases that have favorably construed provisions contained in the form. Editorial comment also is frequently included. Examples of general form books are:

a. *American Jurisprudence Legal Forms 2d* (West, multivolume with annual pocket supplements). This set includes more than 22,000 legal forms. Arranged alphabetically, each title contains form drafting guides, notes on use, and copious sample forms. A two-volume, soft-cover index provides access to the set. Two separate volumes, *Federal Tax Guide to Legal Forms*, serve as a companion to the larger set. This set is available electronically on *Westlaw*.

b. *American Jurisprudence Pleading and Practice Forms Annotated* (West, multivolume with annual pocket supplements). This set contains more than 43,000 state and federal forms. It covers notices, complaints, petitions, declarations, summonses, demurrers, answers, counterclaims, cross-complaints, interrogatories, replies, motions, affidavits, stipulations, bills of particulars, subpoenas, orders, writs, jury instructions, findings of fact, judgments, and bonds. A multivolume index provides access to the set. This set is available electronically on *Westlaw*.

c. *Nichols Cyclopedia of Legal Forms, Annotated* (West, multivolume with annual pocket supplements). This set of transactional forms covers over 230 topics of law, such as contracts, deeds, wills, trusts, articles of incorporation, and merger agreements. It does not contain litigation or pleadings forms. Each subject area contains an overview of topics, tax implications, drafting checklists, and references to other publications. It includes state-specific statutes to help locate provisions and phrasing needed to comply with a state's particular requirements. This set is available electronically on *Westlaw*.

d. Jacob Rabkin & Mark H. Johnson, *Current Legal Forms with Tax Analysis* (LexisNexis, multivolume looseleaf). This set provides forms for corporate, commercial, intellectual property, domestic relations, employment, computer agreements (including e-commerce and Internet agreements), family/estate planning, and real estate matters. It does not cover criminal law or litigation. Each chapter includes a tax background, a practice background, checklists, drafting guidelines, and forms. This set is available electronically on *LexisNexis*.

e. *West's Legal Forms, 3d* (multivolume with annual pocket supplements). In addition to general forms, this set provides forms for topics such as business organizations, retirement plans, debtor-creditor relations, real estate transactions, domestic relations, estate planning, commercial transactions, elder law, patents, copyrights and trademarks, and employee benefit plans. There is a separate soft-cover annual index. This set is available electronically on *Westlaw*.

2. Federal Forms

Some form books are created specifically for practice in the federal courts. Examples include:

a. *Bender's Federal Practice Forms* (Matthew Bender, multivolume looseleaf). This set provides a complete range of litigation forms needed for practice in any federal court from district courts through the Supreme Court of the United States. Twelve volumes cover civil proceedings in federal district courts, from initial complaint through trials and post-trial motions. Two volumes cover criminal prosecutions in the district courts. Additional volumes provide forms for collateral attacks on criminal convictions that may be brought in district courts, civil and criminal appeals to the United States courts of appeals, forms required by the Federal Rules of Evidence, and proceedings in the U.S. Supreme Court. A comprehensive index of all of the forms is included in a separate volume. This set is available electronically on *LexisNexis*.

b. *West's Federal Forms* (multivolume with annual pocket supplements). This set provides federal procedural forms for civil and criminal matters arranged by type of proceeding and the particular court to which they pertain. Bankruptcy and admiralty proceedings also are covered.

Forms developed by the Administrative Office of the United States Courts, bankruptcy court judges, clerks, and United States trustees are included along with an annual index and tables of statutes and court rules. This set is available electronically on *Westlaw*.

c. *Federal Procedural Forms, Lawyers Edition,* (West, multivolume with annual pocket supplements). Arranged by topic, this set provides guidance for drafting forms for use before federal courts and administrative agencies, including extensive procedural checklists, "how to" explanations, and convenient practice aids. This set also reprints the Federal Judicial Center's *Litigation Management Manual.* A three-volume general index aids user access. This set is available electronically on *Westlaw*.

3. Subject Form Books

Many form books are devoted to a particular subject or to a particular phase of the litigation process. Examples are:

a. *National*

(1) *Bender's Forms of Discovery* (Matthew Bender, multivolume, looseleaf). This set includes charts comparing the discovery rules of the 50 states with the various federal discovery rules, as well as appendixes providing the text of the state discovery rules at variance with the federal rules. Sample interrogatories under more than 200 categories are provided. This set is available electronically on *LexisNexis*.

(2) *Fletcher Corporation Forms, Annotated* (4th ed. Clark Boardman Callaghan, multivolume with pocket supplements). This set is divided into 32 categories that cover various areas of corporate law, such as pre-incorporation contracts, bylaws, organization of corporation, corporate financing, directors and meetings, consolidations and mergers, and rolling stock agreements. A separate index volume is included. This set is available electronically on *Westlaw*.

(3) F. Lee Bailey & Kenneth J. Fishman, *Complete Manual of Criminal Forms* (3d ed. Clark Boardman Callaghan, multivolume looseleaf). The set contains over 1,000 federal and state criminal forms covering criminal matters from pre-trial proceedings through the trial to post-trial proceedings. This set is available electronically on *Westlaw*.

(4) Robert P. Wilkins, *Drafting Wills & Trust Agreements* (3d ed. Clark Boardman Callaghan, multivolume looseleaf). This set provides forms for drafting will or trust agreements with a focus on estate planning, federal tax law, and various state laws relevant to estate planning.

b. *State*

There are also many state-specific form books focused on local practice. These are published both by commercial publishers and by state bar associations. They contain the same features as the form books discussed above, but are designed for local use and, therefore, may be more useful for the practitioner. Examples of state-specific form books include:

(1) *California Legal Forms: Transaction Guide* (Matthew Bender, multivolume looseleaf). This set provides forms for business and nonprofit organizations, real estate transactions, commercial transactions, wills and

trusts, contracts and obligations, and personal transactions. This set is available electronically on *LexisNexis*.

(2) *West's Texas Forms* (3d ed., multivolume with pocket supplements). Organized by subject, this set features drafting checklists, client interview worksheets, alternative provisions and clauses, substantive research features, references to tax considerations, and references to applicable federal law. This set is available electronically on *Westlaw*.

4. Other Sources of Forms

a. *Forms in Treatises*. Many treatises include forms, either integrated into the text or in separate volumes.

b. *State Codes*. Some state codes include both substantive and procedural forms. Within a particular state code, consult the general index under "Forms."

c. *Internet*. A wide variety of websites provide legal forms. The providers range from federal agencies (such as the Internal Revenue Service and the Copyright Office), state agencies, and county agencies to public service organizations, law schools, and commercial vendors. General forms on the Internet may or may not accurately reflect the law of a specific jurisdiction.

SECTION C. JURY INSTRUCTIONS; VERDICT AND SETTLEMENT AWARDS

1. Jury Instructions

Before a jury begins deliberations, the judge instructs it on the applicable law. Attorneys often have the opportunity to submit proposed instructions to the judge in advance, tailoring these instructions to the evidence and theory of the case. It is at the judge's discretion whether or not to use these instructions, to modify them, to use his or her own instructions, or to use instructions from other sources.

Numerous publications contain jury instructions characterized as "pattern" or "model" instructions. Some of these are prepared for use in specific states; others are for particular subjects such as antitrust, torts, employment discrimination, or medical malpractice. Still others are designed for use in specific federal courts. The Federal Judicial Center, the Judicial Conference of the United States, and committees of the various circuits often are instrumental in preparing federal circuit instructions. These instructions are published in pamphlet form and often are available on a court's website.[2] Two commercially published sets that contain extensive collections of instructions for use in the federal courts, together with commentary and case references, are:

a. Kevin F. O'Malley et al., *Federal Jury Practice and Instructions: Civil and Criminal* (5th ed., West, multivolume with annual pocket supplements). This set provides instructions for federal civil and criminal trials. Instructions are provided for particular federal crimes, and there are

---

[2] For example, both civil and criminal jury instructions are available on the website of the United States Court of Appeals for the Fifth Circuit: http://www.lb5.uscourts.gov/juryinstruct ions/.

specialized instructions for medical issues, antitrust, patent infringement, and business torts.

b.   Leonard B. Sand et al., *Modern Federal Jury Instructions* (Matthew Bender, multivolume looseleaf). Both civil and criminal instructions are provided along with commentary, case references, and frequent citations to the text of pattern jury instructions of the fifth, seventh, and ninth circuits.

2. Verdict and Settlement Awards

Legal researchers often seek information about the amount of damages that might be awarded in a particular type of case. This information can influence an attorney's decision whether or not to accept a case, to go to trial, or to settle. The following publications provide general information about jury verdicts and settlements:

a.   *JVR Personal Injury Valuation Handbooks* (Jury Verdict Research, Inc., multivolume looseleaf) This set is arranged by type of injury, recovery probabilities, and psychological factors affecting verdicts. Each report focuses on a specific injury or liability and provides comparable case summaries, distribution of settlements and awards, and award medians, means, and probability ranges for recent years.

b.   Heidi Thorson, *What's It Worth: A Guide to Current Personal Injury Awards and Settlements* (Matthew Bender, annual). This publication contains summaries of decisions and settlements during the previous year. Arrangement is by specific type of injury and then alphabetically by state. This title is available electronically on *LexisNexis*.

For state-specific information, the National Association of State Jury Verdict Publishers' website[3] provides links to various regional publications focused on verdicts and settlement awards. *Westlaw* and *LexisNexis* also have extensive verdict and settlement databases that can be searched by specific jurisdiction.

SECTION D. LAW DICTIONARIES

Law dictionaries provide a short definition for each word or phrase. These definitions of legal terms are derived from a variety of sources, usually explained in the introductory matter of the dictionary or in the entries for each word. Some legal dictionaries also provide references that trace the etymology of the word or phrase, a definition from a learned treatise, or citations to judicial opinions.

The multivolume set *Words and Phrases,* discussed in Chapter 7, Section M, includes digests from judicial opinions in which a word or phrase has been judicially interpreted. *Words and Phrases* can also be used as a dictionary, but because it is limited to the definitions of words as set forth in judicial opinions, it is not a comprehensive dictionary of legal terms.

Several law dictionaries currently are available on the Internet and are easily searchable. The Legal Information Institute's website at Cornell

[3] http://www.juryverdicts.com.

University Law School includes an electronic dictionary.[4] Many law school libraries provide an "electronic reference desk" or a "virtual library" at their website that includes links to a variety of reference materials, including online legal dictionaries.

Described below are some of the more commonly used American and British law dictionaries.

1. American Law Dictionaries

a. *Ballentine's Law Dictionary, with Pronunciations* (3d ed., Lawyers Cooperative Publishing Company 1969). This volume often provides citations to *A.L.R. Annotations*, *American Jurisprudence 2d*, and relevant case law. It is available on *LexisNexis*.

b. *Black's Law Dictionary* (Brian A. Garner ed., 8th ed. West 2004). The most widely used of all law dictionaries. Individual entries may contain references to statutes, West key numbers and *Corpus Juris Secondum*. A Table of Legal Abbreviations and a compilation of legal maxims also are included. This edition is available on *Westlaw*. An abridged, paperback version (2005) and a 3d pocket edition (2006) also are available.

c. *Bouvier's Law Dictionary and Concise Encyclopedia* (8th ed., 3d revision, West Publishing Company 1914, 3 volumes; reprinted by William S. Hein & Co., 1984) Although out-of-date in some respects, this is a particularly scholarly work. Many of its definitions are encyclopedic in nature and it remains useful for many historical terms. The first edition was published in 1837. The 8th edition, 3d revision, is available on *HeinOnline*.

d. William C. Burton, *Burton's Legal Thesaurus* (4th ed., McGraw Hill 2006). This volume includes words in legal contexts, words used by the legal community, and words used in legal communications. It includes "associated concepts" and translations of many foreign words and phrases.

e. Susan Ellis Wild, *Webster's New World Law Dictionary* (Wiley 2006). This volume contains definitions of more than 4,000 legal terms, common abbreviations, foreign words and phrases, and the United States Constitution.

f. James E. Clapp, *Webster's Dictionary of the Law* (Random House 2000). This volume attempts to define legal terms in context, and includes cross-references to related terms.

g. Bryan A. Garner, *A Dictionary of Modern Legal Usage* (2d ed., Oxford University Press 1995). Containing definitions, spelling rules, and grammar guidelines, this volume is perhaps most valuable for its "authoritative guidance on many matters of usage that are unique to legal writing."[5] The 1987 first edition is available on *LexisNexis*.

h. *The Law Dictionary* (7th ed. Anderson Publishing Company 1997). This volume is a condensed dictionary including a Table of Abbreviations and is available on *LexisNexis*.

---

[4] The dictionary is named *Wex*. It can be accessed at http://topics.law.cornell.edu/wex/Main_Page.

[5] Charles Alan Wright, *Book Review*, Townes Hall Notes, Spring 1988, at 5 (reviewing the first edition).

i. Daniel Oran, *Oran's Dictionary of the Law* (4th ed., Thomson/Delmar Learning 2008). This dictionary is written for a wide audience; the definitions are concise and contemporary. A brief introduction to legal research is also included.

j. Kenneth R. Redden & Gerry W. Beyer, *Modern Dictionary for the Legal Profession* (3d ed., William S. Hein & Co., 2001). This work focuses on modern terminology and includes slang and colloquialisms.

2. British Law Dictionaries

a. *A Dictionary of Law* (Elizabeth A. Martin & Jonathan Law eds., 6th ed., Oxford University Press 2006). This volume emphasizes accessible language and includes citations to relevant cases.

b.William A. Jowitt & Clifford Walsh, *Jowitt's Dictionary of English Law* (John Burke ed., 2d ed., Sweet & Maxwell 1977, 2 volumes, supplemented periodically). This set aims to provide a comprehensive lexicon of English law, and includes citations to relevant cases and statutes.

c. J.E. Penner, *Mozley & Whiteley's Law Dictionary* (12th ed. Oxford University Press 2005). This volume reflects changes in English legal terminology resulting from the final report and implementation of Lord Woolf's reform of civil justice.

d. Percy G. Osborn, *Osborn's Concise Law Dictionary* (Sheila Bone ed., 10th ed., Sweet & Maxwell 2005). This volume includes a Table of Law Reports, Journals and Abbreviations.

e. *Stroud's Judicial Dictionary of Words and Phrases* (Daniel Greenberg & Alexandra Millbrook eds., 6th ed., Sweet & Maxwell 2000, 3 volumes, supplemented periodically). This multivolume set includes numerous case citations and references to statutes.

3. Special Law Dictionaries

A number of bilingual and multilingual law dictionaries are available, such as English–Spanish, English–Portuguese, English–Japanese, and English–French–German. A dictionary that explains the use of Latin terminology with respect to the broader context is Russ VerSteeg's *Essential Latin for Lawyers* (Carolina Academic Press 1990). Some legal dictionaries are devoted to specific subjects, such as labor law, family law, environmental law, and taxation. Listed below are several subject-specific legal dictionaries:

a. James R. Fox, *Dictionary of International & Comparative Law* (3d ed., Oceana Publications 2003).

b. Bryan A. Garner, *A Handbook of Family Law Terms* (West 2001).

c. Bryan A. Garner, *A Handbook of Criminal Law Terms* (West 2000).

d. James J. King, *The Environmental Dictionary and Regulatory Cross–Reference* (3d ed., Wiley 1995).

e. Robert Sellers Smith, *West's Tax Dictionary* (West 2007).

f. Richard A. Westin, *WG & L Tax Dictionary* (Warren, Gorham & Lamont 2006).

SECTION E.   LEGAL ABBREVIATIONS

Many legal dictionaries and books about legal research contain tables of abbreviations. The following resources also are especially useful in determining the meaning of legal abbreviations:

a. Mary Miles Prince, *Bieber's Dictionary of Legal Abbreviations* (5th ed., William S. Hein & Co., 2001). This volume is divided in two parts. The first part sets forth the abbreviation followed by the word or words represented. The second part sets forth the word or words followed by the abbreviation. The fourth edition is available on *LexisNexis*.

b. Mary Miles Prince, *Prince's Dictionary of Legal Citations* (7th ed., William S. Hein & Co., 2006). This volume provides examples of statutes, reporters, and legal periodicals in *Bluebook* form.

c. Donald Raistrick, *Index to Legal Citations and Abbreviations* (2d ed., Professional Books 1993). Although the focus of this publication is the United Kingdom, Ireland, the Commonwealth and the United States, it also includes entries for select countries in Europe, Africa, Asia and South America.

d. *World Dictionary of Legal Abbreviations* (Igor I. Kavass & Mary Miles Prince, eds., William S. Hein & Co., 1991, 4 volumes with looseleaf updates). Includes abbreviations and acronyms from English, Bulgarian, French, German, Hebrew, Italian, Japanese, Korean, Portuguese, and Spanish legal literature. Volume 4 provides abbreviations by subjects, such as environment, maritime, military, and taxation.

SECTION F.   LAW DIRECTORIES

Law directories are useful for locating information about lawyers, law firms, courts, and administrative agencies. Law directories vary in their scope of coverage. Some directories attempt to list all lawyers; others are limited to a region, state, municipality, or practice specialty.

Increasingly, law directories are available electronically on the Internet, where they can be updated more frequently than an annual printed publication. Some publishers of print directories also provide electronic versions of the directory. In addition, the websites of organizations such as state bar associations may provide access to databases, which often give current contact information and may provide biographical information about members.

1.   General Directories

a. *Martindale–Hubbell Law Directory* (Martindale–Hubbell, annual). This multivolume set is a comprehensive, annual directory of lawyers, law firms, and other related information.

The United States Lawyer volumes are arranged alphabetically by state with each volume containing Practice Profiles and Professional Biographies. All lawyers admitted to the bar of any jurisdiction are eligible for a general listing in the Practice Profiles at no charge. For each state, an Index of Towns and Cities by County is followed by an alphabetical list of lawyers and law firms within each city. For each listed attorney, information is given regarding date of birth, date of admission to the bar, college and law school attended, and degrees obtained. Ratings obtained through confidential inquiries made to members of the bar also are given. A key to the ratings is included in the preliminary pages of each volume, along with the numeric codes for the List of Colleges, Universities, and Law Schools. These ratings attempt to evaluate legal ability and provide general recommendations.

The Professional Biographies are not comprehensive because inclusion in this section requires payment. These biographies are arranged by state, listing the cities within each state and the law firms within each city. Each entry may set forth the address and telephone number of the firm, names and short biographies of its members, representative clients, areas of practice, and references.

A Patent and Trademark Practice Profiles section at the end of each Practice Profiles section provides a listing of patent and trademark attorneys for the specific jurisdictions covered in the volume's Practice Profiles. Listings of United States government lawyers located in Washington, D.C., are grouped by department, agency, commission, etc., and follow the general Practice Profiles for Washington, D.C.

Martindale–Hubbell includes several other specialized listings. The Corporate Law Departments section includes Practice Profiles and Professional Biographies of attorneys working for corporations. The Law School section includes addresses, phone numbers, key contacts, descriptions of the institution and its academic programs, and biographical summaries of the law faculty. As a fee is required for inclusion in the Law School section, the list is not comprehensive.

Martindale–Hubbell's law digests summarize various areas of statutory law. Digests cover every state, the District of Columbia, Puerto Rico, and the Virgin Islands along with a general federal law digest, digests for copyright, trademark and patent law, and international law, and summaries of selected laws from more than 80 foreign countries and the European Union.

Lastly, the *Martindale–Hubbell International Law Directory* covers Europe, Asia, Australasia, the Middle East, Africa, North America, the Caribbean, and Central and South America and includes a Professional Biographies section.

In addition to the print edition, *Martindale–Hubbell* is available on *LexisNexis* and as a CD–ROM. Additionally, the *Martindale–Hubbell* website provides access to some of the information found in the other formats.[6]

b. *West Legal Directory.* This directory, available on *Westlaw*, contains profiles of law firms, a listing of branch offices, and biographical records of lawyers from all states and the District of Columbia, Puerto Rico, the Virgin Islands, Canada, England, and Europe. Numerous topical directories are available within the main database. Comprised of more than 1,000,000 profiles, this directory is also available as a CD–ROM.

c. *Who's Who in American Law* (Marquis Who's Who, biennial). This compilation contains biographical information on approximately 25,000

---

[6] http://www.martindale.com.

attorneys selected for their prominence as judges, educators, or practitioners. Despite the large number of entries, no claim is made to comprehensiveness in any area of the profession. In fact, the content is often a function of attorneys' willingness to complete the paperwork necessary for inclusion. The format is similar to that used in other Marquis *Who's Who* publications.

d. *Chambers USA: America's Leading Lawyers for Business* (Chambers & Partners, annual). This volume begins with national rankings by practice areas and then is organized alphabetically by state. Firms and individual lawyers are ranked based upon over 10,000 telephone interviews. The volume also includes a firm index and lawyer index. The *Chambers & Partners* website provides access to some of the information found in the print edition.[7]

e. *Chambers Global: The World's Leading Lawyers* (Chambers & Partners, annual). This volume is organized alphabetically by country and only covers firms and lawyers engaged in global areas of practice. It provides a firm index and leading lawyers index. The *Chambers & Partners* website, mentioned above, provides access to some of the information found in the print edition.

f. *Martindale-Hubbell Canadian Law Directory* (Martindale–Hubbell, annual). This one-volume directory, in a format similar to its American counterpart, is a guide to Canada's legal profession. The *Martindale–Hubbell* website provides access to some of the information found in the print edition.

g. *The American Bar including The Canadian Bar, The Mexican Bar and The International Bar* (Forster-Long, Inc., annual). These are annual biographical directories of prestigious United States and foreign lawyers. The set profiles certain North American law firms and provides individual biographical data. In addition to the profiles for the United States, Canada, and Mexico, there is also a brief international section. An individual attorney index, firm name and location index, and practice areas index are also included to aid users.

A paperback reference handbook provides an abridged version of the main set, and includes firm name, members, location, and contact information, including website address and attorney email addresses when provided. Additionally, the American Bar website (http://www.americanbar.com/) provides access to some of the information found in the print edition.

h. *Other International Directories.* Many other companies publish directories that can be used to locate attorneys in particular countries. Among these directories are *The Canadian Law List* (Canada Law Book), *The International Law List* (L. Corper–Mordaunt & Co.), *Kime's International Law Directory* (Sweet & Maxwell), and *Waterlow's Solicitors' & Barristers' Directory* (Waterlow).

2. State and Regional Directories

Directories of the attorneys practicing within a specific state also are available. Legal Directories Publishing Co., publishes directories for 22

---

[7] http://www.chambersandpartners.com.

states. These directories list attorneys by county and city, and also contain some biographical data. Their website provides attorney, firm, and mediator listings.[8] In addition to print resources, many state bar organizations now make membership information available on the Internet.

3. Judicial Directories and Biographies

  a. *Directories*

  (1) *BNA's Directory of State and Federal Courts, Judges, and Clerks* (Bureau of National Affairs, annual). This volume provides federal court information along with court information for each state in alphabetical order. For each court system, a flow chart of the court system is provided along with contact information for each individual court.

  (2) *Federal-State Court Directory* (CQ Press, annual). This volume includes contact information for all federal courts, U.S. bankruptcy trustees, federal administrative law judges, and state bar associations. For each state court system, a flow chart of the court system is provided along with limited contact information.

  (3) *Judicial Staff Directory* (CQ Press, annual). This volume provides information on the court structure for the federal and state courts along with contact information for each court. A flow chart of the Department of Justice along with contact information for its various branches, a chart correlating counties and all cities with population over 1,500 with their federal circuit and district courts, an index of Article III judges, biographies for key judicial personnel, and an index to individuals are added features of the volume. An electronic version is available for a subscription fee.

  (4) *United States Court Directory* (Administrative Office of the U.S. Courts). The print version of this title has been replaced by the Court Links page of U.S. Courts website which provides links to contact information for all federal courts.[9]

  b. *Biographical Directories*

  (1) *Historical*

  (a) *Biographical Directory of the Federal Judiciary* (Bernan 2001). The print volume covers 1789–2000 and includes the legislative history of each court, including its creation, addition of judgeships, and abolishment if applicable. Sections cover the Supreme Court, the circuit courts of appeals, the district courts, and courts of special jurisdiction. There are lists of every judge to serve on a specific court. A separate section provides biographical information for each of the judges. The texts of landmark legislation also are included.

  An electronic version is available through the Federal Judicial Center.[10] While the print version only provides coverage through 2000, the electronic version provides updated information and is searchable by judge name.

---

[8] http://www.legaldirectories.com.

[9] http://www.uscourts.gov/courtlinks/.

[10] http://www.fjc.gov/public/home.nsf/hisj.

(b) Iris J. Wildman & Mark J. Handler, *Federal Judges and Justices: A Current Listing of Nominations, Confirmations, Elevations, Resignations, Retirements* (Fred B. Rothman & Co., 1987–2001, looseleaf). A compilation of judicial nominations, confirmations, resignations, and retirement divided by Congress from the 99th Congress (1985–1986) to the 107th Congress (2001–2002). Although the directory ceased publication in 2001, it contains useful information on judges that is not as easily found elsewhere.

(2) *Current*

(a) *The Almanac of the Federal Judiciary* (Aspen Law & Business, 2 volumes looseleaf, biennial updates). This is the most thorough source for biographical information on federal judges. In addition to the basic data found in other sources, such as address, education, and work experience, this directory includes descriptions of judges' noteworthy rulings and media coverage along with lawyers' anonymous evaluations of the judges' ability and temperament. This title is available through *Westlaw*.

(b) *The American Bench: Judges of the Nation* (Forster–Long, Inc., annual). This directory has biographical information about over 18,000 judges at all levels of federal, state, and local courts with jurisdictional, structural, and geographical facts about the courts. Biographical information about state judges is organized alphabetically by state. An alphabetical name index and a gender ratio summary also are included.

4. Academic Directories

The Association of American Law Schools compiles the *AALS Directory of Law Teachers* to serve the academic legal community. This annual volume provides addresses and phone numbers and biographical information about law school faculty, as well as a listing of faculty members arranged by teaching specialty. This publication is available on *Westlaw*.

The American Association of Law Libraries' *AALL Directory and Handbook* lists member law libraries in the United States and Canada, arranged geographically, and the law librarians employed by the member law libraries. A separate alphabetical list of law library personnel also is included. This directory can be accessed by AALL members from the AALL website.[11]

5. Specialty Directories

Some directories list only attorneys specializing in particular areas of the law. Examples of these directories are *Lawyer's Register International By Specialties and Fields of Law* (Lawyer's Register), *Directory of Corporate Counsel* (Aspen), and Martindale–Hubbell's *International Arbitration and Dispute Resolution Directory*. The *Directory of Corporate Counsel* is available on *LexisNexis*.

SECTION G. LEGAL QUOTATIONS

A number of sources collect and index law-related quotations. Examples include the following:

---

[11] http://www.aallnet.org.

a. Eugene C. Gerhart, *Quote It Completely! World Reference Guide to More Than 5,500 Memorable Quotations from Law and Literature* (William S. Hein & Co., 1998). This is a combined and enlarged edition of two separate collections: *Quote It!*, 1969; and *Quote It II*, 1988. Quotations are arranged by subject, with separate author and word indexes.

b. Simon James & Chantal Stebbings, *A Dictionary of Legal Quotations* (Macmillan Publishing Company 1987). This volume is arranged under 160 key words and includes indexes of authors, sources, and key words.

c. M. Frances McNamara, *2,000 Classic Legal Quotations* (Aqueduct Books 1967). Quotations are arranged by subject; a general index also is included.

d. *The New Lawyer's Wit and Wisdom: Quotations on the Legal Profession, In Brief* (Bruce Nash and Allan Zullo eds., Running Press 2001). This volume contains quotations and brief anecdotes organized into 23 topical categories.

e. *Respectfully Quoted: A Dictionary of Quotations Requested from the Congressional Research Service* (Suzy Platt ed., Library of Congress 1989). This volume contains 2,100 quotations, a significant number of which are law-related, gathered in response to congressional inquiries to the Congressional Research Service for quotations.

f. Fred R. Shapiro, *The Oxford Dictionary of American Legal Quotations* (Oxford University Press 1993). The most scholarly of the quotation books, this source contains more than 3,500 quotations by Americans about law or by non-Americans about United States law. It is arranged alphabetically by subject and chronologically within each subject. The volume also includes cross-references and author and keyword indexes.

g. David S. Shrager & Elizabeth Frost–Knappman, *The Quotable Lawyer* (rev. ed. Checkmark Books 1998). This volume contains more than 3,000 quotations arranged under 157 major subject headings. Author and subject indexes are included.

SECTION H. BRIEFS, RECORDS, AND ORAL ARGUMENTS

After a trial court or an intermediate court of appeals decides a case, the case may be appealed to a higher court. If the higher court considers the appeal, attorneys for each side submit written briefs in which they set forth the reasons why the appellate court should either affirm or reverse the lower court's decision. These briefs contain discussion and analysis of the law along with citation to authority supporting legal arguments. *Amicus curiae* ("friend of the court") briefs also may be filed by groups or individuals not parties to the case, but supporting one side or the other. Such *amicus curiae* briefs often are filed in cases before state supreme courts and the Supreme Court of the United States.

When available, the record of the trial court typically is submitted with the brief. This record usually contains the preliminary motions and pleadings in the case, transcripts of examination and cross-examination of witnesses, instructions to the jury, the opinion of the lower court, and various other exhibits.

Briefs and records potentially can provide attorneys involved in similar cases with a great deal of information, together with a sense of what arguments have or have not succeeded with an appellate court. Oral arguments reveal the focus of the attorneys and judges during the in-court presentations.[12]

1. Supreme Court of the United States

a. *Records and Briefs.* A small number of libraries receive print copies of briefs and records submitted to the Supreme Court of the United States. Most law school libraries and some large bar association libraries have these briefs and records available in microform or in electronic format. West Court Record Services' *Records and Briefs of the United States Supreme Court*, a microfiche collection, provides coverage of all argued cases since 1832 and non-argued cases since 1984. *CIS US Supreme Court Records & Briefs,* a microfiche collection, includes all argued cases since 1897 and, since 1975, all non-argued cases in which one or more justices wrote a dissent from the *per curiam* decision to deny review. Summaries of some attorneys' briefs are included in the *United States Supreme Court Reports, Lawyers' Edition.*

LexisNexis has briefs on the merits filed with the Supreme Court beginning in January 1979. These merit briefs are available on *Westlaw* beginning with the October 1990 term along with *amicus* briefs beginning with the October 1995 term. *Westlaw* has selected petitions for writ of certiorari beginning in 1990 for granted petitions and beginning in 1995 for denied petitions. *BriefServe* has briefs available for purchase in PDF format from 1984 to the present.[13]

FindLaw provides petitioner, respondent, and *amicus* briefs from October 1999 term at no charge.[14] The American Bar Association provides all merit briefs since the October 2003 term.[15] All briefs filed by the Solicitor General on behalf of the government since the October 1998 term are available on the Department of Justice's website.[16]

For older briefs, Yale University's *Curiae Project* publishes PDF versions of briefs for selected Supreme Court cases.[17] This website is a work in process and will eventually cover over 1,000 cases. Briefs for cases such as *Plessy v. Ferguson* (1896), *Lochner v. New York* (1904), *Brown v. Board of Education* (1954 & 1955), and *Miranda v. Arizona* (1966) already are available.

Gale Cengage Learning's *The Making of Modern Law: U.S. Supreme Court Records and Briefs, 1832–1978*, offers electronic access to historical Supreme Court briefs. This database is searchable by keyword, docket number, party name, or citation to the Court's opinion in *U.S. Reports,*

---

[12] To locate a library whose collection includes briefs, records, and oral arguments, refer to the listings in MICHAEL WHITEMAN & PETER SCOTT CAMPBELL, A UNION LIST OF APPELLATE RECORDS AND BRIEFS: FEDERAL AND STATE (Fred B. Rothman & Co. 1999).

[13] http://www.briefserve.com.

[14] http://supreme.lp.findlaw.com/supreme_court/briefs/index.html.

[15] http://www.abanet.org/publiced/preview/briefs/home.html.

[16] http://www.usdoj.gov/osg/briefs/search.html.

[17] http://curiae.law.yale.edu/.

Supreme Court Reporter, or *United States Supreme Court Reports, Lawyers' Edition.*

 b. *Oral Arguments*

 (1) *Audiotapes.* Oral arguments presented before the Supreme Court have been recorded since 1955. These tapes are available for a fee from the National Archives.[18]

 (2) *The Oyez Project.* This website is a U.S. Supreme Court multimedia database, providing digital audio of Supreme Court oral arguments in many important cases.[19] Currently, the site provides access to more than 2,000 hours of Supreme Court audio, including all audio recorded by the Court since 1995. Before 1995, the audio collection is selective. The site's aim is to create a complete and authoritative archive of Supreme Court audio from October 1955, when the Court began recording its proceedings, through the most recent term. The site also includes biographical information on all Supreme Court justices and a virtual tour of the Supreme Court.

 (3) *Transcripts.* Starting with the 1952 Term, transcripts of oral arguments are available from Congressional Information Service, Inc. in a microfiche set entitled *Oral Arguments of the U.S. Supreme Court.* Beginning with the October 2000 term, transcripts of oral arguments are available on the Supreme Court's Web site.[20] Beginning with the October 2006 term, the Court makes transcripts available on the same day the argument is heard by the Court. *LexisNexis* has transcripts of oral arguments from the October 1979 term, and *Westlaw* has transcripts of oral arguments from the 1990–91 term.

 c. *Landmark Briefs and Arguments of the Supreme Court of the United States: Constitutional Law.* This series, published by LexisNexis, covers cases from 1793 forward. The period 1793 to 1974 consists of 81 volumes. Annual supplements published since 1974 average approximately eight volumes each year. The series is now over 350 volumes. As the title indicates, coverage is selective.

2. Federal Courts of Appeals

 A small number of law libraries receive print copies of briefs and records filed with the federal court of appeals for the circuit in which they

---

[18] Until late 1993, audiotapes were not available until three years after the oral arguments, could only be used for educational or instructional purposes, and could not be copied and disseminated. However, the Supreme Court's policy changed following publication of MAY IT PLEASE THE COURT: THE MOST SIGNIFICANT ORAL ARGUMENTS MADE BEFORE THE SUPREME COURT SINCE 1955 (Peter Irons & Stephanie Guitton eds., 1993). This publication consists of a 370–page book and six 100-minute cassettes, which include 23 edited live recordings of oral arguments, with a voice-over narration by Irons. Publication of these materials created a furor, with charges levied by the Supreme Court that Irons violated contractual arrangements by duplicating and disseminating the tapes. *See, e.g.,* Tony Mauro, *Tapes Project Sparks Clash: Supreme Court to Legal Scholar: Keep Oral Arguments to Yourself,* LEGAL TIMES, Aug. 16, 1993, at 1; Maro Robbins, *"May It Please the Court" Doesn't Please the Court,* NAT'L L.J., Oct. 11, 1993, at 47. The result, however, was to cause the Supreme Court to change its policy and make the tapes readily and immediately available to the public through the National Archives. *See* Linda Greenhouse, *Supreme Court Eases Restrictions on Use of Tapes of Its Arguments,* N.Y. TIMES, Nov. 3, 1993, at A22, col. 1.

[19] http://www.oyez.org.

[20] http://www.supremecourtus.gov.

are located. West Court Records Services publishes microfiche collections of records and briefs for all circuits with coverage beginning in 1891. *Brief-Serve* has briefs available for purchase in PDF format from all circuits, with coverage from 1981.[21] *Westlaw* has selected federal court of appeals briefs from 1972. *LexisNexis* has selected federal court of appeals briefs since 2000.

3. State Courts

Some law libraries also receive print copies of briefs and records from state courts. West Court Record Services publishes microfiche collections of records and briefs from the highest courts of 29 state and the appellate courts of 14 states. The dates of coverage vary by state and court. *LexisNexis* and *Westlaw* have selected state court briefs. The dates of coverage vary by state.

BriefServe, previously mentioned, provides briefs for purchase in PDF format from the New York Court of Appeals and the California Supreme Court since 1996 and Pennsylvania Commonwealth and Supreme Court since 1998.

SECTION I.   ATTORNEY GENERAL OPINIONS

Attorneys general serve as legal advisors to the executive branch of government. As a general rule, the opinions of an attorney general relate to the interpretation of statutes or general legal problems. Some attorneys general limit their advice and will not render opinions regarding the constitutionality of proposed legislation.

This advice is often provided as an official written opinion.[22] While formal opinions, written and signed by an attorney general, are official statements of an executive officer, issued pursuant to his or her authority, the opinions are merely advisory rather than mandatory orders. The recommendations and conclusions set forth in these opinions are persuasive and are often followed by executive officers. These opinions also may influence judicial deliberations.

1. Opinions of the Attorneys General of the United States

Official Opinions of the Attorneys General of the United States compiles all attorney general opinions published between 1791 and 1982 in 43 volumes. This publication is available in many law libraries and also in PDF format from *HeinOnline*. Since 1980, opinions of the attorneys general are included in the annual publication *Opinions of the Office of Legal Counsel*.

---

[21] http://www.briefserve.com.

[22] For additional information on the role of attorneys general, see Scott M. Matheson, Jr., *Constitutional Status and Role of the State Attorney General*, 6 U. FLA. J.L. & PUB. POL'Y 1 (1993); STATE ATTORNEYS GENERAL: POWERS AND RESPONSIBILITIES (Lynne M. Ross ed., 1990) (prepared by the National Association of Attorneys General); 200TH ANNIVERSARY OF THE OFFICE OF THE ATTORNEY GENERAL (1989) (Attorney General of the United States); Peter E. Heiser, Jr., *The Opinion Writing Function of Attorneys General*, 18 IDAHO L. REV. 9 (1982); and William N. Thompson, *Transmission or Resistance: Opinions of State Attorneys General and the Impact of the Supreme Court*, 9 VAL. U. L. REV. 55 (1974).

A selection of 104 United States attorneys general opinions is contained in H. Jefferson Powell, *The Constitution and the Attorneys General* (Carolina Academic Press 1999). These opinions were selected for their enduring significance. This volume also contains a listing of all U.S. attorneys general from 1791 to 1999.

The full texts of the opinions of the attorneys general are available on *LexisNexis* and *Westlaw*. The *United States Code Annotated* and the *United States Code Service* include digests of U.S. attorneys general opinions in their annotations.

2. Opinions of the Office of Legal Counsel

Pursuant to 28 U.S.C. § 510 and 28 C.F.R. § 0.25, the U.S. attorney general has delegated to the Office of Legal Counsel the duties of preparing formal opinions of the attorney general, rendering informal opinions to the various federal agencies, assisting the attorney general in the performance of his or her function as adviser to the president, and rendering opinions to the attorney general and the various organizational units of the U.S. Department of Justice.

Opinions of the Office of Legal Counsel has been published annually since 1977 and includes the opinions written by various attorneys in the office on matters referred to that office for response, as well as formal Attorneys General opinions. Only a small portion of the Office of Legal Counsel's opinions are actually published because the addressee of the opinion must agree to publication. The opinions are first published in a paperback preliminary print and are subject to revision until the bound volume is issued. Like the opinions of the Attorney General, the opinions of the Office of Legal Counsel are merely advisory statements and are not mandatory orders.

The print publication, *Opinions of the Office of Legal Counsel*, is available in PDF format on *HeinOnline*. Due to the delay in publication of the print edition of the *Opinions of the Office of Legal Counsel*, researchers seeking more recent opinions should consult the Department of Justice's website, which provides opinions issued since 1992.[23] Published opinions also are available on *LexisNexis* and *Westlaw*. *LexisNexis* and *Westlaw* include published opinions and recent opinions available from the Department of Justice's website.

3. Opinions of State Attorneys General

Almost every state publishes the opinions of its attorney general. A checklist of published opinions of state attorneys general is included in *Pimsleur's Checklists of Basic American Legal Publications* (Marcia S. Zubrow ed., William S. Hein & Co., looseleaf). *BNA's Directory of State Administrative Codes and Registers* (Judith A. Miller & Kamla J. King comps., 2d ed., 1995) includes an appendix detailing the availability of opinions of state attorneys general, including those of U.S. territories and of the District of Columbia's corporation counsel.

---

[23] http://www.usdoj.gov/olc/opinions.htm.

References to state attorney general opinions are included in many annotated state codes. *Westlaw* and *LexisNexis* also contain opinions of state attorneys general. Coverage varies by state, often with selective coverage beginning as early as the 1940s or as late as the 1970s.

Increasingly, state attorney general opinions are available on the Internet at the website of the state attorney general's office. The National Association of Attorneys General website provides links to websites of state attorneys general.[24] While not all of these websites contain the full text of the opinions, many have added this information and some state attorneys general websites provide greater coverage than *LexisNexis* or *Westlaw*.

SECTION J. RESEARCHING LEGAL ETHICS

Norms of conduct developed by the American Bar Association have influenced the conduct of lawyers since the *Canons of Professional Ethics* was first adopted in 1908. In 1969, the *Model Code of Professional Responsibility* replaced the *Canons.* In 1983, the *Model Rules of Professional Conduct* was promulgated, and it is the *Model Rules* that are intended to constitute the national standard of conduct for attorneys.[25] The *Model Rules* and their related comments have been amended numerous times.

While the ABA promulgates the model codes and rules, each state must decide whether to adopt those norms or some variation of them as its standard. Although over three-fourth of the states have adopted the *Model Rules,* some states have adopted only portions of them; other states continue to follow the *Model Code*; and still others, such as California, have their own set of rules.

The ABA also has promulgated rules of conduct for the judiciary, beginning with the *Canons of Judicial Ethics* in 1924. In 1972, the *Model Code of Judicial Conduct* was promulgated. In 1990, it was replaced with an updated version. As with the *Model Rules,* it is up to each state to determine its own rules of judicial conduct.

Through its website, the American Bar Association provides electronic access to the *Model Rules*[26] and the *Model Code of Judicial Conduct.*[27] The current versions also are included in the *Martindale–Hubbell Law Directory.* Annotated print versions, *Annotated Model Rules of Profession Conduct* (6th ed. Center for Professional Responsibility, American Bar Association 2007) and *Annotated Model Code of Judicial Conduct* (Center for Professional Responsibility, American Bar Association 2004), also are available. Some states include their rules of professional and judicial conduct in their compiled statutes. The websites of many state bar organizations provide electronic access to these rules.

Enforcement of these rules and the power to discipline lawyers and judges is the responsibility of the state legislature or the highest court in the state; the ABA, as a voluntary association, has no authority over these

---

[24] http://www.naag.org.

[25] For information pertaining to the development of the MODEL RULES, see CENTER FOR PROFESSIONAL RESPONSIBILITY, AMERICAN BAR ASSOCIATION, A LEGISLATIVE HISTORY: THE DEVELOPMENT OF THE ABA MODEL RULES OF PROFESSIONAL CONDUCT, 1982–1988 (2d ed., 1999).

[26] http://www.abanet.org/cpr/mrpc/home.html.

[27] http://www.abanet.org/cpr/mcjc/home.html.

matters. The procedure for disciplining lawyers varies from state to state. The rules governing discipline can be located by consulting the indexes of the state codes. Disciplinary actions frequently are reported in state legal newspapers and in bar association journals.

1. Opinions on Legal Ethics

The American Bar Association has a Standing Committee on Ethics and Professional Responsibility, which is charged with interpreting the ABA's codes of conduct and recommending appropriate amendments and clarifications. Lawyers and judges can request an opinion from the committee about the propriety of a proposed action.

These opinions are published in *Opinions on Professional Ethics* (1967), *Informal Ethics Opinions* (1975), *Formal and Informal Ethics Opinions* (1984), and a current looseleaf service, *Recent Ethics Opinions*. ABA ethics opinions are also available on *Westlaw* and *LexisNexis*. New opinions are published in the *ABA Journal*.

Most state bar associations have committees similar to the ABA Standing Committee. The opinions of these committees, along with other information on professional responsibility, can be located in the following sources:

a. *ABA/BNA Lawyer's Manual on Professional Conduct* (BNA, looseleaf). A joint project of the American Bar Association and the Bureau of National Affairs, this multivolume set is the most comprehensive source for a wide range of materials dealing with the legal profession. It includes judicial opinions involving lawyer discipline and the text of state ethics opinions. It also is available from BNA as a fee-based electronic service.

b. *National Reporter on Legal Ethics and Professional Responsibility* (University Publications of America, looseleaf). This multivolume service includes the full text of both court cases on legal ethics and ethics opinions from state and local bar associations. This publication also is available electronically on *LexisNexis*.

c. *State and Local Bar Journals.* These publications often print recently issued opinions of state and local ethics committees.

d. *State Ethics Sources on the Internet.* Many state bar associations have published their ethics codes and opinions online or provide links to websites that provide this information.

LexisNexis has an ethics library, which includes state case law relevant to ethical issues, ethics rules from each state, and related ABA publications on professional responsibility. *Westlaw* contains ethics opinions for select states. These opinions can be searched by state.

2. Shepard's Professional and Judicial Conduct Citations

This citator covers citations to judicial opinions from state and federal courts and to secondary sources that have cited the various codes of conduct and the ABA's formal and informal opinions.

Chapter 21

INTERNATIONAL LAW*

This chapter deals with research in the field known as public international law—the law governing relations among sovereign states and other actors on the international scene. In today's globalized world an understanding of how to conduct research in international law is essential. Moreover, international law forms part of the law of the United States.

All the main sources of international law are covered: international agreements (treaties); customary international law; general principles of law; adjudications; and commentary by leading writers. The chapter also discusses research on international organizations, focusing on two of the most important organizations, the United Nations and the European Union. The concluding section covers research on a substantive area of international law—international protection of human rights.

SECTION A. INTRODUCTION

1. International Law in United States Law

International law is part of our law, and must be ascertained and administered by the courts of justice of appropriate jurisdiction as often as questions of right depending upon it are duly presented for their determination.[1]

International law and international agreements of the United States are law of the United States and supreme over the law of the several States. Cases arising under international law or international agreements of the United States are within the Judicial Power of the United States, and subject to Constitutional and statutory limitations and requirements of justiciability, are within the jurisdiction of the federal courts.[2]

These two quotations, one classic and one contemporary, accurately state the relation between international law and the law of the United States. The Supremacy Clause of the Constitution (Art. VI, § 2) declares:

This Constitution, and the Laws of the United States which shall be made in Pursuance thereof, *and all Treaties made, or which shall be made, under the Authority of the United States,* shall be the supreme Law of the Land; and the Judges in every State shall be bound thereby,

---

* Jonathan Pratter, Foreign and International Law Librarian, Tarlton Law Library, Jamail Center for Legal Research, University of Texas School of Law, wrote this chapter.

[1] The Paquete Habana, 175 U.S. 677, 700 (1900).

[2] RESTATEMENT OF THE LAW THIRD, THE FOREIGN RELATIONS LAW OF THE UNITED STATES §§ 111(1), (2) (1987).

419

any Thing in the Constitution or Laws of any State to the Contrary notwithstanding.[3]

To give practical impact to these broad statements of law, consider the fact that since 1988 an agreement for the sale of goods, the most common of all commercial transactions, between a seller in the United States and a buyer in any of over 60 other countries will be governed by an international agreement, the United Nations Convention on Contracts for the International Sale of Goods,[4] unless the parties provide otherwise. In an increasingly globalized world, lawyers practicing anywhere should consider an understanding of international law and its research methods to be fundamental.

2. Definition of International Law

"International law ... consists of rules and principles of general application dealing with the conduct of states and of international organizations and with their relations *inter se,* as well as with some of their relations with persons, whether natural or juridical."[5] Two points arise from this definition. First, the focus is on legal relations among sovereign states. For this reason the subject is sometimes known as the law of nations, and sometimes as *public* international law. The latter term is often contrasted with *private* international law, or as more commonly known in the United States, conflict of laws. Private international law concerns legal relations between and among individuals where the law of more than one nation may be involved.

The second point to be made about the definition of international law is that sovereign states are not the only actors involved. Obviously, international organizations, such as the United Nations or the Organization of American States, are not nations. But their structure, powers, and activities are a significant topic of international law. Moreover, the individual is by no means excluded from participation, although the understanding of exactly how persons (either natural or legal) participate in international law is not a well-settled question. Nevertheless, it is clear that a topic like the protection of human rights in international law is centrally concerned with the position of the individual.

3. The Sources of International Law

International law lacks a formal mechanism for making law, an obvious characteristic of a national legal system. There is no duly constituted legislature, executive, or judiciary, although more or less distant analogs of each of these can be found. In the absence of such mechanisms, the question of where international law comes from has to receive much attention.

Article 38(1) of the Statute of the International Court of Justice[6] is considered to be an authoritative statement of the sources of international law. Article 38(1) provides:

---

[3] Emphasis added.

[4] Apr. 11, 1980, 1489 U.N.T.S. 3, *reprinted in* 19 I.L.M. 671 (1980).

[5] Restatement of the Law Third, The Foreign Relations Law of the United States § 101 (1987).

[6] 59 Stat. 1055 (1945), T.S. No. 993.

The Court, whose function is to decide in accordance with international law such disputes as are submitted to it, shall apply:

(a) international conventions, whether general or particular, establishing rules expressly recognized by the contesting states;

(b) international custom, as evidence of a general practice accepted as law;

(c) the general principles of law recognized by civilized nations;

(d) . . . judicial decisions and the teachings of the most highly qualified publicists of the various nations, as subsidiary means for the determination of rules of law.

We can then identify five broad categories of sources:

a. *International Conventions.* These conventions include treaties and other international agreements of all kinds. ("Convention," as used here, is a synonym for agreement.) The category includes bilateral agreements (between two parties) and multilateral agreements (having three or more parties).

b. *Customary International Law.* Rules that arise out of the general and consistent practice of states acting out of a sense of legal obligation are referred to as *customary international law.*

c. *General Principles of Law.* Examples of such general principles "common to the major legal systems" (to use the contemporary formulation) include the doctrine of laches or the passage of time as a bar to a claim, principles of due process in the administration of justice, and the doctrine of *res judicata.*[7]

d. *Judicial Decisions.* This category includes the decisions of both international tribunals and national courts, when the latter deal with questions of international law. An international tribunal covers various kinds of judicial fora, ranging from the International Court of Justice to an ad hoc arbitral panel constituted to resolve a particular international dispute.

e. *Writings of International Law Scholars.* This phrase is the modern substitute for the archaic language found in Article 38 ("teachings of the most highly qualified publicists"). This category covers treatises and textbooks of leading scholars, the draft conventions and reports of the International Law Commission of the United Nations ("formed for the purpose of encouraging the progressive development of international law and its codification"), and the reports and resolutions of such non-governmental groups as the American Society of International Law, the International Law Association, and the Institut de Droit International.

Lawyers and scholars often use the term "secondary sources" to describe such materials because they are commentaries on or discussion of the law rather than primary sources of law. This description is consistent with the usage of Article 38(1), which calls such materials "subsidiary

---

[7] *See generally* Bin Cheng, General Principles of Law as Applied by International Courts and Tribunals (1994).

means." Judicial decisions, ordinarily considered primary sources, are, under Article 38(1), subsidiary means.[8]

4. Impact of the Internet and the World Wide Web

The era of electronic information, and the advent of the Internet and the development of websites in particular, have not altered the sources of international law as described here.[9] However, the vast and constantly expanding amount of information available electronically, much of it without cost other than access to a computer and to the Internet, promises to have a profound effect on research on international law. Consider research on state practice as an example. Many national governments, and their foreign ministries in particular, maintain websites. These websites publish official statements of position on a host of issues, in speeches and in other statements by high officials, in press releases, in programmatic documents, and in other announcements and notices. It is often possible to assemble evidence of state practice of national governments simply by consulting official web pages.

Information published on the Internet achieves the widest possible dissemination in the shortest time imaginable. Documentation that once was difficult or impossible to access is now readily available. Examples are manifold. Documents of the United Nations are now freely accessible on the World Wide Web. This is a revolutionary development. The European Commission maintains a freely accessible web portal devoted to European Union law. Reference will be made throughout this chapter to useful sources on the World Wide Web.

A useful Web-based resource is called *EISIL*,[10] which stands for Electronic Information System for International Law. It is sponsored by the American Society of International Law. *EISIL* is best described as a moderated portal or gateway to international legal information on the World Wide Web. Because *EISIL* is moderated, i.e., the content is authenticated and checked for accuracy, the researcher can have confidence that the sources she finds through *EISIL* are reliable.

Also of use as a complement to *EISIL* is the *ASIL Guide to Electronic Resources for International Law*,[11] which covers in a narrative fashion several fields of current interest (e.g., human rights, international environmental law, and international criminal law).

An innovative and creative use of the World Wide Web for the free dissemination of information about international law is the *Audiovisual*

---

[8] To avoid confusion, the reader should note that in discussions of researching international law the word "sources" can have two different senses. The first sense refers to the formal sources of international law as described in Article 38(1). The other sense refers to published sources, i.e., the publications and other resources described in this chapter that make up the documentation of international law.

[9] For an ambitious contrasting view, see John King Gamble, *New Information Technologies and the Sources of International Law: Convergence, Divergence, Obsolescence and/or Transformation*, 41 GERMAN Y.B. INT'L L. 170 (1998).

[10] http://www.eisil.org.

[11] http://www.asil.org/resource/home.htm. ("ASIL" stands for American Society of International Law).

Library of International Law, produced by the United Nations.[12] It has three components: (1) the Historical Archives, containing documents on the adoption of significant international legal instruments; (2) the Lecture Series, containing video lectures on various international legal topics given by leading scholars in the field; and (3) the Research Library, containing a broad array of links to international legal resources available for free on the World Wide Web.

There are at least four weblogs ("blogs") in English on international law that are worthy of note. They are written by law professors in the U.S. One is called *Opinio Juris*;[13] one is called *International Law Reporter*;[14] one is called *International Law Prof Blog*;[15] and one is called simply *International Law*.[16] Developments in international law take place constantly all over the world. Blogs function as excellent sources of news and comment on these developments.

SECTION B.   INTERNATIONAL AGREEMENTS: UNITED STATES SOURCES

1.   Introduction[17]

A *treaty* is "an international agreement concluded between States in written form and governed by international law ... whatever its particular designation."[18] Any number of terms can be used to refer to international agreements, e.g., treaty, convention, protocol, covenant, charter, statute, act, declaration, concordat, exchange of notes, agreed minute, memorandum of agreement, and memorandum of understanding. The definition given above makes the important point that the terminology describing a particular international agreement does not affect its legal status as an agreement binding in international law.

The subject of treaties is complicated in the United States by the frequent use made of the *executive agreement*. Under the Constitution, the President has the "Power, by and with the Advice and Consent of the Senate, to make Treaties, provided two thirds of the Senators present concur...."[19] But this formal treaty-making power does not exhaust the federal government's authority to negotiate international agreements. In fact, there are far more executive agreements in force between the United States and other countries than there are treaties.[20] The difference between the two kinds of agreement is a subject for the substantive course in

[12] http://www.un.org/law/avl/. The department responsible is the Codification Division of the Office of Legal Affairs in the UN Secretariat.

[13] http://www.opiniojuris.org.

[14] http://ilreports.blogspot.com.

[15] http://lawprofessors.typepad.com/international_law.

[16] http://blogs.law.harvard.edu/internationallaw.

[17] *See generally* Jonathan Pratter, *Treaty Research Basics*, 89 Law Libr. J. 407 (1997). *See also Guide to Treaty Research* (Columbia Law Library), http://www.law.columbia.edu/library/Research_Guides/internat_law/treaty_research.

[18] Vienna Convention on the Law of Treaties, May 23, 1969, art. 2(1)(a), 1155 U.N.T.S. 331.

[19] U.S. Const. art. II, § 2.

[20] *See* John C. Yoo, *Laws as Treaties?: The Constitutionality of Congressional–Executive Agreements*, 99 Mich. L. Rev. 757, 765–68 (2001).

international law.[21] For our purposes it is enough to know that both treaties and executive agreements constitute binding international agreements of the United States.[22]

2. Current Sources

a. *T.I.A.S. and U.S.T.* Since 1945, the State Department has published the international agreements of the United States in a series of pamphlets called *Treaties and Other International Acts Series (T.I.A.S.).* The series began with number 1501 and as of this writing has reached *T.I.A.S.* 12854, an agreement concluded in 1997. Since 1950, the State Department has published the agreements that first appear in *T.I.A.S.* in a series of bound volumes entitled *United States Treaties and Other International Agreements (U.S.T.). U.S.T.* currently consists of 35 volumes; each volume may have as many as five or six separately bound parts. Volume 35, part 6, the most recently issued as of this writing, ends with *T.I.A.S.* 11059, an agreement concluded in 1984. By statute, both *U.S.T.* and *T.I.A.S.* are authoritative sources for the text of agreements published there.[23]

b. *Internet.* Both *T.I.A.S.* and *U.S.T.* are available in full-text image files on *HeinOnline* in the Treaties and Agreements Library.[24] However, the great delay in publishing both of the official treaty series has been noted. Such a delay causes obvious problems for the researcher. These are primary sources of law containing binding international obligations of the United States. Moreover, *The Bluebook* prefers citation to one of these sources when the U.S. is a party,[25] something that is clearly impossible in the case of more recent international agreements. Given the lengthy time lag in the publication of the official treaty series, finding a substitute source for more recent U.S. international agreements is essential.

In 2004 the statute 1 U.S.C. § 112a was amended to add subsection (d):

> The Secretary of State shall make publicly available through the Internet website of the Department of State each treaty or international agreement proposed to be published in the compilation entitled "United States Treaties and Other International Agreements" not later than 180 days after the date on which the treaty or agreement enters into force.

Recent international agreements of the U.S. can now be found on the State Department's website.[26] It is necessary to start at the Treaty Affairs

---

[21] *See generally* SEAN D. MURPHY, PRINCIPLES OF INTERNATIONAL LAW 208–10 (2006).

[22] *See* CONGRESSIONAL RESEARCH SERVICE, LIBRARY OF CONGRESS, TREATIES AND OTHER INTERNATIONAL AGREEMENTS: THE ROLE OF THE UNITED STATES SENATE, S. PRT. NO. 106–71, 77 (2001) (providing a thorough treatment of United States treaty practice). This document is available in full text from *GPO Access,* http://www.gpoaccess.gov. Under Legislative Resources, click View All. Click on Congressional Committee Prints. Search the 106th Congress, Senate Committee Prints, using keyword "treaties." The first hit is this document.

[23] 1 U.S.C. §§ 112a, 113 (2000).

[24] http://www.heinonline.org/HOL/Index?collection=ustreaties.

[25] THE BLUEBOOK: A UNIFORM SYSTEM OF CITATION, R. 21.4.5 (18th ed. 2005) [hereinafter THE BLUEBOOK].

[26] http://www.state.gov.

page of the website.[27] This page is maintained by the Office of the Assistant Legal Adviser for Treaty Affairs; it is the gateway to a great deal of valuable information. In the sidebar is a link titled "Reporting International Agreements to Congress under Case Act (Text of Agreements)."[28]

At the Case Act page,[29] the researcher will find some explanatory text, but more significantly, a sidebar with links for 2009, 2008, 2007, 2006, and "2005–1997 (FOIA Site.)"[30] Clicking on the 2008 link takes the researcher to a long list of agreements posted in numerical order, according to numeration that will be unfamiliar even to experienced international legal researchers. The numeration runs from 2008–001 to 2008–221. [Illustration 21–1] Each number is accompanied by the name of a country, which safely may be assumed to be the other party. If there is more than one other party, the term "Multilateral" is used. The number and name combination is the link to the full text of the agreements in PDF format. These are scanned originals.

For example, agreement 2008–012 is with China and is titled "Agreement on the safety of food, with annex. Signed at Beijing December 11, 2007. Entered into force December 11, 2007." Clicking the link brings up a scan of the rather badly printed original document. The researcher finds stamped at the top of the first page the number "08–12." This is the State Department's internal numbering for identifying and citing agreements before they are published officially. This numbering is essential because of the enormous time lag in official publication. Note, however, that *The Bluebook* does not recognize the State Department's internal number as an acceptable citation.

To complicate matters, clicking the link "2005–1997 (FOIA Site)" takes the researcher out of the Treaty Affairs area and into the Freedom of Information Act sector of the State Department's website. This is another telling indicator of the bad state of publication of international agreements in the U.S.

Some U.S. government agencies make available on the World Wide Web collections of international agreements related to their work. Examples are:

- Trade Agreements (Office of the United States Trade Representative)[31]

---

[27] http://www.state.gov/s/l/treaty.

[28] The Case Act is codified at 1 U.S.C. § 112b. Essentially, it requires the Secretary of State to "transmit to the Congress the text of any international agreement . . ., other than a treaty, to which the United States is a party as soon as practicable after such agreement has entered into force with respect to the United States. . . ." 1 U.S.C. § 112b(a). As we have seen, the Secretary of State is also bound by statute to publish U.S. international agreements on the State Department's website. That disclosure and publication of U.S. international agreements depend on these kinds of statutory injunctions is indicative of the serious deficiencies in official publication of U.S. international agreements.

[29] http://www.state.gov/s/l/treaty/caseact.

[30] No doubt, future years will be added in due course.

[31] http://www.ustr.gov/Trade_Agreements/Section_Index.html. For more information and updates, try the website *TradeAgreements.gov*, http://tradeagreements.gov.

- Income Tax Treaties (Internal Revenue Service)[32]

- International Antitrust and Consumer Protection Cooperation Agreements (Federal Trade Commission)[33]

- Private International Law (State Department)[34]

- Treaties and Agreements [Arms Control] (State Department)[35]

A commercial collection called *Treaties and International Agreements Online* is available.[36]

c. *Westlaw and LexisNexis*. These commercial legal databases provide relatively easy access to U.S. international agreements. Both systems combine recent and historical documents in one file. On *Westlaw* the database identifier is "USTREATIES." On *LexisNexis*, a similar database called "U.S. Treaties on Lexis" will be found under "Area of Law–By Topic–International Law."

d. *Other formats*. In print there is a series titled *Consolidated Treaties & International Agreements: Current Document Service*.[37] In microfiche there is a set called *Hein's United States Treaties and Other International Agreements: Current Service*. The electronic analogy to this is available on *HeinOnline's* "Treaties and Agreements Library".

e. *U.S.C., U.S.C.A., U.S.C.S.*, and *Federal Register*. There might be a tendency to think that U.S. international agreements would be found in the official *U.S.C.*, the *Federal Register*, or in the annotated federal codes. In general, that is *not* true. *U.S.C.* does not include treaties. The annotated codes, *U.S.C.A.* and *U.S.C.S.*, publish a few treaties of general interest. For example, the United Nations Convention on Contracts for the International Sale of Goods appears in the Appendix volume to Title 15 of *U.S.C.A.* *U.S.C.S.* has an unnumbered volume entitled "International Agreements" containing the text of 40 miscellaneous multilateral agreements to which the U.S. is a party. Case notes and references to secondary sources are appended to some agreements. Another volume of *U.S.C.S.* entitled "Annotations to Uncodified Laws and Treaties" contains case notes to Native American treaties and to an additional group of miscellaneous international agreements. The *Federal Register* rarely publishes U.S. international agreements. Research for the text of U.S. international agreements *should not* begin with any of these sources. On the other hand, they *should* be consulted in order to find implementing legislation and judicial interpretation, as noted below in Section B–7 of this chapter.

3. Earlier Publications

a. *United States Statutes at Large*. International agreements of the United States were published in *United States Statutes at Large* from

---

[32] http://www.irs.gov/businesses/international/article/0,,id=96739,00.html. (The double comma in the URL is not a typo.)

[33] http://www.ftc.gov/oia/agreements.shtm.

[34] http://www.state.gov/s/l/c3452.htm.

[35] http://www.state.gov/t/ac/trt/.

[36] For more information, see http://www.oceanalaw.com.

[37] (Oceana Publications 1990–).

volume 8 through volume 64 (1949). Volume 8 includes agreements entered into between 1776 and 1845. Beginning with volume 47, executive agreements were included. Volume 64, part 3 (1950–51), contains an index of all the agreements in *United States Statutes at Large.*

b. *T.S. and E.A.S.* The current pamphlet series, *T.I.A.S.*, was preceded by the *Treaty Series (T.S.)* and the *Executive Agreement Series (E.A.S.).* The *Treaty Series* reached pamphlet number 994 and the *Executive Agreement Series* went to pamphlet number 506, for a total of 1500. Thus, *T.I.A.S.* begins at 1501.[38]

c. *Bevans.* A useful collection published by the State Department is *Treaties and Other International Agreements of the United States of America, 1776–1949,*[39] known as "Bevans" from the name of the compiler. This series collects, in 13 volumes, the international agreements of the United States up to the beginning of *U.S.T.* Multilateral treaties are arranged chronologically in volumes 1–4. Bilateral treaties are arranged alphabetically by the name of the other country in volumes 5–12. Volume 13 is a general index. Two other collections published by the State Department are also known by the names of their respective compilers: *Treaties, Conventions, International Acts, Protocols, and Agreements Between the United States of America and Other Powers*[40] ("Malloy"), and *Treaties and Other International Acts of the United States of America*[41] ("Miller"). For most purposes Bevans supersedes both of the earlier collections. In Table 4, Treaty Sources, Unofficial treaty sources, *The Bluebook* allows citation to Bevans. All three compilations are available in *HeinOnline* in the Treaties and Agreements Library.

4. United States Treaties in Congressional Documents

a. *Senate Treaty Documents and Senate Executive Reports.* After a treaty for which the advice and consent of the Senate will be sought has been negotiated and signed, the president submits it to the Senate in a message from the president, with the text of the agreement annexed to it. The proposed treaty is referred to the Committee on Foreign Relations for hearings and a recommendation to the full Senate. Until the 97th Congress (1981–82), the Senate printed the proposed treaty under the name *Senate Executive Document* with a letter designation.

Beginning with the 97th Congress, the printed treaties are called *Treaty Documents* and receive a number, the first part of which indicates the Congress that considered the treaty. For example, the message from the President of July 2007 transmitting the International Convention for the Suppression of Acts of Nuclear Terrorism, signed by the U.S. in September 2005, is the *Senate Treaty Document* designated 110–4.

The Committee on Foreign Relations then makes its recommendation to the full Senate in a report printed in the numbered series of *Senate Executive Reports.* For example, the Committee's report of December 2007

---

[38] For detailed information on these series and on the bibliography of the early publication of United States international agreements, see 1 Hunter Miller, Treaties and Other International Acts of the United States of America 35–138 (1931).

[39] (Charles I. Bevans comp., U.S.G.P.O. 1968–76).

[40] (William M. Malloy comp., U.S.G.P.O. 1910–38).

[41] (Hunter Miller ed., U.S.G.P.O. 1931–48).

favorably reporting the United Nations Convention on the Law of the Sea is *Senate Executive Report* 110–9. Again, the first part of the number reflects the Congress that considered the treaty.

Researchers should note the significance of these congressional treaty documents. The message of transmittal from the President in the *Treaty Document* series always includes the text of the agreement in an annex, as well as the letter of submittal from the Secretary of State to the President, which itself contains a detailed article-by-article analysis of the agreement. The report of the Senate Foreign Relations Committee in the *Executive Report* series has the Committee's analysis of the agreement, discussion of needed implementing legislation, and a statement of minority views, as the case may be, along with other useful information. Given the serious delay in the standard official publication of U.S. international agreements, these congressional treaty documents often furnish the sole official source of publication for purposes of citation.[42]

Moreover, in the case of agreements that have generated disagreement or controversy in the Senate, the Foreign Relations Committee often appends statements of "conditions," "declarations," "understandings," or "provisos" to its recommendation of advice and consent to the full Senate. If the full Senate gives its advice and consent to ratification subject to these conditions, important consequences for the correct understanding of the treaty text and of the legal obligations it imposes will follow, at least from the point of view of the United States. The committee report in the *Executive Report* series is often the only place to find the text of these appended statements. They are also printed in the *Congressional Record* where the Senate's vote on advice and consent to ratification is published.

Treaty Documents and *Executive Reports* beginning with the 104th Congress (1995–96) are available from the United States Government Printing Office website (*GPO Access*).[43]

The recent publication, *Treaties Submitted to the United States Senate: Legislative History, 1989–2004*,[44] compiles the information on Senate treaty consideration. It is organized chronologically. Each entry begins with the title of the agreement and then gives the references to the relevant Treaty Document, committee hearing, and Executive Report. Information on advice and consent by the full Senate as found in the *Congressional Record* is also given.

b. *Pending Treaties.* Treaties submitted to the Senate for advice and consent can be held over from year to year. Some international agreements remain pending in the Senate for a long period of time. For example, the Vienna Convention on the Law of Treaties,[45] one of the more significant international agreements of the modern era, was submitted as *Executive Document L* during the 92d Congress, 1st Session (1971). It has remained pending before the Senate Committee on Foreign Relations, without action of any kind, ever since.

---

[42] *See* THE BLUEBOOK, R. 21.4.5(a)(i) (18th ed. 2005) (allows citation to Senate *Treaty Documents* for the text of agreements not found in *U.S.T., Stat., T.I.A.S., T.S.,* or *E.A.S.*).

[43] http://www.gpoaccess.gov/serialset/cdocuments/index.html and http://www.gpoaccess.gov/serialset/creports/index.html.

[44] CHRISTIAN L. WIKTOR (Martinus Nijhoff 2006).

[45] 1155 U.N.T.S. 331 (1969).

The Treaty Affairs sector of the State Department website has a page titled "Treaties Pending in the Senate."[46] This page is frequently updated and is probably the best source to consult for the purpose of tracking pending treaties. The website of the U.S. Senate Committee on Foreign Relations has a link to "Pending Treaties."[47] This leads to an updated statement of treaties pending before the committee.[48] Volume 1 (Senate) of the *Congressional Index* has a "Treaties" tab that is useful for tracking treaties pending in the Senate. There is a subject index.

5. Other Publications

a. *Unperfected Treaties of the United States, 1776–1976.*[49] This multivolume set is an annotated collection of treaties to which the United States was a signatory, but which never went into force.

b. *Extradition Laws and Treaties of the United States.*[50] This looseleaf set contains extradition treaties currently in force between the United States and other countries, arranged alphabetically by the name of the other country. Additional volumes in this set reprint U.S. agreements concerning international judicial assistance in criminal matters.

c. *Indian Affairs: Laws and Treaties.*[51] Volume 2 contains treaties made by the United States with Indian tribes between 1778 and 1883. It was reprinted under the title *Indian Treaties.*[52] Volume 7 of *United States Statutes at Large* also includes a compilation of Indian treaties. Treaties concluded with Indian tribes before the independence of the United States are in *Early American Indian Documents: Treaties and Law, 1607–1789.*[53]

d. *Tax Treaties.*[54] This looseleaf publication provides comprehensive coverage with annotations and background material of the income and estate tax treaties of the United States currently in force and of those pending ratification. This is now online as part of the *CCH Tax Research NetWork.*[55] Under the "International" tab, there is a link to *Tax Treaties Reporter.*

6. Finding United States International Agreements and Verifying Their Status

The process of locating international agreements requires skills quite different from those utilized in researching other legal materials. As is the

---

[46] http://foreign.state.gov/s/l/treaty/pending/index.htm.

[47] http://foreign.senate.gov/legislation.html.

[48] http://www.senate.gov/treaties.pdf.

[49] Christian L. Wiktor (Oceana Publications 1976).

[50] (Igor I. Kavass & Adolph Sprudzs eds., William S. Hein & Co. 1979–).

[51] (Charles J. Kappler ed., U.S.G.P.O. 1903–41). This is available on *HeinOnline* in the "Treaties and Agreements Library" and on the Oklahoma State University Library Electronic Publishing Center, http://digital.library.okstate.edu/kappler/index.htm.

[52] (Interland Publishing 1972). *See also* the website *Early Recognized Treaties with American Indian Nations*, http://earlytreaties.unl.edu.

[53] (Aldent T. Vaughn ed., U.P.A. 1979–89).

[54] (Commerce Clearing House 1952 to present).

[55] http://tax.cchgroup.com/TRN/default.

case for other primary sources of law, after locating the text of an international agreement, the current status of that document must be verified.

Multilateral agreements do not come into force once they are negotiated. A minimum number of countries must agree to join a multilateral treaty before it goes into effect; this may take years. Moreover, only those countries that agree to become parties to a multilateral agreement are bound by it, thus making it essential to know what the "states party" are. States may accede to (join) a multilateral treaty long after it is first negotiated. As a final complication, states may denounce (terminate) their participation in either a multilateral or bilateral agreement at some time after becoming a party. Obviously, the process of verification is crucial. The finding tools noted in this section refer to the location of the text of international agreements. They also provide critical additional information for verifying current status.

a.   *Treaties in Force.*[56] The full title of this publication is *Treaties in Force: A List of Treaties and Other International Agreements in Force on [date]*. It is published by the State Department and appears in hardcopy several months after the date on the cover. It is divided into bilateral and multilateral sections. The bilateral section is organized alphabetically by the name of the other country and subdivided by subject matter; the multilateral section is organized alphabetically by subject matter and chronologically within each subject heading.

Each entry begins with the name of the agreement, followed by the place and date it was concluded, the date it entered into force (if multilateral, the date of entry into force in general and for the United States in particular), the citation (with parallel citations), a list of the other states party to the agreement (if multilateral), and brief notes regarding such points as whether a state entered a reservation or declaration to a multilateral agreement.

Treaties in Force can answer several questions: (a) what international agreements are currently in place between the United States and a particular country or on a particular subject; (b) is a particular international agreement in force for the United States; (c) where can the text of the agreement be found; and (d) what other countries are parties to a multilateral agreement. As of the 2007 edition, the depositaries of multilateral agreements are listed and URLs for the online version of the text are given, although these often turn out not to work.

The hard copy *Treaties in Force* is current to the date on the cover and needs updating to catch developments that have occurred since it was last issued.

The current edition of *Treaties in Force* in PDF is now part of the Treaty Affairs section of the State Department's website.[57] [Illustration 21–2] In fact, although this is not clearly stated, the Web is now the chief mode of publication of *Treaties in Force*. The introductory text to the 2007 edition in both hard copy and on the Web says:

---

[56] (U.S.G.P.O. 1944–).

[57] http://www.state.gov/s/l/treaty/treaties/2007/index.htm.

The electronic edition of *Treaties in Force* may be updated periodically throughout the year on the Treaty Affairs webpage.... The print edition of *Treaties in Force* is published annually in limited quantities to meet the needs of certain users who are unable to consult the online version. Because the print edition is updated only annually, the electronic edition will, in most cases, better reflect the current status of U.S. treaties and international agreements.

Indeed, as of December 2008, the cover date of the online edition was November 1, 2007, an eleven month improvement over the hard copy cover date.

Treaties in Force does not provide all information that may be required. For example, when an agreement has not been published in *T.I.A.S.* or *U.S.T.*, there may be no citation, merely the unhelpful indication "TIAS ___." When for multilateral agreements the U.S. or another party has entered a declaration or reservation, this will be noted, but the text is not reproduced. When all else fails, the researcher should use the information and follow the instructions found at the Contact Information page in the Treaty Affairs section of the State Department's website.[58]

b. *Treaty Actions.* The Treaty Affairs section of the State Department's website also has a page called "Treaty Actions," which is meant to update *Treaties in Force*.[59] As of December 2008, there was a Treaty Actions document for November 2007, a four-month update of the online version of *Treaties in Force*.

c. *A Guide to the United States Treaties in Force.*[60] This commercial publication contains essentially the same information as that found in *Treaties in Force*. However, as it is more heavily indexed, it can be used to find references to agreements that might be hard to locate in *Treaties in Force*. For example, it contains lists of agreements newly added to the current *Treaties in Force*, as well as of agreements no longer found in *Treaties in Force* (as compared to the previous year).

d. *United States Treaty Index.*[61] This is a commercial index of international agreements of the United States entered into from 1776 through 2004. The set consists of a "master guide" in numerical order, a chronological guide, a country index, a subject index, and a "geographical subject index." This set is very confusingly organized. Even a law librarian will have difficulty putting it to use.

e. *Current Treaty Index.*[62] This is a semiannual supplement to the *United States Treaty Index.*

The three commercial publications mentioned above (c, d, and e) contain a fair amount of useful information. However, their organization can be confusing, making them cumbersome and difficult to use. Research-

---

[58] http://www.state.gov/s/l/treaty/contact. Experience has shown that the more the researcher knows about the question she has, the more helpful the Treaty Affairs Office is likely to be.

[59] http://www.state.gov/s/l/treaty/c3428.htm.

[60] (Igor I. Kavass ed., William S. Hein & Co. 1983–).

[61] (Igor I. Kavass ed., William S. Hein & Co. 1991–).

[62] (Igor I. Kavass ed., William S. Hein & Co. 1982–).

ers should, therefore, always try to start with *Treaties in Force*, and then turn to the commercial publications for additional information.

7.   Implementation and Judicial Interpretation of United States Treaties

a.   *U.S.C., U.S.C.A., U.S.C.S., C.F.R.,* and *Federal Register.* Often the terms of a U.S. international agreement require implementing legislation in order to become effective as part of U.S. law. For example, the Convention on the Recognition and Enforcement of Foreign Arbitral Awards[63] is enacted as chapter 2 of the Federal Arbitration Act.[64] Moreover, when a branch of the federal executive is charged with carrying out various responsibilities of the United States under a treaty and its implementing legislation, there are implementing administrative regulations as well. Under the UNESCO Convention on the Means of Prohibiting and Preventing the Illicit Import, Export and Transfer of Ownership of Cultural Property[65] and its implementing legislation,[66] the U.S. Customs Service issues regulations to restrict the import of various kinds of cultural property. These regulations are first published in the *Federal Register* and later summarized in a list at 19 C.F.R. § 12.104g. Therefore, when researching a U.S. international agreement, checking for federal legislation and administrative regulations on point is essential.

b.   *Judicial Decisions.* Finding cases decided under and interpreting U.S. international agreements requires creative research along various lines. Three lines of inquiry are suggested here.

(1) Use of the *Westlaw* and *LexisNexis* databases is a good way to find U.S. cases arising under or interpreting U.S. international agreements. Courts typically identify international agreements by name, though with some variation. Therefore, search queries can be formulated using key words from the formal and popular name of the agreement, e.g., *(convention +3 contracts +3 "international sale of goods")* or *cisg*.[67]

(2) The West key number digests include a topic, "Treaties," that collects cases involving the interpretation and application of U.S. international agreements.

(3) *U.S.C.S.* includes a volume entitled *Uncodified: Notes to Uncodified Laws and Treaties,* which collects case notes to various multilateral, bilateral, and Indian treaties of the United States.

SECTION C.   INTERNATIONAL AGREEMENTS: ADDITIONAL SOURCES

1.   General Treaty Collections

a.   *United Nations Treaty Series (U.N.T.S.).* Under Article 102 of the United Nations Charter, every member of the United Nations is required to

---

[63] 21 U.S.T. 2517, 330 U.N.T.S. 38.

[64] 9 U.S.C. § 201 *et seq.* (2000).

[65] 823 U.N.T.S. 231.

[66] Convention on Cultural Property Implementation Act, 19 U.S.C. § 2601 *et seq.* (2000).

[67] As of April 2008, this search returned 78 cases in the DCT database on *Westlaw.*

register its international agreements with the Secretariat, which, in turn, is required to publish them. Compulsory registration and publication are intended in part to prevent secret diplomacy. Begun in 1946, *U.N.T.S.* now has over 2,300 volumes and contains many thousands of agreements. However, *U.N.T.S.* also runs years behind in terms of publishing agreements. Its index volumes likewise run behind and are difficult to use. The researcher should note that the formal title by which libraries catalog this source is *Treaty Series (United Nations)*.

Agreements published in *U.N.T.S.* are now available on the *United Nations Treaty Collection* website.[68] Text is presented in an image format as the document appears in *U.N.T.S.* While this image format ensures authenticity, it is often difficult to determine the volume and page number of *U.N.T.S.* Unfortunately, it is not possible to search by citation to *U.N.T.S.* This is a serious drawback.

The website now has a file of recent multilateral agreements not yet published in *U.N.T.S.*

For more information on the registration and publication of international agreements by the United Nations, see the *Treaty Handbook* prepared by the Treaty Section of the United Nations Office of Legal Affairs.[69]

b. *League of Nations Treaty Series (L.N.T.S.)*. This is the predecessor of *U.N.T.S.*, having been published under the auspices of the League of Nations. In 205 volumes covering the period 1920–1946, the *Series* published the treaties registered with the Secretariat of the League. The set is often cataloged under the title *Treaty Series (League of Nations)*.

L.N.T.S. is now included in the *United Nations Treaty Collection* website. Unfortunately, *L.N.T.S.* is integrated into the main database, which makes it very difficult to search separately from *U.N.T.S.*

c. *Consolidated Treaty Series (C.T.S.)*.[70] This commercially published series, 243 volumes covering the period 1648–1919, is valuable for locating the text of historically important international agreements.

Note that the three treaty series mentioned here (*C.T.S., L.N.T.S.,* and *U.N.T.S.*) cover a continuous period from 1648 to the present.

2. Other Treaty Collections

a. *Council of Europe Treaty Series (C.E.T.S)*. The Council of Europe, an international organization of 47 European nations, has as one of its main purposes the drafting and sponsoring of multilateral agreements on subjects of mutual interest. The most significant treaty sponsored by the Council of Europe is the Convention for the Protection of Human Rights and Fundamental Freedoms.[71] The Council of Europe's treaties are first published as individual documents in the *Council of Europe Treaty Series*. (The former title was *European Treaty Series (E.T.S.)*.) They have also

---

[68] http://treaties.un.org.

[69] (United Nations 2002). The Treaty Handbook is available in PDF on the *United Nations Treaty Collection* website (http://treaties.un.org/doc/source/publications/THB/English.pdf).

[70] (Oceana Publications 1969–81).

[71] C.E.T.S. No. 5, 213 U.N.T.S. 221.

been collected and republished (through 1998) in the seven volumes of *European Conventions and Agreements.*[72]

Today the clearly superior method for researching Council of Europe agreements is on the World Wide Web, using the Council of Europe's conventions website.[73]

b. *International Legal Materials (I.L.M.).* Published since 1962 by the American Society of International Law, this is a leading source for the text of recent international agreements of note. *I.L.M.* is published six times a year and is probably the best source for recent international documents of significance, including international agreements. A distinguished editorial board makes the selection. *I.L.M.* contains many other kinds of documents, e.g., judicial decisions, arbitral awards, and the documents of international organizations. *I.L.M.* is available on both *Westlaw* and *LexisNexis.*

c. *O.A.S. Treaty Series.* Like the Council of Europe, the Organization of American States drafts and sponsors multilateral agreements of mutual interest to member states. These are published in the *O.A.S. Treaty Series.*[74] Its formal title, under which it is cataloged in libraries, is *Treaty Series (Organization of American States).*

Multilateral international agreements sponsored by the O.A.S. can now be conveniently consulted on the O.A.S. website.[75] They are organized both by year and by subject. Status information can also be found.

d. *National Treaty Series.* Like the United States, many other countries publish their international agreements in a special series. Examples are the *United Kingdom Treaty Series, Canada Treaty Series,* and *Recueil des Traits et Accords de la France.*

The *United Kingdom Treaty Series* is technically a subset of documents called "command papers." The *Treaty Series* command papers are now available as PDF documents from January 2002 forward at the website of the Foreign & Commonwealth Office.[76] The Australian government makes available an online source of its international agreements, the *Australian Treaties Library.*[77] This is a comprehensive database of all international agreements to which Australia is a party, and which are published in hard copy in the *Australian Treaty Series.* France now has a good database of its international agreements, both bilateral and multilateral, called *Base Pacte.*[78] The *Irish Treaty Series* is now online.[79] As part of its systematic collection of legislation online, Switzerland has a classified database of its international agreements.[80] The Canadian government maintains a database concerning its international agreements called *Canada Treaty Infor-*

---

[72] (Council of Europe 1971–).

[73] http://conventions.coe.int/.

[74] This is the name usually applied to the series. THE BLUEBOOK (18th. ed. 2005) mistakenly continues to use the former title, *Pan–American Treaty Series.*

[75] http://www.oas.org/DIL/treaties.htm.

[76] http://www.fco.gov.uk/en/about-the-fco/publications/treaty-command-papers-ems.

[77] http://www.ustlii.edu.au/au/other/dfat.

[78] http://www.doc.diplomatie.gouv.fr/pacte/index.html.

[79] http://foreignaffairs.gov.ie/home/index.aspx?id=42915.

[80] http://www.admin.ch/index.html?lang=en.

mation.[81] Rather than the full text of agreements, it provides citations to *Canada Treaty Series* and other sources, in addition to full status information.

Countries that have official gazettes (this generally does not include the common-law jurisdictions) will as a general practice publish international agreements of any significance in the official gazette. An excellent example is Germany, which devotes an entire part of its official gazette to the publication of international agreements—the *Bundesgesetzblatt, Teil II.*

e. *Subject Compilations.* Many publishers, both governmental and commercial, have compiled collections of international agreements. These collections can be very useful because they bring together documents that otherwise are scattered in several sources. There are too many of these collections to list comprehensively here, but some leading recent examples are:

- *Basic Documents on International Migration Law*[82]

- *Basic Documents on International Trade Law*[83]

- *Collection of International Instruments and Legal Texts Concerning Refugees and Others of Concern to UNHCR.*[84]

- *Copyright and Related Rights: Laws and Treaties*[85]

- *Documents on the Laws of War*[86]

- *Industrial Property Laws and Treaties*[87]

- *International Criminal Law: A Collection of International and European Instruments*[88]

- *International Environmental Law: Multilateral Treaties*[89]

f. *Historical Collections.* There are many collections of international agreements, both bilateral and multilateral, that are now chiefly of historical interest. To locate these, refer to the publication *Treaties, Treaty Collections and Documents on Foreign Affairs: From Sun King Suppilulima I to the Hague Peace Conferences of 1899 & 1907: An Annotated Bibliography.*[90] Also of use is the online *Guide to Researching Historical Treaties.*[91]

[81] http://www.accord-treaty.gc.ca/.

[82] RICHARD PLENDER (Martinus Nijhoff 3d ed. 2007).

[83] CHIA-JUI CHENG (Kluwer Law International 3d ed. 1999).

[84] (United Nations High Commissioner for Refugees 2007). This is also available online, http://www.unhcr.org/publ/PUBL/455c460b2.html.

[85] (World Intellectual Property Organization 1987–).

[86] ADAM ROBERTS & RICHARD GUELF (Oxford University Press 3d ed. 2000).

[87] (World Intellectual Property Organization 1976–).

[88] (Christine Van den Wyngaert ed. Martinus Nijhoff 2005).

[89] (W.E. Burhenne ed., Kluwer Law International 1974–).

[90] PETER MACALISTER-SMITH & JOACHIM SCHWIETZKE (Arbeitsgemeinschaft für Juristisches Bibliotheks-und Dokumentationswesen 2002).

[91] http://www.law.columbia.edu/library/Research_Guides/internat_law/hist_treaties.

3. International Agreements on the Internet

a. *Agreements Sponsored by International Organizations.* Several international organizations maintain excellent websites with collections of international agreements for which they are responsible. Some outstanding examples are:

- Council of Europe[92]
- Hague Conference on Private International Law[93]
- International Committee of the Red Cross[94]
- International Institute for the Unification of Private Law (UNIDROIT)[95]
- International Labor Organization (ILO)(ILOLEX)[96]
- Organization of American States (OAS)[97]
- United Nations Commission on International Trade Law (UNCITRAL)[98]
- United Nations Environment Programme (UNEP)[99]
- United Nations High Commissioner for Human Rights (UNHCHR)[100]
- World Intellectual Property Organization (WIPO)[101]

b. *Treaty Secretariats.* Many important international agreements provide for the establishment of secretariats to deal with administrative matters related to the operation of the agreement. Two examples are the Secretariat of the Convention on International Trade in Endangered Species of Wild Fauna and Flora[102] and the Secretariat of the Convention on Biological Diversity.[103] The secretariats' tasks include organizing periodic meetings of the states party to the agreement, preparing reports and technical studies, and distributing public information about the operation of the agreement. In addition, the secretariats often produce excellent websites for the use of the public. These websites invariably include a text of the agreement and related documents, along with much other current and relevant information.

c. *Other Internet Sources.* Creative use of Internet search engines will locate a multitude of other sites reproducing all kinds of international agreements. Subjects covered run the range of topics in international law,

---

[92] http://conventions.coe.int.

[93] http://www.hcch.net/index_en.php?act=conventions.listing.

[94] http://www.icrc.org/ihl.

[95] http://www.unidroit.org/english/conventions/c-main.htm.

[96] http://www.ilo.org/ilolex/.

[97] http://www.oas.org/juridico/english/treaties.html.

[98] http://www.uncitral.org/uncitral/en/uncitral_texts.html.

[99] http://www.unep.org/Law/Law_instruments/multilateral_instruments.asp.

[100] http://www2.ohchr.org/english/law/index.htm.

[101] http://www.wipo.int/treaties/en/.

[102] http://www.cites.org.

[103] http://www.biodiv.org.

e.g., international trade, the environment, disarmament, and humanitarian law. A word of caution is in order. The accuracy and authority of texts reproduced on Internet websites vary significantly from site to site. It is dangerous to rely, without verifying their accuracy, on texts retrieved from unofficial Internet sites. Texts available in official sources, either print or electronic, should be preferred. The Internet often does make available texts of international agreements not available elsewhere, however.

d. *LexisNexis and Westlaw. LexisNexis* has a variety of files containing international agreements. They are most easily found under "Area of Law–By Topic," then under "International Law–Treaties and International Agreements." These files are of varying degrees of usefulness. At the positive end of the spectrum is "Tax Analysts Worldwide Tax Treaties." At the negative end is a file of European Community treaties that is obsolete.

Westlaw has scattered collections of international agreements. The best way to find them is to search the directory using the term "treaties". The *Westlaw* databases also vary in quality.

4. Finding and Updating International Agreements (When the United States May Not Be a Party)

In addition to the finding tools mentioned in Section B–6 of this chapter, several sources can help in locating international agreements and determining their current status, regardless of whether the United States is a party. A convenient online source for quick consultation is *Frequently–Cited Treaties and Other International Instruments*,[104] prepared by the University of Minnesota Law Library, which covers 70 multilateral agreements.

a. *Multilateral Treaties Deposited with the Secretary–General.* This annual publication from the United Nations tracks the status of more than 500 international agreements drafted under the auspices of the United Nations and League of Nations for which the Secretary–General performs depositary functions. The entry for each treaty gives complete information (as of December 31) regarding the states party to the treaty and the relevant dates. This is one of the few sources that publishes the text of various declarations and reservations entered by states at the time of becoming a party.

Multilateral Treaties Deposited with the Secretary–General is now available in a frequently updated version on the *United Nations Treaty Collection* website.

b. *Multilateral Treaties: Index and Current Status.*[105] This useful but now dated volume provides information on about 1,000 treaties. Each entry sets out the date of conclusion, citations to the location of the text in multiple sources, date of entry into force, states party to the treaty, and states signatory. A notes section describes the agreement and makes reference to related documents. A supplement updates the volume to January 1, 1994.

---

[104] http://local.law.umn.edu/library/pathfinders/most-cited.html.

[105] (M.J. Bowman & D.J. Harris eds., Butterworth 1984).

c. *Multilateral Treaty Calendar, 1648–1995.*[106] This is a chronological listing of over 6,000 agreements in over a hundred sources. Each entry gives the full name of the agreement in English and French, date of conclusion, original parties, multiple citations, and notes. Several appendices and an extensive index are provided.

d. *World Treaty Index.*[107] The advantage of this five-volume index is that it covers bilateral as well as multilateral agreements. The disadvantage is that it does not go beyond 1980.

5. Finding Travaux Préparatoires

The French phrase "travaux préparatoires" is used in international law to describe the documents making up the drafting history or negotiating history of an international agreement. Travaux préparatoires can play an important role in treaty interpretation. Finding them can be a challenge.[108]

SECTION D.   CUSTOMARY INTERNATIONAL LAW

1. Introduction

Article 38 of the Statute of the International Court of Justice speaks of "international custom, as evidence of a general practice accepted as law." Several questions arise from this formulation. The first must be, *"Whose* custom?" Many actors have roles to play in the creation of international law. However, when it comes to the creation of a binding norm of customary international law, it is usually *state* practice that counts. The next question must be, *"What* is international custom?" The text of Article 38 gives the germ of an answer: "a general practice accepted as law." Customary international law, then, has a dual character. It derives (1) from the general practice of states and other subjects of international law that are (2) acting from a sense of legal obligation.

The definition of international custom simply pushes the difficulty back a step. Now the question becomes, "How does the researcher go about establishing the existence of something that by definition is unwritten and the evidence of which might be found in any number of sources?"

A leading scholarly work on this question has a chapter titled "Phenomenology of State Practice." Here the author draws up a catalog of possibilities, including:

- Diplomatic correspondence;

- Advice of the legal advisor to the foreign ministry (in the case of the U.S., the State Department);

- General statements of policy on international legal questions;

[106] CHRISTIAN L. WIKTOR (Martinus Nijhoff 1998).

[107] (Peter H. Rohn ed., ABC–Clio Information Services 2d ed. 1983).

[108] For detailed information on how to do research on travaux préparatoires, see the article published electronically on *GlobaLex* by the author of this chapter. Jonathan Pratter, *A la Recherche des Travaux Préparatoires: An Approach to Researching the Drafting History of International Agreements,* http://www.nyulawglobal.org/globalex/Travaux_Preparatoires1.htm.

- Parliamentary practice (e.g., statements or documents from the Senate Committee on Foreign Relations);

- National legislation on international legal questions;

- Administrative practice on international legal questions; and

- Decisions of national courts on international legal questions.[109]

This list makes the point that the search for evidence of state practice as an element of customary international law must go forward on several fronts. Despite the difficulties, some well-established sources are available with which the researcher can begin the process.

It is also apparent from the list that actions and statements by government officials, especially those charged with responsibility in foreign relations, carry substantial weight as components of state practice. This means that it is essential to observe what foreign ministries around the world do and say. Today, this kind of research is greatly facilitated by the fact that foreign ministries have good websites, which they use to disseminate information about the policies and positions of their governments on the full range of international issues. For example, on the home page of Japan's Ministry of Foreign Affairs[110] the researcher finds under the heading "Foreign Policy" a set of 30 links to information on international issues, everything from Agriculture to Women's Issues.

Two good collections of Web links to foreign ministries around the world are done by the United States Institute of Peace[111] and by *Google*.[112]

2. Digests of Practice: United States Publications

The United States government traditionally has done a good job of publishing digests of international law or digests of practice in international law. The first of these was published in 1877.[113] Digests of practice bring together references and quotations from a huge array of sources and organize them according to the main topics of public international law. Usually a digest will focus on the practice of a particular nation. The digests produced in the United States (under the auspices of the State Department) draw their material from a broad range of U.S. source documents. These digests are frequently referred to by the name of the preparer.

a. *Digest of International Law*.[114] Whiteman's is the most recent of the U.S. digests. It consists of 14 volumes plus an index volume.

b. *Digest of International Law*.[115] Hackworth's digest, in eight volumes, covers the period 1906–1939.

[109] Luigi Ferrari Bravo, *Méthodes de Recherche de la Coutume Internationale dans la Pratique des États*, 192 (1985 III) Recueil des Cours 233 (1986).

[110] http://www.mofa.go.jp.

[111] http://www.usip.org/library/formin.html.

[112] http://www.google.com/Top/Society/Government/Foreign_Ministries.

[113] John L. Cadwalader, Digest of the Published Opinions of the Attorneys-General, and of the Leading Decisions of the Federal Courts, with Reference to International Law, Treaties and Kindred Subjects (U.S.G.P.O. 1877).

[114] (Marjorie M. Whiteman comp., U.S.G.P.O. 1963–73).

[115] (Green H. Hackworth comp., U.S.G.P.O. 1940–44).

c. *A Digest of International Law as Embodied in Diplomatic Discussions, Treaties and Other International Agreements, International Awards, the Decisions of Municipal Courts, and the Writings of Jurists....*[116] Moore's digest, in eight volumes, sets the pattern for its successors and supersedes Wharton's (below).

d. *A Digest of the International Law of the United States Taken from Documents Issued by Presidents and Secretaries of State, and from Decisions of Federal Courts and Opinions of Attorneys–General.*[117] Wharton's digest, in three volumes, was the first to adopt a subject arrangement according to the main topics of international law.

e. *Updating the U.S. Digests.* Whiteman's digest completed publication in 1973. The next year the State Department began a new project of preparing an annual *Digest of United States Practice in International Law.* Eight volumes covering the period 1973–1980 are followed by a three-volume set for the years 1981–1988.[118] After a long delay, annual volumes for 2000–2007 have been published as well as a volume for 1989–90. Finally, two volumes covering the period 1991–1999 were published.[119] It is expected that future volumes will be published in a timely fashion. Cumulative indexes for 1973–1980 and for 1989–2006 have been issued.

The print *Digest* is supplemented on the State Department's website at the "Digest of International Law" page.[120] The explanatory text says: "The full text of documents excerpted in the *Digest*, but not readily available in hard copy or electronic format are made available on this website."

Starting with volume 53 (1959), the *American Journal of International Law* publishes in each quarterly issue a section entitled "Contemporary Practice of the United States Relating to International Law."

3. Digests of Practice from Other Countries

Digests relating to the practices of other countries in international law are available. Some leading examples are given here.

a. *A British Digest of International Law.*[121] This was to be a major project in two phases. Five volumes of the first phase, covering the years 1860–1914, were published, but nothing has appeared since 1967. Fortunately, the *British Yearbook of International Law*[122] includes a section entitled "United Kingdom Materials on International Law." Oxford University Press has published a CD–ROM titled *United Kingdom Materials on International Law: 1975–2001.*[123]

[116] (John B. Moore comp., U.S.G.P.O. 1906).

[117] (Francis Wharton ed., U.S.G.P.O. 1886).

[118] The last volume was published in 1995.

[119] The DIGEST for the recent years is published by the International Law Institute under an agreement with the State Department, which produces the content. Oxford University Press now participates, too. Cambridge University Press has published two volumes of UNITED STATES PRACTICE IN INTERNATIONAL LAW, covering the years 1999–2001 and 2002–2004.

[120] http://www.state.gov/s/l/c8183.htm.

[121] (Clive Parry ed., Stevens & Sons 1967–).

[122] (Oxford University Press 1920–).

[123] (Geoffrey Marston ed., 2004).

b. *Répertoire de la Pratique Française en Matière de Droit International Publique.*[124] This digest of practice from France can be supplemented with the sections of the *Annuaire Français de Droit International*[125] entitled "Pratique Française du Droit International" and "Chronologie des Faits Internationaux d'Intérêt Juridique."

c. *Yearbooks.*[126] Yearbooks of international law can prove very useful because they typically contain sections documenting state practice for the country in which they are published. Some examples in English are *Australian Year Book of International Law,*[127] *Canadian Yearbook of International Law,*[128] *Japanese Annual of International Law,*[129] and *Netherlands Yearbook of International Law.*[130] There are also some regional yearbooks, such as the *African Yearbook of International Law,*[131] the *Asian Yearbook of International Law,*[132] and the *Baltic Yearbook of International Law.*[133]

4. Additional Sources Documenting State Practice

a. *Foreign Relations of the United States.*[134] This multivolume series prepared by the State Department constitutes the official record of the foreign policy and diplomacy of the United States. Supplemental documents in this series are now published in microform.

b. *American Foreign Policy: Current Documents.*[135] This is an annual series prepared by the State Department since 1956. The last volume published was for 1990. Each volume is organized into topical and regional chapters. These collections published by the government can be supplemented with the privately or commercially published series, *The United States in World Affairs,*[136] *Documents on American Foreign Relations,*[137] and *American Foreign Relations.*[138]

c. *British and Foreign State Papers.*[139] The British equivalent of *Foreign Relations of the United States,* this series covers the period 1812–1968. For the period 1945–1950, *Documents on British Policy Overseas*[140]

[124] (Alexandre C. Kiss ed., C.N.R.S. 1962–72).

[125] (CNRS Editions 1956 to present).

[126] *See also* Section G–4, below.

[127] (Centre for International and Public Law, Faculty of Law, Australian National University 1966 to present).

[128] (University of British Columbia Press 1963 to present).

[129] (International Law Association of Japan 1957 to present).

[130] (Martinus Nijhoff 1971 to present).

[131] (Martinus Nijhoff 1994 to present).

[132] (Martinus Nijhoff 1993 to present).

[133] (Kluwer Law International 2002–   ).

[134] (U.S.G.P.O. 1861 to present). This is now available in its entirety on *HeinOnline.*

[135] (U.S.G.P.O. 1956 to present).

[136] (Council on Foreign Relations 1931–71).

[137] (Council on Foreign Relations 1939–70).

[138] (New York University Press 1971–78).

[139] (H.M.S.O. 1928–77).

[140] (H.M.S.O. 1984–89).

provides supplemental coverage, as does *Documents on International Affairs*[141] for the period 1926–1963.

d. *United Nations Legislative Series.* This is the title for a group of materials published by the United Nations containing national legislation and other elements of state practice in areas of interest to the United Nations. The series includes: *Laws Concerning Nationality; Laws and Regulations Regarding Diplomatic and Consular Privileges and Immunities; Legislative Texts and Treaty Provisions Concerning the Legal Status, Privileges and Immunities of International Organizations; Legislative Texts and Treaty Provisions Concerning the Utilization of International Rivers for Purposes Other than Navigation; Materials on Succession of States; National Legislation and Treaties Relating to the Territorial Sea, the Contiguous Zone, the Continental Shelf, the High Seas, and to Fishing and Conservation of the Living Resources of the Sea; Materials on Succession of States in Respect of Matters other than Treaties; National Legislation and Treaties Relating to the Law of the Sea; Materials on Jurisdictional Immunities of States and Their Property;* and *National Laws and Regulations on the Prevention and Suppression of International Terrorism.*

e. *Bibliography.* The publication *Sources of State Practice in International Law*[142] documents treaty collections, diplomatic documents, international law yearbooks, and digests of state practice for 14 jurisdictions. There is also a chapter on "Multi–Jurisdictional Collections by Subject."

A good online guide is on *GlobaLex*, titled *Researching Customary International Law, State Practice and the Pronouncements of States regarding International Law.*[143] Another worthwhile online guide is titled *International & Foreign Legal Research: Researching Customary International Law and Generally Recognized Principles.*[144]

SECTION E.   GENERAL PRINCIPLES OF LAW

General principles of law, the third main source set out in Article 38 of the Statute of the International Court of Justice, presents some of the same kinds of difficulties as those encountered in researching customary international law; there is no authoritative collection of general principles. The evidence for the existence of a general principle of law must be developed from a variety of authorities. Some of these may be primary sources, but general principles are more likely discovered through authoritative secondary sources, such as leading treatises.

A conceptual difficulty has to be resolved before research can begin. Does this source have to do with general principles of law as found in *national* legal systems or does it refer to general principles that are peculiar to *international* law? There is substantial overlap, for example, where ideas such as good faith in the performance of agreements or the duty to compensate for causing harm are concerned. There is some disagreement, but the prevailing opinion is that "general principles of law" refers to those

---

[141] (Oxford University Press 1929–73).

[142] (Ralph Gaebler & Maria Smolka–Day eds., Transnational Publishers 2002).

[143] http://www.nyuglobal.org/globalex/Customary_International_Law.htm. By Silke Sahl, International, Comparative & Foreign Law Librarian, Columbia University Law School.

[144] http://www.law.berkeley.edu/library/classes/iflr/customary.html.

general principles common to the major *domestic* legal systems. Therefore, the phrase "general principles of law" has to be distinguished from another one, "general principles of *international* law"; the latter are principles derived from customary international law.[145]

Given the emphasis on domestic law, some understanding of *comparative* law, the comparative study of national legal systems, is important. Fortunately, there exists a wealth of information on international law discussing general principles of law applied in the international arena.[146] Researchers can enlist the assistance of virtually this entire book as part of a project to discover a general principle of law common to major legal systems, starting with the United States.

SECTION F. ADJUDICATIONS

States may settle their differences in a variety of peaceful ways, ranging from diplomatic negotiation to compulsory submission of a dispute to the World Court,[147] with such mechanisms as mediation, conciliation, and binding arbitration in between.[148] Article 38 of the Statute of the International Court of Justice accepts "judicial decisions" as a "subsidiary means for the determination of rules of law." The phrase "subsidiary means" does not capture the true significance of the work of various judicial fora in the contemporary development of international law. Moreover, the phrase "judicial decisions" is too narrow, because it does not indicate that decisions of international arbitral tribunals and decisions of national courts on international legal questions are also included in the category.

This section focuses on the leading sources for decisions of the main international tribunals. It then discusses the ways of finding domestic judicial decisions dealing with questions of international law.

1. International Court of Justice

The International Court of Justice (I.C.J.) is the principal judicial organ of the United Nations. It was founded in 1945 at the same time as the United Nations. The governing instrument of the Court is the Statute of the International Court of Justice, which is an international agreement.[149] The seat of the Court is the Peace Palace at The Hague, Netherlands. The Court is composed of fifteen judges elected by the General

---

[145] *See generally* RESTATEMENT OF THE LAW THIRD, THE FOREIGN RELATIONS LAW OF THE UNITED STATES § 102 cmt. 1, reporter's note 7 (1987); IAN BROWNLIE, PRINCIPLES OF PUBLIC INTERNATIONAL LAW 16–19 (7th ed. 2008); Giorgio Gaja, *General Principles of Law, in* MAX PLANCK ENCYCLOPEDIA OF PUBLIC INTERNATIONAL LAW (online ed.) (article updated March 2007).

[146] In addition to the references already noted, see generally BIN CHENG, GENERAL PRINCIPLES OF LAW AS APPLIED BY INTERNATIONAL COURTS AND TRIBUNALS (Stevens 1953); Arnold D. McNair, *The General Principles of Law Recognized by Civilized Nations,* 33 BRIT. Y.B. INT'L L. 1 (1957).

[147] This is the informal name of the International Court of Justice and of its predecessor, the Permanent Court of International Justice.

[148] *See generally* J.G. MERRILLS, INTERNATIONAL DISPUTE SETTLEMENT (Cambridge University Press 4th ed. 2005); JOHN G. COLLIER & VAUGHAN LOWE, THE SETTLEMENT OF DISPUTES IN INTERNATIONAL LAW: INSTITUTIONS AND PROCEDURES (Oxford University Press 1999).

[149] 59 Stat. 1055, 3 Bevans 1179 (1945). *See* THE STATUTE OF THE INTERNATIONAL COURT OF JUSTICE: A COMMENTARY (Andreas Zimmermann et al. eds., Oxford University Press 2006).

Assembly and Security Council of the United Nations. Only states may be parties to a proceeding before the I.C.J. The I.C.J. takes jurisdiction of a dispute either by agreement of the parties, or because the parties have made a declaration under Article 36(2) of the Statute of the International Court of Justice that they accept the "compulsory jurisdiction" of the Court in any legal dispute involving a state that has made the same declaration. The Court is authorized to issue advisory opinions on legal questions to the General Assembly and Security Council. The judgments of the I.C.J. are the single most significant component of the source of international law known as judicial decisions. The publications of the I.C.J., and related materials, are described below.

a. *Reports of Judgments, Advisory Opinions and Orders.* Along with other documents, the final decisions (judgments on the merits) of the Court are published in this series. The text of a final judgment, including separate and dissenting opinions, may extend to several hundred pages. Judgments appear even longer because the English and French texts are printed together on facing pages. Decisions are first published individually; then the collected decisions for each year are published together in a single volume.

b. *Pleadings, Oral Arguments, Documents.* Volumes in this series are published after the end of a case, sometimes years after the judgment. They contain the pleadings, memorials (briefs), record of oral proceedings, and other documents, such as maps, that may be submitted to the Court. For each case, several volumes may be published.

c. *Acts and Documents Concerning the Organization of the Court.* This is a single volume that was updated in 2007. It is a useful place to find the United Nations Charter and the Statute and Rules of the Court.

d. *Yearbook.* This annual publication has chapters on the organization of the Court and its work during the year and useful biographies of the judges.

e. *Bibliography of the International Court of Justice.* Each year the Registry of the Court issues this bibliography listing works relating to the Court.

f. *International Court of Justice Website.* The website of the Court[150] vastly improves timely access to the Court's documentation, including its judgments and associated documents. [Illustration 21–3] Under "Decisions" are links to documentation relating to all cases in the Court since its inception in 1945. This documentation includes pleadings that otherwise would not be published until long after a case has been decided.

An example demonstrates the fruitfulness of consulting the Court's website. In the case *Sovereignty over Pedra Branca . . . and South Ledge* (Malaysia v. Singapore), the I.C.J. handed down its judgment on the merits in May 2008. Within hours the full text of the judgment and all dissenting and separate opinions was loaded on the I.C.J. website in PDF. Ordinarily it would take months for the judgment in hardcopy to reach libraries. That is not all. Ever since the case was first brought in 2003, the Court has posted important documents in the case, including the special agreement,

---

[150] http://www.icj-cij.org.

the memorials (briefs), and even transcripts of oral argument. Normally these documents would not have appeared for years in the series *Pleadings, Oral Arguments, Documents*.[151]

g. *Secondary Literature*. Secondary literature concerning the Court is extensive. It can be researched using the subject heading "International Court of Justice" in library catalogs and journal indexes.[152]

2. Permanent Court of International Justice

The predecessor to the I.C.J. was the Permanent Court of International Justice (P.C.I.J.), established under the League of Nations. It heard cases from 1922 to early 1940 and was dissolved in 1946 when the I.C.J. was inaugurated. Many decisions of the P.C.I.J. continue to be of significance in international law. The publications of the P.C.I.J. were issued in series much like those of the I.C.J.:

Series A. *Collection of Judgments* (up to 1930)

Series B. *Collection of Advisory Opinions* (up to 1930)

Series A/B. *Judgments, Orders and Advisory Opinions* (after 1930)

Series C. *Acts and Documents Relating to Judgments and Advisory Opinions* (up to 1930)/*Pleadings, Oral Statements and Documents* (after 1930)

Series D. *Acts and Documents Concerning the Organization of the Court*

Series E. *Annual Reports*

Series F. *Indexes*

The judgments of the P.C.I.J. are also available in *World Court Reports: A Collection of the Judgments, Orders and Opinions of the Permanent Court of International Justice* (Manley O. Hudson ed., Carnegie Endowment for International Peace 1934–43). Note that the complete set of P.C.I.J. documentation set out above is now available in PDF format on the I.C.J. website.

3. Digests of I.C.J. and P.C.I.J. Decisions

The use of the digests noted below facilitates research by providing detailed references and extensive excerpts from those parts of often very lengthy I.C.J. and P.C.I.J. judgments dealing with particular points of international law.

---

[151] Databases of I.C.J. documents are also available on *Westlaw* (INT–ICJ) and on *LexisNexis* under International Law—Cases, but they are not as current as the I.C.J. website.

[152] Recent publications in English concerning the I.C.J. include TERRY D. GILL, ROSENNE'S THE WORLD COURT: WHAT IT IS AND HOW IT WORKS (Martinus Nijhoff 6th ed. 2003), SHABTAI ROSENNE, THE LAW AND PRACTICE OF THE INTERNATIONAL COURT, 1920–2005 (Martinus Nijhoff 4th ed. 2006), MOHAMED SAMEH M. AMR, THE ROLE OF THE INTERNATIONAL COURT OF JUSTICE AS THE PRINCIPAL JUDICIAL ORGAN OF THE UNITED NATIONS (Kluwer Law International 2003), and HOWARD N. MEYER, THE WORLD COURT IN ACTION: JUDGING AMONG THE NATIONS (Rowman & Littlefield 2002).

a.   *The Case Law of the International Court.*[153]

b.   *World Court Digest.*[154]

c.   A *Digest of the Decisions of the* International Court.[155]

4.   International Criminal Tribunal for the Former Yugoslavia[156]

The Tribunal was established in 1993 by United Nations Security Council Resolution 827. The Tribunal sits in The Hague, The Netherlands. The mandate of the Tribunal is to prosecute persons responsible for serious violations of international humanitarian law (including war crimes and genocide) committed in the territory of the former Yugoslavia since 1991.

To date the Tribunal has produced much important documentation as a result of its work, including many judgments. Substantial amounts of Tribunal documentation, including the full text of judgments and orders, are available on the Tribunal's website.[157]

Volumes of the official series, *Judicial Reports*, have been published for the years 1994–1995 to 2000.[158]

5.   International Criminal Court

The Rome Statute of the International Criminal Court of 1998,[159] an international agreement, establishes the International Criminal Court. The Court, seated at The Hague, has jurisdiction to try cases charging the most serious crimes of concern to the international community–genocide, crimes against humanity, war crimes, and aggression.

The best way to follow the activities of the Court and to gain access to its documentation is through its website.[160] During December 2008, four cases were underway. To go to the case documentation, click the link "Situations and Cases." The documentation can usefully be divided into two main categories: public court records and transcripts. The former are plentiful and allow the researcher to follow cases and learn a great deal about procedure. The latter are not as accessible because only transcripts of hearings in open session are available, and many hearings are held in closed session.[161]

---

[153] (Edvard Hambro ed., A.W. Sijthoff 1952–76).

[154] RAINER HOFMANN ET AL. (Springer 1993–). Before 1993 the title was DIGEST OF THE DECISIONS OF THE INTERNATIONAL COURT OF JUSTICE. Earlier volumes in the series deal with the P.C.I.J.

[155] (Krystyna Marek ed., Martinus Nijhoff 1974–78).

[156] There is also an International Criminal Tribunal for Rwanda. It has produced some important decisions, which can be found at the Court's website, http://www.ictr.org. There is an official series, REPORTS OF ORDERS, DECISIONS AND JUDGMENTS (Bruylant 2000–).

[157] http://www.un.org/icty/cases-e/index-e.htm.

[158] (Martinus Nijhoff 1999–).

[159] 2197 U.N.T.S. 90, 37 I.L.M. 999 (1998).

[160] http://www.icc-cpi.int.

[161] A quasi-international criminal court worthy of note is the Special Court for Sierra Leone. Four cases are under way. Trial chamber judgments on the merits have been rendered in two cases. Substantial documentation is available through the Court's website, http://www.sc-sl. org. Click on "Cases." *See also* CYRIL LAUCCI, DIGEST OF JURISPRUDENCE OF THE SPECIAL COURT FOR SIERRA LEONE, 2003–2005 (Martinus Nijhoff 2007). Another international court worthy of mention is the International Tribunal for the Law of the Sea. Although the Tribunal has heard only 15 cases, it is a significant component of the dispute resolution framework set up in the United Nations Convention on the Law of the Sea, Dec. 10, 1982, 1833 U.N.T.S. 3. Judgments and other documents produced in the Tribunal's cases are posted on the Tribunal's

6. Project on International Courts and Tribunals (PICT)[162]

This well-designed website is a freely available, non-profit joint venture of study centers at University College London and New York University, supported by several foundations. *PICT* tracks the work of no fewer than 25 international adjudicatory bodies. The website is a good way to follow developments in the field of international adjudication, although it could be more frequently updated.[163] Also to be noted is the creation of a sister website, *African International Courts and Tribunals (AICT)*,[164] that covers 13 international adjudicatory institutions specific to the region of Africa.

7. International Arbitrations: Collections and Digests of Decisions

Finding published decisions of international arbitral tribunals is notoriously troublesome. Several circumstances contribute to this situation. Most international arbitrations are ad hoc. The tribunal is constituted to resolve the particular dispute, and there is no sponsoring institution to deal with publication.... It has fallen to scholars working in their private capacity to prepare collections and digests. The result is that the documentation in this field is widely scattered.[165]

The difficulties of finding international arbitral decisions should not discourage the researcher. The sources noted below and in the following section make the task less frustrating.[166]

a. *Reports of International Arbitral Awards (R.I.A.A.).*[167] Published by the United Nations, this is probably the leading current source for the text of *selected* international arbitral awards. Volume XXVIII, the most recent, was published in 2007 and contains a great miscellany of awards and decisions in 34 different dispute-settlement procedures from the late eighteenth to the mid–twentieth century, all dealing with international boundary delimitation. Each volume is indexed, but there is no overall index or table of cases. This means that *R.I.A.A.* must be used together with one of the finding tools noted in the next section. *R.I.A.A.* is available online without charge through volume XXV from the United Nations.[168]

b. *International Law Reports.*[169] Because it contains the reports of many kinds of international adjudications, this series could be mentioned

---

website, http://www.itlos.org. The official publication is the series REPORTS OF JUDGMENTS, ADVISORY OPINIONS AND ORDERS (Kluwer 2000–).

[162] http://www.pict-pcti.org.

[163] At the time of writing, the Latest News section was six months behind.

[164] http://www.aict-ctia.org.

[165] Jonathan Pratter, Book Review, 26 TEX. INT'L L.J. 597, 603 (1991). On the substantive law of international arbitration, see generally J. GILLIS WETTER, THE INTERNATIONAL ARBITRAL PROCESS: PUBLIC AND PRIVATE (Oceana Publications 1979).

[166] Two collections of arbitral decisions, both in French, also deserve mention: A. DE LAPRADELLE & N. POLITIS, RECUEIL DES ARBITRAGES INTERNATIONAUX (Pedone 1905–54); HENRI LA FONTAINE, PASICRISIE INTERNATIONALE: HISTOIRE DOCUMENTAIRE DES ARBITRAGES INTERNATIONAUX (Stämpfli 1902, reprinted in 1997 by Kluwer).

[167] (United Nations 1948–).

[168] http://www.un.org/law/riaa. It is also available through vol. XXII on *HeinOnline*.

[169] (Cambridge University Press 1932–). Until 1949 the title was ANNUAL DIGEST AND REPORTS OF PUBLIC INTERNATIONAL CASES.

under any of several headings. It appears here because it is particularly valuable for its publication of substantial extracts from arbitral decisions difficult to find elsewhere.[170]

c. *International Legal Materials (I.L.M.).*[171] Significant arbitral awards often are published first in *I.L.M.*

d. *History and Digest of the International Arbitrations to Which the United States Has Been a Party.*[172] The United States has long been an active participant in the process of international arbitration. In fact, a leading commentator notes that "[m]odern arbitration begins with the Jay Treaty of 1794 between the United States and Great Britain...."[173] In many cases, the government would publish the results of the early arbitrations in which the United States participated; these books are very difficult to find today. Therefore, Moore's *History and Digest* in six volumes continues to be a valuable source for reports of arbitrations of the United States from the late eighteenth to the end of the nineteenth century.

e. *International Adjudications: Ancient and Modern: History and Documents.*[174] This ambitious project was never completed, but six volumes were issued between 1929 and 1936.

f. *The Hague Court Reports*[175] and *The Hague Arbitration Cases.*[176] These titles refer to an institution known formally as the Permanent Court of Arbitration (P.C.A.). It is not a court, but a mechanism for establishing arbitral panels. Between 1900 and 1932 twenty cases were heard. The decisions, some of them still significant in international law, are published in these collections.[177]

g. *Iran–United States Claims Tribunal Reports.*[178] Following the resolution of the Iran Hostage Crisis in late 1980, an arbitral tribunal was established to decide outstanding claims between United States citizens and companies and the government of Iran. Although its work has now wound down, the Iran–United States Claims Tribunal probably has been the most notable arbitral institution in recent years. To date, its decisions are reported in the 37 volumes of this series and on *Westlaw* in the INT–IRAN database, which contains some documents that are more recent than the hardcopy *Reports*. A recent development is the official website of the

---

[170] At the time of writing, plans are afoot to make INTERNATIONAL LAW REPORTS commercially available online.

[171] *See* the main discussion of *I.L.M.* at Section C–2–b of this chapter.

[172] JOHN B. MOORE (U.S.G.P.O. 1898).

[173] IAN BROWNLIE, PRINCIPLES OF PUBLIC INTERNATIONAL LAW 702 (7th ed. 2008). The arbitrations under the Jay Treaty concerned both boundaries and claims for compensation following the Revolutionary War.

[174] (John B. Moore ed., Oxford University Press 1929–36).

[175] (James B. Scott ed., Oxford University Press 1916–32).

[176] (George G. Wilson comp., Ginn 1915).

[177] The activity of the P.C.A. has recently increased. There are several recent or pending cases. Information, including some documentation, can be found at the P.C.A.'s website, http://www.pca-cpa.org.

[178] (Cambridge University Press 1983–).

Tribunal.[179] It has a link to a free database of Tribunal documents, including awards.

h. *Investment Arbitrations*. Disputes between foreign investors and host states are often settled by arbitration. These arbitrations have substantial jurisprudential and practical significance. Finding these arbitral awards and associated documents can be difficult. A selection of awards made under the auspices of the International Centre for the Settlement of Investment Disputes (ICSID) can be found on the Centre's website[180] and in the hard copy *ICSID Reports*.[181] Similar awards made under Chapter 11 of the North American Free Trade Agreement are on the website of the U.S. State Department,[182] of Canada's Department of Foreign Affairs and International Trade,[183] and of Mexico's Secretaría de Economía.[184]

A valuable development in this field is the *Investment Treaty Arbitration*, or *ITA*, website, sponsored by the University of Victoria (Canada) Faculty of Law.[185] A wealth of primary-source documents is available on the site. These are documents that in many cases would be either unknown or impossible to find.

The United Nations Conference on Trade and Development (UNCTAD) offers a similar service called *Database of Treaty–Based Investor–State Dispute Settlement Cases*.[186] A commercial service called *Investment Claims* is available from Oxford University Press.[187]

8. Finding Tools for International Arbitrations

Research in international arbitration would be much more difficult without the use of the finding tools noted in this section.

a. *Survey of International Arbitrations, 1794–1989*.[188] This book covers approximately 600 international disputes that resulted in agreements to arbitrate, although in some cases awards were never rendered. The one-page entries for each case give all the critical information, including the names of the parties; a brief description of the dispute; a note on the agreement to arbitrate and its location, if available; and notes on the disposition, with citations to the text of the award if it is published.

b. *Repertory of International Arbitral Jurisprudence*.[189] This is a comprehensive collection of excerpts from hundreds of arbitral decisions organized according to a detailed outline of international law. Each extract refers to a table of awards where the researcher will find essential informa-

---

[179] http://www.iusct.org/index-english.html. *See also* CHRISTOPHER R. DRAHOZAL & CHRISTOPHER S. GIBSON, THE IRAN–U.S. CLAIMS TRIBUNAL AT 25: THE CASES EVERYONE NEEDS TO KNOW FOR INVESTOR–STATE AND INTERNATIONAL ARBITRATION (Oxford University Press 2007).

[180] http://icsid.worldbank.org. Click "Cases," then "Search Online Decisions and Awards."

[181] (Cambridge University Press 1993–).

[182] http://www.state.gov/s/l/c3439.htm.

[183] http://www.international.gc.ca/trade-agreements-accords-commerciaux/disp-diff/nafta. aspx?lang=en.

[184] http://economia.gob.mx/?P=2259.

[185] http://ita.law.uvic.ca.

[186] http://www.unctad.org/iia-dbcases.

[187] http://www.investmentclaims.com/index.html. *See also* the *KluwerArbitration* online service, http://www.kluwerarbitration.com/arbitration.

[188] (A.M. Stuyt ed., Martinus Nijhoff 3d ed. 1990).

[189] (Vincent Coussirat–Coustère & Pierre M. Eisemann eds., Martinus Nijhoff 1989–91).

tion about the decision, including a citation to the publication of the full text.[190] In three volumes, the *Repertory* covers the period 1794–1988.

9.   International Law in U.S. Courts

a.   *General Sources.* Using fundamental techniques of legal research introduced in this book, the researcher can find cases in United States courts, usually federal courts, on questions of international law. For example, the West digests have two topics, "International Law" and "Treaties," that collect cases on several points of international law as applied in the courts of the United States. The first topic is useful for such questions as the sources of international law and its relation to United States law, territorial sovereignty, foreign sovereign immunity, the act of state doctrine, and extraterritoriality. The second topic deals with the negotiation, operation, and interpretation of international agreements in United States law. Another topic on point in a specialized area is "Ambassadors and Consuls."

American Law Reports, Federal (A.L.R. Fed.) increasingly publishes annotations on international legal issues in U.S. courts. Some recent examples are: *Effect of World Trade Organization (WTO) Decisions upon United States,*[191] *Construction and Application of International Covenant on Civil and Political Rights,*[192] and *Applicability of Immunity under Vienna Convention and Diplomatic Relations Act.*[193]

In this area of research, the benefits of using CALR systems such as *Westlaw* and *LexisNexis* cannot be overstated. Cases in a United States court raising a question of international law might arise in almost any field of law. Significant cases having international legal implications could start life as a suit on a bill of lading[194] or promissory note.[195] Obviously, the digests do not deal adequately with this possibility. A well-designed search on *Westlaw* or *LexisNexis* is an indispensable step in the research process when looking for cases with an international legal component.

b.   *American International Law Cases.*[196] This set of reports is now in a fourth series. As a general matter, it reprints cases available elsewhere.[197]

10.   International Law in National Courts of Other Countries

Domestic courts in other countries also decide cases involving issues of public international law. Finding these decisions is to a large extent a matter of researching *foreign law.* For common law jurisdictions such as

---

[190] The researcher should be aware that sometimes the text of arbitral awards is never published in completely unabridged form. Instead, for example, lengthy extracts are published in one of the leading journals of international law.

[191] 17 A.L.R. Fed. 2d 1 (2007).

[192] 11 A.L.R. Fed. 2d 751 (2006).

[193] 1 A.L.R. Fed. 2d 351 (2005).

[194] *See, e.g.,* Banco Nacional de Cuba v. Sabbatino, 376 U.S. 398 (1964) (act of state doctrine).

[195] *See, e.g.,* Gau Shan Co., Ltd. v. Bankers Trust Co., 956 F.2d 1349 (6th Cir. 1992) (injunction against suit in a foreign court and international comity).

[196] (Oceana Publications 1971 to present).

[197] *See also* Commonwealth International Law Cases (Oceana Publications 1974–95).

the United Kingdom and Canada, which are well-represented on *Westlaw*, *LexisNexis*, and the Web, the difficulty is not so great. Outside the leading common law jurisdictions, this research presents greater challenges. A good approach is to consult the digests of practice in international law discussed in Sections D–2 and D–3 of this chapter. The digests include summaries of judicial decisions.

Ideally, every country would be as well-served as Germany. There the Max Planck Institute for Comparative Public Law and International Law publishes annual online installments of *Deutsche Rechtsprechung in völkerrechtlichen Fragen (German Judicial Decisions on Questions of International Law).*[198] This covers the years 1986–2001. Beginning with 2003, judicial decisions are included in the annual online installments of *Völkerrechtliche Praxis der Bundesrepublik Deutschland (German Practice in International Law).*[199]

A recent entrant in this field is the commercial online resource from Oxford University Press called *International Law in Domestic Courts (ILDC).*[200] Each case in the database receives careful editorial treatment, including translation into English and commentary. However, at the time of writing the database contained a total of only 335 cases. Fifty-nine countries are represented, but many by only one or two cases: one case for France, one for Mexico, none for Argentina, and none for Japan.

SECTION G.   SECONDARY SOURCES

Article 38 of the Statute of the International Court of Justice expressly acknowledges secondary sources ("the teachings of the most highly qualified publicists") as means for the "determination of rules of law."[201] A strong argument can be made that the researcher in international law, especially the beginner, should *start* work with a good secondary source, such as a leading textbook, because the beginner has not yet learned what are the significant primary sources of law for a specific question. A good secondary source refers to, cites, and analyzes crucial primary sources as part of the discussion of an issue. Therefore, a good secondary source can efficiently orient and give direction to research. The secondary literature of international law is massive and expanding rapidly. Moreover, it is multilingual. This section can give only an overview of available resources, with indications of specific titles that are particularly useful to researchers who are getting underway in their work.

1.   Treatises and Textbooks

a.   A good treatise (meaning a major, comprehensive work) on general international law, and usually having chapters on some subtopics (known as the "special part" of international law) is an indispensable starting point for research. A textbook (meaning a less comprehensive work) is almost as

---

[198] http://www.mpil.de/ww/en/pub/research/details/publications/institute/rspr.cfm.

[199] http://www.mpil.de/ww/en/pub/research/details/publications/institute/prax.cfm. For the years 1961–1985, the researcher can consult the hard copy DECISIONS OF GERMAN COURTS RELATING TO PUBLIC INTERNATIONAL LAW (Springer 1978–89).

[200] http://ildc.oxfordlawreports.com.

[201] *See* the discussion in Section A–3.

good for starters. In fact, works on international law lie along a continuum with the introduction at one end, and the multivolume set at the other.[202] Treatises and textbooks on both the general part and special branches of international law are found by consulting the appropriate subject headings in the law library catalog. A caveat is in order here: a search on the subject "international law" may return thousands of hits. Limiting by date, language, or keyword will be necessary. As to browsing for international law in the library stacks, note that the Library of Congress classification for international law is "KZ."[203]

There is space here to mention only some of the better recent works on general public international law. In English, we may cite *Principles of Public International Law* by Ian Brownlie,[204] *International Law* by Antonio Cassese,[205] *International Law* by Malcolm D. Evans (editor),[206] and *International Law* by Malcolm N. Shaw.[207] A classic in English is *Oppenheim's International Law: Vol. 1: Peace*.[208] An older work, recommended for researchers in the U.S., is Charles Cheney Hyde's *International Law: Chiefly as Interpreted and Applied by the United States*.[209] International law scholars in the U.S. have not recently produced a major treatise on general public international law. On the other hand there are good recent introductions, such as *Public International Law in a Nutshell* by Thomas Buergenthal and Sean Murphy[210] or *International Law* by Mark Janis.[211]

Doing research in international law necessarily means going beyond English, if possible. Recent works in other languages that can be recommended include *Droit International Public* by Dinh Nguyen Quoc, Patrick Daillier and Alain Pellet,[212] *Droit International Public* by Jean Combacau and Serge Sur,[213] *Völkerrecht* by Wolfgang Vitzthum (general editor),[214] *Völkerrecht: ein Studienbuch* by Knut Ipsen (general editor),[215] and *Derecho Internacional* by Antonio Remiro Brotóns et al.[216]

b. *Restatement of the Law Third, The Foreign Relations Law of the* United States.[217] Usually known as the *Restatement, Third,* this is probably

---

[202] The multivolume treatise is more frequent in languages other than English. Good examples are CHARLES ROUSSEAU, DROIT INTERNATIONAL PUBLIC (Sirey 1970–1983) and GEORG DAHM, JOST DELBRÜCK & RÜDIGER WOLFRUM, VÖLKERRECHT (W. de Gruyter 2d ed. 1989–).

[203] It was preceded by the "JX" classification, where older materials may still be found.

[204] (Oxford University Press 7th ed. 2008).

[205] (Oxford University Press 2d ed. 2005).

[206] (Oxford University Press 2d ed. 2006).

[207] (Cambridge University Press 5th ed. 2003).

[208] (Robert Jennings & Arthur Watts eds., Oxford University Press 9th ed. 2008).

[209] (Little, Brown 2d ed. 1945).

[210] (Thomson/West 4th ed. 2007). Buergenthal is a judge of the International Court of Justice.

[211] (Aspen Publishers 5th ed. 2008).

[212] (L.G.D.J. 7th ed. 2002).

[213] (Montchrestien 8th ed. 2008).

[214] (de Gruyter 4th ed. 2007).

[215] (Beck 5th ed. 2004).

[216] (Tirant lo Blanch 2007).

[217] (American Law Institute 1987).

the secondary source in the United States that can claim the greatest influence and authority in the field of international law. Its "black-letter rules" provide a clear and concise statement of the contemporary view of the leading international law scholars in the United States on a wide range of issues, both in general public international law and in the foreign relations law of the U.S. The comments and reporter's notes add background and depth. Given the immense changes in both fields that have taken place in the two decades since publication, it is clearly time to undertake the drafting of a new *Restatement*.

c. *Collected Courses of* the Hague Academy of International Law.[218] Every summer, the Hague Academy of International Law offers a series of advanced courses on both public and private international law. This extensive series of collected monographs (often book-length essays devoted to a particular subject) is usually known by its title in French, *Recueil des Cours*. Not all contributions are in English (the other official language is French), but many are, and they are valuable secondary sources on current aspects of international law. Several volumes are published each year, along with indexes that appear at irregular intervals. Starting in 2008, the entire series is available commercially in full text online.[219]

2. Dictionaries and Encyclopedias

a. *Max Planck Encyclopedia of Public International Law*. This comprehensive encyclopedia is now available online from Oxford University Press.[220] Editorial responsibility lies with the Max Planck Institute for Comparative Public Law and International Law in Heidelberg, Germany. Several hundred articles of a much larger universe of planned articles have been published online. Hardcopy publication begins in 2009. For most purposes, the earlier *Encyclopedia of Public International Law*[221] is now superseded.

b. *Parry and Grant Encyclopaedic Dictionary of International Law*.[222] There are several dictionaries of international law, some of varying quality. The one mentioned here is accurate and useful.

3. Journals

Many journals are devoted to international law. The advantage of using journals is that they reflect current developments and opinions in the field. Of course, law journal articles are filled with footnotes containing copious citations to primary sources or to other secondary authority on point. The explanation for the proliferation of law journals in international law can be traced in part to the phenomenon of law school publication of student-edited law journals in the United States. There are over 90 international law journals currently in publication. Leading examples are the

[218] (Martinus Nijhoff 1992–).

[219] http://www.nijhoffonline.nl/pages/recueil-courses.

[220] http://www.mpepil.com.

[221] (North–Holland 1992–2003).

[222] (John P. Grant & J. Craig Barker eds., 2d ed. Oceana Publications 2004).

Harvard International Law Journal,[223] *Columbia Journal of Transnational Law*,[224] and *Texas International Law Journal*.[225]

The most important journal of international law in the United States is the *American Journal of International Law*,[226] published by the American Society of International Law. Of course, many outstanding international law journals are published outside the United States. The leading example in English is the *International and Comparative Law Quarterly*,[227] published by the British Institute of International and Comparative Law.

Quite possibly the most prestigious journals of international law are not published in English. (As already noted, international law is a field in which a working knowledge of more than one language is a valuable asset.) Candidates for the position include the *Journal du Droit International*[228] and the *Zeitschrift für Ausländisches öffentliches Recht und Völkerrecht*.[229]

4. Yearbooks[230]

A yearbook of international law is an annual publication, generally sponsored and edited by a national association of international law, a university institute of international law, or an editorial committee of international law scholars from one country. Unfortunately, no yearbook of international law is produced in the United States. The usual format of a yearbook begins with lead articles followed by shorter notes and book reviews. Almost invariably, a yearbook has sections covering developments in international law in the courts of the country and in the practices of the government. These sections make yearbooks very useful for keeping up with the latest developments as surveyed by leading scholars. There are roughly 15 yearbooks from various countries. Three of the most prestigious are *British Yearbook of International Law*,[231] *Annuaire Français de Droit International*,[232] and *German Yearbook of International Law*.[233]

5. Indexes and Bibliographies

The standard periodical indexes in law, *LegalTrac* and *Index to Legal Periodicals & Books,* are satisfactory resources for locating articles on international law published in the United States. In addition, they capture a fair percentage of articles on international law published in British law reviews. However, a substantial amount of writing on international law *in English* is done in sources published in Europe, Asia, and other parts of the world not covered by the usual indexes. Therefore, in-depth research requires the use of some creativity and unfamiliar resources.

[223] (1967–).
[224] (1961–).
[225] (1965–).
[226] (1907–).
[227] (1955–).
[228] (Editions Techniques 1874–).
[229] (Kohlhammer 1929–).
[230] *See also* Section D–3–c.
[231] (Oxford University Press 1921–).
[232] (C.N.R.S. 1956–).
[233] (Duncker & Humblot 1954–).

Public International Law: A Current Bibliography of Books and Articles[234] is the only source that can make a claim to broad, transnational coverage. It is prepared at the Max Planck Institute for Comparative Public Law and International Law in Heidelberg, Germany. References are entered under 33 topics of international law. The hardcopy bibliography is supposed to be published twice a year. Unfortunately, it runs over a year behind. A free online version of the article references in the bibliography is available at the website of the Institute.[235]

Another valuable resource is the *Index to Foreign Legal Periodicals*,[236] which covers dozens of journals and other serials in public international law.

SECTION H. DOCUMENTS OF INTERNATIONAL ORGANIZATIONS

1. Introduction[237]

The term *international organization* refers to an association of states established by a treaty. The organization pursues the common aims of its member states as set out in the founding treaty. An international organization has a legal personality separate from its member states, and the founding treaty provides for decision-making and administrative structures to allow the organization to carry out its work. *Universal* international organizations, such as the United Nations, have wide-ranging purposes; membership is open to any state. Conversely, there are international organizations devoted to special purposes, e.g., the World Health Organization, or to particular regions of the world, e.g., the Organization of American States. The organizations addressed in this section are sometimes known as international *governmental* organizations (IGOs) to distinguish them from international *non-governmental* organizations (NGOs), such as Amnesty International or Greenpeace.

For our purposes, the significance of international organizations lies in the fact that they produce documents of great interest in international law. Documents of international organizations are interesting because the constitution and law of international organizations, and their methods of deliberation and modes of action, are themselves part of the study of international law. Moreover, their documentation is significant because the substantive issues addressed by international organizations are at the forefront of contemporary international law.

Even experienced researchers have difficulty with the documents of international organizations for several reasons. First, a surprisingly large

---

[234] (Springer 1975–).

[235] http://www.mpil.de. (Click on "Research," then "Publications of the Institute.")

[236] (University of California Press/American Association of Law Libraries 1964–).

[237] *See generally* C.F. AMERASINGHE, PRINCIPLES OF THE INSTITUTIONAL LAW OF INTERNATIONAL ORGANIZATIONS (Cambridge University Press 2d ed. 2005); JOSÉ E. ALVAREZ, INTERNATIONAL ORGANIZATIONS AS LAW-MAKERS (Oxford University Press 2005); PHILIPPE SANDS, PIERRE KLEIN, BOWETTS LAW OF INTERNATIONAL INSTITUTIONS (Sweet & Maxwell, 5th ed. 2001); Rudolf L. Bindschedler, *International Organizations, General Aspects*, *in* 2 ENCYCLOPEDIA OF PUBLIC INTERNATIONAL LAW 1289 (North–Holland 1995). *See also* the journal INTERNATIONAL ORGANIZATIONS LAW REVIEW (Martinus Nijhoff 2004–).

number of international organizations exist. Within the United Nations system alone there are twenty affiliated international organizations, known collectively as *specialized agencies,* each autonomous, with its own founding treaty and membership. Next, each IGO has its own publishing program and method of organizing its documents. Then, there may be deficiencies in distribution. Finally, libraries sometimes inconsistently organize collections and have different means of providing access. Thus, it can be hard to find a particular document of a particular international organization.

An accurate citation that includes the name of the document or a clear indication of its subject matter, the document "symbol" or number assigned by the organization, and the date the document was issued are especially helpful in international organization documents research.[238]

2. United Nations

a. *Introduction.* The United Nations (UN) carries out its work through a complex organizational structure. The wide range of UN concerns has led to the establishment of an equally wide range of commissions, committees, and conferences. The key to understanding United Nations documentation is to understand both the organization of the UN and its operation. Most UN documentation is the product of the UN's official work, and documents are identified with the particular body within the UN structure that produced them. Those unfamiliar with the UN should consult the "About the United Nations" section of the UN website[239] and print sources, such as *Basic Facts About the United Nations,*[240] *Encyclopedia of the United Nations,*[241] *Encyclopedia of the United Nations and International Agreements,*[242] *Guide to United Nations Organization, Documentation & Publishing for Students, Researchers, Librarians,*[243] and *Introduction to International Organizations.*[244]

b. *United Nations Charter.* The Charter is the constitutive document of the United Nations, as well as a binding international agreement that is acknowledged to state fundamental principles of international law. The text of the Charter can be found in many places, including the United Nations website,[245] and print sources, such as *Basic Documents in International Law,*[246] *Yearbook of the United Nations,*[247] and any of the documentary supplements to the leading casebooks on international law. There are

---

[238] *See* INTERNATIONAL INFORMATION: DOCUMENTS, PUBLICATIONS, AND ELECTRONIC INFORMATION OF INTERNATIONAL GOVERNMENTAL ORGANIZATIONS (Peter I. Hajnal ed., Libraries Unlimited 2d ed. 1997) for a good overview of issues concerning the use of documents produced by international organizations.

[239] http://www.un.org/aboutun/index.html. The UN website also has a useful organization chart, at http://www.un.org/aboutun/chart.html.

[240] (United Nations 2004).

[241] JOHN A. MOORE & JERRY PUBANTZ (Facts On File 2d ed. 2008).

[242] EDMUND J. OSMANCZYK (Routledge 3d ed. 2003).

[243] PETER I. HAJNAL (Oceana Publications 1978).

[244] (Lyonette Louis–Jacques & Jeanne S. Korman eds., Oceana Publications 1996).

[245] http://www.un.org/aboutun/charter/index.html.

[246] (Ian Brownlie ed., Oxford University Press 6th ed. 2009).

[247] (United Nations; Martinus Nijhoff 1947–).

excellent recent commentaries on the Charter in English[248] and French.[249] The other article-by-article commentary in English is out-of-date but still of some use.[250]

    c. *United Nations Document Symbols.*[251] The United Nations uses a system of document symbols, based on the issuing body, to identify and organize its documentation. Each document symbol identifies the source of that document within the UN hierarchy of organization. Two examples illustrate both the system of document symbols as well as its range and complexity. A typical symbol is A/CN.9/654. The forward slash is a distinguishing characteristic in all UN document symbols. This example is the 654th document issued by the United Nations Commission on International Trade Law (CN.9), a body established by the General Assembly (A).[252] A more complicated example is A/CN.9/WG.VI/WP.3/Add.1. This is also a Commission document (A/CN.9), but it is the first addendum (Add.1) to Working Paper 3 (WP.3) produced by Working Group VI (WG.VI).[253]

    The salient components of the system of United Nations document symbols are:

    (1) *Leading elements,* denoting the four major United Nations organs that use the system (the International Court of Justice does not):

A/–	General Assembly
E/–	Economic and Social Council
S/–	Security Council
ST/–	Secretariat

    (2) *Special leading symbols* have been created for other bodies. Some important examples are:

CCPR/–	Human Rights Committee (under the International Covenant on Civil and Political Rights)
CERD/–	International Convention on the Elimination of All Forms of Racial Discrimination
TD/–	United Nations Conference on Trade and Development (UNCTAD)
UNEP/–	United Nations Environment Programme

---

[248] THE CHARTER OF THE UNITED NATIONS: A COMMENTARY (Bruno Simma ed., Oxford University Press 2d ed. 2002).

[249] JEAN-PIERRE COT & ALAIN PELLET, LA CHARTE DES NATIONS UNIES: COMMENTAIRE ARTICLE PAR ARTICLE (Economica 3d ed. 2005).

[250] LELAND M. GOODRICH ET AL., CHARTER OF THE UNITED NATIONS: COMMENTARY AND DOCUMENTS (Columbia University Press 3d ed. 1969).

[251] *See generally* "United Nations Documentation: Research Guide" on the United Nations website, http://www.un.org/Depts/dhl/resguide.

[252] Examination of the document shows that it was issued in February 2008 and is titled "Facilitation of cooperation, direct communication, and coordination in cross-border insolvency proceedings: Note by the Secretariat."

[253] Examination of this document shows that it was issued in March 2008, that WG.VI is the Working Group on Security Interests, and that the title is "Security rights in intellectual property rights."

(3) Elements denoting the *subsidiary organ*:

–/AC./–	Ad hoc committee
–/C./–	Standing or main sessional committee
–/CN./–	Commission
–/CONF./–	Conference
–/WG./–	Working Group

(4) Elements denoting the *nature of the document*:

–/PV...	Verbatim records of meetings ("procès verbaux")
–/RES/–	Preliminary text of adopted resolutions
–/SR...	Summary records of meetings

(5) Elements indicating a *change in an earlier document*:

–/Add...	Addendum
–/Corr...	Corrigendum
–/Rev...	Revision

(6) Elements indicating *distribution*:

–/L...	Limited
–R...	Restricted

A good description of the system can be found on the website of the UN's Dag Hammarskjöld Library.[254]

Detailed information on UN document symbols in use is contained in *United Nations Document Series Symbols, 1946–1996*.[255]

d. *United Nations Working Documents and Official Records.* UN bodies produce vast amounts of documents relating to their work. Some of these documents receive the name *official records*. The main organs of the United Nations—the General Assembly and its seven committees, the Security Council, the Secretariat and the Economic and Social Council—issue official records. Both working documents and official records are issued with a document symbol as described above. Official records come out in both *provisional* and *final* form.

In provisional form, official records are published individually on plain white paper. Official records are later collected together and republished in bound form, with tan paper covers for the General Assembly, yellow for the Security Council, and light blue for the Economic and Social Council. In final form, official records contain meeting records, annexes, and supplements. Note that significant working documents often reappear in the annexes and supplements to the official records.

A collection of UN documents is available on microfiche from Readex/Newsbank.

e. *Publications for Sale.* The United Nations has an active publishing program through which it offers for sale a wide array of publications. This includes subscriptions to working documents and official records. Many titles in the fields of international relations, population issues, environmen-

---

[254] http://www.un.org/Depts/dhl/resguide/symbol.htm.

[255] (United Nations 1998).

tal policy, international trade and economics, and statistics are also available. These publications receive a sales number, such as 08.III.B.7, which is used only for ordering and should not be confused with the document symbol.[256]

f. *Tools for Researching United Nations Documents.*

(1) *ODS.*[257] "*ODS*" stands for Official Document System of the United Nations. The UN describes *ODS* as "the premier full-text web resource for official United Nations documentation." Access to *ODS* is open. Coverage on *ODS* for recent years is excellent and quite good back to 1993. New documents are added continuously and retrospective additions to the database are underway. Searching by document symbol is possible. Several kinds of full-text searching also are possible.

(2) *UNBISnet.* The free online index to UN documentation published since 1979 is called *UNBISnet.*[258] It doubles as the online catalog of the Dag Hammarskjöld Library in New York and the UN library in Geneva. Subject and keyword searching, as well as searching by document symbol, are possible. Records often link to the full text of indexed documents on *ODS.* *UNBISnet* practically supersedes the hardcopy indexes. For research before 1979 it will be necessary to use *UNDEX*[259] and *United Nations Document Index.*[260] These hardcopy indexes are succeeded by *UNDOC: Current Index* for 1979–1996, and since 1998 by the currently published *United Nations Documents Index.*

(3) *UN–I–QUE.*[261] This is another documents research database provided by the Dag Hammarskjöld Library. It focuses on UN documents of a recurring nature. For example, the researcher learns that the United Nations Conference on Disarmament publishes its annual report in the General Assembly Official Records, Supplement No. 27. Similarly, the report of the Conference of the Parties to the United Nations Framework Convention on Climate Change is issued under the symbol FCCC/CP/[year].

(4) *UN Pulse.*[262] This is a blog that provides alerts of selected, just-released UN online information—major reports, publications, and documents. It is produced by the Dag Hammarskjöld Library.

(5) *United Nations website.*[263] This is the main gateway to the UN on the World Wide Web. It provides a variety of access points, including access to the webpages of each of the main bodies. There are also subject sectors: Peace & Security, Economic and Social Development, Human Rights, Humanitarian Affairs, and International Law. The UN website also provides access to official documents, but it should be used together with *ODS* for this purpose.

[256] The United Nations publications catalog is available at the website, http://unp.un.org.

[257] http://documents.un.org.

[258] http://unbisnet.un.org.

[259] (United Nations 1970–78).

[260] (United Nations 1950–73).

[261] http://lib-unique.un.org/lib/unique.nsf.

[262] http://unhq-appspub–01.un.org/lib/dhlrefweblog.nsf.

[263] http://www.un.org/english/.

(6) *Yearbook of the United Nations.*[264] The *Yearbook* describes the activities of both the UN and its specialized agencies. It is organized in broad subject categories, such as Political and Security Questions, Regional Questions, and Economic and Social Questions. Under each subtopic the action of UN organs is summarized and important resolutions are reproduced. Particularly valuable are the references (by document symbol) to UN documents relating to the points discussed. The UN now makes the full-text of all volumes of the *Yearbook* freely available on the World Wide Web in PDF format.[265]

(7) *Index to Proceedings of the General Assembly, Index to Proceedings of the Security Council,* and *Index to Proceedings of the Economic and Social Council.* The indexes are not as easy to use as *UNDOC,* but they are valuable resources that should be consulted for comprehensive research.

g. *Secondary Sources.* The secondary literature on the UN and its work is enormous. Searching in both the library catalog and in journal indexes in law and related disciplines is necessary. Of the latter, *PAIS International* is recommended. On the law of the UN, two sources for starting research are mentioned here: *Law and Practice of the United Nations: Documents and Commentary*[266] and *Max Planck Yearbook of United Nations Law.*[267]

3. European Union

a. *Introduction.* The European Union (EU) is an international organization composed of 27 European countries—Austria, Belgium, Bulgaria, Cyprus, the Czech Republic, Denmark, Estonia, Finland, France, Germany, Greece, Hungary, Ireland, Italy, Latvia, Lithuania, Luxembourg, Malta, The Netherlands, Poland, Portugal, Romania, Slovakia, Slovenia, Spain, Sweden, and the United Kingdom.[268] The main seat of EU institutions is Brussels. It also has a presence in Luxembourg[269] and Strasbourg.[270] The EU is sometimes called a *supranational* organization because it has authority under its founding treaties to make law binding on the member states.

A source of confusion is the similarity between the names of the EU and of the Council of Europe, a different organization. The Council of Europe is responsible, among other things, for the administration of the European Convention for the Protection of Human Rights and Fundamental Freedoms.[271] The European Court of Human Rights is an arm of the Council of Europe, *not* of the EU.[272]

---

[264] (United Nations 1947–).

[265] http://unyearbook.un.org.

[266] SIMON CHESTERMAN, THOMAS M. FRANCK & DAVID M. MALONE (Oxford University Press 2008).

[267] (Kluwer Law International 1998–).

[268] Croatia, Turkey and the former Yugoslav Republic of Macedonia are candidates for membership.

[269] The European Court of Justice sits in Luxembourg.

[270] The European Parliament holds some of it sessions in Strasbourg.

[271] C.E.T.S. No. 5.

[272] *See* Section I–2 of this chapter for detailed discussion of European human rights research.

Again, the importance of the European Union for our purposes is, first, that it holds great law-making power that affects not only the member states, but may also have an impact on third states, such as the U.S., and, second, that it produces many documents important to the study of the EU itself and of subjects with which the EU is concerned. The EU carries out its work through four main institutions—Council, Commission, European Parliament, and Court of Justice. Of lesser importance for legal research are the Economic and Social Committee, Court of Auditors, and the Committee of the Regions. Each institution produces documentation that can appear in a variety of forms. An understanding of the institutional structure and law-making process of the EU will make the research process easier. For this purpose, a leading treatise on the law and institutions of the EU is indispensable.[273]

b. *EUR–Lex*. The *EUR–Lex* website[274] provides access to European Union law. Today *EUR–Lex* should be the starting point for European Union legal research. It is freely accessible. The main content of *EUR–Lex* includes the following kinds of legal and other information, which are considered in more detail below:

- Founding treaties and other treaties relating to the establishment and functioning of the European Union
- *Official Journal of the European Union*
- Legislation in force
- Preparatory acts
- Case-law

c. *Founding treaties and other treaties*. The European Union is based on a group of what are called founding treaties. Chief among these are the Treaty Establishing the European Community and the Treaty on European Union. An important amending agreement, the Treaty of Lisbon, was signed in December 2007. Under it the new name of the Treaty Establishing the European Community will be the Treaty on the Functioning of the European Union. The founding treaties and amending treaties, together with the accession treaties, are found on *EUR–Lex* under the "Treaties" link.[275]

d. *Official Journal of the European Union*.[276] The *Official Journal* is the central gazette of EU legal information. The *Official Journal* is

---

[273] *See, e.g.,* ANTHONY ARNULL ET AL., WYATT AND DASHWOOD'S EUROPEAN UNION LAW (Sweet & Maxwell 5th ed. 2006); JOHN FAIRHURST, LAW OF THE EUROPEAN UNION (Pearson Longman 5th ed. 2006); KOEN LENAERTS & PIET VAN NUFFEL, CONSTITUTIONAL LAW OF THE EUROPEAN UNION (Sweet & Maxwell 2d ed. 2005); P.S.R.F. MATHIJSEN, A GUIDE TO EUROPEAN UNION LAW (Sweet & Maxwell 8th ed. 2004); TREVOR HARTLEY, THE FOUNDATIONS OF EUROPEAN COMMUNITY LAW: AN INTRODUCTION TO THE CONSTITUTIONAL AND ADMINISTRATIVE LAW OF THE EUROPEAN COMMUNITY (Oxford University Press 5th ed. 2003).

[274] http://eur-lex.europa.eu/en/index.htm.

[275] These are the versions as published in the OFFICIAL JOURNAL. Consolidated versions of the Treaty on European Union and the Treaty on the Functioning of the European Union are found in O.J. C115/1 (2008), as posted on *EUR–Lex*.

[276] (1973–). The OFFICIAL JOURNAL was not published in English before 1973. There is an OFFICIAL JOURNAL SPECIAL EDITION (1972–73) of translations of EC law enacted before the United Kingdom and Ireland became members.

published every business day in all European Union member languages. The *Official Journal* has more than one part. Most important are the "L" series (containing final legislative acts, such as directives, regulations, decisions, opinions, and recommendations) and the "C" series (containing information and notices, proposals for legislation, European Parliament resolutions, opinions of the Economic and Social Committee, and excerpts from the judgments of the Court of Justice). Every issue of the *Official Journal* is numbered separately. Knowing the relevant part and number is essential to locating a particular document within the *Official Journal*. A typical reference would be "O.J. L146/10 (2008)." This refers to issue 146 of the L series for 2008, page 10.

The *Official Journal* is available in full-text PDF since January 1998 on *EUR–Lex*. Libraries that hold the *Official Journal* in their collections now receive it in CD–ROM format. Before that the *Official Journal* was distributed in microfiche.

e. *Legislation in force*. The European Union legislates using various kinds of enactments. These include directives, regulations, and decisions, among others. These appear first in the *Official Journal*. There is no code or compilation of European Union Law currently in force. The closest such source is the database of *Legislation in force* as found on *EUR–Lex*. *Legislation in force* can be searched by type of enactment, by search term in full text, or by date. Recent legislation (back to 1998) is produced in PDF as published in the *Official Journal*. Prior to 1998, legislation is in HTML with a full reference to the *Official Journal*. Searching is also possible using the classified scheme in the *Directory of Community legislation in force* as available on *EUR–Lex*.

f. *Preparatory acts*. Proposals for European Union legislation usually originate with the European Commission. *EUR–Lex* calls these "Preparatory acts." However, in practice, these documents are usually called "COM" documents (COM=Commission). For example, the "Proposal for a Directive of the European Parliament and of the Council facilitating cross-border enforcement in the field of road safety of March 2008" is COM(2008)151. Before *EUR–Lex*, COM documents were difficult to find. *EUR–Lex* now has COM documents in full text from January 1999.

Not all COM documents are proposals for legislation. For example, COM(2008)165 is titled "WHITE PAPER on Damages actions for breach of EC antitrust rules." This type of COM document is also available on *EUR–Lex* in the "Preparatory acts" sector.

g. *Case-law*. The European Court of Justice (E.C.J.) is one of the most important institutions of the European Union. Its decisions have far-reaching significance for the development of European Union law. The name of the official reporter for the E.C.J. is *Reports of Cases Before the Court*. The informal name is *European Court Reports* and the usual citation is "*E.C.R.*" The official reports appear late. The solution to this delay is to use the respected commercially published reporter *Common Market Law Reports* (*C.M.L.R.*),[277] which appears in weekly advance sheets.

---

277 (Sweet & Maxwell 1962 to present). There is a companion series called C.M.L.R. ANTITRUST REPORTS (Sweet & Maxwell 1991 to present).

Judgments of the E.C.J. are available on *EUR–Lex*. However, the database of the E.C.J. on *EUR–Lex* lacks good search functionality, and for that reason use of the Court's own website[278] is preferable.

The European Court of First Instance was established in 1989. It has initial jurisdiction over a number of types of direct actions brought by individuals and member states. Appeals go to the E.C.J. Judgments of the Court of First Instance are also reported in *Reports of Cases Before the Court (E.C.R.)*. The Treaty of Lisbon renames the Court of First Instance the General Court.

h. *PreLex*.[279] This is the European Commission's database for tracking decision-making in the European Union institutions regarding Commission proposals. It has links to relevant documents, including enacted legislation.

i. *Legislative Observatory (European Parliament)*.[280] This is a database for tracking the progress of European Union legislation as it makes its way through the European Parliament. It has links to relevant documents, including enacted legislation.

j. *Europa*.[281] *Europa* is called the "Gateway to the European Union." It is the main web portal to European Union information. There are links to the websites of all European Union institutions. There are over 30 links to web pages on various topics relating to European Union activities. Use *EUR–Lex* in conjunction with *Europa* for the broadest and deepest access to European Union legal and other information online for free.

k. *Westlaw and LexisNexis*. Both *Westlaw* and *LexisNexis* have databases of European Union law. Both services provide access to the text of the EU treaties and legislation, and to decisions of the European Court of Justice. For most purposes, the free access to EU legal materials provided by *EUR–Lex* remains the preferred source. There may be occasions, however, when *Westlaw* or *LexisNexis* has material not available on *EUR–Lex*.

l. *Publications about the European Union*.

(1) *Bulletin of the European Union*. This is a monthly bulletin that reports on the work of the EU institutions. It is a good place to begin research on current developments in the European Union. It contains numerous references to European Union documents on point. The *Bulletin* is available in full text from 1996 forward at the *Europa* website.[282]

(2) *General Report on the Activities of the European Union*. This is an annual account of the work of the European Union. It too is useful for researching current developments across the full range of EU activity. The footnotes refer to documents published in the *Official Journal*. The *General Report* is available in full text from 1997 forward at the *Europa* website.[283]

---

[278] http://curia.europa.eu/en/transitpage.htm.

[279] http://ec.europa.eu/prelex/apcnet.cfm?CL=en.

[280] http://www.europarl.eu.int/oeil/index.jsp?language=en.

[281] http://europa.eu/index_en.htm.

[282] http://europa.eu/bulletin/en/welcome.htm.

[283] http://europa.eu/generalreport/en/welcome.htm.

(3) *Other sources.* A mass of secondary literature is published about the European Union, much of it dealing specifically with legal issues. A large amount of literature on the EU also is available from the perspective of political science and international relations. The more recent Library of Congress subject headings for general works on the EU include: "European Union," "Europe-Economic integration," "European Union countries-Politics and government," and "European Federation." Works on EU law in general receive the subject heading "Law-European Union countries." The subject subheading used in the last example can be used to narrow a search to specific fields of law, e.g., "Antitrust law-European Union countries."

Journal articles on European Union law can appear in virtually any law review published in the United States and Britain, as well as the rest of Europe. Therefore, research in the standard journal indexes will prove fruitful. Several English-language journals are devoted to EU law: *Common Market Law Review*,[284] *European Law Review*,[285] *Legal Issues of European Integration*,[286] *Columbia Journal of European Law*,[287] and *European Law Journal*.[288] A journal from the perspective of political science is *Journal of Common Market Studies*.[289] An annual publication of interest is the *Yearbook of European Law*.[290]

SECTION I. INTERNATIONAL PROTECTION OF HUMAN RIGHTS

So far in this chapter we have presented a general methodology for researching international law. In this section we turn to a substantive field of international law, one that has consistently gained in significance as we enter further into the twenty-first century. This is the field known as the international legal protection of human rights.

The idea of fundamental human dignity is as old as civilization itself and is common to all cultures and religions. However, it was not until the Age of the Enlightenment in the late seventeenth century, and even more strongly, in the eighteenth century that the idea of individual *rights* became a central concept of our *political* vocabulary. While there are several candidates for the honor, we can refer to two documents of the late eighteenth century as canonical expressions of the concept of individual rights: the U.S. Declaration of Independence[291] and the French Declaration of the Rights of Man and Citizen.[292]

It was not until after the horrors of the Second World War that the idea of the protection of human rights in international law gained traction.

---

[284] (Martinus Nijhoff 1963–).

[285] (Sweet & Maxwell 1975–).

[286] (Kluwer 1974–).

[287] (Parker School of Foreign & Comparative Law 1994–).

[288] (Blackwell 1995–).

[289] (Blackwell 1962–).

[290] (Oxford University Press 1982–).

[291] Declaration of Independence para. 2 (U.S. 1776) ("[A]ll men are created equal.... [T]hey are endowed, by their Creator, with certain unalienable rights....").

[292] Declaration of the Rights of Man and Citizen (Fr. 1789), *reprinted in* THE FRENCH REVOLUTION AND HUMAN RIGHTS: A BRIEF DOCUMENTARY HISTORY 77–79 (Lynn Hunt ed., 1996).

The main obstacle had been the entrenched doctrine of domestic jurisdiction, according to which the way a state treated its own citizens was not a matter for the intervention of international law. Thanks mainly to the momentum gained from the founding of the United Nations, the doctrine gave way to the belief that the violation of human rights by a state against its own citizens was indeed a matter of concern for the international community and for international law.[293]

Today, the edifice of human rights protection built by international law is imposing. There will be space here to consider only the broad outline of this structure. We will consider the three major international systems of human rights protection: the United Nations system, the European system, and the Inter–American system.[294] We also will touch on developments in Africa and on the indispensable work carried out by the international non-governmental organizations ("NGOs").[295] The focus will always be on the ways and means of conducting research; the substantive descriptions will provide a backdrop to research method.

1. The United Nations System[296]

The United Nations Charter mentions human rights briefly seven times. Significantly, the phrase occurs in both the preamble[297] and in article 1.[298] As one of its first major actions, the United Nations Economic and Social Council established the Commission on Human Rights in 1946. The Commission began immediately to draft the Universal Declaration of Human Rights, which was adopted by a resolution of the General Assembly.[299] From these beginnings the United Nations has over the course of sixty years built up an extensive machinery of human rights protection. The Office of the UN High Commissioner for Human Rights has prepared a good online collection of mostly United Nations human rights instruments.[300]

In the United Nations human rights system the first step in the correct approach to doing research is to divide the system into its two main functional components: the Charter-based bodies and the treaty-based

---

[293] For an interesting interpretation of the historical development, see MICHELINE R. ISHAY, THE HISTORY OF HUMAN RIGHTS: FROM ANCIENT TIMES TO THE GLOBALIZATION ERA (2004).

[294] A comprehensive collection of materials on the regional systems is DINAH SHELTON, REGIONAL PROTECTION OF HUMAN RIGHTS (Oxford University Press 2008).

[295] The other approach to take would be *thematic*, meaning keyed to the full range of substantive rights, rather than to the systems of protection. For example, we could look at researching the right of self-determination, the rights of indigenous peoples and minorities, the rights of persons with disabilities, the rights of migrants, of refugees, or of children, labor rights, torture, the death penalty, and so on. Unfortunately, there is no room here to explore the thematic approach more fully.

[296] A recent introduction in hardcopy is JULIE MERTUS, THE UNITED NATIONS AND HUMAN RIGHTS: A GUIDE FOR A NEW ERA (Routledge 2005).

[297] "We the peoples of the United Nations determined . . . to reaffirm faith in fundamental human rights. . . ."

[298] "The purposes of the United Nations are . . . to achieve international co-operation . . . in promoting and encouraging respect for human rights. . . ."

[299] G.A. Res. 217A (III), U.N. Doc. A/810 (Dec. 12, 1948).

[300] http://www2.ohchr.org/english/law.

bodies. These two main elements are bridged by the Office of the United Nations High Commissioner for Human Rights, which is a department of the United Nations Secretariat.

a. *Charter-based bodies.* In 2006 the General Assembly established the Human Rights Council.[301] This was a fundamental change in the United Nations human rights system. The Council replaced the Commission on Human Rights, which was a dependency of the Economic and Social Council, rather than the General Assembly. The Commission had come under criticism for being politicized and ineffective and for having members who were guilty of serious human rights violations.[302]

The new Human Rights Council has 47 seats. Each member state must be elected individually by a majority of the General Assembly. Member states are required to uphold the highest standards of human rights. A two-thirds majority of the General Assembly may suspend a member if it commits serious abuses of human rights.

The Human Rights Council sits in Geneva, Switzerland. It holds at least three sessions a year for a total of at least ten weeks. It may and does also hold special sessions.

The Council's UN document symbol is A/HRC/-. For example, document A/HRC/7/22, dated March 2008, is the 22nd document of the Council's seventh session, and is titled "Human Rights Situations that Require the Council's Attention: Report of the Special Rapporteur on the Situation of Human Rights in the Sudan."

The Council is assisted in its work by the Advisory Committee made up of 18 human rights experts who serve independently in their personal capacities. The Advisory Committee replaces the old Sub–Commission on the Promotion and Protection of Human Rights. Unlike the Sub–Commission, the Advisory Committee does not have its own document symbol.

In establishing the Human Rights Council, the General Assembly mandated that it "undertake a universal periodic review ... of the fulfillment by each state of its human rights obligations and commitments ... such a mechanism shall complement and not duplicate the work of treaty bodies."[303] In 2007 the Council adopted its resolution 5/1 that sets up the framework and main procedures of the Universal Periodic Review (UPR). The UPR will be carried out by the Working Group on the Universal Periodic Review, which, oddly, is composed of all 47 member states of the Council. The document symbol of the working group is A/HRC/WG.6/. There will be a "troika" of three rapporteurs who will facilitate each review and help with the drafting of the final report. The Council adopted a calendar that sets up a four-year cycle for the UPR, which means that each member of the UN will be reviewed every four years. The first session of the working group on the UPR took place in April 2008. The first reviews have been conducted and the first reports issued.[304] The best way to follow

---

[301] G.A. Res. 60/251, U.N. Doc. A/RES/60/251 (Mar. 15, 2006).

[302] *See, e.g.,* Eric Heinze, *Even-handedness and the Politics of Human Rights*, 21 HARV. HUM. RTS. J. 7, 41 (2008).

[303] G.A. Res. 60/251, U.N. Doc. A/RES/60/251 (Mar. 15, 2006).

[304] *See, e.g.,* U.N. Doc. A/HRC/WG.6/1/CZE/4 (report on the Czech Republic).

the progress of the UPR and to find the reports is at the website of the High Commissioner for Human Rights.[305] It is also necessary to search the document symbol of the working group on the *ODS* system.

The Human Rights Council has decided to continue for the present some of the working methods developed under the old Commission. Much important work is carried out using what are called "special procedures." Two of these are called "country mandates" and "thematic mandates." As of May 2008, there are nine country mandates and 28 thematic mandates in place.

Examples of thematic mandates are the Special Rapporteur on the right to education, the Working Group on Arbitrary Detention, and the Independent Expert on Human Rights and Extreme Poverty. Follow work on both country and thematic mandates on the High Commissioner's website[306] and on the *ODS* system.

The Council reviewed, revised, and reinstituted the mechanism for making individualized complaints. It is now known formally as the Complaint Procedure. It is meant "to address consistent patterns of gross and reliably attested violations of all human rights and all fundamental freedoms occurring in any part of the world and under any circumstances." Communications under the Complaint Procedure must come from victims or from "persons, including non-governmental organizations, acting in good faith ... and claiming to have direct and reliable knowledge of the violations concerned." The Complaint Procedure operates through two working groups. Note that the Complaint Procedure is *confidential*, which means that it produces no public documents.

b.   *Treaty-based mechanisms.* The nine core international human rights agreements in the United Nations system are:

- International Covenant on Civil and Political Rights[307]
- International Covenant on Economic, Social and Cultural Rights[308]
- International Convention on the Elimination of All Forms of Racial Discrimination[309]
- Convention on the Elimination of All Forms of Discrimination against Women[310]
- Convention against Torture and Other Cruel, Inhuman or Degrading Treatment or Punishment[311]

[305] http://www.ohchr.org/EN/HRBodies/UPR/Pages/UPRMain.aspx.

[306] http://www2.ohchr.org/english/bodies/chr/special/countries.htm   and   http://www2.ohchr.org/english/bodies/chr/special/themes.htm.

[307] Dec. 16, 1966, 999 U.N.T.S. 171. (Also cited to G.A. Res. 2200A (XXI), U.N. GAOR, 21st Sess., Supp. No. 16, at 52, U.N. Doc. A/6316 (1966)). *See generally* MANFRED NOWAK, U.N. COVENANT ON CIVIL AND POLITICAL RIGHTS: CCPR COMMENTARY (N.P. Engel 2d ed. 2005).

[308] Dec. 16, 1966, 993 U.N.T.S. 3. (Also cited to G.A. Res. 2200A (XXI), U.N. GAOR, 21st Sess., Supp. No. 16, at 49, U.N. Doc. A/6316 (1966)).

[309] Dec. 21, 1965, 660 U.N.T.S. 195. (Also cited to G.A. Res. 2106 (XX), U.N. GAOR, 20th Sess., Supp. No. 14, U.N. Doc. A/6014 (1965)).

[310] Dec. 18, 1979, 1249 U.N.T.S. 13. (Also cited to G.A. Res. 34/180, U.N. GAOR, 34th Sess., Supp. No. 46, at 193, U.N. Doc. A/34/46 (1981)).

[311] Dec. 10, 1984, 1465 U.N.T.S. 85. (Also cited to G.A. Res. 39/46, U.N. GAOR, Supp. No. 51, U.N. Doc. A/39/51 (1984)).

- Convention on the Rights of the Child[312]
- International Convention on the Protection of the Rights of All Migrant Workers and Members of their Families[313]
- Convention on the Rights of Persons with Disabilities[314]
- International Convention for the Protection of All Persons from Enforced Disappearances[315]

The human rights treaty bodies are committees of independent experts that monitor the implementation of the UN human rights treaties.[316] The committees meet in Geneva or New York and have from one to three sessions a year.

One of the main tasks of the committees is the consideration of state party reports. Every state party to any of the UN core agreements is under an obligation to submit regular reports to the respective monitoring committee. Thus, this system of monitoring by means of obligatory state reporting is common to the core treaties. Draft harmonized guidelines on state reporting for use by all committees were adopted in 2006.[317]

The first report is due usually one year after becoming a party and then periodically according to the requirements of each agreement (usually every four or five years). Also, the treaty committees may receive information on the human rights situation in a state party from other sources, including non-governmental human rights organizations ("NGOs"), UN agencies, or other international organizations. The treaty committee examines the state report and then publishes its concerns, criticisms, and recommendations in a document called "Concluding Observations."

Every core treaty committee drafts interpretations of provisions of the agreement that it monitors. These are called "general comments." (CERD and CEDAW use the term "general recommendations.") The Human Rights Committee has adopted 31 general comments. For example, there is General Comment No. 29, States of Emergency (Article 4).[318] The general comments of six treaty committees have been compiled as of 2006 in UN document HRI/GEN/1/Rev. 8.

---

[312] Nov. 20, 1989, 1577 U.N.T.S. 3. (Also cited to G.A. Res. 44/25, U.N. GAOR, 44th Sess., Supp. No. 49, U.N. Doc. A/44/49 (1989)).

[313] G.A. Res. 45/158, U.N. GAOR, 45th Sess., Supp. No. 49A, at 262, U.N. Doc. A/45/49 (1990), 2220 U.N.T.S. 3.

[314] G.A. Res. 61/106, U.N. GAOR, 61st Sess., Supp. No. 49 (vol. I), at 65, U.N. Doc. A/61/49 (2006), 46 I.L.M. 443.

[315] G.A. Res. 61/177, U.N. GAOR, 61st Sess., Supp. No. 49 (vol. I), at 408, U.N. Doc. A/61/49 (2006).

[316] The name of a committee coincides with the name of the agreement for which it is responsible: Human Rights Committee (HRC) for the International Covenant on Civil and Political Rights, Committee on Economic, Social and Cultural Rights (CESCR), Committee on the Elimination of All Forms of Racial Discrimination (CERD), Committee on the Elimination of All Forms of Discrimination against Women (CEDAW), Committee against Torture (CAT), and Committee on the Rights of the Child (CRC). Also, the U.N. document symbol for a committee coincides with the name of the agreement: CCPR/- for the HRC, E/C.12/- for the CESCR, CAT/- for the CAT, CEDAW/- for CEDAW, CERD/- for CERD, and CRC/- for CRC.

[317] U.N. Doc. HRI/MC/2006/3.

[318] U.N. Doc. CCPR/C/21/Rev. 1/Add. 11 (August 2001).

Four of the treaty bodies (HRC, CEDAW, CERD and CAT) have the authority to receive individual "communications" (complaints) alleging specific violations of an agreement by a state party. The state must have agreed to participate in the individual complaints procedure, either by joining an optional protocol or by making a declaration according to the terms of the treaty.

The individual communication initiates a quasi-judicial proceeding in the relevant committee. It is quasi-judicial because, although the committee has the authority to make findings of fact and conclusions of law about specific violations, it has no firm enforcement power. If the committee concludes that there has been a violation, the state party is "invited" to supply information on the steps it has taken to give effect to the committee's views on the appropriate remedy. In case a state's remedial action is inadequate, there is the possibility of a follow-up procedure.[319]

Significantly for research purposes, the texts of final committee decisions on individual communications are posted on the website of the Office of the United Nations High Commissioner for Human Rights. These decisions make up what is referred to as the committee's "jurisprudence."

c. *Website of the Office of the UN High Commissioner for Human Rights.* Today, research on the United Nations human rights system should begin with the website of the Office of the United Nations High Commissioner for Human Rights (OHCHR).[320] [Illustration 21–4] In fact, the OHCHR website marks a major advance in United Nations human rights research. By clicking on the link for "Human Rights Bodies," it is possible to do research that perfectly tracks the bipartite functional structure of the United Nations human rights system that has been sketched here.

A large amount of essential documentation is available on the website. For example, under "Treaty Bodies" there is a link to "Treaty body document search." The researcher can then select the desired agreement and type of document. Types of documents that can be located include:[321]

- State party reports;
- Concluding observations of the committee;
- General comments by the committee;
- Jurisprudence (decisions on individual communications);
- Summary records of committee meetings; and
- Sessional or annual reports of the committee to the General Assembly.

The same kind of research is possible for all of the core treaty bodies. Similarly, in-depth research is possible for the Charter-based bodies. If a desired document is not available on the OHCHR website, the researcher can turn to the Official Documents System of the United Nations, as described in Section H–2–c.

---

[319] See the detailed overview of the individual communications procedure on the website of the Office of the United Nations High Commissioner for Human Rights, http://www2.ohchr.org/english/bodies/petitions/index.htm.

[320] http://www.ohchr.org/.

[321] This is a partial list for illustration.

It is important to note that human rights are referred to in the United Nations as a "cross-cutting issue." This means that human rights are supposed to be taken into account in virtually everything the United Nations does and so could be taken up by any of the United Nations organs or programs. Therefore, human rights research in the United Nations system requires application of the general principles of United Nations research covered in Section H–2 of this chapter.

2. The European System

The heart of the European system of human rights protection is the Convention for the Protection of Human Rights and Fundamental Freedoms[322] adopted in 1950 under the auspices of the Council of Europe.[323] The Convention is usually called the European Convention on Human Rights. It is the first international human rights instrument in the form of a legally binding treaty. All 47 states that are members of the Council of Europe are also parties to the Convention. All states of Europe, including Russia and Turkey, are covered.

The negotiating history of the Convention has been published in eight volumes titled *Collected Edition of the "Travaux Préparatoires."*[324]

The Convention creates the European Court of Human Rights, which sits in Strasbourg, France. In terms of the number of cases it has decided, the range of issues it has dealt with, and the amount of commentary devoted to it, this is the most important court in the world in the field of human rights. All states party to the Convention must accept the jurisdiction of the Court to decide cases involving individual complaints.

In 2007 alone the Court delivered over 1,500 judgments. Judgments are published selectively in the official reports of the Court. From 1996 these are titled simply *Reports of Judgments and Decisions*. Up to 1996 the title was *Publications of the European Court of Human Rights. Series A: Judgments and Decisions*.[325] There is an unofficial commercial set of reports titled *European Human Rights Reports*.[326] At one time there was a *Series B: Pleadings, Oral Arguments and Documents*. This ceased publication in 1995 with volume 104.

Until 1998 there was a subsidiary body called the European Commission on Human Rights. It performed a screening function for the Court, which is now carried out by the Court itself. Selected decisions of the Commission were published in a series titled *Decisions and Reports*.[327]

---

[322] C.E.T.S. No. 5, 213 U.N.T.S. 221. The U.N.T.S. citation is to the Convention in its original form. However, the Convention has been amended and altered several times by protocol. To locate an authoritative current version of the Convention, the Council of Europe's treaty website is recommended. The URL for the Convention is http://conventions.coe.int/Treaty/en/Treaties/Html/005.htm.

[323] Note that the Council of Europe is a completely different international organization from the European Union. It is true that fundamental rights play a role in European Union law, but in the field of human rights in Europe the Council of Europe plays the leading role.

[324] (Martinus Nijhoff 1975–1985).

[325] The former title ceased with volume 338.

[326] (Sweet & Maxwell 1979–).

[327] (Strasbourg, The Commission 1975–98).

Today research on the European Court of Human Rights should begin with its website,[328] and specifically with the database of the case law of the court, which is called *HUDOC*.[329] Full-text searching is possible, as are searching by the name of applicant, name of respondent state, application number, and relevant article of the Convention. Search results can be sorted in various ways, including by relevance and by date.

Both *Westlaw* and *LexisNexis* can be used to search the case law of the Court. The *Westlaw* database derives from the *European Human Rights Reports*. The database identifier is EHR–RPTS. On *LexisNexis*, the file is called Human Rights Cases. Confusingly, it is located with the databases for the European Union. Equally confusingly, the file contains material from a variety of human rights organs besides the European Court of Human Rights.

The secondary literature on the European Convention on Human Rights and the European Court of Human Rights is enormous. The leading treatise in English is *Jacobs and White: The European Convention on Human Rights*.[330] The leading journal in English is *European Human Rights Law Review*.[331] A useful subject heading for use in library catalogs is "Human Rights–Europe." A valuable reference source is the *Yearbook of the European Convention on Human Rights*.[332] Two brief introductions have recently been published: *Short Guide to the European Convention on Human Rights*[333] and *Introduction to the European Convention on Human Rights: The Rights Guaranteed and the Protection Mechanism*.[334]

The European Convention on Human Rights by no means exhausts the human rights work of the Council of Europe. There is a set of other human rights treaties and organs. There is space here only to name and cite them and to give a reference to the relevant page on the Council of Europe's website:

- European Social Charter[335]
- European Social Charter (revised)[336]
- European Convention for the Prevention of Torture and Inhuman or Degrading Treatment or Punishment[337]
- Framework Convention for the Protection of National Minorities[338]

---

[328] http://www.echr.coe.int/echr.

[329] http://cmiskp.echr.coe.int/tkp197/search.asp?skin=hudoc-en.

[330] CLARE OVEY & ROBIN WHITE (Oxford University Press 4th ed. 2006).

[331] (Sweet & Maxwell, 1996–).

[332] (Martinus Nijhoff, 1960–).

[333] DONNA GOMIEN (Council of Europe Publishing 3d ed. 2005).

[334] JEAN-FRANÇOIS RENUCCI (Council of Europe Publishing 2005).

[335] Oct. 18, 1961, C.E.T.S. No. 35, 529 U.N.T.S. 89.

[336] May 3, 1996, C.E.T.S. No. 163. *See* http://www.coe.int/T/DGHL/Monitoring/SocialCharter/.

[337] Nov. 26, 1987, C.E.T.S. No. 126, 27 I.L.M. 1152. *See* the large amount of information, including official documents and a database of information, available at http://www.cpt.coe.int/en/.

[338] Feb. 1, 1995, C.E.T.S. No. 157, 34 I.L.M. 351. *See* http://www.coe.int/t/dghl/monitoring/minorities/default_en.asp. *See also*, THE RIGHTS OF MINORITIES IN EUROPE: A COMMENTARY ON THE

- European Charter for Regional or Minority Languages[339]
- Convention for the Protection of Human Rights and Dignity of the Human Being with Regard to the Application of Biology and Medicine (Convention on Human Rights and Biomedicine)[340]
- Commissioner for Human Rights[341]
- European Commission Against Racism and Intolerance[342]

In addition to the Council of Europe, the European Union makes the protection of human rights a high-profile issue. The best way to begin researching the multi-faceted European Union approach to human rights is to consult the human rights page of the *Europa* website.[343]

In 2000, the member states of the European Union agreed on a Charter of Fundamental Rights.[344] In 2007 the European Union Agency for Fundamental Rights was established.[345] The main activities of the Agency are to give advice to the EU institutions and member states, to gather information and do research and analysis, and to cooperate with civil society while raising awareness of fundamental rights in the EU. In 2008 the Agency's Multi-annual Framework for its work was adopted.[346] Thematic areas to receive special attention are: racism and xenophobia, unlawful discrimination, compensation of victims, rights of the child, asylum and immigration, visa and border control, citizen participation in the democratic functioning of the EU, information society (including privacy and personal data protection), and access to justice. The best way to follow the Agency's work is through its website.[347]

There is an *EU Annual Report on Human Rights* that surveys EU action on human rights in all dimensions.[348]

Another European entity that devotes substantial attention to human rights is the Organization for Security and Co-operation in Europe (OSCE).[349] The OSCE focuses on Eastern Europe, South-Eastern Europe (the Balkans), the Caucasus, and Central Asia. The OSCE's main field of action is international peace and security in these regions.[350] However, the

European Framework Convention for the Protection of National Minorities (MARC WELLER ED., OXFORD UNIVERSITY PRESS 2005).

[339] Nov. 5, 1992, C.E.T.S. No. 148. *See* http://www.coe.int/T/E/Legal_Affairs/Local_and_regional_Democracy/Regional_or_Minority_languages/.

[340] April 4, 1997, C.E.T.S. No. 164. See the Bioethics page of the Council of Europe website at http://www.coe.int/t/dg3/healthbioethic/default_en.asp.

[341] *See* the large amount of information, including official documents, on the Commissioner's page of the Council of Europe website at http://www.coe.int/t/commissioner/default_en.asp.

[342] http://www.coe.int/t/dghlmonitoring/ecri/default_en.asp.

[343] http://europa.eu/pol/rights/index_en.htm.

[344] O.J. C364/1 (2000).

[345] O.J. L53/1 (2007).

[346] O.J. L63/14 (2008).

[347] http://fra.europa.eu.

[348] *See, for example*, the 2007 report, http://ec.europa.eu/external_relations/human_rights/doc/report07_en.pdf.

[349] http://www.osce.org/.

[350] The OSCE speaks of the "politico-military" dimension.

OSCE has established an Office for Democratic Institutions and Human Rights (ODIHR), based in Warsaw, Poland. The best way to begin research on OSCE/ODIHR human rights activities is to go to the ODIHR website.[351] Note should also be made of the OSCE's High Commissioner on National Minorities[352] and its Special Representative on Combating Trafficking in Human Beings.[353]

3. The Inter–American System

Like the European system, the Inter–American system is regional. However, in structure it resembles the United Nations system because it has both an O.A.S. Charter-based body and a treaty-based body. The Charter-based body is the Inter–American Commission on Human Rights.[354] The treaty-based body is the Inter–American Court of Human Rights.[355]

The first key document is the American Declaration of the Rights and Duties of Man.[356] It was adopted in May 1948 and so predates the Universal Declaration of Human Rights by several months. The key human rights agreement is the American Convention on Human Rights.[357] The Convention has two important supplementary agreements: the Additional Protocol to the American Convention on Human Rights in the Area of Economic, Social and Cultural Rights ("Protocol of San Salvador")[358] and the Protocol to the American Convention on Human Rights to Abolish the Death Penalty.[359]

The Commission has a wide scope of activity. It is authorized to receive individual complaints charging violations of both the American Declaration and the American Convention. The Commission also carries out country studies and situation reports. An example of the former is the 2007 report titled *Access to Justice and Social Inclusion: the Road towards Strengthening Democracy in Bolivia*.[360] An example of the latter is the 2006 *Report on the Situation of Human Rights Defenders in the Americas*.[361]

---

[351] http://www.osce.org/odihr/.

[352] http://www.osce.org/hcnm/.

[353] http://www.osce.org/cthb/.

[354] The Commission's website is http://www.cidh.org/.

[355] The Court's website is http://www.corteidh.or.cr/.

[356] Strictly speaking, the American Declaration is cited as Res. XXX, Final Act of the Ninth International Conference of American States, Bogotá, Colombia, Mar. 30–May 2, 1948. This document is almost impossible to find. Therefore, it is recommended that the citation include a "reprinted in" element referring to the quasi-official O.A.S. publication titled BASIC DOCUMENTS PERTAINING TO HUMAN RIGHTS IN THE INTER-AMERICAN SYSTEM (O.A.S. General Secretariat 2007). The O.A.S. document symbol is OEA/Ser. L/V/I.4 rev.9 Eng. The publication is available in PDF format at http://www.corteidh.or.cr/docs/libros/Basingl01.pdf, and in HTML format at http://www.cidh.org/basicos/english/basic.toc.htm.

[357] Nov. 22, 1969, O.A.S.T.S. No. 36, 1144 U.N.T.S. 123. It should be noted that the U.S. is not party to the American Convention.

[358] Nov. 17, 1988, O.A.S.T.S. No. 69, 28 I.L.M. 161.

[359] Aug. 28, 1991, O.A.S.T.S. No. 73, 29 I.L.M. 1447.

[360] O.A.S. doc. OEA/Ser.L/V/II. doc. 34 (June 28, 2007).

[361] O.A.S. doc. OEA/Ser.L/V/II.124 doc. 5 rev.1 (March 7, 2006).

Unfortunately, individual Commission documents can be difficult to find. Therefore, it is recommended that the researcher refer to the *Annual Report of the Inter–American Commission on Human Rights to the General Assembly*.[362] The annual report is current to within one year, and is comprehensive and detailed, dealing with all aspects of the Commission's work. The Commission's website also carries a substantial amount of documentation.

The Court is a true judicial body, comparable to its European counterpart, although it has does not have the same caseload. The Court exercises both contentious and advisory jurisdiction.

Currently, the Court publishes its work in four official series. The most important of these are *Series A–Judgments and Opinions*[363] and *Series C–Decisions and Judgments*. Editorial work and the requirement of translation delay publication in final form. Fortunately, the jurisprudence of the Court is available comprehensively on the Court's website. The Court also issues its *Annual Report of the Inter–American Court of Human Rights*, although it is not as comprehensive as the Commission's report. These are available from 1980 almost to the present in Spanish, sometimes in English, on the Court's website.[364]

Also to be consulted is the *Inter–American Yearbook on Human Rights*,[365] although this appears several years behind.

Unfortunately, the secondary literature (books) in English on the Inter–American human rights system is somewhat sparse. A recent exception is *The Practice and Procedure of the Inter–American Court of Human Rights*.[366] Two standard, but now somewhat dated, treatments are *The Inter–American System of Human Rights*[367] and *The Inter–American Human Rights System*.[368]

The Inter–American human rights system includes several other specialized agreements for which there is room here only to give their titles and citation:

- Inter–American Convention to Prevent and Punish Torture[369]
- Inter–American Convention on Forced Disappearance of Persons[370]
- Inter–American Convention on the Prevention, Punishment and Eradication of Violence Against Women[371]
- Inter–American Convention on the Elimination of all Forms of Discrimination against Persons with Disabilities[372]

[362] (O.A.S. General Secretariat 1970–). (Early volumes are available in Spanish only.)

[363] This is a confusing title. Series A actually publishes the *advisory opinions* of the Court.

[364] http://www.corteidh.or.cr/informes.cfm.

[365] (O.A.S. General Secretariat 1973–).

[366] Jo M. PASQUALUCCI, Cambridge University Press 2003.

[367] David J. Harris & Stephen Livingstone eds., Oxford University Press 1998.

[368] J. SCOTT DAVIDSON, Dartmouth 1997.

[369] Dec. 9, 1985, O.A.S.T.S. No. 67, 25 I.L.M. 519.

[370] June 9, 1994, O.A.S. doc. OEA/Ser.P, AG, doc. 3114/94 rev.1, 33 I.L.M. 1529.

[371] June 9, 1994, O.A.S. doc. OEA/Ser.P, AG/doc. 3115/94 rev.2, 33 I.L.M. 1534.

[372] June 7, 1999, O.A.S. A.G. Res. 1608, 29th Sess., O.A.S. doc. OEA/Ser. AG/doc. 3826/99.

Other organizations under the O.A.S. umbrella that address human rights include:

- Inter–American Commission of Women[373]
- Inter–American Children's Institute[374]
- Inter–American Indian Institute[375]
- Inter–American Institute of Human Rights[376]

4. Developments in Africa

The key document is the African Charter on Human and Peoples' Rights,[377] adopted under the auspices of the Organization of African Unity (O.A.U.). Related instruments of note are the Convention Governing the Specific Aspects of Refugee Problems in Africa,[378] the African Charter on the Rights and Welfare of the Child,[379] and the Protocol to the African Charter on the Rights of Women in Africa.[380]

The key body established by the African Charter is the African Commission on Human and Peoples' Rights. The Commission has a protective mandate, which it carries out by exercising its authority to hear individual communications alleging specific violations of the African Charter. The Commission also has a promotional mandate which it carries out by considering and critiquing states' reports on their adherence to the African Charter. The Commission also acts through its special mechanisms, which include special rapporteurs and working groups, as well as missions to examine the human rights situation in particular countries. The Commission also adopts resolutions concerning significant human rights issues.

Research on the Commission's work can begin with its website.[381] There the researcher will find various Commission documents, including state reports, the Commission's Activity Reports, and reports produced by the special mechanisms. The other valuable Web resource is the University of Minnesota Human Rights Library. It has a page devoted to the Commission[382] that includes final communiqués from the Commission's sessions, Commission resolutions, and a good number of Commission decisions on individual communications.[383]

---

[373] http://portal.oas.org/Default.aspx?tabid=621&language=en-US.

[374] http://www.iin.oea.org/default_ingles.htm.

[375] http://www.indigenista.org/web.

[376] http://www.iidh.ed.cr/default_eng.htm.

[377] June 27, 1981, 1520 U.N.T.S. 217.

[378] Sept. 10, 1969, 1001 U.N.T.S. 45, 8 I.L.M. 1288.

[379] July 11, 1990, O.A.U. Doc. CAB/LEG/24.9/49, at http://www1.umn.edu/humanrts/africa/afchild.htm. *See also* the website of the African Committee of Experts on the Rights and Welfare of the Child, at http://www.africa-union.org/child/home.htm.

[380] July 11, 2003, http://www1.umn.edu/humanrts/africa/protocol-women2003.html.

[381] http://www.achpr.org.

[382] http://www1.umn.edu/humanrts/africa/comision.html.

[383] http://www1.umn.edu/humanrts/africa/comcases/comcases.html.

Recommended secondary sources are *International Human Rights Law in Africa* by Frans Viljoen[384] and *The African Charter on Human and Peoples' Rights: the System in Practice, 1986–2000.*[385] To find more, use the subject heading "Human rights–Africa" in the library catalog. Journals of note are *African Human Rights Law Journal,*[386] *East African Journal of Peace and Human Rights,*[387] and *South African Journal on Human Rights.*[388]

In 1998 the O.A.U. decided to establish an African Court on Human and Peoples' Rights. In 2002 the African Union (A.U.), successor to the O.A.U., was established. The judicial organ of the A.U. was to be the African Court of Justice. Then, in 2004 the A.U. decided to merge the two courts into one, to be called the African Court of Justice and Human Rights. If and when it comes into existence, the Court will have 15 judges and will sit in two sections, the General Affairs Section and the Human and Peoples' Rights Section. As of 2008, this had not yet happened.

5. Human Rights NGOs, Country Reports, and Secondary Sources

"NGO" is the abbreviation for "non-governmental organization." These are private associations of like-minded people that act on the international scene. NGOs are sometimes referred to as the main component of "international civil society." Human rights NGOs play an important role. They report in detail on human rights abuses around the world, they advocate for victims, they keep human rights issues in the public eye, and they assist and often criticize the performance of the official international human rights bodies. Two outstanding examples of human rights NGOs are Amnesty International[389] and Human Rights Watch.[390] There are many more. Directories of human rights NGOs are available on the World Wide Web.[391]

Both Amnesty International and Human Rights Watch publish annual reports on the human rights situation internationally and in virtually every country in the world. These are often called country reports. They are available in both hardcopy and on the World Wide Web.[392] In addition, the U.S. State Department is required to submit to Congress annual human rights country reports. These are most easily consulted at the State

---

[384] (Oxford University Press 2007).

[385] (Cambridge University Press 2d ed. 2008).

[386] (Juta Law 2001–).

[387] (Makerere University, Human Rights and Peace Centre 1993–).

[388] (Ravan Press 1985–).

[389] http://www.amnesty.org.

[390] http://www.hrw.org.

[391] *See, e.g.,* the link collections of the University of Minnesota Human Rights Library (http://www1.umn.edu/humanrts/links/ngolinks.html) and the Derechos NGO (http://www.derechos.net/links/ngo/all.html). *See also* HUMAN RIGHTS ORGANIZATIONS AND PERIODICALS DIRECTORY (Meiklejohn Civil Liberties Institute 12th ed. 2007).

[392] The formal titles are AMNESTY INTERNATIONAL REPORT and HUMAN RIGHTS WATCH WORLD REPORT. On the World Wide Web go to http://thereport.amnesty.org/eng/Homepage and http://www.hrw.org/wr2k5.

Department's website.[393] The State Department also submits annual reports on religious freedom[394] and trafficking in persons.[395]

Both Amnesty International and Human Rights Watch maintain extensive online libraries of their publications, usually available in full text without charge.

The secondary literature is massive. An efficient solution is to use the Library of Congress subject heading "Human rights." This heading can be subdivided by country, e.g., "Human rights–Colombia." As well, thematic searching is possible using Library of Congress subject headings or keyword searches, e.g., "Children's rights," "Detention of persons," "Disappeared persons," "Fair trial," "Freedom of expression," "Freedom of religion," "Political prisoners," and so on.

As to finding information on the World Wide Web, recommended is *HuriSearch*, which is a dedicated human rights search engine.[396] At the time of this writing (December 2008) it covers 4,500 human rights websites.

There are many journals devoted to human rights, and to their international legal protection in particular. There is space here only to mention some of the more significant or interesting ones in English:

- *Asia–Pacific Journal on Human Rights and the Law*[397]
- *East European Human Rights Review*[398]
- *Harvard Human Rights Journal*[399]
- *Human Rights Law Journal: HRLJ*[400]
- *Human Rights Law Review*[401]
- *Human Rights Quarterly*[402]
- *International Review of the Red Cross*[403]
- *Journal of Human Rights*[404]
- *Muslim World Journal of Human Rights*[405]
- *Netherlands Quarterly of Human Rights*[406]
- *Religion and Human Rights: An International Journal*[407]

---

[393] http://www.state.gov/g/drl/rls/hrrpt/. The hard copy can be found in collections of U.S. government documents, but it is published late.

[394] http://www.state.gov/g/drl/rls/irf.

[395] http://www.state.gov/g/tip/rls/tiprpt.

[396] http://www.hurisearch.org.

[397] (Kluwer Law 2000–).

[398] (BookWorld Publications 1995–).

[399] (Harvard Law School 1990–).

[400] (N.P. Engel 1980–).

[401] (Oxford University Press 2001–).

[402] (Johns Hopkins University Press 1981–).

[403] (International Committee of the Red Cross 1961–).

[404] (Carfax 2002–).

[405] This is a solely electronic publication. The URL is http://www.bepress.com/mwjhr/.

[406] (Kluwer Law 1989–).

[407] (Martinus Nijhoff 2006–).

- *Security and Human Rights*[408]

- *Yale Human Rights and Development Law Journal*[409]

In addition, the journals of general international law publish many articles on human rights. Use the standard law review research techniques to find these articles.

SECTION J.   ILLUSTRATIONS

21–1.   Unpublished International Agreements of the U.S. on the State Department Website

21–2.   Pages from Multilateral Section of Treaties in Force as Found on State Department Website

21–3.   Judgment of the International Court of Justice as Posted on the Court's Website

21–4.   Website of the United Nations High Commissioner for Human Rights

[408] (Martinus Nijhoff 2008–).

[409] (Yale Law School 1998–).

[Illustration 21–1]

UNPUBLISHED INTERNATIONAL AGREEMENTS OF THE U.S. ON THE STATE DEPARTMENT WEBSITE

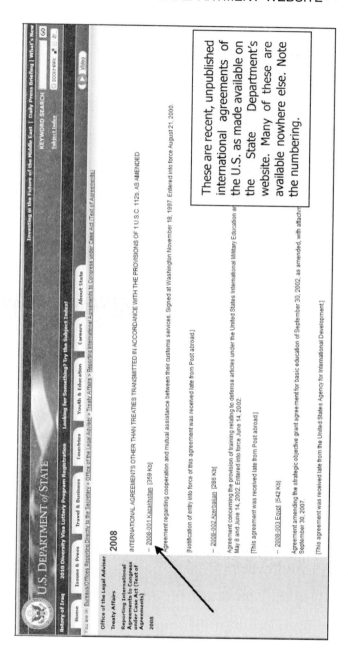

[Illustration 21–2]

PAGES FROM MULTILATERAL SECTION OF TREATIES IN FORCE AS FOUND ON STATE DEPARTMENT WEBSITE

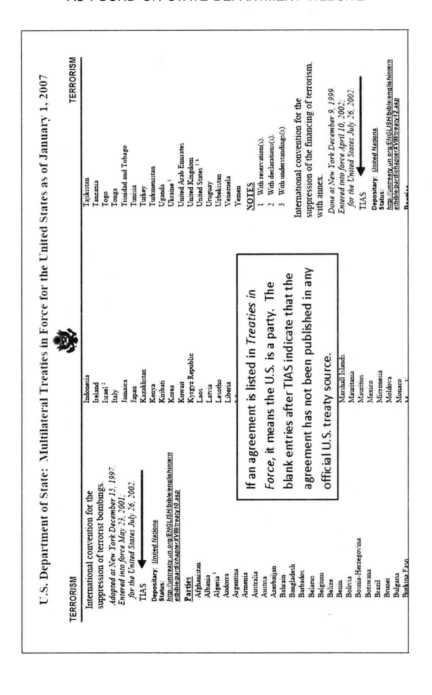

[Illustration 21–3]

JUDGMENT OF THE INTERNATIONAL COURT OF JUSTICE
AS POSTED ON THE COURT'S WEBSITE

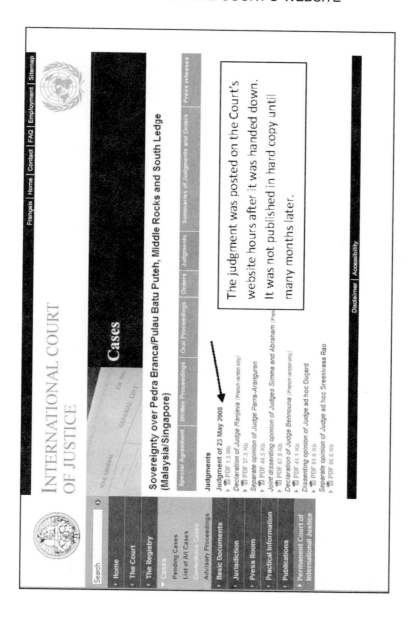

[Illustration 21–4]

WEBSITE OF THE UNITED NATIONS HIGH COMMISSIONER FOR HUMAN RIGHTS

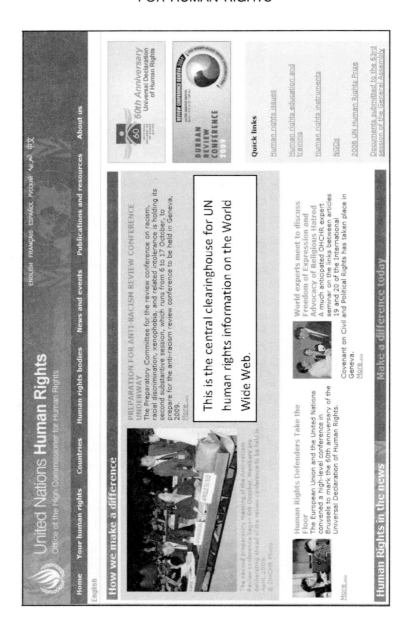

Chapter 22

LEGAL RESEARCH IN THE
UNITED KINGDOM*

The United Kingdom of Great Britain and Northern Ireland comprises four countries and three distinct legal systems. The countries, England, Wales, Scotland, and Northern Ireland, all share the same head of state, the Monarch. The existence of three legal systems is the result of arrangements made when the states unified (Wales with the 1535 *Laws in Wales Act*, Scotland with the 1707 *Act of Union*, and Northern Ireland in 1921 with the *Government of Ireland Act*).

Scotland and Northern Ireland have retained separate legal systems, evidenced by their different court structures, different legal professions, and, as a result of recent changes, different legislative bodies. Wales has some variances from England, but for the purposes of this chapter Wales is largely incorporated into the discussion of English legal research. The 1997 devolution[1] referendums changed the degree to which Scotland and, to a lesser extent, Wales are independent of the United Kingdom. As a result of the referendums and subsequent legislation, both Scotland and Wales now have their own legislative bodies with varying amounts of devolved authority.[2] The National Assembly for Wales and the Scottish Parliament opened in 1999. However, the U.K. Parliament in London, frequently referred to as "Westminster," continues to legislate on a variety of matters affecting the regions and all matters affecting the nation as a whole.

Following the 1998 "Good Friday" agreement,[3] the new Northern Ireland Assembly, a multiparty legislative body, was established to legislate over certain matters specific to that country. Disagreement between representatives of the Unionists and the Nationalists led to the suspension of the Assembly in October 2002. Following the acceptance of the St. Andrews Agreement and the successful Assembly elections in early 2007, full power was restored to the Assembly in May 2007.[4] In light of the recent history of Northern Ireland, it is difficult to assess the long-term implications of the new Assembly. The result of these relatively recent constitutional changes

---

* Stephen Young, Reference Librarian, Judge Kathryn J. DuFour Law Library, Catholic University of America, Columbus School of Law, Washington, D.C., wrote this chapter.

[1] Devolution has been defined as "The delegation by the central government to a regional authority of legislative or executive functions (or both) relating to domestic issues within the region." Oxford Dictionary of Law 140 (1997).

[2] The process of devolution is explored in Noreen Burrows, Devolution (2000).

[3] Agreement Reached in the Multi–Party Negotiations, April 10, 1998, 37 I.L.M. 751 (1998) [hereinafter Good Friday Agreement].

[4] http://niassembly.gov.uk/.

is a United Kingdom that resembles a federal system of government, and a legal research methodology not unfamiliar to researchers in the United States.

SECTION A. ENGLISH LAW

The sources of English law can be divided into four main categories: statutes and treaties; case law; custom and convention; and the laws of the European Union.[5] Perhaps the most fundamental difference between English law and the law of the United States is the lack of a written constitution. However, it would be incorrect to assume that a constitution does not exist. The reality is that all of the sources described above comprise the country's constitution, albeit unwritten. Constitutional law is, therefore, a melting pot of legislation enacted by Parliament, decisions rendered by the courts of law, various customs and conventions that must be adhered to, and laws imposed on member countries by the European Union.

SECTION B. ENGLISH PRIMARY LEGISLATION

1. The Parliamentary Process

Parliament is a bicameral legislative body consisting of the House of Commons and the House of Lords. The House of Commons is comprised of 646 elected Members of Parliament. The House of Lords, recently a subject of reform, is comprised of 91 hereditary peers (elected and appointed), 629 life peers, and 26 bishops. Some of the most useful sources of authoritative and up-to-date information on the Houses of Parliament are the *House of Commons Factsheets*. These are published on the Parliament website by the House of Commons Information Office and cover a variety of topics, including the workings of committees, the passage of legislation, and even the history of the House of Commons building.[6]

Bills are introduced into either the House of Commons or the House of Lords. Three classes of bills exist: public bills, which affect the general public; private bills, which affect either an individual or a company; and hybrid bills, which combine elements of public and private bills. Public bills introduced by a minister are referred to as *government bills*; those introduced by backbenchers[7] are referred to as *private members' bills*. Government bills usually survive the parliamentary process; only ten percent of private members' bills make it through both houses.

Copies of bills are printed by The Stationery Office and are made available on the Parliament website shortly after their initial reading.[8] Once introduced, bills must then undergo a second reading (where floor debate may occur), a committee (in the Commons it will usually be one of perhaps ten standing committees lettered A–J), a report, and a third reading. The bill is then referred to the second house, where it is again

---

[5] Gary Slapper & David Kelly, The English Legal System (7th ed. 2004).

[6] http://www.parliament.uk/parliamentary_publications_and_archives/factsheets.cfm.

[7] Members of Parliament who do not hold ministerial or shadow ministerial office are known as "backbenchers." They are so-called because they sit on the back benches of the House of Commons.

[8] http://www.parliament.uk/bills/bills.cfm.

considered and, if approved, sent back to the originating house for final approval. If approved, the bill then receives the Royal Assent[9] and becomes an act of Parliament. Amendments are usually made after the second reading, in committee, or after being referred to the second house for approval. A bill will fail if it does not pass through all these stages before the end of the parliamentary session. If, however, the bill is introduced in two successive sessions and is approved by the House of Commons, but not by the House of Lords, the bill may still become an act of Parliament (e.g., *The War Crimes Act 1991*).[10]

Citations to bills include the initials of the House in which the bill had its initial reading, the session of Parliament, and the bill number. A bill receives a new number when it undergoes substantial changes and when it is referred to the second chamber of Parliament. *The Weekly Information Bulletin of the House of Commons* is the most complete source for tracking amendments and bill numbers and for determining where in the parliamentary process the bill is at any given moment in time.

Legislation also can be traced through the parliamentary process by using *The Official Report of Debates ("Hansard")*, or by using the "Progress of Bills" section in *Current Law Monthly Digest*. *The Weekly Information Bulletin* and *Hansard* are available in full text on the Parliament website and are updated on a daily basis.[11] Major pieces of legislation are often accompanied by a research paper prepared by the House of Commons Library. These documents, available through the Parliament website, can provide valuable insights into the origins and purpose of the bill.

2. Acts of Parliament

Acts passed by Parliament are classified as either "private and local" or "public and general" acts.[12] Once they receive the Royal Assent, they are published individually by Her Majesty's Stationery Office (H.M.S.O.), a division of the Office of Public Sector Information, in a format known as the Queen's Printer's Copy. Full-text copies are made available on the O.P.S.I. website on the day of publication.[13] Acts passed during the year are bound together in annual, not sessional, volumes. The public acts, together with any General Synod Measures, have been published annually since 1831 as *The Public General Acts and Measures*. The last volume for each year contains an index and tables listing the acts alphabetically and chronologically. In addition, this last volume also contains tables that show *derivations and destinations* of the consolidated acts and the effect of each statute upon earlier measures.[14] Some libraries own *The Law Reports Statutes and Public General Acts,* a verbatim reprint of *The Public General*

---

[9] The Royal Assent is the equivalent to the presidential signature on an act of Congress; however, the Royal Assent has not been refused since 1707.

[10] A full discussion of the progress of a bill through Parliament is available in *Factsheet L1, The Parliamentary Stages of a Government Bill*, at http://www.parliament.uk/documents/upload/l01.pdf.

[11] http://www.publications.parliament.uk/pa/cm/cmpubns.htm.

[12] A more comprehensive treatment of acts of Parliament is available in DONALD GIFFORD, HOW TO UNDERSTAND AN ACT OF PARLIAMENT (1996).

[13] http://www.opsi.gov.uk/acts.htm.

[14] Measures are akin to acts passed by the Congress of the United States.

Acts and Measures published by the Incorporated Council of Law Reporting.

3. Compilations of Statutes

England has no official codification of all enactments of Parliament comparable to the *United States Code*. There is, however, current interest in codifying particular branches of the law, such as criminal law and family law. For this purpose, and to make recommendations for reform of various areas of the law, a Law Commission for England and Wales has been created.[15] In addition, from time to time Parliament passes a consolidated statute in which relevant acts and amendments thereto are consolidated into one act. A number of official and commercial compilations of statutes also are available to the researcher.

a. *The U.K. Statute Law Database (SLD).*[16] This is the official revised edition of the primary legislation of the United Kingdom. It takes over from its predecessor, *Statutes In Force: Official Revised Edition* which was last published in 1996. *SLD* is the official collection of all acts in force, as amended. It contains all acts since 1235 in effect and incorporates all amendments that add to or change the language of the original act.

b. *Halsbury's Statutes of England & Wales*, 4th ed. (1985). This commercially published set is a compilation of statutes in force arranged by subject, and is considered the principal hard-copy source of primary legislation in England and Wales. [Illustration 22–1] Valuable features include the liberal use of annotations and the frequency of revisions that reflect recent changes in legislation. Annotations follow each section of an act and provide references to several kinds of information, including administrative regulations passed under the authority of the act and cases interpreting language used in the act. The fourth edition of this set is comprised of the following components:

(1) *The 50 volumes of the main set.* Volumes are reissued from time to time to reflect amendments and incorporate additions.

(2) *Cumulative Supplement.* This volume is issued annually and compiles changes and additions to material in the main volumes. [Illustration 22–2]

(3) *Consolidated Index volume.* This volume is issued annually. It contains a general subject index to the entire set and an alphabetical and chronological table of statutes.

(4) *Noter-up service.* This looseleaf volume, used together with the *Cumulative Supplement,* updates the main set to within a few weeks of the most recent legislation.

(5) *Current Statutes Service binders.* These looseleaf volumes (lettered A–F) contain the full, annotated text of new acts that have not yet been incorporated into the main set. [Illustration 22–3]

---

[15] http://www.lawcom.gov.uk/index.htm.

[16] http://www.dca.gov.uk/lawdatfr.htm.

(6) *Destination Tables and Consolidated Table of Cases volumes*. These are the most recent additions to the set and provide useful information on the treatment and history of a statute.

(7) *Statutes Citator volume*. This is another recent addition to the set and serves to record changes to statutes by subsequent statutes.

c. *Current Law Statutes Service*. This set publishes the full text of all public and private acts once they have received the Royal Assent. The acts first appear in booklet format one month after publication by The Stationery Office and are filed in the Service File. Later, annotated versions of the acts for the current year are cumulated and published in annual volumes. The set includes a table of statutes dating back to 1700 and a table of parliamentary debates dating back to 1950.

d. *Butterworth's Annotated Guides to Legislation*. This is a very selective series that reprints the full text of acts considered important by the editors, together with extensive annotations and commentary. Individual acts constitute a single volume.

4. In Force Legislation

An act of Parliament may not necessarily become law, even though it has received the Royal Assent and has not been repealed. Acts of Parliament, either in part or in whole, are required to be "in force" before they are considered part of the law of the land. Therefore, an essential component of English legislative research is determining whether the act, either in whole or in part, is currently "in force" (i.e., carries with it the force of law).

Most acts contain within them a commencement provision. This provision is usually set forth near the end of the act alongside the short title and extent information (i.e., indicating that sections of the act do not apply to Scotland or Northern Ireland); it is possible, however, for commencement information to be spread throughout an act (thereby making research difficult). Section 4 of the *Interpretation Act 1978* (c. 30) states that a commencement provision may provide a date, either a fixed date or a date after an elapsed period of time (most commonly two months), on which either the whole act or designated sections of the act come into force. Or the provision may provide for a Minister of the Crown to determine when the act, or sections of it, should be brought into force (this is done through a piece of delegated legislation known as a "commencement order"). (See Section C for a discussion of delegated legislation.) If an act does not provide a commencement provision, it is assumed that the entire act comes into force on the date of the Royal Assent. Such assumptions are usually only necessary in the case of short or uncomplicated acts.

Determining whether an act or part of an act has been brought into force can be as simple as examining the commencement provision of the original act. There are other sources, however, that not only provide information on whether the act is yet in force but also whether it remains in force. Among these, the most widely used is the companion volume to *Halsbury's Statutes of England & Wales*, 4th ed., appropriately entitled *Is It In Force?* This single volume outlines the commencement status, section by section, of all acts passed in the last 25 years. The 25–year cut-off date can present some difficulties to the researcher needing to know whether a section of an older act has commenced, but most questions regarding the commencement of legislation can be answered using this source. An annual publication like *Is It In Force?* also has another limitation—very recent action is not included. In order to span this gap, the researcher must consult the *Statutes Citator* volume of *Halsbury's Statutes*.

The *SLD* provides the researcher with a new alternative to *Halsbury's*. The *SLD* contains commencement, repeal, and amendment information for acts.

5. Early English Statutes

Early English laws were published in many editions; the following statutory compilations comprise those most likely to be found in a law library in the United States.

a. *Statutes of the Realm*, 12 folio volumes, reproducing statutes enacted in the period 1225–1713. Published by the Record Commissioners, this set is considered the authoritative source for pre–1714 legislation (excluding the period of the Commonwealth). Some early statutes are reproduced in their original Latin or Norman French in addition to the English translation.

b. *Statutes at Large*. This series provides coverage of legislation for the period 1225–1869. The title is a generic term for a number of compilations of the early statutes. The original compilation is entitled *The Whole Volume of Statutes at Large* (1587); however a number of additional compilations share the same generic title. Arguably the most used compilation is by Danby Pickering and entitled *Statutes at Large from Magna Charta, to the End of the Eleventh Parliament of Great Britain, Anno 1761* [continued to 1806] (1807). This compilation is commonly referred to as "Pickering's Statutes." Another frequently cited compilation is the nine-volume set published by Owen Ruffhead between 1763 and 1765.[17]

6. Acts and Ordinances of the Interregnum, 1642–1660

This is a selected three-volume integration of the laws enacted during the Interregnum.[18] The third volume of this set includes a Chronological Table of Acts and Ordinances, an Index to Subjects, and an Index of Names, Places, and Things.

7. Electronic Access to English Statutes

The formation of The Stationery Office in 1996 not only led to an overhaul of the way in which official print material was made available, but also began a revolution in the availability of official government material on the World Wide Web.

Very soon after the creation of The Stationery Office, legislative documents, including official, full-text versions of parliamentary bills and

[17] A more complete discussion of the early statute compilations is available in WILLIAM HOLDSWORTH, 11 A HISTORY OF ENGLISH LAW 287 (1938).

[18] The Interregnum is the interval between the end of the reign of Charles I and the beginning of the reign of his successor, Charles II. During this period the country was governed as a commonwealth.

acts of Parliament, appeared on the Internet. Over the past few years websites, such as *parliament.uk*[19] and *official-documents.co.uk*,[20] have developed rapidly and now publish a wide variety of legislative material, including debate from both houses of Parliament, reports from committees, bill-tracking information, bills, acts, and other parliamentary documents. Although the Parliament website provides extensive coverage of the workings of Parliament and thus serves as an indispensable tool in tracking legislation, it does not provide the text of acts. The full text of acts can be located on the Office of Public Sector Information's *Legislation* website.[21]

The most recent development in the area of online access to statutory information was the release of the aforementioned *U.K. Statute Law Database* in late 2006. The *SLD* is maintained by the Department for Constitutional Affairs and provides free access to most types of legislation, both primary and secondary. The legislation is offered in revised form, meaning that it incorporates any amendments made to it by subsequent legislation. The database includes legislation dating back to 1267's *Statute of Marlborough*, the oldest statute containing provisions still in force.

The following services, all but one of which are fee-based, also provide access to valuable legislative material.[22]

a. *LexisNexis. LexisNexis*, a fee-based service, has a file of U.K. statutes comprising the full, amended text of all public general acts that are currently in force. Legislation that has been recently enacted but is not yet in force is also included.

b. *Westlaw. Westlaw*, a fee-based service, has developed a useful database of in-force English primary legislation. *Westlaw* provides coverage of current and historic legislation. The Law In Force coverage for statutes begins in 1267 and is consolidated through the current year.

c. *BAILII.* In 2000, the British and Irish Legal Information Institute (BAILII) began electronic publication of a database designed to provide hypertext-linked, full-text versions of primary legislation and case law for the United Kingdom.[23] The legislative content for this database is obtained from the Office of Public Sector Information and is therefore essentially identical to the material found on the O.P.S.I.'s *Legislation* website.

d. *LexisNexis Butterworth's Legislation Direct.* This is a fee-based service providing users with the full text of in-force statutes.[24] A bill-tracking service is also available.

e. *Justis.* This is a fee-based database containing all acts of Parliament for England, Wales, and Scotland dating back to 1235.[25]

[19] http://www.parliament.uk/.

[20] http://www.official-documents.gov.uk/.

[21] *See supra* note 13.

[22] Throughout this chapter references to *Westlaw* and *LexisNexis* refer to the content available through U.S. subscriptions to these services. It should be noted that separate U.K. subscriptions may contain different content.

[23] http://www.bailii.org.

[24] http://www.butterworths.com/butterworths.asp.

[25] http://www.justis.com/titles/titles.html.

8. Citation of English Statutes

Prior to 1963, English statutes were cited by name, regnal year (the year of the sovereign's reign spanned by the parliamentary session in which the statute was passed), and chapter, e.g., *National Services Act, 11 & 12 Geo. 6*, c. 64. In this example the act was passed during the parliamentary session that spanned the 11th and 12th years of the reign of King George VI. It should be noted that a parliamentary session usually begins in November and concludes either the following autumn or earlier in an election year. The regnal year citation form requires that the year of passage of a statute be determined. As all legal writing on English law prior to 1963 cited to regnal year, a table of regnal years is set forth below for convenience.

TABLE OF REGNAL YEARS

Sovereign	Reign Began
William I	Oct. 14, 1066
William II	Sept. 26, 1087
Henry I	Aug. 5, 1100
Stephen	Dec. 26, 1135
Henry II	Dec. 19, 1154
Richard I	Sept. 3, 1189
John	May 27, 1199
Henry III	Oct. 28, 1216
Edward I	Nov. 20, 1272
Edward II	July 8, 1307
Edward III	Jan. 25, 1327
Richard II	June 22, 1377
Henry IV	Sept. 30, 1399
Henry V	Mar. 21, 1413
Henry VI	Sept. 1, 1422
Edward IV	Mar. 4, 1461
Edward V	Apr. 9, 1483
Richard III	June 26, 1483
Henry VII	Aug. 22, 1485
Henry VIII	Apr. 22, 1509
Edward VI	Jan. 28, 1547
Mary	July 6, 1553
Elizabeth I	Nov. 17, 1558
James I	Mar. 24, 1603
Charles I	Mar. 27, 1625
The Commonwealth	Jan. 30, 1649
Charles II	May 29, 1660
James II	Feb. 6, 1685
William & Mary	Feb. 13, 1689
Anne	Mar. 8, 1702
George I	Aug. 1, 1714
George II	June 11, 1727
George III	Oct. 25, 1760
George IV	Jan. 29, 1820
William IV	June 26, 1830
Victoria	June 20, 1837
Edward VII	Jan. 22, 1901
George V	May 6, 1910
Edward VIII	Jan. 20, 1936
George VI	Dec. 11, 1936
Elizabeth II	Feb. 6, 1952

The Acts of Parliament Numbering and Citation Act 1962, which came into force in 1963, changed this form of citation. Under provisions of this statute, citation to an act is to the short name of the act and calendar year in which it was passed, e.g., *The Football Spectators Act 1999*. Since 1898, each act of Parliament includes a section indicating the title of the act by which it is to be cited.

SECTION C. ENGLISH SECONDARY LEGISLATION

The term *secondary legislation*, sometimes known as *delegated legislation*, comprises the body of law referred to as administrative law in the United States. The Statutory Instruments (formerly called Statutory Rules and Orders) made[26] by Ministers of the Crown are the English equivalent to the rules and regulations published in the United States in the *Federal Register* and compiled in the *Code of Federal Regulations*. Statutory Instruments are orders, rules, and regulations promulgated by the Ministers under authority delegated to them by Parliament. Bylaws made by local governmental or other authorities exercising power conferred upon them by Parliament also are included in this body of material.

1. Publication of Statutory Instruments

Statutory Instrument (or SI) is a generic term derived from the *Statutory Instruments Act 1946*,[27] applicable to four types of delegated legislation: orders; rules; regulations; and bylaws. Prior to 1948 (when the act came into force), SIs were referred to as S.R. & O.s (Statutory Rules and Orders); prior to 1894, orders and proclamations were cited by their title and date. It should be noted that the use of Statutory Instruments has grown rapidly and reflects the increasing complexity of society.[28] Prior to the middle of the nineteenth century, relatively few pieces of secondary legislation were promulgated. Typically, The Stationery Office, on any given weekday, publishes numerous SIs, and almost 3,000 annually are brought into force. Each SI is assigned a number based on the sequential order in which it is passed in the calendar year, (e.g., SI 2008/1068 is the 1,068th SI passed in 2008). A letter may appear in parenthesis after the citation indicating a particular subseries of SI. The main subseries are: C (commencement orders); L (legal matters, e.g., court rules); and W (Welsh only).

a. *Statutory Instruments*. SIs are first listed in the *Daily List of Government Publications* (available in hard copy and on the Internet),[29] and are then made available online and in full text on the O.P.S.I.'s website.[30] SIs are also often listed in the major legal periodicals, e.g., *Solicitor's*

---

[26] The word "made" is a term of art used to describe the creation or promulgation of delegated legislation.

[27] Statutory Instruments Act, 9 & 10 Geo. 6, c. 36 (1946).

[28] PETER CLINCH, USING A LAW LIBRARY: A STUDENT'S GUIDE TO LEGAL RESEARCH SKILLS 71 (2d ed. 2001).

[29] http://www.tsoshop.co.uk/.

[30] http://www.opsi.gov.uk/stat.htm.

Journal and *New Law Journal*. Digests of SIs are available in the monthly issues of *Current Law*; the full text of SIs appear in unannotated, annual bound volumes published by H.M.S.O., entitled simply *Statutory Instruments* (this set dates back to 1946). The *List of Statutory Instruments*, which is published monthly and cumulated annually, provides helpful tables and summaries of new SIs.

b. *Halsbury's Statutory Instruments*. Although this set is selective in providing the full text of delegated legislation, it does at least offer a summary of all SIs currently in force. SIs are selected for full-text inclusion based on their relative importance to the legal community. This multivolume work is arranged alphabetically by subject-based titles and contains, in addition to the 22 base volumes (nine of which are reissued annually), a Consolidated Index and Alphabetical List of Statutory Instruments volume, an E.C. Legislation Implementation volume, and a looseleaf service binder. The looseleaf binder contains useful tables (list of authorizing statutes, chronological list of SIs, commencement orders), an annual supplement to the base volumes, a monthly survey with an accompanying key to the base volumes, and the full text of selected new SIs arranged in numerical order.

Halsbury's Statutory Instruments is useful in tracing delegated legislation on a particular subject; the set can also be used to trace SIs by their title and even their citation (although the O.P.S.I. website may prove to be more convenient for this type of search). Each SI is annotated with case citations, and an overview of the relevant SIs is provided at the beginning of each title. Each title also contains a complete list of the SIs that have been summarized and a list of SIs no longer in force, e.g., those that have been repealed or superseded. New volumes are published periodically and may not be indexed until the following the annual index.

2. Electronic Access to Statutory Instruments

Since 1997, the most convenient way to locate individual SIs is the O.P.S.I. website, which now contains the full text of individual SIs promulgated since 1987 (explanatory memorandum are available for early 2004 to present).[31] A search engine is available on the website to assist in the location of instruments. Welsh and Scottish SIs are available on separate websites. Secondary legislation for Northern Ireland is discussed in Section O of this chapter.

a. *LexisNexis*. The *LexisNexis* Library of UK materials contains the full, amended text of all public general SIs currently in force. It is updated weekly and is a fee-based service.

b. *Westlaw*. *Westlaw* coverage for SIs begins with 1948 and is kept relatively up-to-date. In addition to the in force SIs, a separate database contains historical versions of certain SIs beginning with 1992. *Westlaw* is a fee-based service.

c. *BAILII*. Coverage of SIs corresponds to the coverage on the official O.P.S.I. website.

[31] *Id.*

d. *Justis.* This is a fee-based service providing users with coverage of secondary legislation from 1671 to the present.[32]

3. The National Assembly for Wales

The National Assembly for Wales, located in the principality's capital, Cardiff, came into existence on July 1, 1999. Although the Assembly was not initially granted powers under the *Government of Wales Act 1998* to make primary legislation, it has recently been granted very limited primary law making authority under the *Government of Wales Act 2006.*[33]

The Assembly is comprised of 60 elected members. It is led by the Presiding Officer, who is elected by Assembly members, and an Assembly Commission comprised of seven others. The proceedings of the Assembly, including background information and documents presented to the Assembly, are available on the National Assembly of Wales website.[34] Legislation made by the Assembly, in the form of Statutory Instruments or Assembly Measures, is published by O.P.S.I. on the Welsh Legislation website.[35] All documents produced by or on behalf of the Assembly are available in English and Welsh. Welsh SIs are identified by a parenthetical reference to Wales in the title and number of the citation, e.g., SI 2000/1079 (W. 72) *The Homelessness (Wales) Regulations 2000. Westlaw* and *LexisNexis* provide coverage of legislation made by the National Assembly.

SECTION D. ENGLISH CASE LAW

1. English Court Organization

The modern organization of the English court system began with *The Judicature Act 1873* and continued into the twentieth century with subsequent Parliamentary legislation, such as the *Courts Act of 1971,* and the handover of the administration of the courts to The Court Service in 1995.[36] In addition, significant changes in the civil justice system followed the Woolf Inquiry in 1996 and the adoption of the new *Civil Procedure Rules 1998.*[37] Recent changes include the passage of the *Courts Act 2003* and the proposal for a new Supreme Court of the United Kingdom.[38]

a. *House of Lords.* This body, in addition to its legislative function, serves as the supreme court of appeal for the United Kingdom in civil cases and the final court of appeal for criminal cases from England, Wales, and Northern Ireland.

[32] http://www.justis.com/titles/uk_statutory_instruments.html.

[33] For a more complete discussion of the Assembly's powers, see http://www.assemblywales.org.htm.

[34] http://new.wales.gov.uk/?lang=en.

[35] http://www.opsi.gov.uk/legislation/wales/w-stat.htm.

[36] The Court Service merged with the Magistrates' Courts Service on April 1, 2005, forming Her Majesty's Courts Service.

[37] The most useful source for timely, authoritative information on rules of procedure and changes in the justice system is the Ministry of Justice website, at http://www.justice.gov.uk/guidance/guidance.htm.

[38] *See* http://www.justice.gov.uk/whatwedo/supremecourt.htm.

b. *Supreme Court of Judicature.* This is the name given to three different courts: Court of Appeal; High Court of Justice; and Crown Court.

(1) Court of Appeal. This court has two divisions—civil and criminal. It hears appeals from the High Court of Justice and certain other inferior courts.

(2) High Court of Justice. This court now consists of three divisions: Queen's Bench Division (including the Admiralty Court and Commercial Court); Chancery Division; and Family Division.[39] In practice, each division acts as a separate court.

(3) Crown Court. This court was created by the *Courts Act 1971*. It is a criminal court with general jurisdiction. As the main criminal court of England, it tries serious criminal cases and hears appeals from the Magistrates' Courts.

c. *County Courts.* There are 218 County Courts. These courts have broad first-instance civil jurisdiction.

d. *Magistrates' Courts.* The Magistrates' Courts play a significant role in the criminal courts structure. These courts handle the majority of minor criminal cases and some "either way" cases (criminal cases in which a "hybrid" offense has occurred).

2. Development of English Court Reports

The history of court reporting in England dates back to the thirteenth century.[40] The reporting of English cases can be divided into three distinct periods.

a. *Year Books*, 1272–1537. The *Year Books*, originally written in Law French,[41] are the first available law reports. Their purpose and function are still disputed by legal historians, although it is widely believed that their original purpose was more educational than practical. Cases from the *Year Books* are still cited on occasion, but the *Year Books* are now largely used for historical research. The Selden Society has reprinted most of the *Year Books*, together with English translations.[42]

b. *Nominate* Reports, 1537–1865. During the period from 1535 to 1865 there was no officially recognized system of court reporting. Any reporter could publish court reports, and although commentators argue over the exact number that were published, what we do know with some

---

[39] Prior to the enactment of the *Courts Act 1971*, the High Court of Justice consisted of: Queen's Bench Division; Probate, Divorce, and Admiralty Division; and Chancery Division.

[40] For a detailed treatment of the development of English court reporting, see RICHARD WARD, WALKER & WALKER'S ENGLISH LEGAL SYSTEM (10th ed. 2008). *See also* John H. Baker, *Dr. Thomas Fastoff and the History of Law Reporting*, 45 CAMBRIDGE L.J. 84 (1986); WILLIAM SEARLE HOLDSWORTH, SOURCES AND LITERATURE OF ENGLISH LAW (1925). Law students who think reading old English cases is a useless exercise should read David V. Stivison, *The Practical Uses of Legal History*, 33 PRAC. LAW. 27 (1987). The author discusses how some of these old cases can be useful in a modern practice of law.

[41] Law French refers to "[t]he corrupted form of the Norman French language that arose in England in the centuries after William the Conqueror invaded England in 1066 and that was used for several centuries as the primary language of the English legal system." BRIAN A. GARNER, BLACK'S LAW DICTIONARY 902 (8th ed. 2004).

[42] http://www.selden-society.qmw.ac.uk/.

certainty is that many of them covered the same period of time and the same courts with varying degrees of accuracy.[43] It has been customary to refer to these reports by the names of the reporters—hence their generic name, *nominate reports*. Many of the cases reported in the various nominate reports have been reprinted in the following sets.

(1) *English Reports, Full Reprint.* This is a reprint of the nominate reports and some *Year Books* from 1220 to 1865. When there were competing sets of reports, the editors included only the set they deemed most accurate. There are 176 volumes in this set, including a two-volume Table of Cases and a separate wall chart that lists all the nominate reports with reference to their location in the *Full Reprint.* This set is more widely available in American law libraries than many of the individual nominate reports and is considered the standard source for pre–1865 English cases. The entire set, together with accompanying charts and indexes, is available electronically in full text on *HeinOnline.*

(2) *The Revised Reports.* The Revised Reports are in 149 volumes and cover the period 1785 to 1865. Although this set largely duplicates *The English Reports, Full Reprint,* its value lies in the contributions of its editor, Sir Frederick Pollock, a distinguished legal scholar. Pollock not only selected cases, he also edited and combined cases to provide a more accurate reflection of the law.

(3) *The All England Law Reports Reprint.* This set covers selected cases from 1558 to 1935. The cases, arranged in 36 volumes, are chosen from the nominate reports and *The Law Times Reports* (a Victorian weekly periodical that selectively published reports of cases). Those cases selected were deemed to be of most use to the legal profession at the time of publication.

c. *The Law Reports,* 1865 to present. As a result of the inconsistent and overlapping nature of many of the nominate reports, the Incorporated Council of Law Reporting for England and Wales was formed in 1865. The Incorporated Council is a registered charity consisting of members nominated by the Inns of Court and by the General Counsel of the bar. As such, it has quasi-official status. Shortly after formation, the Council began publication of *The Law Reports.* This series, discussed more fully below, has become the preeminent series of court reports in England and Wales and is available electronically on both *LexisNexis* and *Westlaw.*

3. Modern Law Reports

As previously mentioned, cases reported before 1865 are available in each of *The English Reports, Full Reprint* or *The Revised Reports.* English cases decided since 1865 can be found in the following:

a. *The Law Reports.* This set reports selected decisions since 1865; it includes decisions of permanent significance of the House of Lords, the Judicial Committee of the Privy Council, the Court of Appeal, and the High Court of Justice. In addition to the opinions of the judges, it also includes the legal arguments presented to the courts. Although originally published

---

[43] The most useful treatments of the nominate reports are Van Vechten Veeder, *The English Reports 1292–1865*, 15 HARV. L. REV. 1 (1901), and Van Vechten Veeder, *The English Reports 1292–1865 II*, 15 HARV. L. REV. 109 (1901).

in 11 different series, *The Law Reports* are now published in four series: (1) *Appeal Cases* (includes decisions of the House of Lords and of the Judicial Committee of the Privy Council); (2) *Queen's Bench*; (3) *Chancery*; and (4) *Family Division*. Decisions of the Court of Appeal are published in the last three series.

b.   *Weekly Law Reports.* This set is also published by the Incorporated Council of Law Reporting and includes many cases that will ultimately be published in *The Law Reports*. It is issued first in weekly pamphlets and then in annual bound volumes. *The Weekly Law Reports* also include cases not intended for publication in *The Law Reports*. These cases appear in the first of the three volumes published each year. It should be noted that arguments of counsel are not included in *The Weekly Law Reports*.

c.   *The All England Law Reports and Other Sets of Reports.* Although the Incorporated Council of Law Reporting assumed responsibility for systematizing court reporting, there is no prohibition of private reporting and many such sets are published. The most important of the private reports is *The All England Law Reports*. This set began in 1936 and incorporated both *The Law Journal Reports* and *The Times Law Reports* (reports of cases published in *The Times* newspaper). *The All England Law Reports* includes the decisions of the House of Lords, Court of Appeal, High Court of Justice, and courts of special jurisdiction. The opinions are released in advance sheets and then in bound volumes. [Illustration 22–4] A great number of cases are reported only in either the daily newspapers or in professional journals. Accordingly, it is not uncommon to see citations to *The Times* or *The Law Society Gazette*.

4.   Electronic Access to English Cases

a.   *LexisNexis. LexisNexis* includes a library of English cases dating back to 1558, including all cases decided after 1865 and reported in *The All England Law Reports, The Law Reports, Lloyd's Law Reports* (a reporter for maritime and commercial cases), and a number of specialized reporters. Otherwise unreported decisions may also be available in *LexisNexis*.

b.   *Westlaw.* Included in *Westlaw*'s U.K. materials is a database of case reports, including *The Law Reports* and *The Weekly Law Reports* dating back to 1865.

c.   *BAILII.* The British and Irish Legal Information Institute's website includes High Court of Justice, Court of Appeal, and House of Lords decisions dating back to 1996.[44]

d.   *Additional Electronic Resources.* Judgments from the House of Lords are made available in full text on the Parliament website within two hours of the decision being rendered.[45] Among the many commercial databases providing access to case law, *Justis* has one of the more complete collections, including access to *The English Reports, The Law Reports, The Times Law Reports*, and a number of specialist reporters.[46] *HeinOnline*

---

[44] *Supra* note 23.

[45] House of Lords judgments are available on the Parliament website, at http://www. publications.parliament.uk/pa/ld/ldjudgmt.htm.

[46] *Supra* note 25.

provides the only searchable full-text version of *The English Reports, Full Reprint*.

5. Citation of English Cases

Many American legal researchers are uncomfortable researching English case law due to a lack of familiarity with English case citation rules. Some general rules that apply to English case law research are set forth below.[47]

a. Cites include the year in brackets when it is essential to finding the case, e.g., [1969] 1 All E.R. 210, and the year in parenthesis when the volume number is sequential from year to year. All of *The Law Reports* series and many of the other major reports adopt the bracketed style of citation.

b. In the United States the government is identified in the style of the case by the terms "State" or "United States" or "U.S." In the United Kingdom, by contrast, the government (i.e., The Crown) is usually identified by the letter "R." (the R indicating Regina or Rex depending on which monarch is reigning at the time the action is brought). Cases involving the Crown are thus cited as R. v defendant.

c. When speaking of the parties in civil cases, they are referred to as Smith *and* Jones rather than Smith *versus* Jones, although they are cited in the written form as *Smith* v *Jones*. In criminal cases the parties are referred to as the Crown *against* Williams, not *versus*; citation would take the form *R.* v *Williams*. Most case indexes use the initial letter "R." When citing English cases, the names of the parties are in italics, the "v" is not in italics, and the "v" is not followed by a period.

d. Some of the more common reporter abbreviations include:[48]

AC–Law Reports Appeal Cases [2001] AC 53

QB–Law Reports Queens Bench Division [2001] 1 QB 53

Ch–Law Reports Chancery Division [2001] 1 Ch 53

Fam–Law Reports Family Division [2001] Fam 53

All ER–All England Law Reports [2001] 2 All ER 53

ER–English Reports, Full Reprint (1802) 3 Bos. & Pul. 116, 127 ER 62[49]

JP–Justice of the Peace Reports (2001) 165 JP 53

e. Beginning in 2001, the Court of Appeal and parts of the High Court adopted a format-neutral citation system, which cites to the case name, year, case number, court, and paragraph number (e.g., W [2004] EWHC 1000 (Ch) [5]–[7]). A Practice Direction issued in 2002 by the Lord

---

[47] For more complete information on citing legal materials from the U.K., see DEREK FRENCH, HOW TO CITE LEGAL AUTHORITIES (1996).

[48] A fairly comprehensive index of abbreviations and citations is described in Section G–3 of this chapter.

[49] Note that citations to THE ENGLISH REPORTS, FULL REPRINT should also include a full reference to the original nominate report.

Chief Justice further extended the format-neutral citation system to all parts of the High Court.[50]

SECTION E. DIGESTS AND ENCYCLOPEDIAS

1. Digests

The Digest: Annotated British, Commonwealth and European Cases. Prior to 1981, this set was entitled *The English and Empire Digest.* It is a comprehensive digest of over 500,000 English cases reported from the earliest times to the present and consists of 99 volumes. It also includes cases from the courts of Scotland, Ireland, Canada, and other countries of the British Commonwealth and South Africa. Cases of only historical interest are excluded from the publication. *The Digest* is arranged topically and has a detailed outline at the beginning of each major subject area and an index at the end of each volume. Cases on a particular aspect of a general topic are grouped in chronological order and assigned case numbers.

The Digest has an annotated index that provides subsequent citation information. Each case annotation is followed by notes of subsequent citing cases, if any, indicating whether the annotated case has been approved, followed, distinguished, overruled, or otherwise mentioned. Under each section or subsection of *The Digest*, cross-references and references to pertinent statutes and to *Halsbury's Laws of England & Wales*, 4th ed. (described below) are given. There is a three volume Consolidated Table of Cases and a two volume Consolidated Index. *The Digest* is updated with reissue volumes, annual cumulative supplements, and quarterly surveys (i.e., updates).

2. Encyclopedias

The premier English encyclopedia for both statutory and case law is *Halsbury's Laws of England,* 4th edition (a 5th edition of this set began publication in 2008). This set should not be confused with *Halsbury's Statutes of England & Wales,* a previously described collection of legislation.

Halsbury's Laws of England, consisting of over 80 volumes, is alphabetically arranged by topic. Each topic is subdivided into parts, sections, subsections, and paragraphs with appropriate footnote references to cases, statutes, and statutory instruments. An annual cumulative supplement, an Annual Abridgment volume, and two Current Service looseleaf volumes containing a noter-up service and monthly reviews update the set. The electronic version of *Halsbury's Laws of England, Halsbury's Laws Direct,* is available as part of the *Butterworth's LexisNexis Direct* suite of databases. [Illustration 22–5]

3. Current Law

Current Law, dating from 1947, provides a digest of English law. It is arranged topically and, under each topic, sets forth annotations of cases,

---

[50] http://www.hmcourts-service.gov.uk/cms/816.htm.

statutes, statutory instruments, and recent books and periodical articles. The publications consist of the following:

a. *Current Law Monthly Digest.* This is a monthly pamphlet advance sheet service that includes a number of useful case, statute, and statutory instrument tables.

b. *Current Law Year Book.* This annual cumulation includes, among other information, a cumulative subject index, table of cases, tables of statutory instruments and instruments affected, and digests of unreported cases.

c. *Master Volume.* The *Current Law Year Books* were consolidated into a 1947–51 volume; since then, a five-year cumulative *Year Book* entitled the *Master Volume* is published every five years.

d. *Current Law Citators.* These volumes are discussed in Section F of this chapter.

Elements of the *Current Law* suite of publications also form part of *Current Legal Information (CLI)*, an electronic service from Sweet & Maxwell which also includes *Legal Journals Index.*

SECTION F. CITATORS/NOTING UP

Nothing exactly corresponding to *Shepard's Citations* materials exists for English law. There are, however, several methods of obtaining later citations or, to use the correct term, *noting up* cases or statutes.[51]

1. Statutes

Citators for statutes are arranged chronologically. As a general rule, citations are given to each subsequent statute that amends or repeals the cited statute, and to each case that cites the statute. The primary resource for determining the status of legislation is the *U.K. Statute Law Database,* described in Section B of this chapter; however additional citators for statutes are contained in the resources described below:

a. *Chronological Tables of the Statutes.* This publication consists of a detailed status table of all English statutes giving their status section-by-section. The researcher can tell whether a particular part of a statute of interest has been repealed, amended, or otherwise modified (but not what cites to it). A more specialized tool, *The Chronological Tables of Local and of Private Acts,* covering the period 1539–2006, is available online on the O.P.S.I. website.[52]

b. *Current Law Statute Citator.* These volumes update legislation between specified dates, while paperback volumes bring the set up to date. Citations to cases construing legislation are included. Statutory Instruments have also been included in this set since 1993. The content from these publications is available electronically as part of the *CLI* suite of databases.

---

[51] For a more detailed description of this topic, see Stephen Young, *"Shepardizing" English Law,* 90 LAW LIBR. J. 209 (1998).

[52] http://www.opsi.gov.uk/chron-tables/chron-index.htm.

c. *The All England Law Reports, Consolidated Tables and Index.* The Tables volumes contain an extensive listing of statutes considered, with citations to cases in the *The All England Law Reports.*

2. Cases

a. *The Digest.* This publication works both as a tool for finding cases by subject and as a citator. When there are later cases of note, the digest summary of the main case is followed immediately by an annotations paragraph citing to later cases that consider or cite to the main case.

b. *Current Law Case Citator.* A variety of volumes are used in conjunction with each other to cover the period from 1947 to the present. References set forth the citation to the main case and to the paragraph of the *Current Law Yearbook* containing annotations of later cases on point. The content from these publications is available electronically as part of the *CLI* suite of databases.

c. *The All England Law Reports, Consolidated Tables and Index 1936–2007.* Volume 1 contains a cumulative table of cases reported and considered. Cases are listed alphabetically with each case followed by citations to later cases reported in *The All England Law Reports.*

d. *The Index to The Law Reports. The Index to The Law Reports* (popularly known as the "Red" and "Pink" indexes) provides a table of Cases Judicially Considered and a table of Statutes Judicially Considered. Despite their official title, the "Red" and "Pink" indexes do much more than merely index cases to *The Law Reports.* Also included are references to cases reported in *Industrial Cases, Lloyd's Law Reports, Road Traffic Reports, Tax Cases, Criminal Appeal Reports, Local Government Reports,* and *The All England Law Reports.* The advance sheets to *The Weekly Law Reports* also include lists of cases judicially considered.

SECTION G.   REFERENCE TOOLS

1. Court Rules

The *Civil Procedure Rules* are published biennially in the traditional "White Book" (formally known as *Supreme Court Practice*) and are available, together with Practice Directions and recent updates, on the Ministry of Justice website.[53] The *Criminal Procedure Rules* are also available from the Ministry of Justice website.[54]

2. Directories

The *Waterlow's Solicitors' and Barristers' Directory* is an extensive directory, published annually, that is arranged by geographical location (London first), name of individual, and name of firm. Areas of specialization for law firms are provided. After the listings for solicitors are entries for barristers by chambers (London followed by the provinces) and by name. This is the *Martindale–Hubbell* of Britain (Scotland is also represented). A limited version of *Waterlow's* is also available on the Internet.[55]

---

[53] http://www.justice.gov.uk/civil/procrules_fin/index.htm.

[54] http://www.justice.gov.uk/criminal/procrules_fin/index.htm.

[55] http://www.waterlowlegal.com/index.htm.

The Law Society also provides a web-based directory for locating solicitors in England and Wales.[56]

3. Abbreviations

The *Cardiff Index to Legal Abbreviations* is a relatively recent addition to the growing list of web-based legal reference sources.[57] This resource is particularly useful and has quickly become an indispensable tool for all legal researchers. The *Index to Legal Citations and Abbreviations* (2d ed. 1993) is the most comprehensive hardcopy listing of abbreviations used in English legal research. It is often referred to by the author's last name, "Raistrick's."

4. Words and Phrases

A number of the standard English legal publications include definitions of words and phrases. Many of these publications are discussed in the preceding sections. Several other sources exclusively treat judicial interpretations of words and phrases.

a. *Stroud's Judicial Dictionary of Words and Phrases* (7th ed. 2007). This three-volume publication includes not only definitions but also references to cases and statutes from which they are derived. It is kept current by annual supplements.

b. *Words and Phrases Legally Defined* (4th ed. 2007). A revision of Burrow's *Words and Phrases Judicially Defined,* this work has been expanded to include treatise and statutory, as well as judicial, definitions. A cumulative supplement is published annually.

5. Internet Resources

The nature of Internet resources is such that it is difficult to provide a listing that contains both authoritative and stable websites. The following selective list includes only those websites that have stood the test of time and have provided reliable, authoritative information.

a. *Lawlinks*.[58] Compiled by the Library staff at the University of Kent at Canterbury, this is one of the most extensive "legal portals" for U.K. material. Information is organized by type of material and by jurisdiction. This website is regularly updated and logically arranged.

b. *Official Documents*.[59] The Stationery Office administers this useful compilation of links to official websites. The material can be accessed by document title, date of publication, or category of material.

c. *Legal Resources in the U.K. & Ireland*.[60] Delia Venables maintains this portal to legal material of the United Kingdom. The material on this comprehensive website is arranged according to the type of user. The comprehensive nature of this website makes it a "must visit" among the U.K. Internet resources.

[56] http://www.lawsociety.org.uk/choosingandusing/findasolicitor.law.

[57] http://www.legalabbrevs.cardiff.ac.uk/.

[58] http://www.kent.ac.uk/lawlinks/.

[59] http://www.official-documents.gov.uk/.

[60] http://www.venables.co.uk/.

d. *BAILII.*[61] The British and Irish Legal Information Institute has created one of the most comprehensive databases of legislation and judgments for the various jurisdictions within the United Kingdom.

SECTION H. SCOTLAND

Scotland has been a member country of the United Kingdom since the 1707 *Act of Union*. The country has retained its own legal system and has recently been granted a certain amount of home rule.[62] The origins and sources of Scottish law are different from those associated with English law. A heavy reliance on the Civil and Roman law tradition encouraged the development of a different legal system and, therefore, a different system of legal research.[63] In recent years the establishment of a new Scottish Parliament has dramatically changed the constitutional status of Scotland and its role as a member of the United Kingdom.[64]

SECTION I. SCOTTISH PRIMARY LEGISLATION

1. The Scottish Parliament

Since July 1, 1999, when the Scottish Parliament assumed its powers granted under *The Scotland Act 1998*, primary legislation affecting Scotland has been issued either by the U.K. Parliament in London or the Scottish Parliament sitting in Edinburgh.[65] Certain matters are "reserved" by the U.K. Parliament, i.e., deemed to be outside of the legislative competence of the Scottish Parliament; other matters are "devolved" to the Scottish Parliament, i.e., deemed to be within the legislative competence of the Scottish Parliament. Reserved matters include the U.K. constitution, foreign policy, national security, fiscal policy, international trade policy, nuclear safety, certain areas of social security and employment policy, and certain areas of health policy. Devolved matters include education, local government, housing, tourism, civil and criminal law, emergency services, economic development, agriculture, and sports.

2. Sources of Scottish Legislation

The source for Scottish primary legislation depends on which legislative body is responsible for producing the legislation. Acts of the U.K. Parliament extending to Scotland are available in *The Public & General Acts and Measures*, *The Law Reports Statutes*, *Current Law Statutes*, *Statutes In Force*, and *Halsbury's Statutes of England & Wales*, 4th ed. U.K. acts are available online at the official O.P.S.I. U.K. Legislation website, the U.K. Statute Law Database, and BAILII's U.K. Legislation website; *Westlaw* and *LexisNexis* also provide access to U.K. acts. The

---

[61] http://www.bailii.org/.

[62] The Scotland Act 1998, c. 46.

[63] DAVID M. WALKER, THE SCOTTISH LEGAL SYSTEM: AN INTRODUCTION TO THE STUDY OF SCOTS LAW (8th ed. rev. 2001).

[64] For a more complete discussion of the impact of devolution on Scottish legal research, see Stephen Young, *Devolution in the United Kingdom: A Revolution in Online Legal Research*, *LLRX.com*, June 1, 2001, at www.llrx.com/features/devolution.htm.

[65] The determination as to which areas are governed by which legislative body is outlined in sections 29 and 30 and schedules 4 and 5 of the act.

extent section of U.K. acts, usually located toward the end of the act, details the geographical extent of the act; however, it is presumed that the act extends nationwide unless the extent section indicates otherwise.

For those matters that reside within the scope of Scotland's devolved legislative powers, the source of primary legislation is the Scottish Parliament.

3. The Scottish Parliamentary Process

The passage of legislation through the Scottish Parliament differs from the process followed in the U.K. Parliament (see Section B–1 of this chapter). The Scottish Parliament website provides researchers with comprehensive information concerning the workings of this new institution.[66] Because the Scottish Parliament is a unicameral body, the passage of a bill in Scotland is understandably less complex than the corresponding process in Westminister.

The passage of a bill through the Scottish Parliament entails four stages. *The Scotland Act 1998* originally called for bills to proceed through a three-stage process. However, the Consultative Steering Group on the Scottish Parliament indicated in their report, *Shaping Scotland's Parliament*, that a four-stage process should be employed. Stage 1 involves the deliberation on the principles of the bill by a lead committee. At this stage a determination is made as to whether the scope and purpose of the bill is acceptable. This determination is then reported to a plenary session of Parliament. In Stage 2 Parliament, in plenary session, debates and votes on the principles of the bill. The details of the bill are discussed in Stage 3. In Stage 3 the bill is assigned to one or more committees of Parliament. At this stage amendments to the bill can be made. Stage 4, held in plenary session, is the final debate and voting stage. Once again amendments can be made; however, there are strict guidelines concerning the extent of amendments at this stage. The *Official Report* includes transcripts of committee discussions and floor debates from plenary sessions.[67]

The passage of a bill can be tracked using the *Business Bulletin*[68] (a resource very similar in style to the *Weekly Information Bulletin* of the House of Commons) in conjunction with *This Week in the Scottish Parliament*, a weekly publication providing information on the workings of the Scottish Parliament.[69]

4. Acts of the Scottish Parliament

Acts passed by the Scottish Parliament ("ASP") can be located using the following sources.

a. *The Scottish Legislation Website.* This website contains full-text versions of ASPs. The aim of the O.P.S.I. is "to publish these documents on the Internet simultaneously or at least within 24 hours of their publication

---

[66] http://www.scottish.parliament.uk/.

[67] http://www.scottish.parliament.uk/business/officialReports/index.htm.

[68] http://www.scottish.parliament.uk/business/businessBulletin/index.htm.

[69] http://www.scottish.parliament.uk/nmCentre/twisp.htm.

in printed form. However, any document which is especially complex in terms of its size or its typography may take longer to prepare."[70]

b. *Print Versions.* Full-text versions of ASPs can be located in sessional volumes published by The Stationery Office and in *Current Law Statutes*. In addition, selected ASPs are reproduced in the *Parliament House Book*, a five-volume looseleaf set published by W. Green & Son Ltd.

c. *Additional Online Resources.* ASPs are often first listed on The Stationery Office's *Daily List*. This website also provides information on other Scottish Parliamentary publications. A complete run of ASPs in full text are also available through *BAILII*. A series of *Westlaw* databases contain Scottish law, including one database containing legislation specifically or primarily affecting Scotland (UKSCO–ST). This database includes acts of both the U.K. government and the Scottish Parliament. Other databases in this series include Scottish legislation in force since 1706 (UKSCO–LIF), a Scottish legislative locator (UKSCO–LEGISLOC), and Scottish delegated legislation (UKSCO–SI). *LexisNexis* provides coverage of Scottish legislation in its SCOSTA file.

SECTION J. SCOTTISH SECONDARY LEGISLATION

Delegated or secondary legislation comprises the body of law often referred to in the United States as administrative law. In Scotland this law takes the form of either Statutory Instruments made under powers granted by a U.K. act, or a Scottish Statutory Instrument (SSI) made under powers granted by an act of the Scottish Parliament. Devolution, therefore, created not only two levels of primary legislation for the region, but also two levels of secondary legislation. Delegated legislation made under powers not devolved to the Scottish Parliament continues to originate in London. Such delegated legislation can be most easily located by using the resources described in Section C of this chapter.

The Scottish Executive carries out Scottish delegated legislation under powers granted by acts of the Scottish Parliament. The Scottish Executive is comprised of the First Minister, six Cabinet Secretaries and ten Ministers appointed by the First Minister, the Lord Advocate, and the Solicitor General. The Scottish Executive can make delegated legislation only on matters that are within its devolved competence as defined by section 54 of *The Scotland Act 1998*. Prior to coming into force, the majority of SSIs are reviewed by the Scottish Parliament.

SSIs are cited by their title and are assigned a sequential number according to the chronological order in which the Queen's Printer receives the SSIs. For example, *The Smoke Control Areas (Exempt Fireplaces) (Scotland) Order 2001* SSI 2001/16 refers to the 16th Scottish Statutory Instrument made in 2001.

a. *Scottish Legislation Website.*[71] SSIs, together with their Executive Notes, are made available in full text on the Scottish Legislation website either instantaneously or within 24 hours of their print publication. Draft

---

[70] http://www.opsi.gov.uk/legislation/scotland/about.htm.

[71] *Id.*

SSIs also are made available at this website. The Stationery Office *Daily List* often provides the first notification of new SSIs.

b. *Print Versions.* The Queen's Printer publishes print versions of SSIs, in both individual and cumulative bound versions. The *Parliament House Book* publishes select SSIs following the authorizing ASP.

c. *Additional Online Resources. Westlaw* makes SSIs available in the UKSCO–SI database, together with U.K. statutory instruments affecting Scotland. *BAILII* also provides the full-text of all SSIs in its Scotland database.[72] *LexisNexis* provides coverage of Scottish delegated legislation in its SCOSI file.

SECTION K.　SCOTTISH CASE LAW

1.　The Scottish Court System

　　a.　*Civil*

(1) The Sheriff Court (49 Sheriff courts in six regional Sheriffdoms headed by a Sheriff Principal) is the inferior court and, consequently, handles most civil cases. Appeals are made to the Sheriff Principal.

(2) The Court of Session, which is both a court of first instance and a court of appeal, is divided into the Inner House and the Outer House (The Lords Ordinary). The Inner House, which is divided further into First and Second Divisions of equal authority, functions solely as an appeal court.

(3) The House of Lords is the court of first instance for certain actions, but generally is the court of appeal for cases appealed from the Court of Session.

Other specialized courts in civil actions include, among others, the Court of the Lord Lyon and the Scottish Land Court.

　　b.　*Criminal*

(1) The District Court. This court of first instance is presided over by justices of the peace and magistrates. Beginning in 2007 the District courts are slowly being replaced by Justice of the Peace Courts.[73]

(2) The Sheriff Courts (see above).

(3) The High Court of Justiciary. This court functions as a court of first instance and a court of appeal. Criminal actions are not appealed to the House of Lords; however, the European Court of Justice can review them.

2.　Modern Scottish Reporters

　　a.　*Session Cases*, 1821 to present. Published since 1957 by the Scottish Council of Law Reporting (SCLR), this reporter includes civil matters from Scotland appealed to the House of Lords, criminal cases in the Court of Justiciary, and civil cases heard in the Court of Session. This reporter is considered official for citation purposes. In the first 85 years of publication the *Session Cases* appeared as five nominate series: Shaw (1821–38);

---

[72] http://www.bailii.org/scot/legis/num_reg/.

[73] *See* http://www.scotcourts.gov.uk/summary_justice_reform/index.asp for a detailed summary of the revisions to the Scottish criminal justice system.

Dunlop (1838–62); Macpherson (1862–73); Rettie (1873–98); and Fraser (1898–1906). From 1906 to 1957 the Faculty of Advocates published *Session Cases* until SCLR began publishing it. *Session Cases* reports cases from three courts, and each volume contains three separate page number sequences corresponding to the different courts being reported. The Justiciary cases may be bound separately from the rest of the series. Citation form to an opinion within the set varies depending on whether a volume from a nominate series is being cited and on which court issued the opinion.

b.   *Scots Law Times*, 1893 to present. Coverage includes the Court of Session, the High Court of Justiciary, and the House of Lords. Cases from various other courts (see below) are also reported. The series is published weekly and cumulates annually. Each volume is divided into two sections—Notes and Reports. The Reports section sets forth reports from recent decisions of the courts listed above and is consecutively paged. The Notes section includes articles, news, and Acts of Sederunt.[74] Also included in this section are reports of cases from the following courts: Sheriff Court Reports (beginning in 1922); Scottish Land Court Reports (beginning in 1964), and Land Tribunals for Scotland Reports (beginning in 1971); Poor Law Reports (1932–1941); and Lyon Court Reports (1950–1959, 1966, and 1977).

c.   *Scottish Civil Law Reports*, 1987 to present. This publication reports cases from the Court of Session and the Sheriff Courts.

d.   *Scottish Criminal Case Reports*, 1981 to present. Coverage includes cases from the Sheriff Courts and the High Court of Justiciary.

3.   Older Scottish Reporters

a.   *Practicks*. Often these are the only reports available for very old cases (approximately 1469 to 1754). These volumes, frequently setting forth only rough notes of cases, are known by the name of the jurist responsible for the material. The most well known are Balfour, Spotiswoode, and Hope. These have been reprinted by the Stair Society.

b.   *Private Reports*. Twenty-two private reports were published in the seventeenth and eighteenth centuries covering material from the Court of Session (1621–1833). Ten private reports cover the early Scottish cases decided in the House of Lords (1707–1865). Ten private reports also cover the early Justiciary (criminal) cases (1819–1916).

c.   *The Faculty Collection*. This set was published in three series: the old series (1752–1808); the new series (1808–1825); and the Octavo series (1825–1841). This set was the official reporter for the Court of Session for the periods indicated. The Octavo series is also known by the name *Faculty Decisions*.

d.   *Other Reports*. Other reporter sets include *The Scottish Jurist* (1829–1873), *Scottish Law Reporter* (1865–1924), and *Scottish Law Review and Sheriff Court Reports* (1885–1963).

e.   *Collections*. Two major collections of early reports are Kames & Woodhouselee, *Decisions of the Court of Session* (five volumes covering 1540 to 1796), and Morison, *Decisions, Court of Session in the Form of a*

---

[74] Acts of Sederunt govern procedure in the Scottish civil courts. The equivalent rules for Scottish criminal courts are known as Acts of Adjournal.

Dictionary (38 volumes covering 1540 to 1808). A five-volume supplement by Brown and an additional *Synopsis* by Morison add material omitted from the original work. Morison contains some reports dated before 1540 taken from the *Practicks*. A more recently published collection of older reports is *Scots Revised Reports* (45 volumes covering Scottish decisions prior to 1873).

4. Electronic Access to Scottish Cases

a. *Scottish Courts Website.* Beginning in 1998 opinions from the Supreme Courts (Court of Session for civil cases and High Court of Justiciary for criminal cases), and the Sheriff Courts are available on the Scottish Courts website.[75]

b. *BAILII.* Scottish decisions since 1998 are available on BAILII. Coverage includes material from the Court of Session, the High Court of Justiciary, and the Sheriff Courts. The information on the BAILII site is sourced from the Scottish Courts website and is therefore identical.

c. *Westlaw.* This fee-based service provides coverage of cases reported in the *Scots Law Times* since 1893 and *Session Cases* since 1930.

d. *LexisNexis.* Coverage in this fee-based service includes *Session Cases* from 1930, *Scottish Criminal Case Reports* from January 1981, and *Scottish Civil Law Reports* from February 1986.

e. *Justis.* In collaboration with the Scottish Council of Law Reporting, Justis has made available in PDF format *Session Cases* dating back to 1873. The database includes access to Rettie's and Fraser's *Session Cases*. This is a fee-based service.

5. Digests and Indexes to Scottish Cases

a. *Green's Weekly Digest.* The cases digested in *Green's* later appear in *Scots Law Times*.

b. *The Faculty of Advocates' Digest.* This digest was published from 1868 to 1922 and supplemented through 1990.

c. *The Scots Digest.* Coverage varies depending on the court, but generally is from 1800 to 1944.

d. *Current Law*, 1948 to present. A separate Scottish edition ceased publication in 1991. Scottish cases are now incorporated, albeit in a separate section, into the monthly digests.

e. *The Digest.* This is the same tool used to locate English (and Commonwealth) case law. For a more complete description, see Section E–1 of this chapter.

SECTION L. NORTHERN IRELAND

The province of Northern Ireland was formed when the *Government of Ireland Act 1920* divided Ireland into two regions. The act called for the creation of two separate parliaments, one in Dublin (to govern the 26 southern counties) and one in Belfast (to govern the six counties in the north loyal to Britain). In 1921 the Anglo–Irish Treaty was signed, thereby

---

[75] http://www.scotcourts.gov.uk/opinionsApp/index.asp?txt=False.

creating the Irish Free State and leading to the eventual creation of the Republic of Ireland in 1949. Since 1921 the responsibility for governing Northern Ireland has varied. At times, the province has experienced home rule; at other times it has fallen under direct rule from the U.K. Parliament in London. In order to research Northern Ireland materials, an understanding of the history of the constitutional basis of the province is necessary.

Northern Ireland experienced home rule in the period between 1921, when the *Government of Ireland Act 1920* created the province, and 1972, when the British government declared an end to home rule and instituted direct rule from Westminster. During this period the Northern Ireland Parliament ("Stormont")[76] operated as a devolved legislative body; it was perceived as a body more representative of the Protestants' interests than the Catholics'. The escalation of violence in the province during the late 1960s and early 1970s resulted in the suspension of home rule and the vesting of wide discretionary powers in the Secretary of State for Northern Ireland under direct rule. In 1974, a second attempt at devolution was made with the creation of the first Northern Ireland Assembly. This Assembly lasted only five months, although in that time it did manage to pass a number of measures. Direct rule of the province resumed in the summer of 1974 as a result of increased sectarian violence.

During the 1980s and 1990s continued negotiations between the British government and various parties attempted to bring an end to the violence and establish a system of home rule. The breakthrough occurred in 1998 with the signing of the Good Friday Agreement.[77] This document formed the basis for the style of devolution currently experienced in Northern Ireland. Included within the agreement is a provision for a democratically elected legislative body for Northern Ireland. The *Northern Ireland (Elections) Act 1998* lays out the process for electing the Assembly members, while the *Northern Ireland Act 1998* provides for the peaceful transfer of functions to the new Northern Ireland Assembly. In December 1999, the Assembly was eventually granted the devolved powers. Since 1999 the Northern Ireland Assembly has been suspended on a number of occasions, the longest period of suspension being almost 5 years. However, recent times appear to hold out the promise of a less turbulent future for the Assembly and for the province in general.

SECTION M. NORTHERN IRELAND PRIMARY LEGISLATION

1. The New Northern Ireland Assembly

The powers conferred on the new Northern Ireland Assembly include the power to adopt primary legislation for the province. However, the *Northern Ireland Act 1998* clearly distinguishes between matters within the legislative competence of the Assembly and matters outside of its competence, and therefore leaves legislation subject to judicial review.[78] Drawing distinctions between transferred, entrenched, excepted, and reserved mat-

---

[76] Stormont is the popular name given to Parliament Buildings on the Stormont Estate near Belfast.

[77] Good Friday Agreement, *supra* note 3.

[78] The Northern Ireland Act 1998, c. 47.

ters, the *Northern Ireland Act 1998* defines the scope of the Assembly's powers. Entrenched matters include the *Human Rights Act 1998*, the *European Communities Act 1972*, and other basic constitutional documents outlined in section 7 of the act. The Assembly cannot amend these documents. Excepted matters are defined in section 6 as matters that are outside the legislative competence of the Assembly, and are listed in schedule 2 of the *Northern Ireland Act 1998*. Reserved matters are matters that are within the legislative competence of the Assembly, but can only be acted upon with the consent of the Secretary of State for Northern Ireland. Reserved matters are outlined in schedule 3. All other matters are considered transferred matters and are deemed within the legislative competence of the Assembly.

The Northern Ireland Assembly website provides researchers with access to a variety of information, including general information concerning the body, a calendar of events, and services for tracking legislation (primary and secondary) through the Assembly.[79] Bills can be tracked through the various legislative stages and accessed in full text; committee reports are also available. Transcripts of floor debates can be found using the *Official Report*, a daily Hansard publication. The legislative process adopted by the Assembly is very similar in practice to the one described above for the Scottish Parliament. As with acts passed by other legislative bodies in the United Kingdom, the acts of the Northern Ireland Assembly are published by the O.P.S.I. on behalf of the Government Printer for Northern Ireland and are, therefore, not located on the Assembly's website.[80]

2. Forms of Legislation for Northern Ireland

a.   The various forms of legislation for Northern Ireland are a direct result of the complex history of the province. Prior to 1999, Northern Ireland was subject to the following:

(1) *Acts of the Northern Ireland Parliament ("Stormont")*, 1921–1972. These acts are available in the *Statutes Revised Northern Ireland 2d*. This multivolume looseleaf set includes all legislation in force in the province, except U.K. legislation, up to 1981.

(2) *Acts of the U.K. Parliament Extending to Northern Ireland and Orders in Council*, 1972–1973. Acts of the U.K. Parliament extending to Northern Ireland can be located in sources traditionally used to locate acts of Parliament (see Section B–2 for a description of these traditional sources). The Orders in Council passed for the province, although considered a form of delegated legislation, are made available in the *Statutes Revised Northern Ireland 2d* and in session volumes in *Northern Ireland Statutes*.

(3) *Measures of the Northern Ireland Assembly*, January 1974–May 1974. The few measures passed by the first Northern Ireland Assembly in its five-month existence are made available in the *Statutes Revised Northern Ireland 2d*.

---

[79] http://www.ni-assembly.gov.uk/.

[80] http://www.opsi.gov.uk/legislation/northernireland/ni_legislation.htm.

(4) *Acts of the U.K. Parliament and Orders in Council*, June 1974–1999. Availability of this material is the same as described in (2) above; however, recent legislation is also available on the O.P.S.I. Legislation website.

b.   Since 1999, primary legislation for Northern Ireland has included:

(1) *Legislation promulgated by the new Northern Ireland Assembly.* Acts of the new Northern Ireland Assembly are published by the O.P.S.I. on the Northern Ireland Legislation website and by the H.M.S.O in hard copy.

(2) *Acts of the U.K. government Extending to Northern Ireland.* Acts of the U.K. government that extend to Northern Ireland can be located in the traditional U.K. primary legislation sources described above. Acts of the U.K. government that apply primarily or exclusively to Northern Ireland can be located on the Northern Ireland Legislation website.

(3) *Orders in Council made for the province by the U.K. government.* Orders in Council are a form of secondary legislation considered primary legislation for Northern Ireland. They have been promulgated since the first period of direct rule in 1972; since 1998 their use has been limited to periods when the Assembly has been suspended. U.K. Orders in Council, made by and with the advice of the Privy Council, are published in full text on the Northern Ireland Legislation website.

BAILII provides coverage of Orders in Council and Statutes of the New Northern Ireland Assembly. *LexisNexis* and *Westlaw* do not provide coverage of Northern Ireland Assembly legislation. Initial notification of the publication of official documents for Northern Ireland is in The Stationery Office *Daily List*.

SECTION N.   NORTHERN IRELAND SECONDARY LEGISLATION

The publication of delegated legislation for Northern Ireland is as complex as publication of Northern Ireland's primary legislation. Since 1998 delegated legislation for the province has taken any one of four forms. It has been issued as (1) U.K. statutory instruments extending to Northern Ireland, (2) U.K. statutory instruments made primarily or exclusively for Northern Ireland, (3) statutory rules made under the authority of an act of the U.K. government, or (4) statutory rules made under the authority of an act of the Northern Ireland Assembly.

1.   United Kingdom Statutory Instruments

U.K. statutory instruments extending to Northern Ireland can be located using the online resources described above, i.e., *LexisNexis, Westlaw, BAILII,* and the O.P.S.I. Statutory Instruments website. U.K. statutory instruments made primarily or exclusively for Northern Ireland are located on a separate Northern Ireland Legislation website.

2.   Northern Ireland Statutory Rules

Delegated legislation made for Northern Ireland takes the form of statutory rules. The Northern Ireland Assembly details on its website the processes by which a statutory rule becomes law. Statutory rules presented to the Assembly are subject to affirmative resolution, confirmatory resolution, or negative resolution. Once a rule becomes law, O.P.S.I. publishes it on the Statutory Rules of Northern Ireland website, together with statutory rules passed by the U.K. Parliament. *BAILII* includes a section for Northern Ireland Statutory Rules for the period 2001 to the present. *LexisNexis* and *Westlaw* do not provide access to Northern Ireland statutory rules.

SECTION O.   NORTHERN IRELAND CASE LAW

1.   The Northern Ireland Court System

Fortunately, the complexities associated with performing legislative research in the province are not carried over into case law. The court system of Northern Ireland is very similar to the court system in England and Wales. A simplified outline of the system follows.

- The House of Lords is the final court of appeal for Northern Ireland.
- The Court of Appeal handles both civil and criminal appeals.
- The High Court of Justice, comprised of the Queen's Bench, Family, and Chancery divisions, handles civil matters.
- The Crown Court handles serious criminal matters.
- The inferior courts are the County Courts (7 divisions) and the Magistrates' Courts (21 districts).

2.   Northern Ireland Reporters

a.   *The Northern Ireland Law Reports (NILR)*, 1925 to present. Issued in quarterly installments by *LexisNexis Butterworth's*, this reporter covers cases in the High Court of Justice and the Court of Appeal in Northern Ireland. Since 1970 reports of cases on appeal to the House of Lords are also included (*Law Reports Appeal Cases* also includes Northern Ireland decisions on appeal to the House of Lords). This publication is cited as: [year] NI page. Prior to 1925 Northern Ireland cases are reported in *Irish Reports*, along side cases from the Irish Free State.

b.   *Northern Ireland Judgements Bulletin (NIJB)*, 1972 to present. This publication is also published twice a year by *LexisNexis Butterworth*'s. It includes reports of civil judgments from the High Court of Justice and the Court of Appeal. It also includes material not always available in *NILR*. This publication is cited as: [year] vol. NIJB page.

c.   *Northern Ireland Legal Quarterly*, 1936 to present. This journal contains notes on decisions, rather than the full text of decisions. It is published by the Law Faculty at Queen's University, Belfast.

3.   Electronic Access to Northern Ireland Cases

a.   *Northern Ireland Court Service Website*. This website has recently started to make available the text of judgments dating back to 1999. It is also a useful website for information concerning the Northern Ireland courts and their business.[81]

---

[81] http://www.courtsni.gov.uk.

b. *BAILII.* The British and Irish Legal Information Institute website has full-text coverage of Court of Appeal, High Court of Justice, and Crown Court decisions since 1999.

c. *LexisNexis.* This service provides coverage of reported Northern Ireland cases since 1945 and unreported cases since 1984. *Westlaw* does not provide coverage of either Northern Ireland case law or legislation exclusive to Northern Ireland.

4. Digests and Indexes to Northern Ireland Cases

Index to Cases Decided in the Courts of Northern Ireland and Reported During the Period 1921–1970. This set is supplemented through 1975. It provides an index to Northern Ireland case materials, and also acts as a citator service for legislation, both primary and delegated.

SECTION P. ILLUSTRATIONS

Problem: Is it illegal to possess indecent images of a minor?

22–1. **Page from Halsbury's Statutes of England & Wales, 4th ed., Volume 12**

22–2. **Page from Halsbury's Statutes of England & Wales, 4th ed., Cumulative Supplement**

22–3. **Page from Halsbury's Statutes of England & Wales, 4th ed., Current Statutes Service**

22–4. **Page from R v Bowden [2000] 2 All ER 418**

22–5. **Paragraph 365 from Halsbury's Laws of England, 4th ed., Volume 11(1)**

[Illustration 22–1]

PAGE FROM HALSBURY'S STATUTES OF ENGLAND & WALES, 4TH ED., VOLUME 12

6 Enactment of same provisions for Northern Ireland

An Order in Council under paragraph 1(1)(b) of Schedule 1 to the Northern Ireland Act 1974 (legislation for Northern Ireland in the interim period) which contains a statement that it operates only so as to make for Northern Ireland provision corresponding to this Act—

  (a) shall not be subject to paragraph 1(4) and (5) of that Schedule (affirmative resolution of both Houses of Parliament); but

  (b) shall be subject to annulment by resolution of either House.

NOTES

  Order in Council . . . which contains a statement, etc. The power to make Orders in Council is exercisable by statutory instrument; see the Statutory Instruments Act 1946, s 1(1), V‹ l 41, title Statutes.

  Subject to annulment. For provisions as to annulment of statutory instruments in pursuance of a resolution of either House of Parliament, see the Statutory Instruments Act 1946, ss 5(1), 7(1), Vol 41, title Statutes.

  Northern Ireland Act 1974, Sch 1, para 1. See Vol 31, title Northern Ireland (Pt 2).

7 Short title, commencement and extent

  (1) This Act may be cited as the Theft Act 1978.

  (2) This Act shall come into force at the expiration of three months beginning with the date on which it is passed.

  (3) This Act except section 5(3), shall not extend to Scotland; and except for that subsection, and subject also to section 6, it shall not extend to Northern Ireland.

NOTE

  Three months beginning, etc. "Month" means a calendar month; see the Interpretation Act 1978, s 5, Sch 1, Vol 41, title Statutes. In calculating this period, the date (ie 20 July 1978) on which the Act was passed (ie received the Royal Assent) is reckoned; see *Hare v Gocher* [1962] 2 QB 641,

> The full text of the *Protection of Children Act 1978* is reproduced along with notes referring to commencement, regulations, and other statutes.

PROTECTION OF CHILDREN ACT 1978

(1978 c 37)

ARRANGEMENT OF SECTIONS

An Act to prevent the exploitation of children by making indecent photographs of them; and to penalise the distribution, showing and advertisement of such indecent photographs

[20 July 1978]

[Illustration 22–2]

PAGE FROM HALSBURY'S STATUTES OF ENGLAND & WALES, 4TH ED., CUMULATIVE SUPPLEMENT

VOLUME 12 (1997 Reissue) HALSBURY'S STATUTES (4TH EDN) SUPPLEMENT

PAGE **Criminal Law Act 1977 (c 45)** — *continued*

the Water Act 1989, s 190(3), Sch 27, Pt I; the Opticians Act 1989, s 37(4), Sch 2; and the Water Consolidation (Consequential Provisions) Act 1991, s 3(1), Sch 3, Pt I."

"Sch 5: para 1(1)(a), (2)(c) repealed by the Customs and Excise Management Act 1979, s 177(3), Sch 6, Pt I; para 1(1)(b), (c), (1A), (3) amend certain entries relating to penalties in the Misuse of Drugs Act 1971, Sch 4, Vol 28, title Medicine and Pharmacy (Pt 2), which have been further affected by the Criminal Justice Act 1982, Vol 27, title Magistrates; para 1(2)(a), (b) repealed by the Magistrates' Courts Act 1980, s 154, Sch 9; para 2 repealed in part by the Criminal Justice Act 1988, s 170(2), Sch 16, remainder repealed by the Road Traffic (Consequential Provisions) Act 1988, s 3(1), Sch 1, Pt I."

"Sch 6, which increased fines for certain summary offences, was superseded by the Criminal Justice Act 1982, Vol 27, title Magistrates; much of this Schedule has, however, been repealed by the following enactments: the Nurses, Midwives and Health Visitors Act 1979, s 23(5), Sch 8; the Merchant Shipping Act 1979, s 50(4), Sch 7; the Child Care Act 1980, s 89, Sch 6; the Residential Homes Act 1980, s 11(5), Sch 2; the Housing Act 1980, ss 145, 152, Sch 23, paras 6(2), 8(2); the Highways Act 1980, s 343(3), Sch 25; the Wildlife and Countryside Act 1981, s 73, Sch 17, Pt II; the Mental Health Act 1983, s 148(3), Sch 6; the Telecommunications Act 1984, s 109(6), Sch 7, Pt IV; the

This volume is arranged according to the volume and page number of the base volumes. This supplement indicates that the original act has been amended by the *Sexual Offenses (Protected Material) Act of 1997.*

(Consequential Provisions) Act 1988, s 3(1), Sch 1, Pt I; the Water Act 1989, s 190(3), Sch 27, Pt I; the Water Consolidation (Consequential Provisions) Act 1991, s 3(1), Sch 3, Pt I; the Education Act 1993, s 307(1), (3), Sch 19, para 68, Sch 21, Pt I; the Criminal Procedure (Consequential Provisions) Act 1995, ss 4, 6(1), Schs 3, 5; the Police Act 1996, s 103(3), Sch 9, Pt I; and the Housing Grants, Construction and Regeneration Act 1996, s 147, Sch 3, Pt II."

692 **Schedules 1–12**

Schedule 12 amended by Powers of Criminal Courts (Sentencing) Act 2000, s 165(4), Sch 12, Pt I, Vol 12, title Criminal Law.

Theft Act 1978 (c 31)

701 **Section 1**

Deception. See also *R v Rai* [2000] 1 Cr App R 242.

Protection of Children Act 1978 (c 37) ◄———

706 *Prohibition on cross-examination in person of protected witnesses.* The Youth Justice and Criminal Evidence Act 1999, s 35, applies to any offence under this Act; see s 35(3) thereof, Vol 17, title Evidence.

706 **Section 1**

Sub-s (1): It is an offence. An offence under this section, including an offence of conspiring, attempting or inciting another to commit such an offence, is a "sexual offence" for the purposes of the Sexual Offences (Protected Material) Act 1997; see s 2 of, and Schedule, paras 5–8 to, the 1997 Act, Vol 12, title Criminal Law.

[Illustration 22–3]

PAGE FROM HALSBURY'S STATUTES OF ENGLAND & WALES, 4TH ED., CURRENT STATUTES SERVICE

SEXUAL OFFENCES (PROTECTED MATERIAL) ACT 1997

(1997 c 39)

Preliminary Note

This Act, which received Royal Assent on 21 March 1997 and comes into force on a day to be appointed under s 11(2), regulates access by the defendant and others to victim statements and certain other material disclosed by the prosecutor in connection with proceedings relating to the sexual and other offences specified in the Schedule.

S 1 principally defines "protected material", in relation to proceedings for a sexual offence, as a copy (in whatever form) of statements relating to that or any other offence made by any victim of the offence, a photograph or pseudo-photograph of any such victim, or a report of a medical examination of the physical condition of any such victim, which is given by the prosecutor to any person under the Act.

S 2 defines other expressions used in the Act, including the expression "proceedings in relation to a sexual offence".

S 3 requires a prosecutor to disclose such material by giving a copy of it to the defendant's legal representative, if he has one and where the representative gives the prosecutor the undertaking required by s 4, or by giving a copy of it to the "appropriate person" for the purposes of s 5, in order for that person to show the

> The full text of the *Sexual Offenses (Protected Material) Act* is reproduced together with notes. This act will be incorporated into base volume 12 when the volume is reissued.

material or make a copy of it.

S 5 defines the "appropriate person" as a prison governor or officer in charge of a police station (or their nominee), and requires that person to give the defendant access to the protected material under the same conditions as are specified in s 4. Provision is also made for the prosecutor to give a copy of protected material to another person at the defendant's request.

S 6 provides for the further disclosure of material by the prosecutor where the defendant's legal representative ceases to act as such or dies, or where a previously undefended defendant becomes represented.

S 7 makes similar provision for the disclosure of material by the Criminal Cases Review Committee.

S 8 creates offences in connection with the unauthorised disclosure or possession of protected material.

S 9 modifies or amends certain other enactments; s 10 makes financial provision; and s 11 gives the short title, commencement and extent of the Act.

ARRANGEMENT OF SECTIONS

Introductory

[Illustration 22–4]

PAGE FROM R V BOWDEN [2000] 2 ALL ER 418

418	All England Law Reports	[2000] 2 All ER

R v Bowden

a

COURT OF APPEAL, CRIMINAL DIVISION

OTTON LJ, SMITH AND COLLINS JJ

2 SEPTEMBER, 10 NOVEMBER 1999

b

Criminal law – Indecent photographs or pseudo-photographs of children – Making indecent photographs of children – Whether offence encompassing downloading or printing out of computer data – Protection of Children Act 1978, ss 1(1)(a), 7.

c

The appellant, B, downloaded indecent photographs of young boys from the Internet, and either printed them out or stored them on his computer disks. He was charged, inter alia, with 12 counts of having 'made an indecent photograph' of children contrary to s 1(1)(a)[a] of the Protection of Children Act 1978. Under s 7[b] of that Act, the term 'indecent photograph' included a copy of such a photograph, and references to 'a photograph' included data stored on a computer disk which was capable of conversion into a photograph. Although B initially pleaded not

d

The defendant in this case was charged with "making" indecent photographs of children. This case cites extensively to the 1978 act. See Illustration 22-1.

Held – The offence of making an indecent photograph of a child contrary to s 1(1)(a) of the 1978 Act was not confined to original photographs. Rather, by virtue of s 7 of that Act, it also applied to negatives, copies of photographs and data stored on computer disks. Thus a person who downloaded images onto a disk or printed them off was making them within the meaning of s 1(1)(a) of the 1978 Act. That Act was concerned not only with the original creation of images, but also with their proliferation. Photographs or pseudo-photographs found on the Internet could have originated from outside the United Kingdom, and downloading or printing them within the jurisdiction created new material that might not have hitherto existed therein. Accordingly, the appeal would be dismissed (see p 423 *e* to *h* and p 424 *e*, post).

f

g

Notes

For offences concerning indecent photographs of children, see 11(1) *Halsbury's Laws* (4th edn reissue) paras 365–366.

For the Protection of Children Act 1978, ss 1, 7, see 12 *Halsbury's Statutes* (4th edn) (1997 reissue) 706, 711.

h

Cases referred to in judgment

Pepper (Inspector of Taxes) v Hart [1993] 1 All ER 42, [1993] AC 593, [1992] 3 WLR 1032, HL.

j

R v Fellows, R v Arnold [1997] 2 All ER 548, CA.

a   Section 1, so far as material, is set out at p 420 *h* to p 421 *a*, post
b   Section 7, so far as material, is set out at p 421 *b* to *d*, post

[Illustration 22–5]

PARAGRAPH 365 FROM HALSBURY'S LAWS
OF ENGLAND, 4TH ED., VOLUME 11(1)

| Para 364 | *Vol 11(1): Criminal Law, Evidence and Procedure* | 282 |

---

as the contrary is shown by evidence given on behalf of the same or any other party[6].

1 For the meaning of 'play' see para 362 note 3 ante.
2 'Script' in relation to the performance of a play, means the text of the play, whether expressed in words or in musical or other notation, together with any stage or other directions for its performance, whether contained in a single document or not: Theatres Act 1968 s 9 (2).
3 Ie under ibid s 2 (as amended) (see para 362 ante) or s 6 (public performance of a play provoking a breach of the peace: see THEATRES vol 45 para 956).
4 A police officer of or above the rank of superintendent, who has reasonable grounds for suspecting that any such offence has been committed by any person in respect of the performance of a play, or that the performance of a play is to be given and that any such offence is likely to be committed by a person in respect of it, may make a written order in relation to that person and that performance: ibid

> This encyclopedic tool outlines the law relating to a particular topic. In this section are references to the relevant acts and commentary on their interpretation.

s 10 (3). Any person who without reasonable excuse fails to comply with any such requirement is liable on summary conviction to a fine not exceeding level 3 on the standard scale: s 10 (4) (amended by the Criminal Justice 1982 ss 38, 46). For the meaning of 'the standard scale' see para 808 post.
5 Theatres Act 1968 ss 9 (1) (a), 10 (5) (amended by the Public Order Act 1986 s 40 (3), Sch 3).
6 Theatres Act 1968 ss 9 (1) (b), 10 (5).

(iii) Indecent Photographs of Children

365. Taking and distributing indecent photographs of children. It is an offence for a person[1]:
   (1) to take[2], or permit to be taken, any indecent[3] photograph[4] of a child[5]; or
   (2) to distribute[6] or show such indecent photographs; or
   (3) to have in his possession such indecent photographs, with a view to their being distributed or shown by himself or others; or
   (4) to publish or cause to be published any advertisement likely to be understood as conveying that the advertiser distributes or shows such indecent photographs, or intends to do so[7].

Proceedings for any such offence may not be instituted except by or with the consent of the Director of Public Prosecutions[8]. A person guilty of any such offence is liable on conviction on indictment to imprisonment for a term not exceeding three years or a fine, or to both, or on summary conviction to imprisonment for a term not exceeding six months or a fine not exceeding the prescribed sum, or to both[9].

Where a person is charged with an offence under heads (2) or (3) above, it is a defence for him to prove (a) that he had a legitimate reason for distributing or showing the photographs or, as the case may be, having them in his possession; or (b) that he had not himself seen the photographs and did not know, nor had any cause to suspect, them to be indecent[10].

1 Where a body corporate is guilty of an offence under the Protection of Children Act 1978 and it is proved that the offence occurred with the consent or connivance of, or was attributable to any neglect on the part of, any director, manager, secretary or other officer of the body, or any person who was purporting to act in any such capacity, he, as well as the body corporate, is deemed to be guilty of that offence and is liable to be proceeded against and punished accordingly: s 3 (1). Where the affairs of a body corporate are managed by its members, s 3 (1) applies in relation to the acts and defaults of a member in connection with his functions of management as if he were a director of the body corporate: s 3 (2).

Chapter 23

ELECTRONIC LEGAL RESEARCH*

Legal information is published in a variety of formats—print, electronic, and microform. Electronic resources have emerged as an important and complex research platform. *Westlaw* and *LexisNexis*—the two dominant, national commercial legal information services—provide access to a wide variety of primary and secondary legal databases, along with news, business, public records and other non-legal databases. Other electronic research products and services are offered to researchers through per-use or ongoing licenses. Legal research materials also are available through the Internet, often at no cost. Advances in technology are occurring rapidly; research technology and resources available today may be changed tomorrow as new materials are added to databases, enhancements are made to search tools, additional databases are created, the Internet expands, and new products are developed.

SECTION A. INTRODUCTION: THE INTERFACE OF TECHNOLOGY AND LEGAL INFORMATION

Electronic legal information is stored in several ways. Most legal information systems are now available through the Internet, eliminating the need for proprietary network-based telecommunications systems. Another storage option is local storage formats, available on CD–ROM or DVD–ROM. The scope of legal information available through these media, however, is limited compared to online services such as *Westlaw*, *LexisNexis*, and others, and to what is available through the free or open Internet. The Internet has proven to be a more efficient delivery mechanism than the compact disk.

Both *Westlaw*[1] and *LexisNexis*[2] are primarily accessed through the Internet. In the past, researchers accessed *Westlaw* and *LexisNexis* via a dial-up telephone connection, whereby a researcher's computer dialed up, or called, a *Westlaw* or *LexisNexis* network connected to their respective mainframe computers. However, over the last few years, *Westlaw* and *LexisNexis* have been transitioning from proprietary research software to Web format. Although proprietary access is still available, neither *LexisNexis* nor *Westlaw* is actively supporting this access, nor are current law

---

* George H. Pike, Director of the Barco Law Library, and Assistant Professor of Law, University of Pittsburgh School of Law, revised this chapter. Pat Newcombe, Associate Director, Western New England School of Law Library, prepared the previous version of this chapter.

[1] http://www.westlaw.com.

[2] http://www.lexis.com.

students being taught to use it.[3] Internet-based access provides the researcher with the flexibility to access *Westlaw* or *LexisNexis* services from any computer with a Web browser and an Internet connection. *Westlaw* and *LexisNexis* also provide access to selected resources using a mobile device, such as a personal digital assistant (PDA), and a text-only edition for slower Internet connections.

SECTION B. THE WESTLAW AND LEXISNEXIS SERVICES

The two most widely used electronic legal research services are *Westlaw*, owned by Thomson Reuters, and *LexisNexis*,[4] a product of Reed Elsevier.[5] Since the development of computer-assisted legal research (CALR) in the early 1970s, the scope of *Westlaw* and *LexisNexis* has grown consistently with the legal profession's acceptance of electronic research. Today, both services serve as comprehensive and complex sources of legal information, providing primary source materials, including cases, statutes, and regulations; and secondary sources, such as legal periodicals and treatises. Both services also have been expanding their holdings of non-legal resources, including current and archived news, public records, and corporate and business information. Materials provided by *Westlaw* and *LexisNexis* are constantly undergoing expansion and refinement.[6]

Some of the content of *Westlaw* and *LexisNexis* databases is determined by the contractual agreements between those services and the owners or providers of proprietary information. Therefore, a vendor may eliminate or restrict information on *Westlaw* or *LexisNexis* when licensing costs reduce the profitability of placing material in an online environment, when a vendor enters into an exclusive arrangement with a different service provider, or when a vendor develops its own online product.[7]

---

[3] Both *LexisNexis* and *Westlaw* are phasing out their proprietary software access. Many new *LexisNexis* and *Westlaw* features are not available to proprietary software users. *Westlaw*'s software is used by less than 10% of *Westlaw* users and is no longer being updated. *LexisNexis* is charging for access through its proprietary software. Both companies exclusively use their Web formats for law student training. References to, and illustrations of, *Westlaw* and *LexisNexis* in this chapter are based on the Web versions.

[4] The official brand name of the *LexisNexis* online service is: *LexisNexis Total Research System*. Many users simply refer to it as "*Lexis*." This chapter will refer to it as *LexisNexis*.

[5] Although this chapter focuses on *LexisNexis* and *Westlaw*, the two largest and most common computer-assisted legal research services, it must be noted that numerous other CALR services are available. These services, some of which are listed in Section E of this chapter, vary in size and scope of their databases, editorial enhancements, the power of their search engines, and their cost. The basic concepts of searching, however, are applicable from service to service.

[6] The size of these services is vast. For example, as of December 2008 *Westlaw* contained over 32,000 databases and 200 million documents. With its extensive collection of news and information resources, *LexisNexis* contained over 40,000 databases with over 5 billion searchable documents.

[7] After *LexisNexis* merged with Reed Elsevier, Inc., in 1994, and Thomson Publishing Company (now Thomson Reuters) purchased West Publishing Company, including *Westlaw*, in 1996, a number of databases have been moved or removed from one or the other service. Among the most prominent of these changes was the removal of *Shepard's Citations* (also owned by Reed Elsevier) from *Westlaw*, which in turn led to the development of *Westlaw*'s *KeyCite* citation service.

Although a particular research resource or title may appear in *Westlaw* or *LexisNexis*, it is necessary to determine the scope of the materials that actually are available online. Typically, when legal information vendors introduce a resource, they do not provide a complete retrospective file of the collection. Sometimes only selected content from the resource may be provided. A researcher should evaluate very carefully the scope and content of any database before relying on that database as the primary access for legal information. Database directories or menu screens on *Westlaw* and *LexisNexis* provide instructions for determining the content of a file.

The following summaries of *Westlaw* and *LexisNexis* provide a general overview of the coverage of these two services. Numerous chapters in this book discuss, more specifically, relevant *Westlaw* and *LexisNexis* databases in particular substantive areas of law and jurisdictions.

1. Westlaw

Westlaw organizes its materials into general categories, such as U.S. Federal Materials, U.S. State Materials, Topical Practice Areas, International/Worldwide Materials, etc. [Illustration 23–1] Each category includes a variety of databases. To view a detailed description of each database, researchers can utilize the Scope feature, identified by a small-case letter "i" inside a circle. Scope displays information about what is available in a database, along with the coverage dates, and may also contain search tips and other valuable information.

Primary federal and state legal information, including case law, statutes, and administrative materials are each located in U.S. Federal Materials and U.S. State Materials, respectively. The cases in *Westlaw* contain not only the actual text of each case, but also all of the additional editorial features of West's *National Reporter System*, including the synopsis, headnotes, and key numbers.

Over 40 different topical database collections, such as Antitrust & Trade Regulation, Estate Planning & Probate, Intellectual Property, Securities, Taxation, and Workers' Compensation, are included in Topical Practice Areas. Each topical database collection provides access to primary and secondary resources related to that subject, thus making the use of these database collections extremely useful and cost effective to the specialist.

Business & News includes comprehensive coverage of news, business, and financial information, including local and national newspapers, legal newspapers, business and trade journals, and a number of magazines. Public Records includes public records, litigation filings, asset locators, and people finders.[8]

Legal Periodicals & Current Awareness and the related Treatises, CLEs, Practice Guides includes documents from law reviews, legal encyclopedias, continuing legal education materials, bar journals, practice guides, restatements, *American Law Reports* (*A.L.R.*), etc. *Westlaw* offers full text access to nearly 600 legal periodicals, with a mix of comprehensive

---

[8] Many of these databases are not included in the educational license provided to law schools and, therefore, are unavailable to law students.

and selective coverage of articles. Access to online versions of the *Index to Legal Periodicals & Books*, *Legal Resource Index*, and *Current Index to Legal Periodicals* is also available.[9]

Westlaw also has increased its International/Worldwide resources to now include international, multinational, and foreign legal primary and secondary sources.[10] The materials are organized by region of the world and country. The content varies by country but will usually include business news with some coverage of case law, legislation and patents and trademarks. A separate database provides extensive access to European Union materials.[11]

Other specialized materials on *Westlaw* include: *KeyCite*, an online citation research service[12]; materials from the American Bar Association; news, research, and statistical databases from DIALOG; dockets and litigation materials from state and appellate courts; materials from other legal publishers, including practitioner-oriented publications of the Practising Law Institute (PLI); an array of Warren, Gorham & Lamont tax and estate planning materials; MEDLINE, a medical information service from the National Library of Medicine; Disclosure, providing financial information on thousands of companies; and major treatises published by West and other Thomson Reuters brands.

The *West Legal Directory* provides information about attorneys, judicial clerkships, and subject-specific information throughout the United States.[13]

For specialized areas of legal research, consult the individual chapters in this book regarding the appropriate *Westlaw* databases. *Westlaw* produces a newsletter that reports additions and changes to its databases. Online and print database directories also are available.

2. LexisNexis

LexisNexis organizes its expansive collection of databases into tabs. Tabs such as "Legal," "News and Business," "Public Records," and "Find a Source" are standard. [Illustration 23–2] Users can also designate specialized tabs by jurisdiction or subject area. For general legal research needs, the "Legal" and "News and Business" tabs will contain the most relevant materials.

LexisNexis organizes the materials in its "Legal" tab into general categories, such as Cases–U.S., Federal Legal–U.S., States Legal–U.S., Legislation & Politics–U.S. & U.K., etc. *LexisNexis* uses a system of database folders, similar to Windows folders, which allows easy navigation

---

[9] *See* Chapter 18.

[10] *See* Chapter 21 for an extensive discussion of international legal resources.

[11] Thomson Reuters also offers several foreign editions of *Westlaw*, including *Westlaw China*, Westlaw *ES* (Spain), *WestlawCARSWELL* (Canada), *La Ley Online* (Argentina), and others. These editions are not included in the U.S. edition of *Westlaw* and require separate subscriptions.

[12] *KeyCite* is described in more detail in Chapter 15.

[13] The WEST LEGAL DIRECTORY is also available through *FindLaw*, another Thomson Reuters service, as the *FindLaw Legal Directory* at http://lawyers.findlaw.com, and as a stand-alone CD–ROM product.

within each category. Each category includes a variety of sources. To view a detailed description of each source, researchers can utilize Source Information (designated by the letter "i" within a small box), which provides a summary of the source's content, coverage information, search tips, and a sample document.

Case law from the combined federal and combined state courts is located in the Cases–U.S. folder. Case law from combined or individual federal courts, along with statutes and administrative materials, are each located in Federal Legal–U.S. The States Legal–U.S. folder contains cases, legislative material, and administrative law from individual states organized in folders by state. Cases on *LexisNexis* may include editorial features such as Case Summaries—concise, targeted synopses of cases—along with Core Concepts, which identify the key legal points of a case. A new feature is *LexisNexis* headnotes, numbered key points of law drawn from the language of the court, that summarize the holding of the case and provide a hierarchical structure for finding other cases with similar holdings.

Researchers also can also access Area of Law—by Topic. These specialized menus cover such diverse subjects as admiralty, copyright law, insurance, and securities. These sources provide access to both primary and secondary sources related to that topic, thus making the use of these sources extremely useful and cost effective to the specialist.

Secondary Legal includes the full text of law reviews, bar journals, restatements, etc. *LexisNexis* makes available the full text of over 400 legal periodicals online and continues to add new titles. *LexisNexis* also provides online access to the leading legal periodical indexes—*Index to Legal Periodicals & Books* and *Legal Resource Index*.[14]

Electronic versions of major looseleaf publications[15] comprise many of the specialized sources on *LexisNexis*. Major looseleaf vendors contributing information to the *LexisNexis* service include Bureau of National Affairs (BNA), Mealey Reports and Conferences, Tax Analysts, and numerous treatises, practice guides, and form books from Matthew Bender & Company, another subsidiary of Reed Elsevier.

Other folders in the "Legal" collection include Legal News, organized by practice area, jurisdiction, or information vendor, and Reference, with a variety of directories, dictionaries, and other reference tools. *LexisNexis* continues to expand the scope of its sources devoted to foreign law. The "Legal (excluding U.S.)" folder lists over 100 countries and regions focusing on business and political news, company information, country reports, and primary authority, including selected case and statutory law.

The other major *LexisNexis* categories include News & Business, a current awareness news and information service with over 22,000 worldwide full-text sources from newspapers, magazines, journals, newsletters, wire services, and broadcast transcripts. The Company & Financial databases include information on public and private businesses and Public

---

[14] *See* Chapter 18, Section B.

[15] *See* Chapter 14.

Records with people finders, bankruptcy and other court filings, and tax and property records, among other sources.[16]

Other *LexisNexis* specialized sources include: *Shepard's,* an online version of the traditional citator[17]; *MEDLINE*, covering medical and health information; Legislation & Politics, providing the full text of state and federal legislation, pending legislation, and bill tracking; Deed Transfers & Tax Assessor Records, providing selective national coverage of real estate assessments and deed transfers; and Martindale–Hubbell Law Directory Listings, with law firm profiles and basic biographical information on lawyers throughout the United State, Canada, and around the world.

For specialized areas of legal research, consult the individual chapters in this book for information about the appropriate *LexisNexis* sources. There are several ways to keep up-to-date with the wide variety of sources available on *LexisNexis*. *LexisNexis* provides a newsletter that describes the changes and additions to its databases. The researcher can review the *LexisNexis* introductory screen and the searchable *LexisNexis Directory of Online Sources* to identify new databases.[18]

3. Selecting a Source or Database

a. *Westlaw*. Like *LexisNexis*, the *Westlaw* front page has several tabs for accessing its information resources. Academic users will default to Law School, while other users can select Westlaw or Business & News, or they can select a jurisdiction or topic area.

Westlaw offers the user a variety of methods for selecting individual or combined databases. From the *Westlaw* main page, users can access all the resources available. [Illustration 23–3] Researchers who know specific database names can select the Search for a Database textbox and enter the database name. However, a researcher may also use the Search the Westlaw Directory textbox to search with only a keyword, e.g., bankruptcy. *Westlaw* will retrieve a list of suggested databases. An additional access point is *Westlaw*'s Directory, located on the toolbar, which displays all the databases. Other database-finding features, such as Recent Databases, Favorite Databases, and Find a Database Wizard, can all be accessed through the *Westlaw* main page. The Recent Databases feature maintains a list in a drop-down menu of the last 20 databases accessed by the user. The Favorite Databases feature allows the user to customize a list of frequently used databases in a drop-down menu format, and it allows the user to save, organize, rename, and delete databases from a customized interface as necessary.

When a novice researcher needs assistance in choosing a source, the Directory provides a hierarchical arrangement of databases by subject or type, such as U.S. State Materials, U.S. Federal Materials, Topical Practice Areas, Legal Periodicals, Litigation, Business & News, Public Records, etc. The Find a Database Wizard is also an easy way to select a database. Users are asked a series of questions regarding the type of material they are

---

[16] As with *Westlaw*, many of the public records databases are not available to academic users under the *LexisNexis* educational contract.

[17] *See* Chapter 15 for a discussion of *Shepard's* and other citators.

[18] http://w3.nexis.com/sources/.

seeking. *Westlaw* then suggests databases to search. After the selection process is completed, the Database Wizard displays either the Search page for a specific database or the section in *Westlaw*'s Directory that contains the databases relevant to one's research.

Another search option, KeySearch, is powered by West's key number system, which assists researchers in finding relevant documents. [Illustration 23–4] KeySearch is extremely helpful when the user is unfamiliar with a specific area of law or is unable to identify an appropriate key number. KeySearch identifies key numbers and terms related to particular legal issues and creates an appropriate search query. The user either selects from a list of topics and subtopics by clicking relevant folder icons or types specific terms in the text box. Search results include not only West-reported cases that contain key numbers, but also documents, such as unpublished cases and law review articles, which do not contain key numbers.

Users can access *KeyCite*, *Westlaw*'s citator research service, directly from the main page. A textbox allows the researcher to enter a citation and quickly determine whether a case, statute, administrative decision, or regulation is good law and retrieve citing references.[19]

Researchers can also utilize My Westlaw, a feature that allows users to design up to 50 customized *Westlaw* pages. My Westlaw is useful when a researcher frequently searches in a particular jurisdiction or in a particular area of law. By customizing these tabs, researchers can quickly access frequently needed databases.

b. *LexisNexis*. *LexisNexis* offers several methods for selecting a source. The method chosen depends upon the individual's expertise with *LexisNexis* and the knowledge of the topic and issue being researched.

After the researcher signs on to www.lexis.com, *LexisNexis* defaults to the Total Research System page. [Illustration 23–2] The Search by Source page features three methods from which to select a source: Recently Used Sources; Look for a Source; and Find a Source. The Recently Used Sources option provides an historical listing of the last 20 sources accessed. This method is helpful when the researcher frequently uses the same sources. The Look for a Source option has a hierarchical directory of major category tabs and database folders. The Find a Source option offers searching in two distinct categories: an alphabetical directory and a natural language search engine that searches by keyword or phrase.

Two additional database selection mechanisms are provided using tabs at the top of the Total Research System page. The by Guided Search Forms tab connects to a list of a number of collections of databases by subject, including Federal Legal, States Legal, Area of Law, Cases, Codes, etc. Selecting one of these collections brings up a new page with a search box and a drop down box with a list of combined and individual databases within the collection. An additional search option—by Dot Command—is useful for researchers more accustomed to the proprietary version of *LexisNexis*. If a researcher knows the library and file name of the source desired, the user can go directly to the particular source instead of navigating through the source hierarchy. In command searching, users can

---

[19] *See* Chapter 15 for an in-depth discussion of *KeyCite*.

utilize "dot commands" and "command stacking"—search methods familiar to users of the traditional proprietary version of *LexisNexis*.[20]

A less direct method of choosing a source is to select the *LexisNexis* by Topic or Headnote subtab located under Search. [Illustration 23–5] This method is a useful place to begin a search when a user is unfamiliar with the area of law and is unsure where to start. by Topic or Headnote targets legal issues, suggests alternative research paths, identifies appropriate sources, and formulates search requests. by Topic or Headnote is a classification system of approximately 16,000 topics and subtopics. Upon accessing by Topic or Headnote, the user can choose from two different options— Find a Legal Topic and Explore Legal Topics. The Find a Legal Topic option is ideal when the user has a legal issue or keyword and wants to find all the possible areas of law in which it could be included. Explore Legal Topics is similar to the Explore Sources option in Search Sources; topics are arranged in a hierarchal format with each legal topic broken down into subtopics. This method is useful when the researcher knows the area of law; the user can then navigate through the hierarchical layers of topics and examine possible issues and alternative research paths.

For practitioners, a useful tool offered by *LexisNexis* is Research Tasks pages, providing access to a variety of information for individual practice areas in one location. Two methods of accessing this tool are to search by area of law or to search by jurisdiction.

Users can access *Shepard's* citation service directly from the main page by clicking on Shepard's. A textbox allows the researcher to enter a citation and quickly determine whether a case, statute, administrative decision, or regulation is good law and retrieve citing references.

4. Document Retrieval

At times, a researcher needs to retrieve a document by a known category of information, e.g., party name, citation, or docket number. By utilizing *Westlaw*'s Find & Print feature, or *LexisNexis'* Get a Document feature, a user can quickly and efficiently retrieve the needed source. This technique avoids the necessity of determining the appropriate database and formulating a query. When utilizing these features, template screens on both *Westlaw* and *LexisNexis* make it easy for the user to enter the known information.[21]

Both *Westlaw* and *LexisNexis* offer a Table of Contents feature. *Westlaw*'s Table of Contents, located on the toolbar, allows users to select from a directory of publications that offer a table of contents for viewing, browse the table of contents for a specific publication, view a document in the context of the sections surrounding it, and quickly retrieve related sections. While *LexisNexis* also offers a Table of Contents feature for particular

---

[20] Dot commands are used as a shorthand method to display formats, e.g., .ci (cite view) or .fu (full view). Command stacking is used when the researcher wants to quickly select a source and enter a search query at the same time, e.g., *GENFED; 5CIR; employment discrimination and pregnancy.*

[21] *LexisNexis* and *Westlaw* commercial users are charged a modest flat fee for finding documents using a specific citation. However, locating documents by party name, docket number or other access point will actually run a database search, for which a per-search or per-minute charge will apply.

publications, it is available only after a user has selected the specific publication; the user cannot use the Table of Contents feature to select a source, as one can in *Westlaw*.

SECTION C. FORMULATING SEARCH REQUESTS ON WESTLAW AND LEXISNEXIS[22]

1. Costs of Searching

Mastering search strategy techniques is essential to make the most efficient use of online legal research services. Pricing options for *Westlaw* and *LexisNexis* vary considerably; a representative of each company must be consulted for pricing information. Charges to commercial accounts often are based on the amount of time spent online, the number of searches executed, or both, although many organizations negotiate flat rates for use of these services. Premiums may be charged for accessing certain sources or databases, especially those containing multiple types of authority. Both vendors have price structures that reward efficiency.

"Educational" subscriptions enable students, faculty, librarians, and other qualified individuals at law schools and universities to have unlimited access to these services.[23] The educational discount limits student use of *Westlaw* and *LexisNexis* to research associated with the curricular and co-curricular activities of the school's program.

One method of reducing costs is to construct a search and plan a research path in advance. Deciding in advance which databases or sources are most appropriate for a search, instead of automatically searching in the premium databases, makes research more cost effective. Regardless of billing concerns, a thoughtful search strategy planned before going online is more likely to lead to successful results.[24]

For non-subscribers who want to access *Westlaw*, the company offers *Westlaw by Credit Card*, a service that allows non-subscribers to access *Westlaw* document retrieval and *KeyCite* services on the Internet with the use of a credit card. *LexisNexis* offers a similar service for non-subscribers—*lexisOne*—available online.[25]

2. Traditional Search Strategies—Terms and Connectors

Traditionally, searching on *Westlaw* and *LexisNexis* has been accomplished almost exclusively by using words and phrases within a framework of instructions to the database. The search mechanisms employed are

---

[22] This portion of the chapter is designed as a brief overview for computerized legal research search strategy. *Westlaw* and *LexisNexis* produce extensive materials to assist the legal researcher. Both services have online tutorials to assist in learning computerized legal research skills, as well as the specifics of each service. *See also* JUDITH A. LONG, LEGAL RESEARCH USING WESTLAW (2001); ADAM J. PIACENTE, WESTLAW.COM UNPLUGGED: THE USER-FRIENDLY GUIDE TO WESTLAW ON THE INTERNET (2008).

[23] "Unlimited" refers to the absence of restrictions on or fees tied to how much time a user spends on the service. As noted, the educational subscriptions do not provide access to every resource available. Public records and some looseleaf and other third-party databases often are not included.

[24] For a discussion of efficient query formulation, see Section C–4 below.

[25] http://www.lexisone.com.

similar for both services and are referred to as "terms and connectors." As an alternative to term searching, both *Westlaw* and *LexisNexis* offer natural language searching, which is discussed in Section C–3 below.

In a terms and connectors search, the researcher focuses on words or phrases that express a legal issue and are likely to be found in relevant documents. These words and phrases are combined with connectors to link the terms the user is seeking in the documents.

a. *Plurals, Possessives, Word Truncation, Universal Character.* *Westlaw* and *LexisNexis* both automatically generate regular plural forms when the word's singular form is searched. For example, *dog* also retrieves *dogs*. *Westlaw*, however, also retrieves most irregular plural forms. Both services automatically retrieve the singular possessive and plural possessive forms of nouns.

To retrieve variant spellings, the *universal character,* an asterisk (*), is available. For example, to retrieve *compact disk* or *compact disc, compact dis** should be entered. Universal characters can be placed in the middle or at the end of a term, but not at the beginning. When a universal character is used at the end of a term, the maximum length of that term is specified. For example, *eat*** retrieves all forms of the root "eat" that have up to two additional characters, such as *eaten* and *eats*, but not *eating*.

Words may also be truncated. Truncation identifies a particular word root. For example, a researcher may wish to retrieve documents that include either *tort* or *tortious*. A user can choose to place both terms in a search or capture any expression using the root "tort" followed by the root expander, an exclamation point (!). Therefore, *tort!* isolates all these expressions, including *tort, tortious, tortiously*, and *torte*. Torte may not have any legal relevance, although it tastes good; however, the search software performs literal search requests.

b. *Boolean Logic Connectors.* Boolean logic is a technique that allows the researcher to link words or phrases in order to define a relationship between them.

The connector "AND" requires a word or phrase and another word or phrase to be located in the same document. "AND" does not require the two elements in the search to appear in any particular proximity to each other or in any particular portion of the document.

The "OR" connector requires either or both words or phrases to appear in a document or in any particular portion of the document. If one word or phrase is located, it may appear in any portion of a document. If both words or phrases appear in the same document, they need not appear in any particular proximity to one another. "OR" as a connector is commonly used when a word has a synonym or when a phrase may be expressed in several ways. A space between two terms is understood by *Westlaw* to imply an "OR" connector. *LexisNexis* treats the words on either side of a space as a phrase, as if they were in quotation marks.[26]

---

[26] There are other slight variations between *Westlaw*'s Boolean search syntax and *LexisNexis*' Boolean search syntax. Generally, both services will either accept the syntax from the other service, or provide a pop-up error message to prompt a correction.

In *Westlaw* phrases are identified by quotation marks to avoid an implied "OR" connector. Consider these two alternative search strategies on *Westlaw*:

#1: *res ipsa loquitor*

#2: *"res ipsa loquitor"*

In the first example, *Westlaw* locates documents that contain either *res* or *ipsa* or *loquitor*. The second query, *"res ipsa loquitor,"* locates only documents where the words *res ipsa loquitor,* the legal phrase, appear. *LexisNexis* recognizes *res ipsa loquitor* as a phrase; no quotations or connectors are necessary.

Boolean connectors are also utilized to exclude documents that contain certain terms. *Westlaw*'s "BUT NOT" or *LexisNexis*' "AND NOT" connectors should be used judiciously, as they eliminate any words that follow and can change the intent of the search request. For example, *trust AND NOT "charitable trust"* finds trust anywhere in the document, but "charitable trust" cannot appear in the document.

c. *Proximity Connectors.* Both *Westlaw* and *LexisNexis* permit users to conduct a search looking for terms located in proximity to one another. This is accomplished using grammatical and numerical connectors to locate two or more words or phrases within a certain number of words of each other or in a particular order within a defined number of words.

The relationship of words and their physical juxtaposition imparts ideas and concepts that words, when expressed independently, do not. For instance, a researcher examining the jurisprudence of criminal procedure would be interested in documents that place *reasonable* and *doubt* in close proximity to one another. Simply searching the database for all occurrences of *reasonable* and *doubt* in a document using the "AND" connector would yield an unwieldy number of irrelevant cases. However, looking for the phrase *reasonable doubt*, or *reasonable* and *doubt* within the same sentence or paragraph, or within a defined number of words of one another, or in a specific order, will produce better results.

Both companies use numerical proximity connectors to search for words within a designated number "W/#" of words apart. "#" can be any number up to 255, although if you would expect your search terms to be more than 100 words apart, you might consider using "AND." Lower numbers, such as 1 to 5 are often used for phrases such as "assum! w/5 risk," which will locate both "assumption of the risk" and "the risk was assumed by." A range of 10 to 25 can be used to locate terms within a sentence or two, helpful for finding linkages between an issue and a specific fact or facts. A range of 30 to 100 can be used to locate terms within a paragraph or section.

The basic proximity connector, "W/#", searches for the words in any order no more than "#" words apart. "Pre/#" (on *LexisNexis*) or " + #" (*on Westlaw*) are used when the terms must be in a specific order with the first term preceding the second term. "W/s" and "W/p" are used to find terms within a specific text sentence or paragraph respectively. "W/seg" (on *LexisNexis* only) is used to find terms within a specific segment of the document. In *LexisNexis*, adding the word "NOT" to a proximity connector (e.g., "NOT w/#" or "NOT w/s") allows the elimination of one term when proximate with another, but not the elimination the term entirely, such as "rico NOT w/2 puerto." In contrast, *Westlaw* treats "NOT" as a word. To achieve the same result on *Westlaw*, use "rico & puerto % puerto rico."

d. *Field or Segment Searching.* Besides conducting a search looking for terms in proximity, both *Westlaw* and *LexisNexis* permit users to look for words or phrases within a certain predefined section of a document. Electronically stored documents are broken into identifiable parts, such as citation, date, and body. *Westlaw* and *LexisNexis* both enable a user to search these particular predefined portions of a document. *Westlaw* calls this feature field searching; *LexisNexis* calls it segment searching.

When a full-text search is conducted, the system normally searches all parts of a document. Alternatively, a user can restrict a search to one or more fields or segments. A field or segment search can enhance the quality of search results and often eliminates the retrieval of irrelevant information.

Westlaw and *LexisNexis* users can select field restrictions/segments when accessing a particular database/source to view the various fields/segments available for searching. For example, for court decisions, *Westlaw* defines its fields by the physical sections of a document. Because all West's *National Reporter System* cases appear in similar formats, that format established the defined fields in *Westlaw*.

e. *Additional search strategies.* Three additional research tools are capitalization, singular and plural, and frequency searching.

Capitalization permits a search for terms in all upper or lower case. This is useful when searching for acronyms, country and state abbreviations, agencies, and alphabetical characters in state statutes and codes.

Singular specificity avoids both services' automatic searching for regular plural forms of words. Plural specificity is helpful to locate only the plural form of a noun. For example, if one is looking for references to the New York Yankees baseball team, a user can combine plural specificity with capitalization to produce a search request.

Finally, frequency searching determines if a specific term appears within a document a certain minimum of times. For example, to find a document containing 15 occurrences of the word "redundant," the search request would read as *atleast15(redundant)*.

3. Natural Language Searching

In 1992, *Westlaw* introduced a natural language search mechanism as an alternative to the terms and connectors search method. In preparing a natural language search, the *Westlaw* database is queried in the simple form of a question. In 1993, *LexisNexis* released its version of natural language referred to then as "freestyle." Today, "natural language" searching is the term used by both vendors for this approach to research. Natural language searching works best (1) when the researcher is searching for broad concepts, rather than very specific topics, (2) is unfamiliar with the issue, (3) when the issue is complex and a terms and connector query would be difficult to construct, or (4) when the researcher is a new or infrequent user.

a. *Westlaw*. The natural language search method on *Westlaw* uses "an editorially created phrase list to automatically recognize certain phrases in the query and puts them inside quotation marks."[27] A user can also create phrases by enclosing terms in quotation marks, e.g., *"reasonable person standard."*

To expand the accuracy of a query, *Westlaw* natural language searching allows the user to add additional related terms to the search by placing them parenthetically after specific words. Westlaw also provides an online legal thesaurus that recognizes the query's search phrases and suggests related terms or phrases.

In the example: *Are universities liable for injuries to students participating in intramural sports?*, the user could add the term "colleges" as a related term for "universities", and add the word "athletics" as a related term for "intramural sports." The search would then read, *Are universities (colleges) liable for injuries to students participating in intramural sports (athletics)?*

Using the thesaurus, the natural language search recognized the following search concepts, and the thesaurus augmented those terms by providing the suggestions appearing below in parenthesis:

university and college (higher education)

liable (accountable, culpable, responsible, etc.)

injury (harm, damage, wrong, etc.)

student (pupil, undergraduate, etc.)

sport (athletics, competition, match, event, etc.)

The researcher can select some or all of the terms identified by the thesaurus to add to the search.

The next step in a *Westlaw* natural language search is that the chosen database is searched for "hits." A "hit" occurs when an occurrence of words or phrases or roots of words are compared with a statistical-linguistic algorithm, indicating that the "hit" is statistically relevant to the query. The results of the statistical analysis are then ranked by frequency of occurrence and statistical relevance using the algorithm. By default, a natural language search retrieves the 20 documents containing the most closely matching concepts to those specified in the user's description. A maximum of 100 documents can be retrieved.

b. *LexisNexis*. Just as in *Westlaw*, a researcher can enter a natural language search in *LexisNexis*, by using plain English without connectors. Users can type in a research issue as an individual term, phrase, list, or sentence. The system automatically checks for common legal phrases. It is also possible to create phrases by enclosing words in quotes. Unlike a terms and connectors search, where terms must appear in every document, in natural language searches, relevant documents may not contain all search terms. Therefore, to specify that a particular search word or phrase must

---

[27] Nancy Johnson et al., Discovering Winning Research Skills 80 (West 2004).

appear in retrieved documents, it should be set forth as a mandatory term by entering it into a "Restrict Using Mandatory Terms" text box on the screen. The Suggest Terms for My Search Feature, *LexisNexis'* version of an online thesaurus, allows a user to select from a list of words or concepts related to the user's search terms. As with *Westlaw*, a user can restrict results by date.

Natural language in *LexisNexis* analyzes the words and phrases in the search request, eliminates irrelevant terms, and then ranks in importance the remaining terms in that query. The natural language search mechanism then provides the user the opportunity to make revisions to the search. Search results can be limited to 10 to 250 documents and sorted by either relevance or date.

4. Efficient Query Formulation

In developing a search strategy, a user should keep in mind the following steps.

First, try to identify in advance which sources are likely to contain the information needed. This allows a more quick and efficient search. Searching the narrowest source that meets a researcher's need makes evaluating search results easier, which in turn reduces the amount of time spent online. In addition, it is more costly to access sources that contain multiple types of authority, such as those containing all federal or state cases.

Next, recognizing the ambiguous nature of language, a researcher should consider all the ways in which an idea may be expressed. Use the TARP analysis (thing, action, relief, and parties) outlined in Chapter 2 of this book when trying to isolate an appropriate keyword.

Think in terms of the idiomatic nature of language and the use of synonyms. Keep in mind terms of art, or "legalese," frequently used in legal writing.[28] Try to express a query according to the way the words or phrases might appear in the variety of documents that the computer searches and in what relationship, both physical and syntactical, the words and phrases may be used. Recognize that no search strategy is perfect, and understand that there is no assurance that every document retrieved will satisfy the user's information needs.

A thesaurus indicates a variety of ways that a particular concept may be expressed. *Westlaw* permits the use of its online thesaurus not only in natural language searching, but also in terms and connectors searching. *LexisNexis* users can access the Suggest Terms for My Search feature in both terms and connectors and natural language searching, providing searchers with ideas for synonyms and related concepts. Researchers may also consider using a print thesaurus.[29]

Structure the search efficiently. Use fields and segments to limit the search to appropriate portions of the document. It may be especially difficult to research emerging areas of the law if no consistent forms of expression or "buzz-words" have developed. There are ways of overcoming the imprecise nature of language using the software capabilities inherent in

---

[28] *See* BLACK'S LAW DICTIONARY (Bryan A. Garner ed., 8th ed. 2004) for legal definitions.

[29] WILLIAM C. BURTON, BURTON'S LEGAL THESAURUS (4th ed. rev. 2006).

Westlaw and *LexisNexis*. When "buzz-words" are not readily available, opting for the use of a natural language search may be helpful.

Once search results are retrieved, a researcher must determine the success of a search query based on the researcher's level of expertise with the subject area. A user's individual analysis should be similar to the TARP analysis undertaken when developing the initial search request. Several methods can be used to review search results.

Westlaw and *LexisNexis* both offer basic browsing techniques. *Westlaw*'s Term Mode and *LexisNexis*' KWIC (Key Words in Context) format assist the researcher in quickly assessing the validity of the search results. Term Mode allows a user to quickly scan each document's sections where the highlighted search terms appear. KWIC format in *LexisNexis* automatically displays 25 words appearing directly before and after the highlighted search terms. A user can alter this number from 1 to 999 in Variable KWIC format. In addition, in both *Westlaw* and *LexisNexis*, search results can be viewed in full text, citation, or field and segment formats.

Another useful method to determine the relevancy of search results is to review the synopses of individual cases. Synopses set forth a summary of the case and may include a review of the facts presented, the holding of the lower court, and the disposition of the case.

When a researcher locates an on-point document, *Westlaw* offers features that help locate additional relevant documents. Users may utilize the West key number as a component of a search. By examining the headnotes and related key numbers of relevant documents, the researcher can identify concepts and hyperlink to other documents with the same key number(s). The key number system on *Westlaw* is the same classification of legal concepts used in the *American Digest System*.[30] Keep in mind, however, that the key number system has changed over the years and is not always consistent, and it is based on the judgment of West editors.

Another useful *Westlaw* feature is Most Cited Cases. After identifying a relevant digest topic and key number from a case, this feature allows researchers to retrieve a list of the cases cited most frequently for that particular point of law. The cases are listed in order of citation frequency, with the case most often cited listed first. Researchers can then choose to narrow or broaden their jurisdiction, add additional search terms, or use a date restriction.

LexisNexis provides case summaries, similar to the synopses available on *Westlaw*, which assist the researcher in evaluating the relevancy of search results. The summaries are concise synopses of cases and contain three sections: Procedural Posture (describes the case's procedural history); Overview (provides a brief review of the court's holding on the legal issues raised); and Outcome (reviews the procedural disposition of the case). *LexisNexis* assigns headnotes that identify the key legal points of a case. *LexisNexis*' legal editors assign these headnotes after examining the language of the court. This is similar to the manner in which West's legal editors assign key numbers. Headnotes allow a user to link to relevant text within a case and to other relevant documents.

---

[30] *See* Chapter 7.

In *LexisNexis*, when a searcher locates a relevant document, a user can utilize the More Like This feature. This feature makes it easy to locate additional documents quickly by looking for documents with similar language patterns. The computer generates language patterns, e.g., keywords called Core Terms, and citation patterns called Core Cites, directly from the case. More Like This creates a new search using your original search words, Core Terms or Core Cites, and other information from the original document. Searchers are allowed to change sources, use Core Cites, select particular Core Terms, add mandatory terms, and change a date restriction. The More Like This feature works with case law, statutes, law reviews, and news article databases. A related search option is More Like Selected Text. This option allows a researcher to find more documents that contain language like the highlighted text selected within a case.

One of the best methods to assess the relevancy of search results and, if necessary, narrow a search result that is too large is to perform a Locate or Focus search. *Westlaw*'s Locate and *LexisNexis*' Focus allow a researcher to search for terms within the documents retrieved in the initial query. The terms can either be part of the original search query or new terms selected by the user. This operation is performed without altering the original search request. In effect, it operates as a search within a search. Commercial users of Locate and Focus do not incur additional charges for these searches.

5.   Westlaw and LexisNexis Alert Services

For ongoing research, both companies provide alert services which allow a researcher to monitor the service for new cases, statutes, or other developments. An alert is a pre-set search, including search terms and database selection, that the researcher programs to run on a periodic basis. The alert automatically runs the search, and then identifies any new documents that have been added to the database since the last alert search—or indicates that no new documents have been added. The researcher can program the alert to send an email notification to the researcher of the search results, have the results sent directly to a printer, or save the results for later review.

Westlaw uses its Alert Center and Westlaw Watch services to allow users to create and monitor alert searches in a number of categories. Westclip is the primary alert category, which allows the researcher to monitor developments in most case, statute, regulatory, law review or other publication databases. Results are delivered to the destination specified by the user, i.e., printer, fax, or email address. Other categories allow alerts to be established for *KeyCite* results and for specialized categories such as federal and state court dockets, federal agency filings, people profilers, and Dun and Bradstreet reports.[31]

Alert is *LexisNexis*' electronic monitoring service, which reruns searches at daily, weekly, or monthly intervals. *LexisNexis* Alert results can be viewed online, printed, or emailed. Alerts are available with terms and connectors searches but not with natural language searches.

Both services provide RSS alerts to commercial subscribers.

---

[31] Some of these alert resources are not available to law students under the *Westlaw* educational contract.

6. Using Westlaw and LexisNexis as Citators

In addition to either *KeyCite* and *Shepard's*, *Westlaw* and *LexisNexis* both provide methods for using their databases as citators, i.e., to locate documents that have cited specific sources, whether cases, statutes, journal articles, or any other source. It should be noted that commercial users may incur search charges that are more expensive than *KeyCite* or *Shepard's* charges. The use of the CALR services as citators is most efficient and effective when searching for citations that are not included in *KeyCite* or *Shepard's*.

a. Westlaw and LexisNexis Numerical Connectors as Citators. *Westlaw* and *LexisNexis* can be used as citators to locate documents that have cited specific cases, statutes, and other sources. This can be done by accessing a database and typing a terms and connectors query that includes citation information from the document for which a user wants to find citing references. Numerical connectors, discussed earlier, may be used so that numbers must appear within a document in a particular sequence or proximity. For example, 42 U.S.C. § 12101, may be cited in the following formats: 42 U.S.C. § 12101, 42 U.S.C.A. § 12101, Section 12101 of Title 42, etc. An effective search may simply be "42 w/5 12101".

b. KeyCite and Shepard's. *KeyCite* is *Westlaw*'s proprietary citation research service that helps quickly determine whether a case, statute, administrative decision, or regulation is good law and retrieves citing references for these materials as well as secondary sources. *KeyCite* provides information regarding a case's history, including prior and subsequent history, negative indirect history (cases that have a negative impact on the cited case, but are not within the cited case's appellate history), and citing references that cite to and discuss the cited case.

LexisNexis provides electronic access to its own citation service, *Shepard's,* covering a wide variety of legal information, including federal and state case law, federal and state statutory materials, law review articles, federal administrative regulations, patents, and federal rules. *Shepard's* on *LexisNexis* offers full treatment and history analysis needed to verify the status of a case. A user may verify the correct name and official and parallel citations for a case, check the current validity of a case, and review a case's prior and subsequent history, including negative indirect history.[32]

SECTION D.   ILLUSTRATIONS: WESTLAW AND LEXISNEXIS

23–1. **Screen Print, Westlaw Directory and Main Page**
23–2. **Screen Print, LexisNexis Directory and Main Page**
23–3. **Screen Print, Westlaw Search Sources Page**
23–4. **Screen Print, Westlaw KeySearch Page**
23–5. **Screen Print, LexisNexis Search Advisor Page**

[32] *See* Chapter 15 for a discussion of *KeyCite* and *Shepard's.*

[Illustration 23–1]

SCREEN PRINT, WESTLAW DIRECTORY AND MAIN PAGE

[Illustration 23–2]

SCREEN PRINT, LEXISNEXIS DIRECTORY AND MAIN PAGE

[Illustration 23–3]

SCREEN PRINT, WESTLAW SEARCH SOURCES PAGE

[Illustration 23–4]

SCREEN PRINT, WESTLAW KEYSEARCH PAGE

[Illustration 23–5]

SCREEN PRINT, LEXISNEXIS SEARCH ADVISOR PAGE

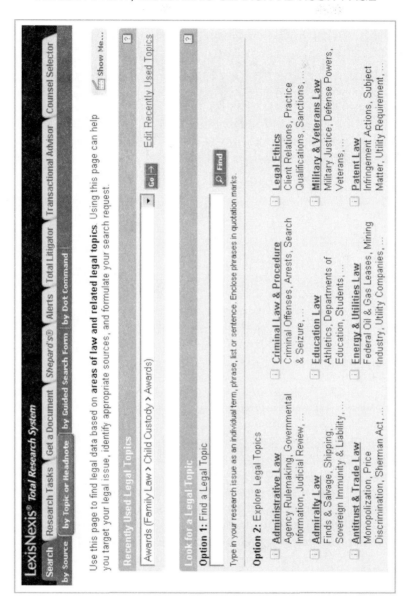

SECTION E. OTHER COMMERCIAL LEGAL INFORMATION PROVIDERS

LexisNexis and *Westlaw* are not the only vendors providing electronic access to primary and secondary legal information. A number of other companies provide access to commercial, restricted-access databases containing content that is often not available through *LexisNexis* and *Westlaw*. While some of these databases are available on CD–ROM, or occasionally DVD–ROM, most of them are accessed directly through the Internet.

Unlike Internet resources to be discussed in Section F, these databases are available only to subscribers, or in some cases on a fee-for-use basis. They utilize digital rights management (DRM) technologies to restrict access to authorized users, and they often use detailed licensing agreements to control who may use the services and how they may be used.

Starting in the late 1980s, legal publishers began to publish secondary authority, and later, primary authority on CD–ROM. The cost of these CD–ROM products was often less than online access, eliminating researchers' concerns regarding the costly per minute charges of *Westlaw* and *LexisNexis*, while still providing hyperlink ability. The CD–ROM format, however, clearly limited the amount of data that can be stored and also required continual updating.

Most legal publishers have since turned to the Internet as the preferred vehicle for providing access to electronic legal research resources. Using the World Wide Web and Web browser software, legal publishers are able to provide access that is faster and offers an easier updating process than CD–ROMs. Web technology also helps resolve many of the problems that existed with CD–ROM networks, such as the lack of standards, multiple search interfaces, and proprietary components. Bureau of National Affairs (BNA) for example, now offers many of its publications in full text on the Web, with email alerts for their newsletters; Commerce Clearing House (CCH) offers many of its looseleaf services via the Internet, and Matthew Bender provides many of its popular treatises like *Nimmer on Copyright* on the Web through *Matthew Bender Online*.[33]

Commercial and restricted-access websites rely upon DRM technology to admit only authorized or licensed users to the information contained in the site. There are two primary methods to accomplish this: (1) individual passwords; and (2) Internet Protocol (IP) address authentication. For a database controlled by password access, individual passwords; are issued to authorized users by the database vendor, such as in the cases of *Westlaw* and *LexisNexis*. For IP authentication, the vendor accepts requests from users of specific computers with an IP address within a pre-approved range, such as a law school or law firm. IP addresses uniquely identify a computer that the vendor's server is programmed to recognize and allow access to the vendor's content. Keep in mind that restricted-access websites accessible through IP authentication may not be available from home or offsite locations.

Among the more popular commercial providers of Web-based legal information are:[34]

---

[33] *See* Chapter 14 for a discussion of BNA and CCH looseleaf services and Chapter 19 for a discussion of treatises.

[34] This is a selective list of commercial, Web-based databases to which most academic law libraries and many larger firm libraries subscribe, including both full-text databases and bibliographic databases. There are many specialty databases and pay-as-you-go services that are available through the Web as well. Check with your law library for information about what subscription services are available to you, or go online to the particular service's home page for subscription information.

Bloomberg Law, http://www.bloomberg.com

While Bloomberg has been a long-time provider of business, financial, and media information, *Bloomberg Law* is a relatively new entrant into the electronic legal information marketplace. *Bloomberg Law*'s primary products are their subject-specific *Law Reports*, which are comprehensive analyses of legal and regulatory developments in a wide variety of topical areas. *Law Reports* are published periodically, often weekly or monthly. *Bloomberg Law* also delivers legal news, court dockets and filings, regulatory information, court opinions, company and biographical information, and other legal content. *Bloomberg Law* is presently available via dedicated terminals within law school, law firm, and corporate law department libraries.

BNA, http://www.bna.com

The Bureau of National Affairs is a major publisher of looseleaf services, now available online. The major collections include Antitrust and Trade, Bankruptcy, Criminal Law, Employment Discrimination, Environmental Law, Family Law, Health and Medical Law, Intellectual Property, International Trade, Labor Law, Securities Regulation, and Taxation. BNA provides full-text access to the content of its looseleaf services. Some collections have an email service to provide daily or weekly highlights to users.

Casemaker, http://www.casemaker.us
CasemakerX, http://www.casemakerx.com

Both of these related services provide access to a wide collection of state and federal legal research resources. *Casemaker* works with a consortium of state bar associations to provide access to current and archived state and federal caselaw, statutes, court rules, and regulations, plus additional state content including attorney general opinions, ethics opinions, and jury instructions. Members of bar associations that participate in the *Casemaker* consortium have free access to these resources. *CasemakerX* provides access to the *Casemaker* databases to law students. *CasemakerX* provides an additional social networking service which allows students to connect with other students as well as attorney members of the *Casemaker* consortium by setting up *Facebook*-style profiles.

CCH Internet Research NetWork, http://www.cch.com
CCH Tax Research NetWork, http://www.tax.cch.com

The *CCH Internet Research NetWork* offers Web-based research services, including a business compliance network containing full-text looseleaf services and treaties in the health care and human services areas; a business and finance network with corporate, securities, banking, trade regulation, and other business-related information; and a computer and Internet online network with treatises on Internet and e-commerce law. The *CCH Tax Research NetWork* contains primary and secondary sources for both federal and state tax systems, including the full-text of CCH's *Standard Federal Tax Reporter*, state tax guides, IRS publications, and other materials.

Fastcase, http://fastcase.com

Fastcase is a more economically priced legal research service available by subscription and in some states through the state bar association. The search engine provides for keyword and natural language searching. Cases can be retrieved by citation, and there is an authority check function. The depth and breadth of the database is expanding.

HeinOnline, http://www.heinonline.org

HeinOnline is a rapidly expanding collection of primary and secondary source libraries. Its initial and most used library is its Law Journal Library, which contains full-text law review and journal articles from most U.S. published law reviews. Coverage generally goes much further back in time than *LexisNexis* or *Westlaw*, often back to the journal's inception. However, *HeinOnline* may not provide the most recent six months to a year of journal content. *HeinOnline* also has online collections of treaties, the *Federal Register* and *Code of Federal Regulations*, Supreme Court and attorney general opinions, selected legislative histories, *U.S. Statutes at Large* and state session laws, and a growing collection of classic legal treatises. *HeinOnline* is also expanding into international and foreign materials, including English reports, international yearbooks, decisions of international tribunals, and some international and foreign law journals. Most of the documents are available as PDFs of the original printed documents and are searchable in full text. This is particularly helpful in providing pagination and other information for citation purposes.

Index to Legal Periodicals (ILP), http://www.hwwilson.com
LegalTrac, http://www.infotrac.galegroup.com

H.W. Wilson's *Index to Legal Periodicals & Books (ILP)* is a bibliographic index to law reviews, bar association and journal publications, and government publications. Some online subscriptions also provide access to selected full-text articles.[35] H.W. Wilson also provides the *Index to Legal Periodicals Retrospective: 1908–1981*, which is the only online bibliographic index to journal articles published prior to 1980. *LegalTrac* is a bibliographic database which indexes law reviews, bar journals and legal newspapers back to 1980.

LLMC Digital, http://www.llmc-digital.org

LLMC (The Law Library Microform Consortium) *Digital* is an online collection of state and federal primary materials, including an extensive collection of federal agency documents, early American state and federal case law and statutory compilations, territorial legal materials, and selected Anglo–American and foreign legal materials. Many of the documents are searchable and are presented as scanned images of document pages.

Loislaw, http://www.loislaw.com

Loislaw is accessible solely over the Internet via the World Wide Web and is an alternative to *Westlaw* and *LexisNexis*. *Loislaw* provides searchable, full-text access to federal and state primary law, including appellate court opinions, statutes, regulations, constitutions, administrative law, and court rules. Case law dates back to 1899 for the U.S. Supreme Court, 1950 for federal appellate courts, and 1921 for district courts. Boolean searching and proximity connectors are available tools for the researcher. *Loislaw* also provides searchable, full-text access to personal and corporate public

---

[35] *See* Chapter 18 for more discussion of law journals and journal indexes.

records, libraries of treatises and legal forms, and bar publications for selected states.

The Making of Modern Law, http://www.gale.cengage.com/ModernLaw/

This is an archival collection of over 21,000 18th, 19th and early 20th century legal treatises, casebooks, practice manuals, forms, letters and speeches, and other documents that have been scanned from library collections in the U.S. and England and are available in PDF format. Full-text searching of the collection is available and the collection is separated into 99 different subject areas for browsing. Additional resources that have been recently added to *The Making of Modern Law* "brand" are *Supreme Court Records and Brief*s from 1832 to 1978 and *Trials*, a collection of treatises about trials, trial transcripts, and related material from 1600 to 1926.

Matthew Bender Online, http://bender.lexisnexis.com

Matthew Bender, now part of *LexisNexis*, is a publisher of multivolume treatises in a number of areas. The online service provides full-text electronic access to those treatises. The service is broken down into libraries, including civil procedure, elder law, federal litigation, intellectual property law, labor and employment, and securities.

West's *Rise of American Law*

This is a new electronic collection of legal resources from West covering the period from 1820 to 1970. It provides access to over 1,700 out-of-print volumes in PDF format, including multivolume sets and multiple editions. Searching is by keyword, author, or title.

VersusLaw, http://www.versuslaw.com

VersusLaw is a Web-based research service focusing on federal and state case law from all states and the District of Columbia. *VersusLaw* is not as comprehensive a research system as *Loislaw*, *Westlaw*, and *Lexis-Nexis*. However, the company is expanding its product offerings to include statutes and regulations. *VersusLaw* utilizes Boolean searching or natural language searching. It was founded in 1985 and migrated to the Web in 1995. United States Supreme Court cases are available from 1900, while most federal appellate court cases are available since 1930. *VersusLaw* has begun to add case law from the federal district courts. State court appellate decisions date back to the 1920s to 1950s for most states. *VersusLaw* also provides links from its website to law school and law-related websites, legal forms, and state websites.

SECTION F. THE INTERNET[36]

1. Introduction

The Internet began in the 1960s as an experimental wide-area network maintained by the U.S. Department of Defense. In the Internet's early

---

[36] The Internet has created a new specialty in the practice of law. If you are interested in legal issues involving the Internet, see GEORGE B. DELTA & JEFFREY H. MATSUURA, LAW OF THE INTERNET (1998 to date); JANINE HILLER, INTERNET LAW AND POLICY (2002); PIKE & FISCHER: INTERNET LAW & REGULATION (1999 to date); F. LAWRENCE STREET, LAW OF THE INTERNET (2001); KENT D. STUCKEY, INTERNET AND ONLINE LAW (2000 to date).

years, the military, scientific and academic communities were the exclusive users. By the mid–1990s, commercial interests were becoming dominant, and by the twenty-first century the Internet became a ubiquitous global presence. The Internet is technically a global collection of computers and networks using a series of standard communication protocols to exchange information.

As a communications platform, the Internet utilizes a number of specific tools for exchanging information, including: email, chat, and instant messaging; peer-to-peer and other forms of file exchange; and, most important for legal research purposes, the World Wide Web.[37] The World Wide Web (often abbreviated WWW or just "the Web") uses hyperlinks to access documents, even individual elements of documents such as images or audio, that are otherwise scattered among disconnected computer servers. The Web was designed to make the Internet more user-friendly and simplify the sharing of information. The Web's hypertext and multimedia capabilities allow the dissemination of information in ways that were not previously possible.

Using the Web, researchers can access a massive body of information on an array of subjects. Over 165 million distinct websites[38] containing billions of individual webpages, documents, and media files, are maintained by individuals, for-profit and not-for-profit organizations, governmental units, and educational institutions. The Web is a powerful tool that supplements traditional sources of legal research and increases the researcher's chances of locating needed information. The Web provides users with access to a growing wealth of information, available in a cost-effective manner, and provides information not available through traditional online services such as *Westlaw* and *LexisNexis*. For example, some legal materials, such as city or county ordinances, are only accessible through the Web.[39]

Once the domain of free information, the Web now provides a combination of free and fee-for-use websites. While many high-quality Internet sources are available free of charge, a growing number are fee-based, either by subscription or as pay-as-you-go (usually by credit card) services. As previously discussed, commercial legal information providers use the Internet and the Web to distribute their products. This avoids both the maintenance costs of dedicated network communication systems and technical problems inherent in CD–ROM and DVD–ROM technology.[40]

---

[37] It is quite common for researchers to use the phrase "the Internet" interchangeably with "the Web," i.e., "I found the case on the Internet"—referring to a case found on a court's website. (See, e.g., CAROLE A. LEVITT AND MARK E ROSCH, THE LAWYER'S GUIDE TO FACT FINDING ON THE INTERNET (3rd ed. 2006) in which all of the content focuses on various websites.) This chapter will use the phrases, "the Web" or "the World Wide Web", unless specifically referring to the broader Internet network or one of the other communication tools.

[38] *Netcraft: April 2008 Web Server Survey*; http://news.netcraft.com/archives/2008/04/14/april_2008_web_server_survey.html (last visited May 14, 2008).

[39] For example, the Seattle Public Library's website provides municipal codes online at http://www.spl.org/default.asp?pageID=collection_municodes, offering links to many ordinances available throughout the country.

[40] An example of a dedicated network communication system would be a bulletin board system, where the user uses a telephone modem to dial directly into the bulletin board's

2. Getting to the Internet

Most researchers will access the Internet through their law firm, employer, or academic institution, or through subscription access to an Internet Service Provider (ISP). Basic subscription access was originally through a dial-up ISP, which connects through a telephone line and a computer modem. Higher speed, or "broadband," access is usually provided by law firms, employers, and academic institutions and is available by subscription through most cable, telecommunications, and satellite providers.

To access the Internet, a computer must have a telephone, DSL or cable modem, wired/wireless ethernet cards, and software that can communicate with the Internet.[41] Most computers are sold with this software preloaded. Microsoft's Internet Explorer and Apple Safari are the Web browsers provided with Windows and Apple computers, respectively. Other browsers include Opera and Mozilla Firefox, which can usually be downloaded from the Web.[42]

Navigation of the Web is accomplished through the use of menu bars and buttons at the top of the browser screen that execute a variety of tasks. The browser software provides an address line on the screen that indicates the Web address of the site currently being viewed. A user can maintain a list of frequently referenced websites with the browser's bookmark or favorites feature, or through "social bookmarking" websites.

Browsers will often use software "plug-ins" to access certain types of Web content, such as PDF documents, audio and video files, and interactive content. These applications may be bundled with the browser software or be downloaded when needed.

3. Navigating the World Wide Web

a. *Website Addresses or Uniform Resource Locators.* Under Internet protocols, each Web page receives a unique address or Uniform Resource Locator, commonly known as a URL, which permits direct access to that particular Web page. A URL is comprised of the domain name, indicating the website's sponsor and the nature of the sponsoring organization. For example, the address for the website at the Legal Information Institute at Cornell Law School is:

server. In the 1970s and 1980s, *Lexis* and *Westlaw* used dedicated systems to connect to their services. By the 1990s, both companies were transitioning to the Internet and access via the Web using desktop Web browser software.

[41] Different desktop software applications are used to access the Internet's different communications tools. These include e-mail applications such as *Outlook* or *GroupWise*, peer-to-peer applications such as *LimeWire*, and World Wide Web browsers, discussed *supra*. Many of the applications are bundled into software "suites" and pre-installed on most new computers; others are downloaded from the Internet as needed.

[42] All browsers will have the same basic capabilities. However, some websites are configured for optimum use with specific browsers (usually Microsoft Internet Explorer) and may not be fully functional when viewed with another browser. Also, Web browsers are frequently updated as new features are developed or security, bugs, or other problems identified.

http://www.law.cornell.edu

Each element of the address stands for the following:

http	=	hypertext transfer protocol[43]
://	=	a separator between the transfer protocol and the URL
www	=	indicates the World Wide Web
law	=	the subdivision at the Cornell University Web server that maintains the website, e.g., the University's law school (technically known as the "subdomain")
cornell	=	the website's sponsoring institution (the "domain")
edu	=	an indicator that the sponsoring institution is an educational institution (the "top-level domain")

The phrase "http://" may precede a website address. "http://" instructs the computer to look for a website address on the Internet that utilizes the hypertext transfer protocol, which supports links to other websites that complement or expand upon the information available at the initial website. As Web browsers have become more sophisticated, including "http://" in the address is no longer necessary.

URLs might be further divided into discrete components with a forward slash (/) separating each component. The distinct components of a URL direct the computer to the particular location of a specific Web page on a server and represent either a directory path or a filename. For example, http://www.law.pitt.edu/library/legal/index.php brings the user to a specific Web page containing an index of legal websites on the University of Pittsburgh School of Law's server.

Note that in the Cornell and Pitt examples the top-level domain, ".edu," identifies an educational institution. Other types of organizational indicators within website addresses include ".org" for non-profit organizations and associations, ".gov" for federal and (now) state government agencies, ".com" for commercial entities, and ".net" for computer-related organizations or communications networks. Due to the explosion of ".com" website addresses, additional new Internet suffixes have been created: ".info" for general information, ".biz" for business, ".name" for individuals, ".pro" for professionals, ".museum" for museums, ".coop" for business cooperatives, and ".aero" for the aviation industry. Researchers may also find website addresses with a national designation; for example, "gov.au" indicates the government-sponsored site is located in Australia, "amazon.de" indicates the German (*Deutschland)* version of Amazon.com.

b. *Search Engines.* A search engine is a specific Web service that examines a collection of Web pages for specified search terms. A massive database of Web pages is created and updated regularly by a computer-indexing program known as a crawler or spider that continuously crawls the Web or follows its links looking for new Web pages to add to the database.

Each search engine explores its own database of Web pages; the engines do not perform a search of the entire Web.[44] Every search engine

---

[43] Some websites require a high degree of secured access, including the use of passwords and encryption. Commercial databases, as well as online banking and other financial services websites are examples. These websites will often use the prefix "https" to identify them as "secured" websites utilizing a secured and encrypted http connection.

[44] Even the most powerful search engines can reach only a small portion of the resources on the Internet. The "deep" or "invisible" Web—that part of the Web not accessible by general

utilizes its own rules for finding, organizing, and delivering the Web pages upon query. While search engines differ in some elements, they also have many similarities. All search engines contain a textbox for typing search terms, which are words or phrases that the researcher thinks will lead to needed information. A search engine compares the search terms to the language used in various Web pages. It then furnishes users with a list of Web pages that contain those specified words or phrases.

Search engines are often the starting point in research to locate websites when the actual URLs are not known. A wide variety of search engines are available. *Google*[45] claims to have the Web's largest index and has emerged as the most dominant Web search engine.[46] Some of the other top-ranked search engines are *Yahoo*,[47] *MSN Search*,[48] *AlltheWeb*,[49] *Ask*,[50] and *Hotbot*.[51] Many of the better search engines provide advanced searching capability and may allow sophisticated Boolean searching. Others utilize natural language algorithms to generate a suitable query, similar to the natural language search engines available on *Westlaw* and *LexisNexis*. Researchers should be aware that each search engine uses different algorithms for finding and organizing retrieved material and that some websites will pay for better placement on search engine retrieval lists.

With the variety of search engines to choose from on the Web, there is yet another option for the researcher. A metasearch tool takes a query and submits it to several search engines simultaneously. *Metacrawler*[52] and *Dogpile*[53] are among the oldest and most well-known Web metasearch tools, simultaneously searching seven or eight popular search engines, including *Google*, *Yahoo*, and *MSN*. While metasearch tools are useful because they link several search engines together, they also may slow the search considerably, and prevent use of advanced search capabilities.

In addition to the general search engines, there are a number of specialty search tools for locating legal information. *FindLaw*'s *LawCrawler*, powered by the *Google* search engine, is available through the *FindLaw*[54] website. *LawCrawler* searches materials found on *FindLaw* and can be set (using a pulldown menu) to search "All Legal Websites," as well as

---

search engines—is of substantial consequence to researchers. Web pages not located by search engines may comprise: (1) websites lacking static URLs; (2) password-protected pages; and (3) collections of information contained within a database. In this case the search engine may locate the database but not the content contained in the database.

[45] http://www.google.com.

[46] As of February 2008, 59.2% of searches done in the US were done on *Google*. *Yahoo's* search engine and directory was second with 21.6% of searches. *U.S. Core Search Rankings*, February 2008, at http://searchenginewatch.com/showPage.html?page=3628837 (last visited May 15, 2008).

[47] http://www.yahoo.com.

[48] Also known as the Microsoft Network, at http://www.msnsearch.com.

[49] http://www.alltheweb.com.

[50] Formerly *Ask Jeeves,* at http://www.ask.com.

[51] http://www.hotbot.com.

[52] http://www.metacrawler.com.

[53] http://www.dogpile.com.

[54] http://lawcrawler.findlaw.com. *FindLaw* is owned by Thomson Reuters.

U.S. government-sponsored websites. *Justia.com* also provides a specialty search engine for legal information.

c. *Search Directories.* Search directories differ from search engines in that they organize information by category and allow the searcher to browse from broad, general categories down to the specific category containing the information they require. Web-wide directories have largely been supplanted by search engines, although *Yahoo* continues to maintain a directory with about 20 broad categories. Directories that focus on specific subjects, however, remain a very popular tool for locating information within that subject.

There are a number of legal directories available from both commercial and nonprofit sources. Among the commercial directories are *Findlaw for Legal Professionals*,[55] *Justia.com*,[56] *Hieros Gamos*,[57] *AllLaw.com*,[58] and *Lawsonline.com*.[59] Many law schools and law libraries provide legal directories as well. Among the oldest and most prominent are the *Legal Information Institute*[60] at Cornell School of Law, and *WashLaw: Legal Research on the Web*[61] from Washburn University School of Law.

d. *Searching Strategies.*[62] Because of the huge volume of content being indexed by the major search engines, locating information on the Internet is both easier and more complex than on *LexisNexis* or *Westlaw*. Basic searching is generally by keyword. Entering one word will obtain results containing that word. Search queries of multiple words presume a Boolean "AND" connector between the words. The algorithms used by the search engines generally give results containing the terms as a phrase first, followed by the terms in close proximity, followed by terms occurring anywhere within the page, followed by occurrences of one of the terms.[63] Using the Boolean "OR" command is possible on most search engines but may not be advisable unless the alternate terms are very specific.

[55] http://www.findlaw.com. *FindLaw* and *FindLaw for Legal Professionals* (http://lp.findlaw.com) are owned by Thomson Reuters. The *FindLaw* site is oriented toward consumers and the general public, whereas *FindLaw for Legal Professionals* is oriented toward lawyers, law students, paralegals, etc.

[56] http://www.justia.com.

[57] http://www.hg.org.

[58] http://www.alllaw.com.

[59] http://www.lawsonline.com.

[60] http://www.law.cornell.edu.

[61] http://www.washlaw.edu.

[62] Many guides and tutorials on the Internet identify techniques essential to good information retrieval. Some excellent examples are: *Bare Bones 101: A Basic Tutorial on Searching the Web*, published by the Beaufort Library at the University of South Carolina and found online at http://www.sc.edu/beaufort/library/pages/bones/bones.shtml, and the University of California at Berkeley's *Finding Information on the Internet: A Tutorial*, at http://www.lib.berkeley.edu/TeachingLib/Guides/Internet/FindInfo.html.

[63] Because of the billions of search pages that are indexed, it is not uncommon for a multi-word search to return thousands to millions of results. E.g., a search for "George Pike" (without quotes) returned 3,190,000 results. The proprietary algorithms used by the search engines are intended to return the most likely relevant searches first, becoming less likely relevant as the results continue. While *Google* will report the total number of results, it only presents the first 1,000 hits.

Google has an Advanced Search capability that allows more sophisticated searching. The Advanced Search page allows you to enter both individual terms as well as phrases and permits you to exclude words (similar to the Boolean "NOT" command). The Advanced Search feature also allows you to limit your search by language, file format (such as PDF files only), date, number of occurrences of your search term, and domain name.

Google also offers a number of other techniques for advanced Web searching, including the use of quotation marks ("") for specific phrases, truncation and wildcards (using the character (*) in place of a letter or at the end of the word), synonym searching (using a tilde (~) prior to the search term), and segment searching by title (intitle:), URL (inurl:), and website (site:).[64]

4. Legal Research on the Internet

As good as *Google* and the other search engines are, they cannot change one fundamental challenge of doing legal research on the World Wide Web: The Web works best when searching for specific information and is not as useful when trying to gather comprehensive information on a specific subject. For example, the Web is an effective (and free) tool for finding a copy of *Roe v. Wade* or the text of proposed legislation on a partial-birth abortion ban. It is less effective for doing comprehensive legal research on abortion law. As such, the Web and other Internet tools supplement, but do not replace the other print and electronic research skills outlined in this book.

Part of the challenge is the nature of the Web. While *LexisNexis* and *Westlaw* are now available via the Web, they remain dedicated research services controlled by their respective parent companies. The millions of websites available through the World Wide Web are owned or controlled by millions of different entities. Each website is provided by an independent host who alone decides what content to make available. There are very few content providers who have the ability to aggregate or combine information from separate websites or filter out substantive analysis from incidental material. For example, a *Google* search for "abortion law cases" does not focus on finding United States court decisions dealing with abortion but on whatever abortion-related content the algorithm generates.[65]

The other challenge is the free nature of a multitude of the resources on the World Wide Web. Many of the electronic tools that are covered in this book are written, organized, edited, updated, and published by commercial services. Because of marketing, copyright, and other considerations, these resources are rarely if ever made available for free on the Web. While one can find the text of the *U.S. Code* and state statutory codes on the Web, the Web will not have annotated state codes with their notes of

---

[64] Information about these and other Google search techniques can be found through *Google's Web Search Guides*, available online at www.google.com/support.

[65] A Google search for "abortion law cases" (without quotes) returned 2,380,000 hits. Most of the first 20 hits were to news articles, articles from advocacy groups and bloggers, and *Wikipedia*, with one link to *Roe v. Wade*. Changing the search to "abortion law cases" (with quotes) yielded 192 total hits, including one substantive journal article, but otherwise were primarily news articles and advocacy group materials. With some digging, a few of the sources did have links to a few major court decisions. (Searches conducted on June 10, 2008.)

decisions and other value-added content. The Web may have access to federal and state court decisions, but not the West digest and key number system, or collected *LexisNexis* databases for finding cases dealing with a particular issue. The Web will have some law journal articles from selected journals that publish online, and open access providers like *SSRN*, but will not have *LegalTrac* or other comprehensive bibliographic indexes.

5. Relying on Internet Sources

The legal scholar Karl Llewellyn once cautioned about the *"threat of the available"* and the *"threat from apparent simplicity,"* in discussing the traditional approach to law and its research methods.[66] The former threat warns of the tendency to turn to and study the most available material, then make the mistake of assuming that is all that there is to see. The latter threat cautions against the assumption that all things *must* be simple.

Llewellyn did not know it, but he may have been talking about the World Wide Web. The sheer volume of information available on the Web is both its strongest asset and its greatest liability. The volume of information can make it exceedingly easy (available and simple) to find *some* relevant information, but very difficult to locate *all* relevant material.

Even when a researcher locates potentially valuable information, the next hurdle is to determine whether the information can be relied upon. The traditional legal research methods and resources described in this book generally have long and distinguished pedigrees. Even though the court decisions published in West case reporters, and statutes published in annotated codes are "unofficial," researchers generally do not hesitate to rely on them. Legal researchers have a similar level of comfort using treatises, law review articles, legal encyclopedias, and similar secondary tools. While you may not (or may) wish to cite to them as authority, most researchers are very comfortable using them as research tools to locate, explain, summarize, or clarify their research.

The reason that researchers are comfortable doing this is that the legal publishing industry has developed a track record of authority, accuracy, objectivity, and reliability that researchers rarely find need to question. Such indicia of reliability can be much more difficult to discern with Internet resources. The World Wide Web itself is only about 10 to 12 years old as a practical research source. Its "youth" does not give it the track record of a long standing legal publisher such as West, BNA, or LexisNexis. The Internet, by its nature, is very fluid, with content coming and going quite rapidly. The Internet, being a global and very cheap (comparatively) means of publishing that is available to anyone with a computer and some rudimentary computer skills, has a lot of questionable, unverifiable, and potentially misleading information sources among its billions of Web pages. Legal researchers need information to be accurate, authoritative, objective, and current in order to rely on it. Confirming that a particular Internet

---

[66] Karl N. Llewellyn, *Legal Tradition and Social Science Method—A Realist's Critique*, originally published in Brookings Institution, Essays on Research in the Social Sciences (1931), reprinted in Karl N. Llewellyn, Jurisprudence: Realism in Theory and Practice 77, 82–84 (1962). (Emphasis in original.)

source meets these criteria will depend on a mix of objective and subjective indicators.

Accuracy requires that a source be a correct representation of what it purports to represent, e.g., a case, statute, regulation, fact, etc. Absent direct knowledge of the underlying circumstance (e.g., you know "X" to be true), you can objectively determine accuracy by verification of the information in multiple places. You can subjectively determine accuracy by a careful evaluation of the source.

The legal research world is fortunate that most of its more important research materials are the primary resources—statutes, cases, regulations—that come directly from federal and state government institutions. Websites provided by those government institutions are often considered to be an "official" source for that content.[67] Provided the researcher confirms that the information comes from the government source, there is very little reason not to rely on the online source to the same degree that you would rely on the printed source.

What about non-governmental sources? In these cases, the more information you know about the source provider the more you can determine the accuracy and reliability of the information. Websites of known "brick and mortar" content[68] providers, such as the *New York Times*, *Harvard Law Review*, *Dun and Bradstreet*, or well-known organizations like the United Nations or academic institutions, will have that history and can be relied on for accuracy equal to their traditional print counterparts.

Sources that do not have a historical "brick and mortar" counterpart may need additional verification. An important way to verify the accuracy of a suspect website is to confirm the information through another source. This is not only an essential part of the Web information verification process but also a good research practice.

The next question is whether the information is authoritative. Primary sources obtained from government sources generally have that high level of authority as having been drafted by the institution of government ultimately responsible for the information, e.g., the courts, the legislature, or executive agencies. With secondary materials, the best indicator of authority is the reputation of the content author or provider. An obvious first step in verifying the authority of Web content is to determine if the author or

---

[67] Concern has been raised about whether "official" online resources are also "authentic." Whereas "official" is generally defined as a source that has been mandated or approved by the relevant state or federal government, "authentic" requires that the source be verified by the government as "complete and unaltered" when compared with the original or "official" text and be certified as such. A recent study by the American Association of Law Libraries determined that many of the "official" online legal sources have not been verified as "authentic." STATE BY STATE REPORT ON AUTHENTICATION OF ONLINE LEGAL RESOURCES (American Association of Law Libraries 2007), available online at http://www.aallnet.org/aallwash/authen_rprt/AuthenFinalReport.pdf. This does not reduce the value of these online resources as research tools, but may suggest verifying against another official source at some point in the research process.

[68] The phrase, "Brick and Mortar" has come to refer to a service provider that provided a physical product from a physical location—a "brick and mortar" building—in contrast with services that are only available through the Web. It is also quite common for "brick and mortar" companies to have a significant presence on the Web, such as the NEW YORK TIMES newspaper and http://www.nyt.com.

provider is identified. This is not a guaranteed process because a number of websites do not indicate the authority or source of their content. Clues to look for in the absence of a named author are a named source provider, some "About us" information, a means of contacting the provider (usually email, occasionally by phone), or a corporate affiliation.

Other newer sources of Internet legal information are blogs, podcasts, wikis, and "open access" journal archives.

Blogs, short for "Web logs," are maintained by individuals or groups and usually consist of commentary on a particular topic.[69] They are often enhanced with links to related Web documents or articles, graphics, or audio files. Many blogs invite interested readers to respond to particular blog entries, often leading to an ongoing discussion of the issue raised in the original entry. In addition to providing secondary content, a well-run blog, like many "traditional" secondary sources, can be an effective research tool through the publication of links or citations to primary sources, news articles, and other relevant materials.

Many legal blogs[70] are from the same scholars, policymakers, and attorneys that are behind many of the better secondary sources.[71] It should be remembered, however, that blogs are secondary sources and should be carefully reviewed for authenticity and authority. Also, while many blogs are created, far fewer are maintained, so care should be taken to archive (online or in print) any blog material being relied on for your research.

Podcasts are similar to blogs in that they provide a forum for commentators and organizations to offer streaming or downloadable audio discussions on topics of interest.

"Open access" journal archives and repositories are websites that provide a forum for authors to publish their work directly on the Web instead of (or increasingly in addition to) publishing through a traditional law journal or commercial publishers.[72] The *Legal Scholarship Network* of the *Social Science Research Network (SSRN)*[73] and the *Berkeley Electronic Press (bepress)*[74] publish articles from identified legal scholars and named researchers from other disciplines.

A "Wiki" is a website created around a particular subject or project, with the content contributed by a number of authorized users. *Wikipedia*[75]

---

[69] Many personal blogs will not focus on a particular topic, allowing the blogger to address whatever topic he or she wishes.

[70] The phrase "blawg" has been used to refer to blogs dealing with legal issues. Directories of legal blogs can be found at *Justia's BlawgSearch*, at http://blawgsearch.justia.com; *Law Professor Blogs*, at http://www.lawprofessorblogs.com; and *Blawg: Legal Blogs*, at http://www.blawg.com.

[71] For example, Harvard University Law Professor Lawrence Lessig writes one of the most widely read blogs on intellectual property at http://www.lessig.org.

[72] *See* Chapter 18 for a discussion of law reviews and other legal scholarship.

[73] http://www.ssrn.com/lsn/index.html. The *Social Science Research Network* also maintains open source repositories for other disciplines including economics, marketing, management, politics, entrepreneurship, social and environmental impact, literature and classics, and philosophy. The main directory of repositories can be found at http://www.ssrn.com.

[74] http://www.bepress.com.

[75] http://www.wikipedia.org.

is the most prominent example. *Wikipedia* is an online encyclopedia that covers virtually any and every subject imaginable. The content, however, is written by unknown individuals who have—or purport to have—knowledge of a particular subject. While *Wikipedia* has a reputation for general accuracy, the absence of identifying information about the content authors limits *Wikipedia* as authoritative source.[76]

A final, critical element to evaluate is whether the information is up-to-date. As noted, websites come and go, and they add and delete information all the time. Websites also go stale as the website developer discontinues its efforts or goes out of business. This is an area where even governmental primary source materials should be viewed with scrutiny. Many statutory and administrative codes, even those published by "official" government sources, may not be updated in the same way that commercially published annotated codes are updated through pocket parts or supplementation. For example, the "official" version of the *Code of Federal Regulations*, as published on the Government Printing Office's website,[77] is no more current than the print version. The presence of a "last modified" or "last updated" notation on a particular website is helpful, but it does not end the inquiry. It may be difficult to determine exactly what content has been updated and what has not. Some particular items may be dated, which is beneficial, but it is also not uncommon for websites to use automatic date generators, which put "today's" date on every page of the website.

6.   Noteworthy Legal and Law–Related Websites

Staying up-to-date with the Web's ever-growing resources is an overwhelming task for even the most industrious legal researcher. The search engines and directories listed in this chapter are among the best sources for keeping up-to-date. Other current awareness aids, including *LLRX: The Law Librarians' Resource Exchange*[78] and *Inter Alia: An Internet Legal Research Weblog*,[79] assist researchers in evaluating Internet sources.

Especially noteworthy law and law-related cyber-research print resources include: Dittakavi Rao's *101 Legal Research Web Sites Every Attorney Should Know About* (2005); Stacy Gordon's *Online Legal Research: A Guide to Legal Research Services and Other Internet Tools* (Hein 2003); Simonsen & Anderson's *Computer–Aided Legal Research on the Internet* (2d ed. 2005); and Carole Levitt's *The Cybersleuth's Guide to the Internet: Conducting Effective Investigative and Legal Research on the Web* (2008). If interest is limited to information distributed on the Internet through the United States Federal Depository Act, consider Peggy Garvin's *United States Government Internet Manual, 2005–2006* (Bernan Press

---

[76] There are a number of court decisions that have cited to *Wikipedia* articles. However, this is usually in support of non-critical factual points and is often cited as a "see" or "see also" reference. *See* Phillips v. Pembroke Real Estate, Inc., 459 F.3d 128, 133 (1st Cir. 2006). Some *Wikipedia* articles will cite to references in support of the points in the *Wikipedia* article. Those references can and should be checked for authority and may be cited if they prove to be an independently authoritative source.

[77] http://www.gpoaccess.gov/cfr/index.html.

[78] http://www.llrx.com.

[79] http://www.inter-alia.net.

2005) and Peter Hernon's *U.S. Government on the Web* (Libraries Unlimited 2003).

Periodicals and newsletters helpful in identifying useful law and law-related websites include: *Internet Law Researcher* (West–Glasser Legal Works); *The Internet Lawyer: Navigating the Internet for the Legal Profession* (GoAhead Publications); and *Internet Reference Services Quarterly* (Haworth Press).

There is a substantial and continuing proliferation of legal information websites. Many of the major sites are sponsored by academic institutions, notably law schools and their libraries, nonprofit organizations, and government agencies and provide information and links to other websites that support their academic programs. However, there also are several excellent websites of a comprehensive nature that are not affiliated with any educational institution. Major legal research websites of note include:

a.   *Search Directories and Portals*[80]

FindLaw for Legal Professionals, http://lp.findlaw.com

FindLaw for Legal Professionals is a comprehensive website providing case law, codes and statutes, law reviews, legal organizations, and specific legal subjects, including constitutional, intellectual property, and labor law, along with access to foreign and international resources. It claims to be the most heavily visited free legal portal. *FindLaw* is owned by Thomson Reuters, the parent company of *Westlaw*. *FindLaw* content generally does not come directly from *Westlaw* (e.g., court decisions on *FindLaw* are generally text or PDF versions of slip opinions, not scans or text from *Westlaw*.) However, there are occasionally links to *Westlaw*-by-credit-card to obtain an "enhanced" case or statute or to *KeyCite* the case or statute.

FirstGov, http://www.firstgov.gov

This site is the U.S. government's portal to government information on the Web. The site includes an A–Z directory of government agency websites and a search engine that searches over 2.7 million government Web pages. This site is a great starting place for locating any information originating from a federal government body.

Hieros Gamos, http://www.hg.org

Hieros Gamos is one of the oldest and most comprehensive legal websites, boasting more than two million links. International in scope, it is organized under a very detailed index of topics and sources.

Justia, http://www.justia.com

Justia is a well organized site with a search engine that has selection options for searching within the site, within the "legal Web" of other legal information websites, within legal blogs, for legal podcasts. *Justia*'s directory is organized both by topical legal practice area as well as by legal research source. Many federal resources are directly available through *Justia*, including federal appellate and Supreme Court decisions, the United States Constitution and *U.S. Code,* the *CFR,* and some state content. Other

---

[80] A Web "portal" is generally defined as a website that serves primarily as a point of access to other information on the World Wide Web. Portals will often be collections of hyperlinks to other content providers, usually organized by category and subcategory.

sources are linked to the original provider, with *Justia* providing an information screen about the source and its content.

Law Library of Congress, *Guide to Law Online*, http://www.loc.gov/law/public/law-guide.html

This directory focuses on sites that offer the full texts of laws, regulations, and court decisions, along with commentary from lawyers writing primarily for other lawyers. It also contains a comprehensive directory of foreign law sites arranged by country.

The *Legal Information Institute,* http://www.law.cornell.edu

Provided by Cornell University Law School, this was one of the first comprehensive legal information sites on the Web. It is organized by type of information and subject area as well as jurisdiction.

State and Local Government on the Net, http://www.statelocalgov.net

This is an excellent directory of official state and local governmental websites organized by jurisdiction and topic, with some national organizations for agency officials.

Washlaw (Washburn University School of Law), http://www.washlaw.edu

Basic alphabetical arrangement by topic as well as jurisdiction makes this site among the easiest to navigate.

b. *Government Sources for Primary Law*

Administrative Office of U.S. Courts, http://www.uscourts.gov

This is the central site for accessing all United States federal courts, including the Supreme Court, federal circuit courts, district and bankruptcy courts, and special courts. Individual court websites will provide access to current and archived opinions (generally going back to the mid 1990s); dockets; court rules, forms, policies and procedures; and judicial directories and other contact information.

Administrative Office of the Pennsylvania Courts, http://www.aopc.org

Each state will have its own website for court opinions. This site is typical, providing access to opinions of the Pennsylvania Supreme Court and appellate courts, access to court rules and forms, local rules, links to state dockets, and other court resources.

FedStats, http://www.fedstats.gov

This site provides a gateway to statistical information from over 100 federal agencies, including the U.S. Census Bureau, Bureau of Labor Statistics and Bureau of Justice Statistics. The links are arranged by agency, topic, or geographically.

GPO Access, http://www.access.gpo.gov

Produced by the U.S. Government Printing office, *GPO Access* provides official electronic versions of the *Federal Register* (updated daily), the *List of Sections Affected (LSA)* and the *Code of Federal Regulations (CFR)*. There is also a version of the *CFR* called the *e-CFR* which while unofficial, is updated daily. This site provides links to the official version of the *United States Code*, *Statutes at Large*, and presidential materials. *GPO Access* will be replaced during 2009 by the *Federal Digital System* (*FDsys*).

Office of the Law Revision Council, United States Code, http://uscode.house.gov

The Law Revision Council of the U.S. House of Representatives prepares and publishes the *U.S. Code*. This version is fully searchable with Boolean and proximity connectors. It is usually the most current version available of the *U.S. Code*. A related set of classification tables at http://uscode.house.gov/classification/tables.shtml allows the researcher to update the online version of the *U.S. Code* by providing tables of current public law numbers and sections which affect *U.S. Code* sections.

Office of the President, http://www.whitehouse.gov

This resource includes presidential executive orders and proclamations, speeches, and press conferences. It also includes a topical list of subjects such as budget management, health care, and national security with related documents in each topic.

Public Access to Court Electronic Records, http://pacer.login.uscourts.gov

Known as *PACER*, this site provides access to dockets from most federal district, bankruptcy, and appellate courts. Dockets are accessed by jurisdiction, then by party name or docket number and may provide PDF copies of pleadings, orders, and opinions that often are not available on the general court websites or other websites. You must register to access *PACER*, and there is a small per-page charge for accessing PDF documents.

THOMAS: Legislative Information on the Internet, http://thomas.loc.gov

THOMAS, from the Library of Congress, should be any researcher's first stop for federal legislative information. Researchers can access current and archived bills with bill tracking, current and archived public laws, committee reports, the *Congressional Record*, and major documents such as the Constitution, Bill of Rights, and Declaration of Independence. *THOMAS* also provides links to other legislative sites including the U.S. House and Senate webpages, which in turn link to individual Senators and Representatives' websites, committee sites containing legislative hearings and business sessions, and party caucus sites.

c.　*Other Sources of Primary Law*

Open access caselaw databases: There are several websites that provide open access to federal court decisions which had not been previously available on the Web. The core content of these websites are U.S. Supreme Court decisions from 1789 to 2005 and U.S. Court of Appeals decisions from 1950 to 2007.[81] The decisions are provided with their *United States Reports* or *Federal Reporter* citation, although they do not have their original pagination. Some of these websites feature search engines and browseable directories, and several have additional legal resources includ-

---

[81] These decisions are available as of June 2008. It is likely, but not presently certain, that additional decisions will be added.

ing state court decisions. Open access federal court decisions are available from *Public.Resource.Org*,[82] *Justia.com*,[83] *Public Library of Law*,[84] *Altlaw*,[85] and *Precydent*.[86]

Law Librarians' Society of Washington, D.C., Legislative Sourcebook, http://www.llsdc.org/sourcebook

The *Legislative Sourcebook* is a portal to legislative information from a number of government and non-governmental sources. Included are links to selected legislative histories, government documents, related regulatory filings, and articles on conducting legislative research.

lexisONE, http://www.lexisONE.com

lexisONE is a Web service of *LexisNexis* that supplies practice resources for solo and small-firm practitioners on a pay-as-you-go basis. It offers a selection of free material, including caselaw, legal forms, legal news, and practice management resources. *lexisONE* provides U.S. Supreme Court cases dating back to 1790, selected federal and state cases from 2000 to the present, and a "Legal Internet Guide" with links to more than 20,000 law-related websites organized by category. *lexisONE* does not offer the full range of services that are available through the paid *LexisNexis* service.

Municode.com, http://www.municode.com

Municipal Code Corporation publishes print and online codes for cities around the nation. Their online library has links to all of the online codes that they publish, arranged by state and then city.

National Center for State Courts, http://www.ncsconline.org

This is a valuable source for finding information on courts, including coverage of juries and caseloads, statistics and extensive links to state court sites.

OYEZ, http://www.oyez.org/oyez/frontpage

OYEZ is a non-profit service that provides a wide variety of material about the U.S. Supreme Court, including streaming audio and transcription of current and historical oral arguments.

Seattle Public Library: Municipal Codes Online, http://www.spl.org/default.asp?pageID=collection_municodes

This service of the Seattle Public Library provides access to several dozen municipal codes published in cities around the country. It also provides links to other publishers of municipal codes.

United States Code at LII, http://www.law.cornell.edu/uscode

This online version of the *United States Code* is provided by the Legal Information Institute at Cornell. It provides searching by title and section,

---

[82] http://public.resource.org.

[83] http://www.justia.com.

[84] http://www.plol.org.

[85] http://www.altlaw.org.

[86] http://www.precydent.com.

or keyword searching by title with links to updating information, CFR and other cross-references, notes, a popular name table, and additional content.

d. *Topical Websites*

American Bar Association (ABA) Network, http://www.abanet.org

Provides a variety of information about the ABA, its activities and publications. Also provides access to briefs for current U.S. Supreme Court cases. Individual ABA section websites often include extensive resources related to specific areas of law, although most limit access to members only.

Blawg.com, http://www.blawg.com

A comprehensive directory of legal and law-related blogs, podcasts, and RSS feeds.

Electronic Information System for International Law, http://www.eisil.org

A directory of international resources, includes links to both primary and secondary sources from governments, NGOs, IGOs, academic institutions, and other organizations.

FindLaw's Forms, Forms Collections and Forms Indexes, http://forms.lp.findlaw.com/, http://forms.lp.findlaw.com/collections.html

These pages on the *FindLaw* site features links to several dozen free and fee-based forms and form services categorized by issue and jurisdiction.

Jurist: Legal News and Research, http://jurist.law.pitt.edu

Jurist is a legal news and real-time legal research service that tracks important legal news stories and annotates them with documents, commentary, and links to other resources.

Law Librarians Resource Exchange, http://www.llrx.com

Primarily consists of articles and pathfinders written by law firm and academic librarians. Somewhat like working with *American Law Reports* (*A.L.R.*) annotations, if you find one on point you will get a wealth of information resources. Notable for its comprehensive directory of online court rules.

Search Systems Public Record Database, http://www.searchsystems.net

Search Systems provides links to over 1,700 free "public record" databases. Many of the databases are genealogical in nature or provide names and addresses of contact persons for found records, rather than the providing access to the records themselves. National records are in alphabetical order; state records are organized by state.

SEC Filings and Forms (EDGAR), http://www.sec.gov/edgar.shtml

EDGAR provides access to financial and other filings for publicly traded companies in the U.S. Searchable by company name, most recent filings, or full text.

Social Science Research Network, http://www.ssrn.com
Legal Scholarship Network, http://www.ssrn.com/lsn/index.html

Both of these services focus on publishing scholarly papers and abstracts in all disciplines. This can include pre-publication works, working papers, and peer-reviewed materials.

Wex, http://topics.law.cornell.edu/wex

Wex is a collaboratively created, public-access law dictionary and encyclopedia. It is sponsored and hosted by the Legal Information Institute at Cornell Law School.

Wikipedia, http://www.wikipedia.org

Wikipedia is a comprehensive online encyclopedia with articles written by contributors from around the world. It currently has over 4,000,000 entries in several languages covering virtually any subject. Because the authors are generally not named, *Wikipedia* articles should be verified for accuracy.

Zimmerman's Research Guide: An Online Encyclopedia for Legal Researchers,
http://www.lexisnexis.com/infopro/zimmerman/

A comprehensive guide to Web and Internet resources, print resources, or telephone contact information broken down into several hundred subjects and jurisdictions. The encyclopedia can be searched by keyword, or the researcher can browse through the entries. Many entries also have "see also" references to direct the researcher to related information.

7. Citation to Internet Resources[87]

The Bluebook: A Uniform System of Citation, 18th ed., Rule 18.2 et seq., requires the use and citation of "traditional printed resources" or a "widely available commercial database" (e.g., *LexisNexis* or *Westlaw*) if available, but otherwise permits citation to World Wide Web and Internet resources. *The Bluebook* allows Web citation when the source is "unavailable" in a traditional printed format or commercial database, and when "the content of the Internet source is identical to that of the printed version and a parallel citation to the Web resource will substantially improve access to the source cited." *The Bluebook* also mandates the citation to PDF versions of documents when available.[88]

A challenging part of a Web citation is the URL. *The Bluebook* requires that the URL "should point readers directly to the source cited rather than to an intervening page of links." While this will often be straightforward,[89] some URLs can be long and full of nontextual characters.[90] In this case the researcher should cite to the most practical URL closest to the specific

---

[87] *See also* Chapter 24 of this book.

[88] "If a document is available both in HTML format and in a widely used format that preserves pagination and other attributes of printed work (such as Adobe's portable document format, or 'PDF'), the latter should always be cited in lieu of an HTML document." THE BLUEBOOK: A UNIFORM SYSTEM OF CITATION R. 18.2.1(c), at 154 (Columbia Law Review Ass'n et al. eds., 18th ed. 2005).

[89] E.g., "http://jurist.law.pitt.edu/forum/forumnew40.htm," locates a specific page on the *Jurist* website for a comment by Prof. Susan Herman on the USA Patriot Act.

[90] For example, "http://www.nytimes.com/2006/07/31/world/middleeast/31cnd-mideast.html? ex=1311998400 & en=19b863a569140283 & ei=5089 & partner=rssyahoo & emc=rss" locates a July 31, 2006, NEW YORK TIMES article about the situation in the Middle East.

document, then describe the step(s) needed to locate the document. (See Rule 18.2.1.)

Author, title, case name, code section, date, and similar items generally follow *Bluebook* standards as much as possible. When citing a source from the Internet as a parallel citation, use the author, title, case name, docket number, date, pagination, etc., of the original printed source, then use the comment *"available at"* and provide the URL. When citing to an Internet or Web document as the direct source, *Bluebook* Rule 18.2.3 provides that you should cite the author and title as they "appear in the window of a browser viewing the site." If this is unwieldy or uninformative, then "an alternative title that better describes the source should be used." If authorship of a specific item is not clearly stated, then the title alone may be used or the item may be described. Pinpoint citation to a specific page can be done if the document itself is paginated, e.g., for PDF documents that preserve pagination. Paragraph numbers may be used only if utilized by the source document. Screen numbers or other software-based numbers should not be used.

Court decisions provide a particular challenge because many Web-published case decisions may not contain traditional West reporter citations. (e.g., to "F.2d", "F. Supp", "A.2d", etc.)[91] *The Bluebook* makes it clear that if the case is available in print, or through *LexisNexis* or *Westlaw*, then that citation should be provided, with a parallel citation to the Internet. If the case is not available in print or through *LexisNexis* or *Westlaw* (as may often be the case for very recent decisions, trial court decisions, or interim court orders), the closest standard for citing the case would be as an unreported case or slip opinion (*Bluebook* Rule 10.8.1) which utilizes the case name, docket number, court and date, with an *"available at"* reference to the Internet source.

If a document obtained from the Web provides a specific publication date, then that date should be used (year only) in the citation. If no date is provided, the date should be the date on which you last visited the website. The current edition of *The Bluebook* specifically disapproves using a website's "last modified" or "last updated" date.

8.   The Future of the Internet and Cyberspace

Legal information is being transformed from print to electronic format. An increasing number of legal resources are now accessible to Internet users at any location in the world. These resources are available from vast proprietary online services with extremely powerful search engines, such as *Westlaw* and *LexisNexis*, and from smaller open access websites supported by educational institutions with simple or no search engines.

The availability of robust Internet technology is raising the bar on the quality and diversity of research materials. It is less costly to publish electronically than in paper format. In the future, states that currently

[91] The open access federal court decisions discussed in Section F–6–c will often provide the West reporter citation for the particular decision. However, the decisions are not PDF documents from West reporters and generally do not have the pagination needed for pinpoint citations. Decisions found on court websites will have the court's docket number but will generally not provide the West reporter citation.

publish official reporters in paper may discontinue publishing in this format. Some even suggest that West may stop publishing printed reporters and digests.[92] CD–ROM discs also will probably become obsolete, as they lack the currency and breadth of resources published on the Internet. There will be continued advancements in Internet speed and security, and pricing structures will continue to diversify. All in all, with the growing reliance on the development of Internet technology, the future of online electronic services looks promising for the legal researcher.

[92] Robert C. Berring, *Legal Information and the Search for Cognitive Authority*, 88 CALIF. L. REV. 1673, 1703 (2000). Even if materials remain in print, many libraries are electing to discontinue print copies in favor of online access.

Chapter 24

LEGAL CITATION FORM*

Citation form in all legal writing requires uniformity and consistency for two fundamental reasons. First, individuals relying on legal research need to be able to accurately and efficiently locate and verify the information referenced. Second, a uniform system of citation provides the reader with information concerning the manner in which the source supports the text for which it is cited.

This chapter offers an overview of basic legal citation form. The chapter refers to the 18th edition of *The Bluebook: A Uniform System of Citation*, which represents the most commonly accepted and referenced form of legal citation. Additionally, the chapter includes a discussion of the third edition of the *ALWD Citation Manual: A Professional System of Citation*, an alternative citation manual which has gained acceptance primarily in the academic legal community. Finally, the chapter considers citation to electronic information, as well as neutral citation standards designed to uniformly and consistently reference legal information available in both electronic and print formats. Neutral citation refers to a citation that is medium neutral (applicable to book or electronic form) and vendor neutral (does not require vendor-specific information). Neutral citation can be used with the resources of multiple publishers and information producers, eliminating the conflicts that arise in having one or two dominant providers of legal information. Throughout the chapter, examples of case law citation form are used to illustrate the various citation systems.

SECTION A. THE BLUEBOOK: A UNIFORM SYSTEM OF CITATION

1. Historical Development of The Bluebook: A Uniform System of Citation

Citation form developed along with the growth of the common law case reporting system. Its development reflected the legal system's dependency on case law under the concept of *stare decisis* and the use of precedent.[1] With the development of American legal education during the nineteenth century, law schools provided intensive writing opportunities for their

---

* Pat Newcombe, Associate Director, Western New England College School of Law Library, Springfield, Massachusetts, wrote this chapter.

[1] For an excellent historical summary of citation form, see Byron D. Cooper, *Anglo–American Legal Citation: Historical Development and Library Implications*, 75 LAW LIBR. J. 3 (1982). For a general discussion of the advent of the footnote in scholarly writing, see ANTHONY GRAFTON, THE FOOTNOTE: A CURIOUS HISTORY (1997).

students and began to publish scholarly works and commentary, early versions of today's law reviews.

In 1926, the law review editorial boards of Harvard, Yale, Columbia, and the University of Pennsylvania produced the first edition of *A Uniform System of Citation* to offset the expenses incurred in printing the law reviews.[2] At the time, the costs associated with typesetting detailed footnotes were greater than the costs of typesetting the text of the article. By developing a consistent shorthand expression for citation form, these early law review editors were able to reduce both typesetting costs and the space required for footnotes.

Over time, *The Bluebook: A Uniform System of Citation*,[3] now in its 18th edition, became the most widely used and accepted standard for legal citation form.[4] Typically, a law student's rite of passage into the legal profession required a detailed and accurate understanding of the variety of citation rules set forth in this citation manual.

2.   The Rules of The Bluebook: A Uniform System of Citation

The Bluebook: A Uniform System of Citation is a lengthy (416 pages), complex, and self-proclaimed complete rendition of legal citation form.[5] *The Bluebook* serves two functions: it acts as a guide to citation form and as a style manual for legal publication. Its periodic revisions, including rule changes, are a frequent source of frustration for those attempting to

---

[2] Cooper, *supra note* 1, at 21. With the 15th edition, the editors added "The Bluebook" to the UNIFORM SYSTEM's title to more accurately reflect the common shorthand expression for the citation system. THE BLUEBOOK derives its name from its traditional blue cover.

[3] THE BLUEBOOK: A UNIFORM SYSTEM OF CITATION (18th ed. 2005) [THE BLUEBOOK]. References to editions other than the most recent will be designated by edition number.

[4] Some jurisdictions and several law reviews believed their individual jurisdictional citation needs were not adequately addressed by THE BLUEBOOK. Consequently, alternative citation manuals have developed to attempt to satisfy these perceived deficiencies. An example of such a manual is that produced by the UNIVERSITY OF CHICAGO LAW REVIEW and the UNIVERSITY OF CHICAGO LAW FORUM. *See* The University of Chicago Law Review & The University of Chicago Legal Forum, *The University of Chicago Manual of Legal Citation*, 53 U. CHI. L. REV. 1353 (1986). This manual was subsequently published in 1989 (its first and only edition) by Lawyers Cooperative Publishing, Bancroft–Whitney Company, and Mead Data Central, Inc., as a 63-page pamphlet with a maroon cover, hence its common name, the MAROON BOOK. Rather than being a complete guide to citation form, like that provided by THE BLUEBOOK, the MAROON BOOK offered a guiding philosophy of citation form. Editorial discretion, rather than consistent uniform citation form, was the MAROON BOOK's guiding principle. It never gained wide acceptance and failed perhaps because it overreached its goal of being flexible, leaving the reader without clear guidance. Melissa H. Weresh, *The ALWD Citation Manual: A Coup De Grace*, 23 U. ARK. LITTLE ROCK L. REV. 775, 781–82 (2001). Some law reviews have developed their own particularized style manuals and rules of citation form.

[5] For a restatement of the rules set out in the 18th edition of THE BLUEBOOK, see ALAN L. DWORSKY, USER'S GUIDE TO THE BLUEBOOK (rev. ed. 2006). For a discussion and illustration of the rules of THE BLUEBOOK and ALWD, see LARRY L. TEPLY, LEGAL WRITING CITATION IN A NUTSHELL (2008). For a learning tool for citation form, see, e.g., TRACY L. McGAUGH & CHRISTINE HURT, INTERACTIVE CITATION WORKBOOK FOR THE BLUEBOOK: A UNIFORM SYSTEM OF CITATION (2007 ed.); Peter W. Martin, *Introduction to Basic Legal Citation* (LII 2007 ed.), http://www.law.cornell.edu/citation/. The Center for Computer–Assisted Legal Instruction (CALI) also provides computer-based programs offering self-directed instruction in the use of THE BLUEBOOK at http://www.cali.org.

conform their citation practices to those in the latest edition of *The Bluebook*.[6]

The most recent edition of *The Bluebook* is organized into three major parts. The first part is the Bluepages, printed on light blue paper, directly after the Introduction. The Bluepages, a new feature of the 18th edition, provides basic legal citation guidance suitable for the requirements of first-year law students, law clerks, and legal practitioners. Examples provided in the Bluepages are printed using ordinary typeface conventions typically used in legal practice. This 43–page section summarizes main citation rules and is designed to act as a practical guidebook for the most common citation forms. A useful feature is the Bluepages Tips, which appear throughout the Bluepages, and offer helpful explanations and provide references to the complete rules if more specificity is required. The tips are printed in blue to draw the reader's attention. This section also includes a table of suggested abbreviations for words commonly found in the titles of court documents and a table listing jurisdiction-specific citation rules and style manuals.

The second part, printed on white paper, contains the main body of *The Bluebook*. This section provides the rules of citation and style in more detail appropriate to meet the complex and nuanced requirements of law review writing. Rules 1 through 9 provide general standards of citation and style used to cite any type of authority in legal writing, while rules 10 through 21 provide specific rules for citations to cases, statutes, books, periodicals, foreign materials, and international materials. Examples provided throughout this part are printed using typeface conventions standard in law journal footnotes.

The third part of *The Bluebook*, printed on white paper with a blue border, provides tables used in conjunction with the rules. The tables include outlines of United States federal and state jurisdictions with appropriate abbreviations for primary source materials, similar information for foreign nations and intergovernmental organizations, and abbreviations for case names, court names, geographical terms, periodicals, looseleaf services, and other frequently referenced items.

The Bluebook also is available on the Internet as *The Bluebook Online*.[7] Subscribers to the online version access the full content of *The Bluebook* with searching capability, and are able to make and share notes and bookmarks. Even without a subscription to this Internet version, researchers who access this website may consult the Blue Tips, where the editors provide guidance on subjects covered by *The Bluebook*. The most helpful answers are compiled and organized by subject. These tips are regularly updated, searchable, and linked to *The Bluebook* content to which they refer.

a. *Style and Typeface.* Bluepages B13 and Rule 2 deal with typeface conventions and style issues. *The Bluebook* serves both the more pragmatic

---

[6] For reviews and reaction to the 18th edition of THE BLUEBOOK, see J. James Christian, *The New Bluebook: Bigger, Better and Bluer*, ARIZ. ATT'Y, Nov. 2005, at 26; K.K. DuVivier, *The Bluebook No. 18—"Thank God for Competition . . . ,"* COLO. LAW., Nov. 2005, at 111; Ellen K. Boegel, *"Bluebook" Strikes Back*, THE NAT'L L.J., July 25, 2005, at 23.

[7] http://www.legalbluebook.com.

practitioner-oriented concerns regarding style in legal briefs and memoranda and the more formal legal publication needs of law reviews. The most common typeface conventions are outlined in the Bluepages for practitioners. A more complex collection of typeface conventions, including ordinary roman type, italics, and large and small capitals, conceived prior to the electronic word processing environment, is detailed in the alternative rules applicable for law reviews, found in the body of *The Bluebook*. If a practitioner is using the Bluepages for citation and cannot locate the rule governing a particular authority, the practitioner may need to consult the body of *The Bluebook* for guidance. The practitioner must then remember to convert the typeface in the rule examples and tables into the correct format for practitioners in accordance with Bluepages B13.

The Bluebook references local court rules concerning the style of documents to be filed as well as a number of jurisdiction-specific manuals that offer guidance specific to local citation practice. In addition to *The Bluebook*, many legal publications use style manuals designed for the social sciences, arts and humanities, or federal government publications to supplement *The Bluebook* rules.[8]

b. *Citation Form.* All other sections of *The Bluebook* are devoted exclusively to legal citation form. The organizational structure and a variety of finding tools help users locate material and properly use the rules set out in *The Bluebook*. The inside front cover and first page provide a basic outline with examples of commonly used citations in the format used in law review footnotes. The last page and inside back cover provide the same examples of commonly used citations in the form used by practitioners in legal memoranda and court documents. The examples are accompanied by references to the appropriate rules that detail the finer points and subtleties of the rules and provide additional examples. A detailed index at the end of *The Bluebook* provides direct access by subject to specific aspects of citation form.

c. *Differences Between Editions.* The preface to the 18th edition provides a brief discussion of *The Bluebook*'s purpose; it includes a listing of the changes from the 17th edition. This feature is a welcome assistant in highlighting revisions between editions. Minute alterations may be made to *The Bluebook* between printings of the same edition.

d. *Priority Within Citations: Citation Structure.* Bluebook Rules 10 through 18 are ordered according to the perceived influence of the legal authority cited, i.e., a discussion of citation to primary sources precedes the discussion of secondary authority.[9] Each rule begins with a basic example. Within the rules for particular types of sources, individual rules are ordered according to the information conveyed within the citation, i.e., information set forth first in the citation is addressed by the first rule.

---

[8] THE CHICAGO MANUAL OF STYLE (15th ed. 2003), U.S. GOVERNMENT PRINTING OFFICE, STYLE MANUAL, 2000 (29th ed. 2000), and KATE L. TURABIAN, A MANUAL FOR WRITERS OF RESEARCH PAPERS, THESES, AND DISSERTATIONS (7th ed. 2007), are the manuals most commonly used for this purpose.

[9] Notice how Rules 1.3 and 1.4 relate to the order of information within a signal (*e.g., accord, see, see also, cf.*), moving from primary to secondary sources of legal information, while the ordering of signals themselves moves from direct support of a legal proposition to contradictory sources of legal information.

This perceived-influence approach to legal information applies to Rules 10 through 18. This technique can be applied to the most frequent type of citation—cases. The elements of a case citation, moving from left to right, are:

- case name
- volume number of the reporter
- abbreviated name of the reporter
- page number on which the opinion begins
- abbreviated name of the court, including its geographic jurisdiction (if not apparent from the name of the reporter)
- date or year of decision (give exact date of decision for unreported cases or slip opinions)
- parenthetical information regarding the case
- prior and subsequent case histories
- special or unique citation forms
- citation ends with a period

Or, as is illustrated by this hypothetical example:[10]

Belbin v. Laviolette, 455 F. Supp. 2d 55 (S.D. Cal. 2007) (Stone, J., dissenting), *aff'd*, No. 06–4099, 2008 WL 24484 (9th Cir. August 24, 2008).

Look at the elements of this citation and sequence of rules in *The Bluebook* following the basic citation form set out at Rule 10.1. Note that all citation examples provided in this chapter are in the format used by practitioners, not in the format used for law reviews. Therefore, relevant Bluepages rules are provided in addition to the rules found in the white pages of *The Bluebook*.

Belbin v. Laviolette,	case name	Rule 10.2/B5.1.1
455 F. Supp. 2d 55	reporter information	Rule 10.3/B5.1.2
(S.D. Cal. 2007)	court and jurisdiction, date or year	Rules 10.4–10.5/B5.1.3
(Stone, J., dissenting),	parenthetical information	Rule 10.6/B5.1.4
aff'd,	prior and subsequent history	Rule 10.7/B5.1.5
No. 06–4099, 2008 WL 24484 (9th Cir. Aug. 24, 2008).	special citation forms	Rule 10.8[11]/B5.1.3

3. Additional Aids for Using The Bluebook

Several additional citation tools have been developed to assist in understanding the complexities and nuances of *The Bluebook*. *Prince's*

---

[10] Note that all citation examples used in this chapter are hypothetical and used for illustrative purposes only.

[11] The special form of citation for unreported cases available on commercial electronic databases is set forth in Rule 18.1.1., which is cross-referenced from Rule 10.8.1(a).

Dictionary of Legal Citations[12] provides an alphabetical list of citation examples prepared according to the rules appearing in *The Bluebook*.

LexisNexis has developed, for use with standard word processing programs, a software application that checks citation forms for correctness. *Shepard's StyleCheck* (formerly known as *CiteRite*) checks citations in word-processed documents to ensure compliance with either *The Bluebook* or California citation forms. *Shepard's StyleCheck* checks for improper underlining and punctuation, typographical errors, incorrect reporter abbreviations, and missing parallel citations. It is capable of checking forms of citations to federal and state cases in official and unofficial case reporters, federal and state statute codifications, law review articles, federal legislative histories, model codes, and uniform acts. *Shepard's StyleCheck* does not correct the information in the word-processed text; rather, it highlights the problems in a report that displays the errors with reference to the appropriate rule.

West has developed a similar product called *CiteAdvisor* that suggests correct citation format following *The Bluebook* format, *ALWD Citation Manual* format, and state or local rules. With both *StyleCheck* and *CiteAdvisor* the researcher must still verify all components of a citation for accuracy. Although the correct citation format is suggested, the actual volume number, page number, and date are not verified.

SECTION B.   ALWD CITATION MANUAL: A PROFESSIONAL SYSTEM OF CITATION

1.   Historical Development of the ALWD Citation Manual: A Professional System of Citation

The *ALWD Citation Manual: A Professional System of Citation*[13] was produced as an alternative to *The Bluebook* and was designed to remedy some of the perceived complexities of *The Bluebook*. It was the perception of many professionals teaching legal writing and citation throughout the country that *The Bluebook* was unnecessarily complex, outdated, and of limited value to the majority of legal writers—law students and practitioners. Additionally, the Association of Legal Writing Directors (ALWD), an association dedicated to improving the analytic, reasoning, and writing abilities of law students and lawyers, sought to unify and simplify the teaching and use of citations. The *ALWD Citation Manual* contains one system for all legal documents, making no distinction between law review articles and other types of legal writing. The manual has been adopted by instructors at more than 90 law schools, many paralegal programs, and a number of law reviews, moot court competitions, and courts.

---

[12] MARY MILES PRINCE, PRINCE'S DICTIONARY OF LEGAL CITATIONS: A REFERENCE GUIDE FOR ATTORNEYS, LEGAL SECRETARIES, PARALEGALS, AND LAW STUDENTS (7th ed. 2006).

[13] Darby Dickerson of the Stetson University College of Law, an expert in legal citation, served as the lead author of the ALWD CITATION MANUAL. A draft manuscript was prepared by Dickerson and reviewed by the ALWD Citation Manual Advisory Committee. ASSOCIATION OF LEGAL WRITING DIRECTORS & DARBY DICKERSON, ALWD CITATION MANUAL: A PROFESSIONAL SYSTEM OF CITATION (3d ed. 2006) [ALWD CITATION MANUAL]. Unless otherwise stated, all references to the ALWD CITATION MANUAL will be from the third edition.

One of the main catalysts to the development of the *ALWD Citation Manual* was the 16th edition of *The Bluebook*, in which the editors substantially altered the meaning of citation signals. Citation signals (for example, *accord, see, see also, contra, e.g.*) are terms used to introduce a citation and operate as a shorthand method of indicating to the reader the manner in which an authority supports or contradicts an assertion. The most significant modification in the 16th edition of *The Bluebook* concerned the frequently used "see" signal. The 16th edition required "see" to be used with any direct support authority. Because the "see" signal had previously signified indirect support for a proposition, the new meaning of the signal created a strong likelihood that an author's use of authority would be misinterpreted.

The 16th edition's signal changes drew a strongly negative response from the legal community.[14] This was compounded by longstanding general dissatisfaction with origins of *The Bluebook* rules, i.e., students at select law reviews imposing citation rules on practitioners and academicians without input from any other interested constituencies. The concern in the legal community about changes in the meaning of citation signals was so strong that the Association of American Law Schools (AALS) passed a plenary resolution at the 1997 Annual Meeting to formally request that the editors of *The Bluebook* reinstate the introductory signals definitions from the 15th edition of *The Bluebook*.[15] The resolution also advocated that law reviews continue to use the 15th edition's introductory signal rules.[16]

The Association of Legal Writing Directors was encouraged by the AALS resolution and decided to move ahead with publication of a citation guide, written by professional legal educators, to provide an alternative to *The Bluebook*. ALWD sought to simplify the teaching and use of the system of citation. The *AWLD Citation Manual* simplifies some of the rules so that the rules are easier to find, interpret, and apply. The *ALWD Citation Manual* also provides more examples of how to apply each rule, and decreases inconsistencies in citation form, generally making it a more user-friendly and effective teaching tool.[17] The goals were not to alter citation format radically, but to develop a system that addressed specific deficiencies, while retaining those rules that functioned well,[18] and present a more pleasing, accessible format.[19]

[14] Darby Dickerson, *An Un–Uniform System of Citation: Surviving with the New Bluebook*, 26 STETSON L. REV. 53, 56–57 (1996).

[15] Darby Dickerson, *Seeing Blue: Ten Notable Changes in the New* Bluebook, 6 SCRIBES J. LEGAL WRITING 75 (1996–97) (outlining the action taken by the Association of American Law Schools).

[16] Not surprisingly, THE BLUEBOOK editors reverted back to the introductory signal rules from the 15th edition in the 17th edition, with minor changes.

[17] Steven D. Jamar, *The ALWD Citation Manual—A Professional System of Citation for the Law*, 8 PERSP.: TEACHING LEGAL RES. & WRITING 65, 66 (Winter 2000).

[18] Darby Dickerson, *It's Time for a New Citation System*, THE SCRIVENER, Summer 1998, at 2. For example, authors of the ALWD CITATION MANUAL note that present word processing capabilities have removed the archaic differentiation THE BLUEBOOK made between law review articles and legal and court memoranda. Furthermore, they recognize there is no valid rationale to use different typeface styles for footnote text versus main text or to make Form of Persp. distinctions between citations in textual sentences and citations in footnotes. *Id.*

[19] Suzanne E. Rowe, *The Bluebook Blues: AWLD Introduces a Superior Citation Reference Book for Lawyers*, OR. ST. B. BULL., June 2004, at 31.

The *ALWD Citation Manual* (generally called *"ALWD"*) (pronounced ALL-wood or ALL-wid) was first published in March 2000; the third edition was released in 2006.

2. Organization, Format, and Features of the ALWD Citation Manual

a. *Organization.* The *ALWD Citation Manual* is organized into seven parts. Part one contains introductory material explaining the importance and purpose of legal citation, the organization of the manual, the role of local citation rules, and instructions as to the method of changing default settings on a word processing program so that citations are not affected. Part two (Rules 1–11), "Citation Basics," contains rules applicable to citation to all types of authority, such as issues relating to typeface, abbreviations, spelling, capitalization, footnotes, and endnotes. Part three (Rules 12–37), discusses print citation formats for primary and secondary authorities, and part four (Rules 38–42) sets forth the rules regarding electronic citation formats. Part five (Rules 43–46) details the incorporation of citations into documents. Part six (Rules 47–49) addresses quotations. The last section, part seven, comprises a variety of appendices that provide information on state and federal primary sources, local court citation rules, abbreviations, and federal taxation materials, and sets forth a sample of a legal memorandum—a helpful inclusion that demonstrates correct usage and placement of legal citations in a document.

b. *Format.* The *ALWD Citation Manual*, at 572 pages, is longer than *The Bluebook*. Its pages are larger and easier to read, with larger type. Green icons illustrate spacing rules clearly. Although the spacing rules in the *ALWD Citation Manual* are not significantly different from those in *The Bluebook*, the ALWD manual makes it easier to determine the number of spaces required within a particular citation. The *ALWD Citation Manual* uses color changes in the text to emphasize points and clarify distinctions, and is written in a tabular style to more easily highlight every aspect of each rule.

c. *Features.* A useful feature employed in the *ALWD Citation Manual* is the "Sidebar," a teaching tool that provides supplementary background information on key points to help users avoid common problems. The Bluepages Tips, included in the new edition of *The Bluebook* is similar to the "Sidebar" feature pioneered by ALWD. The *ALWD Citation Manual* also contains a "Fast Formats" section at the beginning of chapters that cover specific sources, e.g., cases, statutes, treatises, and legal periodicals. These Fast Formats are useful to researchers when checking citations to common sources, as they include detailed examples. The Fast Formats are comparable to *The Bluebook*'s Quick Reference feature set forth inside both the front and back covers. Although the *ALWD Citation Manual* presents a wider range of examples of proper citation format, it does not collect in one location examples of citations to different sources; rather, the researcher must locate the correct rule in the manual to find the appropriate example. *The Bluebook*'s citation examples, while more limited in number, are more readily accessed inside the book's covers.

A website supplements the *ALWD Citation Manual* and posts updates to the text, frequently asked questions, and any necessary clarifications.[20]

3.   **Rules of the ALWD Citation Manual**[21]

The *ALWD Citation Manual* incorporates customary forms of citation, and many commentators observe that it simplifies the rules and achieves more consistency.[22] While the citation rules in the *ALWD Citation Manual* and *The Bluebook* overlap substantially, they are not identical.[23] Among the various simplifications outlined in the *ALWD Citation Manual*, two are most noteworthy. First is the provision of one consistent body of rules for all types of legal writing, regardless of where the citation appears. This eliminates confusion and complexity when using distinct citation methods for law review footnotes, the text of law review articles, and practitioners' memoranda and briefs, as *The Bluebook* does.

The second notable simplification in the *ALWD Citation Manual* involves the elimination of the use of large and small capitals in citations that are required by *The Bluebook*. There are only two type systems required in the *ALWD Citation Manual*: italics and regular type.[24]

The *ALWD Citation Manual* rules for citing cases have some minor differences from *The Bluebook*. The *ALWD Citation Manual* permits, but does not require, abbreviations within case names, unlike *The Bluebook* which requires abbreviations. One exception to this is that the *ALWD Citation Manual* requires the abbreviation of "United States" when it is a named party to a case, instead of spelling out the party as "United States," as required by *The Bluebook*. Some of the abbreviations in the *ALWD Citation Manual* deviate from *The Bluebook*. For example, the *ALWD Citation Manual* eliminates the apostrophe in abbreviations in case names. So when *The Bluebook* abbreviates Memorial as Mem'l, the *ALWD Citation Manual* abbreviates it as Meml. The *ALWD Citation Manual* requires that when a state case is cited, the citation must include available information about departments, districts, or divisions that decided the case. *The Bluebook* generally does not allow this information. Another difference in case citation is that the *ALWD Citation Manual* drops the unnecessary abbreviation "Ct." in parentheticals within state appellate court citations.

The hypothetical citation discussed previously in the *The Bluebook* section of this chapter appears almost identical using the *AWLD Citation Manual*. The only difference is that the *Westlaw* portion of the citation does not require the docket number, as illustrated in the following citation:

---

[20] The *ALWD Citation Manual* Web address is http://www.alwd.org.

[21] For a learning tool to citation form, see TRACY L. MCGAUGH & CHRISTINE HURT, INTERACTIVE CITATION WORKBOOK FOR ALWD CITATION MANUAL (2007 ed.). The Center for Computer–Assisted Legal Instruction also provides an interactive computer-based program in using the ALWD CITATION MANUAL at http://www.cali.org.

[22] Andrea Kaufman, *Uncomplicating the Citation Process*, 87 ILL. B.J. 675, 675 (1999) (book review).

[23] Section C of this chapter provides a comparison of selected ALWD (3d edition) and THE BLUEBOOK (18th edition) rules.

[24] Underlining may be substituted for italics in both manuals.

Belbin v. Laviolette, 455 F. Supp. 2d 55 (S.D. Cal. 2007) (Stone, J., dissenting), *aff'd*, 2008 WL 24484 (9th Cir. August 24, 2008).

Belbin v. Laviolette,	case name	Rule 12.2
455 F. Supp. 2d 55	reporter information	Rule 12.3–12.5
(S.D. Cal. 2007)	court and jurisdiction, date or year	Rule 12.6–12.7
(Stone, J., dissenting),	parenthetical informa-tion	Rule 12.11
aff'd,	prior and subsequent history	Rule 12.8–12.10
2008 WL 24484 (9th Cir. Aug. 24, 2008).	cases published only on *LexisNexis* or *West-law*	Rule 12.12

4. The Future of the ALWD Citation Manual

Although other competitors to *The Bluebook* have failed to gain wide acceptance, the *ALWD Citation Manual* may have a chance of survival due to its overall quality and consistency, the fact that it does not depart radically from *The Bluebook* tradition, and the fact that it is an excellent and effective teaching tool. Because many legal writing directors are members of the Association of Legal Writing Directors, the *ALWD Citation Manual* has been integrated into many first year law school writing curricula, and future lawyers are becoming familiar with it.

However, the legal profession is steeped in tradition and is slow to change, and most practicing legal professionals learned *The Bluebook* system for citation form. Therefore, it is very unlikely that the *ALWD Citation Manual* will ever rival *The Bluebook* in popularity. It is more appropriate, however, to consider whether there is room for both of these citation manuals. One issue to consider is whether the *ALWD Citation Manual*'s utility as a teaching resource will have lasting impact on *The Bluebook*'s use as a legal citation manual. The *ALWD Citation Manual* is expressly tailored to teach law students citation form and is predominately focused on citation form used by practitioners. Conversely, *The Bluebook* is primarily tailored for use by editors of scholarly writing.

It is important to remember that while the editors of the *ALWD Citation Manual* made some modifications to citation form, these modifications are relatively marginal to the basic design of legal citation. The *ALWD Citation Manual* was prepared largely as a restatement of citation,[25] and was not intended to deviate substantially from conventional form. Rather, changes were made only to promote consistency or flexibility on matters that do not affect the reader's ability to locate or interpret the cited material. In sum, students learning citation form with the *ALWD Citation Manual* are learning standard form. In fact, most practitioners and judges are unlikely to notice whether the *ALWD Citation Manual* or *The Bluebook* was used to prepare a specific citation or document.[26]

[25] Darby Dickerson, *Professionalizing Legal Citation*: The ALWD Citation Manual, 47 FED. LAW. 20, 22 Nov./Dec. 2000.

[26] Jennifer L. Cordle, ALWD Citation Manual: *A Grammar Guide to the Language of Legal Citation*, 26 U. ARK. LITTLE ROCK. L.REV. 573 (2004).

Only a few jurisdictions designate *The Bluebook* as the required citation form.[27] Most jurisdictions do not specify which citation form to follow.[28] Of the sixteen court systems that have adopted *The Bluebook* as an acceptable citation guide, five of them also have adopted *ALWD* as an acceptable citation guide.[29] Therefore, court adoption may not be a significant issue if the two citation guides continue to coexist.[30]

Regardless of how the role of, and the relationship between, the two citation manuals evolves over time, it is clear that competition from the *ALWD Citation Manual* has prompted *The Bluebook* editors to respond by improving *The Bluebook*'s 18th edition's format and quality of instruction to make it more user-friendly than prior editions. The 18th edition of *The Bluebook* now uses a larger font size; is formatted in a larger book size; comes with stronger covers for improved durability; includes color for key terms, headings and references; includes Bluepages—a new feature that includes numerous examples and is geared toward first year law students and practitioners; and now cites local court rules. Additionally, in preparation for the 18th edition, *The Bluebook* editors began a user survey to solicit input from interested parties. These changes from prior editions address several of *The Bluebook* criticisms and incorporate many of the elements admired by *ALWD Citation Manual* users.

It has been wisely suggested that the similarity between the two citation guides and the citations they generate indicates that it would not be difficult to integrate the best features of both guides to produce a truly exceptional citation manual.[31] ALWD could decide to join forces with *The Bluebook*'s student editors in a collaborative endeavor that would assist in the guidance of legal citation's progressive evolution.[32] This type of collaboration would serve the needs of the profession.

---

[27] The jurisdictions that have officially adopted THE BLUEBOOK are: U.S. Court of Appeals for the Eleventh Circuit, U.S. Court of Appeals for the Armed Forces, U.S. District Court for the District of Montana, U.S. District Court for the District of Delaware, U.S. Bankruptcy Court for the District of Montana, and the state courts of Alabama, California, Delaware, Florida, Idaho, Indiana, New Mexico, North Carolina, Texas, Washington, and Wisconsin.

[28] For example, the rules of the U.S. Supreme Court set forth requirements for nearly every aspect of documents submitted to the Court, from size of paper used to font size for footnotes, yet do not articulate a requirement for citation form. Use of THE BLUEBOOK is clearly assumed and traditional.

[29] The jurisdictions that have officially adopted the ALWD CITATION MANUAL are: U.S. Court of Appeals for the Eleventh Circuit, U.S. District Court for the District of Montana, U.S. Bankruptcy Court for the District of Montana, and the state courts of Alabama and Idaho.

[30] There is some evidence that law school Legal Research and Writing (LRW) directors and faculty are currently being pressured to teach THE BLUEBOOK alone, or teach the ALWD CITATION MANUAL only in conjunction with THE BLUEBOOK. Julie Cheslik, *The Battle Over Citation Form Brings Notice to LRW Faculty: Will Power Follow*? 73 UMKC L. REV. 237, 249 (2004). If one looks at the history of the number of LRW programs that planned to teach *only* the ALWD CITATION MANUAL, the numbers have decreased from 66 in 2001 to 40 in 2008. The number of LRW programs that planned to teach *only* THE BLUEBOOK increased from 52 to 108, respectively. Interestingly, the number of LRW programs planning to teach both the ALWD CITATION MANUAL and THE BLUEBOOK together increased from 14 programs in 2001, to 17 programs in 2008. Association of Legal Writing Directors/Legal Writing Institute, 2001–2008 Survey Results, Question 27, http://www.alwd.org. It is important to keep in mind, however, that until the ALWD CITATION MANUAL was published in 2000 essentially every LRW program taught only THE BLUEBOOK.

[31] Eric Shimamoto, *Comment: To Take Arms Against a Sea of Troubles: Legal Citation and the Reassertion of Hierarchy*, 73 UMKC L. REV. 443, 463 (2004).

[32] *Id.* at 465.

SECTION C.   COMPARISON OF SELECTED ALWD 3D EDITION RULES AND BLUEBOOK 18TH EDITION RULES

RULE	ALWD CITATION	BLUEBOOK CITATION	DIFFERENCES
Typeface **ALWD:** Rule 1 **BB:** B13 & Rule 2.0	Ordinary type and *italics* (or <u>underlining</u>). No distinctions based on type of document (law review v. court document) or placement of citation within the paper. Rule 1.1 in the third edition indicates that some journals and book publishers that do not follow ALWD require the use of large and small capital letters; Sidebar 23.2 provides examples of how to use large and small capital letters in various circumstances.	Ordinary type, *italics* (or <u>underlining</u>), and SMALL CAPS. Different fonts required depending on type of document and where source is cited within the paper.	ALWD has one set of conventions, not two. ALWD does not use small caps as a typeface.
Abbreviations and Spacing **ALWD:** Rule 2 **BB:** B5.1.1(v), B10.1, & Rule 6.1	F. Supp. F.3d Corp. Govt. Intl. Petr. In citations, ALWD gives the writer the flexibility to abbreviate words found in the appendices.	F. Supp. F.3d Corp. Gov't Int'l Pet'r In citations, the Bluebook requires that words in a case citation (as opposed to a case name used in a textual sentence) be abbreviated if the words appear in the Tables.	No substantial differences on spacing. ALWD abbreviations end with periods; some Bluebook abbreviations include apostrophes. ALWD provides flexibility regarding use of abbreviations.

RULE	ALWD CITATION	BLUEBOOK CITATION	DIFFERENCES
Capitalization **ALWD:** Rule 3 **BB:** B10.6 & Rule 8	*Federal Civil Procedure before Trial*	*Federal Civil Procedure Before Trial*	ALWD eliminates the "and prepositions of four or fewer letters" part of the Bluebook, which brings legal citation closer to non-legal style.
Numbers **ALWD:** Rule 4 **BB:** Rule 6.2	Indicates that the convention in law is to use words for zero through ninety-nine in all text and notes. However, ALWD provides flexibility on whether to designate numbers with words or numerals. Ordinal contractions are presented as follows: 1st, 2d, 3d, 4th, etc.	Use words for zero through ninety-nine in all text and notes. Ordinal contractions are presented as follows: 1st, 2d, 3d, 4th, etc.	No substantial differences, other than ALWD allows for more flexibility. However, ALWD inserts a comma in some four-digit numerals: 3,000.
Page spans **ALWD:** Rule 5 **BB:** Rule 3.2(a)	125-126 **or** 125-26	125-26	ALWD gives a choice on how to present a page span; you may retain all digits or drop repetitive digits and retain two digits on the right-hand side of the span, as in Bluebook 3.2(a).

RULE	ALWD CITATION	BLUEBOOK CITATION	DIFFERENCES
Footnotes and endnotes **ALWD**: Rule 7 **BB:** Rule 3.2(b)-(c)	n. 7 nn. 12-13	n.7 nn.12-13	ALWD requires a space after n. or nn. abbreviation.
Supra* and *infra **ALWD**: Rule 10 **BB**: Rule 3.5	*Supra* n. 45.	*Supra* note 45.	Under ALWD, abbreviate note as "n." and place a space after the period.
Id. **ALWD:** Rule 11.3 **BB**: B5.2, Rules 4.1, 10.9 & 12.9	*Id.* at 500.	*Id.* at 500.	Basically similar rules. ALWD eliminates the "5 *id.* in a row" rule found in Bluebook Rule 10.9. In the ALWD Manual, *id.* cannot be used with Practitioner and Court documents. Rule 29.6.

RULE	ALWD CITATION	BLUEBOOK CITATION	DIFFERENCES
Cases **ALWD:** Rule 12 **BB:** B5 & Rule 10	*Brown v. Bd. of Educ.*, 349 U.S. 294, 297 (1955). *MBNA Am. Bank, N.A. v. Cardoso*, 707 N.E.2d 189 (Ill. App. 1st Dist. 1998). [required inclusion of district court information]	*Brown v. Bd. of Educ.*, 349 U.S. 294, 297 (1955). *MBNA Am. Bank, N.A. v. Cardoso*, 707 N.E.2d 189 (Ill. App. Ct. 1st Dist. 1998). [permissive inclusion of district information]	Under ALWD, case names are always italicized or underlined. Under ALWD, you do not have to abbreviate words in case names. For those who want to abbreviate, Appendix 3 provides a longer list of words that are abbreviated. ALWD requires division and district information for state appellate courts, and eliminates "Ct." from most court abbreviations. For cases cited from Westlaw or LexisNexis, ALWD does not require the docket number of the case. ALWD also requires two asterisks to identify multiple pages of a pinpoint cite.

RULE	ALWD CITATION	BLUEBOOK CITATION	DIFFERENCES
Constitutions **ALWD:** Rule 13 **BB:** B7 & Rule 11	U.S. Const. amend. V.	U.S. Const. amend. V.	No substantial differences.
Statutes **ALWD:** Rule 14 **BB:** B6.1.1, B6.1.2 & Rule 12	18 U.S.C. § 1965 (2000).	18 U.S.C. § 1965 (2000).	No substantial differences.
Legislative Materials **ALWD:** Rules 15 & 16 **BB:** B6.1.6 & Rule 13	Sen. Res. 146, 109th Cong. (2005).	S. Res. 146, 109th Cong. (2005).	ALWD abbreviates Senate as "Sen." instead of "S." to avoid confusion with other abbreviations. Most forms are relatively consistent.
Court Rules **ALWD:** Rule 17 **BB:** B6.1.3 & Rule 12.8	Fed. R. Civ. P. 11.	Fed. R. Civ. P. 11.	No substantial differences.

RULE	ALWD CITATION	BLUEBOOK CITATION	DIFFERENCES
Administrative Materials **ALWD:** Rules 19 and 20 **BB:** B6.1.4 & Rule 14.2	34 C.F.R. § 607.1 (2006). 70 Fed. Reg. 10868 (Mar. 5, 2005).	34 C.F.R. § 607.1 (2006). 70 Fed. Reg. 10868 (Mar. 5, 2005).	C.F.R. citation is the same. Both require an exact date for Fed. Reg. citations. ALWD includes guidance about how to cite C.F.R. references found on unofficial electronic databases, such as Westlaw and LexisNexis. Rule 19.1(d).
Books and Treatises **ALWD:** Rule 22 **BB:** B8 & Rule 15	Charles Alan Wright, Arthur R. Miller & Mary Kay Kane, *Federal Practice and Procedure* vol. 7A, § 1751, 10-17 (3d ed., West 2005). OR Charles Alan Wright et al., *Federal Practice and Procedure* vol. 7A, § 1751, 10-17 (3d ed., West 2005).	7A Charles Alan Wright, Arthur R. Miller & Mary Kay Kane, *Federal Practice and Procedure* § 1751, at 10-17 (3d ed. 2005). OR 7A Charles Alan Wright et al., *Federal Practice and Procedure* § 1751, at 10-17 (3d ed. 2005).	ALWD places volume information after the title, just like any other subdivisions. ALWD separates subdivisions separated with a comma, but no "at." ALWD requires that the publisher be included, no matter what type of document. ALWD uses et al. for three authors or more, compared with the Bluebook which uses et al. for two authors or more.

RULE	ALWD CITATION	BLUEBOOK CITATION	DIFFERENCES
Legal Periodicals **ALWD:** Rule 23 **BB:** B9 & Rule 16	Geoffrey P. Miller, *Bad Judges*, 83 Tex. L. Rev. 431 (2004). Margaret Graham Tebo, *Duty Calls*, 91 ABA J. 35 (Apr. 2005). Carrie Ann Wozniak, Student Author, *Difficult Problems Call for New Solutions: Are Guardians Proper for Viable Fetuses of Mentally Incompetent Mothers in State Custody?* 34 Stetson L. Rev. 193 (2004). Jodi Wilgoren, *Prosecution Lays out Case for Harsh Sentencing of B.T.K. Killer in Gory Detail*, 154 N.Y. Times A14 (Aug. 18, 2005).	Geoffrey P. Miller, *Bad Judges*, 83 Tex. L. Rev. 431 (2004). Margaret Graham Tebo, *Duty Calls*, A.B.A. J., Apr. 2005, at 35. Carrie Ann Wozniak, Comment, *Difficult Problems Call for New Solutions: Are Guardians Proper for Viable Fetuses of Mentally Incompetent Mothers in State Custody?* 34 Stetson L. Rev. 193 (2004). Jodi Wilgoren, *Prosecution Lays out Case for Harsh Sentencing of B.T.K. Killer in Gory Detail*, N.Y. Times, Aug. 18, 2005, at A14.	ALWD eliminates most distinctions between consecutively and non-consecutively paginated articles. Include longer [exact] date for non-consecutively paginated journals, but do so within the parenthetical. ALWD uses the term "Student Author" to replace Note, Comment, Recent Development, etc.

RULE	ALWD CITATION	BLUEBOOK CITATION	DIFFERENCES
A.L.R. Annotations **ALWD:** Rule 24 **BB:** Rule 16.6.6	Carolyn Kelly MacWilliam, *Individual and Corporate Liability for Libel and Slander in Electronic Communications, Including E-mail, Internet and Websites,* 3 A.L.R.6th 153 (2005).	Carolyn Kelly MacWilliam, Annotation, *Individual and Corporate Liability for Libel and Slander in Electronic Communications, Including E-mail, Internet and Websites,* 3 A.L.R.6th 153 (2005).	ALWD eliminates the "Annotation" reference.
Legal Dictionaries **ALWD:** Rule 25 **BB:** Rule 15.8	*Black's Law Dictionary* 87 (Bryan A. Garner ed., 8th ed., West 2004).	*Black's Law Dictionary* 87 (8th ed. 2004).	ALWD treats dictionaries like books.
Legal Encyclopedias **ALWD:** Rule 26 **BB:** Rule 15.8	98 C.J.S. *Witnesses* § 397 (2002). 68 Am. Jur. 2d *Schools* §§ 20-24 (2000 & Supp. 2005).	98 C.J.S. *Witnesses* § 397 (2002). 68 Am. Jur. 2d *Schools* §§ 20-24 (2000 & Supp. 2005).	No substantial differences; however, ALWD provides expanded coverage and includes a list of many abbreviations for state encyclopedias.

RULE	ALWD CITATION	BLUEBOOK CITATION	DIFFERENCES
Internet **ALWD:** Rule 40 **BB:** Rule 18.2.3	Fed. Jud. Ctr., *History of the Federal Judiciary*, http://www.fjc. gov/history/home.nsf (accessed Aug. 18, 2005).	Federal Judicial Center, *History of the Federal Judiciary* (visited Aug. 18, 2005), *at* http://www. fjc.gov/history/home. nsf	ALWD permits the abbreviation of an organizational author's name, to save space. ALWD uses "accessed" instead of "visited" to be consistent with non-legal citation guides. The Bluebook contains different formats for material that appears only on the Web and for material that appears on the Web and in other medium. The position of the date parenthetical moves depending on the type of information cited.

RULE	ALWD CITATION	BLUEBOOK CITATION	DIFFERENCES
Signals **ALWD:** Rule 44 **BB:** B4 & Rule 1.2	Signals are *e.g.,* *accord, see, see also, cf., contra, compare . . . with, but see, but cf.,* and *see generally.*	Signals are *e.g.,* *accord, see, see also, cf., contra, compare . . . with, but see, but cf.,* and *see generally.*	Under ALWD, all signals may be separated with semicolons. Under the Bluebook, a new citation sentence must start when there is a new type of signal. (Signals are categorized by type in the Bluebook-supportive, comparative, contradictory, or background-whereas in ALWD, the signals are ordered individually.) ALWD does not use any punctuation after a signal.

RULE	ALWD CITATION	BLUEBOOK CITATION	DIFFERENCES
Order of Cited Authority **ALWD:** Rule 45 **BB:** B4.5 & Rule 1.4	ALWD lists federal, state, and foreign court cases first by jurisdiction, then in reverse chronological order.	Federal (appellate and trial) court cases are ordered in reverse chronological order. State court cases are first, alphabetized by state, and then ranked within each state.	Minor differences in the order when looking at the list of specific sources: (1) Under ALWD, statutes (federal and state) come before rules of evidence and procedure, whereas in the Bluebook, federal statutes and rules of evidence and procedure come before state statutes and rules of evidence and procedure. (2) Under the ALWD, the student-authored articles are classified with all other material in law reviews, law journals, and other periodicals, whereas in the Bluebook, the student-authored articles are separate, and cited after the non-student authored articles.

RULE	ALWD CITATION	BLUEBOOK CITATION	DIFFERENCES
Quotations **ALWD:** Rule 47 **BB:** B12 & Rule 5	ALWD says to block indent passages if they contain at least fifty words OR if they exceed four lines of typed text.	The *Bluebook* says to block indent passages if they contain at least 50 words.	ALWD does not require you to count the exact number of words in long quotations.

The above chart was prepared by Darby Dickerson, Vice President, Dean, and Professor of Law at Stetson University College of Law. ©2006 by Darby Dickerson.[33]

SECTION D. ELECTRONIC CITATION SYSTEMS AND NEUTRAL CITATION SYSTEMS

1. Citation to Electronic Resources

The Bluebook and the *ALWD Citation Manual* both require the researcher to cite to print sources whenever possible. Citation to electronic sources alone, such as *Westlaw, LexisNexis*, or the Internet, is permitted only when the information is unavailable in traditional print form, or the source cannot be located because it is so obscure that it is practically unavailable. Researchers may add an electronic source as a parallel citation, if it will help readers access the information more easily. Proponents of neutral citation systems, discussed later in this chapter, encourage citation to an electronic version of a source, regardless of the availability of the information in print.

a. *Citation to Westlaw and LexisNexis.* Both *The Bluebook* and the *ALWD Citation Manual* have adopted online citation forms developed by *Westlaw* and *LexisNexis*. A *Westlaw* or *LexisNexis* citation to a case in an electronic database is available from the moment a case appears on *Westlaw* or *LexisNexis*. The citation provides a precise method for referring to that case in the database. Because most cases are available within 24 to 72 hours after the court's ruling, *Westlaw* and *LexisNexis* citations might be the only available means for referring to recently created materials during the traditional editorial and publication process.

(1) *The Bluebook*

A typical *Westlaw* citation, according to *Bluebook* Rule 18.1 would appear as:

Burkhard v. Fradette, No. 06–1234, 2008 WL 4672, at *5 (D. Mass. Oct. 17, 2008).

---

[33] ALWD–Bluebook Comparison Charts; http://www.alwdmanual.com/books/dickerson_alwd/updates/ALWD-BluebookComparisonCharts.pdf.

Burkhard v. Fradette,	case name
No.06-1234,	docket number
2008 WL 4672,	database identifier: year, name of database, and unique document number
at *5	pinpoint reference
(D. Mass. Oct. 17, 2008).	jurisdictional information and date of decision

Similarly, a typical *LexisNexis* citation, according to *Bluebook* Rule 18.1, would appear as:

Burkhard v. Fradette, No. 06–1234, 2008 U.S. Dist. LEXIS 19523, at *5 (D. Mass. Oct. 17, 2008).

Note that the only difference between the *Westlaw* and *LexisNexis Bluebook* citations is in the database identifier portion of the citation.

(2) *ALWD*

Westlaw and *LexisNexis* case citations conforming to the *ALWD Citation Manual* rules are slightly different from those using *The Bluebook*. *ALWD* Rule 12.12 does not require a docket number, and does not require a comma before a pinpoint reference.

A typical *Westlaw* citation, according to the *ALWD Citation Manual* rules, would appear as:

Burkhard v. Fradette, 2008 WL 4672 at *5 (D. Mass. Oct. 17, 2008).

Similarly, a typical *LexisNexis* citation, according to the *ALWD Citation Manual* rules, would appear as:

Burkhard v. Fradette, 2008 U.S. Dist. LEXIS 19523 at *5 (D. Mass. Oct. 17, 2008).

b. *Citation to Information on the Internet. The Bluebook* and the *ALWD Citation Manual* recognize that information is available in multiple formats, although both clearly prefer citation to print sources. According to both citation manuals, the Internet may be cited only when information is not available in print form, or when a print source exists but a parallel citation to the Internet will substantially improve access to the information cited.

(1) *The Bluebook*

According to *Bluebook* Rule 18.2, when a source is unavailable in a print format or on a widely available commercial database, direct citation to the Internet is allowed without an explanatory phrase. However, when a source is available in a print format, but increased accessibility to the source will be provided in the form of a parallel citation to the Internet source with identical content, citation must include the explanatory phrase "*available at*" before the URL. For example, the citation to a recent case on the U.S. District Court for the District of Maryland's website, which has not yet appeared in print or on a widely available commercial database, would appear as:

Bobowicz v. Cardona, No. 06–1983 (D. Md. Nov. 5, 2008), http://www.mdd.uscourts.gov/Opinions/Opinions/Bobowicz1105.pdf.

Bobowicz v. Cardona	case name
No. 06-1983	docket number
(D. Md. Nov. 5, 2008),	court and jurisdiction, date or year:
http://www.mdd.uscourts.gov/Opinions/ Opinions/Bobowicz1105.pdf.	URL (generally not under- lined)

(2) *ALWD*

ALWD Rule 40 covers general citation to information on the Internet, while Rule 12.15 specifically provides for citing cases on the Internet. According to Rule 12.15, a researcher may cite the Internet only if a case is not available in a reporter, an online database such as *Westlaw* or *Lexis-Nexis*, or a looseleaf service. The *ALWD Citation Manual* requires the case name with the URL and a parenthetical with the court abbreviation and exact date. A citation to a case that is available only on the Internet would appear as:

Bobowicz v. Cardona, http://www.mdd.uscourts.gov/Opinions/Opinions/ Bobowicz1105.pdf (D. Md. Nov. 5, 2008).

Notice that, unlike *The Bluebook*, the docket number is not required by the *ALWD Citation Manual*, and the date is placed at the end of the citation.

2. Neutral Citation

The development of information technology caused significant changes in the ways that legal information is published and disseminated. A number of courts began to report their most recent decisions electronically. New providers of legal information entered a market that was no longer exclusively controlled by the traditional publishers.

Traditional citation rules limited the use of electronic resources and hampered their acceptance in the marketplace. The rules for citing primary sources in electronic formats had not kept pace with the enhanced access made possible by technology. In response, the American Association of Law Libraries (AALL) and the American Bar Association (ABA) each developed "neutral" citation formats, incorporating developing technology with legal citation.[34] Neutral citation refers to a citation that is medium neutral (applicable to print or electronic formats) and vendor neutral (does not require vendor-specific information). Citation would be identical whether the researcher located the case in print, *Westlaw*, *LexisNexis*, or on the Internet. Other terms used to refer to this same concept are "universal"

---

[34] AALL published the first edition of its Universal Citation Guide (*UCG*) in 1999, with rules that covered cases, statutes, constitutions, and administrative regulations. Citation Formats Comm., Am. Ass'n of Law Libraries, Universal Citation Guide (1999). The second edition was published in 2004, providing formats for law reviews, court rules, and administrative decisions. Citation Formats Comm., Am. Ass'n of Law Libraries, Universal Citation Guide (2d ed. 2004). *See also* Special Committee on Citation Issues, American Bar Ass'n, Report and Recommendation (May 23, 1996) (approved by the ABA House of Delegates on August 6, 1996). In February 2003, the ABA House of Delegates passed the Universal Citation Facilitation resolution reaffirming its commitment to universal citation. The text of both the 1996 report and the 2003 reaffirmation resolution are available on the Internet at http://www.abanet.org/tech/ltrc/research/citation/.

citation form, or "public domain" citation form—usable by any publisher without reference to products of any other publisher. Neutral citations are created when the court assigns a sequential number to an opinion and numbers the paragraphs in the opinion. Support for neutral citation developed because knowledge of a case name, decision number, court, and date would allow the researcher to locate a case in any medium.

a. *Neutral Case Citation.* The basic citation form for neutral citation of court opinions, according to both *The Bluebook* and the *ALWD Citation Manual*, comprises the following components: case name, year of decision, the state's two-character postal code, the court abbreviation (unless it is the state's highest court), and the sequential number of the decision. There is much variation among adopting states concerning spacing and punctuation in neutral citations, so researchers must follow the examples given by local rule.

(1) *The Bluebook*

The Bluebook has weighed into the controversy by recommending a format for public domain citation (the term *The Bluebook* employs for neutral citation) in Rule 10.3.3. However, *The Bluebook* remains deeply committed to print sources and requires, if available, a parallel citation to the appropriate regional reporter. When referencing specific material within a decision, the pinpoint citation should be made to the paragraph number where the material appears, along with the page number in the regional reporter, if available. *The Bluebook*'s format requires that if a decision is unpublished, a capital "U" is placed after the sequential number of the decision. *The Bluebook* makes clear that if a jurisdiction adopts a public domain format differing from *The Bluebook*'s recommended form, the jurisdiction's format should be observed. Table 1 of *The Bluebook* identifies jurisdictions that have adopted a public domain format and provides examples.

The following is an example representative of *The Bluebook*'s recommended public domain citation format for a North Dakota Supreme Court case:

Barney v. Licht, 2008 ND 112, ¶ 11, 749 N.W.2d 158, 160.

Barney v. Licht,	case name
2008	year of decision
ND	state's two-character postal abbreviation
112,	sequential number of decision
¶ 11,	pinpoint paragraph
749 N.W.2d 158,	parallel citation to regional reporter
160.	pinpoint reference in regional reporter

(2) *ALWD*

The *ALWD Citation Manual* (Rule 12.16) informs researchers to use neutral citation when required by local rule. Appendix 2 should be consulted to determine whether a particular court requires neutral citation. If a court does not require a neutral citation, a researcher still may include one as a parallel citation by using the format adopted by the court or the following format: case name, year of decision, court abbreviation, opinion number, and citation to reporter or online source. Therefore, the above example of neutral case citation according to *The Bluebook* also conforms to the *ALWD Citation Manual*.

b. *The Future of Neutral Citation Reform.* An effective neutral citation system for legal materials would not be dependent on commercial vendors, and would facilitate precise pinpoint citations to material in all formats. Citations would not rely on a specific volume and page number and, therefore, would be immediately available when an opinion is released from the court. The citation would remain consistent despite the format. Consequently, researchers would find the system easy to use, and readers would be able to identify legal citations with clarity.

Opponents of neutral citation argue two points: (1) there would be increased expense to the court and (2) there would be diminished access to law because cases without identifying sources would be difficult to locate. In response to these arguments, proponents of neutral citation note the reduced cost to researchers, because a public domain system fosters competition among vendors, making legal information available at a lower cost. Proponents of neutral citation counter that access to legal material will actually increase, as the citation, now in the public domain, facilitates wider dissemination of information on the law.[35]

At the time this is written, fourteen state court systems have adopted some form of neutral citation.[36]

---

[35] The Conference of Chief Justices report notes that those court systems that are adding sequential opinion numbers or paragraph numbers state that no additional costs are associated with this process. CONFERENCE OF CHIEF JUSTICES, REPORT OF THE COMMITTEE ON OPINIONS CITATION (National Center for State Courts 1999), http://ccj.ncsc.dni.us/finalrpt.pdf.

[36] Arizona, Louisiana, Maine, Mississippi, Montana, New Mexico, North Dakota, Ohio, Oklahoma, South Dakota, Utah, Vermont, Wisconsin, and Wyoming. For additional discussion, see Ian Gallacher, *Cite Unseen: How Neutral Citation and America's Law Schools Can Cure Our Strange Devotion to Bibliographical Orthodoxy and the Constriction of Open and Equal Access to the Law*, 70 ALB. L. REV. 491, 528 (2007); Peter W. Martin, *Neutral Citation, Court Web Sites, and Access to Authoritative Case Law*, 99 LAW LIBR. J. 329, 348 (2007).

Chapter 25

FEDERAL TAX RESEARCH*

This chapter discusses primary and secondary sources of federal tax law and provides information about research materials containing these items. The chapter also suggests methods for evaluating and updating results.

SECTION A. INTRODUCTION

Many researchers erroneously believe federal tax research has little or nothing in common with traditional legal research methods. That belief is incorrect. Researchers can solve problems involving federal taxation using techniques mastered in a basic legal research course and often can use traditional materials.[1] Many library collections include sources dealing solely with federal taxation. Because those tax-specific sources are more comprehensive and cover topics more thoroughly than do general legal research sources, they are better-suited for tax research. Whether shelved together in a "tax alcove," dispersed throughout the collection, or accessed online, tax-specific materials are no more difficult to locate or use than are traditional research tools.

This chapter focuses on general tax research principles. Because so many items are available, a library may lack a source described in this chapter, contain materials omitted here, or include particular materials in a different format (e.g., CD–ROM or DVD). Because the publishing industry continues to consolidate, and many formerly independent publishers are now commonly owned,[2] researchers should not be surprised if a publication described in this chapter is dropped or renamed. Researchers who understand basic tax research techniques will be able to adapt to these changes.

---

* Gail Levin Richmond, Professor, Nova Southeastern University Shepard Broad Law Center, Fort Lauderdale, Florida, wrote this chapter. An expanded version is separately published under the title FEDERAL TAX RESEARCH: GUIDE TO MATERIALS AND TECHNIQUES (7th ed. 2007) (Foundation Press).

[1] This chapter devotes very little space to traditional legal research tools. If the library lacks a tax-oriented tool, researchers may want to consult traditional materials. References to the appropriate chapters in this book assist in locating such materials.

[2] Thomson Reuters is the parent for West Publishing, West Group, *Westlaw*, *FindLaw*, Foundation Press, Research Institute of America (RIA), Warren, Gorham & Lamont, Lawyers Cooperative, and Clark Boardman Callahan; subgroups exist within this group. Reed Elsevier owns Michie, Butterworths, Shepard's, Matthew Bender, and LexisNexis. Wolters Kluwer owns Commerce Clearing House, Aspen, *Loislaw*, and Kleinrock; Aspen has acquired several titles formerly published by Little, Brown. New editions frequently carry the imprint of the parent rather than of the original publisher.

SECTION B. RESEARCH METHODOLOGY

Tax research follows general legal research procedures. Using a set of facts presented in a problem, researchers must ascertain the issues raised by these facts and determine if any additional facts might be relevant. To resolve the issues, they must locate governing statutory language and sources that interpret that language. Legislative history, administrative pronouncements, and judicial decisions are three sources for guidance in interpreting the statute. Judicial decisions are also important in assessing the validity of any administrative pronouncements. Although most decisions relate to interpretation, courts may also hear constitutional challenges to a statute or to an administrative interpretation. If foreign-source income or noncitizens are involved, research must also include applicable treaties.

Researchers who are familiar with the subject matter involved can often locate these items without resort to any secondary authority other than a citator. Researchers who lack such familiarity might proceed in an entirely different manner. They would begin with secondary materials, which will help them determine which Code sections are involved and will explain the underlying issues. Looseleaf services, treatises, and periodical articles are particularly useful in this phase of one's research.

SECTION C. CONSTITUTION

The Constitution contains several specific provisions for taxation. These include the apportionment clauses (Article I, section 2, clause 3, and Article I, section 9, clause 4), the origination clause (Article I, section 7, clause 1), the uniformity clause (Article 1, section 8, clause 1), and the export clause (Article I, section 9, clause 5). Because the income tax is specifically authorized by the Constitution's sixteenth amendment, it avoids an earlier holding that it was a direct tax subject to apportionment based on population.[3] The estate and gift taxes, on the other hand, are indirect taxes subject only to the requirement that they be uniform throughout the United States.

Because substantive tax research rarely involves the Constitution, tax-oriented research tools focusing on the Constitution are limited. In fact, none of the tax-oriented citators (Section L) includes the Constitution as cited material. Constitutional research is best performed using traditional materials.[4] Alternatively, online tax services (Section T) may be searched, using either a specific constitutional provision or a common term (e.g., due process). The *Standard Federal Tax Reporter* volume 1 (Section M) includes materials on litigation involving constitutional claims. Because constitutional litigation often involves provisions that do not specifically mention taxation, secondary materials are an important part of initial constitutional tax research.

---

[3] Pollock v. Farmers' Loan & Trust Co., 158 U.S. 601 (1895); *cf.* Springer v. United States, 102 U.S. 586 (1881), concluding the Civil War income tax was indirect.

[4] The most useful materials are annotated constitutions, such as those included in UNITED STATES CODE ANNOTATED and UNITED STATES CODE SERVICE, and digests. See Chapters 8 and 9 of this book. For a discussion of tax litigation involving constitutional claims, see 1 BORIS I. BITTKER & LAWRENCE LOKKEN, FEDERAL TAXATION OF INCOME, ESTATES AND GIFTS ch. 1 (3d ed. 1999 & most recent Cum. Supp.).

SECTION D. STATUTORY SCHEME

United States Code Title 26, more commonly referred to as the Internal Revenue Code of 1986, contains the vast majority of statutes covering income, estate and gift, excise, and employment taxes. Throughout this chapter these materials are referred to as the Code. References to the two previous Codes—1939 and 1954—include the year.[5] The Code has numerous subdivisions, including subtitle, chapter, and subchapter. Researchers must keep these in mind, as many Code sections apply only for purposes of particular subdivisions.

Some tax-related provisions are set forth outside the Internal Revenue Code. These include provisions codified in other *U.S.C.* titles and uncodified provisions. For example, many rules affecting retirement benefits appear in Title 29. Statutory relief rules in the employee/independent contractor area have been amended several times but have never been codified.[6]

SECTION E. LOCATING CURRENT, REPEALED, AND PENDING LEGISLATION

In researching a tax problem, the time frame involved is quite important. If, for example, the research involves a contemplated transaction, current statutory provisions are certainly important. If the current statutory language is of recent vintage, research into its meaning might include the repealed statute it replaced. And, because tax provisions change frequently, researchers ignore pending legislation at their peril. A bill changing the tax consequences of a proposed transaction might be enacted before a client negotiates a binding contract.[7] Finally, some provisions have specific sunset dates, which usually appear within the Code. When working with Code provisions, researchers must be mindful of the distinctions between enactment date, effective date, and sunset date.

The following sections discuss sources containing the text of relevant legislation. Legislative histories (Section G) may also be useful.

1. Current Code—Codifications

Several publishers produce annual versions of the Internal Revenue Code.[8] Those publishing in a looseleaf format regularly integrate new

[5] Before 1939, tax statutes were reenacted in their entirety, or with necessary changes, on a regular basis. Because many current provisions can be traced back to the 1939 Code or even earlier—I.R.C. § 263, for example, contains language taken almost verbatim from § 117 of the 1864 Act, 13 Stat. 282—cross-references to these earlier materials are extremely useful. Section G discusses materials used to trace statutory language.

[6] Revenue Act of 1978, Pub. L. No. 95–600, § 530, 92 Stat. 2763, 2885, *extended indefinitely by* Tax Equity and Fiscal Responsibility Act of 1982, Pub. L. No. 97–248, § 269(c), 96 Stat. 324, 552, *and amended by* Small Business Job Protection Act of 1996, Pub. L. No. 104–188, § 1122, 110 Stat. 1755, 1766, *and by* Pension Protection Act of 2006, Pub. L. No. 109–280, § 864, 120 Stat. 780, 1024.

[7] Effective dates for new legislation frequently precede the actual enactment date. However, transactions subject to binding contracts on an act's effective date are often exempted. In other cases, transactions that occur after a statute is enacted may be disqualified because the contract was entered into before the enactment. *See, e.g.,* Gulf Opportunity Zone Act of 2005, Pub. L. No. 109–135, § 405(a)(1), 119 Stat. 2577, 2634. Polone v. Commissioner, 505 F.3d 966 (9th Cir. 2007), *cert. denied,* 128 S. Ct. 1720 (2008), illustrates how a change in the law can affect a multi-year transaction.

[8] Non-tax-oriented codifications such as UNITED STATES CODE, UNITED STATES CODE ANNOTATED, and UNITED STATES CODE SERVICE are discussed in Chapter 9 of this book.

material into the codification volumes. Publishers of bound volumes may use supplements for new matter or may not supplement at all during the year. CD–ROM (Section S) and online services (Section T) insert new material directly into the relevant database. The two listed below publish in looseleaf form; both services are discussed in Section M.

- *CCH Standard Federal Tax Reporter (SFTR)*[9]

- *RIA United States Tax Reporter (USTR)*[10]

2. Individual Revenue Acts

Acts are first published as slip laws and then bound in Public Law number order into the appropriate volume of *United States Statutes at Large*. Although looseleaf services integrate the text of recent statutes into their codifications, the slip law version of an act remains valuable. Slip laws include effective dates and congressional instructions to the IRS. Codifications omit this information or reproduce it in relatively small print.

A researcher can locate these acts in various non-tax services[11] and in CD–ROM (Section S) and online services (Section T). The IRS-produced *Cumulative Bulletin* (Section Q) included revenue acts, but it ceased publishing this material after the *Cumulative Bulletin* for 2003; *Internal Revenue Acts—Text and Legislative History* (Section Q) also includes statutory text. Online services, both government and commercial, are the best sources for the text of recent laws.

3. Previous Law

The materials listed in subsection 2 contain individual acts. Those listed below provide both earlier versions of amended sections and the text of legislation that has been repealed altogether. The first three items provide the most compact means of tracing changes. The others use a multivolume format that makes the tracing process tedious.

- *RIA Cumulative Changes* (Section Q) (1939 to date)

- *Barton's Federal Tax Laws Correlated* (Section Q) (1913–52)

- *Seidman's Legislative History of Federal Income and Excess Profits Tax Laws* (Section Q) (1861–1953)

---

[9] STANDARD FEDERAL TAX REPORTER includes all federal taxes in its two Code volumes but covers only income and employment taxes in the remainder of the set. CCH also publishes FEDERAL ESTATE AND GIFT TAX REPORTER and FEDERAL EXCISE TAX REPORTER. Because their formats resemble that of *SFTR*, this chapter includes few separate references to those services. The Code provisions also appear in each looseleaf service's compilation volumes.

[10] All federal taxes are covered in the two UNITED STATES TAX REPORTER Code volumes, but this service is otherwise limited to income and employment taxes. Because USTR—ESTATE & GIFT TAXES and USTR—EXCISE TAXES cover their respective subject matters in a similar format, they are rarely referenced separately in this chapter. The Code provisions also appear in each looseleaf service's compilation volumes.

[11] Sources such as U.S. CODE CONGRESSIONAL AND ADMINISTRATIVE NEWS (USCCAN) and UNITED STATES CODE SERVICE, ADVANCE SERVICE, are discussed in Chapters 9 and 10 of this book.

- Mertens, *Law of Federal Income Taxation—Code* (Section M) (1954–85)

- *Internal Revenue Acts—Text and Legislative History* (Section Q)

- *Tax Management Primary Sources* (Section Q) (1969–2003)

- *The Internal Revenue Acts of the United States: 1909–1950; 1950–1972; 1973–* (Section Q)

Eldridge, *The United States Internal Revenue System* (Section Q), provides annotated text for revenue acts prior to 1894. It can be used if *Seidman's* is unavailable, but it does not contain as much information.

4. Pending and Potential Legislation

Even before a bill is introduced, taxpayers may receive hints that it is on the horizon. In presidential election years, for example, party platforms include potential legislative agendas. Presidential budget messages may also serve this function. Items of this nature appear in newsletters (Section P) as well as in general interest newspapers.

Researchers can track pending legislation online or by using print sources. Online services (Section T) are usually the best means for following pending bills. The Library of Congress *THOMAS* website is one such source. In addition, both *LexisNexis* and *Westlaw* provide bill-tracking services.

The weekly *CCH Congressional Index* is an excellent print source for locating and tracking pending items. It provides a brief digest of pending bills. It also indicates a bill's progress, listing hearings and other pertinent information.[12]

Although looseleaf services (Section M) and newsletters (Section P) cover pending legislation, only *Daily Tax Report* and *Tax Notes* list a significant number of bills introduced in the current Congress; their descriptions of most items are cursory. Looseleaf services are generally less valuable than newsletters; they generally cover fewer bills and are likely to provide less detailed information.

SECTION F. CITATORS FOR STATUTES

Researchers can use citators to determine if a federal court considered a statute's constitutionality. Citators are discussed in Section L.

SECTION G. LEGISLATIVE HISTORIES

The process for enacting tax legislation is virtually identical to that followed in the enactment of any federal law.[13] Because there are many steps and groups involved, the number of documents comprising the history of a major tax statute is likely to be extensive.

---

[12] Chapter 10 of this book describes services such as those available from CONGRESSIONAL INFORMATION SERVICE (CIS), which follow a bill's progress through Congress, and the WEEKLY COMPILATION OF PRESIDENTIAL DOCUMENTS.

[13] With one constitutional limitation—revenue-raising bills must originate in the House of Representatives—the enactment process follows that described in Chapters 9 and 10 of this book.

The House Committee on Ways and Means and the Senate Committee on Finance have primary jurisdiction over revenue bills. Each committee (or subcommittees thereof) may hold hearings, which will be published, and issue a committee report when a bill is reported out of committee.[14] If House and Senate versions differ, a Conference Committee meets to resolve these differences. This group generates a third report, which explains the resolution of those differences.

Five members each from Ways and Means and from Finance sit on a separate Joint Committee on Taxation (JCT).[15] While proposals and reports may emanate from this committee, it is not charged with drafting legislation and its reports lack the interpretive significance of those issued by the Ways and Means and Finance Committees. In addition to studies for use in the hearings or drafting process, the JCT's staff publishes a post-enactment *General Explanation* (the *"Blue Book"*). The staff published no *Blue Books* after the one for the 1986 Act; it resumed issuing them for 1996 and subsequent legislation.

Bills reported out by committee are debated on the floor of the appropriate house. Although Senate rules permit more extensive debate and floor amendments than do House procedures, each chamber can change the bill. Discussion of the bill during any congressional debate appears in the *Congressional Record*.[16]

Unlike treaties, bills die when a Congress's second session ends. Members work under extreme time pressure to complete major legislation by that date. Under these circumstances, a conference report's version of a bill may contain errors, which Congress passes along with the rest of the bill. If both houses agree, a Concurrent Resolution can be used to make necessary changes before the act is enrolled for submission to the president. If they cannot agree, or they find the errors too late, a technical corrections bill is inevitable.[17]

---

[14] Committee reports can include explanatory language omitted from the act itself. *See, e.g.,* H.R. REP. No. 104–737, 104TH CONG., 2D SESS. 301 (1996): "The House bill provides that the exclusion from gross income only applies to damages received on account of a personal physical injury or physical sickness. If an action has its origin in a physical injury or physical sickness, then all damages (other than punitive damages) that flow therefrom are treated as payments received on account of physical injury or physical sickness whether or not the recipient of the damages is the injured party. For example, damages (other than punitive damages) received by an individual on account of a claim for loss of consortium due to the physical injury or physical sickness of such individual's spouse are excludable from gross income." The IRS has cited this language in response to taxpayer requests for rulings. *See, e.g.,* Private Letter Ruling 200121031 (May 25, 2001).

[15] I.R.C. §§ 8001–8023. The Committee is charged with investigating the operation and effects of the tax system, its administration, and means of simplifying it. *Id.* § 8022. The Joint Committee also reviews tax refunds exceeding $2,000,000. *Id.* § 6405.

[16] In Ashburn v. United States, 740 F.2d 843 (11th Cir. 1984), the court referred to committee reports and to congressional debates as evidence of the meaning of a phrase in the Equal Access to Justice Act. *See also* Commissioner v. Engle, 464 U.S. 206 (1984) (citing to testimony at hearings, floor debates, and committee reports to assist in interpreting I.R.C. § 613A). Researchers should be aware that the Supreme Court has become less receptive to using legislative history in interpreting statutes.

[17] H.R. Con. Res. 528, 108th Cong., 2d Sess. (2004), removed language relating to access to tax returns from the Consolidated Appropriations Act, 2005. H.R. Con. Res. 395, 99th Cong.,

The president can sign or veto an act in its entirety (or allow it to become law without signing it); Congress can override a veto by a two-thirds vote of each house.[18] After an act becomes law, the interpretive process begins. If no Treasury regulations are available, researchers may consult legislative history materials to ascertain congressional intent. Even after regulations are issued, they may use legislative history materials to challenge a regulation's validity.[19] Legislative history includes testimony at hearings, committee reports, and floor debate. It also includes presidential messages, statements of sponsors, and reports by the Joint Committee staff. Courts and agencies vary in the degree of weight accorded to legislative history materials.[20]

The materials below aid in determining which sections of prior laws may be applicable. They are also useful for locating committee reports and other legislative history materials.

1. Cross–References to Prior Codes and Revenue Acts

Code cross-reference tables provide section cross-references between the 1939 and 1954 Codes. [Illustration 25–1] However, limitations apply. First, Congress changed section numbers (generally by inserting new subsections and moving old ones) after enacting the 1954 Code and again in the 1986 Code. Because cross-reference tables may not reflect these changes, researchers should determine when each provision was assigned its current section number. The section number in effect when the table was compiled must be consulted. A second limitation is also important. These tables reflect their compilers' opinions as to the appropriate cross-references. Different publishers' tables may yield different results.

United States Statutes at Large (Appendix in volume 68A following text of 1954 Code) includes cross-reference tables. The tax-oriented services below also provide tables cross-referencing the 1954 and 1939 Codes.

- *CCH Standard Federal Tax Reporter* (Section M) (Code volume I)
- Rabkin & Johnson, *Federal Income, Gift and Estate Taxation* (Section M) (volume 7B)
- Mertens, *Law of Federal Income Taxation—Code* (Section M) (1954–58 Code volume) (1954 to 1939 only)
- *RIA Cumulative Changes* (Section Q) (1954 Code volume I)
- *Barton's Federal Tax Laws Correlated* (Section Q) (looseleaf volume)

2d Sess. (1986), failed to pass, thus leaving flaws in the 1986 Act. Technical corrections provisions often appear as titles within acts passed for other purposes.

[18] The Line Item Veto Act, Pub. L. No. 104–130, 110 Stat. 1200 (1996), would have allowed the President to veto only parts of a piece of legislation. This act was ruled unconstitutional in Clinton v. City of New York, 524 U.S. 417 (1998).

[19] *See, e.g.,* United States v. Nesline, 590 F. Supp. 884 (D. Md. 1984) (holding invalid a regulation that varied from the plain language of the statute and had no support in the committee reports); *cf.* Tutor–Saliba Corp. v. Commissioner, 115 T.C. 1 (2000) (holding that a regulation comported with congressional intent).

[20] The Treasury Department and IRS cite to legislative history in administrative documents. *See, e.g.,* T.D. 9194, 70 Fed. Reg. 18920, 18924 (2005) (H.R. Rep. No. 108–755); Rev. Rul. 2006–1, 2006–2 I.R.B. 262, 263–64 (Senate floor amendment and other legislative history items).

- *Seidman's Legislative History of Federal Income and Excess Profits Tax Laws* (Section Q) (1939–53 volume II)

- Joint Committee on Taxation, *Derivations of Code Sections of the Internal Revenue Codes of 1939 and 1954* (JCS–1–92), Jan. 21, 1992, reprinted in DAILY TAX REPORT, Jan. 23, 1992 (Special Supplement)

Provisions that predate the 1939 Code can be traced using *Barton's Federal Tax Laws Correlated* (Section Q), *Seidman's Legislative History of Federal Income and Excess Profits Tax Laws* (Section Q), or the Joint Committee on Taxation report listed above. There are also tables in *United States Statutes at Large* (Appendix in volume 53 (pt. 1) following text of 1939 Code).

[Illustration 25–1]

EXCERPT FROM 1939—1954 CROSS REFERENCE TABLE STANDARD FEDERAL TAX REPORTER CODE VOLUME I

46	442
47(a)	443, 6011(a)
47(c)	443
47(e)	443
47(g)	443
48(a)	441, 7701(a)(23)

☐ This version of the *SFTR* table appears in the *CCH Tax Research NetWork*. The 1939 Code sections are on the left; the 1954 Code sections are on the right.

2. Committee Reports

Major tax legislation involves at least three committee reports. The Conference Committee issues a report in addition to those already issued by the relevant House and Senate committees. These reports are numbered sequentially by Congress, not by committee, and use the issuing house's initials as an identifier.[21] The Conference Committee report is issued as a House report. Not every act is sufficiently important (or involves sufficient inter-chamber differences) as to require all three reports.

a. *Citations to Committee Reports.* A citation to a committee report enables a researcher to easily locate its text in one of the services discussed in the next paragraph or in the library's government documents (or microform) collection. Online services, such as *THOMAS* and *LexisNexis Congressional* [Illustration 25–2], provide both citations and links to the documents themselves.

---

[21] The House Ways and Means Committee report for the Safe, Accountable, Flexible, Efficient Transportation Equity Act: A Legacy for Users, Pub. L. No. 109–59, 119 Stat. 1144, is H.R. REP. No. 109–12, 109TH CONG., 1ST SESS. (2005). The Senate Finance report for the same act is S. REP. No. 109–53, 109TH CONG., 1ST SESS. (2005). The Conference Committee report is H.R. REP. No. 109–203, 109TH CONG., 1ST SESS. (2005). Although this act's primary focus was on transportation issues, it included several tax provisions.

Several print services provide citations to committee reports. The *Bulletin Index–Digest System* covers the 1954 and 1986 Codes but ceased publication in 1994. *Barton's Federal Tax Laws Correlated* covers legislation through 1969. Both are discussed in Section Q.[22] *CCH Standard Federal Tax Reporter—Citator* (Section L) sets forth citations to 1954 and 1986 Code reports printed in the *Cumulative Bulletin*. Citations appear in Code section order in the citator's Finding Lists section. *TaxCite*, published in 1995 by the ABA Section of Taxation in conjunction with student editors from three law reviews, provides this information for commonly cited statutes enacted between 1913 and 1993.

b. *Text of Committee Reports.* The following services provide at least partial texts of relevant committee reports.

- *CCH Standard Federal Tax Reporter* (Section M) (limited coverage)
- *RIA United States Tax Reporter* (Section M) (limited coverage)
- Rabkin & Johnson, *Federal Income, Gift and Estate Taxation* (Section M) (1954 Code only)
- *Cumulative Bulletin* (Section Q) (1913–2003)[23]
- *Internal Revenue Acts–Text and Legislative History* (Section Q) (since 1954)
- *Tax Management Primary Sources* (Section Q) (1969–2003)
- *Seidman's Legislative History of Federal Income and Excess Profits Tax Laws* (Section Q) (1863–1953)
- *The Internal Revenue Acts of the United States: 1909–1950; 1950–1972; 1973–* (Section Q)

The Internal Revenue Acts of the United States: 1909–1950; 1950–1972; 1973– volumes provide full text with original pagination for all materials. *Seidman's*, which includes at least partial texts, should be consulted for material dated before 1909. Unfortunately, *Seidman's* does not cover estate and gift taxes.

A researcher can also find recent legislative history materials in CD–ROM format (Section S) and online (Section T).

3. Other Documents

a. *Blue Book and Other Staff Documents.* The *General Explanation* ("*Blue Book*") issued by the staff of the Joint Committee on Taxation is not an official committee report. As such, it is not covered by materials giving citations to committee reports. The same is true for other Joint Committee staff reports and for reports of subcommittees of legislative committees. These reports are published as committee prints. These items can be

---

[22] The government itself occasionally prepares citations to legislative history materials. *See, e.g.*, JOINT COMMITTEE ON TAXATION, LISTING OF SELECTED FEDERAL TAX LEGISLATION REPRINTED IN THE IRS CUMULATIVE BULLETIN, 1913–1990 (JCS–19–91), Dec. 19, 1991. This study appeared as a supplement to DAILY TAX REPORT. It can also be accessed on the Tax Analysts database in *LexisNexis* at 91 TNT 258–17.

[23] Committee reports for 1913 through 1938 appear in 1939–1 (pt. 2) C.B. With the exception of the 1954 Code, for which none are included, committee reports for most other acts appeared in the CUMULATIVE BULLETINS as they were issued. William S. Hein & Co., has issued a one-volume work, INTERNAL REVENUE CODE OF 1954: CONGRESSIONAL COMMITTEE REPORTS, covering the 1954 Code's history. In addition, Professor Bernard Reams has compiled a multivolume work containing texts of committee reports, hearings, and debates. This set is available from Hein as part of *The Internal Revenue Acts of the United States* series (Section Q).

located online (Section T), in microform collections (Section R), or in the library's government documents section.

b.   *Hearings.* Transcripts of hearings can be located in the government documents section or in microform in most libraries. In addition, their full text appears in *The Internal Revenue Acts of the United States: 1909–1950; 1950–1972; 1973–* (Section Q). Excerpts are in *Tax Management Primary Sources* (Section Q) (1969–2003) and in *Seidman's Legislative History of Federal Income and Excess Profits Tax Laws* (Section Q) (1863–1953). Transcripts are also available online (Section T). The *Lexis-Nexis Congressional* service [Illustration 25–2] provides citations to hearings and links to the actual testimony. If a committee releases a hearings transcript to the Government Printing Office, it will be available on *GPO Access.* The relevant House and Senate committee websites may also include hearings transcripts.

[Illustration 25–2]

PARTIAL LEGISLATIVE HISTORY FOR PUB. L. NO. 109–222 FROM LEXISNEXIS CONGRESSIONAL

DEBATE:

151 Congressional Record, 109th Congress, 1st Session - 2005
  Nov. 16, Senate consideration of S. 2020, p. S12923, S12925.
  Nov. 17, Senate consideration and passage of S. 2020, p. S13072.
  Dec. 7, House consideration and passage of H.R. 4096, p. H11141.
  Dec. 8, House consideration and passage of H. Res. 588 and H.R. 4297, p. H11227, H11234.

152 Congressional Record, 109th Congress, 2nd Session - 2006
  Feb. 1, Senate consideration of H.R. 4297, p. S387.
  Feb. 2, Senate consideration and passage of H.R. 4297 with an amendment, p. S466.
  Feb. 8, House disagreement to the Senate amendment to H.R. 4297, request for a conference, and appointment of conferees, p. H185, H195.
  Feb. 13, Senate insistence on its amendments to H.R. 4297, agreement to a conference, and appointment of conferees, p. S1079.
  May 9, Submission in the House of the conference report on H.R. 4297, p. H2209.
  May 10, House agreement to H. Res. 805 and the conference report on H.R. 4297, p. H2353, H2454, H2367.
  May 11, Senate agreement to the conference report on H.R. 4297, p. S4385.

REPORTS:

109th Congress

H. Rpt. 109-304 on H.R. 4297, "Tax Relief Extension Reconciliation Act of 2005," Nov. 17, 2005.
  CIS NO: 05-H783-7
  LENGTH: 99 p.
  SUDOC: Y1.1/8:109-304

H. Rpt. 109-330 on H. Res. 588, "Providing for Consideration of H.R. 4297, Tax Relief Extension Reconciliation Act of 2005," Dec. 7, 2005.
  CIS NO: 05-H683-100
  LENGTH: 13 p.
  SUDOC: Y1.1/8:109-330

H. Rpt. 109-455, conference report on H.R. 4297, "Tax Increase Prevention and Reconciliation Act of 2005," May 9, 2006.
  CIS NO: 06-H783-2
  LENGTH: 320 p.
  SUDOC: Y1.1/8:109-455

☐ This service links to *Congressional Record* and provides CIS information about reports. Note how the act's name changed from Tax Relief Extension Reconciliation Act to Tax Increase Prevention and Reconciliation Act.

c. *Floor Statements.* Floor statements include sponsors' speeches at a bill's introduction and presidential messages accompanying an administration bill. In addition, questions and answers and other statements made during floor debate may illuminate the meaning of an act provision.

The *Congressional Record* includes full text of floor statements. Excerpts appear in *Tax Management Primary Sources* (Section Q) (1969–2003), *Internal Revenue Acts—Text and Legislative History* (Section Q) (since 1954), and *Seidman's Legislative History of Federal Income and Excess Profits Tax Laws* (Section Q) (1863–1953). A researcher can use *Barton's Federal Tax Laws Correlated* (Section Q) as a shortcut for citations to material appearing from 1953 through 1969. Citations and links to full text can also be obtained from an online service such as *LexisNexis Congressional* [Illustration 25–2].

SECTION H. TREATIES

Although United States citizens residing in another country pay United States income tax on both domestic and foreign-source income, they may also be subject to taxation in the foreign country of residence. Congress has enacted several mechanisms to mitigate the resulting double taxation. These include foreign tax credits, deductions for foreign taxes, and exclusions for certain foreign source income.[24] Treaties between the United States and other countries are another means of preventing double taxation or other harsh tax consequences.

In determining what authority governs a transaction, neither a treaty nor a statute automatically receives preferential treatment by virtue of its status. Article VI, clause 2, of the Constitution includes both statutes and treaties as the "supreme Law of the Land." However, Congress can decide that treaty provisions will override Code rules governing income earned (or property transferred) abroad by a United States citizen or resident or transactions undertaken in this country by a foreign national.[25] In addition, treaties can be overruled by a later statute, a later treaty, or treaty termination.

Treaties are considered by the Senate Foreign Affairs Committee and then by the Senate as a whole. Unlike bills, treaties do not die if the Senate fails to ratify them before the end of a session of Congress.

There are several important dates to note in doing treaty research. The first is the date on which the treaty is signed. The second is the date on which it is ratified by the Senate. The third is the date on which the countries exchange instruments of ratification. The fourth is the date (or dates) on which treaty provisions become effective.

1. Locating Treaties and Their Histories

Once a treaty goes into force, it is added to the State Department's *Treaties and Other International Acts Series* (*T.I.A.S.*). *T.I.A.S.* is the

---

[24] I.R.C. §§ 27, 164(a), 911, 912 & 2014.

[25] *See* I.R.C. §§ 894(a) & 7852(d). Disclosure requirements apply to taxpayers who claim that a tax treaty overrules or modifies an internal revenue law. I.R.C. § 6114; Treas. Reg. § 301.6114–1; IRS Form 8833.

treaty equivalent of *Statutes at Large*; the treaty document equivalent of *United States Code* is *United States Treaties and Other International Agreements* (*U.S.T.*). Because these treaty compilations are not revised nearly as quickly as their statutory counterparts, a researcher should use other sources to obtain the text of recent treaties.

Although tax treaties and their revising protocols and supplements are published in various places, several tax-oriented resources cover tax treaties. In addition to the services below, a researcher can obtain tax treaties on *LexisNexis*, *Westlaw*, and on government websites.[26]

- Tax Analysts publications (*OneDisc Premium DVD;* online and DVD *Worldwide Tax Treaties Service*)

- Thomson Reuters publications (print and online RIA *Federal Tax Coordinator 2d* and online *Checkpoint* and *Westlaw* services)

- *Legislative History of United States Tax Conventions* (Roberts & Holland Collection) (William S. Hein & Co.) (looseleaf)

- *CCH Tax Treaties* (looseleaf, CD–ROM, and online *Tax Research NetWork*)

- Rhoades & Langer, *U.S. International Taxation and Tax Treaties* (Matthew Bender) (looseleaf, CD–ROM, and online *LexisNexis* service)

- BNA *Tax Management–Foreign Income* (looseleaf and online) (Section M)

In addition to treaty texts, these services may also include Senate Executive Reports and Treasury Department Technical Explanations prepared for the Senate.

2. Citators for Tax Treaties

Shepard's Federal Statute Citations covered court decisions involving treaties through 1995; *U.S.T.* and *T.I.A.S.* citations are necessary in order to use this service. Pre–1994 IRS pronouncements were covered in the Service's *Bulletin Index–Digest System*, discussed in Section Q. Looseleaf services (Section M), CD–ROMs (Section S), and online services (Section T) are the best current sources for locating administrative and judicial rulings involving treaties.

SECTION I. TREASURY REGULATIONS

Code section 7805(a) authorizes the Secretary of the Treasury to "prescribe all needful rules and regulations for the enforcement" of the tax

---

[26] Researchers using government sites to search for treaty documents may have to use *GPO Access*, the IRS website (http://www.irs.gov), and the Treasury Department of Tax Policy website (http://www.ustreas.gov/offices/tax-policy/treaties.shtml) because no one site includes all relevant information. The IRS site includes treaty texts and Treasury Technical Explanations as well as the text of INTERNAL REVENUE BULLETINS. The Treasury site includes testimony at hearings, press releases, and Joint Committee on Taxation materials. *GPO Access* provides access to hearings, committee reports, and floor debate. Publications such as JOINT COMMITTEE ON TAXATION, LISTING OF SELECTED INTERNATIONAL TAX CONVENTIONS AND OTHER AGREEMENTS REPRINTED IN THE IRS CUMULATIVE BULLETIN, 1913–1990 (JCS–20–91), Dec. 31, 1991, can be used to obtain citations to older treaty documents and administrative guidance.

statutes.[27] General authority regulations issued pursuant to this authorization are referred to as interpretive (or interpretive). In contrast, there are so-called legislative regulations, issued for Code sections in which Congress has included a specific grant of authority, allowing IRS experts to write rules for highly technical areas.[28] When a regulation is issued or proposed, the transmittal includes a paragraph indicating the Treasury's authority for issuing the regulation, either a specific Code section (legislative) or Code section 7805 (interpretative). Courts uphold interpretive regulations unless these regulations clearly contravene congressional intent; legislative regulations are virtually unassailable.[29]

The type of regulation is apparent from its citation form. A proposed regulation includes "Prop." (e.g., Prop. Treas. Reg. § 1.801–4(g)); a temporary regulation includes a "T" (e.g., Treas. Reg. § 1.71–1T); a final regulation has no special identifier (e.g., Treas. Reg. § 1.106–1). These designations are used for both interpretive and legislative regulations.

The researcher may need to locate a current regulation and one or more prior versions. The researcher may also need to determine if a regulation is about to be proposed or may wish to read the explanatory preambles that accompany proposed, temporary, or final regulations.

1. Final and Temporary Regulations

Temporary and final regulations, which are issued as Treasury Decisions (T.D.), can be found in title 26 of the *Code of Federal Regulations*. The services below print them in Code section order. The print versions of the first two services are updated more frequently than the print versions of the other two.

- *CCH Standard Federal Tax Reporter* (Section M)
- *RIA United States Tax Reporter* (Section M)
- *United States Code Annotated—Federal Tax Regulations* (Section Q)
- Mertens, *Federal Tax Regulations*

Online (Section T) and CD–ROM (Section S) materials provide easy access to the language of regulations.

2. Proposed Regulations and Regulations Under Development[30]

Because final and temporary regulations are numbered based on the underlying Code section, they are easy to locate in a tax service or in the *C.F.R.* itself. This is not necessarily true for proposed regulations. Their

---

[27] Regulations are formulated by the IRS and approved by Treasury Department personnel. *See* 26 C.F.R. § 601.601(a)(1).

[28] For example, I.R.C. § 42(n) provides: "The Secretary shall prescribe such regulations as may be necessary or appropriate to carry out the purposes of this section . . . ."

[29] In Rite Aid Corp. v. United States, 255 F.3d 1357 (Fed. Cir. 2001), the court rejected a legislative regulation for being manifestly contrary to the statute. Taxpayers may litigate a regulation's status as legislative or interpretive. *See, e.g.*, Newborn v. Commissioner, 94 T.C. 610 (1990).

[30] Background memoranda prepared during a regulation's development are relevant if the regulation being litigated is ambiguous. *Compare* Jewett v. Commissioner, 455 U.S. 305 (1982), *with* Sidell v. Commissioner, 225 F.3d 103 (1st Cir. 2000), Armco, Inc. v. Commissioner, 87 T.C. 865 (1986), *and* Deluxe Check Printers, Inc. v. United States, 5 Cl. Ct. 498 (1984).

project numbers (e.g., REG–119518–07) do not reflect the underlying Code section, and they do not appear in *C.F.R.* Many looseleaf services include proposed regulations along with final and temporary regulations. Services that set forth proposed regulations in a separate volume usually include a Code section cross-reference table. Using CD–ROMs (Section S) or online services (Section T), a researcher can easily locate a proposed regulation by searching for the Code section, project number, or subject matter.

Because Congress enacts new statutes and amends old ones frequently, many Code sections lack regulations. Others have regulations that fail to reflect current law. The Treasury Department and IRS issue an annual regulatory plan (*Priority Guidance Plan*) indicating projects that should yield regulations or other guidance during the coming year. The *Treasury Semiannual Agenda of Regulations* provides extensive information about the status of pending items; it appears in the *Reginfo.gov* website.[31] The *Priority Guidance Plan* is available on the IRS website.

3.   Prior Regulations

Prior regulatory language may be relevant if a researcher is evaluating recent changes or if the research involves a completed transaction. Prior language can be obtained from Mertens, *Law of Federal Income Taxation— Regulations* (Section M) (1954–1985 material); *United States Code Annotated—Federal Tax Regulations* (Section Q); and *RIA Cumulative Changes* (Section Q) (libraries are more likely to have the 1954 and 1986 Code versions than the 1939 Code version).

If a 1954 Code regulation was originally published before 1960, it was republished that year in T.D. 6498, 6500, or 6516. The *United States Code Annotated* service ignores the original publication in its history notes; *Cumulative Changes* omits the 1960 T.D.s; the Mertens bound volumes cite only the most recent change in a regulation. IRS *Cumulative Bulletins* include regulations for the 1939 Code.

4.   Citators for Regulations

Regulations rarely keep pace with congressional activity. When a Code section changes, existing regulations may no longer be valid. If a regulation appears to contradict statutory language, a researcher should check the date of issue of the most recent T.D. to determine if it predates the Code section involved.

If an existing regulation affects a transaction, it is important to determine if courts upheld or invalidated that regulation in previous litigation. The Treasury Department is not bound by adverse decisions in any tribunal other than the Supreme Court. As a result, it will not withdraw a regulation merely because one or more lower courts invalidate it. Researchers should use a citator indicating judicial action to determine the outcome of challenges to a regulation's validity. Both the *Shepard's* and *KeyCite* citators will provide more accurate information than their CCH and RIA counterparts. *Shepard's* and *KeyCite* use the regulation section as the cited material; the other two citators use the T.D. number. The latter

---

[31] Items are categorized by status, such as proposed rule stage and final rule stage, in the listing at http://www.reginfo.gov/public/do/eAgendaMain.

may give misleading results, as a single T.D. often involves several regulations sections. Citators are discussed further in Section L.

SECTION J.   INTERNAL REVENUE SERVICE PRONOUNCEMENTS

1.   Types of IRS Pronouncements

There are several methods of categorizing IRS pronouncements. One method looks to the means of publication. The IRS officially publishes several pronouncements, most notably revenue rulings, revenue procedures, notices, and announcements, in the weekly *Internal Revenue Bulletin* and the semiannual *Cumulative Bulletin*. Other items, including private letter rulings, technical advice memoranda, actions on decisions, and chief counsel advice, are not published officially but are available to the public. Most documents in this group are currently released because of Freedom of Information Act (FOIA) litigation.

Another method of categorization involves a document's initial audience. Revenue rulings and other items published in the *Internal Revenue Bulletin* are directed to all taxpayers and their representatives. Private letter rulings, on the other hand, are directed to a specific taxpayer; the IRS makes them available to other readers after deleting identifying material. Still other documents are written for government personnel. Although many of these, such as technical advice memoranda, are publicly available, the IRS resists releasing some other internal documents. In part because of privacy concerns, there are extensive deletions in most released documents.

2.   Officially Published IRS Pronouncements

a.   *Revenue Rulings (Rev. Rul.).* The IRS issues rulings that apply the law to particular factual situations taxpayers have presented. Rulings fall into two categories—revenue rulings and private letter rulings. If the IRS determines a ruling to be of general interest, it publishes it in the *Internal Revenue Bulletin* and *Cumulative Bulletin* as a revenue ruling.[32] Newsletters (Section P) and online systems (Section T) may report on a ruling several weeks before the ruling appears in the *Internal Revenue Bulletin.*

Although a revenue ruling is not as authoritative as a Treasury regulation, any taxpayer whose circumstances are substantially the same as those described in the ruling can rely upon it.[33] Subject to the limitations in Code section 7805(b), rulings can apply retroactively unless their text indicates otherwise. [See Illustration 25–3 for an excerpt from a revenue ruling.]

---

[32] The IRS occasionally issues a revenue ruling to indicate it will not follow an adverse appellate court decision. *See, e.g.,* Rev. Rul. 95–74, 1995–2 C.B. 36. Since 1993, it has primarily used nonacquiescences for this purpose.

[33] The IRS has occasionally issued adverse rulings based on facts encountered in an audit or refund claim and then attempted to assert the ruling as authority when the taxpayer litigates. *See* Niles v. United States, 710 F.2d 1391 (9th Cir. 1983) (discussing Rev. Rul. 79–427, 1979–2 C.B. 120); AMP Inc. v. United States, 185 F.3d 1333, 1338–39 (Fed. Cir. 1999) (discussing Rev. Rul. 91–21, 1991–1 C.B. 112).

[Illustration 25–3]

EXCERPT FROM REV. RUL. 2005–24, 2005–16 I.R.B. 892

Part I. Rulings and Decisions Under the Internal Revenue Code of 1986

Section 105.—Amounts Received Under Accident and Health Plans

(Also Section 106.)

Health reimbursement arrangements. This ruling addresses the income tax treatment under section 105 of the Code of amounts received by employees from employer-provided reimbursement plans. Notice 2002–45 amplified.

Rev. Rul. 2005–24

ISSUE

Are amounts paid to an employee under a reimbursement plan that provides for the payment of unused reimbursement amounts in cash or other benefits excludable from gross income under § 105(b) of the Internal Revenue Code (the Code)?

FACTS

Situation 1

Employer sponsors a reimbursement plan (the Plan) that reimburses an employee solely for medical care expenses (as defined in § 213(d)) that are substantiated before the reimbursements are

is the plan year. The Plan reimburses medical care expenses only to the extent that the employee or the employee's spouse or dependents have not been reimbursed for the expense from any other plan.

Under the Plan, a portion of each employee's reimbursement amount available at the end of each plan year is forfeited if not used to reimburse medical expenses. The remaining unused reimbursement amount is carried forward for use in subsequent plan years. Neither the employee nor any other person has the right, currently or for any future year, to receive cash or any taxable or nontaxable benefit other than the reimbursement of medical care expenses incurred by the employee and his or her spouse and dependents.

When an employee retires, Employer automatically and on a mandatory basis (as determined under the Plan) contributes an amount to the reimbursement plan equal to the value of all or a portion of the retired employee's accumulated unused vacation and sick leave. Under no circumstances may the retired employee or the retired employee's spouse or dependents receive any of the designated amount in cash or other benefits.

The Plan satisfies the nondiscrimination requirements of § 105(h) for a self-insured medical expense reimburse-

Situation 4

Same facts as in *Situation 1*, except the Employer has an "option plan" which purports to be separate and apart from the reimbursement plan. Under the "option plan," an employee elects, prior to the beginning of the plan year, to participate in the "option plan." If an employee elects to participate in the "option plan," any unused reimbursement amount available at the end of the plan year is "forfeited." However, the "option plan" provides that the employee may elect to transfer all or a portion of the "forfeited" amount to one of several retirement plans or to receive the amount as a cash payment. If an employee does not elect to participate in the "option plan," any reimbursement amount unused at the end of the plan year is carried forward for use in future plan years.

LAW AND ANALYSIS

Section 61(a)(1) provides that, except as otherwise provided in Subtitle A, gross income includes compensation for services, including fees, commissions, fringe benefits, and similar items. Section 1.61–21(a)(3) and (4) of the Income Tax Regulations state that a fringe benefit provided in connection with the performance of services shall be considered to have

---

The IRS numbers revenue rulings chronologically.[34] Ruling numbers do not indicate which Code section is involved. The IRS began issuing numbered revenue rulings in 1953 and adopted the current numbering system in 1954. Earlier revenue rulings, with different names [Table 1], were also published in the *Bulletin*.

Revenue rulings indicate the Code and regulations sections involved; their text is divided into segments. Commonly used segments include Issue, Facts, Law, Analysis (or a combined Law and Analysis segment), Holding, and Effective Date. An Effect on Other Documents segment appears if the current ruling revokes, modifies, obsoletes, or otherwise affects a prior holding. Rulings also include information about the IRS official who drafted them.

---

[34] Rev. Rul. 2009–1 denotes the first revenue ruling issued in 2009; Rev. Rul. 99–1, the first revenue ruling issued in 1999. The IRS used two digits to indicate the year until 2000. Each week's rulings are numbered sequentially, generally in Code section order. The number of rulings varies from year to year. The IRS issued over 700 in 1955; it released only 72 in 2007.

Table 1
Pre–1953 Titles of Cumulative Bulletin Pronouncements

A.R.M.	Committee on Appeals and Review Memorandum
A.R.R.	Committee on Appeals and Review Recommendation
A.T.	Alcohol Tax Unit; Alcohol and Tobacco Tax Division
C.L.T.	Child–Labor Tax Division
C.S.T.	Capital–Stock Tax Division
C.T.	Carriers Taxing Act of 1937; Taxes on Employment by Carriers
D.C.	Treasury Department Circular
Dept.Cir.	Treasury Department Circular
E.P.C.	Excess Profits Tax Council Ruling or Memorandum
E.T.	Estate and Gift Tax Division or Ruling
Em.T.	Employment Taxes
G.C.M.	Chief Counsel's Memorandum; General Counsel's Memorandum; Assistant General Counsel's Memorandum
I.T.	Income Tax Unit or Division
L.O.	Solicitor's Law Opinion
MS.	Miscellaneous Unit or Division or Branch
M.T.	Miscellaneous Division or Branch
Mim.	Mimeographed Letter; Mimeograph
O.	Solicitor's Law Opinion
O.D.	Office Decision
Op.A.G.	Opinion of Attorney General
P.T.	Processing Tax Decision or Division
S.	Solicitor's Memorandum
S.M.	Solicitor's Memorandum
S.R.	Solicitor's Recommendation
S.S.T.	Social Security Tax and Carriers' Tax; Social Security Tax; Taxes on Employment by Other than Carriers
S.T.	Sales Tax Unit or Division or Branch
Sil.	Silver Tax Division
Sol.Op.	Solicitor's Opinion
T.	Tobacco Division
T.B.M.	Advisory Tax Board Memorandum
T.B.R.	Advisory Tax Board Recommendation
Tob.	Tobacco Branch

b. *Revenue Procedures (Rev. Proc.) and Procedural Rules.* Revenue procedures are published statements of IRS practices and procedures, numbered chronologically since 1955, and published in the *Internal Revenue Bulletin* and *Cumulative Bulletin*. Procedures of general applicability may be added to the IRS Statement of Procedural Rules and published in the *Code of Federal Regulations*.

Several regularly issued revenue procedures are particularly important. The first one issued each year (e.g., Rev. Proc. 2009–1) establishes procedures for obtaining letter rulings, determination letters, and closing agreements. It also includes a sample ruling request format and a schedule of user fees. The second revenue procedure each year deals with requests for technical advice, discussed in Section J–3. The third, which is supplemented during the year, contains a cumulative list of areas in which the IRS will not grant rulings.

Revenue procedures include several subdivisions, which vary in number based on the procedure's scope and complexity. The following subdivisions are commonly used: Purpose; Background; Scope; Effect on Other Documents; and Effective Date. Drafting information also appears.

c. *Notices, Announcements, and Other Items.* The IRS issues notices to provide guidance before revenue rulings and regulations are available. Notices can describe future regulations in a manner that will pass muster under the Code section 7805(b) rules on retroactivity. Notices are numbered by year; their number does not indicate the Code section involved. Notices appear in both the *I.R.B.* and *C.B.*

Announcements appear in the *I.R.B.* but did not appear in the *C.B.* until 1998. They alert taxpayers to time-sensitive information and are numbered by year.

The *Bulletins* also contain disbarment notices and IRS acquiescences (and nonacquiescences) in unfavorable court decisions.[35] Non–IRS material includes Treasury regulations and Supreme Court decisions.

Instructions accompanying tax return forms and explanatory booklets are published on a regular basis. However, they contain few, if any, citations to authority and do not indicate if the IRS position has been disputed. Further, even if they are misleading, taxpayers who rely on them cannot cite them as authority against a contrary IRS position.[36] These items do not appear in the *I.R.B.* or *C.B.* They are available on the IRS website.

3. Publicly Released Pronouncements

The items below are useful in determining IRS positions on relevant issues; some constitute authority for avoiding the Code section 6662 substantial understatement penalty. Unless otherwise indicated, they use a common numbering system (e.g., 2006–50–023). The first digits indicate the year, and the next two the week, of release; the final numbers indicate the item number for that week. Unless the identifying letters are added (e.g., P.L.R.), readers will not know the type of document being cited. Note that CD–ROM and online services may omit periods or hyphens (e.g., PLR 200650023 or TAM 200648028). The IRS website also omits the hyphens.

These and other IRS guidance documents have been released because of Freedom of Information Act Litigation.[37] Although the public has access

---

[35] Although these materials appear in the I.R.B., the C.B.s published through 1997 include only disbarment information and acquiescences and nonacquiescences. The IRS announced a policy change effective in 1991 and began including acquiescence notices for all courts beginning with 1993–1 C.B. Previously, it included this information only for Tax Court regular decisions.

[36] *See* Osborne v. Commissioner, 97–2 U.S.T.C. ¶ 50,524, 79 A.F.T.R.2d 97–3011 (6th Cir. 1997). *See also* T.A.M. 83–50–008 (involving IRS refusal to allow a taxpayer to claim reliance on a portion of the INTERNAL REVENUE MANUAL or on the 1982 version of IRS PUBLICATION 544). *But see* Gehl Co. v. Commissioner, 795 F.2d 1324 (7th Cir. 1986) (government decision not to seek *certiorari* explained in A.O.D. 1988–002).

[37] Freedom of Information Act, 5 U.S.C. § 552, litigation led to the release of letter rulings and technical advice memoranda issued after October 31, 1976, and to the enactment of I.R.C. § 6110. *See* Tax Analysts and Advocates v. Internal Revenue Service, 405 F. Supp. 1065 (D.D.C. 1975). Letter rulings have been released as issued since mid-March 1977. I.R.C. § 6110(h) authorizes inspection of documents issued after July 4, 1967. Additional Tax

to them, generally subject to the limitations of Code section 6610, the IRS is not bound by them in its dealings with taxpayers as a group.[38]

a. *Private Letter Rulings (P.L.R.; PLR; Ltr. Rul.; Priv. Ltr. Rul.).* Private letter rulings[39] illustrate IRS policy and often indicate areas where future guidance is likely. As noted above, the IRS may ultimately publish those of general interest as revenue rulings. A researcher can request IRS release of background documents, including IRS-taxpayer correspondence with regard to a particular ruling. The cost of such items can be substantial.[40]

The requesting taxpayer receives a private letter ruling approximately three months before its release to the public. As a result, the actual week of release is later than that shown in the letter.

b. *Technical Advice Memoranda (T.A.M.; TAM; Tech. Adv. Mem.).* Technical advice memoranda are issued by the IRS National Office in response to IRS requests arising out of tax return examinations; private letter ruling requests focus on proposed transactions.

c. *Actions on Decisions (A.O.D.; AOD; action on decision; action on dec.).* A.O.D.s indicate the reasoning behind the Service's recommendation whether or not to appeal an adverse decision by a trial or appellate court[41] and whether to acquiesce or nonacquiesce in that decision.[42] A.O.D.s are numbered sequentially by year (e.g., A.O.D. 2008–01); the numbering provides no information about the underlying case name or issue.

d. *General Counsel Memoranda (G.C.M.; GCM; Gen. Couns. Mem.).*[43] These memoranda emanate from the Office of Chief Counsel. They indicate the reasoning and authority used in revenue rulings, private letter rulings, and technical advice memoranda. IRS personnel can use them as guides in formulating positions.

Analysts' lawsuits led to the release of other IRS documents, including G.C.M.s, A.O.D.s, F.S.A.s, and tax-exemption denials and revocations.

[38] *But see* Ogiony v. Commissioner, 617 F.2d 14, 17–18 (2d Cir. 1980) (Oakes, J., concurring). Although noting that they had no precedential value, courts have cited letter rulings as evidence of IRS inconsistent interpretation. *See* Rowan Cos., Inc. v. United States, 452 U.S. 247, 261 n.17 (1981); Transco Exploration Co. v. Commissioner, 949 F.2d 837, 840 (5th Cir. 1992).

[39] Determination letters are similar to letter rulings but do not emanate from one of the national office associate chief counsel offices. Directors issue determination letters only if they can be based on clearly established rules that apply to the issues presented. Otherwise, the national office is the appropriate venue. Letter rulings generally involve proposed transactions; determination letters, completed transactions.

[40] *See* I.R.C. § 6110. The IRS imposes a search fee and a per-page fee for the effort in deleting identifying and other confidential information from background documents. Rev. Proc. 95–15, 1995–1 C.B. 523; I.R.M. 11.3.5.9.5(3) (May 24, 2005).

[41] Even the IRS has a sense of humor. *See* A.O.D. 1984–022 for a poetic rejoinder to the Tax Court's "Ode to Conway Twitty" footnote in Jenkins v. Commissioner, 47 T.C.M. (CCH) 238, 247 n.14 (1983).

[42] The IRS originally issued notices of acquiescence and nonacquiescence only for Tax Court regular decisions. Beginning with 1993–1 C.B., it now issues these notices for decisions by other courts as well. A.O.D.s were never limited to Tax Court decisions.

[43] Do not confuse current G.C.M.s with revenue rulings issued before 1953, which were also called G.C.M.s. *See* Table 1.

G.C.M.s are numbered sequentially (e.g., G.C.M. 39890). The numbering system does not indicate the year of issue, the relevant Code section, or the document about which they supply information. The number issued has declined significantly in recent years; none has appeared since 2007.

e. *Internal Revenue Manual (I.R.M.; IRM).* A tax problem may require knowledge of IRS operating policies. The *Internal Revenue Manual (I.R.M.)* is the best source of information about such topics as which IRS office is responsible for various types of guidance, the examining process, or procedures for dealing with rewards to informants. The *Manual* has its own numbering system based on topics.

f. *Chief Counsel Advice (C.C.A.; CCA).*[44] These documents provide information about taxpayers to IRS field or service center employees. They may respond to a field office query or may provide information about a taxpayer (such as a taxpayer's request to change accounting method being denied). Several items classified as chief counsel advice have been issued under other names. These include field service advice (*F.S.A; FSA*) and service center advice (*S.C.A; SCA*).

g. *Chief Counsel Bulletins.* This category includes several documents, many of which are no longer published.[45] *Collection, Bankruptcy and Summonses Bulletins (C.B.S.; CBS)* contain summaries of recent court cases. They were called *General Litigation Bulletins (G.L.B.; GLB)* through June 2000. Although the *Bulletins* are numbered in a series, they also share the common numbering system used for other documents (e.g., Bulletin No. 490 is also C.B.S. 2001–39–029). *Criminal Tax Bulletins (C.T.B.; CTB)* are compilations of cases pertaining to criminal tax matters. They share the common numbering system. *Disclosure Litigation Bulletins (D.L.B.; DLB)* discuss litigation and other developments involving FOIA and related litigation. They are separately numbered (e.g., D.L.B. 2000–3). *Tax Litigation Bulletins (T.L.B.; TLB)* summarize recent court decisions and briefs and publish recommendations for appellate action; they are numbered by year (e.g., T.L.B. 96–5).

h. *Litigation Guideline Memoranda (L.G.M.; LGM).* Litigation guideline memoranda discuss variations on fact patterns and tactical approaches that might be used in litigation. In mid–1999, the IRS released those issued between January 1, 1986, and October 20, 1998. The numbering system initially reflected the area of the IRS involved in the guidelines (e.g., INTL–1 involved the foreign tax credit). Later items use the common numbering system (e.g., L.G.M. 2000–18–050).

i. *Industry Specialization Program (I.S.P.); Market Segment Specialization Papers (M.S.S.P.); Market Segment Understandings (M.S.U.).* The IRS has issued documents providing guidance to agents auditing returns in various types of business (I.S.P.), describing how it reviews tax returns for

[44] These documents are classified as IRS Legal Memoranda (ILM) in Tax Analysts publications; the IRS, *Westlaw*, and *LexisNexis* use the Chief Counsel Advice (CCA) designation. They appear in the IRS Written Determinations section of the IRS website, at http://www.irs.gov (electronic reading room option on the Freedom of Information Act page). *See also* INTERNAL REVENUE MANUAL pt. 33, at http://www.irs.gov/irm/part33/index.html.

[45] The last posted C.B.S. was Bulletin 496 (January 2002); the last posted D.L.B. was 2000–3; the last G.L.B. was Bulletin 477 (June 2000). The IRS website no longer includes T.L.B.s.

various types of businesses (M.S.S.P. Audit Technique Guides), and discussing employer/independent contractor issues in various industries (M.S.U.). For example, a coordinated issue paper issued in 2005 discussed like kind exchanges of FCC licenses.

4. Unreleased Documents

Closing agreements memorialize the agreement regarding specific IRS-taxpayer disputes. The IRS has forced publication of certain agreements with exempt organizations but has otherwise resisted releasing these agreements to the public. Advance pricing agreements are made between taxpayers and the IRS regarding income allocation between commonly controlled entities. They are important for companies that segment their operations between countries with different tax rates. Code section 6110(b)(1)(B) exempts closing agreements and advance pricing agreements from disclosure.

5. Locating and Evaluating IRS Pronouncements

a. *Internal Revenue Bulletin Items—Citations and Texts.* Because IRS materials do not carry numbers that correspond to the Code sections they discuss, CD–ROMs (Section S) and online services (Section T) are excellent sources for finding these items; each database can be searched by topic, Code or regulations section, or prior ruling.

The following publications can also be used to locate and read relevant items.

- *CCH Standard Federal Tax Reporter* (Section M)

- *RIA United States Tax Reporter* (Section M) [Illustration 25–4]

- *Federal Tax Coordinator 2d* (Section M)

- Mertens, *Law of Federal Income Taxation* (Section M) (does not print text of notices and announcements) [Illustration 25–5]

- Rabkin & Johnson, *Federal Income, Gift and Estate Taxation* (Section M) (does not print texts)

- *Tax Management Portfolios* (Section M) (does not print texts)

- *Bulletin Index–Digest System* (Section Q) (pre–1994) (full texts appear in *Internal Revenue Bulletin* and *Cumulative Bulletin*)

Mertens and the *Cumulative Bulletin* cumulate prior years' rulings in bound volumes. Because it contains only rulings and procedures, Mertens may be slightly easier to use for a project involving multiple years. However, its coverage from 1954 until 1987 is limited to the income tax. Electronic services are probably the best tools for finding rulings for a particular Code section.

[Illustration 25–4]

EXCERPT FROM RIA UNITED STATES TAX REPORTER

ANN ¶1055.01(40) Unused reimbursement amounts.
Income (USTR)

▶ **Expl** | ▶ **IRC** | ▶ **Regs** | ▶ **Com Rpts** | ▶ **Hist**

Ann ¶ 1055.01(40). Unused reimbursement amounts.

Amounts paid under employer-sponsored employee medical expense reimbursement plan are excludable from employee's gross income only if payments are limited to reimbursements of substantiated medical care expenses incurred by current and former employees, spouses, and dependents, and no one has right to receive unused reimbursement amounts as cash or any other benefit under plan. Other plans discussed (involving cash payout of unused reimbursement amounts at end of year; payout of unused amount as death benefit; option to transfer unused amounts to retirement plan, take it as cash, or carry it forward to following year) didn't meet requirements for favorable tax treatment and no amounts paid from those plans, even for qualified medical expenses, would be excludable from gross income: plans pay "irrespective" of whether medical care expenses have been incurred.

Rev. Rul. 2005-24, 2005-1 CB 892 , amplifying *Notice 2002-45, 2002-2 CB 93* , as modified by *Notice 2007-22, 2007-10 IRB* , below.

Employer-provided health care reimbursement plan in which unused reimbursement amounts are carried forward for use in later years, including expenses incurred by employee, spouse, or family after employee terminates employment or retires, qualify as employer-provided health coverage and are excludable from gross income under *Code Sec. 105* and *Code Sec. 106* .

☐ Revenue Ruling 2005-24 [Illustration 25-3] could be located using annotations in a looseleaf service such as *United States Tax Reporter*, where it appears in ¶ 1055.01(40). The excerpt above is from the *Checkpoint* version of *USTR*. Note how *Checkpoint* indicates how Revenue Ruling 2005-24 was modified by subsequent IRS action.

[Illustration 25–5]

EXCERPT FROM MERTENS CODE–RULINGS TABLE

MERTENS RULINGS

Code Sec.	Rev. Rul.
104(a)	56-42, 58-578, 59-269, 64-10, 65-29, 96-65
104(a)(1)	56-83, 57-399, 59-269, 68-10, 72-44, 72-45, 72-136, 72-291, 72-400, 73-346, 78-416, 79-147, 79-322, 80-14, 80-44, 80-84, 80-137, 81-47, 83-77, 83-91, 85-104, 85-105
104(a)(2)	58-578, 61-1, 65-29, 68-649, 79-220, 79-313, 79-427, 83-25, 84-108, 85-97, 85-98, 85-143, 93-88, 96-65, 2003-115
104(a)(3)	58-90, 58-602, 59-159, 63-181, 69-154, 73-155
104(a)(4)	56-42, 58-43, 58-599, 59-26, 62-14, 77-318, 78-161, 80-9
104(b)(2)(B)	80-9
104(b)(4)	80-9
105	55-245, 55-263, 56-83, 56-514, 59-158, 59-159, 60-184, 61-192, 64-10, 69-154, 71-105, 71-403, 71-588, 72-401, 73-347, 74-65, 74-185, 74-603, 75-119, 75-479, 76-173, 76-174, 76-343, 77-15, 77-28, 77-65, 77-123, 78-249, 81-121, 82-196, 85-121, 2002-3, 2002-41, 2002-58, 2003-43, 2003-102, 2004-55, 2004-98, → 2005-24, 2005-55, 2006-36
105(a)	56-326, 58-90, 58-371, 58-462, 59-158

Cumulative Code/Rulings Table

Code Sec.	Rev. Rul.
	59-159, 59-323, 60-203, 60-219, 61-192, 63-181, 85-121, 2002-41, 2002-58, 2003-43, 2003-102
105(b)	59-159, 59-323, 60-203, 63-181, 69-141, 71-588, 2002-3, 2002-32, 2002-41, 2002-58, 2002-80, 2003-43, 2003-102
105(c)	59-159, 59-170, 59-323, 60-203, 63-181
105(c)(1)	63-181
105(c)(2)	63-181
105(d)	55-85, 55-283, 55-366, 56-83, 56-326, 57-76, 57-101, 57-152, 57-178, 57-359, 57-360, 57-384, 57-399, 58-43, 58-90, 58-91, 58-163, 58-178, 58-371, 58-462, 58-544, 58-599, 59-26, 59-64, 59-158, 59-159, 59-170, 59-265, 59-323, 60-203, 60-219, 61-6, 61-161, 61-192, 63-181, 63-219, 64-150, 66-182, 66-319, 67-222, 68-385, 68-578, 69-12, 71-105, 72-44, 78-416, 79-322, 80-44, 87-84
105(d)(1)	81-121
105(d)(3)	78-249
105(d)(6)	81-121
105(e)	57-76, 59-159, 71-588, 85-44, 85-121, 2002-41, 2002-58, 2002-80, 2003-43, 2003-102
105(h)	2002-41, 2003-43
105(h)(1)	2002-41
105(h)(2)	2002-41

☐ Revenue Ruling 2005-24 [Illustration 25–3] could be located using the Mertens Code-Rulings Table. Check the current year's table for the most recent rulings.

b. *Forms and Publications.* The IRS website carries IRS publications and IRS forms and accompanying instructions. Researchers can search for these items by number or topic or can use the website's Advanced Search feature to search by word or phrase. These items are also available in other online (Section T) and CD–ROM (Section S) services.

c. *Other IRS Documents.* The IRS releases letter rulings and other documents on a weekly basis. It makes them available in the Electronic Reading Room area of its website, http://www.irs.gov/foia/article/0,,id= 110353,00.html. In most cases, it presents them in numerical order or in Uniform Issue List order, which reflects the underlying Code section. Because neither format is user-friendly, researchers generally prefer other methods for locating these documents. Other sources include citators

(Section L), online commercial services (Section T) and CD–ROMs (Section S). Researchers can also use online versions of newsletters (Section P).

In addition to the above sources, Commerce Clearing House publishes looseleaf services that include full texts of IRS documents. These include:

- *IRS Letter Rulings Reporter* (print or CD–ROM)
- *IRS Positions* (print or CD–ROM)
- *Internal Revenue Manual* (print, CD–ROM, or online)

6. Citators for IRS Materials

The IRS reviews revenue rulings and procedures for continued relevance. In addition, some rulings have been subjected to judicial scrutiny. The status of these items can be determined from citators (Section L), CD–ROMs (Section S), and online services (Section T).

[Illustration 25–6]

EXCERPT FROM MERTENS RULINGS STATUS TABLE

Cumulative Rulings Status Table		*MERTENS* RULINGS
Previous Ruling	**Action**	**Current Ruling**
Rev. Rul. 2002-78	Supplemented & Superseded	Rev. Rul. 2003-118
Rev. Rul. 2002-79	Supplemented & Superseded	Rev. Rul. 2003-119
Rev. Rul. 2002-80	Distinguished	Rev. Rul. 2003-43
Rev. Rul. 2003-2	Revoked	Rev. Rul. 2003-22
Rev. Rul. 2003-58	Distinguished	Rev. Rul. 2003-102
Rev. Rul. 2003-92	Clar & Amp	Rev. Rul. 2007-7
Rev. Rul. 2003-109	Superseded	Rev. Rul. 2007-28
Rev. Rul. 2004-38	Suspended	Rev. Proc. 2004-22
Rev. Rul. 2004-43	Revoked	Rev. Rul. 2005-10
Rev. Rul. 2004-75	Amplified	Rev. Proc. 2004-97
Rev. Rul. 2004-103	Superseded	Rev. Rul. 2005-3
Rev. Rul. 2004-107	Supplemented & Superseded	Rev. Rul. 2005-76
Rev. Rul. 2004-108	Supplemented & Superseded	Rev. Rul. 2005-75
Rev. Rul. 2005-76	Supp & Super	Rev. Rul. 2007-4
Rev. Rul. 2006-1	Modified	Rev. Rul. 2006-31
Rev. Rul. 2007-54	Superseded	Rev. Rul. 2007-61

☐ Consult both the cumulative and current year's Rulings Status Tables to determine if the IRS has taken action on a revenue ruling or revenue procedure. The Mertens tables indicated no action on Revenue Ruling 2005-24 in the release issued in March 2008. However, this ruling was amplified by Revenue Ruling 2006-36 (which is listed in Illustration 25-5) and modified by Notice 2007-22. Citators gave more accurate information.

Two other services, listed below, have significant limitations. First, they ignore judicial action and letter rulings. Second, they are not sufficiently current. The Mertens service is not updated as frequently as are other services; the *Bulletin Index–Digest System* is useful only for historical research.

- Mertens, *Law of Federal Income Taxation—Rulings* (Section M) [Illustration 25–6]

- *Bulletin Index–Digest System* (Section Q) (pre–1994 items only)

SECTION K.   JUDICIAL REPORTS

1.   Court Organization

Four federal courts serve as trial courts for most tax disputes: district courts; the Court of Federal Claims; the Tax Court; and bankruptcy courts.

a.   *United States District Courts.* Because federal district courts are courts of general jurisdiction, their judges rarely develop as high a level of expertise on tax law questions as do judges of the Tax Court or even of the Court of Federal Claims. Taxpayers must pay the amount in dispute and sue for a refund before litigating in district court, the only tribunal where a jury trial is available.

b.   *United States Court of Federal Claims.* Although the Court of Federal Claims does not hear tax cases exclusively, the percentage of such cases it hears is greater than that heard in the average federal district court. As in the district court, a taxpayer must first pay the disputed amount before bringing suit. Prior to October 1, 1982, this court was named the United States Court of Claims. Trials were conducted by a trial judge (formerly called a commissioner). Trial judges' decisions were reviewed by Court of Claims judges; only the Supreme Court had jurisdiction over appeals from Court of Claims decisions. Between October 1, 1982, and October 29, 1992, this court was named the United States Claims Court.

c.   *United States Tax Court.* Because Tax Court judges hear only tax cases, their expertise is substantially greater than that of judges in the other trial courts. Tax Court cases are tried by one judge, who submits an opinion to the chief judge for consideration. The chief judge can allow the decision to stand or refer it to the full court for review. The published decision indicates if it has been reviewed; dissenting opinions, if any, are included. In some instances, special trial judges hear disputes and issue opinions.

Two types of Tax Court decisions can be cited as precedent:[46] the court officially publishes decisions presenting important legal issues (regular decisions); other publishers print decisions involving well-established legal issues (memorandum decisions). A taxpayer can sue in the Tax Court without paying the amount in dispute prior to litigating. Taxpayers also had this privilege in the Tax Court's predecessor, the Board of Tax Appeals.

d.   *United States Bankruptcy Court.* In addition to deciding priority of liens and related matters, United States bankruptcy courts may also issue substantive tax rulings.[47] Most bankruptcy court decisions are reviewed by district court judges or by Bankruptcy Appellate Panels; some are reviewed directly by federal courts of appeals.[48]

---

[46] The Tax Court also has a Small Cases division that taxpayers can elect to use for disputes of $50,000 or less. Decisions in such cases cannot be appealed, cannot be used as precedents, and were not generally available before 2001. I.R.C. § 7463. The Tax Court began public release of these opinions in January 2001. Booth v. Commissioner, T.C. Summary Opinion 2001–1 (Jan. 3, 2001), was the first such opinion released.

[47] *See, e.g.,* United States v. Yellin (*In re* Weinstein), 251 B.R. 174 (B.A.P. 1st Cir. 2000), *aff'g In re* Weinstein, 237 B.R. 4 (Bankr. D. Mass. 1999).

[48] 28 U.S.C. § 158.

e. *Appellate Review.* When research uncovers conflicting decisions at the trial court level, those decisions should be traced to the appellate court level. If no appeals have been taken, the Tax Court's specialized knowledge may cause greater weight to be accorded to its decisions than to decisions from the other trial courts.[49] In addition, if a court has ruled against the government and the IRS has issued a notice of acquiescence, the precedential value of the decision is further enhanced.[50]

Decisions of federal district courts and the Tax Court are appealed to the court of appeals for the taxpayer's geographical residence[51] and from there to the Supreme Court. Decisions of the Court of Federal Claims are appealed to the court of appeals for the Federal Circuit. Because the Supreme Court reviews so few court of appeals decisions, the Court of Federal Claims—Federal Circuit route offers a forum-shopping opportunity to taxpayers living in circuits where appellate court decisions involving similar issues are adverse.[52]

2. Locating Decisions

a. *Finding Lists.* Researchers can compile a preliminary reading list of decisions involving a particular statute, treaty, regulation, or ruling by using the citators discussed in Section L or the looseleaf services discussed in Section M.

b. *Texts of Decisions.*[53] Federal court decisions involving taxation appear in the sets listed below. They may also be found online (Section T), in microform (Section R), and in CD–ROM format (Section S). Various newsletters (Section P) also print full texts or digests.

(1) *Supreme Court* (since 1796): *United States Reports (U.S.)* (official); *United States Supreme Court Reports, Lawyers' Edition (L. Ed.; L. Ed. 2d)*; *Supreme Court Reporter (S. Ct.)* (since 1882); *American Federal Tax Reports*; *U.S. Tax Cases* (since 1913); *Internal Revenue Bulletin (I.R.B.)*; *Cumulative Bulletin (C.B.)* (since 1920).

(2) *Courts of Appeals* (since 1880): *Federal Reporter (F.; F.2d; F.3d)*; *American Federal Tax Reports*; *U.S. Tax Cases* (since 1915).

(3) *District Courts* (since 1882): *Federal Supplement (F. Supp.; F. Supp. 2d)* (since 1932); *Federal Reporter* (from 1882 until 1932); *American Federal Tax Reports*; *U.S. Tax Cases* (since 1915).

---

[49] *But see* Baizer v. Commissioner, 204 F.3d 1231, 1233 (9th Cir. 2000) ("Although a presumption exists that the tax court correctly applied the law, no special deference is given to the tax court's decisions.").

[50] Always check to see if the IRS issued an A.O.D. (Section J) giving its rationale for appealing or acquiescing.

[51] From 1924 to 1926, decisions of the Board of Tax Appeals (the Tax Court's predecessor) were appealed to a district court. Revenue Act of 1924, ch. 234, § 900(g), 43 Stat. 253, 336; Revenue Act of 1926, ch. 27, § 1001(a), 44 Stat. 9, 109.

[52] Ginsburg v. United States, 184 Ct. Cl. 444, 449, 396 F.2d 983, 986 (1968), discusses this phenomenon in the court's predecessor, the Court of Claims.

[53] Relevant dates of coverage are indicated for each court. Separate indications are noted for unofficial reports if their coverage dates are different. Early Cumulative Bulletins included lower federal court decisions either as Court Decisions (Ct. D.) or as Miscellaneous Rulings. Because the disparate labels make these items virtually impossible to locate, they are omitted from these lists. Case reporter services are discussed in Chapter 5 of this book.

(4) *Court of Federal Claims* (since 1884): *U.S. Court of Claims Reports (Ct. Cl.)* (official) (until October 1, 1982); *Federal Reporter* (from 1929 until 1932; from 1960 until October 1, 1982); *Federal Supplement* (between 1932 and 1960); *United States Claims Court Reporter (Cl. Ct.)* (from October 1, 1982, until October 29, 1992); *United States Court of Federal Claims Reporter (Fed. Cl.)* (since October 30, 1992); *American Federal Tax Reports*; *U.S. Tax Cases* (since 1924).

(5) *Tax Court* (since 1942): *Tax Court of the United States Reports; United States Tax Court Reports (T.C.)* (official); *CCH Tax Court Reports (regular and memorandum decisions)*; *RIA Tax Court Reports* (formerly *P–H*); *RIA Tax Court Memorandum Decisions* (formerly *P–H*).

(6) *Board of Tax Appeals* (between 1924 and 1942; memorandum decisions between 1928 and 1942): *Board of Tax Appeals Reports (B.T.A.)* (official); *P–H B.T.A. Memorandum Decisions*.

(7) *Bankruptcy Courts* (since 1979): *West's Bankruptcy Reporter (B.R.)*; *American Federal Tax Reports*; *U.S. Tax Cases*.

3. Tax–Oriented Case Reporter Services

Most of the sets listed above are published by the Government Printing Office or by Thomson Reuters (West) and are used similarly for tax research as for non-tax research. The sets published by Research Institute of America and Commerce Clearing House differ enough from the others to warrant further discussion. The discussion below covers print versions of these services. Researchers can also access these reporter services and related looseleaf services in their publishers' tax-oriented web services (*Checkpoint* and *CCH Tax Research NetWork*).

a. *American Federal Tax Reports (A.F.T.R.)* and *U.S. Tax Cases (U.S.T.C.)* The use of these sets can be coordinated with the use of each publisher's looseleaf reporting service, *A.F.T.R.* with *RIA United States Tax Reporter* and *U.S.T.C.* with *CCH Standard Federal Tax Reporter*. Each service publishes decisions from all courts except the Tax Court, and each may include "unpublished" decisions omitted from *Federal Supplement* and *Federal Reporter*.[54] Decisions initially appear in an Advance Sheets volume of the related looseleaf reporting service. As a result, recent decisions are available in print on a weekly basis although each service occasionally prints decisions before the other does.

These very recently decided cases also appear in the listings of new material in the services' update volumes (Recent Developments for *RIA United States Tax Reporter*; New Matters for *CCH Standard Federal Tax Reporter*). The listings appear in Code section order and are cross-referenced to discussions in the services' compilation volumes. As a result, a recent case can be located when the Code section involved is known but not the taxpayer's name, and a researcher can immediately find a discussion of the topic involved in the compilation volumes. The daily newsletters (Section P), which are probably the only more current print source of these cases, print only partial texts and lack a weekly index.

---

[54] The earliest volumes of this service print all Supreme Court decisions and those lower court decisions of "genuine precedent value...." *Foreword* to 1 U.S.T.C. (1938). When CCH began issuing two volumes per year, it expanded coverage to all decisions.

When using these reporter services, note the reference method being used. *U.S.T.C.* uses paragraph numbers for cross-references to the Advance Sheets and bound volumes (e.g., 2000–2 U.S.T.C. ¶ 50,579). RIA cites decisions in the *A.F.T.R.* Advance Sheets and bound volumes by page number (e.g., 86 A.F.T.R.2d 2000–5001). The services sometimes differ in their captions for bankruptcy cases.[55] Captions may also differ for non-bankruptcy cases involving a decedent's estate. A reporter service might name the decedent or the personal representative. [Illustrations 25–8 and 25–9]

The bound volumes include all types of tax cases—income, estate and gift, and excise; the individual Advance Sheets volumes do not. The different types of cases appear in Advance Sheets sections accompanying each publisher's looseleaf service for the particular area of tax law.

b. *Tax Court Reports.* CCH *Tax Court Reports* has three looseleaf volumes. Volume 1 contains memorandum decisions and volume 2 contains regular decisions. Volume 3, which is discussed below, contains case digests and information about pending litigation. Volume 1 has an alphabetical Table of Decisions, while volume 2 provides cross-references from the reporter service to CCH case numbers. Updating is weekly.

4. Pending Litigation, Briefs, and Petitions

Either the *RIA United States Tax Reporter* Tables volume or the *CCH Standard Federal Tax Reporter* New Matters volume can be used to determine if appeals have been filed in recent tax cases. *United States Tax Reporter* has an alphabetical Table of Cases in which appeals are noted; the *SFTR* version is the current year's Case Table.

Cases pending decision by the Tax Court appear in volume 3 of *CCH Tax Court Reports.* This service contains abstracts of petitions deemed noteworthy by the editors. These digests identify cases whose eventual outcome might affect the results of a current research effort. CCH arranges cases by docket numbers; these numbers appear in the alphabetical Petitioners Table. The *CCH Tax Court Reporter* also contains Motion and Trial Calendars.

Researchers who know the taxpayer's name or the docket number can also obtain information about pending Tax Court cases by consulting the court's website, www.ustaxcourt.gov.

Because the IRS often indicates its recommendation about appealing adverse decisions in actions on decisions (Section J), these documents should be consulted before deciding if appeals are likely in cases of interest.

5. Citators for Decisions

There are four citators commonly used for judging the relative authority of any tax decision; many libraries offer access to all of them. With the exception of *KeyCite*, all are also available in print versions. All four are discussed in Section L.

---

[55] *Compare In re* Guardian Trust Company, 99–2 U.S.T.C. ¶ 50,819 (Bankr. S.D. Miss. 1999), *with* Henderson v. United States, 84 A.F.T.R.2d 99–5940 (Bankr. S.D. Miss. 1999).

- *Shepard's Citations* (*LexisNexis*)
- *KeyCite* (*Westlaw*)
- *RIA Citator 2nd* (*Checkpoint* and *Westlaw*)
- *CCH Standard Federal Tax Reporter—Citator* (*CCH Tax Research NetWork*)

In addition, the IRS website AOD section indicates IRS action with regard to cases it has lost. This information is also available, and easier to locate, in subscription-based online services (Section T).

SECTION L. CITATORS

Four Web-based citators can be used to judge whether a particular statute, regulation, ruling, or judicial decision was criticized, approved, or otherwise commented upon in a more recent proceeding. The material being evaluated is referred to as the *cited* item; any later material that refers to it is a *citing* item. The four services are *Shepard's Citations*; West's *KeyCite*; *RIA Citator 2nd*[56]; and *CCH Standard Federal Tax Reporter—Citator*. With the exception of *KeyCite*, these services are also available in print versions. The online versions are much easier to use and more up-to-date. [See Illustrations 25–7 through 25–10 for partial lists of citations to Estate of Mitchell v. Commissioner, 250 F.3d 696 (9th Cir. 2001).]

Both *Shepard's* and *KeyCite* provide citations to secondary source material. Researchers can use each to determine if an article has cited a judicial decision and vice versa. When citing judicial decisions, these citators use syllabus numbers to indicate issues, but each uses its own headnote numbering system. These citators also indicate whether the later item followed or disagreed with the earlier item.

RIA also indicates issue number and indicates how the citing item treated the cited item. Unlike *Shepard's* and *KeyCite*, *RIA* does not provide citations for secondary material. In addition, it does not provide citations for the Constitution or statutes.

CCH uses fewer citing cases than do the others. As was true for *RIA*, it does not provide citations for articles, the Constitution, or statutes. Although *CCH* indicates if a later decision cited an earlier one, it does not indicate if the later item agreed with the earlier item.

Researchers using the print citators must keep in mind that *Shepard's* is arranged by numerical reporter citations. *CCH* and *RIA* arrange cited cases by taxpayer name. The taxpayer's first name should be noted, particularly if the taxpayer has a common surname.

Mertens, *Law of Federal Income Taxation* (Section M) and the IRS *Bulletin Index–Digest System* (Section Q) also include citator features, but these are limited to IRS action on revenue rulings and procedures.

---

[56] The first series of the RIA CITATOR is available only in print. That imprint was initially published by Prentice–Hall.

[Illustration 25–7]

EXCERPT FROM SHEPARD'S CITATOR

[Illustration 25–8]

EXCERPT FROM RIA CITATOR 2ND

RIA

MITCHELL, PAUL, EST OF, v. COM., 87 AFTR 2d 2001-2043, 250 F3d 696, 2001-1 USTC ¶60,403, (CA9, 5/2/2001)
Citator 2nd (RIA)

Related case : AOD 2005-001 , 2005 USTR ¶86,273 .

Cited In

Cited favorably : Trompeter, Emanuel, Est of v. Com., <u>89 AFTR 2d 2002-736</u>, 279 F3d 770 (CA9, 1/30/2002) *[See 87 AFTR 2d 2001-2049, 250 F3d 703-704]*

Cited favorably : Blodgett, Diane S. v. Com., <u>95 AFTR 2d 2005-451</u>, 394 F3d 1035 (CA8, 1/12/2005) *[See 87 AFTR 2d 2001-2047, 250 F3d 701]*

Cited favorably : Dunia, Michel, Est of, 2004 <u>RIA TC Memo 2004-805</u> (5/20/2004) *[See 87 AFTR 2d 2001-2048, 250 F3d 702]*

Cited favorably : Chin, Kaing & Baek, Hae Kyung, 2004 <u>RIA TC Memo 2004-1138</u> (8/24/2004) *[See 87 AFTR 2d 2001-2047-2001-2048, 250 F3d 701-702]*

☐ This excerpt is from *Checkpoint*; the *RIA Citator* is also available on Westlaw.

[Illustration 25–9]

EXCERPT FROM CCH STANDARD FEDERAL TAX REPORTER—CITATOR

CCH–CITATOR, FEGT, Main Citator Table, Fujieki, Patrick T., Exr.

Fujieki, Patrick T., Exr.

ANNOTATED AT ... FEGT ¶220.075, ¶220.382, ¶220.37J, ¶220.403, ¶220.405, ¶220.46, ¶220.468, ¶220.476, ¶220.476, ¶220.83, ¶21.575.40, ¶21.790.30, ¶22.501.44, ¶22.520.59

- ● CA-9–(aff'g TC in an unpublished memorandum), 200¢–1 USTC ¶60.475; 83 FedAppx 987
- ● TC–(supplemental opinion), Dec. 54.715(M), 83 TCM 1524, TC Memo. 2002-38, (Mitchell Est., Paul)
- Hess, TC, Dec. 55.274(M), 86 TCM 303, TC Memo. 2003-251
- ● CA-9–(aff'g, vac'g and rem'g TC), 2001-1 USTC ¶50.403; 250 F3d 696; (Mitchell Est., Paul; Nonacq, IRB 2005-23, June 6, 2005)

Trompeler Est., CA-9, 2002-1 USTC ¶60.428, 279 F3d 767

Dunia Est., TC, Dec. 55.643(M), 87 TCM 1353, TC Memo. 2004-123

Harper Est., TC, Dec. 54.745(M), 33 TCM 1641, TC Memo. 2002-121

☐ Note that *CCH* lists the executor's name rather than the name of the decedent's estate. The FEGT notation indicates that this case is covered in the *CCH Federal Estate and Gift Tax Reporter.* This information is relevant to researchers using the print citator and reporter services.

[Illustration 25–10]

EXCERPT FROM KEYCITE

Graphical History

△

FOR EDUCATIONAL USE ONLY

↳ SELECT TO PRINT, EMAIL, ETC.

Estate of Mitchell v. C.I.R.
250 F.3d 696
C.A.9,2001.
May 02, 2001

Citing References

(Showing 198 documents)

Positive Cases (U.S.A.)

★ ★ ★ **Discussed**

☐ H 1 Estate of Trompeter v. C.I.R., 279 F.3d 767, 770+, 89 A.F.T.R.2d 2002-734, 2002-734+, 2002-1 USTC P 60,428, 60428+, 02 Cal. Daily Op. Serv. 892, 892+, 2002 Daily Journal D.A.R. 1137, 1137+ (9th Cir. Jan 30, 2002) (NO. 99-70805) ▸▸ HN: 9,10 (F.3d)

☐ △ 2 Harper v. C.I.R., 2002 WL 992347, *2+, T.C. Memo. 2002-121, 2002-121+, 83 T.C.M. (CCH) 1641, 1641+, T.C.M. (RIA) 2002-121, 2002-121+, 2002 RIA TC Memo 2002-121, 2002-121+ (U.S.Tax Ct. May 15, 2002) (NO. 19336-98) HN: 7,8 (F.3d)

★ ★ **Cited**

☐ H 3 Blodgett v. C.I.R., 394 F.3d 1030, 1035, 95 A.F.T.R.2d 2005-448, 2005-448, 2005-1 USTC P 50,146, 50146 (8th Cir. Jan 12, 2005) (NO. 03-3917) HN: 5 (F.3d)

☐ C 4 Fujieki v. C.I.R., 83 Fed.Appx. 987, 988+, 93 A.F.T.R.2d 2004-362, 2004-362+, 2004-1 USTC P 60,475, 60475+ (9th Cir. Dec 29, 2003) (Table, text in WESTLAW, NO. 02-72043) HN: 7,8 (F.3d)

☐ C 5 Chin v. C.I.R., 2004 WL 1879830, *2, T.C. Memo. 2004-189, 2004-189, T.C.M. (RIA) 2004-189, 2004-189, 2004 RIA TC Memo 2004-189, 2004-189 (U.S.Tax Ct. Aug 24, 2004) (NO. 8740-03) HN: 7 (F.3d)

SECTION M. LOOSELEAF SERVICES, ENCYCLOPEDIAS, AND TREATISES

It may be necessary to consult explanatory materials early in the research effort, perhaps even before reading the relevant statutes. The texts described in this chapter often provide insight into the problem being researched, and their liberal use of citations is a useful introduction to the relevant cases and administrative pronouncements. Each is updated at frequent intervals, and most have at least one related newsletter (Section P).

While general research texts would categorize some of these materials as looseleaf services and others as legal encyclopedias or treatises,[57] those

---

[57] *See* Chapters 14, 16, and 19 of this book for further discussion of these research tools. The annotated law reports discussed in Chapter 17 also provide textual material.

classifications are less significant than are classifications based upon their formats. Most of them take a subject matter approach, but two of the best-known services are arranged in Code section order.

Before using a looseleaf service, a researcher should become familiar with the service's format for designating materials. Cross-references to updating items use that format.

1. Code Section Arrangement

The *Standard Federal Tax Reporter*[58] and the *United States Tax Reporter*[59] looseleaf services take essentially the same approach. Compilation volumes provide the full texts of Code sections and Treasury regulations along with editorial explanations. An annotation section lists cases and rulings for each Code section. Users wanting ready access to the text of the law while they are reading explanations of it will appreciate this format.

Because of the arrangement described above, however, problems involving multiple Code sections do not receive comprehensive discussion in the Code compilations. Although the publishers supplement these services with newsletters and other aids, Code-based services are not the best tools for learning about a particular topic. Researchers who are unfamiliar with a particular area may find it easier to begin research in a looseleaf that is arranged by subject matter.

Although each service is arranged in Code section order, all materials are assigned paragraph numbers; *USTR* uses the Code section numbers in its paragraph numbering system; *SFTR* does not. A "paragraph" can be several pages long or the size of a traditional paragraph. Each service generally cross-references between paragraph numbers, not between page numbers. New developments are indexed according to the paragraph in the main compilation to which they relate, i.e., in Code section order. Both services provide information about pending litigation, proposed regulations, and other matters of interest to researchers.

Libraries often carry both *SFTR* and *USTR* in looseleaf and subscribe to their online versions. Users eventually develop a preference for one or the other. As each service's annotations are editorially selected, use of both can reduce the risk of missing a valuable annotation although it may substantially increase research time. The extra material obtained is unlikely to justify the additional time involved.

These services contain the following features. In addition, each has a variety of other useful tables and finding lists.

a. *Code Volumes*. These volumes print, in Code section order, all provisions involving income, gift and estate, employment, and excise taxes, as well as procedural provisions. *SFTR's* Code volume I includes a table cross-referencing Code sections to each other. This table is quite useful,

---

[58] CCH STANDARD FEDERAL TAX REPORTER (income tax); CCH FEDERAL ESTATE AND GIFT TAX REPORTER; CCH FEDERAL EXCISE TAX REPORTER.

[59] UNITED STATES TAX REPORTER—INCOME TAXES; UNITED STATES TAX REPORTER—ESTATE & GIFT TAXES; UNITED STATES TAX REPORTER—EXCISE TAXES. RIA also publishes a subject matter format service (*Federal Tax Coordinator 2d*).

particularly for researching an unfamiliar area. Unfortunately, it is not updated frequently; in December 2008, it was current as of January 19, 2004. In addition, the cross-reference table will not help if relevant Code sections do not specifically refer to each other. *SFTR* also contains tables that cross-reference between the 1939 and 1954 Codes. [Illustration 25–1]

   b.   *Compilation Volumes.* These volumes contain, in Code section order, the full text of the Code, excerpts from congressional committee reports, proposed, temporary, and final regulations, and digest-annotations to judicial decisions, revenue rulings, and other IRS guidance. [Illustration 25–11]

   c.   *Updating Volumes.* Recent material is indexed in the New Matters volume (*SFTR*) or Recent Developments volume (*USTR*). These materials are arranged according to the paragraph numbers used in the Compilation volumes, making it easy to find recent rulings and decisions in any area of interest.[60] These volumes also provide limited coverage of pending legislation. The updating volumes print full text of recent IRS materials.

---

[60] Because USTR updates the Compilation volumes throughout the year, there is far less material included in its updating volume.

[Illustration 25–11]

EXCERPT FROM CCH STANDARD FEDERAL TAX REPORTER

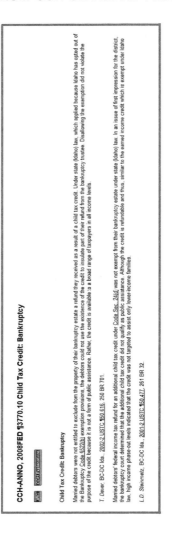

d.   *Advance Sheets Volumes.* These volumes contain the texts of income tax decisions rendered by courts other than the Tax Court. Decisions involving estate and gift taxes or excise taxes appear in the CCH and RIA services covering those topics. Court decisions covering all taxes will later be issued in hardbound volumes as part of the *U.S.T.C.* and *A.F.T.R.*

reporter services discussed in Section K. *SFTR* includes preambles to proposed regulations in the Advance Sheets volume; *USTR* has a separate Proposed Regulation Preambles volume.

e. *Citator Volumes.* The CCH and RIA citators, which cover both judicial decisions and IRS materials, are discussed in Section L. The RIA citator is more comprehensive than its CCH counterpart.

2. Subject Matter Arrangement—Multiple Topics

The materials described in this section cover a wide range of topics, using a subject matter arrangement. Most of them include tables indicating where a researcher can find discussion of judicial decisions and other primary source material. These services also have topical indexes.[61]

a. *Federal Tax Coordinator 2d (Research Institute of America).* This weekly service contains excellent discussions of all areas of taxation, with minimal coverage of employment taxes. Discussions in each chapter of the text volumes include liberal use of citations, cross-references to topics of potential relevance discussed in other chapters, and analysis of as yet unresolved matters.

Each chapter has the following arrangement: a Detailed Reference Table for topics included; discussion of each topic, with extensive footnotes; and text of Code and regulations sections applicable to the chapters being discussed. Topics in each chapter are further subdivided into "paragraphs."

The service has an extensive Topical Index and cross-reference tables for discussions of primary source material. A variety of practice aids, such as sample client letters and annuity tables, are also included.

Volumes 20 and 20A contain the texts of United States tax treaties and lists of signatory countries, in addition to textual material dealing with the treaties. Volumes 27 and 27A contain proposed regulations reproduced in the order in which they were issued, along with preambles and *Federal Register* citations. Volume 28 contains reprints of the weekly *Internal Revenue Bulletin* (Section Q).

b. *Tax Management Portfolios (Bureau of National Affairs).* BNA issues three series of *Tax Management Portfolios*: *U.S. Income; Foreign Income;* and *Estates, Gifts, and Trusts.* Each series is subdivided into several softbound *Portfolios* that cover narrow areas of tax law in great depth.[62]

Each *Portfolio* has three sections: (1) Detailed Analysis; (2) Worksheets—checklists, forms that can be used as models in drafting documents, and texts of relevant congressional and IRS materials; and (3) Bibliography—citations to regulations, legislative history, court decisions, IRS materials, books, and articles. BNA updates the *Portfolios* with Changes & Analysis sheets, or completely revises them, as warranted by new developments.

[61] TAX MANAGEMENT PORTFOLIOS lack case and rulings tables. They have excellent Code and topical indexes.

[62] Subdivisions are so narrow that several PORTFOLIOS may cover any one Code section; for example, *Portfolios* 370, 389, 397, and 506 cover § 22. The index indicates the primary *Portfolio(s)* for each Code section with a "Main discussion" designation.

BNA provides several methods for locating relevant *Portfolios*. The looseleaf Portfolio Index includes the Classification Guides, lists of *Portfolios* in each series arranged by major category (e.g., Real Estate), and a more detailed Key Word Index (Master Index). Each series also has an index covering the worksheets (Working Papers Index). A Code section index covers all series. IRS forms and publications are cross-referenced numerically to appropriate *Portfolios*.

c. *Mertens, Law of Federal Income Taxation (Clark Boardman Callaghan)*. The original Mertens service contained five sets of volumes: treatise; rulings; Code; Code commentary; and regulations. Although only the treatise and rulings materials have been continued in their original format, the archival Code and regulations materials are useful for historical research.

(1) *Treatise*. The treatise volumes closely resemble general encyclopedias such as *Am. Jur. 2d* and *C.J.S.* in format.[63] Discussion includes historical background and extensive footnoting.

Tables volumes contain tables indicating where primary source materials are discussed. IRS materials include items printed in the *Cumulative Bulletin* and letter rulings.

The Index volume contains a detailed subject matter index. Treatise materials are supplemented monthly; supplements are cumulated semiannually.

(2) *Code*. Each Code volume contains all income tax provisions enacted or amended during a particular time period (one or more years). Textual notations (diamond shapes and brackets) indicate additions and deletions. A historical note indicates act, section, and effective date and can be used to reconstruct the prior language. The subject matter index in a looseleaf volume cross-references each topic to applicable Code sections. This material covers only the 1954 Code.

(3) *Code Commentary*. Looseleaf volumes of Code Commentary initially provided useful short explanations of statutory provisions and cross-references to the discussions in the treatise materials. More recent items are limited to references to statutory changes or to recent cases and rulings for the particular Code section.

(4) *Regulations*. Regulations materials have undergone change since the mid–1990s. In a separate service, but using the Mertens name, the publisher currently issues an annual softbound set of regulations in force (volumes 1 through 6) and proposed regulations (volume 7). Regulations appear in Code section order, and there is a subject-matter index. New material is issued throughout the year and filed in a looseleaf Current Developments and Status Table binder. The service also includes looseleaf volumes containing the preambles to proposed, temporary, and final regulations.

Many libraries also contain hardbound volumes that include the texts and preambles of all income tax regulations issued or amended during a

---

[63] Encyclopedias are discussed in Chapter 16 of this book. Within each encyclopedia, discussions of taxation appear in separate volumes and are quite accessible.

particular time period (two or more years). Publication is made in Code section order. Textual notations indicate deletions, additions, and other changes in amended regulations. Historical notes permit the determination of the regulation's prior wording. These volumes are no longer being updated.

(5) *Rulings.* The Rulings volumes in this service contain the texts of revenue rulings and procedures. Each volume covers a particular time period and includes rulings in numerical order, followed by procedures in numerical order. Mertens adds current items monthly.

The looseleaf current volume has Code-Rulings and Code-Procedures Tables [Illustration 25–5], which provide chronological listings of every revenue ruling and procedure involving Code sections or subsections. In addition, a Rulings Status Table [Illustration 25–6] lists the most recent revenue ruling or procedure affecting the validity of a previously published item. Mertens indicates the effect on the earlier item (e.g., modified, revoked). A separate section includes *Cumulative Bulletin* citations for this material.

d. *Rabkin & Johnson, Federal Income, Gift and Estate Taxation (Matthew Bender).* The discussions in this service's treatise volumes do not purport to cover all types of authority. Letter rulings are rarely discussed or cited as authority "[b]ecause they lack precedential value."[64] New Matter pages appear near the beginning of each volume in text section number order.

Some libraries carry volumes that are no longer being updated; these cover legislative history and regulations for the 1954 Code.

3. Subject Matter Arrangement—Limited Scope

Various publishers issue textual materials discussing a limited number of Code sections, such as those covering S corporations. These texts are particularly useful for research involving complex topics. Researchers can find texts on almost any topic, from tax problems of the elderly to taxation of inventories. Although these materials are periodically supplemented, their updating is rarely as frequent as that for the looseleaf services in subsections 1 and 2.

SECTION N.   LEGAL PERIODICALS

Commentary on particular tax problems appears in various legal periodicals, several of which focus on taxation.[65] This group includes such offerings as *Journal of Taxation, Tax Lawyer, TAXES—The Tax Magazine,* and *Tax Law Review.* Many publications adopt a narrower focus within taxation, e.g., *Real Estate Taxation.*

---

[64] 1A RABKIN & JOHNSON, FEDERAL INCOME, GIFT AND ESTATE TAXATION § G 1.03[6], at G–11. This service is also available on *LexisNexis.*

[65] While not technically periodicals, annual institutes, such as those given at New York University (taxation) and the University of Miami (estate planning), are extraordinarily useful sources of information, have their own excellent indexes, and are covered in several periodical indexes.

In addition to the services discussed in this section, researchers can obtain lists of articles online using sources such as *Google Scholar*, *Hein-Online*, and *Social Science Research Network (SSRN)*.

The first two services discussed below focus exclusively on taxation. Unfortunately, neither is available electronically.

1. CCH Federal Tax Articles

This monthly looseleaf reporter contains summaries of articles on federal taxes appearing in legal, accounting, business, and related periodicals. Each month's contents appear in Code section order; each item receives a paragraph cross-reference number. [Illustration 25–12] Contents are cumulated and given new paragraph numbers at six-month intervals.

There are topic and author indexes. Hardbound volumes cover materials since 1954; the looseleaf volume contains the most recent material. Coverage in recent volumes is not as extensive as it was in earlier years.

[Illustration 25–12]

EXCERPT FROM CCH FEDERAL TAX ARTICLES

---

546   2-2008   **4431**

¶ 6770 Taxation of REMIC's (Code Sec. 860A)

2004 Article Summaries

¶6770.016 **Should It Stay or Should It Go—The Tax Considerations of Modifying REMIC-Held Mortgages.** Marshall Feiring and Carol Schwartz.. Journal of Taxation of Financial Products, Vol. 5, No. 1, Winter 2004.

Helps trustees or servicers determine whether changes to a mortgage are considered significant modifications with respect to debt modification and Real Estate Mortgage Investment Conduit (REMIC) purposes. Indicates that current home refinance abatement may be the likely cause for mortgagor or lender to ask for modifications in mortgages. Offers examples of qualified mortgages to ensure that REMICs do not hold nonpermitted assets and that they are not subject to the prohibited transaction tax. Explains how significant modifications differ with respect to being treated as taxable exchanges under debt modification rules, and with respect to threatening a REMIC's tax status or imposing a prohibited transactions tax.

2008 Article Summaries

¶6770.018 **IRS Relieves Some of a REMIC's Distress from Relieving Distressed Mortgages.** Alan S Lederman and Milton A Vescovacci. 24 Tax Management Real Estate Journal 2, Feb 6, 2008.

Provides a brief history of REMICs (Real Estate Mortgage Investment Conduits) and the role of these pass-through entities in the subprime mortgage crisis. Discusses how loan modifications have affected REMICs and includes solutions from both the SEC and the IRS to ensure the entities' continued use to securitize mortgages. Views the American Securitization Forum's (ASF) foreclosure and loss avoidance framework as a guide to mortgage servers. Considers three types of subprime borrowers from individuals who can refinance their loans, lenders in the fast loan modification class and those who may face foreclosure. Notes that the IRS relief applies only to first-lien residential ARM loans that originated between January 1, 2005 and July 31, 2007, have an initial fixed rate period of 36 months or less and have an initial interest rate reset between January 1, 2008 and July 31, 2010.

2. Index to Federal Tax Articles (Warren, Gorham & Lamont)

This multivolume work covers the literature on federal income, gift, and estate taxation contained in legal, specialized tax, accounting, and economics journals, as well as in nonperiodical publications.

Coverage begins with 1913, making this an important tool for locating discussions of pre–1954 Code developments. Current material appears in the quarterly cumulative supplement volume. There are separate topical and author listings but no Code section index. The most recent entry appears first in each listing of articles. [Illustration 25–13]

[Illustration 25–13]

EXCERPT FROM INDEX TO FEDERAL TAX ARTICLES

SPRING 2008 CUMULATIVE SUPPLEMENT

FICA Tax—*Cont'd*

How Increasing the Payroll Tax Base Affects Tax Burdens, Thomas L. Hungerford, 115 Tax Notes No. 7, 643 (2007)

The Student FICA Exception and Medical Residents. Richard M. Weber, Jr., 114 Tax Notes No. 4, 453 (2007)

The Application of Employment Taxes to S Corporation Shareholders—What Is "Unreasonably Low" Compensation?, Timothy R. Koski, 85 Taxes No. 1, 19 (2007)

Weigh Reducing Social Security Tax Payments Against Lower Benefits, James Parker and Claire Y. Nash, 77 Practical Tax Strategies No. 12, 350 (2006)

Individuals and Passthrough Entities: Self-Employment Tax and Passthrough Entities: Proposals for Reform, Susan Kalinka, 84 Taxes No. 3, 17 (2006)

Financial Products (See also Bonds, Debentures and Notes; Securities)

International Tax Watch: To Integrate or Not to Integrate? That is the Question, Stewart R. Lipeles and John D. McDonald, 86 Taxes No. 1, 5 (2008)

Equity Derivatives, Inbound Capital and Outbound Withholding Tax, David P. Hariton, 60 Tax Lawyer No. 2, 313 (2007)

The Cost of Norms: Tax Effects of Tacit Understandings, Alex Raskolnikov, 74 University of Chicago Law Review No. 2, 601 (2007)

Subprime Woes Necessitate a Reevaluation of Cash Investments, William M. Vandenburgh, Philip J. Harmelink, and Christopher J. Burke, 79 Practical Tax Strategies No. 5, 282 (2007)

3. Current Law Index; Legal Resource Index (Gale)

The *Current Law Index* is the most convenient print-based general periodical index for federal tax research. Although its subject matter listing is not geared to Code sections, its Table of Statutes includes a separate heading for "Internal Revenue Code." This section lists articles in Code section order. In addition to indexing by statutes, this service also indexes articles by subject, author/title, and case name. It covers several tax-oriented periodicals, including *Tax Notes*.

The *Legal Resource Index* can be accessed online through both *Lexis-Nexis* and *Westlaw*. These services cover material since 1980.

4. Index to Legal Periodicals; WilsonWeb (H.W. Wilson Company)

Index to Legal Periodicals & Books (ILP) includes tax articles in its subject matter listings. Because its Table of Statutes arranges articles by act, it is not accessible by Code section. *ILP* indexes articles by subject/author, case name, and act name. It indexes somewhat fewer publications than *Current Law Index* does (e.g., it does not include *Tax Notes*), and it imposes page minimums for indexed material. Because *ILP* began publication in 1908, it is better than the *Current Law Index* for extensive historical research.

WilsonWeb is available online, and *ILP* is carried on *LexisNexis* and *Westlaw*; Both cover material indexed since mid–1981. A recent *WilsonWeb* addition, *Index to Legal Periodicals Retrospective: 1908–1981,* should be useful for historical tax research.

5. HeinOnline (William S. Hein & Co.)

HeinOnline provides full-text access to the periodicals it covers. Researchers can search for articles by author, title, or words in text. This service includes numerous tax-oriented periodicals.

6. Tax Management Portfolios (Bureau of National Affairs)

The Bibliography section of each *Portfolio* contains articles listings, arranged by year of publication. The *Portfolios* are discussed further in Section M.

7. Mertens, Law of Federal Income Taxation (Clark Boardman Callahan)

Mertens lists current articles by topic in the Recent Tax Articles section of its monthly *Developments & Highlights* newsletter. Although Mertens is an income tax service, the lists include articles on estate planning. Mertens is discussed further in Section M. Unfortunately, the articles listings are not cumulated.

8. NYU Institute on Federal Taxation (Matthew Bender)

Although limited to the NYU Institute in their scope, this set's Consolidated Indexes offer ready access to numerous significant articles. Consolidated indexes, which are published irregularly, are arranged by subject, author, title, cases, statutes, regulations, and rulings. Current indexes and tables appear in the second volume of each annual Institute.

9. Tax Policy in the United States: A Selective Bibliography with Annotations (1960–84)

Published by the Vanderbilt Law School Library in cooperation with the ABA Section of Taxation, this looseleaf covers articles, books, and government documents dealing with tax policy. Each item is explained briefly. There are author and subject indexes.

10. WG & L Tax Journal Digest (Warren, Gorham & Lamont)

Previously published as the *Journal of Taxation Digest*, this service covers articles published in the *Journal of Taxation* and several other Warren, Gorham & Lamont publications. Coverage begins with 1977, and the titles covered have varied over time. The digests are arranged by topic; cross-references are given to relevant articles digested under other topical headings.

SECTION O. FORM BOOKS

Form books are useful aids in drafting documents, particularly if tax consequences will be determined by the drafter's choice of language. Authors often include references to primary authority. Many form books are available online and as CD–ROMs; users can download and customize forms for their clients' needs.

Available titles include Bittker, Emory & Streng, *Federal Income Taxation of Corporations and Shareholders: Forms* (Warren, Gorham & Lamont); Mancoff & Steinberg, *Qualified Deferred Compensation Plans–Forms* (Clark Boardman Callaghan); and *Murphy's Will Clauses: Annotations and Forms with Tax Effects* (Matthew Bender). In addition, the IRS occasionally publishes prototype language in revenue procedures and notices.

SECTION P.   NEWSLETTERS

Researchers in any area must update their findings or risk citing obsolete sources. When the research involves taxation, the odds of change are higher than in most fields and the number of sources to be consulted may appear endless.

Newsletters are convenient tools for keeping up with changes in the law. While they are no substitute for updating with a citator or the new matter section of a looseleaf service, they offer the opportunity for a leisurely review of changes occurring during a predetermined time period.

1.   Daily Tax Report (BNA) (print and online)

This newsletter, published five times each week, provides extensive coverage of current developments in tax law.[66] [Illustration 25–14] Each issue includes a section describing congressional activity, including bills passed and introduced, committee hearings, and committee reports.

[Illustration 25–14]

EXCERPT FROM BNA DAILY TAX REPORT

(No. 11)   GG-1

Lead Tax Report

Trusts

Trust Investment Advisory Fee Deductions Subject to 2 Percent Floor, High Court Rules

The U.S. Supreme Court Jan. 16 unanimously held that deductions for investment advisory fees paid by a trust are subject to the 2 percent floor under Internal Revenue Code Section 67 (*Knight v. Commissioner*, U.S., No. 06-1286, 1/16/08).

The trust filed a petition in the U.S. Tax Court arguing that the trustee's fiduciary duty to act as a "prudent investor" under the state uniform prudent investor act required the trustee to obtain investment advisory services, and therefore to pay investment advisory fees. The trust argued that such fees were accordingly unique to trusts and therefore fully deductible under tax code Section 67(e)(1).

The Tax Court rejected this argument, holding that tax code Section 67(e)(1) allows full deductibility only for expenses that are not commonly incurred outside

☐ *Daily Tax Report* includes news reports in addition to primary source material. The excerpt above is from the January 17, 2008, print version.

---

[66] BNA also publishes a weekly newsletter, Tax Management Weekly Report.

The *Daily Tax Report* prints full texts or digests of judicial decisions, IRS documents, and Treasury regulations. Subscribers can access full text documents online using Tax Management's *TaxCore*.

2. Tax Notes (Tax Analysts) (print and online)

This weekly newsletter contains a comprehensive collection of recent tax-oriented material.

Tax Notes includes information about significant revenue rulings and procedures, other IRS documents, and court opinions. It also includes information about committee reports, testimony at hearings, bills, and statements in the *Congressional Record*. The editors also cover public hearings on regulations and comments received on proposed regulations. [Illustration 25–15] Each issue of *Tax Notes* includes one or more substantive articles.

Full text information, such as statements at hearings on legislation and regulations, texts of tax articles, and even the IRS *Cumulative Bulletin* are included the Tax Analysts database on *LexisNexis* (Section T). Document cross-references in *Tax Notes* allow a researcher to retrieve these full text documents. Tax Analysts also publishes CD–ROM and DVD services (Section S) covering both primary and secondary source material and offers its own web-based daily service.

[Illustration 25–15]

EXCERPT FROM TAX NOTES (TAX ANALYSTS)

OTHER NEWS

LAWMAKERS, WITNESSES EXPRESS SUPPORT FOR CONSOLIDATING EDUCATION TAX BREAKS. College and university representatives who appeared last week at a House subcommittee hearing on tax incentives to help students afford college strongly backed legislation that would consolidate several of the tax breaks.

Lawmakers and witnesses at the House Ways and Means Select Revenue Measures Subcommittee hearing agreed that the current system of tax credits, deductions, and other tax breaks is complex and confusing and does not help everyone who needs financial assistance to pay for college. Ways and Means member Dave Camp, R-Mich., said that "this is an area of the tax code that is long overdue for reform and simplification." Camp, along with Ways and Means Committee member Rahm Emanuel, D-Ill., is an original sponsor of H.R. 2458, which would consolidate the HOPE and lifetime learning credits and tuition deduction into one credit. (For the bill, see Doc 2007-12453 or 2007 TNT 100-26.)

reasons for the omission, although she said the absence of the reforms should not be taken as a sign the administration does not support simplification. Earlier, when delivering her testimony, she cautioned that revising the tax incentives may lead to unintended consequences.

"Recognizing budgetary constraints, legislative reform of existing tax incentives will almost invariably result in winners and losers," she said. "Further, considering that the population of students spans so many circumstances and situations, there may be no one-size-fits-all solution."

Another problem with higher education tax breaks is that they do not help low-income students. Lawmakers and panelists said. Subcommittee ranking minority member Phil English, R-Pa., said the lifetime learning credit is more helpful to students who attend more expensive schools. Susan Dynarski, associate professor of public policy at Harvard University, agreed. (For Dynarski's testimony, see Doc 2008-9728 or 2008 TNT 86-63.)

☐ As was true for *Daily Tax Report, Tax Notes* includes news items in addition to coverage of primary source materials. Note the references to full-text sources in this article from May 5, 2008.

SECTION Q. COLLECTIONS OF PRIMARY SOURCE MATERIALS

The materials described below, which are referred to at various points in this chapter, print several types of material necessary for tax research. Except as indicated in the following paragraphs, these sets contain no textual discussion of the materials presented.

1. Internal Revenue Bulletin; Cumulative Bulletin; Bulletin Index–Digest System

The first two of these IRS-generated series contain the text of almost every officially published nonjudicial primary authority. Until it ceased publication, the *Bulletin Index–Digest System (Index–Digest)* was an invaluable aid to using the other two series. The primary source materials printed in these volumes are also available in microform (Section R), CD–ROM (Section S), and online services (Section T) offered by a variety of vendors.

a. *Internal Revenue Bulletin.* The weekly *Internal Revenue Bulletin* is divided into four parts. Part I prints all revenue rulings, final regulations, and Supreme Court tax decisions issued during the week. Part II covers treaties and legislative materials. Part III contains notices and revenue procedures, while Part IV, "Items of General Interest," is varied in content. Its coverage ranges from disbarment notices to announcements of proposed regulations. *Federal Register* dates and comment deadlines are provided in addition to the preambles and text of proposed regulations. The *Bulletin* also indicates IRS acquiescence or nonacquiescence in judicial decisions decided against its position.

Although the *Bulletin* has Finding Lists, citators (Section L) are a better means for locating and evaluating IRS material. Every issue contains a Numerical Finding List for each type of item, listing each in numerical order; these Finding Lists lack any tie-in to Code sections. The Finding List of Current Actions on Previously Published Items indicates IRS, but not judicial, action. The quarterly subject matter indexes also lack Code section information.[67] Researchers can search for *Bulletin* items using the IRS website search tool, but searching in subscription-based services is easier. Because of its index format, the *Bulletin* is best used to locate material for which citations are already available or as a tool for staying abreast of recent IRS and Treasury developments.

b. *Cumulative Bulletin.* Every six months the material in the *Internal Revenue Bulletin* is republished in a hardbound *Cumulative Bulletin*. The *Cumulative Bulletin* format through 1997 follows that of the weekly service with three exceptions.[68] First, major tax legislation and committee reports generally appear in a third volume rather than in the two semiannual volumes.[69] Second, only disbarment notices and proposed regulations appear from Part IV. Finally, rulings appear in the *Cumulative Bulletin* in semiannual Code section order; this bears no relation to their numerical order. Beginning in 1998, the *Cumulative Bulletins* reprint the *Internal Revenue Bulletin* verbatim. Items no longer appear in Code section order for the six-month period. After 2003, major legislation is no longer being published.

The *Cumulative Bulletin* indexes are also difficult to use. The 1998 and later *Cumulative Bulletins* provide Code section references to included

---

[67] The indexes are subdivided by type of tax.

[68] Although the CUMULATIVE BULLETIN included preambles, it omitted drafting information before 1998.

[69] Committee reports for 1913 through 1938 appear in 1939–1 (pt. 2) C.B. Committee reports for the 1954 Code's enactment never appeared in the CUMULATIVE BULLETIN.

items in a Code Sections Affected by Current Actions listing; these lists are not cumulated over multiple years.

The *Cumulative Bulletin* has been published since 1919. Volumes initially were given Arabic numerals (1919–1921); the IRS adopted a Roman numeral system in 1922. Since 1937, volumes have been numbered by year (e.g., 1937–1). There have been two volumes annually (with occasional extra volumes for extensive legislative history material) since 1920; the –1, –2 numbering system for each year began in 1922. The *Cumulative Bulletin's* format differed slightly from the above description until the 1974–2 volume. Proposed regulations, which appear as a separate category, were added in the 1981–1 volume.

c. *Bulletin Index–Digest System.* The IRS issued the *Index–Digest* in four services: Income Tax; Estate and Gift Tax; Employment Tax; and Excise Tax until 1994. Because the *Index–Digest* is no longer current, it is best used for pre–1994 research.

The *Index–Digest* provided *Internal Revenue Bulletin* or *Cumulative Bulletin* citations for revenue rulings and procedures, Supreme Court and adverse Tax Court decisions, Public Laws, Treasury Decisions, and treaties. In addition, it digested the rulings, procedures, and court decisions. The digests of IRS materials were arranged by topic. A researcher who did not know the underlying Code section number could still use these digests effectively.

2. United States Code Annotated—Federal Tax Regulations; Internal Revenue Acts—Text and Legislative History (West)

These series can be used in researching the texts and histories of the Code and regulations sections.

The annual *Federal Tax Regulations* volumes contain the text of all income, estate and gift, employment tax, and procedural regulations in force on the first day of the year. These materials include references to the T.D. number, date, and *Federal Register* publication for both original promulgation and all amendments. However, *Federal Tax Regulations* omits T.D. numbers for original promulgation of pre-existing regulations republished in 1960 in T.D. 6498, 6500, or 6516. Both final and temporary regulations are included. The final volume for each year contains a subject matter index. This service was previously published as *U.S. Code Congressional & Administrative News—Federal Tax Regulations*.

Internal Revenue Acts, issued annually in pamphlet form, prints the full text of new tax acts in chronological order. Hardbound volumes cumulate the material in one or more years' pamphlets. Texts of selected committee reports, *Congressional Record* statements, and presidential signing messages appear in the second section of each pamphlet. Each pamphlet includes a subject matter index; tables indicate Code sections affected and cross-reference Public Law section numbers to pages in *Statutes at Large*. The cross-reference table listed acts by name through 1996; beginning in 1997, it has a separate Popular Name Acts table. This series is excerpted from the general *U.S. Code Congressional & Administrative News (USCCAN)* service and cross-references to material printed there but omitted here.

3. Tax Management Primary Sources (Bureau of National Affairs)

Primary Sources is an excellent tool for deriving the legislative history of existing Code sections. It also covers the Employee Retirement Income Security Act (ERISA). It is no longer being updated, so its usefulness is limited to material appearing in 2003 and earlier.

Extensive legislative history excerpts for selected Code sections comprise the remainder of this service. The sections chosen for inclusion in the historical binders are traced back to their original 1954 Code versions[70]; all changes are presented. [Illustration 25–16] Materials presented for each Code section include presidential messages, committee reports, Treasury Department testimony at hearings, and discussion printed in *Congressional Record*.

The legislative histories are published in five series, each of which covers several years. Within each series, material appears in Code section order. Each Series contains a Master Table of Contents in Code section order. *Primary Sources* began its coverage with Code sections affected by the Tax Reform Act of 1969 (with limited 1954 Act coverage).

[Illustration 25–16]

EXCERPT FROM BNA TAX MANAGEMENT PRIMARY SOURCES

```
IV-26                                                          §168 [1981] pg.(i)
 _____

              SEC. 168 — ACCELERATED COST RECOVERY SYSTEM

                            Table of Contents
                                                                    Page

 STATUTE — [As Added by the Economic Recovery Tax Act of 1981
           (P.L. 97-34)] ...................................... §168 [1981] pg. 1

 LEGISLATIVE HISTORY

     Background
         97th Congress, 1st Sess. (H.R. 3849)
             Treasury Dept. Tech. Explanation of H.R. 3849 ......... §168 [1981] pg. 28

     House of Representatives
         Ways and Means Committee
             Committee Hearings
                 Statement of Donald Regan, Sec'y of Treasury ........ §168 [1981] pg. 34
             Committee Report ................................. §168 [1981] pg. 35

     Senate
         Finance Committee
             Committee Hearings
                 Statement of Donald Regan, Sec'y of Treasury ........ §168 [1981] pg. 43
             Committee Press Releases
                 No. 81-19 (June 24, 1981) ..................... §168 [1981] pg. 44
                 No. 81-21 (June 26, 1981) ..................... §168 [1981] pg. 45
             Committee Report ................................. §168 [1981] pg. 46
         Senate Discussion
             Vol. 127 Cong. Rec. (July 20, 1981) .............. §168 [1981] pg. 55
             Vol. 127 Cong. Rec. (July 23, 1981) .............. §168 [1981] pg. 58
```

[70] Series I also includes the 1939 Code version for each section covered.

4. RIA Cumulative Changes

This multivolume looseleaf service allows a researcher to track changes in the Code and Treasury regulations. There are series for the 1939, 1954, and 1986 Codes and regulations. Many libraries lack the 1939 Code series.

The Code and regulations materials appear separately, arranged in Code section order. The 1954 series contains parallel citation tables for the 1939 and 1954 Codes. This service covers groups of changes every quarter. As a result, some changes may not be immediately included in the service.

a. *Internal Revenue Code.* A chart for each Code section indicates its original effective date. The chart includes the Public Law number, section, enactment and effective dates of each amendment, and the act section prescribing the effective date. The chart is particularly useful because it covers Code section subdivisions (subsections, paragraphs, and even smaller subdivisions). It does not include *Statutes at Large* citations. The tables' format changed slightly in the mid–1990s; citations for effective dates are printed instead of the dates themselves. [Illustration 25–17]

The pages following each chart reproduce each version (except the current one) since the provision's original introduction in the relevant Code. The current version can be found in the *RIA United States Tax Reporter* Code and compilation volumes (Section M) or in any other current Code publication.

b. *Treasury Regulations.* Tables of amendments cover all regulations sections for each tax; individual sections do not have their own charts. The table indicates the original and all amending T.D. numbers and filing dates and provides a *Cumulative Bulletin* or *Internal Revenue Bulletin* citation. Cross-references to *RIA United States Tax Reporter* are also given. A Table of Amending TDs, in T.D. number order, indicates the purpose, date, and *Cumulative Bulletin* or *I.R.B.* citation for each regulation issued under each Code.[71]

The 1954 and 1986 series tables list oddly numbered (e.g., not using the normal prefix designations) regulations last rather than in Code section order. The 1954 series includes tables for regulations that have been redesignated or replaced.

Immediately following the tables, the editors print prior versions of each regulation. Older materials note changes in italics and use footnotes to indicate stricken language; recent materials do not use this format. *Cumulative Changes* includes the T.D. number and the dates of approval and filing for each version.

[71] Although T.D. 6500, a 1960 republication of existing income tax regulations is not formally included, the 1954 CUMULATIVE CHANGES does list the original pre–1960 T.D. A cautionary note warns the user to remember that pre–1960 regulations were republished in T.D. 6500. T.D. 6498 (procedure and administration) and T.D. 6516 (withholding tax) receive similar treatment. None of these T.D.s appears in the CUMULATIVE BULLETIN.

[Illustration 25–17]

EXCERPT FROM RIA CUMULATIVE CHANGES

3-2000   **Sec. 51. Amount of Credit**   **§ 51—p. 3**

[See definitions preceding chart on page 1 of this section.]

SEC. 51 '86 I.R.C.	SUBSECTIONS					
	(f)—(h)	**(i)(1)**	**(i)(2)**	**(i)(3)**	**(j)**	**(k)**
Pub. Law 99-514, 10-22-86				Added by 1701(c) 1701(e)* Note 1		Redesig. 1878(f)(1) 1881* Note 1
AMENDING ACTS						
Pub Law 103-66, 8-10-93		13302(d) 13303* 8-10-93				

Public Law	Law Sec.	IRC Sec.	Eff. Date
P.L. 104-188	1201(a)	51(a)	1201(g)*
	1201(e)(1)	51(a)	1201(g)*
	1201(f)	51(c)(1)	1201(g)*
	1201(d)	51(c)(4)	1201(g)*
	1201(b)	51(d)	1201(g)*
	1201(e)(1)	51(g)	1201(g)*
	1201(c)	51(i)(3)	1201(g)*
	1201(e)(5)	51(j) Heading	1201(g)*
P.L. 105-34	603(b)(2)	51(d)(2)(A)	
	603(c)(2)	51(d)(9)-(11) Redes (10)-(12)	
	603(d)(2)	51(i)(3)	
P.L. 105-277	1002(a)	51(c)(4)(B)	1002(b)
	4006(c)(1)	51(d)(6)(B)(i)	
P.L. 106-170	505(a)	51(c)(4)(B)	505(c)
	505(b)	51(i)(2)	505(c)

☐ Note the change in format for more recent amendments to the Code. As of September 2008, the table for section 51 continued through P.L. 108-311.

5. Barton's Federal Tax Laws Correlated (Federal Tax Press, Inc.)

The six volumes of this set trace income, estate, and gift tax provisions from the Revenue Act of 1913[72] through the Tax Reform Act of 1969.

---

[72] The original Second Edition (vol. 1) also contained the text of the income tax laws from 1861 through 1909. This section was omitted in the Reproduced Second Edition.

The five hardbound volumes reproduce in Code or act section order the text of the various tax acts through 1952. Because the acts are lined up in several columns on each page, a researcher can read across a page and see every enacted version of a particular section for the period that volume covers.[73] Whenever possible, *Barton's* uses different typefaces to highlight changes.

The first two volumes provide a citation to *Statutes at Large* for each act. Volume 1 includes case annotations, and each volume includes a subject matter index. The volumes following the 1939 Code include tables indicating amending acts and effective dates for 1939 Code sections. Volume 5 has a retrospective table cross-referencing sections to pages in the four previous volumes.

The looseleaf sixth volume does not print the text of Code sections. Instead it consists of Tables that provide citations to primary sources where desired material appears. Tables A–D are in Code section order; Table E is in Public Law number order.

Table A provides the history of the 1954 Act. It indicates *Statutes at Large* page; House, Senate, and Conference report page (official and *U.S. Code Congressional & Administrative News*); 1939 Code counterpart; Revenue Act where the provision originated; and relevant pages in volumes 1–5. Table C is similar to Table A, but it covers the 1939 Code. It gives the 1954 Code section; the origin of the 1939 Code provision; and cross-references to volumes 1–5.

Table B covers amendments to the 1954 Code. For each section it provides Public Law number, section, and enactment date; *Statutes at Large* citation; House, Senate, and Conference report numbers and location in the *Cumulative Bulletin*; comment (e.g., revision, amendment); and effective date information. Table D is the same as Table B, but it covers post–1953 changes to the 1939 Code.

Table E provides citations to legislative history for all acts from 1953 through 1969. Table E provides the following information provided for each act: Public Law number; date of enactment; congressional session; *Statutes at Large*, *Cumulative Bulletin*, and *USCCAN* citations for the act; congressional sessions, dates, and *Cumulative Bulletin* and *USCCAN* citations for House, Senate, and Conference report numbers; and *Congressional Record* citations for floor debate. Acts are not cited by popular name.

6. Seidman's Legislative History of Federal Income and Excess Profits Tax Laws[74] (Prentice–Hall)

Although *Seidman's* coverage stops in 1953, it remains useful for determining the legislative history of provisions that originated in the 1939 Code or even earlier.[75] This series follows each act in reverse chronological

---

[73] Volume 1 covers 1913–1924; volume 2 covers 1926–38; volume 3 covers 1939–43; volume 4 covers 1944–49; volume 5 covers 1950–52.

[74] The two volumes covering 1939 through 1953 include both taxes. Separate volumes for the income tax and the excess profits tax were used for the earlier materials, covering 1861 through 1938 and 1917 through 1947, respectively.

[75] I.R.C. § 263, for example, contains language taken almost verbatim from the 1864 Act, § 117. *See* 13 Stat. 282.

order, presenting the text of Code sections, followed by relevant committee reports and citations to hearings[76] and the *Congressional Record*.[77] Because *Seidman's* uses different type styles, a researcher can easily determine where in Congress a particular provision originated or was deleted. [Illustration 25–18]

[Illustration 25–18]

EXCERPT FROM SEIDMAN'S LEGISLATIVE HISTORY OF FEDERAL INCOME TAX LAWS

for key to statute type]	1934 ACT	381

SEC. 164 DIFFERENT TAXABLE YEARS.   Sec. 164

If the taxable year of a beneficiary is different from that of the estate or trust, the amount which he is required, under section 162 (b), to include in computing his net income, shall be based upon the income of the estate or trust for any taxable year of the estate or trust (whether beginning on, before, or after January 1, 1934) ending within his taxable year.

Committee Reports

Report—Ways and Means Committee (73d Cong., 2d Sess., H. Rept. 704).—Section 164. Different taxable years: The present law requires a beneficiary of an estate or trust to include in his income amounts allowed as a deduction to the estate or trust under section 162 (b). In order to continue this policy, it is necessary in view of the policy adopted in section 1 to add additional language to provide for cases where the estate or trust has a taxable year beginning in 1933 and ending in 1934 (p.32)

Report—Senate Finance Committee (73d Cong., 2d Sess., S. Rept. 558).—Same as Ways and Means Committee Report. (p.40)

SEC. 166 REVOCABLE TRUSTS.   Sec. 166

Where at any time (96) <during-the-taxable-year>the power to revest in the grantor title to any part of the corpus of the trust is vested—

Seidman's prints proposed sections that were not enacted along with relevant history explaining their omission. Such information can aid in interpreting those provisions Congress actually adopted. Although its coverage has great breadth, *Seidman's* does not print every Code section. It omits provisions with no legislative history, items lacking substantial interpretative significance, and provisions the editor considered long outmoded. *Seidman's* does not cover gift, estate, or excise taxes.

Seidman's has three indexes and a Code cross-reference table. The Code section index lists each section by act and assigns it a key number. The same key number is assigned to corresponding sections in subsequent acts. The key number index indicates every act, by section number and page in the text, where the item involved appears. A subject index lists key numbers by topic. Volume II of the 1939–1953 set contains a table cross-referencing 1953 and 1954 Code sections covered in *Seidman's*. *Seidman's* is available in the *HeinOnline* service (Section M), which covers legislative history materials in addition to periodicals.

---

[76] SEIDMAN'S cites relevant page numbers in the hearings and indicates appearances by Treasury representatives.

[77] SEIDMAN'S cites to relevant pages and reproduces the text itself in some instances.

7. The Internal Revenue Acts of the United States: 1909–1950; 1950–1972; 1973–(William S. Hein & Co.)

a. *Original Series.* This set, edited by Bernard D. Reams, Jr., provides the most comprehensive legislative histories of all materials discussed in this section. In addition to each congressional version of revenue bills, the 144 original volumes (1909–1950) contain the full texts of hearings, committee reports, Treasury studies, and regulations. Official pagination is retained for relevant documents. In addition to income and excise taxes, this set includes estate and gift, social security, railroad retirement, and unemployment taxes. This set is available in hard copy and microfiche.

An Index volume contains several indexes that a researcher can use in locating relevant materials. [Illustration 25–19] The longest index, which is chronological, lists each act and every item comprising its legislative history. A volume reference is given for each item. Other indexes cover Miscellaneous Subjects, such as hearings on items that did not result in legislation; Treasury studies; Joint Committee reports; regulations; congressional reports; congressional documents; bill numbers; and hearings. Unfortunately, there is neither a Code section nor a subject matter index.

[Illustration 25–19]

EXCERPT FROM THE INTERNAL REVENUE ACTS OF THE UNITED STATES

REVENUE ACT OF 1916	Volume
BILL IN ITS VARIOUS FORMS	
Passed Senate, 64th Cong., 1st session, H.R. 16763. In the House of Representatives. September 6, 1916. Ordered to be printed with the amendments of the Senate numbered	61
SLIP LAW	
Public No. 271, 64th Cong., (H.R. 16763), an act to increase the revenue, and for other purposes. Approved September 8, 1916. 39 Stat. 756	91
REPORTS	
To increase the revenue, and for other purposes, report, H.Rpt. 64-922, July 5, 1916	93

Full text materials appear by type of document rather than by the act involved. All hearings are printed together, as are all bills, laws (accompanied by committee reports), studies, and regulations. The researcher must access several volumes to assemble all materials for a particular law or provision. This is by no means a substantial drawback to using this set; assembling the same materials from elsewhere in the collection (assuming they are all available) would be far more difficult.

b. *Subsequent Series.* Professor Reams subsequently compiled materials to extend this set's coverage to later years. The later volumes are similar in coverage and format to the 1909–50 materials, although hearings receive less attention.

The 1954 volumes include committee reports, hearings, debates, and the final act. Revenue bills and Treasury studies do not appear. Because the IRS *Cumulative Bulletins* do not cover the 1954 Act, these materials are particularly valuable. A two-volume update published in 1993 includes fifty House and Senate bills missing from the original volumes.

Additional sets compiled by Professor Reams cover legislative histories for 1950–51, 1953–72, 1969, 1971, 1975, 1976, 1978, 1980, 1984, 1985 (Balanced Budget), 1986, 1987 (Balanced Budget), 1988, 1990, and 1993 acts. Two other sets, covering the Taxpayer Relief Act of 1997 and the Economic Growth and Tax Relief Reconciliation Act of 2001, were edited by William Manz. Several of these sets are currently available only in microfiche.

8. Eldridge, The United States Internal Revenue System (William S. Hein & Co.)

This reprint of early legislative materials is a useful complement to *Internal Revenue Acts of the United States*, discussed in the immediately preceding paragraphs. It includes texts of revenue acts passed through 1894. There is extensive textual material as well as annotations for the various acts. It also contains a descriptive history of the various acts.

SECTION R. MICROFORMS

As primary and secondary source materials proliferate, many libraries seek alternatives to bound volumes. Microforms provide one option for expanding the collection within space limitations. In addition, libraries may be limited to microform acquisitions for out-of-print materials. Check the library's microform file before abandoning a search for a particular item.

An important caveat is in order. Many publishers that previously offered products in microform format have switched to CD–ROM, DVD, and online services, all of which are easier to navigate. As a result, their microform materials may no longer be current; they do remain valuable for historical research. For example, the *Tax Analysts Microfiche Database* provided access to primary sources and selected commentary. It included full texts of *Tax Notes* and other Tax Analysts publications in addition to primary source materials. Tax Analysts' print publications provided document numbers that facilitated access to the *Microfiche Database*. Tax Analysts now publishes this material on DVD and online instead of in microfiche.

Several government publications remain available in microform. These include *Congressional Record*, *Federal Register*, *Code of Federal Regulations*, IRS *Cumulative Bulletins*, and Tax Court and Supreme Court case reporter services. Many libraries include briefs filed with the United States Supreme Court in their microform collections.

Publishers offering legislative histories in microform include Congressional Information Service (part of LexisNexis) and William S. Hein & Co. Some libraries may own BNA's *Tax Management Primary Sources–Series I* (Section Q) in ultrafiche.

SECTION S. CD–ROMS

Compact discs store significant amounts of information yet require little storage space. Thus, they offer another means for libraries to maintain large amounts of data in a small area. In many areas of research, CD–ROM has supplanted microform as an alternative to print materials. Unfortunately, unless a CD–ROM is networked, only one researcher can use it at a time. In addition, a single CD–ROM has relatively limited capacity. Many publishers have responded to this limitation by publishing in DVD format. Because web-based services allow more than one simultaneous user and have space for significantly more material, they are likely to supplant both CD–ROM and DVD. The paragraphs below list representative titles available in CD–ROM or DVD.

1. Tax Analysts

The *OneDisc Premium* (quarterly or monthly DVD) includes a full array of legislative, administrative and judicial primary source materials.

2. Commerce Clearing House

- *Tax Court Decisions* (monthly)
- *IRS Letter Rulings Reporter* and *IRS Positions* (monthly)
- *Internal Revenue Manual* (periodic)

3. LexisNexis

- *Rhoades and Langer*, U.S. International Taxation and Tax Treaties
- Rabkin & Johnson, *Current Legal Forms*
- *Tax Institutes* (New York University; University of Miami; University of Southern California)

LexisNexis offers many of its publications (e.g., *Murphy's Will Clauses*) on various LexisNexis CD services.

4. Research Institute of America

The *OnPoint* System offers several combinations of sources on DVD. Materials available include primary source, citator, looseleaf service, and treatise materials.

SECTION T. ONLINE LEGAL RESEARCH

Online legal research systems have several useful features. First, they bring the research materials together in one readily accessible location. Libraries with tax alcoves require several rows of shelves to house relevant information; libraries without this arrangement may shelve relevant items on several floors. An online system requires only a computer with Internet access.

The Internet provides a means for communicating both text and graphics anywhere in the world. In addition to primary and secondary source material, Internet sites may include email, blogs, and online discussion groups.

More important than the time saved in gathering the material is the ability to do searches that are virtually impossible to accomplish using print materials. Because the service responds to queries based on words appearing or not appearing in its database, an online system can be used to compile a list of all opinions by a particular judge. Likewise, the computer can quickly locate all decisions rendered in 2008, at every court level, involving the medical expense deduction. Although CD–ROM searches can yield similar results, an online service generally includes far more material than does a single CD–ROM disc.

A variety of services are available on the Internet. Some commercial services include tax materials in a general database. Others focus exclusively on tax materials. Sites that can be accessed without a fee vary in their coverage; they may include data from a variety of sources or may focus on a single type of information. Many of these sites provide online links to relevant materials rather than including the material itself in their databases.

Materials available online are also available in print or on CD–ROM, often from the publisher that makes them available online. Coverage dates for each format may vary, which can affect the researcher's choice of format. Coverage for a source may begin at a later date online than it does in print. This is particularly likely for government websites.

1.　Online Commercial Services—General Focus

Although they do not focus on tax, two commercial services, *LexisNexis* and *Westlaw*, have extensive tax databases.[78] The researcher can customize each by adding a Tax tab to the opening page. These services frequently expand the number of sources and time periods covered. They also delete sources, generally substituting others. Such changes often reflect the parent companies' acquisitions of other publishers.

LexisNexis and *Westlaw* differ slightly in their coverage and in the search terms a researcher would use while online. Both allow the researcher to specify particular words that must appear or be absent in a document; if the words must be in a desired proximity, that limitation may be specified as well. For example, they can be used to locate decisions involving damages within five words of the term personal injury, or for decisions involving damages that do not involve personal injury. Searches can be limited to particular types of authority (e.g., only Tax Court) or to particular dates.

Before formulating a search query, the researcher should become familiar with the search term symbols used on the system being accessed. In addition to each service's explanatory texts, other guides are available for this purpose.

a.　*Westlaw*. The *Westlaw* tax library, FTX–ALL, gives access to virtually every type of primary source material. These materials can also be accessed separately through individual files (e.g., FTX–CSRELS for judicial decisions and IRS material; FTX–CODREG for statutes and regulations).

---

[78] Chapter 23 of this book includes extensive coverage of these and other electronic resources. In some instances (e.g., finding law review articles), *Westlaw* and *LexisNexis* searches should be extended to their non-tax libraries.

Secondary source files cover tax-oriented law reviews, looseleaf services, newsletters, and various materials published by Bureau of National Affairs/Tax Management, Research Institute of America, and Warren, Gorham & Lamont. *Westlaw* includes *RIA Citator 2nd* and West's *KeyCite*. No knowledge of library names is necessary to gain access to the web-based *Westlaw* system. [Illustration 25–20]

   b.   *LexisNexis.* The *LexisNexis* tax library, FEDTAX, is divided into files. The OMNI file gives access to virtually every type of primary source material. These materials can also be accessed separately through individual files (e.g., CASREL for judicial decisions and IRS material; TXLAWS for statutes and regulations). Secondary source files cover tax-oriented law reviews, looseleaf services, newsletters, and various materials published by Matthew Bender, Kleinrock, Tax Analysts, and other publishers. *Shepard's Citations* is part of LexisNexis. No knowledge of library or file names is necessary to gain access to the web-based *LexisNexis* system. [Illustration 25–21]

[Illustration 25–20]

SCREEN PRINT FROM WESTLAW

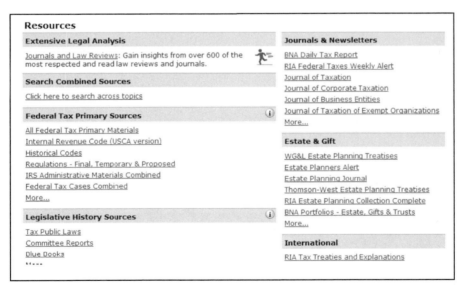

☐ This screen print shows part of the *Westlaw* tax database contents.

[Illustration 25–21]

SCREEN PRINT FROM LEXISNEXIS

Tax Center -Specialized Tax Research Interface

☐ Click to launch LexisNexis® Tax Center ⓘ

Search Tax Services

LexisNexis

Find Federal Statutes & Regulations

☐ USCS-Title 26;Internal Revenue Code Annotated ⓘ

☐ Final & Temporary Regulations ⓘ

☐ Legislative Impact® & Regulatory Impact® ⓘ

Find Legislative History

    View more sources

Find Federal Administrative Materials

☐ IRS Advance Releases ⓘ

☐ IRS Cumulative Bulletin and Internal Revenue Bulletin ⓘ

☐ IRS Private Letter Rulings and Technical Advice Memoranda ⓘ

    View more sources

Access Directories

☐ Martindale-Hubbell(R) Law Directory - Tax Law Listings ⓘ

    View more sources

Search Analysis, Law Reviews & Journals

☐ LexisNexis® Tax Advisor - Federal Topical ⓘ

☐ LexisNexis IRC (Internal Revenue Code) Explanations ⓘ

☐ Rabkin & Johnson, Federal Tax Guidebook ⓘ

☐ Federal Tax Practice and Procedure ⓘ

☐ New York University Annual Institute on Federal Taxation ⓘ

☐ Major Tax Planning-USC Annual Institute on Federal Taxation ⓘ

☐ Tax Controversies: Audits, Investigations, Trials ⓘ

☐ Federal Income Taxation of Corporations Filing Consolidated Returns ⓘ

☐ Tax Planning For Corporations and Shareholders ⓘ

☐ This screen print shows part of the *LexisNexis* tax database contents.

2. Online Subscription Services—Tax Focus

The services listed below provide access to a variety of primary and secondary source materials.

a. *Commerce Clearing House (Wolters Kluwer)*. The *CCH Tax Research NetWork* includes the Code, committee reports, regulations, treaties, IRS materials (including items such as letter rulings and the *Internal Revenue Manual*), and judicial decisions. The service includes *Standard Federal Tax Reporter*, CCH newsletters and journals, the CCH citator, and various practice aids. The service does not include *CCH Federal Tax Articles*. [Illustration 25–22]

b. *Research Institute of America*. Materials from RIA are included on *Westlaw*. RIA's parent (Thomson Reuters) also offers its own service, *Checkpoint*. This service includes the Code, committee reports, regulations, treaties, IRS materials, judicial decisions, *Federal Tax Coordinator 2d*, *United States Tax Reporter*, and the *RIA Citator 2nd*. [Illustration 25–23]

c. *Tax Analysts*. Materials from Tax Analysts are included in *Lexis-Nexis*. Tax Analysts also offers its own subscription-based service, *Federal Research Library*. This service includes the Code, regulations, IRS materials, and judicial decisions. Tax Analysts also offers a web-based treaty service and web-based access to its newsletters.

d. *BNA Tax Management*. Materials from Tax Management are included in *Westlaw*. Tax Management also offers *TaxCore*, which has links from the web-based *Daily Tax Report*. Available sources include the Code, committee reports, testimony at hearings, regulations, IRS materials, and judicial decisions.

e. *Kleinrock*. Kleinrock publications are currently carried on *Lexis-Nexis*. Because Kleinrock has been acquired by Wolters Kluwer, the parent of CCH, it is possible that this situation will change. Kleinrock also offers its own web-based service, *Federal TaxExpert*. This service covers the Code, committee reports, regulations, treaties, IRS materials, and judicial decisions.

[Illustration 25–22]

SCREEN PRINT FROM CCH TAX RESEARCH NETWORK

☐ This screen print shows part of the *CCH Tax Research NetWork* database contents.

[Illustration 25–23]

SCREEN PRINT FROM CHECKPOINT

Choose Sources from: All Federal > Save

Editorial Materials
+ Citator 2nd (RIA)
Federal Tax Handbook (RIA)
+ Federal Tax Coordinator (RIA)
+ Form/Line Finders (RIA)
Tables & Rates (RIA)
+ Tax Alerts (RIA)
Tax Planning and Practice Guides (Special Studies) (RIA)
+ United States Tax Reporter - Annotations (RIA)
+ United States Tax Reporter - Explanations (RIA)

News/Current Awareness
+ Cummings' Corporate Tax Insights (RIA)
+ Federal Taxes Weekly Alert Newsletter (RIA)
+ WG&L Journals

Primary Source Materials
+ Internal Revenue Code, Treasury Regulations, Committee Reports (RIA)
+ Federal Tax Cases (RIA)
IRS Publications (RIA)
+ IRS Rulings and Releases (RIA)
U.S. Tax Treaties in Force (RIA)

Legislation (Editorial Analysis and Source Material)
Complete Analysis of the Tax Provisions of H.R. 1424 (Including the Emergency Economic Stabilization, Energy Improvement and Extension, and Tax Extenders and AMT Relief Acts of 2008)
Complete Analysis of the Housing Assistance Tax Act of 2008
Complete Analysis of the Heartland, Habitat, Harvest, and Horticulture Act of 2008
Complete Analysis of the Heroes Earnings Assistance and Relief Tax Act of 2008
Complete Analysis of the Economic Stimulus Act of 2008

This screen print shows part of the *Checkpoint* database contents.

3. Other Internet Services

There are a variety of useful websites available for tax research. Some provide primary source material directly; others provide hypertext links to other websites; some sites perform both functions. Unfortunately, websites often change address or cease to exist altogether. Thus, a researcher is likely to find links to at least a few nonexistent sites.[79]

The following list, which includes a sampling of these sites, includes the current URL for each site.

a. *Sites Maintained by the Federal Government.* Many government sites also link to each other.

- Internal Revenue Service (http://www.irs.gov)—includes text of tax forms and publications, *Internal Revenue Bulletins*, the *Internal Revenue Manual*, treaties, and IRS releases that are not included in the *I.R.B.* It provides links to *United States Code*, *Code of Federal Regulations*, *Federal Register*, and additional treaty documents. This site could be better-organized; location of the material is not intuitively obvious.

- Treasury Department (http://www.ustreas.gov)—the Office of Tax Policy page provides text for tax treaty materials and Treasury department testimony at congressional hearings; the Office of Tax Analysis page includes analytical reports on tax policy issues.

- Library of Congress (http://thomas.loc.gov)—users can find texts of bills, note the progress of bills in Congress, and gain access to the *Congressional Record* and committee reports.

- House Ways & Means Committee (http://waysandmeans.house.gov), Senate Finance Committee (http://finance.senate.gov), and Joint Committee on Taxation (http://jct.gov)—the first two sites provide information about committee activities, including hearings transcripts; the JCT site provides full text access to reports on proposed and enacted legislation.

- United States Tax Court Home Page (http://ustaxcourt.gov)— provides text of regular, memorandum, and summary opinions. This site can be searched by judge, date, taxpayer name, or words and phrases.

- White House Home Page (http://www.whitehouse.gov)—provides text of presidential speeches, including bill-signing messages.

- Government Printing Office (http://www.gpoaccess.gov)—provides text of, or links to, documents generated by all branches of the federal government.

b. *Other Sites.* The sites below are a sample of those available. Each provides access to a variety of primary and secondary source materials.

- Cornell Law School's *Legal Information Institute* (http://www.law.

- *WashLaw: Legal Research on the Web* (http://www.washlaw.edu)

- *A Taxing Matter* (http://ataxingmatter.blogs.com/tax/)

- *MauledAgain* (http://mauledagain.blogspot.com/)

- *TaxProf Blog* (http://taxprof.typepad.com/)

---

[79] In that case, the correct address might be located by using a general Internet search engine; *see* Chapter 23.

Appendix A

TABLE OF LEGAL ABBREVIATIONS*

Even the legal scholar may occasionally encounter an abbreviation whose complete title is difficult to identify. In such instances, researchers may have to consult a specialized source such as William H. Bryson's *Dictionary of Sigla and Abbreviations to and in Law Books Before 1607* (Buffalo: William S. Hein & Co. 1996); Mary Miles Prince's *Bieber's Dictionary of Legal Abbreviations* (Hein 5th ed. 2001—also on *LexisNexis* in the BIEBLA database); *World Dictionary of Legal Abbreviations,* edited by Igor I. Kavass and Mary Miles Prince (Hein 1991, 4 vols., looseleaf format and irregularly updated—vol. 3 Appx. A includes Bryson's *Dictionary of Sigla*); or Donald Raistrick's *Index to Legal Citations and Abbreviations* (London: Bowker–Saur 2d ed. 1993). Researchers may also need to check Colin Fong and Alan Edward's *Australian and New Zealand Legal Abbreviations* (Sydney: Australian Law Librarians Group, NSW Division 2d ed. 1995).[1] One of the largest listings of periodical abbreviations, including legal periodicals, is *Periodical Title Abbreviations* (Detroit: Thomson Gale 17th ed. 2007). Finally, among the many abbreviations lists on the internet, the most notable list may be the *Cardiff Index to Legal Abbreviations.*[2]

As primary and secondary legal materials continue to proliferate each year, it is extremely difficult to include in one place all their abbreviations and titles. Appendix A is restricted primarily to the English language periodicals, court reports, and looseleaf services that one could expect to find in a large American law library as of December 31, 2008. In addition, Appendix A includes many esoteric and historical citations. This appendix is not presumed to be authoritative in any official sense, but to reflect past and current usage by editors and publishers of English language legal materials. Superseded titles have been retained because they are never out-of-date as possible citations.

This table uses a strictly alphabetical arrangement. The entries for the abbreviation are to be read letter-by-letter and the ampersand is to be read as the word "and."

---

* Daniel W. Martin, Director of the Law Library and Professor of Law, Loyola Law School, Los Angeles, revised and updated this appendix with the assistance of Adriana Dulic, 2001 graduate of Pepperdine University School of Law, and Frank Park, 2008 graduate of Loyola Law School.

[1] http://www.nzlla.org.nz/documents/anzla2ded.pdf.

[2] http://www.legalabbrevs.cardiff.ac.uk/index.jsp.

A

a.	Atlantic Reporter	A.B.A.J.	American Bar Association Journal
A.	Same	A.B.A.Rep.	American Bar Association Reports
a2d	Same, Second Series	A.B.A.Sect.	American Bar Association Section of Insurance, Negligence and Compensation Law Proceedings
A.2d	Same	Ins.N. & C.	
A. & E.	Adolphus & Ellis Queen's Bench (Eng.)	L.Proc.	
A. & E.Ann. Cas.	American & English Annotated Cases	Abb	Abbott's United States Circuit and District Court Reports
A. & E.Anno.	Same		
A. & E.Cas.	Same		
A. & E.Corp. Cas.	American & English Corporation Cases		
A. & E.Corp. Cas. (N.S.)	Same, New Series	Abb.	Same
A. & E.Enc. L. & Pr.	American & English Encyclopedia of Law and Practice	Abbadm	Abbott's Admiralty (U.S.)
		Abb.Adm.	Same
A. & E.Ency.	American & English Encyclopedia of Law	Abb.App.Dec.	Abbott's Appeal Decisions (NY)
		Abb.Dec.	Abbott's Decisions (NY)
A. & E.Ency. Law	Same	Abb.Dict.	Abbott's Dictionary
A. & E.P. & P.	American & English Pleading and Practice	Abb.N.Cas.	Abbott's New Cases (NY)
		Abb.Prac.	Abbott's Practice (NY)
A. & E.R.Cas.	American & English Railroad Cases	Abb.Prac. N.S.	Same, New Series
A. & E.R.Cas. (N.S.)	Same, New Series	Abb.R.P.S.	Abbott's Real Property Statutes (WA)
A. & E.R.R. Cas.	American & English Railroad Cases	A.B.C.Newsl.	International Association of Accident Boards and Commissions Newsletter
A. & E.R.R. Cas. (N.S.)	Same, New Series		
AB	American Bankruptcy Reports Assembly Bill (CA)	AbD	Abbott's Court of Appeals Decisions (NY)
A.B.	Anonymous Reports at end of Benloe, or Bendloe (Eng.)	A'Beck.Res. Judgm.	A'Beckett's Reserved Judgments (Vict.)
		A.B.F.Research Reptr.	American Bar Foundation Research Reporter
A.B.A. Canon	American Bar Association Canons of Judicial Ethics		
		A.B.F.Res.J.	American Bar Foundation Research Journal
A.B.A. Code	American Bar Association Code of Professional Responsibility		
		AbN.	Abstracts, Treasury Decisions, New Series
A.B.A. Code, DR	American Bar Association Code of Professional Responsibility (Disciplinary Rules)	ABn	American Bankruptcy Reports, New Series
		Abogada Int'l	Abogada Internacional
A.B.A. Code, EC	American Bar Association Code of Professional Responsibility (Ethical Considerations)	AbPn	Abbott's Practice Reports, New Series
		Abr	Halsbury's Abridgment

Abs.	Abstracts, Treasury Decisions	adcbna	American with Disabilities Cases (BNA)
	Ohio Law Abstract	ADCBNA	Same
Abstr.Crim. & Pen.	Abstracts on Criminology and Penology	Ad.Ct.Dig.	Administrative Court Digest
AC	American Annotated Cases	Add.	Addison's Reports (PA)
A.C.	Advance California Reports	Add.Eccl.Rep.	Addams' Ecclesiastical Reports (Eng.)
	Appeal Cases (Can.)	addison	Addison Reports (PA)
	Law Reports Appeal Cases (Eng.)	Add.Penn.	Addison (PA)
ACA	Assembly Constitutional Amendment (CA)	Add.Rep.	Same
		Adel.L.Rev.	Adelaide Law Review
A.C.A.	Advance California Appellate Reports	Ad.L.	Pike and Fischer, Administrative Law
Acad.Pol.Sci. Proc.	Academy of Political Science Proceedings	Ad.L.2d	Same, Second Series
		Ad.L.Bull.	Administrative Law Bulletin
Acct. for L. Firms	Accounting for Law Firms	Ad.L.News	Administrative Law News
A.C.L.U.Leg. Action Bull.	American Civil Liberties Union Legislative Action Bulletin	Ad.L.Newsl.	Administrative Law Newsletter
		Ad.L.Rev.	Administrative Law Review
ACR	Assembly Concurrent Resolution (CA)	Adm. & Ecc.	Admiralty & Ecclesiastical (Eng.)
A.C.R.	American Criminal Reports	Adm. C.	California Administrative Code
Act.	Acton Prize Cases, Privy Council (Eng.)	Admin. L.J.	Administrative Law Journal
		Admin.L.J. Am.U.	Administrative Law Journal of the American University
Acta Cancelariae	English Chancery Reports		
Acta Crim.	Acta Criminologica	Admin.L.Rev.	Administrative Law Review
Acta Jur.	Acta Juridica	Adm Rules	Rules Regulating Admission to Practice Law in California
Acton	Acton Prize Cases, Privy Council (Eng.)		
ACTR	Australian Capital Territory Reports	ADRLJ	Arbitration and Dispute Resolution Law Journal
ad	Appellate Division Reports (NY)		
AD	American Decisions	Advocates' Q.	Advocates' Quarterly
A.D.	Same	advsheets	Massachusetts Advance Sheets
ad2d	Appellate Division Reports, Second Series (NY)	A/E Legal Newsl.	A/E Legal Newsletter
Adams	Adams (ME)	AELE Legal Liab.Rep.	AELE Legal Liability Reporter
	Adams (NH)		
Ad. & El.	Adolphus & Ellis, Queen's Bench (Eng.)	A.F.L.Rev.	Air Force Law Review
		Afr. J. Int'l L.	African Journal of International Law
Ad. & El. (N.S.)	Same, New Series	Afr.L.Dig.	African Law Digest
ADC	U.S. Court of Appeals for the District of Columbia Reports	Afr.L.R.	African Law Reports
		Afr.L.R., Mal. Ser.	African Law Reports, Malawi Series

Afr.L.R., Sierre L.Ser.	African Law Reports, Sierre Leone Series	Ala.St.B. Found. Bull.	Alabama State Bar Foundation Bulletin
Afr.L.Stud.	African Law Studies	Alb	Albany Law Review
aftr	American Federal Tax Reports	Albany L.Rev.	Same
		Alb.L.J.	Albany Law Journal
AFTR	Same	Alb.L.J.Sci. & Tech.	Albany Law Journal of Science and Technology
aftr2d	Same, Second Series		
AFTR2d	Same	Alb.L.Rev.	Albany Law Review
Agric. C.	Agricultural Code (renamed Food and Agricultural Code) (CA)	Albuquerque B.J.	Albuquerque Bar Journal
		Alc. & N.	Alcock & Napier, King's Bench (Ir.)
Agric.Dec.	Agriculture Decisions	Alcohol. Treat.Q.	Alcoholism Treatment Quarterly
Agric.L.J.	Agriculture Law Journal	Alc.Reg.Cas.	Alcock Registry Cases (Ir.)
A.I.D.	Accident/Injury/Damages	Ald.	Alden's Condensed Reports (PA)
AIDS L. Rep.	AIDS Law Reporter	Aleyn	Aleyn, King's Bench (Eng.)
AIDS L.Rev. Q.	AIDS Law Review Quarterly		
AIDS Litigation Rep.	AIDS Litigation Reporter	AlF	Alaska Federal Reports
aik	Aiken's Reports (VT)	A.L.I.	American Law Institute
Aik.	Same		
A.I.L.C.	American International Law Cases 1783–1968	ALI–ABA CLE Rev.	American Law Institute–American Bar Association–Continuing Legal Education Review
Air & Space L.	Air and Space Law		
Air L.	Air Law		
Air L.Rev.	Air Law Review	Alison Pr.	Alison Practice (Scot.)
AJ	Assembly Daily Journal (CA)	ALJ	Australian Law Journal
AJB	Assembly Joint Resolution (CA)	ALJR	Australian Law Journal Reports
AkA	Arkansas Appellate Reports	Allen	Allen's Reports (MA)
A.K.Marsh.	A.K. Marshall (KY)	Allen N.B.	Allen (N.B.)
Akron L.Rev.	Akron Law Review	All E.R.	All England Law Reports
Akron Tax J.	Akron Tax Journal		
ala	Alabama Reporter	All ER (EC)	All England Law Reports European Cases
Ala.	Alabama Appellate Reports		
alaapp	Alabama Appellate Court Reports	All India Crim. Dec.	All India Criminal Decisions
Ala.App.	Alabama Court of Appeals	All India Rptr.	All India Reporter
Ala.Law.	Alabama Lawyer	Allinson	Allinson, Pa. Superior District Courts
Ala.L.J.	Alabama Law Journal		
Ala.L.Rev.	Alabama Law Review	All N.L.R.	All Nigeria Law Reports
Ala.Sel.Cas.	Alabama Select Cases	All Pak.Leg. Dec.	All Pakistan Legal Decisions
alaska	Alaska Reports	Alr	American Law Reports
Alaska	Same		
Alaska B.Brief	Alaska Bar Brief	ALR	Australian Law Reports
Alaska B.J.	Alaska Bar Journal	A.L.R.	American Law Reports
Alaska L.J.	Alaska Law Journal		
Alaska L.Rev.	Alaska Law Review	Alr(2d)	Same, Second Series

A.L.R.2d	Same
A.L.R.3d	Same, Third Series
A.L.R.4th	Same, Fourth Series
A.L.R.5th	Same, Fifth Series
A.L.Rec.	American Law Record
A.L.Reg. (N.S.)	American Law Register, New Series
A.L.Reg. (O.S.)	Same, Old Series
A.L.R.Fed.	American Law Reports Federal
Alta.	Alberta Law Reports
Alta.L.	Alberta Law
Alta.L.Q.	Alberta Law Quarterly
Alta.L.Rev.	Alberta Law Review
Am.Acad. Matri.Law. J.	American Academy of Matrimonial Lawyers Journal
Am. & E. Corp. Cas.	American & English Corporation Cases
Am. & E. Corp. Cas. (N.S.)	Same, New Series
Am. & Eng. Ann.Cas.	American & English Annotated Cases
Am. & Eng. Eq.D.	American & English Decisions in Equity
Am. & Eng. Pat. Cas.	American & English Patent Cases
Am. & E.R. Cas.	American & English Railroad Cases
Am. & E.R. Cas. (N.S.)	Same, New Series
A.M. & O.	Armstrong, Macartney & Ogle Nisi Prius (Ir.)
Amb.	Ambler, Chancery (Eng.)
Am.Bankr. L.J.	American Bankruptcy Law Journal
Am.Bankr. Reg.	American Bankruptcy Register
Am.Bankr. Rep.	American Bankruptcy Reports
Am.Bankr. Rev.	American Bankruptcy Review
Am.B.Found. Res.J.	American Bar Foundation Research Journal
Am.B.News	American Bar News
Am.B.R. (N.S.)	American Bankruptcy Reports, New Series
Am.Bus.L.J.	American Business Law Journal
amc	American Maritime Cases
A.M.C.	Same
Am.Corp.Cas.	American Corporation Cases
Am.Cr.	American Criminal Reports
Am.Crim. L.Q.	American Criminal Law Quarterly
Am.Crim. L.Rev.	American Criminal Law Review
amdd	Americans with Disabilities Decisions (LCP)
Am.Dec.	American Decisions
Am.Elect. Cas.	American Electrical Cases
Ames	Ames (MN)
	Ames (RI)
Ames K. & B.	Ames, Knowles & Bradley (RI)
Am.Fed.Tax R.	American Federal Tax Reports
Am.Fed.Tax R.2d	Same, Second Series
Am.For.L. Ass'n Newsl.	American Foreign Law Association Newsletter
Am.Hist.Rev.	American Historical Review
Amicus	Amicus (South Bend, IN)
	Amicus (Thousand Oaks, CA)
Am.Indian L.Rev.	American Indian Law Review
Am. Ind.J.	American Indian Journal
Am.Ind.L. Newsl.	American Indian Law Newsletter
Am.Insolv. Rep.	American Insolvency Reports
Am.J.Comp. L.	American Journal of Comparative Law
Am.J.Crim. L.	American Journal of Criminal Law
Am.J.Fam. L.	American Journal of Family Law
Am.J.For.Psych.	American Journal of Forensic Psychiatry
Am.J.Int'l Arb.	American Journal of International Arbitration
Am.J.Int'l L.	American Journal of International Law
Am.J.Juris.	American Journal of Jurisprudence
Am.J.L. & Med.	American Journal of Law and Medicine
Am.J.Legal Hist.	American Journal of Legal History
Am.J.Police Sci.	American Journal of Police Science

Am.J.Tax Pol'y	American Journal of Tax Policy	Am.Railw. Cas.	American Railway Cases (Smith & Bates)
Am.J.Trial Advoc.	American Journal of Trial Advocacy	Am.R. & Corp.	American Railroad Corporation
Am.Jur.	American Jurisprudence	Am.Rep.	American Reports
	American Jurist	Am.R.Rep.	American Railway Reports
Am.Jur.2d	American Jurisprudence, Second Series	Am.Ry.Rep.	American Railway Reports
Am.Lab.Leg. Rev.	American Labor Legislation Review	Am.Soc'y Int'l L.Proc.	American Society of International Law Proceedings
Am.Law.	American Lawyer	Am.St.R.	American State Reports
Am.Law Rec.	American Law Record (OH)	Am.St.R.D.	American Street Railway Decisions
Am.Law Reg.	American Law Register	Am.St.Rep.	American State Reports
Am.L.Ins.	American Law Institute	Am.Trial Law.J.	American Trial Lawyers Journal
Am.L.J.	American Law Journal (OH)	Am.Trial Law. L.J.	American Trial Lawyers Law Journal
	American Law Journal (PA)	Am.Tr.M. Cas.	American Trademark Cases (Cox)
Am.L.J. (N.S.)	Same, New Series	Am.U.Intra. L.Rev.	American University Intramural Law Review
Am.L.Mag.	American Law Magazine	Am.U.J. Gender & L.	American University Journal of Gender and the Law
Am.L.Rec.	American Law Record (OH)		
Am.L.Reg.	American Law Register	Am.U.J.Int'l L. & Pol'y	American University Journal of International Law and Policy
Am.L.Reg. (N.S.)	Same, New Series		
Am.L.Reg. (O.S.)	Same, Old Series	Am.U.L.Rev.	American University Law Review
Am.L.Rev.	American Law Review	AN	Abbott's New Cases
Am.L.Sch. Rev.	American Law School Review	An.B.	Anonymous Reports at end of Benloe, or Bendloe (Eng.)
Am. L. T.	American Law Times United States Courts	AnC	New York Annotated Cases
Am.L.T. Bankr.	American Law Times Bankruptcy Reports	And.	Anderson, Common Pleas (Eng.)
Am.Mar.Cas.	American Maritime Cases	Anderson 2d; 3d	Anderson Uniform Commercial Code (2d and 3d ed.)
Am.Negl.Cas.	American Negligence Cases	Anderson Legal Forms 2d	Anderson Legal Forms (2d ed.)
Am.Negl.Rep.	American Negligence Reports	Anderson P.P. Forms 2d	Anderson Pleading and Practice Forms (2d ed.)
Am.Notary	American Notary		
Am.Pol.Sci. Rev.	American Political Science Review	Andr.	Andrews, King's Bench (Eng.)
Am.Prob.	American Probate Reports	Ang.	Angell (RI)
		Ang. & Dur.	Angell & Durfee (RI)
Am.Prob. (N.S.)	Same, New Series	Anglo–Am.L. Rev.	Anglo–American Law Review
Am.Pr.Rep.	American Practice Reports (DC)	Animal Rights L.Rep.	Animal Rights Law Reporter
Am.R.	American Reports		

Ann.	Annaly's Hardwicke King's Bench (Eng.)
Annals	Annals of the American Academy of Political and Social Science
Annals Air & Space	Annals of Air and Space Law
Annaly	Annaly's Hardwicke King's Bench (Eng.)
Ann.Cas.	American Annotated Cases
Ann.Dig.	Annual Digest and Reports of International Law Cases
Ann.Indus. Prop.L.	Annual of Industrial Property Law
Ann.Leg. Forms Mag.	Annotated Legal Forms Magazine
Ann.L.Reg. U.S.	Annual Law Register of the United States
Ann.Rev.Int'l Aff.	Annual Review of International Affairs
Ann.Surv. Afr.L.	Annual Survey of African Law
Ann.Surv. Am.L.	Annual Survey of American Law
Ann.Surv. Banking L.	Annual Survey of Banking Law
Ann.Surv. Colo.L.	Annual Survey of Colorado Law
Ann.Surv. Commonw. L.	Annual Survey of Commonwealth Law
Ann.Surv. Ind.L.	Annual Survey of Indian Law
Ann.Surv. S.Afr.L.	Annual Survey of South African Law
Ann.Tax Cas.	Annotated Tax Cases
anp	Anthon's Nisi Prius Cases
anp2	Same, Second Series
Anst.	Ansthruther, Exchequer (Eng.)
Anth.N.P.	Anthon's Nisi Prius (NY)
Antitrust Bull.	Antitrust Bulletin
Antitrust L. & Econ.Rev.	Antitrust Law and Economics Review
Antitrust L.J.	Antitrust Law Journal
Antitrust L.Sym.	Antitrust Law Symposium
AntNP	Anthon's Nisi Prius Cases(NY)
AntNP2d	Same, Second Series

AOA	Anderson's Ohio Appellate Unreported Decisions
A.O.C.Newsl.	Administrative Office of the Courts Newsletter
ApDC	Court of Appeals for District of Columbia
APLA Q.J.	American Patent Law Association Quarterly Journal
App.	Appleton (ME) California District Courts of Appeal
App.Cas.	Law Reports, Appeal Cases (Eng.)
App.Cas.2d	Same, Second Series
App.Court Ad. Rev.	Appellate Court Administration Review
appdc	Appeal Cases (DC)
App.D.C.	Same
App.Div.	Appellate Division (NY)
App.Div.2d	Same, Second Series
App.N.Z.	Appeal Reports (N.Z.)
App.R.N.Z.	Same, Second Series
App.Rep.Ont.	Ontario Appeal Reports
A.P.R.	Atlantic Provinces Reports
AR	American Reports
A.R.	Alberta Reports
Arb.J.	Arbitration Journal
Arb.J. (N.S.)	Same, New Series
Arb.J. (O.S.)	Same, Old Series
Arb.L.Dig.	Arbitration Law: A Digest of Court Decisions
A.R.C.	American Ruling Cases
Archer	Archer (FL)
Archer & H.	Archer & Hogue (FL)
Argus L.R.	Argus Law Reports (Austl.)
ariz	Arizona Reports
Ariz.	Same
arizadvrep	Arizona Advance Reports
arizapp	Arizona Appeals Reports
Ariz.App.	Same
Ariz.B.J.	Arizona Bar Journal
Ariz.J.Int'l & Comp.L.	Arizona Journal of International and Comparative Law
Ariz.Law.	Arizona Lawyer
Ariz.L.Rev.	Arizona Law Review

Ariz.St.L.J.	Arizona State Law Journal	At	Atlantic Reporter
ark	Arkansas Reports	A.T.	Alcohol Tax Unit (I.R.B.)
Ark.	Same	Ateneo L.J.	Ateneo Law Journal
arkapp	Arkansas Court of Appeals Reports	Atk.	Atkyns, Chancery (Eng.)
Ark.Just.	Arkley's Justiciary (Scot.)	Atl.	Atlantic Reporter
Ark.L.J.	Arkansas Law Journal	A.T.L.A.J.	American Trial Lawyers Association Journal
Ark.Law.	Arkansas Lawyer	ATLA L.J.	Journal of the Association of Trial Lawyers of America
Ark.Law.Q.	Arkansas Lawyer Quarterly		
Ark.L.Rev.	Arkansas Law Review		
A.R.M.	Appeals & Review Memorandum Committee (I.R.B.)	Atom.Energy L.J.	Atomic Energy Law Journal
		Att'y Gen.	Attorney General
Armour	Queen's Bench, Manitoba Tempere Wood, by Armour	Att'y Gen.L.J.	Attorney General's Law Journal
		Att'y Gen.Rep.	United States Attorneys General's Reports
Arms.Con. Elec.	Armstrong's Contested Elections (NY)		
		Atwater	Atwater (MN)
Army Law.	Army Lawyer	Auckland U.L.Rev.	Auckland University Law Review
Arn.	Arnold, Common Pleas (Eng.)	Aust.Jur.	Australian Jurist
Arn. & H.	Arnold & Hodges, Queen's Bench (Eng.)	Austl. & N.Z. J.Crim.	Australian and New Zealand Journal of Criminology
Arnold	Arnold, Common Pleas (Eng.)	Austl.Argus L.R.	Australian Argus Law Reports
A.R.R.	Appeals & Review Recommendation (I.R.B.)	Austl.Bankr. Cas.	Australian Bankruptcy Cases
		Austl.Bus. L.Rev.	Australian Business Law Review
Art.	Article		
Art & L.	Art and the Law	Austl.Com.J.	Australian Commercial Journal
AS	American State Reports	Austl.Convey. & Sol.J.	Australian Conveyancer and Solicitors Journal
	Annual Survey of American Law		
A.S.A.Newsl.	Association for the Study of Abortion Newsletter	Austl.Current L.Rev.	Australian Current Law Review
		Austl.J.For. Sci.	Australian Journal of Forensic Sciences
Ashm.	Ashmead (PA)		
Asian Comp. L.Rev.	Asian Comparative Law Review		
Asian Pac. Comm.Law.	Asian Pacific Commercial Lawyer	Austl.J.L. Soc'y	Australian Journal of Law and Society
ASILS Int'l L.J.	Association of Student International Law Society's International Law Journal	Austl.Jr.	Australian Jurist
		Austl.L.J.	Australian Law Journal
		Austl.L.J. Rep.	Australian Law Journal Reports
Aspin.	Aspinall's Maritime Cases (Eng.)	Aust.L.T.	Australian Law Times
A.S.R.	American State Reports	Austl.L. Times	Australian Law Times
Ass'n Trial Law.Am. Newsl.	Association of Trial Lawyers of America Newsletter	Austl.Law.	Australian Lawyer
		Austl.Tax	Australian Tax Decisions

Austl.Tax Rev.	Australian Tax Review	Av.Cas.	Aviation Cases
Austl.Y.B. Int'l L.	Australian Yearbook of International Law	Av.L.Rep.	Aviation Law Reporter (CCH)
Austr.C.L.R.	Commonwealth Law Reports, Australia	AVMA	AVMA Medical & Legal Journal
Auto.Cas.	Automobile Cases	Az	Arizona Reports
Auto.Cas.2d	Same, Second Series	AzA	Arizona Court of Appeals Reports
Auto.L.Rep.	Automobile Law Reporter (CCH)		

B

B.	Weekly Law Bulletin	B. & A.	Barnewall & Alderson, King's Bench (Eng.)
Bac.Abr.	Bacon's Abridgment (Eng.)		
Bag. & Har.	Bagley & Harman (CA)	Ban. & A.	Banning & Arden, Patent Cases (U.S.)
Bagl.	Bagley (CA)		
Bagl. & H.	Bagley & Harman (CA)	B. & Ad.	Barnewall & Adolphus, King's Bench (Eng.)
Bail Ct.Cas.	Lowndes & Maxwell, Bail Court Cases (Eng.)	B. & Ald.	Barnewall & Alderson, King's Bench (Eng.)
Baild.	Baildon's Select Cases in Chancery (Eng.)	B. & Arn.	Barron & Arnold, Election Cases (Eng.)
Bail.Eq.	Bailey's Equity (SC)	B. & Aust.	Barron & Austin Election Cases (Eng.)
Bailey	Bailey's Law (SC)		
BAJI	California Jury Instructions, Civil (7th rev. ed.)	B. & B.	Ball & Beatty's Chancery (Ir.)
Bal.Ann. Codes	Ballinger's Annotated Codes & Statutes (WA)		Broderip & Bingham, Common Pleas (Eng.)
Bal.Pay't Rep.	Balance of Payments Reports (CCH)	B. & C.	Barnewall & Cresswell's King's Bench (Eng.)
baldw	Baldwin's United States Circuit Court Reports	B. & C.R.	Reports of Bankruptcy & Companies Winding up Cases (Eng.)
Baldw.	Baldwin (U.S.)		
Balf.Pr.	Balfour's Practice (Scot.)	B. & D.	Benloe & Dalison, Common Pleas (Eng.)
Ball & B.	Ball & Beatty, Chancery (Ir.)	B. & F.	Broderip & Freemantle's Ecclesiastical (Eng.)
Ballantine	Ballantine & Sterling, California Corporation Laws (4th ed.)	B. & H.Cr. Cas.	Bennet & Heard's Criminal Cases (Eng.)
Balt.L.T.	Baltimore Law Transcript	B. & H.Crim. Cas.	Same
bamsl	Bankruptcy Reporter by Bar Association of Metropolitan St. Louis	B. & Macn.	Brown & Macnamara, Railway Cases (Eng.)
bana	Banning & Arden's Patent Cases	B. & P.	Bosanquet & Puller, Common Pleas (Eng.)

B & PC	Business and Professions Code (CA)	Barnes	Barnes, Practice Cases (Eng.)
B. & P.N.R.	Bosanquet & Puller's New Reports (Eng.)	Barnes' Notes	Barnes' Notes (Eng.)
		Barnet	Barnet, Common Pleas (Eng.)
B. & S.	Best & Smith, Queen's Bench (Eng.)	Barr	Barr (PA)
		Barr.Ch.Pr.	Barroll, Chancery Practice (MD)
Bank. & Ins.R.	Bankruptcy & Insolvency Reports (Eng.)	Bar Regs	Rules and Regulations of State Bar
Bank C	Banking Code (CA)	Barrister	Barrister (Chicago)
Bank.Cas.	Banking Cases		Barrister (Coral Gables, FL)
Bank.Ct.Rep.	Bankrupt Court Reports		Barrister (Davis, CA)
Banking L.J.	Banking Law Journal		Barrister (Fort Lauderdale, FL)
Banking L. Rev.	Banking Law Review		Barrister (Toronto)
Bankr.B.Bull.	Bankruptcy Bar Bulletin	Barr.MSS.	Barradall, Manuscript Reports (VA)
Bankr.Dev.J.	Bankruptcy Developments Journal	Bart.Elec. Cas.	Bartlett's Election Cases
Bankr.L.Rep.	Bankruptcy Law Reporter (CCH)	Bates Ch.	Bates, Chancery (DE)
Bankr.Reg.	National Bankruptcy Register (NY)	Batty	Batty, King's Bench (Ir.)
Banks	Banks (KS)	Baxt.	Baxter (TN)
Bann.	Bannister's Common Pleas (Eng.)	baxttn	Same
		Bay	Bay (MO)
Bann. & A.	Banning & Arden, Patent Cases (U.S.)		Bay (SC)
		Baylor L.Rev.	Baylor Law Review
Bann. & Ard.	Same	B.Bull.	Bar Bulletin
Bar	Barbour's Supreme Court Reports (NY)	B.C.	British Columbia
		bca	Board of Contract Appeals Decisions (U.S.)
Bar. & Arn.	Barron & Arnold, Election Cases (Eng.)	B.C.Branch Lec.	Canadian Bar Association, British Columbia Branch Meeting Program Reports
Bar. & Aust.	Barron & Austin, Election Cases (Eng.)		
Barb.	Barber (AR)	B.C.C.	Bail Court Cases (Eng.)
	Barbour (NY)	bcd	Bankruptcy Court Decisions
Barb.Ch.	Barbour's Chancery (NY)	BCD	Same
Barber	Barber (NY)	B.C.Envtl. Aff. L.Rev.	Boston College Environmental Affairs Law Review
Barn.	Barnardiston, King's Bench (Eng.)		
Barn. & Ad.	Barnewall & Adolphus, King's Bench (Eng.)	BCh	Barbour's Chancery Reports (NY)
Barn. & Ald.	Barnewall & Alderson, King's Bench (Eng.)	B.C.Indus. & Com.L.Rev.	Boston College Industrial and Commercial Law Review
Barn. & C.	Barnewall & Cresswell, King's Bench (Eng.)		
Barn. & Cress.	Same	B.C.Int'l & Comp.L.J.	Boston College International and Comparative Law Journal
Barn.Ch.	Barnardiston, Chancery (Eng.)		

B.C. Int'l & Comp. L. Rev.	Boston College International and Comparative Law Review	Bell H.L.	Bell's Appeal Cases, House of Lords (Scot.)
BCLC	Butterworths Company Law Cases	Bell P.C.	Bell's Parliament Cases (Scot.)
B.C.L. Notes	British Columbia Law Notes	Bell Sc.Cas.	Bell's Scotch Court of Sessions Cases
B.C.L.Rev.	Boston College Law Review	Bell Ses.Cas.	Same
bcr	Bankruptcy Court Reporter (CO)	ben	Benedict's District Court Reporter
BCR	Same	Ben.	Same
B.C. Third World L.J.	Boston College Third World Law Journal	Ben. & H.L.C.	Bennett & Heard, Leading Criminal Cases (Eng.)
B.D. & O.	Blackham, Dundas & Osborne, Nisi Prius (Ir.)	Bendl.	Bendloe's English Common Pleas
Beale	Beale, The Conflict of Laws	Bened.	Benedict (U.S. District Court)
Beasl.	Beasley (NJ)	Benl.	Benloe's Common Pleas (Eng.)
Beav.	Beavan, Rolls Court (Eng.)		Benloe's King's Bench (Eng.)
Beav. & W. Ry. Cas.	Beavan & Walford's Railway & Canal Cases (Eng.)	Benl. & D.	Benloe & Dalison, Common Pleas (Eng.)
Beav.R. & C.Cas.	Beavan, Railway & Canal Cases (Eng.)	Benl. & Dal.	Same
		Benl.K.B.	Benloe's King's Bench (Eng.)
Beaw.Lex Mer.	Beawes Lex Mercatoria (Eng.)	Benl.Old	Benloe, Old English Common Pleas
Bee	Bee's (U.S.)	Benn.	Bennett (CA)
Bee Adm.	Bee's Admiralty, United States District Court (SC)		Bennett (Dakota) Bennett (MO)
		Bent.	Bentley's Chancery (Ir.)
Bee C.C.R.	Bee's Crown Cases Reserved (Eng.)	Berkeley Women's L.J.	Berkeley Women's Law Journal
Behav.Sci. & L.	Behavioral Sciences and the Law	Berry	Berry (MO)
Belg.Rev.Int'l L.	Belgian Review of International Law	Bev Hills BJ	Beverly Hills Bar Journal
Bell.	Bellewe, King's Bench (Eng.)	B.Exam.	Bar Examiner
		B.Exam.J.	Bar Examination Journal
Bell App.Cas.	Bell's Appeal Cases, House of Lords (Scot.)	bibb	Bibb (KY)
		Bibb	Same
		Bibl.Cott.	Cotton Manuscripts
Bell Cas.	Bell's Cases (Scot.)	B.I.C.I.L. Newsl.	British Institute of International and Comparative Law Newsletter
Bell.Cas.t.H. VIII	Bellewe, King's Bench, tempore Henry VIII (Eng.)		
Bell.Cas.t.R. II	Same, tempore Richard II (Eng.)	Bick.	Bicknell (NV)
Bell C.C.	Bell's Crown Cases Reserved (Eng.)	Bick. & H.	Bicknell & Hawley (NV)
Bell Comm.	Bell's Commentaries (Eng.)	Big.Ov.Cas.	Bigelow's Overruled Cases
Bell Cr.C.	Bell's Crown Cases Reserved (Eng.)	B.I.L.C.	British International Law Cases
Bellewe (Eng.)	Bellewe, King's Bench	Bill Rights J.	Bill of Rights Journal
		Bill Rights Rev.	Bill of Rights Review

Bin	Binney's Reports (PA)	Blake & H.	Blake & Hedge (MT)
Bing.	Bingham, New Cases, Common Pleas (Eng.)	Bland	Bland's Chancery Reports (MD)
binn	Binney's Reports (PA)	blandch	Same
		blatch	Blatchford's U.S. Circuit Court Reports
Binn.	Same		
biss	Bissell's U.S. Circuit Court Reports	Blatchf.	Blatchford (U.S.)
		Blatchf. & H.	Blatchford & Howland (U.S. District Court)
Biss.	Same		
Bitt.Rep. in Ch.	Bittleson's Reports, Queen's Bench (Eng.)	Blatchf.Prize Cas.	Blatchford's Prize Cases (U.S.)
		Bla.W.	William Blackstone's King's Bench (Eng.)
Bitt.W. & P.	Bittleson, Wise & Parnell Practice Cases (Eng.)		
Bk.	Black (U.S.)	B.Leader	Bar Leader
Bl.	William Blackstone's King's Bench (Eng.)	Bleckley	Bleckley (GA)
		blh	Blatchford & Howland (U.S. District Court)
Bla.	Same		
black	Black's U.S. Supreme Court Reporter	Bl.H.	Henry Blackstone's Common Pleas (Eng.)
Black	Black (IN) Black (U.S.) Blackford's Reports (IN)	Bli.	Bligh, House of Lords (Eng.)
		Bli. (N.S.)	Same, New Series
		Bligh	Same
Black.	William Blackstone's King's Bench (Eng.)	Bligh (N.S.)	Same, New Series
		Bliss	Bliss, Delaware County Reports (PA)
Black.Cond.	Blackwell's Condensed Reports (IL)		
		BLR	Building Law Reports
Black.Cond. Rep.	Same	BLRev	Business Law Review
Black.D. & O.	Blackham, Dandas & Osborne, Nisi Prius (Ir.)	Blue Sky L.Rep.	Blue Sky Law Reporter (CCH)
		Bluett	Bluett's Isle of Man Cases
blackf	Blackford's Reports (IN)		
Blackf.	Blackford (IN)	Bl.W.	William Blackstone's King's Bench (Eng.)
Black.H.	Henry Blackstone's Common Pleas (Eng.)		
		BMLR	Butterworths Medico–Legal Reports
Black.Jus.	Blackerby's Justices' Cases (Eng.)	B.Mon.	Ben Monroe (KY)
Black L.J.	Black Law Journal	BNA	Bureau of National Affairs
Blackst.R.	William Blackstone's King's Bench (Eng.)	BNA Banking Rep.	BNA's Banking Report
Blackw.Cond.	Blackwell's Condensed Reports (IL)	BNA Sec.Reg.	Securities Regulation & Law Report
Bla.H.	Henry Blackstone's Common Pleas (Eng.)	Bogert	Bogert, The Law of Trusts and Trustees (2d ed.)
Blair Co.	Blair County Law Reports (PA)	Bombay L.J.	Bombay Law Journal
		bond	Bond's U.S. Circuit Court Reports
Blake	Blake (MT)	Bond	Same

Book of Judg.	Book of Judgments (Eng.)
Boor.	Booraem (CA)
Bos	Bosworth's Reports (NY)
Bos.	Bosworth, Superior Court (NY)
Bos. & P.	Bosanquet & Puller, Common Pleas (Eng.)
Bos. & P. N.R.	Same
Bos. & Pul.	Same
Bos.Pol.Rep.	Boston Police Reports
Bost.L.R.	Boston Law Reporter
Boston B.J.	Boston Bar Journal
Bosw.	Boswell (Scot.)
	Bosworth, Superior Court (NY)
Bott Poor Law Cas.	Bott's Poor Laws Settlement Cases (Eng.)
Bott's Set. Cas.	Same
Bould.	Bouldin (AL)
Bouv.	Bouvier Law Dictionary
Bov.Pat.Cas.	Bovill's Patent Cases
Boy	Boyce's Reports (DE)
Boyce	Boyce (DE)
boycede	Same
bpc	Blatchford's Prize Cases
br	Bankruptcy Reporter
BR	Same
	Brooklyn Law Review
B.R. (Army)	Board of Review (Army)
Bract.	Bracton De Legibus et Consuetudinibus Angliae (Eng.)
Bracton L.J.	Bracton Law Journal
Bradb	Bradbury's Pleading and Practice Reports (NY)
Bradf	Bradford's Surrogate Court Reports (NY)
Bradf.	Bradford (IA)
Bradf.Surr.	Bradford's Surrogate Court (NY)
Bradl.	Bradley (RI)
Bradw.	Bradwell (IL)
Brady (Bailey) (5th ed.)	Brady on Bank Checks (5th ed.) (Bailey)
Brame	Brame (MS)
Branch	Branch (FL)
Br. & B.	Broderip & Bingham, Common Pleas (Eng.)
Br. & Col.	British & Colonial Prize Cases
Br. & F.Ecc.	Broderick & Freemantle's Ecclesiastical Cases (Eng.)
Br. & Gold.	Browndow & Goldesborough's Common Pleas (Eng.)
Br. & L.	Brownlow & Lushington's Admiralty Cases (Eng.)
Br. & Lush.	Same
Brantly	Brantly (MD)
Bray	Brayton's Reports (VT)
Brayt.	Brayton (VT)
brayton	Same
B.R.C.	British Ruling Cases
brcc	Brunner's Collected Cases
Br.Eccl.	Brown's Ecclesiastical (Eng.)
Breese	Breese's Reports (IL)
Breese App.	Breese Appendix
breeseappx	Same, Appendix (IL)
Brev.	Brevard (SC)
Brew.	Brewer (MD)
	Brewster (PA)
Brews.	Brewster (PA)
Bridg.	J. Bridgmore, Common Pleas (Eng.)
Bridgeport L.Rev.	Bridgeport Law Review
Bridg.J.	Sir J. Bridgman, Common Pleas (Eng.)
Bridg.O.	Sir Orlando Bridgman, Common Pleas (Eng.)
Brief/Case (S.F. Bar)	Brief/Case (San Francisco Bar Law Review)
Brightly	Brightly (PA)
Brightly El.Cas.	Brightly's Leading Election Cases (PA)
Brisb.	Brisbin (MN)
Brit.Cr.Cas.	British Crown Cases
Brit.J.Ad.L.	British Journal of Administrative Law
Brit.J. Criminol.	British Journal of Criminology
Brit.J.Law & Soc'y	British Journal of Law and Society
Brit.Prac. Int'l L.	British Practice in International Law
Brit.Ship.L.	British Shipping Laws (Stevens)
Brit.Tax Rev.	British Tax Review

Brit.Y.B.Int'l L.	British Year Book of International Law	Brown Ch.	Brown's Chancery (Eng.)
B.R.–J.C. (Army)	Board of Review and Judicial Council of the Army	Brown Dict.	Brown's Law Dictionary
Br.N.C.	Brooke's New Cases, King's Bench (Eng.)	Browne	Browne (MA) Browne, Common Pleas (PA)
Br.N.Cas.	Same	Browne & G.	Browne & Gray (MA)
Bro. & F.	Broderick & Freemantle's Ecclesiastical (Eng.)	Browne & H.	Browne & Hemingway (MS)
Bro. & Fr.	Same	Browne Bank Cas.	Browne's National Bank Cases
Bro. & Lush.	Browning & Lushington's Admiralty (Eng.)	Brown Ecc.	Brown's Ecclesiastical (Eng.)
Brock.	Brockenbrough (U.S.)	brownes	Browne's Reports (PA)
Brock. & Hol. Cas.	Brockenbrough & Holmes' Cases (VA)	Brownl. & G.	Brownlow & Goldesborough, Common Pleas (Eng.)
Brock.Cas.	Brockenbrough's Cases (VA)	Brown N.P.	Brown's Nisi Prius (MI)
Brod. & F. Ecc. Cas.	Broderick & Freemantle's Ecclesiastical Cases (Eng.)	Brown Parl. Cas.	Brown's House of Lords Cases (Eng.)
Brod. & Fr. Ecc. Cas.	Same	Brown P.C.	Same
		brownsadm	Brown's U.S. Admiralty Reports
Brodix Am. & El.Pat.Cas.	Brodix's American & English Patent Cases	Bruce	Bruce (Scot.)
		Brunn.Coll. Cas.	Brunner's Collected Cases (U.S.)
Bro.Just.	Brown's Justiciary (Scot.)	BRW	Bankruptcy Reporter (West)
Brook Abr.	Brook's Abridgment (Eng.)	bstockton	B. Stockton's New Jersey Equity Reports
Brook. Barrister	Brooklyn Barrister		
Brook.J.Int'l L.	Brooklyn Journal of International Law	Bt.	Benedict (U.S.)
Brook.L.Rev.	Brooklyn Law Review	bta	Board of Tax Appeals (U.S.)
Brook N.Cas.	Brook's New Cases, King's Bench (Eng.)	B.T.A.	Same
		btr	Brief Times Reporter (CO)
Brooks	Brooks (MI)	BTR	British Tax Review
Brown	Brown (MS) Brown (MO) Brown (NE)	BTW	United States Board of Tax Appeals Reports
Brown A. & R.	Brown's United States District Court Admiralty & Revenue Cases	Buck	Buck (MT) Buck, Bankrupt Cases (Eng.)
Brown Adm.	Brown's Admiralty (U.S.)	Buck.	Bucknill's Cooke's Cases of Practice, Common Pleas (Eng.)
Brown. & L.	Browning & Lushington, Admiralty (Eng.)		
Brown & MacN.	Brown & MacNamara, Railway Cases (Eng.)	Buck.Dec.	Buckner's Decisions (in Freeman's Chancery Reports) (MS)
Brown & R.	Brown & Rader (MO)	Buf	Buffalo Law Review
		Buff.L.Rev.	Same

B.U.Int'l L.J.	Boston University International Law Journal	Burgess	Burgess (OH)
		Burk	Burk (VA)
B.U.J.Tax L.	Boston University Journal of Tax Law	Burlesque Rep.	Skillman's New York Police Reports
		Burnett	Burnett (OR)
Bull.	Weekly Law Bulletin		Burnett (WI)
Bull.Am. Acad. Psych. & L.	Bulletin of the American Academy of Psychiatry and the Law	Burr.	Burrow, King's Bench (Eng.)
		Burr.S.Cases	Burrow's Settlement Cases (Eng.)
Bull.Can. Welfare L.	Bulletin of Canadian Welfare Law	Burr.t.M.	Burrow's Reports, tempore Mansfield (Eng.)
Bull.Copyright Soc'y	Bulletin of the Copyright Society of the United States of America	Bus. & L.	Business and Law
		Bus. & Prof. C.	Business and Professions Code (CA)
		Busb.Eq.	Busbee, Equity (NC)
Bull.Czech.L.	Bulletin of Czechoslovak Law	Busb.L.	Busbee, Law (NC)
		Bush	Bush (KY)
Buller N.P.	Buller's Nisi Prius (Eng.)	Bus.Law.	Business Lawyer
		Bus.L.J.	Business Law Journal
Bull.Int'l Fiscal Doc.	Bulletin for International Fiscal Documentation	Bus.L.Rev.	Business Law Review (Eng.)
Bull.Legal Devel.	Bulletin of Legal Developments		Business Law Review (U.S.)
Bull.L.Science & Tech.	Bulletin of Law, Science and Technology	Bus.Reg.L. Rep.	Business Regulation Law Report
		Buxton	Buxton (NC)
Bull.Waseda U.Inst. Comp.L.	Bulletin, Waseda University Institute of Comparative Law	B–W Cal Civ Prac	Bancroft–Whitney California Civil Practice
		B.W.C.C.	Butterworths Workmen's Compensation Cases (Eng.)
B.U.L.Rev.	Boston University Law Review	B.Y.U.J.L. & Educ.	Brigham Young University Journal of Law and Education
Bulstr.	Bulstrode, King's Bench (Eng.)		
Bunb.	Bunbury, Exchequer (Eng.)	BYU J.Pub.L.	Brigham Young University Journal of Public Law
B.U.Pub.Int. L.J.	Boston University Public Interest Law Journal	B.Y.U.L.Rev.	Brigham Young University Law Review
Bur	Burnett's Reports (WI)		
Burf.	Burford (OK)		

C

c	California Reports	C.A.	Same
C.	Same	[ ] C.A.	Recueils de Jurisprudence du Quebec, Cour d'appel. 1970
	Cowen (NY)		
c2d	California Reports, Second	ca2d	California Appellate Reports, Second
C.2d	Same		
c3d	Same, Third	C.A.2d	Same
C.3d	Same	ca2ds	California Appellate Reports, Supplement, Second
c4th	Same, Fourth		
C.4th	Same		
ca	California Appellate Reports	C.A.2d Supp.	Same

ca3d	California Appellate Reports, Third	Cal. Comp. Cases	Same
C.A.3d	Same	Cal. Const.	California Constitution
ca3ds	California Appellate Reports, Supplement, Third	Calcutta W.N.	Calcutta Weekly Notes
C.A.3d Supp.	Same	Cald.	Caldecott's Magistrate's and Settlement Cases (Eng.)
ca4bcr	Fourth Circuit and District of Columbia Bankruptcy Court Reporter		Caldwell (WV)
		Cal.Dec.	California Decisions
CA4S	California Appellate Reports, Fourth Series, Supplement	Cald.J.P.	Caldecott's Magistrate's and Settlement Cases (Eng.)
		Cald.M.Cas.	Same
ca4th	California Appellate Reports, Fourth	Cald.Mag. Cas.	Same
		Cald.S.C.	Same
ca4ths	California Appellate Reports, Supplement, Fourth	Cald.Sett. Cas.	Same
		Cal. Forms	California Legal Forms
C.A.A.	Civil Aeronautics Authority Reports	Cal.Ind. Acci.Dec.	California Industrial Accidents Decisions
C.A.B.	Civil Aeronautics Board Reports	CALJIC	California Jury Instructions, Criminal
Cab. & E.	Cababe & Ellis, Queen's Bench (Eng.)	Cal.Jur.	California Jurisprudence
CACJ	California Attorneys for Criminal Justice Forum	Cal.Jur.2d	Same, Second Edition
		Cal.Jur.3d	Same, Third Edition
cad	Customs Appeals Decisions (by number)	Call	Call (VA)
		Cal. Law.	California Lawyer
		Cal.Leg.Rec.	California Legal Record
C.A.D.	Same		
Cahiers	Les Cahiers de Droit	Cal LR	California Law Review
Cai.	Caines' Reports (NY)		
Cai.Cas.	Caines' Cases	Cal.L.Rev.	Same
CaiCs	Caines' Cases (NY)	Cal.Prac.	California Practice
Cai.R.	Caines' Reports	Cal. P.U.C.	Decisions of California Public Utilities Commission
CaL	California Law Review		
Cal.	California Supreme Court Reports	Cal Real Prop J	California Real Property Journal
	California Reports	Cal.Reg.L. Rep.	California Regulatory Law Reporter
Cal.2d	Same, Second Series		
Cal.3d	Same, Third Series	calrptr	West's California Reporter
Cal 4th	Same, Fourth Series		
Cal. Adm. Code	California Administrative Code	Cal.Rptr.	Same
		calrptr2d	Same, Second Series
Cal.App.	California Appellate Reports	Cal.Rptr.2d	Same
		Cal. Rules of Court	California Rules of Court
Cal.App.2d	Same, Second Series		
Cal.App.3d	Same, Third Series	Cal.St.B.J.	California State Bar Journal
Cal.App.4th	Same, Fourth Series		
Cal.App.Dec.	California Appellate Decisions	Calthr.	Calthrop, King's Bench (Eng.)
Cal Code Reg	California Code of Regulations	Cal Trial LJ	California Trial Law Journal
calcompcas	California Compensation Cases	calunrep	California Unreported Cases

Cal Unrep	Same	Can.Community	Canadian Communi-
Cal.Unrep. Cas.	Same	L.J.	ty Law Journal
Cal Western Int LJ	California Western International Law Journal	Can.Com.R.	Canadian Commercial Law Reports
		Can.Cr.Cas.	Canadian Criminal Cases
Cal Western LR	California Western Law Review	Can.Crim.	Criminal Reports (Can.)
Cal. Western L. Rev.	Same	Can.Crim. Cas. (N.S.)	Canadian Criminal Cases, New Series
Cal.W.Int'l L.J.	California Western International Law Journal	Can.Crim. Cas. Ann.	Canadian Criminal Cases Annotated
Cal.W.L.Rev.	California Western Law Review	C. & A.	Cooke & Alcock, King's Bench and Exchequer (Ir.)
Cam.	Cameron's Privy Council Decisions	C. & C.	Case and Comment
Cam. & N.	Cameron & Norwood's Conference Reports (NC)		Colemand & Caines' Cases (NY)
Cambrian L.Rev.	Cambrian Law Review	C. & D.	Corbett & Daniel's Election Cases (Eng.)
Cambridge L.J.	Cambridge Law Journal		Crawford & Dix's Abridged Cases (Ir.)
Cam.Cas.	Cameron's Cases (Can.)	C. & D.A.C.	Crawford & Dix's Abridged Cases (Ir.)
Cameron	Cameron's Supreme Court Cases	C. & D.C.C.	Crawford & Dix's Circuit Cases (Ir.)
Cameron Pr.	Cameron's Practice (Can.)		Crawford & Dix's Criminal Cases (Ir.)
Camp	Camp (ND)		
Campaign L.Rep.	Campaign Law Reporter	C. & E.	Cababe & Ellis, Queen's Bench (Eng.)
Campb.	Campbell (NE) Campbell's Nisi Prius (Eng.)	C. & F.	Clark & Finelly, House of Lords (Eng.)
Campb.L.G.	Campbell's Legal Gazette (PA)	C. & J.	Crompton & Jervis, Exchequer (Eng.)
Campbell L.Rev.	Campbell Law Review	C. & K.	Carrington & Kirwan, Nisi Prius (Eng.)
Can.App.Cas.	Canadian Appeal Cases	C. & L.	Connor & Lawson's Chancery (Ir.)
Can.B.A.J.	Canadian Bar Association Journal	C. & L.C.C.	Caines & Leigh, Crown Cases (Eng.)
Can.Bankr. Ann.	Canadian Bankruptcy Reports Annotated	C. & M.	Carrington & Marshman's Nisi Prius (Eng.)
Can.Bankr. Ann. (N.S.)	Same, New Series		Crompton & Meeson's Exchequer (Eng.)
Can.B.Ass'n Y.B.	Canadian Bar Association: Year Book	C. & Marsh.	Carrington & Marshman's Nisi Prius (Eng.)
Can.B.J.	Canadian Bar Journal		
Can.B.R.	Canadian Bar Review	C. & N.	Cameron & Norwood's North Carolina Conference
Can.B.Rev.	Same		
Can.Bus.L.J.	Canadian Business Law Journal		
Can.Com.L. Rev.	Canadian Communications Law Review		

C. & P.	Carrington & Payne's Nisi Prius (Eng.)	Can.S.C.	Canada Supreme Court
	Craig & Phillips, Chancery (Eng.)	Can.S.Ct.	Canada Supreme Court Reports
C. & R.	Cockburn & Rowe's Election Cases	Can.Tax App. Bd.	Canada Tax Appeal Board Cases
C. & S.	Clarke & Scully's Drainage Cases (Ont.)	Can.Tax Cas. Ann.	Canada Tax Cases Annotated
Cane & L.	Cane & Leigh's Crown Cases Reserved (Eng.)	Can.Tax Found. Rep. Proc.Tax Conf.	Canadian Tax Foundation Report of Proceedings of the Tax Conference
Can. Env.L.News	Canadian Environmental Law News	Can.Tax J.	Canadian Tax Journal
Can.Exch.	Canadian Exchequer	Can.Tax News	Canadian Tax News
Can.Green Bag	Canadian Green Bag	Can.-U.S.L.J.	Canada–United States Law Journal
Can.Human Rights Rep.	Canadian Human Rights Reporter		
Can.Hum. Rts.Advocate	Canadian Human Rights Advocate	Can.Wel.	Canadian Welfare
Can. J. Admin. L. & Prac.	Canadian Journal of Administrative Law & Practice	Can.Y.B.Int'l L.	Canadian Yearbook of International Law
Can.J.Correction	Canadian Journal of Correction	Cap.U.L.Rev.	Capital University Law Review
Can.J.Crim & Corr.	Canadian Journal of Criminology and Corrections	CaR	California Reporter
		CaR2d	Same, Second Series
		CaR3d	Same, Third Series
Can.J.Fam.L.	Canadian Journal of Family Law	Car. & K.	Carrington & Kirwan, Nisi Prius (Eng.)
Can. J. L. & Juris.	Canadian Journal of Law and Jurisprudence	Car. & P.	Carrington & Payne, Nisi Prius (Eng.)
		Cardozo Arts & Entertainment L.J.	Cardozo Arts & Entertainment Law Journal
Can.Lab.	Canadian Labour	Cardozo L.Rev.	Cardozo Law Review
Can.Law.	Canadian Lawyer	Car.H. & A.	Carrow, Hamerton & Allen, New Sessions Cases (Eng.)
Can.Legal Stud.	Canadian Legal Studies		
Can.L.J.	Canadian Law Journal	carlrepos	Carolina Law Repository (NC)
Can.L.J. (N.S.)	Same, New Series		
Can.L.R.B.R.	Canadian Labour Relations Board Reports	Carolina L.J.	Carolina Law Journal
Can.L.Rev.	Canadian Law Review	Carolina L.Repos.	Carolina Law Repository
Can.L.T. Occ.N.	Canadian Law Times Occasional Notes	Carp.	Carpenter (CA)
		Carp.P.C.	Carpmael, Patent Cases (Eng.)
Can.L.Times	Canadian Law Times		
Can.Mun.J.	Canadian Municipal Journal	Caribbean L.J.	Caribbean Law Journal
Can.Native L.Rep.	Canadian Native Law Reporter	Caribbean L.Libr.	Caribbean Law Librarian
Can.Oil & Gas	Canadian Oil and Gas (Butterworths)	Cart.B.N.A.	Cartwright's Constitutional Cases (Can.)
Can.Pub.Ad.	Canadian Public Administration	Carter	Carter (IN)
			Carter, Common Pleas (Eng.)
Can.R.Cas.	Canadian Railway Cases	Carth.	Carthew, King's Bench (Eng.)
Can.Ry.Cas.	Same		

Cartwr.Cas.	Cartwright's Cases (Can.)	CBA Rec.	Chicago Bar Association Record
Cary	Cary Chancery (Eng.)	cbc	Collier Bankruptcy Cases
cas	California Appellate Reports, Supplement	C.B.C.	Same
		cbc2d	Same, Second Series
Cas.C.L.	Cases in Crown Law (Eng.)	C.B.R.	Canadian Bankruptcy Reports
Case & Com.	Case & Comment	CC	Civil Code, United States Circuit Court
Case W.Res. J.Int'l L.	Case Western Reserve Journal of International Law		
		C.C.	Ohio Circuit Court Reports
Case W.Res. L.Rev.	Case Western Reserve Law Review	C.C.A.	Circuit Court of Appeals (U.S.)
Casey	Casey (PA)	CCA	Court of Customs and Patent Appeals Reports (Customs)
Cass.Prac. Cas.	Cassels' Practice Cases (Can.)		
Cass.S.C.	Cassels' Supreme Court Decisions		
Cas.Tak. & Adj. Cases	Taken and Adjudged (Report in Chancery, First Edition) (Eng.)	C.C.C.	Canadian Criminal Cases
		Ccf	Federal Contract Cases
Cas.t.Hardw.	Cases tempore Hardwicke, King's Bench (Eng.)	CCF	Same
		CCH	Commerce Clearing House
Cas.t.Holt	Cases tempore Holt, King's Bench (Eng.)	CCH Atomic En.L.Rep.	Atomic Energy Law Reporter (CCH)
		cchblr	Bankruptcy Law Reporter (CCH)
Cas.t.King	Cases tempore King, Chancery (Eng.)	CCH Comm. Mkt.Rep.	Common Market Reporter (CCH)
Cas.t.Northington	Cases tempore Northington, Chancery Reports (Eng.)	cchepd	Employment Practices Decisions (CCH)
Cas.t.Talb.	Cases tempore Talbot, Chancery (Eng.)	CCH Fed.Federal Banking L.Rep.	Banking Law Reporter (CCH)
Cas.t.Wm. III	Cases tempore William III (Eng.)	CCH Fed.Sec. L.Rep.	Federal Securities Law Reporter (CCH)
C.A. Supp.	California Appellate Reports, Supplement	cchfslr	Federal Securities Law Reporter (CCH)
CaU	California Unreported Cases	CCH Inh.Est. & Gift Tax Rep.	Inheritance, Estate, and Gift Tax Reporter (CCH)
Cates	Cates (TN)		
Cath.Law.	Catholic Lawyer	CCH Lab. Arb. Awards	Labor Arbitration Awards (CCH)
Cath.U.L.Rev.	Catholic University of America Law Review	CCH Lab.Cas.	Labor Cases (CCH)
		CCH Lab.L. Rep.	Labor Law Reporter (CCH)
cb	Cumulative Bulletin (IRS)	cchlc	Labor Cases (CCH)
C.B.	Same	cchnlrb	National Labor Relations Board Decisions (CCH)
	Manning, Granger & Scott, Common Bench (Eng.)		
C.B. (N.S.)	Manning, Granger & Scott, Common Bench (New Series) (Eng.)	cchoshd	Occupational Safety and Health Decisions (CCH)

cchplr	Products Liability Reports (CCH)
CCH Stand. Fed.Tax Rep.	Standard Federal Tax Reporter (CCH)
CCH State Tax Cas.Rep.	State Tax Cases Reporter (CCH)
CCH State Tax Rev.	State Tax Review (CCH)
CCH Tax Ct. Mem.	Tax Court Memorandum Decisions (CCH)
CCH Tax Ct. Rep.	Tax Court Reporter (CCH)
cchtc	Trade Cases (CCH)
cchuir	Unemployment Insurance Reporter (CCH)
CCL	Court of Claims Reports
C.C.L.T.	Canadian Cases on the Law of Torts
C.C. (N.S.)	Ohio Circuit Court Reports, New Series
CCP	Code of Civil Procedure
ccpa	Court of Customs and Patent Appeals
C.C.P.A.	Same
C.C.Supp.	City Court Reports Supplement (NY)
CD	Decisions of the Commissioner of Patents
C.D.	Commissioner's Decisions, United States Patent Office
	Ohio Circuit Decisions
	United States Customs Court Decisions
cdos	California Daily Opinion Service
CEB	Continuing Education of the Bar (CA)
C.E.Gr.	C.E. Greene's Equity (NJ)
C.E.Greene	Same
Cent.Dig.	Century Digest
Centr.L.J.	Central Law Journal
Cert Rules	State Bar Program for Certifying Legal Specialists
Ceylon L.Rev.	Ceylon Law Review
C.F.R.	Code of Federal Regulations

Ch.	Law Reports, Chancery (Eng.)
	Chapter
Cha.App.	English Law Reports, Chancery Appeal Cases
Chamb.Rep.	Chancery Chambers (Ont.)
Chand	Chandler's Reports (WI)
Chandl.	Chandler (NH)
	Chandler (WI)
Chaney	Chaney (MI)
Charley Pr.Cas.	Charley's Practice Cases (Eng.)
Charlt.	R.M. Charlton (GA)
	T.U.P. Charlton (GA)
chase	Chase (U.S. District Court)
Chase	Same
Ch.Cal.	Calendar of Proceedings in Chancery (Eng.)
Ch.Cas.	Cases in Chancery (Eng.)
Ch.Chamb.	Chancery Chambers (Upper Can.)
Ch.Col.Op.	Chalmers' Colonial Opinions
Ch.D.	Law Reports, Chancery Division (Eng.)
Ch.D.2d	Same, Second Series
Chest.Co.	Chester County (PA)
Chev.Ch.	Cheves' Chancery (SC)
Chev.Eq.	Same
Cheves	Cheves' Law (SC)
Chi.B.Record	Chicago Bar Record
Chicago L.B.	Chicago Law Bulletin
Chicago L.J.	Chicago Law Journal
Chicago L.Rec.	Chicago Law Record
Chicano–Latino L.Rev.	Chicano–Latino Law Review
Chicano LR	Chicano Law Review
Chicano L.Rev.	Same
Chic.L.T.	Chicago Law Times
Chi.-Kent L.Rev.	Chicago–Kent Law Review
Chi.Leg.N.	Chicago Legal News
China L.Rev.	China Law Review
Chin.L. & Gov't	Chinese Law and Government
Chip.	Chipman (N.Bruns.)
	Chipman (VT)
ChipD	D. Chipman's Reports (VT)

ChipN	N. Chipman's Reports (VT)	Cir	Connecticut Circuit Court Reports
Chit.	Chitty's Bail Court (Eng.)	Cir.Ct.Dec.	Circuit Court Decisions (OH)
Chit.B.C.	Same	Cir. DC	U.S. Court of Appeals, District of Columbia Circuit
Chitt.	Same		
Chitty's L.J.	Chitty's Law Journal		
ChL	University of Chicago Law Review	Cir. Fed.	U.S. Court of Appeals, Federal Circuit
Choyce Cas.Ch.	Choyce's Cases in Chancery (Eng.)	Cir.(number)	United States Court of Appeals, United States District Court Circuit (number)
Ch.Prec.	Precedents in Chancery		
Ch.R.	Upper Canada Chambers Reports		
Ch.Rep.	Chancery Reports (Eng.)	cit	U.S. Court of International Trade
	Chancery Reports (Ir.)	CIT	Same
Ch.R.M.	R.M. Charlton (GA)	City Ct.R.	City Court Reports (NY)
Chr.Rep.	Chamber Reports (Upper Can.)	City Ct.R. Supp.	Same, Supplement
Chr.Rob.	Christopher Robinson's Admiralty (Eng.)	City Hall Rec.	City Hall Recorder (NY)
		City Hall Rep.	City Hall Reporter, Lomas (NY)
ChS	Chancery Sentinel Reports	Civ. & Mil. L.J.	Civil and Military Law Journal
ChS(2)	Same, No. 2	Civ. C.	Civil Code (CA)
Ch.Sent.	Chancery Sentinel (NY)	Civ.Just.Q.	Civil Justice Quarterly
Ch.T.U.P.	T.U.P. Charlton (GA)	Civ.Lib.	Civil Liberty
		Civ.Lib.Dock.	Civil Liberties Docket
Chy.Chrs.	Upper Canada Chancery Chambers Reports	Civ.Lib.Rev.	Civil Liberties Review
		Civ.Lib.Rptr.	Civil Liberties Reporter
C.I.L.C.	Commonwealth International Law Cases	Civ.Litigation Rep.	Civil Litigation Reporter (CEB)
C.I.L.J.S.A.	Comparative and International Law Journal of Southern Africa	civprocns	Civil Procedure Reports, New Series (NY)
Cin.B.Ass'n J.	Cincinnati Bar Association Journal	Civ.Proc.R.	Civil Procedure Reports (NY)
Cincinnati Law Bull.	Weekly Law Bulletin (OH)	Civ.Rights Dig.	Civil Rights Digest
		C.J.	Corpus Juris
Cinc.L.Bul.	Cincinnati Law Bulletin	C.J.Ann.	Corpus Juris Annotations
Cinc.Sup.Ct. Rep.	Cincinnati Superior Court Reporter	CJQ	Civil Justice Quarterly
Cin.Law Bull.	Weekly Law Bulletin (OH)	C.J.S.	Corpus Juris Secundum
Cin.L.Rev.	Cincinnati Law Review	CLA	University of California at Los Angeles Law Review
Cin.Mun.Dec.	Cincinnati Municipal Decisions	C.L.A.I.T.	Constitutions and Laws of the American Indian Tribes (Scholarly Resources)
Cin.R.	Cincinnati Superior Court Reporter		
Cin.S.C.R.	Same		
Cin.S.C.Rep.	Same		

Cl. & F.	Clark & Finnelly, House of Lords (Eng.)
Clark	Clark (AL)
	Clark (PA)
Clark & F.	Clark & Finnelly, House of Lords (Eng.)
Clark & F. (N.S.)	Same, New Series
Clark App.	Clark, Appeals Cases House of Lords (Eng.)
Clark Col.Law	Clark Colonial Law
Clarke	Clarke (IA)
	Clarke (MI)
	Clarke's Chancery Reports (NY)
Clarke & S. Dr. Cas.	Clarke & Scully's Drainage Cases (Ont.)
Clarke Ch.	Clarke, Chancery (NY)
C.L.A.S.	Criminal Law Audio Series
Class Act. Rep.	Class Action Reports
Clayt.	Clayton's Reports York Assizes (Eng.)
ClC	Claims Court Reporter
C.L.Chambers	Chambers' Common Law (Upper Can.)
clct	Claims Court Reporter
ClCt	Same
	United States Claims Court and United States Court of Federal Claims
Clearinghouse Rev.	Clearinghouse Review
C. Leg. Rec.	California Legal Record
CLE J. & Reg.	Continuing Legal Education Journal and Register
Clemens	Clemens (KS)
Clev.Bar Ass'n J.	Cleveland Bar Association Journal
Cleve.Law R.	Cleveland Law Reporter (OH)
Cleve.Law Rec.	Cleveland Law Record (OH)
Cleve.Law Reg.	Cleveland Law Register (OH)
Cleve.L.Rec.	Cleveland Law Record (OH)
Cleve.L.Reg.	Cleveland Law Register (OH)

Cleve.L.Rep.	Cleveland Law Reporter (OH)
Clev.Mar.L. Rev.	Cleveland Marshall Law Review
Clev.St.L. Rev.	Cleveland State Law Review
cliff	Clifford's U.S. Circuit Court Reports
Cliff.	Same
Clif.South.El. Cas.	Clifford, Southwick Election Cases
C.L.J.	California Law Journal
	Cambridge Law Journal
C.L.J. & Lit. Rev.	California Law Journal and Literary Review
Clk's Mag.	Clerk's Magazine (London)
	Clerk's Magazine (RI)
	Clerk's Magazine (Upper Can.)
C.L.L.C.	Canadian Labour Law Cases
C.L.L.R.	Canadian Labor Law Reports (CCH)
CLP	Computer Law and Practice
CLQ	Cornell Law Quarterly
C.L.R.	Common Law Reports (Eng.)
	Commonwealth Law Reports (Austl.)
	Cyprus Law Reports
C.L.Rec.	Cleveland Law Record
C.L.Reg.	Cleveland Law Register
C.L.Rep.	Cleveland Law Reporter
C.L. Rev.	California Law Review
CLSR	Computer Law and Security Report
C.L.S.R.	Computer Law Service Reporter
CLU J.	Chartered Life Underwriter Journal
C.L.W.	Commercial Laws of the World (Oceana)
CLY	Current Law Yearbook
C.M. & R.	Crompton, Meeson & Roscoe, Exchequer (Eng.)

C.M.A.R.	Canadian Court Martial Appeal Reports
CMLR	Common Market Law Reports
C.M.R.	Court–Martial Reports
C.M.R. (Air Force)	Court–Martial Reports of the Judge Advocate General of the Air Force
CoA	Colorado Court of Appeals Reports
Cobb	Cobb (AL)
	Cobb (GA)
CoCai	Coleman and Caines' Cases (NY)
Cochr.	Cochran (Nova Scotia)
	Cochrane (ND)
Cockb. & R.	Cockburn & Rowe's Election Cases (Eng.)
Cocke	Cocke (AL)
	Cocke (FL)
CoCs	Coleman's Cases
Co.Ct.Cas.	County Court Cases (Eng.)
Co.Ct.Ch.	County Court Chronicle (Eng.)
Co.Ct.Rep.	Pennsylvania County Court Reports
Code Am.	Code Amendments (CA)
coderep	Code Reporter (NY)
Code Rep.	Same
Code Rep. (N.S.)	Same, New Series
CodR	Code Reporter (NY)
CodRn	Same, New Series
Cof	Coffey's Probate Decisions
Coff.Prob.	Coffey's Probate (CA)
Co.Inst.	Coke's Institutes (Eng.)
Coke	Coke, King's Bench (Eng.)
Col	Colorado Supreme Court Reports
Col.	Coleman (AL)
Col. & C.Cas.	Coleman & Caine's Cases (NY)
Col.Cas.	Coleman's Cases (NY)
Cold.	Coldwell (TN)
coldtn	Same
Coldw.	Same
Cole	Cole (AL)
	Cole (IA)

Cole. & Cai. Cas.	Coleman & Caines' Cases
Cole.Cas.	Coleman's Cases
Col.Int'l Dr. Comp.	Colioque International de Droit Compare
Co.Litt.	Coke on Littleton (Eng.)
Coll.	Collyer's Chancery (Eng.)
Coll. & E. Bank	Collier's & Eaton's American Bankruptcy Reports
Colles	Colles Cases in Parliament (Eng.)
Coll.L.Bull.	College Law Bulletin
Coll.L.Dig.	College Law Digest
Col.L.Rev.	Columbia Law Review
colo	Colorado Reports
Colo.	Same
coloapp	Colorado Appeals Reports
Colo.App.	Same
colobcr	Colorado Bankruptcy Court Reporter
Colo.J. Int'l Envtl.L. & Pol'y	Colorado Journal of International Environmental Law and Policy
Colo.Law.	Colorado Lawyer
Colo.Law Rep.	Colorado Law Reporter
Colombo L.Rev.	Colombo Law Review (Ceylon)
Colonial Law.	Colonial Lawyer
Colq.	Colquit (Modern) (Eng.)
Coltm.	Coltman Registration Appeal Cases (Eng.)
Colum.Bus.L. Rev.	Columbia Business Law Review
Colum.Hum. Rts.L.Rev.	Columbia Human Rights Law Review
Colum.J. Envtl.L.	Columbia Journal of Environmental Law
Colum.J.Gender & L.	Columbia Journal of Gender and Law
Colum.J.Int'l Aff.	Columbia Journal of International Affairs
Colum.J.L. & Arts	Columbia Journal of Law and the Arts
Colum.J.L. & Soc.Probs.	Columbia Journal of Law and Social Problems
Colum.J. Transnat'l L.	Columbia Journal of Transnational Law

Colum.L.Rev.	Columbia Law Review	Comp.Gen.	United States Comptroller General Decisions
Colum. Soc'y Int'l L.Bull.	Columbia Society of International Law Bulletin	Comp.Jurid. Rev.	Comparative Juridical Review
Colum.Survey Human Rights L.	Columbia Survey of Human Rights Law	Comp.Lab.L.J.	Comparative Labor Law Journal
Colum.–VLA J.L. & Arts	Columbia Volunteer Lawyers for the Arts Journal of Law & the Arts	Comp Lawyer	Company Lawyer
		Compleat Law.	Compleat Lawyer
		Comp.L.J.	Company Law Journal
Com. & L.	Communications and the Law	Com.P.Reptr.	Common Pleas Reporter (Scranton, PA)
Com. & Mun. L.Rep.	Commercial & Municipal Law Reporter	Comptr. Treas. Dec.	United States Comptroller of Treasury Decisions
Co.Mass.Pr.	Colby Massachusetts Practice	Computer L. & Prac.	Computer Law & Practice
Comb.	Comberbach, King's Bench (Eng.)	Computer L. & Tax	Computer Law and Tax Report
Com.B.	Manning, Granger & Scott, Common Bench (Eng.)	Computer L.J.	Computer Law Journal
Com. C.	Commercial Code (CA)	Computers & L.	Computers and Law
Com.Cas.	Commercial Cases Since 1895 (Eng.)	Comst.	Comstock, Appeals (NY)
Com.Dec.	Commissioners' Decisions (Patent)	Comyns	Comyn's King's Bench and Common Pleas (Eng.)
Com.L.	Commercial Law (Can.)	Comyns Dig.	Comyn's Digest (Eng.)
Com.L.J.	Commercial Law Journal	Con.B.J.	Connecticut Bar Journal
Com. L. Rep.	Commercial Law Report	Condee	Condee, California Probate Court Practice (2d ed.)
Comm.B.	Manning, Granger & Scott, Common Bench (Eng.)	Condit.Sale— Chat.Mort. Rep.	Conditional Sale— Chattel Mortgage (CCH)
Comm.Cause	Common Cause	conf	North Carolina Conference Reports
Comm.Mkt.L.R.	Common Market Law Reports	Conf.	Same
Commodity Futures L.Rep.	Commodity Futures Law Reporter (CCH)	ConfR	Conference by Cameron and Norwood (NC)
Common Mkt. L.Rev.	Common Market Law Review	Conf.Teach. Int'l L.	Conference of Teachers of International Law
Community Prop.J.	Community Property Journal	Cong.Dig.	Congressional Digest
Commw.Arb.	Commonwealth Arbitration Reports	Cong.Rec.	Congressional Record (U.S.)
Commw.L.R.	Commonwealth Law Reports	conn	Connecticut Reports
		Conn.	Same
Comparisons in L. & Monet.Com.	Comparisons in Law and Monetary Comments	connapp	Connecticut Appellate Reports
		Conn.B.J.	Connecticut Bar Journal
Comp.Dec.	United States Comptroller of Treasury Decisions	conncir	Connecticut Circuit Reports
		Conn.Cir.Ct.	Same

Conn.J.Int'l L.	Connecticut Journal of International Law	Coop.	Cooper (FL)
			Cooper's Chancery (Eng.)
Conn.L.Rev.	Connecticut Law Review		Cooper's Chancery (TN)
connoly	Connolly's Surrogate's Court Reporter (NY)	Coop.C. & P.R.	Cooper's Chancery Practice Reporter (U.S.)
Conn.Prob. L.J.	Connecticut Probate Law Journal	Cooper	Cooper, State Administrative Law
Connsupp	Connecticut Supplement	Coop.Pr.Cas.	Cooper's Practice Cases (Eng.)
Conn.Supp.	Same		
Conn.Surr.	Connolly's Surrogate (NY)	Coop.t. Brough.	Cooper's Cases tempore Brougham, Chancery (Eng.)
Conov.	Conover (WI)		
Const.Afr.States	Constitutions of African States (Oceana)	Coop.t.Cott.	Cooper's Cases tempore Cottenham, Chancery (Eng.)
Const. Commentary	Constitutional Commentary	Coop.t.Eldon	Cooper's Reports tempore Eldon, Chancery (Eng.)
Const.Dep. & Sp.Sov.	Constitutions of Dependencies and Special Sovereignties	Co.P.C.	Coke Pleas of the Crown (Eng.)
		Cope	Cope (CA)
Const. Nations	Constitutions of Nations (Nijhoff)	Copp Min. Dec.	Copp's Mining Decisions (U.S.)
Const.Rep.	Constitutional Reports (SC)	Copp's Land Owner	Copp's Land Owner
Const.Rev.	Constitutional Review	Copy.	Copyright
		Copy.Bull.	Copyright Bulletin
Const.World	Constitutions of the Countries of the World (Oceana)	Copyright L.Sym.	Copyright Law Symposium (American Society of Composers, Authors, and Publishers)
Consumer Fin. L.Q. Rep.	Consumer Finance Law Quarterly Report		
		Cor	Cornell Law Review
Consumer Prod. Saf'y Guide	Consumer Product Safety Guide (CCH)	Corb. & D.	Corbett & Daniels Election Cases (Eng.)
Contemp. Drug Prob.	Contemporary Drug Problems	Cornell Int'l L.J.	Cornell International Law Journal
Conv	Conveyancer and Property Lawyer	Cornell J.L. & Pub.Pol'y	Cornell Journal of Law and Public Policy
Conv. & Prop. Law	Same	Cornell L.F.	Cornell Law Forum
Convey.	Conveyancer	Cornell L.J.	Cornell Law Journal
Convey. (N.S.)	Conveyancer & Property Lawyer, New Series	Cornell L.Q.	Cornell Law Quarterly
		Cornell L.Rev.	Cornell Law Review
Cooke	Cooke, Cases of Practice, Common Pleas (Eng.)	Corp C	Corporations Code (CA)
	Cooke (TN)	Corp.Counsel Rev.	Corporate Counsel Review
Cooke & A.	Cooke & Alcock, King's Bench (Ir.)	Corp.Couns. Rep.	Corporate Counsel Reporter
cooketn	Cooke's Tennessee Reports	Corp.J.	Corporation Journal
		Corp.L.Rev.	Corporation Law Review
Cook Vice–Adm.	Cook's Vice–Admiralty (Lower Can.)	Corp.Pract. Comment.	Corporate Practice Commentator
Cooley L.Rev.	Cooley Law Review		

Corp.Pract. Rev.	Corporate Practice Review	C.P.Rep.	Common Pleas Reporter (PA)
Corp.Reorg.	Corporate Reorganizations	CR	Columbia Law Review
Corp.Reorg. & Am.Bank. Rev.	Corporate Reorganization & American Bankruptcy Review		Clinical Risk
			California Reporter
		C.R.	Criminal Reports (Canada)
Coup.	Couper's Justiciary (Scot.)	crabbe	Crabbe (U.S. District Court)
Court. & MacL.	Courtenay & MacLean (Scot.)	Crabbe	Same
Coutlea	Coutlea's Supreme Court Cases	C.R.A.C.	Canadian Reports, Appeal Cases
Cow.	Cowen's Reports (NY)	Craig & Ph.	Craig & Phillips, Chancery (Eng.)
Cow.Cr.	Cowen's Criminal Reports (NY)	cranch	Cranch's U.S. Supreme Court Reports
Cowp.	Cowper King's Bench (Eng.)	Cranch	Same
Cowp.Cas.	Cowper (Eng.)	Cranch C.C.	Cranch's Circuit Court (U.S.)
Cox	Cox (AR)		
Cox Am.T. Cas.	Cox's American Trademark Cases	Cranch Pat. Dec.	Cranch's Patent Decisions (U.S.)
Cox & Atk.	Cox & Atkinson, Registration Appeals (Eng.)	Cr. & M.	Crompton & Meeson, Exchequer (Eng.)
		Cr. & Ph.	Craig & Phillips, Chancery (Eng.)
Cox C.C.	Cox's Criminal Cases (Eng.)	Crane	Crane (Mont.)
Cox Ch.	Cox's Chancery (Eng.)	Cr.App.	Criminal Appeals (Eng.)
Cox Crim. Cas.	Cox's Criminal Cases	Cr App Rep (S)	Criminal Appeal Reports (Sentencing)
Coxe	Coxe (NJ)		
Cox Eq.	Cox's Equity	Cr.App.R.(S.)	Same
Cox J.S.Cas.	Cox's Joint Stock Cases (Eng.)	Craw.	Crawford (AR)
		Crawf. & D. Abr.Cas.	Crawford & Dix's Abridged Cases (Ir.)
CP	Civil Procedure Reports (NY)		
CPA	Court of Customs Appeals Reports	Crawf. & Dix's	Crawford & Dix's Circuit Cases (Ir.)
	Court of Customs & Patent Appeals Reports (Customs)		Crawford & Dix's Criminal Cases (Ir.)
CP(B)	Civil Procedure Reports (NY) (Browne)	CRC	California Rules of Court
C.P.C.	Carswell's Practice Cases		Decisions of California Railroad Commission
C.P.Coop.	C.P. Cooper, Chancery (Eng.)	C.R.C.	Canadian Railway Cases
CPD	Customs Penalty Decisions	Cr.Cas.Res.	Law Reports, Crown Cases Reserved (Eng.)
C.P.D.	Law Reports, Common Pleas Division (Eng.)		
		CRD	Customs Rules Decisions
CP(M)	Civil Procedure Reports (McCarty) (NY)	Creighton L.Rev.	Creighton Law Review
CPn	Same, New Series	Crim.	Criminologie
C.P.R.	Canadian Patent Reporter	Crim. & Soc. Just.	Crime and Social Justice

Crim.App.	Criminal Appeal Reports	C.Rob.	Christopher Robinson's Admiralty (Eng.)
Crim.App. Rep.	Cohen's Criminal Appeals Reports (Eng.)	Cro.Car.	Croke tempore Charles I (Eng.)
Crim.Case & Com.	Criminal Case and Comment	Cro.Eliz.	Croke tempore Elizabeth (Eng.)
Crim.Def.	Criminal Defense	Cro.Jac.	Croke tempore James I, King's Bench (Eng.)
Crime & Delin'cy	Crime & Delinquency		
Crime & Delin'cy Abst.	Crime and Delinquency Abstracts	Cromp.	Star Chamber Cases (Eng.)
Crime & Delin'cy Lit.	Crime and Delinquency Literature	Cromp. & J.	Crompton & Jervis, Exchequer (Eng.)
Crim.Just.	Criminal Justice	Cromp. & M.	Crompton & Meeson, Exchequer (Eng.)
Crim.Just. & Behav.	Criminal Justice and Behavior	Cromp.M. & R.	Crompton, Meeson & Roscoe, Exchequer (Eng.)
Crim.Just. Ethics	Criminal Justice Ethics	Crosw.Pat. Cas.	Croswell's Collection of Patent Cases (U.S.)
Crim.Just.J.	Criminal Justice Journal		
Crim.Just. Newsl.	Criminal Justice Newsletter	Crounse	Crounse (NE)
Crim.Just.Q.	Criminal Justice Quarterly	C.R.T.C.	Canadian Railway & Transport Cases
Crim.Just. Rev.	Criminal Justice Review	Crumrine	Crumrine (PA)
		CS	Connecticut Supplement
Crim.L.Bull.	Criminal Law Bulletin	C.S.C.R.	Cincinnati Superior Court Reporter
Crim.L.F. Int'l J.	Criminal Law Forum: An International Journal	CSD	Customs Service Decisions
Crim.L.J.	Criminal Law Journal	C.S.T.	Capital Stock Tax Division (I.R.B.)
Crim.L.Mag.	Criminal Law Magazine (NJ)	C.T.	Carrier's Taxing Ruling (I.R.B.)
Crim.L.Mag. & Rep.	Criminal Law Magazine and Reporter	Ct	Connecticut Reports
Crim.L.Q.	Criminal Law Quarterly	CtA	Connecticut Appellate Reports
Crim LR	Criminal Law Review	C.T.C.	Canada Tax Cases
Crim.L.Rec.	Criminal Law Recorder	ctcl	U.S. Court of Claims Reports
Crim.L.Rep.	Criminal Law Reporter	Ct.Cl.	Same
		Ct.Cust & Pat. App.	Court of Customs & Patent Appeals
Crim.L.Rev.	Criminal Law Review (Manhattan)	ctcustapp	U.S. Court of Customs Appeals Reports
Crim.L.Rev. (Eng.)	Criminal Law Review (Eng.)		
Crim.L.Rptr.	Criminal Law Reporter	Ct.Cust.App.	Same
Crim. Prac. L. Rev.	Criminal Practice Law Review	C.T.L.J.	California Trial Lawyers Journal
Crim.Rep. (N.S.)	Criminal Reports, New Series	CTLR	Computer and Telecommunications Law Review
Cripp Ch.Cas.	Cripp's Church & Clergy Cases	Ct.Rev.	Court Review
Critch.	Critchfield (OH)	C.T.S.	Consolidated Treaty Series
Cro.	Croke's King's Bench (Eng.)	C.U.	California Unreported Cases

CuCt	Customs Court Reports	Curry	Curry (LA)
CuD	Customs Court Decisions	curt	Curtis Circuit Court (U.S.)
Cumb.L.Rev.	Cumberland Law Review	Curt.	Same
Cum.Bull.	Cumulative Bulletin	Curt. Eccl.	Curtis, Eccelesiastical (Eng.)
Cum.L.Rev.	Cumberland Law Review	Cush.	Cushing's Reports (MA)
Cummins	Cummins (ID)	cushma	Same
Cum.Sam.L. Rev.	Cumberland–Samford Law Review	Cust.App.	United States Customs Appeals
Cunn.	Cunningham King's Bench (Eng.)	Cust.Ct.	Custom Court Reports (U.S.)
Cur.Leg. Thought	Current Legal Thought	C.W.Dud.	C.W. Dudley's Law or Equity (SC)
Current Com. & Leg.Mis.	Current Comment and Legal Miscellany	C.W.Dudl.Eq.	C.W. Dudley's Equity (SC)
		C.W.L. Rev.	California Western Law Review
Current L.	Current Law	Cy	Connoly's Surrogate's Court Reports (NY)
Current L. & Soc.Prob.	Current Law and Social Problems		
Current Legal Prob.	Current Legal Problems	Cyc.	Cyclopedia of Law & Procedure
Current L.Y.B.	Current Law Yearbook	Czech.J. Int'l L.	Czechoslovak Journal of International Law
Current Med. for Atty's	Current Medicine for Attorneys		
Currents: Int'l Trade L.J.	Currents: International Trade Law Journal	Czech.Y.B. Int'l L.	Czechoslovak Yearbook of International Law

D

D.	Disney (OH)	daly	Daly's Reports (NY)
Dak.	Dakota Reports	Daly	Same
Dak.L.Rev.	Dakota Law Review	Dan.	Daniell's Exchequer & Equity (Eng.)
Dal	Daly's Reports (NY)		
Dal.C.P.	Dallson's Common Pleas (Eng.)	Dana	Dana (KY)
Dale	Dale (OK)	D. & B.	Dearsley & Bell's Crown Cases (Eng.)
Dale Ecc.	Dale's Ecclesiastical (Eng.)		
Dale Eccl.	Same	D. & B.C.C.	Same
Dale Leg.Rit.	Dale's Legal Ritual (Eng.)	D. & C.	Deacon & Chitty's Bankruptcy Cases (Eng.)
Dalhousie L.J.	Dalhousie Law Journal		Dow & Clark's Parliamentary Cases (Eng.)
Dal. in Keil.	Dallison in Keilway's King's Bench (Eng.)		
Dall.	Dallam (TX)	D. & Ch.	Same
	Dallas (PA)	D. & Chit.	Same
	Dallas (U.S.)	D. & E.	Dwinford & East's King's Bench, Term Reports (Eng.)
Dallam	Dallam's Decisions (TX)		
dallassc	Dallas' U.S. Supreme Court Reports	D. & J.	De Gex & Jones, Chancery (Eng.)
Dalr.	Dalrymple's Decisions (S.C.)	D. & J.B.	De Gex & Jones, Bankruptcy (Eng.)

D. & L.	Dowling & Lowndes, Bail Court (Eng.)
D. & M.	Davison & Merivale's Queen's Bench (Eng.)
D. & P.	Denison & Pearce's Crown Cases (Eng.)
D. & R.	Dowling & Ryland's King's Bench (Eng.)
D. & R.Mag. Cas.	Same
D. & R.M.C.	Dowling & Ryland's Magistrates' Cases (Eng.)
D. & R.N.P.	Dowling & Ryland's Nisi Prius Cases (Eng.)
D. & R.N. P.C.	Same
D. & S.	Deane & Swabey's Ecclesiastical (Eng.)
	Drewry & Smale's Chancery (Eng.)
D. & Sm.	Drewry & Smale's Chancery (Eng.)
D. & Sw.	Deane & Swabey Ecclesiastical (Eng.)
D. & W.	Drewry & Walsh's Chancery (Ir.)
	Drewry & Warren's Chancery (Ir.)
D. & War.	Drewry & Warren's Chancery (Ir.)
Dane Abr.	Dane's Abridgment of American Law (Eng.)
Dann	Dann (AZ)
	Dann (CA)
Dann.	Danner (AL)
Dans. & L.	Danson & Lloyd's Mercantile Cases (Eng.)
Dans. & Lld.	Same
D'Anv.Abr.	D'Anver's Abridgment (Eng.)
dar	Daily Appellate Report (CA)
Dass.Ed.	Dassler (KS)
Dauph.Co.	Dauphin County (PA)
Dav. & M.	Davison & Merivale, Queen's Bench (Eng.)
Dav. & Mer.	Same
Daveis	Daveis (Ware) (U.S.)
Davies	Davis, King's Bench (Ir.)
Davis	Daveis (Ware) (U.S.)
	Davis (HI)
	Davis, King's Bench (Ir.)

Davys	Davys, King's Bench
day	Day's Reports (CT)
Day	Same
Dayton	3 Ohio Miscellaneous Decisions
Dayton Term Rep.	Iddings' Term Reports (OH)
Dayton T.R.	Same
D.B.	Domesday Book
D.B. & M.	Dunlop, Bell & Murray (Scot.)
D.C.	District of Columbia Reports
	Treasury Department Circular (I.R.B.)
DC2d	Pennsylvania District and County Reports, Second Series
DC3d	Same, Third Series
DC4d	Same, Fourth Series
D.C.A.	Dorion's Queen's Bench (Can.)
D.C.App.	District of Columbia Appeals
D.C.B.J.	District of Columbia Bar Journal
D.C.Cir.	District of Columbia Court of Appeals Cases
DCh	Delaware Chancery Reports
DCH	Reports of the United States District Court of Hawaii
dchip	D. Chipman's Reports (VT)
D.Chip.	Same
D.Chipm.	Same
D.C.L.Rev.	District of Columbia Law Review
D.D.C.	District Court, District of Columbia
D.Dec.	Dix's School Decisions (NY)
Dea.	Deady, United States Circuit & District Courts (CA & OR)
Dea. & Chit.	Deacon & Chitty (Eng.)
Dea. & Sw.	Deane & Swabey's Ecclesiastical (Eng.)
	Deane & Swabey's Probate & Divorce (Eng.)

Deac.	Deacon, Bankruptcy (Eng.)	De G.F. & J.	De Gex, Fisher & Jones, Chancery (Eng.)
Deac. & C.	Deacon & Chitty, Bankruptcy (Eng.)	De G.J. & S.	De Gex, Jones & Smith, Chancery (Eng.)
Deac. & Chit.	Same		
Deacon & C.	Same	De G.M. & G.	De Gex, Macnaghten & Gordon, Chancery (Eng.)
Deacon, Bankr. Cas.	Deacon, Bankruptcy (Eng.)		
deady	Deady's United States Circuit Court Reports	del	Delaware Reports
		Del.	Same
		delch	Delaware Chancery Reports
Deady	Deady, United States Circuit and District Courts (CA & OR)	Del.Ch.	Same
		Del.Co.	Delaware County (PA)
Deane	Deane (VT) Deane & Swabey's Probate & Divorce (Eng.)	Del.County	Delaware County Reports
		Del.Cr.Cas.	Delaware Criminal Cases
Deane & S.Eccl.Rep.	Deane & Swabey's Ecclesiastical (Eng.)	Del.J.Corp.L.	Delaware Journal of Corporate Law
		Dem.	Demarest's Surrogate Court Reports (NY)
Deane & Sw.	Same		
Deane Ecc.	Same		
Deane Ecc.Rep.	Same	Dem.Surr.	Same
Dears.	Dearsley & Bell, Crown Cases (Eng.)	Den.	Denio's Reports (NY) Denis (LA)
Dears. & B.	Same	Den. & P.	Denison & Pearce's Crown Cases (Eng.)
Dears. & B.C.C.	Same		
Dears.C.C.	Same	Den. & P.C.C.	Same
Deas & A.	Deas & Anderson (Scot.)	Den.C.C.	Denison's Crown Cases (Eng.)
Deas & And.	Same	Denio	Denio (NY)
Decalogue	Decalogue Journal	Denis	Denis (LA)
Dec.Com.Pat.	Decisions of Commissioner of Patents	Den.J. Int'l L. & Policy	Denver Journal of International Law and Policy
Dec.Dig.	Decennial Digest	Den.L.J.	Denver Law Journal
Decisions and Reports	Decisions and Reports of European Commission on Human Rights	Den.L.N.	Denver Legal News
		Denning L.Rev.	Denning Law Review
		Den.U.L.Rev.	Denver University Law Review
Dec.Rep.	Ohio Decisions Reprint	Denv.J.Int'l L. & Pol'y	Denver Journal of International Law and Policy
Dec.U.S. Compt. Gen.	Decisions of United States Comptroller General		
		Denv.U.L.Rev.	Denver University Law Review
Deering's Gen Laws	Deering's General Laws (CA)	DePaul Bus.L.J.	DePaul Business Law Journal
Def. Couns. J.	Defense Counsel Journal	DePaul L.Rev.	DePaul Law Review
		Dept.State Bull.	Department of State Bulletin (U.S.)
Def.L.J.	Defense Law Journal	Des.	Dessaussure's Equity (SC)
De G. & J.	De Gex & Jones, Chancery (Eng.)		
		Desaus.Eq.	Same
De G. & Sm.	De Gex & Smale, Chancery (Eng.)	Dess.	Same
		Dessaus.	Same
De Gex	De Gex, Bankruptcy (Eng.)	Det.C.L.Rev.	Detroit College of Law Review

Det.Leg.N.	Detroit Legal News
Det.L.J.	Detroit Law Journal
Det.L.Rev.	Detroit Law Review
Detroit Coll L Rev	Detroit College of Law Review
Detroit L.Rev.	Detroit Law Review
Dev	Devereux's Reports
Dev.	Devereux's Equity (NC)
	Devereux's Law (NC)
	Devereux's United States Court of Claims
Dev. & B.	Devereux & Battle's Equity (NC)
	Devereux & Battle's Law (NC)
Dev.Ct.Cl.	Devereux's Court of Claims (U.S.)
Dew.	Dewey (KS)
De Witt	De Witt (OH)
Di.	Dyer's King's Bench (Eng.)
Dice	Dice (IN)
Dick.	Dickens' Chancery (Eng.)
	Dickinson's Equity (NJ)
Dick.J.Envtl. L. & Pol'y	Dickinson Journal of Environmental Law and Policy
Dick.J.Int'l L.	Dickinson Journal of International Law
Dick. Law.	Dickinson Lawyers
Dick.L.Rev.	Dickinson Law Review
Dicta	Dicta of Denver Bar Association
	Dicta Magazine, San Diego Bar Association
Dig.C.L.W.	Digest of Commercial Law of the World (Oceana)
D.I.L. (Hack.)	Digest of International Law (Hackworth)
D.I.L. (Moore)	Digest of International Law (Moore)
D.I.L. (White.)	Digest of International Law (Whiteman)
dill	Dillon's U.S. Circuit Court Reports
Dill.	Same
Dirl.Dec.	Direlton's Decisions (Scot.)
Disn.	Disney (OH)
Disney	Same

Dispute Res.N.	Dispute Resolution Notes
Dist.	California District Court
distcol	District of Columbia Reports
D.L.R.	Dominion Law Reports (Can.)
D.L.R.2d	Same, Second Series
D.L.R.3d	Same, Third Series
Docket	Docket (Lebanon, PA)
	Docket (St. Paul, MN)
	Docket Magazine, Sacramento Bar Association
Dod.	Dodson's Admiralty (Eng.)
Dod.Adm.	Same
Dods.	Same
Dom.L.R.	Dominion Law Reports (Can.)
Donaker	Donaker (IN)
Donn.	Donnelly's Chancery (Eng.)
	Donnelly's Irish Land Cases
Donnelly	Same
Dorion	Dorion (Lower Can.)
Doshisha L.Rev.	Doshisha Law Review
Doug.	Douglas' Reports (MI)
	Douglas' King's Bench (Eng.)
dougl	Douglas Reports (MI)
Dougl.	Same
Dougl.El.Cas.	Douglas, Election Cases (Eng.)
Dougl.K.B.	Douglas, King's Bench (Eng.)
Dow	Dow's House of Lords Parliamentary Cases (Eng.)
Dow.	Dowling's Practice Cases (Eng.)
Dow & Cl.	Dow & Clark's House of Lords Cases (Eng.)
Dow. & L.	Dowling & Lowndes' Bail Court (Eng.)
Dowl. & Lownd.	Dowling & Lowndes' Practice Cases (Eng.)
Dowl. & R.	Dowling & Ryland's King's Bench (Eng.)

	Dowling & Ryland's Queen's Bench & Magistrates' Cases (Eng.)	Duer	Duer's Superior Court Reports (NY)
Dowl.P.C. (N.S.)	Dowling, Practice Cases, New Series (Eng.)	Duke B. Ass'n J.	Duke Bar Association Journal
Dowl.Pr.Cas.	Dowling, Practice Cases (Eng.)	Duke Envtl. L. & Pol'y F.	Duke Environmental Law and Policy Forum
Down. & Lud.	Downton & Luder's Election Cases (Eng.)	Duke J.Comp. & Int'l L.	Duke Journal of Comparative & International Law
D.P.R.	Decisiones de Puerto Rico	Duke L.J.	Duke Law Journal
Drake L.Rev.	Drake Law Review	Duke's Charitable Uses	Duke's Charitable Uses (Eng.)
Draper	Draper (Upper Can.)	Dunc.Ent. Cas.	Duncan Entail Cases (Scot.)
D.Rep.	Ohio Decisions Reprint	Dunc.N.P.	Duncombe, Nisi Prius
D.Repr.	Same	Dunl.	Dunlop, Bell & Murray (Scot.)
Drew	Drew (FL)		
Drew.	Drewry's Chancery (Eng.)	Dunl.B. & M.	Same
		Dunlop	Dunlop (Scot.)
Drew. & S.	Drewry & Smale's Chancery (Eng.)	Dunn.	Dunning's King's Bench (Eng.)
Drinkw.	Drinkwater Common Pleas (Eng.)	Duq.L.Rev.	Duquesne Law Review
Drug Abuse L.Rev.	Drug Abuse Law Review	Duq.U.L.Rev.	Duquesne University Law Review
Drug L.J.	Drug Law Journal	Durf.	Durfee (RI)
Drury	Drury's Chancery (Ir.)	Durfee	Same
		Durie	Durie (Scot.)
D.T.C.	Dominion Tax Cases	Durn. & E.	Durnford & East's King's Bench, Term Report (Eng.)
Dublin U.L.J.	Dublin University Law Journal		
Dublin U.L.Rev.	Dublin University Law Review	Dutch.	Dutcher's Law (NJ)
Dud	Dudley's Reports (GA)	Duv.	Duval's Reports (Can.)
Dudl.	Dudley (GA)		Duval's Supreme Court (Can.)
	Dudley's Equity (SC)		
	Dudley's Law (SC)	Dy.	Dyer's King's Bench (Eng.)
dudley	Dudley's Georgia Reports	Dyer	Same

E

E.	East's King's Bench (Eng.)	E. & A.	Grant Error & Appeal Reports (Upper Can.)
Ea.	Same		Spink's Ecclesiastical & Admiralty (Eng.)
E.Afr.L.J.	East African Law Journal		
E.Afr.L.R.	East Africa Law Reports	E. & B.	Ellis & Blackburn's Queen's Bench (Eng.)
E.Afr.L.Rev.	Eastern Africa Law Review	E. & E.	Ellis & Ellis' Queen's Bench (Eng.)
Eag. & Y.	Eagle & Young's Tithe Cases (Eng.)		
Eag.T.	Eagle's Commutation of Tithes (Eng.)	E. & I.	English & Irish Appeals, House of Lords (Eng.)

Earth L.J.	Earth Law Journal	Edm	Edmond's Select Cases (NY)
E.A.S.	Executive Agreement Series (U.S.)	Edm.Sel.Cas.	Edmond's Select Cases (NY)
East	East's King's Bench (Eng.)	EDR	Education Department Reports
East.	Eastern Reporter (U.S.)	E.D.S.	E.D. Smith's Reports (NY)
East.J.Int'l L.	Eastern Journal of International Law	EDSm	Same
East.L.R.	Eastern Law Reporter (Can.)	E.D.Smith	Same
		Educ. C.	Education Code (CA)
East P.C.	East's Pleas of the Crown (Eng.)	Edw.	Edwards (MO)
East.Rep.	Eastern Reporter (U.S.)		Edward's Chancery (NY)
East.T.	Eastern Term (Eng.)	Edw.Abr.	Edward's Abridgment, Prerogative Court Cases
East. U.S. Bus. L.Rev.	Eastern United States Business Law Review		Edward's Abridgment, Privy Council
E.A.W.R.	Employment–At–Will Reporter	Edw.Adm.	Edward's Admiralty (Eng.)
E.B. & E.	Ellis, Blackburn & Ellis' Queen's Bench (Eng.)	Edw.Ch.	Edward's Chancery (NY)
E.B. & S.	Ellis, Best & Smith's Queen's Bench (Eng.)	Edw.Lead. Dec.	Edward's Leading Decisions in Admiralty
ebc	Employee Benefits Cases (BNA)	Edw.Pr.Cas.	Edward's Prize Cases, Admiralty (Eng.)
Ebersole	Ebersole (IA)	Edw.Pr.Ct. Cas.	Edward's Abridgement of Prerogative Court Cases
E.C.	English Chancery		
ECA	Temporary Emergency Court of Appeals	E.E.	English Exchequer
Eccl. & Adm.	Spink's Ecclesiastical & Admiralty (Upper Can.)	E.E.C.J.O.	Official Journal of the European Communities
Eccl.R.	Ecclesiastical Reports (Eng.)	E.E.C.L.	Encyclopedia of European Community Law (Bender)
Eccl.Rep.	Same	E.E.O.C.Compliance Manual	Equal Employment Opportunity Commission Compliance Manual (CCH)
E.C.L.	English Common Law		
E.C.L.R.	European Competition Law Review		
Ecology L.Q.	Ecology Law Quarterly		
E.C.R.	Reports of Cases before the Court of Justice of the European Communities	E.E.R.	English Ecclesiastical Reports
		Efird	Efird (SC)
		EG	Estates Gazette
		EGCS	Estates Gazette Case Summaries
Ed.	Eden's Chancery (Eng.)	E.G.L.	Encyclopedia of Georgia Law
Ed C	Education Code		
Ed.Ch.	Edward's Chancery Reports (NY)	EGLR	Estates Gazette Law Reports
Eden	Eden's Chancery (Eng.)	Ehrman 3d	Ehrman & Flavin, Taxing California Property (3d ed.)
Edg.	Edgar (Scot.)		
Edinb.L.J.	Edinburgh Law Journal	EHRR	European Human Rights Reports

EIPR	European Intellectual Property Review	Empl.Saf'y & Health Guide	Employment Safety and Health Guide (CCH)
El.	Elchie's Decisions (Scot.)	Enc.Pl. & Pr.	Encyclopedia of Pleading & Practice
El. & B.	Ellis & Blackburn's Queen's Bench (Eng.)	Enc.U.S.Sup. Ct.Rep.	Encyclopedia of United States Supreme Court Reports
El. & Bl.	Same		
El. & El.	Ellis & Ellis, Queen's Bench (Eng.)	Energy Controls	Energy Controls (P–H)
E.L. & Eq.	English Law & Equity Reports	Energy L.J.	Energy Law Journal
		Eng.	English (AR)
El.B. & E.	Ellis, Blackburn & Ellis' Queen's Bench (Eng.)	Eng.Adm.	English Admiralty
		Eng.Adm.R.	English Admiralty Reports
El.B. & El.	Same	Eng.C.C.	English Crown Cases
El.B. & S.	Ellis, Best & Smith's Queen's Bench (Eng.)	Eng.Ch.	Condensed English Chancery
			English Chancery
El.Bl. & El.	Ellis, Blackburn & Ellis' Queen's Bench (Eng.)	Eng.C.L.	English Common Law Reports
		Eng.Com.L.R.	Same
El.Cas.	Election Cases	Eng.Cr.Cas.	English Crown Cases
Elchies'	Elchies' Decisions (Scot.)	Eng.Eccl.	English Ecclesiastical Reports
Elec C	Elections Code (CA)	Eng.Ecc.R.	Same
Elect.Cas. (N.Y.)	Election Cases, Armstrong, NY	Eng.Exch.	English Exchequer
		Eng.Hist. Rev.	English Historical Review
Elect.Rep.	Election Reports (Ont.)	Eng.Ir.App.	Law Reports English & Irish Appeals
ELJ	Ecclesiastical Law Journal	Eng.Judg.	English Judges (Scot.)
Ell. & Bl.	Ellis & Blackburn's Queen's Bench (Eng.)	Eng.L. & Eq.	English Law & Equity Reports
		Eng.L. & Eq.R.	Same
Ell.Bl. & Ell.	Ellis, Blackburn & Ellis' Queen's Bench (Eng.)	Eng.Rep.	English Reports, Full Reprint
		Eng.Rep.R.	Same
El Paso Trial Law.Rev.	El Paso Trial Lawyers Review	Eng.Ry. & C.Cas.	English Railway and Canal Cases
Elr	Environmental Law Reporter	Eng.Sc.Ecc.	English & Scotch Ecclesiastical Reports
E.L.R.	Eastern Law Reporter (Can.)	Entertainment & Med.L.	Entertainment & Media Law
Els.W.Bl.	Elsley's Edition of William Blackstone's King's Bench (Eng.)	Entertainment L.J.	Entertainment Law Journal
		Envir.L.	Environmental Law
		Envtl.Affairs	Environmental Affairs
Em.App.	Emergency Court of Appeals (U.S.)	Envtl.F.	Environmental Forum
Emory Int'l L.Rev.	Emory International Law Review	Envtl.L.	Environmental Law
		Envtl.L.J.	Environmental Law Journal
Emory J. Int'l Disp.Resol.	Emory Journal of International Dispute Resolution	Envtl.L.Rev.	Environmental Law Review
Emory L.J.	Emory Law Journal	Envtl.L.Rptr.	Environmental Law Reporter
Empl.Rel.L.J.	Employee Relations Law Journal		

Envtl.Pol'y & L.	Environmental Policy and Law	Eur.L.Dig.	European Law Digest
Env't Rptr.	Environment Reporter (BNA)	Eur.L.Newsl.	European Law Newsletter
E.P.D.	Employment Practices Decisions (CCH)	Eur.L.Rev.	European Law Review
Eq.Cas.Abr.	Equity Cases Abridged (Eng.)	Eurolaw Com.Intel.	Eurolaw Commercial Intelligence
Eq.Rep.	Harper's Equity (SC)	Europ.T.S.	European Treaty Series
Equity Rep.	English Chancery Appeals	Eur.Parl. Deb.	Debates of the European Parliament
	Gilbert, Equity (Eng.)	Eur.Parl. Docs.	European Parliament Working Documents
	Harper's Equity (SC)		
E.R.	East's King's Bench (Eng.)	Eur.Tax.	European Taxation
erc	Environment Reporter Cases (BNA)	Eur.Trans.L.	European Transport Law
E.R.C.	English Ruling Cases	Eur.Y.B.	European Yearbook
	Environmental Reporter Cases	Evans	Evans, Washington Territory Reports
Err. & App.	Error & Appeals (Upper Can.)	Ev C	Evidence Code (CA)
Ersk.	Erskine (U.S. Circuit Court)	Evid. C.	Same
		Ex.	Exchequer Reports (Eng.)
E.School L.Rev.	Eastern School Law Review	Examiner	Examiner (NY)
Esp.	Espinasse's Nisi Prius (Eng.)		Examiner (Que.)
Esp.N.P.	Same	Excerpta Crim.	Excerpta Criminologica
Est. & Tr.J.	Estates & Trusts Journal	Exch.	Exchequer (Scot.)
Est. & Tr.Q.	Estates and Trusts Quarterly		Welsby, Hurlstone & Gordon, Exchequer (Eng.)
Est. Gifts & Tr.J.	Estates, Gifts & Trusts Journal	Exch.Can.	Exchequer Reports (Can.)
Est.Plan.	Estate Planning	Exch.Cas.	Exchequer Cases (Scot.)
Est.Plan.Rev.	Estate Planning Review (CCH)	Exch.Rep.	Exchequer Reports
E.T.	Estate Tax Division (I.R.B.)	Ex.C.R.	Exchequer Court Reports (Can.)
E.T.R.	Estates & Trusts Reports	Ex.D.	Law Reports, Exchequer Division (Eng.)
Euer	Euer Doctrina Placitandi (Eng.)	Ex.Div.	Same
Eur.Consult. Ass.Deb.	Council of Europe Consultative Assembly, Official Report of Debates	Exec.Order	Executive Order
		Eyre	Eyre's King's Bench (Eng.)

F

f	Federal Reporter (U.S.)	f2d	Federal Reporter, Second Series (U.S.)
F.	Same	F.2d	Same
F. (Ct.Sess.)	Fraser's Court of Sessions Cases (Scot.)	f3d	Same, Third Series
		F.3d	Same

Fac.L.Rev.	Faculty of Law Review (Toronto)	fcdr	Fulton County Daily Report (GA)
F.A.D.	Federal Anti–Trust Decisions	FCirT	Trade Cases in the U.S. Court of Appeals for the Federal Circuit
Fairf.	Fairfield (ME)		
Falc.	Falconer's Court of Sessions Cases (Scot.)	FCR	Family Court Reporter
Falc. & F.	Falconer & Fitzherbert's Election Cases (Eng.)	Fd & Ag C	Food and Agricultural Code
Fam (preceded by date)	Law Reports (Family Division)	F.D.Cosm.L. Rep.	Food, Drug, Cosmetic Law Reporter (CCH)
Fam C	Family Code (CA)	Fed.	Federal Reporter (U.S.)
Family Law Service	California Family Law Service		
Family L News	Family Law News	fedapp	Federal Appeals
Family LQ	Family Law Quarterly	Fed.Appx.	West's Federal Appendix
Fam Law	Family Law (journal)	Fed.B.A.J.	Federal Bar Association Journal
Fam.L. Commtr.	Family Law Commentator	Fed.B.J.	Federal Bar Journal
Fam.L. Newsl.	Family Law Newsletter	Fed.B.News	Federal Bar News
		Fed.Carr. Rep.	Federal Carriers Reporter (CCH)
Fam.L.Q.	Family Law Quarterly	Fed.Cas.	Federal Cases (U.S.)
Fam.L.Rep.	Family Law Reporter (BNA)	fedcir	Federal Circuit Trade Cases
Fam.L.Rev.	Family Law Review	fedcl	Federal Claims Reporter
F. & F.	Foster & Finlason, Nisi Prius (Eng.)	Fed.Com.B.J.	Federal Communications Bar Journal
F & G C	Fish and Game Code	Fed.Com.L.J.	Federal Communications Law Journal
F.App.	West's Federal Appendix		
Far.	Farresley's King's Bench (Eng.)	Fed.Crim.L. Rep.	Federal Criminal Law Report
Far East.L.Rev.	Far Eastern Law Review	Fed.Ct.Rep.	Federal Court Reports (Aust.)
F.B.C.	Fonblanque's Bankruptcy Cases (Eng.)	Fed.Est. & Gift Tax Rep.	Federal Estate and Gift Tax Reporter (CCH)
FBILEB	Federal Bureau of Investigation Law Enforcement Bulletin	Fed.Juror	Federal Juror
		Fed.L.Rep.	Federal Law Reports
FC	Federal Cases	Fed.L.Rev.	Federal Law Review
F.C.	Faculty Collection of Decisions (Scot.) Canada Federal Court Reports	Fed'n Ins. Counsel Q.	Federation of Insurance Counsel Quarterly
		Fed.Prob.	Federal Probation
F.C.A.	Federal Code Annotated	Fed RCP	Federal Rules of Civil Procedure
F.Carr.Cas.	Federal Carriers Cases (CCH)	Fed.Reg.	Federal Register
fcas	Federal Cases	Fed.Rules Serv.	Federal Rules Service
F.C.C.	Federal Communication Commission Reports	Fed.Rules Serv.2d	Same, Second Series
FCCR	Federal Communications Commission Record	Fee Arb Rules	Rules of Procedure for the Hearing of Fee Arbitrations by the State Bar of California

Fee Arb Stds	State Bar Guidelines and Minimum Standards for Mandatory Fee Arbitration Programs	Fla.St.U. L.Rev.	Florida State University Law Review
fep	Fair Employment Practices (BNA)	flasupp	Florida Supplement
		Fla.Supp.	Same
F.E.P.Cas.	Fair Employment Practices Cases	flasupp2d	Same, Second Series
ferc	Federal Energy Regulatory Commission Reporter (CCH)	Fletcher F. World Aff.	Fletcher Forum of World Affairs
		flip	Flippin's U.S. Circuit Court Reports
Ferg.Cons.	Fergusson's Consistory, Divorce (Scot.)	Flipp.	Same
		F.L.J.	Forum Law Journal (U. of Baltimore)
Fergusson	Fergusson (of Kilkeran) (Scot.)	F.L.P.	Florida Law and Practice
F.H.L.	Fraser, House of Lords (Scot.)	FLR	Family Law Reports
		FLS	Florida Supplement
Fin C	Financial Code	FLS2d	Same, Second Series
Finch	Finch's Chancery (Eng.)	flw	Florida Law Weekly
		flwfeds	Florida Law Weekly–Federal
Fin. L. R.	Financial Law Reports	F.M.C.	Federal Maritime Commission Reports
Fin.Tax. & Comp.L.	Finance Taxation and Company Law (Pak.)	Fogg	Fogg (NH)
		F.O.I.C.R.	Freedom of Information Center Reports
Fire & Casualty Cas.	Fire and Casualty Cases (CCH)	F.O.I.Dig.	Freedom of Information Digest
Fish & Game C.	Fish and Game Code (CA)	Fonbl.	Fonblanque's Bankruptcy (Eng.)
Fish & G.C.	Same	Food & Ag. C.	Food and Agricultural Code (CA)
fishpatcas	Fisher's U.S. Patent Cases	Food & Agric. C.	Same
Fish.Pat.Cas.	Same	Food Drug Cosm.L.J.	Food, Drug, Cosmetic Law Journal
Fish.Pat.R.	Fisher's Patent Reports (U.S.)	Fordham Ent.Media & Intell. Prop. L.F.	Fordham Entertainment Media & Intellectual Property Law Forum
fishpr	Fisher's U.S. Prize Cases		
Fish.Prize Cas.	Same	Fordham Envtl. L.Rep.	Fordham Environmental Law Report
Fitzh.	Fitzherbert's Abridgment (Eng.)		
Fitzh.N.Br.	Fitzherbert's Natura Brevium (Eng.)	Fordham Int'l L.F.	Fordham International Law Forum
fla	Florida Reports	Fordham Int'l L.J.	Fordham International Law Journal
Fla.	Same		
Fla. & K.	Flanagan & Kelly, Rolls (Ir.)	Fordham L.Rev.	Fordham Law Review
Fla.B.J.	Florida Bar Journal	Fordham Urb. L.J.	Fordham Urban Law Journal
Fla.Int'l L.J.	Florida International Law Journal	Form.	Forman (IL)
Fla.J.Int'l L.	Florida Journal of International Law	Forr.	Forrest's Exchequer (Eng.)
Fla.Jur.	Florida Jurisprudence	Forrester	Forrester's Chancery Cases Tempore Talbot (Eng.)
Fla. L.J.	Florida Law Journal		
Fla. L. Rev.	Florida Law Review		
Flan. & Kel.	Flanagan & Kelly, Rolls (Ir.)	For.Sci.	Forensic Science

For.Tax Bull.	Foreign Tax Law Bi–Weekly Bulletin	France	France (CO)
Fortesc.	Fortescue's King's Bench (Eng.)	Franchise L. Rev.	Franchise Law Review
Fort.L.J.	Fortnightly Law Journal	Fran.Coll.L.J.	Franciso College Law Journal
Forum	The Forum	Fraser	Fraser, Court of Session Cases (Scot.)
Fost.	Foster (HI)		
	Foster (NH)	FRCh	Freeman's Chancery Reports (MS)
	Foster's Crown Cases (Eng.)	frd	Federal Rules Decisions
	Foster's Legal Chronicle Reports (PA)	F.R.D.	Same
Found.L.Rev.	Foundation Law Review	Freem.	Freeman (IL)
Fount.Dec.	Fountainhall's Decisions (Scot.)	freemch	Freeman's Mississippi Chancery Reports
Fox	Fox's Registration Cases (Eng.)	Freem.Ch.	Same
	Fox's Decisions (ME)	Freem.K.B.	Freeman's King's Bench (Eng.)
Fox & S.	Fox & Smith's King's Bench (Ir.)	French	French (NH)
Fox Pat.C.	Fox's Patent, Trade Mark, Design and Copyright Cases	freserv	Federal Rules of Evidence Service
		FS	Federal Supplement
		FS2d	Same, Second Series
		FSR	Fleet Street Reports
F.P.C.	Federal Power Commission Decisions	fsupp	Federal Supplement
FPC	Federal Power Commission Reports	F.Supp.	Same
		F.Supp.2d	Same, 2d
FR	Federal Register	ftc	Federal Trade Commission Decisions
FR	Fordham Law Review	F.T.C.	Same
		Fuller	Fuller (MI)

G

ga	Georgia Reports	Gale & Dav.	Same
GA	Decisions of General Appraisers (U.S.)	Ga.L.J.	Georgia Law Journal
		gall	Gallison's U.S. Circuit Court Reports
Ga.	Georgia Reports		
GaA	Georgia Appeals Reports	Gall.	Same
		Ga.L.Rep.	Georgia Law Reports
gaapp	Same	Ga.L.Rev.	Georgia Law Review
Ga.App.	Same	G. & D.	Gale & Davison's Queen's Bench (Eng.)
Ga.B.J.	Georgia Bar Journal		
Ga.Bus.Law.	Georgia Business Lawyer		
Ga.Dec.	Georgia Decisions	G. & G.	Goldsmith & Guthrie (MO)
gadecpt1; gadecpt2	Same, Part 1; Part 2	G. & J.	Gill & Johnson (MD)
Ga.J.Int'l & Comp.L.	Georgia Journal of International & Comparative Law		Glyn & Jameson's Bankruptcy (Eng.)
		G. & R.	Geldert & Russell (Nova Scotia)
Galb.	Galbraith (FL)		
Galb. & M.	Galbraith & Meek (FL)	Garden.	Gardenhire (MO)
		Gard.N.Y. Reptr.	Gardenier's New York Reporter
Gale	Gale's Exchequer (Eng.)	GaS	Georgia Reports, Supplement
Gale & D.	Gale & Davison's Queen's Bench (Eng.)	Ga.St.B.J.	Georgia State Bar Journal

Ga.St.U. L.Rev.	Georgia State University Law Review	Gibb.Surr.	Gibbon's Surrogate (NY)
gasupp	Lester's Supplement (GA)	Giff.	Giffard's Chancery (Eng.)
Ga.Supp.	Same	Giff. & H.	Giffard & Hemming's Chancery (Eng.)
Gaz.	Gazette		
	Weekly Law Gazette (U.S.)	Gil.	Gilman (Ill.)
Gaz.Bankr.	Gazette of Bankruptcy	Gilb.	Gilbert's Chancery (Eng.)
Gaz.L.R.	Gazette Law Reports	Gilb.Cas.	Gilbert's Cases, Law & Equity (Eng.)
G.C.M.	General Counsel's Memorandum (I.R.B.)	Gilb.C.P.	Gilbert's Common Pleas (Eng.)
		Gilb.Exch.	Gilbert's Exchequer (Eng.)
G.Coop.	G. Cooper's Chancery (Eng.)	Gildr.	Gildersleeve (NM)
GD(1)	Georgia Decisions, Part 1	Gilf.	Gilfillan (MN)
		gill	Gill's Reports (MD)
GD(2)	Same, Part 2	Gill	Same
Geld. & M.	Geldart & Maddock's Chancery (Eng.)	gill & j	Gill & Johnson Maryland Reports
Geld. & O.	Geldert & Oxley (Nova Scotia)	Gill & J.	Same
		Gill & Johns.	Same
Geo	Georgetown Law Journal	Gilm.	Gilmer (VA)
		Gilm. & Falc.	Gilmour & Falconer (Scot.)
Geo.Immigr. L.J.	Georgetown Immigration Law Journal	gilp	Gilpin's U.S. District Court Reports
Geo.Int'l Envtl. L.Rev.	Georgetown International Environmental Law Review	Gilp.	Same
		GJ	Gill & Johnson Reports (MD)
		Gl. & J.	Glyn & Jameson's Bankruptcy Cases (Eng.)
Geo.J.Legal Ethics	Georgetown Journal of Legal Ethics	Glanv.	Glanville De Legibus et Consuetudinibus Angliae (Eng.)
Geo.L.J.	Georgetown Law Journal		
Geo.Mason L. Rev.	George Mason Law Review	Glanv.El.Cas.	Glanville's Election Cases (Eng.)
Geo.Mason U.Civ.Rts. L.J.	George Mason University Civil Rights Law Journal	Glasc.	Glascock (Ir.)
		Glendale LR	Glendale Law Review
Geo.Mason U.L.Rev.	George Mason University Law Review	Glendale L.Rev.	Same
		Glenn	Glenn (LA)
George	George (MS)	Glyn & J.	Glyn & Jameson's Bankruptcy Cases (Eng.)
Geo.Wash.J. Int'l L. & Econ.	George Washington Journal of International Law and Economics	Glyn & Jam.	Same
		Godb.	Godbolt's King's Bench (Eng.)
Geo.Wash. L.Rev.	George Washington Law Review	Godson	Godson, Mining Commissioner's Cases
ggreene	George Greene's Iowa Reports	Goebel	Goebel's Probate (OH)
gib	Gibbons' Surrogate Court Reports (NY)	Gold. & G.	Goldsmith & Guthrie (MO)
Gib	Same	Golden Gate LR	Golden Gate Law Review
Gibbs	Gibbs (MI)		

Golden Gate L.Rev.	Same	grayma	Gray's Massachusetts Reports
Golden Gate U.L.Rev.	Golden Gate University Law Review	Gre	G. Greene's Reports (IA)
Gonz.L.Rev.	Gonzaga Law Review	Green	Green (OK)
Gonz.Pub. Lab. L.Rep.	Gonzaga Special Report: Public Sector Labor Law		Green (RI) Green Equity (NJ) Green Law (NJ)
Gottschall	Gottschall (OH)	Green Cr.	Green's Criminal Law (Eng.)
Gouldsb.	Gouldsborough's King's Bench (Eng.)	Greene	Greene (IA) Greene's Annotated Cases (NY)
Gov C	Government Code (CA)	Greenl.	Greenleaf (ME)
Govt. C.	Same	Greenl.Ov. Cas.	Greenleaf's Overruled Cases
Gov't Cont.Rep.	Government Contracts Reporter (CCH)	Grein.Pr.	Greiner, Practice (LA)
Gow	Gow's Nisi Prius (Eng.)	Griffith	Griffith (IN)
		Gris.	Griswold (OH)
GR	Grant's Cases (PA)	Griswold	Same
Gr.	Grant, Chancery Reports (Upper Can.)	Group Legal Rev.	Group Legal Review
Granger	Granger (OH)	G.S.R.	Gongwer's State Reports (OH)
Grant	Grant's Cases (PA)		
grantcas	Same	Guild Prac.	Guild Practitioner
Grant Err. & App.	Grant's Error & Appeal (Upper Can.)	Guthrie	Guthrie (MO)
		G.W.D.	Green's Weekly Digest
Gratt.	Grattan (VA)		
Gray	Gray's Reports (MA) Gray (NC)	Gwill.T.Cas.	Gwillim's Tithe Cases (Eng.)

H

H.	Handy (OH)	Hale P.C.	Hale's Pleas of the Crown (Eng.)
Ha.	Hare's Vice–Chancery (Eng.)	Hall	Hall (NH)
HA	Hawaii Appellate Reports		Hall's Superior Court (NY)
Ha. & Tw.	Hall & Twell's Chancery (Eng.)	Hall.	Hallett (CO)
		Hall & Tw.	Hall & Twell's Chancery (Eng.)
HAC	Howard's Appeal Cases (NY)	Halst.	Halsted's Equity (NJ)
Had.	Hadley (NH)		Halsted's Law (NJ)
Hadd.	Haddington Manuscript Reports (Scot.)	Ham.	Hammond (GA) Hammond (OH)
		Ham.A. & O.	Hamerton, Allen & Otter, New Session Cases (Eng.)
Hadl.	Hadley (NH)		
Hagan	Hagan (UT)		
Hagans	Hagans (WV)	Ham. & J.	Hammond & Jackson (GA)
Hagg.Adm.	Haggard's Admiralty (Eng.)	Hamlin	Hamlin (ME)
Hagn. & M.	Hagner & Miller (MD)	Hamline J.Pub.L. & Pol'y	Hamline Journal of Public Law and Policy
Hailes Dec.	Hailes' Decisions (Scot.)	Hamline L.Rev.	Hamline Law Review
Hale	Hale (CA)	Hammond	Hammond (OH)
	Hale's Common Law (Eng.)	Han.	Handy (OH)
		Hand	Hand (NY)

H. & B.	Hudson & Brooke's King's Bench (Ir.)	Harb. & Nav. C.	Harbors and Navigation Code (CA)
H. & C.	Hurlstone & Coltman's Exchequer (Eng.)	Harc.	Harcarse, Decisions (Scot.)
		HarCh	Harrington's Chancery Reports (MI)
H. & D.	Hill & Denio, Lalor's Supplement (NY)	Hard.	Hardesty, Term Reports (DE)
H. & G.	Harris & Gill (MD)	Hardes.	Same
	Hurlstone & Gordon's Exchequer (Eng.)	Hardin	Hardin (KY)
		hardky	Same
H. & H.	Harrison & Hodgin's Municipal Reports (Upper Can.)	Hardres	Hardres' Exchequer (Eng.)
	Horn & Hurlstone's Exchequer (Eng.)	Hare	Hare's Vice–Chancery (Eng.)
H. & J.	Harris & Johason (MD)	Hare & W.	American Leading Cases, Hare & Wallace
	Hayes & Jones' Exchequer (Ir.)	Harg.	Hargrove (NC)
H. & J.Ir.	Same	Harp.	Harper's Equity (SC)
H. & M.	Hemming & Miller's Vice Chancery (Eng.)		Harper's Law (SC)
		Harper	Harper's Conspiracy Cases (MD)
	Hening & Munford (VA)	Harr.	Harrington's Reports (DE)
H. & M.Ch.	Hemming & Miller's Vice Chancery (Eng.)		Harrison (IN)
			Harrison (NJ)
		harr & g	Harris & Gill's Reports (MD)
H. & McH.	Harris & McHenry (MD)	Harr. & H.	Harrison & Hodgins' Municipal Reports (Upper Can.)
H. & N.	Hurlstone & Norman's Exchequer (Eng.)		
		Harr. & Hodg.	Same
H & N C	Harbors and Navigation Code (CA)	harr & j	Harris & Johnson's Reports (MD)
H. & R.	Harrison & Rutherford's Common Pleas (Eng.)	Harr. & J.	Same
		Harr. & M.	Harris & McHenry (MD)
H. & S.	Harris & Simrall (MS)	harr & mch	Same
		Harr. & R.	Harrison & Rutherford's Common Pleas (Eng.)
H & S C	Health and Safety Code (CA)		
H. & T.	Hall & Twell's Chancery (Eng.)	Harr. & W.	Harrison & Wollaston's King's Bench (Eng.)
H. & W.	Harrison & Wollaston's King's Bench (Eng.)		
		harrch	Harrington's Michigan Chancery Reports
	Hurlstone & Wahnsley's Exchequer (Eng.)	Harr.Ch.	Harrison's Chancery (Eng.)
Handy	Handy (OH)	harrde	Harrington's Delaware Reports
Han.N.B.	Hannay's Reports (N.B.)		
Hans.	Hansbrough (VA)	Harris	Harris (PA)
Har.	Harrington (DE)	Harris & G.	Harris & Gill (MD)
	Harrington's Chancery (MI)	Harris & S.	Harris & Simrall (MS)
	Harrison (LA)	Hart.	Hartley (TX)
	Harrison's Chancery (MI)	Hart. & H.	Hartley & Hartley (TX)

Harv.Blackletter J.	Harvard Blackletter Journal	Hast LJ	Hastings Law Journal
Harv.Bus.Rev.	Harvard Business Review	Havil.	Haviland (P.E.I.)
Harv.C.R.–C.L.L.Rev.	Harvard Civil Rights—Civil Liberties Law Review	Haw.	Hawaii Reports
		hawaii	Same
		Hawaii	Same
Harv. Envtl.L.Rev.	Harvard Environmental Law Review	Hawaii B.J.	Hawaii Bar Journal
		hawapp	Hawaii Appellate Reports
Harv.Hum. Rts.J.	Harvard Human Rights Journal	Hawk.	Hawkins' Louisiana Annual
Harv.Int'l L.J.	Harvard International Law Journal	Hawk.P.C.	Hawkins' Pleas of the Crown
Harv.J.L. & Pub.Pol'y	Harvard Journal of Law and Public Policy	Hawks	Hawks (NC)
		Hawl.	Hawley (NV)
		Hay.	Haywood (NC)
Harv. J. L. & Tech.	Harvard Journal of Law & Technology		Haywood (TN)
		Hay & H.	Hay & Hazelton (U.S.)
Harv.J. on Legis.	Harvard Journal on Legislation	Hay & M.	Hay & Marriott's Admiralty (Eng.)
Harv. L. R.	Harvard Law Review	Hayes	Hayes (Scot.)
Harv.L.Rev.	Same		Hayes' Exchequer (Ir.)
Harv.L.S. Bull.	Harvard Law School Bulletin	Hayes & J.	Hayes & Jones' Exchequer (Ir.)
Harv.Women's L.J.	Harvard's Women's Law Journal	hayw	Haywood's North Carolina Reports
Harv.W.Tax Ser.	Harvard World Tax Series (CCH)	Hayw.	Same
Hasb.	Hasbrouck (ID)		Haywood (TN)
Hask.	Haskell's Reports for United States Courts in Maine (Fox's Decisions)	haywtn	Haywood's Tennessee Reports
		Haz.Reg.	Hazard's Register (PA)
haskcc	Haskell's U.S. Circuit Court Reports	H.Bl.	Henry Blackstone's Common Pleas (Eng.)
Hast.	Hastings (ME)	hc	Hayward & Hazelton's U.S. Circuit Court Reports
Hast Comm/Ent LJ	Hastings Communications/Entertainment Law Journal		
Hast Const LQ	Hastings Constitutional Law Quarterly	HC	House of Commons Paper
		H.C.L.M.	Health Care Labor Manual
Hastings Comm. & Ent.L.J.	Hastings Communications and Environmental Law Journal	HCr	Houston's Criminal Reports (DE)
		Head	Head (TN)
		headtn	Head's Tennessee Reports
Hastings Const. L.Q.	Hastings Constitutional Law Quarterly	Health & Saf. C.	Health & Safety Code (CA)
Hastings Int'l & Comp.L. Rev.	Hastings International and Comparative Law Review	Health & S.C.	Same
		Health Matrix: J.L.-Med.	Health Matrix: Journal of Law–Medicine
Hastings L.J.	Hastings Law Journal	Heath	Heath (ME)
Hastings Women's L.J.	Hastings Women's Law Journal	Hedges	Hedges (MT)
Hast Intl & Comp LR	Hastings International and Comparative Law Review	heisk	Heiskell's Tennessee Reports

Heisk.	Same
Helm	Helm (NV)
Hem. & M.	Heming & Miller's Vice–Chancery (Eng.)
Heming.	Hemingway (MS)
Hemp.	Hempstead (U.S. Circuit Court)
hempst	Same
Hempst.	Same
Hen. & M.	Hening & Munford (VA)
Henning CLE Rep.	Henning Continuing Legal Education Reporter
Henn.Law.	Hennepin Lawyer (MN)
Hepb.	Hepburn (CO)
Het.	Hetley's Common Pleas (Eng.)
HG	Harris & Gill's Reports (MD)
HH	Hayward and Hazeleton's Reports
Hibb.	Hibbard (NH)
Hight	Hight (IA)
High Tech. L.J.	High Technology Law Journal
Hill	Hill (IL)
	Hill's Reports (NY)
	Hill's Equity (SC)
	Hill's Law (SC)
Hill & D.	Hill & Denio (NY)
Hillyer	Hillyer (CA)
Hil.T.	Hilary Tenn (Eng.)
Hilt.	Hilton's Reports (NY)
Hines	Hines (KY)
Hitotsubashi J.L. & Pol.	Hitotsubashi Journal of Law and Politics
HJ	Harris & Johnson's Reports (MD)
H.L.Cas.	House of Lords Cases (Eng.)
H.L.N.R.	Health Lawyers News Report
HLR	Harvard Law Review
	Housing Law Reports (Eng.)
HM	Harris & McHenry's Reports (MD)
Hob.	Hobart's Common Pleas & Chancery (Eng.)
Hobart	Hobart's King's Bench (Eng.)
Hod.	Hodges' Common Pleas (Eng.)
Hodg.El.	Hodgin's Election (Upper Can.)
Hodges	Hodges' Common Pleas (Eng.)
Hof	Hofstra Law Review
HofCh	Hoffman's Chancery Reports (NY)
hoff	Hoffman's Decisions
Hoff. Dec.	Same
hofflc	Hoffman's Land Cases (U.S. District Court)
Hoff. L. Cas.	Hoffman's Land Cases
Hoffm.	Hoffman's Chancery (NY)
	Hoffman's Land Cases (U.S.)
Hoff. Op.	Hoffman's Opinions
Hofstra Lab. L.F.	Hofstra Labor Law Forum
Hofstra Lab.L.J.	Hofstra Labor Law Journal
Hofstra L.Rev.	Hofstra Law Review
Hofstra Prop. L.J.	Hofstra Property Law Journal
Hog.	Hogan's Rolls Court (Ir.)
Hogoboom & King	Hogoboom & King, California Practice Guide Family Law
Hogue	Hogue (FL)
Holl.	Holligshead (MN)
holmes	Holmes (U.S. Circuit Court)
Holmes	Holmes (OR)
	Holmes (U.S.)
Holt Adm.	Holt's Admiralty Cases (Eng.)
Holt Eq.	Holt's Equity (Eng.)
	Holt's Vice Chancery (Eng.)
Holt K.B.	Holt's King's Bench (Eng.)
Holt N.P.	Holt's Nisi Prius (Eng.)
Home	Home Manuscript, Decisions, Court of Sessions (Scot.)
Hong Kong L.J.	Hong Kong Law Journal
Hook.	Hooker (CT)
Hope Dec.	Hope's Decisions (Scot.)
Hopk.	Hopkins' Chancery Reports (NY)
Hopk.Dec.	Hopkinson's Admiralty Decisions (PA)
Hopw. & C.	Hopwood & Coltman's Registration Appeal Cases (Eng.)

Hopw. & P.	Hopwood & Philbrick's Registration Appeal Cases (Eng.)	HP	Howard's Practice Reports (NY)
		HPns	Same, New Series
Horner	Horner (SD)	HPr	Same
Horw.Y.B.	(Horwood) Year Book of Edward I	H.R.J.	Human Rights Journal (Revue des droits de l'homme)
Hosea	Hosea (OH)	H.R.L.J.	Human Rights Law Journal
Hoskins	Hoskins (ND)		
Hou	Houston's Reports (DE)	Hubb.	Hubbard (ME)
		Hud. & B.	Hudson & Brooke's King's Bench (Ir.)
Houghton	Houghton (AL)		
Housing & Devel.Rep.	Housing and Development Reporter (BNA)	Hughes	Hughes (KY) Hughes (U.S.)
		hughescc	Hughes' U.S. Circuit Court Reports
Hous.J.Int'l L.	Houston Journal of International Law	hughesky	Hughes' Kentucky Reports
Hous.Law.	Houston Lawyer	Hume	Hume's Decisions (Scot.)
Hous.L.Rev.	Houston Law Review		
Houst.	Houston (DE)	Humph.	Humphrey
Houst.Cr.	Houston, Criminal Cases (DE)	Humphr.	Humphrey's (TN)
houstcrim	Same	Hum.Rts.	Human Rights
houstde	Houston's Delaware Reports	Hum.Rts.J.	Human Rights Journal
Houst.L.Rev.	Houston Law Review	Hum.Rts.L.J.	Human Rights Law Journal
Houston Law.	Houston Lawyer		
Hov.	Hovenden's Supplement, Vesey's Chancery (Eng.)	Hum.Rts.Q.	Human Rights Quarterly
		Hum.Rts.Rev.	Human Rights Review
How.	Howard (MS) Howard (U.S.) Howell (NV)	Hum.Rts. U.S.S.R.	Human Rights in Union of Soviet Socialist Republics
How.A.Cas.	Howard's Appeal Cases (NY)	humtn	Humphrey's Tennessee Reports
How. & Beat.	Howell & Beatty (NV)	hun	Hun New York Supreme Court Reports
How. & N.	Howell & Norcross (NV)	Hun	Same
howard	Howard's U.S. Supreme Court Reporter	Hung.L.Rev.	Hungarian Law Review
		Hunt.Torrens	Hunter's Torrens Cases
Howard Journal	Howard Journal of Criminal Justice	Hurl. & G.	Hurlstone & Gordon's Exchequer (Eng.)
Howard L.J.	Howard Law Journal		
How.Ch.	Howard's Chancery (Ir.)	Hurl. & W.	Hurlstone & Wahnsley's Exchequer (Eng.)
How.L.J.	Howard Law Journal		
hownp	Howell, Nisi Prius (MI)	Hutch.	Hutcheson (AL)
How.N.P.	Same	Hutt.	Hutton's Common Pleas (Eng.)
How.Pr.	Howard's Practice (NY)		
How.Pr. (N.S.)	Same, New Series	H.W.Gr.	H.W. Green's Equity (NJ)
How.St.Tr.	Howell's State Trials (Eng.)		

I

Ia	Iowa Reports	Idaho L.J.	Idaho Law Journal
I.A.C.	Immigration Appeal Cases	Idaho L.Rev.	Idaho Law Review
	Industrial Accident Commission Decisions	Idding	Idding's Term Reports (Dayton, OH)
IALS Bull.	Institute of Advanced Legal Studies, Bulletin	Iddings T.R.D.	Same
		Idd.T.R.	Same
i & ndec	Immigration and Nationality Laws, Administrative Decisions Under Immigration and Naturalization Interim Decisions	ier	Individual Employment Rights Cases (BNA)
		I.F.L. Rev.	International Financial Law Review
		IIC	International Review of Industrial Property and Copyright Law
I. & N.Dec.	Immigration and Nationality Decisions	IlLR	University of Illinois Law Review
I.B.L.	International Business Lawyer	I.J.E.C.L.	International Journal of Estuarine and Coastal Law
I.Bull.	Interights Bulletin		
ICC	Interstate Commerce Commission Reports	IlA	Illinois Appellate Court Reports
ICC2d	Same, Second Series	I.L. & P.	Insolvency Law and Practice
I.C.C.L.R.	International Company and Commercial Law Review	IlCC	Illinois Circuit Court Reports
I.C.C.Pract.J.	Interstate Commerce Commission Practitioners' Journal	IlCCl	Illinois Court of Claims Reports
ICCR	International Company and Commercial Law Review	I.L.C. Newsl.	International Legal Center Newsletter
		I.L.E.	Indiana Law Encyclopedia
I.C.J.	International Court of Justice Reports	ILJ	Industrial Law Journal
ICJ Reports	International Court of Justice Reports	ill	Illinois Supreme Court Reports
I.C.J.Y.B.	Yearbook of the International Court of Justice	Ill.	Same
		ill2d	Same, Second Series
		Ill.2d	Same
ICLQ	International and Comparative Law Quarterly	ill3d	Same, Third Series
		illapp	Illinois Appellate Court Reports
I.C.L.R.	International Construction Law Review	Ill.App.	Same
		illapp2d	Same, Second Series
ICR	Industrial Cases Reports	Ill.App.2d	Same
		illapp3d	Same, Third Series
ID	Decisions of the Department of the Interior	Ill.App.3d	Same
		Ill.B.J.	Illinois Bar Journal
I.D.	Interior Department Decisions, Public Land	illcc	Illinois Circuit Court Reports
		Ill.Cir.	Same
Ida	Idaho Reports	Ill.Cont.L.Ed.	Illinois Continuing Legal Education
idaho	Same	Ill.Cont.Legal Ed.	Same
Idaho	Same		

Ill.Ct.Cl.	Illinois Court of Claims Reports	Indian L.J.	Indian Law Journal
IlD	Illinois Decisions	Indian L.R.	Indian Law Reports
illdec	Same	Indian Rul.	Indian Rulings
Ill.L.B.	Illinois Law Bulletin	indianterr	Indian Territory Reports
Ill.L.Q.	Illinois Law Quarterly	Indian Terr.	Same
IlLR	University of Illinois Law Review	India S.Ct.	India Supreme Court Reports
Ill.L.Rev.	Illinois Law Review	Ind.Int'l & Comp.L. Rev.	Indiana International & Comparative Law Review
I.L.M.	International Legal Materials		
I.L.P.	Illinois Law and Practice	Ind.J. Int'l L.	Indian Journal of International Law
	International Legal Practitioner	Ind.Legal F.	Indiana Legal Forum
		Ind.L.J.	Indiana Law Journal
I.L.R.	Insurance Law Reporter (Can.)	Ind.L.Q.Rev.	Indian Law Quarterly Review
	International Labour Review	Ind.L.Rev.	Indian Law Review
	International Law Reports		Indiana Law Review
		Ind.L.Stud.	Indiana Law Student
I.L.R.M.	Irish Law Reports Monthly	Ind.Prop.	Industrial Property
		Ind.Prop.Q.	Industrial Property Quarterly
I.L.W.	Investment Laws of the World (Oceana)	Ind.Rel.J. Econ. & Soc.	Industrial Relations: Journal of Economy and Society
I.M.L.	International Media Law	Ind.S.C.	Indiana Superior Court
Imm. and Nat. L. & P.	Immigration and Nationality Law and Practice	Ind. Sol.	Independent Solicitor
		IndT	Indian Territory Reports
Imm AR	Immigration Appeal Reports	Indus. & Lab. Rel.Rev.	Industrial and Labor Relations Review
Immig.B.Bull.	Immigration Bar Bulletin	Indus.L.J.	Industrial Law Journal
Immig. L. & Bus.News	Immigration Law & Business News	Indus.L.Rev.	Industrial Law Review
Immig.Newsl.	Immigration Newsletter	Indus.Rel.L.J.	Industrial Relations Law Journal
InA	Indiana Appellate Court Reports	Ind.Y.B.Int'l Aff.	Indian Yearbook of International Affairs
	Indiana Court of Appeals Reports		
ind	Indiana Supreme Court Reports	Inequal.Ed.	Inequality in Education
Ind.	Same	INLP	Immigration and Nationality Law and Practice
Ind.Advocate	Indian Advocate		
Ind. & Intell. Prop.Austl.	Industrial and Intellectual Property in Australia		
		Ins. C.	Insurance Code (CA)
Ind. & Lab. Rel. Rev.	Industrial and Labor Relations Review	Ins.Counsel J.	Insurance Counsel Journal
indapp	Indiana Appellate Court Reports	Ins. L. & P.	Insolvency Law and Practice
Ind.App.	Same	Ins.Liability Rep.	Insurance Liability Reporter
Ind.Cl.Comm.	Indian Claims Commission Decisions	Ins.L.J.	Insurance Law Journal (PA)
India Crim.L. J.R.	India Criminal Law Journal Reports	Ins.L.Rep.	Insurance Law Reporter (CCH)
Indian Cas.	Indian Cases		

Inst.Ad.Legal Stud.Ann.	Institute of Advanced Legal Studies Annual
Inst.Est.Plan.	Institute on Estate Planning (U. of Miami)
Inst.Lab.Rel. Bull.	Institute for Labor Relations Bulletin
Inst.Min.L.	Institute on Mineral Law (La. State University)
Inst. on Fed. Tax'n	Institute on Federal Taxation
Inst.Plan. & Zoning	Institute on Planning and Zoning
Inst.Plan. Zoning & E.D.	Institute on Planning, Zoning and Eminent Domain
Inst.Sec.Reg.	Institute on Securities Regulation (PLI)
INT	United States Court of International Trade
intdecno	Immigration and Naturalization Interim Decisions
Int. J. Comp. L.L.I.R.	International Journal of Comparative Law and Industrial Relations
Int. J. Law & Fam.	International Journal of Law and the Family
Int. J. Soc. L.	International Journal of the Sociology of Law
Int. Rel.	International Relations
Int.Rev.Bull.	Internal Revenue Bulletin
Int.Rev.Code	Internal Revenue Code
Int.Rev.Code of 1954	Internal Revenue Code of 1954
Int.Rev.Rec.	Internal Revenue Record
Intell.Prop. L.Rev.	Intellectual Property Law Review
Inter–Am. L.Rev.	Inter–American Law Review
Interior Dec.	United States Interior Department Decisions
Int'l Aff.	International Affairs
Int'l & Comp. L.Bull.	International and Comparative Law Bulletin
Int'l & Comp. L.Q.	International and Comparative Law Quarterly
Int'l Arb. Awards	Reports of International Arbitral Awards
Int'l Arb.J.	International Arbitration Journal
Int'l B.J.	International Bar Journal
Int'l Bus. & Trade L.Rep.	International Business & Trade Law Reporter
Int'l Bus. Lawyer	International Business Lawyer
Int'l Bus.Ser.	International Business Series (Ernst & Ernst)
Int'l Concil.	International Conciliation
Int'l Crim. Pol. Rev.	International Criminal Police Review
Int'l Dig. Health Leg.	International Digest of Health Legislation
Int'l Encycl. Comp.L.	International Encyclopedia of Comparative Law
Int'l J.	International Journal
Int'l J.Crim. & Pen.	International Journal of Criminology and Penology
Int'l J.L. & Fam.	International Journal of Law and the Family
Int'l J.L. & Psych.	International Journal of Law and Psychiatry
Int'l J.Legal Res.	International Journal of Legal Research
Int'l J.L.Lib.	International Journal of Law Libraries
Int'l J.Off. Ther. & Comp.Crim.	International Journal of Offender Therapy and Comparative Criminology
Int'l J.Pol.	International Journal of Politics
Int'l J.Soc.L.	International Journal of the Sociology of the Law
Int'l Jurid. Ass'n Bull.	International Juridical Association Monthly Bulletin
Int'l J.World Peace	International Journal on World Peace
Int'l Lab.Rev.	International Labour Review

Int'l L. & Trade Persp.	International Law & Trade Perspective	I.P.D.	Intellectual Property Decisions
Int'l Law.	International Lawyer	Ir.	Law Reports (Ir.)
		IR	Irish Reports
Int'l L.Doc.	International Law Documents	I.R.	Internal Revenue Decisions
Int'l Legal Ed. Newsl.	International Legal Education Newsletter	irb	Internal Revenue Bulletin
		I.R.B.	Same
Int'l Legal Materials	International Legal Materials	I.R.C.	Internal Revenue Code
Int'l L.News	International Law News	Ir.Ch.	Irish Chancery
		Ir.Cir.	Irish Circuit Reports
Int'l L.Persp.	International Law Perspective	Ir.C.L.	Irish Common Law
		Ir.Eccl.	Irish Ecclesiastical Reports
Int'l L.Q.	International Law Quarterly	Ired.	Iredell's Law (NC)
Int'l L.Stud.	International Law Studies	Ired.Eq.	Iredell's Equity (NC)
		Ir.Eq.	Irish Equity
Int'l Prop. Inv.J.	International Property Investment Journal	Ir.Jur.	Irish Jurist
		Ir. Jur. Rep.	Irish Jurist Reports
		Ir.L. & Eq.	Irish Law & Equity
Int'l Rev.Ad. Sci.	International Review of Administrative Sciences	I.R.L.I.B.	Industrial Relations Legal Information Bulletin
Int'l Rev. Crim.Policy	International Review of Criminal Policy	IRLR	Industrial Relations Law Reports
Int'l Rev.L. & Econ.	International Review of Law and Economics	Ir.L.T.R.	Irish Law Times Reports
Int'l Soc'y of Barr.Q.	International Society of Barristers Quarterly	Ir.R.	Irish Reports
		Ir.R.C.L.	Irish Reports Common Law
Int'l Surv.L. D.L.L.	International Survey of Legal Decisions on Labour Laws	Ir.R.Eq.	Irish Reports Equity
		I.R.R.Newsl.	Individual Rights and Responsibilities Newsletter
Int'l Sym. Comp.L.	International Symposium on Comparative Law	Ir.Soc'y for Lab. L.J.	Irish Society for Labor Law Journal
Int'l Tax & Bus. Law.	International Tax & Business Lawyer	Irv.Just.	Irvine's Justiciary (Scot.)
Int'l Tax J.	International Tax Journal	ISL L.Rev.	International School of Law Law Review
Int'l Trade L.J.	International Trade Law Journal	Israel L.Rev.	Israel Law Review
Int'l Woman Law.	International Woman Lawyer	Israel Y.B. Human Rights	Israel Yearbook on Human Rights
Intramural L.J.	Intramural Law Journal	Issues Crim.	Issues in Criminology
Intramural L.Rev.	Intramural Law Review	I.T.R.	Ridgeway, Lapp & Schoaler, Term Reports (Ir.)
I.O.C.C.Bull.	Interstate Oil Compact Commission Bulletin		Industrial Tribunal Reports
iowa	Iowa Reports	itrd	International Trade Reporter Decisions (BNA)
Iowa	Same		
Iowa L.B.	Iowa Law Bulletin		
Iowa L.Rev.	Iowa Law Review	Iustitia	Iustitia

J

Jac.	Jacob's Chancery (Eng.)	J. & L.	Jones & La Touche's Chancery (Ir.)
Jac. & W.	Jacob & Walker's Chancery (Eng.)	J. & La. T.	Same
Jac. & Walk.	Same	J. & S.	Jones & Spencer's Superior Court (NY)
J.Accountancy	Journal of Accountancy		
Jack.	Jackson (GA)	J. & W.	Jacob & Walker's Chancery (Eng.)
Jack. & L.	Jackson & Lumpkin (GA)	Japan Ann.L. & Pol.	Japan Annual of Law and Politics
Jack.Tex. App.	Jackson's Texas Appeals	Jap.Ann.Int'l L.	Japanese Annual of International Law
Jac.L.Dict.	Jacob's Law Dictionary	J.Art & Ent.L.	Journal of Art and Entertainment Law
J.Afr.L.	Journal of African Law	J.Arts Mgmt.L. Soc'y	Journal of Arts Management, Law and Society
JAG Bull.	Judge Advocate General Bulletin, United States Air Force	J.Ass'n L.Teachers	Journal of the Association of Law Teachers
JAG J.	Judge Advocate General Journal	J.B.Ass'n D.C.	Journal of the Bar Association of the District of Columbia
JAG L.Rev.	Judge Advocate General Law Review, United States Air Force	J.B.Ass'n St. Kan.	Journal of the Bar Association of the State of Kansas
J.Agric.Tax. & L.	Journal of Agricultural Taxation and the Law	J.Beverly Hills B.Ass'n	Journal of the Beverly Hills Bar Association
J.Agr.Tax'n & L.	Same	J.B.L.	Journal of Business Law
J.Air L. & Com.	Journal of Air Law and Commerce	J.B.Moore	J.B. Moore's Common Pleas (Eng.)
J.A.L.	Journal of African Law	J.Bridg.	Sir John Bridgman's Common Pleas (Eng.)
JAMA	Journal of the American Medical Association	J.Bridgm.	Same
J.Am.Acad. Matrim. Law.	Journal of American Academy of Matrimonial Lawyers	J.Bus.L.	Journal of Business Law
James	James' Reports (Nova Scotia)	J.C.	Johnson's Cases (NY)
James. & Mont.	Jameson & Montagu's Bankruptcy (Eng.)	J.Can.B. Ass'n	Journal of the Canadian Bar Association
J.Am.Jud. Soc'y	Journal of the American Judicature Society	J.C. & U.L.	Journal of College & University Law
J.Am.Soc'y C.L.U.	Journal of the American Society of Chartered Life Underwriters	J.Ceylon L.	Journal of Ceylon Law
		JCh	Johnson's Chancery Reports (NY)
J. & C.	Jones & Cary's Exchequer (Ir.)	J.Ch.	Same
J. & H.	Johnson & Hemming's Chancery (Eng.)	J. Chinese L.	Journal of Chinese Law
		J.Church & St.	Journal of Church and State

J.C.L.	Journal of Criminal Law	J.Denning L.Soc'y	Journal of the Denning Law Society
J.C.L. & Crim.	Journal of Criminal Law and Criminology	J. Disp.Resol.	Journal of Dispute Resolution
J.C.M.S.	Journal of Common Market Studies	Jebb	Jebb's Crown Cases (Ir.)
J.C.N.P.S.	Journal of Collective Negotiations in the Public Sector	Jebb & B.	Jebb & Bourke's Queen's Bench (Ir.)
J.Coll. & U.L.	Journal of College and University Law	Jebb & S.	Jebb & Symes' Queen's Bench (Ir.)
		Jebb & Sym.	Same
J.Comm.Mt. Stud.	Journal of Common Market Studies	Jebb C.C.	Jebb's Crown Cases (Ir.)
J.Comp.Leg. & Int'l L.3d	Journal of Comparative Legislation and International Law, Third Series	jeff	Jefferson's Reports (VA)
		Jeff.	Same
		J.Energy & Devel.	Journal of Energy and Development
J.Confl.Res.	Journal of Conflict Resolution	J.Energy L. & Pol'y	Journal of Energy Law & Policy
J.Cons.Affairs	Journal of Consumer Affairs	Jenk.	Jenkins' Exchequer (Eng.)
J.Const. & Parl. Stud.	Journal of Constitutional and Parliamentary Studies	Jenk.Cent.	Same
		Jenks	Jenks (NH)
		Jenn.	Jennison (MI)
J.Contemp. Health L. & Pol'y	Journal of Contemporary Health Law and Policy	J.Env. L.	Journal of Environmental Law
J.Contemp.L.	Journal of Contemporary Law	J.Envtl.L. & Litig.	Journal of Environment Law and Litigation
J.Contemp. Legal Issues	Journal of Contemporary Legal Issues	J.E.R.L.	Journal of Energy and Natural Resources Law
J.Contemp. R.D.L.	Journal of Contemporary Roman–Dutch Law	J.Eth.L.	Journal of Ethiopian Law
J.Copyright Entertainment Sports L.	Journal of Copyright Entertainment and Sports Law	Jew.Y.B.Int'l L.	Jewish Yearbook of International Law
J.Corp.L.	Journal of Corporation Law	J.Fam.L.	Journal of Family Law
J.Corp.Tax'n	Journal of Corporate Taxation	JFK U L Record	John F. Kennedy University Law Record
J.C.R.	Johnson's Chancery (NY)	J.For.Med.	Journal of Forensic Medicine
J.Crim.Just.	Journal of Criminal Justice	J.For.Med. Soc'y	Journal of the Forensic Medicine Society
J.Crim.L. (Eng.)	Journal of Criminal Law (Eng.)	J.For.Sci.	Journal of the Forensic Sciences
J.Crim.L. & Criminology	Journal of Criminal Law and Criminology	J.For.Sci. Soc'y	Journal of the Forensic Science Society
J.Crim.L., C. & P.S.	Journal of Criminal Law, Criminology and Police Science	J.Health Pol. Pol'y & L.	Journal of Health, Politics, Policy & Law
J.Crim.Sci.	Journal of Criminal Science	JIBFL	Journal of International Banking and Financial Law
JCs	Johnson's Cases (NY)		
J.D.	Juris Doctor		

J.I.B.L.	Journal of International Banking Law	J.Land Use & Envtl.L.	Journal of Land Use & Environmental Law
J.I.F.D.L.	Journal of International Franchising and Distribution Law	J.Law & Econ.	Journal of Law and Economics
		J.Law & Econ. Dev.	Journal of Law and Economic Development
J.Ind.L.Inst.	Journal of the Indian Law Institute	J.Law & Health	Journal of Law and Health
J.Int'l Aff.	Journal of International Affairs	J.Law & Soc.	Journal of Law and Society
J.Int'l Arb.	Journal of International Arbitration	J.Law, Econ. & Org.	Journal of Law, Economics and Organization
J.Int'l Comm. Jur.	Journal of the International Commission of Jurists	J.Law Reform	Journal of Law Reform
J.Int'l L. & Dipl.	Journal of International Law and Diplomacy	J.Legal Educ.	Journal of Legal Education
		J.Legal Hist.	Journal of Legal History
J.Int'l L. & Econ.	Journal of International Law and Economics	J.Legal Med.	Journal of Legal Medicine
J.Int'l L. & Pol.	Journal of International Law and Politics	J.Legal Prof.	Journal of the Legal Profession
		J.Legal Stud.	Journal of Legal Studies
J.Int'l L. & Prac.	Journal of International Law and Practice	J.Leg. Hist.	Journal of Legal History
J.Ir.Soc. Lab.L.	Journal of the Irish Society for Labour Law	J.Legis.	Journal of Legislation
		J.L.H.	Journal of Legal History
J.Islam. & Comp.L.	Journal of Islamic and Comparative Law	J.L.Soc'y	Journal of the Law Society of Scotland
J.J.	Jersey Judgements	J.L.S.S.	Same
J.J.Mar.	J.J. Marshall (KY)	J.Mar.J.Prac. & Proc.	John Marshall Journal of Practice and Procedure
J.J.Marsh. (KY)	Same		
J.Juris.	Journal of Jurisprudence		
J.Juv.L.	Journal of Juvenile Law	J.Mar.L. & Com.	Journal of Maritime Law and Commerce
J Juvenile L	Same	J.Mar.L.J.	John Marshall Law Journal
J.Kan.B. Ass'n	Journal of the Kansas Bar Association	J.Mar.L.Q.	John Marshall Law Quarterly
J.L.	Journal of Law	J.Marshall L.Rev.	John Marshall Law Review
J.Land & P.U.Econ.	Journal of Land and Public Utility Economics	J.Min.L. & Pol'y	Journal of Mineral Law and Policy
J.L. & Com.	Journal of Law and Commerce	J.M.L. & P.	Journal of Media Law and Practice
J.L. & Econ.	Journal of Law & Economics	J.M.L.C.	Journal of Maritime Law and Commerce
J.L. & Educ.	Journal of Law and Education	J.Mo.Bar	Journal of the Missouri Bar
J.L. & Pol.	Journal of Law and Politics	J.N.A.A.L.J.	Journal of the National Association of Administrative Law Judges at Pepperdine University
J.L. & Religion	Journal of Law and Religion		
J.L. & Tech.	Journal of Law and Technology		

Jo. & La T.	Jones & La Touche's Chancery (Ir.)	Jones & S.	Jones & Spencer's Superior Court (NY)
John.	Johnson's Reports (NY)	JP	Justice of the Peace Reports
	Johnson's Vice–Chancery (Eng.)	J.P.	Justice of the Peace (Eng.)
John Mar.J. Prac. & Proc.	John Marshall Journal of Practice and Procedure	J.Pat. & Trademark Off.Soc.	Journal of the Patent and Trademark Office Society
John Marsh. L.J.	John Marshall Law Journal	J.Pat.Off. Soc'y	Journal of the Patent Office Society
John Marsh. L.Q.	John Marshall Law Quarterly	J.Pension Plan. & Compliance	Journal of Pension Planning & Compliance
Johns.	Johnson (NY)		
	Johnson's Vice–Chancery (Eng.)	JP Jo	Justice of the Peace Journal
Johns. & H.	Johnson & Hemming's Chancery (Eng.)	J.P.L.	Journal of Planning and Environmental Law
Johns. & Hem.	Same		
Johns.Cas.	Johnson's Cases (NY)	J.Plan. & Env.L.	Journal of Planning and Environment Law
Johns.Ch.	Johnson's Chancery (MD)	J.P.N.	Justice of the Peace Journal
	Johnson's Chancery (NY)	J.Pol.Sci. & Admin.	Journal of Police Science and Administration
Johns.Ct.Err.	Johnson's Court of Errors (NY)		
Johns.Dec.	Johnson's Chancery Decisions (MD)	J.Prod. & Toxics Liab.	Journal of Products and Toxics Liability
Johns.N.Z.	Johnson's New Zealand Reports	J.Prod.Liab.	Journal of Products Liability
Johns.U.S.	Johnson's United States Circuit Court Decisions	J.P.Sm.	J.P. Smith's King's Bench (Eng.)
Jon. & L.	Jones & La Touche's Chancery (Ir.)	J.Psych. & L.	Journal of Psychiatry and Law
Jon. & La T.	Same	J.Publ.L.	Journal of Public Law
Jones	Jones (AL)	J.Quantitative Criminology	Journal of Quantitative Criminology
	Jones (MO)		
	Jones (PA)	J.R.	Johnson (NY)
	Jones, T., King's Bench (Eng.)	J.R.	Judicial Review
	Jones, W., King's Bench (Eng.)	J.Radio L.	Journal of Radio Law
	Jones' Exchequer (Ir.)	J.Real Est. Tax.	Journal of Real Estate Taxation
	Jones' Law or Equity	J.Reprints Antitrust L. & Econ.	Journal of Reprints for Antitrust Law and Economics
	Jones' Reports (Upper Can.)		
Jones & C.	Jones & Cary's Exchequer (Ir.)	JS	Jones and Spencer's Superior Court Reports (NY)
Jones & L.	Jones & La Touche's Chancery (Ir.)	J.S.Gr. (N.J.)	J.S. Green (NJ)
Jones & La T.	Same	J.Soc.Welfare L.	Journal of Social Welfare Law
Jones & McM. (PA)	Jones & McMurtrie (PA)	J.Soc'y Comp. Leg.	Journal of the Society of Comparative Legislation

J.Soc'y Pub. Tchrs.L.	Journal of the Society of Public Teachers of Law	Jur.	Jurist (Eng.)
		Jurid.Rev.	Juridical Review
		Jurimetrics J.	Jurimetrics Journal
J.Space L.	Journal of Space Law	Juris.	Jurisprudence
J.St.Tax'n	Journal of State Taxation	Jurist	Jurist (DC)
		Jur. (N.S.)	Same, New Series
JSWFL	Journal of Social Welfare and Family Law	Just.Cas.	Justiciary Cases
		Just.L.R.	Justice's Law Reporter (PA)
J.Tax'n	Journal of Taxation	Just.P.	Justice of the Peace and Local Government Review
J.Transnat'l L. & Pol'y	Journal of Transnational Law and Policy		
		Just.Syst.J.	Justice System Journal
Jud.Conduct Rep.	Judicial Conduct Reporter		
Judd	Judd (HI)	Juv. & Fam. Courts J.	Juvenile and Family Courts Journal
Judge Advoc.J.	Judge Advocate Journal	Juv.Ct.J.	Juvenile Court Journal
Judges' J.	Judges' Journal		
Judge's J.	Judge's Journal	Juv.Ct.Judges J.	Juvenile Court Judges Journal
Judicature	Journal of the American Judicature Society	Juv.Just.	Juvenile Justice
		J.World Trade L.	Journal of World Trade Law
	Judicature	J.W.T.	Journal of Word Trade
Jud Nom Rules	Rules and Procedures of Commission on Judicial Nominees Evaluation (CA State Bar)		

K

KA2d	Kansas Court of Appeals Reports, Second Series	K.& G.R.C.	Same
		Kan.J.L. & Pub. Pol'y	Kansas Journal of Law and Public Policy
Kames Dec.	Kames' Decisions (Scot.)		
		Kan.L.J.	Kansas Law Journal
Kames Elucid.	Kames' Elucidation (Scot.)	Kan.L.Rev.	University of Kansas Law Review
Kames Rem. Dec.	Kames' Remarkable Decisions (Scot.)	Kan.St.L.J.	Kansas State Law Journal
Kames Sel.Dec.	Kames' Select Decisions (Scot.)	Karachi L.J.	Karachi Law Journal (Pak.)
kan	Kansas Reports	Kay	Kay's Vice–Chancery (Eng.)
Kan.	Same		
KanA	Kansas Court of Appeals Reports	Kay & J.	Kay & Johnson's Chancery (Eng.)
kanapp	Kansas Appeals Reports	K.B.	Law Reports King's Bench (Eng.)
Kan.App.	Same	K.C.L.J.	Kings College Law Journal
kanapp2d	Same, Second Series		
Kan.B.Ass'n J.	Kansas Bar Association Journal	K.Counsel	King's Counsel
		Ke.	Keen's Rolls Court (Eng.)
Kan.City L.Rev.	Kansas City Law Review		
Kan.C.L.Rep.	Kansas City Law Reporter	Keane & Gr.	Keane & Grant's Registration Appeal Cases (Eng.)
K.& G.	Keane & Grant's Registration Appeal Cas	Keane & G.R.C.	Same
		Keb.	Keble's King's Bench (Eng.)
K.& Gr.	Same		

Keen	Keen's Rolls Court (Eng.)	K.L.R.	Kenya Law Reports
Keil.	Keilway's King's Bench (Eng.)	Knapp	Knapp & Ombler's Election Cases (Eng.)
Kel.C.C.	Kelyng's Crown Cases (Eng.)	Knapp & O.	Same
Kellen	Kellen (MA)	Knight's Ind.	Knight's Industrial Reports
Kelly	Kelly (GA)	Knowles	Knowles (RI)
Kelly & C.	Kelly & Cobb (GA)	Knox	Knox (N.S.W.)
Kel.W.	Kelyng's Chancery (Eng.)	Knox & F.	Knox & Fitzhardinge (N.S.W.)
Kenan	Kenan (NC)	Kn.P.C.	Knapp's Privy Council (Eng.)
Keny.	Kenyon (Lord) King's Bench (Eng.)	Kobe U.L.Rev.	Kobe University Law Review
	Kenyon's Notes of King's Bench Reports (Eng.)	Korea L.Rev.	Korea Law Review
		Korean J.Comp.L.	Korean Journal of Comparative Law
Kenya L.R.	Kenya Law Reports	Korean J.Int'l L.	Korean Journal of International Law
Keny.Ch.	Kenyon's Chancery (Eng.)	Korean L.	Korean Law
Kerala L.J.	Kerala Law Journal	Kreider	Kreider (WA)
Kern	Kern (MD)	Kress	Kress (PA)
Kern.	Kernan (NY)	Kulp	Kulp (PA)
Kerr	Kerr (IN)	Kwansei Gak. L.Rev.	Kwansei Gaknin Law Review
	Kerr (N.B.)	ky	Kentucky Reports
	Kerr's Civil Procedure (NY)	Ky.	Same
Key	Keyes' Reports (NY)	Ky.Bench & B.	Kentucky Bench and Bar
Keyes	Same		
Kilk.	Kilkerran's Decisions (Scot.)	Ky.Comment'r	Kentucky Commentator
Kilkerran	Same	Ky.Dec.	Kentucky Decisions
King	King's Civil Practice Cases (CO)	Ky.L.J.	Kentucky Law Journal
	King's Louisiana Annual	kylr	Kentucky Law Reporter
Kingston L.R.	Kingston Law Review	Ky.L.R.	Same
		Ky.L.Rptr.	Same
Kingston L.Rev.	Same	Ky.Op.	Kentucky Opinions
K.I.R.	Knight's Industrial Reports	kyops	Kentucky Court of Appeals Opinions
kirby	Kirby's Reports and Supplement (CT)	Kyoto L.Rev.	Kyoto Law Review
Kirby	Same	Ky.St.B.J.	Kentucky State Bar Journal

L

la	Louisiana Reports	Lab.	Labatt's District Court (CA)
La.	Same		
LA	Legal Action	Lab. & Auto. Bull.	Labor and Automation Bulletin
laann	Louisiana Annual Reports	Lab.Arb.	Labor Arbitration Reports (BNA)
La.Ann.	Same		
laapp	Louisiana Court of Appeals Reports	LA Bar B	Los Angeles Bar Bulletin
La.App.	Same	Lab C	Labor Code
La.App. (Orleans)	Court of Appeal, Parish of Orleans	La.B.J.	Louisiana Bar Journal

L.A.B.J.	Los Angeles Bar Journal	Land Dec.	Land Decisions (U.S.)
Lab.Law.	Labor Lawyer	L. & E.	English Law & Equity Reports (Boston)
Lab.L.J.	Labor Law Journal		
Labor C.	Labor Code		
Lab.Rel.L.Letter	Labor Relations Law Letter	L. & E.Rep.	Law & Equity Reporter (NY)
Lab.Rel.Rep.	Labor Relations Reporter	L. & Just.	Law and Justice
		L. & Leg. GDR	Law and Legislation in the German Democratic Republic
L.A.C.	Labour Arbitration Cases		
Lackawanna B.	Lackawanna Bar (PA)		
		L. & Lib.	Law and Liberty
Lack.Jur.	Lackawanna Jurist (PA)	L. & M.	Lowndes & Maxwell, Bail Cases (Eng.)
Lack.Leg.N.	Lackawanna Legal News (PA)	L. & Order	Law and Order
		L. & Psych.Rev.	Law and Psychology Review
Lack.Leg.Rec.	Lackawanna Legal Record (PA)		
		L. & Soc.Inquiry: J. Am. B. Found.	Law and Social Inquiry: Journal of the American Bar Foundation
Ladd	Ladd (NH)		
L.Advertiser	Law Advertiser		
L.A.G.Bull.	Legal Act Group Bulletin		
		Land Use & Env.L.Rev.	Land Use and Environment Law Review
L.A.J.P.E.L.	Latin American Journal of Politics, Economics and Law		
		Lane	Lane's Exchequer (Eng.)
LA Law	Los Angeles Lawyer	Lans.	Lansing (MI)
L.A. Lawyer	Same	LAp	Louisiana Courts of Appeal Reports
La.L.J.	Louisiana Law Journal		
		La Raza L.J.	La Raza Law Journal
Lalor	Lalor's Supplement to Hill & Denio (NY)		
		Larson	Larson, Workmen's Compensation Practice
La.L.Rev.	Louisiana Law Review		
Lamar	Lamar (FL)	Latch	Latch's King's Bench (Eng.)
Lamb	Lamb (WI)		
L.Am.Soc'y	Law in American Society	Lath.	Lathrop (MA)
		La.T.R.	Martin's Louisiana Term Reports
Lan	Lansing's Supreme Court's Reports		
LAn	Louisiana Annual Reports	Law.	Lawyer
		Law.Am.	Lawyer of the Americas
Lanc.Bar	Lancaster Bar (PA)		
Lanc.L.Rev.	Lancaster Law Review (PA)	Law & Bk.Bull.	Weekly Law and Bank Bulletin (OH)
Land & Water L.Rev.	Land and Water Law Review	Law & Computer Tech.	Law and Computer Technology
L. & B.Bull.	Weekly Law and Bank Bulletin (OH)	Law & Contemp.Probs.	Law and Contemporary Problems
		Law & Housing J.	Law and Housing Journal
L. & C.	Lefroy and Cassels' Practice Cases (Ont.)	Law & Hum. Behav.	Law and Human Behavior
	Leigh & Cave's Crown Cases Reserved (Eng.)	Law & Just.	Law and Justice
		Law. & Magis.Mag.	Lawyer's and Magistrate's Magazine
L. & Computer Tech.	Law and Computer Technology	Law & Phil.	Law & Philosophy
		Law & Pol.	Law and Policy

Law & Pol'y Int'l Bus.	Law and Policy in International Business	LCA	New York Leading Cases Annotated
Law & Pol'y Q.	Law and Policy Quarterly	L.C.D.	Ohio Lower Court Decisions
Law & Psych. Rev.	Law and Psychology Review	LCh	Lansing's Chancery Reports
Law & Soc. Ord.	Law and the Social Order (Arizona State Law Journal)	L.Chron.	Law Chronicle
		L.Chron. & L.Stud.Mag.	Law Chronicle and Law Students' Magazine
Law & Soc'y Rev.	Law and Society Review	L.Chron. & L.Stud.Mag., (N.S.)	Same, New Series
Lawasia	Lawasia, Journal of the Law Association for Asia and the Western Pacific	L.C.Jur.	Lower Canada Jurist
		L.C.L.J.	Lower Canada Law Journal
		L.Coach	Law Coach
		L.Comment'y	Law Commentary
Law Cases	Law Cases, William I to Richard I (Eng.) (Placita Anglo–Normannica)	LCP	Law and Contemporary Problems
		L.C.R.	Land Compensation Reports
Law.Committee News	Lawyers Committee News	L.C.Rep. S.Qu.	Lower Canada Reports Seignorial Questions
Law Corp Rules	Law Corporation Rules of State Bar	LD	Decisions of the Department of the Interior (Public Land Decisions)
Law Inst.J.	Law Institute Journal		
Law Lib.	Law Librarian		
Law Libr.J.	Law Library Journal	L.D.	Land Office Decisions (U.S.)
Law.Med.J.	Lawyer's Medical Journal	L.D.L.R.	Land Development Law Reporter
Law Notes	Law Notes	Ld.Raym.	Lord Raymond's King's Bench (Eng.)
Law Q.Rev.	Law Quarterly Review		
Lawr.	Lawrence (OH)		
Lawrence	Same	LE	United States Supreme Court Reports, Lawyers' Edition
Law Rep.	Law Reporter (MA) Law Reports (Eng.)		
Law Rep. (N.S.)	Law Reports, New Series (NY)		
Law Rev. Com	Law Revision Commission	LE2d	Same, Second Series
		Lea	Lea (TN)
Law Rev.J.	Law Review Journal	Leach C.C.	Leach's Crown Cases, King's Bench (Eng.)
Law Soc'y Gaz.	Law Society Gazette (Toronto)		
	Law Society's Gazette (London)	League of Nations Off.J.	League of Nations Official Journal
Law Soc'y J.	Law Society Journal (Boston)	Learn. & L.	Learning and the Law
	Law Society Journal (N.S.W.)	L.East.Eur.	Law in Eastern Europe
Lawyer & Banker	Lawyer and Banker and Central Law Journal	leatn	Lea's Tennessee Reports
		Lect.L.S.U.C.	Special Lectures of the Law Society of Upper Canada
Lawyer's Med.J.	Lawyer's Medical Journal		
L.Book Adviser	Law Book Adviser	led	Lawyers' Edition, United States Supreme Court Reports
L.C.	Lower Canada Lord Chancellor		
L.C. News	Law Centres News		

L.Ed.	Same	Lex & Sci.	Lex et Scientia
led2d	Same, Second Series	L. Exec.	Legal Executive
L.Ed.2d	Same	Ley	Ley, King's Bench (Eng.)
Lee	Lee (CA)		Common Pleas (Eng.)
Lee Eccl.	Lee's Ecclesiastical (Eng.)		Exchequer (Eng.)
Leese	Leese (NE)		Court of Wards (Eng.)
Lee t.Hardw.	Lee tempore Hardwicke, King's Bench (Eng.)		Court of Star Chamber (Eng.)
Legal Aspects Med.Prac.	Legal Aspects of Medical Practice	LF	University of Illinois Law Forum
Legal Med.Ann.	Legal Medicine Annual	L.G.	Law Glossary
Legal Med.Q.	Legal Medical Quarterly	L.Gaz.	Law Gazette
Legal Obser.	Legal Observer	LGR	Local Government Reports
Legal Res.J.	Legal Research Journal	LG Rev	Local Government Review
Legal Resp. Child Adv. Protection	Legal Response: Child Advocacy and Protection	L.Guard.	Law Guardian
Legal Stud.Forum	Legal Studies Forum	Liberian L.J.	Liberian Law Journal
Legal Video Rev.	Legal Video Review	L.I.E.I.	Legal Issues of European Integration
Leg. & Ins.R.	Legal & Insurance Reporter (PA)	Life Cas.	Life, Health & Accident Cases (CCH)
Leg.Chron.	Legal Chronicle (PA)	Life Cas.2d	Same, Second Series
Leg.Gaz.	Legal Gazette Reports (PA)	Lincoln LR	Lincoln Law Review
Leg.Int.	Legal Intelligencer (PA)	Lincoln L.Rev.	Same
		L. in Soc'y	Law in Society
Leg.Op.	Legal Opinions (PA)	L.Inst.J.	Law Institute Journal
Leg.Rec.	Legal Record (PA)		
Leg.Rep.	Legal Reporter (TN)	L.Inst.J.Vict.	Law Institute Journal of Victoria
Leg.Rev.	Legal Review (Eng.)		
Lehigh Co. L.J.	Lehigh County Law Journal (PA)	L. in Trans.Q.	Law in Transition Quarterly
Lehigh Val. L.R.	Lehigh Valley Law Reporter (PA)	Liquor Liab.J.	Liquor Liability Journal
Leigh	Leigh (PA)	Lit.	Litigation
Leigh & C.	Leigh & Cave's Crown Cases (Eng.)	Litig.	Same
		Livingston's M.L.Mag.	Livingston's Monthly Law Magazine
Leigh & C.C.C.	Same	L.J.	Law Journal
Leo.	Leonard, King's Bench, Common Pleas, Exchequer (Eng.)	L.J.Adm.	Law Journal, Admiralty (Eng.)
Leon.	Same	L.Japan	Law in Japan
Lester	Lester (GA)	L.J.Bankr.	Law Journal, Bankruptcy (Eng.)
Lester & B.	Lester & Butler's Supplement (GA)	L.J.Ch.	Law Journal, Chancery, New Series (Eng.)
Lev.	Leving, King's Bench, Common Pleas (Eng.)		
		L.J.Ch.(O.S.)	Same, Old Series
Lew.C.C.	Lewin's Crown Cases (Eng.)	L.J.C.P.	Law Journal, Common Pleas (Eng.)
Lewis	Lewis (MO)	L.J.C.P. (O.S.)	Same, Old Series
	Lewis (NV)	L.J.Eccl.	Law Journal, Ecclesiastical (Eng.)
	Lewis' Kentucky Law Reporter		

L.J.Exch.	Law Journal, Exchequer, New Series (Eng.)
L.J.Exch. (O.S.)	Same, Old Series
L.J.H.L.	Law Journal House of Lords, New Series (Eng.)
L.J.K.B.	Law Journal, King's Bench, New Series (Eng.)
L.J.Mag.	Law Journal, New Series Common Law, Magistrates Cases
L.J.M.C.	Law Journal, Magistrate Cases, New Series (Eng.)
L.J.M.C. (O.S.)	Same, Old Series (Eng.)
L.J.N.C.	Law Journal, Notes of Cases (Eng.)
L.J.O.S.	Law Journal, Old Series
L.J.P. & M.	Law Journal, Probate & Matrimonial (Eng.)
L.J.P.C.	Law Journal, Privy Council (Eng.)
L.J.P.C. (N.S.)	Same, New Series
L.J.P.D. & Adm.	Law Journal, Probate, Divorce & Admiralty (Eng.)
L.J.Q.B.	Law Journal, Queen's Bench, New Series (Eng.)
L.J.R.	Law Journal Reports
Ll. & G.t.Pl.	Lloyd & Goold tempore Plunkett, Chancery (Ir.)
Ll. & G.t.S.	Lloyd & Goold tempore Sugden, Chancery (Ir.)
Ll. & W.	Lloyd & Welsby Mercantile Cases (Eng.)
L.Lib.	Law Librarian
L.Libr.J.	Law Library Journal
L.L.J.	Same
Ll.L.Rep.	Lloyd's List Reports (Eng.)
Lloyd's L.Rep.	Lloyd's Law Reports
Lloyds Mar. & Com.L.Q.	Lloyds Maritime and Commercial Law Quarterly
Lloyd's Rep.	Lloyd's List Law Reports Admiralty
llrm	Labor Relations Reference Manual (BNA)
L.Mag. & Rev.	Law Magazine and Review
L.M. & P.	Lowndes, Maxwell & Pollock's Bail Cases (Eng.)
L.M.C.L.Q.	Lloyd's Maritime and Commercial Law Quarterly
L.M.E.L.R.	Land Management and Environmental Law Report
L.Notes Gen. Pract.	Law Notes for the General Practitioner
Lns	Lawyers Reports Annotated, New Series
L.N.T.S.	League of Nations Treaty Series
Local Ct. & Mun.Gaz.	Local Courts and Municipal Gazette
Local Gov't	Local Government and Magisterial Reports
Local Gov't R.Austl.	Local Government Reports of Australia
Lock.Rev.Cas.	Lockwood's Reversed Cases (NY)
L.Off.Econ. & Mgt.	Law Office Economics and Management
Lofft	Lofft's King's Bench (Eng.)
Lois Rec.	Lois Recentes du Canada
London L.Rev.	City of London Law Review
Long & R.	Long & Russell's Election Cases (MA)
Long Beach Bar B	Long Beach Bar Bulletin
Long Beach B.Bull.	Same
Longf. & T.	Longfield & Townsend's Exchequer (Ir.)
Los Angeles Bar J.	Los Angels Bar Journal
Louisville Law.	Louisville Lawyer
low	Lowell's U.S. District Court Reports
Low.Can. Jurist	Lower Canada Jurist
Low.Can.L.J.	Lower Canada Law Journal
Low.Can.R.	Lower Canadian Reports
Lowell	Lowell (U.S.)
Lower Ct.Dec.	Lower Court Decisions (OH)

Loy.Cons. Prot.J.	Loyola of Los Angeles Consumer Protection Journal	L.R.Ch.	Law Reports, Chancery Appeal Cases (Eng.)
Loy. Consumer L. Rep.	Loyola of Los Angeles Consumer Law Reporter	L.R.Ch.D.	Law Reports, Chancery Division (Eng.)
Loy.Dig.	Loyola Digest	L.R.C.P.	Law Reports, Common Pleas Cases (Eng.)
Loy. Ent.L. J.	Loyola of Los Angeles Entertainment Law Journal		
Loy.L.A.Int'l & Comp.L.Ann.	Loyola of Los Angeles International & Comparative Law Annual	L.R.C.P.D.	Law Reports, Common Pleas Division (Eng.)
		L.Record.	Law Recorder
		L.R.Eq.	Law Reports, Equity Cases (Eng.)
Loy.L.A. Int'l & Comp.L.J.	Loyola of Los Angeles International and Comparative Law Journal	L.Rev.Dig.	Law Review Digest
		L.R.Exch.	Law Reports, Exchequer Cases (Eng.)
Loy.L.A.L. Rev.	Loyola of Los Angeles Law Review	L.R.Exch.D.	Law Reports, Exchequer Division (Eng.)
Loy.Law.	Loyola Lawyer		
Loy.L.Rev.	Loyola Law Review (New Orleans)	L.R.H.L.	Law Reports, House of Lords (English & Irish Appeal Cases)
Loyola Consumer Protection J	Loyola Consumer Protection Journal		
Loyola L. Rev.	Loyola University of Los Angels Law Review	L.R.H.L.Sc.	Law Reports, House of Lords (Scotch Appeal Cases)
Loyola U of LA LR	Loyola University of Los Angeles Law Review	L.R.Indian App.	Law Reports, Indian Appeals (Eng.)
		L.R.Ir.	Law Reports (Ir.)
Loy.U.Chi. L.J.	Loyola University of Chicago Law Journal	L.R.N.S.W.	Law Reports, New South Wales
Loy.U.L.J.	Same	L.R.P. & D.	Law Reports, Probate & Divorce (Eng.)
L.Q.	Law Quarterly		
LQR	Law Quarterly Review	L.R.P.C.	Law Reports, Privy Council (Eng.)
L.Q.Rev.	Same	L.R.Q.B.	Law Reports, Queen's Bench (Eng.)
L.R.	Law Recorder (Ir.) Law Reports (Eng.) Ohio Law Reporter		
		L.R.Q.B.Div.	Law Reports, Queen's Bench Division (Eng.)
L.R. (N.S.)	Irish Law Recorder, New Series		
L.R.A.	Lawyers' Reports Annotated (U.S.)	L.R.R.	Labor Relations Reporter
L.R.A. & E.	Law Reports, Admiralty & Ecclesiastical (Eng.)	L.R.R.M.	Labor Relations Reference Manual (BNA)
L.R.A. (N.S.)	Lawyers' Reports Annotated, New Series (U.S.)	L.R.R.P.	Reports of Restrictive Practices Cases
L.R.App.Cas.	Law Reports, House of Lords Appeal Cases (Eng.)	L.R.S.A.	Law Reports, South Australia
		L.S.	Legal Studies
L.R.C.C.	Law Reports, Crown Cases (Eng.)	L.S.G.	Law Society Gazette (Eng.)
L.R.C.C.R.	Law Reports, Crown Cases Reserved (Eng.)	L.S. Gaz.	Same
		LS Gaz Rep	Law Society Gazette Reports

L.Stud.Helper	Law Student's Helper	Ludd.	Ludden (ME)
L.Stud.J.	Law Students' Journal	Lump.	Lumpkin (GA)
L.T.	Law Times (PA)	Lush.	Lushington's Admiralty (Eng.)
L.T. (N.S.)	Law Times, New Series (Eng.)	Lutw.	Lutwyche's Common Pleas (Eng.)
L.T. (O.S.)	Same, Old Series (Eng.)	Lutw.Reg.Cas.	Lutwyche's Registration Cases (Eng.)
L.T.G.F. Newsl.	Lawyers' Title Guaranty Funds Newsletter	Luz.Leg.Obs.	Luzerne Legal Observer (PA)
L.T.R. (N.S.)	Law Times, Reports, New Series (Eng.)	Luz.Leg.Reg.	Luzerne Legal Register (PA)
L.T.Rep.N.S.	Same	Luz.L.J.	Luzerne Law Journal (PA)
L. Teach.	Law Teacher	Luz.L.T.	Luzerne Law Times (PA)
L.Teacher	Same	Lynd.	Lyndwoode, Provinciale (Eng.)
L.Trans.Q.	Law in Transition Quarterly	Lyne	Lyne's Chancery (Ir.)

M

MA	Missouri Appeal Reports	mackey	Mackey's Reports (DC)
MaA	Massachusetts Appeals Court Reports	Mackey	Same
		MacL.	MacLean (U.S. Circuit Court)
Mac.	Macnaghten's Chancery (Eng.)	MacL. & R.	MacLean & Robinson's House of Lords (Eng.)
MacAll.	MacAllister (U.S.)		
Mac. & G.	Macnaghten & Gordon's Chancery (Eng.)	Macn. & G.	Macnaghten & Gordon's Chancery (Eng.)
Mac. & Rob.	Maclean & Robinson's Appeals, House of Lords (Scot.)	Macph.	Macpherson, Court of Sessions (Scot.)
		Macph.L. & B.	Macpherson, Lee & Bell (Scot.)
MacAr.	MacArthur (DC) MacArthur's Patent Cases (DC)	Macph.S. & L.	Macpherson, Shireff & Lee (Scot.)
		Macq.	Macqueen's Scotch Appeal Cases
MacAr. & M.	MacArthur & Mackey's District of Columbia Supreme Court	Macr.	Macrory's Patent Cases (Eng.)
		Madd.	Maddock (MT) Maddock's Chancery (Eng.)
MacAr. & Mackey	Same		
MacAr.Pat. Cas.	MacArthur's Patent Cases (DC)	Madd. & B.	Maddock & Back (MT)
macarth	MacArthur's Reports (DC)	Madd.Ch.Pr.	Maddock's Chancery Practice (Eng.)
MacArth.	Same MacArthur's Patent Cases (DC)	MADR	Massachusetts Appellate Division Reports
macarth & m	MacArthur's and Mackey's Reports (DC)	Madras L.J.	Madras Law Journal
		Madras L.J. Crim.	Madras Law Journal Criminal
MacArth. & M.	Same	Mag.	Magruder (MD)
MacFarl.	MacFarlane, Jury Court (Scot.)	Mag. & Const.	Magistrate and Constable
		Mag.Cas.	Magisterial Cases

Mag.Mun. Par. Law.	Magistrate and Municipal and Parochial Lawyer
Maine L.Rev.	Maine Law Review
M.A.L.C.M.	Mercantile Adjuster and the Lawyer and Credit Man
Mal.L.J	Malayan Law Journal
Malloy	Malloy's Chancery (Ir.)
Mal.L.Rev.	Malaya Law Review
Malone	Malone's Heiskell (TN)
Man.	Manitoba Law Manning (MI)
Man. & G.	Manning & Granger's Common Pleas (Eng.)
Man. & Ry.Mag.	Manning & Ryland's Magistrates' Cases (Eng.)
Man. & S.	Manning & Scott's Common Bench (Old Series) (Eng.)
Man.B.News	Manitoba Bar News
M. & A.	Montagu & Ayrton's Bankruptcy Reports (Eng.)
M. & Ayr.	Same
M. & B.	Montague & Bligh's Bankruptcy (Eng.)
M. & C.	Montague & Chitty's Bankruptcy (Eng.) Mylne & Craig's Chancery (Eng.)
M. & Cht. Bankr.	Montague & Chitty's Bankruptcy (Eng.)
M. & G.	Maddock & Geldhart's Chancery (Eng.) Manning & Granger's Common Pleas (Eng.)
M. & Gel.	Maddock & Geldhart's Chancery (Eng.)
M. & Gord.	Macnaghten & Gordon's Chancery (Eng.)
M. & H.	Murphy & Hurlstone's Exchequer (Eng.)
M. & K.	Mylne & Keen's Chancery (Eng.)
M. & M.	Moody & Malkin's Nisi Prius (Eng.)
M. & McA.	Montague & McArthur's Bankruptcy (Eng.)
M. & P.	Moore & Payne's Common Pleas & Exchequer (Eng.)
M. & R.	Maclean & Robinson's Appeal Cases (Scot.) Manning & Ryland's King's Bench (Eng.) Moody & Robinson's Nisi Prius (Eng.)
M. & R.M.C.	Manning & Ryland's Magistrates' Cases, King's Bench (Eng.)
M. & Rob.	Moody & Robinson's Nisi Prius (Eng.)
M. & S.	Manning & Scott's Common Pleas (Eng.) Maule & Selwyn's King's Bench (Eng.) Moore & Scott's Common Pleas (Eng.)
M. & Scott	Same
M. & W.	Meeson & Welsby's Exchequer (Eng.)
M. & W.Cas.	Mining & Water Cases Annotated (U.S)
M. & Y.	Martin & Yerger (TN)
Man.G. & S.	Manning, Granger & Scott's Common Bench (Eng.)
Man.Gr. & S.	Same
Man.L.J.	Manitoba Law Journal
Mann.	Manning (MI)
Mann. & G.	Manning & Granger's Common Pleas (Eng.)
Mansf.	Mansfield (AR)
Manson	Manson's Bankruptcy (Eng.)
Man.t.Wood	Manitoba tempore Wood
manunrep	Manning's Unreported Cases (LA)
Man.Unrep. Cas.	Same
March	March's King's Bench (Eng.)
MarD	Martin's Decisions in Equity (AR)
Marijuana Rev.	Marijuana Review
Maritime L.J.	Maritime Law Journal

Mark's & Sayre's	Mark's & Sayre's (AL)	Mass.App. Div.	Massachusetts Appellate Division Reports
Mar.Law.	Maritime Lawyer		
Mar.L.Cas. (N.S.)	Maritime Law Cases, New Series	Mass.App. Rep.	Massachusetts Appeals Court Reports
Mar.N. & Q.	Maritime Notes and Queries	Mass.L.Q.	Massachusetts Law Quarterly
Mar.Prov.	Maritime Provinces Reports (Can.)	Mass.L.Rev.	Massachusetts Law Review
Marq.L.Rev.	Marquette Law Review	Mathews	Mathews (WV)
Marq. Sports L.J.	Marquette Sports Law Journal	Matson	Matson (CT)
		MC	American Maritime Cases
Mars.Adm.	Marsden's Admiralty (Eng.)	McA	Michigan Court of Appeals Reports
Marsh.	Marshall (U.S.)	mcall	McAllister's U.S. Circuit Court Reports
	Marshall (UT)		
	Marshall, A.K. (KY)		
	Marshall, J.J. (KY)		
	Marshall's Common Pleas (Eng.)	McAll	Same
		McBride	McBride (MO)
mart	Martin's Reports (LA)	McC.	McCahon's Reports (KS)
Mart. & Y.	Martin & Yerger (TN)	M.C.C.	Mixed Claims Commission
martin	Martin's North Carolina Reports		Motor Carriers' Cases (I.C.C.)
Martin	Martin (GA)	McCah.	McCahon's Reports (KS)
	Martin (IN)		
	Martin (LA)	mccahon	Same
	Martin (U.S.)	McCarter	McCarter's Chancery (NJ)
	Martin's Decisions (Law) (NC)	McCartney	McCartney's Civil Procedure (NY)
Martin Mining	Martin Mining Cases	McClell.	McClelland's Exchequer (Eng.)
	Martin's New Series (LA)		
martns	Martin's Louisiana Reports, New Series	McClell. & Y.	McClelland & Younge's Exchequer (Eng.)
martyertn	Martin & Yerger's Tennessee Reports	McCook	McCook (OH)
		McCord	McCord's Chancery (SC)
marv	Marvel's Reports (DE)		
Marv.	Same	McCork.	McCorkle (NC)
Mas	Massachusetts Reports	McCrary	McCrary (U.S.)
		mccrcc	Same
Mason	Mason (U.S.)	McG.	McGloin's Court of Appeals Reports (LA)
masoncc	Mason's U.S. Circuit Court Reports		
		McGill L.J.	McGill Law Journal
mass	Massachusetts Reports	mcgloin	McGloin's Court of Appeals Reports (LA)
Mass.	Same		
massad	Massachusetts Appellate Division	Mch	Michigan Reports
		M.C.J.	Michigan Civil Jurisprudence
massapp	Massachusetts Appellate Reports		
		McL	McLean's U.S. Circuit Court Reports
massappdec	Massachusetts Appellate Decisions	mclcc	Same
Mass.App. Dec.	Same	McLean	Same

MCLE Rules	MCLE Rules and Regulations (CA State Bar)	Meigs	Meigs (TN)
McMul.	McMullan's Chancery (SC)	meigstn	Same
		Melanesian L.J.	Melanesian Law Journal (Papua N.G.)
	McMullan's Law (SC)	Melb.U.L. Rev.	Melbourne University Law Review
M.C.R.	Montreal Condensed Reports	Me.L.Rev.	Maine Law Review
McWillie	McWillie (MS)	Mem.L.J.	Memphis Law Journal (TN)
md	Maryland Reports		
Md.	Same	Mem.St.U.L. Rev.	Memphis State University Law Review
M.D.	Master's Decisions (Patents)		
MdA	Maryland Appellate Reports	Menken	Menken's Civil Procedure (NY)
mdapp	Same	Mercer Beasley L.Rev.	Mercer Beasley Law Review
Md.App.	Same		
Md.B.J.	Maryland Bar Journal	Mercer L.Rev.	Mercer Law Review
		Meredith Lect.	W.C.J. Meredith Memorial Lectures
mdch	Maryland Chancery Reports	Meriv.	Merivale's Chancery (Eng.)
Md.Ch.	Same		
Md.J. Contemp. Legal Issues	Maryland Journal of Contemporary Legal Issues	met	Metcalf's Reports (MA)
		Met.	Metcalf (KY)
Md. J. Int'l L. & Trade	Maryland Journal of International Law and Trade		Metcalf (MA)
		Metc.	Same
		M.F.P.D.	Modern Federal Practice Digest
Md.L.F.	Maryland Law Forum	Miami L.Q.	Miami Law Quarterly
Md.L.Rec.	Maryland Law Record		
Md.L.Rep.	Maryland Law Reporter	mich	Michigan Reports
		Mich.	Same
Md.L.Rev.	Maryland Law Review	michapp	Michigan Court of Appeals Reports
me	Maine Reports		
Me.	Same	Mich.App.	Same
Mean's	Mean's Reports (KS)	Michie's Jur.	Michie's Jurisprudence of Va. and W.Va.
Medd.	Meddaugh (MI)		
Media L.Notes	Media Law Notes		
medialr	Media Law Reporter	Mich. J. Int'l L.	Michigan Journal of International Law
Medico–Legal J.	Medico–Legal Journal	Mich.L.Rev.	Michigan Law Review
Med.L. & Pub. Pol.	Medicine, Law and Public Policy		
		michnp	Michigan Nisi Prius
Med.-Legal Crim.Rev.	Medico–Legal and Criminological Review	Mich.N.P.	Same
		Mich.St.B.J.	Michigan State Bar Journal
Med.-Legal J.	Medico–Legal Journal	Mich.T.	Michaelmas Term (Eng.)
Med.-Legal Soc'y Trans.	Medico–Legal Society Transactions	Mid.East L.Rev.	Middle East Law Review
Med LR	Medical Law Reports	Mil & Vet C	Military and Veterans Code
Med.Sci. & L.	Medicine, Science and the Law	Miles	Miles (PA)
			Miles' Philadelphia District Court
Med.Trial Tech.Q.	Medical Trial Technique Quarterly	Mill Const.	Mill's Constitutional Reports (SC)
Meg.	Megone Company Cases (Eng.)	Mill.Dec.	Miller's Decisions (U.S.)

Mil.L.Rev.	Military Law Review	MnL	Minnesota Law Review
Mills	Mill's Surrogate's Court Reports (NY)	mo	Missouri Supreme Court Reports
Milw.	Milward's Ecclesiastical (Ir.)	Mo.	Same
		Moak	Moak (Eng.)
Min	Minnesota Reports	moapp	Missouri Appeals
Min.	Minor (AL)	Mo.App.	Same
minn	Minnesota Reports	Mo.A.R.	Missouri Appellate Reporter
Minn.	Same		
Minn.Cont. L.Ed.	Minnesota Continuing Legal Education	Mo.B.J.	Missouri Bar Journal
		Mod.	Modern (Eng.)
		Mo.Dec.	Missouri Decisions
Minn.Cont.Legal Ed.	Same	Mod.L. & Soc'y	Modern Law and Society
Minn.L.Rev.	Minnesota Law Review	Mod.L.Rev.	Modern Law Review
minor	Minor's Reports (AL)	Mod.Pract. Comm.	Modern Practice Commentator
Mis	Mississippi Reports	Mo.J.Dispute Res.	Missouri Journal of Dispute Resolution
misc	Miscellaneous (NY)		
Misc.	Same	Moll.	Molloy's Chancery (Ir.)
misc2d	Same, Second Series		
Misc.Dec.	Ohio Miscellaneous Decisions	Mo.L.Rev.	Missouri Law Review
		Mon.	B. Monroe (KY)
miss	Mississippi Reports		T.B. Monroe (KY)
Miss.	Same	Monag	Monaghan's Reports (PA)
Miss.C.L.Rev.	Mississippi College Law Review		
Miss.Dec.	Mississippi Decisions (Jackson)	monaghan	Same
		Monash U.L. Rev.	Monash University Law Review
Miss.L.J.	Mississippi Law Journal	mont	Montana Reports
Miss.St.Cas.	Mississippi State Cases	Mont.	Same
		Mont. & Ayr.	Montagu & Ayrton's Bankruptcy (Eng.)
Mister	Mister (MO)		
Mitchell's Mar. Reg.	Mitchell's Maritime Register	Mont. & M.	Montagu & McArthur's Bankruptcy (Eng.)
mj	Military Justice Reporter		
MJ	Same	Month.Dig. Tax Articles	Monthly Digest of Tax Articles
ML	Judicial Panel on Multidistrict Litigation	Month.Leg. Exam.	Monthly Legal Examiner (NY)
Ml.	Miller (Law) (MD)	Month.L.J.	Monthly Journal of Law (WA)
M.L.Dig. & R.	Monthly Digest & Reporter (Que.)		
		Month.L.Mag.	Monthly Law Magazine (London)
M.L.E.	Maryland Law Encyclopedia	Month.L.Rep.	Monthly Law Reporter (Boston)
M.L.P.	Michigan Law and Practice		Monthly Law Reports (Can.)
M.L.R.	Military Law Reporter	Month.L.Rev.	Monthly Law Review
	Modern Law Review	Month.West. Jur.	Monthly Western Journal (Bloomington, IN)
M.L.R. (Q.B.)	Montreal Law Reports, Queen's Bench		
		Mont.L.Rev.	Montana Law Review
M.L.R. (S.C.)	Montreal Law Reports, Superior Court		
		Montr.Cond. Rep.	Montreal Condensed Reports
mlw	Massachusetts Lawyers Weekly	Montr.Leg.N.	Montreal Legal News

Montr.Q.B.	Montreal Law Reports, Queen's Bench	Moult.Ch.	Moulton's Chancery Practice (NY)
Mont.Super.	Montreal Law Reports (Superior Court)	M.P.L.R.	Municipal and Planning Law Reports
Moo.C.C.	Moody's Crown Cases Reserved (Eng.)	M.P.R.	Maritime Province Reports
Mood. & Mack.	Moody & Mackin's Nisi Prius (Eng.)	M.P.T.M.H.	Major Peace Treaties of Modern History
Mood. & Malk.	Moody & Malkin's Nisi Prius (Eng.)	Mrt	Martin's Reports (LA)
Mood. & Rob.	Moody & Robinson's Nisi Prius (Eng.)	MrtN	Same, New Series
Moody Cr.C.	Moody's Crown Cases Reserved (Eng.)	mspr	U.S. Merit Systems Protection Board Reporter
Moon	Moon (IN)	Mt	Montana Reports
Moo.P.C.	Moore, Privy Council	Mtg Rules	Rules Governing Open Meetings, Closed Sessions and Records of Board of Governors of State Bar (CA)
Moo.P.C. (N.S.)	Moore, New Series		
Moore	Moore (AL) Moore (AR) Moore (TX)		
Moore & S.	Moore & Scott's Common Pleas (Eng.)	Mun.	Munford (VA)
		Mun.Att'y	Municipal Attorney
Moore & W.	Moore & Walker (TX)	Mun.Corp. Cas.	Municipal Corporation Cases
Moore B.B.	Moore's King's Bench (Eng.)	Munf.	Munford (VA)
		Munic. & P.L.	Municipal & Parish Law Cases (Eng.)
Moore C.P.	Moore's Common Pleas (Eng.)	Mun.L.Ct. Dec.	Municipal Law Court Decisions
Moore Indian App.	Moore's Indian Appeals (Eng.)	Mun.L.J.	Municipal Law Journal
Moore P.C.C.	Moore's Privy Council Cases (Eng.)	Mun.Ord. Rev.	Municipal Ordinance Review
Mor	Morris' Reports (IA)	Mun.Rep.	Municipal Reports (Can.)
Morg.	Morgan's Chancery Acts & Orders (Eng.)	Mur.	Murray's New South Wales Reports Murray's Scotch Jury Court Reports
Morr.	Morrill's Bankruptcy Cases (Eng.) Morris (CA) Morris (IA) Morris (MS)	Mur. & H.	Murphy & Hurlstone's Exchequer (Eng.)
morris	Morrissett (AL)	Mur. & Hurl.	Same
Morris.	Same	Murph.	Murphy (NC)
Morr. Min. Rep.	Morrison's Mining Reports	Murph. & H.	Murphy & Hurlstone's Exchequer (Eng.)
Morrow	Morrow (OR)	Murr.	Murray's Scotch Jury Court Reports
Morr.St.Cas.	Morris State Cases (MS)		
Morr.Trans.	Morrison's Transcript United States Supreme Court Decisions	Murr.Over. Cas.	Murray's Overruled Cases
Morse Exch. Rep.	Morse's Exchequer Reports (Can.)	M.V.R.	Motor Vehicle Reports
Mosely	Mosely's Chancery (Eng.)	Myer Fed. Dec.	Myer's Federal Decisions

Myl. & C.	Mylne & Craig's Chancery (Eng.)	Myr.	Myrick's Probate (CA)
Myl. & Cr.	Same	Myrick (CA)	Same
Myl. & K.	Mylne & Keen's Chancery (Eng.)	Myr.Prob.	Same
Mylne & K.	Same	Mysore L.J.	Mysore Law Journal

N

NACCA L.J.	National Association of Claimant's Compensation Attorneys Law Journal	Nat'l School L.Rptr.	National School Law Reporter
		Nat'l Taiwan U.L.J.	National Taiwan University Law Journal
N. & Dr.	Nevile & Manning's King's Bench (Eng.)	Nat'l Tax J.	National Tax Journal
N. & H.	Nott & Huntington's U.S. Court of Claims	Nat.Munic. Rev.	National Municipal Review
		Nat.Reg.	National Register (Mead)
N. & Macn.	Nevile & Macnamara Railway & Canal Cases (Eng.)	Nat.Resources & Env't	Natural Resources & Environment
N. & Mc.	Nott & McCord (SC)	Nat.Resources J.	Natural Resources Journal
N. & McC.	Same	Nat.Resources Law.	Natural Resources Lawyer
N. & P.	Nevile & Perry's King's Bench (Eng.)	Nat.Resources L.Newsl.	Natural Resources Law Newsletter
Napt.	Napton (MO)	Nat U LR	National University Law Review
Napton	Same		
Narcotics Control Dig.	Narcotics Control Digest	N.B.	New Brunswick
Narcotics L.Bull.	Narcotics Law Bulletin	N.Benl.	New Benloe, King's Bench (Eng.)
Nat.Bankr. Reg.	National Bankruptcy Register (U.S.)	N.B.Eq.	New Brunswick Equity
Nat.Corp. Rep.	National Corporation Reporter	N.B.Rep.	New Brunswick Reports
Nat. Jewish L. Rev.	National Jewish Law Review	nc	North Carolina Reports
N.Atlantic Reg. Bus. L.Rev.	North Atlantic Regional Business Law Review	N.C.	Same
		nca	Decisions of Nebraska Court of Appeals
Nat'l Black L.J.	National Black Law Journal	NCA	North Carolina Court of Appeals Reports
Nat'l Civic Rev.	National Civic Review	ncapp	Same
Nat.L.F.	Natural Law Forum	N.C.App.	Same
Nat'l Income Tax Mag.	National Income Tax Magazine	N.C.C.	New Chancery Cases (Eng.)
Nat'l J.Crim. Def.	National Journal of Criminal Defense	N.C.C.A.	Negligence & Compensation Cases Annotated
Nat'l Legal Mag.	National Legal Magazine	N.C.Cent.L.J.	North Carolina Central Law Journal
Nat'l Mun. Rev.	National Municipal Review	N.C.Conf.	North Carolina Conference Reports
Nat'l Prison Project J.	National Prison Project Journal	N.Cent. School L.Rev.	North Central School Law Review
Nat.L.Rep.	National Law Reporter		

nchip	North Chipman's Reports (VT)	N.Eng.L.Rev.	New England Law Review
N.Chipm.	Same	Neth.Int'l L.Rev.	Netherlands International Law Review
N.C.J.Int'l L. & Com. Reg.	North Carolina Journal of International Law and Commercial Regulation	Neth.Y.B. Int'l.Law	Netherlands Yearbook of International Law
N.C.L.Rev.	North Carolina Law Review	nev	Nevada Reports
NCr	New York Criminal Reports	Nev.	Same
		Nev. & P.	Nevile & Perry's King's Bench (Eng.)
nctermrep	North Carolina Term Reports	Nev.St.Bar J.	Nevada State Bar Journal
N.C.T.Rep.	Same	New.	Newell (IL)
nd	North Dakota Reports	newbadm	Newberry's Admiralty (U.S. District Court)
N.D.	Same		
N.D.J.Legis.	North Dakota Journal of Legislation	Newb.Adm.	Same
N.D.L.Rev.	North Dakota Law Review	New Eng.L. Rev.	New England Law Review
ne	North Eastern Reporter	New Eng.J. Prison L.	New England Journal of Prison Law
N.E.	Same	Newfoundl.	Newfoundland
ne2d	Same, Second Series	Newf.S.Ct.	Newfoundland Supreme Court Decisions
N.E.2d	Same		
neb	Nebraska Reports		
Neb.	Same	New L.J.	New Law Journal
NebA	Nebraska Advance Reports	New Rep.	New Reports in All Courts (Eng.)
nebapp	Nebraska Appeals Decisions	New Sess. Cas.	New Session Cases (Eng.)
Neb.L.Bull.	Nebraska Law Bulletin	New Yugo.L.	New Yugoslav Law
Neb.L.Rev.	Nebraska Law Review	New Zeal.L.	New Zealand Law
		Nfld. & P.E.I.R.	Newfoundland and Prince Edward Island Reports
Neb.St.B.J.	Nebraska State Bar Journal		
nebunof	Nebraska Unofficial Reports	Nfld.R.	Newfoundland Reports
Neb. (Unoff.)	Same	Nfld.Sel.Cas.	Tucker's Select Cases (Nfld.)
Negl. & Comp. Cas. Ann.	Negligence & Compensation Cases Annotated	nh	New Hampshire Reports
Negl. & Comp. Cas. Ann. (N.S.)	Same, New Series	N.H.	Same
		N.H.B.J.	New Hampshire Bar Journal
Negl. & Comp. Cas. Ann.3d	Same, Third Series	NI	Northern Ireland Law Reports
Negl.Cas.	Negligence Cases (CCH)	Nigeria L.R.	Nigeria Law Reports
Negl.Cas.2d	Same, Second Series	Nigerian Ann. Int'l L.	Nigerian Annual of International Law
Negotiation J.	Negotiation Journal	Nigerian L.J.	Nigerian Law Journal
Negro.Cas.	Bloomfield's Manumission (NJ)	N.Ill.U.L. Rev.	Northern Illinois University Law Review
Nels.	Nelson's Chancery (Eng.)		
Nels.Abr.	Nelson's Abridgment (Lag.)	N.I.M.L.O. Mun.L.Rev.	N.I.M.L.O. Municipal Law Review
N.Eng.J.Prison L.	New England Journal on Prison Law	N.Ir.L.Q.	Northern Ireland Legal Quarterly

N.Ir.L.R.	Northern Ireland Law Reports	Nolan	Nolan, Magistrate Cases (Eng.)
nj	New Jersey Reports	NOLPE Sch. L.J.	National Organization on Problems of Education School Law Journal
N.J.	Same		
NJE	New Jersey Equity Reports		
njeq	Same	NOLPE School L. Rep.	National Organization on Problems of Education School Law Reporter
N.J.Eq.	Same		
njl	New Jersey Law Reports		
N.J.L.	Same		
N.J.Law	Same		
N.J.L.J.	New Jersey Law Journal	Norc.	Norcross (NV)
		Norris	Norris (PA)
N.J.L.Rev.	New Jersey Law Review	North	North (IL)
		North.	Northington's Chancery (Eng.)
NJM	New Jersey Miscellaneous Reports	North & G.	North & Guthrie (MO)
njmisc	Same		
N.J.Misc.	Same	North.Co.	Northampton County Legal News (PA)
NJS	New Jersey Superior Court Reports		
N.J.St.B.J.	New Jersey State Bar Journal	Northrop U.L.J.Aerospace Energy & Env.	Northrop University Law Journal of Aerospace, Energy and the Environment
njsuper	New Jersey Superior and County Court Reports		
N.J.Super.	Same	Northumb. Co. Leg. News	Northumberland County Legal News (PA)
NJT	New Jersey Tax Court Reports		
njtax	Same	Northumb. Legal J.	Northumberland Legal Journal
N.Ky.L.Rev.	Northern Kentucky Law Review	Notes of Cas.	Notes of Cases (Eng.)
N.Ky.St.L.F.	Northern Kentucky State Law Forum	Notre Dame Int'l & Comp. L.J.	Notre Dame International and Comparative Law Journal
NLADA Brief.	National Legal Aid and Defender Association Briefcase		
NLJ	New Law Journal	Notre Dame J.L.Ethics & Pub.Pol'y	Notre Dame Journal of Law, Ethics & Public Policy
NLJR	New Law Journal Reports		
nlrb	National Labor Relations Board Reports	Notre Dame Law.	Notre Dame Lawyer
		Notre Dame L. Rev.	Notre Dame Law Review
N.L.R.B.	Same	Nova L.J.	Nova Law Journal
nlrbno	National Labor Relations Board, Decisions and Orders of National Labor Relations Board	Nova L.Rev.	Nova Law Review
		Noy	Noy, King's Bench (Eng.)
		N.P.	Ohio Nisi Prius Reports
nm	New Mexico Reports		
N.M.	Same	N.P. (N.S.)	Same, New Series
NM(J)	New Mexico Reports (Johnson)	N.P. & G.T. Rep.	Nisi Prius & General Term Reports (OH)
N.M.L.R.	Nigerian Monthly Law Reports	N.R.	National Reporter
N.M.L.Rev.	New Mexico Law Review	N.R.A.B. (4th Div.)	National Railroad Adjustment Board Awards
Noise Reg. Rep.	Noise Regulation Reporter (BNA)	N.S.	Nova Scotia

N.S.Dec.	Nova Scotia Decisions	N.Y.Ch.Sent.	Chancery Sentinel (NY)
N.S.R.	Nova Scotia Reports	N.Y.City Ct.	New York City Court
N.S.W.	New South Wales State Reports	N.Y.City Ct. Supp.	New York City Court Supplement
N.S.Wales	New South Wales	N.Y.City H.Rec.	New York City Hall Recorder
N.S.Wales L.	New South Wales Law	N.Y.Civ.Proc.	New York Civil Procedure
N.S.Wales L.R.Eq.	New South Wales Law Reports Equity	N.Y.Civ.Proc. (N.S.)	Same, New Series
N.S.W.St.R.	New South Wales State Reports	N.Y.Civ.Pro. R.	New York Civil Procedure Reports
NTR	Northern Territory Reports	N.Y.Civ. Pro.R. (N.S.)	Same, New Series
NU	Nebraska Unofficial Reports	N.Y.Code Rep.	New York Code Reporter
Nuclear L.Bull.	Nuclear Law Bulletin	N.Y.Code Rep. (N.S.)	Same, New Series
Nuclear Reg. Rep.	Nuclear Regulation Reporter (CCH)	N.Y.Cond.	New York Condensed Reports
NVAdv	Nevada Advance Opinion Number	N.Y.Cont. L.Ed.	New York Continuing Legal Education
nw	North Western Reporter	N.Y.Cont. Legal Ed.	Same
N.W.	Same	N.Y.County Law. Ass'n B.Bull.	New York County Lawyers Association Bar Bulletin
nw2d	Same, Second Series		
N.W.2d	Same	N.Y.Cr.R.	New York Criminal Reports
Nw.J.Int'l L. & Bus.	Northwestern Journal of International Law & Business	N.Y.Crim.	Same
		NYCS	New York City Court Reports, Supplement
NwL	Northwestern University Law Review		
		N.Y.Daily L.Gaz.	New York Daily Law Gazette
N.W.Terr.	Northwest Territories Supreme Court Reports	N.Y.Daily L.Reg.	New York Daily Law Register
N.W.T.L.R.	North West Territories Law Reports	N.Y.Dep't R.	New York Department Reports
Nw.U.L.Rev.	Northwestern University Law Review	N.Y.Elec.Cas.	New York Election Cases
ny	New York Reports	N.Y.Jud. Repos.	New York Judicial Repository
N.Y.	Same	N.Y.Jur.	New York Jurisprudence
ny2d	Same, Second Series		
N.Y.2d	Same, Second Series		New York Jurist
NYAD	New York Appellate Division Reports	NYL	New York University Law Review
NYAD2d	Same, Second Series	N.Y.L.Cas.	New York Leading Cases
N.Y.Anno. Cas.	New York Annotated Cases	N.Y.Leg.N.	New York Legal News
N.Y.Anno. Dig.	New York Annotated Digest	N.Y.Leg.Obs.	New York Legal Observer
N.Y.App.Div.	New York Supreme Court Appellate Division Reports	N.Y.L.F.	New York Law Forum
NYC	New York City Court Reports	N.Y.L.J.	New York Law Journal
N.Y.Cas.Err.	New York Cases in Error (Claim Cases)		

N.Y.L.Rec.	New York Law Record	N.Y.Super.	New York Superior Court
N.Y.L.Rev.	New York Law Review	N.Y.Supp.	New York Supplement
N.Y.L.Sch. Int'l L.Soc'y J.	New York Law School International Law Society Journal	N.Y.U.Conf. Charitable	New York University Conference on Charitable Foundations Proceedings
N.Y.L.Sch.J. Hum.Rts.	New York Law School Journal of Human Rights	N.Y.U.Conf. Lab.	New York University Conference on Labor
N.Y.L.Sch.J. Int'l & Comp.L.	New York Law School Journal of International and Comparative Law	N.Y.U. Envtl. L.J.	New York University Environmental Law Journal
N.Y.L.Sch. L.Rev.	New York Law School Law Review	N.Y.U. Inst. on Fed. Tax.	New York University Institute on Federal Taxation
NYM	New York Miscellaneous Reports	N.Y.U.Intra.L.Rev.	New York Intramural Law Review
N.Y.Misc.	Same	N.Y.U.J.Int'l L. & Pol.	New York University Journal of International Law and Politics
N.Y.Misc.2d	Same, Second Series		
N.Y.Month. L.Rep.	New York Monthly Law Reports		
N.Y.Mun. Gaz.	New York Municipal Gazette	N.Y.U.L.Center Bull.	New York University Law Center Bulletin
N.Y.P.R.	New York Practice Reports	N.Y.U.L.Q. Rev.	New York University Law Quarterly Review
N.Y.Pr.Rep.	Same		
N.Y.Rec.	New York Record	N.Y.U.L.Rev.	New York University Law Review
nys	New York Supplement		
N.Y.S.	Same	N.Y.U.Rev.L. & Soc. Change	New York University Review of Law and Social Change
nys2d	Same, Second Series		
N.Y.S.2d	Same		
NYSD	New York State Department Reports	N.Y.Wkly. Dig.	New York Weekly Digest
N.Y.Sea Grant L. & Pol'y J.	New York Sea Grant Law and Policy Journal	N.Z.L.J.	New Zealand Law Journal
N.Y.St.	New York State Reporter	N.Z.L.R.	New Zealand Law Reports
N.Y.St.B.J.	New York State Bar Journal	N.Z.U.L.Rev.	New Zealand Universities Law Review

O

O.	Ohio	oapp2d	Same, Second Series
	Oklahoma	oapp3d	Same, Third Series
	Oregon	O.A.R.	Ohio Appellate Reports
O.A.	Ohio Appellate Reports		Ontario Appeal Reports
OA2d	same, Second Series		
OA3d	same, Third Series	O.B. & F.N.Z.	Olliver, Bell & Fitzgerald's New Zealand Reports
OAG	Opinions of the Attorneys General of the United States		
		O.Ben.	Old Benloe, Common Pleas (Eng.)
oapp	Ohio Appellate Reports	O.Benl.	Same
O.App.	Same	Obiter Dictum	Obiter Dictum

O.Bridgm.	Orlando Bridgman, Common Pleas (Eng.)	Oh.Dec. (Reprint)	Same (Reprint)
O.C.A.	Ohio Courts of Appeals Reports	Oh.F.Dec.	Ohio Federal Decisions
O.C.C.	Ohio Circuit Court Decisions	ohio	Ohio Reports
	Ohio Circuit Court Reports	Ohio	Same
		Ohio (N.S.)	Same, New Series
O.C.C. (N.S.)	Ohio Circuit Court Reports, New Series	Ohio App.	Ohio Appellate Reports
OCCns	Same	Ohio App.2d	Same, Second Series
O.C.D.	Ohio Circuit Decisions	Ohio Bar	Ohio State Bar Association Reports
Ocean Dev. & Int'l L.J.	Ocean Development and International Law Journal	ohiobr	Same
		Ohio C.A.	Ohio Courts of Appeals Reports
OCr	Oklahoma Criminal Reports	Ohio C.C.	Ohio Circuit Court Reports
O.C.S.	Office of Contract Settlement Decisions	Ohio C.C.R.	Same
		Ohio C.C.R. (N.S.)	Same, New Series
O.D.	Office Decisions (I.R.B.)	Ohio C.Dec.	Ohio Circuit Decisions
	Ohio Decisions	Ohio Cir.Ct.	Ohio Circuit Court Decisions
O.D.C.C.	Ohio Circuit Decisions	Ohio Cir.Ct. (N.S.)	Ohio Circuit Court Reports, New Series
O.Dec.Rep.	Ohio Decisions Reprint	Ohio Cir.Ct.R.	Ohio Circuit Court Reports
Odeneal	Odeneal (OR)		
O.D.N.P.	Ohio Decisions, Nisi Prius	Ohio Cir.Ct.R. (N.S.)	Same, New Series
O.E.M.	Office of Emergency Management	Ohio Ct.App.	Ohio Courts of Appeals Reports
O.F.D.	Ohio Federal Decisions	ohiodec	Ohio Decisions
		Ohio Dec.	Same
Off.Brev.	Officina Brevium	Ohio Dec. Repr.	Same, Reprint
Off.Gaz.	Official Gazette, United States Patent Office	Ohio F.Dec.	Ohio Federal Decisions
		Ohio Fed.Dec.	Same
Officer	Officer (MN)	Ohio Jur.	Ohio Jurisprudence
Official Rep. Ill. Courts Commission	Official Reports: Illinois Courts Commission	Ohio Jur.2d	Same, Second Edition
O.G.	Official Gazette, United States Patent Office	ohiolabs	Ohio Law Abstract
		Ohio L.Abs.	Same
		Ohio Law Abst.	Same
Ogd.	Ogden (LA)	Ohio Law Bull.	Weekly Law Bulletin (OH)
O.G.Pat.Off.	Same		
ogr	Oil and Gas Reporter	Ohio Law J.	Ohio Law Journal
Oh.	Ohio Reports	Ohio Law R.	Ohio Law Reporter
Oh.A.	Ohio Court of Appeals	Ohio L.B.	Weekly Law Bulletin (OH)
Oh.Cir.Ct.	Ohio Circuit Court	Ohio Legal N.	Ohio Legal News
Oh.Cir.Ct. (N.S.)	Same, New Series	Ohio Leg.N.	Same
		Ohio L.J.	Ohio Law Journal
Oh.Cir.Dec.	Ohio Circuit Decisions	Ohio Lower Dec.	Ohio Lower Court Decisions
Oh.Dec.	Ohio Decisions	Ohio L.R.	Ohio Law Reporter
		Ohio Misc.	Ohio Miscellaneous Reports
		Ohio Misc. Dec.	Ohio Miscellaneous Decisions

ohionp	Ohio Nisi Prius Reports	Oil & Gas Inst.	Oil and Gas Institute
Ohio N.P.	Same	Oil & Gas J.	Oil and Gas Journal
ohionpns	Same, New Series	Oil & Gas L. & Tax.Inst. (Sw.Legal Fdn.)	Oil & Gas Law & Taxation Institute (Southwestern Legal Foundation)
Ohio N.P. (N.S.)	Same		
Ohio N.U. L.Rev.	Ohio Northern University Law Review		
		Oil & Gas Rptr.	Oil and Gas Reporter
Ohio Op.	Ohio Opinions	Oil & Gas Tax Q.	Oil and Gas Tax Quarterly
Ohio Op.2d	Same, Second Series		
Ohio Prob.	Goebel's Ohio Probate Reports	OJ C	Official Journal of the European Communities–Communications and Information Series
Ohio R.Cond.	Ohio Reports Condensed		
Ohio S. & C.P.Dec.	Ohio Superior & Common Pleas Decisions		
		OJ L	Same–Legislation Series
Ohio St.	Ohio State Reports	Okl	Oklahoma Reports
Ohio St. (N.S.)	Same, New Series	okla	Same
Ohio St.2d	Same, Second Series	Okla.	Same
Ohio St.J. on Disp.Resol.	Ohio State Journal on Dispute Resolution	Okla.B.Ass'n J.	Oklahoma Bar Association Journal
		Okla.City U.L.Rev.	Oklahoma City University Law Review
Ohio St.L.J.	Ohio State Law Journal		
Ohio S.U.	Ohio Supreme Court Decisions (Unreported Cases)	Okla.Cr.	Oklahoma Criminal Reports
		oklacrim	Same
Ohio Sup. & C.P.Dec.	Ohio Decisions	Okla.Crim.	Same
		Okla.L.J.	Oklahoma Law Journal
Ohio Supp.	Ohio Supplement		
Ohio Tax Rev.	Ohio Tax Review	Okla.L.Rev.	Oklahoma Law Review
Ohio Unrep. Jud.Dec.	Pollack's Ohio Unreported Judicial Decisions Prior to 1823	Okla.S.B.J.	Oklahoma State Bar Journal
		O.L.A.	Ohio Law Abstract
Ohio Unrept. Cas.	Ohio Supreme Court Decisions, Unreported Cases	O.L.B.	Weekly Law Bulletin (OH)
		olcott	Olcott (U.S.)
Oh.Jur.	Ohio Jurisprudence	Olcott	Same
Oh.L.Bull.	Ohio Law Bulletin	O.L.D.	Ohio Lower Court Decisions
Oh.L.Ct.D.	Ohio Lower Court Decisions		
		O.Legal News	Ohio Legal News
Oh.Leg.N.	Ohio Legal News	Oliv.B. & L.	Oliver, Beavan & Lefroy, English Railway & Canal Cases
Oh.L.J.	Ohio Law Journal		
Oh.L.Rep.	Ohio Law Reporter		
OhM	Ohio Miscellaneous Reports	O.L.J.	Ohio Law Journal
OhM2d	Same, Second Series	O.L.Jour.	Same
Oh.N.P.	Ohio Nisi Prius	Olliv.B. & F.	Olliver, Bell & Fitzgerald (New Zealand)
Oh.N.P. (N.S.)	Same, New Series		
Oh.Prob.	Ohio Probate		
Oh.S. & C.P.	Ohio Superior & Common Pleas Decisions	O.L.N.	Ohio Legal News
		O.Lower D.	Ohio (Lower) Decisions
Oh.S.C.D.	Ohio Supreme Court Decisions (Unreported Cases)	O.L.R.	Ohio Law Reporter Ontario Law Reports
		O.L.R.B.	Ontario Labour Relations Board Monthly Report
Oh.St.	Ohio State Reports		
Oil & Gas Compact Bull.	Oil and Gas Compact Bulletin	O.L.Rep.	Ohio Law Reporter

O'M. & H.El. Cas.	O'Malley & Hardcastle, Election Cases (Eng.)	orleansapp	Louisiana Court of Appeals, Parish of Orleans
O.M.B.R.	Ontario Municipal Board Reports	Orleans' App.	Same
omisc	Ohio Miscellaneous Reports; Ohio Miscellaneous Reports	Orleans Tr.	Orleans Term Reports (LA)
		Or.L.Rev.	Oregon Law Review
omisc2d	Same, Second Series	Ormond	Ormond (AL)
O.N.P.	Ohio, Nisi Prius	os	Ohio State Reports
O.N.P. (N.S.)	Same, New Series	O.S.	Same
Ont.	Ontario Reports	os2d	Same, Second Series
Ont.A.	Ontario Appeals	os3d	Same, Third Series
Ont.El.Cas.	Ontario Election Cases	Osaka Pref. Bull.	University of Osaka Prefecture Bulletin
Ont.Elec.	Same	Osaka U.L. Rev.	Osaka University Law Review
Ont.L.	Ontario Law		
Ont.L.J.	Ontario Law Journal	oscd	Ohio Supreme Court Decisions (Unreported Cases)
Ont.L.J. (N.S.)	Same, New Series		
Ont.L.R.	Ontario Law Reports		
Ont.Pr.	Ontario Practice	O.S.C.D.	Same
Ont.W.N.	Ontario Weekly Notes	Osgoode Hall L.J.	Osgoode Hall Law Journal
Ont.W.R.Op.	Ontario Weekly Reporter Opinions of Attorneys General (U.S.)	oshc	Occupational Safety and Health Cases (BNA)
		O.S.H.Dec.	Occupational, Safety, and Health Decisions (CCH)
O.O.	Ohio Opinions		
oops	Same		
oops2d	Same, Second Series	O.S.H.Rep.	Occupational, Safety, and Health Reporter (BNA)
oops3d	Same, Third Series		
Op.Att'y Gen.	Opinions of the Attorney General, United States	O.S.L.J.	Ohio State Law Journal
Op. Leg. Counsel	Opinions of Legislative Counsel (CA)	O.St.	Ohio State Reports
		O.Su.	Ohio Supplement
Ops.Atty. Gen.	Opinions of Attorneys General (U.S.)	O.S.U.	Ohio Supreme Court Decisions, Unreported Cases
Op.Sol.Dept.	Opinions of the Solicitor, U.S. Department of Labor	OSUC	Same
		Otago L.Rev.	Otago Law Review
or	Oregon Reports	otr	Oregon Tax Reports
Or.	Same	Ottawa L.Rev.	Ottawa Law Review
O.R.	Ontario Reports	otto	Otto (U.S.)
OrA	Oregon Court of Appeals Reports	Otto	Same
		Out.	Outerbridge (PA)
Orange County B.J.	Orange County Bar Journal	Outerbridge	Same
		Over.	Overton (TN)
Orange County Law	Orange County Lawyer	Overt.	Same
		Overton	Same
orapp	Oregon Appeals Reports	overttn	Same
		Ow.	Owen's King's Bench (Eng.)
Ore.	Oregon Reports		
Ore.App.	Oregon Court of Appeals Reports	Ow.	Owen's Common Pleas (Eng.)
Ore.L.Rev.	Oregon Law Review	Owen	Same
Ore.St.B. Bull.	Oregon State Bar Bulletin	O.W.N.	Ontario Weekly Notes
Ore.Tax Ct.	Oregon Tax Court Reports	O.W.R.	Ontario Weekly Reporter

| Oxford Law. | Oxford Lawyer | Oxley | Oxley, Young's Vice Admiralty Decisions (Nova Scotia) |

P

p	Pacific Reporter	pad & c2d	Same, Second Series
P.	Law Reports Probate, Divorce & Admiralty Division, Third Series	Pa.D. & C.2d	Same
		pad & c3d	Same, Third Series
		pad & c4th	Same, Fourth Series
	Pacific Reporter	Pa.Dist.	Pennsylvania District Reporter
	Pickering (MA)		
	Probate	PaDC	Pennsylvania District and County Reports
p2d	Pacific Reporter, Second Series		
		Pa.Fid.Reporter	Pennsylvania Fiduciary
P.2d	Same		
P.3d	Pacific Reporter, Third Series	Pai	Paige's Chancery Reports (NY)
pa	Pennsylvania Reports	Paige	Paige's Chancery (NY)
Pa.	Same	paine	Paine's U.S. Circuit Court Reports
Pa.B.A.Q.	Pennsylvania Bar Association Quarterly		
		Paine	Same
		Pak.Crim. L.J.	Pakistan Criminal Law Journal
Pa.B.Brief	Pennsylvania Bar Brief		
		Pak.L.R.	Pakistan Law Reports
Pac.	Pacific Reporter		
PaC	Pennsylvania Commonwealth Court Reports	PaL	University of Pennsylvania Law Review
Pa.Cas.	Sadler (PA)	Pa.L.J.	Pennsylvania Law Journal
Pac. Basin Int'l L.J.	Pacific Basin International Law Journal	Pa.L.J.R.	Clark's Pennsylvania Law Journal Reports
Pace Envtl. L.Rev.	Pace Environmental Law Review	Palm.	Palmer (NH)
			Palmer (VT)
Pace J.Int'l & Corp.L.	Pace Journal of International and Comparative Law		Palmer, King's Bench & Common Pleas (Eng.)
Pace L. Rev.	Pace Law Review	Pa.L.Rec.	Pennsylvania Law Record
Pace Y.B. Int'l L.	Pace Yearbook of International Law		
		Pa.Misc.	Pennsylvania Miscellaneous Reports
Pacific LJ	Pacific Law Journal		
Pac.L.J.	Same	Pan–Am.T.S.	Pan–American Treaty Series
pacmwlth	Pennsylvania Commonwealth Reports		
		P. & B.	Pugsley & Burbridge's Reports (N.B.)
Pa.Co.Ct.	Pennsylvania County Court		
		P. & C.	Prideaux & Cole's New Sessions Cases (Eng.)
Pa.C.P.	Common Pleas Reporter		
Pa.C.Pl.	Pennsylvania Common Pleas	P & CR	Property and Compensation Reports
Pac.Rim.L. & Pol'y J.	Pacific Rim Law & Policy Journal	P. & D.	Perry & Davison's Queen's Bench (Eng.)
pad & c	Pennsylvania District & County Reports		
		P. & F.Radio Reg.	Pike & Fischer's Radio Regulation Reporter
Pa.D. & C.	Same		

P. & H.	Patton's & Heath's Reports (VA)
P. & K.	Perry & Knapp, Election Cases (Eng.)
P. & W.	Penrose & Watts (PA)
Papua & N.G.	Papua and New Guinea Law Reports
Papy	Papy (FL)
Park	Parker's Criminal Reports (NY)
Park.	Parker's Exchequer (Eng.)
Park.Cr.	Parker's Criminal Reports (NY)
Park.Cr.Cas.	Same
Parker	Parker (NH)
Parker Cr.Cas.	Parker's Criminal Reports (NY)
Park.Ins.	Parker's Insurance
Pars.Dec.	Parson's Decisions (MA)
Pars.Eq.Cas.	Parsons' Select Equity Cases (PA)
PaS	Pennsylvania Superior Court Reports
Pasch.	Paschal (TX)
Pa.State	Pennsylvania State Reports
pasuper	Pennsylvania Superior Court Reports
Pa.Super.	Same
Pat. & T.M.Rev.	Patent & Trade Mark Review
Pat. & Tr. Mk.Rev.	Same
Pat.Cas.	Reports of Patent, Design and Trade Mark Cases
Pater. Ap. Cas.	Paterson's Appeal Cases (Scot.)
Pat.L.Rev.	Patent Law Review
Pat.Off.Rep.	Patent Office Reports
Paton App. Cas.	Paton's Appeal Cases (Can.)
Patr.Elec. Ca.	Patrick, Contested Elections (Ont.)
Patt. & H.	Patton & Heath's Reports (VA)
PattH	Patton Jr. & Heath's Reports (VA)
Pat.T.M. & Copy.J.	Patent, Trademark & Copyright Journal
patton & h	Patton & Heath's Reports (VA)
P.C.	Price Control Cases (CCH)

P.C.I.J.	Permanent Court of International Justice Advisory Opinions, Cases, Judgments, Pronouncements
P.C.I.J. Ann.R.	Permanent Court of International Justice Annual Reports
P.C.L.J.	Pacific Coast Law Journal
P.Coast L.J.	Same
P.D.	Law Reports, Probate, Divorce & Admiralty Division, Second Series Division
	Pension and Bounty (U.S. Dept. of Interior)
P.Div.	Law Reports, Probate Division (Eng.)
Peab.L.Rev.	Peabody Law Review
Peake N.P.	Peake's Nisi Prius (Eng.)
Peake N.P. Add. Cas.	Peake, Additional Cases, Nisi Prius (Eng.)
PEAL	Publishing, Entertainment, Advertising and Allied Fields Law Quarterly
Pearce C.C.	Pearce's Reports in Dearsley's Crown Cases (Eng.)
Pearson	Pearson, Common Pleas (PA)
peck	Peck (TN)
Peck	Peck (IL)
	Peck (TN)
Peck.El.Cas.	Peckwell's Election Cases (Eng.)
Peeples	Peeples (GA)
Peeples & Stevens	Peeples & Stevens (GA)
Peere Williams	Peere Williams' Chancery (Eng.)
Peere Wms.	Same
P.E.I.	Haszard & Warburton's Reports (Prince Edward Island)
Pel	Pennewill's Reports (DE)
Pen.	Pennington's Law (NJ)

Pen	Pennypacker's Reports (PA)	P–H Corp.	Corporation (P–H)
		Pheney Rep.	Pheney's New Term Reports (Eng.)
Pen. & W.	Penrose and Watts (PA)	P–H Est. Plan.	Estate Planning (P–H)
Pen C	Penal Code (CA)		
Penn.B.A.Q.	Pennsylvania Bar Association Quarterly	P–H Fed. Taxes	Federal Taxes (P–H)
		P–H Fed. Wage & Hour	Federal Wage and Hour (P–H)
Penn.Del.	Pennewill (DE)	Phil.	Phillips' (IL)
pennede	Same		Phillips' Chancery (Eng.)
pennyp	Pennypacker (PA)		Phillips' Equity (NC)
Pennyp.	Same		Phillips' Law (NC)
Pennyp.Col. Cas.	Pennypacker's Colonial Cases	Phila.	Philadelphia (PA)
penr & w	Penrose & Watts (PA)	Philanthrop.	Philanthropist
		Phil.El.Cas.	Phillips Election Cases (Eng.)
Penr. & W.	Same	Phil.Int'l L.J.	Philippine International Law Journal
Pension Plan. & Tax'n	Pension Planning and Taxation		
Pension Rep.	Pension Reporter (BNA)	Phillim.	Phillimore Ecclesiastical (Eng.)
Pepp. Disp. Res. L.J.	Pepperdine Dispute Resolution Law Journal	Phil.L.J.	Philippine Law Journal
		P–H Ind. Rel. Lab. Arb.	Industrial Relations, American Labor Arbitration (P–H)
Pepperdine LR	Pepperdine Law Review		
Pepperdine L.Rev.	Same	P–H Ind. Rel.Union Conts.	Industrial Relations, Union Contracts and Collective Bargaining (P–H)
Pepp.L.Rev.	Same		
Perry & K.	Perry & Knapp's Election Cases (Eng.)	P–H Soc.Sec. Taxes	Social Security Taxes (P–H)
		P–H State & Local Taxes	State and Local Taxes (P–H)
Pers.Finance L.Q.	Personal Finance Law Quarterly Report	P–H Tax Ct. Mem.	Tax Court Memorandum Decisions (P–H)
Pers.Inj. Comment'r	Personal Injury Commentator		
Pers.Inj. Def. Rep.	Personal Injury Defense Reporter	P–H Tax Ct. Rep. & Mem. Dec.	Tax Court Reported and Memorandum Decisions (P–H)
Pet.	Peters (U.S)	Pick.	Pickering's Reports (MA)
Pet.Ab.	Petersdorf's Abridgment		
petadm	Peters' Admiralty (U.S.)	Pickle	Pickle (TN)
		Pig. & R.	Pigott & Rodwell's Registration Cases (Eng.)
Pet.Adm.	Same		
Pet.Br.	Petit (or Little) Brook (Brooke) New Cases King's Bench (Eng.)	Pike	Pike's Reports (AR)
		Pin.	Pinney's Reports (WI)
petcc	Peters' Circuit Court (U.S.)	Pinn.	Same
		pinney	Same
Pet.C.C.	Same	Pipe Roll Soc'y	Publications of the Pipe Roll Society
peters	Peters (U.S.)		
Peters	Same	Pipe Roll Soc'y (N.S.)	Same, New Series
P.F.Smith	P.F. Smith (PA)	PIQR	Personal Injuries and Quantum Reports
P–H	Prentice–Hall		
P–H Am.Lab. Arb.Awards	American Labor Arbitration Awards (P–H)	Pitblado Lect.	Isaac Pitblado Lectures on Continuing Legal Education
P–H Am.Lab. Cas.	American Labor Cases (P–H)		

Pittsb.	Pittsburgh (PA)	Poly L.Rev.	Poly Law Review
Pittsb.Leg.J.	Pittsburgh Legal Journal (PA)	Pomeroy	Pomeroy (CA)
Pittsb.R. (PA)	Pittsburgh Reporter (PA)	Poor L. & Local Gov't	Poor Law and Local Government Magazine
Pitts.Leg.J. (N.S.)	Pittsburgh Legal Journal, New Series (PA)	Poph.	Popham, King's Bench (Eng.)
Pitts.L.J.	Pittsburgh Legal Journal		Chancery (Eng.)
Pitts.Rep.	Pittsburgh Reports (PA)		Common Pleas (Eng.)
P.Jr. & H.	Patton, Jr., & Heath (VA)	por	Pending Opinion Reports (OH)
Plan. & Comp.	Planning and Compensation Reports	Por	Porter's Reports (AL)
Pl.Ang.-Norm.	Placitca Anglo–Normannica Cases (Bigelow)	port	Porter (IN)
		Port.	Porter (AL)
			Porter (IN)
Plan.Zoning & E.D.Inst.	Planning, Zoning & Eminent Domain Institute	Portia L.J.	Portia Law Journal
		Portland U.L.Rev.	Portland University Law Review
P.L.E.	Pennsylvania Law Encyclopedia	Porto Rico Fed.	Porto Rico Federal Reports
PLI	Practising Law Institute	Posey	Posey's Unreported Commissioner Cases (TX)
P.L.M.	Pacific Law Magazine	poseyunrep	Same
P.L.Mag.	Same	Posey Unrep. Cas.	Same
Plowd.	Plowden, King's Bench (Eng.)	Post	Post (MI)
PLR	(Estates Gazette) Planning Law Reports		Post (MO)
	Pacific Law Reporter	Potomac L.Rev.	Potomac Law Review
P.L.Rep.	Pacific Law Reporter	Potter	Potter (WY)
Plt	Peltier's Orleans Appeals Decisions (LA)	Pow	Power's Surrogate's Court Reports (NY)
plw	Pennsylvania Law Weekly	Pow.Surr.	Same
Pol.	Pollack's Ohio Unreported Judicial Decisions Prior to 1823	PQ	United States Patents Quarterly
		PQ2d	Same, Second Series
	Pollexfen, King's Bench (Eng.)	Pr.	Price, Exchequer (Eng.)
Pol C	Political Code (CA)	P.R.	Parliamentary Reports
Police J.	Police Journal		Practice Reports (Ont.)
Police L.Q.	Police Law Quarterly		Probate Reports
Poll.Contr. Guide	Pollution Control Guide (CCH)		Puerto Rico Supreme Court Reports
Pollexf.	Pollexfen, King's Bench (Eng.)	Prac.Law.	Practical Lawyer
Pollution Abs.	Pollution Abstracts	Prac.Real Est. Law.	Practical Real Estate Lawyer
Pol.Sci.Q.	Political Science Quarterly	P.R. & D.El. Cas.	Power, Rodwell & Dew's Election Cases (Eng.)
Pol.Y.B.Int'l L.	Polish Yearbook of International Law	Prec.Ch.	Precedents in Chancery (Eng.)
		Pr.Edw.Isl.	Prince Edward Island

Preview	Preview of United States Supreme Court Cases	P.T.	Processing Tax Division (I.R.B.)
P.R.H.	Puerto Rico Federal Reports	Pub.Ad.Rev.	Public Administration Review
Price	Price, Exchequer (Eng.)	Pub Con C	Public Contract Code (CA)
	Price's Mining Commissioner's Cases (Ont.)	Pub Con LJ	Public Contract Law Journal
Price Pr.Cas.	Price's Notes of Practice Cases (Eng.)	Pub.Cont. L.J.	Same
		Pub.Cont. Newsl.	Public Contract Newsletter
Prick.	Prickett (ID)	Pub.Employee Rel.Rep.	Public Employee Relations Reports
Prin.Dec.	Sneed's Printed Decisions (KY)	Pub. Interest L.J.	Public Interest Law Journal
Prison L.Reptr.	Prison Law Reporter	Pub.Int'l L.	Public International Law
Prob. & Prop.	Probate and Property		
Probation & Parole L.Rep.	Probation and Parole Law Reports	Pub.L.	Public Law
		Pub.Land & Res.L.Dig.	Public Land and Resources Law Digest
Probation & Parole L.Sum.	Probation and Parole Law Summaries	Pub. Res. C.	Public Resources Code (CA)
Prob C	Probate Code	Pub. Util. C.	Public Utilities Code (CA)
Prob.Law.	Probate Lawyer		
Prob.L.J.	Probate Law Journal	Pub.Util. Fort.	Public Utilities Fortnightly
Prob.Rep.	Probate Reports (OH)	P.U.Fort.	Same
Prod.Liab. Int'l	Product Liability International	Pugs.	Pugsley (N.B.)
		Pugs. & B.	Pugsley & Burbridge (N.B.)
Prod.Safety & Liab.Rep.	Product Safety and Liability Reporter (BNA)	Pugs. & T.	Pugsley & Truenian (N.B.)
Prop. & Comp.	Property and Compensation Reports	Puls.	Pulsifer (ME)
		Pulsifer	Same
Prop.Law.	Property Lawyer	P.U.R.	Public Utilities Reports
Prouty	Prouty (VT)		
P.R.R.	Puerto Rico Reports	P.U.R. (N.S.)	Same, New Series
Pr.Reg.B.C.	Practical Register, Bail Court (Eng.)	P.U.R.3d	Same, Third Series
		pur4th	Same, Fourth Series
Pr.Reg.Ch.	Practical Register, Chancery (Eng.)	PW	Penrose & Watts' Reports (PA)
Pr.Reg.C.P.	Practical Register, Common Pleas (Eng.)	P.Wms.	Peere–Williams, Chancery (Eng.)
Pr.Rep.	Practice Reports (Eng.)	Pyke	Pyke (Lower Can.)
	Practice Reports (Upper Can.)		Pyke's Reports, King's Bench (Que.)

Q

Q.B.	Law Reports, Queen's Bench	Q.B.U.C.	Queen's Bench (Upper Can.)
Q.B.D.	Law Reports, Queen's Bench Division	Q.Intramural L.J.	Queen's Intramural Law Journal
		Q.L.	Quebec Law
Q.B.L.C.	Queen's Bench (Lower Can.)	Q.L.J.	Queen's Law Journal
		Q.L.R.	Quebec Law Reports

Q.L.Rev.	Quarterly Law Review	Queensl. S.C.R.	Queensland Supreme Court Reports
Q.Newsl.-Spec. Comm. Env.L.	Quarterly Newsletter–Special Committee on Environmental Law	Queensl. St. Rep.	Queensland State Reports
		Queensl.W.N.	Queensland Weekly Notes
Que.B.R.; Que. C.S.	Quebec Rapports Judicaires Officiels (Banc de la Reine; Cour superieure)	Que.K.B.	Quebec Official Reports, King's Bench
		Que.L.	Quebec Law
Que.C.A.	Quebec Official Reports (Court of Appeal)	Que.L.R.	Quebec Law Reports
		Que.Pr.	Quebec Practice
		Que.Prac.	Quebec Practice Reports
Queens B.Bull.	Queens Bar Bulletin		
Queensl.	Queensland Reports	Que.Q.B.	Quebec Official Reports, Queen's Bench
Queensl.J.P.	Queensland Justice of the Peace		
Queensl.J.P. Rep.	Queensland Justice of the Peace Reports	Que.Rev.Jud.	Quebec Revised Judicial
		Que.S.C.	Quebec Official Reports, Superior Court
Queensl.L.	Queensland Law		
Queensl.Law.	Queensland Lawyer	Que.Super.	Quebec Reports Superior Court
Queensl.L.J.	Queensland Law Journal	quincy	Quincy (MA)
Queensl.L. Soc'y J.	Queensland Law Society Journal	Quincy	Same
		Quis Cust.	Quis Custodiet

R

R.	Rawle (PA)	R. & Can. Tr. Cas.	Railway & Canal Traffic Cases (Eng.)
	The Reports, Coke's King's Bench (Eng.)	R. & M.	Russell & Mylne's Chancery (Eng.)
R. 1 Cro.	Croke, Elizabeth		
R. 2 Cro.	Croke, James I.	R. & M.C.C.	Ryan & Moody's Crown Cases (Eng.)
R. 3 Cro.	Croke, Charles I.		
RA	Rating Appeals (Eng.)	R. & N.L.R.	Rhodesia and Nyasaland Law Reports
R.A.C.	Ramsay's Appeal Cases (Que.)	R. & R.	Russell & Ryan, Crown Cases (Eng.)
Race Rel.L. Rep.	Race Relations Law Reporter		
Rac.Rel.L. Survey	Race Relations Law Survey	Raney	Raney (FL)
		rawle	Rawle (Pa.)
Rader	Rader (MO)	Rawle	Same
Rag.	Ragland California Superior Court Decisions	Raym.	Raymond (IA)
		R.C.L.	Ruling Case Law
		RD	Reappraisement Decisions
Rand	Rand (OH)		
Rand.	Randall (OH)	R. de D. McGill	Revue de Droit De McGill
	Randolph (KS)		
	Randolph (VA)	R.D.F.Q.	Recueil de droit fiscal Quebecois
Rand.Ann.	Randolph Annual (LA)	R.D.T.	Revue de Droit du Travail
R. & C.	Russell & Chesley (Nova Scotia)	Real Est.Fin. L.J.	Real Estate Finance Law Journal
R. & Can. Cas.	Railway & Canal Cases (Eng.)	Real Est.L.J.	Real Estate Law Journal

Real Est. L.Rep.	Real Estate Law Report	Rept.t.Holt	Cases tempore Holt, King's Bench (Eng.)
Real Est.Rev.	Real Estate Review		
Real Prop. Prob. & Tr.J.	Real Property, Probate and Trust Journal	Res. & Eq. Judgm.	Reserved & Equity Judgments (N.S.W.)
Reap.Dec.	U.S. Customs Court Reappraisement Decisions	Res. Ch.	Resolution Chapter (CA)
		Res Ipsa	Res Ipsa Loquitur
Rec.L.	Recent Law	Res Judic.	Res Judicatae
Rec.Laws	Recent Laws in Canada	Res.L. & Econ.	Research in Law and Economics
Record of N.Y.C.B.A.	Record of the Association of the Bar of the City of New York	Res.L. & Soc.	Research in Law and Sociology
		Restric.Prac.	Reports of Restrictive Practices Cases
R.E.D.	Russell's Equity Decisions (Nova Scotia)	Rettie	Rettie, Crawford & Melville's Session Cases (Scot.)
Redf	Redfield's Surrogate's Court Reports	Rev. & T. C.	Revenue and Tax Code (CA)
Redf. & B.	Redfield & Bigelow's Leading Cases (Eng.)	Rev & Tax C	Same
		Rev.Bar.	Revue du Barreau
		Rev.Barreau Que.	Revue de Barreau de Quebec
Redf.Surr.	Redfield's Surrogate (NY)	Rev.C.Abo. Pr.	Revista de Derecho del Colegio de Abogados de Puerto Rico
Reding.	Redington (ME)		
Reese	Reese, Heiskell's (TN)		
Reeve Eng.L.	Reeve's English Law	Rev.Contemp.L.	Review of Contemporary Law
Ref.J.	Referees' Journal (Journal of National Association of Referees in Bankruptcy)	Rev.Crit.	Revue Critique (Can.)
		Rev. de Legis.	Revue de Legislation (Can.)
Ref Svc	Minimum Standards for Lawyer Referral Service in California (State Bar)	Rev.D.P.R.	Revista de Derecho Puertorriqueno
		Rev.D.U.S.	Revue de Droit Universite de Sherbrooke
Regent U.L. Rev.	Regent University Law Review	Rev.Gen.D.	Revue Generale de Droit
Rel. & Pub. Order	Religion and the Public Order	Rev.Ghana L.	Review of Ghana Law
Remy	Remy (IN)	Rev. Int'l Bus. L.	Review of International Business Law
Rep.Atty. Gen.	Attorneys General's Reports (U.S.)		
Reports	Coke's King's Bench (Eng.)	Rev.Int'l Comm. Jur.	Review of the International Commission of Jurists
Rep.Pat.Cas.	Reports of Patent Cases (Eng.)		
Rep.Pat.Des. & Tr.Cas.	Reports of Patents Designs & Trademark Cases	Revised Rep.	Revised Reports (Eng.)
		Rev., Jud., & Police J.	Revenue, Judicial, and Police Journal
Reprint	English Reports, Full Reprint	Rev.Jur.U. Inter.P.R.	Revista Juridica de law Universidad Interamericana de Puerto Rico
Rept.t.Finch	Cases tempore Finch, Chancery (Eng.)		

Rev.Jur.U. P.R.	Revista Juridica de la Universidad de Puerto Rico	Ridg.Ap.	Ridgeway's Appeals Parliament Cases (Ir.)
Rev.L. & Soc. Change	Review of Law and Social Change	Ridg.App.	Same
Rev.Leg.	Revue Legale (Can.)	Ridg.L. & S.	Ridgeway, Lapp & Schoales' King's Bench (Ir.)
Rev.Legale	Same		
Rev.Leg. (N.S.)	Same, New Series	Ridg.P.C.	Ridgeway's Parliamentary Cases (Ir.)
Rev.Leg. (O.S.)	Same, Old Series		
Rev.Litig.	Review of Litigation		
Rev.Not.	Revue de Notariat Revue du Notariat	Ridg.t.Hardw.	Ridgeway tempore Hardwicke, Chancery, King's Bench
Rev.Pol.L.	Review of Polish Law	Ried.	Riedell (NH)
		Riley	Riley (WV)
Rev.P.R.	Revista de Derecho Puertorriqueno		Riley's Equity (SC) Riley's Law (SC)
revproc	Revenue Procedures	rilw	Rhode Island Lawyers Weekly
Rev.R.	Revised Reports (Eng.)		
Rev.Rep.	Same	Ritchie	Ritchie's Equity (Can.)
revrul	Revenue Rulings		
Rev.Sec. & Commodities Reg.	Review of Securities and Commodities Regulation	R.J.R.Q.	Quebec Revised Reports
		R.L. & S.	Ridgeway, Lapp & Schoales, King's Bench (Ir.)
Rev.Sec.Reg.	Review of Securities Regulation		
Rev.Sel.Code Leg.	Review of Selected Code Legislation	R.L. & W.	Robert, Leaming & Wallis County Court (Eng.)
Rev.Soc.L.	Review of Socialist Law	R.L.B.	United States Railroad Labor Board Decisions
Rev.Stat.	Revised Statutes		
Rev. Tax'n of Indiv.	Review of Taxation for Individuals	R.M.C.C.	Ryan & Moody's Crown Cases (Eng.)
Reyn.	Reynolds (MS)		
Rhodesian L.J.	Rhodesian Law Journal	R.M.C.C.R.	Same
		rmcharlt	R.M. Charlton's Reports (GA)
ri	Rhode Island Reports		
R.I.	Same	R.M.Charlt.	Same
riatcm	U.S. Tax Court Memorandum Decisions (RIA)	rob	Robinson (CA)
		Rob.	Robard (MO) Robard, Conscript Cases (TX)
R.I.B.J.	Rhode Island Bar Journal		Robert's Louisiana Annual
Rice	Rice's Equity (SC) Rice's Law (SC)		Robertson (HI)
Rich.	Richardson (NH) Richardson's Equity (SC) Richardson's Law (SC)		Robertson's Marine Court (NY) Robertson's Superior Court (NY)
Rich. & H.	Richardson & Hook's Street Railway Decisions		Robinson (CA) Robinson (CO) Robinson's Reports (LA)
Rich. & W.	Richardson & Woodbury (NH)		Robinson (NV) Robinson (Upper Can.)
Rich.C.P.	Richardson's Practice, Common Pleas (Eng.)		Robinson (VA) Robinson's Annual (LA)
Rich.Ct.Cl.	Richardson's Court of Claims		

Rob.Adm.	Robinson, Admiralty (Eng.)	Rowell El.Cas.	Rowell, Election Cases (U.S.)
Rob. & J.	Robard & Jackson (TX)	R.P.	Rapports des Pratique de Quebec/Quebec Practice Reports
	Robertson & Jacob's Marine Court (NY)		
Robb Pat. Cas.	Robb's Patent Cases (U.S.)	R.P. & W.	Rawle, Penrose & Watt (PA)
Rob.Eccl.	Robertson's Ecclesiastical (Eng.)	R.P.C.	Reports of Patent Cases
Robert.App. Cas.	Robertson's Appeal Cases (Scot.)	R.P.R.	Real Property Reports
Robin.App. Cas.	Robinson's Appeal Cases, House of Lords (Scot.)	R.P.W.	Rawle, Penrose & Watt
Rob.L. & W.	Robert, Leaming & Wallis' County Court (Eng.)	R.R.	Pike & Fischer Radio Regulation Revised Reports
Rocky Mt. L.Rev.	Rocky Mountain Law Review	R.R.2d	Same, Second Series
Rocky Mt. Miner.L. Rev.	Rocky Mountain Mineral Law Review	RRC	Ryde's Rating Cases
		RRR	Special Court Regional Rail Reorganization Act of 1973
Rocky Mt. Min.L. Inst.	Rocky Mountain Mineral Law Institute	RSCR	Robertson's Superior Court Reports (NY)
Rocky Mt. Min.L. Newsl.	Rocky Mountain Mineral Law Newsletter	RTR	Road Traffic Reports
Rodm.	Rodman (KY)	Rucker	Rucker (WV)
Rogers	Rogers Annual (LA)	Ruff. & H.	Ruffin & Hawks (NC)
Roll.	Rolle, King's Bench (Eng.)	Runn.	Runnell (IA)
Rolle	Same	Rus.	Russell's Election Cases (Nova Scotia)
Rolle Abr.	Rolle's Abridgment (Eng.)		
Rom.Cas.	Romilly's Notes of Cases (Eng.)	Rus. & C.Eq. Cas.	Russell & Chesley's Equity Cases (Nova Scotia)
root	Root's Reports (CT)		
Root	Same	Russ. & Geld.	Russell & Geldert (Nova Scotia)
Rose	Rose, Bankruptcy (Eng.)	Russ. & M.	Russell & Mylne, Chancery (Eng.)
Rose's Notes (U.S.)	Rose's Notes on United States Reports	Russ. & Ry.	Russell & Ryan, Crown Cases (Eng.)
Ross Lead. Cas.	Ross's Leading Cases (Eng.)	Russ.El.Cas.	Russell's Election Cases (MA)
Rot.Chart.	Rotulus Chartarum (The Charter Roll)		Russell's Election Reports (Can.)
Rot.Claus.	Rotuli Clause (The Close Roll)	Russell	Russell's Chancery (Eng.)
Rot.Parl.	Rotulae Parliamentarum	Russ.Eq.Cas.	Russell's Equity Cases (Nova Scotia)
Rot.Pat.	Rotuli Patenes		
Rot.Plac.	Rotuli Placitorum	Russ.t.Eld.	Russell's Chancery tempore Eldon (Eng.)
Rotuli Curiae Reg.	Rotuli Curiae Regis (Eng.)		
Rowe	Rowe, Parliament & Military Cases (Eng.)	Rut.Cam.L.J.	Rutgers–Camden Law Journal
Rowell	Rowell (VT)		

Rutgers Computer & Tech. L.J.	Rutgers Computer and Technology Law Journal	Rutgers U.L.Rev.	Rutgers University Law Review
Rutgers J. Computers & Law	Rutgers Journal of Computers and the Law	RVR	Rating and Valuation Reporter
Rutgers J. Computers Tech. & L.	Rutgers Journal of Computers, Technology and the Law	Ryan & M.	Ryan & Moody's Nisi Prius (Eng.)
		Ry. & M.	Ryan & Moody's Nisi Prius (Eng.)
		Ryde	Ryde's Rating Appeals (Eng.)
Rutgers L.J.	Rutgers Law Journal	Ry.M.C.C.	Ryan & Moody's Crown Cases (Eng.)
Rutgers L.Rev.	Rutgers Law Review		

S

S.	Shaw, Dunlop & Bell, Court of Sessions (Scot.)	San	Sanford's Chancery Reports (NY)
	Shaw's Appeal Cases, House of Lords (Scot.)	S. & B.	Smith & Batty's King's Bench (Ir.)
		S. & C.	Saunders & Cole's Bail Court (Eng.)
	Southern Reporter	S. & C.P.Dec.	Ohio Decisions
SA	Silvernail's Court of Appeal Reports, (NY)	S. & D.	Shaw, Dunlop & Bell, Court of Sessions, 1st Series (Scot.)
	South African Law Reports	Sandf.	Sandford's Superior Court (NY)
Sad	Sadler's Supreme Court Cases (PA)	Sandf.Ch.	Sandford, Chancery Reports (NY)
sadler	Sadler's Cases (PA)	San Diego LR	San Diego Law Review
Sadler	Same		
S.Afr.J.Hum. Rts.	South African Journal on Human Rights	San Diego L.Rev.	Same
		Sand.I.Rep.	Sandwich Islands Reports (HI)
S.Afr.L.J.	South African Law Journal	S. & L.	Schoales & Lefroy's Chancery (Ir.)
S.Afr.L.R.	South African Law Reports	S. & M.	Smedes & Maclean's Appeal Cases, House of Lords (Scot.)
S.Afr.L.R. App.	South African Law Reports Appellate		
S.Afr.L.Rev.	South African Law Review		Smedes & Marshall (MS)
S.Afr.L.T.	South African Law Times	S. & Mar.	Same
		S. & Mar.Ch.	Smedes & Marshall's Chancery (MS)
S.Afr.Tax Cas.	South African Tax Cases	S & M.Ch.	Same
S.A.G.	Sentencis arbitrales de griefs (Que.)	S. & R.	Sergeant & Rawle's Reports (PA)
Sal.	Salinger (IA)	S. & S.	Sausse & Scully's Rolls Court (Ir.)
Salk.	Salkeld, King's Bench, Common Pleas & Exchequer (Eng.)		Simons & Stuart's Vice Chancery (Eng.)
SALT News	Strategic Arms Limitation Treaty News	S. & Sc.	Sausse & Scully's Rolls Court (Ir.)
Samoan P.L.J.	Samoan Pacific Law Journal	S. & Sm.	Searle & Smith's Probate & Divorce Cases (Eng.)

S. & T.	Swabey & Tristram's Probate & Divorce Cases (Eng.)	S.C.	Court of Session Cases (Scot.)
Sanf.	Sanford (AL)		South Carolina Reports
San Fern.V. L.Rev.	San Fernando Valley Law Review		Supreme Court Reporter
San Fran.L.Rev.	San Francisco Law Review	SCA	Senate Constitutional Amendment
Santa Clara Computer & High Tech. L.J.	Santa Clara Computer and High Technology Law Journal	S.Calif.Law Rev.	Southern California Law Review
		S.Cal.L.Rev.	Same
Santa Clara L.	Santa Clara Lawyer	S.Cal.Rev.L. & Women's Stud.	Southern California Review of Law and Women's Studies
Santa Clara Law.	Same	Scam.	Scammon (IL)
Santa Clara LR	Santa Clara Law Review	S.C.Cas.	Cameron's Supreme Court (Can.)
Santa Clara L.Rev.	Same	SC–DCA Rule	Rules on Appeal to California Supreme Court and District Courts of Appeal
Santo Tomas L.Rev.	University of Santo Tomas Law Review		
Sar.Ch.Sen.	Saratoga Chancery Sentinel	SCE	South Carolina Equity Reports
Sask.	Saskatchewan Law Reports	sceq	South Carolina Equity
Sask.B.Rev.	Saskatchewan Bar Review	S.C.Eq.	Same
Sask.L.	Saskatchewan Law	Sch. & Lef.	Schoales & Lefroy, Equity (Ir.)
Sask.L.Rev.	Saskatchewan Law Review	Scher.	Scherer's Miscellaneous Reports (NY)
Sau. & Sc.	Sausee & Scully, Rolls Court (Ir.)	Schm.L.J.	Schmidt's Law Journal (New Orleans)
Sauls.	Saulsbury (DE)	School C.	School Code (CA)
Saund.	Saunders, King's Bench (Eng.)	Schuyl.L.Rec.	Schuylkill Legal Record (PA)
Saund. & Cole	Saunders & Cole, Bail Court (Eng.)	scl	South Carolina Law Reports
S.Aust.L.	South Australian Law	S.C.L.Q.	South Carolina Law Quarterly
S.Austl.	South Australia State Reports	SCLR	Southern California Law Review
S.Austl.L.R.	South Australian Law Reports		South Carolina Law Reports
Sav.	Savile, Common Pleas & Exchequer (Eng.)	S.C.L.Rev.	South Carolina Law Review
		Scot.Jur.	Scottish Jurist
sawcc	Sawyer's U.S. Circuit Court Reports	Scot.L.J.	Scottish Law Journal and Sheriff Court Record
Sawy.	Same	Scot.L.Mag.	Scottish Law Magazine and Sheriff Court Reporter
Sax.	Saxton's Chancery (NJ)		
Say.	Sayer, King's Bench (Eng.)	Scot.L.Rep.	Scottish Law Report
		Scot.L.Rev.	Scottish Law Review and Sheriff Court Report
S. Bar. J.	California State Bar Journal		
S.B.J.	Same	Scot.L.T.	Scottish Law Times
sc	South Carolina Reports	Scots L.T.R.	Scots Law Times Reports
		Scott	Scott, Common Pleas (Eng.)

Scott N.R.	Scott's New Reports, Common Pleas (Eng.)
SCR	Senate Concurrent Resolution (CA)
S.C.R.	Supreme Court Reports (Can.)
Scr.L.T.	Scranton Law Times (PA)
Sc.Sess.Cas.	Scotch Court of Sessions Cases
Sc.St.Crim.	Scandinavian Studies in Criminology
Sc.St.L.	Scandinavian Studies in Law
sct	Supreme Court Reporter (U.S.)
S.Ct.	Same
S.Ct.Rev.	Supreme Court Review
sd	South Dakota Reports
S.D.	Same
SDC	Supreme Court, District of Columbia Reports, New Series
S.D.L.Rev.	South Dakota Law Review
S.D.St.B.J.	South Dakota State Bar Journal
se	South Eastern Reporter
S.E.	Same
se2d	Same, Second Series
S.E.2d	Same
Sea Grant L. & Pol'y J.	Sea Grant Law and Policy Journal
Sea Grant L.J.	Sea Grant Law Journal
S.E.C.	United States Securities and Exchange Commission Decisions
Sec Fd Rules	Rules of Procedure Client Security Fund Matters
Sec.L.Rev.	Securities Law Review
Sec.Reg. & Trans.	Securities Regulation and Transfer Report
Sec.Reg.L.J.	Securities Regulation Law Journal
Sel.Cas.	Yates' Select Cases (NY)
Sel.Cas.Ch.	Select Cases in Chancery (Eng.)
Seld.	Selden's Notes (NY)
Selden	Selden's Court of Appeals (NY)

Sel.Serv. L.Rptr.	Selective Service Law Reporter
Selw.N.P.	Selwyn's Nisi Prius (Eng.)
Senior Law.	Senior Lawyer
Seoul L.J.	Seoul Law Journal
serg & r	Sergeant's & Rawle's Reports (PA)
Serg. & R.	Same
Sess.Ca.	Sessions Cases, King's Bench (Eng.)
Sess.Cas.	Court of Sessions Cases (Scot.) Sessions Cases King's Bench (Eng.)
Sess.Laws	Session Laws
Seton Hall Const.L.J.	Seton Hall Constitutional Law Journal
Seton Hall J. Sport L.	Seton Hall Journal of Sport Law
Seton Hall Legis.J.	Seton Hall Legislative Journal
Seton Hall L.Rev.	Seton Hall Law Review
Sex.L.Rep.	Sexual Law Reporter
Sex Prob.Ct. Dig.	Sex Problems Court Digest
S.F.L.J.	San Francisco Law Journal
Shad.	Shadford's Victoria Reports
Shan.	Shannon's Unreported Cases (TN)
Shand	Shand (SC)
Shand Pr.	Shand Practice, Court of Sessions (Scot.)
shannoncas	Shannon's Unreported Tennessee Cases
Shaw	Shaw (VT) Shaw, Appeal Cases, English House of Lords from Scotland Shaw, Scotch Justiciary Cases Shaw, Scotch Teind Reports, Court of Sessions
Shaw & D.	Shaw & Dunlop (Scot.)
Shaw & Dunl.	Same
Shaw & M.	Shaw & MacLean, Appeals, House of Lords (Scot.)
Shaw & Macl.	Same
Shaw App.	Shaw Appeal Cases

Shaw Crim. Cas.	Shaw's Criminal Cases Justiciary Court (Scot.)	Silv.Sup.	Silvernail's Supreme Court (NY)
Shaw, D. & B.	Shaw, Dunlop & Bell's Court of Sessions (1st Series) (Scot.)	Silv.Unrep.	Silvernail's Unreported Cases (NY)
		Sim.	Simmons (WI)
	Shaw, Dunlop & Bell's Session Cases (Scot.)		Simon's Vice–Chancery (Eng.)
		Sim. & C.	Simmons & Conover (WI)
Shaw, D. & B.Supp.	Shaw, Dunlop & Bell's Supplement, House of Lords Decisions (Scot.)	Sim. & St.	Simons & Stuart's Vice–Chancery (Eng.)
		Simes	Simes, Handbook of the Law of Future Interest (2d ed.)
Shaw Dec.	Shaw's Decisions in Scotch Court of Sessions (1st Series)	Sim. (N.S.)	Simon's Vice–Chancery, New Series (Eng.)
Shaw, Dunl. & B.	Shaw, Dunlop & Bell's Sessions Cases (Scot.)	Singapore L.Rev.	Singapore Law Review
		SJ	Solicitors' Journal
Shaw, W. & C.	Shaw, Wilson & Courtnay, House of Lords (Scot.)	SJR	Senate Joint Resolution
Sheld	Sheldon's Buffalo Superior Court Reports (NY)	Skill.Pol.Rep.	Skillman's Police Reports (NY)
		Skin.	Skinner, King's Bench (Eng.)
Shep.	Shepherd (AL)	Skink.	Skinker (MO)
Shep.Abr.	Sheppard's Abridgment	S.L.C.	Stuart's Appeal Cases (Lower Can.)
Shep.Sel.Cas.	Shepherd's Select Case (AL)	S.L.J.R.	Sudan Law Journal and Reports
Sher.Ct.Rep.	Sheriff Court Reports (Scot.)	SLT	Scots Law Times
Shingle	The Shingle, Philadelphia Bar Association	SLU LJ	Saint Louis University Law Journal
		S.M.	Solicitor's Memorandum (Treasury) (I.R.B.)
Shipp	Shipp (NC)		
Shirl.	Shirley (NH)	Smale & G.	Smale & Gifford's Vice–Chancery (Eng.)
Shirl.L.C.	Shirley's Leading Crown Cases (Eng.)		
		Small Bus. Tax'n	Small Business Taxation
Show.	Shower, King's Bench (Eng.)	Sm. & M.	Smedes & Marshall (MS)
Show.P.C.	Shower's Parliamentary Cases (Eng.)	Sm. & M.Ch.	Smedes & Marshall, Chancery (MS)
Sick.	Sickel's Court of Appeals (Eng.)	Sm. & S.	Smith & Sager's Drainage Cases (Ont.)
Sid.	Siderfin, King's Bench (Eng.)	SMCh	Smedes & Marshall's Chancery Reports (MS)
Sil.	Silver Tax Division (I.R.B.)		
S.Ill.U.L.J.	Southern Illinois University Law Journal	smedes & mch	Smedes & Marshall's Mississippi Chancery
S.Ill.U.L.Rev.	Southern Illinois University Law Review	Smith	Smith (CA)
			Smith (Eng.)
Silv.A.	Silvernail's Appeals (NY)		Smith's Supreme Court Reports (IN)

	Smith (ME)	SoC	South Carolina Reports
	Smith (MO)		
	Smith (NH)	Soc.Action & L.	Social Action and the Law
	Smith (SD)		
	Smith (WI)	So.Calif. L.Rev.	Southern California Law Review
	Smith, E.B. (IL)		
	Smith, E.D., Common Pleas (NY)	So. Cal. L.R.	Same
		So. Cal. L. Rev.	Same
	Smith, E.H., Court of Appeals (NY)	Soc. & Lab. Bull.	Social and Labour Bulletin
	Smith, E.P., Court of Appeals (NY)	So.Car.Const.	South Carolina Constitutional Reports
	Smith, P.F. (PA)	So.Car.L.J.	South Carolina Law Journal
Smith & B.	Smith & Batty, King's Bench (Ir.)	Soc.Just.	Social Justice
Smith & B.R.C.	Smith & Bates, American Railway Cases	Soc.Sec.Bull.	Social Security Bulletin
		Software L.J.	Software Law Journal
Smith & G.	Smith & Guthrie (MO)	Sol.	Solicitor
		Solar L.Rep.	Solar Law Reporter
Smith & H.	Smith & Heiskell (TN)	So.Law T.	Southern Law Times
Smith C.C.M.	Smith, Circuit Courts–Martial (ME)	So.L.J.	Southern Law Journal (Nashville)
		Sol.J.	Solicitor's Journal (Eng.)
Smith Cond.	Smith's Condensed Alabama Reports	Sol.Op.	Solicitor's Opinions (I.R.B.)
smith(ind)	Smith's Reports (IN)		
Smith K.B.	Smith's King's Bench (Eng.)	So.L.Q.	Southern Law Quarterly
Smith Lead. Cas.	Smith's Leading Cases (Eng.)	Sol.Q.	Solicitor Quarterly
		So.L.Rev.	Southern Law Review (Nashville)
Smith L.J.	Smith's Law Journal		
Smith Reg. Cas.	Smith's Registration Cases (Eng.)		Southern Law Review (St. Louis)
smithtn	Smith's Tennessee Reports	So.L.Rev. (N.S.)	Same, New Series
		Somerset L.J.	Somerset Legal Journal
SmithR	Smith's Reports (NH)	So.Tex.L.J.	South Texas Law Journal
SMU L.Rev.	Southern Methodist University Law Review	So.U.L.Rev.	Southern University Law Review
Smy.	Smythe, Common Pleas (Ir.)	Southard	Southard (NJ)
		Southwestern L.J.	Southwestern Law Journal
Smythe	Same	Southwestern L. Rev.	Southwestern University Law Review
SN	Selden's Notes (NY)		
Sneed	Sneed (TN)		
	Sneed's Decisions (KY)	Southwestern U LR	Same
Sneed Dec.	Sneed's Kentucky Decisions	Soviet Jewry L.Rev.	Soviet Jewry Law Review
sneedky	Sneed's Kentucky Reports	Soviet L. & Gov't	Soviet Law and Government
sneedtn	Sneed's Tennessee Reports	Soviet Stat. & Dec.	Soviet Statutes and Decisions
Snow	Snow (UT)	Soviet Y.B. Int'l L.	Soviet Year–Book of International Law
so	Southern Reporter		
So.	Same	SP	Stewart & Porter's Reports (AL)
so2d	Same, Second Series		
So.2d	Same		

S.Pac.L.Rev.	South Pacific Law Review	Stan.J.Int'l Stud.	Stanford Journal of International Studies
Spaulding	Spaulding (ME)		
Spear	Spear's Law (SC)	Stan.J.L. Gender & Sex. Orient.	Stanford Journal of Law, Gender & Sexual Orientation
Spear Ch.	Spear's (or Speer) Chancery (SC)	Stan J of Int Studies	Stanford Journal of International Studies
Spear Eq.	Spear's Equity (SC)		
Speer	Spear's Law (SC)		
Spenc.	Spencer (MN) Spencer, Law (NJ)	Stan.L. & Pol'y Rev.	Stanford Law & Policy Review
Spencer	Same	Stan LR	Stanford Law Review
Spinks	Spinks, Ecclesiastical and Admiralty (Eng.)	Stan.L.Rev.	Same
		Stan.Pa.Prac.	Standard Pennsylvania Practice
Spinks Eccl. & Adm.	Same	Stant.	Stanton (OH)
Spoon.	Spooner (WI)	Stanton	Same
Spooner	Same	Star Ch.Cas.	Star Chamber Cases (Eng.)
Spott.	Spottiswoode (Scot.)		
Spott.C.L. & Eq.Rep.	Common Law & Equity Reports published by Spottiswoode	Stark.	Starkie's Nisi Prius (Eng.)
		Stat.	Statutes at Large (U.S.)
Spottis.Eq.	Spottiswoode's Equity (Scot.)	Stat. at L.	Same
spr	Sprague (U.S. District Court Admiralty)	State Court J.	State Court Journal
		State Gov't	State Government
		State Tr.	State Trials (Eng.)
Sprague	Same	Stath.Abr.	Statham's Abridgment
SR	Syracuse Law Review		
S.R.	Solicitor's Recommendation (I.R.B.)	St BJ	State Bar Journal (CA)
		STC	Simon's Tax Cases
S.R. & O. and S.I.Rev.	Statutory Rules & Orders and Statutory Instruments Revised	STC (SCD)	Same (Special Commissioners' Decisions)
		Stetson L.Rev.	Stetson Law Review
SS	Silvernail's Supreme Court Reports (NY)	Stev. & G.	Stevens & Graham (GA)
		stew	Stewart's Reports (AL)
S.S.L.R.	Selective Service Law Reporter	Stew.	Same Stewart (SD)
ssrs	Social Security Reporting Service		Stewart's Reports (N.S.)
S.S.T.	Social Security Tax Ruling (I.R.B.)	Stew.Admr.	Stewart's Admiralty (N.S.)
S.T.	Sales Tax Division (I.R.B.)	stew & p	Stewart's and Porter's Reporter (AL)
Stafford	Stafford (VT)	Stew. & P.	Same
Stair	Stair (Scot.)	Stewart	Stewart's Vice–Admiralty Reports (N.S.)
Stan.Envt'l L.Ann.	Stanford Environmental Law Annual		
Stan.Envtl.L.J.	Stanford Environmental Law Journal	Stew.Eq.	Stewart's Equity (NJ)
		S.Tex.L.J.	South Texas Law Journal
Stanf. L. Rev.	Stanford Law Review	S.Tex.L.Rev.	South Texas Law Review
Stan.J.Int'l L.	Stanford Journal of International Law	STI	Simon's Tax Intelligence

Stiles	Stiles (IA)	St. Thomas L.Rev.	St. Thomas Law Review
Still.Eccl.Cas.	Stillingfleet's Ecclesiastical Cases (Eng.)	Stuart	Stuart's King's Bench (Lower Can.)
Stiness	Stiness (RI)	Stuart Vice–Adm.	Stuart's Vice–Admiralty (Lower Can.)
StJ	St. John's Law Review	Student Law.	Student Lawyer
St. John's J. Legal Comment.	St. John's Journal of Legal Commentary	Student Law. J.	Student Lawyer Journal
St. John's L.Rev.	St. John's Law Review	Stud.Int'l Fiscal L.	Studies on International Fiscal Law
St. Louis L.Rev.	St. Louis Law Review	Stud.L. & Econ. Dev.	Studies in Law and Economic Development
St. Louis U.L.J.	St. Louis University Law Journal	Stu.M. & P.	Stuart, Milne & Peddie (Scot.)
St. Louis U.Pub.L.F.	St. Louis University Public Law Forum	Stu.Mil. & Ped.	Same
St. Louis U.Pub.L.Rev.	St. Louis University Public Law Review	Style	Style, King's Bench (Eng.)
St. Mary's L.J.	St. Mary's Law Journal	Suffolk Transnat'l L.J.	Suffolk Transnational Law Journal
StnL	Stanford Law Review	Suffolk U.L. Rev.	Suffolk University Law Review
Sto	Storey's Reports (DE)	S.U.L.Rev.	Southern University Law Review
stock	Stockton's New Jersey Equity Reports	Summerfield	Summerfield (NV)
Stockett	Stockett (MD)	Sumn.	Sumner, Circuit Court (U.S.)
Stockt.	Stockton's Equity (NJ)	sumnercc	Same
Stockton	Stockton's Vice–Admiralty (N.B.)	Sup. & C.P. Dec.	Ohio Decisions
Stockt.Vice–Adm.	Same	Sup.Ct.	Superior Court (PA)
Story	Story (U.S.)	Sup.Ct.Hist. Soc'y Q.	Supreme Court Historical Society Quarterly
storycc	Story's U.S. Circuit Court Reports	Sup.Ct.Hist. Soc'y Y.B.	Supreme Court Historical Society Yearbook
Story Eq.Jur.	Story on Equity Jurisprudence	Sup.Ct.Rep.	Supreme Court Reporter (U.S.)
Str.	Strange's King's Bench (Eng.)	Sup.Ct.Rev.	Supreme Court Review
StR	New York State Reporter	Super.	California Superior Court
Stra.	Strange's King's Bench (Eng.)	Susq.Leg. Chron.	Susquehanna Legal Chronical (PA)
Strahan	Strahan (OR)	sw	South Western Reporter
Straits L.J. & Rep.	Straits Law Journal and Reporter	S.W.	Same
Str. & H.C.	Streets and Highways Code (CA)	sw2d	Same, Second Series
		S.W.2d	Same
Stratton	Stratton (OR)	Swab.	Swabey's Admiralty (Eng.)
St.Rep.	State Reporter		
St.Rep.N. S.W.	State Reports (N.S.W.)	Swab. & Tr.	Swabey's & Tristram, Probate & Divorce (Eng.)
Stringf.	Stringfellow (MO)		
Strob.	Strobhart's Law (SC)	Swan	Swan (TN)
Strob.Eq.	Strobhart's Equity (SC)	Swanst.	Swanston, Chancery (Eng.)
Sts & H C	Streets and Highways Code	swantn	Swan's Tennessee Reports

Sween.	Sweeney's Superior Court (NY)	Sydney L.Rev.	Sydney Law Review
Swin.	Swinton's Registration Appeal Cases (Scot.)	Syme	Syme's Justiciary Cases (Scot.)
Swiss Rev.Int'l Competition L.	Swiss Review of International Competition Law	Symposium Jun.B.	Symposium l'Association de Jeune Barreau de Montreal
S.W.L.J.	South Western Law Journal (Nashville)	Syn.Ser.	Synopsis Series of Treasury Decisions (U.S.)
Sw.L.J.	Southwestern Law Journal	Syracuse J. Int'l L. & Com.	Syracuse Journal of International Law and Commerce
Sw.U.L.Rev.	Southwestern University Law Review	Syracuse L.Rev.	Syracuse Law Review

T

T.	Tappan (OH) Tobacco Division (I.R.B.)	Tasm.U.L. Rev.	Tasmania University Law Review
Tait	Tait's Manuscript Decisions (Scot.)	Taun.	Taunton, Common Pleas (Eng.)
Tal.	Cases tempore Talbot, Chancery (Eng.)	Taunt.	Same
		Tax A.B.C.	Canada Tax Appeal Board Cases
Talb.	Same	Tax Adm'rs News	Tax Administrators News
Tam.	Tamlyn, Rolls Court (Eng.)	Tax Cas.	Tax Cases (Eng.)
Taml.	Same	Tax Counselor's Q.	Tax Counselor's Quarterly
Tamlyn	Tamlyn's Chancery (Eng.)	Taxes	Taxes, The Tax Magazine (CCH)
Tamlyn Ch.	Same	Tax. for Law.	Taxation for Lawyers
T. & C.	Thompson & Cook, Supreme Court (NY)	Tax Law.	Tax Lawyer
		Tax L.Rep.	Tax Law Reporter
T. & G.	Tyrwhitt & Granger's Exchequer (Eng.)	Tax L.Rev.	Tax Law Review
		Tax Mag.	Tax Magazine
T. & M.	Temple & Mew's Crown Cases (Eng.)	Tax Mgmt. Est. Gifts & Tr.J.	Tax Management Estates, Gifts and Trusts Journal
T. & P.	Turner & Phillips' Chancery (Eng.)	Tax Pract. Forum	Tax Practitioners Forum
T. & R.	Turner & Russell's Chancery (Eng.)	Tax.R.	Taxation Reports
taney	Taney, Circuit Court (U.S.)	Tay.	Taylor's Carolina Reports (NC)
Taney	Same		Taylor's King's Bench (Can.)
Tann.	Tanner (IN)		Taylor's Term Reports (NC)
Tanner	Same	taylor	Taylor's Reports (NC)
Tap	Tappan's Reports (OH)	Taylor	Same
Tapp.	Tappan (OH)	Taylor, U.C.	Taylor, King's Bench (Ont.)
Tappan	Same	T.B. & M.	Tracewell, Bowers & Mitchell, Comptroller's Decisions (U.S.)
Tasm.	Tasmanian State Reports		
Tasm.L.R.	Tasmania Law Reports		

T.B.M.	Tax Board Memorandum (I.R.B.)	Temp.Wood	Manitoba Reports tempore Wood (Can.)
T.B.Mon.	T.B. Monroe (KY)	Ten	Tennessee Reports
T.B.R.	Advisory Tax Board Recommendation (I.R.B.)	tenn	Same
		Tenn.	Same
		tennapp	Tennessee Appeals
	Tariff Board Reports	Tenn.App.	Same
TC	Tax Court of the United States Reports	Tenn.App. Bull.	Tennessee Appellate Bulletin
	Tax Cases (Eng.)	Tenn.B.J.	Tennessee Bar Journal
T.C.	Tax Court of the United States Reports	Tenn.Cas.	Shannon's Tennessee Cases
TCh	Tennessee Chancery Reports	tenncca	Tennessee Court of Civil Appeals
TChA	Tennessee Chancery Appeals Reports	Tenn.C.C.A.	Same
		tennch	Cooper, Chancery (TN)
tcm	U.S. Tax Court Memorandum Decisions (CCH)	Tenn.Ch.	Same
		tennchapp	Tennessee Chancery Appeals
tcmemo	Same (P–H)	Tenn.Ch. App.	Same
TCR	Tribal Court Reporter	Tenn.Civ. App.	Tennessee Court of Civil Appeals
TCSR	Thompson & Cook's Supreme Court Reports (NY)	tenncrim	Tennessee Criminal Court
TCSRA	Same, Addenda	Tenn.Crim. App.	Tennessee Criminal Appeals Reports
TCt	Tax Court of the United States Reports	Tenn.Leg. Rep.	Tennessee Legal Reporter
	United States Tax Court Reports	Tenn.L.Rev.	Tennessee Law Review
td	Treasury Decisions	Ter	Terry's Reports (DE)
T.D.	Same	Term	Durnford & East, Term Reports, King's Bench (Eng.)
Tel–Aviv U.Stud.L.	Tel–Aviv University Studies in Law		
Temp.	tempore	Term N.C.	Taylor, Term Reports
Temp. & M.	Temple & Mew, Crown Cases (Eng.)	Term R.	Durnford and East, Term Reports, King's Bench (Eng.)
Temp.Envtl. L. & Tech.J.	Temple Environmental Law and Technology Journal		
		Term.Rep.	Same
Temp.Geo.II	Cases in Chancery tempore Geo. II. (Eng.)	Terr.	Terrell (TX)
		Terr. & Wal.	Terrell & Walker (TX)
Temp.Int'l & Comp. L.J.	Temple International and Comparative Law Journal	Terr.L.R.	Territories' Law Reports (N.W.T.)
		tex	Texas Reports
Temple & M.	Temple & Mew, Crown Cases (Eng.)	Tex.	Same
		Tex.A.Civ. Cas.	White & Wilson's Civil Cases (TX)
Temple L.Q.	Temple Law Quarterly	Tex.A.Civ. Cas. (Wilson)	Texas Court of Appeal Civil Cases
Temp.L.Q.	Same	texapp	Texas Court of Appeals Cases
Temp.L.Rev.	Temple Law Review	Tex.App.	Texas Civil Appeals Cases
Temp.Pol. & Civ.Rts. L.Rev.	Temple Political and Civil Rights Law Review		Texas Court of Appeals Cases

texappciv	Texas Civil Appeals	Themis	La Revue Juridique Themis
texbcr	Texas Bankruptcy Court Reporter	T.Holt	Holt, Modern Cases (Eng.)
Tex.B.J.	Texas Bar Journal	Thom.	Thomson's Reports (Nova Scotia)
texcivapp	Texas Civil Appeals		
Tex.Civ.App.	Same	Thomas & Fr.	Thomas & Franklin Chancery (MD)
Tex.Civ.Rep.	Texas Civil Appeals		
Tex.Com. App.	Texas Commission Appeals	Thomp.	Thompson (CA)
		Thompson & C.	Thompson & Cook, Supreme Court (NY)
Tex.Cr.App.	Texas Criminal Appeals		
texcrim	Texas Criminal Reports	thomptenn	Thompson's Unreported Tennessee Cases
Tex.Crim.	Same		
Tex.Cr.R.	Same	Thomp.Tenn. Cas.	Same
Tex.Ct. App.R.	Texas Court of Appeals Reports	Thomson	Thomson's Reports (Nova Scotia)
Tex.Dec.	Texas Decisions	Thor.	Thorington (AL)
Tex.Int.L. Forum	Texas International Law Forum	Thorpe	Thorpe's Louisiana Annual
Tex.Int'l L.F.	Same	Thur.Marsh. L.J.	Thurgood Marshall Law Journal
Tex.Int'l L.J.	Texas International Law Journal	T.I.Agree.	Treaties and Other International Agreements of the United States of America
Tex.Jur.	Texas Jurisprudence		
Tex.Jur.2d	Same, Second Series		
Tex.J. Women & L.	Texas Journal of Women and the Law		
		T.I.A.S.	Treaties and Other International Acts Series (U.S.)
Tex.Law.	Texas Lawman		
Tex.Lawyer	Texas Lawyer	T.I.F.	Treaties in Force
Tex.L.J.	Texas Law Journal	Tiff.	Tiffany, Court of Appeals (NY)
Tex.L.Rev.	Texas Law Review		
Tex. Oil & Gas L.J.	Texas Oil and Gas Journal	Tiffany	Same
		Till.	Tillman (AL)
Tex.Real Est. L.Rep.	Texas Real Estate Law Reporter	Tillman	Same
		Timber Tax J.	Timber Tax Journal
TexS	Texas Supreme Court Reports, Supplement	Tinw.	Tinwald (Scot.)
		T.Jones	Thomas Jones, King's Bench and Common Pleas (Eng.)
Tex.S.Ct.	Texas Supreme Court Reporter		
Tex.So.U. L.Rev.	Texas Southern University Law Review		
		T.L.R.	Times Law Reports (Eng.)
texsupp	Texas Supplement		
Tex.Supp.	Same	T. Marshall L.J.	Thurgood Marshall Law Journal
texsupcj	Texas Supreme Court Journal		
		T. Marshall L.Rev.	Thurgood Marshall Law Review
Tex.Tech L.Rev.	Texas Tech Law Review		
		T.M.Bull.	Trade Mark Bulletin (U.S.)
Tex.Unrep. Cas.	Posey Unreported Cases (TX)		
		T.M.Bull. (N.S.)	Same, New Series
Th. & C.	Thompson & Cook's (NY) Supreme Court (NY)	T.M.M.	Tax Management Memorandum (BNA)
thatchercrim	Thatcher's Criminal Cases (MA)	T.M.Rep.	Trade Mark Reporter
Thatcher Cr.	Same	TnA	Tennessee Appeals Reports
Thayer	Thayer (OR)		

TnCr	Tennessee Criminal Appeals Reports	Trends L. Libr. Mgmt. & Tech.	Trends in Law Library Management and Technology
T.N.E.C.	Temporary National Economic Committee	Trent L.J.	Trent Law Journal
		Trial	Trial
tnt	Tax Notes Today	Trial Advoc.Q.	Trial Advocate Quarterly
Tobey	Tobey (RI)		
Tort L.Rev.	Tort Law Review	Trial Law. Forum	Trial Lawyers Forum
Toth.	Tothill's Chancery (Eng.)	Trial Law. Guide	Trial Lawyer's Guide
Touro J. Transnat'l L.	Touro Journal of Transnational Law	Trial Law.Q.	Trial Lawyers' Quarterly
Touro L.Rev.	Touro Law Review		
TPR	Official Translations of the Opinions of the Supreme Court of Puerto Rico	Trial Prac. Newsl.	Trial Practice Newsletter
		Trin.T.	Trinity Term (Eng.)
		Tripp	Tripp (Dak.Terr.)
		Tru.	Trueman's Equity Cases (N.B.)
TR	Taxation Reports		
T.R.	Durnford & East, Term Reports, King's Bench (Eng.)	Trust Bull.	Trust Bulletin
		Trust Terr.	Trust Territory Reports
		T.S.	Treaty Series (U.S.)
TrA	Transcript Appeals Reports (NY)	TSCR	Tucker's Surrogate's Court Reports (NY)
Trace. & M.	Tracefell & Mitchell, Comptroller's Decisions (U.S.)	T.T.	Jurisprudence de droit de Travail
Trade Cas.	Trade Cases (CCH)	tuc	Tucker & Clephane
Trademark Rep.	Trade–Mark Reporter	Tuck.	Tucker (MA)
		Tuck. & C.	Tucker & Clephane (DC)
Trade Reg. Rep.	Trade Regulation Reporter (CCH)	Tuck.Dist. of Col.	Tucker's Appeals (DC)
Trade Reg. Rev.	Trade Regulation Review	Tuck.Sel.Cas.	Tucker's Select Cases (Nfld.)
Tr. & Est.	Trusts & Estates		
Tr. & H.Pr.	Troubat & Haly's Practice (PA)	Tuck.Surr.	Tucker's Surrogate (NY)
Trans. & Wit.	Transvaal & Witswatersrand Reports	Tulane L.Rev.	Tulane Law Review
		Tul.Civ.L.F.	Tulane Civil Law Forum
Transc.A.	Transcript Appeals (NY)		
Transit L.Rev.	Transit Law Review	Tul.Envtl.L. J.	Tulane Environmental Law Journal
Transnat'l L.Contemp. Probs.	Transnational Law & Contemporary Problems	Tul.L.Rev.	Tulane Law Review
		Tul.Mar.L.J.	Tulane Maritime Law Journal
Transp.L.J.	Transportation Law Journal	Tulsa L.J.	Tulsa Law Journal
		Tul.Tax Inst.	Tulane Tax Institute
Trauma	Trauma	tupcharlt	T.U.P. Charlton's Reports (GA)
T.Raym.	Thomas Raymond, King's Bench (Eng.)	T.U.P.Charlt.	Same
		Tupp.App.	Tupper's Appeal Reports (Ont.)
Tread. Const.	Treadway's Constitutional Reports (SC)	Turn.	Turner (AR)
			Turner (KY)
Treas.Dec.	Treasury Decisions (U.S.)		Turner & Russell's Chancery (Eng.)
Trem.P.C.	Tremaine, Pleas of Crown (Eng.)	Turn. & P.	Turner & Phillips' Chancery (Eng.)

Turn. & Ph.	Same	TxCr	Texas Criminal Appeals Reports
Turn. & R.	Turner & Russell's Chancery (Eng.)	TxL	Texas Law Review
Turn. & Rus.	Same	Tyl	Tyler's Reports (VT)
Turn. & Russ.	Same	tyler	Same
Tutt.	Tuttle (CA)	Tyler	Same
Tutt. & C.	Tuttle & Carpenter (CA)	Tyng	Tyng (MA)
		Tyrw.	Tyrwhitt, Exchequer (Eng.)
Tutt. & Carp.	Same		
TxCi	Texas Civil Appeals Reports	Tyrw. & G.	Tyrwhitt & Granger, Exchequer (Eng.)

U

U.Ark.Little Rock L.J.	University of Arkansas at Little Rock Law Journal	U.C.C.Rep. Serv.	Uniform Commercial Code Reporting Service
U.Balt.J. Envtl.L.	University of Baltimore Journal of Environmental Law	uccrs	Same
		uccrs2d	Same, Second Series
		U.C.Davis L.Rev.	University of California at Davis Law Review
U.Balt.L.F.	University of Baltimore Law Forum	UCD LR	Same
U.Balt.L.Rev.	University of Baltimore Law Review	U.C.E. & A.	Upper Canada Error & Appeals Reports
U.B.C.L.Rev.	University of British Columbia Law Review	U.C.Err. & App.	Same
		U.Chi.Legal F.	University of Chicago Legal Forum
U.B.C.Notes	University of British Columbia Legal Notes	U.Chi.L.Rec.	University of Chicago Law School Record
U.Bridgeport L.Rev.	University of Bridgeport Law Review	U.Chi.L.Rev.	University of Chicago Law Review
U.C.	Upper Canada	U.Cin.L.Rev.	University of Cincinnati Law Review
U.C. (O.S.)	Upper Canada Queen's Bench Reports, Old Series	U.C.I.S.	Unemployment Compensation Interpretation Service, Benefit Series
U.C.App.	Upper Canada Appeal Reports		Unemployment Compensation Interpretation Service, Federal Series
U.C.App.Rep.	Same		
U.C.C.	Uniform Commercial Code		
U.C.Ch.	Upper Canada Chancery Reports		Unemployment Compensation Interpretation Service, State Series
U.C.Cham.	Upper Canada Chamber Reports		
U.C.Chamb. Rep.	Same		
U.C.Chan.	Upper Canada Chancery Reports	U.C.Jur.	Upper Canada Jurist
		U.C.K.B.	Upper Canada King's Bench Reports, Old Series
U.C.Ch.Rep.	Same		
U.C.C.Law Letter	Uniform Commercial Code Law Letter	UCLA–Alaska L.Rev.	UCLA Alaska Law Review
U.C.C.L.J.	Uniform Commercial Code Law Journal	UCLA Intra.L.Rev.	UCLA Intramural Law Review
U.C.C.P.	Upper Canada Common Pleas Reports	UCLA J.Envtl.L. & Pol'y	UCLA Journal of Environmental Law & Policy
U.C.C.P.D.	Upper Canada Common Pleas Division Reports (Ont.)	UCLA L.Rev.	UCLA Law Review

UCLA Pac. Basin L.J.	UCLA Pacific Basin Law Journal	U.Miami Ent. & Sports L.Rev.	University of Miami Entertainment and Sports Law Review
UCLA Women's L.J.	UCLA Women's Law Journal	U.Miami Inter–Am. L.Rev.	University of Miami Inter–American Law Review
U.C.L.J.	Upper Canada Law Journal		
U.C.L.J. (N.S.)	Same, New Series	U.Miami L.Rev.	University of Miami Law Review
U.Colo.L.Rev.	University of Colorado Law Review	U.Miami Y.B.Int'l L.	University of Miami Yearbook of International Law
U.C.Pr.	Upper Canada Practice Reports		
U.C.P.R.	Same	U.Mich.J. L.Ref.	University of Michigan Journal of Law Reform
U.C.Q.B.	Upper Canada Queen's Bench Reports		
U.C.Q.B. (O.S.)	Same, Old Series	U.Mo.Bull. L.Ser.	University of Missouri Bulletin Law Series
U.C.R.	Upper Canada Reports		
UCR2d	Uniform Commercial Code Reporting Service, Second Series	U.N.	United Nations Law Reports
		U.N.B.L.J.	University of New Brunswick Law Journal
U.C.Rep.	Upper Canada Reports		
Udal	Fiji Law Reports	Uncod Meas	Uncodified Initiative Measures and Statutes (CA)
U.Dayton L.Rev.	University of Dayton Law Review		
U.Det.J. Urb.L.	University of Detroit Journal of Urban Law	U.N.Comm. Int'l Trade L.Y.B.	United Nations Commission on International Trade Law Yearbook
U.Det.L.J.	University of Detroit Law Journal	U.N.Doc.	United Nations Documents
U.Det.L.Rev.	University of Detroit Law Review	U.N.ECOSOC	United Nations Economic and Social Council Records
U.Det.Mercy L.Rev.	University of Detroit Mercy Law Review		
U.East.L.J.	University of the East Law Journal	Unemp. Ins. C.	Unemployment Insurance Code (CA)
U.Fla.J.L. & Pub.Pol'y	University of Florida Journal of Law and Public Policy	Unempl.Ins. Rep.	Unemployment Insurance Reporter (CCH)
U.Fla.L.Rev.	University of Florida Law Review	U.Newark L.Rev.	University of Newark Law Review
Uganda L.Foc.	Uganda Law Focus	U.New S.Wales L.J.	University of New South Wales Law Journal
U.Ghana L.J.	University of Ghana Law Journal		
U.Hawaii L.Rev.	University of Hawaii Law Review	U.N.GAOR	United Nations General Assembly Official Records
U.Ill.L.F.	University of Illinois Law Forum		
U.Ill.L.Rev.	University of Illinois Law Review	Unific.L.Y.B.	Unification of Law Yearbook
U.I.L.R.	University of IFE Law Reports (Nigeria)	Unif.L.Conf. Can.	Uniform Law Conference of Canada
		Uniform L.Rev.	Uniform Law Review
U.Kan.City L.Rev.	University of Kansas City Law Review	Unif. Prof. C.	Uniform Probate Code
U.Kan.L.Rev.	University of Kansas Law Review	Un. Ins. C.	Unemployment Insurance Code (CA)
U.L.A. (Master Ed.)	Uniform Laws Annotated (Master Ed.)	U.N.Jur.Y.B.	United Nations Juridical Yearbook

U.N.M.T.	United Nations Multilateral Treaties
Unof.	Unofficial Reports
Un.Prac.News	Unauthorized Practice News
U.N.Res., Ser. I	United Nations Resolutions, Series I
U.N.R.I.A.A.	United Nations Reports of International Arbitral Awards
U.N.SCOR	United Nations Security Council Official Records
U.N.T.S.	United Nations Treaty Series
U.Pa.J.Int'l Bus.L.	University of Pennsylvania Journal of International Business Law
U.Pa.L.Rev.	University of Pennsylvania Law Review
Up.Can.L.J.	Upper Canada Law Journal
U.Pitt.L.Rev.	University of Pittsburgh Law Review
U.Puget Sound L.Rev.	University of Puget Sound Law Review
U.Queensl. L.J.	University of Queensland Law Journal
Urban Affairs Rep.	Urban Affairs Reporter (CCH)
Urban L.Rev.	Urban Law Review
Urb.L. & Pol'y	Urban Law and Policy
Urb.L.Ann.	Urban Law Annual
Urb.Law.	Urban Lawyer
U.Rich. L.Rev.	University of Richmond Law Review
us	United States Reports
U.S.	Same
U.S. & Can.Av.	United States and Canadian Aviation Reports
U San Fernando V LR	University of San Fernando Valley Law Review
U.San Fernando V.L.Rev.	Same
U.S.App.	United States Appeals
usappdc	U.S. Circuit Court Reports (D.C. Circuit)
usappx	United States Reports Appendix Cases
USApx	Same
U.S.Aviation	Aviation Reports (U.S.)
U.S.Av.R.	Same
U.S.C.	United States Code
U.S.C. (Supp.)	Same, Supplement
U.S.C.A.	United States Code Annotated
U.S.C.A. Const.	Same, Constitution
U.S.C.Govt'l Rev.	University of South Carolina Governmental Review
U.S.C.M.A.	United States Court of Military Appeals
U.S.Code Cong. & Ad.News	United States Code Congressional & Administrative News
U.S.C.S.	United States Code Service
U.S.Ct.Cl.	United States Court of Claims Reports
U.S.D.C.	United States District Court
U.S. Dept. Int.	United States Department of Interior
USF LR	University of San Francisco Law Review
U.S.F.L.Rev.	Same
U.S.F.Mar. L.J.	University of San Francisco Maritime Law Journal
U.S.I.C.C. V.R.	United States Interstate Commerce Commission Valuation Reports
U.S.Jur.	United States Jurist (DC)
U.S.Law.Ed.	United States Supreme Court Reports, Lawyers' Edition
U.S.L.Ed.	Same
U.S.L.J.	United States Law Journal
U.S.L.Mag.	United States Law Magazine
U.S.L.Rev.	United States Law Review
uslw	U.S. Law Week
U.S.L.W.	Same
U.S.L.Week	Same
U.S.M.C.	United States Maritime Commission
U.S.M.L.Mag.	United States Monthly Law Magazine

U.So. Cal.1955 Tax Inst.	University of Southern California Tax Institute
uspq	U.S. Patents Quarterly,
U.S.P.Q.	Same
uspq2d	Same, Second Series
U.S.S.B.	United States Shipping Board
U.S.S.C.Rep.	United States Supreme Court Reports
U.S.Sup.Ct. Rep.	United States Supreme Court Reporter (West)
U.S.T.	United States Treaties and Other International Agreements
U.S.Tax Cas.	United States Tax Cases (CCH)
ustc	Same
U.S.T.D.	United States Treaty Development
U.S.V.A.A.D.	United States Veterans Administration Administrator's Decisions
U.S.V.B.D.D.	United States Veterans Bureau Director's Decisions
Ut	Utah Reports
Ut2d	Same, Second Series
utah	Utah Reports
Utah	Same
utah2d	Same, Second Series
Utah 2d	Same
utahadvrep	Utah Advance Reports
Utah L.Rev.	Utah Law Review
U.Tasm. L.Rev.	University of Tasmania Law Review (or Tasmania University Law Review)
Util.L.Rep.	Utilities Law Reporter (CCH)
Util.Sect. Newsl.	Utility Section Newsletter
U.Tol.L.Rev.	University of Toledo Law Review
U.Tor.Fac. L.Rev.	University of Toronto Faculty of Law Review
U.Tor.L.Rev.	University of Toronto School of Law Review
U.Toronto Fac. L.Rev.	University of Toronto Faculty of Law Review
U.Toronto L.J.	University of Toronto Law Journal
U.Toronto Sch. L.Rev.	University of Toronto School of Law Review
U.Wash. L.Rev.	University of Washington Law Review
U.W.Austl. L.Rev.	University of Western Australia Law Review
U.West L.A. L.Rev.	University of West Los Angeles Law Review
U.Windsor L.Rev.	University of Windsor Law Review
UWLA LR	University of West Los Angeles Law Review
U.W.L.A. L.Rev.	Same

V

va	Virginia Reports
Va.	Same
VaA	Virginia Court of Appeals Reports
vaapp	Same
Va.Bar News	Virginia Bar News
Va.Cas.	Virginia Cases
Va.Ch.Dec.	Chancery Decisions (VA)
VaD	Virginia Decisions
vadec	Same
Va.Dec.	Same
Va.Envtl.L.J.	Virginia Environmental Law Journal
Va.J.Int'l L.	Virginia Journal of International Law
Va.J.Nat.Resources L.	Virginia Journal of Natural Resources Law
Va.J.Soc. Pol'y & L.	Virginia Journal of Social Policy and the Law
VaL	Virginia Law Review
Va.L.J.	Virginia Law Journal
Val.R. (I.C.C.)	Interstate Commerce Commission Valuation Reports
Va.L.Reg.	Virginia Law Register
Va.L.Reg. (N.S.)	Same, New Series
Va.L.Rev.	Virginia Law Review
Val.U.L.Rev.	Valparaiso University Law Review

Vand.J.Transnat'l L.	Vanderbilt Journal of Transnational Law	Ves.Jun.	Same
		Ves.Jun. Supp.	Same, Supplement
Vand.L.Rev.	Vanderbilt Law Review	Ves.Sen.	Vesey, Senior, Chancery (Eng.)
Van K.	Van Koughnett's Common Pleas (Upper Can.)	Ves.Sr.	Same
		Ves.Supp.	Vesey, Senior, Supplement, Chancery (Eng.)
vannes	Van Ness, Prize Cases (U.S.)	vetapp	Veterans Appeals Reporter
Van Ness Prize Cas.	Same	Vez.	Vezey, (Vesey) Chancery (Eng.)
Va.R.	Gilmer's Virginia Reports	vi	Virgin Islands Reports
VATTR	Value Added Tax Tribunal Reports	V.I.	Same
Vaug.	Vaughan, Common Pleas (Eng.)	V.I.B.J.	Virgin Islands Bar Journal
Vaugh.	Same	Vict.	Victoria
Vaughan	Same	Vict.Admr.	Victorian Admiralty
Vaux	Vaux, Decisions (PA)	Vict.Eq.	Victorian Equity
	Vaux, Recorder's Decisions (PA)	Vict.L.	Victorian Law
		Vict.L.R.	Victorian Law Reports
VCO	Virginia Circuit Court Opinions	Vict.L.R.Min.	Victorian Law Mining Reports
V.C.Rep.	Vice Chancellor's Reports (Eng.)	Vict.L.T.	Victorian Law Times
Ve.	Vesey, Chancery Reports (Eng.)	Vict.Rev.	Victorian Review
	Vesey, Senior, Chancery (Eng.)	Vict.St.Tr.	Victorian State Trials
Ve. & B.	Vesey & Beames, Chancery (Eng.)	Vict.U.L.Rev.	Victoria University Law Review
Veaz.	Veazey (VT)	Vict.U.Well. L.Rev.	Victoria University of Wellington Law Review
Veazey	Same		
Veh C	Vehicle Code (CA)	Vil. & Br.	Vilas & Bryant's Reports (WI)
Vent.	Ventris, Common Pleas (Eng.)	Vilas	Vilas' Criminal Reports (NY)
	Ventris, King's Bench (Eng.)	Vill.Envtl. L.J.	Villanova Environmental Law Journal
Ventr.	Same		
Ver.	Vermont	Vill.L.Rev.	Villanova Law Review
Vern.	Vernon's Cases (Eng.)	Vin.Abr.	Viner's Abridgment (Eng.)
Vern. & S.	Vernor & Scriven, King's Bench (Ir.)	Vin.Supp.	Same, Supplement
Vern. & Sc.	Same	vir	Virginia Law Reports
Vern. & Scr.	Same	Vir.	Virgin (ME)
Vern. & Scriv.	Same	Virgin	Same
Vern.Ch.	Vernon's Chancery (Eng.)	Virgin Is.	Virgin Islands
Ves.	Vesey, Chancery (Eng.)	VJNRL	Virginia Journal of Natural Resources Law
	Vesey, Senior, Chancery (Eng.)		
Ves. & B.	Vesey & Beames' Chancery (Eng.)	Vr.	Vroom's Law Reports (NJ)
Ves. & Bea.	Same	VR	Valuation Reports, Interstate Commerce Commission
Ves. & Beam.	Same		
Ves.Jr.	Vesey, Junior, Chancery (Eng.)		Victorian Reports

Vroom	Vroom's Law Reports (NJ)	vt	Vermont Reports
Vroom (G.D.W.)	G.D.W., Vroom (NJ)	Vt.	Same
Vroom (P.D.)	P.D., Vroom (NJ)	Vt.L.Rev.	Vermont Law Review

W

W.	Wandell (NY)	walljr	Wallace, Junior (U.S.)
	Watts (PA)		
	Wheaton's Supreme Court (U.S.)	Wall.Jr.	Same
	Wright (OH)	Wall.Rep.	Wallace on the Reporters
Wa.	Wage and Hour Reporter		
			Wallace's Supreme Court Reports (U.S.)
W.A'B. & W.	Webb, A'Beckett & Williams (Vict.)		
W.A.C.A.	Selected Judgments of the West African Court of Appeals	wallsr	Wallace, Senior (U.S.)
		Wall.Sr.	Same
		Walsh	Walsh's Registry Cases (Ir.)
W.Afr.App.	West African Court of Appeal Reports	W. & C.	Wilson & Courtenay's Appeal Cases
Wage & Hour Cas.	Wage and Hour Cases (BNA)	W & I C	Welfare and Institutions Code
Wage & Hour Rep.	Wage & Hour Reporter	W. & M.	Woodbury & Minot, Circuit Court (U.S.)
Wage–Price L. & Econ.Rev.	Wage–Price Law and Economics Review	W. & S.	Watts & Sergeant (PA)
Wake Forest Intra.L.Rev.	Wake Forest Intramural Law Review		Wilson & Shaw's Appeal Cases (Scot.)
Wake Forest L.Rev.	Wake Forest Law Review	W. & W.	White & Webb's Victorian Reports
Wake For. L.Rev.	Same	W. & W.Vict.	Wyatt & Webb's Victorian Reports
Wal.By L.	Wallis, Irish Chancery (By Lyne)	WAp	Washington Appellate Reports
Wal.Jr.	Wallace, Junior (U.S.)	Ward.	Warden (OH)
walk	Walker (MI)	Ward. & Sm.	Warden & Smith (OH)
Walk.	Walker (AL)		
	Walker (MS)	Warden's Law & Bk.Bull.	Weekly Law & Bank Bulletin (OH)
	Walker's Supreme Court Reports (PA)	ware	Ware, District Court (U.S.)
	Walker (TX)	Ware	Same
WalkC	Walker's Chancery Reports (MI)	wash	Washington Reports
walkch	Same	Wash.	Same
Walk.Ch.	Same		Washington Reports (VA)
Walk.Ch.Cas.	Same	wash2d	Washington Reports, Second Series
Wall.	Wallace (U.S.)(Philadelphia)	Wash.2d	Same
	Wallis (Philadelphia)	Wash. & Haz. P.E.I.	Washburton & Hazard's Reports (P.E.I.)
Wall.C.C.	Wallace, Circuit Court (U.S.)		
Wallis	Wallis' Chancery (Ir.)	Wash. & Lee L.Rev.	Washington & Lee Law Review
Wallis by L.	Wallis, Irish Chancery (By Lyne)	washapp	Washington Appellate Reports
		Wash.App.	Same

Washb.	Washburn (VT)	Webb, A'B. &	Webb, A'Beckett &
Washburn L.J.	Washburn Law Journal	W.	Williams' Reports
			(Austl.)
washcc	Washington Circuit	Webb & D.	Webb & Duval (TX)
	Court (U.S.)	Webb & Duval	Same
Wash.C.C.	Same	Webs.Pat. Cas.	Webster's Patent
Wash.L.Rep.	Washington Law Reporter (DC)		Cases (Eng.)
		Week.Cin. L.B.	Weekly Law Bulletin
Wash.L.Rev.	Washington Law Review		(OH)
		Week.Dig.	Weekly Digest (NY)
washterr	Washington Territory	Week.Jur.	Weekly Jurist (IL)
		Week.Law Bull.	Weekly Law Bulletin
Wash.Terr.	Same		(OH)
Wash. Terr.(N.S.)	Same, New Series	Week.Law Gaz.	Weekly Law Gazette
			(OH)
Wash.Ty.	Same	Week.L.Gaz.	Same
Wash.U.J. Urb. & Contemp.L.	Washington University Journal of Urban and Contemporary Law	Week.L.Rec.	Weekly Law Record
		Weekly L.R.	Weekly Law Reports
			(Eng.)
		Week.Notes Cas.	Weekly Notes of
			Cases (London)
Wash.U.L.Q.	Washington University Law Quarterly		Weekly Notes of
			Cases (PA)
Wat	Watts' Reports (PA)	Week.Rep.	Weekly Reporter
Wat C	Water Code (CA)		(Eng.)
Water C.	Same	Week.Trans.	Weekly Transcript
Water C. App.	Same, Appendix	Rep.	Reports (NY)
watts	Watts (PA)	Welf. & Inst. C.	Welfare and Institutions Code (CA)
Watts	Same		
	Watts (WV)	Welfare L.Bull.	Welfare Law Bulletin
watts & s	Watts & Sergeant (PA)	Welfare L.News	Welfare Law News
		Welf. C.	Welfare Code (CA)
Watts & S.	Same	Welf. R. Bull.	Welfare Rights Bulletin
Watts & Ser.	Same		
Watts & Serg.	Same	Welsb.H. & G.	Welsby, Hurlstone &
W.Austl.Ind. Gaz.	Western Australia Industrial Gazette		Gordon's Exchequer (Eng.)
W.Austl.J.P.	Western Australia Justice of the Peace	Welsby H. & G.	Same
		Welsh (Ir.)	Welsh's Registry Cases
W.Austl.L.R.	Western Australia Law Reports	Wen	Wendell's Reports (NY)
Wayne L.Rev.	Wayne Law Review	Wend.	Same
W.Bl.	Sir William Blackstone's King's Bench & Common Pleas (Eng.)	Wenz.	Wenzell (MN)
		Wes.C.L.J.	Westmoreland County Law Journal
		West	West Publishing or West Group
W.Bla.	Same		West's Chancery (Eng.)
W.C.C.	Washington's Circuit Court (U.S.)	West.	Weston (VT)
	Workmen's Compensation Cases	West.Austl.	Western Australian Reports
W.C.Ins.Rep.	Workmen's Compensation & Insurance Reports	West Ch.	West's Chancery (Eng.)
W.Coast Rep.	West Coast Reporter	Western Res. L.Rev.	Western Reserve Law Review
W.C.Rep.	Workmen's Compensation Reports	Western State L. Rev.	Western State University Law Review
Webb	Webb (KS)		
	Webb (TX)		
	Webb's Civil Appeals (TX)		

Western St LR	Same	Whart.St.Tr.	Wharton's State Trials (U.S.)
West.Jur.	Western Jurist (Des Moines, IA)	W.H.Cases	Wage & Hour Cases
West L.A. L. Rev.	West Los Angeles Law Review	WhCr	Wheeler's Criminal Cases (NY)
West.Law J.	Western Law Journal	Wheat.	Wheaton (U.S.)
		wheatr	Same
West.Law M.	Western Law Monthly (OH)	Wheel.	Wheeler's Criminal Cases (NY)
West.Legal Obser.	Western Legal Observer		Wheelock (TX)
		Wheeler Abr.	Wheeler's Abridgment
West.L.Gaz.	Western Law Gazette (OH)	Wheeler C.C.	Wheeler's Criminal Cases (NY)
West.L.J.	Western Law Journal	White	White (TX)
West.L.M.	Western Law Monthly (OH)		White (WV)
			White's Justiciary Cases (Scot.)
West.L.Mo.	Same	White & T. Lead.Cas. Eq.	White & Tudor's Leading Cases in Equity (Eng.)
West.L. Month.	Same		
West.L.R.	Western Law Reporter (Can.)	White & W.	White & Wilson (TX)
West.L.Rev.	Western Law Review	Whitm.Lib. Cas.	Whitman's Libel Cases (MA)
Westm.	State of Westminster (Eng.)	Whit.Pat.Cas.	Whitman's Patent Cases (U.S.)
Westm.L.J.	Westmoreland Law Journal (PA)	Whitt.	Whittlesey (MO)
West.R.	Western Reporter	Whittier LR	Whittier Law Review
West.School L.Rev.	Western School Law Review	Whittier L.Rev.	Same
		W.H.Man.	Wages & Hours Manual
West. St. L. R.	Western State Law Review	W.H.R.	Wage & Hour Reporter
West.St.U. L.Rev.	Western State University Law Review	Widener J.Pub.L.	Widener Journal of Public Law
		Wight	Wight's Section Cases (Scot.)
West t.Hardw.	West tempore Hardwicke, Chancery (Eng.)	Wight.	Wightwick, Exchequer (Eng.)
West Va.	West Virginia	Wightw.	Same
West.Week. Rep.	Western Weekly Reports (Can.)	Wilc.	Wilcox (OH)
West.Wkly.	Western Weekly (Can.)	Wilc.Cond.	Wilcox, Condensed Ohio Reports
Wethey	Wethey's Queen's Bench (Upper Can.)	Wilcox	Wilcox (OH)
			Wilcox (PA)
W.F.P.D.2d	West's Federal Practice Digest, Second Series	Wilcox Cond.	Wilcox, Condensed Ohio Reports
		Wilk.	Wilkinson (Austl.)
wh	Wages and Hours Cases (BNA)		Wilkinson, Court of Appeals and Civil Appeals (TX)
wh2d	Same, Second Series		
W.H. & G.	Welsby, Hurlstone & Gordon's Exchequer (Eng.)	Will.	Williams (MA)
			Willson (TX)
Whar	Wharton's Reports (PA)	Willamette L.J.	Willamette Law Journal
whart	Same	Willamette L.Rev.	Willamette Law Review
Whart.	Same		
Whart.Law Dict.	Wharton's Law Lexicon	Willes	Willes, King's Bench & Common Pleas (Eng.)

Williams	Peere–Williams' English Chancery Reports	Winch	Winch, Common Pleas (Eng.)
	Williams (MA)	Winst.	Winston (NC)
	Williams (UT)	W.I.R.	West Indian Reports
	Williams (VT)	wis	Wisconsin Reports
Williams & Bruce Ad.Pr.	Williams & Bruce's Admiralty Practice	Wis.	Same
		wis2d	Same, Second Series
Williams P.	Peere–Williams' English Chancery Reports	Wis.2d	Same
		Wis.B.Bull.	Wisconsin Bar Bulletin
Williams–Peere	Same	Wis.B.T.A.	Wisconsin Board of Tax Appeals Reports
Will.L.J.	Willamette Law Journal		
Willm.W. & D.	Willmore, Wollaston & Davison's Queen's Bench (Eng.)	Wisc.Stud. B.J.	Wisconsin Student Bar Journal
		Wis.Int'l L.J.	Wisconsin International Law Journal
Willm.W. & H.	Willmore, Wollaston & Hodges' Queen's Bench (Eng.)	Wis.Law.	Wisconsin Lawyer
		Wis.L.N.	Wisconsin Legal News
Wills	Willson's Reports (TX)	Wis.L.Rev.	Wisconsin Law Review
Willson	Willson, Civil Cases (TX)	Wis.Multi–Cultural L.J.	Wisconsin Multi–Cultural Law Journal
Willson, Civ. Cas.Ct.App.	Same		
Will.Woll. & Dav.	Willmore, Wollaston & Davison, Queen's Bench (Eng.)	Wis.Tax App.C.	Wisconsin Tax Appeals Commission Reports
		Wis.Women's L.J.	Wisconsin Women's Law Journal
Will.Woll. & H.	Willmore, Wollaston & Hodges' Queen's Bench (Eng.)	Withrow	Withrow (IA)
		W.Jo.	William Jones King's Bench, Common Pleas, House of Lords and Exchequer (Eng.)
Will.Woll. & Hodg.	Same		
Wilm.	Wilmot's Notes (Eng.)		
Wils.	Wilson (CA)	W.Jones	Same
	Wilson (MN)	W.Kel.	William Kellynge, King's Bench & Chancery (Eng.)
	Wilson (OR)		
	Wilson, Superior Court Reports (IN)	Wkly.Dig.	Weekly Digest (NY)
	Wilson's King's Bench & Common Pleas (Eng.)	Wkly.Law Bull.	Weekly Law Bulletin (OH)
		Wkly.L.Bul.	Same
Wils. & S.	Wilson & Shaw, House of Lords (Scot.)	Wkly.L.Gaz.	Weekly Law Gazette (OH)
Wils.Ch.	Wilson's Chancery (Eng.)	Wkly.N.C.	Weekly Notes of Cases (PA)
Wils.C.P.	Wilson's Common Pleas (Eng.)	Wkly.Rep.	Weekly Reporter (Eng.)
Wils.Exch.	Wilson's Exchequer (Eng.)	W.L.A.C.	Western Labour Arbitration Cases
Wils.K.B.	Wilson's King's Bench (Eng.)	W.L.Bull.	Weekly Law Bulletin
		W.L.G.	Weekly Law Gazette (OH)
Wils.P.C.	Wilson's Privy Council (Eng.)	W.L.Gaz.	Same
wilssuper	Wilson Superior Court Reports (IN)	W.L.J.	Western Law Journal
		W.L.Jour.	Weekly Law Journal

W.L.M.	Western Law Monthly (OH)	Woods	Woods, Circuit Court (U.S.)
WLR	Wisconsin Law Review	Woodw.	Woodward's Decisions (PA)
W.L.R.	Weekly Law Reports (Eng.)	wool	Woolworth's U.S. Circuit Court Reports
	Western Law Reporter	Woolw.	Woolworth (NE)
	Women Law Reporter		Woolworth, Circuit Court (U.S.)
W.L.T.	Western Law Times and Reports	Workmen's Comp. L.Rev.	Workmen's Compensation Law Review
Wm. & Mary Bill Rts.J.	William and Mary Bill of Rights Journal	World Jurist	World Jurist
		World Pol.	World Polity
		W.R.	Weekly Reports
Wm. & Mary J.Envtl.L.	William & Mary Journal of Environmental Law	W.Res.L.Rev.	Western Reserve Law Review
		Wri	Wright's Supreme Court Reports (OH)
Wm. & Mary L.Rev.	William & Mary Law Review	Wright	Wright (OH)
Wm. & Mary Rev.Va.L.	William and Mary Review of Virginia Law		Wright (PA)
		W.Rob.	William Robinson's Admiralty (Eng.)
Wm.Mitchell L.Rev.	William Mitchell Law Review	WS	Watts & Sergeant's Reports (PA)
W.N.	Weekly Notes (Eng.)	Wsh	Washington State Reports
W.New Eng. L.Rev.	Western New England Law Review	Wsh2	Same, Second Series
Wol.	Wolcott's Chancery (DE)	W.St.U. L.Rev.	Western State University Law Review
	Wollaston's English Bail Court Reports (Eng.)	WT	Washington Territory Reports
Wolf. & B.	Wolferstan & Bristow's Election Cases (Eng.)	WV	West Virginia Reports
		wva	Same
Wolf. & D.	Wolferstan & Dew's Election Cases (Eng.)	W.Va.Crim. Just.Rev.	West Virginia Reports Criminal Justice Review
Woll.	Wollaston's English Bail Court Reports (Practice Cases)	W.Va.L.Q.	West Virginia Law Quarterly
		W.Va.L.Rev.	West Virginia Law Review
Woll.P.C.	Same	WW	White & Willson's Reports (TX)
Women & L	Women and Law		
Woman Offend.Rep.	Woman Offender Report	W.W. & D.	Willmore, Wollaston & Davison, Queen's Bench (Eng.)
Women Law.J.	Women Lawyer's Journal	W.W. & H.	Willmore, Wollaston & Hodges' Queen's Bench (Eng.)
Women's Rights L.Rptr.	Women's Rights Law Reporter		
W.Ont.L.Rev.	Western Ontario Law Review	W.W.D.	Western Weekly Digests
wood	Wood's U.S. Circuit Court Reports	WWH	W. W. Harrington's Reports (DE)
Wood.	Woodbury & Minot, Circuit Court (U.S.)	W.W.Harr.	W.W. Harrington (DE)
Wood. & M.	Same	W.W.R.	Western Weekly Report (Can.)
Woodb. & M.	Same		
woodm	Same	W.W.R.(N.S.)	Same, New Series

Wy. & W.	Wyatt & Webb (Vict.)	Wythe	Wythe's Chancery Reports (VA)
wyo	Wyoming Reports	wythech	Same
Wyo.	Same	Wy.W. & A'Beck	Wyatt, Webb & A'Beckett (Vict.)
Wyo.L.J.	Wyoming Law Journal		

Y

Y.	Yeates (PA)	Y.B.Ed. I	Year Books, Edward I
Y.A.D.	Young's Admiralty Decisions (Nova Scotia)	Y.B.Eur. Conv. on Human Rights	Yearbook of the European Convention on Human Rights
Yale J.Int'l L.	Yale Journal of International Law	Y.B.Eur.L.	Yearbook of European Law
Yale J.L. & Feminism	Yale Journal of Law & Feminism	Y.B.Human Rights	Yearbook on Human Rights
Yale J.L. & Humanities	Yale Journal of Law & the Humanities	Y.B.Int'l L.Comm'n	Yearbook of the International Law Commission
Yale J.L. & Lib.	Yale Journal of Law & Liberation	Y.B.Int'l Org.	Yearbook of International Organizations
Yale J. on Reg.	Yale Journal on Regulation		
Yale J.World Pub.Ord.	Yale Journal of World Public Order	Y.B.League of Nations	Yearbook of the League of Nations
Yale L. & Pol'y Rev.	Yale Law & Policy Review	Y.B.P.1, Edw. II	Year Books, Part 1, Edward II
Yale L.J.	Yale Law Journal	Y.B.S.C.	Year Books, Selected Cases
Yale Rev.Law & Soc.Act'n	Yale Review of Law and Social Action	Y.B.U.N.	Yearbook of the United Nations
Yale Stud. World Pub. Ord.	Yale Studies in World Public Order	Y.B.W.A.	Yearbook of World Affairs
Y. & C.	Younge & Collyer's Chancery (Eng.)	Y.B.World Pol.	Yearbook of World Polity
Y. & C.C.C.	Same	Yea.	Yeates' Reports (PA)
Y. & J.	Younge & Jervis' Exchequer (Eng.)	Yearb.	Year Book, King's Bench (Eng.)
Yannacone & Cohen	Yannacone & Cohen, Environmental Rights and Remedies	Yearb.P.7, Hen.VI	Year Books, Part 7, Henry VI
		yeates	Yeates' Reports (PA)
Yates	Yates' Select Cases	Yeates	Same
Yates Sel. Cas.	Yates' Select Cases (NY)	Yel.	Yelverton, King's Bench (Eng.)
Y.B.	Year Book, King's Bench (Eng.)	Yelv.	Same
Y.B. (Rolls Series)	Same, Rolls Series (Eng.)	Yerg.	Yerger (TN)
		yertn	Same
Y.B. (Sel. Soc.)	Same, Selden Society (Eng.)	Y.L.C.T.	Yearbook of Law, Computers, and Technology
Y.B.A.A.A.	Yearbook of the Association of Attenders and Alumni of the Hague Academy of International Law	YLJ	Yale Law Journal
		Yorke Ass.	Clayton Reports, Yorke Assizes
		York Leg. Rec.	York Legal Record (PA)
Y.B.A.S.L.	Yearbook of Air and Space Law	You.	Younge's Exchequer (Eng.)

You. & Coll. Ch.	Younge & Collyer's Exchequer (Eng.)	Younge & C. Exch.	Younge & Collyer's Exchequer Equity (Eng.)
You. & Coll. Ex.	Same		
You. & Jerv.	Younge & Jervis, Exchequer (Eng.)	Younge & Coll. Ex.	Same
Young	Young (MN)	Younge & J.	Younge & Jervis, Exchequer (Eng.)
Young Adm.	Young, Admiralty (N.S.)		
		Younge & Je.	Same
Young Adm. Dec.	Same	Younge Exch.	Younge, Exchequer (Eng.)
Younge	Younge's Exchequer (Eng.)	Younge M.L. Cas.	Younge, Maritime Law Cases (Eng.)
Younge & C. Ch.Cas.	Younge & Collyer's Chancery or Exchequer Equity (Eng.)	Young Naut. Dict.	Young's Nautical Dictionary
		Yugo.L.	Yugoslav Law

Z

Zab.	Zabriskie (NJ)	Zane	Zane (UT)
Zambia L.J	Zambia Law Journal		

Appendix B

STATE GUIDES TO LEGAL RESEARCH*

As discussed in Chapter 1, the United States consists of 51 major legal systems—one for each state and the federal government. Although the state legal systems have much in common, each is the product of a unique legal history and background. Methods of legislating, codifying, and court reporting vary from state to state. Consequently, where possible, researcher's should learn the unique aspects of legal research in each state in which they are conducting extended research.

In many states, law librarians and other professionals familiar with legal research have written guides that explain their state's legal system. The list below is a compilation of these guides. It includes books as well as shorter bibliographic sources from the American Association of Law Libraries (AALL), but excludes sources that appear in legal periodicals. In addition, the list includes titles from Carolina Academic Press' Legal Research Series. A researcher contemplating or beginning any research in one of the states listed below should consult the guides first. Such a first step could save much time and effort.

Historical
Michael Chiorazzi & Marguerite Most, *Prestatehood Legal Materials: A Fifty–State Research Guide*, 2 v. (Haworth Information Press, 2005).

Alabama
Gary Orlando Lewis, *Legal Research in Alabama: How to Find and Understand the Law in Alabama* (2001).

Hazel L. Johnson & Timothy L. Coggins, *Guide to Alabama State Documents and Selected Law–Related Materials* (AALL, 1993).

George D. Schrader, *Alabama Law Bibliography* (Barrister Press, 1989).

Alaska
Aimee Ruzicka, *Alaska Legal and Law–Related Publications: A Guide for Law Libraries* (AALL, 1984).

Arizona
Tamara S. Herrera, *Arizona Legal Research* (Carolina Academic Press, 2008).

Arizona: A Survey of Arizona State Legal and Law–Related Documents (AALL, 2006).

* This guide was revised and updated by Bonnie Shucha, Head of Reference, University of Wisconsin Law Library.

Kathy Shimpock–Vieweg & Marianne Sidorski Alcorn, *Arizona Legal Research Guide* (Hein, 1992).

Arkansas

Coleen M. Barger, *Arkansas Legal Research* (Carolina Academic Press, 2007).

Lynn Foster, *Arkansas Legal Bibliography: Documents and Selected Commercial Titles* (AALL, 1988).

California

Larry D. Dershem, *California Legal Research Handbook* (Hein, 2008).

Hether C. Macfarlane & Suzanne E. Rowe, *California Legal Research* (Carolina Academic Press, 2008).

John K. Hanft, *Legal Research in California*, 6th ed. (Thomson/West, 2007).

Daniel Martin & Dan F. Henke, *Henke's California Law Guide*, 8th ed. (LexisNexis Matthew Bender, 2006).

Janet Fischer & Steven Feller, *California State Documents: A Bibliography of Legal Publications and Related Materials* (AALL, 2005).

Colorado

Robert C. Richards & Barbara Bintliff, *Colorado Legal Resources: An Annotated Bibliography* (AALL, 2004).

Connecticut

Jessica G. Hynes, *Connecticut Legal Research* (Carolina Academic Press, 2009).

Lawrence Cheeseman & Arlene G. Bielefield, *The Connecticut Legal Research Handbook* (Connecticut Law Book Company, 1992).

Shirley R. Bysiewicz, *Sources of Connecticut Law* (Butterworth, 1987).

David R. Voisinet et al., *Connecticut State Legal Documents: A Selective Bibliography* (AALL, 1985).

Delaware

Selective Annotated Bibliography of Delaware State Documents and Other Resources Used in Delaware Legal Research (AALL, 2008).

District of Columbia

State Documents Bibliography: Washington, D.C. (AALL, 2008).

Leah F. Chanin, Pamela J. Gregory & Sarah K. Wiant, *Legal Research in the District of Columbia, Maryland, and Virginia*, 2d ed. (Hein, 2000).

Florida

Betsy L. Stupski, *Guide to Florida Legal Research*, 7th ed. (Florida Bar, Continuing Legal Education, 2008).

Barbara J. Busharis & Suzanne E. Rowe, *Florida Legal Research*, 3d ed. (Carolina Academic Press, 2007).

Georgia

Nancy P. Johnson, Elizabeth G. Adelman & Nancy J. Adams, *Georgia Legal Research* (Carolina Academic Press, 2007).

Rebecca Simmons Stillwagon, *Georgia Legal Documents: An Annotated Bibliography* (AALL, 1991).

Leah F. Chanin & Suzanne L. Cassidy, *Guide to Georgia Legal Research and Legal History* (Harrison, 1990).

Hawaii

Richard F. Kahle, *How to Research Constitutional Legislative and Statutory History in Hawaii*, 3d ed. (Hawaii Legislative Reference Bureau, 2004).

Jerry Dupont & Beverly D. Keever, *The Citizens' Guide: How to Use Legal Materials in Hawaii* (1983).

Idaho

Tenielle Fordyce–Ruff & Suzanne E. Rowe, *Idaho Legal Research* (Carolina Academic Press, 2008).

Michael J. Greenlee, *Idaho State Documents: A Bibliography of Legal Publications and Related Materials* (AALL, 2003).

Illinois

Laurel Wendt, *Illinois Legal Research Guide*, 2d ed. (Hein, 2006).

Mark E. Wojcik, *Illinois Legal Research* (Carolina Academic Press, 2003).

Cheryl R. Nyberg et al., *Illinois State Documents: A Selective Annotated Bibliography for Law Librarians* (AALL, 1986).

Indiana

Linda K. Fariss & Keith A. Buckley, *An Introduction to Indiana State Publications for the Law Librarian* (AALL, 1982).

Iowa

John D. Edwards, *Iowa Legal Research* Guide (Hein, 2003).

Angela K. Secrest, *Iowa Legal Documents Bibliography* (AALL, 1990).

Kansas

Joseph A. Custer & Christopher L. Steadham, *Kansas Legal Research* (Carolina Academic Press, 2008).

Joseph A. Custer, Barbara J. Ginzburg & Robert A. Mead, *Kansas Legal Research and Reference Guide*, 3d ed. (Kansas Bar Association, 2003).

Martin E. Wisneski, *Kansas State Documents for Law Libraries: Publications Related to Law and State Government* (AALL, 1984).

Kentucky

Kurt X. Metzmeier, Amy Beckham Osborne & Shaun Esposito, *Kentucky Legal Research Manual*, 3d ed. (Office of Continuing Legal Education, University of Kentucky College of Law, 2005).

Ryan Valentin & Michelle Cosby, *Kentucky State Documents: A Bibliography of Legal & Law–Related Material* (AALL, 2008).

Wesley Gilmer, Jr., *Guide to Kentucky Legal Research: A State Bibliography*, 2d ed. (Kentucky State Law Library, 1985).

Louisiana

Mary Garvey Algero, *Louisiana Legal Research* (Carolina Academic Press, 2009).

Charlene Cain & Madeline Hebert, *Louisiana Legal Documents and Related Publications*, 3d ed. (AALL, 2001).

Win–Shin S. Chiang, *Louisiana Legal Research,* 2d ed. (Butterworth, 1990).

Maine

Christine I. Hepler & Maureen P. Quinlan, *Maine State Documents: A Bibliography of Legal and Law Related Material* (AALL, 2003).

William W. Wells, Jr., *Maine Legal Research Guide* (Tower Publishing, 1989).

Maryland

Leah F. Chanin, Pamela J. Gregory & Sarah K. Wiant, *Legal Research in the District of Columbia, Maryland, and Virginia*, 2d ed. (Hein, 2000).

William L. Taylor, *Maryland State Publications in Law and Related Fields: A Selective Bibliography with Annotations* (AALL, 1996).

Michael S. Miller, *Ghost Hunting: Finding Legislative Intent in Maryland* (Maryland State Law Library, 1984).

Massachusetts

Mary Ann Neary, Ruth G. Matz & Margot Botsford, *Handbook of Legal Research in Massachusetts* (Massachusetts Continuing Legal Education, 2002).

Virginia J. Wise, *How to Do Massachusetts Legal Research: Maximizing Efficiency in the Print and Online Environment* (Massachusetts CLE, Inc., 1998).

Leo McAuliffe & Susan Z. Steinway, *Massachusetts State Documents Bibliography* (AALL, 1985).

Michigan

Pamela Lysaght, *Michigan Legal Research* (Carolina Academic Press, 2006).

Michael W. Tillman–Davis & Christopher T. Bloodworth, *Michigan Legal Documents: A Bibliography of Legal & Law–Related Materials* (AALL, 2006).

Richard L. Beer & Judith J. Field, *Michigan Legal Literature: An Annotated Guide,* 2d ed. (Hein, 1991).

Minnesota

John Tessner et al., *Minnesota Legal Research Guide*, 2d ed. (Hein, 2002).

Marsha L. Baum & Mary Ann Nelson, *Guide to Minnesota State Documents and Selected Law Related Materials* (AALL, 1985).

Mississippi

Ben Cole, *Mississippi Legal Documents and Related Publications: A Selected Annotated Bibliography* (AALL, 1987).

Missouri

Wanda M. Temm & Julie M. Cheslik, *Missouri Legal Research* (Carolina Academic Press, 2007).

Introduction to Legal Materials: A Manual for Non–Law Librarians in Missouri (Missouri Bar, 2006).

Mary Ann Nelson, *Guide to Missouri State Documents and Selected Law–Related Materials* (AALL, 1991).

Montana

Margaret Ann Chansler, *Montana State Documents: A Bibliography of Legal and Law–Related Material* (AALL, 2004).

Robert K. Whelan, Meredith Hoffman & Stephen R. Jordan, *A Guide to Montana Legal Research*, 8th ed. (State Law Library of Montana, 2003).

Nebraska

Kay L. Andrus, *Research Guide to Nebraska Law* (LexisNexis, 2006).

Patrick H. Charles, *Lexis Publishing's Research Guide to Nebraska Law* (Lexis Publishing, 2001).

Mitchell J. Fontenot et al., *Nebraska State Documents Bibliography* (AALL, 1988).

Nevada

Jennifer Larraguibel Gross, Thomas Blake Gross & Tom Boone, *Nevada Legal Research Guide* (Hein, 2005).

Ann S. Jarrell & G. LeGrande Fletcher, *Nevada State Documents Bibliography: Legal Publications and Related Material*, 2d ed. (AALL, 2000).

New Jersey

Paul Axel–Lute, *New Jersey Legal Research Handbook*, 4th ed. (New Jersey Institute for CLE, 1998).

Christina M. Senezak, *New Jersey State Publications: A Guide for Law Libraries* (AALL, 1984).

New Mexico

Patricia D. Wagner & Mary Woodward, *Guide to New Mexico State Publications,* 2d ed. (AALL, 1991).

Arie W. Poldervaart, *Manual for Effective New Mexico Legal Research* (Univ. of New Mexico Press, 1955).

New York

Elizabeth G. Adelman & Suzanne E. Rowe, *New York Legal Research* (Carolina Academic Press, 2008).

Gail F. Whittemore & Susan L. Dow, *New York Legal Documents 2007: A Selective Annotated Bibliography* (AALL, 2007).

William H. Manz, Ellen M. Gibson & Karen L. Spencer, *Gibson's New York Legal Research Guide*, 3d ed. (Hein, 2004).

Robert Allan Carter, *New York State Constitution: Sources of Legislative Intent*, 2d ed. (Rothman, 2001).

North Carolina

Miriam J. Baer & James C. Ray, *Legal Research in North Carolina* (Carolina Academic Press, 2006).

Mary Louise Corbett, Marguerite Most & Thomas M. Steele, *Guide to North Carolina Legal and Law–Related Materials*, 2d ed. (AALL, 1996).

Ohio

Katherine L. Hall & Sara A. Sampson, *Ohio Legal Research* (Carolina Academic Press, 2008).

Melanie K. Putnam & Susan M. Schaefgen, *Ohio Legal Research Guide* (Hein, 1997).

Ann S. McFarland, *Ohio Legal Resources: An Annotated Bibliography and Guide,* 4th ed. (Ohio Regional Association of Law Libraries, 1996).

Christine Corcas, *Ohio State Legal Documents and Related Publications: A Selected Annotated Bibliography* (AALL, 1987).

David M. Gold & Marcia A. Cooper, *A Guide to Legislative History in Ohio* (Ohio Legislative Service Commission, 1985).

Oklahoma

Marilyn K. Nicely, *Oklahoma Legal and Law–Related Documents and Publications: A Selected Bibliography,* 2d ed. (AALL, 1995).

Oregon

Suzanne E. Rowe, *Oregon Legal Research*, 2d ed. (Carolina Academic Press, 2007).

Lesley Ann Buhman et al., *Bibliography of Law Related Oregon Documents* (AALL, 1986).

Pennsylvania

Frank Y. Liu, *Pennsylvania Legal Research Handbook* (American Lawyer Media, 2008).

Barbara J. Busharis & Bonny L. Tavares, *Pennsylvania Legal Research* (Carolina Academic Press, 2007).

Joel Fishman, *Pennsylvania State Documents: A Bibliography of Legal & Law–Related Material* (AALL, 2007).

Rhode Island

Gail I. Winson, *State of Rhode Island and Providence Plantations: Survey of State Documents and Law–Related Materials* (AALL, 2004).

Legal Research in Rhode Island (Rhode Island Law Institute, 1989).

South Carolina

Paula Gail Benson & Deborah Ann Davis, A *Guide to South Carolina Legal Research and Citation* (South Carolina Bar, CLE Division, 1991).

Robin K. Mills & Jon S. Schultz, *South Carolina Legal Research Handbook* (Hein, 1976).

South Dakota

Delores A. Jorgensen, *South Dakota Legal Research Guide*, 2d ed. (Hein, 1999).

Delores A. Jorgensen, *South Dakota Legal Documents: A Selective Bibliography* (AALL, 1988).

Tennessee

Sibyl Marshall & Carol McCrehan Parker, *Tennessee Legal Research* (Carolina Academic Press, 2007).

D. Cheryn Picquet & Reba A. Best, *Law and Government Publications of the State of Tennessee: A Bibliographic Guide* (AALL, 1988).

Lewis L. Laska, *Tennessee Legal Research Handbook* (Hein, 1977).

Texas

Brandon D. Quarles & Matthew C. Cordon, *Researching Texas Law*, 2d ed. (Hein, 2008).

Matthew C. Cordon & Brandon D. Quarles, *Specialized Topics in Texas Legal Research* (Hein, 2005).

Pamela R. Tepper & Peggy N. Kerley, *Texas Legal Research*, 2d ed. (Delmar Publishers, 1997).

Lydia M.V. Brandt et al., *Texas Legal Research: An Essential Lawyering Skill* (Texas Lawyer Press, 1995).

Karl T. Gruben & James E. Hambleton, *A Reference Guide to Texas Law and Legal History: Sources and Documentation,* 2d ed. (Butterworth, 1987).

Paris Permenter & Susan Fischer Ratliff, *Guide to Texas Legislative History* (Legislative Reference Library, 1986).

Malinda Allison & Kay Schleuter, *Texas State Documents for Law Libraries* (AALL, 1983).

Vermont

Virginia J. Wise, *A Bibliographic Guide to the Vermont Legal System,* 2d ed. rev. (AALL, 1991).

Virginia

John D. Eure & Gail F. Zwirner, *A Guide to Legal Research in Virginia*, 6th ed. (Virginia CLE Publications, 2008).

Leah F. Chanin, Pamela J. Gregory & Sarah K. Wiant, *Legal Research in the District of Columbia, Maryland, and Virginia*, 2d ed. (Hein, 2000).

Jacqueline Lichtman & Judy Stinson, *A Law Librarian's Introduction to Virginia State Publications* (AALL, 1988).

Washington

Julie A. Heintz, *Washington Legal Research* (Carolina Academic Press, 2005).

Penny Hazelton et al., *Washington Legal Researcher's Deskbook,* 3d ed. (Gallagher Law Library, 2002).

Peggy Roebuck Jarrett & Cheryl Rae Nyberg, *Washington State Documents: A Bibliography of Legal and Law–Related Material* (AALL, 1997).

West Virginia

Sandra Stemple et al., *West Virginia Legal Bibliography* (AALL, 1990).

Wisconsin

Theodore A. Potter & Jane Colwin, *Legal Research in Wisconsin,* 2d ed. (Hein, 2008).

Ellen J. Platt & Mary J. Koshollek, *Wisconsin Practice Materials: A Selective, Annotated Bibliography* (Hein, 1999).

Janet Oberla, *An Introduction to Wisconsin State Documents and Law Related Materials* (AALL, 1987).

Richard A. Danner, *Legal Research in Wisconsin* (University of Wisconsin–Extension, Law Department, 1980).

Wyoming

Debora A. Person, *Wyoming State Documents: A Bibliography of State Publications and Related Materials* (AALL, 2006).

Appendix C

LEGAL RESEARCH IN TERRITORIES
OF THE UNITED STATES*

The United States exercises sovereignty, in varying degrees, over a small number of places outside the 50 states and the District of Columbia. These are all island jurisdictions found in either the Caribbean or the Pacific. These jurisdictions can usefully be grouped as either territories or possessions of the United States on the one hand, or as states in free association with the United States on the other hand.[1]

Each of the jurisdictions discussed in this appendix has substantial local autonomy and lawmaking power. Therefore, legal research in these jurisdictions requires the use of the locally published materials described in this appendix, in conjunction with research in the applicable federal law as described elsewhere in this book.

The World Wide Web has revolutionized research in the law of the jurisdictions discussed in this appendix. These developments are noted throughout. This change is so fundamental that, as a general matter, research should begin with the World Wide Web resources mentioned in this appendix, even when hard copy counterparts exist.[2]

SECTION A.   TERRITORIES OF THE UNITED STATES

"Incorporated" or "unincorporated" and "organized" or "unorganized" denote two sets of ideas used to describe the political status of territories of the United States. The first set refers to the application of the United States Constitution. Given that by definition a territory does not have the status of a state, it is also thought not to be fully a part of the United States, with the further consequence that the federal Constitution is held not to apply there fully. Territories are said to be unincorporated. The second set of terms refers to the existence of an organic act passed by Congress for the governance of a territory. If Congress has passed such an "organic act," the territory is said to be organized.[3]

---

* Jonathan Pratter, Foreign and International Law Librarian, Tarlton Law Library, Jamail Center for Legal Research, University of Texas School of Law, revised and updated this appendix.

[1] *See* STANLEY K. LAUGHLIN, JR., THE LAW OF UNITED STATES TERRITORIES AND AFFILIATED JURISDICTIONS (1995), for a full discussion of the legal status of these jurisdictions.

[2] Several of the jurisdictions discussed in this appendix are in the South Pacific. Readers working with these jurisdictions are advised always to see what is available on the website of the Pacific Islands Legal Information Institute, http://www.paclii.org.

[3] *See generally Definitions of Insular Area Political Organizations* (U.S. Dept. of Interior, Office of Insular Affairs), at http://www.doi.gov/oia/Islandpages/politicaltypes.htm.

AMERICAN SAMOA

American Samoa is an unincorporated and unorganized territory of the United States. The United States gained sovereignty over American Samoa by a treaty in 1899 with Germany and Great Britain,[4] and by cessions in 1900 and 1904 from the indigenous Samoans. American Samoa's status as a territory was confirmed by statute in 1929.[5] The Department of the Interior is responsible for the administration of American Samoa.[6]

While American Samoa does not have an organic act, it does have a Constitution of 1967 approved by the voters and by the Secretary of the Interior. The text of the Constitution as amended is contained in volume 10 of *Constitutions of Dependencies and Special Sovereignties*[7] and at the beginning of the *American Samoa Code Annotated*. The Constitution can also be found at the website of the American Samoa Bar Association.[8] The Constitution provides American Samoa with a legislature, a judiciary, and an executive, so that American Samoa enjoys substantial local lawmaking authority.

Statutes

American Samoa Code Annotated. Pago Pago, American Samoa: The Bureau, 2004.

The code is edited, indexed, and published by the Legislative Reference Bureau of American Samoa. It is organized in titles. The code is available online at the website of the American Samoa Bar Association.[9]

Court Reports

American Samoa Reports. Orford, NH: Equity Pub. Corp., 1977–1982.

Complete in four volumes and a digest, this series reports the decisions of the High Court of American Samoa from 1900 to 1975.

American Samoa Reports, 2d series. Pago Pago, American Samoa: The Court, 1983–1997.

This series contains decisions of the Trial, Land and Titles, and Appellate Divisions of the High Court of American Samoa. The second series is complete in 31 volumes. The third series of *American Samoa Reports* began publication in 1997. To date, only a few volumes have been published.

All series of the *American Samoa Reports* are available online in HTML format at the website of the American Samoa Bar Association. Cases are organized alphabetically by the name of the first party.

[4] Convention on Adjustment of Jurisdiction in Samoa, 31 Stat. 1878, T.S. 314, 1 Bevans 276.

[5] Act of Feb. 20, 1929, ch. 281, 45 Stat. 1253 (1929), codified as amended at 48 U.S.C. § 1661 (1994). Additional foundational documents establishing American Samoa's political status can be found at the website of the American Samoa Bar Association, www.asbar.org.

[6] Exec. Order No. 10,264, 16 Fed. Reg. 6419 (1951).

[7] (Albert P. Blaustein ed., Oceana Publications 1975–).

[8] http://www.asbar.org. Click "Legal Resources." (This URL and instruction applies to all legal materials available on the website of the American Samoa Bar Association.)

[9] http://www.asbar.org.

Digests

American Samoa Digest. 2007 ed. Pago Pago, American Samoa: High Court of American Samoa, 2007.

The digest covers the first and second series of *American Samoa Reports.* It is available in both PDF and HTML format on the website of the American Samoa Bar Association. A separate digest in HTML covering *American Samoa Reports, 3d series,* is on the website of the American Samoa Bar Association.

Administrative Regulations

The *American Samoa Administrative Code* is available in part on the website of the American Samoa Bar Association.

GUAM

Guam was ceded to the United States by treaty following the Spanish–American War.[10] Guam is an unincorporated but organized territory of the United States. Guam received its organic act in 1950.[11] The act establishes a legislature, judiciary, and executive for Guam. In addition to territorial courts, there is a United States District Court of Guam from which appeal lies to the United States Court of Appeals for the Ninth Circuit. Negotiations with Congress and successive administrations on commonwealth status have been underway for years.

Statutes

The *Guam Code Annotated,* current through mid–2008, is available in PDF at the website of the Compiler of Laws.[12] Some academic law libraries will have the *Guam Code Annotated* in hard copy, but it is not as current as the online version.

Both *Westlaw* and *LexisNexis* have Guam legislation. *Westlaw* has a database called Guam Statutes–Annotated (GU–ST–ANN) that includes the *Guam Code Annotated.* The same is true for *LexisNexis.*

Guam public laws are available at the website of the Guam Legislature.[13] The information is current.

Court Reports

The decisions of the Supreme Court of Guam from 1996 to the present are found on the website of the Compiler of Laws.[14] They can also be found on the website of the Unified Courts of Guam.[15] Note that the Supreme Court of Guam has adopted format-neutral citation of its decisions. *Westlaw* has a database called Guam Cases (GU–CS) that has the decisions of the Supreme Court from 1996, as well as the decisions of the U.S. District

---

[10] Treaty of Peace, Spain–U.S., December 10, 1898, 30 Stat. 1754, T.S. 343, 11 Bevans 615.

[11] Act of Aug. 1, 1950, ch. 512, 64 Stat. 384, codified as amended at 48 U.S.C. § 1421 *et seq.* (2000).

[12] http://www.guamcourts.org/compileroflaws/gca.html.

[13] http://www.guamlegislature.com. Click "Public Laws."

[14] http://www.guamcourts.org/compileroflaws/supremeop.html.

[15] http://www.justice.gov.gu/Opinions/opinions.html.

Court of Guam from 1951. *LexisNexis* has Guam Supreme Court cases from 1996.

Administrative Regulations

The *Guam Administrative Rules and Regulations*, current as of April 2004, are available on the website of the Compiler of Laws.[16] *LexisNexis* has a file of the Guam administrative regulations, but it is out of date.

NORTHERN MARIANA ISLANDS

This island group in the Pacific north of Guam was part of the Trust Territory of the Pacific Islands created in 1947 by the United Nations and administered by the United States. Negotiations on status led to the signing in 1975 of the Covenant to Establish a Commonwealth of the Northern Mariana Islands in Political Union with the United States of America, approved by Congress in 1976.[17] Under the Covenant, the Northern Mariana Islands are a self-governing Commonwealth "in political union with and under the sovereignty of the United States." The Commonwealth exercises authority of local self-government, while the United States retains sole responsibility for defense and foreign affairs. Under section 105 of the Covenant, general federal legislation applies in the Northern Mariana Islands.

The Covenant calls for the drafting and approval of a Constitution, which was promulgated in 1977. It establishes a legislature, judiciary, and executive. The text of the Constitution is contained in volume 10 of *Constitutions of Dependencies and Special Sovereignties* and at the beginning of the *Commonwealth Code*. An annotated text of the Constitution, published in 1995, is available from the Commonwealth Law Revision.

The Covenant establishes a United States District Court of the Northern Mariana Islands, the jurisdiction of which tracks that of its counterpart for Guam. Appeal lies to the Ninth Circuit.

Statutes

Northern Mariana Islands Commonwealth Code. Saipan, Northern Mariana Islands: Commonwealth Law Revision Commission, 2007.

This edition of the code is available in both hard copy and CD–ROM format from the Commonwealth Law Revision Commission.[18]

Court Reports

Decisions of the Commonwealth Supreme Court from 1996 to the present and of the Commonwealth Superior Court from 1989 to the present are found on the website of the Commonwealth Law Revision Commission.[19] Note that the Supreme Court has adopted format-neutral citation.

The hard copy *Northern Mariana Islands Reporter* publishes decisions of the Supreme Court from 1989 to 1999. The hard copy *Commonwealth*

[16] http://www.guamcourts.org/compileroflaws/gar.html.

[17] Act of March 24, 1976, Pub.L.No. 94–241, 90 Stat. 263.

[18] http://www.cnmilaw.org.

[19] http://www.cnmilaw.org/court_opinions.htm.

Reporter publishes decisions of the Commonwealth Superior Court (formerly the Trial Court) and of the District Court of the Northern Mariana Islands from 1978 to 1989.

Westlaw has a Northern Mariana Islands Cases database (MP–CS) that has the decisions of the Supreme Court from 1990 and a separate database (DCTMP) with decisions of the U.S. District Court of the Northern Mariana Islands from 1981. *LexisNexis* has files with similar coverage.

PUERTO RICO[20]

Puerto Rico is the largest of the territories associated with the United States, both in terms of land area and population (over 3.8 million in 2000). The United States acquired Puerto Rico from Spain following the Spanish–American War. The law governing Puerto Rico's current political status is found in federal legislation,[21] the Constitution of Puerto Rico,[22] and judicial decisions, both federal and territorial. In its Constitution, Puerto Rico is denominated a Commonwealth. Puerto Rico exercises a degree of sovereignty approaching that of a state of the United States. In addition to a fully developed Commonwealth judiciary, there is a United States District Court for Puerto Rico from which appeals lie to the United States Court of Appeals for the First Circuit.

Statutes

Leyes de Puerto Rico/Laws of Puerto Rico. San Juan, Puerto Rico: LexisNexis of Puerto Rico, 1900–.

The session laws are published in separate Spanish and English series. They are also available on microfiche in the William S. Hein & Co., Inc., series of state session laws. Because of the substantial delay in the publication of bound session law volumes, there are advance session law services thru the Internet. There are currently various competing services, which will be discussed under the Computer Databases topic at the end of this section.

Leyes de Puerto Rico Anotadas/Laws of Puerto Rico Annotated. San Juan, Puerto Rico: LexisNexis of Puerto Rico, 1954–.

This is the standard compilation of the Puerto Rican statutes. It is updated with pocket parts and replacement supplements. The annotations include not only court cases but also cross-references to *Rules and Regulations of Puerto Rico.* There are historical notes to trace the development of various sections. *Laws of Puerto Rico Annotated* is published in separate English and Spanish editions, as both languages are official.

Court Reports

Puerto Rico Reports. San Juan, Puerto Rico: Equity Publishing Corp., vols. 1–100, 1900–1972.

---

[20] The authors thank Maria M. Otero, M.L.I.S., J.D., Director, University of Puerto Rico Law Library, for revising and updating the Puerto Rico section of Appendix C.

[21] *See generally* 48 U.S.C. § 731 *et seq.*

[22] The current text in English is found in Title 1, LAWS OF PUERTO RICO.

This English-language set includes all cases from the Supreme Court of Puerto Rico from 1900 to 1972. The English version suspended publication with volume 100. The decisions of the Supreme Court since 1972 are available in translation, but unpublished, from the Court with the title *Official Translations of the Decisions of the Supreme Court of Puerto Rico.* Certified or plain copies of translations prepared by the Court can be requested from Secretaría del Tribunal Supremo, Negociado de Traducciones, Apartado 9022392, San Juan, Puerto Rico 00902–2392, phone (787) 723–6033, ext.2090, 2091

Decisiones de Puerto Rico. San Juan, Puerto Rico: West Group de Puerto Rico, 1900–.

The Spanish version of the reports of the Supreme Court of Puerto Rico continues to be published, but there is approximately a two-year delay before a volume of decisions is published.

Jurisprudencia del Tribunal Supremo de Puerto Rico. San Juan, Puerto Rico: Publicaciones JTS, 1977–.

These are weekly advance sheets of the decisions of the Supreme Court, published only in Spanish, with quarterly indexes and case tables.

Opiniones Avanzadas del Tribunal Supremo. San Juan, Puerto Rico: Colegio de Abogados de Puerto Rico, 1963–.

The *Puerto Rico Bar Association* publishes these advance sheets of the decisions of the Supreme Court of Puerto Rico. There is an annual index. Its website[23] includes the complete text of the decisions of the Supreme Court of Puerto Rico since 1998 and other useful information.

Decisiones del Tribunal de Circuito de Apelaciones de Puerto Rico. San Juan, Puerto Rico: Publicaciones JTS, 1995–.

These advance sheets of the decisions of the Puerto Rico Appellate Circuit Court are published twice monthly, in Spanish. They include annual indexes.

Digests

Digesto de Puerto Rico. San Juan, Puerto Rico: LexisNexis of Puerto Rico, 1974–1996.

This was the topical digest to the decisions of the Supreme Court of Puerto Rico. It was published in Spanish only. Organization is analogous to the West digests. Updating was by cumulative annual pocket parts, but it has not been updated since 1996.

Administrative Regulations

Administrative regulations are no longer published in print. The following print publications are not updated.

Rules and Regulations of Puerto Rico. San Juan, Puerto Rico: Commonwealth of Puerto Rico, Department of State, 1957–1972.

This looseleaf service contained the English-language codification of all regulations adopted by the executive branch of Puerto Rico.

---

[23] http://www.capr.org.

Puerto Rico Register. San Juan, Puerto Rico: Commonwealth of Puerto Rico, Department of State, 1957–1982.

This looseleaf service was published periodically (about seven times a year), and contained new regulations and amendments to existing regulations, thus keeping the *Rules and Regulations of Puerto Rico* up-to-date.

Catalog of Regulations of Puerto Rico. San Juan, Puerto Rico: Michie Co., 1991–1998.

This was a looseleaf compilation of Puerto Rican administrative regulations in force. It contains an abstract of the regulations. Updating was by replacement pages.

Reglamentos del Estado Libre Asociado de Puerto Rico. San Juan, Puerto Rico: LexisNexis of Puerto Rico, 1995–2000.

This publication contains the code of administrative regulations of the governmental agencies in Puerto Rico. Currently, 27 volumes are published, but the set is not complete.

Updated regulation information can be obtained using commercial computer databases such as *MicroJuris, Lexjuris, JTS Online, Consulta Legislativa* and the administrative agencies websites, which now offer a wealth of information thru the Internet.[24] The Departamento de Estado website publishes the regulations, searchable by title, number, and agency.[25] The regulations are in Spanish, and many of them are available in English.

Executive Opinions

Opiniones del Secretario de Justicia de Puerto Rico. San Juan, Puerto Rico: Thomson–West, 1903–.

The *Opiniones* are more or less equivalent to state attorneys general opinions. They come out irregularly but are kept up-to-date. They are also published in the William S. Hein & Co., microfiche set of attorneys general opinions. The Departamento de Justicia publishes the opinions, from 2003 to present on the World Wide Web.[26]

Law Reviews

Revista de Derecho Puertorriqueño. Quarterly publication of the Universidad Católica de Puerto Rico, School of Law, Ponce, Puerto Rico, 1961–.

Revista del Colegio de Abogados de Puerto Rico. Quarterly publication of the Colegio de Abogados de Puerto Rico, San Juan, Puerto Rico, 1939–.

Revista Jurídica de la Universidad de Puerto Rico. Quarterly publication of the Escuela de Derecho de la Universidad de Puerto Rico, Ro Piedras, Puerto Rico, 1932–.

Revista Jurídica de la Universidad Interamericana de Puerto Rico. A triannual publication of the Universidad Interamericana de Puerto Rico, Santurce, Puerto Rico, 1964–.

[24] http://www.gobierno.pr.

[25] http://www.estado.gobierno.pr.

[26] http://www.justicia.gobierno.pr.

Revista de Derecho Puertorriqueño, *Revista del Colegio de Abogados de Puerto Rico*, and *Revista Jurídica de la Universidad de Puerto Rico* are available on *Westlaw* and *LexisNexis*. All of them are indexed in *LegalTrac* and in *Index to Legal Periodicals*.

Citation Index

Shepard's Puerto Rico Citations. Colorado Springs, CO.: LexisNexis, 1968–.

This is a complete citation service showing all citations by the Puerto Rico and federal courts to the Puerto Rico cases reported in the various series of Puerto Rico reports. It includes all citations by the Puerto Rico and federal courts to the Constitution of the Commonwealth of Puerto Rico, the Organic Acts, and codes and laws, acts, ordinances, and court rules. All citations by the Puerto Rico courts to the United States Constitution and federal statutes are also shown.

Computer Databases

Westlaw has the Puerto Rico statutes annotated (PR–ST–ANN), both in English and in Spanish, the rules of court, and a legislative database called Recent Laws that purports to have the text of recently passed laws (last two years). There is a database of decisions from the First Circuit and from the U.S. District Court for the District of Puerto Rico. It contains many decisions from the District Court that are not published in the *Federal Supplement*. *Westlaw* includes the decisions of the Supreme Court of Puerto Rico, in Spanish, since 1899 to present in the database (PRS–CS), a selection of translations of the opinions of the Supreme Court of Puerto Rico, in English, since 1986 and the Appellate Circuit Court of Puerto Rico decisions, in Spanish, since September 2001. For additional information on these and other Puerto Rico databases, the researcher should consult the current edition of the *Westlaw Database Directory*.

LexisNexis has a Puerto Rico library that contains files for the annotated statutes, both in English and Spanish, and a file that purports to have the text of recently passed laws, though it does not appear to contain anything more recent than the other statutory databases. There are separate case files that contain the decisions of the Supreme Court of Puerto Rico, since 1899, and the decisions of the Appellate Circuit Court of Puerto Rico since 1995, both in Spanish. *LexisNexis* also includes the full text of Puerto Rico administrative regulations, although not all the administrative agencies are covered.

Both *Westlaw* and *LexisNexis* now carry the complete decisions of the Supreme Court of Puerto Rico since its first volume in 1899.

Leyes y Reglamentos de Puerto Rico (West CD–ROM Libraries). Thompson/West, 1992–.

This is a database in CD–ROM format containing the full text in Spanish of *Leyes de Puerto Rico Anotadas (Laws of Puerto Rico Annotated)* and, in a separate CD, the decisions of the Supreme Court of Puerto Rico, from 1899 to the present. It also contains Puerto Rico administrative regulations, although not all the administrative agencies are covered.

Microjuris. San Juan, Puerto Rico: Microjuris, Inc. 1989–.

This database is available through the Internet on a subscription basis. It contains the opinions of the Supreme Court of Puerto Rico since 1949 and the Appellate Circuit Court of Puerto Rico since 1995. It also includes the *Laws of Puerto Rico Annotated* and the *Opinions of the Attorney General of Puerto Rico*. It includes the most complete collection of government regulations organized by subject and agency names and other useful indexes. The information is in Spanish and is updated on a daily basis. A database for legislative information, which contains an abstract of the bills and resolutions introduced in the Legislative Assembly of Puerto Rico since 1985, includes information about the history and status of the bills, organized by subject, bill number, and other indexes.

LexisNexis Puerto Rico Primary Law. LexisNexis, 1995–.

This database in CD–ROM format contains the opinions of the Supreme Court of Puerto Rico since 1948, the opinions of the Appellate Circuit Court of Puerto Rico since 1995, the *Laws of Puerto Rico Annotated*, and a file containing the regulations of Puerto Rico organized by government agency.

Lexjuris.[27] *LexJuris* de Puerto Rico.

This is a commercial Internet database with free access for the basic collection, which contains the text of Puerto Rico cases, statutes, and regulations and other useful information. They also offer a fee-based subscription for more specialized research.

Other free access databases are *Colegio de Abogados de Puerto Rico* (Puerto Rico Bar Association)[28] and *PRLex*.[29]

JTS Online[30] and *Consulta Legislativa*[31] are commercial access databases for Puerto Rico legal research in Spanish. Both include statutes, cases and regulations. *JTS Online* includes the complete text of various legal books. *Consulta Legislativa* includes complete information about the legislative process, the text of bills and resolutions, and the legislative calendar, updated daily.

Administración de Tribunales de Puerto Rico.

Administración de Tribunales de Puerto Rico (Puerto Rico Courts Administration) has a website,[32] with information and texts of the Supreme Court cases from 1998. It also contains other useful information about the court system and judges. Case status information is searchable by parties. The information is in Spanish.

Legislative Library, Legislative Assembly of Puerto Rico.

It publishes bills, resolutions, and statutes in Spanish and English with free access on its website,[33] along with other useful information about the legislative process in Puerto Rico.

---

[27] http://www.lexjuris.com.

[28] http://www.capr.org.

[29] http://www.prlex.com.

[30] http://www.pub-jts.com.

[31] http://consultalegislative.com.

[32] http://www.tribunalpr.org.

[33] http://www.oslpr.org/english/.

Legal Research Guides

Carlos I. Gorrín Peralta, *Fuentes y Proceso de Investigación Jurídica.* Orford, NH: Butterworth Legal Publishers, Equity Publishing Division, 1991.

Luis Muñiz Arguelles & Migdalia Fraticelli Torres. *La Investigación Jurídica: Fuentes Puertorriqueñas, Norteamericanas y Españolas.* 4th ed. Bogotá, Colombia: Editorial Temis S.A., 2006.

VIRGIN ISLANDS

The United States Virgin Islands were acquired by purchase from Denmark in 1916.[34] The Virgin Islands are an unincorporated, organized territory. The new organic act was adopted in 1954.[35] There is a unicameral legislature, an elected governor, and a Territorial Court for the Virgin Islands. The United States District Court for the Virgin Islands exercises jurisdiction along the lines of other territorial federal courts, but in addition hears appeals from the Territorial Court. In 1976 Congress authorized the adoption of a constitution, but two attempts to do so failed with the voters, as did a 1993 referendum on political status.

Statutes

Virgin Islands Code Annotated. Charlottesville, Va.: LexisNexis, 1970–.

Annotated and updated annually with pocket parts and replacement volumes, this is the standard commercial edition of the Virgin Islands statutes in compiled form. Unnumbered index and tables volumes, a volume of court rules, and an advance session law service complete the set.

The *Virgin Islands Code*, unannotated, except for basic source information, is available freely on the World Wide Web.[36]

Westlaw has the current Virgin Islands statutes in a database called VI–ST–ANN. This is a version of the *Virgin Islands Code Annotated. LexisNexis* also has the current *Virgin Islands Code Annotated.*

Session Laws of the Virgin Islands. Charlotte Amalie, Virgin Islands: Law Revision Commission, 1955–.

Published annually, the session laws contain the text of laws and resolutions enacted by the legislature and approved by the governor. The session laws are also published in the series of state session laws produced in microfiche by William S. Hein & Co., Inc.

On *Westlaw* current Virgin Islands session laws are found in the VI–LEGIS database. *LexisNexis* has a file called Virgin Islands Advance Legislative Service that contains both historical and recent session laws.

---

[34] Convention on Cession of Danish West Indies, Denmark–U.S., Aug. 4, 1916, 39 Stat. 1706, T.S. 629, 7 Bevans 56.

[35] Act of July 22, 1954, ch. 558, 68 Stat. 497, codified as amended at 48 U.S.C. §§ 1541 *et seq.* (2000).

[36] http://www.michie.com/virginislands.

Court Reports

Virgin Islands Reports. Charlottesville, Va.: LexisNexis, 1959–.

Covering the period from 1917, and now in 48 volumes, this is the standard series of reports for the courts of the Virgin Islands. It publishes the decisions of the Territorial Court, the District Court of the Virgin Islands, and the United States Court of Appeals for the Third Circuit.

The *Westlaw* database VI–CS has the decisions of the Supreme Court of the Virgin Islands from 2007, the Superior Court from 1996, and the U.S. District Court for the Virgin Islands from 1946. *LexisNexis* has the decisions of the Superior (formerly Territorial) Court back to 1959 and coverage similar to *Westlaw* for the other courts.

Both the Supreme Court of the Virgin Islands and the Superior Court have good websites.[37]

Digests

Virgin Islands Digest. Charlottesville, Va.: LexisNexis, 1991–.

In six volumes, including a descriptive-word index and table of cases, this set gives topical access to decisions published in *Virgin Islands Reports.* Coverage in the bound volumes is through 1990 and updating is done by means of pocket parts.

SECTION B.   STATES IN FREE ASSOCIATION WITH THE UNITED STATES

The freely associated states are the Federated States of Micronesia, Palau, and the Republic of the Marshall Islands, all in the western Pacific. The fundamental distinction between a territory and a freely associated state is that in international law the latter has the status of a sovereign nation. Each of the freely associated states is a member of the United Nations.

The freely associated states formerly were part of the Trust Territory of the Pacific Islands created by the United Nations in 1947 and administered by the United States. Negotiations on political status led to the signing and approval of Compacts of Free Association with the United States in the 1980s.[38] The compacts are in the nature of international agreements. The freely associated states have much of the status of independent sovereign states. Under the compacts, the United States takes on responsibility for military security and defense and receives exclusive military authority. However, in consultation with the United States, the freely associated states retain the authority to conduct their foreign affairs.

FEDERATED STATES OF MICRONESIA

Today, the place to do research on the law of the Federated States of Micronesia (FSM) is on the World Wide Web, at the site of the Legal Information System (LIS) of the FSM.[39] The LIS is funded primarily by a technical assistance grant from the Asian Development Bank, with coordi-

---

[37] http://www.visupremecourt.org; http://www.visuperiorcourt.org.

[38] For the Marshall Islands and Micronesia, see 48 U.S.C. § 1901. For Palau, see 48 U.S.C. § 1931. The texts of the Compacts of Free Association are found in the notes following these sections in the annotated editions of the UNITED STATES CODE.

[39] http://www.fsmlaw.org/index.htm.

nation and support from the FSM Supreme Court. The LIS has primary legal sources for the FSM National Government and for the four states, Chuuk, Kosrae, Pohnpei, and Yap.

Constitutions

The Constitutions of the FSM National Government and of the four states are on the LIS.

Statutes

The FSM Code, current to August 2001, is on the LIS. Source notes and case notes are included. Recent public laws are on the website of the FSM Congress.[40] The hard copy *Federated States of Micronesia Code Annotated* has not been published since 1999.

The state codes, in varying degrees of currentness, are on the LIS.[41]

Court Reports

Federated States of Micronesia Supreme Court Interim Reporter. Kolonia, Pohnpei, FSM: The Court, 1997–.

Volumes 1–15 of the *Interim Reporter* are available in HTML format on the LIS. The hard copy version of the *Interim Reporter* can be found in some large academic law libraries. Some state court decisions not published in the *Interim Reporter* can be found in the LIS. More state court decisions are available on the Pacific Islands Legal Information Institute website.[42]

PALAU

Constitution

The Constitution of Palau is available on the World Wide Web in PDF on the website of the Embassy of Palau to the U.S.,[43] and in HTML format on the website of the Pacific Islands Legal Information Institute.[44] It is available commercially in *Constitutions of the Countries of the World*.

Statutes

Palau National Code Annotated: PNCA. Koror, Palau: Palau Publication and Law Access Unit, 1995–.

In four looseleaf volumes the code was prepared by the Palau National Code Commission. It is annotated with case citations and source notes. It has been supplemented to 2003. Unfortunately, no version of the code, available either commercially or for free, is available online.

[40] http://www.fsmcongress.fm.

[41] The Chuuk State Code is a 2001 draft version.

[42] http://www.paclii.org.

[43] http://www.palauembassy.com/Documents/ConstituionE.pdf.

[44] http://www.paclii.org/pw/legis/consol_act/cotrop359/.

Court Reports

Republic of Palau Reports. Koror, Palau: Republic of Palau Supreme Court, 1987–.

The former title was *Courts of the Republic of Palau Interim Reporter.* This looseleaf in 12 volumes publishes the decisions of the Supreme Court, Appellate Division, and selected decisions of the Supreme Court, Trial Division. It can be found in a small number of large academic law libraries. Unfortunately, there is no online counterpart available.

REPUBLIC OF THE MARSHALL ISLANDS

Constitution

The Constitution of the Marshall Islands is available in PDF on the website of the Electoral Knowledge Network[45] and in HTML on the website of the Pacific Islands Legal Information Network.[46] It is available commercially in *Constitutions of the Countries of the World.*

Statutes

Marshall Islands Revised Code. 2004 ed. Majuro: Office of Legislative Counsel, Nitijela of the Marshall Islands, 2004–.

This two-volume loose-leaf is held by very few law libraries. An unofficial version of the code is available on the website of the Pacific Islands Legal Information Institute.[47] Interestingly, the code as amended to August 2007, which is more recent than will be found elsewhere, is available on the website of the Republic of the Marshall Islands Judiciary.[48]

Court Reports

Marshall Islands Law Reports. Majuro, Marshall Islands: Supreme Court, 1993–.

The full formal title is *Republic of the Marshall Islands Law Reports.* It contains the decisions of the Supreme Court of the Marshall Islands. Both the publication history and responsibility are difficult to ascertain. The difficulty arises from the fact that the reports were reformatted and republished in 2007. In essence, the reports consist of a revised volume 1, a volume 2 that says it was revised at the bottom of the title page, but not in the title proper, and an interim volume 3. The reports are available in PDF on the website of the Republic of the Marshall Islands Judiciary and in HTML on the website of the Pacific Islands Legal Information Institute.

---

[45] http://aceproject.org/ero-en/regions/pacific/MH/MarshallIslandsConstitution1990.pdf/.

[46] http://www.paclii.org/mh/legis/consol_act/cotmi363/.

[47] http://www.paclii.org/mh/legis/consol_act/.

[48] http://rmicourts.org.

Appendix D

STATE REPORTS

A. YEAR OF FIRST REPORTED CASE DECIDED IN THE STATES' APPELLATE COURTS

Many of the states were colonies or territories when their first appellate decisions were issued. Pennsylvania was a commonwealth. In 1840, what is now the state of Texas was an independent republic.

Although printing began in the colonies in 1638, the first reported case appears to be the *Trial of Thomas Sutherland* for murder, printed in 1692. Prior to the American Revolution, approximately 30 of the 150 English reports were being used in this country as the written case law; only about 35 to 40 legal books or pamphlets had been printed here.

Connecticut was the first state to publish an official law report after a 1784 statute entitled *An Act Establishing the Wages of the Judges of the Superior Court* was enacted requiring judges of the supreme and superior courts to file written opinions. The first volume, known as *Kirby's Reports,* was published in 1789 by Ephraim Kirby in Litchfield, Connecticut; its first case is from 1785. Next to be published were Dallas' *Pennsylvania Cases* (1790), Hopkinson's *Admiralty Reports* (1792), and Chipman's *Vermont Reports* (1793). Through the early 1800s, reports commenced in North Carolina, Virginia, Kentucky, New Jersey, Maryland, Louisiana, New York, and Tennessee. Some of these early reports gathered and published cases much older than the publication date of the reporter. For example, the *Harris & McHenry Reports* from the General Court of Maryland contains a case decided in 1658.

State	Date	State	Date
Alabama	1820	Louisiana	1809
Alaska	1869	Maine	1820
Arizona	1866	Maryland	1658
Arkansas	1837	Massachusetts	1804
California	1850	Michigan	1805
Colorado	1864	Minnesota	1851
Connecticut	1785	Mississippi	1818
Delaware	1792	Missouri	1821
District of Columbia	1801	Montana	1868
Florida	1846	Nebraska	1860
Georgia	1846	Nevada	1865
Hawaii	1847	New Hampshire	1796
Idaho	1866	New Jersey	1789
Illinois	1819	New Mexico	1852
Indiana	1817	New York	1791
Iowa	1839	North Carolina	1778
Kansas	1858	North Dakota	1867
Kentucky	1785	Ohio	1821

State	Date	State	Date
Oklahoma	1890	Texas	1840
Oregon	1853	Utah	1855
Pennsylvania	1754	Vermont	1789
Rhode Island	1828	Virginia	1729
South Carolina	1783	Washington	1854
South Dakota	1867	West Virginia	1864
Tennessee	1791	Wisconsin	1839
		Wyoming	1870

B. STATES THAT HAVE DISCONTINUED PUBLISHING OFFICIAL STATE REPORTS

Except for Louisiana, all states that have discontinued their official reports have adopted West's *National Reporter System*, or an offprint of the *National Reporter System*, as official. Alaska has used the *Pacific Reporter* as its official reporter since it became a state.

State	Last Published Volume	Year of Last Case	First Volume Only in National Reporter System
Alabama	295	1976	331 So. 2d
Ala. App.	57	1976	331 So. 2d
Colorado	200	1980	616 P.2d
Colo. App.	44	1980	616 P.2d
Delaware	59	1966	220 A.2d
Florida	160	1948	37 So. 2d
Indiana	275	1981	419 N.E.2d
Ind. App.	182	1979	366 N.E.2d
Iowa	261	1968	158 N.W.2d
Kentucky	314	1951	237 S.W.2d
Louisiana	263	1972	270 So. 2d
Maine	161	1965	215 A.2d
Minnesota	312	1977	254 N.W.2d
Mississippi	254	1966	183 So. 2d
Missouri	365	1956	295 S.W.2d
Mo. App.	241	1952	274 S.W.2d
North Dakota	79	1953	60 N.W.2d
Oklahoma	208	1953	265 P.2d
Okla. Crim.	97	1953	265 P.2d
Rhode Island	122	1980	501 A.2d
South Dakota	90	1976	245 N.W.2d
Tennessee	225	1971	476 S.W.2d
Tenn. App.	63	1972	480 S.W.2d
Tenn. Crim. App.	4	1970	475 S.W.2d
Texas	163	1962	358 S.W.2d
Tex. Crim. App.	172	1963	363 S.W.2d
Tex. Civ. App.	63	1911	134 S.W.
Utah 2d	30	1974	519 P.2d
Wyoming	80	1959	346 P.2d

Appendix E

COVERAGE OF THE NATIONAL REPORTER SYSTEM

The entire system, with its beginning year of coverage and its jurisdictional coverage is outlined below:

Reporter	Began in	Jurisdictional Coverage (start date varies by state)
Atlantic Reporter	1885	Conn., Del., Me., Md., N.H., N.J., Pa., R.I., Vt., and D.C.
California Reporter	1959	Calif. Sup. Ct., courts of appeal, and Appellate Division, Superior Ct.
Illinois Decisions	1976	Ill. (all state appellate courts).
New York Supplement	1888	N.Y. (all appellate courts to 1932). Since 1932, the N.Y. Court of Appeals opinions are published here as well as in the North Eastern Reporter.
North Eastern Reporter	1885	Ill., Ind., Mass., N.Y., and Ohio.
North Western Reporter	1879	Iowa, Mich., Minn., Neb., N.D., S.D., and Wis.
Pacific Reporter	1883	Alaska, Ariz., Cal. to 1960, Calif. Sup. Ct. since 1960, Colo., Hawaii, Idaho, Kan., Mont., Nev., N.M., Okla., Or., Utah, Wash., and Wyo.
South Eastern Reporter	1887	Ga., N.C., S.C., Va., and W.Va.
South Western Reporter	1886	Ark., Ky., Mo., Tenn., and Tex.
Southern Reporter	1887	Ala., Fla., La., and Miss.
Supreme Court Reporter	1882	Supreme Court of the United States.
Federal Reporter	1880	From 1880 to 1911: U.S. Circuit Court (abolished in 1912). From 1880 to 1932: U.S. district courts (coverage transferred to Federal Supplement). 1891 to present: U.S. Court of Appeals (formerly U.S. Circuit Court of Appeals). 1911 to 1913: Commerce Court of the U.S. (abolished in 1913). 1929 to 1932 and 1960 to 1982: U.S. Court of Claims (abolished in 1982). 1929 to 1982: U.S. Court of Customs and Patent Appeals.[1] 1943 to 1961: U.S. Emergency Court of Appeals. 1972 to 1993: Temporary Emergency Court of Appeals.
Federal Appendix	2001	2001 to present: Unreported cases from the U.S. courts of appeals.

[1] Since 1983, jurisdiction of the U.S. Court of Customs and Patent Appeals and the appellate division of the U.S. Court of Claims transferred to U.S. Court of Appeals for the Federal Circuit.

Reporter	Began in	Jurisdictional Coverage (start date varies by state)
Federal Supplement	1932	1932 to present: U.S. district courts.
		1932 to 1960: U.S. Court of Claims.
		1954 to 1980: United States Customs Court (replaced by U.S. Court of International Trade).
		1980 to present: U.S. Court of International Trade.
		1968 to present: Judicial Panel on Multidistrict Litigation.
		1974 to 1997: Special Court under the Regional Rail Reorganization Act of 1973.
Federal Claims Reporter	1982	1982 to 1992: Formerly U.S. Claims Court Reporter through vol. 26, covering U.S. Claims Court.[2]
		1992 to present: U.S. Court of Federal Claims. Commences with vol. 27.
Federal Rules Decisions	1939	1939 to present: U.S. district courts construing Federal Rules of Civil Procedure (1939 to present) and Federal Rules of Criminal Procedure (1946 to present).
Military Justice Reporter	1975	1975 to present: U.S. Court of Appeals for the Armed Forces (formerly the Court of Military Appeals) and courts of criminal appeals (formerly courts of military review) for the Army, Navy–Marine Corps, Air Force, and Coast Guard.
Bankruptcy Reporter	1979	1979 to present: Bankruptcy cases from U.S. bankruptcy courts, U.S. district courts dealing with bankruptcy matters (cases not printed in Federal Supplement), U.S. courts of appeals (reprinted from Federal Reporter), and U.S. Supreme Court (reprinted from Supreme Court Reporter).
Veterans Appeals Reporter	1989	1989 to present: Veterans appeals cases from the U.S. Court of Veterans Appeals, U.S. district courts, U.S. courts of appeals, and U.S. Supreme Court (in review of the Court of Veterans Appeals).

[2] This court changed its name in 1992 to the U.S. Court of Federal Claims.

Appendix F

A FUNDAMENTAL LAWYERING SKILL

In 1989 the American Bar Association's Section of Legal Education and Admissions to the Bar created the Task Force on Law Schools and the Profession: Narrowing the Gap. Its purpose was to study and improve the processes by which new members of the profession are prepared for the practice of law. In August 1992, the Task Force issued its final report, *Legal Education and Professional Development—An Educational Continuum.* The report includes a "Statement of Fundamental Skills and Values," which identifies "Legal Research" as one of the ten fundamental skills that a lawyer should possess. The task force was chaired by former ABA president Robert MacCrate, and its report is commonly referred to as the "MacCrate Report." Reproduced below is the section of the report that discusses legal research.[1]

FUNDAMENTAL LAWYERING SKILLS § 3 LEGAL RESEARCH[2]

In order to conduct legal research effectively, a lawyer should have a working knowledge of the nature of legal rules and legal institutions, the fundamental tools of legal research, and the process of devising and implementing a coherent and effective research design:

3.1 *Knowledge of the Nature of Legal Rules and Institutions.* The identification of the issues and sources to be researched in any particular situation requires an understanding of:
   (a) The various sources of legal rules and the processes by which these rules are made, including:
      (i) Caselaw. Every lawyer should have a basic familiarity with: (A) The organization and structure of the federal and state courts of general jurisdiction; general concepts of jurisdiction and venue; the rudiments of civil and criminal procedure; the historical separation between courts of law and equity and the modern vestiges of this dual court system; (B) The nature of common law decisionmaking by courts and the doctrine of *stare decisis*; (C) The degree of "authoritativeness" of constitutional and common law decisions made by courts at the various levels of the federal and state judicial systems;
      (ii) Statutes. Every lawyer should have a basic familiarity with: (A) The legislative processes at the federal, state, and local levels, including the procedures for preparing, introducing, amending, and enacting legislation; (B) The relationship be-

---

[1] For additional discussion of the implications for legal research of the MacCrate Report, see Donald J. Dunn, *Legal Research: A Fundamental Lawyering Skill,* 1 Persp.: Teaching Legal Res. & Writing 2 (1992); Donald J. Dunn, *Are Legal Research Skills Essential? "It Can Hardly Be Doubted . . .",* 1 Persp.: Teaching Legal Res. & Writing 34 (1993); Steven M. Barkan, *Should Legal Research Be Included on the Bar Exam? An Exploration of the Question,* 99 Law Libr. J. 403 (2007); *reprinted in* 77 (2) The Bar Examiner, May 2008, at 35.

[2] Reprinted by permission of the American Bar Association.

tween the legislative and judicial branches, including the power of the courts to construe ambiguous statutory language and the power of the courts to strike down unconstitutional statutory provisions;

(iii) Administrative regulations and decisions of administrative agencies. Every lawyer should have a basic familiarity with the rudiments of administrative law, including: (A) The procedures for administrative and executive rulemaking and adjudication; (B) The relationship between the executive and judicial branches, including the power of the courts to construe and pass on the validity and constitutionality of administrative regulations and the actions of administrative agencies;

(iv) Rules of court;

(v) Restatements and similar codifications (covering non-official expositions of legal rules that courts tend to view as authoritative);

(b) Which of the sources of legal rules identified in § 3.1(a) *supra* tend to provide the controlling principles for resolution of various kinds of issues in various substantive fields;

(c) The variety of legal remedies available in any given situation, including: litigation; legislative remedies (such as drafting and/or lobbying for new legislation; lobbying to defeat pending legislative bills; and lobbying for the repeal or amendment of existing legislation); administrative remedies (such as presenting testimony in support of, or lobbying for, the adoption, repeal, or amendment of administrative regulations; and lobbying of an administrator to resolve an individual case in a particular way); and alternative dispute-resolution mechanisms (formal mechanisms such as arbitration, mediation, and conciliation; and informal mechanisms such as self-help);

3.2 *Knowledge of and Ability to Use the Most Fundamental Tools of Legal Research*:

(a) With respect to each of the following fundamental tools of legal research, a lawyer should be generally familiar with the nature of the tool, its likely location in a law library, and the ways in which the tool is used:

(i) Primary legal texts (the written or recorded texts of legal rules), including: caselaw reporters, looseleaf services, and other collections of court decisions; codifications of federal, state, and local legislation; collections of administrative regulations and decisions of administrative agencies;

(ii) Secondary legal materials (the variety of aids to researching the primary legal texts), including treatises, digests, annotated versions of statutory compilations, commentaries in looseleaf services, law reviews, and Shepard's Compilations of citations to cases and statutes;

(iii) Sources of ethical obligations of lawyers, including the standards of professional conduct (the Code of Professional Responsibility and the Model Rules of Professional Conduct), and collections of ethical opinions of the American Bar Association and of state and local bar associations;

(b) With respect to the primary legal texts described in § 3.2(a)(i) *supra*, a lawyer should be familiar with:

    (i) Specialized techniques for reading or using the text, including:

        (A) Techniques of reading and analyzing court decisions, such as: the analysis of which portions of the decision are holdings and which are *dicta*; the identification of narrower and broader possible formulations of the holdings of the case; the evaluation of a case's relative precedential value; and the reconciliation of doctrinal inconsistencies between cases;

        (B) Techniques of construing statutes by employing well-accepted rules of statutory construction or by referring to secondary sources (such as legislative history);

    (ii) Specialized rules and customs permitting or prohibiting reliance on alternative versions of the primary legal texts (such as unofficial case reporters or unofficial statutory codes);

(c) With respect to the secondary legal materials described in § 3.2(a)(ii) *supra*, a lawyer should have a general familiarity with the breadth, depth, detail and currency of coverage, the particular perspectives, and the relative strengths and weaknesses that tend to be found in the various kinds of secondary sources so that he or she can make an informed judgment about which source is most suitable for a particular research purpose;

(d) With respect to both the primary legal materials described in § 3.2(a)(i) *supra*, and the secondary legal materials described in § 3.2(a)(ii) *supra*, a lawyer should be familiar with alternative forms of accessing the materials, including hard copy, microfiche and other miniaturization services, and computerized services (such as LEXIS and WESTLAW);

3.3 *Understanding of the Process of Devising and Implementing a Coherent and Effective Research Design*: A lawyer should be familiar with the skills and concepts involved in:

(a) Formulating the issues for research:

    (i) Determining the full range of legal issues to be researched (*see* Skill § 2.1 *supra*);

    (ii) Determining the kinds of answers to the legal issues that are needed for various purposes;

    (iii) Determining the degree of confidence in the answers that is needed for various purposes;

    (iv) Determining the extent of documentation of the answers that is needed for various purposes;

    (v) Conceptualizing the issues to be researched in terms that are conducive to effective legal research (including a consideration of which conceptualizations or verbalizations of issues or rules will make them most accessible to various types of search strategies);

(b) Identifying the full range of search strategies that could be used to research the issues, as well as alternatives to research, such as, in appropriate cases, seeking the information from other people who have expertise regarding the issues to be researched (for example, other attorneys or, in the case of procedural issues, clerks of court);

(c) Evaluating the various search strategies and settling upon a research design, which should take into account:

    (i) The degree of thoroughness of research that would be necessary in order to adequately resolve the legal issues (*i.e.*, in order to find an answer if there is one to be found, or, in cases where the issue is still open, to determine to a reasonable degree of certainty that it is still unresolved and gather analogous authorities);

(ii) The degree of thoroughness that is necessary in the light of the uses to which the research will be put (*e.g.,* the greater degree of thoroughness necessary if the information to be researched will be used at trial or at a legislative hearing; the lesser degree of thoroughness necessary if the information will be used in an informal negotiation with opposing counsel or lobbying of an administrator);

(iii) An estimation of the amount of time that will be necessary to conduct research of the desired degree of thoroughness;

(iv) An assessment of the feasibility of conducting research of the desired degree of thoroughness, taking into account:

(A) The amount of time available for research in the light of the other tasks to be performed, their relative importance, and their relative urgency;

(B) The extent of the client's resources that can be allocated to the process of legal research; and

(C) The availability of techniques for reducing the cost of research (such as, for example, using manual research methods to gain basic familiarity with the relevant area before using the more expensive resource of computerized services);

(v) If there is insufficient time for, or the client lacks adequate resources for, research that is thorough enough to adequately resolve the legal issues, a further assessment of the ways in which the scope of the research can be curtailed with the minimum degree of risk of undermining the accuracy of the research or otherwise impairing the client's interests;

(vi) Strategies for double-checking the accuracy of the research, such as using different secondary sources to research the same issue; or, when possible, conferring with practitioners or academics with expertise in the area;

(d) Implementing the research design, including:

(i) Informing the client of the precise extent to which the scope of the research has been curtailed for the sake of time or conservation of the client's resources (*see* § 3.3(c)(v) *supra*); the reasons for these curtailments; and the possible consequences of deciding not to pursue additional research;

(ii) Monitoring the results of the research and periodically considering:

(A) Whether the research design should be modified;

(B) Whether it is appropriate to end the research, because it has fully answered the questions posed; or, even though it has not fully answered the questions posed, further research will not produce additional information; or the information that is likely to be produced is not worth the time and resources that would be expended;

(iii) Ensuring that any cases that will be relied upon or cited have not been overruled, limited, or called into question; and that any statutes or administrative regulations that will be relied upon or cited have not been repealed or amended and have not been struck down by the courts.

INDEX

References are to Pages

CITATORS—Cont'd
Subject-specific citators, 307
Non-legal citators, 316
Tax regulations, 602, 617
Tax treaties, 600
United Kingdom legal research, 486, 487, 499
Updating print citators, 303
Using CALR services as citators, 283, 534

CIVIL AND COMMON LAW LEGAL SYSTEMS
    Generally, 3
Legislation, role of, 7
Treatises, authoritative value, 10

CLIENT LETTERS
Generally, 23, 27

CODES
See also Legislation, this index; Statutes, this index
Annotated codes, 197
Annotated constitutions, 108
Code of Federal Regulations. See Administrative Law, this index
Common law codifications, 8
Common law vs civil law authority, 3
Electronic access to state codes, 199
Federal regulations. See Administrative Law, this index
Internal Revenue Code, 591, 636
Interpretation of Statutes, this index
Model acts, 390
Municipal, 209
Official and unofficial publications, 11
Rules of court in, 212
State constitutions, 124
State legislation, 196
Statutes and positive law, 133
Statutes distinguished, 7
Tax research, 591, 636
Uniform laws, 390
United Kingdom legal research, 486
United States Code, 133

COMMON LAW
    Generally, 2
Civil law compared
        Generally, 3
    Legislation, role of, 7
    Treatises, authoritative value, 10
Hypothetical questions, 5
Restatements
        Generally, 381
    See also Restatements, this index
Statutes codifying, 8

COMPACTS, INTERSTATE
Generally, 207

COMPLAINTS
Sources of filings, 3
Writing, 25

COMPUTER–ASSISTED LEGAL RESEARCH (CALR)
    Generally, 33, 518 et seq.
CD–ROM Publications, this index
Electronic Research, this index
Internet Tools and Resources, this index

CONSTITUTIONAL LAW RESEARCH
    Generally, 108 et seq.
See also Supreme Court of United States, this index
ALR, 110

†